PSYCHOLOGY
A NEW INTRODUCTION

Richard Gross
and
Rob McIlveen

Hodder & Stoughton

A MEMBER OF THE HODDER HEADLINE GROUP

British Library Cataloguing in Publication Data

ISBN 0 340 65539 9

First published 1998

Impression number 10 9 8 7 6 5 4 3 2 1
Year   2002 2001 2000 1999 1998

Typeset by GreenGate Publishing Services, Tonbridge, Kent.

Printed and bound in Great Britain for Hodder and Stoughton Educational,
a division of Hodder Headline plc, 338 Euston Road, London NW1 3BH,
by Redwood Books Limited, Trowbridge, Wiltshire.

PSYCHOLOGY

A NEW INTRODUCTION

CONTENTS

Part 2 Memory

Part 3 Language and thought

Unit 4 Developmental Psychology

Part 1 Early socialisation

PREFACE

Our aim in this book is to provide a comprehensive and detailed, yet readable and accessible, introduction to the diverse and constantly changing discipline of psychology. To achieve this, the book is divided into seven units.

Unit 1 (Approaches and Methods) comprises two chapters the first dealing with definitions and sub-divisions of psychology (including major theoretical orientations), and the second outlining the major methods of research used by psychologists

Unit 2 (Biopsychology) comprises Chapters 3–20. These cover basic neural and hormonal processes and their influence on behaviour (3–5), cortical functions (6–10), awareness (11–15), and motivation, emotion and stress (16–20)

Unit 3 (Cognitive Psychology) consists of Chapters 21–37. These discuss perception and attention (21–26), memory and learning (27–31), and language and thought (32–37),

Unit 4 (Developmental Psychology) comprises Chapters 38–50. These consider early socialisation (38–40), cognitive development (41–43), social behaviour and diversity in development (44–46), and adolescence, adulthood and old age (47–50).

Unit 5 (Social Psychology) consists of Chapters 51–64. These discuss social cognition (51–54), social relationships (55–57), social influence (58–61), and pro- and anti-social behaviour (62–64).

Unit 6 (Abnormal Psychology and Atypical Development) comprises Chapters 65–80. These cover conceptions and models of abnormality (65–67), psychopathology (68–71), therapeutic approaches (72–77), and atypical development (78–80).

Finally, **Unit 7** (Perspectives) consists of Chapters 81–85. Chapter 81 considers free will and determinism, and reductionism. Chapters 82–84 discuss controversies in psychology, and ethical issues are discussed in Chapter 85.

Whilst the sequence of chapters and much of the content is based on the AEB A/AS level syllabus (0675/0975), we believe that the book will also prove valuable to those studying the NEAB and OCEAC A/AS syllabuses, as well as undergraduate students seeking a general introductory textbook.

Each chapter includes an introduction and overview, conclusions, and a detailed summary, designed to help with revision of the chapter's major aspects. In addition, the Perspectives chapters include several exercises, aimed at helping students to draw on (and revise) their knowledge of the subject as a whole so as to meet the demands of this synoptic section. Also for revision purposes, the Index contains page numbers in **bold** which refer to definitions and main explanations of particular concepts for easy reference.

We won't pretend that psychology is easy, and there is no substitute for hard work. We hope – and believe – that this book will make the task of studying psychology both less arduous and even a little more enjoyable than it would otherwise be. Good luck!

Richard Gross

Rob McIlveen

DEDICATION

To Jan, Tanya and Jo, with my love. Here's to the future, which promises even more than the past has so far delivered.
R.G.

To Gill, Willy, and Katie, with all my love.
R.M.

ACKNOWLEDGEMENTS

We would like to thank Dave Mackin, Anna Churchman and Denise Stewart at GreenGate Publishing for the excellent job they have made of preparing the text. Also, thanks to Tim Gregson-Williams and Marie Jones for their help and support during what has been an enormous and sometimes extremely demanding project. We got there in the end!

UNIT 1

Introduction

AN INTRODUCTION TO PSYCHOLOGY
AND ITS APPROACHES

Introduction and overview

Clearly, the first chapter in any textbook is intended to 'set the scene' for what follows, and this normally involves defining the subject or discipline. In most disciplines, this is usually a fairly simple task. With psychology, however, it is far from straightforward.

Definitions of psychology have changed frequently during its relatively short history as a separate field of study. This reflects different, and sometimes conflicting, theoretical views regarding the nature of human beings and the most appropriate methods for investigating them. Whilst there have been (and still are) many such theoretical approaches, three of the most important are the *behaviourist, psychodynamic* and *humanistic*. These, and the *neurobiological* (*biogenic*) and *cognitive* approaches, recur throughout this book and together form the core of what is commonly referred to as *mainstream* psychology.

Before looking at these approaches in detail, this chapter considers the discipline of psychology as a whole by looking at major areas of academic research and applied psychology. Throughout, we shall identify where these approaches and areas are discussed in the 84 chapters that follow.

What is psychology?

The word *psychology* is derived from the Greek *psyche* (mind, soul or spirit) and *logos* (discourse or study). Literally, then, psychology is the 'study of the mind'. The emergence of psychology as a separate discipline is generally dated at 1879, when Wilhelm Wundt opened the first psychological laboratory at the University of Leipzig in Germany. Wundt and his co-workers were attempting to investigate 'the mind' through *introspection* (observing and analysing the structure of their own conscious mental processes). Introspection's aim was to analyse conscious thought into its basic elements and perception into its constituent sensations, much as chemists analyse compounds into elements. This attempt to identify the structure of conscious thought is called *structuralism*.

Wundt and his co-workers recorded and measured the results of their introspections under controlled conditions, using the same physical surroundings, the same 'stimulus' (such as a clicking metronome), the same verbal instructions to each participant, and so on. This emphasis on measurement and control marked the separation of the 'new psychology' from its parent discipline of philosophy.

For hundreds of years, philosophers discussed 'the mind'. For the first time, scientists (Wundt was actually a physiologist by training) applied some of scientific investigation's basic methods to the study of mental processes. This was reflected in James's (1890) definition of psychology as:

' ... the Science of Mental Life, both of its phenomena and of their conditions ... The Phenomena are such things as we call feelings, desires, cognition, reasoning, decisions and the like'.

However, by the early twentieth century, the validity and usefulness of introspection were being seriously questioned, particularly by an American psychologist, John B. Watson. Watson believed that the results of introspection could never be proved or disproved, since if one person's introspection produced different results from another's, how could we ever decide which was correct? *Objectively*, of course, we cannot, since it is impossible to 'get behind' an introspective report to check its accuracy. Introspection is *subjective* and only the individual can observe his/her own mental processes.

Consequently, Watson (1913) proposed that psychologists should confine themselves to studying *behaviour*, since only this is measurable and observable by more than one person. Watson's form of psychology was known as *behaviourism*. It largely replaced introspectionism and advocated that people should be regarded as complex animals and studied using the same scientific methods as used by chemistry and physics. For Watson, the only way psychology could make any claims to being scientific was to emulate the natural sciences, and adopt its own objective methods. He defined psychology as:

' ... that division of Natural Science which takes human behaviour – the doings and sayings, both learned and unlearned – as its subject matter' (Watson, 1919).

The study of inaccessible, private, mental processes was to have no place in a truly scientific psychology.

Especially in America, behaviourism (in one form or another) remained the dominant force in psychology for the next 40 years or so. The emphasis on the role of learning (in the form of *conditioning*) was to make that topic one of the central areas of psychological research as a whole (see Box 1.8 and Chapter 32).

Box 1.1   Psychoanalytic theory and Gestalt psychology

In 1900, Sigmund Freud, a neurologist living in Vienna, first published his *psychoanalytic theory* of personality in which the *unconscious* mind played a crucial role. In parallel with this theory, he developed a form of psychotherapy called *psychoanalysis*. Freud's theory (which forms the basis of the *psychodynamic* approach) represented a challenge and a major alternative, to behaviourism (see this chapter, pages 11–12).

A reaction against both structuralism and behaviourism came from the *Gestalt* school of psychology, which emerged in the 1920s in Austria and Germany. Gestalt psychologists were mainly interested in perception, and believed that perceptions could not be broken down in the way that Wundt proposed (see Chapter 83) and behaviourists advocated for behaviour (see Chapters 32 and 83). Gestalt psychologists identified several 'laws' or principles of perceptual organisation (such as 'the whole is greater than the sum of its parts') which have made a lasting contribution to our understanding of the perceptual process (see Chapter 21 for a detailed discussion).

In the late 1950s, many British and American psychologists began looking to the work of computer scientists to try to understand more complex behaviours which, they felt, had been either neglected altogether or greatly oversimplified by learning theory (conditioning). These complex behaviours were what Wundt, James and other early scientific psychologists had called '*mind*' or mental processes, but which were now referred to as *cognition* or *cognitive processes* (all the ways in which we come to know the world around us, how we attain, retain and regain information, through the processes of perception, attention, memory, problem-solving, language and thinking in general).

Cognitive psychologists see people as *information-processors* and cognitive psychology has been heavily influenced by computer science, with human cognitive processes being compared with the operation of computer programs (the *computer analogy*). Cognitive psychology now forms part of *cognitive science*, which emerged in the late 1970s (see

Figure 1.1, page 4). The events which together constitute the 'cognitive revolution' are described in Chapter 83 (page 713).

Although mental or cognitive processes can only be inferred from what a person does (they cannot be observed literally or directly), mental processes are now accepted as being valid subject-matter for psychology, provided they can be made 'public' (as in memory tests or problem-solving tasks). Consequently, what people say and do are perfectly acceptable sources of information about their cognitive processes, although the processes themselves remain inaccessible to the observer, who can study them only indirectly.

The influence of both behaviourism and cognitive psychology is reflected in Clark & Miller's (1970) definition of psychology as:

> ' ... the scientific study of behaviour. Its subject matter includes behavioural processes that are observable, such as gestures, speech and physiological changes, and processes that can only be inferred, such as thoughts and dreams'.

Similarly, Zimbardo (1992) states that:

> '*Psychology* is formally defined as the scientific study of the behaviour of individuals and their mental processes ... '.

Classifying the work of psychologists

Despite behaviourist and cognitive psychology's influence on psychology's general direction in the last 80 years or so, much more goes on within psychology than has been outlined so far. There are other theoretical approaches or orientations, other aspects of human (and non-human) activity that constitute the special focus of study, and different kinds of work, that different psychologists do. A useful, but not hard and fast, distinction is that between the *academic* and *applied* branches of psychology (see Figure 1.3, page 9). Academic psychologists carry out research in a particular area and are attached to a university or research establishment where they will also teach undergraduates and supervise the research of postgraduates. Research is *pure* (done for its own sake and intended, primarily, to increase our knowledge and understanding) and *applied* (aimed at solving a particular problem). Applied research is usually funded by a government institution like the Home Office or the Department of Education and Employment, or by some commercial or industrial institution. The range of topics that may be investigated is as wide as psychology itself, but they may be classified as focusing either on the

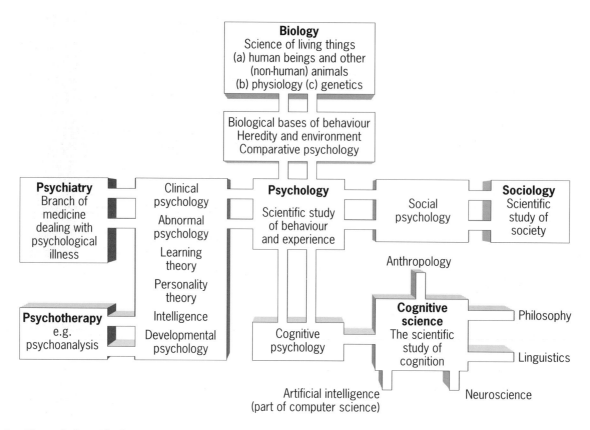

Figure 1.1   The relationship between psychology and other scientific disciplines

processes or *mechanisms* underlying various aspects of behaviour, or more directly on the *person* (Legge, 1975).

THE PROCESS APPROACH

This divides into four main areas: the biological bases of behaviour (or biopsychology), learning, cognitive processes and comparative psychology (the study of the behaviour of non-humans).

Biopsychology (Chapters 3–20)

Biopsychologists are interested in the physical basis of behaviour, how the functions of the nervous system (in particular the brain) and the endocrine (hormonal) system are related to and influence behaviour *and* mental processes. For example, are there parts of the brain specifically concerned with particular behaviours and abilities (*localisation of brain function*)? What role do hormones play in the experience of emotion and how are these linked to brain processes? What is the relationship between brain activity and different *states of consciousness* (including *sleep*)?

A fundamentally important biological process with important implications for psychology is genetic trans-mission. The *heredity* and *environment* (or *nature–nurture*) *issue* draws on what geneticists have discovered about the characteristics that can be passed from parents to off-spring, how this takes place and how genetic factors interact with environmental ones (see Chapters 43 and 68). Other biopsychological topics include *motivation* and *stress*. Sensory processes are also biological processes, but because of their close connection with perception are dealt with in Chapter 21.

Cognitive psychology (Chapters 21–37)

As was seen on page 3, cognitive (or mental) processes include *attention, memory, perception, language, thinking, prob-lem-solving, reasoning* and *concept-formation* ('higher-order' mental activities). Although these are often studied for their own sake, they may have important practical impli-cations too, such as understanding the memory processes involved in eye-witness testimony. Much of social psy-chology (classified here as belonging to the person category) is cognitive in flavour, that is, concerned with the mental processes involved in interpersonal perception (e.g. stereotyping) and is known as *social cognition*. Also, Piaget's theory (again, belonging to the person category) is concerned with *cognitive development*.

4

The investigation of *learning* permeates most areas of psychology, which partly reflects the influence of behaviourism (see above). However, whilst social learning theorists (see Chapter 32) accept many of the basic principles of conditioning theory, they believe that conditioning alone cannot account for most human social behaviour, and have focused on *observational learning* (*modelling*) as an important additional learning process, especially in children (see also Chapters 44 and 45). Most human learning is closely related to cognitive processes, such as language and perception, and *cognitive learning* is also displayed by chimpanzees (*insight learning*) and rats ('*mental maps*') (see Chapter 32).

THE PERSON APPROACH

Developmental psychology (Chapters 38–50)

Developmental psychologists study the biological, cognitive, social and emotional changes that occur in people over time. One significant change within developmental psychology during the past 25 years or so is the recognition that development is not confined to childhood and adolescence, but is a lifelong process (the *lifespan approach*). It is now generally accepted that adulthood is a developmental stage, distinct from childhood, adolescence and old age.

Developmental psychology is not an isolated or independent field and advances in it depend on progress within psychology as a whole, such as behavioural genetics, (neuro)physiological psychology, learning, perception and motivation. Conversely, although Piaget's theory of cognitive development, for example, was meant to map the changes that take place up to about 15 years of age, he is considered to have made a major contribution to psychology as a whole (see Chapter 42).

Social psychology (Chapters 51–64)

Some psychologists would claim that 'all psychology is social psychology' because all behaviour takes place within a social context and, even when we are alone, our behaviour continues to be influenced by others. However, other people usually have a more immediate and direct influence upon us when we are actually in their presence (as in *leadership*, *conformity* and *obedience*: see Chapters 58–60).

Social psychology is also concerned with *interpersonal perception* (forming impressions of others and judging the causes of their behaviour), interpersonal attraction and intimate relationships, prejudice and discrimination, and pro- and anti-social behaviour (especially aggression).

Figure 1.2   Jean Piaget (1896–1980)

Abnormal psychology and atypical development (Chapters 65–80)

These areas study the underlying causes of deviant behaviour and psychological abnormality. The focus in this book is on *mental disorders* such as schizophrenia, depression, anxiety disorders and eating disorders. Abnormal psychology is closely linked with *clinical psychology*, one of the major *applied* areas of psychology (see below). Psychologists who study abnormality and clinical psychologists are also concerned with the effectiveness of different forms of treatment and therapies. As will be seen later, each major theoretical approach has contributed to both the explanation and treatment of mental disorders. Whilst the focus of Chapters 65–77 is on *adult* disorders, Chapters 78–80 are concerned with childhood and adolescent disorders and other aspects of *atypical development*.

Comparing the process and person approaches

In practice, it is very difficult to separate the two approaches, even if it can be done theoretically. However, there are important *relative* differences between them.

Box 1.2   Some important differences between the process and person approaches

- The *process approach* is typically confined to the laboratory (where experiments are the method of choice), makes far greater experimental use of non-humans and assumes that psychological processes (particularly learning) are essentially the same in *all* species and that any differences between species are only *quantitative* (differences of degree).

- The *person approach* makes much greater use of field studies (such as observing behaviour in its natural environment) and of non-experimental methods (e.g. correlational studies: see Chapter 2). Typically, human participants are studied, and it is assumed that there are *qualitative* differences (differences in kind) between humans and non-humans.

AREAS OF APPLIED PSYCHOLOGY

Discussion of the person/process approaches has been largely concerned with the *academic* branch of psychology. Since the various areas of *applied* psychology are all concerned with people, they can be thought of as the applied aspects of the person approach. According to Hartley & Branthwaite (1997), most applied psychologists work in four main areas: *clinical, educational, occupational* and *government service* (such as prison psychologists). Additionally, Coolican (1996) identifies *criminological* (or *forensic*), *sports, health* and *environmental* psychologists. Hartley and Branthwaite argue that the work psychologists do in these different areas has much in common: it is the subject matters of their jobs which differ, rather than the skills they employ. Consequently, they consider an applied psychologist to be a person who can deploy specialised skills appropriately in different situations.

Box 1.3   Seven major skills (or roles) used by applied psychologists

- *The psychologist as counsellor:* helping people to talk openly, express their feelings, explore problems more deeply and see these problems from different perspectives. Problems may include school phobia, marriage crises and traumatic experiences (such as being the victim of a hijacking), and the counsellor can adopt a more or less *directive* approach (see page 15 and Chapter 76).

- *The psychologist as colleague:* working as a member of a team and bringing a particular perspective to a task, namely drawing attention to the human issues, such as the point of view of the individual end-user (be it a product or a service of some kind).

- *The psychologist as expert:* drawing upon psychologists' specialised knowledge, ideas, theories and practical knowledge to advise on issues ranging from incentive schemes in industry to appearing as an 'expert witness' in a court case.

- *The psychologist as toolmaker:* using and developing appropriate measures and techniques to help in the analysis and assessment of problems. These include

questionnaire and interview schedules, computer-based ability and aptitude tests and other *psychometric* tests (see Chapter 82).

- *The psychologist as detached investigator:* many applied psychologists carry out evaluation studies to assess the evidence for and against a particular point of view. This reflects the view of psychology as an objective science, which should use controlled experimentation whenever possible. The validity of this view is a recurrent theme throughout psychology (see, in particular, Chapter 83).

- *The psychologist as theoretician:* theories try to explain observed phenomena, suggesting possible underlying mechanisms or processes. They can suggest where to look for causes and how to design specific studies which will produce evidence for or against a particular point of view. Results from applied psychology can influence theoretical psychology and vice versa.

- *The psychologist as agent for change:* applied psychologists are involved in helping people, institutions and organisations, based on the belief that their work will change people and society for the better. However, some changes are much more controversial than others, such as the use of psychometric tests to determine educational and occupational opportunities (see Chapter 82) and the use of behaviour therapy and modification techniques to change abnormal behaviour (see Chapters 74 and 85).

(Based on Hartley & Branthwaite, 1997)

Clinical psychology

Clinical psychologists are the largest single group of psychologists, both in the UK (Coolican, 1996) and America (Atkinson *et al.*, 1990). A related group is '*counselling psychologists*', who tend to work with younger clients in colleges and universities rather than in hospitals (see page 15).

Box 1.4   The major functions of the clinical psychologist

Clinical psychologists have had three years post-graduate training and their functions include:

- assessing people with learning difficulties, administering psychological tests to brain-damaged patients, devising rehabilitation programmes for long-term psychiatric patients, and assessing the elderly for their fitness to live independently.

- planning and carrying out programmes of therapy, usually *behaviour therapy/modification* (both derived from learning theory principles), or *psychotherapy* (group or individual) in preference to, or in addition to, behavioural techniques (see Chapters 73–76);

- carrying out research into abnormal psychology, including the effectiveness of different treatment methods ('outcome' studies). Patients are usually adults, many of whom will be elderly, in psychiatric hospitals, psychiatric wards in general hospitals and psychiatric clinics;

- involvement in community care as psychiatric care in general moves out of the large psychiatric hospitals;

- teaching other groups of professionals, such as nurses, psychiatrists and social workers.

Psychotherapy is usually carried out by *psychiatrists* (medically qualified doctors specialising in psychological medicine) or *psychotherapists* (who have undergone special training, including their own psychotherapy). In all its various forms, psychotherapy is derived from Freud's psychoanalysis (see below) and is distinguished both from behavioural treatments and physical treatments (those based on the medical model: see Chapter 72).

Criminological (or forensic) psychology

This is a branch of psychology which attempts to apply psychological principles to the criminal justice system. It is rooted in empirical research and draws on cognitive, developmental, social and clinical psychology. One main focus is the study of criminal behaviour and its management, but in recent years research interests have expanded to other areas, most notably those with a high media profile.

Box 1.5   Some recent areas of research interest among criminological psychologists

- Jury selection

- The presentation of evidence

- Eyewitness testimony (see Chapter 31)

- Improving the recall of child witnesses

- False memory syndrome and recovered memory (see Chapter 30)

- Offender profiling

- Crime prevention

- Devising treatment programmes (such as anger management)

- Assessing the risk of releasing prisoners

(From Coolican, 1996)

Criminological psychologists work in a wide range of contexts, including psychiatric hospitals and special hospitals for the criminally insane (such as Broadmoor and Rampton), young offender institutions and prisons. Like clinical psychologists, a crucial part of their work involves research and evaluation of what constitutes successful treatment.

Educational psychology

Educational psychologists have had at least two years teaching experience and gained a postgraduate qualification in educational or child psychology.

Box 1.6   Some of the responsibilities of the educational psychologist

- administering psychometric tests, particularly intelligence (or IQ) tests, as part of the assessment of learning difficulties (see Chapters 43 and 82);

- planning and supervising remedial teaching;

- research into teaching methods, the curriculum (subjects taught), interviewing and counselling methods and techniques;

- planning educational programmes for those with mental and physical impairments (including the visually impaired and autistic), and other groups of children and adolescents who are not attending ordinary schools (*special educational needs:* see Chapters 78–80);

- advising parents and teachers how to deal with children and adolescents with physical impairments, behaviour problems or learning difficulties;

- teacher training.

Educational psychologists are usually employed by a Local Education Authority (LEA) and work in one or more of the following: child and family centre teams (what was called 'child guidance'), the Schools Psychological Service, hospitals, day nurseries, nursery schools, special schools (day and residential) and residential children's homes. Clients are aged up to 18 years, but most fall into the 5 to 16 age-group.

Occupational (work or organisational) psychology

Occupational psychologists are involved in the selection and training of individuals for jobs and vocational guidance, including administration of aptitude tests and tests of interest. (This overlaps with the work of those trained in *personnel management*).

Box 1.7   Other responsibilities of the occupational psychologist

- helping people who, for reasons of illness, accident or redundancy, need to choose and re-train for a new career (industrial rehabilitation);

- designing training schemes, as part of *'fitting the person to the job'*. Teaching machines and simulators (such as of an aeroplane cockpit) often feature prominently in these;

- *'fitting the job to the person'* (*human engineering/ engineering psychology* or *ergonomics*), wherein applications from experimental psychology are made to the design of equipment and machinery in order to make the best use of human resources and to minimise accidents and fatigue. Examples include telephone dialling codes (memory and attention) and the design of decimal coinage (tactile and visual discrimination);

- advising on working conditions in order to maximise productivity (another facet of *ergonomics* – the study of people's efficiency in their working environments). Occupational groups involved include computer/VDU operators, production line workers and air traffic controllers;

- helping the flow of communication between departments in government institutions, or 'industrial relations' in commerce and industry (*organisational psychology*). The emphasis is on the social, rather than the physical or practical, aspects of the working environment;

- helping to sell products and services through advertising and promotions. Many psychologists are employed in the advertising industry, where they draw on what experimental psychologists have discovered about human motivation, attitudes, cognition and so on (see Chapter 82).

CHARTERED PSYCHOLOGISTS

Since 1987, the British Psychological Society (BPS), the only professional body for British psychologists incorporated by Royal Charter, has been authorised under its Charter to keep a Register of Chartered Psychologists. Entry to the Register is restricted to members of the Society who have applied for registration and who have the necessary qualifications or experience to have reached a standard sufficient for professional practice in psychology without supervision (Gale, 1990).

Major theoretical approaches in psychology

Different psychologists make different assumptions about what particular aspects of a person are worthy of study, and this helps to determine an underlying model or image of what people are like. In turn, this model or image determines a view of psychological normality, the nature of development, preferred methods of study, the major cause(s) of abnormality, and the preferred methods and goals of treatment.

An approach is a perspective which is not as clearly outlined as a theory and which:

> ' ... provides a general orientation to a view of humankind. It says, in effect, 'we see people as operating according to these basic principles and we therefore see explanations of human behaviour as needing to be set within these limits and with these or those principles understood ... ' (Coolican, 1996).

As will be seen in the remainder of this chapter, all the major approaches include two or more distinguishable theories, but within an approach, they share certain basic principles and assumptions which give them a distinct 'flavour' or identity. The focus here is on the *behaviourist*, *psychodynamic* and *humanistic* approaches.

THE BEHAVIOURIST APPROACH

Basic principles and assumptions

As seen on pages 2–3, Watson (1913) revolutionised psychology by rejecting the introspectionist approach and advocating the study of observable behaviour. Only by modelling itself on the natural sciences could psychology legitimately call itself a science. Watson was seeking to transform the very subject matter of psychology (from 'mind' to behaviour) and this is often called *methodological behaviourism*. According to Skinner (1987),

> "Methodological' behaviourists often accept the existence of feelings and states of mind, but do not deal with them because they are not public and hence statements about them are not subject to confirmation by more than one person ... '.

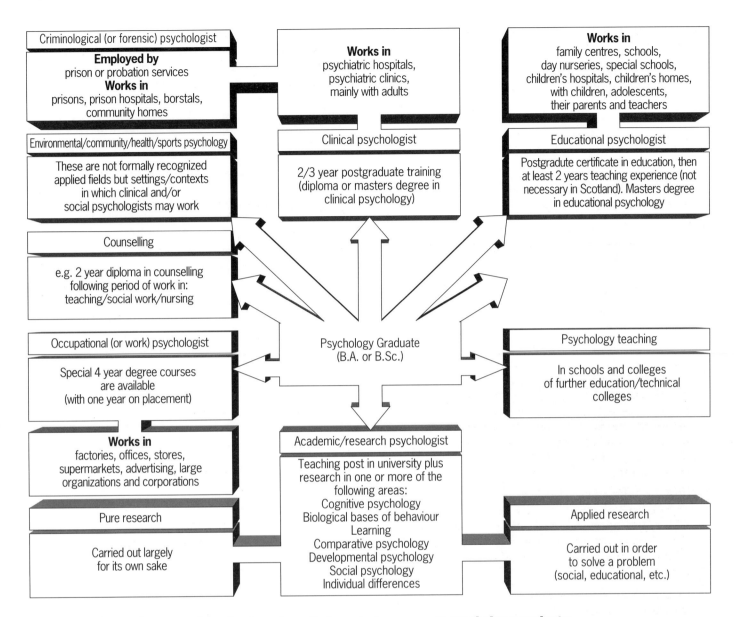

Figure 1.3   The main areas of academic and applied psychology open to psychology graduates

Figure 1.4   B.F. Skinner (1904–90)

In this sense, what was revolutionary when Watson (1913) first delivered his 'behaviourist manifesto' has become almost taken-for-granted, 'orthodox' psychology. It could be argued that *all* psychologists are methodological behaviourists (Blackman, 1980). Belief in the importance of empirical methods, especially the experiment, as a way of collecting data about humans (and non-humans), which can be quantified and statistically analysed, is a major feature of mainstream psychology (see Chapter 83). By contrast, as Skinner (1987) asserts:

' ... 'Radical' behaviourists ... recognise the role of private events (accessible in varying degrees to self-observation and physiological research), but contend that so-called mental activities are metaphors or explanatory fictions

9

and that behaviour attributed to them can be more effectively explained in other ways ... '.

For Skinner, these more effective explanations of behaviour come in the form of the principles of reinforcement derived from his experimental work with rats and pigeons. What is 'radical' about Skinner's radical behaviourism is the claim that feelings, sensations and other private events cannot be used to explain behaviour but are to *be explained* in an analysis of behaviour. Whilst methodological behaviourism proposes to ignore such inner states (they are *inaccessible*), Skinner ignores them only as variables used for explaining behaviour (they are *irrelevant*) and argues that they can be translated into the language of reinforcement theory (Garrett, 1996).

Given this important distinction between methodological and radical behaviourism, we need to consider some principles and assumptions that apply to behaviourism in general.

Box 1.8 Basic principles and assumptions made by the behaviourist approach

- Emphasis on the role of environmental factors in influencing behaviour, to the near exclusion of innate or inherited factors. This amounts essentially to a focus on learning. The key form of learning is *conditioning*, either classical (*Pavlovian* or *respondent*), which formed the basis of Watson's behaviourism, or *operant* (*instrumental*), which is at the centre of Skinner's radical behaviourism. Classical and operant conditioning are often referred to (collectively) as *learning theory*, as opposed to 'theories of learning' (which usually implies theories other than conditioning theories, that is, non-behaviourist theories: see Chapter 32).

- Behaviourism is often referred to as 'S–R' psychology ('S' standing for 'stimulus' and 'R' for 'response'). Whilst classical and operant conditioning account for observable behaviour (responses) in terms of environmental events (stimuli), the stimulus and response relationship is seen in fundamentally different ways. Only in classical conditioning is the stimulus seen as triggering a response in a predictable, automatic way, and it is this which is conveyed by 'S–R' psychology. It is, therefore, a mistake to describe operant conditioning as a 'S–R' approach (see Chapter 32).

- Both types of conditioning are forms of *associative learning*, whereby associations or connections are formed between stimuli and responses that did not exist before learning took place. This reflects the philosophical roots of behaviourism, namely the empirist

philosophy of John Locke, which was a major influence on the development of science in general, as well as on behaviourism in particular (see Chapter 83).

- Part of Watson's rejection of introspectionism was his belief that it invoked too many vague concepts that are difficult, if not impossible, to define and measure. According to the *law of parsimony* (or 'Occam's razor'), the fewer assumptions a theory makes the better (more 'economical' explanations are superior).

- The mechanisms proposed by a theory should be as simple as possible. Behaviourists stress the use of *operational definitions* (defining concepts in terms of observable, measurable, events: see Chapter 2).

- The aim of a science of behaviour is to *predict* and *control* behaviour. This raises both *conceptual* questions (about the nature of science, in particular the role of theory: see Chapter 83) and *ethical* questions (for example, about power and the role of psychologists as agents of change: see Chapter 85).

Theoretical contributions

Behaviourism made a massive contribution to psychology, at least up to the 1950s, and explanations of behaviour in conditioning terms recur throughout this book. For example, apart from a whole chapter on learning and conditioning (32), imagery as a form of organisation in memory and as a memory aid is based on the principle of association (Chapters 29 and 31), and the interference theory of forgetting is largely couched in stimulus–response terms (Chapter 30). Language, moral and gender development (Chapters 34, 44 and 45) have all been explained in terms of conditioning, and some influential theories of the formation and maintenance of relationships focus on the concept of reinforcement (Chapter 56). The behaviourist approach also offers one of the major models of abnormal behaviour (Chapter 66). Finally, Skinner's notorious views on free will are discussed in detail in Chapter 81.

As with Freud's psychoanalytic theory (see below), theorists and researchers critical of the original, 'orthodox' theories have modified and built on them, making a huge contribution in the process. Noteworthy examples are Tolman's *cognitive behaviourism* (see Chapter 32) and *social learning theory* (see Chapters 32, 44 and 45).

Practical contributions

We may think of *methodological behaviourism*, with its emphasis on experimentation, operational definitions, the measurement of observable events (see Box 1.8), as a major influence on the practice of scientific psychology in general (what Skinner, 1974, called the 'science of behaviour'), quite unrelated to any views about the nature and role of mental events. Other, more 'tangible' contributions include:

- *behaviour therapy* and *behaviour modification* (based on *classical* and *operant conditioning* respectively) as major approaches to the treatment of abnormal behaviour (see Chapter 74) and one of the main tools in the 'kit bag' of the clinical psychologist (see Box 1.4);
- *biofeedback* as a non-medical treatment for stress-related symptoms, derived from attempts to change rats' autonomic physiological functions through the use of operant techniques (see Chapters 20 and 32);
- *teaching machines* and *programmed learning*, which now commonly take the form of *computer assisted learning* (CAL).

An evaluation of behaviourism

In addition to the criticisms – both general and specific – which occur in the particular chapters where behaviourist explanations are given, two evaluative points will be made here. The first concerns the famous 'Skinner box', the 'auto-environmental chamber' in which rats and pigeons' environment can be totally controlled by the experimenter (see Chapter 32). Since pressing the lever was intended to be equivalent to a cat operating an escape latch in Thorndike's puzzle box, counting the number of lever presses (frequency of response) became the standard measure of operant learning. Despite Skinner's claims to not having a *theory*, 'the response' in operant conditioning has largely considered *only* the frequency of behaviour, ignoring intensity, duration and quality. As Glassman (1995) observes,

'While the focus on frequency was a practical consideration, it eventually became part of the overall conceptual framework as well – a case of research methods directing theory'.

But in everyday life, frequency is not always the most meaningful aspect of behaviour. For example, should we judge an artist's worth by *how many* paintings he or she produces, rather than their *content*?

The second criticism relates to Skinner's claim that human behaviour can be predicted and controlled in the same way as the behaviour of non-humans. Possessing language allows us to communicate with each other and to think about 'things' that have never been observed (and may not even exist), including rules, laws and principles (Garrett, 1996). Whilst these can only be expressed in words or thought about by means of words, much of people's behaviour is governed by them. According to Garrett, when this happens,

' ... behaviour is now shaped by what goes on inside their [people's] heads ... and not simply by what goes on in the external environment ... '.

What people *think* is among the important variables determining what they do and say, the very opposite of what Skinner's radical behaviourism claims.

THE PSYCHODYNAMIC APPROACH

The term 'psychodynamic' denotes the active forces within the personality that motivate behaviour and the inner causes of behaviour (in particular the unconscious conflict between the different structures that compose the whole personality). Whilst Freud's was the original psychodynamic theory, the approach includes all those theories based on his ideas, such as those of Jung, Adler and Erikson. Freud's *psychoanalytic theory* (sometimes called 'psychoanalysis') is psychodynamic, but the psychodynamic theories of Jung and so on, are not psychoanalytic. So the two terms are not synonymous. However, because of their enormous influence, Freud's ideas will be emphasised in the rest of this section.

Basic principles and assumptions

Freud's concepts are closely interwoven, making it difficult to know where their description should begin (Jacobs, 1992). Fortunately, Freud himself stressed acceptance of certain key theories as essential to the practice of psychoanalysis, the form of psychotherapy he pioneered and from which most others are derived (see below).

Box 1.9   The major principles and assumptions of psychoanalytic theory

- Much of our behaviour is determined by *unconscious* thoughts, wishes, memories and so on. What we are consciously aware of at any one time represents the tip of an iceberg: most of our thoughts and ideas are either not accessible at that moment (*pre-conscious*) or are totally inaccessible (*unconscious*). These unconscious causes can become conscious through the use of special techniques, such as *free association*, *dream interpretation* and *transference*, the cornerstones of *psychoanalysis* (see text below and Chapter 73).

- Much of what is unconscious has been made so through *repression*, whereby threatening or unpleasant experiences are 'forgotten'. They become inaccessible, locked away from our conscious awareness. This is a major form of *ego defence* (see Chapter 66). Freud singled it out as a special cornerstone 'on which the whole structure of psychoanalysis rests. It is the most essential part of it ... ' (Freud, 1914). Repression is closely related to *resistance*, interpretation of which is another key technique used in psychoanalysis (see Chapter 73).

- According to the *theory of infantile sexuality*, the sexual instinct or drive is active from birth and develops through a series of five *psychosexual stages*. The most important of these is the *phallic stage* (spanning the ages 3–5/6), during which all children experience the *Oedipus complex* (see Chapters 44 and 66). In fact, Freud used the German word '*Trieb*' , which translates as 'drive', rather than '*Instinkt*', which was meant to imply that experience played a crucial role in determining the 'fate' of sexual (and aggressive) energy.

- Related to infantile sexuality is the general impact of early experience on later personality. According to Freud (1949),

  'It seems that the neuroses are only acquired during early childhood (up to the age of six), even though their symptoms may not make their appearance until much later ... the child is psychologically father of the man and ... the events of its first years are of paramount importance for its whole subsequent life.'

Figure 1.5 Sigmund Freud (1856–1939)

Theoretical contributions

As with behaviourist accounts of conditioning, many of Freud's ideas and concepts have become part of mainstream psychology's vocabulary. You do not have to be a 'Freudian' to use concepts such as repression, unconscious and so on, and many of the vast number of studies of different aspects of the theory have been conducted by critics hoping to discredit it (such as Eysenck, 1985; Eysenck and Wilson, 1973).

Like behaviourist theories, Freud's can also be found throughout psychology as a whole. His contribution is extremely rich and diverse, offering theories of motivation (see Chapter 17), dreams and the relationship between sleep and dreams (Chapters 12 and 13), forgetting (Chapter 30), attachment and the effects of early experience (Chapters 38 and 39), moral and gender development (Chapters 44 and 45), aggression (see Chapter 63) and abnormality (Chapter 66).

Psychoanalytic theory has also influenced Gould's (1978, 1980) theory of the evolution of adult consciousness (Chapter 48) and Adorno *et al.*'s (1950) theory of the authoritarian personality (a major account of prejudice: see Chapter 53).

Finally, and as noted earlier, Freud's theories have stimulated the development of alternative theories, often resulting from the rejection of some of his fundamental principles and assumptions, but reflecting his influence enough for them to be described as psychodynamic.

Box 1.10   Some major alternative psychodynamic theories to Freud's psychoanalytic theory

- *Ego psychology*, promoted by Freud's daughter, Anna, focused on the mechanisms used by the ego to deal with the world, especially the *ego defence mechanisms*. Freud, by contrast, stressed the influence of the id's innate drives (especially sexuality and aggression) and is often described as an instinct theorist (but see Box 1.9, point 3).

- Erik Erikson, trained by Anna Freud as a child psychoanalyst, also stressed the importance of the ego, as well as the influence of social and cultural factors on individual development. He pioneered the *lifespan approach* to development, proposing eight *psychosocial* stages, in contrast with Freud's five *psychosexual* stages that end with physical maturity (see Chapters 47, 48 and 50).

- Two of Freud's original 'disciples', Carl Jung and Alfred Adler, broke ranks with Freud and formed their own 'schools' ('*analytical psychology*' and '*individual psychology*' respectively). Jung attached relatively little importance to childhood experiences (and the associated *personal* unconscious) but considerable importance to the *collective* (or racial) unconscious, which stems from the evolutionary history of human beings as a whole.

- Like Jung, Adler rejected Freud's emphasis on sexuality, stressing instead the will to power or striving for superiority, which he saw as an attempt to overcome feelings of inferiority faced by all children as they grow up (see Chapter 60). He also shared Jung's view of the person as an indivisible unity or whole, and Erikson's emphasis on the social nature of human beings.

- Melanie Klein is often seen as a key transitional figure between Freud's instinct theory and the object relations school (see below). Like Anna Freud, she adapted Freud's techniques (such as pioneering *play therapy*) in order to tap a young child's unconscious, and maintained that the superego and Oedipus complex appear as early as the first and second years of life (see Chapter 73).

Figure 1.6
a Anna Freud (1895–1982)
b Erik Erikson (1902–1994)
c Carl Gustav Jung (1875–1961)
d Alfred Adler (1870–1937)

- The object relations school (the 'British school') was greatly influenced by Klein's emphasis on the infant's earliest relationships with its mother. It places far less emphasis on the role of instincts and more on the relationship with particular love objects (especially the mother), seeing early *relationships* as crucial for later development. Fairbairn (1952), for example, saw the aim of the libido as *object-seeking* (as opposed to pleasure-seeking), and this was extended by Bowlby in his *attachment theory* (see Chapters 38 and 39).

(Based on Jacobs, 1992; Holmes, 1993; Glassman, 1995; Fancher, 1996)

Practical contributions

The current psychotherapy scene is highly diverse, with only a minority using Freudian techniques (see Chapter 73), but, as Fancher (1996) points out,

'Most modern therapists use techniques that were developed either by Freud and his followers or by dissidents in explicit reaction against his theories. Freud remains a dominating figure, for or against whom virtually all therapists feel compelled to take a stand'.

Both Rogers, the major humanistic therapist (see below and Chapter 76) and Wolpe, who developed *systematic desensitisation* (a major form of behaviour therapy: see Chapter 74), were originally trained in Freudian techniques. Perls, the founder of *Gestalt therapy* (see Chapter 76), Ellis, the founder of *rational emotive therapy* (RET) (see Chapter 75) and Berne, who devised *transactional analysis* (see Chapter 73) were also trained psychoanalysts.

Even Freud's fiercest critics concede his influence, not just within world psychiatry but in philosophy, literary criticism, history, theology, sociology and art and literature generally. Freudian terminology is commonly used in conversations between therapists well beyond Freudian circles, and his influence is brought daily to therapy sessions as part of the cultural background and experience of nearly every client (Jacobs, 1992).

An evaluation of the psychodynamic approach

A criticism repeatedly made of Freudian (and other psychodynamic) theories is that they are unscientific because they are *unfalsifiable* (incapable of being disproved). For example, if the Freudian prediction that 'dependent' men will prefer big-breasted women is confirmed, then the theory is supported, but if such men actually prefer small-breasted women (Scodel, 1957), Freudians can use the concept of *reaction formation* (an ego defence mechanism: see Box 66.4) to argue that an unconscious fixation with big breasts may manifest itself as a conscious preference for the opposite, a clear case of ' heads I win, tails you lose' (Popper, 1959; Eysenck, 1985).

Figure 1.7   Hans J. Eysenck (1916–1997), a major critic of Freud)

However, it is probably a mistake to see reaction formation as typical of Freudian theory as a whole. According to Kline (1989), for example, the theory comprises a collection of hypotheses, some of which are more easily tested than others, some of which are more central to the theory than others, and some of which have more supporting evidence than others.

Furthermore, Freud's theory provides methods and concepts which enable us to interpret and 'unpack' underlying meanings (it has great *hermeneutic strength*). Popper's and Eysenck's criticism help to underline the fact that these meanings (both conscious and unconscious) cannot be measured in any precise way. Freud offers a way of understanding that is different from theories that are easily testable and which may actually be more appropriate for capturing the nature of human experience and action (Stevens, 1995: see Chapter 83). According to Fancher (1996),

'Although always controversial, Freud struck a responsive chord with his basic image of human beings as creatures in conflict, beset by irreconcilable and often unconscious demands from within as well as without. His ideas about repression, the importance of early experience and sexuality, and the inaccessibility of much of human nature to ordinary conscious introspection have become part of the standard Western intellectual currency'.

THE HUMANISTIC APPROACH

Basic principles and assumptions

As has been seen, Rogers, a leading humanistic psychologist (and therapist) was trained as a psychoanalyst. Although the term 'humanistic psychology' was coined by Cohen (1958), a British psychologist, this approach emerged mainly in the USA during the 1950s. Maslow

(1968), in particular, gave wide currency to the term 'humanistic' in America, calling it a 'third force' (the other two being behaviourism and Freudianism). However, Maslow did not reject these approaches but hoped to unify them, thus integrating both subjective and objective, the private and public aspects of the person, and providing a complete, holistic psychology.

> **Box 1.11   Some basic principles and assumptions of the humanistic approach**
>
> - Both the psychoanalytic and behaviourist approaches are *deterministic*. People are driven by forces beyond their control, either unconscious forces from within (Freud) or reinforcements from without (Skinner). Humanistic psychologists believe in *free will* and people's ability to *choose* how they act (see Chapter 81).
>
> - A truly scientific psychology must treat its subject matter as fully human, which means acknowledging individuals as interpreters of themselves and their world. Behaviour, therefore, must be understood in terms of the individual's *subjective experience*, from the perspective of the actor (a *phenomenological* approach, which explains why this is sometimes called the 'humanistic-phenomenological' approach). This contrasts with the *positivist* approach (of the natural sciences), which tries to study people from the position of a detached observer. Only the individual can explain the meaning of a particular behaviour and is the 'expert' – not the investigator or therapist.
>
> - Maslow argued that Freud supplied the 'sick half' of psychology, through his belief in the inevitability of conflict, neurosis, innate self-destructiveness and so on, while he (and Rogers) stressed the 'healthy half'. Maslow saw *'self-actualisation'* at the peak of a hierarchy of needs (see below and Chapter 17), whilst Rogers talked about the *actualising tendency*, an intrinsic property of life, reflecting the desire to grow, develop and enhance our capacities. A fully functioning person is the ideal of growth. Personality development naturally moves towards healthy growth, unless it is blocked by external factors, and should be considered the norm.
>
> - Maslow's contacts with Wertheimer and other Gestalt psychologists (see Chapter 21) led him to stress the importance of understanding the *whole person*, rather than separate 'bits' of behaviour.
>
> (From Glassman, 1995)

Theoretical contributions

Maslow's *hierarchy of needs* (see Chapter 17, pages 142–143) distinguishes between motives shared by both humans and non-humans and those that are uniquely human, and can be seen as an extension of the psycho-dynamic approach. Freud's id would represent physiological needs (at the hierarchy's base), Horney (a major critic of the male bias in Freud's theory: see Chapter 84) focused on the need for safety and love (corresponding to the next two levels), and Adler stressed esteem needs (at the next, fourth level). Maslow added self-actualisation to the peak of the hierarchy (Glassman, 1995).

Figure 1.8   Abraham H. Maslow (1908–1970)

According to Rogers (1951), whilst awareness of being alive is the most basic of human experiences, we each fundamentally live in a world of our own creation and have a unique perception of the world (the *phenomenal field*). It is our *perception* of external reality which shapes our lives (not external reality itself). Within our phenomenal field, the most significant element is our sense of *self*, 'an organised consistent gestalt, constantly in the process of forming and reforming' (Rogers, 1959). This view contrasts with many other self theorists who see it as a central, unchanging core of personality (see Chapter 46).

Practical contributions

By far the most significant practical influence of any humanistic psychologist is Rogers' *client-* (or *person-*) *centred therapy* (see Chapter 76). Less well known is the prolific research that Rogers undertook during the 1940s, 50s and 60s into this form of therapy. According to Thorne (1992),

'This body of research constituted the most intensive investigation of psychotherapy attempted anywhere in the world up to that time ... The major achievement of these studies was to establish beyond all question that psychotherapy could and should be subjected to the rigours of scientific enquiry'.

Figure 1.9   Carl Rogers (1902–1987)

Rogers helped develop research designs (such as Q-sorts: see Box 76.4) which enable objective measurement of the self-concept, ideal self, and their relationship over the course of therapy, as well as methodologies (such as rating scales and the use of external 'consultants') for exploring the importance of therapist *qualities*. These innovations continue to influence therapeutic practice, and many therapists are now concerned that their work should be subjected to research scrutiny. Research findings are now more likely than ever before to affect training procedures and clinical practice across many different therapeutic orientations (Thorne, 1992).

By emphasising the therapist's personal qualities, Rogers opened up psychotherapy to psychologists and contributed to the development of therapy provided by non-medically qualified thereapists (*lay therapy*). This is especially significant in the USA, where psychoanalysts *must* be psychiatrists (medically qualified). Rogers originally used the term 'counselling' as a strategy for silencing psychiatrists who objected to psychologists practising 'psychotherapy'. In the UK, the outcome of Rogers' campaign has been the evolution of a counselling profession whose practitioners are drawn from a wide variety of disciplines, with neither psychiatrists nor psychologists dominating. Counselling skills are used in a variety of settings throughout education, the health professions, social work, industry and commerce, the armed services and international organisations (Thorne, 1992).

Evaluation of the humanistic approach

According to Wilson *et al.* (1996), the humanistic approach is not an elaborate or comprehensive theory of personality, but should be seen as a set of uniquely personal theories of living created by humane people optimistic about human potential. It has wide appeal to those who seek an alternative to the more mechanistic, deterministic theories. However, like Freud's theory, many of its concepts are difficult to test empirically (such as self-actualisation), and it cannot account for the origins of personality. Since it describes but does not explain personality, it is subject to the *nominal fallacy* (Carlson & Buskist, 1997).

Nevertheless, for all its shortcomings, the humanistic approach represents a counterbalance to the psychodynamic (especially Freud) and the behaviourist approaches, and has helped to bring the 'person' back into psychology. Crucially, it recognises that people help determine their own behaviour and are not simply slaves to environmental contingencies or to their past. The self, personal responsibility and agency, choice and free will are now legitimate issues for psychological investigation.

Conclusions

Psychology is a diverse discipline. Psychologists investigate a huge range of behaviours and mental or cognitive processes. There is a growing number of applied areas, in which theory and research findings are brought to bear in trying to improve people's lives in a variety of ways. During the course of its life as a separate discipline, definitions of psychology have changed quite fundamentally, reflecting the influence of different theoretical approaches. This chapter has considered in detail the basic principles and assumptions of the behaviourist, psychodynamic and humanistic approaches, together with their theoretical and practical contributions to the discipline of psychology as a whole.

Summary

■ Early psychologists, such as Wundt, attempted to study the mind through **introspection** under controlled conditions, aiming to analyse conscious thought into its basic elements (**structuralism**).

■ Watson rejected introspectionism's subjectivity and replaced it with **behaviourism**. Only by regarding people as complex animals, using the methods of natural science and studying observable behaviour, could psychology become a true science.

■ **Gestalt** psychologists criticised both structuralism and behaviourism, advocating that 'the whole is greater than the sum of its parts'. Freud's **psychoanalytic theory** was another major alternative to behaviourism.

■ Following the **cognitive revolution**, people came to be seen as **information-processors**, based on the **computer analogy**. Cognitive processes, such as perception and memory, became an acceptable part of psychology's subject-matter, even though they can only be inferred from behaviour.

■ **Academic** psychologists are mainly concerned with conducting either **pure** or **applied research**, which may focus on underlying processes/mechanisms or on the person. The **process approach** consists of biopsychology, learning, cognitive processes and comparative psychology, whilst the **person approach** covers developmental, social and abnormal psychology.

■ Whilst the process approach is largely confined to laboratory experiments using non-humans, the person approach makes greater use of field studies and non-experimental methods involving humans. The two approaches see species differences as **quantitative** or **qualitative** respectively.

■ Most **applied** psychologists work in clinical, educational, occupational or government service, with newer fields including criminological/forensic, sports, health and environmental psychology. Common skills or roles shared by all these practitioners include counsellor, expert, toolmaker, detached investigator, theoretician and agent for change.

■ **Clinical** psychologists are the most numerous group of applied psychologists. Their functions include planning and carrying out behaviour therapy/modification, as well as psychotherapy, which is more commonly carried out by psychiatrists and psychotherapists.

■ The British Psychological Society keeps a Register of **Chartered Psychologists**, restricted to those with the necessary qualifications or experience for unsupervised professional practice.

■ Different theoretical **approaches/perspectives** are based on different models/images of the nature of human beings.

■ Watson's **methodological behaviourism** removes mental processes from the science of psychology and focuses on what can be quantified and observed by different researchers. Skinner's **radical behaviourism** regards mental processes as both **inaccessible** and **irrelevant** for explaining behaviour, but which can be **explained** by the principles of reinforcement.

■ The behaviourist approach stresses the role of environmental influences (learning), especially classical and operant **conditioning**. Behaviourists also advocate the **law of parsimony** and the use of **operational definitions**. Psychology's aim is to **predict** and **control** behaviour.

■ Tolman's **cognitive behaviourism** and **social learning theory** represent modifications of 'orthodox' learning (conditioning) theory and have made huge contributions in their own right.

■ Methodological behaviourism has influenced the practice of scientific psychology in general. Other practical contributions include behaviour therapy and modification, biofeedback and teaching machines/programmed learning.

■ While not formally part of a 'theory' of conditioning, counting the **frequency of response** in the Skinner box has become part of the overall conceptual framework of operant learning. This ignores intensity, duration and quality of response. Also, Skinner's claim that human behaviour can be predicted and controlled in the same way as that of non-humans is contradicted by the fact that thinking through language actually determines people's behaviour.

■ The **psychodynamic approach** is based on Freud's **psychoanalytic theory**. Central aspects of Freud's theory are the **unconscious** (especially **repression**), **infantile sexuality** and the **impact of early experience** on later personality. The cornerstones of psychoanalysis are **free association, dream interpretation** and **transference**.

■ Freud identified five stages of **psychosexual development**, the most important being the **phallic stage**, during which all children experience the **Oedipus complex**. This is relevant to explaining moral and gender development. Freud's ideas have become part of mainstream psychology, contributing to our understanding of motivation, sleep and dreams, forgetting, attachment, aggression and abnormality.

■ Major modifications/alternatives to Freudian theory include **ego psychology**, Erikson's **psychosocial** developmental theory, Jung's 'analytical psychology', Adler's 'individual psychology' and the **object relations school**, influenced by Klein's focus on the infant's earliest relationship with the mother.

■ All forms of psychotherapy stem directly or indirectly from psychoanalysis, and many trained psychoanalysts have been responsible for developing radically different therapeutic approaches, including Rogers, Perls and Wolpe.

■ Freud's influence on a wide range of disciplines outside psychology and psychotherapy is undeniable, as is his more general impact on Western culture. Whilst his theory is often dismissed as **unfalsifiable** (and, therefore, unscientific), the criticism fails to acknowledge its great **hermeneutic strength**.

■ Maslow called the **humanistic approach** the 'third force' in psychology. It believes in **free will**, the importance of taking the actor's perspective (the **phenomenological approach**), understanding the **whole person**, the positive aspects of human personality, and the natural tendency towards healthy growth.

■ **Self-actualisation** is at the top of Maslow's hierarchy of needs, while for Rogers, the **self** is the most significant part of our **phenomenal field**, the only true reality for the individual.

■ Rogers developed **client/person-centred therapy**. He was also a prolific researcher into the effectiveness of his therapy, inspiring others to do the same and influencing both therapist training and clinical practice. He opened up psychotherapy to psychologists and other non-medically qualified practitioners, and created a counselling profession that operates within a wide diversity of settings.

■ The humanistic approach may be very difficult to test empirically, but it represents a major alternative to deterministic theories and has helped to bring the 'person' back into psychology.

2

PSYCHOLOGY AND ITS METHODS

Introduction and overview

As well as being diverse in terms of its content, psychology also uses a wide range of methods to study its subject matter. Five main methods can be identified. These are experiments, observation, case studies, surveys and correlation. Each of these is useful in gathering data, but each gives rise to a different type of conclusion. The experiment, for example, is the only method which allows cause and effect to be inferred. Other methods allow only general and tentative conclusions to be drawn. However, each method has its own strengths and limitations. This chapter examines the five main methods and considers their strengths and limitations.

Experiments in psychology

One of Wundt's and Watson's desires was to establish psychology as an empirical, research-based discipline separate from philosophy (see Chapter 1). To do this, they adopted the *experiment*, the main method of the natural sciences. By using experiments, 'mainstream' psychology became firmly established within the boundaries of 'positivism' (see Chapter 83).

The experimental method's logic is delightfully simple, and is based on abstraction, control and manipulation. Experimenters rarely study events as they occur in real life. Instead, they extract one *variable* for close scrutiny and manipulation, a variable being any element that can change or vary from one time or person to another. Having abstracted the variable, experimenters then work according to what the philosopher J.S. Mill called 'the rule of one variable': if two groups of people are equal in all respects save one, and are not similar with respect to the behaviour being measured, then the difference between them *must* be attributable to the one way in which they were different.

Only the experimental method permits psychologists to talk in terms of *cause and effect*, that is, one variable producing a change in another. This is an extremely powerful reason for using the experimental method in *any* discipline. The amount of control the experimental method provides has given the experiment a respectability not afforded to other methods.

Experimentation begins with the formulation of an *experimental hypothesis*. A hypothesis is an unambiguously phrased prediction about behaviour or mental processes that can be empirically tested, and the goal of an experiment is to test that hypothesis. The one factor which will be different between the groups of participants in an experiment is called the *independent variable* (IV). Its name derives from the fact that it is independently under the experimenter's control. The behaviour measured in an experiment is called the *dependent variable* (DV), and its name derives from the fact that it cannot be manipulated, since it is the outcome of the manipulation of the independent variable and dependent upon it.

Box 2.1 Operational definitions

As noted in the text, a hypothesis is an unambiguously phrased prediction. Suppose an experimenter hypothesises that alcohol affects performance. The IV which will be manipulated is 'alcohol', and the DV, the variable that will be measured, is 'performance'. To test the hypothesis, the experimenter must *operationally define* what is meant by 'alcohol' and 'performance'. 'Alcohol' could refer to beer, wine or spirits, and the experimenter needs to decide how much alcohol will be consumed and over what time period. 'Performance', too, must be operationally defined. It could refer to how quickly or accurately a task is performed, and the task could involve reaction time, memory, and many other things.

An operational definition narrows down what will be investigated, and provides an unambiguous description of what particular terms mean. Other experimenters might not agree with particular operational definitions, but this is unimportant. What is important is that other researchers *understand* what terms mean as they are used in the experiment.

Experiments always involve some kind of comparison, often between a *control group* (people who are not exposed to the IV being studied) and one or more *experimental groups* (who are exposed to the IV and variations of it). The simplest version of the experiment has two groups or conditions, but more complex experiments have three or more conditions. An experimental design is a way of allocating the people who will take part in the experiment to its various conditions, and three basic experimental designs can be identified.

Box 2.2   Basic experimental designs

- In the *independent* (*unrelated*) *groups design*, participants are randomly allocated to the various conditions, so that each participant has an equal chance of being in any one. Hopefully, differences between participants in the conditions will be minimal, so that any effect is a result of their different experiences (such as receiving or not receiving the IV) rather than differences that existed between them from the start.

- In the *repeated measures design*, each participant is tested in *all* of the conditions. The logic here is that since the same individuals are appearing in all conditions, individual differences between them will not have any effect since each participant acts as his or her own 'control'.

- In the *matched groups design*, different participants are used in the conditions, but pairs of them are *matched* according to some variable(s) that the experimenter suspects might influence the experiment's outcome and therefore wishes to hold constant. Such variables include age, sex and education level.

Box 2.3   Statistical tests in psychological experiments

As long as the differences between participants are random rather than systematic, the effect of the IV may be determined through the use of *statistical tests*. These determine the likelihood of obtaining the observed (or more extreme) results if the independent variable has no effects and chance factors alone are operating. The experimental hypothesis predicts that the IV will affect the DV. The *null hypothesis*, however, predicts that the IV will *not* affect the DV and that any differences between the groups can be attributed to the operation of chance factors alone.

Psychologists accept that, if the likelihood of obtaining the observed (or more extreme) results as predicted by the null hypothesis is sufficiently small (typically less than 5 per cent), then it is reasonable to *reject* the null hypothesis in favour of the experimental hypothesis. Because of what they study, psychologists can only talk in terms of *probabilities* rather than absolutes or certainties. When a statistical test indicates that it is extremely unlikely that a difference between conditions as large as that actually observed would arise from the operation of chance factors alone, the difference is said to be *statistically significant*, and the experimenter concludes that the IV has had an effect on the DV.

(Based on Humphreys, 1992)

LABORATORY EXPERIMENTS

Much research in psychology is conducted in the *psychological laboratory*. This is to provide maximum control for the possibility of extraneous and confounding variables influencing the experiment's outcome (such as variations in noise, light and temperature). By minimising the influence of these variables, a much more confident claim can be made about the effect (if any) of the IV on the DV. The laboratory is not the exclusive preserve of the experiment, however, and many observational studies are also carried out in psychology laboratories, most notably in developmental and social psychology (see, for example, Chapter 38).

As noted, the laboratory facilitates control and reduces the possibility of confounding variables. Many examples of laboratory experimentation using human participants can be found in the Unit on cognitive psychology (see Chapters 21–37). These strengths, though, contribute to the laboratory's principal weakness as a setting for experiments, namely its *artificiality*. Psychologists should not be surprised if people display artificial and contrived behaviour if they are studied in an artificial and contrived environment (Heather, 1976). Additionally, because

Each of the three experimental designs has its own advantages and limitations. In the independent groups design, for example, the experimenter is able to use exactly the same stimulus material in all conditions of the experiment, something which is not possible with the repeated measures design. However, in the repeated measures design, the experimenter knows that there are no individual differences between participants in the conditions. In the independent groups design, the experimenter *hopes* that the random allocation of participants to conditions achieves this. A further discussion of these advantages and disadvantages can be found in Coolican (1995).

In order to maximise comparability between groups or conditions, experimenters also use *standardised experimental procedures and instructions*. These ensure the uniformity of experience and assessment and hopefully eliminate or control for any possible *confounding* (or *extraneous*) *variables* (factors other than the IV) which may operate across conditions. Psychologists are not, however, physicists or chemists and their subject matter cannot be controlled in exactly the same way (Humphreys, 1992). Experimental psychologists must, therefore, accept that there will always be some random fluctuations between the experiences of the participants, though hopefully these will be minor and unimportant (see Chapter 83).

experiments are typically conducted in university psychology departments, undergraduates are frequently used as participants. The findings laboratory experiments generate may not *generalise* to other groups of people because undergraduates are not a *representative sample*.

When people enter a laboratory, they have perceptions and expectations of what will happen to them and possibly how they are expected to behave, which Orne (1962) calls *demand characteristics*. Some participants try to behave in a way that they think will confirm the experimenter's hypothesis. Others, however, behave in a way which they think will disconfirm the experimenter's hypothesis (the 'screw you' effect: Masling, 1966). Experimenters, too, may influence participants' behaviour. Such *experimenter effects* (Rosenthal, 1963) are usually unintentional and include things like non-verbal behaviours (such as a smile or frown) which are detected by participants.

Box 2.4   Single and double blind control

Demand characteristics and experimenter effects can be controlled for by using *single* and *double blind control*. In single blind control, participants are kept in ignorance as to the experiment's real purpose, sometimes by being told that the experiment has one purpose when another is intended (that is, participants are *deceived* in an attempt to control for demand characteristics). The ethical issues surrounding the use of deception in psychological investigation are discussed in detail in Chapter 85.

In double blind control, the experimenter conducting the experiment is unaware of the hypothesis being tested or the condition to which a participant has been allocated. In some research, this is achieved through the use of *placebos* (see Chapter 77, Box 77.6). If the experimenter is unaware of the hypothesis, then he or she cannot intentionally or unintentionally influence participants' behaviour.

FIELD AND NATURAL EXPERIMENTS

Although tightly controlled, the artificiality of the laboratory experiment means that it lacks *ecological validity* (the data from such experiments often have little relevance and application to behaviour in the 'real world'). The *field experiment* takes place in the real world. Like laboratory experiments, field experiments involve the manipulation of an IV to see its effects on a DV. Such experiments produce higher ecological validity, but at the expense of a loss of control over the IV, DV and confounding variables.

Because of this, field experiments are harder to replicate than laboratory experiments. They also raise ethical issues because at least some study people who do not know they are being studied. Finally, the results from field experiments may be difficult to generalise from the setting in which they took place to other settings. Notwithstanding these cautions, field experiments have been used extensively by social psychologists. For example, research into conformity (Chapter 58), obedience to authority (Chapter 59), and altruism and bystander behaviour (Chapter 62) have all made extensive use of the field experiment.

Box 2.5   Natural experiments

The natural experiment is similar to the field experiment in that it takes place in the real world. However, the experimenter does not control or manipulate the IV, but takes advantage of a fortuitous and naturally occurring division. For this reason, some researchers prefer to describe the natural experiment as *quasi-experimental*.

Natural experiments divide participants into different groups which are differentially exposed to the IV, but this division is not made by the experimenter. A good example of an ongoing naturalistic experiment can be found in Chapter 64 (see Box 64.5) in which researchers are investigating the effects on social behaviour of the introduction of television to a society which previously did not have it.

As with field experiments, natural experiments have high ecological validity, but this advantage over the laboratory experiment is offset by the loss of control over possible confounding variables.

Observation

NATURALISTIC OBSERVATION

There are several types of observational study. In *naturalistic observation*, the researcher observes behaviour in its natural environment and does not attempt to interfere with what is being observed. Indeed, the best type of observational research is that in which those being observed are not aware of this, because it avoids *participant reactivity*. Naturalistic observation is very different from an experiment in which researchers deliberately alter an environment and then observe the effects of this on behaviour.

Observers do not rely on their own impressions or memories. Rather, they have some way of recording, as objectively as possible, the behaviour being observed. One of the main weaknesses with naturalistic observation is *observer bias*. As Chapter 31 illustrates, studies of the accuracy of eyewitness testimony indicate that observation is often far from reliable, and that observers may distort what they see so that it conforms to what they expect to see.

Box 2.6   Intra- and inter-observer reliability

By using careful and systematic recording, and having more than one observer observing the same behaviour, researchers are more likely to obtain an accurate and objective description of the observed behaviour. The use of careful and systematic recording increases *intra-observer reliability* (the consistency of observation by the same observer on different occasions). Having more than one observer allows *inter-observer reliability* (consistency of observation between different observers watching the same behaviour) to be assessed.

Naturalistic observation is used extensively in developmental and social psychology, and the chapters in Units 4 and 5 describe the findings of many studies using this method. The observational study of non-humans in their natural environment is called *ethology*, and was pioneered in the 1930s by Lorenz (see Clamp & Russell, 1998). The results of ethologists' observations, which try to give as complete a description of a particular form of non-humans' behaviour as possible, are called *ethograms*.

CONTROLLED OBSERVATION

In *controlled observation*, the researcher attempts to structure or influence the behaviour or response to be observed. As with the distinction between natural and field experiments (see page 20), the emphasis is not on the setting but on the natural occurrence of the event (Humphreys, 1992). A good example of this research is Ainsworth *et al.*'s (1971) study of babies in what is called the 'strange situation' (see Chapter 38, page 329).

PARTICIPANT OBSERVATION

Another observational method involves the researcher becoming a part of the 'thing' being observed. This is called participant observation, and has been extensively employed to investigate the processes occurring in particular groups. An observer might try to 'blend in' with the group and act as another member. For example, Festinger *et al.* (1956) used the former approach to study how an 'end-of-the-world' group would react when the world failed to end on the date they had predicted.

Alternatively, the observer might try to enter the group in a special capacity This was used by Whyte (1943) in his story of an Italian gang in Chicago. Since he was unable to pass himself off as a group member, Whyte told the group's leader he was writing a book on the area and used this as his 'cover'. In both Festinger *et al.*'s and Whyte's research (and other observational research), observers face the ethical issue of *disclosure*. People's behaviour changes when they know they are being observed, so the genuineness of observations can be lost if those being observed are aware of the observer's real intentions. However, by not revealing their intentions, observers are *deceiving* those being observed (see Chapter 85).

An important decision observers have to make is how they will classify, record and analyse behaviour, the *validity* of the observations made (the extent to which they are meaningful) being an obvious and important consideration. Once this decision has been reached, they must then decide how to sample the behaviour to be observed.

Box 2.7   Some ways of categorising behaviour for observation

- In *specimen description*, the observer makes as full an account as possible of behaviour in a chosen segment of an individual's life, by recording what is happening, the context in which it is happening, and the other people involved. This is a time-consuming method and there are frequently problems concerning the reliability of the observation and observer effects.

- *Event sampling* focuses on a specific behaviour and records the number of times it occurs, the context in which it occurs, and the events surrounding it. Event sampling saves time where the behaviour recorded occurs infrequently and is especially good for preserving the context in which the event occurs.

- *Time sampling* is more suitable when the behaviour being observed occurs relatively frequently. The researcher observes for a period and then records the observations for another period. The presence or absence of behaviour during each observation interval can be recorded to give an idea of how frequently it occurs. By varying the time intervals for observations, researchers can give full attention to what they are observing and gain an important impression of how, say, a particular group is operating.

- The *target time method* uses time as a criterion. Observation occurs for a specified time period, and at specified and predetermined times the behaviour occurring is recorded. This technique is particularly

---

useful for reducing distraction, as it ensures that the behaviour is recorded evenly and according to the given criteria.

(Based on Humphreys, 1992)

Observational studies are useful in providing new ideas and suggestions for research which can be systematically tested in the future. They also provide the opportunity to see how particular actions fit into the overall flow of behaviour, and are higher in ecological validity than contrived experimental manipulations (although not all observational studies are non-interventionist or carried out in non-laboratory settings).

However, observers have no control over what they are observing, and cannot tell those being observed to stop behaving in some way because it is not the behaviour the observer wants to study. Also, each natural situation is a once only occurrence, and it is impossible to make general statements based on information from one observational study. Finally, observation is descriptive rather than explanatory, which provides a weak basis for drawing conclusions about why behaviour occurs, and observational studies do not tell us what caused particular behaviours.

Case studies

Case studies are in-depth investigations of a single 'unit'. Typically, the 'unit' is a person, but it can be a single event or community. Data are gathered about a case using various methods such as careful observation, psychometric testing (see Chapter 82), self- and other-report, and so on. The data collected may include all sorts of information relating to the past and present that will help provide insight into the case being investigated.

Case studies may also use the *diary method*. This involves the daily recording of descriptions and observations of the behaviour of a specific person. Piaget kept detailed diaries of the developmental processes he observed in his own children, and from these was able to construct part of his theory of cognitive development (see Chapter 41).

Case studies are used in three main ways. First, the method is an essential part of understanding and helping people with mental disorders. Therapies originated by Freud (see Chapter 73) were developed almost entirely on the basis of case studies. A second use is to illustrate psychological principles. Case studies feature throughout this book precisely for that reason (see, for example,

Boxes 7.6, 29.3 and 30.1). Third, the case study is an important research tool. It is primarily used to suggest theories or hypotheses about behaviour (see Box 27.5).

Box 2.8   Case studies: other advantages and limitations

- Case studies provide in-depth information about a person. They often shed light on things that are unethical or impractical to study in other ways. The extensive evidence gathered may provide an important way of illustrating a theory or supporting an argument. When used clinically and over long periods of time, they enable researchers to explore important variables and relationships between them in detail.

- Case studies lack control over important variables. The 'unit' studied may not be representative or typical and so the findings cannot be generalised. There is the potential for observer and participant bias. The case study is an unconvincing basis for establishing relationships between variables.

Surveys

Case studies generate a great deal of information about a single 'unit'. Surveys provide researchers with a limited amount of information about various groups of people. Survey data are typically collected either through a face-to-face *interview* or in written form using *questionnaires*. Questionnaires may contain a few or thousands of questions, and may be multiple-choice, true–false, or open-ended. They can be completed alone or in the researcher's presence.

Researchers first identify the *population* (those to whom the findings will apply) of people they wish to survey. Then, using statistical methods, a random but *representative sample* of that population is selected. One well-known survey was conducted by Kinsey *et al.* (1948) who were interested in the sexual behaviour of Americans. Amongst other things they asked people about were the types of sexual behaviour they engaged in, the frequency with which they practised them and the number of partners they had had. The data were surprising, and showed that pre-marital sex was more common than generally believed.

Both interviews and questionnaires have advantages and limitations. Because questionnaires are often anonymous, people are more likely to respond truthfully than if the same questions are posed by an interviewer. Questionnaires are also cheaper and quicker than interviews. Interviews, however, have the advantage of being flexible, and an interviewer can clarify questions and vary their sequence. Good interviewers can establish a rapport with their interviewees, although there is the danger of biased interpretation (see, for example, Chapter 76).

When used properly, a survey is a valuable research tool. Like other non-experimental methods, though, the conclusions that can be drawn are primarily descriptive, and surveys do not explain the behaviour they describe.

Box 2.9   Surveys: other advantages and limitations

- Surveys allow researchers to obtain information from more people than can practically be studied in the laboratory. They may also require less investment in terms of time and financial resources. Surveys are an effective means of measuring actions, attitudes, preferences, opinions and intentions.

- The results of a survey can only be generalised to the population from which the sample was drawn. Kinsey *et al.*'s research, for example, under-represented the lower socioeconomic classes and rural segments of America, and the sample contained no black Americans. The reliability of the responses given is difficult to determine, and self-report may be an inaccurate measure of actual behaviour. Surveys provide only limited insights about factors contributing to people's behaviour and attitudes.

Correlation

Strictly speaking, correlation is not a research method. Rather, it is a way of treating or analysing data gathered by other means. However, this does not mean that data cannot be specifically gathered for the purpose of a correlational investigation. Laboratory studies and psychometric tests, for example, can be used to gather data for correlation.

Correlation is a widely used investigative tool which summarises the *relationship* between two (and sometimes more) measurable variables. Basic correlational studies use paired measurements. Sometimes, individual participants provide pairs of measurements. At other times, logical pairs are used, as is the case when the relationship between the intelligence levels of monozygotic twins is assessed (see Chapter 43). Both twins provide an intelligence test score and, with pairs of scores provided by other twins, the correlation between them is examined.

With experiments, it is important to distinguish between the IV and DV. In correlation, this distinction loses its usefulness, since correlational analysis can assess the relationship between DVs or between an IV and a DV. The correlational method does not require the IV/DV distinction to be made.

Two variables are correlated when changes in the value of one are associated with changes in the value of the other. One way to illustrate the strength of a relationship between two variables is by means of a scattergram, in which the data obtained for one variable are plotted against the corresponding data for the other variable.

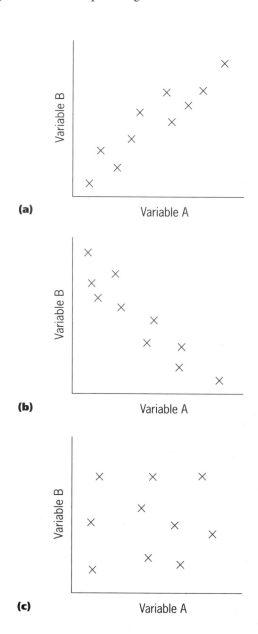

Figure 2.1   Three scattergrams showing (a) positive correlation, (b) negative correlation and (c) no correlation

As Figure 2.1 (a) shows, high scores on one variable (such as the amount of time spent revising) are generally associated with high scores on the other (such as marks obtained in an exam). When a rise or fall in the value of one variable tends to be accompanied by a rise or fall in the other, a *positive* (or *direct*) correlation exists. When a rise or fall on the two variables are exactly related, the correlation is *perfectly positive*.

In Figure 2.1 (b), high values on one variable (such as a measure of interest in money) are associated with low values on the other (such as a measure of interest in sharing and giving to others). When a rise on one variable tends to be accompanied by a fall on the other, a *negative* (or *inverse*) *correlation* exists. When a rise on one variable is accompanied by an exact corresponding fall on the other, the correlation is *perfectly negative*. In Figure 2.1 (c), there is no systematic relationship between the two variables (as would be the case if social security numbers were plotted against intelligence test scores), and no correlation exists. Scattergrams also indicate the strength of correlation between two variables, as shown in Figure 2.2 (a–d).

A more convenient way to describe the strength of correlation between two variables is numerically, using a *correlation coefficient*. Several techniques for determining a correlation coefficient exist (see, for example, Coolican, 1995). The most common techniques produce a coefficient varying between −1.0 and +1.0. The mathematical sign indicates the *direction* of the correlation (negative or positive), whilst the value indicates its *strength*. The correlation coefficient is 0 when there is no correlation between the variables, and 1.0 when the correlation is perfect.

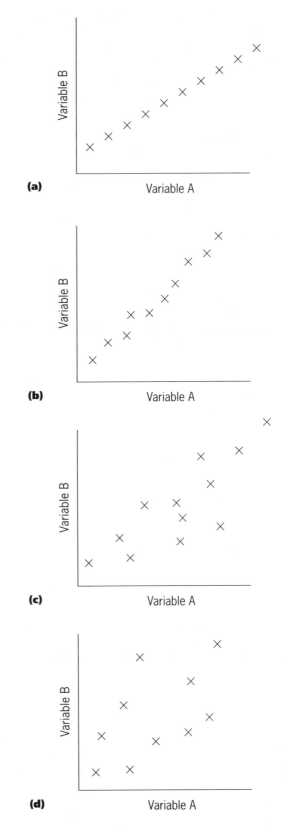

(a) Variable A

(b) Variable A

(c) Variable A

(d) Variable A

Figure 2.2   Four scattergrams showing (a) perfect positive correlation, (b) strong positive correlation, (c) moderate positive correlation and (d) weak positive correlation

---

Box 2.10   Correlation and prediction

The stronger the correlation between two variables, the greater is the accuracy in predicting performance on one variable from a knowledge of performance on the other (irrespective of whether the correlation is positive or negative). The *coefficient of determination* tells us the proportion of the total variance in a data set attributable to the correlation between two variables (Sutherland, 1991) and is obtained by squaring the correlation coefficient, multiplying by one hundred and expressing this as a percentage.

For example, with a correlation of 0.9, 81 per cent of the variance can be accounted for by the correlation. This means that predicting performance on one variable, if performance on the other is known, is quite accurate. A correlation of 0.5, though, means that only 25 per cent of the variance can be accounted for by the correlation and that prediction will be much less accurate.

The correlation coefficient is a descriptive measure of the strength of relationship between two variables, but does not indicate whether the relationship is statistically significant (see Box 2.3). Statistical tests for a correlation do this, but the statistical significance of a correlation is influenced by several factors other than the correlation coefficient (Humphreys, 1992).

Correlation is a useful method when experimentation is not the most practical method to use, and can give important information about the relationship between variables in the real world. However, correlational studies do not allow *causality* to be inferred as the experiment does. Just because two variables are correlated, it does not necessarily mean that changes in one are the cause of changes in the other. The variables may be accidentally correlated and caused by some other, as yet unknown, variable.

Smoking and lung cancer are correlated, and this correlation is very probably causal. On the basis of a correlation alone, however, it is not legitimate to conclude that smoking causes lung cancer (and it would be just as illegitimate to conclude that lung cancer causes people to smoke on the basis of a correlation between them). Both smoking and lung cancer may be due to a third factor (personality) correlated with both, a suggestion first made by Eysenck (Gray, 1997).

Similarly, a correlation exists between being authoritarian, dogmatic and rigid, and being prejudiced against ethnic groups (see Chapter 53). This could mean that being authoritarian causes people to be prejudiced (as some researchers have claimed), but it could also be that other things (such as social class norms) produce both authoritarianism and ethnic prejudice (Brown, 1965).

Box 2.11   Non-linear, multiple and partial correlation

Some variables are correlated in a non-linear (non-straight-line) fashion. In the case of familiarity with and liking for forenames, for example, the relationship is *curvilinear* (Colman *et al.*, 1981).

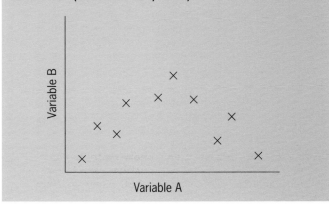

The strength of such correlations cannot be assessed using the techniques that apply to linear (straight-line) correlations, and more sophisticated techniques are required.

Sometimes, researchers are interested in the relationship between three or more variables. Here, *multiple correlational analysis* is necessary. Alternatively, the relationship between two variables, when the effect of a third variable related to them both is controlled for, may be of interest. In this case, a *partial correlational technique* is needed. Again, techniques for assessing multiple and partial correlations exist. As with curvilinear relationships, though, such techniques are quite complex.

Conclusions

This chapter has examined five main methods used in psychological research. The experiment is a powerful tool because it allows cause and effect to be established, which no other method does. However, the experiment also has limitations associated with it. Non-experimental approaches also have limitations, but a great many strengths are associated with them.

Summary

■ Five main methods used in psychological research are experiments, observation, case studies, surveys and correlations. Each has associated strengths and weaknesses.

■ Only **experiments** permit talk of cause and effect. Experimentation begins with the formulation of an operationally defined and testable hypothesis.

■ In the simplest type of experiment, there are two conditions. In one, participants are exposed to the IV, whilst in the other they are not. Because all other factors are held constant, any difference in a behavioural measure (the DV) can be attributed to the IV.

■ **Laboratory experiments** involve a high degree of control over possible extraneous and confounding variables. However, the laboratory is an artificial environment, low in **ecological validity**. Since laboratory experiments often use unrepresentative samples, their data cannot be generalised to other groups.

■ **Field experiments** have greater ecological validity, but lack of control over potential extraneous and confounding variables makes them harder to replicate than laboratory experiments. They also raise ethical issues (because people are sometimes unaware they are part of an experiment), and their findings may not generalise from the setting in which the experiment took place.

■ **Natural experiments** do not involve manipulation of an IV (unlike laboratory and field experiments). Instead, the experimenter takes advantage of a naturally occurring division. Such experiments have high ecological validity, but suffer from the same weaknesses as field experiments.

■ There are several types of **observational study**, including naturalistic, controlled and participant. Good observational research avoids **participant reactivity** and **observer bias**. The use of careful and systematic recording of observational data increases **intra-observer reliability**. **Inter-observer reliability** can be enhanced by having several observers observe the same behaviour.

■ Observational studies provide new ideas and suggestions for further research which can be systematically tested later. They are also higher in ecological validity than contrived experimental manipulations. Weaknesses of observational research include lack of control over what is being observed, and the impossibility of making general statements based on information from one observational study. Observation is descriptive rather than explanatory, and observations cannot tell us what causes particular behaviours to occur.

■ **Case studies** are in-depth investigations of a single 'unit', (a person, event or community). Information is collected about a case using various sources/approaches. One use of case studies is in understanding and helping people with mental disorders. Another is to illustrate psychological principles. They are also important research tools used to suggest theories or hypotheses about behaviour.

■ Although useful in many respects, case studies lack control over important variables (so cannot be used to establish relationships between variables) and are prone to both observer and participant bias. Cases may not be representative and so the findings cannot be generalised.

■ **Surveys** provide researchers with a limited amount of information about various groups of people. Survey data are collected by means of **interviews** or **questionnaires**. Questionnaires are cheaper and quicker than interviews and, because questionnaires are usually anonymous, respondents are more likely to respond truthfully. Interviews, however, are more flexible.

■ Whilst surveys are an effective means of measuring actions, attitudes, opinions and so on, the data they produce can only be generalised to the population from which the sample was drawn. The reliability of survey data is also questionable, and self-reports may be an inaccurate measure of actual behaviour.

■ Whilst **correlation** is not strictly a research method, correlational studies enable researchers to summarise the relationship between variables. Basic correlational research uses paired measurements, sometimes provided by participants and sometimes by logical pairs.

■ Two variables are correlated when changes in the value of one are associated with changes in the value of the other. Correlation can be **positive** (a rise or fall in the value of one variable is associated with a rise or fall in the value of the other), **negative** (a rise in one variable is accompanied by a fall in the other), or of a more complex form (such as **curvilinear**).

■ The direction and strength of a correlation is indicated by the **correlation coefficient**. The stronger the correlation between two variables, the more accurately the value of one can be predicted if the value of the other is known.

■ Unlike the experiment, correlational studies do not allow causality to be inferred, Variables may be accidentally correlated and caused by some other, unknown, variable.

UNIT 2

Biopsychology

PART 1

Basic neural and hormonal processes and their influences on behaviour

3

THE NERVOUS SYSTEM AND NEURONAL ACTIVITY

Introduction and overview

The nervous system (NS) is the network of all the nerve cells in the human body. It enables us to receive, process, and transmit information originating both within and outside the body and is, therefore, our primary communication system. The NS can be divided into two major components, the *central nervous system* (CNS) and the *peripheral nervous system* (PNS). The CNS consists of the *brain* and *spinal cord*, and is the point of origin of all complex commands, decisions and evaluations. The CNS is examined in detail in Chapter 4.

The PNS has two functions. The first is sending information *to* the CNS from the outside world, muscles and organs. The second is sending messages *from* the CNS to all of the body's muscles and glands. The PNS and its interaction with the *endocrine system*, the system that secretes hormones into the body's bloodstream, is considered in Chapter 5.

The NS is a complicated network of electrical and chemical events. This chapter examines the NS's composition and two of the main cell types found in it (*glial cells* and *neurons*). Since neurons are the basic structural units or 'building blocks' of the NS, and involved in all aspects of an organism's behaviour, particular attention will be paid to them. After describing a typical neuron's structure, the chapter looks in depth at the way in which neurons work, that is, how they *function* within the NS. As will be seen, information is communicated between neurons biochemically, involving *neurotransmitters* and *neuromodulators*. The final part of this chapter considers their role in behaviour.

Glial cells and neurons

A neuron is a cell that processes and transmits information. The human NS has ten to twelve billion neurons (or nerve cells) 80 per cent of which are found in the *brain*, particularly its topmost outer layer, the *cerebral cortex* (see Chapter 7). The NS also contains many more smaller cells called *glial cells* whose functions are summarised in Box 3.1.

Box 3.1   Some functions of glial cells

- supplying nutrients and providing structural support to neurons, thereby directing their growth;

- insulating neurons by forming myelin sheaths (see Box 3.2);

- removing debris following a cell's death and providing the brain with a barrier to certain substances from the bloodstream. This protects the brain from

---

the harmful effects of substances sometimes carried in the blood.

There are three main types of neuron. *Sensory* (or *afferent*) neurons respond directly to external stimuli such as light, sound and touch, and transmit this information to the CNS. *Motor* (or *efferent*) neurons carry messages from the CNS to the muscles and glands of the body. *Association* (or *connector*) neurons integrate the activities of these neurons. Any neuron not classified as sensory or motor and which transmits messages to other neurons is an association neuron. They constitute about 97 per cent of the neurons in the CNS, which is the only part of the NS where they are found.

The reflex

The role played by different types of neuron can be illustrated using the *reflex*. Accidentally touching a hot stove is painful, and we react quickly by withdrawing the hand. The temperature change is detected by sensory neurons which pass this information to association neurons. These pass the information to motor neurons which instruct muscles to remove the hand. This *reflex arc* occurs quickly, because of the speed at which information is passed. Some neural impulses travel very slowly, at around two to three miles per hour. In a reflex action, however, the impulses travel at over 200 miles per hour. So, a message takes about one fiftieth of a second to reach the brain from the toe.

The reflex is made even quicker because its production actually bypasses the brain. Of course, information about painful stimuli reaches the brain, but because it takes longer to arrive there than for the reflex arc to be completed, the hand has been withdrawn before pain is felt. In evolutionary terms this is very useful: the hand has been removed before too much damage has been sustained, but because we have experienced *some* pain we learn that certain stimuli (such as hot stoves) should not be touched in the future.

Suppose, however, that you are carrying a very hot plate using worn-out oven gloves. From what has been said, you might expect that motor neurons controlling the hands would cause you to drop the plate. This sometimes happens, but on at least some occasions we are able to carry the plate to a suitable surface before removing our hands. How do you think we achieve this? (see page 32)

The principle used to describe a simple reflex also applies to more complicated behaviours. Consider the neuronal activity involved in responding correctly to a question about, say, neurons. Sensory neurons record the sound waves and the information is interpreted in the part of the brain that deals with auditory information. To recall the answer, association neurons involved in memory are activated. Neurons associated with language formulate an answer and motor neurons in the tongue and mouth excite the correct muscle groups to produce a response.

THE STRUCTURE OF NEURONS

Although no two neurons are identical, most share the same basic structure and work in essentially the same way. A typical neuron is shown in Figure 3.1. The *cell body* (or *soma*) houses the nucleus of the cell (containing the genetic code) and controls the cell's metabolism and maintenance. Branching out from the cell body are *dendrites*. These receive information from other neurons and carry it *towards* the cell body. The *axon* transmits messages *away* from the cell body to other neurons, muscles or gland cells. Axons vary in size. Those running from the brain to the base of the spinal cord, and from the spinal cord to the tip of the thumb, may be three feet in length. By contrast, axons in the cerebral cortex are often less than one ten-thousandth of an inch in length.

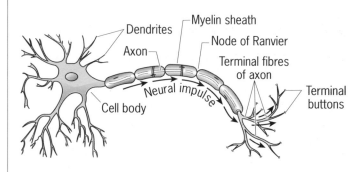

Figure 3.1   A typical neuron

A group of axons bundled together is called a *nerve* if it occurs in the PNS and a *tract* if it occurs in the CNS. Humans have 43 pairs of peripheral nerves, one nerve from each pair on the left side of the body and one on the right. These are considered further in Chapter 5.

Box 3.2   Myelin sheath and Nodes of Ranvier

Some nerves are coated with *myelin sheath*. This is part protein and part fat and consists of the membranes of a type of glial cell called the *Schwann cell*. These expand and wrap repeatedly around the axon. The principal function of myelin sheath is to *insulate* axons from one another and from ions found in the fluids encasing the NS. By insulating axons from one another, myelin sheath helps to prevent neurons from 'scrambling' messages. It also helps them act with greater efficiency, since Schwann cells speed up information transmission. In some people, the myelin sheath surrounding the axon breaks down. This produces *multiple sclerosis*, which is characterised by severe movement disorders and sensory functions, eventually leading to death.

The myelin sheath surrounding an axon is segmented rather than continuous, so that at the *Nodes of Ranvier* the axon is exposed rather than insulated. As will be seen, this also enables information to be transmitted faster than if the myelin sheath was continuous.

THE FUNCTION OF NEURONS

Neurons have three major functions. These are receiving, responding to, and sending messages. To understand these functions, we need to know how information travels *within* a single neuron and how it is transmitted *between* neurons or from neurons to other cells.

The transmission of information within a neuron

Inactive neurons (those not transmitting information) contain positively charged potassium ions and large, negatively charged protein molecules. The fluid surrounding a neuron, however, is richly concentrated in positively charged sodium ions and negatively charged chloride ions. The cell membrane keeps sodium ions out by the action of *sodium-potassium pumps* and the membrane is *impermeable* to sodium ions. However, potassium and chloride ions can move in and out of the cell membrane fairly freely and the membrane is *semipermeable* to them. The net result is that when it is inactive (in its *resting state*) a neuron is *polarised* and the inside of the cell is negatively charged relative to the outside by about 70 millivolts (70 thousandths of a volt).

When a neuron is activated by a stimulus, the sodium channels open for about one millisecond and the neuron becomes *permeable* to sodium ions which flood into it. This causes the neuron to become *depolarised* and the charge inside it momentarily changes from the resting state value of –70 millivolts to an active state of about +40 millivolts. This is called the *action potential* and has a value of 110 millivolts (the difference between –70 and +40 millivolts). A chain reaction is then set off in which the sodium channels open at adjacent sites all the way down the axon. However, almost as soon as these channels open they close again, and potassium channels open

instead. This allows potassium to move *out* through the membrane and restores the resting state potential of –70 millivolts.

This sequence of events applies to *unmyelinated* neurons. As was seen earlier, however, the sheath surrounding the axon of myelinated neurons is segmented with uninsulated Nodes of Ranvier. With myelinated neurons, the electrochemical action potential 'leaps' from one node to another (*saltatory conduction*). This allows information to be conducted faster than if the myelin sheath was continuous or the fibre unmyelinated. An impulse's speed, then, is in part determined by the presence or absence of myelin sheath. It is also determined by an axon's diameter, because impulses travel faster down thick than thin axons.

To cause a neuron to respond, a stimulus must be of a certain intensity. A stimulus which is not strong enough might cause a shift in the electrical charge in a small area of the neuron, a phenomenon called a *graded potential*, and after a very brief time the neuron returns to its normal resting state. However, when a stimulus is sufficiently strong to exceed the neuron's *threshold of excitation* an action potential occurs.

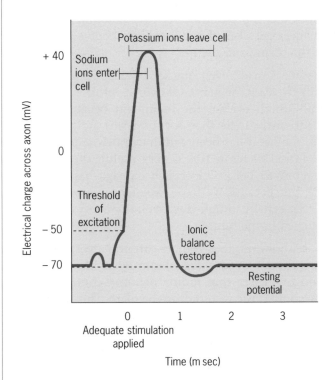

Figure 3.2   The sequence of events when a neuron 'fires'. The small 'bump' on the left represents an incoming message that was not strong enough to cause the neuron to fire

There is always a brief period of one or two milliseconds during which a neuron that has just 'fired' will not 'fire' again irrespective of the size of the stimulus. This is called the *absolute refractory period* (ARP) and is followed by another brief period of a few milliseconds called the *relative refractory period* (RRP). The RRP is a 'time of recovery' for the neuron during which sodium cannot pass through the neuronal membrane. A neuron will fire during the RRP, but only if the stimulus applied to it is considerably stronger than its threshold of response. Some neurons can fire as many as 1000 times a second whereas others can only fire a few times a second.

The transmission of information between neurons

The way neurons communicate with one another can be explained by looking at what happens to the action potential once it has passed down the axon. For a small number of neurons, the axon transmits information *directly* to the cell body of another neuron. However, for most neurons an action potential's journey along the axon ends with its arrival at a *terminal button* (see Figure 3.3). These house tiny sacs called *synaptic vesicles*, which contain between ten and 100,000 molecules of chemical messengers called *neurotransmitters*.

Terminal buttons approach, but do not touch, the other cells of the body (that is, other neurons, muscles or glands). The electrochemical message sent down the axon stimulates the synaptic vesicles to discharge their neuro-transmitters into the microscopic gap between the terminal button and a receiving neuron's dendrite. The gap between them is called the *synaptic cleft* or *synapse* and a neurotransmitter takes only one ten-thousandth of a second to make this journey.

The end of the terminal button releasing the neurotransmitter molecules is called the *pre-synaptic membrane*, and the dendrite of the neuron receiving the molecules the

post-synaptic membrane. The latter contains special *receptor sites* made of complex protein molecules. These act as 'locks' and are precisely tailored to match the shape of the neurotransmitter molecules which act as 'keys'.

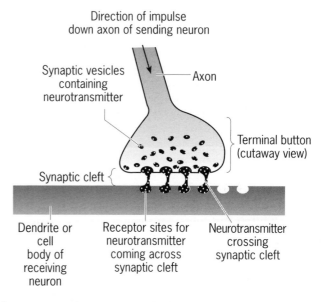

Figure 3.3   The processes involved in synaptic transmission

Several dozen neurotransmitters have been discovered. They are not randomly distributed throughout the brain but are located in specific groups of neurons. Indeed, more than one neurotransmitter can be released from the same terminal button depending on the *pattern* of the action potential which reaches it, a phenomenon called *cotransmission* (McCrohan, 1996).

Neurotransmitters have an *excitatory* and/or *inhibitory* effect on receiving neurons. Excitatory neurotransmitters cause a 'local breakdown' in the cell membrane of a receiving neuron. This allows sodium ions to flood in and potassium ions to flood out and makes the receiving neuron more positively charged and more likely to 'fire'. Inhibitory neurotransmitters have the opposite effect, and so receiving neurons become even more negatively charged and much less likely to 'fire'. The effects of a neurotransmitter depend on how much of it there is. If no more of a neurotransmitter crosses the synaptic cleft, its effects on a receiving neuron quickly fade.

A neuron may have hundreds of dendrites and terminal buttons. As a result, it can be 'in touch' with many other neurons at both its input (dendritic) end and its output (terminal button) end. Some of the neurons that form synapses with a receiving neuron will be excitatory and some inhibitory. The 'decision' to 'fire' or not depends on the *combined* effects of all the neurons with which a receiving neuron forms synapses.

Box 3.4   Summation, excitation and inhibition

An equal number of excitatory and inhibitory neurons cancel each other out and a neuron will not fire. The combined effect of enough excitatory synapses may be sufficient to exceed the threshold of response, a process called *summation*. Inhibitory synapses are important because they help to control the spread of excitation through the highly interconnected NS. This keeps activity channelled in appropriate networks or 'circuits'. Epileptic seizures might be caused by the simultaneous excitation of many different brain circuits. Inhibition may actually prevent all of us from having seizures much of the time. As another (more mundane) example, consider the action of flexing the arm. This could not be achieved if the neurons controlling the triceps were inhibited and those controlling the biceps excited.

Although many neurons communicate exclusively with other neurons, some form synapses with glands and muscles (see page 29). All of the muscle fibres with which a motor neuron forms synapses contract with a brief twitch when an axon transmits a message. The strength of a muscular contraction therefore depends on the number of motor neurons whose action potentials cause the release of neurotransmitters. Whether a muscle contracts or not, or glandular activity is initiated or inhibited, depends on which neurotransmitters are released.

Excitation and inhibition can explain why we are able to carry a very hot plate to a convenient surface rather than reflexively dropping it (see page 29). Hot objects increase the activity of excitatory neurotransmitters that communicate with motor neurons controlling the hand's muscles. However, this excitation is counteracted by neurons in the brain which release inhibitory neurotransmitters. The activity of the inhibitory neurons is greater than that of the excitatory neurons and the brain prevents the withdrawal reflex from occurring. Hence we do not drop the plate.

A neurotransmitter's effect is ended either by *de-activation*, in which it is destroyed by special enzymes, or, much more commonly, by *re-uptake*. Re-uptake occurs very quickly and neurotransmitters have only a very brief time in which to stimulate the post-synaptic receptor sites. The rate at which a terminal button takes back its neurotransmitter determines how long its effects will last for. Psychoactive drugs affect the nervous system by altering the rate of neurotransmitter re-uptake (see Chapter 15). If a drug inhibits the process of re-uptake, the neurotransmitter remains in the synaptic cleft for a longer period of time and continues to stimulate the post-synaptic receptor sites. The inhibition of re-uptake, then, *increases* the effect of the neurotransmitter.

Some neurotransmitters and neuromodulators

NEUROTRANSMITTERS

The vast majority of neurotransmitters play an important role in the communication between neurons in the brain. Neurotransmitters are not, however, found exclusively in the brain. They are found elsewhere in the body, including the spinal cord, peripheral nerves and certain glands.

Acetylcholine

Acetylcholine (ACh) is excitatory at synapses between nerves and muscles that control voluntary movement, and inhibitory at the heart and other locations. ACh occurs at every junction between a motor neuron and a muscle. When it is released to muscle cells, the muscle contracts.

Curare, a poison used in hunting by South American Indians, prevents ACh from lodging in receptor sites. This causes paralysis and death by suffocation since the victim cannot contract the muscles used in breathing. Certain nerve gases and insecticides also affect ACh and cause fatal muscular paralysis. They do this by destroying the enzyme *acetylcholinesterase* (AChE) which ordinarily deactivates ACh. As a result of ACh build-up, further synaptic transmissions are prevented. The *Botulinum toxin*, a poison present in improperly canned food, blocks the release of ACh. Less than one millionth of a gram can paralyse and kill a human. By contrast, the venom of the Black Widow spider causes large amounts of ACh to be released, which induces violent muscle contractions in a victim.

ACh is particularly concentrated in the *hippocampus* (see page 40) which plays a role in memory. ACh has been implicated in *Alzheimer's disease*, which is characterised by a gradual impairment in memory and other cognitive functions as a result of a progressive deterioration of ACh-producing neurons. Drugs that increase the amount of brain ACh (such as *choline*, a chemical found in our diet) facilitate learning and memory. However, drugs that block the post-synaptic ACh receptors and prevent ACh from having any action, appear to disrupt learning and memory.

Dopamine

Dopamine is primarily inhibitory and is involved in voluntary movements, learning, memory and arousal. Deficiencies have been linked to *Parkinson's disease*, a disorder in which the sufferer progressively loses muscle control, and is characterised by muscle tremors and jerky, uncoordinated movements. In Parkinson's disease, dopamine-producing neurons degenerate. The disease cannot be treated using dopamine since it is unable to cross the bloodstream–brain barrier. However, its progress can be slowed by the drug *L-dopa* which the brain converts to dopamine.

Box 3.5 Dopamine and schizophrenia

Dopamine has also been implicated in *schizophrenia*. Schizophrenics might have more receptor sites for dopamine in parts of the brain involved in emotion and thought. Possibly, dopamine is over-utilised in the schizophrenic brain and it is this which causes its characteristic symptoms of hallucinations, thought disorder and emotional disturbances (see Chapter 68). Interestingly, some drugs used to treat schizophrenia block dopamine's action by locking it out of the receptor sites it tries to occupy (see page 31).

Serotonin

Serotonin is primarily inhibitory and believed to play a role in emotional arousal and sleep (see Chapter 12). Deficiencies have been linked to anxiety, mood disorders (see Chapter 69) and insomnia. Elevated levels have also been linked to mood disturbances and other disorders such as *autism* (see Chapter 80). Serotonin's exact role, and whether it acts independently or with other neurotransmitters, is not yet clear.

Noradrenaline

Noradrenaline (or *norepinephrine*) is produced mainly by neurons in the brain stem. It acts as both a neurotransmitter and a *hormone* (see Chapter 5, Box 5.5). Noradrenaline increases heart rate and other bodily processes involved in general arousal. It has also been implicated in learning, memory and the stimulation of eating. Both excesses and deficiencies of noradrenaline have been linked to mood disorders. *Reserpine*, which reduces the amount of noradrenaline by preventing it from being stored in vesicles, has a potent tranquillising effect. *Amphetamines* (see Chapter 15), by contrast, increase the amount of noradrenaline that is released and has a stimulating effect.

Gamma-amino butyric acid

The most common inhibitory neurotransmitter in the NS is *gamma-amino butyric acid* (GABA). Although it is present in all parts of the NS, it is particularly concentrated in the brain, where it can be found in up to one third of terminal buttons. GABA plays a role in motor behaviour and in the inherited disease *Huntington's chorea*, in which involuntary movements are accompanied by a progressive deterioration in cognitive functions. Huntington's chorea may be caused by the degeneration of GABA-producing neurons in the part of the brain involved in motor control. GABA may also be involved in the modulation of *anxiety*, since anxiety-relieving drugs (such as *Valium*, see Chapter 72) increase GABA's activity.

NEUROMODULATORS

The term *neuromodulator* has been used to describe any chemical substance which 'primes' neurons so that they respond by either increasing or decreasing the action of specific neurotransmitters. The most intensely researched of these are *endogenous opioid peptides* or *endorphins* which were discovered during research into the effects of the pain-killing chemical *morphine* (see Chapter 15). Findings suggested that morphine exerts its effects by binding to certain receptor sites in the brain. Pert & Snyder (1973) reasoned that it was unlikely that the brain had evolved specific receptor sites to accommodate molecules from the opium poppy (from where morphine comes). They believed that the body must produce its own internal (or endogenous) morphine-like substance, hence the term endorphins.

Box 3.6 Endorphins and pain relief

Endorphins are inhibitory and once they have locked onto a receptor site, neurotransmitters are prevented from occupying it. Like morphine, endorphins relieve pain. One of them, B–*endorphin*, is 48 times more potent than morphine when injected into the brain, and three times more potent when injected into the bloodstream. Another, *encephalin*, inhibits receptors in the spinal cord and neurons that transmit pain messages. However, whilst encephalin shares the pain-relieving effect of other endorphins, it is somewhat weaker and shorter-acting. The release of endorphins may occur in response to painful stimuli, and endorphin levels have been shown to increase during pregnancy and further increase during labour. As well as relieving pain, endorphins may also play a role in hunger, sexual behaviour, mood regulation and body temperature.

Endorphins might explain the *placebo effect* (see Chapter 77). Inactive substances can relieve pain if a person believes that a pain-relieving drug has been taken. Levine *et al* (1979) studied dental patients shortly after they had been a given a placebo and undergone oral surgery. They were then given *naloxone* which blocks the pain-relieving effects of morphine. Naloxone increased the reported pain of those who had responded to the placebo, suggesting it had somehow caused the brain to release endorphins and naloxone had reversed their effect.

The role of neurotransmitters and neuromodulators is currently the subject of much research. However, the fact that endorphins are sometimes found in the same neurons as other neurotransmitters has complicated our understanding of the way in which neurotransmitters work. There is still a long way to go towards understanding the relationship between neurotransmitters, neuromodulators, mental processes and behaviour.

Conclusions

This chapter has looked at basic neural processes including the structure of neurons and how they transmit and receive information to and from a variety of sources. Neurotransmitters and neuromodulators are involved in the transmission and reception of information, and they affect our behaviour in many ways.

Summary

■ The nervous system (NS) enables us to receive, process and transmit information arising from both within and outside the body. The NS is divided into the **central nervous system (CNS)** and the **peripheral nervous system (PNS)**.

■ The human NS consists of 10–12 billion **neurons** (nerve cells), 80 per cent of which are found in the cerebral cortex. **Glial cells** have several functions, including insulating neurons by forming myelin sheaths and protecting the brain from harmful substances in the bloodstream.

■ **Sensory** (or **afferent**) **neurons** respond directly to external stimuli. **Motor** (or **efferent**) **neurons** carry messages from the CNS to the muscles and glands. **Association** (or **connector**) **neurons** integrate the activities of the first two. In the **reflex arc**, information passes quickly from sensory to association and then motor neurons, which instruct muscles to act.

■ All neurons share the same basic structure which includes the **cell body, dendrites** and the **axon**. Bundles of axons in the PNS are called **nerves**; in the CNS they are called **tracts**.

■ **Myelin sheath** insulates axons from each other and from ions in the surrounding fluid. This speeds up information transmission. The myelin sheath is segmented, with the axon exposed at the **Nodes of Ranvier**. This also speeds up information transmission.

■ Inactive neurons contain positively charged potassium ions and negatively charged protein molecules. The fluid surrounding a neuron contains positively charged sodium ions and negatively charged chloride ions. **Sodium-potassium pumps** keep sodium ions out of the neuron, but it is **semi-permeable** to potassium and chloride ions. This makes the neuron **polarised**.

■ When an unmyelinated neuron is activated, it becomes **permeable** to sodium ions, and the charge inside it changes from −70 millivolts to +40 millivolts (the **action potential**) all the way down the axon. In myelinated neurons, the action potential travels down the axon by **saltatory conduction**.

■ Action potentials only occur if a neuron's **threshold of response** is exceeded. Neurons either 'fire' or don't 'fire' (the **all-or-none rule**), and the stronger the stimulus, the more often a neuron fires. Neurons will not 'fire' during the **absolute refractory period**. They may 'fire' during the **relative refractory period**, depending on the strength of the stimulus.

■ For most neurons, action potentials travel to a terminal button containing **synaptic vesicles**. These release **neurotransmitters** from the **pre-synaptic membrane** into the **synapse**. The neurotransmitters travel to the receptor sites of the **post-synaptic membrane**.

■ Neurotransmitters have an **excitatory** and/or **inhibitory** effect on receiving neurons. A single neuron can be in contact with many other inhibitory or excitatory neurons. If there is an equal number of both kinds, a neuron will not fire. However, if enough excitatory neurons are active, their combined effect (**summation**) may be sufficient to exceed the threshold of response.

■ A neurotransmitter's effect is ended either by **de-activation** or **re-uptake**, the latter being more common. Psychoactive drugs affect the NS by altering the rate of re-uptake. When re-uptake is inhibited, a neurotransmitter's effect is prolonged.

■ **Acetylcholine** (ACh) is excitatory at synapses between nerves and muscles controlling voluntary movement, but inhibitory at the heart and other locations. Substances which destroy acetylcholinesterase (which normally deactivates ACh) produce paralysis. Alzheimer's disease may involve a progressive deterioration of ACh-producing neurons in the hippocampus, since drugs that increase the amount of brain ACh facilitate learning and memory.

■ **Dopamine** is primarily inhibitory and is involved in voluntary movements, learning, memory and arousal. A degeneration of dopamine-producing neurons has been implicated in Parkinson's disease. **L-dopa** is converted to dopamine by the brain. Dopamine has also been implicated in schizophrenia.

■ **Serotonin** is primarily inhibitory and is involved in emotional arousal and sleep. Deficiencies and excesses have been linked with mood disorders.

■ **Noradrenaline** acts as both a neurotransmitter and a **hormone**. It increases heart rate and other bodily processes involved in arousal. Drugs which increase noradrenaline's release, such as amphetamines, have a stimulating effect.

■ **Gamma-amino butyric acid** (GABA) is the most common inhibitory transmitter in the NS. Degeneration of GABA-producing neurons involved in motor control may be the cause of Huntington's chorea.

■ **Neuromodulators** prepare neurons to respond to the action of specific neurotransmitters. **Endogenous opioid peptides (endorphins)** are the body's own internal, morphine-like, painkillers. Their levels increase in response to painful stimuli and they are probably involved in the **placebo effect**.

THE CENTRAL NERVOUS SYSTEM

Introduction and overview

As noted in Chapter 3, the central nervous system (CNS) consists of the brain and spinal cord, and their primary function is to integrate and coordinate all body functions and behaviour. Knowledge of the relationship between the brain and behaviour is not new. In a surgical guide written in 3000 BC, an Egyptian physician described a patient with a fractured skull who displayed difficulty in walking. However, it is only in the last 100 years or so that our knowledge about the brain has advanced significantly.

This chapter looks at the organisation, structure and functioning of the CNS. It begins by looking briefly at the spinal cord, but the majority of this chapter describes what is known about the brain.

The spinal cord

The spinal cord is a thick column of nerve fibres that emerges from the bottom of the brain and runs down the whole length of the back. For protection, it is encased by bony structures called *spinal vertebrae*. There is no precise point at which the spinal cord ends and the brain begins, since the spinal cord widens as it enters the skull and becomes the brain stem.

The spinal cord is the main 'communication cable' between the CNS and PNS (see Chapter 5). Messages from neurons enter and leave the spinal cord by means of 31 pairs of *spinal nerves*, each of which innervates a different and fairly specific part of the body. Mostly, these nerve fibres contain both sensory neurons (to transmit information to the brain) and motor neurons (to convey the brain's response to the muscles and glands). At the junction with the spinal cord itself, however, the nerves divide into two *roots*. The *dorsal root* (towards the back of the body) contains sensory neurons, whereas the *ventral root* (towards the front of the body) contains motor neurons.

From a psychological perspective, the spinal cord is not as interesting as the brain. However, its importance to normal functioning cannot be underestimated. If the spinal cord is severed, paralysis occurs. The further up the spinal cord the damage occurs, the more extensive is the paralysis. The spinal cord is also involved in certain reflex actions. *Spinal reflexes* do not involve the brain and are mainly protective in that they enable the body to avoid serious damage and maintain muscle tone and posture. Some spinal reflexes involve only sensory and motor neurons. Most, however, are more complex than this. The example used in Chapter 3 of touching a hot stove also involves association neurons.

The brain

THE DEVELOPMENT OF THE BRAIN

There are two main ways in which the brain could be 'divided up' in order to examine its structures. Some researchers use MacLean's (1973, 1982) *triune model*. As its name suggests, the model identifies three main parts. The *central core* is the oldest, and MacLean calls it the *reptilian brain* because its structures in humans are virtually identical to those in the brains of existing reptiles. The *limbic system* is more recent than the central core, and developed in early mammals about 100 million years ago. MacLean calls it the *old mammalian brain*. The third part is the most recently evolved. The *cerebral cortex* developed in the last two million years, but only in some mammals. For that reason, MacLean calls it the *new mammalian brain*.

A second way of 'dividing' up the brain is to base the division on what happens during the foetal stage of life. In this, the nervous system's structure emerges from a single tube of neural tissue (the *neural tube*). The lower part will become the spinal cord. As the foetus develops, the lower part also puts out 'streaks' of neural tissue which will eventually become the PNS (see Chapter 5). The top of the tube swells into an enlargement that will become the brain. Growth occurs quickly, and three separate sections can be identified, although in the adult brain these are not as easy to distinguish. The lowest section of the upper end of the neural tube is called the *hindbrain*. The next, immediately above it, is the *midbrain*. The section at the very top is the *forebrain*.

This chapter uses the second way of 'dividing' up the brain as the basis for looking at its structures. All of these structures are present at birth, but require time to develop fully.

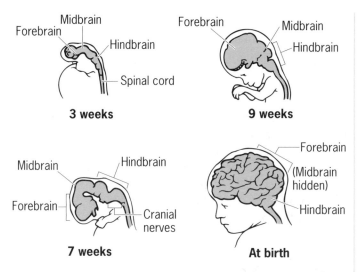

Figure 4.1   The human brain at four stages of development

Box 4.1   Brain size and weight

At birth, the brain has almost its full complement of neurons and is closer then to its adult size than any other organ. Neurons continue to grow after birth in terms of size and complexity rather than number. At six months, the development of synaptic connections between neurons, coupled with the development of glial cells and myelin sheath, results in the brain already being half its eventual adult weight. At one year, the brain is about 60 per cent of its eventual adult weight and by the age of ten this figure has risen to 95 per cent. The brain reaches its maximum weight (between 1200 and 1500 grams) by the age of 20. When fully grown, it loses weight by about one gram per year, the result of neurons dying without being replaced.

It is not the size of the human brain that is its most remarkable feature, since many animals have brains both larger and heavier than ours. What is remarkable is the complexity of interconnections between brain neurons. The number of possible ways in which neurons can be interconnected is enormous and larger than the number of atoms in the universe!

Box 4.2   Meninges, CSF and ventricles

The human brain is extremely soft and fragile. It is encased by three different sets of membranes called *meninges*. The outer one is thick and unstretchable whereas the two inner ones are thinner and more fragile. Between the two inner meninges is *cerebrospinal fluid* (CSF). This is similar to blood plasma, the clear liquid that remains when white and red blood cells are

removed from the blood. CSF is produced continuously by specialised blood vessels in the ventricles or hollow chambers of the brain. As a result of CSF flowing out of the ventricles and into the meninges, the brain is provided with a 'liquid cushion' in which it floats instead of resting against the skull. Without CSF, the brain would be bruised and injured by any movement of the head.

Essentially, the brain has three main functions. These are taking in information from the senses, interpreting this information, and acting on it. The remainder of this chapter, and Chapters 6–10, examine the structures involved in achieving these functions.

Figure 4.2 shows a front-to-back cross section of the brain and identifies the principal structures described in this chapter.

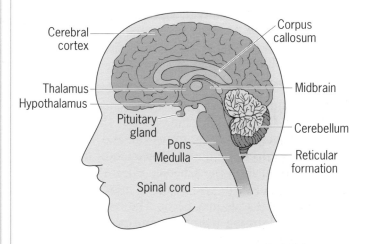

Figure 4.2   A front-to-back cross-section of the brain showing its major structures. The limbic system and basal ganglia surround the areas of the hypothalamus and thalamus, but are difficult to depict in a two-dimensional illustration

The hindbrain

This consists of the *medulla oblongata* (or, for short, the *medulla*), *pons* and *cerebellum*. Since the hindbrain is found in even the most primitive vertebrates, it is the earliest part of the brain to have evolved.

The *medulla* is the first structure that emerges from the spinal cord as it widens on entering the skull. It contains all the nerve fibres connecting the spinal cord to the brain. Most of these cross the medulla so that, generally, the left half of the body is connected to the right half of the brain. This is called a *contralateral connection*, in contrast to an *ipsilateral connection* in which nerve fibres from one half of the body go to the *same* half of the brain.

Although only one and a half inches long, the medulla regulates vital functions such as heart rate, blood pressure, respiration and body temperature via its connections with the ANS (see Chapter 5). The medulla receives sensory information directly from receptors in the body and exerts its effects through the nerve fibres of the PNS. The medulla also plays a role in activities such as vomiting, coughing and sneezing. Overdoses of certain drugs depress its functions and *can* lead to death. A very small lesion in a critical location *does* cause immediate death.

The *pons* is a bulge of white matter lying forward of the medulla. It is an important connection between the midbrain and the medulla, and is vital in integrating the movements of the two halves of the body. The pons also plays a role in functions related to attention, respiration, alertness and sleep (see Chapter 12).

The *cerebellum* lies behind the pons. It consists of two 'creased' or *convoluted* hemispheres which extend outward to the back of the skull on either side of the pons. The cerebellum is involved in maintaining balance and, although it does not initiate movement, is responsible for 'smoothing' muscular movements so they occur in an integrated fashion.

The cerebellum also handles certain reflexes, especially those to do with breathing and balance. The classic signs of drunkenness (poor coordination and balance) are partly due to alcohol-induced depression of neural activity in the cerebellum (see Chapter 15). If the cerebellum is damaged, stumbling and a lack of muscular coordination and muscle tone may occur. The cerebellum is also important in learning and programming motor responses and stores *muscular memories*. The sequence of movements involved in learning to ride a bike, for example, is programmed into the cerebellum so that it is carried out 'automatically' and never forgotten.

Box 4.3   Purkinje cells

For Eccles (1973), the cerebellum is a computer controlling complex motor behaviour, leaving the rest of the brain free for conscious activity. It accounts for about 11 per cent of the brain's entire weight and only the *cerebrum* (see page 40) is heavier. The cerebellum also contains *Purkinje cells*, which are capable of forming synapses with up to 100,000 other neurons. This is more than any other kind of neuron found in the brain and, given the sequence of movements involved in, say, playing a complex piece of music, we can appreciate why such rich potential interconnections between neurons are needed.

The midbrain

The relatively small division of the brain called the midbrain is not really a separate structure that can be easily isolated, since it is essentially an extension of the hindbrain and connects the forebrain to the spinal cord. Its principal structure is the *reticular formation*, a tangle of nerve cells and fibres.

The reticular formation's fibres ascend from the spinal cord to the forebrain carrying mainly motor information. This is important in maintaining muscle tone and controlling various reflexes. The *orienting reflex* is a general response to a novel stimulus, as when a dog pricks up its ears in response to a noise. Animals that use sound as their major sensory system, such as bats, have a very prominent auditory area in the midbrain. In humans, the reticular formation includes an area controlling eye reflexes such as pupil dilation and eye movements. It is also important in hearing, as well as being one of several places in the brain where pain is registered.

The reticular formation is vitally important in maintaining general arousal level. Because it is also involved in sleep and waking (see Chapter 12), it is sometimes called the *reticular activating system* and the 'consciousness system'. Stimulation of the reticular formation causes messages to be sent to the *cerebral cortex* (see Chapter 7) which make us more alert to sensory information. Drugs which lower its activity cause a loss of consciousness, whilst damage to the reticular formation can produce a comatose state.

Box 4.4   The reticular formation and attention

The reticular formation is also involved in screening incoming information, that is, filtering out irrelevant information whilst allowing important information to be sent to other brain areas. Through the reticular formation, we *habituate* to constant sources of uninformative information such as a clock's ticking in a room in which we are reading a book. However, some sudden changes in stimulation will cause the reticular formation to respond even if we happen to be asleep at the time. Sleeping parents, for example, respond to the cries of their baby but not to the sound of a lorry thundering past the window (see Chapter 11).

The forebrain

This consists of the *thalamus*, *hypothalamus*, *basal ganglia*, *limbic system* and *cerebrum*. We possess not one thalamus but two *thalami*. These are joined egg-shaped structures located near the centre of the brain. Each thalamus acts as a 'sensory relay station' for all sensory information except *olfaction* (smell). This has its own sensory relay station, the *olfactory bulb*, which is located in the limbic system (see below). Many of the messages that travel from one part of the brain to another also pass through the thalami.

Nerve fibres from our sensory systems enter the thalami from below and the information carried by them is transmitted to the cerebral cortex by nerve fibres exiting from above. For example, auditory sensory information travels to the cortical area involved in hearing via a part of the thalami called the *medial geniculate body*. Other parts include the *ventrobasal complex*, which transmits information about the sense of touch and body position, and is fed in from the body via the spinal cord, and the *lateral geniculate nucleus*. This is involved in vision and is considered in detail in Chapter 10.

The thalami also receive information from the cortex, mainly dealing with complex limb movements, which is directed to the cerebellum. Along with other brain activities occurring in the reticular formation and other structures, the thalami also play a role in sleep and attention.

The *hypothalamus* is a tiny collection of nuclei located beneath the thalami. The hypothalamus weighs about four grams and occupies less than one cubic centimetre of tissue. For its size, however, it is a remarkable and extremely important part of the brain involved in various complex behaviours. These include helping to regulate the sympathetic branch of the ANS (see pages 43–44) and controlling the *pituitary gland*, which itself controls the body's other *endocrine glands* (see Chapter 5). The interaction between the hypothalamus and pituitary gland is discussed further in Chapter 20.

The hypothalamus also plays a major role in *species-typical behaviours* and *homeostasis*. The former are those behaviours exhibited by most members of a species and are important to survival. These are sometimes called the four Fs: feeding, fighting, fleeing and 'reproduction'. However, other species-typical behaviours controlled by the hypothalamus include drinking, nest-building and caring for offspring. The role of the hypothalamus in some of these behaviours is explored further in Chapter 16.

Box 4.5   The hypothalamus and homeostasis

Homeostasis comes from the Greek 'himos' meaning 'same' and 'stasis' meaning 'stand-still'. Homeostasis is the maintenance of a proper balance of physiological variables such as body temperature, fluid concentration

and the amount of nutrients stored in the body. The hypothalamus receives information from sensory receptors inside the body and is therefore well-informed about changes in physiological status. It also contains specialised receptors that monitor the various characteristics of blood flowing through the brain, such as its temperature, nutrients and the amount of dissolved salts. Hypothalamic functions can involve either non-behavioural physiological changes, such as regulating temperature by sweating or increasing metabolic rate, or actual behaviours, such as taking off or putting on a coat (see Chapter 16).

Damage to the hypothalamus causes various behavioural impairments. These include changes in food intake, sterility and the stunting of growth (see Chapter 5). The major areas of the hypothalamus and their specialised functions are: the *anterior*, *supraoptic* (both involved in water balance), *presupraoptic* (heat control), *ventromedial* (hunger), *posterior* (sex drive) and *dorsal* ('pleasure').

The *basal ganglia* are embedded in the mass of white matter of each cerebral hemisphere and lie in front of the thalami. They are involved in the control of muscular movement and limb coordination. Whilst the cerebellum controls rapid movements, the basal ganglia control slower movements and mediate a movement's beginning and end. If the basal ganglia are damaged, changes in posture and muscle tone occur, leading to jerks, tremors and twitches.

Much of the brain's *dopamine* (see page 33) is produced in the basal ganglia and the degeneration of neurons in this area has been implicated in *Parkinson's disease*. The basal ganglia should really be called the *basal nuclei*. 'Ganglia' is usually used to describe collections of cell bodies *outside* the nervous system, whereas the same collection *inside* the nervous system is usually referred to as 'nuclei'.)

The *limbic system* is a series of structures located near the border between the *cerebrum* and parts of the hindbrain. It is only fully evolved in mammals, and as the *phylogenetic scale* is ascended the proportion of limbic system decreases whilst that of *cerebral cortex* increases.

Limbic system structures include the *olfactory bulbs, hippocampus, amygdala, septum pellucidum, cingulate gyrus, mamillary body, fornix* and *anterior commissure*. The thalamus and hypothalamus are also sometimes included. At one time, the limbic system was called the 'nose brain' because it contains the olfactory bulb. However, many limbic system structures play little or no direct role in olfaction, and as a result the term is no longer used.

The hippocampus is the largest structure in the limbic system and lies between the thalami and the cortex. It is involved in memory, and damage results in the inability to form new memories, although some memories for events occurring prior to the damage are unaffected (see Chapter 27).

The limbic system is particularly involved in behaviours satisfying motivational and emotional needs. Destruction of the *amygdala*, for example, causes monkeys and other mammals to behave in a docile way. Electrical stimulation of this area can, however, sometimes elicit rage and violent attacks from a previously placid animal. Damage to the septum pellucidum leads some mammals to respond aggressively to the slightest provocation. In humans, stimulating the septum results in the experience of pleasant and positive sensations, and septum stimulation has been used therapeutically to bring relief from the physical pain of advanced cancer. Chapters 16 and 18, consider further the limbic system's role and that of other structures (such as the hypothalamus) in motivation and emotion.

The *cerebrum* is virtually non-existent in the lower vertebrates. Fish, for example, have no tissue recognisable as cerebrum. As we move from the lower vertebrates to humans, the growth of the cerebrum accounts for the change in brain weight compared to body weight. Kilogram for kilogram, humans have more brain in comparison to body weight than any other animal, and the cerebrum is the most prominent brain structure which enfolds, and therefore conceals from view, most other brain structures. Over 75 per cent of neurons are located in the cerebrum, and it accounts for about 80 per cent of the brain's weight. The axons filling the cerebrum interconnect with cortical neurons and those of other brain regions.

The cerebrum's surface layer is called the *cerebral cortex*. This is typically one and a half to three millimetres thick, but at its deepest extends to about ten millimetres. The cortex is the most recently evolved and important part of the cerebrum. Indeed, the cerebrum has been described as a 'support system' for the cortex. The cortex is pinkish-grey in colour (hence the term 'grey matter') because it consists of cell bodies, whereas the other parts of the brain and nervous system consist of myelinated axons and are white in appearance.

The cortex is folded into a pattern of 'hills' and 'valleys' called *convolutions*. These are produced during the brain's development when the cortex folds back on itself. The total surface area of the cortex is around 2400 square centimetres, and convolutions are nature's way of confining it to a skull that has to be narrow enough to pass through the birth canal. The convolutions also facilitate the interconnections between different parts of the cortex needed to control complex behaviours.

Although some species possess a cortex, it is much smaller in surface area, shallower, and less complex than a human's. Generally, the greater the proportion of brain devoted to the cortex, the more complex and flexible is an animal's possible range of behaviours. The cortex, then, accounts for our fantastic information processing capabilities. If it ceases to function, a person vegetates without sensory experiences, voluntary movement and consciousness.

The larger 'hills' (or 'bulges') are called *gyri* (the singular being *gyrus*) whilst the deeper 'valleys' are called *fissures* or *sulci* (the singular being *sulcus*). One of these, the *longitudinal fissure*, runs down the middle of the cerebrum and divides it into the two cerebral hemispheres. Two other naturally occurring fissures in each hemisphere are the *lateral fissure* (or *fissure of Sylvius*) and the *central fissure* (or *fissure of Rolando*).

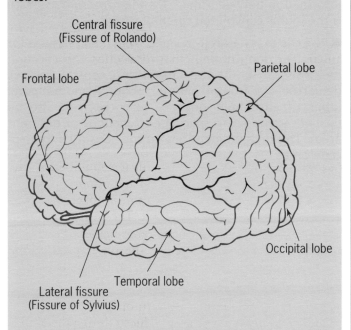
Conclusions

This chapter has looked at the organisation, structure and functioning of the central nervous system, and paid particular attention to the brain. It is possible to identify a number of different structures in the brain and, with some degree of confidence, describe the roles they play.

Summary

■ The central nervous system (CNS) consists of the brain and spinal cord. Their primary function is to integrate and coordinate all body functions and behaviour.

■ The **spinal cord** is a thick column of nerve fibres running from the base of the brain down the entire length of the back. It is the main communication cable between the CNS and PNS. Spinal cord damage causes paralysis. **Spinal reflexes** enable the body to avoid serious damage and maintain muscle tone and position.

■ The **triune model** divides the brain into the **central core (reptilian brain)**, the **limbic system (old mammalian brain)** and the **cerebral cortex (new mammalian brain)**. The brain can also be divided up in terms of foetal development into the **hindbrain**, **midbrain** and **forebrain**.

■ All major brain structures are present at birth, although the brain's neurons continue to grow in size and complexity. Overall brain weight is also due to the development of synaptic connections, glial cells and myelin sheaths. The brain reaches its maximum weight by age 20.

■ The brain is encased by three sets of **meninges**. Between the inner two is **cerebrospinal fluid**. This helps to cushion the brain and protects it against injury.

■ The hindbrain consists of the **medulla oblongata**, **pons** and **cerebellum**. The medulla regulates vital autonomic functions (such as heart rate) and reflexes (such as vomiting). It exerts its effects through connection with the PNS.

■ The pons is vital in integrating the movements of the two sides of the body. It is also involved in attention, respiration, alertness and sleep.

■ The cerebellum is involved in maintaining balance, smoothing muscular movements so that they occur in an integrated manner. Damage can produce a loss of coordination and muscle tone. The cerebellum also stores muscular memories, such as those involved in learning to ride a bike. It is the only part of the brain to contain **Purkinje cells**. These can form connections with 100,000 other neurons.

■ The midbrain is an extension of the hindbrain and connects the forebrain to the spinal cord. Its main structure is the **reticular formation**. This helps maintain muscle tone and controls various reflexes and general level of alertness to stimuli. Damage can cause loss of consciousness or coma.

■ The forebrain consists of the **thalamus, hypothalamus, basal ganglia, limbic system** and **cerebrum**. Each of the two thalami is a relay station for incoming sensory information, with the exception of **olfaction**. Auditory information is transmitted by the **medial geniculate body**, whilst the **ventrobasal complex** does the same for touch and body position. The **lateral geniculate body** is involved in vision.

■ The hypothalamus regulates the sympathetic branch of the ANS, controls the **pituitary gland**, and plays a central role in **species-specific behaviour** and **homeostasis**. It receives information from sensory receptors inside the body and contains specialised receptors which monitor blood flowing through the brain. Damage to the hypothalamus causes various behavioural impairments, depending on the area involved.

■ The basal ganglia are involved in the control of slow muscular movements and a movement's beginning and end. They produce much of the brain's **dopamine**. Degeneration of neurons in the basal ganglia has been implicated in **Parkinson's disease**.

■ The limbic system is a series of structures including the **olfactory bulb, hippocampus, amygdala, septum pellucidum, cingulate gyrus, mamillary body, fornix** and **anterior commissure**. The hippocampus plays a crucial role in memory whilst the limbic system as a whole is involved in motivation and emotion. The amygdala and septum are both involved in the control of aggression.

■ The cerebrum is divided into two **cerebral hemispheres**, joined by the **corpus callosum**, which transmits information between them. On the cerebrum's surface is the highly convoluted **cerebral cortex**.

■ The cortex is naturally divided by **gyri** and **fissures** (or **sulci**). The **longitudinal fissure** divides the cerebral hemispheres whilst the **lateral** and **central fissures** demarcate the **frontal, parietal, occipital** and **temporal lobes** of each hemisphere. The cortex can also be divided according to specialised functions of different areas. This division identifies **motor, sensory** and **associate areas**.

5

THE PERIPHERAL NERVOUS SYSTEM AND THE ENDOCRINE SYSTEM

Introduction and overview

As noted in Chapter 3, the peripheral nervous system (PNS) consists of the nerves connecting the CNS with the sense organs, muscles and glands. It was also noted that the two essential functions of the PNS are to send information to the CNS from the outside world (which it does via the sense organs) and transmit information from the CNS to produce a particular behaviour (which it does through the peripheral nerves to the muscles). Clearly, then, without the PNS, information about the outside world would not reach the brain and the brain would be unable to send instructions to the muscles and glands.

This chapter looks at the way in which the PNS operates and its interaction with the *endocrine system*. Although the endocrine system is not technically a part of the nervous system at all, its interaction with the PNS causes adjustments to internal physiological processes and influences behaviour.

The peripheral nervous system

Some of the nerves constituting the PNS are attached to the spinal cord and serve all of the body below the neck. Humans have 31 pairs of these *spinal nerves*. Other nerves are directly attached to the brain and serve sensory receptors and muscles in the neck and head. We have 12 pairs of these *cranial nerves*. The PNS is divided into the *somatic nervous system* and the *autonomic nervous system*. The former is concerned with the external world, whilst the latter is concerned with the internal world (the function of internal organs).

THE SOMATIC NERVOUS SYSTEM

Sometimes called the *skeletal nervous system*, the somatic nervous system (SNS) connects the CNS to sensory receptors and the skeletal muscles. This allows voluntary movement. Messages to the CNS travel by means of sensory (afferent) neurons. The instructions from the CNS to the muscles travel by means of motor (efferent) neurons (see page 29). Although these neurons send information in different directions, they are bound together in the same nerves for most of their length. Thus, sensory neurons tell the brain what is 'out there', and the brain acts on this information by sending instructions to the skeletal muscles.

If sensory neurons are damaged, we can lose sensation in the body part served by those neurons. If motor neurons are damaged, paralysis of the muscles in the part of the body served by those neurons can occur. Because damaged neurons are not replaced, the loss of sensation and paralysis can be permanent.

THE AUTONOMIC NERVOUS SYSTEM

The nerves of the autonomic nervous system (ANS) connect the CNS to the internal organs (or *viscera*), glands, and 'smooth' muscles (those which are not striped like skeletal muscles are) over which we do not seem to have direct control. Included here, for example, are the muscles involved in the digestive system. The ANS's primary function is to regulate internal bodily processes. However, it does this mainly by sending information to and from the CNS. As important as the ANS is, though, the CNS is ultimately in control.

The ANS is so called because it appears to operate as an independent or *autonomous* control system. Although we learn to control some autonomic functions, such as urination and defecation, these would occur in the absence of control of them. So, many bodily processes are controlled by the ANS without requiring conscious effort. The ANS is divided into two branches which are structurally different and operate in different ways. These are the *sympathetic* and *parasympathetic* branches. Some of the organs affected by them are shown in Figure 5.1 (page 44).

The sympathetic branch

The bundles (or *ganglia*) of neurons comprising the sympathetic branch are interconnected so that they form a long vertical chain on each side of the spinal cord. The sympathetic branch originates in the two middle portions (the thoracic and lumbar regions) of the spinal cord. The interconnections between the neurons allow the sympathetic branch to act as a *unit*. The fact that this branch seemed to make the organs work 'in sympathy' led to its name, although it is now known that it can also act selectively on a single organ.

Essentially, the sympathetic branch prepares the body to expend energy. As well as those effects shown in Figure 5.1, the sympathetic branch increases blood pressure, releases sugar from the liver into the blood (for energy) and increases blood flow to muscles used in physical action. Additionally, it tells the *endocrine system* to release *hormones* into the bloodstream to further strengthen these responses.

Box 5.1 Fight-or-flight

Cannon (1927) suggested that the sympathetic branch's major function was to mobilise the body for an emergency. He called its activation the *fight-or-flight*

response since the physiological changes that occur are designed to help us defend ourselves or flee from a threatening situation. So, when animals are given chemicals that de-activate the neurotransmitters of the sympathetic branch, they find it difficult to learn to escape from an electric shock (Lord *et al.*, 1976). The role played by the sympathetic branch of the ANS in response to stressors is discussed in detail in Chapter 20.

The parasympathetic branch

Parasympathetic ganglia are much more widely distributed than sympathetic branch ganglia. As Figure 5.1 shows, the nerve fibres originate at either end of the spinal cord, and as a general rule nerve fibres are near the organs they affect. However, because the nerve fibres are less interconnected than those of the sympathetic branch, the parasympathetic branch tends to act less as a unit and more on individual organs.

Figure 5.1 shows that the parasympathetic branch operates in the opposite way to the sympathetic branch and

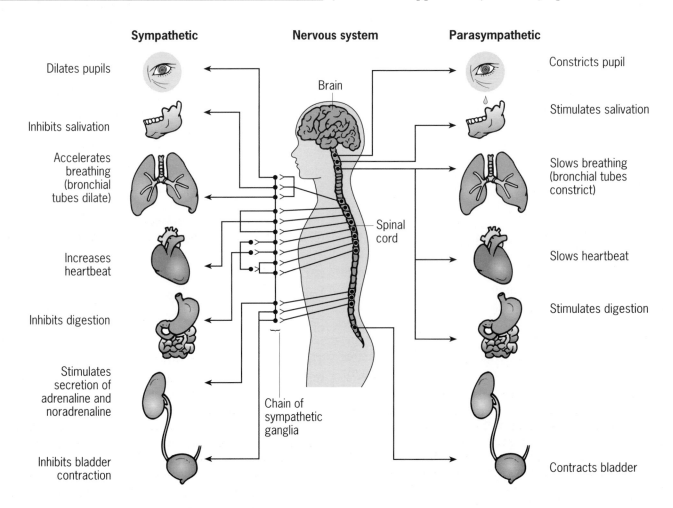

Figure 5.1   Some of the organs affected by the two branches of the ANS (From Hassett & White, 1989)

stimulates processes that serve to restore or conserve energy. It also carries out the body's 'maintenance needs'. As well as promoting digestion, it provides for the elimination of waste products and directs tissue repair. Parasympathetic activity predominates when we are relaxed or inactive, or when an emergency necessitating sympathetic branch activity has passed.

Many internal organs are connected to both branches of the ANS. Because the ANS can influence internal organs in two directions, our internal environment can be kept in a balanced state. As noted in Chapter 4 (see Box 4.5), *homeostasis* refers to the processes by which the body's internal systems are maintained in equilibrium despite variations in external conditions.

The fact that the two branches often oppose each other in order to maintain the balance of the internal organs suggests they are *antagonistic*. Whilst this is generally true, some behaviours are controlled exclusively by one branch or the other. For example, sweating is controlled by the sympathetic branch whereas crying is controlled by the parasympathetic branch. Also, whilst the two branches operate in opposite ways, they can function cooperatively. The male sexual response is a good example of this. For an erection to occur, parasympathetic activity is necessary, but for ejaculation to take place, sympathetic activity is necessary.

Traditionally, the ANS has been regarded as the 'automatic' part of the body's response mechanism. Thus, it was generally believed that the ANS could not be voluntarily speeded up or down. However, some evidence challenges this. For example, Dicara & Miller (1968) reported that rats could be operantly conditioned to alter their heart rates. This effect has also been reported in humans. *Yogis* can apparently slow their heart rate and energy consumption so that they can survive in a sealed box for ordinarily lethal periods of time.

Box 5.2   Biofeedback

Miller pioneered the application of ANS control with *biofeedback*, in which equipment is used to record a particular bodily process (such as heart rate) and to signal (or 'feed back') when the process has changed in the desired direction (see Chapter 20). Whilst there is little doubt that biofeedback can be effective, it is not clear why. Some researchers believe that a reduction in heart rate occurs *indirectly* as a result of the skeletal muscles in the chest being used to slow down breathing (and hence heart rate). To support this, they point to the fact that Dicara and Miller's results have never been replicated (Walker, 1984).

The endocrine system

The ANS exerts its effects by direct neural stimulation of body organs and by stimulating the release of *hormones* from the *endocrine glands*.

The body contains glands with ducts or without them. A duct is a passageway that carries substances to specific locations and secretes them directly onto the body's surface or into body cavities. Glands with ducts are called *exocrine glands*. Tears, sweat and saliva, for example, all reach their destination by means of ducts. Ductless glands secrete their products directly into the bloodstream. These *endocrine glands* are of interest to psychologists because of the role they play in behaviour.

Endocrine glands secrete *hormones*, powerful chemical messengers that have a variety of effects on physical state and behaviour. In some ways, hormones are similar to *neurotransmitters*. Hormones are poured into the bloodstream and circulate throughout the body. However, like neurotransmitters, they act only on receptors in particular locations of the body. Indeed, at least one chemical (*noradrenaline* – see Box 5.5, page 47) can be classified as both a neurotransmitter and a hormone depending on the task it is performing and where it is located.

In other ways, hormones are very different from neurotransmitters. Neurotransmitters can convey a message in a few fractions of a second. Because hormones are discharged into the blood, the endocrine system influences behaviour in a broader but slower way than the nervous system. When immediate behavioural reactions are required (such as a reflexive action), the nervous system plays the major role.

Many hormonal activities enable our bodies to maintain steady states. They achieve this by means of mechanisms that measure current levels and signal glands to release appropriate regulatory chemicals whenever the steady state is disturbed. To maintain the steady state, information must then be fed back to the glands. This is a *negative feedback loop*. Thus, whenever the required amount of a hormone has been secreted, the gland is instructed to stop.

The endocrine and nervous systems interact in complex ways, and the former plays a major role in regulating development and helping to coordinate and integrate complex psychological reactions (this interaction is explained in detail in Chapter 16). Essentially, though, the endocrine system is regulated by the *hypothalamus* (see page 39) which exerts its influence through its effects on the *pituitary gland*. The pituitary is sometimes referred to as the '*master gland*' because the hormones it releases control the secretion of the other endocrine glands.

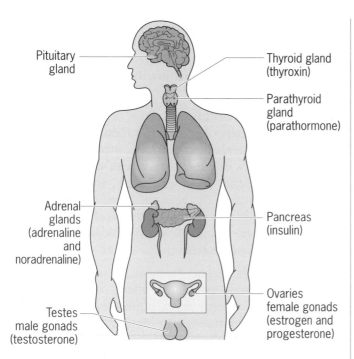

Figure 5.2   Some major glands of the endocrine system and the hormones they produce

THE PITUITARY GLAND

The pituitary gland is located deep within the brain, slightly below the hypothalamus to which it is connected by means of a network of blood vessels called the *infundibulum* or *pituitary stalk*. The pituitary gland consists of two parts, each of which functions separately from the other. The *anterior pituitary* (towards the *front* of the gland) is controlled by *releasing hormones* or *factors* produced by the hypothalamus and transmitted via the infundibulum.

Box 5.3   Some hormones produced by the anterior pituitary

At least eight hormones are produced by the anterior pituitary. One is *somatotrophin* or *growth hormone*. This affects the metabolic functions that determine the growth of muscles, bones and glands. Overproduction can lead to *acromegaly*, a condition in which a person grows two or three feet taller than would be the case if the hormone was produced normally. Underproduction results in arrested growth development and the affected child becomes a *midget*.

Prolactin or *lactogenic hormone* regulates maternal behaviour in mammals such as rats. For example, when blood from a new mother rat is transfused into another female, the recipient displays typical maternal behaviour. In humans, prolactin stimulates the production of milk during pregnancy.

The anterior pituitary is an excellent example of the interaction between the endocrine and nervous systems. As has been shown, the anterior pituitary is controlled by the hypothalamus. One hormone released by the anterior pituitary causes other glands, the *gonads* (see below), to produce yet other hormones. These affect the hypothalamus causing changes in behaviour or feeling. The hypothalamus, then, not only influences the anterior pituitary, but is influenced by it.

Two of the hormones of the *posterior pituitary* (towards the *back* of the gland) are *oxytocin* and *antidiuretic hormone*.

Box 5.4   Oxytocin and antidiuretic hormones

Oxytocin instructs the uterus to contract during childbirth. Shortly after giving birth, the stimulation of nerve endings in and around the nipples sends messages to the brain that cause oxytocin to be released. Oxytocin then causes cells in the breast to eject milk, an example of a *neuroendocrine reflex*. Both prolactin and oxytocin are also secreted in males although their function is not known.

Antidiuretic hormone (ADH) is manufactured in the hypothalamus but stored in the pituitary's posterior lobe. It acts on the kidneys, causing them to decrease the amount of water drawn from body tissues and passed to the bladder. When we are dehydrated, ADH is released to conserve fluid. When we are hydrated and our intake of liquid is excessive, ADH is not released at all and urine production is dramatically increased. The role of ADH in the regulation of drinking is discussed further in Chapter 16.

THE ADRENAL GLANDS

The adrenal glands are located above the kidneys. They have an outer layer (or *cortex*) and an inner core (or *medulla*). The action of the adrenal cortex is regulated by *adrenocorticotrophic hormone* (ACTH), another hormone produced by the anterior pituitary (and is itself released in response to *corticotrophin-releasing hormone* produced by the hypothalamus). The adrenal cortex secretes as many as 20 different hormones called *corticosteroids* or *cortical steroids*. In general, steroids promote muscle development, increase resistance to stress (by fighting inflammation and allergic reaction: see Chapter 20), and stimulate the liver to release stored sugar which influences the body's ability to produce energy quickly. Not surprisingly, steroids are taken by bodybuilders and athletes in order to enhance their performance, although such use is not without danger.

THE THYROID GLAND

The thyroid gland is located just below the larynx. As a
result of the anterior pituitary producing *thyrotrophic hormones*, the thyroid gland produces one primary hormone,
thyroxin. This plays an important role in controlling the
rate at which the body burns food to provide energy. Primarily, thyroxin raises metabolism by increasing oxygen
use and the level of heat production. When thyroxin is
overproduced, a condition called *hyperthyroidism* occurs.
This is characterised by excitability, insomnia and weight
loss (even though the appetite for food is huge). Underproduction produces *hypothyroidism* which is characterised
by the opposite effects to those of hyperthyroidism.
Because thyroxin affects metabolism, untreated hypothyroidism in infants can lead to *cretinism*, a condition
characterised by stunted growth and mental retardation.

THE PARATHYROID GLANDS

The parathyroid glands are embedded in the thyroid
gland. Four small organs secrete *parathormone* which controls calcium and phosphate levels in the blood and
tissue fluids. The amount of calcium in the blood directly
affects the nervous system's excitability. People with too
little parathormone tend to be hypersensitive and suffer
from muscle spasms. People with too much tend to be
lethargic and have poor muscle coordination.

THE PANCREAS

The pancreas plays a major role in controlling blood and
urine sugar levels by secreting the regulating hormones
insulin and *glucagon*. These work against each other to keep
the blood-sugar level properly balanced. When insulin is
oversecreted, there is too little sugar in the blood. This
produces *hypoglycaemia* which is characterised by chronic

fatigue, shakiness and dizziness. These symptoms are
often confused with *anxiety* and when some people seek
help for anxiety they find, through blood tests, that they
are hypoglycaemic (see Chapter 70). Dietary restrictions
are usually used to control the condition.

When insulin is inadequately secreted or is underutilised,
hyperglycaemia occurs. This is characterised by an excess of
sugar in the blood which the kidneys attempt to remove
by secreting more water than usual. As a result, the
body's tissues become dehydrated and poisonous wastes
accumulate in the blood. This condition is called *diabetes
mellitus* and can lead to coma and death. Fortunately, it
can be treated by insulin injections and a special diet
which keeps the blood-sugar level normal.

THE GONADS

The gonads are the sexual glands – *ovaries* in women and
testes in men. Both the ovaries and testes are stimulated
by *luteinising hormone* which is produced by the anterior
pituitary. In addition, *follicle stimulating hormone*, produced by the anterior pituitary, causes egg cells in the
follicles of the ovaries to ripen.

Three main types of sex hormone are secreted by the tissue located within the gonads. All occur in both sexes, but
in different amounts. These hormones control the development of *primary sex characteristics* (those directly involved
in reproduction such as penis growth and the testes' ability to produce sperm). They also control the development
of *secondary sex characteristics* (those characteristics which
differentiate the sexes but which are not directly involved
in reproduction). These include things like the distribution
of body hair and deepening of the voice.

Both estrogen and progesterone regulate the *menstrual cycle*. Estrogen levels rise after menstruation, the monthly sloughing off of the inner lining of the uterus, leading to an egg cell's development. When estrogen reaches peak blood level, the egg cell is released by the ovary. Then, the inner lining of the uterus thickens in response to the secretion of progesterone, eventually gaining the capacity to support an embryo should fertilisation occur. If the egg cell is not fertilised, estrogen and progesterone levels drop, triggering menstruation.

Hormonal changes at the time of menstruation can cause women painful physical problems. For example, the production of *prostoglandins* during menstruation causes uterine contractions. Many of these go unnoticed, but when they are strong and unrelieved, they can be particularly uncomfortable. Fortunately, prostaglandin-inhibiting drugs (such as *Ibuprofen*) can relieve the pain. Much more controversial is the claim that the menstrual cycle can also cause psychological problems such as irritability and poor judgement.

The term *pre-menstrual syndrome* (PMS) has been used as a label for the behavioural and emotional effects associated with menstruation, although its status has been challenged by some writers. As Paige (1973) has observed:

> 'Women, the old argument goes, are eternally subject to the whims and wherefores of their biological clocks. Their raging hormonal cycles make them emotionally unstable and intellectually unreliable. If women have second-class status, we are told, it is because they cannot control the implacable demands of that bouncing estrogen'.

The menstrual cycle is an example of a bodily rhythm called an *infradian rhythm*. Chapter 11 discusses the evidence concerning pre-menstrual syndrome in more detail (see also Chapter 84).

In some people, the sex hormones are unbalanced and this leads to changes in behaviour and physical appearance. Oversecretion of estrogen in males and androgens in females causes the development of secondary sex characteristics of the opposite sex. Females, for example, may grow facial hair, develop a deeper voice and experience shrinkage of the breasts. Males may develop higher pitched voices, begin to grow breasts and lose facial hair.

Box 5.7 Adrenogenital syndrome

In *adrenogenital syndrome* (AGS), the adrenal glands produce a hormone that begins to masculinise the foetus irrespective of its genetically determined sex. Thus, both AGS boys and girls become more masculinised. At birth, the internal reproductive organs of a girl may be female, but their outward appearance is that of a male. Even when surgery is performed and they are raised as females, AGS girls appear to retain some masculine characteristics (if we assume that large amounts of outdoor play, which is enjoyed by AGS girls, is an indicator of 'masculinity'). Money & Erhardt (1972) also suggest that AGS girls prefer to play with boys, describe themselves as 'tomboys' and are less interested in playing with 'typical' girls' toys (such as dolls) and more interested in playing with 'typical' boys' toys (such as trucks and guns). AGS boys seem to be involved in much rougher outdoor activities than their non-AGS counterparts. The development of gender is discussed in detail in Chapter 45.

THE HEART

Traditionally, we think of the heart as being a finely tuned and essential pump. However, it may also be a major endocrine gland. Cantin & Genest (1986) discovered that the heart secretes a powerful peptide hormone called *atrial natriuretic factor* (ANF). According to them, ANF plays an important role in regulating blood pressure and blood volume, and in excreting water, sodium and potassium. The effects exerted are wide, and involve the blood vessels themselves, the kidneys, the adrenal glands and a large number of regulatory glands in the brain. If Cantin and Genest are right in their views about the heart, there is clearly much we have still to learn about the endocrine system.

Conclusions

This chapter has examined the PNS and its interaction with the endocrine system. Its look at the hormones secreted by the endocrine system has been selective rather than exhaustive. However, more hormones will be encountered throughout this part of the book. One of these, *melatonin*, is secreted by the *pineal gland* and plays an important role in the regulation of certain biological rhythms (see Chapter 11).

Summary

■ The peripheral nervous system (PNS) consists of the nerves connecting the CNS with the sense organs, muscles and glands. It sends information to the CNS from the outside world and transmits information from the

CNS to the muscles. The PNS is divided into the **somatic nervous system** (SNS) and the **autonomic nervous system** (ANS).

■ The SNS connects the CNS to sensory receptors and the skeletal muscles, allowing voluntary movement. Damage to sensory and motor neurons of the SNS can cause permanent loss of sensation and paralysis respectively.

■ The nerves of the ANS connect the CNS to viscera, glands and 'smooth' muscled organs. Their main function is to regulate internal bodily processes, although the CNS ultimately controls these. Many bodily processes are controlled by the ANS without the need for conscious effort.

■ The ANS consists of **sympathetic** and **parasympathetic** branches. The former mobilises the body for an emergency (the **fight-or-flight response**). The latter helps the body conserve or reduce energy. It also controls the elimination of waste products and tissue repair. Since most internal organs are connected to both branches, the ANS also plays a major role in **homeostasis**.

■ The ANS exerts its effects by direct neural stimulation of body organs and by stimulating the **endocrine system** to secrete **hormones**, powerful chemical messengers that affect physical state and behaviour. Hormones help maintain the body's steady states through **negative feedback loops**, in which a gland stops secreting when the required amount of hormone has been released.

■ The endocrine system is essentially regulated by the hypothalamus, which exerts its influence by controlling the **pituitary gland**. The anterior and posterior parts of this gland produce several hormones, some of which cause other glands to produce their own hormones. These hormones affect the hypothalamus, an example of the interaction between the endocrine and nervous system.

■ The **adrenal glands** consist of an outer **cortex** and an inner **medulla**. The cortex secretes **corticosteroids** which increase resistance to stress and promote muscle development. The medulla produces **adrenaline** and **noradrenaline**. Epinephrine activates the sympathetic branch of the ANS, whilst noradrenaline stimulates the pituitary to release **adrenocorticotrophic hormone** (ACTH), which regulates the action of the adrenal cortex.

■ The **thyroid gland** produces **thyroxin**, which plays a vital role in metabolism. Overproduction causes **hyperthyroidism** whereas underproduction causes **hypothyroidism**. The latter can lead to **cretinism**.

■ The **parathyroid glands** are embedded in the thyroid gland, and secrete **parathormone** which controls calcium and phosphate levels in the blood. These affect the excitability of the NS.

■ The **pancreas** secretes **insulin** and **glucagon** which are involved in controlling blood-sugar and urine-sugar levels. Oversecretion of insulin causes **hypoglycaemia**. Undersecretion causes **hyperglycaemia**, which is associated with **diabetes mellitus**.

■ The **gonads** (**ovaries** and **testes**) are stimulated by the **luteinizing hormone**. Egg cells ripen as a result of **follicle stimulating hormone**. Three main types of sex hormone are produced in males and females but in different amounts. They control both **primary** and **secondary sex characteristics**. The most potent of the male hormones is **testosterone**. The female hormones are **estrogen** and **progesterone**. They regulate the menstrual cycle.

■ In **adrenogenital syndrome** (AGS), the adrenal glands produce a hormone that masculinises the developing foetus. A genetic female with AGS has a masculine external appearance. AGS girls tend to think and behave in more 'masculine' ways, even when raised as females.

■ The **heart** may be a major endocrine gland. It secretes **atrial natriuretic factor** (ANF), a hormone which regulates blood pressure and volume, and the excretion of water, sodium and potassium.

PART 2
Cortical functions

6

SOME METHODS AND TECHNIQUES USED TO INVESTIGATE CORTICAL FUNCTIONS

Introduction and overview

Chapter 4 examined the human brain and described the relationship between brain structures and behaviour. Although far from completely understanding the brain's mechanisms, our knowledge grows almost daily. But how do we know what we know? This chapter looks at some of the methods and techniques that have advanced our understanding.

The various methods can be discussed under separate headings. *Clinical/anatomical methods* involve 'accidental interventions', such as injury to and disease of the brain. *Invasive methods* involve 'deliberate intervention', such as stimulating the brain either electrically or chemically or causing deliberate injury to it. Finally, *non-invasive methods* involve recording the brain's activity without making deliberate interventions.

Clinical/anatomical methods

Perhaps the most obvious way of studying the brain is to look at the behavioural consequences of *accidental* damage to it. This approach assumes that if damage to a particular brain part causes a behavioural change, then it is reasonable to conclude that the damaged part ordinarily plays a role in the behaviour affected.

Box 6.1   Studies of accidental brain damage

In the late nineteenth century Broca and Wernické studied patients who had suffered a stroke (*cerebrovascular accident*). This occurs when a blood vessel in the brain is damaged or blocked. This causes brain tissue to be deprived of the oxygen and nutrients carried by the blood, and the tissue dies. Broca's patients had difficulty producing speech, but no difficulty understanding it. Wernické's patients, however, could produce speech (although it was often unintelligible), but could not understand it. Post-mortems revealed that Broca's patients had suffered damage in one specific cortical area whilst Wernické's had suffered damage in a different area. The role played by these cortical areas is discussed in detail in Chapter 8.

Clinical and anatomical studies compare what people could do before their brain damage with what they can do afterwards. Unfortunately, in many cases there aren't always precise enough records of people's behaviour before the damage was sustained. As a result, this approach is useful for very obvious behavioural changes (such as the inability to produce language), but less helpful where more subtle effects are involved (such as changes in personality).

Also, it is sometimes difficult to determine the precise location and amount of damage that has been caused by a particular injury. More practically, researchers must wait for the 'right kind' of injury to occur so that a particular brain part can be investigated.

Invasive methods

ABLATION AND LESION PRODUCTION

Ablation involves surgically removing or destroying brain tissue and observing the behavioural consequences. Flourens pioneered the technique in the 1820s, and showed that removal of thin tissue slices from the cerebellum of rabbits, birds and dogs resulted in them displaying a lack of muscular coordination and a poor sense of balance, but no other obvious behavioural difficulties. Flourens concluded that the cerebellum plays a vital role in muscular coordination and balance, a conclusion which was essentially correct (see page 38).

Surgical removal can be achieved by cutting the tissue with a knife, burning it out with electrodes, or sucking it away through a hollow tube attached to a vacuum pump. Although ablation studies are still conducted on non-humans, they are limited in what they can tell us about the human brain. Another problem is the issue of *control* versus *involvement* in behaviour. Behaviour may change when part of the brain is removed, but we cannot be certain that the removed part controlled the behaviour or was merely involved in it. Since many parts of the brain work together to produce a particular behaviour, we cannot be sure what behaviour changes mean when a part is removed.

Lesion production involves deliberately injuring part of the brain and then observing the consequences of the injury (*lesion*) on behaviour. Whilst an animal is under anaesthetic, a hole is drilled in its skull and an electrode inserted into a particular brain site. Then, an electrical impulse of a voltage larger than those occurring naturally in the brain is delivered to the site. This 'burns out' a small area surrounding the electrode. Because the sites involved are usually located deep within the brain, a *stereotaxic apparatus* (see Figure 6.1) is used to precisely locate the area to be lesioned.

Once the animal has recovered, its behaviour is observed to see whether the lesion has produced immediate, delayed, or no apparent changes in behaviour, and whether any changes are permanent or disappear with time, re-training or therapy. Lesion studies have produced some important findings. For example, lesions in one area of the hypothalamus cause extreme overeating in rats and they become grossly overweight. A lesion in a different area, however, produces the opposite effect and, at least initially, they refuse to eat any sort of food (see Chapter 16).

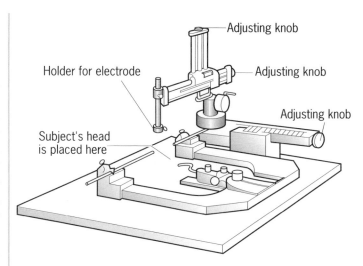

Figure 6.1   A stereotaxic apparatus

Box 6.2   Therapeutic applications of lesion production

Whilst lesion production is not used on humans *purely* for research purposes, lesions have been used therapeutically. In the *split-brain* operation certain nerve fibres are severed to try to reduce the severity of epileptic seizures (see Chapter 9).

Lesion production studies tell us something about how different parts of the brain are *normally* connected. As with ablation studies, however, we must be extremely cautious in interpreting data from them. Again, since the participants are *always* non-humans, findings may not generalise to humans. Additionally, whilst a lesion is produced in a specific area, the possibility that behaviour changes occur as a result of other damage caused by the procedure cannot be ruled out. The problem of 'control versus involvement' in the production of behaviour changes is also a concern with lesion studies.

ELECTRICAL STIMULATION OF THE BRAIN (ESB)

ESB involves inserting one or more electrodes into a living animal's brain and applying an electric current which does not cause any damage. Careful adjustment of the current produces a 'false' nerve impulse which the brain treats as a real impulse from a sensory receptor.

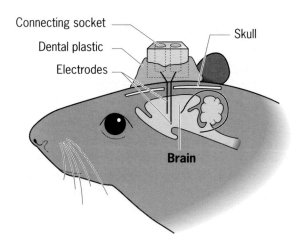

Figure 6.2   Electrical stimulation of the brain

Box 6.3   ESB and the charging bull

ESB has produced some dramatic findings. For example, Delgado (1969) walked into a bullring equipped with a bull fighter's cape and a radio transmitter. Delgado had implanted a radio-controlled electrode into the limbic system of a 'brave bull', a variety bred to respond with a raging charge to the sight of a human being. When the bull charged, Delgado sent an impulse to the electrode in the bull's brain. Fortunately for Delgado, the bull stopped its charge. The implications of this finding is discussed in Chapter 18.

Olds & Milner (1954) found that electrical stimulation of the hypothalamus caused rats to increase the frequency of whatever behaviour they were engaged in. In another experiment they connected the implanted electrode to a control mechanism that the rat could operate. Stimulation of one part of the hypothalamus appeared to be extremely pleasurable for the rat, since it would forego food, water and sex to carry on stimulating its brain at a rate of 100 times a minute and over 1900 times an hour. As well as discovering an apparent 'pleasure centre' in the brain, Olds and Milner also found that placing the electrode in a different location led to an animal that had operated the control mechanism once never operating it again, suggesting the existence of a 'pain centre' (see Chapters 18 and 19).

The studies described above illustrate some of the findings from stimulating structures deep within the brain. However, in other studies the *cerebral cortex* has been electrically stimulated. The classic research in this area was conducted by Penfield in the 1940s and 1950s. Penfield routinely performed surgery on epileptics, and to minimise the disruption of normal functions as a result of his

surgery, he would stimulate the cortex and observe what happened. Because there are no pain receptors in the brain, the person awaiting surgery could be kept conscious whilst the stimulation was given, and could report on the experiences produced by the stimulation (see also Chapter 30, page 261).

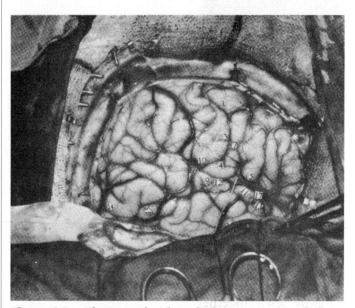

Figure 6.3   Photograph taken during surgery carried out by Penfield. The numbers refer to the parts of the cortex stimulated

(Oxford University Press)

ESB has provided much information about the brain's workings, and has also been used therapeutically. Perhaps its most useful application has been in the reduction of pain. For example, ESB can be used to 'block' pain messages in the spine before they reach the brain, and this relieves the severe pain experienced by people with illnesses such as cancer (Restak, 1975).

Clearly, ESB is a useful way of 'mapping' the connections between areas or structures of the brain since, if stimulation of one area produces increased activity at another, it is reasonable to assume that the two are connected. Equally, if stimulation of a specific brain site produces a behaviour, that site must at least be involved in the behaviour. However, we must be careful about drawing too many conclusions from research findings.

Box 6.4   Some limitations of ESB

Valenstein (1977) offers three cautions. First, no single brain area is likely to be the sole source of any given behaviour or emotion. Second, ESB-provoked behaviour does not perfectly mimic natural behaviour. Rather, it produces compulsive and stereotypical behaviour. For example, an animal whose eating behaviour is initiated by ESB might only eat one type of food. Third, ESB's effects may depend on many other factors, since people exhibit very different behavioural responses to identical stimulation administered at different times. For Valenstein:

'The impression that brain stimulation in humans can repeatedly evoke the same emotional state, the same memory, or the same behaviour is simply a myth. The brain is not organised into neat compartments that correspond to the labels we assign to behaviour'.

MICRO-ELECTRODE RECORDING

Instead of stimulating the brain, some researchers insert tiny electrodes (*micro-electrodes*) to record a single neuron's activity in a living animal's brain. Micro-electrodes are about one ten-thousandth of a millimetre in diameter and enable the 'sound' of a neuron to be recorded without the 'noise' emanating from neighbouring neurons.

Using a stereotaxic apparatus (see pages 51–52), the electrode is inserted into the brain. It is then attached to an electrical connector cemented to the brain. Finally, the scalp is sewn together. The electrical connector is attached to a wire leading to apparatus that records the cell's electrical activity as various tasks are performed. Micro-electrodes are sophisticated enough to detect an electrical charge of one-millionth of a volt.

Recordings of the activity of single neurons have produced interesting findings, particularly into the workings of the visual system. Chapter 10 looks at the research conducted by Hubel and Wiesel into the visual system. These researchers have been able to build up a detailed picture of some of the ways in which the monkey's brain sorts out visual information. However, since the brain has billions of neurons, each of which connects with many others, building up a picture of how the brain works using this method is very slow indeed. Moreover, since micro-electrodes can destroy brain tissue, their use has been confined to non-humans making the generalisation of findings difficult.

CHEMICAL STIMULATION OF THE BRAIN

This technique is used with non-humans and involves introducing a chemical into the brain to determine its behavioural and physiological effects. Typically, a thin tube (or micro-pipette) is inserted into the brain with the open end touching the area being studied. A smaller tube is filled with a few crystals of a chemical substance and inserted into the implanted tube. The chemical is then released at the site being stimulated.

Box 6.5   Chemical stimulation and anatomic pathways

Chemical stimulation has been used to trace anatomic pathways in the brain using radioactive 2-deoxyglucose, a form of sugar. Following the injection, an animal is made to perform a certain task. Those cells involved in the task use more sugar and so radioactivity builds up in them. After the task, the animal is 'sacrificed'. The brain is then frozen and thin slices of it are pressed against photographic film (which is sensitive to radioactivity). This indicates which brain cells were particularly active during the task's performance.

The chemical used depends on the nature of the study. Perhaps the most commonly used chemicals are those believed to affect synaptic transmission. These produce longer-lasting effects than those induced by electrical stimulation, and allow researchers to make their observations over longer periods of time. However, the data are often difficult to interpret, with different non-humans responding differently to the same chemical. Since non-humans respond differently to one another, we should be cautious in generalising the results to humans.

As well as the practical problems involved in the various methods described above there are, of course, serious ethical issues (see Chapter 85). Both practical and ethical issues have led researchers to look for alternative ways of studying the brain which do not involve direct intervention.

Non-invasive methods

RECORDING THE BRAIN'S ELECTRICAL ACTIVITY

Chapter 3 showed that nerve cells in the brain communicate with one another by releasing neurotransmitters. In 1875, it was discovered that these chemical changes also produce recordable electrical discharges. Half a century later, Berger, a German neurologist, devised a technique which allowed the electrical activity to be continuously recorded.

Working on the assumption that the part of the brain which is electrically active during some behaviour is involved in that behaviour, Berger attached two flat silver plates (which acted as electrodes) to his son's scalp. The electrodes were connected to a galvanometer, which measures small electric currents. After much effort, Berger successfully recorded regular electrical activity from the electrodes, and suggested that the activity was affected by *conscious experience*.

Berger's work was largely ignored until 1934 when Adrian and Matthews confirmed his findings using a newly invented device, the *electroencephalogram* (or EEG). An EEG machine measures changes in the electrical activity of different brain parts. There are characteristic patterns of electrical activity which are common to everyone at a particular age or stage of development. However, everyone's individual brain activity is as unique and distinctive as their fingerprint.

Using special jelly, small disc-like electrodes are attached to the scalp. Via wires, these pass electrical information to an amplifier capable of detecting impulses of less than a ten-thousandth of a volt and then magnifying them one million times. The amplifier passes its information to pens which trace the impulses on paper revolving on a drum. This produces a permanent record of the oscillating waves produced by the electrical activity.

Box 6.6   The measurement of 'brain waves'

EEG activity can be described in terms of *frequency* (the number of complete oscillations of a wave that occur in one second which is measured in cycles per second or Hertz (Hz)) and *amplitude* (half the height from the peak to the trough of a single oscillation). Whilst amplitude is important, frequency is more commonly used to describe the brain's electrical activity. The four main types of brain wave are:

- DELTA (1–3 Hz) – mainly found in infants, adults in 'deep' sleep, or adults with brain tumours;

- THETA (4–7 Hz) – commonly seen in children aged between two and five. In adults it has been observed in anti-social personality disorder;

- ALPHA (8–13 Hz) – this wave is seen in adults who are awake, relaxed, and whose eyes are closed;

- BETA (13 Hz and over) – this is found in adults who are awake, alert, have their eyes open, and are concentrating on a task.

The EEG allows researchers to examine the brain's activity in response to specific experiences as they occur, and whilst we are awake the brain's electrical activity changes in response to sights, sounds and other sensory information. The EEG is also extensively used in clinical diagnosis to detect abnormal brain activity, since EEG patterns from tumours and damaged brain tissue, for example, are very distinctive. Indeed, the EEG has been invaluable in the diagnosis of *epilepsy*, a condition characterised by abnormal bursts of electrical activity (which may be 20 times that of normal) occurring in rapidly firing individual nerve cells.

In addition to recording electrical activity in the brain, electrodes can also be attached to the skin beneath the chin and near the outer corners of the eyes. The activity recorded from the chin muscles is called an *electromyogram* (EMG) and provides information about muscle tension or relaxation. The activity recorded from near the outer corner of the eyes is called an *electrooculogram* (EOG) and shows the electrical activity that occurs when the eyes move. A machine that measures more variables than just the electrical activity of the brain is called a *polygraph*.

As well as being used for diagnostic purposes, the EEG is the indispensable tool of those interested in understanding the nature and functions of *sleep* and *dreaming*. Chapters 11–13 discuss sleep and dreaming research and refer extensively to EEG, EMG and EOG measures. As those chapters illustrate, muscle, eye and brain activity is not constant over the course of a night's sleep.

As noted in Chapter 3, the brain contains billions of neurons. Recordings from the scalp therefore reflect the *gross* and simultaneous activity of millions of neurons. For some researchers, the EEG is analogous to standing outside Wembley Stadium on Cup Final day and hearing the crowd roar. A goal could have been scored, but by which side? It could be a penalty, but to whom? It might even be the crowd's response to a streaker running across the pitch! Whilst the EEG reveals that *something* is happening it does not indicate exactly what.

Box 6.7   Computerised electroencephalography

A way of partially overcoming EEG's limitations does exist, however. This involves repeatedly presenting a stimulus and having a computer filter out the activity unrelated to it. This is called *computerised electroencephalography*. The filtering out leaves an *evoked potential* which can be useful in identifying patterns of activity associated with particular behaviours.

For example, Donchin (1975) recorded the EEG activity of participants who were exposed to various familiar or predictable stimuli occasionally interspersed with unfamiliar or unpredictable stimuli. Donchin found that the perception of an unexpected event was consistently associated with the production of an evoked potential called P300. Donchin's research suggests that evoked potentials can be helpful in understanding the relationship between brain activity and mental processes.

More recently, researchers have taken advantage of the fact that the brain's electrical activity creates magnetic fields that can be detected outside the skull (Burne, 1996). *Magnetoencephalograms* (or MEGs) detect these very weak magnetic fields (which are of the order of one billionth of the earth's magnetic field). The brain's electrical signals are distorted when they pass through the skull, making it difficult to identify their point of origin. Magnetic fields are unaffected by bone, and the MEG measures the magnetic field's strength and its source. The biggest weakness of MEG is that the magnetic fields are easily disrupted, and this makes measurement extremely difficult (Charlton, 1996). Despite this, MEG has been used successfully to detect disorders like epilepsy, multiple sclerosis and Alzheimer's disease.

EEG *imaging* is also useful in studying the brain. This technique allows researchers to measure the functioning of the brain 'on a millisecond by millisecond basis' (Fischman, 1985). The activity recorded by 32 electrodes placed on the scalp is fed to a computer which translates it into coloured moving images on a television monitor. The technique was originally developed for research into convulsive seizures. However, it has also been used to predict learning disabilities in children and for mapping the brain activity of people suffering from mental disorders. A similar method, which uses 64 or 128 electrodes and is called a *geodesic sensor net*, has recently been developed for similar purposes (Highfield, 1996a).

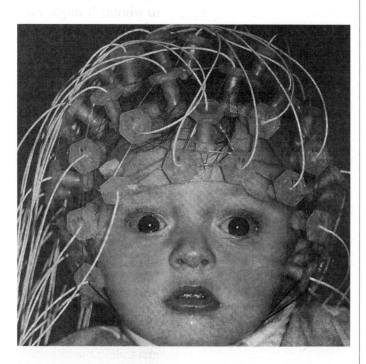

Figure 6.4   A geodesic sensor net being used to study brain activity in an infant

SCANNING AND IMAGING DEVICES

Psychologists know the location of lesions in the brains of laboratory animals because they put them there (Carlson, 1988). Prior to the 1970s, the location of lesions in the human brain could only be identified when the individual died and if the family gave their permission for an autopsy. Since the 1970s, however, a new approach to studying the brain has allowed researchers to identify the location of lesions in *living* individuals, as well as providing other information about the brain's workings.

Computerised axial tomography

For many years, neurologists took X-rays of the head to study brain damage, usually using dyes injected into the circulatory system to make the blood vessels in the brain more visible. However, the flat picture produced by a standard X-ray was not always informative. In the early 1970s, *computerised axial tomography* (CAT) was introduced and made the use of X-rays much more informative.

In CAT, the brain is examined by taking a large number of X-ray photographs of it. A person's head is placed in a large doughnut-shaped apparatus which has an X-ray

The CAT scan

CAT scanning was developed in the early 1970s and was first used for producing scanned images of the brain. Today, the CAT scanner is used to detect abnormalities or injuries in almost any part of the body. Its high cost means that it is not used for detecting simple bone fractures. It is most effective when examining soft tissues in the head or trunk region.

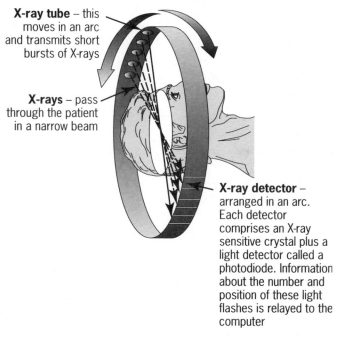

X-ray tube – this moves in an arc and transmits short bursts of X-rays

X-rays – pass through the patient in a narrow beam

X-ray detector – arranged in an arc. Each detector comprises an X-ray sensitive crystal plus a light detector called a photodiode. Information about the number and position of these light flashes is relayed to the computer

Figure 6.5   Diagrammatic representation of CAT

source located on one side and an X-ray detector on the other. As the apparatus is rotated through many different orientations (or axes), the amount by which the X-rays penetrate the brain is recorded by the detector. This information is fed to a computer which creates detailed images – the CAT scan – which are displayed as a three-dimensional representation of the brain's structures.

CAT is helpful to surgeons because it aids decision-making about the procedures that will be followed in an operation on the brain. For psychologists, CAT can help to determine whether a particular behavioural problem has an identifiable physical basis.

Magnetic resonance imaging

A more sophisticated approach than CAT is *magnetic resonance imaging* (MRI). Like CAT, MRI provides a three-dimensional image of brain structures. Although MRI uses similar equipment to CAT, a strong magnetic field rather than X-rays is used to form images of the brain. The person undergoing MRI is placed in a doughnut-shaped tunnel that generates a powerful magnetic field. Then, harmless radio waves are introduced which excite hydrogen atoms in the brain. This causes changes in the magnetic field which are recorded by a computer and then transformed into an image on a television monitor.

MRI is used to identify structural disorders and to study the normal brain. One advantage over CAT is its sensitivity and the clarity of the images produced. MRI can, for example, identify the smallest tumour with pinpoint accuracy, and locate the slightest reduction in blood flow in an artery or vein. Unfortunately, both CAT and MRI can only provide a still image of a cross-section of the brain. Whilst this provides useful information about the brain's structure, it tells us very little about its function. However, *functional MRI (fMRI)*, a variation on MRI in which blood flow in the brain is monitored continuously over time, overcomes MRI's limitations (Spinney, 1997a).

Positron emission tomography

Positron emission tomography (PET) allows researchers to examine the relationship between brain activity and mental processes. PET works by measuring metabolic activity within the brain. A person undergoing PET is first injected with a small amount of harmless radioactive material 'bonded' to a substance, such as glucose, that the body metabolises. Since the brain's primary form of energy is glucose, the areas which are most active absorb more of it.

The glucose is broken down by the brain but the radioactive material is not. As it decays, it emits positively charged particles (*positrons*). These are detected by sensors arranged about the head. This information is then fed to a computer which produces coloured images of the level of activity occurring throughout the brain, different colours indicating different levels of activity. Like CAT and MRI, PET is of great help in diagnosing abnormalities. For example, it is used to locate tumours and growths which gives surgeons vital information about the likelihood of essential brain structures being damaged by surgery.

As noted, PET takes advantage of the fact that at any given time some areas of the brain will be more active than others. PET's biggest advantage over CAT and MRI is that it can be used to provide images of what is going on in the brain *during* various behaviours. For example, when a person shuffles a pack of cards, there is increased activity in the part of the brain concerned with the regulation of skilled performance. When a person looks at a picture, the area of the brain concerned with the processing of visual information becomes active. As was seen in Chapter 4 (see Box 4.6) PET can also be used to identify areas of the brain that are active when we are *thinking*.

PET is useful in revealing differences between the brains of people with and without certain mental disorders. For example, the pattern of neural activity in the schizophrenic brain is different from that in the non-schizophrenic brain, suggesting that this disorder may have a physical cause (see Chapter 68).

Box 6.8 PET and the study of sex differences

Gur *et al.* (1994) showed that men have a more active metabolism than women in the primitive brain centres controlling sex and violence (see also Chapter 18). Although Gur *et al.*'s results are reliable, they only studied the brain at rest. However, the potential applications of PET suggest that it will be a useful way of investigating the brain for many years to come.

Spets and squids

New imaging and scanning devices are presently being developed and tested. These include the *superconducting quantum imaging device* (SQUID) and *single positron emission tomography* (SPET). Like PET, SPET and SQUID are able to map the different brain areas that are either functioning or not functioning during a task's performance. Although very expensive (costing around £350,000), their advantage is that they can focus on very small areas of the brain, occupying less than a fiftieth of a cubic inch in volume.

SPET measures the blood that flows into different brain areas. When mental activity takes place, a great deal of blood is needed. In areas where there is little activity, less blood is required. With SPET, a person is first injected with a small amount of radioactive iodine which makes the blood vessels, including those in the brain, mildly radioactive. The person is then placed so that the head lies in a ring of detectors, each of which turns the radiation emitted by the iodine into a pulse of light which itself is transformed into a minute electronic signal. By carefully analysing the signals, a computer builds up cross-sections of the brain at various depths depending on the part of the brain being studied.

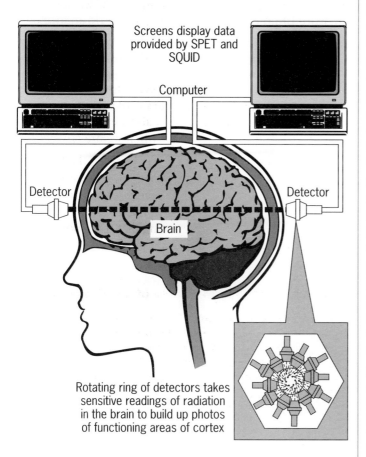

Figure 6.6   Diagrammatic representation of SPET

SPET has already produced some spectacular results. For example, prolonged and heavy use of alcohol causes *Korsakoff's psychosis*, a severe impairment in memory (see Chapter 27). Using SPET, it has been shown that there is a significant loss of functioning in the front part of the brain. SPET is also useful in detecting the brain areas affected in people with learning difficulties (Matthews, 1996a).

Conclusions

This chapter has discussed some ways in which the brain can be investigated. Although the methods and techniques all tell us something about the brain, each has weaknesses which limit the power of the conclusions that can be drawn from them.

Summary

■ Three major ways of investigating the brain are **clinical/anatomical methods**, **invasive methods** and **non-invasive methods**.

■ Studies of the behavioural consequences of accidental brain damage assume that if damage to part of the brain causes a particular behavioural change, the damaged part ordinarily plays a role in that behaviour. This approach was taken by Broca and Wernické in their studies of parts of the brain involved in language production and comprehension.

■ With many cases of accidental damage, however, not enough is known about the individuals before the damage occurred. Also, it can be difficult to determine the precise location and amount of damage, and research requires the 'right kind' of injury to have occurred.

■ **Ablation** involves surgically removing/destroying the brain tissue of non-humans and observing the behavioural effects. However, such research tells us nothing about humans, and because parts of the brain may work together in a behaviour, we do not know whether a part controls or is merely involved in behaviour.

■ The problems with ablation also occur in **lesion production**, in which part of the brain is deliberately injured and the effects observed. Lesion production has been used therapeutically in humans to treat **epilepsy**. These **split-brain** operations have interesting psychological consequences.

■ **Electrical stimulation of the brain** (ESB) involves inserting electrodes into the brain and passing a non-damaging current which the brain treats as a real impulse. Alternatively, the cerebral cortex is stimulated. ESB has been used therapeutically and is a useful way of mapping the connections between various brain structures. However, it is doubtful that brain stimulation in humans can repeatedly evoke the same emotion, memory, or behaviour since the brain is unlikely to be organised into 'neat compartments' that correspond to the labels assigned to behaviour.

■ The activity of single neurons can be studied using **micro-electrode recording**. This has contributed to our understanding of the visual system, but the vast number of neurons in the visual system alone makes it a painstaking method.

■ **Chemical stimulation of the brain** involves the introduction of a chemical to the brain by means of a micro-pipette. The effects produced last longer than in electrical stimulation, but since different non-humans respond differently to the same chemical, interpreting findings is difficult.

■ To overcome the ethical and practical problems of methods using direct intervention, researchers also use non-invasive methods. These involve recording the brain's electrical activity and scanning and imaging it.

■ The **electroencephalogram** (EEG) measures the simultaneous electrical activity of millions of neurons. However, whilst it has been used extensively in research into sleep and dreaming and as a diagnostic tool, it provides only general information about the brain.

Computerised electroencephalography, the **magnetoencephalogram** and **EEG imaging** provide much more specific information, although they too have limitations.

■ A variety of imaging techniques are used to investigate the brain. These include **computerised axial tomography** (CAT) and **magnetic resonance imaging** (MRI). However, both are limited to still images of the brain's structure.

■ **Positron emission tomography** (PET) is an imaging technique that measures the brain's metabolic activity. The advantage of PET over CAT and MRI is that it can measure brain activity *during* a task's performance.

■ The **superconducting quantum imaging device** (SQUID) and **single positron emission tomography** (SPET) are among the most recent imaging and scanning techniques. Both can examine tiny areas of the brain and have already yielded important information.

7

THE CEREBRAL CORTEX

Introduction and overview

As noted in Chapter 4, the cerebral cortex is most developed in humans and is what separates us from other animals. As well as being the last brain part to stop growing and differentiating, it undergoes greater structural change and transformation after birth than any other. As will be seen, certain cortical areas are specialised for particular mental processes and behaviours and this supports *localisation theory*.

This chapter begins by outlining localisation theory. Then, it looks at specific processes and behaviours which have relatively precise and circumscribed cortical locations. The cortex can be conveniently divided up into *primary areas* and *association areas*. After considering the primary *motor area* and the various primary *sensory* areas, the motor and sensory *association* areas (closely related to the primary areas) are examined. The discussion of the cortex concludes by examining other areas which do not seem to be involved in either motor or sensory functions, but appear to play a role in higher cognitive processes such as learning, thinking and memory. The role of the cortex in *language* is considered in Chapter 8.

Localisation theory

According to localisation theory, different areas of the brain and cortex are specialised for different psychological functions. This theory can be traced back to the work of Gall, an Austrian physician. He noticed that some of his friends with particularly good memories also had large protruding eyes. His explanation for this was that the front of their brains (which he believed to be the location of memories) was so well developed that it had pushed out the eyes. On the basis of this and other observations, Gall developed *phrenology*.

Box 7.1   Phrenology

Phrenologists see the brain as being composed of a number of separate organs, each of which is responsible for a different psychological trait. The unusual growth of any of these organs would create a bump on the skull, and people's characters could be determined by the pattern of bumps on their skulls. For example, a bump on the back of the head indicated that a person was 'cautious' whilst a bump on the side of the head indicated a 'secretive' individual. A bump just above the ears apparently meant that a person was 'destructive' and, potentially, a 'criminal'.

Although fashionable in the early nineteenth century, phrenology fell into disrepute on the quite reasonable ground that it was wrong. However, it was 'just right enough' to continue further interest in the idea that psychological functions are localised in certain parts of the brain.

THE PRIMARY MOTOR AREA

As was seen in Chapter 6, electrical stimulation of the brain has been used as a way of attempting to understand its function. One finding briefly described was that some areas of the cortex seem to be specialised in governing motor activity.

Penfield (1947) and Penfield & Roberts (1959) showed that stimulation of part of the frontal lobe near to the central fissure in one cerebral hemisphere caused twitching of specific muscles in the opposite side of the body. Delgado (1969) dramatically illustrated this when he stimulated a part of the primary motor area in a patient's left hemisphere. This caused the patient to form a clenched fist with his right hand. When asked to try to keep his fingers still during the next stimulation, the patient could not achieve this and commented, 'I guess, Doctor, that your electricity is stronger than my will'.

Recall from page 37 that control of one side of the body by the opposite hemisphere is called a *contralateral connection* (and is contrasted with an *ipsilateral connection* in which information from one half of the body is received, processed and acted upon by the same side of the body). Recall also that the crossing over of the nerve fibres connecting each hemisphere to the opposite side of the body takes place in the *medulla oblongata* (see also page 37), a phenomenon called *corticospinal decussation*.

Penfield discovered that when he stimulated the *top* of the primary motor area (or *motor strip*), a twitching in the *lower* part of the body (such as the leg) occurred. However, stimulation of the *bottom* part of the motor strip produced movement in the *upper* part of the body (such as the tongue). Penfield concluded that the body must be represented in an approximately upside-down fashion in the primary motor area. He also found that those body areas which require precise control, such as the fingers and mouth, have more cortical area devoted to them than those requiring less precise control.

Box 7.2   The primary motor area and movement

The primary motor area itself is not responsible for 'commanding' the 600 muscles in the body involved in voluntary movement. These commands are initiated in other cortical locations. However, once a command has been given, neurons in the primary motor area are activated, and send their information to the muscles that perform movements. What Penfield's research identified was exactly where the response messages from the brain start their return trip to the muscles and glands of the body. Damage to the primary motor area does not produce complete paralysis. However, it often results in a loss of control over 'fine' movements (especially of the fingers).

THE PRIMARY SENSORY AREAS

Whilst some cortical parts are specialised for motor functions, others govern sensory functions and receive their information in a precise, orderly way from the thalamus.

The primary somatosensory area

As has just been seen, the primary motor area *transmits* information out to the body. Certain types of incoming information are *received* by the *primary somatosensory area*, located in the parietal lobe, just across the central fissure. It is a thin 'strip' along which information from the skin senses (such as touch, temperature, pressure and so on) is represented. It also receives information concerning *taste*.

Micro-electrode stimulation of the primary somatosensory area might produce the sensation that the arm, for example, is being touched or pinched or that the leg 'feels hot'. Like the primary motor area, the body is represented in an approximately upside-down fashion and those body parts which are more sensitive (such as the face and genitals) have more cortex devoted to them. Relatively insensitive parts of the body, such as the trunk, have considerably less area devoted to them.

Box 7.3   Sensitivity and the primary somatosensory area

There is a clear relationship between the *importance* of a body part and the amount of cortex devoted to it. In animals that use their forepaws to explore the environment (such as the racoon), there is a large amount of forepaw cortical representation. In rats, the amount of primary somatosensory area devoted to the whiskers is very large. If a human is unfortunate enough to lose a finger, the somatosensory part responsible for receiving input from that finger becomes available to receive input from other fingers. As a result, the other fingers become *more sensitive* (Fox, 1984). Similarly, in Braille readers the cortical area devoted to the tip of the right forefinger is considerably enlarged as compared with the left, and is larger than that in non-Braille readers (Robertson, 1995).

As with the primary motor area, the primary somatosensory area in the left hemisphere registers information about the right side of the body. If the primary somatosensory area is damaged, deficits or disturbances in the sense of touch result. The extent of these depends on the amount of damage. With very mild damage, a person might not be able to make fine distinctions between the temperature of objects but could tell the difference between 'hot' and 'cold'. With more severe damage, this might not be possible.

Figure 7.1(a) shows a cross-section through the cerebral cortex just forward of the central fissure. This is the primary motor area. Figure 7.1(b) shows a cross-section through the cortex just behind the central fissure. This is the primary somatosensory area.

The primary auditory area

The primary auditory area lies in the temporal lobe of each hemisphere, along the lateral fissure. When auditory information is detected by the ear it is transmitted via the thalamus to the primary auditory area and causes neurons there to be activated. Penfield discovered that stimulation of these neurons caused his patients to report hearing sounds such as 'the ringing of a door bell' or 'the engine of a car'. The neurons in this area are highly specialised with some responding only to low-pitched sounds and others only to high-pitched sounds.

Most auditory information from one ear travels to the primary auditory area in the hemisphere on the opposite side. However, some information is processed on the same side. In hearing, then, there are both contralateral and ipsilateral connections. Slight damage to the primary auditory area produces 'partial hearing loss'. The more extensive the damage, the greater is the loss.

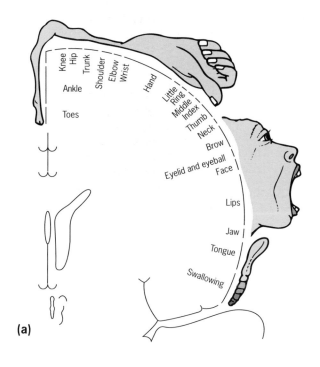

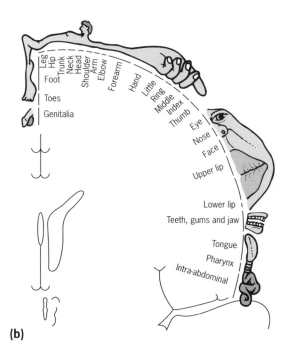

Figure 7.1 (a) and (b)   A cross-section through the cortex. Part (a) shows the primary motor area and the parts of the body it is concerned with. Part (b) shows the same thing for the primary somatosensory area

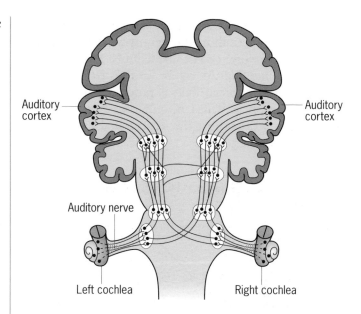

Figure 7.2   The major pathways of the auditory nerve fibres

The primary visual area

One of Penfield's first findings was that parts of the cortex are specialised to receive visual sensory information. For example, when a stimulating electrode was applied to the occipital lobe his patients reported 'seeing' different kinds of visual displays. Penfield (1947) reported the descriptions given by his patients as follows:

'Flickering lights, dancing lights, colours, bright lights, star wheels, blue-, green- and red-coloured discs, fawn and blue lights, radiating grey spots becoming pink and blue, a long white mark, and so on'.

Although his patients never reported a complete picture of the visual displays they experienced, Penfield's findings convinced him that the brain's primary visual area is located in the occipital lobe. When this area is damaged, blindness (or a 'hole') occurs in part of the visual field. The rest of the visual sense is, however, intact. Indeed, by moving the eyes, those parts of the visual world which cannot be seen can be brought into view, although the person will still be blind in some part of the visual field.

Chapter 10 looks in detail at the structures and processes involved in visual perception. However, it is worth briefly describing here how visual information reaches the primary visual area of the cortex. When light strikes the *retina* of the eyes, it is converted into electrical information which then passes along each eye's *optic nerve*. At the *optic chiasma*, the nerve fibres from each eye meet and divide up.

The fibres from the half of each eye's retina closest to the nose cross over and continue their journey in the hemisphere on the opposite side. The fibres from each eye's retina closest to the temples do not cross over and continue their journey in the hemisphere on the same side. The visual world can be divided into a *left visual field* and a *right visual field*. As Figure 7.3 illustrates, information from the left visual field is processed by the right cerebral hemisphere whilst information from the right visual field is processed by the left cerebral hemisphere.

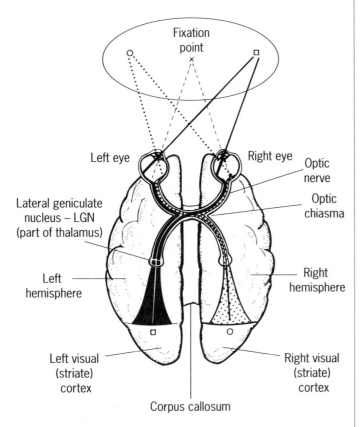

Figure 7.3   The major pathways of the visual nerve fibres

This occurs because of the crossing over of the fibres at the optic chiasma and means that each hemisphere receives information from both eyes. Although it might be simpler if each eye transmitted information to the hemisphere on the same side, damage to one eye would mean that a hemisphere would not receive any visual input. By having the more complex arrangement, damage to one eye does *not* result in a hemisphere 'missing out' on visual information. As mentioned in Chapter 4, visual sensory information travels to the thalami and is sent on from there to the primary visual area via the lateral geniculate nucleus.

ASSOCIATION AREAS IN THE CORTEX

The primary motor and sensory areas account for a relatively small proportion of the cortex's surface area. The primary motor area sends information to adjacent areas of the cortex called the *motor association areas*. Each of the primary sensory areas sends information to adjacent *sensory association areas*.

Motor association areas

These are involved in the planning and execution of movements. Information about which movements are to be executed are sent to the primary motor area. The motor association areas receive their information from several areas and integrate this into plans and actions. One region of the cortex is necessary for the production of spoken language, and is described in detail in Chapter 8.

Left parietal lobe damage makes hand movements difficult. Figure 7.4 shows the attempt of a person with left parietal lobe damage to draw a bicycle. Although the proportions of the elements making up the bicycle are quite good, the drawing looks clumsy and might have been done by a child. The motor association area's ability to integrate information into plans and actions is probably disrupted following left parietal lobe damage.

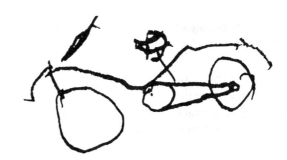

Figure 7.4   Drawing of a bicycle by a person with damage to the left parietal lobe

The motor association areas in the left parietal lobe, then, play an important role in the ability to keep track of the location of the body's moving parts (Carlson, 1988). This view is strengthened by the finding that people with left parietal lobe damage often have difficulty with tasks requiring them to point to a part of the body. They may, for example, point to the shoulder when asked to point to the elbow. Left parietal lobe damage results in 'faulty data' being sent to the primary motor area, which leads to poor execution of movement.

Sensory association areas

Each of the primary sensory areas sends information to adjacent sensory association areas. As was seen earlier on, the primary somatosensory area mediates our awareness of what is happening in the body and on its surface. Severe damage to this area produces *sensory neglect*.

Box 7.4   Sensory neglect

In sensory neglect, the affected person loses all awareness of the opposite side of the body. For example, a person having a shave will shave only one side of the face, eat food on only one side of the plate, and show inadequate representations of one half of something being drawn, (Halligan, 1995).

Figure 7.5   Drawing of a parrot by a person with left-side neglect

Associations in the parietal lobe play a role in *integrating* complex sensory functions as shown in *cross-modal matching*. If an object is placed in your hand but kept out of sight you would, when *shown* an array of objects in which it was included, be able to pick it out. This is because ordinarily we can integrate visual and tactile information. When the parietal lobe association areas are damaged, however, this task is extremely difficult.

The *auditory association area* is located towards the back of the occipital lobes on the side of the temporal lobes. If the left hemisphere's auditory association area is damaged, severe disturbances of language occur. For example, speech comprehension is lost, presumably because the neurons involved in decoding speech sounds have been destroyed. Additionally, the ability to read is lost and whilst the person may still be capable of producing language, its quality is very poor indeed and just a meaningless jumble of words.

Right hemisphere damage, by contrast, does not affect the production or reception of speech to any great degree. It does, however, affect the ability to perceive the *location* of sounds and to recognise non-speech sounds such as rhythms and tones. As noted earlier, the brain areas involved in language are discussed in detail in Chapter 8.

In contrast to the effects produced by damage to the primary visual area, damage to the *visual association area* (which includes parts of the temporal and parietal lobes as well as the occipital lobes) does not produce blindness. However, whilst the primary sensory function of vision is not impaired, the ability to *recognise* objects by sight is, a condition called *visual agnosia*.

For example, Sacks (1985) described a man who could not even recognise his own wife. At the end of one testing session, the man started to look for his hat. He reached over to his wife and began to lift her head, seemingly believing it to be his hat. Evidently, he had mistaken his wife's head for his own hat. Damage to some parts of the visual association area, then, produces deficits in the visual recognition of familiar objects.

Damage to the occipital lobes results in the inability to recognise the elements of a visual scene such as curves and angles. Damage to the right parietal lobe results in great difficulty integrating an object's parts into a consistent whole. In contrast to the drawing of the bicycle produced by a person with left parietal lobe damage (see Figure 7.4) a person with a damaged right parietal lobe produces a drawing which is smoothly executed and well-detailed, but does not have all of the parts placed appropriately.

Figure 7.6   Drawing of a bicycle by a person with right parietal lobe damage

Box 7.5   Higher order analyses of sensory information

As has been seen, sensory association areas are located near to their primary sensory area counterparts and receive information only about one sense modality. However, other sensory association areas receive information from more than one sense modality. These perform higher-order analyses of sensory information and represent abstract information in ways that are independent of individual sense modalities.

When we think about the word 'dog', for example, we can picture a visual image of a particular dog, the sound of its bark, and (perhaps) the pain we felt when it once bit us. We can also think about the visual representation of the word 'd-o-g' and the sound of the word 'dog'. Our thoughts can be stimulated when we see a dog, hear the word being said, or read a book in which the word is printed. The centres of higher-order analysis include areas on the borders between the temporal, parietal and occipital lobes.

Association areas not involved in motor or sensory functions

Even given what has been described, there are still large cortical areas that do not seem to be involved in either motor or sensory aspects of behaviour. Although knowledge is limited, it is known that these other areas are involved in the more complex psychological processes of learning, thinking, memory, and so on. Indeed, the term 'association areas' was originally used to describe them because it was believed that they were used in higher cognitive processes such as forming associations between things.

We may, however, be approaching the limits of our higher cognitive abilities if analyses of the brain's ability to process information conducted by researchers at British Telecom's laboratories are correct. According to them, a significant increase in processing power would require nerve cells to be wider to transmit information more quickly. However, this would require an increase in axon size, amongst other things, which would limit the number of neurons that could occupy the space available. Also, if our brains were larger, neurotransmitters would not cross the synaptic cleft as efficiently or quickly as now (Uhlig, 1997).

The frontal lobe is larger in humans than in any other species. For that reason, it was once thought to be 'the seat of intelligence'. However, frontal lobe damage does not cause significant impairments in intellectual functioning. Rather, it seems to affect the ability to set goals, plan actions and make decisions. Put differently, frontal lobe damage affects *intentions*.

Box 7.6 Perseveration and the frontal lobes

Damage to the frontal lobes results in the inability to change a behaviour in response to a change in a situation. For example, Cotman & McGaugh (1980) described a man who worked in a carpenter's shop. Although he could sand a piece of wood the man did not know to

stop when the sanding was complete. As a result, he sanded completely through the wood and continued sanding the work bench below. Similarly, Luria (1980) reported the case of a man who kept trying to light a match that was already lit. The term *perseveration* has been used to describe these behaviours.

Card-sorting tasks also illustrate perseveration. In these, a person is given a series of cards each of which has one or more patterns on it in one of several colours. People with frontal lobe damage have few difficulties sorting the cards according to colour, but when asked to sort them according to shape, they have great difficulty and continue sorting according to colour. Frontal lobe damage in non-humans results in the inability to remember the solution to a simple problem for more than a few seconds (Rosenkilde & Divac, 1976). Similarly, humans have difficulties in remembering the solutions to problems, especially those which require switching back and forth from one solution to another.

Frontal lobe damage is also associated with changes in personality. For example, a person may react with indifference to emotionally-provoking events, and being informed of the death of a close relative may produce no over-emotional reaction even though the individual understands what has happened. Other consequences of frontal lobe damage include a lack of insight, uncritical acceptance of the failure to solve a task and the inability to perceive sarcasm in written and conversational speech (McDonald & Pearce, 1996). Excessive damage produces *behavioural inertia* in which a person lacks spontaneity, remains motionless and stares vacantly into space.

Surgically damaging the frontal lobes became a 'popular' way of treating some mental disorders in the 1930s and 1940s. *Psychosurgery* is still used to treat some mental disorders and its applications and limitations are discussed further in Chapter 72.

One final consequence of frontal lobe damage is the production of reflexive behaviour normally seen only in babies, such as sucking an object placed near the mouth. Possibly, one role of the frontal lobes is to suppress such activities (which are presumably the result of activity in the more 'primitive' parts of the brain) when they are no longer needed.

Box 7.7 The association areas and memory

The association areas in the temporal lobes play an important role in memory. Penfield (1947) claimed that stimulating these areas causes a person to recall a 'dream-like' reliving of a past event. For example, when he stimulated an area of a young woman's temporal lobe, she said 'I think I heard a mother calling her little boy somewhere. It seemed to be something that happened years ago ... in the neighbourhood where I live'. When the same part was stimulated moments later, she said 'Yes. I hear the same familiar sounds. It seems to be a woman calling; the same lady'. When Penfield moved the electrode slightly and stimulated the woman's cortex she said, 'I hear voices. It is late at night, around the carnival somewhere – some sort of travelling circus. I just saw lots of big wagons that they use to haul animals in'.

Association areas in the temporal lobe also play a role in both social behaviour and certain emotional responses. In some types of temporal lobe damage, a person becomes a compulsive talker who harangues anyone who is (or potentially could be) listening, even if listeners have not the slightest interest in what is being said. This finding suggests that the association areas of the temporal lobe (especially, it seems, of the right hemisphere) play a role in evaluating the appropriateness of thoughts and speech. If the temporal lobes are damaged, the ability to carry out such evaluations is impaired (Carlson, 1988).

Box 7.8   Loser's lobes?

Damasio *et al.* (cited in Matthews, 1997a) gave brain damaged and non-brain damaged people packs of cards. Some individual cards in each pack were worth money whilst some cards in two of the packs carried large financial penalties. Non-brain damaged people quickly learnt to choose cards from packs that did not carry the penalties. Whilst brain-damaged individuals eventually realised the packs were different, they still chose cards from them. Non-brain damaged individuals attributed their decisions to a 'hunch' and Damasio *et al.* suggest that the ventromedial frontal cortices, the parts affected in the damaged individuals, were responsible for these poor decisions since these regions are believed to store information about past rewards and punishment. In the absence of reliable 'hunches', poor decisions invariably occur (see Chapter 36).

Holistic theory as an alternative to localisation theory

The findings relating to cortical areas lend strong support to localisation theory. However, localisation has not been universally accepted. According to *holistic theory*, psychological functions are controlled by neurons throughout the brain. Lashley (1926) studied the effects of destroying various parts of rats' brains on their abilities to remember the way through a complex maze. Although the rats displayed some difficulties, Lashley found that destruction of one particular area did not lead to greater difficulties than destruction of any other area.

In follow-up experiments, Lashley varied the *amount* of cortex destroyed in rats who had learned their way through the maze. He found that the greater the amount of cortex destroyed, the greater the effects, and called this the *law of mass action*. However, he also found that even rats with considerable damage could still find their way through the maze. In 1950, Lashley gave up his search for the part of the brain where memories were stored and remarked that, on the basis of his studies, the only conclusion he could reach after 25 years of research was that 'learning just is not possible!'

From what has been seen in this chapter, it seems undeniable that at least *some* mental processes and behaviours are localised in certain parts of the brain. However, this does not necessarily mean that we can reject holism as an alternative to localisation (see Chapter 8).

Conclusions

The cerebral cortex plays a vital role in behaviours and mental processes. As well as dealing with motor and sensory aspects of behaviour, it is also responsible for higher cognitive processes. When the cortex is damaged, various behavioural deficits occur. With the introduction of the non-invasive methods of studying the brain described in Chapter 6, we can confidently expect knowledge of the cortex and its functions to increase dramatically.

Summary

■ According to **localisation theory**, a scientific successor to **phrenology**, different cortical areas are specialised for different psychological functions.

■ The **primary motor area** is involved in movement, although it is not responsible for 'commanding' the muscles involved in voluntary movement. However, when a command has been given, primary motor area neurons send their information to muscles that perform movements.

■ The body is represented in an approximately upside-down fashion in the primary motor area, and since the area in the left hemisphere sends information to the right side of the body (and vice versa), it is **contralaterally connected**. Parts of the body requiring precise control have more cortical area devoted to them.

■ The **primary somatosensory area** receives information about the skin senses and taste via the thalamus. It is contralaterally connected, and the body is represented in an approximately upside-down fashion. Sensitive and important body parts have more cortex devoted to them. The extent of deficits in the sense of touch depends on the amount of cortical area damaged.

■ The **primary auditory area** is both ipsilaterally and contralaterally connected, and receives auditory information via the thalamus. Stimulation produces the experience of hearing sounds.

■ Light striking the retina is converted to electrical information. This passes along the **optic nerve**. At the **optic chiasma**, the fibres from the half of each retina closest to the nose cross over to the opposite hemisphere. The fibres from the half of each retina closest to the temples continue in the hemisphere on the same side. Since each hemisphere receives information from both eyes, damage to one eye does not result in a hemisphere receiving no visual information.

■ Stimulation of the **primary visual area** results in the experience that something has been seen. If the area is damaged, blindness (or a 'hole') occurs in part of the visual field, although moving the eyes can bring the 'missing' part of the visual world into view.

■ The primary motor and sensory areas send information to adjacent **motor** and **sensory association** areas. Motor association areas are involved in the planning and execution of movements. Damage to these areas produces deficits in the ability to integrate information into plans and actions, and an inability to keep track of the location of the body's moving parts.

■ Damage to the somatosensory association areas produces **sensory neglect**, a loss of awareness of one side of the body. Deficits in **cross-modal matching** can also occur. Damage to the **auditory association area** in the left hemisphere results in severe language disturbances. Right hemisphere damage affects the ability to perceive a sound's location and the recognition of non-speech sounds. When the visual association areas are damaged, **visual agnosia** occurs. The type of agnosia depends on the area damaged.

■ Some association areas receive information from more than one sense modality, and perform higher-order analyses of sensory information as well as representing information in abstract ways.

■ Large areas of the cortex are not obviously involved in either sensory or motor aspects of behaviour. Rather, they are involved in complex psychological processes such as learning, thinking and memory.

■ The **frontal lobes** are involved in setting goals, planning actions and making decisions. Damage to them results in the inability to change behaviour in response to situational change (as in **perseveration**). It is also associated with personality changes and a lack of insight.

■ **Temporal lobe** association areas play an important role in memory, social behaviour and certain emotional responses. Damage impairs the ability to evaluate the appropriateness of thoughts and speech.

■ In contrast to localisation theory, **holism** maintains that psychological functions are controlled by neurons throughout the brain. Whilst some mental processes and behaviours are localised in certain parts of the brain, holism cannot be rejected just on these grounds.

8

LANGUAGE AND THE BRAIN

Introduction and overview

Chapter 7 described the role played by certain cortical areas in mental processes and behaviour. These cortical areas are found in *both* cerebral hemispheres. However, for the overwhelming majority of people, some functions and processes are associated with *one or other* cerebral hemisphere rather than both (see Chapter 9). One of these is the production and comprehension of language. This chapter extends our consideration of the cortex, and looks at the areas of it associated with language and some of the disorders that arise when these are damaged.

Cortical areas, language and language disorders

As noted in Chapter 7, Gall's phrenology fell into disrepute because it was wrong. However, Gall did make some suggestions which were more or less correct. One of these concerned speech. Gall argued that the frontal lobes of the brain were specialised for speech. An admirer who was particularly impressed with phrenology offered the sum of 500 French francs to anyone who could find a person with frontal lobe damage who did *not* have a speech disorder.

Box 8.1   'Tan'

This offer led Broca (see Box 6.1), a French physician, to examine patients who had difficulty producing speech. His first case, 'Tan', was so named because this was the only word he could say. 'Tan' was originally admitted to hospital because he had a serious leg infection, but it was his difficulty in producing speech that most interested Broca.

Shortly after being admitted, 'Tan' died as a result of his infection and Broca conducted a post-mortem on him. This indicated that 'Tan' had suffered strokes which caused multiple *lesions* in a cortical area in the frontal lobe of the left hemisphere. In the next three years, Broca reported a number of other cases, all with the same problem as 'Tan', and all with lesions in a specific part of the left frontal lobe.

Around the same time that Broca was reporting his findings, Wernické (see Box 6.1) described patients who had difficulty in understanding language but were able to produce it, even though what was produced was usually meaningless. Wernické identified a region in the temporal lobe as being responsible for the deficit, and the cortical areas identified by him and Broca are now known called *Wernické's area* and *Broca's area* respectively.

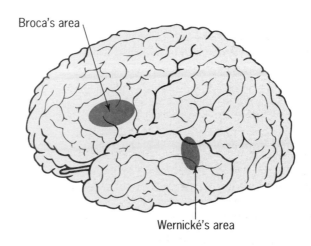

Broca's area

Wernické's area

Figure 8.1   The location of Broca's and Wernické's areas

Language disorders arising from brain damage are called *aphasias*. However, Milner (1971) argues that the term should only be used to describe complete language loss, *dysphasia* being a more accurate term to describe a partial loss of language (the word aphasia comes from the Greek word 'aphitos' which means 'speechless'). Various aphasias, resulting from one or more brain lesions, have been identified and there have been several attempts to classify them. Some classifications are based on the presumed location of the lesion(s), whilst others are based on the general sensory and/or motor functions which are impaired. A third, the *Boston classification* (Kertesz, 1979) is based on the particular linguistic skill that has been lost.

In some cases, where there is a gross disturbance of language abilities, people do not fit neatly into the Boston classification. Such individuals are termed *global aphasics*. In other cases, however, the Boston classification can be used to identify a person as having one of the five types of aphasia identified in Table 8.1.

Table 8.1 The five types of aphasia recognised by the Boston classification and their effects on language

	Type of aphasia				
	Broca's	Wernické's	Conduction	Anomic	Transcortical (MTA)
Is the person fluent?	No	Yes	Reasonably	Yes	No
Is speech and writing normal?	No	No	Yes	Yes	No
Can the person repeat back words?	Limited ability	Limited ability	No	Yes	Yes
Can the person name things?	Limited ability	Limited ability	Limited ability	No	No
Can the person comprehend speech?	Yes	No	Yes	Yes	No

(Adapted from Beaumont, 1988)

BROCA'S APHASIA

A person with damage to Broca's area experiences *Broca's aphasia* (sometimes called *ataxic, expressive, non-fluent* or *motor aphasia*). Usually, a Broca's aphasic can comprehend spoken or written language either normally or nearly normally. However, the person has great difficulty in producing speech (as Broca observed over 100 years ago). Typically, speech production is slow, laboured, non-fluent and difficult for the listener to understand.

For example, Geschwind (1979) reported the case of a Broca's aphasic who was asked about his dental appointment. He replied, 'Yes ... Monday ... Dad and Dick ... Wednesday nine o'clock ... ten o'clock ... doctors ... teeth'. As this example shows, Broca's aphasics find it difficult to produce 'function words', (words with grammatical meaning such as 'a', 'the' and 'about'). Their language consists almost entirely of 'content words' (words which convey meaning such as nouns, verbs, adjectives and adverbs). Consequently, Broca's aphasia has a *telegraphic* quality to it (see Chapter 33, page 288).

Box 8.2   Phonemic paraphrasias and agraphia in Broca's aphasia

In milder cases, the person might be aware that speech is not correct, and may become irritated by being unable to produce the intended words. Another characteristic of Broca's aphasia is the production of *phonemic paraphrasias*. In these, certain words are mispronounced. For example, instead of saying 'lipstick' the person might say 'likstip'. Sometimes, Broca's aphasia is accompanied by difficulty in writing (*agraphia*). Broca's area stores the 'motor plans' for the formulation of words. Normally, these plans are passed to the primary motor area which initiates the processes that will convert them to spoken language. When Broca's area is damaged, 'faulty data' are sent to the primary motor area and this results in the characteristic deficits in speech production described in the text.

WERNICKÉ'S APHASIA

Damage to Wernické's area produces *Wernické's aphasia* (sometimes called *receptive, sensory,* or *fluent aphasia*). Its major characteristic is a difficulty in understanding spoken and written language. Luria (1973), for example, described a person who was puzzled by the question: 'Is an elephant bigger than a fly?' He told Luria that he 'just didn't understand the words smaller or bigger' and that he

'somehow thinks the expression "a fly is smaller than an elephant" means that they're talking about a very small elephant and a big fly'.

In another case, Kertesz (1979) reported the response given by a person who was asked, 'What kind of work did you do before you came into the hospital?' The person replied:

'Never, now mista oyge I wanna tell you this happened when he rent. His – his kell come down here and is – he got ren something. It happened. In these ropiers were with him for hi – is friend – like was. And it just happened so I don't know, he did not bring around anything. And he did not pay for it. And he roden all o these arranjen from the pedis on from his pescid. In these floors now and so. He hadn't had em round here'.

Similarly, Rochford (1974) reports the case of a man who was asked why he had been admitted to hospital. The man replied:

'Boy I'm sweating, I'm awful nervous, you know, once in a while I get caught up, I can't mention the tarripoi, a month ago, quite a little I've done a lot well. I'm pose a lot, while, on the other hand, you know what I mean'.

These examples show that Wernické's aphasics have difficulty in understanding language and the language they produce is, at least in some cases, virtually unintelligible and lacking coherence. Thus, when asked to describe a picture of two boys stealing biscuits behind a woman's back, a patient of Geschwind's replied:

> 'Mother is away here working her work to get better, but when she's looking the two boys looking in the other part. She's working another time' (Geschwind, 1979).

The verbal outpourings of Wernické's aphasics have been described as 'a peculiar and outwardly meaningless language form'. Freud described such utterances as 'an impoverishment of words with an abundance of speech impulse'. Freud might have viewed such verbal behaviour as an indication of a serious mental disorder. However, as Williams (1981) has noted:

> 'The aphasic patient nearly always tries hard to communicate, whereas in [the seriously mentally disturbed individual] communication seems to be irrelevant'.

One characteristic of Wernické's aphasia which is evident in some of the examples given above is the production of *jargon*, that is, nonsense words or *neologisms* (see Chapter 68). For example, when Rochford (1974) asked a Wernické's aphasic to name a picture of an anchor, the person called it a 'martha argeneth'. Similarly, when Kertesz (1979) asked a Wernické's aphasic to name a toothbrush and a pen, the aphasic responded with 'stoktery' and 'minkt'.

Box 8.3   Wernické's aphasia: semantic paraphrasias and comprehension

Merely because a Wernické's aphasic does not answer a question correctly, it cannot be inferred that the question has not been understood. Wernické's aphasia is also characterised by *semantic paraphrasias*, in which the word that is produced does not have the intended meaning although it may be related to the intended word. For example, instead of producing the word 'table', the word 'chair' may be produced. To assess comprehension, *non-verbal* responses must be elicited. One test asks the person to point to various objects on a table. If the person is asked to 'point to the one you unlock a door with' and responds by pointing to an object which is not a key, the request has not been understood.

Wernické's aphasics are capable of using some language including function words, complex verb tenses and subordinate clauses. However, there are few content words and the words that are produced often do not make sense. Since people with damage to Wernické's area have difficulty in understanding language (and may themselves be unaware that they have a speech deficit), it is possible that they are unable to monitor their own language and this accounts for its incoherence.

It is reasonable to propose that Wernické's area stores memories of the sequences of sounds contained in words. This allows us to recognise individual words when we hear them and produce words ourselves. If Wernické's area is damaged, sounds cannot be recognised as speech and so the individual cannot comprehend what has been said.

ANOMIC APHASIA

In terms of producing and understanding language, *anomic* (sometimes called *amnesic* or *nominal*) *aphasics* have few problems. However, they are unable to find correct nouns to name objects. The anomic aphasic will, for example, hesitate whilst nouns are being sought and sometimes produce an inaccurate noun. Alternatively, things may be expressed clumsily as the person tries to get around the difficulty.

Most of us experience this to a degree. For example, ex-president of the USA George Bush's use of phrases such as 'the vision *thing*' and the 'law enforcement *thing*' caused much mirth amongst the American electorate. In severe cases of anomic aphasia, however, the person has difficulty in naming common objects such as a pen or a pair of scissors. In some cases, the anomic aphasic will *circumlocute* or speak in a roundabout way. A shoe, for instance, might be described as 'something to put one's foot in'.

Box 8.4   The angular gyrus

Penfield & Roberts (1959) encountered an anomic aphasic who could not name a comb, but could describe it as 'something I comb my hair with'. Thus, 'comb' could be used as a verb but not as a noun. According to Beaumont (1988), this suggests that:

> 'there is obviously a part of the language system which, given a particular meaning, retrieves the appropriate word from some store and it is this which is disordered in anomic aphasia'.

Anomic aphasia seems to be the result of damage to the *angular gyrus*, which is located in the posterior part of the parietal lobe, and therefore it is this which plays the role described by Beaumont (see Figure 8.2 page 70).

CONDUCTION APHASIA

The typical symptom of *conduction* (or *central*) *aphasia* is difficulty in repeating a sentence that has just been heard. Although conduction aphasics can understand and produce speech relatively well, and give an account of a presented sentence in their own words, *exact* reproduction

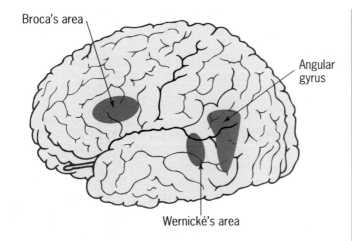

Figure 8.2   The location of the angular gyrus in relation to Broca's and Wernické's areas

is not possible. For example, an American conduction aphasic tested in the 1960s was simply asked to repeat the word 'president'. He replied, 'I know who that is – Kennedy' (Geshwind, 1972). Another aphasic, asked to repeat the sentence, 'The auto's leaking gas tank soiled the roadway', responded with, 'The car tank's leaked and made a mess on the street'. Conduction aphasia probably occurs as a result of lesions interrupting the nerve fibres (the *arcuate fasciculus* or 'arch-shaped bundle') which connect Broca's area with Wernické's area. The arcuate fasciculus, then, is also involved in language.

TRANSCORTICAL APHASIA

The final type of aphasia identified in the Boston classification is called *transcortical aphasia*. Transcortical aphasics have few comprehension skills (*transcortical sensory aphasia* or *TSA*), cannot produce normal speech (*transcortical motor aphasia* or *TMA*) or, more usually, both (*mixed transcortical aphasia* or *MTA*). They are, however, able to repeat back what somebody has said to them. Although TSA is similar to Wernické's aphasia and TMA to Broca's aphasia, the essential difference is that the damage has occurred beyond Wernické's and Broca's areas.

ISOLATION APHASIA

As well as the aphasias recognised by the Boston classification, several other language disorders have been identified. One very rare form is *isolation aphasia*, in which the brain's speech mechanisms receive auditory input and can control the muscles used for speech. However, they receive no information from the other senses or from the neural circuits containing memories about past experiences and the meaning of words. Geschwind *et al.* (1968) studied a female patient who had suffered severe brain damage after inhaling carbon monoxide from a faulty water heater. Although there was no damage to the primary auditory area, Broca's or Wernické's areas, or the connections between them, large parts of the visual association area were damaged and her speech mechanisms were isolated from other parts of the brain.

The woman remained in hospital for nine years until she died. In that time she made few voluntary movements except with her eyes, which were able to follow moving objects. She never said anything meaningful on her own, did not follow verbal commands or otherwise give signs of understanding them. By all available criteria 'she was not conscious of anything that was going on' (Carlson, 1988). However, if somebody recited the first line of a poem such as 'Roses are red, violets are blue', she would respond with 'Sugar is sweet and so are you'.

As well as being able to finish poems, she could also repeat words that were spoken to her. This was not done parrot-fashion since, if someone made a grammatical error while saying something to her, she would repeat what had been said *without* the error. Because she gave no signs of understanding anything she heard or said, her case suggests that:

'consciousness is not simply an activity of the brain's speech mechanisms; it is an activity prompted by information received from other parts of the brain concerning memories or events presently occurring in the environment' (Carlson, 1988).

The relationship between cortical areas and language

Over 100 years ago, Wernické formulated a model of how the brain produces language. This was refined by Geschwind (1979). The *Wernické–Geschwind model* proposes that when asked to repeat a word just heard, the word is passed (via the thalamus and the auditory area of the cortex) to Wernické's area. Activity there allows recognition of the words and understanding of their meaning. The formulation of the word is then passed to Broca's area, where memories of the sequence of movements necessary to produce it are stored. Broca's area then passes this information to the motor area of the cortex which programmes the various muscles in the face, tongue and larynx to reproduce the word (see Figure 8.3). This model explains why damage to Wernické's area leaves speech intact but disrupts language comprehension and the formation of meaningful sentences. It also explains why damage to Broca's area affects language production.

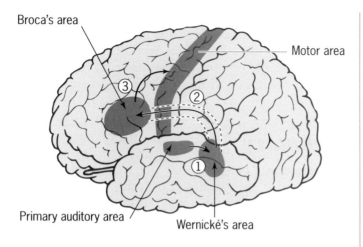

Figure 8.3   The processes involved in speaking a heard word

When asked to repeat a word we have read, a slightly different process occurs. First, the words are registered in the visual area of the cortex. Then, they are sent to the angular gyrus. This cortical area transforms a word's visual appearance into a code which is recognised and understood in Wernické's area (see Box 8.4). Once Wernické's area has received the code and understood the word's meaning, the formulation is then sent to Broca's area and the sequence of events for producing the word is initiated.

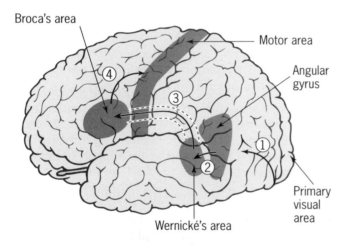

Figure 8.4   The processes involved in speaking a written word

The last two decades have seen significant progress in understanding the brain structures responsible for language (Damasio & Damasio, 1993). Research using PET (see Chapter 6) has been especially revealing. Findings indicate that when people are asked to say a particular word, Broca's area becomes highly active. However,

when asked to generate a verb that would be appropriate for a particular noun (such as 'cook' for 'oven'), other cortical areas are activated.

Language: localisation, lateralisation and holism

Chapter 7 introduced the term *localisation* to describe the fact that some specific functions and processes have relatively precise and circumscribed locations. From what has been said in this chapter, we can consider language to be a localised function along with those described in Chapter 7. At the beginning of this chapter, it was noted that the cortical areas associated with language are, for the vast majority of people, found in one or other cerebral hemispheres rather than both of them. This phenomenon is called *lateralisation*. So, as well as being localised, language is also lateralised.

Box 8.5   Language and handedness

For most of us, language is lateralised in the left hemisphere (Geschwind & Behan, 1984). However, there are some exceptions to this general rule as Satz's (1979) review of research discovered. All but around 5 per cent of us are right-handed, and in around 95 per cent of right-handers language is localised in the left hemisphere. In the remaining 5 per cent of right-handers, language is localised in the *right* hemisphere. In left-handers, Satz found things to be more complex. In about 75 per cent of left-handers, language is localised in the left hemisphere. Although none of the studies reviewed by Satz indicated that left-handers had language localised in the right hemisphere, the remaining 25 per cent showed *bilateral representation*, that is, the language structures were more or less equally represented in *both* hemispheres.

To add to this complex picture, Kimura (1993) has reported that some left-handers show a localisation of language which is exactly the opposite of that observed in the vast majority of right-handers. In other words, some left-handers do have language localised in the right hemisphere.

There also seem to be sex differences in terms of how the brain is organised for speech production. Kimura (1993) has argued that speech is more bilaterally organised in women, and that women are less likely to incur aphasia than men, and evidence exists to support this argument. However, Kimura does not believe that bilateral representation explains this effect. Her research shows that women are more likely to suffer aphasia when the front part of the brain is damaged, whilst in men aphasia is more likely following damage to the back part of the brain. Since restricted damage within a hemisphere more frequently affects the back part of the brain in both men and women, speech functions would be less likely to be disrupted in the latter because the cortical area is less often affected.

Explaining why language sometimes appears in the left and/or right hemispheres is not easy. However, the brain appears to have remarkable *plasticity*. When an area is damaged, other areas are apparently able to reorganise themselves and take over the damaged part's functions. This appears to be particularly the case with language. Lashley (1926) called this phenomenon the *law of equipotentiality* and Luria (1966) argued that the process occurs through *functional reorganisation*. In this, surviving brain circuits reorganise themselves to achieve the same behavioural goal in a different way (Robertson, 1995). This would explain why some victims of a minor stroke recover at least some abilities that were seemingly lost as a result of the stroke.

Box 8.6   Sturge–Weber syndrome and brain plasticity

It appears that the brain is particularly 'plastic' during childhood. In Sturge–Weber syndrome, the blood vessels of the left side of the brain become constricted during foetal development. As a result, the left side becomes shrunken with many calcium deposits. Following removal of the left half of his brain, a ten-year-old boy who was previously mute learnt to speak at an age considered by some researchers to be too late to acquire language (see Chapter 34). A number of explanations for this phenomenon have been proposed, one of the most plausible being that the damaged left side was inhibiting the right from 'taking over' (Connor, 1997).

Holistic theories (which were outlined in Chapter 7 as an alternative to the theory of localisation) are capable of explaining the brain's plasticity. Perhaps, then, both localisation and holism are true to some extent.

Conclusions

The ability to produce and comprehend language is one of many remarkable human abilities. This chapter has identified several cortical structures that play a role in language production and comprehension, and has described the behavioural consequences of damage to them. The cortical areas involved in language are usually found only in the left cerebral hemisphere, although in some people the opposite is the case, and in some the areas are present in both hemispheres.

Summary

■ Phrenologists believed that the frontal lobes were specialised for speech. Based on post-mortems, Broca concluded that lesions in a small cortical area in the left hemisphere (**Broca's area**) were responsible for deficits in **language production**. Wernické identified damage to an area in the temporal lobe (**Wernické's area**) as being responsible for **language comprehension**.

■ **Aphasias** are language disorders arising from brain damage. Classifications of aphasias are based on the presumed location of the lesion(s), the general sensory/motor functions impaired, or the particular linguistic skill lost. The last of these is used in the **Boston classification**.

■ **Broca's aphasia** results in difficulty producing language, and listeners find it difficult to understand. Speech is **telegraphic** and characterised by **phonemic paraphrasias**. Difficulty in writing (**agraphia**) may also occur. Broca's aphasia is a result of Broca's area sending 'faulty data' to the primary motor area.

■ **Wernické's aphasia** is characterised by difficulties in understanding spoken and written language. Speech may be unintelligible and lack coherence. The aphasia is characterised by **jargon** and **semantic paraphrasias** and the absence of content words.

■ Wernické's area stores memories of the sequences of sounds contained in words, which allows us to recognise spoken individual words. Damage to it means that sounds cannot be recognised as speech and so comprehension is absent.

■ **Anomic aphasia** involves the inability to retrieve appropriate words to name things, and **circumlocution** sometimes occurs. The aphasia is the result of damage to the **angular gyrus** which, given a particular meaning, retrieves the appropriate word from some store.

■ In **conduction aphasia**, the person has difficulty in repeating a sentence that has just been heard. The aphasic can, however, put the sentence into his/her own words. Lesions interrupting the **arcuate fasciculus**, which connects Broca's and Wernické's areas, may cause conduction aphasia.

■ **Transcortical motor aphasia** is similar to Broca's aphasia and **transcortical sensory aphasia** to Wernické's aphasia. In **mixed transcortical aphasia**, both the production and comprehension of language are affected.

■ **Isolation aphasia** is extremely rare. In it, the brain's speech mechanisms receive auditory input and can control the muscles used for speech. However, they receive no information from the other senses or from neural circuits containing memories of past experiences and the meaning of words.

■ The **Wernické–Geschwind model** implicates the auditory area, Wernické's area, Broca's area and the motor area in speaking a word that has been heard. When a word that has been read is spoken, the primary visual area, angular gyrus, Wernické's area, Broca's area and the motor area are involved.

■ As well as being **localised**, language is, in most people, **lateralised** as well. For most people it is lateralised in the **left** hemisphere. For a small number it is localised in the **right** hemisphere. For an even smaller number, language is **bilaterally represented**.

■ Speech is more bilaterally organised in women than men, and women are less likely to incur aphasia. However, it is unlikely that bilateral organisation in women explains this.

■ The brain's **plasticity** is particularly marked in the case of language. This flexibility is at its maximum during childhood and even removal of a complete hemisphere does not prevent normal language development. Such a finding is consistent with **holism**.

9

ASYMMETRIES IN THE CEREBRAL HEMISPHERES AND THE 'SPLIT-BRAIN'

Introduction and overview

Chapter 8 noted that for most people language is *lateralised*, that is, the cortical areas associated with it are found in one of the cerebral hemispheres rather than both. Whether the two hemispheres play the same or different roles in other aspects of our mental processes and behaviour has attracted much interest. Although the two hemispheres appear to be mirror images of one another, it has been argued that they are *functionally different*.

This chapter examines what research indicates about the specific abilities of the left and right cerebral hemispheres. However, it will also look at the intriguing question of whether the two cerebral hemispheres represent two kinds of 'mind'.

Cerebral asymmetries and the 'split-brain'

Fechner, one of experimental psychology's pioneers, knew that the brain is *bilaterally symmetrical*, consisting of two hemispheres which are apparently mirror images of each other. In 1860, he asked what would happen if a living person's brain were split in half. His own answer was that each half would have a different conscious experience, that is, he believed that two 'minds' existed inside the one brain.

Fechner thought that the experiment which would answer his question could not be conducted. In the 1960s, however, studying the effects of dividing the brain in two became possible as a by-product of surgery to control epileptic seizures. Up until the 1960s, attempts to control epilepsy involved removing the presumed disordered parts of the brain. However, this approach was limited in its success and researchers sought other treatment methods.

Box 9.1 The commissurotomy

In the early 1960s, Vogel and Bogen (see Bogen, 1969) proposed that epileptic seizures were caused by an amplification of brain activity that 'bounced' back and forth between the hemispheres. As a therapy of last resort, they suggested severing the corpus callosum, an operation called a *commissurotomy*. Their rationale was that severing the corpus callosum's 250 million axons would prevent the reverberation of brain activity, and cause it to be confined to one hemisphere. Since the operation involved splitting the hemispheres apart, people who underwent it became known as *split-brain patients*.

Research with cats and monkeys revealed that commissurotomy did not seem to cause any ill-effects. When the operation was carried out on epileptic patients, the results also suggested that there were no ill-effects apart from, as one patient joked, producing a 'splitting headache'! (Gazzaniga, 1967). As Sperry (1964) remarked:

'In casual conversation over a cup of coffee and a cigarette, one would hardly suspect that there was anything unusual about (the patient)'.

From a therapeutic perspective, the operation was a great success because the severity of the epileptic seizures was dramatically reduced, if not eliminated. From a psychological perspective, the operation provided the opportunity to investigate whether the hemispheres were specialised for particular functions, and allowed Fechner's question to be addressed. As will be seen, the results of many investigations also laid to rest the view that the corpus callosum served no function other than 'to keep the hemispheres from sagging'.

In their research with cats, Sperry *et al.* also severed part of the nerve fibres connecting the eyes and the brain (see page 62). This operation meant that a cat's left and right eyes sent information exclusively to its left and right hemispheres respectively. In one experiment, they placed an eye patch over a cat's left eye and then taught it to perform a particular task. When the task had been learned, the eye patch was switched to the other eye and the cat tested on the task it had just learned. It behaved as though it had *never* learned the task at all.

On the basis of this, the researchers concluded that one half of the brain did not (literally) know what the other half was doing, and that the corpus callosum ordinarily functions as a means by which information can be transmitted back and forth, so that each hemisphere is aware of the sensations and perceptions of the other. Sperry *et al.* wondered if the corpus callosum served the same function in humans. Of course, it would be unethical to sever some of the optic nerve fibres in humans if it could not be justified on therapeutic grounds (and even then, some would still consider it to be unethical).

Normally, we constantly move our eyes and hence both hemispheres receive information about the visual world whether we have experienced a commissurotomy or not. Sperry (1964) devised a way of sending visual information to one hemisphere at a time. Before looking at this methodology, two findings described in Chapter 7 should be recapped.

Box 9.2   The visual system: a recap

Each cerebral hemisphere is primarily connected to the opposite side of the body. So, an object placed in the left hand is sensed by neurons in the right hemisphere. The nerve fibres from the half of each retina closest to the temples send information to the hemisphere on the same side. However, the nerve fibres from each half of the retina closest to the nose send information to the opposite hemisphere. It is possible to divide up the visual world into a left and right visual field. As Figure 7.3 illustrates (see page 62), each hemisphere only receives information about the visual field on its opposite side. Thus, visual sensations in the left visual field are processed only by the right hemisphere, whereas the left hemisphere processes information only from the right visual field.

Normally, each hemisphere more or less immediately shares its information with the other. In 'split-brain' patients, however, the severing of the corpus callosum means that information cannot be conveyed from one hemisphere to another. As noted, we constantly move our eyes, and this allows both hemispheres to receive visual information whether the corpus callosum has been severed or not. Sperry's method of delivering information to only one cerebral hemisphere involved presenting a stimulus to one visual field at a speed that was too quick for eye movements to allow it to enter the other, and hence be perceived by both hemispheres. He discovered that a visual stimulus presented for about one tenth of a second allowed it to be perceived only by one hemisphere.

In the basic procedure, a patient is seated in front of a projector screen with the hands free to handle objects behind the screen, but obscured from sight by it. The patient is asked to gaze at a 'fixation point' in the centre of the screen. Visual stimuli are then 'back-projected' to the left of the fixation point (the left visual field) or to the right of it (the right visual field) for one tenth of a second or less. As noted, this allows the stimulus to be perceived, but is too quick for eye movements to allow it to enter both visual fields.

When a picture of an object is shown to the right visual field and the patient is asked to report verbally what was shown, the task is done easily. However, when a picture of an object is shown to the left visual field, the task cannot be done and the patient typically reports that 'there is nothing there'. Such a finding appears bizarre, but can be easily explained by applying what is known about the organisation of the visual system and what was said in Chapter 8 about the location of the structures responsible for language production and comprehension.

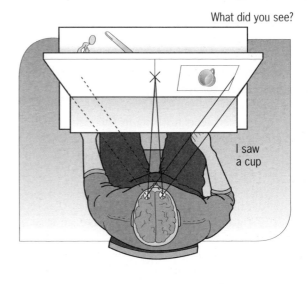

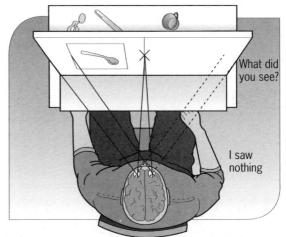

Figure 9.1   Responses given by a split-brain patient when material is presented to the right and left visual fields

All of Sperry *et al.*'s split-brain patients had their language structures in the left hemisphere (to which right visual field information goes). So, when an object was shown in the right visual field, the left hemisphere responded verbally and correctly. However, since the right hemisphere does not contain language structures, it cannot respond verbally. Thus, when an object is shown in the left visual field, the verbal response to the question 'What did you see?' comes from the left hemisphere. Since nothing was presented in the right visual field, the left hemisphere truthfully responds by saying that it saw nothing!

The apparent difference in the left and right hemispheres' abilities to produce spoken language led some researchers to use the terms *major* or *dominant* and *minor* or *subordinate* to describe the left and right respectively, as though the right hemisphere were some sort of 'second-class citizen' (Nebes, 1974). However, whilst the right hemisphere might not be able to respond verbally, it is far from linguistically incompetent.

For example, in another study a picture of an object was shown in the left visual field and hence perceived by the right hemisphere. When the patient was asked what had been presented, the response 'nothing' was given, a response which emanated from the left hemisphere (which had indeed seen nothing in the right visual field). However, when the patient was asked to use the left hand (which was placed beneath the screen so that it could not be seen) to select the object from a variety of objects, it was correctly selected. The left hand is controlled by the right hemisphere and since it was able to select the object, the right hemisphere must have at least some understanding of language (see Figure 9.2).

In a variation of the study just described, a picture of a cigarette was presented to the right hemisphere. The patient was asked to use the left hand (again placed beneath the screen so that it could not be seen) to pick out an object *most closely related* to the picture presented. Of all the objects that could have been selected, an ashtray was the one consistently selected by the patients. However, when asked to verbally identify the picture that had been shown or the object selected by the left hand, the patient was unsuccessful, the right hemisphere being unable to verbalise a response and the left being in complete ignorance of the picture presented.

As well as showing that the right hemisphere has some verbal abilities, even if these cannot be articulated, these findings also suggest that the left hemisphere seemingly has no idea of, or access to, the perceptions and memories of the right hemisphere. This was also shown in studies using the *divided field technique*.

What did you see?

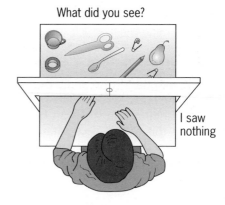

I saw nothing

With your left hand, select the object you saw from those behind the screen

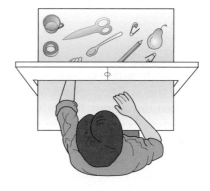

Figure 9.2   Although the right hemishere cannot verbalise a response, the left hand can correctly select an object the patient denies seeing

Box 9.3   The divided field technique

In the divided field technique, a word or picture is presented to the left visual field (right hemisphere) and a different word or picture simultaneously presented to the right visual field (left hemisphere).

In one study using this technique, the word 'case' was presented to the right visual field and the word 'key' simultaneously presented to the left visual field. When asked to report what had been seen, the patient replied 'case'. However, when asked to use the left hand to write the word that had been presented, the patient wrote 'key'. When asked what particular kind of 'case', the patient's left hemisphere would respond with 'in case of fire' or 'the case of the missing corpse' and so on. Any reference to 'key case' was purely fortuitous.

Another study required the patient to find the objects that corresponded to the words shown to the left and right visual fields using the left and right hands (both of which were behind the projector screen and could not be seen). When the right-hemisphere-controlled left hand came across the object that had been shown to the left hemisphere it ignored it completely, as did the left-hemisphere-controlled right hand when it came across the object that the left hand was looking for!

Gazzaniga (1983) claimed that on the basis of 20 years of empirical research:

'the cognitive skills of a normal disconnected right hemisphere without language are vastly inferior to the cognitive skills of a chimpanzee'.

However, the results of many studies have shown that whilst the right hemisphere might not be able to report verbally on its experiences, it has linguistic and cognitive capabilities which far exceed Gazzaniga's claims. As Levy (1983) has remarked, this is hardly surprising because it is unlikely that the 'eons of human evolution' would have left 'half the brain witless'.

An immediate critical response to Gazzaniga's claims came from Zaidel (1983). He developed a technique of presenting stimuli to the left or right visual field using a special contact lens that moves with the eye. This allows a stimulus to be presented for a much longer period than is the case using the original method of studying split-brain patients.

In one study, Zaidel gave vocabulary questions that required the right hemisphere to choose a picture that corresponded to a particular word. Although it did not perform as well as the left hemisphere, its performance was roughly equivalent to that of a ten-year-old child. This, and other findings, led Zaidel to conclude that

'the precise limits of right hemisphere language capacity are not yet known' [and] 'there is increasing evidence for right hemisphere involvement in normal language'.

Indeed, the right hemisphere has been shown to be better than the left at understanding familiar idioms and metaphors such as 'turning over a new leaf'. The right hemisphere may, therefore, play an important (if under-rated) role in language.

The right hemisphere is also superior to the left at copying drawings. Figure 9.3 shows its superior talents. Although the left hand is not as dextrous as the right (the right being the preferred hand in the patients that were studied), it is better able to reproduce the spatial arrangement of the example shown. The more coordinated right hand seems to be incapable of duplicating three-dimensional forms.

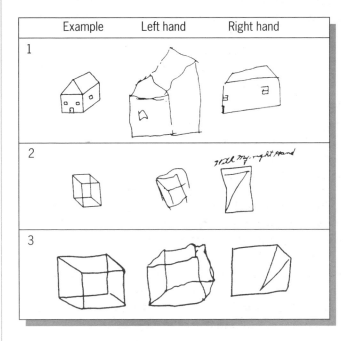

Figure 9.3   The abilities of the right and left hemispheres to reproduce a visual stimulus using the left and right hands respectively

The right hemisphere is also better at recognising faces. Using the divided field technique, pictures of different faces are presented to the left and right visual fields. When asked to select which face had been presented from an array of several other faces, the picture shown to the right hemisphere is consistently chosen whereas the one shown to the left hemisphere is consistently ignored. A slightly different approach to studying face recognition was taken by Levy *et al.* (1972). They showed patients *chimerics* (composite pictures of two different faces) one half of the face being projected to each of the hemispheres. When asked to verbally describe the picture that had been seen, the left hemisphere dominated. When asked to select a picture that had been seen, the right hemisphere dominated. This indicates that the left hemisphere processes information in linguistic terms whereas the right responds to the face as a total picture.

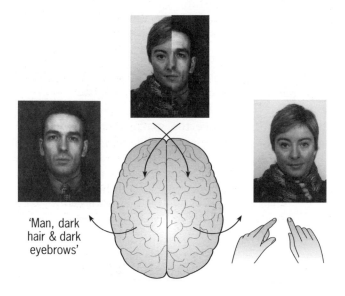

'Man, dark hair & dark eyebrows'

Figure 9.4 Responses given by the left and right hemispheres to a chimeric

Box 9.4 Analytic and synthetic hemispheres?

The terms *analyser* and *synthesiser* have been used to describe the left and right hemispheres respectively. The left hemisphere is evidently skilled at handling discrete information that can be stated verbally in the form of mathematical propositions. Faces, for example, are analysed in terms of their components ('deep-set eyes', 'blonde hair' and so on). The right hemisphere is superior when information cannot be adequately described in words or symbols. With a face, the right hemisphere synthesises all the information and recognises it as a whole. The perceptual superiority of the right hemisphere was also demonstrated by Sperry (1974). When the right hemisphere is instructed to arrange some blocks to match a picture, the left hand is highly competent. When the left hemisphere performs the same task using the right hand, its performance is so bad that, via the left hand, the right hemisphere 'interrupts' and takes over!

Outside the laboratory, the left and right hemispheres occasionally do battle. A female split-brain patient's left hand might pick out a particular dress to wear, only for the right hand to push the dress away and select another. This finding alone supports the view that the left and right hemispheres may be simultaneously conscious in different ways, and partly answers Fechner's question (see page 74 and pages 79–81).

Evidence also suggests that split-brain patients can sometimes perform *better* than people who have not had a commissurotomy. Ellenberg & Sperry (1980) sent one simple decision task to the right hemisphere and another simultaneously to the left. The split-brain patients were much better able to perform both tasks than were people with an intact corpus callosum. Under normal circumstances, then, the two hemispheres work together at solving tasks whereas in split-brain patients they are able to work independently.

As interesting as these data are, it has been suggested that they be treated with caution on the grounds that those who have been studied might not be representative of people in general. It was mentioned earlier that split-brain patients have all had a history of epileptic seizures, and it could be that the differences between the hemispheres occur as a result of changes in brain organisation brought about by the epilepsy. To talk about 'cerebral asymmetries' and 'hemispheric specialisation' requires that the same phenomena occur in people who have not had a history of epilepsy and/or undergone a commissurotomy.

Cerebral asymmetries and the intact brain

There are several ways in which asymmetries in the intact brain can be studied. One of these is the *Wada test*.

Box 9.5 The Wada test

This involves injecting sodium amytal (a barbiturate – see Chapter 15) into the left or right carotid artery. Because this artery sends blood primarily to the cerebral hemisphere on the same side, it is possible to temporarily anaesthetise a hemisphere and observe what happens. Just before the injection, the person is instructed to put his or her arms in the air and begin counting backwards from one hundred. The arm on the opposite side of the artery injected will suddenly fall limp. If the person is able to continue counting backwards, then the language structures must be in the non-injected hemisphere since the injected hemisphere has been temporarily anaesthetised.

The Wada test is only used prior to brain surgery to assess whether language structures might be affected. Other ways of assessing asymmetries include EEG, measurements of blood flow and glucose consumption (see Chapter 6), and studying people who have suffered strokes. It is also possible to use variations of the techniques originally employed to study 'split-brain' patients.

In one of these, different stimuli are simultaneously presented to the left and right visual fields. In some cases, the stimulus to the right visual field will be reported by the person, whereas in others the stimulus presented to the left visual field will be reported. Reporting of the right visual field stimulus implies that the left hemisphere is better at processing the type of information presented. If the left visual field stimulus is reported, this implies that the right hemisphere is better.

This finding is *not* inconsistent with the claim that the right hemisphere cannot verbalise its responses. In the normal brain, the two hemispheres communicate with one another. Information about the stimulus presented to the right hemisphere must cross into the left hemisphere to be verbalised. The fact that the stimulus presented to the right hemisphere is verbally reported first, even though the information has had to travel a greater distance than information presented to the left hemisphere, must mean that the processing has been more efficient.

Similarly, auditory information can be simultaneously presented to the left and right ears. The results of studies using *dichotic listening tasks* (see Chapter 25) indicate a right ear advantage for words, suggesting a left hemisphere superiority for processing verbal material. However, non-verbal auditory material (such as music) tends to produce a left ear advantage, suggesting a right hemisphere superiority in processing this information.

On the basis of many studies using people with intact brains, Ornstein (1986) concluded that the left hemisphere is specialised for analytical and logical thinking, especially in verbal and mathematical functions. It also processes information sequentially (one item at a time) and its mode of operation is linear. By contrast, the right hemisphere is specialised for synthetic thinking in which it is necessary to bring different things together in order to form a whole. This is particularly true for spatial tasks, artistic activities, body image and face recognition. The right hemisphere also processes information more diffusely (several items at once) and its mode of operation is more holistic than linear.

Box 9.6   Left and right brains?

The conclusions drawn by Ornstein, coupled with the results of many studies not described in this chapter, suggest that the hemispheres perform somewhat different functions. This has led to the idea of people being 'logically left-brained' or 'intuitively right-brained' depending on the ways they behave. Indeed, (best-selling) books have been published which claim to show us how to 'unlock the door to the neglected right side of the brain'.

Although hemispheric differences seem to be well-established, psychologists generally believe the claims made in popular books to be both exaggerated and grossly oversimplified. Whilst the terms 'verbal' and 'non-verbal' hemispheres are reasonable first approximations, the data are actually much more complicated. Under normal circumstances, the two hemispheres work together, communicating by means of the corpus callosum, and their functions overlap to at least some degree. Moreover, some of the tasks which are ordinarily dealt with by one hemisphere can be performed by the other. As Sperry (1982) has observed, 'the left-right dichotomy is an idea with which it is very easy to run wild'.

An answer to Fechner's question?

The results from the many studies on split-brain patients seem to agree with Fechner's own answer to the question he posed over 100 years ago. What we see when the brain is bisected is, according to Sperry, essentially a divided organism with two mental units each possessing its own private sensations, perceptions, thoughts, feelings and memories. The mental units are, Sperry argues, each competing for control over the organism.

Ornstein (1986) has asked whether a commissurotomy produces a 'splitting' (or 'doubling') of mind or whether it helps to manifest a duality that is actually present all the time. As has been seen, Sperry and at least some of his colleagues clearly believe the former. Others, however, take the latter view. For example, Pucetti (1977) has argued that split-brain patients are not special in having two minds because even when the hemispheres are connected, we *are* two minds. Normally, Pucetti argues, we appear to be unified and synchronised beings because the separate existence of the two selves is undetectable. All the commissurotomy does is to make apparent the duality that is there all the time. According to this *double brain theory*, the mind, 'self', or personality can be essentially 'reduced' to a hemisphere of the brain.

Parfit (1987) accepts the idea that the split-brain patient has two streams of consciousness, but does not believe that we should regard them as constituting two persons because in a sense, there is *none*. Parfit distinguishes *ego theory* (a theory of what people are) from *bundle theory* (which explains the unity of consciousness by claiming that ordinary people are, at any time, aware of having several different experiences). At any time, split-brain patients do not have one state of awareness of several different experiences. Rather, they have two such states (and *not* two separately existing egos). As Parfit has observed, split-brain patients have great theoretical importance because they 'challenge some of our deepest assumptions about ourselves'.

Conclusions

This chapter has looked at the claim that the two cerebral hemispheres are functionally different. Research with split-brain patients suggests that the left and right hemispheres play different roles in our mental processes and behaviour. However, split-brain patients are not representative of the population in general. Yet, when hemisphere asymmetries in the 'normal' brain are looked at, a similar picture emerges, although some researchers have cautioned against making too much of the left–right hemisphere differences. The question of whether dividing the brain results in a doubling of consciousness has also been examined. There are several viewpoints on this, and further research is needed to assess them.

Summary

■ Whether the cerebral hemispheres play the same or different roles in mental processes and behaviour has long interested psychologists, and can be traced back to a question posed by Fechner in 1860.

■ As a treatment for severe forms of epilepsy, the fibres of the corpus callosum are severed in an operation called a **commissurotomy**. This produces no ill-effects in the **'split-brain' patient**, but allows the roles played by the hemispheres to be investigated.

■ Sperry's method for doing this involves presenting stimuli to either the left or the right visual field only. This is achieved by presenting the stimuli at a speed which is too fast for eye movements to allow it to enter both visual fields.

■ Stimuli presented to the left visual field are perceived by the right hemisphere. Right visual field stimuli are perceived by the left hemisphere. Split-brain patients can verbally report what is presented to the right visual field but verbally deny perceiving anything in the left visual field. This is because the language structures are in the left hemisphere. Since material presented to the left visual field is not perceived by the left hemisphere, this denial is truthful.

■ On the basis of its verbal capabilities, the left hemisphere has been called the **major/dominant hemisphere** and the right the **minor/subordinate hemisphere**. However, because split-brain patients can use the left hand to retrieve an out-of-sight object whose picture was shown in the left visual field, the right hemisphere must have some understanding of language even if it cannot articulate this.

■ The right hemisphere's linguistic ability is roughly equivalent to that of a ten-year-old child. However, with some verbal material, such as idioms and metaphors, the right hemisphere is actually superior to the left.

■ The right hemisphere is superior at copying drawings and, as shown with the **divided field technique** and **chimerics**, recognising faces. The left hemisphere processes pictures of faces linguistically whilst the right responds to the face as a total picture.

■ The left hemisphere has been described as an **analyser** because it is skilled at handling discrete information that can be stated verbally. The right hemisphere has been described as a **synthesiser** since it is superior when information cannot be adequately described in words or symbols (as in recognising a face).

■ Sometimes, split-brain patients can perform tasks better than people with an intact corpus callosum. When two different tasks are presented to the left and right hemispheres, split-brain patients perform better because their hemispheres work independently.

■ Generalising the data from split-brain patients is difficult, since their epilepsy may have caused changes in brain organisation. However, studies of asymmetries in the intact brain, using a variety of methods, have yielded similar findings.

■ The left hemisphere is apparently specialised for **analytical** and **logical** thinking. It processes information sequentially and in a linear fashion. The right hemisphere is apparently specialised for **synthetic** thinking. It processes information more diffusely and in a holistic way. This is a useful first approximation, but the hemispheres normally work together and their abilities tend to overlap.

■ According to Sperry, the bisected brain is two mental units competing for control of the organism. Pucetti believes people have two minds even when the hemispheres are connected, and the commissurotomy simply makes obvious the duality that is there all the time. This is called **double brain theory**.

■ According to **bundle theory**, we are normally aware of having several different experiences, and this accounts for the unity of consciousness. Split-brain patients have two states of awareness of several different experiences, as opposed to being two distinct egos (**ego theory**).

10

THE NEUROPHYSIOLOGICAL BASIS OF VISUAL PERCEPTION

Introduction and overview

Vision is the dominant sense in humans, and much of what we do depends on possessing an adequately functioning visual system. The visual system's importance is reflected by the fact that a greater proportion of the brain is devoted to vision than any other sense. Indeed, such is vision's importance that if lenses that distort a square object into a rectangle are worn, we perceive it as a rectangle even though it can be felt as a square, a phenomenon known as *visual capture*.

This chapter begins by looking briefly at light, the 'messenger' that tells us about the colour, size, shape, location and texture of objects and surfaces. It then discusses the structure of the eye. However, the majority of the chapter examines how light information is transformed by the brain and considers theories of colour vision and colour constancy.

Light

Light consists of energy particles called *photons*. These have both electrical and magnetic properties, and so light is an example of *electromagnetic radiation*. Photons travel in waves that move forward and oscillate up and down. There are two important *characteristics* of light. The number of photons in a pulsating stream determines the *intensity* of a light wave. The distance between successive peaks of a light wave determines its *wavelength*. Wavelength is measured in *nanometres* (nm). One nanometre is one thousand millionth of a metre.

Light has three important *properties*. These are *brightness*, *hue* and *saturation*. The intensity of a light wave determines our experience of *brightness*. The more photons a light source emits, the brighter it appears. *Hue* is the colour we perceive something to be and is partly determined by wavelength. Visible light is a very narrow section of the electromagnetic spectrum that includes radio waves, radar, microwaves and X-rays. Light visible to humans has a wavelength ranging from about 380 nm to 760 nm. Longer wavelengths look red, whereas shorter wavelengths are perceived as violet. In between these extremes, the other colours of the rainbow can be found.

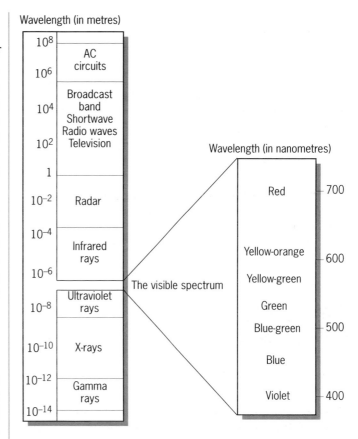

Figure 10.1 The electromagnetic spectrum showing the visible portion to the right

Some colours, such as brown and white, are not in the spectrum of light. Colour, then, cannot be just a matter of wavelength. As will be seen, colours like brown are produced by a complex process in which various wavelengths are mixed by the visual system. White light is, in fact, radiation that includes *all* wavelengths within the visible range. *Saturation* determines how colourful light appears. White is a completely colourless state, and the more white that is present in a colour the less saturated it is. For example, when mint and vanilla chocolate are mixed, the green colour gradually diminishes to a very light green shade. Saturation, then, is the proportion of coloured (or *chromatic*) light to non-coloured (or *achromatic*) light.

Sir Isaac Newton demonstrated that white light is a mixture of wavelengths corresponding to all colours in the visible spectrum. He showed that when light is passed through a prism, the longer wavelengths are refracted least by the prism whilst the shorter wavelengths experience most refraction. By casting this light on to a screen, Newton revealed the full spectrum of colours (see pages 85–86).

The eye

According to Ornstein (1986), the eye 'is the most important avenue of personal consciousness'. About 90 per cent of the information about the external world reaches us through the eye.

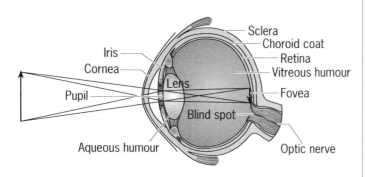

Figure 10.2   Cross-section of the human eye

The eyeball is enclosed by the *sclera*, a tough outer coat. The sclera is opaque, except at the front of the eye where it bulges out to form a transparent membrane (the *cornea*) through which light enters the eye. Via the cornea, light waves pass through a clear, watery fluid (*aqueous humour*), and are refracted to bring them into sharper focus. The *iris* controls the amount of light entering the eye, and contracts or expands to vary the size of the *pupil* (a black aperture in the eye) through which light waves pass. Pupil size adjusts automatically to the amount of light, and is under the control of the ANS (see Chapter 5). In low lighting, the pupil dilates to allow more light to enter. In bright light, it contracts to limit the amount that enters.

Light next strikes the *lens*, a crystalline structure which further focuses light waves. The lens is held in place by *ciliary muscles* that control its shape. Looking into the distance causes the lens to be made thinner. Looking at objects close to us causes it to be made thicker. This process, *accommodation*, brings objects into focus. Abnormalities in eye shape often make it impossible for the lens to accommodate correctly. This causes *short-sightedness* (in which objects can be seen distinctly only over a short distance) or *long-sightedness* (in which distant objects can be seen clearly but near objects cannot).

After being refracted by the lens, light waves pass through a jelly-like substance (*vitreous humour*) before striking the *retina*, a delicate membrane which lines the back of the eye.

Box 10.1   The retina

The main parts of the retina are *cones, rods, bipolar cells and ganglion cells*, all of which are neurons. Rods and cones form one layer of the retina and are *photosensitive cells* (or *photoreceptors*) whose job it is to convert light energy into electrical nerve impulses. Bipolar and ganglion cells form the other two layers of the retina. The bipolar cells are connected to the ganglion cells and to rods and cones. The axons of the ganglion cells form the beginning of the *optic nerve*, the pathway by which information is sent to the brain.

We might expect the photoreceptors to be at the *front* of the retina where they would be in the best position to intercept light waves. However, they are at the *back*. This means that light waves must pass through the other two layers and the blood vessels that serve them. One reason for this arrangement is that the work done by the photoreceptors requires amounts of energy that cannot be supplied by the fluid of the eye. Thus, the photoreceptors are next to the *choroid coat* of the retina, which is rich in blood vessels. Oxygen and other nutrients carried by the blood provide the photoreceptors with the necessary energy.

Each retina has about 120 million rods and 7 million cones. Rods help us to see *achromatic colour* (black, white and intermediate grey), and are specialised for vision in dim light (*scotopic vision*). They are sensitive only to light intensity, and therefore contribute to our perception of brightness but not colour. The photosensitive chemical contained in rods, *rhodopsin*, changes its structure in response to low levels of illumination. Different cones respond to different wavelengths and this helps us see *chromatic colour* (red, green, blue, and so on) and provides us with *photopic vision*. The cones are specialised for bright light vision and contain a chemical called *iodopsin*.

Box 10.2   The distribution of rods and cones

Rods and cones are distributed differently in the retina. Cones are much more numerous towards its centre. The *fovea*, a pit-like depression, is part of a cone-rich area

---

called the *macula lutea* in which around 50,000 cones can be found. This dense packing explains visual *acuity* (or sharpness). The more densely packed the receptors are, the finer are the details of a pattern of light intensity which can be transformed into electrical energy.

Rods are distributed fairly evenly around the retina's periphery and none are found in the fovea. When we want to focus on an object in bright light, our most sharply defined image will be obtained by looking directly at the object so that light is projected on to the cone-rich fovea. In dark light, however, the sharpest image will be obtained if we look slightly to one side of the object in order to stimulate the rods in the retina's periphery.

When a photon strikes a receptor, a *photochemical reaction* occurs. This *transduces* light energy into neural signals. These are passed to bipolar cells which in turn pass them to ganglion cells. These travel across the retina's inner surface and converge to form the optic nerve, which carries signals to the brain. The *optic disc* is the part of the retina where the optic nerve leaves the eye. There are no visual receptors at this point and the optic disc is thus the eye's *blind spot*. Normally, we do not notice the blind spot, one reason being that our eyes are constantly moving. This allows us to receive the image that would fall on the blind spot in another part of the retina.

There are many more rods and cones than there are bipolar cells, and more bipolar cells than ganglion cells. This means that many rods (and cones) send their information to the same bipolar cell, and ganglion cells receive their information from many bipolar cells. Two other kinds of neuron in the retina, *horizontal cells* and *amacrine cells*, transmit information across the retina and allow interactions between adjacent rods, cones, bipolar cells and ganglion cells.

The number of photoreceptors sending information to the same bipolar cell varies. Around the retina's periphery, several hundred rods may send information to one bipolar cell. At the fovea, however, individual bipolar and ganglion cells may serve only one cone. This one-to-one relationship accounts for the better acuity of cone vision as compared with rod vision. However, because many rods send information to one bipolar cell, the cell is more likely to 'fire' and hence rods are better at detecting faint light.

Box 10.3   Receptive fields

Hubel & Wiesel (1962) identified the type of visual stimulus to which individual retinal cells are most sensitive. They inserted micro-electrodes (see Chapter 6) into the optic nerve of an anaesthetised cat. Some cells responded maximally when a spot of light fell on one particular, and usually circular, part of the retina. If the spot was moved to the surrounding part of the retina, the ganglion cells

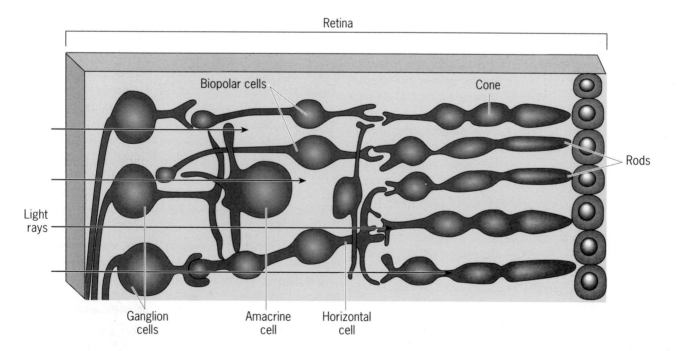

Figure 10.3   The layers of cells in the retina. Note how light must travel through several layers before reaching the photoreceptors

gradually stopped responding. Hubel and Wiesel called the sensitive areas the cell's *receptive field*, and concluded that a ganglion cell is connected to all or most of the rods and cones within a receptive field.

At least three types of ganglion cell exist, each of which has a different kind of receptive field. One has an *on-centre* and an *off-surround*. This cell is more active when light falls in the centre of the receptive field and less active when it falls on the edge. A second has an *off-centre* and *on-surround*. A third has a larger receptive field and seems to respond to movements, especially sudden ones. This is called a *transient cell*. The combined activity of on- and off-centre cells provides a clear definition of contours where there is a sudden change in brightness. Such contours are essential in defining the shape of objects to be perceived (Beaumont, 1988).

From the eye to the brain

As was seen in Chapters 4 and 7, visual sensory information travels to the thalamus and from there to the *primary visual area* of the cortex. Optic nerve fibres terminate at synapses with cells of a part of the thalamus called the *lateral geniculate nucleus* (LGN). The LGN in each of the thalami combines the information from both eyes before sending it to the cortex along the *geniculostriate path*. This and the visual area must be intact for the conscious experience of vision. However, in *blindsight*, the visual area may be extensively damaged but a person can identify objects without being consciously aware of them. Weiskrantz (1986), for example, reported a case in which a person was able to detect whether a visual stimulus had been presented even though he was subjectively blind! This suggests the existence of another pathway which carries enough information to guide some actions in an unconscious way.

Hubel & Wiesel (1965) found that LGN cells had circular receptive fields just like ganglion cells. However, when they investigated cells in the cortex, a slightly different picture emerged. Using micro-electrodes to record the activity of single cells in the primary visual area of monkeys and cats, Hubel and Wiesel suggested the existence of three types of cortical cell that play a role in decoding light information.

Box 10.4   Simple, complex and hypercomplex cells

Simple cells respond only to particular features of a stimulus in a particular orientation and location in the visual field. For example, a vertical straight line in a specific location in the visual field might cause a particular neuron to 'fire'. However, if a horizontal line was in the same part of the visual field, the neuron would not respond.

Complex cells respond to a particular feature of a stimulus in a particular orientation *no matter where* it appears in the visual field. A complex cell, then, might respond to a vertical line wherever it was in the visual field. However, if the line's features or orientation changed, the cell would stop responding. Presumably, complex cells receive inputs from many simple cells which show the same feature and orientation features, and this accounts for their ability to respond to stimuli no matter where they appear in the visual field.

Hypercomplex cells respond to corners, angles, or bars of a particular length moving in a certain direction. Such cells presumably receive inputs from large numbers of complex cells. Although the existence of hypercomplex cells has been questioned (Bruce & Green, 1990), Hubel and Wiesel's research demonstrated that the visual area of the cortex is not a homogeneous mass of tissues with randomly scattered cells. Rather, it shows precise and regular arrangement of different cells which Hubel and Wiesel termed the visual area's *functional architecture*.

Hubel & Wiesel (1977) showed that six main layers of the visual area of the cortex could be identified beneath the microscope. The visual area is apparently divided into roughly 1 mm square blocks of tissue that extend from the surface of the cortex down to the white matter below. These are called *hypercolumns*. Within the hypercolumns, cells have different receptive fields. Although there is a good deal of overlap of these receptive fields, all fall within some single retinal area (or what Hubel and Wiesel term an *aggregate field*).

Two further patterns of organisation are worthy of mention. First, cells fall into two groups according to which eye is most effective in eliciting a response. Although cells in some layers have *binocular fields*, and respond to their optimal stimulus whichever eye it is presented to, they always respond more strongly to the stimulus to one eye or the other (*ocular dominance*). Cells sharing the same ocular dominance are grouped together into bands running across the visual area.

The second pattern of organisation is that cells are arranged in columns about 0.5 mm across according to their 'orientation preference'. If an electrode penetrates the cortex at right angles to the surface, then all the cells it encounters will have the same orientation preference regardless of whether they are simple or complex.

As well as the primary visual area, there are other visual association areas in the occipital, temporal and parietal lobes. Maunsell & Newsome (1987) have suggested the existence of at least 19 visual areas, each of which sends output to several others, and most (if not all) of which are matched by reciprocal connections running in the opposite direction. According to van Essen (1985), there are as many as 92 pathways linking the visual areas!

Each area appears to have its own specialised function. V5, for example, deals with motion. *Visual illusions* (see Chapter 22) might be caused by the breakdown of the rules used by the brain to process signals from the eye. One illusion, 'Enigma', is a painting in blue, black and white by the artist Isia Leviant. Although static, there seems to be a rotating movement within the solid rings of the picture.

Using PET (see Chapter 6), Zeki (cited in Highfield, 1997b) showed that the black and white version of the illusion stimulated V5 and surrounding areas. For some reason, the static picture causes activity in V5 and this accounts for the sensation of the circular movement even though there is no objective motion (see pages 178–179).

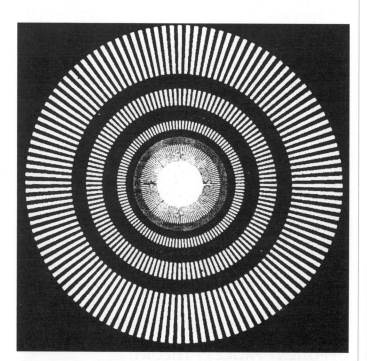

Figure 10.4   A black and white version of 'Enigma'. There appears to be a rotating movement in the solid rings of the picture

Box 10.5   Motion detection in the blind

It used to be thought that retinal signals pass to V1 (the primary visual processing area) which forms an image of a stimulus, and that after this other areas sort out attributes like form (V3), colour (V4) and motion (V5). Zeki has shown that this is not the case. He studied GY, a man blinded in an accident when he was seven. GY could detect fast moving objects, such as cars, and the direction in which they were travelling. Scans confirmed that GY's V5 was active when he was 'seeing' fast motion, but his V1 was not. This suggests that fast movements are first processed by V5 while signals from slow movements arrive in V1 first. In Zeki's view, signals must go through V1 to see clearly, but even the blind can sometimes see through other areas in a rudimentary way.

Colour vision

As noted earlier, one contribution to our knowledge of light made by Sir Isaac Newton. In further experiments, Newton investigated the effects of mixing various components of the spectrum. As well as white light being a mixture of all the colours of the spectrum, Newton found that mixing only two of the colours (such as yellow and violet or red and blue-green) produced white. However, this only occurred with colours far apart in the spectrum. If the light of two colours close together was mixed, light of an intermediate colour was produced. Newton devised a *colour circle* in which colours that produced either white or neutral grey were placed at opposite ends of the circle's diameter (see Figure 10.5, page 86).

The pure colours arranged around the circle are *hues* and those opposite one another are called *complementary colours*. Those of us who have mixed coloured paints may be confused at this point. Surely, blue and yellow produce green, not grey or white. To overcome this confusion, we need to distinguish between *subtractive* and *additive colour mixing*.

Box 10.6   Subtractive and additive colour mixing

Hue is determined by the wavelength of light that is *reflected* rather than the wavelengths that are absorbed. Blue paint appears blue because the light it reflects is predominantly of short-medium wavelength (the blue-green part of the spectrum). The light it absorbs (or 'subtracts') is of a long wavelength. Yellow paint mostly reflects light of long-medium wavelength (the yellow-green part of the spectrum) and absorbs (or 'subtracts') the short wavelength light. When blue and yellow are mixed, *both* short and long wavelength light are absorbed (or 'subtracted') leaving only medium wavelength (or green) light to be reflected. This is *subtractive colour mixing*.

When *lights* with different wavelengths simultaneously stimulate the retina, the combining (or 'adding') of these wavelengths occurs. This is *additive colour mixing*. Thus, subtractive colour mixing takes place in the object we are viewing, whereas additive colour mixing takes place in the visual system. If you were to look closely at a colour television set, for example, you would see that a yellow object was actually composed of red and green.

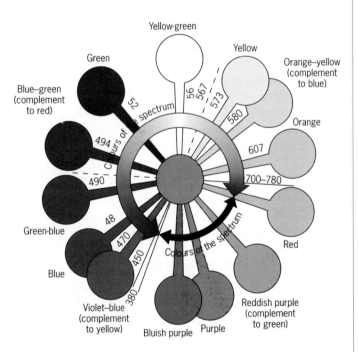

Figure 10.5   The colour circle. When lights of complementary colours such as yellow and violet-blue are mixed, neutral grey is produced

The above raises an interesting question about 'primary colours'. For an artist, these are red, blue and yellow, since all the hues can be produced by a mixture of them. For psychologists, however, the primary colours are red, green and blue *light* since all the various hues can be obtained by mixing these. Humans with normal vision can distinguish up to 150 colours (Bornstein & Marks, 1982) formed from the combination of four basic hues (red, green, blue and yellow) and two hueless colours (black and white). Importantly, whilst wavelengths can be

varied in a *continuous* manner from shorter to longer, changes in colour appear to be *discontinuous*. Thus, our perception of colour may seem to suddenly 'shift' from, say, blue to green, even though the change in wavelength was smaller than that between two 'blues'.

Theories of colour vision

Two major theories of colour vision have been advanced. These are the *Young–Helmholtz theory* and the *opponent-process theory*.

THE YOUNG–HELMHOLTZ THEORY

In 1802, Young demonstrated that the various combinations of red, green and blue light produce all the colours of the spectrum. About 50 years later, von Helmholtz suggested that the eye contains three types of receptor corresponding to red, blue and green, and that the perception of colour is somehow created by combining the information from them. Yellow, for example, would result from the simultaneous stimulation of red and green receptors. According to the Young–Helmholtz theory, then, the ratio of the blue:green:red receptors activated determines the colour perceived.

Because the theory proposes that three types of receptor exist, it is also called the *trichromatic theory of colour vision* ('tri' means 'three' and 'chroma' means 'colour'). Over 100 years after it was proposed, research confirmed the existence of three distinct types of cone in the retina, each of which contains a slightly different *photopigment*. These cones are maximally sensitive to light at 435, 540 and 565 nm, wavelengths corresponding to blue, green and yellow-green (note that to be consistent with earlier convention, the yellow-green receptor is termed 'red'). Nathans (1989) has shown that there are specific genes which direct the three kinds of cones to produce photopigment sensitive to light in the three regions identified above. However, although each type of cone responds maximally to light in the three regions, light of a particular wavelength has been shown to stimulate *more* than one type of receptor (Ohtsuka, 1985).

Whilst the Young–Helmholtz theory can explain the effects of mixing colours of different wavelengths, it has difficulty in explaining *colour blindness* and the phenomenon of *negative after-images* (see Box 10.7). Both of these can be explained more easily by opponent-process theory.

OPPONENT-PROCESS THEORY

In 1870, Hering proposed that we see six primary colours rather than the three identified in the

Young–Helmholtz theory. The additional three colours are yellow, black and white. Like Young and Helmholtz, Hering believed that there were three types of receptor. However, he suggested that each was responsive to *pairs* of colours. Two of these, the red-green and yellow-blue pairs are responsible for the perception of colour. The third, black-white, contributes to the perception of brightness and saturation (see page 81). As its name suggests, *opponent-process theory* proposes that each member of a pair is opposed to the other so that when one (such as red) is excited, the other (green) is inhibited. This explains why we never experience a colour as being 'reddish-green' but do experience colours as 'reddish-yellow'.

Box 10.7   Colour blindness and negative after-images

As noted, Hering's theory can explain colour-blindness. People are *never* colour-blind to red and yellow but able to see green and blue. The most common type of colour-blindness is red-green (one of Hering's pairs). Whilst red and green (and the colours derived from them) cannot be seen, blue and yellow (and the colours derived from them) can. Yellow-blue (another of Hering's pairs) colour-blindness is much rarer but does occur. People who are either red-green or yellow-blue colour-blind are said to be *dichromatic* (whereas normal colour vision is *trichromatic*). People who are totally colour-blind are *monochromatic* and see only black, white and shades of grey.

Opponent-process theory can also explain *negative after-images*. If you stare at a red surface for about 30 seconds and then look at a sheet of white paper, the sheet will appear green. Thus, the persistent sensation of a colour results in the perception of the complementary colour when the colour is removed. According to opponent-process theory, staring at red (say) forces the red-green receptors into 'red phase'. After a while, the red component tires. When our gaze is directed to a neutral surface, the light it reflects stimulates the red and green components equally, but only the green components are 'fresh' enough to fire.

Both theories appear to be correct to a degree, and colour vision may actually be a product of the mechanisms proposed by each. *Microspectrophotometry* research supports the Young–Helmholtz theory by showing that some cones are sensitive to the blue, green and yellow-green parts of the spectrum. Studies of bipolar, ganglion and some cells in the LGN, however, suggest that the messages from the cones are relayed to parts of the brain in opponent-process fashion (DeValois & Jacobs, 1984).

For example, some neurons transmitting information to the brain are excited by red light but inhibited by green light. Others work in the opposite way. A red-sensitive neuron excited by red light for half a minute might switch briefly to 'inhibitory mode' when the light is removed. This would result in us perceiving green as an after-image even if no light was present (Haber & Hershenson, 1980). Opponent-process theory does not seem to operate at the level of the cones, but along the neural path from the cones to the visual area.

Possibly, colour vision may be the result of a trichromatic system working at the level of the photoreceptors and an opponent-process mechanism working at later stages. It may even be that the trichromatic system itself interacts in an opponent-process way. Norman *et al.* (1984), for example, have shown that in the turtle at least, red and green cones are *directly* connected to one another.

Colour constancy

The colours we perceive are not *solely* determined by the wavelength of light reflected from an object. Amongst other factors affecting perception are *familiarity* with, and *knowledge* of, an object's colour. This is part of the phenomenon of *colour constancy*. The visual system is built to tell us about the permanent colours of objects as opposed to the spectral composition of light falling on a local area of the retina (McCann, 1987).

Land (1977) provided a powerful demonstration of colour constancy. He used a *colour Mondrian* consisting of a patchwork of randomly arranged and differently coloured matt papers. The display was illuminated by mixed light from projectors with red, green and blue filters. An independent brightness control was also available for each projector.

Observers then selected one of the colours, and Land measured the amounts of red, green and blue light coming from it. A second colour was then selected and the same measurements taken. The illumination was then changed so that the amount of red, green and blue light coming from the second colour was the *same* as that from the first colour. When all three projectors were turned on, observers were asked to report what colour they saw. All reported seeing the second colour, even though the physical properties of the light coming from it were the same as the first colour!

Box 10.8   Retinex theory

If perceived colour were determined solely by the spectral composition of the reflected light, the second colour would have been seen as the first. However, it was not, and the observers displayed colour constancy. To explain this, Land proposed the *retinex theory of colour constancy* ('retinex' is a combination of 'retina' and 'cortex'). According to this, there are three separate visual systems or retinexes, responsive primarily to long-wavelength light, medium-wavelength light and short-wavelength light. Each produces a separate lightness image and a comparison of these images is carried out.

The comparison determines the colour perceived. The three lightnesses provide the coordinates of a three-dimensional space and, whereas a colour space based on the *absolute* absorptions in the three classes of receptor predicts only whether two stimuli will *match*, a space based on the three lightnesses predicts how colours actually *look*. This is because between them they give the reflectance of the object in different parts of the spectrum (that is, a measure of their *relative absorptions*). Land's theory implies that the formation of lightnesses could occur in the retina or cortex and that the retina-cortical structure acts as a whole.

Conclusions

This chapter has examined the nature of light and the structure of the eye. Light information is transduced into electrical energy in the retina of the eye and then passed on to the brain where it is decoded. Neurons specialised for various functions play an important role in this decoding process, and research has begun to identify areas of the cerebral cortex which are specialised for particular aspects of visual perception. Theories of colour vision and colour constancy have also been presented.

Summary

- Light consists of energy particles called **photons**. Two important characteristics of light are **intensity** and **wavelength**. Three important properties of light are **brightness, hue and saturation**. White light is a mixture of wavelengths corresponding to all colours in the visible spectrum.

- The eye is the organ of vision, and 90 per cent of information about the external world reaches us via the eye. Light ends its journey through the eye at the **retina**, which contains **cones, rods, bipolar cells and ganglion cells**.

- Rods and cones are **photoreceptors** and convert light energy into electrical energy. Each retina contains about 120 million rods. These are distributed around the retina's periphery and help us see **achromatic colour** and are specialised for **scotopic vision**. Seven million cones help us see **chromatic colour** and are specialised for **photopic vision**. Cones are concentrated towards the retina's centre.

- Bipolar cells are connected to ganglion cells and to rods and cones. **Horizontal** and **amacrine** cells transmit information across the retina allowing bipolar and ganglion cells and rods and cones to interact.

- Some ganglion cells have an **on-centre/off-surround** receptive field. Others have an **off-centre/on-surround** receptive field. **Transient cells** have a larger receptive field and are most responsive to sudden movements.

- Information from the eyes travels along the optic nerve to the thalamus, and from there to the primary visual area of the cortex via the **geniculostriate path**. This pathway must be intact for conscious visual experience, but **blindsight** suggests the existence of another pathway allowing 'unconscious vision'.

- **Simple cells** respond only to particular orientations of a stimulus in a certain part of the visual field. **Complex cells** respond to a particular orientation wherever it appears. **Hypercomplex** cells respond to corners, angles or bars of a particular length moving in a certain direction.

- The visual area of the cortex consists of six layers, divided into **hypercolumns**. Cells within these have different receptive fields all falling within an aggregate field. The primary visual field is also organised in terms of **binocular fields, ocular dominance** and **orientation preference**.

- There are many areas within the visual cortex, each of which appears to have its own specialised function. V3, V4 and V5, for example, are concerned with form, colour and motion respectively. If a static image causes activity in V5, the illusion of movement is experienced. Case studies of the blind suggest that signals may have to go through V1 for normal vision, but an intact V5 area may allow the blind to see, albeit in a rudimentary way.

- In Newton's colour circle, pure colours correspond to hues, and those opposite one another are called **complementary colours**. **Subtractive** and **additive colour** mixing explain why mixing coloured paints (for example) results in a different colour from that when light of different wavelengths is mixed.

- People with normal vision can distinguish up to 150 colours formed from four basic hues and two hueless colours. Changes in wavelength can be varied continuously, but changes in colour are discontinuous.

■ The **Young-Helmholtz theory** of colour vision proposes the existence of three types of receptor (cones) corresponding to red, blue and green hues. Colour perception is determined by the ratio of the receptors activated. However, the theory is unable to explain colour blindness and negative after-images.

■ Hering's **opponent-process theory** proposes that three types of receptor are responsive to pairs of colours: red-green, yellow-blue and black-white. When one member of a pair is excited, the other is inhibited. This theory can account for colour blindness and negative after-images.

■ Both theories have some validity and work in a complementary way at different levels or stages. Different cones are sensitive to different wavelengths, although messages from them are relayed to the visual area of the brain in opponent-process fashion.

■ Perceived colour is only partly determined by the wavelength of reflected light from an object. Familiarity with and knowledge of an object's colour are also involved, and play a part in **colour constancy**. According to **Land's retinex theory**, there are three separate visual systems or retinexes, responsive to long-wavelength, medium-wavelength and short-wavelength light. Each produces a separate lightness image and the comparison of these determines the colour perceived.

PART 3

Awareness

BODILY RHYTHMS

Introduction and overview

According to Marks & Folkhard (1985):

> 'rhythmicity is a ubiquitous characteristic of living cells. In the human it is evident within the single cell, in individual behaviour, and at the population level'.

A bodily rhythm is *a cyclical variation over some period of time in physiological or psychological processes*. This chapter looks at five types of bodily rhythm and research findings relating to them.

Circadian rhythms

Circadian rhythms are consistent cyclical variations over a period of about 24 hours (the word circadian comes from the Latin 'circa' meaning 'about' and 'diem' meaning 'a day') and are a feature of human and non-human physiology and behaviour. As Aschoff & Wever (1981) have noted, 'there is hardly a tissue or function that has not been shown to have some 24-hour variation'. These include heart rate, metabolic rate, breathing rate and body temperature, all of which reach maximum values in the late afternoon/early evening and minimum values in the early hours of the morning. It might seem obvious that such a rhythm would occur since we are active during the day and inactive at night. However, the rhythms persist if we suddenly reverse our activity patterns.

The concentration of the body's hormones also varies over the day. However, the time at which a hormone is concentrated varies from one hormone to another. In women, *prolactin* (which stimulates the production of milk) peaks in the middle of the night, and this explains why women are more likely to go into labour then. Certain medications are more effective at different times of the day. Anticoagulant drugs, for example, are more effective at night when the blood is a little thinner in density, and there is a tendency for heart attacks to occur in the morning when the blood is more prone to clotting (Brown, 1996).

Ordinarily, we are surrounded by *external cues* about the time of day. These are called *Zeitgebers* (which comes from the German, meaning 'time-giver') and the process of synchronisation, *entrainment*. Folkhard *et al.* (cited in Huggett & Oldcroft, 1996) had six students spend a month isolated from any external cues. Temperature and activity levels were recorded constantly and mood levels were measured every two hours using computer tasks. One student was asked to play her bagpipes regularly to see if the body's sense of rhythm was affected by the absence of external cues. Folkhard *et al.*'s findings confirmed the existence of several *internal* (or *body*) *clocks* or, more accurately, *oscillators* (Irwin, 1996a).

One of these lies in the *suprachiasmatic nuclei* (SN) located in the hypothalamus. The SN receives information directly from the retina, and this information about light and dark synchronises our biological rhythms with the 24-hour cycle of the outside world. If the SN is damaged, or the connection between it and retina severed, circadian rhythms disappear completely, and rhythmic behaviours become random over the day.

The cycle length of rhythms appears to be dependent on genetic factors. If hamsters are given brain transplants of SN from a mutant strain whose biological rhythms have a shorter cycle than those of the recipients, the recipients adopt the same activity cycles as the mutant strain (Morgan, 1995). Interestingly, the location of the transplant does not appear to be important, suggesting that the SN might rely on chemical signals rather than nerve connections.

> **Box 11.1   The evolution of internal clocks**
>
> According to Loros *et al.* (cited in Highfield, 1996b), primitive bacteria developed an internal clock from molecular machinery that responds to light so they could anticipate the coming of the sun's rays and change their metabolism accordingly. Two proteins, White Collar 1 and 2, regulate light responses, are essential to the circadian rhythm, and work in the dark without light stimulation. The proteins were first discovered in a fungus and then in the fruit fly, and it is likely that all biological clocks share common molecular components.

We can adjust our bodily rhythms if necessary. If our pattern of sleep and waking were reversed, as happens with shift-work, our circadian rhythm would eventually became synchronised to the new set of external cues. Unfortunately, some people take much longer than others to adapt to a change in their activity patterns (and in the case of travelling from one time zone to another we use the term '*jet lag*' to identify this). Indeed, we never achieve a complete reversal (Monk *et al.*, cited in Irwin, 1997). Also, not all physiological functions reverse at the same time. For example, whilst body temperature usually reverses within a week for most people, the rhythm of *adrenocortical hormone* production takes much longer.

The finding that animals transplanted with the SN of others adopt the same activity patterns as their donors, coupled with the fact that the circadian rhythm cannot be experimentally manipulated beyond certain limits, strongly suggests that bodily rhythms are primarily an internal (or *endogenous*) property that do not depend on external (or *exogenous*) cues.

One of the most interesting circadian rhythms is the sleep-waking cycle. Although some people have as little as 45 minutes of sleep each night, the average person has around seven to eight hours per 24-hour day (Meddis *et al.*, 1973). People in all cultures sleep, and even those who take a midday 'siesta' have an extended period of five to eight hours sleep each day.

The need for sleep does not seem to be *determined* by the cycle of light and darkness. For example, Luce & Segal (1966) found that people who live near the Arctic circle, where the sun does not set during the summer months, sleep about seven hours during each 24-hour period.

External cues, then, would not seem to be of primary importance as far as sleep and waking are concerned. Of more importance is the *group two oscillator*, an internal clock which sends us to sleep and wakes us up.

> **Box 11.2   The interval clock**
>
> The interval clock is used to measure *durations,* showing how long it is since an event or process started. We use it when for example, we determine whether there is enough time for us to cross the road before an oncoming car reaches us. The interval clock also governs the perception of time. The *striatum* is responsible for timing short intervals and the *substantia nigra* acts like a metronome, sending pulses to the striatum. These two structures act like a 'gatekeeper', turning on and off awareness of time intervals, and sending this information to the frontal cortex which stores it in memory (Highfield, 1996c).

Infradian rhythms

Infradian rhythms last for *longer* than one day and have been known about for centuries. The infradian rhythm that has attracted most research interest is *menstruation*. Menstruation is an endocrine cycle and several such cycles are experienced by everybody. However, none is as well marked as menstruation and others are much more difficult to study.

Every 28 days or so, female bodies undergo a sequence of changes with two possible outcomes: conception or menstruation. Conventionally, we portray menstruation as the *beginning* of a cycle. In fact, the menstrual period is the end of a four-week cycle of activity during which the womb has prepared for the job of housing and nourishing a fertilised egg (see Chapter 5, page 48).

The onset of the 28-day cycle is often irregular at first, but becomes well established in a matter of months. The cycle can change to fit in with events in the environment. For example, women who spend a lot of time together often find that their menstrual periods become synchronised (Sabbagh & Barnard, 1984). Why this happens is not known, but one hypothesis attributes it to the unconscious detection of some chemical scent secreted at certain times during the menstrual cycle.

As mentioned in Chapter 5, the term *pre-menstrual syndrome* (PMS) has been used to describe a variety of effects occurring at several phases of the menstrual cycle. Typically, these occur around four to five days before the onset of menstruation, and include mild irritation, depression, headaches and a decline in alertness or visual acuity. One commonly reported experience is a day or so of great energy followed by lethargy that disappears with the onset of menstrual bleeding (Luce, 1971). PMS has also been associated with a change in appetite. Some women develop a craving for certain types of food whereas others lose their appetite completely.

Box 11.3   PMS and behaviour change

The most pervasive social impacts of PMS are the psychological and behavioural changes which occur. Dalton (1964) reported that a large proportion of crimes were clustered in the pre-menstrual interval along with suicides, accidents, a decline in the quality of schoolwork and intelligence test scores. However, other research has suggested that whilst a small percentage of women experience effects that are strong enough to interfere with their normal functioning, they are not, contrary to Dalton's claim, more likely to commit crimes or to end up on psychiatric wards. Any effects that do occur are a result of increased stress levels and other health fluctuations (Hardie, 1997).

For a long time, PMS was attributed to a denial of femininity or a resistance to sexual roles. However, the effects of PMS occur in all cultures, indicating a physiological cycle rather than a pattern of behaviour imposed by culture. Support for this comes from the finding that similar effects to those experienced by women occur in primates.

The pituitary gland governs the phases of the menstrual cycle by influencing changes in the *endometrium* (the walls of the uterus) and the preparation of the ovum. Timonen *et al.* (1964) showed that during the lighter months of the year conceptions increased, whilst in the darker months they decreased, suggesting that light levels might have some direct or indirect influence on the pituitary gland which then influenced the menstrual cycle.

Reinberg (1967) studied a young woman who spent three months in a cave relying on only the dim light of a miner's lamp. Her day lengthened to 24.6 hours and her menstrual cycle shortened to 25.7 days. Even though she was in the mine for only three months, it was a year before her menstrual cycle returned to its normal frequency. Reinberg speculated that it was the level of light in the cave which had influenced the menstrual cycle. Consistent with this was his finding that among 600 girls from northern Germany, *menarche* (the onset of menstruation which occurs at puberty) was much more likely to occur in winter. Interestingly, menarche is reached earlier by blind girls than sighted girls. These findings will be considered further later on in this chapter.

Ultradian rhythms

Ultradian rhythms are *shorter* than a day and have been demonstrated in many physiological and behavioural processes including oral activity (such as smoking cigarettes), renal excretion and heart rate. The most well-researched ultradian rhythms are those occurring during *sleep*. Sleep is not a single state, and within a night's sleep several shorter rhythms occur.

Before the EEG's invention (see Chapter 6), sleep could not be studied scientifically because there was no way of accessing what was going on inside the sleeper's head. Loomis *et al.* (1937) used the EEG to record the electrical activity in a sleeping person's brain. They discovered that the brain was electrically active during sleep, and that certain types of activity seemed to be related to changes in the type of sleep. It seemed that the waves tended to get 'bigger' as sleep got 'deeper'.

Box 11.4   REM sleep

In 1952, eight-year-old Armond Aserinsky's father Eugene connected him to an EEG machine to see if repairs carried out on it had been successful. Electrodes were also placed near Armond's eyes to try to record the rolling eye movements believed to occur during sleep. After a while, the EOG started to trace wildly oscillating waves. Aserinsky senior thought that the machine was still broken, but after several minutes the EOG fell silent. Periodically, however, the wildly oscillating waves returned. When Armond was woken by his father during one such period, Armond reported that he had been dreaming.

Aserinsky senior eventually realised that the EOG was indicating fast, jerky eye movements beneath Armond's closed eyelids, and he further observed that whilst the EOG was active, Armond's EEG indicated that his brain was highly active as well, even though the boy was sound asleep. Aserinsky & Kleitman (1953) reported that the same phenomenon occurred when EOG and EEG measurements in adults were recorded. They used the term rapid eye movement sleep (or *REM* sleep) to describe the period of intense EOG activity.

Dement & Kleitman (1957) showed that when people were woken up during REM sleep and asked if they were *dreaming*, they usually replied that they were. When woken at other times during the night, in non-rapid eye movement sleep (or *NREM* sleep), they occasionally reported dream-like experiences, but their descriptions usually lacked the vivid visual images and fantastic themes that were described during REM sleep awakenings.

The EEG allows researchers to measure the electrical activity occurring in the brain over the course of a night's sleep. Rechtschaffen & Kales (1968) devised criteria to describe changes in the brain's electrical activity. These divide NREM sleep into four stages, each of which is characterised by distinct patterns of electrical activity.

When we are awake and alert, the EEG shows the low amplitude and high frequency *beta waves* (see Box 6.6, page 54 for a description of beta waves and the waves that follow). Once we are in bed and relaxed, beta waves are replaced by *alpha waves* of higher amplitude but slower frequency. Gradually, we begin to fall asleep. Breathing and heart rate slow down, body temperature drops and muscles relax. The onset of sleep is marked by the appearance of irregular and slower *theta waves*, and we have entered *Stage 1* of sleep.

The transition from relaxation to Stage 1 is sometimes accompanied by a *hypnagogic state* in which we experience dream-like and hallucinatory images resembling vivid photographs. Such images have been linked to creativity. We may also experience the sensation of falling and our bodies might suddenly jerk. Although the EMG indicates that the muscles are still active, the EOG indicates slow, gentle, rolling eye movements. Because Stage 1 sleep is the lightest stage of sleep, we are easily awakened from it. If this occurs, we might feel that we have not been sleeping at all.

After about a minute, the EEG shows another change which marks the onset of *Stage 2* sleep. Although the waves are of medium amplitude with a frequency of around 4–7 cycles per second (cps), Stage 2 sleep is characterised by brief bursts of activity with a frequency of 12–14 cps. These are called *sleep spindles* and why they appear is not precisely understood.

> **Box 11.5   K-complexes**
>
> Another characteristic of Stage 2 sleep is the presence of *K-complexes*. These are the brain's response to external stimuli such as a sound in the room in which we are sleeping or internal stimuli such as a muscle tightening in the leg. Whilst it is possible to be woken fairly easily from Stage 2 sleep, the EOG registers minimal eye movements and the EMG shows little activity in the muscles (see Figure 11.1).

After around 20 minutes in Stage 2, electrical activity increases in amplitude and becomes even slower, dropping to around 1–3 cps. When these slow *delta waves* account for 20–50 per cent of the EEG, we have entered *Stage 3* sleep. After a brief period of time, delta waves will

account for more than 50 per cent of the EEG and will slow to around ½–2 cps which marks the onset of *Stage 4* sleep. In both Stages 3 and 4 of sleep we are extremely unresponsive to the environment and it is very difficult for us to be woken up. The EOG shows virtually no eye movements and our muscles are completely relaxed. Noises and lights do not disturb us as they would have done in the earlier stages of sleep.

In Stage 4, heart rate, blood pressure and body temperature are at their lowest. We have descended what researchers term the *sleep staircase* and have moved from a very light to a very deep sleep. Our first episode of Stage 4 sleep lasts for around 40 minutes. After this, we begin to 'climb' the sleep staircase, passing briefly through Stage 3, before entering Stage 2 in which we spend around ten minutes.

Instead of re-entering Stage 1, however, something very different registers on the EEG machine and we start showing the irregular eye movements and brain activity first observed by Aserinsky. We are now experiencing our first episode of REM sleep. REM sleep occurs in all mammals except the dolphin and spiny anteater, but does not occur in fish, reptiles and amphibians, and occurs only briefly in a few birds of prey. It is therefore likely that REM sleep is related to the development of brain structures found in mammals.

Interestingly, the EMG in REM sleep indicates that the body's muscles are in a state of *virtual paralysis*, which occurs as a result of inhibitory processes (the occasional twitches of our hands and feet are presumably a result of these processes weakening briefly). The probable function of this paralysis is discussed in Chapter 13. Although our muscles may be paralysed, heart rate and blood pressure begin to fluctuate rapidly, and respiration alters

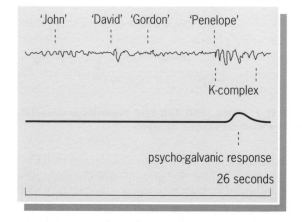

Figure 11.1   EEG response of a person is Stage 2 sleep to the presentation of several names, one of which is his wife's

between shallow breaths and sudden gasps. Males may experience an erection and females corresponding changes in their sexual organs.

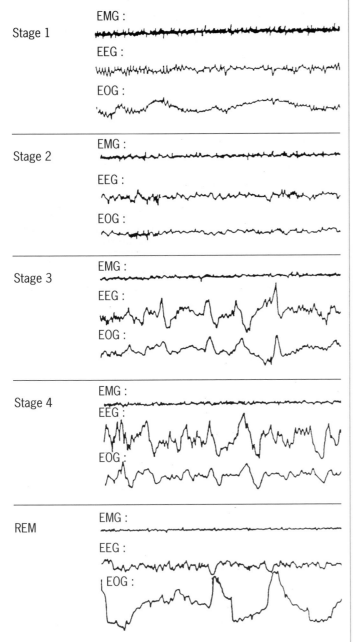

Figure 11.2   EMG, EEG and EOG recordings associated with the various stages of sleep

The fact that the eyes and brain of a person in REM sleep are very *active* whilst the muscles are virtually *paralysed*, coupled with the observation that a person in REM sleep is very difficult to wake up, has led to it also being termed *paradoxical sleep*. Our first period of REM sleep lasts for about 10 minutes. The end of it marks the completion of the first sleep *cycle*.

When REM sleep ends, we enter Stage 2 sleep again and spend around 25 minutes in that stage. After passing briefly through Stage 3, we enter Stage 4 and spend about 30 minutes in a very deep sleep. After ascending the sleep staircase once more, another episode of REM sleep occurs which also lasts for around ten minutes. We have now completed the second sleep cycle.

The entry into Stage 2 sleep marks the beginning of the third cycle. However, instead of descending the sleep staircase (after about an hour in Stage 2), we enter REM sleep and might spend as long as 40 minutes in that stage. Again, the end of REM sleep marks the end of another cycle. Unlike the first two cycles, then, the third cycle does not involve any Stage 3 or 4 sleep. This is also true of the fourth cycle. The cycle begins with around 70 minutes of Stage 2 sleep which is immediately followed by a fourth episode of REM sleep which might last as long as an hour. By the end of the fourth cycle we will have been asleep for around seven hours. The fifth cycle will probably end with us waking up and for that reason it is known as the *emergent cycle* of sleep. We may awake directly from REM sleep or from Stage 2 and might experience *hypnopompic images*, (vivid visual images that occur as we are waking up: cf. the hypnagogic images mentioned earlier). As was true in the third and fourth cycles, the emergent cycle does not consist of any Stage 3 or 4 sleep.

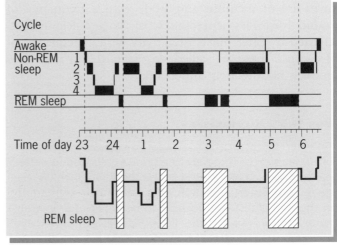

Figure 11.3   A characteristic profile of a night's sleep. (From Borbely, 1986)

Typically, then, we have five or so cycles of sleep, each of which lasts, on average, for around 90 minutes. The exact pattern of sleep varies from person to person, and what has been described is very much an 'average' since the time between REM and NREM sleep varies both between and within people. So, as well as people differing in terms of their sleep cycles, the pattern can vary within the same person from night to night. What does seem to be true for everyone, though, is that Stages 3 and 4 of sleep occur only in the first two cycles of sleep and that whilst REM sleep occurs in every cycle, episodes increase in length over the course of the night.

Our pattern of sleeping also changes as we get older. Newborn infants sleep for around 16 hours a day and spend approximately half this time in REM sleep. One-year-olds sleep for around 12 hours a day and REM sleep occupies about one-third of this time. In adulthood, we spend only around a quarter of an eight-hour period of sleep in REM sleep and in very old age the amount of REM sleep time decreases even further. Stage 4 sleep also changes as we get older. At age 60, Stage 4 sleep has all but disappeared. As a result, we tend to be more easily awakened when we are older even though we may have been very sound sleepers when younger.

Diurnal rhythms

Diurnal rhythms are rhythms which occur during the *waking day*. Whether the time of day at which a task is carried out makes a difference to how well it is performed has been the subject of much research. Because of its potential practical applications, researchers have paid particular attention to how performance of complex 'real-world' tasks varies over the waking day.

Box 11.6   Memory and time of day

Some evidence suggests that immediate memory for realistic events is better in the morning than the afternoon. Gunter *et al.* (cited in Marks & Folkhard, 1985), tested participants for their immediate recall of television news information. There was a decline across the three times of the day that were tested (09.00, 13.00 and 17.00). However, other research has failed to demonstrate such 'time-of-day' effects. Adam (1983), for example, found that the information remembered from lectures did not differ over the day.

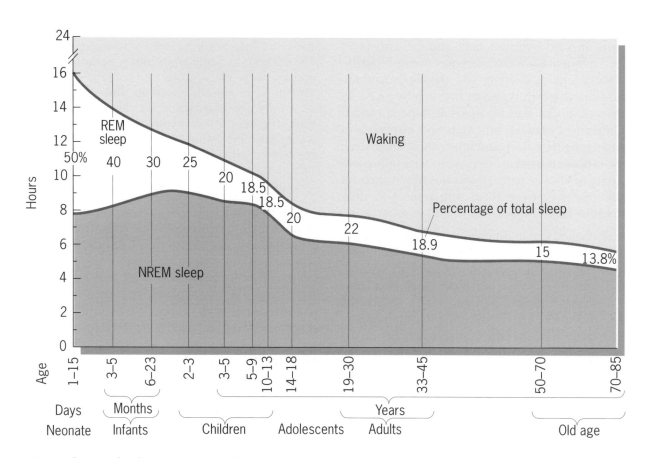

Figure 11.4   Changes in sleep patterns with age

It did not seem to matter whether a lecture was attended first thing in the morning or last thing in the afternoon, there was no difference in how much was remembered (or not remembered). Whilst the time of day did not affect how much was remembered, Adam found that it influenced students' abilities to extract the main *theme* from a lecture. Students were considerably better at this in the afternoon than in the morning. Other research has shown that people tend to be better at short-term memory tasks, such as remembering a telephone number between looking it up and dialling it, in the early morning. Long-term memory seems to function better in the evening (Irwin, 1997).

Using their 'Morningness–Eveningness' questionnaire, Horne & Osterberg (1976) have argued that there are two *diurnal types*. Extreme 'morning types' are characteristically tired in the evening, go to bed early, and wake in the morning feeling alert. By contrast, extreme 'evening types' perform best in the evening, go to bed late, and feel tired in the morning. Marks & Folkhard (1985) have proposed that these differences may be due to a *phase advance* in the circadian system. It seems that morning types 'peak' two or more hours earlier than evening types on a number of variables including body temperature.

Introversion and extroversion may also be associated with diurnal differences. Such differences might be attributable to variations in sleeping and waking behaviour. Whilst the time at which we go to bed is influenced by internal factors, it can also be affected by psychosocial factors. Differences between introverts and extroverts in terms of how long they sleep and how regular their sleep is could be explained in terms of psychosocial influences (such as going to a lot of parties), and this might account for the differences between them with respect to their diurnal rhythms (Blake, 1971).

It is generally believed that differences on cognitive tasks performed during the waking day cannot be *solely* explained in terms of a circadian variation in arousal. Rather, the differences appear to be the result of a combination of many different rhythms which reflect the various cognitive functions contributing to observed performance. Exactly how the different components of the human information processing system change over the course of the day has, however, yet to be determined.

Circannual rhythms

The word circannual describes rhythms that have a period of about a year, and biological circannual clocks regulate migration, the formation of colonies, pair bonding and other seasonal changes in many species. Such changes are found in the behaviour and physiology of most, if not all, animals from temperate latitudes and are adaptive because they promote a species' survival in an environment where the climate fluctuates predictably in a rhythmic sequence (Morgan, 1995).

Box 11.7 The circannual rhythm of the gold-mantled ground squirrel

The most extensively investigated circannual rhythm in mammals is that of the gold-mantled ground squirrel of the Rocky Mountains. The rhythm was first noted by Pengelley & Fisher (1957) while they were studying the hibernation of squirrels. In August, a squirrel was placed in a small, windowless room which was illuminated for a period of 12 hours and then darkened for the same length of time. The temperature of the room was kept constant at 0°C (32°F).

Initially, the squirrel remained active. It ate and drank normally and its temperature remained constant at 37.8°C (98.68°F). In October, the squirrel ceased its activities and hibernated, its body temperature dropping to 1°C (33.8°F). In April, the squirrel became active again and its body temperature rose to 37°C. Finally, in September, it resumed hibernation. The alternating period of activity and hibernation typically lasts for about 300 days. The key to this rhythm seems to be temperature rather than light. This makes sense given that the squirrel, which spends a great deal of time in its burrow, is probably not much affected by changes in the length of the day.

Another rhythm which could be considered circannual is *seasonal affective disorder* (or *SAD*: see also Chapter 69). A growing body of evidence suggests that some mood disorders are under *seasonal* control and regulated by the *pineal gland*. The pineal gland is believed to have evolved by convergence and fusion of a second pair of photoreceptors (Morgan, 1995). It secretes the hormone *melatonin*, which influences the production of the neurotransmitter *serotonin*. Melatonin production is controlled by the presence or absence of direct light stimulation to the eyes. It is produced when it is dark, but its production is suppressed when it is light. In winter SAD, melatonin production may be de-synchronised. One way of treating winter SAD is to re-phase the rhythm of melatonin production, and this is the principle underlying *phototherapy*.

Box 11.8   Photopherapy

In phototherapy, sufferers of winter SAD are seated in front of extremely bright lights (the equivalent to the illumination of 2500 candles on a surface one metre away being the most effective: Wehr & Rosenthal, 1989). Exposure to this light for just over one hour each evening reverses the symptoms within three to four days. Since a pulse of bright light reduces the level of melatonin in the bloodstream and changes the time when it is produced, phototherapy may work by rephasing melatonin's production.

Figure 11.5   Exposure to bright light has been shown to be effective for some individuals in the treatment of seasonal affective disorder (SAD)

The role played by melatonin may also explain some of the findings described earlier concerning infradian rhythms. Recall that Reinberg (1967) hypothesised that the level of light influenced the menstrual cycle of the young woman who spent three months in a cave, and that evidence indicates that menarche is much more likely to occur in winter and occurs earlier in blind than sighted girls. It is reasonable to suggest that the pineal gland is somehow affected by the secretion of melatonin and that this affects both the menstrual cycle and, given the finding concerning increased conceptions during the lighter months of the year, the reproductive system in general.

Conclusions

This chapter has looked at various of bodily rhythms. Several physiological and psychological effects associated with these have been identified, and some of the ways in which disruption of these rhythms can affect behaviour have been discussed.

Summary

■ **Circadian rhythms** are consistent cyclical variations over a period of about 24 hours. Examples include heart rate, metabolic rate, breathing rate and body temperature. These rhythms persist even if activity patterns are reversed or external cues about the time of day removed.

■ One internal clock (or oscillator) lies in the **suprachiasmatic nuclei** (SN). This receives information directly from the retina and synchronises biological rhythms with the 24 hour cycle of the outside world. If the SN is damaged, circadian rhythms disappear.

■ The cycle length of rhythms apparently depends on genetic factors, and internal clocks evolved so that organisms could anticipate the coming of the sun's rays and change their metabolism accordingly. It is likely that all biological clocks share common molecular components.

■ The sleep-waking cycle is largely independent of culture and the cycle of light and dark. It is determined by internal events governed by the **group two oscillator**.

■ The **interval clock** measures durations and governs the perception of time. The **striatum** and **substantia nigra** act like a 'gatekeeper', turning awareness of time on and off. This information is stored in memory by the frontal cortex.

■ **Infradian rhythms** last longer than one day. The most extensively researched of these is menstruation. **Premenstrual syndrome** (PMS) refers to the variety of physical and psychological effects occurring at several phases of the menstrual cycle.

■ PMS does not predispose women to criminal behaviour or mental disorders. Any behaviour changes found are better explained in terms of increased stress levels and other health fluctuations. PMS is evidently a universal physiological cycle, independent of culture.

■ The phases of the menstrual cycle are controlled by the **pituitary gland**. This gland may be influenced by (seasonal) light levels since menarche has been found to be most likely to occur in winter and is reached earlier by blind than sighted girls.

■ **Ultradian rhythms** are shorter than one day. The most well-researched are those that occur during sleep. Sleep consists of a number of cycles lasting around 90 minutes. NREM sleep consists of four stages, each characterised by a distinct pattern of electrical activity.

■ Stage 1 and 2 sleep are the stages of 'light' sleep. Theta waves mark the onset of Stage 1 sleep. Stage 2 sleep is characterised by **sleep spindles** and **K-complexes**. Stages 3 and 4 are the stages of 'deep sleep' and are characterised by delta waves. Stages 3 and 4 only occur in the first two cycles of sleep.

■ REM sleep seems to be related to the development of brain structures found only in mammals. In REM sleep, the musculature is virtually paralysed. The brain is highly active during REM sleep and a person woken from it typically reports experiencing a dream. REM sleep episodes increase in length over the night. In the first cycle, it lasts about ten minutes. In the emergent cycle it lasts about 30 minutes.

■ There are important developmental changes in sleep patterns. Newborns spend about half of their 16 hours of sleep per day in REM sleep. In adulthood, about a quarter of total sleep time is spent in REM sleep. This decreases further in late adulthood which is also accompanied by the virtual disappearance of Stage 4 sleep.

■ **Diurnal rhythms** occur during the waking day. Research indicates that memory varies over the course of the day. Short-term memory tends to be better in the morning whilst long-term memory is better in the evening.

■ Two diurnal types have been proposed. 'Morning types' perform best in the morning and 'evening types' in the evening. These differences may be due to a phase advance in the circadian rhythm. Personality type may also be associated with diurnal differences, though psychosocial influences could be responsible for this.

■ **Circannual rhythms** have a period of about a year. Biological clocks regulate several behaviours including migration, the formation of colonies and pair bonding. These behaviours are adaptive because they promote survival in an environment where the climate fluctuates predictably in a rhythmic sequence.

■ **Seasonal affective disorder** (SAD) can be considered a circannual rhythm. Some mood disorders appear to be under seasonal control and regulated by the pineal gland. This gland secretes melatonin whose production is controlled by the presence or absence of direct light stimulation to the eyes. Desynchronisation of melatonin production may occur in winter SAD. **Phototherapy** is an effective treatment for winter SAD, and may work by re-phasing melatonin's production.

12

THE FUNCTIONS OF SLEEP

Introduction and overview

As was seen in Chapter 11, everyone sleeps at least once a day. Spending approximately seven to eight hours in this altered state of consciousness means that around one third of our lifetime is spent fast asleep! Indeed, we may need to spend as long as ten hours asleep in order to function optimally (Coren, 1996).

This chapter looks at theories of the functions of sleep. One way to study such functions is to deprive people of sleep and observe the consequences. This chapter begins by looking at the effects of total sleep deprivation and theories which have been proposed to explain the functions of sleep in general. Then, it looks at the effects of depriving people of REM sleep, and at theories of this stage's functions. The chapter concludes by looking briefly at some of the physiological processes that occur during sleep.

Studies of total sleep deprivation

It has long been known that depriving people of sleep can have detrimental effects (Borbely, 1986). Indeed, sleep deprivation has served dubious military purposes over the ages. The ancient Romans used *tormentum vigilae* (or the *waking torture*) to extract information from captured enemies, and in the 1950s the Koreans used sleep deprivation as a way of 'brainwashing' captured American airforce pilots (see Chapter 82).

The first experimental study of sleep deprivation was conducted by Patrick & Gilbert (1898). They deprived three 'healthy young men' of sleep for 90 hours. The men reported a gradually increased desire to sleep, and from the second night onwards two of them experienced illusions and other perceptual disorders. When they were allowed to sleep normally, all three slept for longer than they usually did, and the psychological disturbances they reported disappeared.

Box 12.1   The record breakers

In 1959 Peter Tripp, a New York disc-jockey, staged a charity 'wakeathon' in which he did not sleep for eight days. Towards the end of his wakeathon, Tripp showed some disturbing symptoms, including hallucinations and delusions. The delusions were so intense that it was impossible to give him any tests to assess his psychological functioning. In 1965, Randy Gardner, a 17-year-old student, stayed awake for 264 hours and 12 minutes, aiming to get himself into the *Guinness Book of Records*. For the last 90 hours of his record attempt he was studied by sleep researcher William Dement. Although Gardner had difficulty in performing some tasks, his lack of sleep did not produce anything like the disturbances experienced by Peter Tripp.

Afterwards, Gardner spent 14 hours and 40 minutes asleep and when he awoke he appeared to have recovered completely. On subsequent nights, Gardner returned to his usual pattern of sleeping for eight hours per day and did not seem to suffer any permanent physiological or psychological effects from his long period without sleep.

Going without sleep for over 200 hours has subsequently been achieved by a number of people, none of whom appears to have experienced any long-term detrimental effects. This finding has led Webb (1975) to conclude that the major consequence of going without sleep is to make us want to go to sleep!

As interesting as the cases of Tripp, Gardner and others are, they tell us little about the effects of *total sleep deprivation* because they did not take place under carefully controlled conditions. However, many controlled studies have been conducted. The effects of sleep deprivation over time have been summarised by Hüber-Weidman (1976).

Box 12.2   The effects of sleep deprivation over time (after Hüber-Weidman, 1976)

Night 1: Most people are capable of going without sleep for a night. The experience may be uncomfortable, but it is tolerable.

Night 2: The urge to sleep becomes much greater. The period between 3–5 a.m., when body temperature is at its lowest in most of us, is crucial. It is during this period that sleep is most likely to occur.

Night 3: Tasks requiring sustained attention and complex forms of information processing are seriously impaired. This is particularly true if the task is repetitious and boring. If the task is interesting, or the experimenter offers encouragement, performance is less impaired. Again, the early hours of the morning are most crucial.

Night 4: From this night onwards periods of *micro-sleep* occur. We stop what we are doing and stare into space for up to three seconds. The end of micro-sleep is accompanied by a return to full awareness. Confusion, irritability, misperception and the *'hat phenomenon'* occur. In this, a tightening around the head is felt as though a hat that was too small was being worn.

Night 5: As well as the effects described above, delusions may be experienced. However, intellectual and problem-solving abilities are largely unimpaired.

Night 6: Symptoms of *depersonalisation* occur and a clear sense of identity is lost. This is called *sleep deprivation psychosis*.

The effects described above are psychological rather than physiological, and little physical harm follows sleep deparivation. Reflexes are unimpaired and heart rate, respiration, blood pressure and body temperature show little change from normal. Hand tremors, droopy eyelids, problems in focusing the eyes, and heightened sensitivity to pain seem to be the major bodily consequences.

Additionally, the effects of sleep deprivation do not accumulate over time. If we normally sleep for eight hours a day and are deprived of sleep for three days, we do not sleep for 24 hours afterwards. Thus, we do not need to make up for *all* the sleep that has been missed, though we do make up for some.

The experiences of Peter Tripp (see Box 12.1) are unusual. Whilst some temporary psychological disturbances occur following sleep deprivation, sleep deprivation has no significant long-term consequences on normal psychological functioning. Tripp's experiences are, therefore, unlikely to be *solely* attributable to a lack of sleep. It is more likely that *stress*, which sleep deprivation can also cause, produces abnormal behaviour in susceptible individuals.

Whilst it might be tempting to conclude that sleep has little value and a lack of it few harmful effects, such a conclusion is not justified. For example, Rechtschaffen *et al.* (1983) placed a rat on a disc protruding from a small bucket of water with an EEG monitoring its brain activity. Every time brain activity indicated sleep, the disc

rotated. This forced the rat to walk if it wanted to avoid falling in the water.

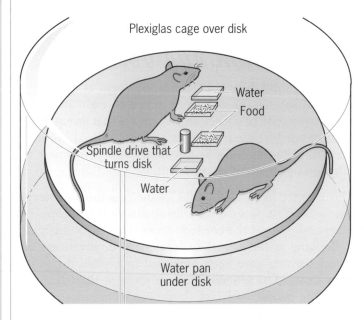

Plexiglas cage over disk
Water
Food
Spindle drive that turns disk
Water
Water pan under disk

Figure 12.1   Apparatus used in the experiment conducted by Rechtschaffen *et al.*

A second rat, also connected to an EEG, was on the disc. However, whenever its brain activity indicated sleep the disc did *not* rotate. Thus, one rat was allowed to sleep normally whereas the other was not. After 33 days, all sleep-deprived rats had died, whereas those that slept normally appeared not to have suffered. The cause of death could not be precisely determined, but given a progressive physical deterioration in the rats, the ability to regulate their own heat may have been fatally impaired.

Unfortunately, the results of sleep deprivation studies on rats tells us little about the effects of sleep deprivation on humans, and there are clearly serious ethical objections to subjecting humans to the length of time the rats were deprived of sleep. However, Lugaressi *et al.* (1986) have reported the case of a man who abruptly began to lose sleep at age 52. He became increasingly exhausted and eventually developed a lung infection from which death resulted. A post-mortem revealed that neurons in areas of the brain linked to sleep and hormonal circadian rhythms were almost completely destroyed.

Irrespective of the effects of sleep deprivation, unless we are constantly encouraged to remain awake, we fall asleep, and we do so in virtually any position anywhere. People do not like to be kept awake and there seems to be a need to sleep even though sleeplessness itself does not, at least as far as we know, appear to be particularly harmful.

Again, as Webb (1975) has suggested, perhaps people sleep in order to avoid feeling sleepy. However, such a suggestion isn't particularly helpful, and researchers have tried to understand sleep's exact functions.

Evolutionary theories of sleep function

Meddis (1975) has pointed to evidence indicating that different species characteristically sleep for different periods of time, and that the amount of time spent asleep is related to an animal's need and method of obtaining food and its exposure to predators. Animals that cannot find a safe place to sleep, have high metabolic rates that require a lot of food gathering, or are at risk from predators, sleep very little.

Box 12.3   The sleeping habits of some non-humans

The short-tailed shrew has a safe burrow, but sleeps very little since its high metabolic rate means that it must eat around the clock or die. Animals that are preyed upon, such as cattle, sheep and deer, sleep only about two hours a day, and even then take only 'brief naps'. By contrast, predator species or those that have safe sleeping places or can satisfy their needs for food and water fairly quickly, sleep for much longer. Like the short-tailed shrew, the ground squirrel has a safe burrow but, being a larger animal, it has a lower metabolic rate and does not need to eat so often. It sleeps for 14 hours a day. The gorilla, which does not need to sleep in a burrow to protect itself, also sleeps for 14 hours a day.

In a variation of Meddis's theory, Webb (1982) has suggested that sleep enables us to conserve energy when there is no need to expend it or when expending energy would probably do more harm than good. Webb argues that sleep is an instinctual behavioural response which does not satisfy a physiological need in the way that food does. Rather, natural selection would favour an organism that kept itself out of danger when danger was most likely to occur. Sleep can therefore be seen as a response which is useful for a species' survival.

Since we usually do not walk or roam about whilst we are asleep and (usually) sleep at night, sleep can be seen as an adaptive instinctual behaviour that keeps us quiet and out of harm's way. This is the *hibernation theory of sleep function*. In our evolutionary past, the enforced inactivity of sleeping allowed us to survive for a least two reasons. First, sleeping at night would reduce the risk of predation

or accidents. Second, since the likelihood of finding food at night would be much reduced, more energy would have been spent hunting than would have been gained by the results of hunting.

However, even though we may be quiet and out of harm's way whilst asleep, we are *potentially* vulnerable. As Evans (1984) has remarked:

'the behaviour patterns involved in sleep are glaringly, almost insanely, at odds with common sense'.

Some evolutionary theorists argue that preyed upon species sleep for short periods because of the constant threat of predation. Others argue that preyed upon species sleep for longer periods in order to keep out of the way of predators. The sleep pattern of any species can be explained in one of these two ways by evolutionary theories which makes them *non-falsifiable* in this respect.

Restoration theories of sleep function

Safety and energy conservation could be two functions of sleep. However, whilst the neural mechanisms for sleep might have evolved to satisfy such needs, they may well have taken on additional functions. Most of us spend around 16 hours a day using up energy. According to Oswald (1966), the purpose of sleep is to restore depleted reserves of energy, eliminate waste products from the muscles, repair cells and recover physical abilities that have been lost during the day.

Box 12.4   Sleep and energy expenditure

The length of time we remain awake is related to how sleepy we feel, and at the end of a busy day we are all 'ready for bed'. Shapiro *et al.* (1981) found that people who had competed in an 'ultra-marathon', a running race of 57 miles, slept an hour and a half longer than they normally did for two nights following the race. The researchers also found that Stage 4 sleep occupied a much greater proportion of total sleep time (about 45 per cent) than normal (about 25 per cent), whilst the proportion of time spent in REM sleep decreased.

The restorative processes that occur during sleep are not precisely known. Some studies have shown that a lack of exercise does *not* substantially reduce sleep, which it might be expected to do if sleep served an exclusively restorative function. Ryback & Lewis (1971) found that healthy individuals who spent six weeks resting in bed showed no changes in their sleep patterns. Adam & Oswald (1977, 1983) have suggested that certain kinds of tissue restoration, such as cell repair, occur during sleep, whilst Webb & Campbell (1983) believe that neurotransmitter levels are restored during sleep.

The pituitary gland releases a hormone during stage 4 sleep which is important for tissue growth, protein and RNA synthesis, and the formation of red blood cells. This suggests that Stage 4 sleep plays a role in the growth process. As noted in Chapter 11, the total time spent in Stage 4 sleep decreases with increasing age and this might be related to a relative lack of need for growth hormone. Disruption of Stage 4 sleep in healthy people produces symptoms similar to those experienced by fibrositis sufferers who are known to experience a chronic lack of Stage 4 sleep (Empson, 1989). Since fibrositis is a disorder which causes acute inflammation of the back muscles and their sheaths, which is experienced as pain and stiffness, it is tempting to accept the suggestion that sleep serves a restorative function.

Box 12.5   Sleep and psychological restoration

A different approach to restoration theory suggests that sleep may serve a psychological as well as (or instead of) a physiological restorative function. For example, Kales *et al.* (1974) have shown that insomniacs suffer from far more psychological problems than healthy people, whilst Hartmann (1973) has reported that we generally need to sleep more during periods of stress, such as occurs when we change a job or move house. Berry & Webb (1983) found a strong correlation between self-reported levels of anxiety and 'sleep efficiency' and also discovered that the better the sleep attained by the participants in their study, the more positive were their moods on the following day.

Although the evidence is not conclusive, it is possible that sleep helps us recover from the psychological as well as the physiological exertions of our waking hours.

Studies of REM sleep deprivation

REM sleep has been of particular interest to researchers, largely because of its paradoxical nature. REM sleep might serve particular functions and much research has investigated this. As with sleep in general, the easiest way to address the role of REM sleep has been to deprive people of it and observe the consequences of the deprivation.

Dement (1960) had volunteers spend several nights at his sleep laboratory. They were allowed to sleep normally but whenever they entered REM sleep they were woken up. A control group of volunteers was woken up the same number of times but only during NREM sleep. Compared with the control group the REM-deprived group became increasingly irritable, aggressive and unable to concentrate on performing various tasks. As the experiment progressed, the REM-deprived group started to show *REM starvation*. After several nights they attempted to go into REM sleep as soon as they went to sleep, and it became increasingly difficult to wake them when they did manage to enter REM.

On the first night, Dement had to wake the REM-deprived sleepers an average of 12 times each, but by the seventh night they had to be woken an average of 26 times, suggesting that the need for REM sleep was steadily increasing. Similarly, Borbely (1986) found that a REM sleep-deprived individual made 31 attempts to enter REM on the first night, 51 attempts on the second, and over 60 on the third!

When people are allowed to sleep normally after REM sleep deprivation most, but not all, show a REM *rebound effect* (they spend longer in REM sleep than is usually the case). This suggests that we try to make up for 'lost' REM sleep time, although firm conclusions cannot be drawn since the rebound effect is *not* observed in everyone. In general, the evidence suggests that we can adjust to REM sleep deprivation in much the same way that we can adjust to not eating for several days if necessary (Webb, 1975). REM sleep seems to be necessary, then, though depriving people of it does not appear to be psychologically harmful.

Box 12.6   REM, anxiety and alcohol

Some researchers have looked at the effects of REM sleep deprivation on the reduction of anxiety. Greenberg *et al.* (1972) had participants watch a film of a circumcision rite performed without anaesthetic. On first viewing, the film elicits a high level of anxiety which gradually subsides on repeated viewing. However, the researchers found that people deprived of REM sleep did *not* show a reduction in their anxiety when they viewed the film on subsequent occasions. This suggests that REM sleep may, at least partly act to reduce the anxiety of events that have occurred during the waking day.

Alcohol (see Chapter 15), suppresses REM sleep without affecting NREM sleep. When heavy alcohol users abstain, a REM rebound effect occurs. The effect can be very disturbing and the sharp increase in dreaming often leads to a resumption of heavy drinking. With severe alcohol abuse, a kind of REM rebound effect may occur during the waking hours. This manifests itself as the disturbing hallucinations experienced during alcohol withdrawal (Greenberg & Pearlman, 1967).

As noted earlier, the evidence generally suggests that there are few harmful effects following REM sleep deprivation. Indeed, according to Dement (1974), research:

'has failed to prove substantial ill-effects result from even prolonged selective REM deprivation'.

Whilst this may be true, the occurrence of the REM rebound effect, and the fact that REM-deprived sleepers try to enter REM more and more over the course of time, suggests that REM sleep may serve important functions.

Restoration theories of REM sleep function

According to Oswald (1966), REM sleep is related to brain 'restoration' and growth. Studies have shown a greater rate of *protein synthesis* during REM sleep than in NREM sleep and protein synthesis may serve as 'an organic basis for new developments in the personality' (Rossi, 1973). However, whether REM sleep *causes* increased protein synthesis or increased protein synthesis is the *result* of the increased activity of nerve cells that occurs during REM sleep is less clear.

REM sleep does, however, differ over the lifespan and accounts for around 50 per cent of the total sleep time (TST) of a newborn baby as compared with only 20 per cent of the TST of an adult (see page 95). Indeed, in almost every mammalian species, adults sleep less than infants and spend less time in REM sleep as they get older. REM sleep may, therefore, promote the protein synthesis necessary for cell manufacture and growth, which is essential to the developing nervous system's maturation. The decline observed in adulthood may reflect a decrease in the rate of development of the brain's information processing capabilities.

REM sleep deprivation has the effect, in non-humans at least, of impairing learning. Bloch (1976) has shown that REM sleep increases when non-humans are given training on a new task and that this increase is greatest during the steepest part of the learning curve. Perhaps, then, the protein synthesis that occurs during REM sleep is a contributory factor in the formation of long-term memories.

In humans, the consequence of a massive 'insult' to the brain by, for example, a drug overdose, results in an increase in the amount of time spent in REM sleep, as though some attempt was being made to repair the damage done.

Even those who support the restoration theory of REM sleep function accept that REM sleep uses a substantial amount of energy (such as increased blood flow to the brain). Such activity would actually *prevent* high levels of protein synthesis. Researchers are still trying to reconcile these contradictory observations.

Some other theories of REM sleep function

MEMORY CONSOLIDATION THEORY

REM sleep may stimulate neural tissue and consolidate information in memory. Empson & Clarke's (1970) participants heard unusual phrases before bedtime and were given a memory test about them the next morning. Those deprived of REM sleep remembered less than those woken the same number of times during the night but from other stages of sleep. This finding has been replicated on a number of occasions using various material (e.g. Tilley & Empson, 1978), although we should note that there is no evidence to suggest that *hypnopaedia* – learning whilst we are asleep – takes place (Rubin, 1968).

As noted in Chapter 11, REM sleep occurs in all mammals except the spiny anteater and dolphin, but not in non-humans such as fish whose behaviour is less influenced by learning. It was also noted that the proportion of time spent in REM sleep declines with increasing age when, possibly, the need to consolidate memories is of less importance. The evidence concerning memory consolidation during REM sleep is mounting, and it may well be that memory consolidation is an important function of REM sleep.

THE SENTINEL THEORY

The observation that EEG activity resembles the patterns of activity observed during waking, and that short periods of wakefulness sometimes occur at the *end* of REM sleep, led Snyder (cited in Borbely, 1986) to suggest that REM serves the function of allowing animals to check their surroundings periodically for signs of danger. Snyder sees the end of REM acting as a *sentinel* (or look-out) to ensure that animals are free from danger. Whilst this is an interesting suggestion, its main weakness lies in the fact that it sees only the end of REM sleep as serving any function. The time spent in REM sleep presumably serves no function at all. It is unlikely that many sleep researchers would agree with this.

THE OCULOMOTOR SYSTEM MAINTENANCE THEORY

Some researchers who might agree with Snyder are those who subscribe to the oculomotor system maintenance theory of REM sleep function. According to this, the function of REM sleep is to keep the eye muscles toned up. About once every 90 minutes during sleep the eye muscles are given some exercise to keep them in trim. Although this theory may be tongue-in-cheek, it highlights one important point about theories of sleep function, namely that they are difficult to test and therefore falsify (as noted earlier, evolutionary theories of sleep seem to be capable of accommodating all of the findings concerning sleep patterns). It is difficult to see how Snyder's theory and the oculomotor system maintenance theory could be tested.

The physiology of sleep

Chapter 11 suggested that external cues are not of primary importance as far as the sleep-waking cycle is concerned. However, external cues do play a role. When night falls, the eyes inform the *supra-chiasmatic nuclei* (*SN*) and, via a neural pathway travelling through the hypothalamus, the *pineal gland*. As noted in Chapter 11, the pineal gland secretes melatonin. Melatonin influences neurons that produce serotonin, which is concentrated in the *raphe nuclei*. Serotonin is then released and acts on the *reticular activating system*.

> ### Box 12.7 Melatonin – the hormone of darkness
>
> Because melatonin is produced mainly at night, it has been called the hormone of darkness. In 1995, a synthetic version of melatonin was produced and marketed in America as a way of overcoming insomnia and jet lag (and, incidentally, as a rejuvenating substance). Although currently banned in the UK, because not enough is known about its effects, it has been used with blind people to resynchronise the biological clock by producing shifts of its timing, an effect probably mediated by the melatonin receptors in the suprachiasmatic nuclei (Minors, 1997).

It has long been known that the RAS is involved in consciousness. Moruzzi & Magoun (1949), for example,

showed that stimulation of the RAS caused a slumbering cat to awaken whereas destruction of the RAS caused a permanent coma. Jouvet (1967) showed that destruction of the raphe nuclei produces sleeplessness and, on the basis of the finding that serotonin is concentrated in this brain structure, he concluded that serotonin must play a role in the induction of sleep. Since serotonin is a *monoamine* neurotransmitter, Jouvet advanced his *monoamine hypothesis of sleep*.

Jouvet discovered that *paracholorophenylalanine* (or *PCPA*), a substance which inhibits serotonin synthesis, prevents sleep. However, if its effects are reversed (by means of *5-hydroxytryptophan*) then sleep is reinstated. This suggests that whilst serotonin may not play *the* role in the induction of sleep, it certainly plays *a* role. Other experiments conducted by Jouvet showed that destruction of the *locus coeruleus* (a small patch of dark cells located in the pons) caused REM sleep to disappear completely, suggesting that the pons plays a role in the regulation of REM sleep. Moreover, if neurons in a different part of the pons were destroyed, REM sleep remained but muscle tension (which is ordinarily absent during REM sleep) was *maintained*. This resulted in a cat moving around during REM sleep, even though it was completely unconscious.

For reasons that are not well understood, the inhibitory processes normally operating during REM sleep do not operate in some people (and this is called *REM behaviour disorder*). Sufferers may 'thrash violently about, leap out of bed, and may even attack their partners' (Chase & Morales, 1990). As mentioned in Chapter 11, dreaming is correlated with REM sleep and, presumably, being paralysed during REM sleep serves the useful biological function of preventing us from acting out dreams. Quite possibly, the cat described above was acting out a dream. 'Sleepwalking', then, cannot occur during REM sleep because the body's musculature is in a state of virtual paralysis. The stage in which it does occur is identified in Box 13.1 (see page 107).

The locus coeruleus produces *noradrenaline* and *acetylcholine*. Jouvet proposed that these were responsible for the onset of REM sleep and the associated loss of muscle tone. The fact that *carbachol*, a chemical which imitates acetylcholine's action but has a more prolonged action, results in much longer periods of REM sleep, supports this view. Moreover, *scopolamine*, a substance which *inhibits* acetylcholine's action, leads to a dramatic *delay* in the onset of REM sleep.

Jouvet (1983) believes that sleep cycles occur as a result of the relationship between the raphe nuclei and locus coeruleus. The raphe nuclei are believed to initiate sleep (by acting on the RAS). Thereafter, interactions between the raphe nuclei and the locus coeruleus generate the NREM-REM sleep cycle. When one structure overcomes the other, wakefulness occurs.

The picture is undoubtedly more complicated than has been painted. For example, stimulation of the *thalamus* can induce sleep, and stimulation of other areas can prevent waking. The ventrolateral preoptic area of the hypothalamus, for example, has been found to provide direct input to neurons which contain *histamine*, *noradrenaline* and *serotonin*. This area might serve as an 'off-switch' for the brain and allow the simultaneous deactivation of all arousal systems. Nonetheless, the view that sleep is a passive process can certainly be dismissed. Both sleeping and waking must be the result of complex interactions between various brain structures.

Conclusions

This chapter has looked at theories of the functions of sleep in general and REM sleep in particular, and has examined what is known about the physiology of sleep. Presently, no theory is firmly supported by experimental evidence. For some, however, the question of why we sleep has a very simple answer. We sleep because we need to dream. If this is the case, another interesting question arises, concerning the function of dreaming. This question is addressed in Chapter 13.

Summary

■ Sleep deprivation is used as a way of studying the functions of sleep. Controlled studies suggest a pattern of psychological reactions whose severity increases with increasing deprivation. After six nights without sleep, **sleep deprivation psychosis** occurs, although this disappears after a period of 'recovery sleep' (which need not last as long as the deprivation). There is little evidence that physical harm follows sleep deprivation.

■ The evidence does not, however, imply that sleep has no value. Long-term sleep deprivation in rats fatally impairs the ability to regulate their own heat. Case studies of humans, who lose sleep as a result of brain damage, also indicate that long-term deprivation is fatal.

■ Theories of sleep function attempt to explain the undeniable need for sleep. Meddis's **evolutionary theory** proposes that sleep time is related to an animal's metabolic rate, method of obtaining food and exposure to predators. Animals with a high metabolic rate, gather food in the open, and are preyed upon, have little sleep.

■ Webb's **hibernation theory** proposes that because natural selection would favour an animal that kept itself out of danger, sleep has survival value. In the evolutionary past of humans, sleeping at night would have reduced the risk of predation/accidents and conserved energy that would have been wasted spent hunting.

■ Some evolutionary theorists argue that preyed-upon species sleep for short periods because of the constant threat of predation. Others argue that such species sleep longer to avoid predation. This account of different sleep times is non-falsifiable.

■ **Restoration theories** propose that sleep restores depleted energy levels, eliminates waste products from the muscles, repairs cells and recovers lost physical abilities. Stage 4 sleep, strongly suspected of being involved in the growth process, increases after excessive physical exertion. Reduced Stage 4 sleep in the elderly may reflect a reduction in the need for growth hormone. Deprivation of Stage 4 sleep produces fibrositis-like symptoms in healthy people. All of these findings are consistent with the view that sleep serves a restorative function.

■ Sleep, especially REM sleep, may also serve a psychological restorative function. Deprivation of REM sleep results in irritability, aggressiveness and the inability to concentrate. People deprived of REM sleep also show REM starvation and try to enter REM as soon as they return to sleep. Most people also show a 'rebound effect' following deprivation of REM sleep, and spend longer in that stage.

■ REM sleep appears to be necessary, but being deprived of it does not appear to be psychologically harmful. It may be involved in brain restoration and growth, since more protein synthesis occurs in it than in NREM sleep. Because REM sleep decreases with age, it may promote maturation of the developing nervous system and increase the brain's information processing capabilities.

■ REM sleep in non-humans increases during learning, especially in the steepest part of the learning curve, and so may be involved in long-term memory formation and consolidation. Studies using humans also point to a role in memory consolidation. However, the fact that increased blood flow to the brain during REM would actually prevent protein synthesis complicates the picture.

■ Snyder's **sentinel theory** proposes that the brief awakenings which sometimes occur at the end of a period of REM sleep allow an animal periodically to monitor its environment for signs of danger. However, this function only concerns the end of REM sleep, not REM sleep itself.

■ The **oculomotor system maintenance theory** proposes that REM sleep's function is to keep the eye muscles toned up. This tongue-in-cheek proposal highlights the lack of falsifiability apparent in many theories of sleep function.

■ Several brain structures, including the supra-chiasmatic nuclei, raphe nuclei, hypothalamus, thalamus, pons, reticular activating system and locus coeruleus have been implicated in sleep. Melatonin, the hormone of darkness, is also involved, as are serotonin, noradrenaline, acetylcholine and histamine. Their roles are described in Jouvet's **monoamine hypothesis of sleep**.

■ The view that sleep is a passive process is incorrect and both sleep and waking are the result of complex interactions occurring in the brain.

13

THE FUNCTIONS OF DREAMING

Introduction and overview

Dreams have long held a fascination for both laypeople and psychologists. Some cultures, for example, believe dreams to be the experiences of a world that is not available during the waking hours. Others see dreams as messages from the gods. Attempts to discover the meaning of dreams can be found in Babylonian records dating back to 5000 BC. The Bible, Talmud, Homer's *Iliad* and *Odyssey* all give accounts of the meaning of dreams. In the Bible, for example, dreams provided revelations. It was during a dream that Joseph learned there was to be a famine in Egypt. This chapter examines theories of the functions of dreaming. It begins, however, by looking at some of the basic findings obtained in this area.

Dreams: some basic findings

The pioneering research of Dement, Aserinsky and Kleitman which was described in Chapter 11 revealed much about dreaming. As noted, REM sleep is correlated with dreaming and so instead of relying on the sometimes hazy recall of a dreamer waking at the end of an eight-hour period of sleep, the waking of a dreamer during a REM episode enabled a vivid account of a dream to be obtained.

Everyone shows the pattern of four to five REM episodes per night. When woken from REM sleep, people report dreaming about 80 per cent of the time. Thus, people who claim that they don't dream really mean that they don't *remember* their dreams. There are wide individual differences in this, but those dreams that are remembered tend to be the ones occurring closest to waking up. People blind from birth also dream and have auditory dreams which are just as vivid and complex as the visual dreams of sighted people.

Dreams may be realistic and well organised, disorganised and uninformed, in black and white or colour, and emotional or unemotional. Although dreaming is most likely to occur in REM sleep, some occurs in NREM sleep. REM sleep dreams tend to be clear, highly detailed, full of vivid images and often reported as fantastic adventures with a clear plot. The eye movements that occur during REM sleep are sometimes correlated with a dream's content, but there is no one-to-one correspondence. NREM dreams typically consist of fleeting images, lack detail,

have vague plots and involve commonplace things.

Most dreams last as long as the events would in real life. Although time seems to expand and contract during a dream, 15 minutes of events occupies about 15 minutes of dream time. The actual content of a dream can be affected by pre-sleep events. For example, people deprived of water often dream of drinking (Bokert, 1970). Also, whilst the brain is relatively insensitive to outside sensory input, some external stimuli can either wake us up (see Box 11.5) or be incorporated into a dream. For example, Dement & Wolpert (1958) lightly sprayed cold water onto dreamers' faces. Compared with sleepers who were not sprayed, they were much more likely to dream about water, incorporating waterfalls, leaky roofs and, occasionally, being sprayed with water into their dreams.

Sex differences in dreaming have also been reported, with females typically dreaming about indoor settings and males about outdoor settings. Male dreams also tend to be more aggressive than female dreams. Contrary to popular belief, only a small proportion (one in ten in men and one in 30 in women) of dreams are clearly sexual in content (Hall & Van de Castle, 1966).

Box 13.1   Lucid dreaming and sleepwalking

Lucid dreamers report having dreams in which they knew they were dreaming and felt as if they were conscious during the dream. They can test their state of consciousness by attempting to perform impossible acts such as floating in the air. If the act can be performed, a lucid dream is occurring. Some lucid dreamers can control the course of events in a dream, and skilled dreamers can signal the onset of a lucid dream by moving their eyes in a way pre-arranged with the sleep researcher. Evidently, the technology now exists for all of us to become lucid dreamers (Hollington, 1995).

Contrary to popular belief, sleepwalking does not occur during REM sleep. It can't, since the musculature is in a state of virtual paralysis during REM sleep (see Chapter 12). As noted, the paralysis presumably prevents us from *acting out* a dream. When the part of the brain responsible for the inhibition of movement is damaged, a cat, for example, will move around during REM sleep. Perhaps, then, non-humans dream too! Sleepwalking occurs during the *deeper stages* of sleep when the musculature is not paralysed.

A great deal is known about the process of dreaming, but what possible functions does it serve? Some researchers believe that dreaming does not have a purpose. Kleitman (1963), for example, has suggested that:

'the low-grade cerebral activity that is dreaming may serve no significant function whatsoever'.

Others believe that dreams have important psychological functions.

Freud's theory of dream function

The first person to seriously consider the psychology of dreaming was Freud (1900) in *The Interpretation of Dreams*. Freud argued that a dream was a sort of 'psychic safety valve' which allowed a person to harmlessly discharge otherwise unacceptable and unconscious wishes and urges.

During the waking hours, these wishes and impulses are excluded from consciousness because of their unacceptable nature. During sleep, they are allowed to be expressed through the medium of dreams. As noted above, Freud saw them as relieving psychic tensions created during the day and gratifying unconscious desires. He also saw them as 'protecting sleep', by providing imagery that would keep disturbing and repressed thoughts out of consciousness.

Box 13.2   Manifest and latent content

Freud argued that unconscious desires are not gratified directly in a dream. What he called the *manifest content* of a dream (the dream as reported by the dreamer) is a censored and symbolic version of its deeper *latent content* (its actual meaning). According to Freud, a dream's meaning has to be 'disguised' because it consists of drives and wishes that would be threatening to us if they were expressed directly. Freud believed that the process of 'censorship' and 'symbolic transformation' accounted for the sometimes bizarre and highly illogical nature of dreams.

For Freud, dreams provide the most valuable insight into the motives that direct a person's behaviour, and he described a dream as 'the royal road to the unconscious'. The task of a dream analyst is to decode the manifest content of a dream into its latent content (see Chapter 73). Analysts call the objects that occur in a dream, and which camouflage its meaning, *symbols*. A gun, for example, might actually be a disguised representation of the penis. A person who dreamt of being *robbed* at gunpoint

might be unconsciously expressing a wish to be sexually dominated. A person who dreamt of *robbing* someone at gunpoint might be unconsciously expressing a wish to be sexually dominant.

Table 13.1   Sexual symbols in Freudian dream interpretation

Symbols for the male genital organs

aeroplanes	fish	neckties	tools	weapons
bullets	hands	poles	trains	
feet	hoses	snakes	trees	
fire	knives	sticks	umbrellas	

Symbols for the female genital organs

bottles	caves	doors	ovens	ships
boxes	chests	hats	pockets	tunnels
cases	closets	jars	pots	

Symbols for sexual intercourse

climbing a ladder	entering a room
climbing a staircase	flying in an aeroplane
crossing a bridge	riding a horse
driving a car	riding a roller coaster
riding a lift	walking into a tunnel or down a hall

Symbols for the breasts

apples	peaches

Freud believed that no matter how absurd a dream appeared to be to the dreamer, it always possessed meaning and logic. However, he did accept that there was a danger in translating the symbols, and warned that dreams had to be analysed in the context of a person's waking life as well as his/her associations with the dream's content: a broken candlestick may well represent a theme of impotence, but as Freud himself (a lover of cigars) famously remarked, 'sometimes a cigar is only a cigar'.

It is, of course, possible that dreams have meaning and might reveal important issues and conflicts in a person's life. However, Freud's view that these issues and conflicts are always disguised has been criticised. For example, a person who is concerned with impotence is just as likely to dream about impotence as s/he is about broken candles. As Fisher & Greenberg (1977) have noted:

'there is no *rationale* for approaching a dream as if it were a container for a secret wish buried under layers of concealment'.

Freud's claim that part of the function of dreaming is to 'protect sleep' has also been challenged. Evidence suggests that disturbing events during the day tend to be followed by related disturbing dreams rather than 'protective imagery' (Foulkes & Cohen, 1973). Hall (1966), amongst others, has noted that the content of most dreams is consistent with a person's waking behaviour. Thus, there is little evidence to support the view that the primary function of dreaming is to act as a release for the expression of unacceptable impulses.

The major problem for Freud's theory of dream function is that the *interpretation* of a dream is not something that can be *objectively* achieved even if the interpreter is a trained psychoanalyst. According to Collee (1993):

> 'Metaphor is a notoriously ambiguous form of communication. You can suggest to me the meaning of having luminous feet, but the image will almost always mean something entirely different to you from what it means to me. So dreams end up in much the same category as tarot cards or tea leaves: just a system of images which the dream expert can manipulate to tell you exactly what they think you need to hear'.

Box 13.3   Dreams and illness

Another theory of dreams developed by Freud derives from practices in ancient Greece. At the Temple of Aesculapius, the physician Epidaurus administered drugs to people who, having slept and dreamt, then told him about their dreams. On the basis of the descriptions provided, Epidaurus was able to tell them the nature of their illness. Like the ancient Greeks, Freud believed that dreams were the body's way of telling us about physical illness. Psychoanalytic interest lies in the finding that dreams may precipitate illness or contribute to the distress of illness (Le Fanu, 1994).

A 'problem-solving' theory of dreaming

Webb & Cartwright (1978) see dreams as a way of dealing with problems relating to work, sex, health, relationships and so on that occur during the waking hours. Cartwright (1978) argues that whatever is symbolised in a dream *is* the dream's true meaning and, unlike Freud, she sees no reason to distinguish between a dream's manifest and latent content. Like Freud, however, Cartwright makes much use of the role of metaphor in dreaming.

Cartwright suggests that a person dreaming of, say, being buried beneath an avalanche whilst carrying several books might be worried about being 'snowed under' with work. Dreaming of a colleague trying to stab you in the neck might indicate that the colleague is a 'pain in the neck'. Cartwright has claimed support for her theory from several studies. In one, participants were presented with common problems which needed solving. Those allowed to sleep uninterrupted generated far more realistic solutions than those deprived of REM sleep.

Additionally, Hartmann (1973) has shown that people experiencing interpersonal or occupational problems enter REM sleep earlier and spend longer in it than people without such problems. For Cartwright, then, dreams are a way of identifying and dealing with many of life's problems. As she has noted, people going through crises need the support of friends and family, a little bit of luck and 'a good dream system'.

'Reprogramming' theories of dreaming

According to Evans (1984), the brain needs to periodically shut itself off from sensory input in order to process and assimilate new information and update information already stored. This shutting off is REM sleep, during which the brain 'mentally reprograms' its memory systems. The dreams we experience are the brain's attempts at interpreting this updating.

Support for this theory has been claimed from studies which show that REM sleep increases following activities requiring intense or unusual mental activity (such as performing complex and frustrating tasks). For example, Herman & Roffwarg (1983) had participants spend the waking day wearing distorting lenses that made the visual world appear upside down. After this experience, which demands considerable mental effort, participants spent longer than usual in REM sleep. Evans' theory would explain this in terms of the brain needing to spend a longer period of time 'off-line', processing and assimilating the experience. The finding that older people spend shorter periods of time dreaming is also consistent with Evans' theory: presumably, the older we get, the less need there is to reprogram our memory systems.

An alternative 'reprogramming' theory has been offered by Foulkes (1985). Like some other sleep researchers, Foulkes argues that dreams occur as a result of spontaneous activity in the nervous system. Foulkes argues that this activity can be related to our cognitive processes. The activation that occurs in the brain may well be spontaneous and random, but our cognitive systems are definitely *not* random. According to Foulkes, these systems, which we use in interpreting new experiences, themselves try to interpret the brain activity that occurs during REM sleep. Because of the structure imposed on the activation by our cognitive systems, dreams consist of events that generally occur in a way that makes at least some sense.

Box 13.4   Foulkes' functions of dreams

For Foulkes, dreams have at least four functions. First, most dreams usually refer to and reflect the memories and knowledge of the dreamer. One function might therefore be to relate *newly* acquired knowledge to one's own self-consciousness. Second, a dream might help integrate and combine specific knowledge and experiences acquired through the various senses with more general knowledge acquired in the past. Third, dreams often contain events that could, or might, have happened to us, but did not. By dreaming about something that has not yet occurred, but which might, a dream may serve the function of programming us to be prepared for dealing with new, unexpected events. Finally, since dreams are shaped by basic cognitive systems, they may reveal important information about the nature of our cognitive processes.

A third 'reprogramming' theory, which is a variation of the second function of dreams proposed by Foulkes, has been proposed by Koukkou & Lehman (1980). They argue that during a dream we combine ideas and strategies of thinking which originated in childhood with recently acquired relevant information. For them, a dream is a restructuring and reinterpretation of data already stored in memory.

Like some other theorists, Koukkou and Lehman clearly see dreams as being *meaningful*. However, some researchers have challenged this view arguing that dreams are a meaningless consequence of brain activity during sleep.

Hobson and McCarley's 'activation-synthesis' theory

One of the best known biopsychological theories of dream function is the 'activation-synthesis' theory proposed by Hobson & McCarley (1977). Hobson (1989) showed that in cats, certain neurons deep within the brain fire in a seemingly random manner during REM sleep. The firing of these neurons *activates* adjacent neurons which are involved in the control of eye movements, gaze, balance, posture and activities such as running and walking.

As noted in Chapter 12, most body movements are inhibited during REM sleep. However, signals are still sent to the parts of the cerebral cortex responsible for visual information processing and voluntary actions when we are awake. Thus, although the body is not moving, the brain receives signals which suggest that it is. In an attempt to make sense of this contradiction, the brain, drawing on memory and other stored information, attempts to *synthesise* the random bursts of neural activity. The result of its efforts is the dream we experience.

The process of synthesis results in the brain imposing some order on the chaotic events caused by the firing of neurons, but it cannot do this in a particularly sophisticated way. This would explain why dreams often comprise shifting and fragmentary images. As Hobson & McCarley (1977) have noted, the dream itself is the brain's effort 'to make the best out of a bad job'. For Hobson and McCarley, then, dream content is the by-product of the random stimulation of nerve cells rather than the unconscious wishes suggested by Freud. Whereas Freud saw dreams as 'the royal road to the unconscious', Hobson and McCarley see them as inherently random and meaningless.

Box 13.5   Giant cells and 'synaptic ammunition'

Hobson (1988) has also offered an explanation of why the brain is periodically activated during the sleep cycle. He argues that *giant cells*, which are found in the reticular activating system and the pons, are responsible for the onset of REM sleep and that these are sensitive to *acetylcholine*. When acetylcholine is available, the giant cells fire in an unrestrained way, but when no more is available they stop.

Hobson uses the analogy of a machine gun which can fire bullets very quickly when the cartridge is full, but can do nothing once it has emptied. The end of REM sleep occurs because there is no more 'synaptic ammunition'. When synaptic ammunition, in the form of acetylcholine, becomes available again, the giant cells start firing and another period of REM sleep begins.

Hobson and McCarley's theory has attracted considerable support because of its apparent explanatory power. For example, our strong tendency to dream about events that have occurred during the day presumably occurs because the most current neural activity of the cortex is that which represents the concerns or events of the day. Commonly experienced dreams about falling are, presumably, the brain attempting to interpret activity in the neurons involved in balance, whilst dreams about floating are the brain's attempt to interpret neural activity in the inner ear.

Activation-synthesis theory is also capable of explaining why we do not experience smells and tastes during a dream. This is because the neurons responsible are not stimulated during REM sleep. Our inability to remember dreams occurs because the neurons in the cortex that control the storage of new memories are turned 'off'. Finally, evidence concerning the role of acetylcholine in REM sleep is also consistent with Hobson and McCarley's theory (see page 104).

Yet whilst Hobson believes that activation synthesis theory has 'opened the door to the molecular biology of sleep' (and closed it on the Freudian approach to dreaming: Bianchi, 1992), it has not escaped criticism. According to Foulkes (1985), the content of dreams is influenced by our waking experiences and therefore dreams cannot be as random and psychologically meaningless as Hobson and McCarley suggest.

In response to this, Hobson (1988) has accepted that:

> 'the brain is so inexorably bent upon the quest for meaning that it attributes and even creates meaning when there is little or none in the data it is asked to process'.

However, although dreams might contain 'unique stylistic psychological features and concerns' which provide us with insights into our 'life strategies' and, perhaps, ways of coping, the activation synthesis theory most definitely sees dreams as the result of brain stem activities rather than unconscious wishes.

Crick and Mitchison's 'reverse learning' theory of dreams

According to Crick & Mitchison (1983), the function of dreaming is to enable the brain to get rid of information it doesn't need by weakening undesirable synaptic connections and erasing 'inappropriate modes of brain activity' which have been produced either by the physical growth of brain cells or experience. Crick and Mitchison propose that during REM sleep, random firing of neurons in the brain sets off undesirable connections, such as hallucinations and fantasies, that have overloaded the cortex. By 'flushing out' the excessive accumulation of 'parasitic information', more space is made available in memory for useful information. 'We dream in order to forget', they write, and call this process *reverse learning* or *unlearning*.

Crick and Mitchison argue that their theory is supported by the finding that all mammals except the spiny anteater and dolphin have REM sleep (when dreaming is most likely to occur). Both of these mammals have an abnormally large cortex for their size, which Crick and Mitchison believe is because they do not dream. Consequently, they need an especially large cortex to accommodate all the useless information they have accumulated, which cannot be disposed of.

For Crick and Mitchison, then, dreams serve a biologically useful process in that they keep the nervous system functioning effectively. However, a dream's content is an accidental result that does not lend itself to meaningful interpretation. Indeed, remembering dreams is *bad* for us because we are storing again the very information we were trying to dispose of!

Box 13.6   Dreams and creativity

One problem for theories which see dreams as meaningless events is that history is littered with stories of discoveries or creations that came to people during a dream. The chemist August Kekulé once dreamed of six snakes chasing each other in such a way that the snake in front was biting the snake behind. From this, he deduced the structure of the benzene ring. Robert Louis Stevenson is said to have dreamed the plot of *Dr Jekyll and Mr Hyde*. His wife told him he was talking in his sleep. Angrily, he replied: 'What did you wake me for? I was dreaming a fine wee bogy tale'.

All theories of dreaming have difficulty in accounting for the observation that something very much like REM sleep occurs in the developing foetus. What unconscious wishes could a developing foetus have? What 'parasitic information' could a foetus be getting rid of? According to Jouvet (1983), the only possible explanation is that REM sleep serves to program processes in the brain necessary for the development and maintenance of genetically determined functions, such as instincts. This theory suggests that REM sleep generates a sensory activity pattern in the brain – the dream – that is independent of the external world (Borbely, 1986). Jouvet sees the activity of nerve cells that occurs in REM sleep as representing a code which is capable of activating information stored in the genes. This inborn instinctive behaviour is 'practiced' during REM sleep. After birth, it is combined with acquired or learned information.

Box 13.7   To sleep, perchance to experience amygdalocortical activation and prefrontal deactivation?

Maquet *et al.* (cited in Highfield, 1996d) persuaded participants connected to an EEG machine to sleep in a PET scanner, their heads pinned in place by a special face mask. The PET scans confirmed the existence of activity in the pons during REM sleep, and also indicated activity in the left thalamus, which receives signals from the brainstem. Of most interest, though, was the activity in the left and right amygdalas. Since one role of these structures is the formation and consolidation of memories of emotional experience, it seems likely that REM sleep is, as theorists like Evans (1984) have proposed, involved in memory processing.

Maquet *et al.* also found reduced activity in the prefrontal cortex, which is involved in self-awareness and the planning of behaviour. They argue that the 'dampening down' of this area may prevent us from realising that a dream is actually unreal, and may be why dreams appear real. The prefrontal cortex's reduced activity may also explain the distortions in time that occur in a dream and the forgetting of a dream after waking.

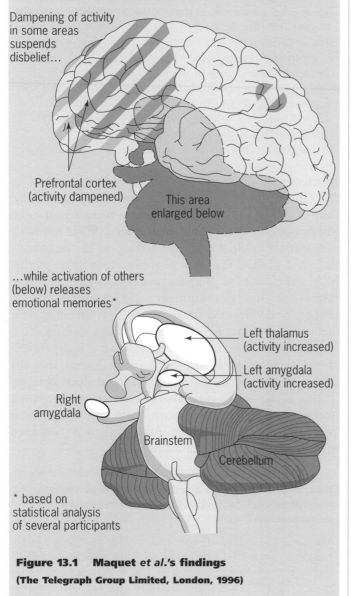

Dampening of activity in some areas suspends disbelief…

Prefrontal cortex (activity dampened)

This area enlarged below

…while activation of others (below) releases emotional memories*

Left thalamus (activity increased)

Left amygdala (activity increased)

Right amygdala

Brainstem

Cerebellum

* based on statistical analysis of several participants

Figure 13.1   Maquet *et al.*'s findings
(The Telegraph Group Limited, London, 1996)

Conclusions

This chapter has reviewed several theories of the function of dreaming. These see dreams as being meaningful *or* meaningless. Because they are difficult to test, none can be disqualified or accepted. A final answer to the question posed at the beginning of the chapter is not, at present, available. As Collee (1993) has observed:

'There is a danger in thinking about the body in teleological terms – imagining that everything has a function, whereas we know that a lot of what happens is accidental. Yawning is one example of such accidents of nature, seeming to be just the useless by-product of various important respiratory reflexes. Dreams might have no function at all or they might have a heap of different functions all jumbled together so that one obscures the other. They might just be the films your brain plays to entertain itself while it is sleeping.'

Summary

■ The correlation between REM sleep and dreaming enables dreams to be studied scientifically. Everyone experiences four to five episodes of REM sleep per night, and when woken from it report dreaming 80 per cent of the time. Some dreams occur in NREM sleep, but there are important differences in quality and content between them and REM dreams.

■ Events in dreams tend to last as long as they would in real life, and a dream's content can be affected by pre-sleep events and events occurring during REM sleep. There are differences in men and women's dreams, although we have fewer dreams about sex than is commonly believed.

■ **Lucid dreamers** are aware that they are having a dream and can sometimes control the events that occur in it. Sleepwalking cannot occur in REM sleep since the musculature is virtually paralysed. Sleepwalking must occur in stages of sleep other than REM.

■ According to Freud, a dream is a 'safety valve' which allows us to harmlessly discharge otherwise unacceptable and unconscious urges and wishes. The dream reported by the dreamer (its **manifest content**) is a censored and symbolic version of its actual meaning (**latent content**).

■ Freud's theory has been widely criticised. For example, there is little evidence to support his view that the function of dreaming is to 'protect sleep', since disturbing events during the day tend to be followed by related disturbing dreams rather than 'protective imagery'. The non-falsifiability of dream interpretation is the theory's major weakness.

■ Dreams have also been proposed as ways of solving problems. Evidence suggests that people experiencing interpersonal/occupational problems enter REM sleep earlier and spend longer in it than those without such problems.

■ Evans' **reprogramming theory** suggests that dreams are the brain's attempt at interpreting the processing and assimilation of new information, and updating information already stored. Support for this comes from the finding that REM sleep time increases following activities requiring intense/unusual mental activity.

■ **Foulkes' reprogramming theory** claims that a dream is an attempt to interpret the random and spontaneous brain activity that occurs in REM sleep. A dream usually makes some sense because our cognitive system imposes its structure on this otherwise meaningless activity. Dreams help integrate specific knowledge and experiences with more general knowledge acquired in the past, and can aid in preparing us for new, unexpected events. They may do this by restructuring data stored in memory in the light of new experiences.

■ **Activation-synthesis theory** suggests that dreams are essentially meaningless and reflect the brain's unsophisticated attempt to make sense of the electrical activity that occurs in REM sleep. A dream occurs when giant cells in the reticular activating system and the pons are activated by acetylcholine. When acetylcholine is no longer available, the giant cells' activity ceases and REM sleep ends.

■ Activation-synthesis theory has much apparent explanatory power. For example, activity in the neurons involved in balance explain dreams about falling, whilst dreams about floating are the brain's attempt to interpret neuronal activity in the inner ear. However, if dreams are influenced by our waking experiences, then dreaming cannot be completely random and meaningless.

■ Crick and Mitchison's **reverse learning theory** proposes that dreams enable the brain to erase information that is no longer needed by weakening certain synaptic connections. Random firing of neurons sets off undesirable connections, such as hallucinations and fantasies, that have overloaded the cortex. The 'flushing out' of 'parasitic information' creates more space in memory for useful information.

■ Crick and Mitchison see the absence of REM sleep in the spiny anteater and dolphin as consistent with their theory, since both of these have abnormally large cortexes for their size. An abnormally large cortex would be needed if there were no way of removing useless information.

■ Historical accounts of discoveries and creations coming to people during dreams are difficult for reverse learning theory to explain. The observation of REM-like sleep in the developing foetus poses problems for all theories of dreaming, although an attempt to account for this phenomenon has been offered by Jouvet.

14

HYPNOSIS AND HYPNOTIC PHENOMENA

Introduction and overview

Like dreaming, hypnosis has long been of fascination to both laypeople and psychologists. This chapter reviews what is known about hypnosis and hypnotic phenomena. It begins by briefly looking at the history of hypnosis and, after describing the induction of a hypnotic state, considers some of its major characteristics. It then looks at two major theories of hypnosis before examining some practical applications of hypnosis and the issue of hypnosis and behaviour control.

A brief history of hypnosis

Serious scientific interest in hypnosis can be traced to 1784, when King Louis XVI of France established a committee to investigate the work of Franz Anton Mesmer. Like some present-day physicists, Mesmer believed that the universe was connected by a mysterious form of 'magnetism'. He also believed that human beings could be drawn to one another by a process called *animal magnetism*.

Box 14.1   Animal magnetism

According to Mesmer, illnesses were caused by imbalances in the body's own magnetic fields. Since he considered himself to possess a very large amount of 'magnetic fluid', Mesmer reasoned that by rechannelling his own magnetism he could cure the sick, because their 'magnetic fluxes' would be restored. *Mesmerism*, the treatment devised by Mesmer, was unusual. In a darkened room, patients, who held iron bars, were seated around wooden barrels filled with water, ground glass and iron filings. With soft music playing in the background Mesmer, dressed in a lilac taffeta robe, would walk around the room and occasionally tap the patients with his bar. Often, they would suffer convulsions and enter a trance-like state. When this occurred, Mesmer's assistants removed them to a mattress-lined room so they would not harm themselves.

Using his techniques, Mesmer apparently cured some minor ailments. However, Louis XVI's committee did not believe that 'animal magnetism' was responsible. In its view, cures probably occurred through 'aroused imagination' or what would today be called the *placebo effect*

(see also Box 77.6). Although the committee's conclusions led to a decline of interest in Mesmer, 'Mesmerism' and 'animal magnetism', physicians remained interested in the possibility that similar techniques had a use, especially to reduce pain during surgery.

In 1842, Long, an American surgeon, operated on an etherised patient, the first instance of anaesthesia being used in medicine. In the same year, Ward, a British physician, reported that he had amputated a man's leg without causing any discomfort and without anything other than 'hypnosis' (a word coined by another British physician, Braid, and taken from the Greek *hypnos* meaning 'sleep'). Between 1845 and 1851, Eskdale performed many operations in India using hypnosis as his only anaesthetic. The technique's success was indicated by the fact that Eskdale's patients appeared to show no sign of suffering during their operations, and no apparent memory for having been in pain.

Inducing a hypnotic state

There are several ways of inducing a 'hypnotic state', the only requirement of any of them being that a person understands hypnosis will take place. Typically, the individual is asked to stare upwards and focus attention on a 'target' such as a small light or a spot on the wall. As attention is focused, the hypnotist makes suggestions of relaxation, tiredness and sleepiness. Contrary to popular belief, hypnotised people are *not* asleep. Although the eyes are closed, EEG recordings do not show the patterns characteristic of the stages of sleep (see Chapter 11) even though rapid eye movements may be seen beneath the closed eyelids.

The hypnotist may also suggest that the arms and legs feel heavy (an *ideomotor* suggestion) or warm (an *ideosensory* suggestion). The *expectation* of bodily changes can be sufficient to produce them. The suggestions probably reduce activity in the sympathetic branch of the ANS and help bring about the relaxed state. If the eyes are still open after ten minutes, the hypnotist will suggest they be closed. After further suggestions of relaxation, hypnotic tests are administered (Heap, 1996).

Characteristics of the hypnotic state

Several characteristics are associated with the hypnotic state, some or all of which may be apparent in a hypnotised person. *Suspension of planning* is a loss of ability to initiate actions. Thus, hypnotised people sit quietly and show little or no activity. If, however, an activity is suggested, the suggestion is responded to. Another characteristic is a *distortion in information processing*. Hypnotised people tend to accept inconsistencies or incongruities that would ordinarily be noticed. A *narrowing of attention* also occurs and results in less awareness of sensory information. For example, a person told to listen to only the hypnotist's voice will apparently hear no other voices. This is interesting because it has been shown that there is no reduction in sensory sensitivity and information is *still* analysed by the brain.

Box 14.2   Sensory information processing and hypnosis

In the Ponzo illusion (a) (see also Chapter 21), the two parallel horizontal lines are the same length, but the top one looks longer than the bottom one. If, through hypnotic suggestion, the slanted lines are made to 'disappear', participants still report the top line as looking longer (Miller *et al.*,1973). This shows that the visual system continues to process sensory information during hypnosis. If this were not the case, the lines would be perceived as being equal in length, as in (b).

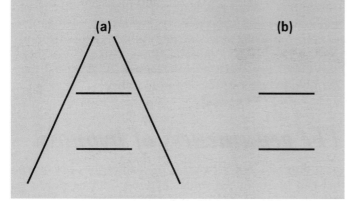

Hypnotised people will also respond to suggestions that their arms are becoming lighter and will rise, or that their hands are becoming 'attracted' to one another. As well as initiating movements, suggestion can inhibit it. A person told that the arm is 'rigid' will report being unable to bend it at all or only with extreme difficulty. Feelings and perceptions suggested by the hypnotist are also experienced, even if they are not consistent with actual external conditions. For example, a person told that the bottle beneath his or her nose contains water may report smelling nothing even though it contains ammonia in the concentration found in household bleach.

Box 14.3   Positive and negative hallucinations

Other perceptual distortions include the uncritical acceptance of hallucinated experiences. For example, hypnotised people may talk to an imaginary person they are told is sitting next to them without checking if this person is real. Responding to something that is not present is called a *positive hallucination*. Failing to respond to something that is present is called a *negative hallucination*.

In *post-hypnotic amnesia*, the hypnotist may instruct the hypnotised individual to forget all that has occurred during the session. On 'awakening', the person may have no knowledge of the session and may not even be aware that hypnosis has occurred. When hypnotised again, however, recall of the original session's events usually occurs.

In *post-hypnotic suggestion*, a person is given an instruction during the session that, for instance, on hearing the word 'sleep' afterwards, he or she will fall into a deep sleep. Responses to post-hypnotic suggestions seem to occur even when a person has been instructed to forget that the suggestions have been made. Of particular interest is the finding that a person eliciting a post-hypnotic response will, in the absence of any reason for making it, attempt to justify it. For example, a person instructed to eat a banana whenever the hypnotist says a particular word may justify the behaviour by saying that he or she 'feels hungry'. Not surprisingly, post-hypnotic suggestion has been used with people who wish to stop smoking but have otherwise been unable to do so. Typically, a *hypnotherapist* will make the suggestion that a lighted cigarette tastes repulsive.

Individual differences in hypnotic susceptibility

Not everyone is susceptible to hypnosis (Bates 1993). Hilgard (1977) estimates that 5–10 per cent of people are highly *resistant* and about 15 per cent highly susceptible. The remaining 75–80 per cent fall somewhere between these two extremes. One device for measuring susceptibility is the *Stanford hypnotic susceptibility scale*. Many of the phenomena included in the scale have already been referred to above.

1 **Arm lowering:** It is suggested to the participant that an outstretched arm is getting heavier and heavier. The arm should be gradually lowered.

2 **Moving hands apart:** The participant sits with arms outstretched in front. The suggestion is made that the hands are repelled from each other as if by magnets. This should lead to them moving part.

3 **Mosquito hallucination:** The suggestion is made to the participant that an annoying mosquito is buzzing around. This should lead to the participant trying to 'shoo' it away.

4 **Taste hallucination:** The participant should respond to the suggestion that a sweet substance and then a sour one is being tasted.

5 **Arm rigidity:** Following the suggestion that an arm held out straight is getting stiffer and stiffer, the participant should be unable to unbend it.

6 **Dream:** The participant is told to have a dream about hypnosis while remaining hypnotised. The contents of the dream should be released by the participant.

7 **Age regression:** The participant is told to imagine being at different school ages. For each of the ages selected, realistic handwriting specimens should be provided.

8 **Arm immobilisation:** Following the suggestion made by the hypnotist, the participant should be unable to lift an arm involuntarily.

9 **Anosmia (loss of smell) to ammonia:** Following suggestions made by the hypnotist, the participant should report being unable to smell household ammonia.

10 **Hallucinated voice:** The participant should answer questions raised by a hallucinated voice.

11 **Negative visual hallucination:** Following suggestions made by the hypnotist, the participant should report the inability to see one of three small coloured boxes.

12 **Post-hypnotic amnesia:** The participant should be unable to recall particular information after hypnosis until given a prearranged signal.

After induction of a hypnotic state, the first suggestion is made. If responded to, it is counted as 'present' and the second suggestion made. The procedure continues until a response is counted as 'absent'. Since the 12 suggestions are ordered in terms of difficulty, a person who does not respond to the first is unlikely to respond to the second, third, and so on.

Hypnotic susceptibility is not related to any particular personality type (Oakley *et al.*, 1996). However, several stable personality traits are correlated with hypnotic susceptibility. These include *absorption* (the tendency to become deeply absorbed in sensory and imaginative experiences), *expectancy* (people are not influenced by hypnotic suggestions if they do not expect to be, and those who do usually are and typically have very positive attitudes towards hypnosis) and *fantasy-proneness* (having frequent and vivid fantasies).

These observations do not, of course, indicate that such characteristics *cause* susceptibility to hypnosis (Kirsch & Council, 1992). Moreover, at least one of them ('absorption') is correlated with hypnotic susceptibility only when people expect to *undergo* hypnosis. In other contexts, the correlation is not obtained (Council *et al.*, 1986). As a general rule, though, a person who becomes deeply absorbed in activities, expects to be influenced by hypnotic suggestions (or 'shows the faith' – Baron, 1989), and has a rich, vivid and active fantasy life, is likely to be more susceptible to hypnotic suggestions.

The genuineness of hypnosis

According to Orne & Evans (1965), all of the phenomena that can be produced under hypnosis can be produced without hypnosis. Spanos *et al.* (1983) have proposed that the essential difference between hypnotised and non-hypnotised people is that the former *believe* their responses are involuntary whereas the latter *know they are pretending*. Although hypnotic phenomena seem to be genuine enough, the genuineness of at least some of them has been questioned.

As noted earlier, in post-hypnotic amnesia people act as though they cannot remember what happened during a hypnotic episode. Spanos *et al.* (1982) have explained this in terms of the suggestion *not* to recall information being an 'invitation' to refrain from attending to retrieval cues. However, when people are given a 'lie detector' test and led to believe that they will be found out if they do not tell the truth, recall of the hypnotic episode increases dramatically! (Coe & Yashinski, 1985). This, along with other findings, has led to the suggestion that hypnotic phenomena are not real but merely a clever act perpetrated by the hypnotist and the participant, the latter pretending to be 'under the influence'.

Several studies have investigated *trance logic*, the difference in performance between the hypnotised and those pretending to be hypnotised. Orne *et al.* (1968) hypnotised one group of participants and instructed a second to act as though they were hypnotised. Both groups were told that in the following 48 hours their right hand would touch their foreheads every time they heard the word 'experiment'. Later, participants encountered a secretary who said the word 'experiment' three times. On average, participants highly susceptible to hypnosis touched their foreheads an average of 70 per cent of the occasions on which the word was said. For the hypnotised participants the figure was 29.5 per cent. For those pretending to be hypnotised it was only 7.7 per cent. Kinnunen *et al.* (1995) have used skin conductance reaction (SCR), a crude but effective measure of deception, to investigate hypnosis. They found significantly higher SCRs for 'simulators' as compared with hypnotised individuals.

Bowers (1976) has shown that participants who are told they cannot see a chair *will* bump into it if they are faking hypnosis, but will walk around it (just as a sleepwalker does) if they have been hypnotised. Other research indicates that hypnotic susceptibility peaks between nine and 12 years of age, decreases until the mid-30s, and then levels off (Hart & Hart, 1996). The finding that hypnotised and non-hypnotised individuals can be shown to differ behaviourally, and that there is no reason why hypnotic susceptibility should change over time if it is faked, suggests that hypnotic phenomena *may* be real.

A 'state' or 'special processes' theory of hypnosis

According to *state* or *special processes* theorists, hypnosis is a unique and altered state of consciousness. Hilgard's (1977) *neo-dissociation theory* proposed that hypnosis is the dissociation (or division) of consciousness into separate channels of mental activity. This division allows us to focus our attention on the hypnotist and, simultaneously, enables us to perceive other events peripherally (or 'subconsciously').

> **Box 14.6   The hidden observer and the cold pressor test**
>
> Central to Hilgard's theory is the *hidden observer* phenomenon. Hilgard (1973) told a male participant that deafness would be induced in him through hypnosis, but that he would be able to hear when a hand was placed on his shoulder. Although 'hypnotically deaf', he was asked to raise a forefinger if there was some part of him that could still hear. To Hilgard's surprise, and that of a watching audience, a forefinger rose.
>
> Hilgard also explored the hidden observer phenomenon using the *cold pressor test* (CPT). In this, one or both forearms is plunged into circulating icy water and the participant is required to keep the forearm(s) submerged for as long as possible. Initially, the sensation is of coldness. After a few seconds, however, this turns to pain which cannot be tolerated by most people for longer than about 25 seconds. Hilgard found that when participants highly susceptible to hypnosis were told that they would feel no pain, they kept their forearm(s) submerged for an average of around 40 seconds.

Although hypnotised participants appear to be able to withstand pain in the CPT for longer than would ordinarily be the case, the hidden observer does not! Thus, when the hidden observer was asked to 'remain out of awareness' and write down ratings of pain on a ten-point scale, the ratings were significantly higher than those reported verbally by the participant. This finding is consistent with Hilgard's theory: the part of consciousness accepting and responding to the hypnotist's suggestions becomes dissociated from the pain whilst the hidden observer, which monitors everything that happens, remains aware of it. This could be explained in terms of neural inhibition preventing information transmission between the verbal system ('consciousness') and the brain's peripheral and motor systems. This might be the 'dissociation' Hilgard refers to.

Earlier, it was noted that hypnosis has a long history as an *analgesic* (or 'pain-reliever'). For example, as well as helping children withstand painful bone marrow transplants for cancer, hypnosis has been used in various surgical procedures including the removal of teeth, tonsils and breast tumours (Hart & Alden, 1994). Indeed, it has been argued that the analgesic effects of hypnosis are more powerful than those of drugs like morphine, and can even act to reduce the emotional upset that accompanies pain as well as the pain itself (Millar, 1996). Hilgard's findings suggest that hypnosis does *not* eliminate pain, but enables it to be tolerated better because there is no conscious awareness of it. Spanos (1991) uses the term *strategic enactment* to refer to the adoption of a strategy (such as mental distraction) which, if the analgesia occurs, can be attributed to hypnosis.

Box 14.7   The analgesic properties of hypnosis

Other ways of explaining the analgesic properties of hypnosis have been advanced. Hypnosis may relax people. By encouraging them to focus on pleasant images, they might be distracted from thoughts of pain. Relaxation itself might allow the brain to produce *endorphins* (see Chapter 3). Whether hypnosis really does have analgesic properties has been the subject of much debate. According to Barber (1970), even if people do experience pain when hypnotised, they might not wish to report this for fear of causing offence! Whether people are simply *acting* as though they are anaesthetised was studied by Pattie (1937). He told participants that they would be unable to feel anything with one hand. They were instructed to cross their wrists as illustrated below.

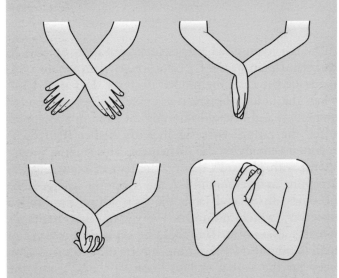

If you try this, and ask someone to touch one of your hands very rapidly, you'll find that it is difficult to determine which hand has been touched. Pattie showed that when he touched the fingers on both hands and asked participants to count the number of times they had been touched, they included touches made to the 'anaesthetised' hand (which should not have been counted if the hand really were anaesthetised). This suggests a difference between local anaesthesia and hypnotic anaesthesia. In the latter, a person behaves *as though* he or she is anaesthetised.

A 'non-state' theory of hypnosis

Barber (1979) takes a very different approach to Hilgard in explaining hypnotic phenomena. Barber argues that if hypnotic phenomena occur only when a person is hypnotised, it is difficult to see why the brain should have evolved in such a way that people *can* be hypnotised. For Barber, the functional analysis of a behavioural phenomenon usually points to a plausible reason for its occurrence. Thus, as far as Barber and other *non-state* theorists are concerned, hypnosis is *not* an altered state of consciousness.

Non-state theorists see hypnotised people as acting out a *social role* which is defined by their own expectations and the situation in which they find themselves. The rules of the situation are governed by the hypnotist's direct instructions or indirectly implied by his or her words and actions (Wagstaff, 1991). In Barber's view, hypnosis is not special but people, and their imagination and ability to play roles, are.

Non-state theorists argue that hypnosis involves the *suspension of self-control*, a phenomenon which occurs when, say, we allow the actors in a film or the author of a book to lead us through some sort of fantasy. Certainly, the finding that 'suggestible' hypnotic participants have (amongst other things) vivid and absorbing imaginations, lends support to a non-state perspective and casts doubt on the claim that hypnosis is an altered state of consciousness.

Non-state theory is also supported by the finding that behaviours possible under hypnosis are also possible in non-hypnotic conditions. The 'human plank' trick, for example, in which a hypnotised person remains suspended from chairs placed at the back of the head and ankles, can be accomplished by most people in a normal waking state. Even Orne (1965), a leading researcher in the area, has acknowledged that the behaviour of non-hypnotised people occasionally fooled him:

'As a clinician who worked extensively with hypnosis, I never doubted it would be easy for me to recognise those who were, in fact, simulating. It came as a complete surprise to find that (people) were able to deceive me'.

According to non-state theorists, the hidden observer phenomenon is simply a product of a *script* which is supplied by the hypnotist. Using the CPT, Spanos *et al.* (1983) told hypnotised participants that they would not experience any pain. Some were also given instructions similar to those used by Hilgard to elicit the hidden observer, whilst others were told that the hidden observer was *less* aware of things going on in and around their bodies. Compared with participants in whom the hidden observer was not elicited, the hidden observer reported more *or* less pain depending on the instructions that had been given.

Spanos *et al.* suggest that these findings reflect the playing of *two roles* rather than a division of consciousness. They argue that participants in Hilgard's experiment ignored the pain when told it would not be perceived and switched attention to it when the hidden observer was requested. Rather than being a part of consciousness remaining aware of reality, Spanos (1986) argues that the hidden observer is an artefact arising from the hypnotist's instructions.

Some practical applications of hypnotic phenomena

Whether hypnosis and hypnotic phenomena have any practical uses has also been the subject of much research. As has been seen, hypnosis can contribute to pain relief. Other applications are described below.

HYPERMNESIA AND CRIMINAL INVESTIGATIONS

Hypermnesia is the apparent ability of a hypnotised person to focus on selected details of an event and reconstruct an entire memory if told to do so. In some police departments, this has been used to prompt the memories of people who have witnessed a crime but cannot recall specific details of the events that occurred. Indeed, in America at least, evidence obtained from hypnotised witnesses has been admitted into court, and some police departments have officers trained in hypnosis.

In the *television technique*, the hypnotised witness is told that he or she will be able to 'zoom in' on details such as a car number plate and 'freeze the frame' to examine the details (Reiser & Nielsen, 1980). Unfortunately, the reports obtained from hypnotised people have not always been helpful. In an American court case (People versus Kempinski, 1980) a hypnotised witness identified Mr Kempinski as a victim's murderer. However, the defence successfully argued that, given the lighting conditions at the time, it would only have been possible to identify the murderer's face from a maximum of eight yards away. Since the witness was some 90 yards away, the defence challenged the validity of the witness' recall under hypnosis. The challenge was accepted and the evidence dismissed.

Box 14.8   Some other cautions against the use of hypnosis in criminal investigations

1 Witnesses may pick up on suggestions communicated by the hypnotist, incorporate these into memory, and recall them as 'factual'. Related to this is the finding that 'leading questions' are even more likely to produce distorted memories under hypnosis.

2 Although the hypnotically suggestible recall more information than non-hypnotised people, this information is frequently incorrect. Hypnotised witnesses sometimes report things that were not there and fail to report things that were.

3 The confidence with which hypnotised people give information is very high (even if it is actually incorrect). This may throw off both the police and a jury.

4 Hypnosis might not actually affect what people remember, but might make them less cautious about what they are willing to guess. If hypnosis does make mental images more vivid, hypnotised people may confuse these images with actual memories.

A panel appointed by the American Medical Association concluded that whilst hypnosis *sometimes* produces additional details, such information is often unreliable. Rather than accepting recall under hypnosis as evidence itself, the police were recommended to limit its use to the investigative stage of an enquiry where it might produce new clues whose details could be checked by other sources of objective evidence.

AGE REGRESSION

Hypnotised people seem to be able to play unusual roles. For example, something requiring increased stamina (such as riding a bicycle) can be done with apparently less fatigue than normal (Banyai & Hilgard, 1976). In *age regression*, people are asked to play themselves as infants or children. Some hypnotised people show excellent recall of childhood memories because hypnosis gives greater *access* to them rather than effecting a literal return to an earlier stage of development (Oakley *et al.*, 1996).

PSYCHOANALYTIC THEORY

Hypnosis made a significant contribution to the development of *psychoanalytic theory* (see Chapter 66). Charcot, for example, believed that hysterical disorders (such as apparent blindness in the absence of any damage to the visual system) were caused by some sort of physical problem. However, his discovery that hysterical symptoms could be simulated under hypnosis led him to conclude that the origins of hysterical disorders were psychological rather than physical.

A little later, Breuer demonstrated that one of his patients could be made to feel better about her problems when she spoke freely of them under hypnosis. Freud believed that hypnosis was useful in gaining access to the unconscious and could be used to uncover the causes of mental disorders. For Freud, psychological problems in adulthood have their origins in early childhood experiences which cannot ordinarily be recalled because the memory of them has been *repressed* (see Chapter 66).

Box 14.9   Regression

Freud believed that hypnotic states produced *regression*. In this, the conscious control (or 'ego functioning') of behaviour is suspended, and it becomes possible to return to childish modes of behaviour. Although Freud later abandoned hypnosis as a method of gaining access to the unconscious (not least for the reason that he felt it elicited childhood *fantasies* rather than *experiences*), it is still used today to help people discuss memories whose apparent inaccessibility is hindering therapeutic progress (Hart & Hart, 1996). However, the approach has been criticised and the recent concerns about *false memory syndrome* have cast doubt on this particular application of hypnosis (see Chapter 30, Box 30.2).

Hypnosis and behaviour control

According to some researchers, hypnotists are able to induce people to act in ways which grossly violate their moral code, and this is sometimes referred to as the *Hollywood theory of hypnosis* (Hayes, 1994). Such behaviours include harming others or doing damage to themselves. Other researchers, however, believe this to be untrue and also feel that it is impossible for a person to be tricked into behaving in such ways (Barber, 1969).

Reports of 'porno-hypnotist' shows in America, the use of 'striptease' in the stage show of at least one British hypnotist, and reports of indecent assaults on patients by hypnotherapists, have raised serious ethical questions about the extent to which hypnotists can control people's behaviour (Rogers, 1994). Because of this, it is hardly surprising that a Federation of Ethical Stage Hypnotists exists!

It is possible to think how a hypnotised person could be tricked into behaving in a way which violates ordinary standards of behaviour. For example, a situation could be misperceived by a hypnotised person who is told to shoot a gun at a 'paper target' which is actually another person (Carlson, 1987). What is much more difficult to determine is whether a particular behaviour occurs because the hypnotist has control or because the person actually wants to behave in that way.

Consider, for example, a person who is instructed to eat raw onions until told to stop. We might find that these instructions are followed and that the person feels angry and embarrassed by having been 'forced' to behave in such a way. Although it would appear that the hypnotist has been successful in producing a behaviour that would ordinarily not have been performed, we cannot rule out the possibility that the person *wanted* to be 'punished' in this way because of some real or imagined misdeed (Baron, 1989). As with all the other phenomena associated with hypnosis, there is still much for us to discover.

Conclusions

Hypnosis has attracted the interest of many researchers and hypnotic phenomena have been the subject of many experimental investigations. How hypnosis can best be explained is an issue yet to be resolved, although Alden (1995) has suggested that more and more researchers are moving towards accepting hypnosis as a 'non-state paradigm'. Whatever the explanation, hypnotic phenomena have been applied in several areas, although whether they contribute anything useful is far from clear.

Summary

■ Serious scientific interest in hypnosis can be traced back to Mesmer and his belief that humans could be drawn together by **animal magnetism**. **Mesmerism**, a treatment for illnesses, supposedly rectified imbalances in the body's magnetic fields. It is likely, though, that any beneficial effects occurred through the **placebo effect**. Nevertheless, hypnosis has been used as an anaesthetic during surgery.

■ There are several ways of inducing a hypnotic state and a number of characteristics associated with it. These include suspension of planning, accepting normally noticed inconsistencies, a narrowing of attention (resulting in less awareness of sensory information) and a responsiveness to suggestions to initiate and inhibit limb movements.

■ Suggestibility also applies to perceptual distortions, including positive and negative hallucinations, post-hypnotic amnesia and post-hypnotic suggestion.

■ There are individual differences in hypnotic susceptibility, and these can be measured using the **Stanford hypnotic susceptibility scale**. Hypnotic susceptibility is correlated with absorption, expectancy and fantasy-proneness, and there are neuropsychophysiological differences associated with hypnotic susceptibility.

■ The genuineness of some hypnotic phenomena has been challenged. However, experimental studies of **trance logic** indicate that hypnotised people do behave differently from those merely pretending to be hypnotised. This, along with the finding that hypnotic susceptibility changes with age, points to hypnotic phenomena being genuine.

■ **State (or special processes) theory** sees hypnosis as a unique and altered state of consciousness. Hilgard's **neo-dissociation theory** proposes that hypnosis is the dissociation (or division) of consciousness into separate channels of mental activity. This allows us to focus attention on the hypnotist and, simultaneously, to perceive other events peripherally (or sub-consciously).

■ The **hidden observer phenomenon** and the **cold-pressor test** support Hilgard's theory. The analgesic properties of hypnosis can be explained by Hilgard's theory, although other explanations (relating to, for example, the production of endorphins) are equally plausible.

■ The **non-state theory** sees hypnotised people as acting out social roles which are defined by their own expectations and the social situations in which they find themselves. It also involves the suspension of self-control.

The theory is supported by the finding that susceptible hypnotic participants have vivid imaginations, and that behaviours possible under hypnosis are also possible in non-hypnotic conditions.

■ The hidden observer phenomenon may simply be a product of a script supplied by the hypnotist. Rather than being a part of consciousness remaining aware of reality, non-state theorists view it as an artefact arising from the hypnotist's instructions.

■ Hypnosis has been applied to criminal investigations, although the claims made by hypnotised people are often unreliable. As a result, evidence gathered under hypnosis must be treated with caution. **Age regression** has been used to recall long-forgotten childhood memories, probably because it gives greater access to them rather than literally returning a person to an earlier stage of development.

■ Freud's **psychoanalytic theory** was influenced by the discovery that hysterical symptoms could be reproduced under hypnosis, and that some people felt better about their problems when speaking freely about them under hypnosis. Hypnosis is still used to help people recover repressed memories, but its use has been criticised because of its implication in **false memory syndrome**.

■ The ethics of using hypnosis to induce behaviour change in public shows has been questioned. Whether it is possible for a hypnotist to cause people to behave in ways which grossly violate their moral code is a question yet to be answered.

15

SOME DRUGS AND THEIR EFFECTS ON BEHAVIOUR

Introduction and overview

For thousands of years, humans have taken drugs to alter their perceptions of reality and for thousands of years societies have limited this kind of drug use by placing various restrictions on it (Weil & Rosen, 1983). This chapter examines the psychological and physiological effects exerted by some *psychoactive drugs*. The word 'psychoactive' is usually taken to mean any chemical that alters perceptions and behaviour by changing conscious awareness. However, most drugs fit into this definition. Aspirin, for example, is psychoactive because when it relieves a headache, it changes conscious experience.

This chapter looks at drugs used to produce a temporarily altered state of consciousness for the purpose of *pleasure*. *Recreational* drugs have no legal restrictions and include alcohol, nicotine and caffeine. *Drugs of abuse* are also taken recreationally, but outside society's approval. These include cannabis, heroin, cocaine, amphetamine and ecstasy (Green, 1996a).

Tolerance, dependence, addiction and withdrawal

All of the drugs discussed in this chapter alter thoughts, feelings and behaviour by affecting the brain. However, the effects of some are *lessened* with continued use, and users need to take increasing amounts to achieve the same initial effect. This phenomenon is called *tolerance*.

Tolerance is sometimes associated with *physiological* (or *physical*) *dependence*. This means that the body cannot do without a drug because it has adjusted to, and becomes dependent on, that drug's presence. When the drug is stopped, various problems occur, such as insomnia, profuse sweating, trembling, and hallucinations. These are symptoms of *withdrawal* (or *abstinence syndrome*). Physical dependence and tolerance together define the medical syndrome called *drug addiction*.

Some drugs are so pleasurable that users feel compelled to continue taking them even though the body is not physically dependent on the drug's presence. This is *psychological dependence*, and being deprived of the drug is anxiety-producing for the user. Since the symptoms of anxiety (e.g. rapid pulse, profuse sweating, and shaking) overlap with withdrawal symptoms, people may mistakenly believe they are physiologically dependent on a drug.

Recreational drugs and drugs of abuse

Four major classes can be identified. *Depressants* (or *sedatives*) depress neural activity, slow down bodily functions, induce calmness and produce sleep. *Stimulants* temporarily excite neural activity, arouse bodily functions, enhance positive feelings, and heighten alertness. The *opiates* also depress activity in the central nervous system, but have an *analgesic* property, and produce pain insensitivity without loss of consciousness. *Hallucinogens* produce alterations in perception and evoke sensory images in the absence of any sensory input. As well as looking at the major drugs in these four classes, we will also consider the effects of *cannabis*, a drug which defies classification as one of the above.

THE DEPRESSANTS

Depressants slow down mental processes and behaviours. The most widely used and abused depressant is *alcohol*, whose effects were known about 10,000 years ago (Hartston, 1996).

Alcohol

Over 90 per cent of adults in Britain drink alcohol to some extent. There are wide individual differences in alcohol's effects, which are at least in part dependent on body weight and sex. The effects of alcohol, and other drugs, also depend on *expectations*. People who believe alcohol has an arousing effect may be more responsive to sexual stimuli even though alcohol *per se* does not increase arousal.

In general, small amounts have a 'stimulating effect' (but alcohol is not a stimulant – see below). These include a lowering of social inhibitions, which interferes with the ability to foresee negative consequences and results in the inability to recall accepted standards of behaviour. Thus, actions may become more extreme and we are likely to 'speak our mind'. Large amounts have a sedative effect.

Box 15.1   Alcohol and cognitive/motor functions

Alcohol affects cognitive functions, such as processing recent experiences into long-term memory. A day after consuming a large amount of alcohol, a person might not remember the events that occurred when it was being taken. Other cognitive impairments include deficits in visual acuity and depth perception, and the subjective experience of time passing more quickly. Alcohol also affects motor functions. Even 10 mg interferes with the ability to follow a moving target with a pointer. 80 mg slows reaction time by about ten per cent. Greater amounts result in staggering and a complete loss of motor coordination caused by depression of neural activity in the cerebellum. Very large amounts can induce a coma or lead to death.

Although short-term use may alleviate depressive feelings, long-term use may augment such feelings. Heavy users suffer malnutrition because they eat less. Alcohol contains many calories, which suppresses appetite. Since alcohol interferes with the absorption of vitamin B from the intestines, it causes vitamin deficiency. The prolonged effect of this is brain damage, and memory is particularly affected (see Chapter 27). Other physical consequences include liver damage, heart disease, increased risk of a stroke, and susceptibility to infections due to a suppressed immune system. Women who drink during pregnancy can produce babies with *foetal alcohol syndrome*. This is characterised by retarded physical growth, intellectual development and motor coordination (see Chapter 79). There are also abnormalities in brain metabolic processes and liver functions.

After prolonged and severe intoxication, physiological dependence and withdrawal occur. The symptoms include restlessness, nausea, fever and the bizarre hallucinations of *delirium tremens*. In some cases, withdrawal produces such a profound shock to the body that death occurs. There is no doubt that tolerance develops, and it is likely that psychological dependence also develops.

Exactly how alcohol exerts its effects is not known. In terms of ANS activity, it has a relaxing effect. Its 'stimulating effects' probably occur from a suppression of the brain mechanisms that normally inhibit behaviour. In large amounts, alcohol decreases neural activity, possibly by acting on the cell membrane of neurons (especially those in the reticular activating system) and reducing their ability to conduct nerve impulses. Alcohol also seems to increase the sensitivity of post-synaptic receptors for the inhibitory neurotransmitter GABA. By increasing the inhibition generated by GABA, alcohol would reduce neural activity in the brain circuits associated with arousal.

Why some people abuse alcohol is also not clear. The *disease model of alcoholism* claims that some people have a weakness for it that cannot be controlled because of a genetic predisposition. If alcoholism is to be cured, the alcoholic must abstain *completely* (the philosophy of *Alcoholics Anonymous*). Alternatively, drinking may be a complex category of behaviour with different causes and hence different cures. According to the *social model of alcoholism*, excessive alcohol consumption can be treated by *controlled drinking* rather than abstinence. This approach implies that people can be taught to maintain consumption at an acceptable (non-damaging) level.

Barbiturates, tranquillisers and solvents

Barbiturates are also depressants and have similar effects to alcohol. Because they depress neural activity, they are often prescribed to induce sleep or reduce anxiety. They exert their effects by reducing the release of excitatory neurotransmitters at synapses in several parts of the nervous system. Barbiturates were first used clinically in 1903. However, their clinical use is limited because of physiological dependence, withdrawal and tolerance. Other depressants include 'minor tranquillisers' (such as *Valium*: see Chapter 72) and *aromatic solvents*. 'Minor tranquillisers' have much milder effects than barbiturates and do not induce sleep. Aromatic solvents include some types of glue and paint thinner. Their use in Britain has been associated with a number of deaths and various surveys have estimated that about six to nine per cent of secondary school children (around 500,000) have abused solvents (Mihill, 1997).

THE STIMULANTS

The general effects of stimulants is to stimulate the CNS by increasing the transmission of nerve impulses. The most widely consumed legal stimulants are *caffeine* and *nicotine*, both of which exert mild effects. *Amphetamines* and *cocaine* exert considerably stronger effects and are illegal, as are the newer 'designer' stimulants such as *methylenedioxymethamphetamine* (or *MDMA*) which is known as *'ecstasy'*. 'Designer' drugs are synthetic substances produced by altering the chemical structure of illegal substances without reducing their potency.

Amphetamines

The amphetamines were first synthesised in the 1920s. Their general effect is to increase energy and enhance self-confidence. As a result, they were used extensively by the military in World War Two to reduce fatigue and give soldiers going into battle more confidence. Another effect is to suppress appetite, and they also found use as 'slimming pills' being marketed under such trade names as Methedrine, Dexedrine and Benzedrine. However, their effects on consciousness and behaviour led to them being widely abused.

Box 15.2 Some uses of amphetamines

Chemically, amphetamines are similar to adrenaline (see page 47). This has led to amphetamines being used as a treatment for asthma, since they open respiratory passages and ease breathing. Amphetamines are also used in the treatment of *narcolepsy*, a disorder characterised by brief and unpredictable periods of sleep.

One other use of amphetamines is in the treatment of attention-deficit/hyperactivity disorder (ADHD) in children. With these children, amphetamines and a related stimulant, methylphenidate hydrochloride (*Ritalin*) increase self-control and attention span and decrease fidgeting. The use of Ritalin in the treatment of ADHD is discussed further in Chapter 80 (see Box 80.3, page 692).

Amphetamines are swallowed in pill form, inhaled through the nose in powder form, or injected in liquid form. Small amounts cause increased wakefulness, alertness and arousal. Users experience a sense of energy and confidence, and feel that any problem can be solved and any task accomplished. This effect is, however, illusory, and problem-solving is no easier with the drug than without it. After the drug wears off, users experience a 'crash' (characterised by extreme fatigue and depression). They counteract this by taking the drug again which can have serious long-term consequences (see below). Large amounts cause restlessness, hallucinations and *paranoid delusions*.

Amphetamine can stimulate aggressive, violent behaviour. This is not due *directly* to the drug itself. Rather, the effect occurs as a result of personality changes that come from excessive use. The paranoid delusions experienced in *amphetamine psychosis* are virtually indistinguishable from those experienced in *paranoid schizophrenia* (see Chapter 68). Long-term use has also been associated with severe depression, suicidal tendencies, disrupted thinking and brain damage.

Tolerance develops quickly as does psychological dependence. The evidence concerning physiological dependence is mixed. However, the amphetamine 'hangover' (characterised by extreme fatigue, depression, prolonged sleep, irritability, disorientation and agitated motor activity) is indicative of a withdrawal effect, suggesting that a physiological dependence has developed (Blum, 1984).

Cocaine

Cocaine, or more properly cocaine hydrochloride, is a powerful CNS stimulant extracted from the leaves of the coca shrub which is native to the Andes Mountains in South America. It was discovered centuries ago by Peruvian Indians who chewed on the plant leaves to increase stamina and relieve fatigue and hunger. Among present-day South Americans, leaf chewing is still practised.

Box 15.3 Cocaine, Coca-Cola and Freud

Cocaine became known in Europe in the middle 1800s, when coca was blended into wine and other drinks. Until 1906, Coca-Cola actually *did* contain cocaine. Today, it is still blended with coca leaves that have had their active ingredient removed! Sigmund Freud used cocaine to fight his own depression and supported its use as, amongst other things, a cure for alcoholism. He eventually became disillusioned with the drug because of its side-effects. One of his friends, however, developed its use as a local anaesthetic: in very high concentrations cocaine blocks the transmission of action potentials in axons. Today, this is still the drug's only legitimate use.

Cocaine is inhaled through the nose in powder form, injected into the veins in liquid form, or smoked. When smoked, the drug reaches the brain in 5–10 seconds, as compared with 30–120 seconds when inhaled and 60–180 seconds when injected (Miller *et al.*, 1989). It can also be swallowed, rubbed on the gums, or blown into the throat.

In general, cocaine's effects are similar to amphetamine, though of a briefer duration (around 15–30 minutes as compared with several hours). This is because cocaine is metabolised much more quickly. Typically, the user experiences a state of euphoria, deadening of pain, increased self-confidence and energy and enhanced attention. As with amphetamines, users experience a 'crash' when the drug wears off. Attempts to offset these effects include taking depressants or opiates.

Even in small amounts, the stimulating effects can result in cardiac arrest and death. Repeated inhalation constricts the blood vessels in the nose. The nasal septum may become perforated, necessitating cosmetic surgery.

Cocaine psychosis (cf. amphetamine psychosis) can also occur with chronic long-term use as can convulsions, respiratory failure and bleeding into the brain. At least in rats, cocaine gradually lowers the tolerance for seizures (Bales, 1986). An interesting effect is *formication*, the sensation that 'insects' ('coke bugs') are crawling beneath the skin. Although this is merely random neural activity, users sometimes try to remove the imaginary insects by cutting deep into themselves with a knife. Cocaine taken in pregnancy has been associated with impaired foetal development.

Whether cocaine produces physiological dependence, tolerance and withdrawal has been the subject of much debate. However, there is no argument that it produces psychological dependence. This probably stems from the user's desire to avoid the severe depression associated with 'crashing' (and some researchers see the symptoms associated with 'crashing' as indicative of physiological dependence: Miller *et al.*, 1989).

Both amphetamine and cocaine stimulate the sympathetic nervous system causing the effects observed with increased ANS activity. The increase in brain activation may be due to heightened activity at synapses that secrete noradrenaline and dopamine. Amphetamine and cocaine facilitate the release of noradrenaline and dopamine, but inhibit their re-uptake by the vesicles that released them. This results in an excess of these neurotransmitters, which increases neuronal activity and leads to a persistent state of arousal.

The euphoric effects are probably the result of the drug's effects on dopamine, whilst the increased energy is probably caused by noradrenaline. According to Carlson (1987), cocaine activates neural circuits that are normally triggered by reinforcing events such as eating or sexual contact. Cocaine can thus be seen as an artificial producer of some of the effects of these activities. The 'crash' associated with cocaine and amphetamine use is held to be a result of the 'rush', depleting the brain of noradrenaline and dopamine.

Box 15.4   Crack

Crack is a form of cocaine which first appeared in the 1980s. It is made using cocaine hydrochloride, ammonia or baking soda, and water. When heated, the baking soda produces a 'cracking' sound. The result is a crystal which has had the hydrochloride base removed (hence the term *free basing* to describe its production). Its effects are more rapid and intense than cocaine. However, the 'crash' is also more intense, and the pleasurable effects wear off more rapidly.

MDMA

MDMA or 'ecstasy' is a chemical relative of amphetamine, first synthesised in 1912, and later patented as an appetite suppressant, though never marketed. It is swallowed in pill or tablet form, and sometimes taken with other mood-altering drugs. Small amounts produce a mild euphoric 'rush', together with feelings of elation. This can last for ten hours. Self-confidence is increased and sexual confidence gained. Large amounts trigger hallucinations. Users report MDMA's effects to be intermediate between amphetamine and LSD (see page 126). Serotonin and dopamine are the neurotransmitters affected.

Ecstasy causes extreme dehydration and hyperthermia which leads to a form of heatstroke. This can produce convulsions, collapse and death. Blood pressure also rises dangerously. If it becomes too high the taker may suffer a stroke and thereafter permanent brain damage. Over 50 deaths in Britain alone have been attributed to the drug (Parrott, 1997). The high temperature dance environment of Britain's 'rave' scene no doubt increases the hyperthermia. Depression and panic attacks are also associated with long-term use, as are kidney and liver failure (Green, 1996b).

As Parrott & Yeomans (1995) have observed, little research has been carried out into the effects of ecstasy, let alone the effects of abstinence, despite the fact that several million doses of the drug are annually consumed worldwide. According to the Department of Health (1994), tolerance occurs but physiological dependence does not.

The opiates

The psychological effects of the sticky resin produced by the unripe seed pods of the opium poppy have been known for centuries. The ancient Sumerians, in 4000 BC, gave the poppy its name: it means 'plant of joy'. One constituent of opium is *morphine*. From morphine, two other opiates can be extracted. These are *codeine* and *heroin*.

Morphine and heroin

In general, the opiates depress neural functioning and suppress physical sensations and responses to stimulation. For reasons which will become clear shortly, the opiates are effective in reducing pain. In Europe, morphine was first used as an analgesic during the Franco-Prussian war. However, it quickly became apparent that it produced physiological dependence, which became known as 'the soldier's disease'. In 1898, in an attempt to cure this physiological dependence, the Bayer Company of Germany developed heroin (so named because it was the 'hero' that would cure the 'soldier's disease'). Unfortunately, heroin also causes physiological dependence and has many unpleasant side-effects.

Heroin can be smoked, inhaled through the nostrils, or intravenously injected. Users term the immediate effects the 'rush', which is described as an overwhelming sensation of pleasure similar to sexual orgasm but affecting the whole body. Subjectively, such effects are so pleasurable that they eradicate any thoughts of food or sex. Heroin rapidly decomposes into morphine which produces feelings of euphoria, well-being, relaxation and drowsiness.

In long-term users, increases in aggressiveness and social isolation have been reported as has a decrease in general physical activity. Although the findings relating to physical damage are mixed, the use of any opiate may damage the body's immune system leading to increased susceptibility to infection. The impurity of heroin sold to users, their lack of an adequate diet, and the risks from contaminated needles also increase the dangers to health. Overdoses are common, but drugs like *naloxone* act as opiate antagonists (see page 34), although their effects are not long-lasting and they cannot control heroin use.

Heroin use produces both physiological and psychological dependence. Tolerance develops very quickly. Withdrawal symptoms initially involve the experience of flu-like symptoms. These progress to tremors, stomach cramps and chills, which alternate with sweating, rapid pulse, high blood pressure, insomnia and diarrhoea. Often, the skin breaks out into goose bumps resembling a plucked turkey (hence the term 'cold turkey' to describe attempts to abstain). The legs also jerk uncontrollably (hence the term 'kicking the habit'). Such symptoms usually disappear within one week.

Box 15.5 Heroin and endorphins

As was seen in Chapter 3, the brain produces its own opiates (*opioid peptides* or *endorphins*). When we engage in behaviours important to our survival, endorphins are released into the fluid that bathes brain cells. Endorphin molecules stimulate *opiate receptors* on some brain neurons. These are similar to those post-synaptic receptors that respond to neurotransmitters. One consequence of this is an intensely pleasurable effect just like that reported by heroin users. This has led some researchers to suggest that endorphins are important in mood regulation. Another consequence is analgesia.

According to Snyder (1977), regularly taking opiates overloads endorphin sites in the brain, and the brain stops its own production of them. When the user abstains, neither the naturally occurring endorphins nor

the opiates are available. The internal mechanism for regulating pain is thus severely disrupted and the person experiences the painful withdrawal symptoms described earlier.

Methadone

To treat the physiological dependence associated with opiate use, several synthetic opiates (or opioids) have been created. One of these is *methadone*, which acts more slowly than heroin and does not produce the 'rush' associated with heroin use. Whether methadone is a suitable substitute is debatable. Whilst methadone users are less likely to take heroin, they are still taking a drug and likely to become at least psychologically dependent on it, so that the withdrawal symptoms associated with heroin can be avoided.

THE HALLUCINOGENS

Hallucinogens produce the most profound effects on consciousness. For that reason they are sometimes called *psychedelics* (which means 'mind expanding' or 'mind manifesting'). Their effects include changes in perception, thought processes and emotions. Two of the most well-researched hallucinogens are naturally derived. *Mescaline* comes from the peyote cactus, whilst *psilocybin* is obtained from the mushroom *Psilocybe mexicana* (the so-called 'magic mushroom'). Others such as *lysergic acid diethylamide* (LSD) and *phencyclidine* (PCP), are chemically synthesised.

LSD

LSD was first synthesised in 1943 by Hoffmann, a Swiss chemist. After accidentally ingesting some of the chemical, Hoffmann reported that he:

> 'perceived an uninterrupted stream of fantastic pictures, extraordinary shapes with intense, kaleidoscopic play of colours'.

In the 1960s, LSD was used for a variety of purposes including the treatment of emotional and behavioural disturbances, and as a pain reliever for the terminally ill. It was also believed that LSD could serve useful military purposes (Neill, 1987).

Its popularity as a 'recreational' drug was largely inspired by Timothy Leary, a Harvard University psychologist, who coined the slogan 'turn on, tune in, and drop out', used by the 1960s' hippy movement.

LSD is usually impregnated on blotting paper and swallowed. Unlike other drugs, the onset of its effects may be delayed for an hour or more. LSD produces heightened and distorted sensory experiences such as sights and sounds being intensified or changing form and colour. Hallucinations may also be tactile. Such effects may be pleasurable or terrifying (a 'bad trip') depending on mood and expectations. The subjective passage of time is distorted and appears to slow dramatically. *Synaesthesia*, the blending of sensory experiences, may also occur. Music, for example, may yield visual sensations. *Depersonalisation* has also been reported and is experienced as a state in which the body is perceived as being separate from the self. Users report being able to see themselves from afar. Impaired judgement also occurs, even though the subjective feeling may be of an 'increased understanding' of the world.

Some long-term users experience *flashbacks*, distorted perceptions or hallucinations occurring days or weeks after the drug was taken. These might be physiological *or* psychological in origin. There is no evidence to suggest that LSD itself can cause death, but there are numerous examples of users being killed as a result of its psychological effects. Reproductive processes also seem to be affected by long-term use, since some women rarely conceive when they are taking the drug. The reason for this is not known.

LSD use does not seem to lead to physiological dependence and withdrawal. However, tolerance can develop rapidly. If taken repeatedly, few effects are produced until its administration is stopped for about a week. Whether LSD produces psychological dependence is hotly debated (McWilliams & Tuttle, 1973).

The chemical structure of some hallucinogens closely resembles dopamine and serotonin. According to Jacobs (1987), hallucinogen molecules compete with the normal activity of these neurotransmitters in the brain. Serotonin may play a role in the production of dream-like activity (see Chapter 11). The inhibition of neural circuits responsible for dreaming at any time other than during sleep might explain why we do not dream during the waking hours. However, suppression of serotonin by hallucinogenic drug molecules might cause 'dream mechanisms' to be activated, with the result that the person experiences a 'waking dream' or hallucination (Carlson, 1988).

Box 15.6   The form of hallucinations

Siegel (1982) has suggested that all hallucinations, whether caused by drugs, oxygen starvation or sensory deprivation, take the same form. Usually they begin with simple geometric forms (such as a spiral), continue with more meaningful images (such as 'replays' of past emotional experiences) and, at the peak of the hallucination, produce a feeling of separation from the body and dream-like experiences which can appear frighteningly real. The fact that all hallucinations seem to take the same form suggests that the same mechanisms may be involved in their production.

Phencyclidine (PCP)

PCP ('angel dust') was first synthesised in the 1950s for use as a surgical anaesthetic. However, this was discontinued when its psychoactive side-effects became apparent. Usually combined with tobacco and smoked, it can be classified as a hallucinogen because it produces distortions in body image and depersonalisation. In small amounts, users report euphoria, heightened awareness, and a sense that all problems have disappeared. With large amounts, however, it has stimulant, depressant, and (not surprisingly given its original purpose) analgesic properties. Effects include violence, panic, psychotic behaviour, disrupted motor activity and chronic depression. These may persist for weeks after the drug has been taken.

Long-term use of PCP is associated with what Smith *et al.* (1978) call the four 'Cs': *combativeness* (agitated or violent behaviour), *catatonia* (muscular rigidity of the body), *convulsions* (epileptic-like seizures) and *coma* (a deep, unresponsive sleep). Users also report difficulty in thinking clearly and emotional blandness. Although PCP does not produce physiological dependence, users may become psychologically dependent (Bolter *et al.*, 1976).

CANNABIS

Cannabis is one of the most widely used drugs, second only in popularity to alcohol. The *cannabis sativa* plant grows wild in many parts of the world and was cultivated over 5000 years ago in China. The plant's psychoactive ingredient is *delta-9-tetrahydrocannabinol* or *THC*. THC is found in the branches and leaves of the male and female plants (*marijuana*), but is highly concentrated in the resin of the female plant. *Hashish* (or 'hash') is derived from the sticky resin and is more potent than marijuana.

Cannabis is usually smoked with tobacco or is eaten. When smoked, THC finds its way to the brain inside seven seconds. Small amounts produce a mild, pleasurable 'high', consisting of relaxation, a loss of social inhibition, intoxication, and a humorous mood. Speech becomes slurred and coordination is impaired. Other effects include increased heart rate, lack of concentration and enhanced appetite. Short-term memory is also affected, and there is an inability to retain information for later use. It is not unusual for a user to begin a sentence and then forget what the sentence was about before it has been completed. As with other drugs, the effects are influenced by social context and other factors. Thus, some users report negative effects such as fear, anxiety and confusion.

Large amounts result in hallucinogenic reactions, including the perceived slowing of time and amplified sensitivity to colours, sounds, tastes and smells. However, these subjective reports are not borne out by objective measures. As well as increased awareness of bodily states (such as heart rate), sexual sensations are also heightened.

THC remains in the body for as long as a month. Cannabis may disrupt the male sex hormones and, in females, influence the menstrual cycle. Its use during pregnancy has been associated with impaired foetal growth, and cannabis is more damaging to the throat and lungs than cigarette smoking. Long-term use may lead to *amotivational syndrome* (a general lack of energy or motivation). However, this may simply reflect the fact that users differ psychologically from non-users.

There is some debate over whether cannabis leads to physiological dependence. Tolerance is a sign of physiological dependence, but with cannabis *reverse tolerance* has been reported. Thus, regular use leads to a *lowering* of the amount needed to achieve the initial effects. This could be due to a build-up of THC which takes a long time to be metabolised. An alternative explanation is that users become more adept at inhaling the drug and therefore perceive its effects more quickly. Withdrawal effects (restlessness, irritability and insomnia) have been reported, but these seem to be associated with the continuous use of very large amounts. Psychological dependence almost certainly occurs in at least some people.

Box 15.7   Some medical uses of cannabis

Cannabis has some *medical* applications. For example, it has been used with glaucoma sufferers because it reduces fluid pressure in the eyes. The fact that cannabis decreases nausea and vomiting has also led to a tablet form (Nabilane) being administered to patients with cancer who must receive chemotherapy, a treatment that induces nausea and vomiting. A third medical application is with multiple sclerosis. Smoking cannabis reduces muscle spasm, tremors, night leg pain and depression (Dillner, 1997).

Cannabis has been classified as a hallucinogen because large amounts produce hallucinations. However, it could also be classified as a stimulant because it also has a stimulant effect. In very large amounts, however, it acts as a depressant.

The precise biochemical mechanisms underlying THC's behavioural effects are not known. It may influence the action of noradrenaline and serotonin. As noted in Chapter 3, acetylcholine plays a role in memory, and the observation that cannabis interferes with the ability to recall previously learned information might be explained in terms of the disruption of normal activity in acetylcholine-utilising neurons in the limbic system.

Conclusions

This chapter has examined the physiological and psychological effects of some of the legal and illegal drugs taken for the purpose of pleasure. The effects produced by the drugs are wide-ranging, as are their effects on brain chemistry.

Summary

■ **Psychoactive drugs** are chemicals which alter perceptions and behaviour by changing conscious awareness. **Recreational drugs** (e.g. alcohol) have no legal restrictions. **Drugs of abuse** (e.g. cannabis) are also taken recreationally, but are outside society's approval.

■ **Physiological (or physical) dependence** is the body's inability to do without a drug. When the drug is stopped, the symptoms of **withdrawal** occur. **Tolerance** is the need for more of a drug to achieve its initial effects. Physical dependence coupled with tolerance defines **drug addiction**. A drug that compels people to take it, even though there is no physical dependence, produces **psychological dependence**.

■ **Depressants** (e.g. alcohol, barbiturates, minor tranquillisers and aromatic solvents) slow down mental processes and behaviour. Small amounts of alcohol suppress brain mechanisms that normally inhibit behaviour. Large amounts relax ANS activity and decrease neural activity, possibly by acting on the cell membranes of neurons and reducing their ability to conduct nerve impulses. Alcohol also reduces neural activity by increasing the sensitivity of post-synaptic receptors for GABA, an inhibitory neurotransmitter.

■ **Stimulants** (e.g. caffeine, nicotine, amphetamine, MDMA and cocaine) stimulate CNS activity by increasing the transmission of nerve impulses. The powerful stimulants increase energy and self-confidence, and produce euphoria and elation.

■ The long-term consequences associated with amphetamine and cocaine include the development of symptoms indistinguishable from paranoid schizophrenia. These stimulants facilitate the release of noradrenaline (associated with increased energy) and dopamine (associated with euphoria), but inhibit their re-uptake by the vesicles that released them.

■ MDMA is a chemical relative of amphetamine. Small amounts produce mild euphoria and increased self- and sexual confidence. Large amounts trigger hallucinations. Long-term consequences include extreme dehydration and hyperthermia, which can result in convulsions and death.

■ The **opiates** include codeine, morphine, heroin and methadone. Their general effect is to depress neural functioning and suppress physical sensations and responses to pain. Regular taking of heroin overloads the brain's opiate receptors and it stops producing endorphins. When the user abstains, the absence of endorphins produces painful withdrawal symptoms.

■ Some **hallucinogens** (e.g. mescaline and psilocybin) are naturally occurring. Others (e.g. LSD and PCP) are chemically synthesised. Hallucinogens cause changes in perception, thought processes and emotions. Hallucinations may be a result of serotonin's suppression by hallucinogenic drug molecules. Synaesthesia and depersonalisation are also associated with LSD use. Long-term consequences include flashbacks and tolerance, although LSD use is not associated with physiological dependence and withdrawal.

■ PCP causes distortions in body image and depersonalisation and, in small amounts, euphoria and heightened awareness. Large amounts have stimulant, depressant and analgesic properties. Behavioural effects include violence, panic, psychotic behaviour, disrupted motor activity and chronic depression. Long-term use is associated with combatitiveness, catatonia, convulsions and coma, as well as psychological dependence.

■ Small amounts of **cannabis** produce relaxation, loss of social inhibition and a humorous mood. However, short-term memory is impaired, concentration is reduced and appetite increased. Large amounts produce a perceived slowing down of time, heightened sensory sensitivity, and an increased awareness of bodily states. Sexual sensations are also increased.

■ THC, the psychoactive chemical in cannabis, can disrupt hormonal activity in both sexes. Used during pregnancy, cannabis can impair foetal growth. Long-term use may produce **amotivational syndrome**, and is associated with **reverse tolerance**. Cannabis may exert its effects by influencing noradrenaline, serotonin and acetylcholine.

PART 4

Motivation, emotion and stress

16

MOTIVATION AND THE BRAIN

Introduction and overview

The word 'motive' comes from the Latin 'movere' which means 'move'. Motives are inner directing forces that arouse an organism and direct its behaviour towards some goal. Geen (1995) describes motivation as 'the processes involved in the initiation, direction, and energisation of individual behaviour'. For Miller (1962), the study of motivation involves:

> 'all those pushes and prods – biological, social, and psychological – that defeat our laziness and move us, either eagerly or reluctantly, to action'.

The study of motivation, then, is the study of the *why* of behaviour which, in a sense is what psychology is all about! This chapter looks at the role played by the brain in the motivational states of hunger and thirst. It also looks at the impact that external factors can have on these behaviours.

Hunger

To survive, the body must have appropriate amounts of food, water, air, sleep and heat. Our bodies contain complex mechanisms that maintain proper levels of these essentials. The body's tendency to maintain a steady state is called *homeostasis* (see Box 4.5, page 39). Homeostasis has been likened to a *thermostat*: when room temperature rises above the *set-point*, the heating system switches off and remains this way until the temperature falls to the set-point. This analogy has dominated much biopsychological thinking and underlies some of the proposals concerning hunger and thirst.

If hunger and eating are at least partially, if not wholly, controlled by some internal homeostatic mechanism, what are the means by which the body's need for food is conveyed to the brain, and what part of the brain receives these messages and sends signals to the body to initiate eating?

When we are hungry, the walls of the stomach contract producing 'hunger pangs'. When the stomach is full we 'feel bloated' or *satiated*. An early theory of eating proposed that the *stomach*, via the *vagus nerve* (the connection between the stomach/gastrointestinal tract and the brain), sent as information to the brain informing it about hunger and satiety.

Box 16.1   Cannon & Washburn's (1912) experiment

Washburn swallowed a balloon which was inflated by air introduced through an attached tube. His stomach contractions forced air out of the balloon and activated a recording device. Whenever Washburn felt a hunger pang he pressed a key which activated another recording device. Each time he reported a hunger pang, a large stomach contraction occurred, suggesting that hunger is controlled by the stomach (see Figure 16.1).

As appealingly simplistic as this common sense approach to hunger is, the picture is actually much more complicated than Cannon and Washburn's findings suggest. For example, people whose stomachs have been surgically removed because of cancer still report feeling hungry, and cutting the connections between the gastrointestinal

130

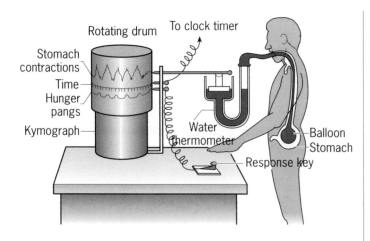

Figure 16.1   Cannon and Washburn's set-up

tract and the brain has little effect on food intake in both humans and non-humans (Pinel, 1993).

Although Cannon exaggerated the importance of stomach contractions in causing hunger, the stomach/gastrointestinal tract does play an influential role. Even if the *vagus nerve* is cut, signals arising from the gut can be communicated to the brain via the circulatory system. Additionally, the presence of food in the stomach (*stomach loading*) is important in the regulation of feeding since if the exit from the stomach to the small intestine is blocked, rats will still eat normal-sized meals. Information about the stretching of the stomach wall must therefore be passed to the brain (via the vagus nerve) and the brain is in some way able to control food intake. As well as the stomach, other internal stimuli involved in eating have been identified.

Box 16.2   Some internal stimuli involved in eating

The mouth: Clearly, chewing and swallowing must provide some sensations of satiety. If they didn't, we might eat for a long time after we had eaten enough, since it takes the digestive tract time to metabolise food and send signals to the brain about food levels. Janowitz & Grossman (1949) found that when a tube was implanted into a dog's throat so that food did not reach the stomach, it stopped eating (although it resumed eating sooner than a normal dog). The secondary taste cortex appears to be responsible for telling us what a pleasant experience tasting food is (Irwin, 1996b).

The liver: Injections of glucose to the liver cause a decrease in eating and specialised cells in the liver convey information to the brain via a nerve connection (Russek, 1971).

Hormones: Eating behaviour may be influenced by hormones. One hormone, *cholecystokinin-8* (CCK-8), is produced by the intestinal walls. Injections of this can cause satiety (Dockray *et al.*, 1978). CCK-8 may, therefore, inform the brain about food levels in the intestines, although exactly how it does this is not yet known (see also Box 16.4).

The depletion of fats, carbohydrates, glucose, vitamins/mineral salts, and proteins/amino acids may all play some role in initiating action in the stimuli identified in Box 16.2. The effects of changes in *blood-glucose* levels and the amounts of *body fat* have received most attention, and several theories have been proposed to explain how such changes relay information about hunger and satiety.

GLUCOSTATIC AND LIPOSTATIC THEORIES

According to *glucostatic theory*, the primary stimulus for hunger is a decrease in the level of blood-glucose *below* a certain *set-point*. Satiety occurs when levels rise above the set-point. Since glucose is the body's (and especially the brain's) primary fuel, this theory is intuitively appealing. It is also supported by evidence. Thus, when glucose is injected into the system, eating is usually inhibited. When insulin injections (which lower blood-glucose levels) are given, eating is stimulated.

Box 16.3   Glucostats

Glucostatic theory proposes the existence of a *glucostat*, an analogue of the thermostat. Mayer & Marshall (1956) injected mice with *gold thioglucose*, reasoning that the glucose would bind to hypothesised *glucoreceptors* (wherever they happened to be) and, because gold is a *neurotoxin*, the tissue would be destroyed. When post-mortems were conducted, damage was found in the *ventromedial hypothalamus* (VMH). Since the injected mice ate large quantities of food following the injection, and since the injection damaged the VMH, Mayer and Marshall concluded that the VMH must be a *satiety centre* which 'tells' mice to stop feeding (and might serve the same function in humans). The role of the VMH in eating is discussed further on page 133.

Glucostatic theory is also supported by the finding that a fall in blood-glucose level before a spontaneous meal is not just related to the onset of eating, but actually causes it. For example, Campfield *et al.* (1985) found that if very small amounts of glucose were injected into the veins of rats as a decline in their blood-glucose levels occurred, the predicted meal they would take was 'postponed' as though the injection had removed the hunger signal.

Mayer and Marshall saw the *rate* of glucose *utilisation*, rather than its *absolute level*, as being the most important factor in eating. However, there is little evidence for this and at least some to contradict it (Geiselman, 1983). Furthermore, although blood-glucose levels might be important, they cannot be the only signal to stop and start eating. An animal that eats a meal low in carbohydrates, but high in fats or protein, still eats a relatively constant amount of calories even though its blood-glucose level is reduced slightly. If eating was exclusively controlled by blood-glucose levels, it would overeat and become fat (Carlson, 1988).

Another explanation of the homeostatic mechanism regulating eating concentrates on the role of fats (or *lipids*) in *adipocytes*. Clumps of adipocytes form the fatty (or *adipose*) tissues of the body, and body fat is normally maintained at a relatively constant level. According to Nisbett's (1972) version of *lipostatic theory*, everyone has a body-weight set-point around which body weight fluctuates within quite narrow limits, and this is determined by fat levels in the adipocytes. Evidence supporting lipostatic theory comes from the observation that short-term dieting programs do *not* produce long-term weight loss. As soon as dieting stops, the lost weight is regained.

Also, when a rat's *lateral hypothalamus* (LH) is damaged, it stops eating, even when food is freely available, to the point of starvation. This condition is called *hypophagia*. Originally, hypophagia was taken to indicate that the LH normally functions to *stimulate* feeding. Keesey & Powley (1975), however, showed that this is not the case. They deprived rats of food so that their body weight was significantly lowered. The LH was then lesioned. Instead of eating less, which should have occurred if the LH does normally stimulate feeding, the rats ate *more*.

The most plausible interpretation of this finding is that the LH affects feeding *indirectly* (rather than directly) by altering the body-weight set-point: when a rat's weight is reduced before the lesion is made, its feeding increases after the lesion in order to reach the new and higher set-point. The role of the LH is discussed further on page 133.

Glucostatic theory was intended to explain the relatively short-term processes of initiating and terminating eating, whereas lipostatic theory was a way of explaining long-term feeding habits and body weight regulation. Both, however, share the belief that pre-determined set-points exist. Some researchers do not agree with this and prefer to see body weight as drifting around a *settling-point*, or a level at which the various factors that influence it try to

achieve equilibrium. Rather than seeing the processes involved in eating as analogous to a thermostat, Pinel (1993) prefers the analogy of a 'leaky barrel' in which the level of fat in the body is regulated around a natural settling-point just as water is in a leaky barrel.

Box 16.4   Glucagon-like peptide and cholecystokinin-8

According to Bloom *et al.* (cited in Nuttall 1996), people prone to gluttony may be underproducing glucagon-like peptide 1 (GLP-1), a substance produced in the brain and intestine after a filling meal. The researchers believe that GLP-1 is produced in response to an extension of the intestine and/or an increase in blood-sugar level. It is also involved in the release of insulin to help digest food.

A synthetic version of GLP-1 may improve treatment for overeating as may substances which affect cholecystokinin-8 (CCK-8). CCK-8 carries messages between nerves in the digestive system and acts within the brain. It dampens appetite and is normally destroyed by a natural enzyme. However, *butabindide*, a synthetic compound, prevents the enzyme from working and allows CCK-8's influence to continue.

EXTERNAL STIMULI FOR HUNGER

As if the picture concerning the internal stimuli for eating were not complex enough, it is also clearly the case that eating can be affected by external factors.

Box 16.5   Some external factors influencing eating

Habit: If we miss a meal, our hunger does not continue to grow indefinitely. Rather, it subsides some time after the meal would normally be taken and then grows just before the scheduled time of the next one. Hunger, then, increases and decreases according to a learned schedule of eating.

Environment: We are much more likely to eat and feel hungry in the presence of others who are eating. Even when we have just eaten, we may join friends for some company only to find ourselves joining in their meal!

Culture: What is accepted as food is shaped by culture (and, indeed, by habits acquired early in life). Ducks' feet and frogs' legs, for example, are enjoyed by members of some cultures but are rarely eaten in our own culture.

Palatability: The sight, smell and taste of food can all influence our eating. For example, children who have just eaten and do not feel at all hungry will still eat M

& Ms (Rodin & Slochower, 1976). Whilst we have an innate preference for sweet tastes, we can also learn the relationship between taste and the post-ingestion consequences of eating food (Pinel, 1993). *Taste aversion studies* show that animals learn to avoid novel tastes which are followed by illness (see Chapter 32). By contrast, a sick rat that tastes a novel food and then recovers will display an acquired preference for that flavour, a phenomenon termed the *medicine preference effect*.

As Box 16.5 indicates, eating is far from a straightforward behaviour to explain. The many internal and external factors interact, often in complex ways. For example, however palatable a food is, several small but different foods are more interesting than one large and specific food. Given access to only one type of food, we demonstrate *sensory-specific satiety*, that is, we become tired of it. Rather than eat four yoghurts of the same flavour, then, we prefer to eat four different flavoured yoghurts. Sensory-specific satiety encourages the consumption of a varied diet, and we are also capable of learning which diets best meet our biological needs. Mexicans, for example, increased the calcium in their bodies by mixing small amounts of mineral lime in their tortillas.

The fact that we sometimes eat when we are not hungry, and some people (such as hunger strikers) do not eat when they are hungry, indicates that hunger is neither necessary nor sufficient for eating even though there is usually a close relationship between them (Blundell & Hill, 1995).

THE HYPOTHALAMUS AND EATING

In 1902, Frolich, a Viennese physician, observed that tumours near the hypothalamus caused overeating (or *hyperphagia*) and *obesity*. In the late 1930s, the introduction of stereotaxic apparatus (see Chapter 6) enabled researchers to assess the effects of experimentally induced damage to areas of the hypothalamus on the eating behaviour of non-humans.

Earlier on, it was noted that Mayer & Marshall's (1956) findings suggested that 'glucoreceptors' might be located in the VMH and that the VMH might act as a satiety centre. In fact, the VMH's role as a satiety centre had been proposed some years previously by Hetherington & Ranson (1942). They showed that a VMH lesioned rat will overeat and become grotesquely fat, doubling or even trebling its normal body weight.

Subsequent research showed that the *VMH hyperphagia syndrome* has two distinct phases. The *dynamic phase* begins as soon as the rat regains consciousness following surgery.

Figure 16.2   A hyperphagic rat

This phase is characterised by several weeks of overeating and rapid weight gain. As the rat approaches its maximum weight, eating gradually declines to a level just sufficient to maintain a stable level of obesity. The *static phase* is a period of stability in which it 'defends' its new body weight. If deprived of food until it loses a substantial amount of weight, the rat will temporarily increase its intake until the lost weight is gained. If, however, it is force-fed, it will temporarily reduce its intake until the excess is lost. Research also revealed that if the VMH is electrically or chemically stimulated (or 'turned on'), rats will terminate eating until the stimulation is stopped.

The role of the LH in eating behaviour earlier on was referred to in the consideration of Keesey & Powley's (1975) findings. The hypophagic effects of LH damage were first reported by Anand & Brobeck (1951) who found that if the damage was extensive enough, rats would actually starve to death. Additionally, electrically stimulating the LH causes a rat to start eating. These findings led to the conclusion that the LH was the 'start feeding' centre in contrast to the VMH's role as the 'stop feeding' centre.

The findings concerning the VMH and the LH led to the *dual hypothalamic control theory of eating*. According to this, the VMH and LH receive information about nutrient levels in the body and operate together to maintain a relatively constant level of satiety. Thus, the LH 'turns' hunger on and the VMH 'turns' it off. It is likely that the hypothalamus can initiate and terminate eating but needs information from peripheral regulatory factors, such as those proposed by glucostatic and lipostatic theories, to do this (Green, 1994). However, the precise interaction between the VMH and LH is still unclear.

Box 16.6 Lipogenesis and lipolysis

Traditionally, biopsychologists have assumed that obesity is a consequence of overeating in VMH lesioned animals. However, obesity may be a *cause* of overeating. VMH lesions might increase *lipogenesis* (the body's tendency to produce fat) and decrease *lipolysis* (its tendency to release fats into the bloodstream). Because this would result in calories being converted to fat at a much higher than normal rate, an animal would be forced to keep eating in order to ensure that it had enough calories in its blood for immediate energy needs. One finding which supports this possibility is that rats with VMH lesions accumulate more fat than controls, even when they eat the same amount of food (Friedman & Stricker, 1976).

The VMH's role is further complicated by the observation that VMH lesioned rats show an increased 'fussiness' about the *taste* of food. Ordinarily, hungry rats will eat food even if it has an unpleasant taste (as, for example, occurs when bitter-tasting quinine is added to it). Such food will not be eaten by VMH lesioned rats even if they become *underweight* (Teitelbaum, 1955). This suggests that such rats become more sensitive to *external cues* (such as the taste of food) than to *internal cues* (such as blood-sugar level), and so the VMH may also play a role in this aspect of eating.

It has also been found that whilst VMH-damaged rats do eat more food than normal, they do so only if food is freely available. If they have to work for food by, for example, having to press a lever or lift a heavy lid, they actually eat less than non-damaged rats. Some obese humans behave in a parallel way and also respond to the availability of food. They are, for example, less willing to find food or prepare it in some way. Although human obesity is almost certain to have physiological correlates, eating is influenced by many other factors, and an account of obesity based only on physiological factors is probably too simplistic.

Findings concerning the LH are also more complex than dual hypothalamic theory proposes. For example, whilst rats with LH lesions initially do not eat, they can be coaxed into eating by first being fed through a tube. After several weeks of this, they begin to eat by themselves provided they are given palatable food (Teitelbaum & Epstein, 1962). These findings challenge the idea that the LH is a discrete 'eating centre', as does the finding that LH damage causes changes in behaviour that are not related to eating. Rats with LH damage fail to groom themselves, have difficulty with balance and show little interest in almost *any* stimuli. The additional finding that eating can be elicited by stimulation of other hypothalamic areas and by the amygdala, hippocampus, thalamus and frontal cortex, also challenges the simple idea that the LH is a discrete 'hunger centre'.

As noted earlier, damage to the LH affects weight indirectly by altering the body-weight set-point and it is possible that this is also the case with the VMH. Such findings seem to indicate that the VMH and LH are not *absolutely* essential for regulating hunger and eating. So whilst the immediate effect of VMH and LH lesions might be to destroy the capacity to regulate eating and body weight, this is not necessarily the case over the long term. However, the fact that lesions in these structures appear to affect the set-point does strongly implicate them in long-term weight control.

The belief that the hypothalamus is the neurological basis of hunger has not, then, always produced data which can be explained simply. The anatomical complexity of the hypothalamus makes it even more difficult to assess its role. For example, VMH lesions also damage the axons connecting the *paraventricular nucleus* (PVN) with certain parts of the brain stem. If CCK (see Box 16.4) is injected into the PVN, food intake is inhibited (Pinel, 1993). Additionally, neurotransmitters in the medial hypothalamus appear to play an important role in eating behaviour. We tend to eat sweet or starchy carbohydrate-laden foods when we are tense or depressed (Carlson, 1987). Carbohydrates help increase *serotonin* levels, and depression is associated with lower than normal levels of it (see Chapter 69). *Noradrenaline*, by contrast, stimulates carbohydrate intake. One potential application of this is the use of food substitutes that mimic the biochemical effects of carbohydrates to treat stress-related food cravings.

With advances in methodology, new information about the processes involved in eating and its regulation by the brain continues to be gained. Current biopsychological thinking views the hypothalamus as just *one part* of a brain system that regulates eating. Other areas (such as the limbic system) also play important roles.

Drinking

As with eating, several theories have been proposed to explain the onset and termination of drinking. According to the *dry mouth theory of thirst*, receptors in the mouth and throat play a major role in determining thirst and satiety. However, 'sham drinking' studies, in which liquid swallowed down the throat does not pass into the stomach, indicate that whilst animals drink a normal amount and then stop, they return to drinking quickly afterwards unless water is placed in the stomach. Thus, internal signals rather than the amount that has been swallowed appear to govern how much is drunk.

THE HYPOTHALAMUS AND DRINKING

One important internal signal in drinking is *cellular dehydration*. Certain cells in the *lateral preoptic area of the hypothalamus* are apparently sensitive to cellular dehydration and their activation causes us to drink until enough has been consumed to restore the balance. The fluid levels inside the cells are affected by salt levels in the blood. When these are high, water leaves the cells by *osmosis* (and hence this type of thirst is often referred to as *osmotic thirst*). It is this that causes the cells to become dehydrated.

The *osmoreceptors*, the name given to the cells, seem to shrink themselves when the brain is fluid-depleted and as a result of this two hypothalamic effects occur. The first is the production of *antidiuretic hormone* (ADH) by the pituitary gland (see Chapter 5, page 46). This causes the kidneys to reabsorb water which would otherwise be excreted as urine. The second is the generation of thirst.

In addition to cellular dehydration, a lowered water level reduces the volume of blood in the body which lowers blood pressure. This *volumetric thirst* stimulates *baroreceptors*

located in the heart, kidneys and veins. Volumetric thirst is caused by bleeding, vomiting, diarrhoea and sweating. The baroreceptors then trigger the secretion of ADH which causes the kidneys to retain water. The kidneys then release the hormone *angiotensin* which circulates to the hypothalamus resulting in the initiation of drinking behaviour.

Whilst we have a reasonable understanding of thirst, our understanding of what stops us drinking is less clear. It is particularly difficult to explain why we normally stop drinking well before the new supply of fluid reaches the *extracellular* (blood plasma) or *intracellular* (the fluid portion of the cell cytoplasm) compartments of the body. However, one plausible hypothesis is that cells in the small intestine send a message to the hypothalamus when enough liquid has been consumed (Rolls, *et al.*, 1980).

Conclusions

Although the relationship between the body and brain is complex, in the motivated behaviours of eating and drinking it has been at least partially explained by biopsychological research. The important brain structure in eating and drinking is the hypothalamus, which receives information from various parts of the body concerning tissue needs. Yet whilst the hypothalamus is important, external factors play an influential role in eating and drinking. Exclusively physiological accounts of these behaviours are, therefore, unlikely to be true.

Summary

■ **Motives** are inner directing forces arousing an organism and directing its behaviour towards a goal. To survive, the body needs food, water, air, sleep and heat. **Homeostasis** provides a balance of these physiological variables.

■ The stomach plays a role in hunger and satiety as do the mouth, liver and various hormones such as cholecystokinin-8 (CCK-8). The depletion of fats, carbohydrates, glucose, vitamins/mineral salts and proteins/amino acids may all initiate action in internal stimuli involved in eating.

■ Theories of hunger and eating have concentrated on changes in blood-glucose levels and the amount of body fat. **Glucostatic theory** proposes that hunger occurs when blood-glucose levels fall below a certain **set-point**; satiety occurs when they rise above the set-point.

■ **Glucostats** (an analogue of a thermostat) may exist in the ventromedial hypothalamus (VMH). However, whilst glucostatic theory is supported by evidence, the view that glucose utilisation is the only factor in eating is unlikely to be true.

■ **Lipostatic theory** proposes that everyone has a body-weight set-point around which body weight fluctuates within quite narrow limits, and that this is determined by fat levels in **adipocytes**. The theory is supported by the finding that short-term dieting does not produce long-term weight loss, and by studies showing that damage to the lateral hypothalamus (LH) affects feeding indirectly by altering the body-weight set-point.

■ Glucostatic and lipostatic theories share the belief that pre-determined set-points exist. However, an alternative view is of a **settling point**, a level at which the various factors that influence body weight try to reach equilibrium.

■ Glucagon-like peptides-1 (GLP-1) and CCK-8 have been linked to overeating. A synthetic version of GLP-1 may offer a treatment for overeating as may substances, such as **butabindide**, which affect the appetite-suppressing effect of CCK-8.

■ Eating is influenced by external factors including habit, the social environment, culture and a food's palatability. We have an innate preference for sweet tastes, but can learn the relationship between taste and the consequences of ingesting certain foods, as demonstrated in **taste aversion studies** and the **medicine preference effect**.

■ Internal and external factors interact in a complex way. For example, access to only one type of (palatable) food produces **sensory-specific satiety**, which encourages the consumption of a varied diet. Hunger is neither necessary nor sufficient for eating, although they are usually correlated.

■ Lesions to the VMH produce **hyperphagia**, which has a dynamic phase (in which maximum weight is attained) and a static phase (in which the new weight is defended). Extensive LH damage causes rats to starve to death, whilst stimulating the LH causes eating to begin.

■ **Dual hypothalamic control theory** sees the LH as a 'start feeding' centre and the VMH as a 'stop feeding' centre. The VMH and LH operate to maintain a relatively constant level of satiety.

■ VMH lesions may increase hypogenesis and decrease lipolysis. Because this would cause calories to be converted to fat at a higher than normal rate, an animal would need to keep eating to ensure it had enough calories for immediate energy needs. This would suggest that obesity is a cause, not a consequence, of overeating.

■ VMH-lesioned rats show increased fussiness about food's taste, suggesting they are more sensitive to external than internal cues. Such rats will only consume more food if they do not have to work for it, which parallels what is seen in obese humans. LH-lesioned rats will eventually eat by themselves, which suggests the LH is not a discrete feeding centre. Eating can occur when other areas of the hypothalamus and structures in the limbic system are stimulated.

■ Obesity may have a genetic cause. Low levels of leptin, a protein produced by fat cells, have been found in cousins who have a small change in the same place in the DNA code in the gene that controls leptin's supply.

■ According to the **dry mouth theory of thirst**, receptors in the mouth and throat play a role in thirst and satiety. However, sham drinking studies suggest that internal signals determine how much is drunk.

■ **Osmoreceptors** in the hypothalamus are sensitive to cellular dehydration, which is caused by high salt levels in the blood that results in water leaving cells by osmosis (**osmotic thirst**). To counter this, ADH is produced and thirst generated.

■ Reduced water levels reduce blood volume which lowers blood pressure. This **volumetric thirst** stimulates **baroreceptors**. These trigger the secretion of ADH, which causes water retention by the kidneys. The kidneys release **angiotensin** to the hypothalamus, leading to drinking. Stopping drinking may be the result of cells in the small intestine sending messages to the hypothalamus.

■ Primary drinking is caused by internal needs whereas secondary drinking is caused by external needs. These needs also determine what is drunk.

17

THEORIES OF MOTIVATION

Introduction and overview

One major aim of psychological research is to explain what motivates us to act in certain ways. Several theories of motivation have been proposed. As might be expected given the findings described in Chapter 16, some of these adopt a distinctly physiological approach. Others, however, are primarily psychological. This chapter examines some physiological and psychological theories of motivation and explores the contrast between them. It begins, however, by looking at different types of motive.

Types of motive

The range of motivation is very broad. As will be seen, some behaviours, such as drinking a glass of water, can be explained in terms of reducing a 'need'. Others, such as smoking cigarettes when we know they cause disease, must have more complex explanations. To assess theories of motivation requires *types* of motive to be identified. Three main categories of human behaviour are *biologically-based motives*, *sensation-seeking motives* and *complex psychosocial motives*.

BIOLOGICALLY-BASED MOTIVES

Biologically-based motives are rooted primarily in body tissue needs (or *drives*) such as those for food, water, air, sleep, temperature regulation and pain avoidance. Although these needs are in-built, their expression is often learned. For example, hunger is caused by food deprivation, and we learn to search the environment effectively for food to satisfy this basic need.

SENSATION-SEEKING MOTIVES

Sensation-seeking motives are apparently largely unlearned needs for certain levels of stimulation. They depend more on external stimuli than biologically-based motives, and their main function is to affect the environment. These motives aim to *increase* rather than decrease the amount of stimulation, and are most evident in the way we attempt to create our own sensations when placed in *sensory isolation*. Other sensation-seeking motives include *activity*, *curiosity*, *exploration* and *manipulation*.

The need to be *active* affects all animals. When an animal is deprived of activity, it is much more active than normal when subsequently released. Whether activity is a separate motive or a combination of motives, unlearned or learned, is unclear. Sensory deprivation studies, in which virtually all sensory input is cut off, indicate that sensory deprivation appears to be intolerable. As well as hallucinations, people have difficulty in thinking clearly. They also experience boredom, anger and frustration. However, voluntary sensory restriction has also been associated with increased ability to gain control over negative habits such as smoking, but this is much milder than studies in which virtually all stimulation is cut off.

Curiosity and *exploration* are activated by the new and unknown, and appear to be directed to no more a specific goal than 'finding out'. For example, children will play with toys even though there is no extrinsic reward for doing so. *Unfamiliarity* and *complexity* are sometimes preferred because they may be more appealing. Thus, a non-human that has just copulated will show an interest in sexual behaviour when presented with a 'novel' partner. Non-humans will learn discrimination problems when the reward is nothing more than a brief look around the laboratory in which they are housed.

Manipulation is directed towards a specific object that must be touched, handled, or played with before we are satisfied. 'Do Not Touch' signs in museums, for example, are there because curators know that the urge to touch things is irresistible. This motive is limited to primates who have agile fingers and toes, and seems to be related to the need to have *tactile experience* and a need to be *soothed*. The 'worry beads' manipulated by Greeks would be an example of the latter. Three other sensation-seeking motives are *play*, *contact* and *control*.

Box 17.1   Play, contact and control

Play: Many species have this innate motive and the young enjoy *practice play*, that is, behaviour which will later be used for 'serious' purposes. Such activity might not appear to have any immediate consequences for the fulfilment of biological needs (Bolles, 1967). Much of the behaviour normally associated with play can be thought of in terms of the drives for curiosity, exploration and manipulation.

Contact: This refers to the need to *touch* other people and is broader and more universal than the need for manipulation. It is not limited to touching with the fingers and toes, and can involve the whole body. Unlike manipulation, which is active, contact can be passive.

Control: The need for control is linked to the need to be free from restrictions from others and to determine our own actions and not to be dictated to. When our freedom is threatened, we tend to react by reasserting it, a phenomenon which Brehm (1966) calls *psychological reactance* (see Chapter 81). *Learned helplessness* (Seligman, 1975: see Chapter 69) is important here. Whilst initial negative experiences produce psychological reactance, further negative experiences produce a state in which we perceive ourselves as being unable to do anything else. All of us have a belief about the things that control events in our everyday lives (Rotter, 1966). Rotter's *locus of control* questionnaire attempts to distinguish between *internals*, who see themselves as being responsible for events in their lives, and *externals*, who see events in the outside world as being particularly influential.

It is generally believed that the motivation to seek stimulation evolved because of its survival value. Organisms motivated to explore their environment, and acquire information about it, would be more likely to survive because of an increased awareness of resources and potential dangers. Such behaviour would allow them to change their environment in beneficial ways.

COMPLEX PSYCHOSOCIAL MOTIVES

These share little if any relationship with biological needs. They are acquired by learning and aroused by psychological events rather than body tissue needs. Unlike the latter, which must be satisfied, there is no biological requirement for complex psychosocial motives to be met (although much of our happiness and misery is associated with them). Murray (1938) identified 20 motives although some have been more extensively researched than others.

Need for achievement (nAch) is the need to meet or exceed some standard of excellence. McClelland (1958) has claimed that nAch can be measured using the *thematic apperception test* which consists of ambiguous pictures about which a story must be told. The story content is then scored for achievement and other important motives held to reflect 'hidden forces' motivating behaviour. Differences between individuals have been correlated with *child rearing practices* (see Chapter 40), such as an emphasis on competition, praise-giving, encouragement to take credit

for success, and *modelling*, where parents serve as models to their children by being high in nAch themselves (see Chapter 40).

Need for affiliation (nAff) is the desire to maintain close, friendly relations with others. Schachter (1959) found that people high in nAff find it painful to make their own decisions or be by themselves over extended periods of time. In anxiety-provoking situations, people high in nAff prefer to be with others provided they are also experiencing anxiety. According to *social comparison theory* (Festinger, 1954), this is because we prefer to affiliate with people we can compare our feelings and behaviours with (see Chapter 56).

Need for power (nPower) is a concern with being in charge, having status and prestige, and bending others to our will. This has both positive and negative features. For example, leaders high in nPower can impede group decision-making by failing to allow full discussion and by not encouraging full consideration of others' proposals. nPower is also linked to child rearing. Children allowed to be aggressive to siblings tend to produce children high in nPower, possibly because allowing children to exercise power at an early age encourages them to continue this later on (see Chapter 40).

Need for approval (nApp) is the desire to gain approval or some kind of sign that others like us and think we are good. The characteristics of people with a high need for approval have been studied using Crowne & Marlowes' (1964) *social desirability scale*. This measures the extent to which people try to gain others' approval by behaving in socially desirable ways. Whilst there are wide individual differences, people high in nApp are conformist and tend to change their behaviour when they know they are being observed (see Chapter 58).

Instinct theories

According to these, we possess *innate* or genetically predetermined dispositions to act in a particular way to a certain stimulus. Instinct theories were popular in the early twentieth century, largely due to Darwin's emphasis on the similarity between humans and other animals. Indeed, James (1890) argued that humans were *more* influenced by instincts because we are motivated by *psychosocial instincts* such as 'jealousy' and 'sympathy', as well as biological instincts. James did not provide any evidence for such instincts, and compiled a list of them from arguments about their evolutionary advantages and observations of his own children's behaviour.

Box 17.2   How many instincts are there?

Several attempts were made to identify instincts fostering self-survival. McDougall (1908) proposed 12 'basic' instincts including 'hunger' and 'sex'. However, lists of instincts grew larger until there were as many instincts as psychologists studying them. Indeed, since around 15,000 instincts were identified, there were probably more (Tolman, 1923). Some instincts (such as 'cleanliness' and 'modesty') had little to do with basic survival, and instinct gradually lost its meaning, becoming a way of *labelling* rather than explaining behaviour. Moreover, an instinct's existence was inferred from the behaviour it was trying to explain. A 'cleanliness' instinct, for example, was inferred from the observation that most people keep themselves clean, and the fact that people keep themselves clean was taken as evidence of this 'cleanliness' instinct. This *circular reasoning* did not enhance instinct theory's reputation.

In the 1930s, instinct theory was revised by *ethologists*. They coined the term *fixed action pattern* to describe an unlearned behaviour, universal to a particular species and occurring (or *released*) in the presence of a naturally occurring stimulus (or *sign stimulus*). Tinbergen (1951), for example, demonstrated that the sign stimulus of a red belly elicited the fixed action pattern of aggressiveness in the three-spined stickleback.

Today's ethologists believe that whilst behaviour is innate or pre-programmed, it can be modified by environmental requirements. The greylag goose, for example, has an innate tendency to retrieve an egg that has rolled from its nest. However, if the egg has rolled to a dangerous place, this behaviour may change.

Whether instincts really are innate is, however, debatable. Some behaviours that ethologists identify as innate are influenced by experiences *before birth*. For example, the duckling's ability to discriminate maternal calls is linked to its behaviour within the egg. At some point, the duckling's bill penetrates the egg's interior membrane and it begins to 'talk to itself'. This self-vocalisation is critical to the duckling's ability at birth to identify the maternal call of its species (Gottlieb, 1975).

Box 17.3   Sociobiology

Sociobiologists argue that innate tendencies play an important role in complex forms of *human* behaviour. Sociobiologists see the primary motivation of all organisms as ensuring the future survival of their *genes*. Our behaviour is basically *selfish*, because it is designed to ensure our genes survive. Far from caring for others and behaving empathically, altruistic acts are actually examples of 'genetic selfishness' designed for gene survival. Although influential, some researchers regard sociobiology as oversimplifying human behaviour. They argue that whilst altruism may have a genetic component, the role of situational and personal variables cannot be ignored (see Chapter 63).

Drive theories

During the 1920s, 'instinct' was replaced by *drive*, a term originated by Woodworth (1918) who likened human behaviour to the operation of a machine. Woodworth saw machines (and hence humans) as being relatively passive and drive was the power that made them (and humans) 'go'. Two major drive theories have been particularly influential. These are *homeostatic drive theory*, which is a physiological theory, and *drive reduction theory* which is primarily a learning theory.

HOMEOSTATIC DRIVE THEORY

Cannon (1929) viewed homeostasis (see Box 4.5) as an optimum level of physiological functioning that maintains an organism in a constant internal state. When imbalance occurs, something must happen to correct it. For example, if body temperature deviates from the normal 98.4°F, sweating occurs to bring it down or shivering occurs to raise it.

When body temperature rises, we do not always need to 'do' anything since sweating is autonomic and physiological. However, with an imbalance caused by a *tissue need* (a physiological need for food or drink), the animal must behave in a way which will procure these. It is here that the concept of a homeostatic drive becomes important: a tissue need leads to an internal imbalance which causes a homeostatic drive. The drive leads to an appropriate behaviour which restores the balance and reduces the tissue need which produced the drive.

The internal environment requires a relatively regular supply of raw materials from the external world. Some of these, such as oxygen intake, are involuntary and continuous. Others, such as eating and drinking, are voluntary and discontinuous. Although we talk about a hunger and thirst drive, we do not talk about an oxygen drive (Green, 1980). Because of eating and drinking's voluntary nature, hunger and thirst have been the most researched homeostatic mechanisms and, as was seen in Chapter 16, they are also the drives most researched in terms of the brain structures involved in them.

DRIVE REDUCTION THEORY

An animal deprived of food is in a state of *need* and experiencing some sort of tissue deficit. Drive reduction theory proposes that this need state leads to an *unpleasant* state of bodily arousal (a *drive state*). Drive states activate behaviour to *reduce* the tension associated with them. Behaviours that achieve this are strengthened, whilst those that do not are weakened. According to drive reduction theory, then, organisms are *pushed* into behaviours arising in connection with tissue needs. A thirsty animal is motivated to reduce the unpleasant drive state by drinking. Once achieved, the behaviour ceases and arousal recedes.

Box 17.4   Drives and needs – always parallel?

Whilst drives and needs are mostly parallel, sometimes they are not. A person who is hungry, for example, might have an overwhelming need for food but may be so weak that the drive to search for nutrition is absent. Originally, drive reduction theory focused on biological needs or *primary drives* such as hunger and thirst. However, through association we also learn *secondary* or *acquired drives* which help reduce primary drives. A drive for money is a secondary drive that enables us to buy food and drink to reduce the primary drives of hunger and thirst and eliminate the tension they produce.

Drive reduction theory is still popular with some researchers, not least because biologically-based motives fit in with it. However, at least four reasons exist for doubting its usefulness as a comprehensive theory of motivation. First, whilst a hunger and thirst drive make sense because they reduce tension or arousal, we would need to invent a drive for all motivated behaviour which reduced a drive. This is as absurd as it is impossible. For example, rats will eat saccharin for hours even though it has no nutritional value and so cannot reduce hunger or thirst (Sheffield & Roby, 1955). To talk of a 'saccharin eating drive' (or, for another behaviour, a 'stamp collecting drive') does not make sense. So, some behaviours are not obviously motivated by drives associated with physiological need states and these are difficult for drive reduction theory to explain.

Second, at least some behaviour *increases* rather than reduces various drives. Some hungry people, for example, will refuse a biscuit with a mid-morning cup of coffee, in order to increase their enjoyment of a lunchtime meal. Others make lengthy efforts to prepare a meal instead of having a snack, even though a snack would quickly reduce the hunger.

Third, the theory proposes that when tension is reduced the behaviour that led to it will itself be reduced. This does not always happen. For example, if given the opportunity to explore our surroundings, we engage in *more* exploration rather than less. All of the sensation motives in Box 17.1 seem to go against drive reduction theory unless there is a 'manipulation drive', 'curiosity drive', and so on, which simply labels rather than explains behaviour (one of the criticisms made of instinct theories).

The fourth, and most compelling evidence against drive reduction theory comes from research into the effects of electrical self-stimulation of the brain.

Box 17.5   Electrical self-stimulation of the brain

Olds & Milner (1954) discovered that placing an electrode in a rat's hypothalamus and allowing it to stimulate its brains results in it doing so thousands of times an hour. This behaviour *never* satiated and was done in preference to anything else. Thus, although exhausted, a rat would continue pressing the lever, cross an electrified grid to gain access to it, and ignore sexually receptive females.

Similar findings were obtained in other species including goldfish, dolphins, monkeys and humans. Olds and Milner proposed the existence of a *pleasure centre* in the brain. Later research suggested that the main reward site for *electrical self-stimulation of the brain* (ES-SB) is the *median forebrain bundle* (MFB), a nerve tract running from the brain stem up to the forebrain and through the lateral hypothalamus.

Olds and Milner also found that placing the electrodes elsewhere in the brain produced the opposite effects. Thus, rats would do everything they could to *avoid* brain stimulation, suggesting the existence of a *pain centre*. This research indicates that reinforcement does *not* consist of drive reduction but appears to *increase* drive levels.

Stimulation of parts of the hypothalamus activates neurons which release dopamine to the *nucleus acumbens*. It is likely that dopamine and the nucleus acumbens are part of some sort of 'reward pathway' and that ES-SB is a 'short cut' to pleasure which eliminates the need for drives and reinforcers. However, although ES-SB has been demonstrated in all species that have been studied, and:

'It remains rather mysterious ... [and] acts as a reminder that however much we may uncover about motivated behaviours ... there are still many aspects of motivation, even in the rat, to be uncovered' (Green, 1994).

(See also Chapter 6, pages 51–52.)

Optimum level of arousal theory

Sometimes we are motivated to reduce tension. As noted, however, on other occasions we behave as though we want to *increase* tension or excitement without the need to satisfy any biological need. Driving a Formula one car at 180 miles per hour, or parachuting from an aeroplane are yet other observations which are difficult for drive reduction theory to explain.

The fact that we sometimes want to decrease and sometimes increase *arousal* suggests we have a preference for an *optimum level* of stimulation that is neither too low nor too high. Like drive reduction theory, optimum level of arousal (OLA) theory proposes that when arousal is too high we try to lower it by decreasing stimulation. Unlike drive reduction theory, OLA theory proposes that when arousal level falls below a certain level we are motivated to raise it by increasing stimulation.

Although most of us fall between the extremes, there are wide individual differences in the OLA we seek. People with low levels may prefer to lead sedentary lives, whereas those with high levels may prefer to engage in activities like driving a Formula one car or parachuting from an aeroplane. Zuckerman (1979) calls such people *sensation-seekers*.

OLA theory's major problem is one that also applies to drive reduction theory. Because we cannot measure an organism's drive or arousal level, we cannot say what its OLA should be. Thus, the theory identifies an organism's optimum level by its behaviour. If it seeks out stimulation it must be functioning below its optimum level, and if it avoids stimulation it must be functioning above it. This is an unsatisfactory and circular way of measuring OLA.

Incentive (or expectancy) theory

The theories considered so far address an animal's internal or biologically-based state and propose that some level of tension or arousal motivates (or *pushes*) it to perform certain behaviours. A different idea is that *external stimuli* motivate (or *pull*) us in certain directions in the absence of known physiological states.

These stimuli are called *incentives*, and according to the incentive (or *expectancy*) theory of motivation, the expectation of a desirable goal motivates us to perform a behaviour. The expectation of an undesirable goal motivates us not to perform a behaviour. Incentive theorists, then, address what induces us to act and what inhibits our actions.

Numerous studies have shown that incentives can act as powerful motivators. As mentioned earlier (see page 140), rats will work hard for a sip of saccharin even though saccharin has no nutritional value and therefore cannot reduce a tissue need. Rats simply like the taste of saccharin and are motivated to experience it! People who are no longer hungry and whose tissue needs have been satisfied will sometimes eat chocolate after a meal.

Incentive theory's most important application is in *work motivation*, our tendency to expend effort and energy on a job. We will demonstrate a high level of work motivation if we believe that (a) hard work will improve performance, (b) good performance will yield rewards (such as a pay increase), and (c) that such rewards are valued (Mitchell & Larson, 1987).

Rotter (1966) has proposed that expectations *and* values affect whether a behaviour is performed or not. For example, whether you ask someone out for the evening is determined to some degree by past experiences. If you have been unsuccessful in the past, your expectations are low and you would be less likely to try again. However, if you assign great value to the goal of taking someone out for the evening, expectations of failure might be overcome.

Box 17.6   Intrinsic and extrinsic motivation

The relationship between *intrinsic* and *extrinsic reward* is also important. Intrinsic refers to the pleasure and satisfaction a task brings. Some tasks themselves are rewarding to us. Extrinsic refers to the rewards that are given beyond a task's intrinsic pleasures. The relationship between these rewards is not straightforward, since being given rewards for behaviours we intrinsically enjoy, *lessens* our enjoyment of them.

Sometimes, then, extrinsic reward can undermine intrinsic motivation. On other occasions, extrinsic rewards can be given without reducing intrinsic motivation. For example, a reward given as a recognition of competence can maintain rather than reduce intrinsic motivation. However, giving rewards for something quite happily done for pleasure can 'rob' a person of that pleasure and reduce intrinsic motivation (see Chapter 81).

Opponent-process theory

Some motives are clearly *acquired* and become powerful and driving forces in our lives. According to Solomon & Corbit (1974), some acquired motives (such as taking drugs) initially bring about a basic pleasure, but each pleasurable experience eventually triggers some kind of 'pain'. In the case of taking drugs, the pain would be the unpleasant symptoms of withdrawal. Equally, other acquired motives, like parachuting from an aeroplane for the first time, bring about an initial suffering (in the form of terror) but eventually trigger a pleasurable experience (the elation of having completed a parachute jump).

Solomon and Corbit's *opponent-process theory* could be considered a theory of emotion since, in essence, they are suggesting that every emotional experience elicits a more intense opposite emotional experience persisting long after the primary emotion has passed. Solomon and Corbit argue that the opposite emotion lasts longer than the primary emotion it developed from, and acts to diminish the primary emotion's intensity. In the case of parachuting from an aeroplane, for example, each successful jump lessens the associated fear whilst the elation of the experience remains. Opponent process theory is considered here, rather than in Chapter 19, because it is similar to theories of motivation that propose the maintenance of 'steady states'.

Box 17.7   Opponent-process theory and drug addiction

Opponent-process theory has been particularly useful in explaining *drug addiction*, although Solomon and Corbit see it as being equally useful in explaining acquired motives such as social attachments and love. With drug addiction, the theory argues that the initial pleasure produced by a drug is followed by a gradual decline and then a minor craving for it. When addiction occurs, the drug is taken to avoid the pain of withdrawal rather than the experience of pleasure and this provides the motivational forces for continued drug-taking.

Opponent-process theory sees behaviour as being influenced by what happens in the long- rather than the short-term. Repeated pleasurable (or unpleasurable) experiences eventually lose their pleasantness (or unpleasantness) and shift the driving force from pleasure to pain or pain to pleasure.

Maslow's theory

According to Maslow (1954), many theories of motivation are 'defensive' and see human behaviour as occurring in a mechanical fashion and aimed at nothing more than survival and tension reduction. In Maslow's view, and that of other *humanistic psychologists*, behaviour is also motivated by the conscious desire for *personal growth* (see Chapter 1, pages 14–16). Maslow argued that our needs could be organised into a *hierarchy*.

At the hierarchy's base are basic physiological needs (such as food and drink) deriving from bodily states that *must* be satisfied. Maslow argues that we all start life at this lowest level (where drive reduction theory operates). As we move up the hierarchy, so the needs become more complex and psychological. The hierarchy culminates in *self-actualisation*, our self-initiated striving to become whatever we believe we are capable of being.

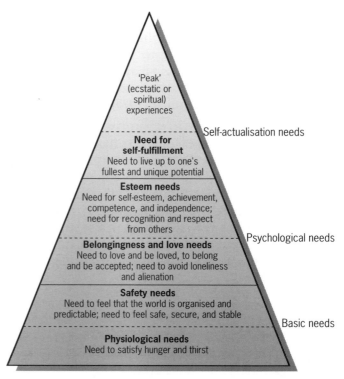

Figure 17.1   One version of Maslow's hierarchy of needs

Maslow labelled behaviours related to survival or deficiency needs '*deficiency*' (*D-motives*) because they satisfy such needs and represent a means to an end. Behaviours relating to self-actualisation are 'growth' or 'being' needs (*B-motives*). Maslow saw them as being performed for their own sake since they are intrinsically satisfying.

Maslow argued that the needs at one level must be 'relatively satisfied' before those at the next level could direct and control behaviour. Before enjoying reading a book for example, the 'stomach pangs' of hunger should ideally be attended to first. Maslow believed that few people achieve self-actualisation because most are stalled along the way by insurmountable social or environmental barriers. However, he also believed that all of us could reach the final level in the hierarchy for brief periods, which he called *peak experiences*.

Maslow's critics have argued that towards the highest level of the hierarchy the ordering is wrong. In a sense, such criticism is trivial because it is the idea of a *need* hierarchy that is useful rather than its exact nature and order. Also, we used the term 'relatively satisfied' with respect to moving from one level to another rather than 'completely satisfied'. Maslow would accept that basic physiological needs do not need to be completely satisfied for higher needs to be addressed and might use the example of the hungry artist working on a 'masterpiece' to illustrate this.

Despite its intuitive appeal, Maslow's theory may be criticised on other grounds. For example, it is difficult to operationally define concepts like self-actualisation, and without such definitions it is impossible to test the theory experimentally. Also, some people don't seem to show any interest in going beyond physiological, safety, and love needs. Thus, it has been proposed that there is too much individual variation for the hierarchy to apply to everyone.

Maslow's conclusions about 'self-actualisation' have also been criticised. These were based on his observations of people he considered to be 'self-actualised' and included historical figures, famous living individuals, and even some of his friends whom he admired greatly. Such an approach does not exactly follow the traditions of the scientific process (Wahba & Bridwell, 1976).

Freud's theory

The theories so far considered assume that motives are *conscious*. Freud, however, argued that behaviour is controlled by *unconscious* motives. Indeed, these could be called 'instincts' and Freud's theory could be discussed as an instinct theory of motivation. Originally, Freud saw all human behaviour as being rooted in *Eros*, the drive for 'bodily pleasure'. After the carnage of World War 1, he argued that behaviour was also directed by a drive for self-destruction (which has been called *Thanatos*).

The view that behaviour is controlled by unconscious motives has attracted much controversy and stimulated considerable theoretical and research interest. However, whether any (let alone all) behaviour is controlled by unconscious motives is difficult to assess because we cannot measure 'unconscious motivation' directly. So, whilst such motives might exist, we do not have direct evidence for them, and for this reason alone Freud's theory is not a plausible explanation of human motivation (see Chapters, 1, 30, 45, 53, 73 and 81).

Conclusions

This chapter has reviewed several theories of motivation. Some are primarily physiological whilst others lay greater emphasis on non-physiological factors. No single theory evidently offers a uniquely correct solution and in any given behaviour (such as hunger), supporting evidence can be found for one or more of the theories presented.

Summary

■ **Motives** are inner forces arousing and directing behaviour towards some goal. The study of motivation is the study of the **why** of behaviour.

■ Several different types of motive exist. **Biologically-based motives** are in-built body tissue needs (or 'drives') such as those for food, water, air, sleep, temperature regulation and pain avoidance.

■ **Sensation-seeking motives** are largely unlearned needs for increasing stimulation. They are most evident in conditions of sensory isolation or deprivation, and include activity, curiosity and exploration, manipulation, play, contact and control. When our freedom is threatened, **psychological reactance** occurs. Repeated negative experiences/loss of control can result in **learned helplessness**.

■ Complex **psychosocial motives** are learned and unrelated to body needs. They include the needs for achievement, affiliation, power and approval.

■ **Instinct theories** explain motivation in terms of innate dispositions. James identified human psychosocial needs whilst McDougall identified 20 basic biological instincts such as hunger and sex. Attempts to identify instincts stopped being useful when they merely acted as descriptive labels for the behaviours they were inferred from.

■ **Ethologists** replaced 'instinct' with **fixed action pattern**, and recognised the role played by environmental stimuli. **Sociobiologists** argue that innate patterns play a crucial role in complex human behaviours, and all animal behaviour is motivated by 'the selfish gene'.

■ Psychologists replaced 'instinct' with 'drive'. Two major approaches are **homeostatic drive theory** and **drive reduction theory**. Some homeostatic needs (e.g. oxygen intake) are involuntary and continuous and satisfied automatically. Tissue needs, however, are involuntary and discontinuous and cause a homeostatic drive which leads to an appropriate behaviour.

■ Drive reduction theory maintains that behaviour successful in reducing unpleasant drive states will be strengthened. However, whilst some behaviours are motivated by drives associated with tissue needs, the majority are not. Also, some behaviours try to increase rather than reduce drives, whilst others continue even when the drive has been apparently reduced. Drive theory cannot explain these findings.

■ Like drive theory, **optimum level of arousal** (OLA) **theory** proposes that arousal is sometimes reduced by decreasing stimulation. Unlike drive theory, however, OLA theory proposes that we sometimes try to increase stimulation. Unfortunately OLA cannot be measured, except in a circular way.

■ **Incentive (or expectancy) theory** sees the expectation of a desirable environmental goal as 'pulling' us towards it. The expectation of an undesirable goal has the opposite effect. The value placed on a goal is also important. A distinction can be made between **intrinsic** and **extrinsic rewards**. Sometimes, extrinsic rewards can reduce the intrinsic enjoyment of certain behaviours.

■ **Opponent-process theory** proposes that every emotional experience triggers an opposite emotional experience which persists longer, is more intense, and reduces the primary emotion's intensity. Drug addiction and other acquired motives which develop over time can be explained in opponent-process ways.

■ **Maslow's hierarchy of needs** places physiological needs at the bottom and **self-actualisation** at the top. Maslow distinguishes between behaviours related to survival or deficiency needs (**D-motives**) and those relating to self-actualisation 'growth' or 'being' (**B-motives**). D-motives are a means to an end, whereas B-motives are intrinsically satisfying. Most people do not achieve self-actualisation but reach the hierarchy's top for brief periods called **peak experiences**.

■ Freud's belief that behaviour is controlled by **unconscious motivation** has attracted much interest. However, it is difficult to assess since unconscious motivation cannot be directly measured.

18

EMOTION AND THE BRAIN

Introduction and overview

The study of emotion has always occupied a prominent position in psychology, with much research devoted to identifying the brain structures involved in emotional experience. This chapter reviews some relevant research findings and begins by looking at data relating to the role played by the hypothalamus and the limbic system. After this, differences between the cerebral hemispheres with respect to the comprehension and communication of emotion are examined. The chapter ends by looking at findings related to sex differences, emotion and the brain.

The hypothalamus and emotion

Bard (1928) found that destroying parts of the cerebral cortex in cats and dogs resulted in a much lowered threshold of emotional excitation. For example, following *decortication* (removal of part or all of the cerebral cortex), a cat would present a typical picture of 'full-blown rage'. It hissed, growled, screamed and spat, arched its back, and displayed elevated heart rate and blood pressure. However, this aggression occurred in response to the slightest provocation and was poorly directed. For example, the responses occurred if the cat had its tail pinched *but* were directed at the ground in front of it rather than the source of the pinching.

Bard concluded that the cortex normally acts as an *inhibitor* of sub-cortical structures and that these structures were responsible for the production of emotional behaviour. The responses elicited by decorticated non-humans were called *sham rage* because they seemed to be the integrated expression of rage but without the awareness and persistence characteristic of normal emotion.

Bard discovered that the rage produced by removal of the cortex largely disappeared if the *hypothalamus* was also removed. The involvement of the hypothalamus in the full expression of emotional behaviour has been shown in many studies of non-humans. For example, destruction of the lateral hypothalamus produces a *quiet biting attack* (which does not appear to be accompanied by strong emotion and which ends when the prey ceases to move), whereas *affective attack* (the behaviours exhibited

by a decorticated cat and described above) is produced by stimulation in the region of the ventromedial nucleus of the hypothalamus. If the *dorsal* part of the hypothalamus is stimulated, a non-human makes frantic attempts to escape the cage in which it is housed, and displays physiological responses indicative of increased activity in the sympathetic branch of the ANS. If it is restrained, it will frequently attack in an attempt to escape.

As well as cats, such findings have also been obtained in rats, monkeys and several other non-humans. In humans, however, the picture is less clear. Sem-Jacobsen (1968) found that hypothalamic stimulation had little effect on emotional experiences, and studies of people with damage to the hypothalamus caused by disease have also reported little change in subjective emotional reactions. The hypothalamus, then, cannot be responsible for the experience of emotion, and it has also been found that it is not uniquely involved in organising emotional behaviour.

> **Box 18.1 Separating the hypothamalmus from the rest of the brain**
>
> Because large hypothalamic lesions will kill an animal by causing severe disruption to the endocrine system, special apparatus is needed to cut around the hypothalamus to sever all the connections between it and the rest of the brain, whilst leaving connections to the pituitary gland intact. Ellison & Flynn's (1968) technique involved two knives that could be rotated around the hypothalamus leaving it as an 'island' in the brain. However, even when the hypothalamus was separated from the rest of the brain, some kinds of aggressive behaviour could still be elicited in cats. These occurred in response to 'natural stimulation' (such as the sight of a mouse) and artificial electrical stimulation of other parts of the brain, although slightly higher levels of electrical current were necessary as compared with those before the isolation.

The limbic system and emotion

Klüver & Bucy (1937) conducted several studies investigating the effects of damage to the temporal lobes in monkeys. Essentially, they found five main consequences which together are known as the *Klüver–Bucy syndrome*. First, the monkeys ate any sort of food that was presented to them, including that which they had rejected prior to the operation, and displayed a tendency to put anything movable into their mouths (*hyperorality*). Second, they displayed *visual agnosia* which, as noted in Chapter 7, is the inability to recognise objects by sight. Third, the monkeys displayed increased, and often inappropriate, sexual activity (*hypersexuality*). A fourth consequence was that they became tamer and safer to handle. Finally, they seemed to display a complete lack of fear. For example, they would repeatedly put their fingers into the flame of a burning match.

Klüver and Bucy also investigated the effects of damage to the limbic system. Much of the early research into the limbic system was concerned with its role in olfaction. However, Klüver and Bucy showed that damage to the limbic system had effects on monkey's emotional behaviour. For example, as well as displaying increased sexuality, they also displayed decreased fearfulness and increased aggression towards one another. Researchers thus began to explore the possibility that limbic system structures may be responsible for emotional expression.

Klüver and Bucy noted that destruction of the *amygdala* (see page 40) made wild and ferocious monkeys tame and placid. Removing the amygdala of a monkey dominant in a social group, for example, caused it to lose its place in the dominance hierarchy when it returned to the colony. When the amygdala was lesioned, stimuli that would normally elicit an aggressive response failed to do so. Such effects were not confined to monkeys, and subsequent research showed that lesions to the amygdala in species such as the rat, wolverine and lynx also resulted in timidity and placidity.

In cats, the effects of electrical stimulation of the amygdala depend on the part stimulated. In one part, stimulation results in the cat arching its back, hissing and showing all the signs of preparing to attack. However, stimulation in another part results in the cat cowering in terror when caged with a small mouse. Of course, there is always a danger in generalising the results obtained with non-humans to human beings. However, some evidence suggests that the amygdala plays a similar role in humans.

Box 18.2   The case of Charles Whitman

Several years ago, Charles Whitman killed his wife and mother before making his way to the University of Texas. Once there, he killed 15 people he did not know and wounded another 24 before being killed himself by

the police. It seems that Whitman was aware of his aggressiveness since, just before he embarked on the killings, he wrote of the agony he was experiencing:

'I don't quite understand what compels me to type this letter ... I am supposed to be an average, reasonable and intelligent young man ... However, lately I have been a victim of many unusual and irrational thoughts ... I talked with a doctor once for about two hours and tried to convey to him my fears that I felt overcome (sick) by overwhelming violent impulses. After one session I never saw the doctor again and since then I have been fighting my mental turmoil alone, and seemingly to no avail. After my death I wish that an autopsy would be performed on me to see if there is any visible physical disorder.' (cited in Johnson, 1972)

An autopsy revealed a small tumour in Whitman's brain. Although the wounds caused by the police gun fire made it difficult to establish the tumour's precise location, it appeared to be in (or at least close to) the amygdala (Sweet *et al.*, 1969).

Klüver, Bucy and others' findings concerning the amygdala were instrumental in the development of *psychosurgery* (see Chapters 7 and 72). In a case study conducted by Mark & Ervin (1970), a young woman called Julia was admitted to hospital after committing, seemingly without any reason, twelve separate attacks on people. Tests suggested that Julia's amygdala was damaged, and her family agreed to surgeons conducting psychosurgery (in the form of a small lesion in the amygdala) to try and reduce her aggressive behaviour. In follow-up studies, Mark and Ervin reported that Julia's aggressive behaviour had been greatly reduced.

As noted in Chapter 7, psychosurgery has many ethical implications. The removal of *damaged* areas of the brain which consequently results in aggression being reduced raises little objection. However, in psychosurgery, brain tissue is removed without there being any direct evidence to suggest that the tissue was in some way damaged (Carlson, 1987).

Despite the ethical issues, some researchers have argued for psychosurgery's use on the grounds that it can produce beneficial effects (given the aim of *improving* rather than *controlling* a person's condition). Others, however, have argued that it is not ethically acceptable to affect behaviour by altering the structure and functioning of the brain. For Breggin (1973), if any country:

'ever falls into the hands of totalitarianism, the dictators will be behavioural scientists and the secret police will be armed with lobotomy and psychosurgery.'

Psychosurgery is discussed in detail in Chapter 72.

Box 18.3   The surgical treatment of emotional disturbances

'Case 34 was admitted and kept in (hospital) ... He was a young man of 25 years ... admitted because he was always violent. He was constantly aggressive and destructive. He could not be kept in general wards and had to be nursed in an isolated cell. It was difficult to establish any sort of communication with him. *Bilateral stereotaxic amygdalectomy* was performed. Following the operation he was very quiet and could be safely left in the general wards. He started answering questions in slow syllables.' (Balasubramamiam *et al.*, 1970)

Balasubramamiam *et al.*'s method of assessing the effectiveness of psychosurgery on the hyperactive or violent behaviour of their patients is presented below (after Carlson, 1977):

Grade	Criteria
A	There is no need of any drug. Patient is able to mingle with others.
B	Very much docile and given to occasional outbursts only.
C	Manageable when given drugs although not leading a useful life.
D	Transient improvement.
E	No change.
F	Died.

According to these criteria, 'Case 34' would be graded as an 'A'. Do you think the patient was cured as a result of psychosurgery or does 'manageability' seem to be the important criterion? Should there be a category for patients whose condition is made *worse* by psychosurgery? (See Chapter 85)

Calder *et al.* (cited in Spinney, 1997b) report the case of D.R., a woman in her early 50s who has suffered from severe epilepsy since the age of 28. D.R. had an operation to treat her epilepsy, which resulted in total destruction of the left amygdala and partial destruction of the right. She seems unable to differentiate whether people are happy, angry or sad from the tone of their voices, and incapable of detecting facial expressions of emotion. Such findings are consistent with the view that the amygdala interprets emotional signals regardless of their source.

D.R. evidently cannot appraise dangerous situations and consequently shows no sense of fear. For example, she finds it difficult to understand television programmes where the plot involves fear or danger, and on one occasion came close to putting her hand into a pot of boiling water before being stopped by her husband. Her response was to shrug the incident off and laugh. D.R. is not

unique, and in other cases where the amygdala has been damaged (through, for instance, encephalitis), similar effects have been observed (Young, 1997).

Another part of the limbic system, the *septum*, has also been implicated in emotional behaviour. Brady & Nauta (1953) found that lesions in the septum resulted in the lowering of a rat's 'rage threshold'. For example, if a person approached the cage in which a septally lesioned rat was housed, it showed signs of extreme emotional arousal such as screaming and jumping wildly. If a person placed a hand into the cage, the rat would launch a vicious attack on it. However, in mice, a septal lesion produces an increase in 'flight' behaviour rather than 'affective rage'. In rats, increased emotionality gradually subsides until within a few weeks it is all but absent. In mice, hyperemotionality remains indefinitely (Carlson, 1977).

As well as these differences, it has been shown that most other non-humans do *not* display emotionality as a result of a septal lesion. Thus, making *general* statements about the septum's role in emotional behaviour is not possible since the effects of lesions apparently depend on the species studied.

On the basis of data obtained from non-human studies and his own investigations of brain-damaged people, Papez (1937) proposed that a complex set of interconnected pathways and centres in the limbic system underlies emotional experience. The *Papez circuit* (see Figure 18.1) forms a closed loop running from the *hippocampus* to the *hypothalamus* and from there to the *anterior thalamus*. The circuit continues via the *cingulate gyrus* and the *entorhinal cortex* back to the hippocampus.

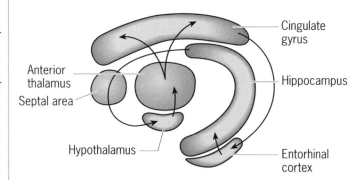

Figure 18.1   The Papez circuit

Unfortunately, Papez's proposals have not stood the test of careful anatomical study. MacLean (1949) modified the circuit and suggested that the amygdala and hippocampus play a central role in the mediation of aggression but the cingulate gyrus does not. Whilst the

Papez–MacLean limbic model has been influential, researchers have cautioned against the idea that there are specific 'emotion centres' (especially 'aggression centres') in the brain, since the brain is not neatly organised into structures that correspond to categories of behaviour.

One who has claimed evidence for an 'aggression centre' is Delgado (1969), whose research was briefly described in Chapter 6 (see Box 6.3, page 52). In a much-publicised demonstration, Delgado showed that stimulating a charging bull's limbic system resulted in the bull stopping in its tracks. However, Valenstein (1973) challenged Delgado's interpretation of his results. After watching film of Delgado's demonstration, Valenstein noted that the bull always circled to the right when Delgado stimulated its brain. Rather than being pacified as a result of the stimulation, Valenstein argues that the bull was simply 'confused' and 'frustrated' and just gave up!

Research has begun to clarify the role that limbic system structures play in emotional behaviour. Much of this has concentrated on the amygdala, and it has been found that the amygdala has direct connections with sensory channels (Connor, 1998). According to LeDoux (1989), when the amygdala receives sensory information, an emotional response can be elicited independently of the cortex. This has been called a pre-cognitive emotional response since it occurs without the cortex having made any appraisal of the appropriateness of a particular emotional response.

Perhaps you have had the experience of someone creeping up on you. On turning round, your initial response is to jump (and perhaps scream), but when the cortex appraises the situation and recognises the person as someone you know, your initial emotional response disappears (sometimes to be replaced by another response – anger!). LeDoux suggests that we can view the initial emotional response as being mediated by the amygdala which acts as a sort of 'early warning system' and allows us to experience emotion without cognition. The cortex then assesses the situation and determines whether the 'system' is responding appropriately or inappropriately.

Box 18.4 Disgust, bad tastes, and the cerebral cortex

Using MRI, it has been found that the sensation of disgust also activates the cortical areas used to recognise unpleasant tastes. Such a finding suggests that disgust (which comes from Latin words meaning 'bad taste') has evolved in higher brain functions as a way of avoiding potentially harmful contamination, especially by decayed food. (From *The Times*, 6 October, 1997)

The cerebral hemispheres and emotion

Since the development of PET and other non-invasive methods of investigating the brain, it has been possible to investigate the activity occurring in the brain during a task's performance (see Chapter 6). As noted in Chapter 9, evidence suggests that the two cerebral hemispheres are not functionally symmetrical but are specialised for the performance of different tasks.

In a case study reported in 1908, a mentally disturbed woman repeatedly tried to choke herself with her left hand. As she did this, her right hand would try to pull the left away from her throat. As well as this self-destructive behaviour, the woman engaged in other destructive behaviours such as ripping her bed pillows and tearing her sheets. However, she only did this with her left hand. After the woman died, a post-mortem was conducted. This revealed that her *corpus callosum* was badly damaged.

As was seen in Chapter 9, the corpus callosum connects the two cerebral hemispheres and allows them to exchange information so that each is aware of the other's activities. When the corpus callosum is surgically divided, the channel of communication is disrupted and the hemispheres are no longer in contact. In a sense, the woman described above was like a split-brain patient and, on the basis of her behaviour, it has been suggested that the two hemispheres might be different in terms of their comprehension and communication of emotion.

Box 18.5 Indifference and catastrophic reactions

Studies of brain damaged people have told us something about the role of the hemispheres in emotion. In Chapter 7 it was noted that damage to the motor area of the right hemisphere leads to paralysis of the body's left side. However, people with right hemisphere damage seem to be completely unmoved by this and continue to make plans as though they could walk normally. This is termed an *indifference reaction*. Damage to the motor area of the left hemisphere causes paralysis of the body's right side. Far from being unmoved by this, people with left hemisphere damage display a *catastrophic reaction*, that is, an episode of severe anxiety and depression which is probably a result of their awareness of the major damage the brain has suffered.

The findings described above suggest that the left and right hemispheres differ in terms of how they react to emotion-provoking stimuli. Because of the undamaged right hemisphere's catastrophic response to the consequences of damage to the left hemisphere, it seems reasonable to propose that the right hemisphere is specialised for recognising emotion-provoking stimuli and for organising the appropriate pattern of emotional responses. Equally, because of the left hemisphere's indifference reaction to the consequences of damage to the right, it seems reasonable to propose that the left hemisphere cannot recognise the emotional significance of this damage and continues to make plans without taking it into consideration. As noted, the left hemisphere is *aware* of the damage, but it does not seem to be 'bothered' by it.

Studies of people with normally functioning left and right hemispheres have *generally* confirmed that the hemispheres do differ in terms of their reactivity to emotion-provoking stimuli. Ley & Bryden (1979) showed participants drawings of faces displaying different emotional expressions. The drawings were presented one at a time to either the left or right hemisphere, using a modified version of the method employed with split-brain patients which enables information to be presented to one hemisphere only (see page 75). After a drawing had been displayed, it was replaced by another which was shown in the centre of the visual field. This meant that it was perceived by both hemispheres. The participants had to decide whether the emotion displayed in the second picture was the same as, or different from, the emotion displayed in the first.

When the drawings displayed *clear* emotional states (such as a big smile), fewer recognition errors were made by the right hemisphere. When the drawing displayed no emotion or a 'mild' emotional state, there was no difference in recognition between the hemispheres. These findings suggest that the right hemisphere has a definite advantage in the recognition of clear or strong facial expressions of emotion. This also appears to be the case when emotions are expressed *paralinguistically*, that is, utterances which convey their meaning in terms of voice tone, emphasis, pausing, and so on (compare the 'Ooh' produced by a soccer crowd when a player makes a valiant effort to score with the 'Ooh' produced when an open goal is missed).

It was noted earlier on that damage to the right hemisphere results in an indifference reaction from the left and, as has just been seen, the right hemisphere seems to be better than the left at recognising facial and paralinguistic expressions of emotion. To suggest that the left hemisphere is completely non-emotional would, however, be incorrect (Davidson, 1992).

Box 18.6   The left hemisphere and positive emotions

Several studies indicate that the left hemisphere is more active during the experience of *positive* emotions. For example, research using PET has indicated that when people are given 'good' news, asked to think about 'positive' events, or required to discriminate happy faces from neutral ones, the left hemisphere is more active than the right (Tomarken & Davidson, 1994; Gur *et al.* 1994). By contrast, the right hemisphere is more active when people are given 'bad' news or asked to think about 'negative' events (and recall from page 148 that the woman who engaged in destructive behaviour did so only with her right-hemisphere-controlled left hand).

Support for the left/right, positive/negative distinction comes from studies of clinically depressed people which show a tendency for the frontal lobes of the right hemisphere to be more active (Miller, 1987).

The different areas of the cortex *within* the right hemisphere may also play slightly different roles. Ross (1981), for example, describes several examples of people with damage to the frontal lobe of the right hemisphere who had difficulty in *producing* facial gestures and tone of voice to express emotion. However, their ability to *recognise* other people's emotional expression appeared to be unaffected. By contrast, people with damage to the right parietal/temporal lobe seemed to be able to produce emotional expressions but unable to recognise those expressed by other people. Damage to both the right frontal and parietal/temporal lobes resulted in the inability to both produce and recognise emotional expression.

There is an interesting similarity between Ross's (1981) findings and those described in Chapter 8 on the localisation and lateralisation of language. Whether there are discrete areas in the right hemisphere for the production and understanding of emotional expression which are analogous to Broca's and Wernicke's areas in the left hemisphere is an interesting possibility, but the findings reported by Ross need to be replicated by other researchers before we can begin to talk about the 'localisation and lateralisation of emotion'.

The apparently differential responses of the right and left hemispheres to positive and negative emotions has also led to much speculation. According to Sackheim (1982), the two hemispheres operate in a *reciprocal* manner with activity in one (caused by either a positive or negative emotion-provoking stimulus) producing reciprocal activity in the other. Such activity might function to ensure that an emotion was not experienced in an inappropriately intense way. Extremely excited reactions might, therefore, be due to the right hemisphere failing to reciprocate the activity in the left hemisphere, whilst extremely sad or angry reactions might result from the left hemisphere failing to reciprocate the activity in the right hemisphere. However, such speculations require considerable investigation to assess their worth.

Box 18.6   Dissocial (psychopathic) personality disorder and the hemispheres

Amongst other things, people with dissocial personality disorder are emotionally cold, superficially charming, and less responsive to facial cues of distress than non-dissocial people (Blair *et al.*, 1997). Day & Wong (1996) measured the time taken by dissocial and non-dissocial individuals to respond to negative emotional words presented to the left and right visual fields (and hence the right and left hemispheres respectively).

Whilst non-dissocial people show a right ('emotional') hemisphere advantage, dissocials exhibited no significant hemisphere advantage. The researchers had predicted the dissocials would show a left ('analytical') hemisphere advantage, so the findings did not completely support their hypotheses. However, the absence of a right hemisphere advantage does suggest differences between dissocials and non-dissocials in the processing of negative information.

Sex differences, emotion and the hemispheres

It has long been known that the average male brain weighs more than the average female brain. Broca, for example, found an average weight of 1235 grams for the 292 male brains he measured, whereas the 140 female brains he measured averaged 1144 grams. For Broca, (cited in Kohn, 1995),

> 'We might ask if the small size of the female brain depends exclusively on her body ... But we must not forget that women are, on the average, a little less intelligent than men, a difference we should not exaggerate but which is nonetheless real'.

Broca saw the smaller female brain as being due to both a 'physical inferiority' and an 'intellectual inferiority'. Although Broca was wrong in claiming that there are sex differences in intelligence (Kohn, 1995), the sexes do appear to differ in some respects (such as spatial ability and language ability – Kimura, 1993: but see Chapter 45). Physiological differences in men and women's brains have also been linked to differences in emotion.

Gur *et al.* (cited in Highfield, 1995a) used PET to study 51 healthy right-handed volunteers of whom 27 were men and 24 women. All participants were studied in a dimly-lit room and instructed to stay quiet and relaxed without closing their eyes or falling asleep. Brain metabolism between the sexes was identical in all regions except two. In the *temporal–limbic system*, metabolism was higher in men than women, whereas in the *cingulate gyrus* the reverse was true.

It has been hypothesised that the temporal–limbic system is associated with 'action-oriented' emotional responses such as sexual arousal and violence, whilst the cingulate gyrus is involved in 'symbolic' modes of expression. Gur *et al.* have proposed that their findings point to the possibility that men are more biologically inclined to express themselves physically (through, for example, aggressive behaviour) whilst women are biologically disposed to 'talk things through'.

We should, however, recognise that Gur *et al.s*' findings concern the brain *at rest*, and before firm conclusions can be drawn it needs to be shown that there are consistent differences between the sexes with respect to activity in the brain during the processing of emotion-provoking stimuli.

Conclusions

This chapter has looked at the role played by specific brain structures in the experience of emotion, and at hemisphere differences with respect to the communication and comprehension of emotion. It has also looked at how male and female brains might differ in terms of emotional expression. Unfortunately, simple conclusions cannot be drawn about any of the research described. The existence of 'emotional centres' (especially 'aggression centres') has yet to be completely supported by experimental evidence.

Summary

■ Bard found that decortication in cats and dogs produced a lower threshold of poorly directed emotional excitation in response to the slightest provocation **(sham rage)**. This suggests that the cortex normally inhibits sub-cortical structures which are actually responsible for emotional behaviour.

■ In non-humans, sham rage largely disappears if the hypothalamus is removed. Destruction of the lateral hypothalamus produces a **quiet biting attack** whilst stimulation near the ventromedial nucleus causes the sham rage (or affective attack) originally reported by

Bard. Stimulation of the dorsal hypothalamus produces aggressive escape behaviours and increased activity in the sympathetic branch of the ANS.

■ When the hypothalamus is separated from the rest of the brain, some kinds of aggressive behaviour are still elicited in cats. In humans, the role of the hypothalamus in emotion is less clear. Neither stimulation nor damage has much effect on subjective emotional reactions.

■ The **Klüver–Bucy syndrome** was first observed in monkeys and is the result of temporal lobe damage. The syndrome is characterised by hyperorality, visual agnosia, hypersexuality, placidity when handled, and a total lack of fear.

■ Damage to the limbic system in monkeys causes increased sexuality, decreased fear and increased aggression. Destruction of the amygdala changes wild and ferocious monkeys into tame and placid ones. Similar effects occur in other species. Electrical stimulation of part of the amygdala in cats causes preparation for attack. Stimulation of a nearby area causes cats to experience fear, even when caged with a small mouse.

■ Damage to the amygdala in humans is also associated with increased aggressiveness. Lesioning of the amygdala has been used to control violent behaviour, although the use of such surgery raises serious ethical issues. The amygdala evidently functions to interpret emotional signals regardless of their source. In rare cases of damage to the amygdala in humans, the individual appears unable to appraise dangerous situations and consequently shows no signs of fear.

■ The amygdala has direct connections with sensory channels, allowing emotional responses to be elicited independently of the cortex (**pre-cognitive emotional response**). This acts as an 'early warning system', after which the cortex appraises the appropriateness of an emotional response.

■ Lesions in the rat septum lowers the 'rage threshold' for a brief period. In mice, lesions produce an increase in 'flight' behaviour which remains indefinitely. In other species, however, emotionality does not follow septal lesions.

■ The **Papez circuit** is a closed loop in the limbic system which may underlie emotional experience. However, anatomical study has failed to confirm the circuit's existence. The **Papez–MacLean limbic model** sees the amygdala and hippocampus as being of major importance. However, the brain might not actually have specific aggression centres as some researchers have claimed.

■ Damage to the motor area of the right hemisphere produces left-side paralysis, but an affected person often displays an **indifference reaction** to this. Damage to the left hemisphere produces a **catastrophic reaction** to the paralysis and brain damage. This suggests that the right hemisphere is specialised for recognising emotion-provoking stimuli and for organising an appropriate pattern of emotional responses. Although the left hemisphere is aware of the damage to the right, it continues to make plans without allowing for this.

■ When facial or paralinguistic expressions of emotion are presented to the left and right hemispheres of people with intact brains, the right hemisphere is better able to recognise these. However, the left hemisphere is more active when people experience positive emotions, and the right more active when negative emotions are experienced. Different areas of the right hemisphere may control the production of emotional reactions and their recognition, and the hemispheres may work in a reciprocal way.

■ Dissocial personalities do not show the right hemisphere advantage for the processing of negative emotional words that non-dissocials exhibit. This absence suggests that dissocials process information differently from non-dissocials.

■ Sex differences have been reported in metabolism in the temporal–limbic system and the cingulate gyrus, with males showing higher levels in the former and females higher levels in the latter. The **temporal–limbic system** may be involved in 'action-oriented' emotional responses such as sexual arousal and violence. The **cingulate gyrus** may be involved in 'symbolic' modes of emotional expression such as 'talking things through'.

19

THEORIES OF EMOTION

Introduction and overview

Some theories of emotion attempt to explain how emotion-provoking events produce subjective emotional experiences. Others attempt to explain how emotions develop. This chapter critically considers theories of *emotional experience*. In everyday language, we use the words 'emotions' and 'feelings' interchangably. However, 'feelings' are but one element of an emotion, and it is possible to identify four integral components of human emotions. These are *subjective feelings*, *cognitive processes*, *physiological arousal* and *behavioural reactions*. The relationship between these components, and the relative emphasis given to one or more of them, distinguishes the various theories.

The chapter begins by looking at two theories which emphasise the role of physiological factors in emotion. We then consider two approaches which emphasise the role of non-physiological factors, in the form of cognitive processes, as important determinants in emotional experience.

The James–Lange theory

Common sense tells us that bodily changes (such as crying) occur because an emotion-arousing stimulus (receiving bad news) produces an emotion (feeling sorry). However, James and, independently, Lange offered a theory running counter to common sense. According to the *James–Lange theory* of emotion, emotional experience is the result rather than the cause of bodily and/or behavioural changes to some emotion-provoking stimulus.

Box 19.1   James on emotion

According to James:

'The bodily changes follow directly the perception of the exciting fact, and ... our feelings of the same changes as they occur is the emotion. Common sense says that we ... are sorry, and weep. The hypothesis to be defended here says that this order of sequence is incorrect, that the one mental state is not immediately induced by the other and that the bodily manifestations must first be interposed between. The more rational statement is that we feel sorry because we cry'.

When we experience some stimulus, then, physiological reactions and behavioural responses occur, and trigger the emotional experience. For the James–Lange theory, emotions are a *by-product* (or *cognitive representation*) of automatic physiological and behavioural responses.

James and Lange argued that the brain receives *sensory feedback* from the body's internal organs *and* parts that respond to emotion-provoking stimuli. The feedback the brain receives is recognised and then labelled appropriately. Although running counter to common sense, you might be able to think of a situation in which you reacted in a fairly automatic way. An example would be slipping down the stairs and grabbing the bannisters. Only when you had stopped yourself would you become aware of feeling frightened, as though the sudden change in your behaviour *caused* the fear, quite apart from *why* you grabbed the bannisters.

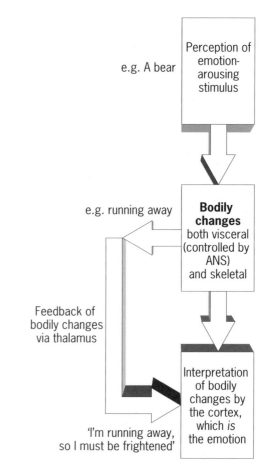

Figure 19.1   The James–Lange theory of emotion

Because it was counter-intuitive, the theory received much attention. Cannon (1927) identified three major problems. The first concerned the pattern of physiological activity fed back to the brain. Cannon argued that each emotion would need its own distinct pattern of activity otherwise the cortex would not be able to 'determine' which emotion should be experienced. Many studies have found distinct patterns of physiological activity associated with different emotional states. However, many other studies have reported the absence of such differences.

Ax (1953) and Schwartz *et al.* (1981) are amongst those who reported data supportive of the James–Lange theory. They showed that emotions like fear, anger, happiness, and sadness are different in terms of heart rate and body temperature, muscular activity in the face, blood pressure, and neural activity in the frontal lobes.

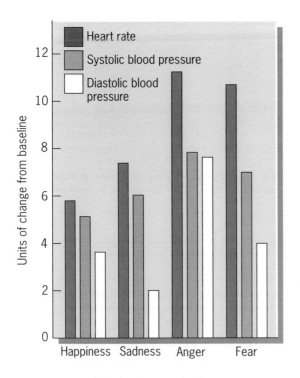

Figure 19.2   Data reported by Schwartz *et al.* (1981) concerning physiological changes when participants recall particular emotion-provoking events

Wolf & Wolff (1947) and Mandler (1962) have supported Cannon's criticisms by showing that different people may display different patterns of physiological activity when experiencing the same emotion, and that the same person may respond differently when experiencing the same emotion on several occasions.

Cannon also argued that James and Lange were wrong to propose that physiological changes themselves produce changes in emotional states. This criticism was based on Marañon's (1924) study in which participants were injected with *adrenaline* which increases ANS activity. Following the injection, participants were asked to describe their emotional state. Most reported a physical change with *no* emotional overtones, and those who did report a change described it as an 'as if' change in emotional state rather than an actual change.

Cannon's third criticism was that total separation of the viscera from the CNS did *not* result in the absence of emotional experience (the James–Lange theory predicts that emotional experience *would* be absent in such conditions). Cannon based this criticism on his own and other researchers' findings indicating that when visceral feedback was abolished in dogs and cats, emotional experience was not affected. However, apart from the fact that we do not know about the emotional experiences of non-humans, Cannon seems to have ignored James's views about the body, and in particular the *muscles*, as well as the viscera. Even if visceral feedback were abolished, an animal would still receive feedback from the muscles and this might contribute to some sort of emotional experience.

If feedback from the internal organs through the ANS were important, then humans with spinal cord damage would not be capable of experiencing emotion of the same intensity they experienced before the damage (if, indeed, they experienced *any* sort of emotion). Hohmann (1966) studied several patients with spinal cord injuries. Some had damaged relatively low portions of the spinal cord which meant that feedback from the internal organs still reached the brain through the higher undamaged portions. Others had spinal cord damage much further up and received little or no information from the internal organs (see page 44).

Box 19.2   Hohmann's study

Hohmann asked his patients to recall an event that had aroused fear, anger, grief, or sexual excitement before their injury and a comparable event that had occurred after it. As measured by self-reports of emotional intensity, there was a diminishing of emotional experience for events after the injury. Also, the higher up the spinal cord the injury was, the less intense were the emotional experiences reported in terms of their *feelings* but not necessarily their *behaviours*. As one patient put it:

'I was at home alone in bed and dropped a cigarette where I couldn't reach it. I finally managed to scrounge around and put it out. I could have burnt up right there, but the funny thing is, I didn't get all shook up about it. I just didn't feel afraid at all, like you would suppose. Now I don't get a feeling of physical animation, it's a sort of cold anger. Sometimes I cry when I see some injustice. I yell and cuss and raise hell, because if you don't do it sometimes I've learned people will take advantage of you, but it doesn't have the heat that it used to. It's a mental kind of anger'. (Reported in Hohmann, 1966)

Hohmann's data cast doubt on Cannon's criticism. However, Hohmann's and other studies finding similar effects (e.g. Jasnos & Hakmiller, 1975) have been criticised on the grounds that they are liable to experimenter and social desirability effects, and the possibility that patients might suppress their feelings as a way of coping with their extreme circumstances (Trieschmann, 1980). Generously, the findings concerning the lack of emotional response in the absence of visceral feedback can be seen as supporting the James–Lange theory, but the potential methodological shortcomings in supportive studies should be acknowledged.

Despite the criticisms levelled at it, the James–Lange theory has stood the test of time remarkably well. In discussing its relevance, James (1890) suggested that it had practical importance as well. Since emotions are no more than the perception of physiological and behavioural responses, we could:

' ... conquer undesirable emotional tendencies ... by assiduously, and in the first instance cold-bloodedly, going through ... the *outward movements* of those contrary dispositions which we prefer to cultivate'.

For James, then, by smiling at someone who makes us angry our anger would eventually disappear. It is generally agreed that emotional states are *reflected* by our facial expressions, but some researchers believe that the reverse may be true as well. Tomkins (1962) has argued that specific facial displays are *universally* associated with neural programmes linked to various emotions.

Certainly, some facial expressions of emotion seem to be recognised by people in all cultures irrespective of their experiences, and studies which induce people to express facially a particular emotion (smiling, for example) are associated with self-reported changes in emotional state and distinct patterns of physiological activity (as Schwartz *et al.*'s study showed – see page 153) comparable to those that occur during actual emotional experiences.

Facial feedback theory argues that facial expressions can *produce* changes in emotional state as well as mirror them. As

James suggested, we do seem to feel happier when we smile, sadder when we frown, and so on. In several studies people have been asked to imagine a pleasurable event such as winning a large sum of money or an unpleasurable event such as being placed in a fear-provoking situation. Then, they are asked to enhance or suppress tension in certain facial muscles. Consistent with facial feedback theory, subjective reports of emotional experience have been shown to change (McCanne & Anderson, 1987).

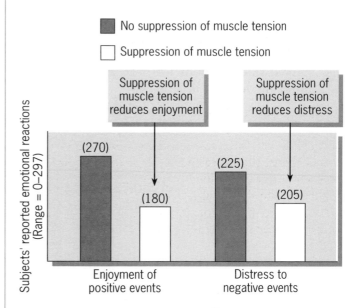

Figure 19.3   Data reported by McCanne & Anderson (1987) supporting the facial feedback hypothesis

Contraction of the facial muscles apparently heightens physiological arousal and this possibly leads us to report changes in perceived emotional state. It has been proposed that contraction of the facial muscles affects blood flow to the brain and this influences the release of serotonin and noradrenaline which are believed to play a role in emotion (see Chapter 69). However, irrespective of the mechanisms involved, it is not hard to see how facial feedback theory could have applications as a potential treatment for certain emotional disorders.

There is, of course, a danger in exaggerating the claims from any area of research. Critics of facial feedback theory have identified several methodological problems with some studies (such as the possibility that the participants' expectations and distracting elements in the experimental setting may affect their emotional states), and while research may show statistically significant effects, these could be *behaviourally* insignificant. Nonetheless, the possibility that the British 'stiff upper lip' may influence our emotional experiences cannot be entirely ruled out!

The Cannon–Bard thalamic theory

As shown in the previous section, Cannon did not believe that different emotions are associated with different patterns of physiological and bodily activity. He saw all emotions as producing the *same* pattern of responses which correspond to the *fight-or-flight* response (see page 44) which prepares us to deal with an emergency. According to Cannon and Bard, external stimuli activate the *thalamus* which sends sensory information to the cortex for interpretation, and simultaneously sends *activation messages* through the PNS to the viscera and skeletal muscles.

The Cannon–Bard theory claims that information sent to the cortex produces the sensations of emotion at the same time as physiological and behavioural responses are produced. However, these are seen as being *independent* of one another. Thus, the experience of emotion neither causes nor is a result of physiological and behavioural responses. Heightened physiological and behavioural activity occurs in response to the emotion-provoking stimulus rather than the experience of emotion it produces.

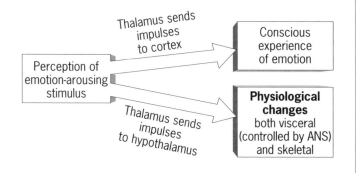

Figure 19.4   The Cannon–Bard thalamic theory of emotion

The claim that physiological and bodily activity is a 'side-effect' of emotion and plays no role in it is, as was seen earlier on, not supported by the evidence. Also, Cannon was almost certainly wrong to ascribe a central role to the thalamus. As noted in Chapter 18, other brain structures, principally the hypothalamus and limbic system, appear to be much more directly involved in emotional experience. However, despite the theory's limitations, it does at least highlight the important role played by the brain in emotional responses.

Schachter's theory

According to Schachter (1964), Cannon was wrong in believing that bodily changes and emotional experiences are independent. He also saw the James–Lange theory as being mistaken in its claim that changes in physiological activity cause emotional experience. Schachter's theory proposes that emotional experience depends on two factors. The first is physiological arousal in the ANS. The second is the *cognitive appraisal* (or interpretation) of the physiological arousal.

Thus, like James and Lange, Schachter sees arousal as preceding emotional experience and being necessary for it. However, physiological arousal itself is not sufficient. If an emotion is to be experienced, the arousal must be appraised in an emotional way. In Marañon's study, (see page 153) the participants had a clear explanation for their physiological arousal, namely the injections they were given. For Schachter, it is hardly surprising they did not report emotional experiences because their cognitive appraisals of the heightened physiological activity could be explained in a non-emotional way.

Schachter argues that the degree of arousal determines an emotion's intensity, provided that arousal is interpreted in an emotional way. The interpretation itself determines the emotion that is experienced. Notice how different this is from the James–Lange theory. That theory sees each emotional state as being determined by a *different* pattern of physiological activity. Schachter's theory assumes that the same physiological changes underlie all emotions and that it is the *meaning* attributed to them that generates different emotions. Because the theory proposes arousal *and* cognition as the central elements in emotional experience, it is sometimes referred to as the *two-factor theory of emotion*.

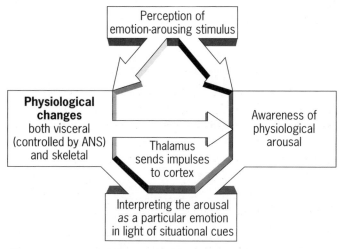

Figure 19.5   Schachter's theory of emotion

Schachter tested his theory in an ingenious experiment (Schachter & Singer, 1962). Male college students were informed that they would be participating in an experiment looking at the effects of the vitamin compound 'Suproxin' on vision, and that this would necessitate them receiving vitamin injections. In fact, they were given injections of *epinephrine* (or *adrenaline*), a hormone that causes an increase in heart rate, respiration rate, blood pressure, and produces muscle tremors (see page 47).

Participants in the *epinephrine-informed condition* were told of these effects, whilst participants in the *epinephrine-misinformed condition* were given *false* information about epinephrine's effects. These participants were told that the injection would cause 'itching', 'facial numbness' and a 'headache'. In a third (*epinephrine-ignorant*) condition, participants were given no information at all about the injection's effects. Participants in a *control condition* were injected with a saline solution, which did not cause changes in physiological activity, and were told nothing about this injection's effects.

After receiving his injection, the participant was taken to a 'waiting room' before supposedly having his vision tested. Once there, he was introduced to another 'participant' (actually a 'stooge') who was part of the experimental set-up. With some participants, the stooge pretended to fill out a questionnaire, a copy of which was also given to the genuine participant to complete. As he completed the questionnaire, the stooge began to act 'angrily' and complain loudly about the personal nature of the questions it contained. After a while, he ripped up the questionnaire and stormed out of the room. With other participants, the stooge pretended to behave 'euphorically', according to a pre-determined script of behaviours, including making paper aeroplanes, throwing crumpled up paper into a basket, and generally 'messing around'.

Box 19.3   Hypothesised effects of the various manipulations in Schachter & Singer's (1962) experiment

Epinephrine-informed condition: These participants have been told of the real effects the 'vitamin' injection will have. Whilst they will show increases in physiological arousal, they will interpret this in a non-emotional way because the effects they are experiencing are the effects they have been told to expect. Factor 1 (arousal) is present, but Factor 2 (cognitive appraisal in an emotional way) is not. Therefore, participants should not experience any change in their emotional states.

Epinephrine-misinformed condition: These participants have been given *false* information about the effects the 'vitamin' injection will have. An increase in physiological arousal will occur, but the participants will not be able to explain it in terms of the injection's effects, since the effects they are experiencing are not those they have been told to expect. Factor 1 (arousal) is present as is Factor 2 (cognitive appraisal potentially explaining the arousal in an emotional way). In the absence of a suitable non-emotional explanation for their arousal, participants would be expected to cognitively appraise their environment for a logical explanation and a suitable label for the arousal they are experiencing. In a room with somebody behaving 'angrily' or 'euphorically', the participant might conclude that he too was feeling angry or euphoric. Participants in this condition should experience change in their emotional states.

Epinephrine-ignorant condition: These participants have been given no information about the effects the 'vitamin' injection will have. Like participants in the epinephrine-misinformed condition, they will experience arousal and will have no obvious explanation for it since they have not been told that the injection will produce any change in their physiological activity. Since both Factor 1 (arousal) and Factor 2 (cognitive appraisal potentially explaining the arousal in an emotional way) are present, these participants too should experience changes in their emotional states.

Control condition: Participants in this condition have received 'vitamin' injections, but the substance they have been injected with produces no change in physiological activity (it is merely a saline solution). Therefore Factor 1 (arousal) is not present. Since arousal is necessary for the experience of emotion, participants should not show any change in their emotional states.

The participant's emotional responses were assessed by observers who watched through a one-way mirror and coded the responses according to a pre-determined schedule, which included the extent to which the stooge's behaviours were copied. At the end of the stooge's 'routine', the genuine participant was given a questionnaire to fill in that included questions about his emotional state. The results provided *some* support for Schachter's theory with participants showing emotional changes generally in line with the experimental predictions.

Thus, in the 'epinephrine-misinformed' and 'epinephrine-ignorant' conditions, participants appeared to use the stooge's behaviour as a cue for identifying and labelling their own emotional states, at least as regards the observers' measurements. Participants in the 'epinephrine-informed' condition had a ready explanation for their arousal and showed little change in their emotional states. The finding that participants' emotional states seemed to change irrespective of whether they were in the 'angry' or 'euphoric' condition is also important because it supports the view that the same type of physiological arousal can be associated with different emotions (recall James and Lange's view concerning different patterns of physiological activity being associated with different emotions).

Other research also supports Schachter's theory. In Dutton & Aron's (1974) experiment, participants were unsuspecting males aged between 18 and 35 who happened to be visiting the Capilano Canyon in British Columbia, Canada. Whilst they were on the extremely unstable suspension bridge 230 feet above the canyon, participants were interviewed by an attractive female who asked them questions as part of a survey she was allegedly conducting on reactions to scenic attractions. In a comparison condition, different participants were interviewed by the same female, but on a solid wooden bridge upstream of the canyon.

In both conditions, participants were asked to invent a short story about an ambiguous picture of a woman. This was later scored for amount of sexual content, taken to reflect a participant's sexual attraction towards the interviewer. Those interviewed on the suspension bridge (the 'high arousal' condition) invented stories with significantly more sexual imagery than those interviewed on the solid wooden bridge (the 'low arousal' condition). This study seems to confirm the view that the physiological arousal accompanying all emotions is similar, and that it is the interpretation of the arousal which is important, even though we may occasionally *misidentify* an emotional state. In this case, the participants seemed to mislabel their fear as sexual attraction towards the interviewer.

Box 19.4   Misattribution therapy

Findings such as those reported by Dutton and Aron have led to Schachter's theory being applied as a form of therapy. Although Schachter did not explicitly say so, his theory really identifies *two* cognitive components that must be present for emotion to be experienced (Reisenzein, 1983). First, cognitive appraisal must interpret the situation in an emotional way. Second this appraisal must 'connect up' (Gordon, 1978) with the arousal and be attributed to the emotional source.

In *misattribution therapy*, people are taught to attribute their arousal to some other source. For example, a therapist dealing with a person who is afraid of spiders might give that person a pill and tell him/her that the pill causes heightened physiological activity. When the person is in the presence of a spider, the heightened physiological activity occurring as a result of fear is attributed to the effects of the pill (even though the pill actually produces no effects). By misattributing increased physiological activity to the pill rather than the spider, it would not be labelled as 'fear'. After a programme of exposure to spiders under these conditions, spiders would become much less frightening to the person.

Schachter's influential theory has been described as a 'juke box' theory of emotion in which arousal is the coin we put into the juke box and cognition is the button we press to select an 'emotional tune'. However, although the theory highlights the important role played by cognition in the experience of emotion, we should be cautious about accepting it uncritically.

One important problem concerns the *replication* of the original findings reported by Schachter & Singer (1962). Some studies (e.g. Marshall & Zimbardo, 1979) have failed to report *any* effects of the arousal and cognition manipulations. Others (e.g. Maslach, 1978) have found different effects to those reported by Schachter and Singer. In her experiment, Maslach discovered that participants were less likely to imitate the stooge's behaviour and more likely to apply negative emotional labels to their arousal irrespective of the social situation in which they were placed.

Hilgard *et al.* (1979) have documented several specific criticisms concerning Schachter and Singer's original experiment. First, epinephrine does not affect everyone in exactly the same way. Indeed, Schachter and Singer actually eliminated from their analysis the data provided by five participants who later reported they experienced no physiological effects. When the data from these discarded participants are included in the analysis, the difference between conditions disappears! Second, Schachter and Singer omitted to assess the mood of the participants *before* they were given the injection. It is possible that a participant in a good mood to begin with might have responded more positively to the stooge irrespective of any injection. Third, some people are extremely afraid of injections. Schachter and Singer appear to have mistakenly assumed that receiving an injection is affectively neutral.

We should also note that everyday experience suggests that many of our emotions are triggered spontaneously and do not result from interpreting and labelling unexplained arousal. Some sorts of stimuli might produce the emotion of fear long before we have any opportunity to cognitively assess the reason for an increased heart rate.

A more complete theory of emotion, then, needs to take this consideration into account.

Lazarus's theory

Of several cognitively-oriented theories that use cognitive appraisal as a central component, the most well-known is that proposed by Lazarus (1982), who argues that some cognitive processing is an essential pre-requisite for the experience of emotion.

Box 19.5:   Lazarus on emotion

According to Lazarus:

'Emotion reflects a constantly changing person–environment relationship. When central life agendas (e.g. biological survival, personal and social values and goals) are engaged, this relationship becomes a source of emotion ... Cognitive activity is a necessary pre-condition of emotion because to experience an emotion, people must comprehend – whether in the form of a primitive evaluative perception or a highly differentiated symbolic process – that their well-being is implicated in a transaction, for better or worse'.

With some emotions, in some situations, cognitive appraisal occurs in a conscious, rational and deliberate way, and up to a point we are able to exercise conscious control over our emotions. However, the view that cognition has primacy over emotion has been disputed. Zajonc (1984), for example, has argued that cognition and emotion operate as independent systems. He believes that in certain circumstances an emotional response may *precede* the onset of cognition and, in other circumstances, an emotional response may occur in the *absence* of any type of cognitive appraisal. For example, when we meet a person for the first time, we often form a positive or negative impression even though we have processed very little information about that person. In Zajonc's view, we have evolved the capacity to detect affective qualities *without* cognitive mediation (see LeDoux's, 1989, research described on page 148).

Lazarus, however, disagrees and argues that primitive emotional responses (such as fear) might not involve any conscious processing, but certainly do involve rapid and unconscious appraisal (and as illustrated in the quote above, Lazarus uses the term *primitive evaluative perception* to describe this). Zajonc has also been criticised on the grounds that some of the things he identifies as emotional states are not emotional states at all. One of these, 'startle', is essentially a *reflex* response, and Lazarus would

not disagree with the view that it occurs in the absence of any cognitive appraisal!

In support of Lazarus, Ekman *et al.* (1985) have noted that whilst 'startle' is a response to a sudden loud noise which is produced automatically in *all people*, there is no known stimulus which reliably produces the same emotion in everybody. As Eysenck & Keane (1990) have noted:

> 'There is no doubt that Lazarus's studies have far more direct relevance to everyday emotional experiences than do those of Zajonc. This provides grounds for assuming (albeit tentatively) that emotional experience is generally preceded by cognitive processes, even if that is not invariably the case'.

Conclusions

This chapter has critically considered theories of emotional experience. Whilst some are almost certainly untrue, others have evidence which generally supports their claims. However, at present there is no single comprehensive theory of emotional experience. Nor, perhaps, are we ever likely to have one. Ethical considerations preclude inducing strong emotions as part of psychological research. Whilst we can ask participants to make facial expressions corresponding to a particular emotion, we cannot expect them to actually experience strong emotions. Only those situations which are motivationally relevant for a person can reliably produce strong emotions, and it would be unethical to create these in laboratory settings.

Summary

■ The four integral components of emotion are subjective feelings, cognitive processes, physiological arousal and behavioural reactions. The relationship between these, and emphasis placed on them, distinguishes theories of emotional experience.

■ The **James–Lange theory** proposes that emotional experience is the result, rather than cause, of bodily/behavioural changes to an emotion-arousing stimulus. Emotions are therefore a by-product (or cognitive representation) of automatic physiological and behavioural responses. The theory proposes that sensory feedback from the internal organs and viscera is sent to the brain, which labels this feedback as a particular emotion.

■ Some studies have found that different patterns of physiological activity are associated with different emotions. However, others have failed in this respect, and indicate that different people show different physiological activity when experiencing the same emotion, and that the same person can show different physiological reactions when experiencing the same emotion on different occasions. In other respects, the James–Lange theory has sometimes been supported and sometimes not.

■ One implication of the theory is that changes in facial expression may induce changes in emotional state and physiological activity. This **facial feedback theory** is supported by experimental evidence, and plausible mechanisms to account for emotional changes have been advanced. However, there are methodological problems associated with research in this area.

■ The **Cannon–Bard thalamic theory** of emotion proposes that external stimuli activate the thalamus, which sends sensory information to the cortex for interpretation and simultaneously, but independently, sends activation messages to the viscera and skeletal muscles. In this theory, emotional experience neither causes, nor is caused by, physiological/behavioural responses. However, there is no evidence to support the theory, and it is unlikely that the thalamus plays a central role in emotion.

■ Schachter's **two-process theory** of emotion sees physiological arousal in the ANS as being a necessary but not sufficient condition for emotional experience. For an emotion to be experienced, the arousal must be interpreted in an emotional way. The same physiological changes underlie all emotions, but the meaning attributed to them determines the emotion experienced.

■ Schachter and Singer tested this theory in an experiment in which participants' arousal levels and their likely explanations for the arousal were manipulated.

The results provided some support for the theory, as have studies conducted by other researchers.

■ The **misattribution of arousal** has been used therapeutically. In **misattribution therapy**, people are taught to attribute their arousal to a source other than the one causing it. Therapists direct arachnophobics, for example, to attribute the arousal that occurs when they come into contact with a spider to a pill given to them by the therapist.

■ Despite its influence, Schachter's theory has been criticised. Importantly, researchers have been unable to replicate the findings from the original experiment. Other criticisms relating to methodology have also been made, all of which cast doubt on the theory.

■ A further criticism is that many emotions are triggered spontaneously, and do not arise from interpreting and labelling unexplained arousal. The possibility that some stimuli elicit emotions before there is opportunity to cognitively assess physiological change has been addressed by Lazarus.

■ Lazarus proposes that some cognitive processing is a prerequisite for emotional experience, and that sometimes this occurs in a conscious, rational and deliberate way. This view that cognition has primacy over emotion has been disputed by Zajonc.

■ Zajonc claims that cognition and emotion operate independently, so that an emotional response sometimes precedes cognition or occurs in the absence of cognitive appraisal. Lazarus claims that emotional responses such as fear may not involve conscious appraisal, but do involve primitive evaluative perception. However, Lazarus and Zajonc agree that reflex emotional responses (such as the universal startle response) do not involve cognitive appraisal.

20

STRESS

Introduction and overview

Many years ago, Selye (1936) conducted experiments aiming to discover a new sex hormone. In one, rats were injected with ovary tissue extracts. This caused the adrenal cortex to enlarge, the thymus gland to shrink, and ulcers in the stomach and small intestine. Since no known hormone produced such effects, Selye believed he had discovered a new one. However, when he injected extracts from other tissues or toxic fluids that did not come from tissues, the results were identical.

Instead of abandoning his research, Selye changed direction. As he noted:

'it suddenly struck me that one could look at [the experiments] from an entirely different angle. [Perhaps] there was such a thing as a non-specific reaction of the body to damage of any kind' (Selye, 1976).

Later, he showed that when rats were exposed to adverse conditions like extreme cold, fatigue, electric shocks, or surgical trauma, the same pattern of physiological responses occurred.

Although Selye's research was undertaken on non-humans, he pioneered research into stress. This chapter looks at what stress is, and at theory and research findings concerning its effects on the body. It also examines the relationship between stress and illness, and some of the ways in which stress can be reduced and its impact on our health minimised.

What is stress?

Defining 'stress' is not easy. Physicists see stress as the pressure or force exerted on a body. Psychologists take a similar view, but look at stress in terms of its demands on an organism and the organism's efforts to adapt, cope, or adjust to them. An adequate definition of stress must, therefore, include the interaction between external *stressors* and physiological and psychological responses to them. It must also acknowledge the role of cognitive factors, since how a potential stressor is *appraised* influences its effects. Finally, since some stress (what Selye, 1980, terms *eustress*) is healthy and necessary to keep us alert, an adequate definition must also acknowledge that stress can be beneficial.

A generally accepted definition which meets these requirements has been offered by Lazarus & Folkman (1984). They define stress as:

'a pattern of negative physiological states and psychological responses occurring in situations where people perceive threats to their well-being which they may be unable to meet'.

The effects of stress on the body

As noted earlier, Selye's rats appeared to respond identically irrespective of the adverse conditions to which they were exposed. Selye concluded that the body's response to a stressor is *non-specific*, and when an organism is confronted with a stressor, the body mobilises for action to defend itself. If the stressor can be adequately managed, the body returns to its original state. However, if repeated or prolonged exposure to the stressor cannot be managed, the organism suffers tissue damage, increased susceptibility to disease and, in extreme cases, death.

THE GENERAL ADAPTATION SYNDROME

Selye called the non-specific response the *general adaptation syndrome* or GAS (also known as the *pituitary-adrenal stress syndrome*). The GAS consists of three distinct stages, representing an example of the interaction between the CNS, ANS and endocrine system.

The alarm reaction

The first stage, the *alarm reaction,* is triggered by the perception of a stressor. The body is mobilised for action. In the *shock phase,* the body initially responds with a drop in blood pressure and muscle tension. This very brief phase is replaced by the *counter-shock phase,* an alerting response to possible threat or physical injury. The bodily reactions in this phase are initiated by the hypothalamus and regulated by the sympathetic branch of the ANS and the endocrine system.

Box 20.1   Major processes occurring in the alarm reaction

The perception of a stressor results in the *hypothalamus*:

(a) releasing *corticotrophic-releasing hormone*. This stimulates the pituitary gland to secrete *adrenocorticotrophic hormone* (ACTH). ACTH acts on the adrenal cortex of the adrenal gland, causing it to enlarge and release corticosteroids. These help to fight inflammation and allergic reactions (e.g. difficulty in breathing);

(b) activating the sympathetic branch of the ANS. This causes the *adrenal medulla* to enlarge and release *adrenaline* and *noradrenaline* (the 'stress hormones'). This initiates a heightened pattern of physiological activity which includes:

- accelerated heart rate and increased blood pressure, which sends blood to parts of the body that will need it for strenuous activity;

- the release of glucose from the liver to provide fuel for quick energy;

- accelerated respiration rate to supply more oxygen to the muscles;

- a tensing of the muscles in preparation for an adaptive response (such as running away);

- an increase in blood coaguability so that blood will clot more quickly if injury occurs;

- perspiration to cool the body and allow more energy to be burned;

- curtailing digestion, which makes more blood available to the muscles and brain;

- the breaking down of some tissue to provide energy-giving sugars;

- the movement of blood from the internal organs to the skeletal musculature.

The physiological activity shown in Box 20.1 (which Cannon, 1927, termed the *fight-or-flight response* – see Chapters 5 and 19) cannot be maintained for long. If the stressor is removed, activity returns to baseline levels (although the noradrenaline released by the adrenal gland *prolongs* adrenaline's action, and so sympathetic arousal continues for a period even if the stressor is removed). However, if the stressor continues, then at some point the *parasympathetic branch* of the ANS is activated to try to slow down the internal organs (such as the heart).

The resistance stage

Although endocrine and sympathetic activities drop slightly, they are still higher than normal as the body continues to draw on its resources. This is the *resistance stage*. If the stressor can be adequately dealt with or is terminated, physiological damage is unlikely to be suffered. However, the action of corticosteroids aggravates the natural inflammatory reaction and the *immune system's* reaction to infection or physical damage is reduced. Additionally, the repair of cells which have a high turnover is inhibited. So, whilst an organism *appears* to be able to defend itself against the stressor, its body's resources are depleted because they are used faster than they are replaced.

The exhaustion stage

If the stressor continues, the adrenal glands enlarge and lose their stores of adrenal hormones. Tissues show signs of wear-and-tear, muscles become fatigued, and the endocrine glands, kidneys and other internal organs are damaged. This is the *exhaustion stage* and what Selye calls *diseases of adaptation* (or *stress-related illnesses*) occur here (see pages 163–166).

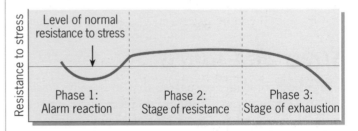

Figure 20.1   The three stages of the GAS and their relationship with levels of resistance to a stressor

Selye's GAS is a useful approach to the physiology of stress. However, his claim about the non-specific responses produced by stressors has been challenged. Some stressors produce patterns of physiological activity different from those of other stressors (Taylor, 1990). Also, Selye's GAS was based on non-humans' responses to stressors, and fails to consider *psychological factors* in the production of the stress response as well as the psychological effects of stressors.

Box 20.2   Psychological responses to a stressor

Stressors exert several effects on cognitive processes. Some of these are negative. For example, a person experiencing a stressor might be easily distracted from a task and perform poorly. However, and as Selye acknowledges, eustress can be beneficial, at least up to a point.

The *primary appraisal* of a stressor involves deciding whether it has positive, neutral or negative implications. If it is decided that the stressor has negative implications, it is assessed according to how challenging, threatening or harmful it is. After this, *secondary appraisal* occurs. This involves considering whether our abilities will allow us to overcome the challenge, threat or harm assessed earlier. The experience of stress depends on these two appraisals.

Stress is also associated with *negative emotional states*, including anger, hostility, embarrassment, depression, helplessness and anxiety. People who cannot cope effectively with anxiety are more susceptible to a variety of mental and physical disorders.

Stress affects *behaviour* in several ways. Some behaviours involve an attempt to confront the stressor whilst others involve withdrawing from it (and the terms 'fight' and 'flight' respectively can be used to describe these). Yet other behaviours involve attempts to adapt to the stressor by, for example, taking avoiding action whenever it occurs. All of these are attempts to manage or reduce the effects of stressors (see pages 164–167).

Stress and illness

A large body of evidence suggests that stress plays a *causal* role in certain types of illness. Indeed, stress may be involved in around 50–70 per cent of *all* physical illnesses (Frese, 1985). A link evidently exists between stress and headaches, asthma, cancer, cardiovascular disorders, hypertension and the malfunctioning of the immune system.

STRESS AND THE IMMUNE SYSTEM

The immune system helps to combat disease. When bacteria, viruses, and other hazardous foreign bodies (or *antigens*) are detected, the immune system stimulates white blood cells (or *leucocytes*) to seek and destroy them. It also produces *antibodies* which bind to antigens and identify them as targets for destruction, and forms a 'memory' of how to fight the antigens it encounters by maintaining them in the bloodstream.

Another role is in *inflammation*. In an injury, blood vessels first contract in order to stem bleeding. Shortly afterwards they dilate, allowing more blood to flow to the damaged area (hence the redness and warmth that characterises inflammation). The blood carries leucocytes to combat foreign bodies that might use the injured area to gain access to the body. However, if the immune system is suppressed, we are much more vulnerable to the effects of foreign bodies, and if it becomes over-reactive, it turns on itself and attacks healthy body tissues.

Box 20.3   Psychoneuroimmunology

The study of psychological factors (especially stress) and their effects on the immune system is called *psychoneuroimmunology*. As noted earlier, steroid production increases when the body is exposed to a stressor. Although an intermittent secretion of steroids has negligible effects on the immune system, persistent secretion (as occurs in the GAS) impairs its functioning by interfering with antibody production. This decreases inflammation and suppresses leucocyte activity.

Stressful events have been linked to several infectious diseases including influenza, herpes and the Epstein–Barr virus. Stressors that apparently compromise or 'downregulate' the immune system include the death of a spouse and marital discord (Evans *et al.*, 1997: see Chapters 49, 50 and 57.) In non-humans, separation from the mother, electric shocks, and exposure to loud noise have all been shown to cause immunological deficiencies (Esterling & Rabin, 1987).

Given the immune system's role and the effect of prolonged exposure to stressors on it, it is hardly surprising a link exists between stress and illness. Steroid production is but one factor involved. Others include *immunoglobulin A*, one of the body's first defenders against influenza, and *interleukin-b*, a protein produced soon after tissue injury which regulates the remodelling of the connective tissue in wounds and the production of collagen, the tough fibrous tissue in scars. Sweeney (1995) describes a study in which two groups of participants underwent a small skin biopsy on their arms. Compared to a non-stressed control group, it took significantly longer for the wound to heal in people caring for relatives with dementia. This suggests that stress impairs the body's ability to heal and its response to infectious diseases, with potentially important consequences for people undergoing major surgery.

Box 20.4   Acute and chronic stressors and the immune system

Acute stressors include things like speaking in public and working to deadlines, whilst chronic stressors include things like separation and divorce. Interestingly, whilst chronic stressors are associated with a decrease in

---

defensive agents like immunoglobulin A (Evans *et al.*, 1995), acute stressors are associated with an *increase* in those agents (Naliboff *et al.*, 1995). Evans *et al.* (1997) speculate that the sympathetic adrenal medullary (SAM) system regulates the defence system in response to acute stressors, and that this may be a normal part of the body's adaptation to life's psychological challenges. With chronic stressors, the hypothalamic pituitary adrenal (HPA) axis takes over and causes immunosuppressive effects via corticosteroid production.

STRESS AND CANCER

Cancer's essential feature is the rapid development of abnormal cells which deplete the body's nutrients. The link between stress and cancer is far from conclusive. However, Visintainer *et al.* (1983) found that the injection of cancerous cells followed by exposure to an uncontrollable stressor dramatically weakened non-humans' abilities to resist the cells' effects. Additionally, exposure to a stressor was linked to a higher incidence of malignancy than was observed in non-stressful conditions.

In humans, Jacobs & Charles (1980) reported that cancer patients have often experienced high levels of stress prior to the onset of their illnesses. A significant percentage of children with cancer, for example, had experienced severe changes in their lives, such as the death of a loved one, in the year preceding the diagnosis. Tache *et al.* (1979) suggest that cancer occurs more frequently among widowed, divorced or separated adults as compared with those who are married. The stress caused by the absence of a *social support network* (see page 167) might play an important role in cancer's development.

Unfortunately, studies of the relationship between stress and cancer tend to be *retrospective*, and patients are asked to discuss events that occurred before they developed their illnesses. This might be inaccurate for several reasons (Herbert & Cohen, 1993). Additionally, stress may be the *result* of cancer developing rather than its cause.

There is also the further problem of identifying the physiological mechanism linking stress and cancer (if it exists). According to Levy (1983), the immune system plays a key role. As has been seen, it guards against hazardous foreign bodies and may even produce chemicals specifically designed to defend against cancer cells (Rogers *et al.*, 1979). Since the relationship between stress and the immune system seems to be well established, the immune system may be the mechanism linking stress and cancer.

At least one other possibility concerning the stress–cancer relationship exists, however. As with some illnesses, there appears to be an inherited predisposition towards developing cancer, and certain behaviours (such as smoking cigarettes) heighten the risks for certain types of cancer. Stressful experiences might lead people to engage in behaviours heightening this risk. Cigarette smokers, for example, might smoke even more in stressful circumstances and increase yet further their risk of developing cancer.

STRESS AND CARDIOVASCULAR DISORDERS

Cardiovascular disorders, such as heart diseases and disorders of the circulatory system, are known to be associated with certain 'risk factors'. These include diet, alcohol consumption, smoking, obesity and lack of physical activity. However, since these risk factors account for only 50 per cent of all diagnosed cases, others must be involved. One of these appears to be stress.

In the late 1950s, Friedman and Rosenman looked at the relationship between diet and cardiovascular disorders. They found that men were far more susceptible to heart disease than women, even though there seemed to be no differences between the sexes in terms of diet. Friedman and Rosenman speculated that job-related stress might be a factor since most of the men worked but most of the women did not. When questioned about what they thought had caused their own heart attacks and those of colleagues, respondents apparently shared Meyer and Friedman's speculation.

In a follow-up study, 40 tax accountants had their blood-clotting speed and serum cholesterol levels (two warning signs in coronary heart disease) monitored over several months. For a time, the levels were within normal range. However, as the deadline for filing tax returns approached, they rose dangerously and then returned to normal after the deadline.

Box 20.5   Type A and B

Friedman & Rosenman (1974) undertook a nine year study involving several thousand 39–59-year-old initially healthy men. On the basis of their responses about eating habits and ways of dealing with stressful conditions, the participants were divided into two roughly equal groups called 'type A' and 'type B'. Type A individuals tended to be ambitious, competitive, easily angered, time-conscious, hard-driving and demanding of perfection in both themselves and others. Type B individuals tended to be relaxed, easy-going, not driven to achieve perfection, understanding, forgiving and not easily angered.

Friedman and Rosenman found that 70 per cent of the 257 who died in the nine years after the study began were type A individuals. Other research has generally confirmed the finding that type A individuals have a greater risk of developing heart disease. However, the role of the *type A personality* in 'coronary proneness' has been debated. Hicks & Pellegrini (1982) propose that type A people engage more frequently in behaviours that are known risk factors, whilst Krantz & Manuck (1984) have suggested that type A people are more psychologically reactive to stress and this contributes to their coronary proneness.

Type A behaviour may, however, be a response to, rather than a cause of, physiological reactivity. Even when they are unconscious and undergoing surgery, type A people show higher blood pressure levels than type B people experiencing the same surgery. This suggests a predisposition to respond with heightened physiological activity to a stressor's presence. If so, type A behaviour could be interpreted as a way of *coping* with heightened physiological activity.

Ragland & Brand (1988) argue that there is actually no difference between the incidence of heart attacks and death rates between type A and type B men. Indeed, they argue that type A men might actually be at a *lower risk* of recurrent heart attacks than type B men (Cramb, 1997). The contradictory findings might be reconciled if some type A characteristics are actually more influential than others. According to Wright (1988), the most important aspects of type A behaviour are *hostility* and an *aggressively reactive temperament*, whilst Carson (1989) proposes that *cynicism* is the most important factor.

Clearly, the relationship between stress and cardiovascular disorders is not straightforward. Stress itself cannot cause cardiovascular disorders, and exactly how it is linked is the subject of much research. However, it seems likely that activity in the sympathetic branch of the ANS is involved.

STRESS AND HYPERTENSION

Consistent with the likely role played by the sympathetic branch of the ANS, stress might be linked to cardiovascular disorders because of its apparent role in hypertension (high blood pressure). Blood flow through the veins increases when ANS activity is heightened. This can cause both a hardening and a general deterioration in the tissue of the blood vessels. Although several factors contribute to hypertension, the role of stress has been demonstrated in several studies.

Box 20.6   Hypertension in the community

Harburg *et al.* (1973) measured the blood pressure of people from 'high' and 'low' stress areas of Detroit, defining high stress areas as those in which population density, crime rates, poverty and divorce were greatest. The highest blood pressures were found in those living in the highest stress areas, although considerable caution should always be exercised in interpreting health and demographic data.

It seems reasonable to conclude that stress almost certainly plays a role in certain types of illness. Given that illnesses are unpleasant, most of us would seek ways of minimising them. If stress can cause illness, it is important to find ways in which it can be reduced and its impact on health minimised.

Reducing stress

One way to reduce stress is to eliminate the factors causing it. However, since so many factors can cause stress this is not realistic. Many ways of managing and reducing stress have been devised. Dixon (1980), for example, has suggested that humour can help because it stimulates the output of *endorphins* (see Chapter 3). This section examines some more orthodox approaches to the management and reduction of stress.

REDUCING PHYSIOLOGICAL RESPONSES TO STRESS

Psychotherapeutic drugs

As has been seen, the stress response involves the activation of the sympathetic branch of the ANS. There are several methods for reducing the physiological effects of stress. One is the use of *drugs* which act directly on the ANS. Commonly used are the *benzodiazepine anti-anxiety* (or *anxiolytic*) *drugs* (such as *Librium* and *Valium*). However, whilst drugs may reduce the physiological effects of stress, they lead to physical dependence in at least some people and also have unpleasant side-effects (see Chapters 15 and 72). For this reason alone, other methods of reducing physiological responses would seem preferable.

Biofeedback

The body is not designed to allow us to be consciously aware of subtle feedback about internal physiological states occurring when we experience stress. *Biofeedback* aims to provide this information so that we can, at least to a degree, learn how to modify or control internal physiological states. A biofeedback machine produces precise information (or feedback) about bodily processes such as heart rate and/or blood pressure. This may be presented in visual or auditory form (or both). For example, heart rate changes may be indicated by a tone whose pitch varies and/or a line on a television monitor that rises or falls when heart rate increases or decreases.

The fact that some people can apparently regulate some internal bodily processes has led to biofeedback being used with many types of stress-related disorders. These include migraine headaches, tension headaches and high blood pressure. However, whilst biofeedback might be useful, several disadvantages are associated with it. First, unlike some methods, biofeedback requires physiological measuring devices. Because biofeedback and techniques not requiring specialised equipment are equally effective in stress reduction, biofeedback would seem to be least preferable.

Another disadvantage is that regular practice appears to be needed for the development and maintenance of any beneficial effects (although this is also true of some other methods). Finally, whilst biofeedback may eventually enable a person to learn to recognise the symptoms of, say, high blood pressure without the need for the biofeedback machine, it is not known exactly how biofeedback works. Some sceptics argue that biofeedback itself exerts no effects, and that the important thing is a person's commitment to reducing stress and the active involvement of a stress therapist!

Relaxation

Physiological responses to stress may also be reduced through *relaxation*. Jacobson (1938) observed that people experiencing stress tended to add to their discomfort by tensing their muscles. To overcome this, Jacobson devised *progressive relaxation*. In this, the muscles in some area of the body are first tightened and relaxed. Then, another group of muscles is tightened and relaxed and so on until, progressively, the entire body is relaxed.

Once a person becomes aware of muscle tension and can differentiate between feelings of tension and relaxation, the technique can be used to control stress-induced effects. Progressive relaxation lowers the arousal associated with the alarm reaction (see page 160) and reduces the number of recurrent heart attacks. However, progressive relaxation only has long-term benefits if it is incorporated into a person's lifestyle as a regular procedure (Green, 1994).

Box 20.7 Meditation

Another relaxation technique is *meditation*. In this, a person assumes a comfortable position and, with eyes closed, attempts to clear all disturbing thoughts from the mind. A single syllable, or *mantra*, is then silently repeated. Although meditation has attracted controversy, at least some people who use it believe it helps them to relax. Indeed, Wallace & Fisher (1987) found that meditation reduces oxygen consumption and induces electrical activity in the brain indicative of a calm, mental state. Both progressive relaxation and meditation reduce blood pressure more than placebos do (Jacob *et al.*, 1977), and the fact that both techniques do not require specialised equipment gives them, as noted earlier, an advantage over biofeedback.

Physical activity and exercise

In a study of London bus drivers and conductors, Morris (1953) found that the conductors, who moved around the bus collecting fares, were far less likely to suffer from cardiovascular disorders than the sedentary drivers. Although Morris' study was correlational, subsequent research has confirmed that *physical activity* and *exercise* are beneficial in stress reduction (Anshel, 1996).

All physical activity seems to be useful in reducing the incidence of stress-related illnesses. Physiologically, exercise promotes fitness. Although fitness is a complex concept, one benefit of being fit is that the body uses more oxygen during vigorous exercise and pumps more blood with each heart beat. Consequently, circulation is improved and the heart muscles strengthened. Psychologically, exercise might also be therapeutic, since sustained exercise can reduce depression and boost feelings of self-esteem (Sonstroem, 1984).

REDUCING STRESS BY CHANGING COGNITIONS

Hardiness

People evidently differ widely in terms of their abilities to resist a stressor's effects. One characteristic that apparently helps resist stress is *hardiness* (Kobasa, 1979). According to Kobasa, 'hardy' and 'non-hardy' individuals differ in three main ways.

Box 20.8 The hardy individual

Hardy people

- are highly *committed* or more deeply involved in

---

whatever they do and see activities associated with their endeavours as being meaningful;

- view change as a *challenge* for growth and development rather than a threat or burden;

- see themselves as having a stronger *sense of control* over events in their lives, and feel they can overcome their experiences (in Rotter's, 1966, terms, they have a *high internal locus of control*).

By choosing to be in stress-producing situations, interpreting any stress as making life more interesting, and being in control, the amount of stress experienced can be regulated. People high in hardiness tend to be healthier than those low in hardiness, even though the amount of stressful experiences they have been exposed to does not differ (Pines, 1984).

Kobasa suggests that stress can be reduced if hardiness is increased. One approach to this is teaching people to identify the physical signs of stress, since a stressor can hardly be dealt with if it cannot be identified. Even if we can identify stressors, the way they are dealt with might not necessarily be beneficial. Another approach is to try to make a more realistic assessment of life's stresses. This involves examining a stressful experience in terms of the ways in which it could have been more and less effectively dealt with.

Kobasa's third approach derives from her view that perceived abilities to bring about change have important effects on our capacity to withstand stress. Kobasa proposes that when a stressor's effects cannot be avoided, we should take on some other challenge which can be dealt with in order to experience the *positive* aspects of coping with a stressor. What Bandura (1984) calls *self-efficacy expectations* regulate problem-solving and allow us to 'bounce back' more readily from failure so that life's stressors are actually experienced as being less stressful.

Coping strategies

Another way in which people differ in their abilities to resist stress is related to the *coping strategies* used in trying to manage it. Coping is the cognitive and behavioural efforts to manage specific external and/or internal demands that are appraised as taxing or exceeding our resources. Lazarus & Folkman (1984) distinguish between *problem-focused* and *emotion-focused* coping strategies. In the former, some specific plan for dealing with a stressor is made and implemented, and other activities are postponed until the stressor has been reduced or terminated. The latter involves implementing strategies that are effective in the

short term, but do little to reduce or eliminate a stressor's long-term effects.

Box 20.9   Using coping strategies

Consider, for example, revising for an examination as a potential stressor. A problem-focused coping strategy would be to organise a revision plan and then adhere to it until the examination. What Moos (1988) calls a *behavioural* emotion-focused coping strategy might be to go out drinking every night, which would avoid confronting the stressor. When the examination results are published, the stress caused by failure could be reduced by using a *cognitive* emotion-focused coping strategy, such as claiming there was no opportunity to revise. Most of us use combinations of problem- and emotion-focused strategies, but some people rely almost exclusively on the latter. By teaching them more effective strategies for dealing with stressors, the amount of stress a problem engenders can be significantly reduced.

Another approach to reducing stress by changing cognition has been devised by Meichenbaum (1976, 1985). This is discussed in detail in Chapter 75.

REDUCING STRESS BY CHANGING BEHAVIOUR

Stress management

At least some everyday stresses could be reduced if we simply changed some of our behaviours. *Stress management programmes* use various techniques for dealing with the stress occurring as a consequence of behaviour. For example, some people tend to leave things until the last minute and then find themselves under extreme pressure to get a job done.

Time management and assertiveness training

Time management training aims to help people pace themselves to avoid leaving too much to the last minute. Somebody who takes on many tasks and finds it difficult to accomplish any one of them is suffering from *superperson syndrome*. Time management helps us to recognise our limits so that we (a) do not take on more than we can accomplish and (b) delegate at least some of the work to others. It can also be used to help people organise themselves more effectively. This involves training in how to establish goals, avoid wasting time, and become more task-oriented. For those who find it difficult to 'stand up for their rights' and who may be 'boiling inside', *assertiveness training* can be used, the aim being to help people *confront* stress-provoking situations.

Social support

A final approach to stress reduction stems from the fact that facing stress alone can be more damaging than facing it with the support of others. *Social support* refers to the resources provided by others when stress is experienced. Evidence suggests that social support can be beneficial in stress reduction even if the stressful situation remains unchanged. For example, Fleming *et al.* (1984) found that residents affected by the nuclear near-accident at Pennsylvania's Three Mile Island reactor plant reported less stress if they had solid networks of social supports, such as close friends or relatives, with whom they could share their experiences.

The effect of social support can be very powerful. Berkman (1984) found that people with fewer family, friendship and community ties were significantly more likely to die at a given age than those who had strong ties, irrespective of their physical health. Wolf & Bruhn (1993) showed that social support can be of considerable help with people suffering from coronary heart disease.

Box 20.10   Some major types of social support

Showing emotional concern: This involves listening to a person's concerns and expressing feelings of sympathy, care, reassurance and understanding.

Providing information: This involves giving information that will enhance a person's ability to cope. Some people, for example, turn to religious personnel or psychotherapists for such guidance.

Giving instructional aid: In some cases, people may require material support in order to cope with stress. When national disasters occur, government and other aid agencies provide relief support to reduce the stress experienced by the victims. Even those not directly involved in a disaster can be affected by it. Dixon *et al.* (1993), for example, showed that cross-channel ferry workers not involved in the *Herald of Free Enterprise* disaster were strongly affected by it (see Chapter 70).

Providing feedback: This involves an appraisal of how the individual experiencing stress is doing. This kind of support can help people to interpret or 'make sense' of what has happened to them.

Socialising: The provision of social companionship can help even if it is not designed to solve any problems. Such support ranges from simple conversation to accompanying a person on, say, a shopping trip.

The evidence relating social support and stress reduction is primarily *correlational*. Social support is a situational variable, but people can *choose* whether or not they seek such support. Those who do might be better at coping anyway.

Type A management

Finally, we should also mention those strategies for reducing stress with people identified as 'type A' (see page 163). Friedman & Ulmer (1984) have advocated approaches based on altering time urgency, hostility and self-destructive tendencies. According to Friedman and Ulmer, when behaviour patterns can be successfully changed, the likelihood of recurrent heart attacks is significantly reduced.

Conclusions

Stress exerts physiological and psychological effects. Research into the link between stress and various illnesses suggests almost beyond doubt that a causal link exists between them. Given the negative effects of stress, we should not be surprised to find that there are many approaches to reducing stress. These involve altering physiological responses and changing cognitions and behaviours.

Summary

■ Stress can be defined as a pattern of negative physiological states and psychological processes occurring in situations where people perceive threats to their well-being which they may be unable to meet.

■ On the basis of his finding that non-humans respond in a physiologically non-specific way to any stressor, Selye proposed the **general adaptation syndrome** (GAS). The **alarm reaction** is characterised by physiological activity that prepares the body for 'fight-or-flight'. In the **resistance stage**, the body is less aroused but continues to draw on its resources above the normal level. The **exhaustion stage** occurs when a stressor can no longer be managed. This results in bodily damage and the development of **diseases of adaptation**.

■ Although the GAS is a useful concept, its application to humans is weaker than to non-humans largely because it ignores the role played by cognitive processes in the stress response. These include **primary appraisal**, in which negative implications of a potential stressor are assessed, and **secondary appraisal** which involves an assessment of the ability to overcome the potential stressor's challenge.

■ Cognitive responses to a stressor include distractability and impaired task performance. Emotional responses include anger, hostility, embarrassment, depression, helplessness, hostility and anxiety. Stressors produce various behavioural responses including confrontation, withdrawal, adaptation and avoidance, all of which are attempts to manage/reduce the effects of stressors.

■ Stress may be a contributor to several types of illness including malfunctioning of the immune system, cancer, cardiovascular disorders and hypertension.

■ **Psychoneuroimmunology** is the study of the effects of psychological factors (especially stress) on immune system functioning. The production of **steroids**, **immunoglobulin A** and **interleukin-b** have all been shown to be 'down-regulated' by chronic stressors. Acute stressors, however, are associated with 'up-regulation' of these, and this may be a normal part of the body's adaptation to psychological challenges.

■ The relationship between stress and cancer is far from conclusive, and it has yet to be established whether cancer is a consequence or cause of stress. If the relationship is causal, the precise physiological mechanism needs to be identified, and interest would probably focus on the immune system.

■ The relationship between stress and cardiovascular disorders could be a consequence of personality type, and some evidence supports this. However, other evidence disputes the relationship, and if a relationship does exist it is a far from straightforward one.

■ Stress may be linked to cardiovascular disorders because of its apparent role in hypertension. Increased blood flow through the veins can cause both a hardening and a general deterioration in the tissue of the blood vessels. Certainly, some studies have reported an apparent link between hypertension and stress.

■ Reducing physiological responses to stress can be achieved through **psychotherapeutic drugs** such as **anxiolytics**, which act directly on the ANS. However, such drugs are associated with physical dependence and unpleasant side effects.

■ **Biofeedback** is another way of reducing physiological responses, and it has been shown to be successful in the treatment of migraine headaches and hypertension. However, because regular practice is needed for beneficial effects and it is not precisely known how it works, its use is limited.

■ **Relaxation** (including **meditation**) and **physical activity and exercise** are other ways of reducing physiological responses. Such practices exert a number of physiological effects which presumably combat those caused by a stressor.

■ Stress can also be reduced by changing cognitions. Kobasa distinguishes between 'hardy' and 'non-hardy' individuals, the former adopting cognitive strategies which enable them to deal with stressors much more effectively. These include being able to identify the physical signs of stress, realistically assessing stressors, and taking on other challenges to experience the positive aspects of coping with a stressor.

■ **Problem-focused coping strategies** involve devising some specific plan for dealing with a stressor and then adhering to it until the stressor has been reduced or terminated. **Emotion-focused coping strategies** involve behaviours that are effective in the short-term, but do little to reduce a stressor's long-term effects. Most people use a combination of the two, but some rely exclusively on emotion-focused coping strategies.

■ **Time management** and **assertiveness training** are other behavioural ways of reducing stress. **Social support** can reduce stress because a person does not have to face the stress alone, even if the stressor itself remains unchanged. Assuming that personality is a factor in stress, stress can be reduced by changing the characteristics associated with coronary-prone individuals.

UNIT 3

Cognitive Psychology

PART 1

Perception and attention

21

VISUAL PERCEPTION AND PERCEPTUAL

ORGANISATION

Introduction and overview

When we compare our experience of the world (one in which objects remain stable and constant) with what our sense organs receive in the form of physical stimulation (a state of near continuous flux), it is almost as if there are two entirely different 'worlds'. Psychologists call these *sensation* and *perception* respectively. Sensations are the experiences that physical stimuli elicit in the sense organs. Perception is the organisation and interpretation of incoming sensory information to form inner representations of the external world.

This chapter looks at some basic visual perceptual phenomena and how visual perception is organised. (Other visual perceptual phenomena will be discussed in relation to theories of visual perception in Chapter 22.) Vision is the dominant sense modality in humans and much more is known about visual perception than any other sense modality (Eysenck, 1993). Many of the principles that govern human visual perception were first uncovered by the German 'school' of *Gestalt psychology*. This chapter begins by examining their contribution to our knowledge of visual perception.

Gestalt psychology and visual perception

Ehrenfels (1890) claimed that many groups of stimuli acquire a pattern quality which is greater than the sum of their parts. A square, for example, is more than a simple assembly of lines – it has 'squareness'. Ehrenfels called this 'emergent property' *Gestalt qualität* (or form quality). In the early twentieth century, Gestalt psychologists (notably Wertheimer, Koffka and Köhler) attempted to discover the principles through which sensory information is interpreted. They argued that as well as creating a coherent perceptual experience that is more than the sum of its parts, the brain does this in regular and predictable ways, and that these organisational principles are largely innately determined. The claim about innateness is discussed in Chapters 23 and 24.

Form perception

In order to structure incoming sensory information, we must perceive objects as being separate from other stimuli and as having a meaningful form.

FIGURE AND GROUND

The first perceptual task when confronted with an object (or *figure*) is to recognise it. To do this, we must perceive the figure as being distinct from the surroundings (or *ground*) against which it appears. A figure's *familiarity* is one 'role' that determines whether it is perceived as figure or ground. However, unfamiliar and even meaningless forms are also seen as figures.

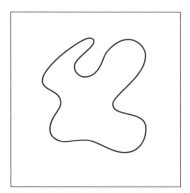

Figure 21.1   Even unfamiliar objects are immediately perceived when the outline is closed

Figure 21.1 illustrates that familiarity is not necessary for form perception. If it were, we would have difficulty perceiving objects we had never seen before (Carlson, 1987). One of the strongest determinants of figure and ground is *surroundedness*. Areas enclosed by a *contour* are generally seen as figures, whereas the surrounding area is generally seen as ground. *Size*, *orientation* and *symmetry* also play a role in figure–ground separation.

Sometimes, though, there may not be enough information in a pattern to allow us to easily distinguish between figure and ground. A good example of this is shown in Figure 21.2 which illustrates the principle underlying *camouflage*.

Figure 21.2   The dalmation dog (the figure) is difficult to distinguish from the ground because it has few visible contours of its own

In *figure–ground reversal*, a figure may have clear contours, but is capable of being perceived in two very different ways because it is not clear which part of it is the figure and which the ground. A famous example is Rubin's vase (Rubin, 1915).

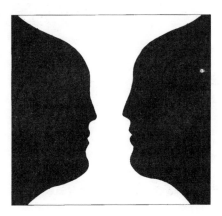

Figure 21.3   A white vase on a black background or two faces in silhouette?

In Rubin's vase, the figure–ground relationship continually reverses, so that it is perceived as either a white vase with a black background or two black profiles on a white background. However, the stimulus is *always* organised into a figure seen against a ground, and the reversal indicates that the same stimulus can trigger more than one perception (see page 177).

Figures 21.4 (a) and (b) show two examples of the ways in which figure–ground reversal has been used by artists.

(a)

Figure 21.4 (a)   The use of reversible ground by a potter. The vase, a commemoratiion of the Queen's Silver Jubilee (1977), can also be perceived as the profiles of the Duke of Edinburgh (left) and the Queen (right)

171

(b)

Figure 21.4 (b)   A woodcut by the artist M.C. Escher. Either black devils or white angels can be seen in the ring

GROUPING

Once we have discriminated figure from ground, the figure can be organised into a meaningful form. Gestalt psychologists believed that objects are perceived as *gestalten* ('organised wholes', 'configurations' or 'patterns') rather than combinations of isolated sensations. They identified several 'laws' of perceptual organisation or grouping which illustrate their view that the perceived whole of an object is more than the sum of its parts.

These laws can be summarised under one heading, *the law of prägnanz*, according to which:

> 'psychological organisation will always be as good as the prevailing conditions allow. In this definition, "good" is undefined' (Koffka, 1935).

'Good' can be defined as possessing a high degree of internal redundancy, that is, the structure of an unseen part is highly predictable from the visible parts (Attneave, 1954). Similarly, according to Hochberg's (1978) *minimum principle*, if there is more than one way of organising a given visual stimulus, we are most likely to perceive the one requiring the least amount of information to perceive it.

In practice, the 'best' way of perceiving is to see things as symmetrical, uniform and stable, and this is achieved by following the laws of prägnanz.

Box 21.1   Gestalt laws of perception

Proximity: Elements appearing close together – in space or time – tend to be perceived together, so that different spacings of dots produce four vertical lines or four horizontal lines:

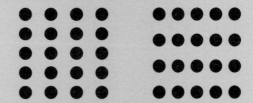

An auditory example would be the perception of a series of musical notes as a melody because they occur soon after one another in time.

Similarity: Similar figures tend to be grouped together. So, the triangles and circles below are seen as columns of similar shapes rather than rows of dissimilar shapes.

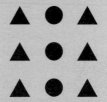

When we hear all the separate voices in a choir as an entity, the principle of similarity is operating.

Good continuation: We tend to perceive smooth, continuous patterns rather than discontinuous ones. The pattern below could be seen as a series of alternating semi-circles, but tends to be perceived as a wavy line and a straight line.

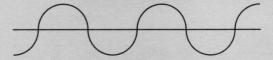

Music and speech are perceived as continuous rather than a series of separate sounds.

Closure: The law of closure says that we often supply missing information to close a figure and separate it from its background. By filling in the gaps, the illustrations are seen as a triangle and a seashell.

Part–whole relationship: As well as illustrating continuity and proximity, the three figures below illustrate the principle that 'the whole is greater than the sum of its parts'. Each pattern is composed of 12 crosses, but the gestalten are different, despite the similarity of the parts.

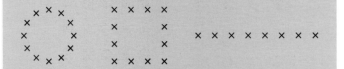

The same melody can be recognised when hummed, whistled or played with different instruments and in different keys.

Simplicity: According to this law, a stimulus pattern will be organised into its simplest components. The figure below is usually perceived as a rectangle with an overlapping triangle rather than as a complex and nameless geometric shape.

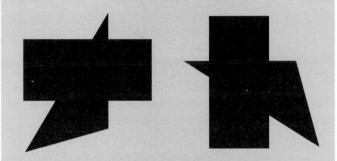

Common fate: Elements seen moving together are perceived as belonging together. This is why a group of people running in the same direction appear to be unified in their purpose.

AN EVALUATION OF THE GESTALT CONTRIBUTION

A major philosophical influence on Gestalt psychology was *phenomenology*. This sees the world as we ordinarily experience it as being of central concern. Koffka, for example, believed that the most important question for perceptual psychologists was 'Why do things look as they do?', and for Köhler:

> 'there seems to be a single starting point for psychology, exactly as for all the other sciences: the world as we find it, naïvely and uncritically'.

The most comprehensive account of perceptual grouping is still that provided by the Gestaltists (Roth, 1986), and in Gordon's (1989) view, Gestalt psychology's discoveries 'are now part of our permanent knowledge of perception'.

Many contemporary researchers, (e.g. Greene, 1990) however, have argued that, as originally expressed, the various Gestalt 'laws' are at best only descriptive and at worst extremely imprecise and difficult to measure (what, for example, makes a circle or square a 'good' figure?). Several studies (e.g. Navon, 1977) have attempted to address the various criticisms made of the Gestalt laws.

Box 21.2   Navon's (1977) experimental test of Gestalt laws

Navon tested the idea that the whole is perceived before the parts that make it up by presenting participants with various stimuli as shown below.

```
  H     H        H        HHH
  H     H          H H   H    H
  H     H         H        H
  H     H          H
  HHHHHHHHHH       H
  H     H           HHHH
  H     H              H H
  H     H        H        H
  H     H         H      H
  H     H          HHHHH
  H     H
```

Navon distinguished between the *global* (or 'whole-like' features of a stimulus) and the *local* (or more specific and 'part-like' features). Each stimulus consisted of a large (global) letter made up of many small (local) letters. In some cases, the global and local letters matched (as shown in the stimulus on the left) and in some cases they did not (as shown on the right).

Participants had to identify either the large or the small letter as quickly as possible. Navon found that the time taken to identify the large letter was unaffected by whether the small letters matched or not. However, the time taken to identify the small letters *was* affected by whether the large letter matched or not, such that when the large letter was different, response times were longer. This suggests that it is difficult to avoid processing the whole and that global processing necessarily occurs before any more detailed perceptual analysis.

(Adapted from Eysenck & Keane, 1995)

Navon's data support claims made by Gestaltists. However, Gestalt laws are difficult to apply to the perception of solid (three-dimensional/3-D) objects (as opposed to two-dimensional/2-D drawings). Our eyes evolved to see 3-D objects, and when 3-D arrays have been studied, Gestalt laws have not been consistently upheld (Eysenck,

1993). The world around us comprises 'whole' scenes in which single objects are but 'parts' (Humphreys & Riddoch, 1987). As a result, many of the Gestalt displays, which involve *single* objects, have very low *ecological validity* in that they are not representative of 'the objects and events which organisms must deal with in order to survive' (Gordon, 1989).

Depth perception

From the 2-D images that fall on our retinas, we manage to organise 3-D perceptions. This ability is called *depth perception*, and it allows us to estimate an object's distance from us. Some of the cues used to transform 2-D retinal images into 3-D perceptions involve both eyes and rely on their working together. These are called *binocular cues*. *Monocular cues* are available to each eye separately.

BINOCULAR CUES

Most preyed upon non-humans (such as rabbits) have their eyes on the side of the head, allowing them to see danger approaching over a wide area. Most predators (such as lions) have their eyes set close together on the front of the head, equipping them with binocular vision, which helps in hunting prey. Like non-human predators, humans have predatory vision, which influences the way we perceive the world. Four important binocular cues are *retinal disparity*, *stereopsis*, *accommodation* and *convergence*.

Because our eyes are nearly three inches apart, each retina receives a slightly different image of the world. The amount of *retinal disparity* (the difference between the two images) detected by the brain provides an important cue to distance. For example, if you hold your finger directly in front of your nose, the difference between the two retinal images is large (and this can be shown by looking at your finger first with the left eye closed and then with the right eye closed). When the finger is held at arm's length, retinal disparity is much smaller.

Ordinarily, we do not see double images, because the brain combines the two images in a process called *stereopsis*. This allows us to experience one 3-D sensation rather than two different images. In *accommodation*, which is a muscular cue, the lenses of the eyes change shape when we focus on an object, thickening for nearby objects and flattening for distant objects. *Convergence*, another muscular cue to distance, is the process by which the eyes point more and more inward as an object gets closer. By noting the angle of convergence, the brain provides us with depth information over distances from about six to 20 feet (Hochberg, 1971).

MONOCULAR CUES

Except with relatively near objects, each eye receives a very similar retinal image whilst looking ahead. At greater distances, we depend on monocular cues.

Box 21.3   Some monocular cues to depth

Relative size: The larger an object's image is on the retina, the larger it is judged to be. Larger objects are also judged to be closer.

Overlap (or Superimposition): If one object is partially covered by another, it is perceived as being further away. When a smaller object partially obscures a larger one, they seem closer together than if their position is reversed (a combination of overlap and relative size).

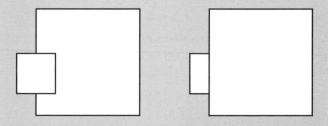

Relative height: Objects *below* the horizon and *lower down* in our field of vision are perceived as being closer. Objects *above* the horizon and *higher up* in our field of vision are perceived as being further away.

Texture gradient: This refers to the fact that textured surfaces nearby appear rougher than distant surfaces. Thus, at increasing distances the details of the surface blend together and the texture appears increasingly smooth.

Linear perspective: The apparent convergence of parallel lines is interpreted as a distance cue. The greater the convergence, the greater the perceived distance.

Shadowing: Opaque objects block light and produce shadows. Shadows and highlights give us information about an object's 3-D shape. In the illustration below, the object on the left is perceived as a 2-D circle. The object on the right is perceived as a 3-D sphere because of the highlight on the surface and the shadow underneath.

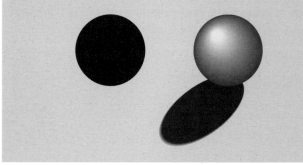

Relative brightness: Objects that are close to us reflect more light to the eyes. The dimmer of two identical objects appears to be further away.

Aerial haze: Objects that are hazy are perceived to be further away than objects more in focus.

Aerial perspective: Objects at a greater distance appear to have a different colour (such as the bluish tint of a distant mountain).

Motion parallax: If we move, objects near to us appear to move more than objects far away from us. When we move past objects located at different distances from us, they appear to move across the visual field at different speeds, with those nearest us moving most rapidly. Such differences in speed help us to judge both distance and depth.

Perceptual constancy

Having perceived an object as a coherent form and located it in space, we must next recognise the object without being 'fooled' by changes in its size, shape, location, brightness and colour. The ability to perceive an object as unchanging despite changes in the sensory information that reaches our eyes is called *perceptual constancy*.

SIZE CONSTANCY

As people move away from us, the size of image they project on the retina decreases. However, rather than seeing people as 'growing smaller', we perceive them as being of a fixed height moving away from us. *Size constancy* occurs because the perceptual system takes into account an object's distance from the perceiver. So, perceived size is equal to retinal image size taking distance into account. When people move away from us, their images on our retinas decrease in size as their distances increase. Our perceptual system interprets these changes as resulting from the change in location of an object of constant size.

The perception of an *after-image* demonstrates how distance can be varied *without* changing the retinal image's size. If you stare at a bright light for a few seconds and then look away, you will experience an after-image. This has a fixed size, shape and position on the retina. However, if you quickly look at a nearby object and then an object further away, the after-image appears to shrink and swell, appearing to be largest when you look at a more distant object. Real objects cast a smaller image the further away they are and to maintain perceptual constancy, the brain 'scales-up' the image (*constancy scaling*). The same constancy scaling is applied to an after-image, producing changes in its apparent size.

SHAPE CONSTANCY

We often view objects from angles at which their 'true' shapes are not reflected in the retinal image they project. For example, rectangular doors often project trapezoid shapes and round cups often project elliptical-shaped images. Just as with size constancy, the perceptual system maintains constancy in terms of shape.

Figure 21.5   No matter what angle a door is viewed from, it remains a door

However, shape and size constancy do not always work. When we look down at people from the top of a very tall building, they do *look* more like ants to us, even though we know they are people.

LOCATION CONSTANCY

Moving our heads around produces a constantly changing pattern of retinal images. However, we do not perceive the world as spinning around. This is because *kinaesthetic feedback* from the muscles and balance organs in the ear are integrated with the changing retinal stimulation in the brain to inhibit perception of movement. To keep the world from moving crazily every time we move our eyes, the brain subtracts the eye-movement commands from the resulting changes on the retina which helps to keep objects in a constant location.

BRIGHTNESS CONSTANCY

We see objects as having a more or less constant brightness even though the amount of light they reflect changes according to the level of illumination. For example, white paper reflects 90 per cent of light falling on it, whereas black paper reflects only ten per cent. In bright sunlight, however, black paper still looks black even though it may reflect 100 times more light than does white paper indoors (McBurney & Collins, 1984). Perceived brightness depends on how much light an object reflects relative to its surroundings (*relative luminance*). If sunlit black paper is viewed through a narrow tube such that nothing else is visible, it will appear greyish because in bright sunlight it reflects a fair amount of light. When viewed without the tube it is again black, because it reflects much less light than the colourful objects around it.

COLOUR CONSTANCY

Familiar objects retain their colour (or, more correctly, their *hue*) under a variety of lighting conditions (including night light), provided there is sufficient contrast and shadow. However, when we do not already know an object's colour, colour constancy is less effective (Delk & Fillenbaum, 1965). If you have purchased new clothes under fluorescent light without viewing them in ordinary lighting conditions, you will no doubt agree.

Illusions

Although perception is usually reliable, our perceptions sometimes misrepresent the world. When our perception of an object does not match its true physical characteristics, we have experienced an *illusion*. Some illusions are due to the *physical distortion* of stimuli whereas others are due to our *misperception* of stimuli (Coren & Girgus, 1978). An example of a *physical illusion* is the bent appearance of a stick when placed in water.

Gregory (1983) identifies four types of *perceptual illusion*. These are *distortions* (or *geometric illusions*), *ambiguous* (or *reversible) figures*, *paradoxical figures* (or *improbable and impossible objects*) and *fictions*.

DISTORTIONS

Figure 21.6 shows several examples of distortions. The Poggendorf illusion (Figure 21.6 (b)) is accentuated when the diagonal line is more steeply slanted and when the parallel bars are more separated. As the line is brought closer to the horizontal, the illusion disappears (MacKay & Newbigging, 1977). The horizontal–vertical illusion (Figure 21.6 (d)) illustrates our tendency to overestimate the size of vertical objects. This helps to explain why a small tree we have chopped down looks shorter than it did when it was standing (Coren & Girgus, 1978).

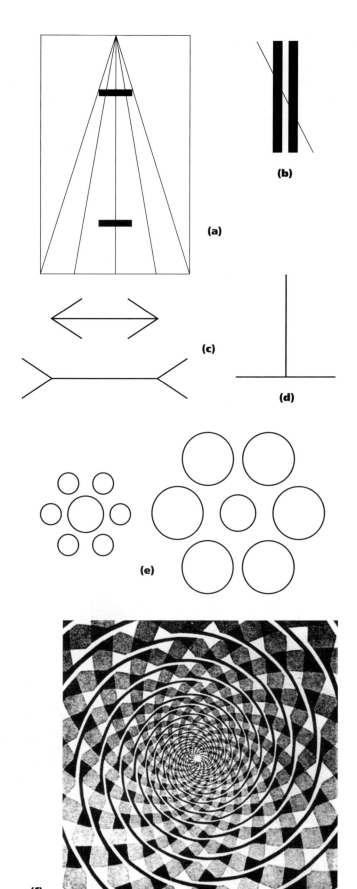

Figure 21.6   Distortions (or geometric illusions). In the Ponzo illusion (a), the horizontal bar at the top is seen as being longer than the horizontal line at the bottom, even though they are both the same length. The Poggendorf illusion (b) suggests that the segments of the diagonal line are offset, even though they are not. The line with the outgoing fins in the Müller–Lyer illusion (c) appears to be longer than the line with the ingoing fins, but in fact they are the same length. In the horizontal–vertical illusion (d), the vertical line is seen as being longer, although it is the same as the horizontal line. In Titchener's circles (e), the central circle in the left-hand group is seen as being larger than the central circle of the right-hand group, but they are both the same size. Finally, in the twisted card illusion (f), the twisted cards appear to be a spiral pattern, but the circles are, in fact, concentric

AMBIGUOUS FIGURES

In addition to Rubin's vase (see page 171), three other well-known reversible figures are shown in Figure 21.7 (a–c). In the Necker cube (Figure 21.7 (a)), the figure undergoes a *depth reversal*. The cube can be perceived with the crosses being drawn either on the back side of the cube or on the top side looking down. Although our perceptual system interprets this 2-D line drawing as a 3-D object, it seems undecided as to which of the two orientations should be perceived, and hence the cube spontaneously reverses in depth orientation if looked at for about 30 seconds.

Figure 21.7 (b) shows Boring's 'Old/Young woman'. This (and Figure 21.7(c)) are examples of reversible figures in which the change in perception illustrates *object reversal*. The figure can be perceived as the profile of a young woman's face with the tip of her nose just visible or the young woman's chin can be perceived as the nose of the face of a much older woman. In Jastrow's reversible duck/rabbit head (Figure 21.7(c)), the object can be perceived either as the head of a duck with its beak pointing to the left or as a rabbit (the duck's beak becomes the rabbit's ears).

PARADOXICAL FIGURES

Whilst paradoxical figures look ordinary enough at first, on closer inspection we realise that they cannot exist in reality (hence 'paradoxical'). Figure 21.8 (a–d) illustrates four such paradoxical figures.

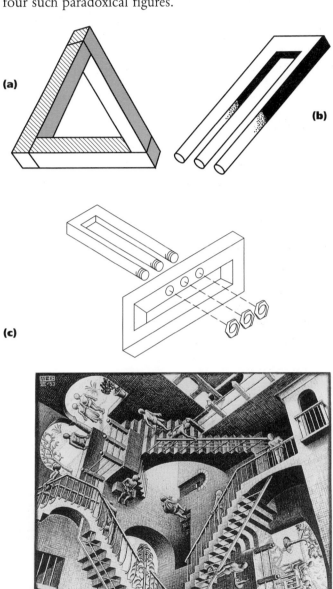

Figure 21.8   Four impossible objects. (a) is the Penrose impossible triangle and (b) is variously known as 'Trident' and 'The devil's pitchfork'. In (c), Trident has been combined with another impossible object. (d) is M.C. Escher's *Relativity*. Although working in two dimensions, Escher has used perceptual cues in such a way as to encourage the viewer to perceive a three-dimensional figure (see Chapter 24)

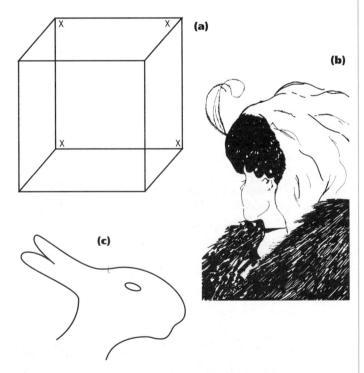

Figure 21.7   Three ambiguous/reversible figures: (a) the Necker cube; (b) Boring's 'Old/Young Woman'; and (c) Jastrow's duck/rabbit head

According to Hochberg (1970), it takes us a few seconds to realise that a figure is impossible because we need time to fully examine or scan it and organise its parts into a meaningful whole. When we look at a figure, our eyes move from place to place at the rate of about three changes per second (Yarbus, 1967). So when we look at an impossible figure, it takes time to scan it and perceive its form, and only after this scanning can we appreciate its impossible nature. The painting by Escher (Figure 21.8 (d)) uses perceptual cues in such a way as to encourage us to perceive a 3-D figure even though the artist is working only in two dimensions.

FICTIONS

Fictions help explain how we perceive that objects possess a specific shape. The idea that shape is determined by the *physical contours* of an object (which cause edge-detectors in the cells of the visual system to fire) has been challenged by the existence of *subjective contours*, which are the boundaries of a shape perceived in the absence of physical contours (Kanizsa, 1976).

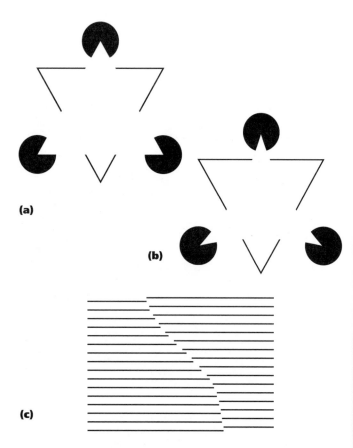

(a)

(b)

(c)

Figure 21.9   Three fictions. In (a), the 'white triangle' is banded by a subjective contour, rather than a continuous physical one. In (b), the subjective contours are curved. In (c), lines of different orientation produce a subjective contour

In Figure 21.9 (a), although no white triangular contour is physically present, we perceive the shape of a white triangle which appears to be opaque and lighter than the background. There are *some* contours that are physically present (the overlap of the triangle and the disc) and these *might* cause enough edge-detector cells to fire. However, this explanation cannot account for the fact that in Figure 21.9 (b), the partial and straight physical contours give rise to a *curved* triangle. Nor can it explain the subjective contour in Figure 21.9 (c) which is marked by lines in a totally different orientation (Krebs & Blackman, 1988).

It is the *relationship between its parts* that is the defining characteristic of a shape rather than its physical contours (Rock, 1984). Physical contours are, of course, usually indicative of the location of an object's parts. However, the location of the parts can also be determined by subjective contours. As a result, the perception of shape must involve more than simply detecting the elements of a pattern (Krebs & Blackman, 1988).

We are surrounded by illusions in our everyday life. The use of perspective cues by artists leads us to infer depth and distance, that is, we add something to a picture which is not physically present, just as we do to the images projected on our television screens. Television pictures also use the *illusion of movement*.

The perception of movement

As we turn our heads and look around a room, the light from various objects stimulates successive and different parts of the retina. Despite this, we perceive the objects to be stationary. At a soccer match, we move our heads so that the light reflected by the players and ball is directed at the same area of the retina, but we know that the players and ball are moving. Cues used to perceive movement include the movement of the head and eyes, and knowledge about certain objects. Unfortunately, there is no single (and simple) way in which movement is perceived, and our conclusions about movement using environmental cues depend on how such cues are interpreted (Poggio & Koch, 1987).

Just as it is possible for changes in patterns of retinal stimulation not to be accompanied by the perception of movement, so it is possible to perceive movement without a successive pattern of retinal stimulation (Ramachandron & Anstis, 1986). This is called *apparent movement*.

Box 21.4   Some examples of apparent movement

The autokinetic effect: If you look at a stationary spot of light in an otherwise completely dark room, the light will appear to move. According to Gregory (1973), this illusion of apparent movement is produced by small and uncontrollable eye movements. Another explanation suggests that it is caused by the absence of a stimulating background to provide a frame of reference by which movement is gauged. This is supported by the fact that the autokinetic effect disappears if other lights are introduced (see also Chapter 58, page 499)

Stroboscopic motion: The illusion of movement is created by the rapid succession of slightly different stationary images. If these are presented sufficiently quickly (around 16 to 22 frames per second), an illusory impression of continuous movement is produced, and this is the mechanism by which moving pictures operate. With fewer than 16 frames per second, the moving picture looks jumpy and unnatural. Smooth *slow motion* is achieved by filming at a rate of 100 or more frames per second and then playing back at about 20 frames per second.

The phi phenomenon: This is a simpler form of stroboscopic motion in which a number of separate lights are turned on and off in quick succession. This gives the impression of a single light moving from one position to another. Both stroboscopic motion and the phi phenomenon can be explained by the law of continuity (see page 172).

Induced movement: This occurs when we perceive an object to be moving, although in reality it is stationary and its surroundings are moving. Movie stars, for example, are often filmed in a stationary car with a projection of a moving background behind them. Similarly, when the moon is seen through a thin cover of moving clouds, we sometimes perceive it to be moving very quickly. Another example is the experience of sitting in a car at traffic lights and noticing that we are 'moving backwards', when in fact the car at our side is moving forwards.

Motion after-effects: People who work on inspection belts in factories experience movement after-effects when the belt suddenly stops but is perceived as now moving backwards. Similarly, if you stare at a waterfall and then switch your gaze to the ground surrounding it, the ground appears to be moving in the opposite direction.

Such after-effects are generally accepted as being due to the overstimulation of particular movement-detector cells in the visual system. Because cells sensitive to, say, downward movement have been overstimulated, they are momentarily insensitive when the stimulation ceases. However, the cells sensitive to, say, upward movement are relatively more active, resulting in a motion after-effect.

At least some examples of apparent movement can be termed *intelligent errors*, because they result from perceptual strategies that work most of the time (Rock, 1983). Motion after-effects, however, can be more easily explained in physiological terms.

Pattern recognition

According to Eysenck (1993):

'one of the most crucial functions of visual perception is to assign meaning to the objects in the visual field by recognising or identifying them'.

The ease with which we are able to recognise the letter 'T', say, whether it is printed on paper, handwritten or spoken 'is so ingrained in our experience that we rarely even notice that we do it' (Houston *et al.*, 1991). As Figure 21.10 shows, the letter 'T' can be presented in many different ways.

Figure 21.10   Anyone for T?

TEMPLATE-MATCHING HYPOTHESIS

According to the *template-matching hypothesis* (TMH), incoming sensory information is matched against miniature copies (or templates) of previously presented patterns or objects which are stored in long-term memory. Template-matching is used by computerised cash registers, which identify a product and its cost by matching a bar code with some stored representation of that code.

Given the complexity of the environment, we would need to possess an incredibly large number of templates, each corresponding to a specific visual input. Even if we were able to use a wheelbarrow to carry around the cerebrum needed for this, the time needed to search for a specific template would be inordinately long, and we would never recognise unfamiliar patterns (Solso, 1995).

Biederman's (1987) *geon theory of pattern recognition* ('geon' stands for 'geometrical icons') is intended to overcome the TMH's limitations. According to Biederman, we use a limited number of simple geometric 'primitives' that may be applied to all complex shapes (an idea similar to Marr's theory of perception: see Chapter 22). Geons can be combined to produce more complex ones. The identification of any visual object is determined by whichever stored representation provides the best fit with the component- or geon-based information obtained from the visual object. In order to establish the number of parts or components making up an object, Biederman believes that the *concave* parts of the contour are particularly important (Solso, 1995).

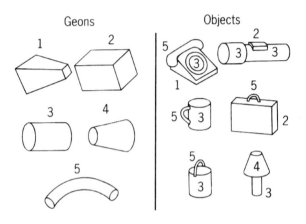

Figure 21.11 Biederman's geons (left) and some of the objects they can combine to make (right)

PROTOTYPE THEORIES OF PATTERN RECOGNITION

Prototype theories propose that instead of storing templates, we store a smaller number of *prototypes* which are 'abstract forms representing the basic elements of a set of stimuli' (Eysenck, 1993). Whereas TMH treats each stimulus as a separate entity, prototype theories maintain that similarities between related stimuli play an important part in pattern recognition. So, each stimulus is a member of a *category* of stimuli and shares basic properties with other members of the category.

The main weakness of prototype theories is their inability to explain how pattern recognition is affected by the context as well as by the stimulus itself (Eysenck, 1993). Knowing just what properties are shared by a category of stimuli is important, but not specified by the theories. What, for example, is an 'idealised' letter 'T' and what is the 'best' representation of the pattern? This question has been addressed by *feature detection theories*.

FEATURE DETECTION THEORIES

These are the most influential approach to pattern recognition, maintaining that each stimulus pattern can be thought of as a configuration of elementary features. Gibson *et al.* (1968) argue that the letters of the alphabet, for example, are composed of combinations of 12 basic features (such as vertical lines, horizontal lines and closed curves).

> **Box 21.5   Some experimental findings supporting feature detection theories**
>
> In *visual scanning tasks*, participants search lists of letters as quickly as possible to find a randomly placed target letter. Since finding a target letter entails detecting its elementary features, the task should be more difficult when the target and non-target letters have more features in common. This is exactly what researchers have found (e.g. Rabbit, 1967). Additional support comes from *studies of eye movements and fixation*. Presumably, the more a feature in a pattern is looked at, the more information is being extracted from it. The perception of features within complex patterns depends on higher cognitive processes (such as attention and purpose) as well as the nature of the physical stimuli being looked at (Yarbus, 1967).

It is also well established that the visual systems of some vertebrates contain both peripheral (retinal) and central (cortical) cells that respond only to particular features of visual stimuli. In their pioneering research, Hubel & Wiesel (1968) identified three kinds of cortical cell (which they called 'simple', 'complex' and 'hypercomplex' to refer to the stimuli the cells respond to: see Chapter 10, Box 10.4.) More recently, it has been claimed that there are face-specific cells in the infero-temporal cortex of the monkey (Ono *et al.*, 1993).

In humans, Perrett (cited in Messer, 1995) has identified cells that respond to specific aspects of a face or to a set of features. There may also be cells which respond to many different views of a face 'summing' inputs from a variety of sources.

Whether such cells constitute the feature detectors postulated by feature detection theories is unclear. These neurological detectors may be a necessary pre-condition for higher-level (or cognitive) pattern task analysis. However, feature detection theories typically assume a *serial* form of processing, with feature extraction being followed by feature combination, which itself is then followed by pattern recognition (Eysenck, 1993). However, it is generally accepted that *parallel* (or non-serial) processing uses the visual cortex and that the relationship between different kinds of cortical cell is more complex than originally believed. An early example of a non-serial processing computer program is Selfridge's (1959) *Pandemonium model.*

Box 21.6   Selfridge's (1959) Pandemonium model

Selfridge's computer program was designed to recognise Morse code and a small set of handwritten letters. The components of the model are known as *demons*, of which there are four kinds. *Image demons* simply copy the pattern presented (and these are analogous to the retina). *Feature demons* analyse the information from the image demons in terms of combinations of features. *Cognitive demons* are specialised for particular letters and 'scream' according to how much the input from the feature demons matches their special letter. Finally, a *decision demon* chooses the 'loudest scream' and identifies the letter as shown below.

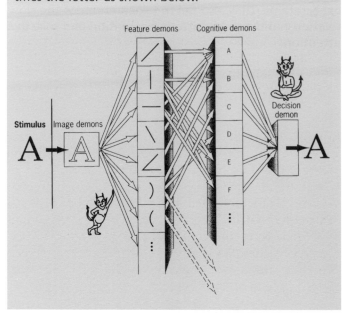

Like prototype theories, feature detection theories have been criticised for failing to take sufficient account of the role played by context and certain perceiver characteristics (such as expectations: see Chapter 22, page 186). An ambiguous feature can produce different patterns, and different features can produce the same pattern depending on the context. This can tell us what patterns are likely to be present and hence what to expect. Pattern recognition involves *selectively attending* to some aspects of the presented stimuli but not to others, aided by context. Pattern recognition and *selective attention* are therefore closely related (Solso, 1995: see Chapters 25 and 26.)

Conclusions

This chapter has looked at some aspects of visual perception and perceptual organisation that have captured and maintained the interest of cognitive psychologists. Attempts have been made to account for various aspects of visual perception, some of which have been more successful than others. Chapter 22 looks at attempts to explain the processes by which perception itself takes place.

Summary

■ **Sensation** involves physical stimulation of the sense organs, while **perception** is the **organisation** and **interpretation** of incoming sensory information. Vision is the dominant sense modality in humans.

■ **Gestalt psychologists** identified innately determined **principles** through which sensory information is interpreted and organised, the most basic being **form perception** which organises incoming sensory information into **figure and ground**.

■ Laws for **grouping** stimuli together all rest on the belief that 'the whole is greater than the sum of its parts'. These laws can be summarised under Koffka's law of **prägnanz**. Major Gestalt laws of perception include **proximity**, **similarity**, **good continuation**, **closure**, **part-whole relationship**, **simplicity** and **common fate**.

■ Gestalt psychology has provided the most comprehensive account of perceptual grouping. However, the various 'laws' are merely descriptive and often imprecise and difficult to measure. Despite empirical support, Gestalt laws are difficult to apply to 3-D perception and to whole scenes (they lack **ecological validity**).

■ **Depth perception** allows us to estimate the distance of objects from us. **Monocular cues** are important for judging objects at greater distances. They include **relative size**, **overlap/superimposition**, **relative height**, **texture gradient**, **linear perspective**, **shadowing**, **relative brightness**, **aerial haze**, **aerial perspective** and **motion parallax**.

■ **Perceptual constancy** refers to the ability to recognise an object as unchanging despite changes in its **size**, **shape**, **location**, **brightness** and **colour**. **Location constancy** is achieved through the brain's integration of **kinaesthetic feedback** from the muscles and balance organs in the ear with the changing pattern of retinal stimulation produced as we move our heads around. **Colour constancy** is most effective in relation to **familiar** objects and, strictly speaking, refers to the object's **hue**.

■ **Physical illusions** are caused by some physical distortion of the stimulus itself, while **perceptual illusions** occur when a stimulus contains misleading perceptual cues. **Fictions**, such as the Kanizsa triangles, suggest that **subjective contours** are at least as important as **physical contours** in determining an object's perceived shape. Shape perception is defined by the relationship between the elements of a pattern, not simply by detection of the elements.

■ Four main kinds of perceptual illusion are **distortions/geometric illusions, ambiguous/reversible figures, paradoxical figures,** and **fictions.**

■ Other illusions include **perception of depth** in paintings/drawings and the **perception of movement** in television pictures. **Apparent movement** refers to movement perception in the absence of changes in patterns of retinal stimulation. Examples include the **autokinetic effect, stroboscopic motion,** the **phi phenomenon, induced movement** and **motion after-effects.**

■ According to the **template matching hypothesis** (TMH), incoming sensory information is matched against miniature copies/templates of previously encountered patterns/objects stored in long-term memory. TMH fails to explain our ability to recognise unfamiliar patterns.

Biederman's **geon theory** attempts to overcome this limitation.

■ According to **prototype theories**, we store **prototypes** rather than templates, such that individual stimuli belong to a category and share basic properties with other members of the category.

■ **Feature detection theories** specify the properties shared by members of a stimulus category. Support comes from **visual scanning tasks** and **studies of eye movements** and **fixation**. Simple, complex and hyper-complex cells in the cortex, and the face-specific cells in the cortex of monkeys, may constitute the necessary neurological pre-condition for higher-level/cognitive pattern task analysis.

■ While feature detection theories typically assume a **serial** form of processing, the visual cortex involves **parallel** processing as represented by Selfridge's **Pandemonium model**. Both prototype and feature detection theories fail to take sufficient account of the context and certain perceiver characteristics, such as expectations. They also fail to take account of the close relationship between pattern recognition and **selective attention**.

22

SOME THEORIES OF VISUAL PERCEPTION

Introduction and overview

Sensation and perception are closely related, though different, processes often taken for granted in everyday life. Explaining visual perception is, however, no straightforward task. Some psychologists have addressed the question of whether our perception of the world is the result of learning and experience or essentially an inbuilt ability which requires little, if any, learning. This is discussed in Chapters 23 and 24. Others have concerned themselves with explaining the processes by which *physical energy* received by the sense organs forms the basis of *perceptual experience* (the sensation/perception distinction).

As Dodwell (1995) has observed:

> 'to perceive seems effortless. To understand perception is nevertheless a great challenge'.

One response to this challenge claims that our perception of the world is the end result of a process which also involves making *inferences* about what things are like. Those who subscribe to this 'end result' view, such as Bruner (1957), Neisser (1967) and Gregory (1972, 1980), are called *top-down* (or *conceptually-driven*) *perceptual processing theorists*. Making inferences about what things are like means that we perceive them *indirectly*, drawing on our knowledge and expectations of the world. Others argue that our perception of the world is essentially determined by the information presented to the sensory receptors, so that things are perceived in a fairly *direct* way. The most influential of these *bottom-up* (or *data-driven*) *perceptual processing theorists* is Gibson (1966, 1979).

This chapter considers the evidence relating to bottom-up and top-down accounts of perception. Although these theories have received much attention, a major alternative also discussed is Marr's (1982) *computational theory of vision*.

Gregory's 'constructivist' theory

According to Gregory (1966):

> 'perception is not determined simply by stimulus patterns. Rather, it is a dynamic searching for the best interpretation of the available data ... [which] involves going beyond the immediately given evidence of the senses'.

To avoid *sensory overload*, we need to select from all the sensory stimulation which surrounds us. Often, we also need to supplement sensory information because the total information that we need might not be directly available to the senses. This is what Gregory means by 'going beyond the immediately given evidence of the senses' and it is why his theory is known as constructivist. For Gregory, we make *inferences* about the information the senses receive (based on Helmholtz's nineteenth century view of perception as *unconscious inferences*).

GREGORY'S THEORY AND PERCEPTUAL CONSTANCIES

Perceptual constancies (see Chapter 21, pages 175–176) tell us that visual information from the retinal image is sketchy and incomplete and that the visual system has to 'go beyond' the retinal image in order to test hypotheses which fill in the 'gaps' (Greene, 1990). To make sense of the various sensory inputs to the retina, the visual system must draw on all kinds of evidence, including distance cues, information from other senses, and expectations based on past experience. For all these reasons, Gregory argues that perception must be an indirect process involving a construction based on physical sources of energy.

GREGORY'S THEORY AND ILLUSIONS

Gregory argues that when we experience a visual illusion (see pages 176–178), what we perceive may not be physically present in the stimulus (and hence not present in the retinal image). Essentially, an illusion can be explained in terms of a *perceptual hypothesis* which is not confirmed by the data, so that our attempt to interpret the stimulus figure turns out to be inappropriate. An illusion, then, occurs when we attempt to construe the stimulus in keeping with how we normally construe the world and are misled by this.

Box 22.1 Explaining the Ponzo illusion

In the Ponzo illusion, for example (see Figure 21.6 (a) on page 176), our system can accept the equal lengths of the two central bars as drawn on a flat 2-D surface (which would involve assuming that the bars are equidistant from us) or it can 'read' the whole figure as a railway track converging into the distance (so that

---

the two horizontal bars represent sleepers, the top one of which would be further away from an observer but appears longer since it 'must' be longer in order to produce the same length image on the retina).

The second interpretation is clearly inappropriate, since the figure is drawn on a flat piece of paper and there are no actual distance differences. As a result, an illusion is experienced.

All illusions illustrate how the perceptual system normally operates by forming a 'best guess' which is then tested against sensory inputs. For Gregory, illusions show that perception is an active process of using information to suggest and test hypotheses. What we perceive are not the data but the interpretation of them so that

'a perceived object is a hypothesis, suggested and tested by sensory data' (Gregory, 1966).

As Gregory (1996) has noted, '… this makes the basis of knowledge indirect and inherently doubtful'.

Gregory argues that when we view a 3-D scene with many distance cues, the perceptual system can quickly select the hypothesis that best interprets the sensory data. However, reversible figures supply few distance cues to guide the system. For example, the Necker cube (see page 177) provides sensory evidence which fits the hypothesis of either orientation *equally* well. The spontaneous reversal of the cube occurs because the perceptual system continually tests two equally plausible hypotheses about the nature of the object represented in the drawing.

One striking illusion is the *rotating hollow mask* (Gregory, 1970: see Figure 22.1). There is sufficient information for us to see the mask as hollow, but it is impossible not to see it as a normal face. The perceptual system dismisses the hypothesis that the mask is an inside-out face because it is so improbable, and note that in this case, the hypothesis we select is strongly influenced by our *past experiences of faces* (Gregory, 1970). With the impossible triangle (see Figure 21.8 (a) on page 177), our perceptual system makes reasonable, but actually incorrect, judgements about the distance of different parts of the triangle.

According to Gregory's *misapplied size constancy theory*, the Müller–Lyer illusion (see Figure 21.6 (c) on page 176) can be explained in terms of the arrow with the ingoing fins providing linear perspective cues suggesting that it could be the outside corner of a building and the ingoing fins the walls receding from us. This would make the arrow appear to be 'close'. In the arrow with the outgoing fins, the cues suggest that it could be the inside corner of a room and the

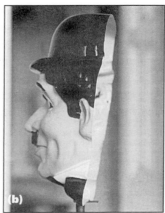

Figure 22.1   The rotating hollow mask. (a) shows the normal face which is rotated to (d), which is a hollow face. However, (d) appears like a normal face rotating in the opposite direction

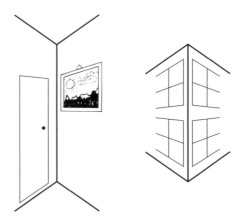

Figure 22.2   A representation of the Müller–Lyer illusion as suggested by Gregory's misplaced size constancy theory

outgoing fins as walls approaching us. This would make the shaft appear to be 'distant' (see Figure 22.2).

However, the retinal images produced by the arrows are equal and, according to size constancy, if equally sized images are produced by two lines, one of which is further away from us than the other, then the line which is furthest from us must be longer! Because this interpretation is taking place unconsciously and quickly, we immediately perceive the illusion. Evidence suggests, though, that if the perspective cues are removed, the illusion remains suggesting that the misapplied size constancy theory is itself misapplied (see Figure 22.3). Alternatively, the apparent distance of the arrow could be caused by the apparent size of the arrows rather than, as Gregory claims, the other way around (Robinson, 1972).

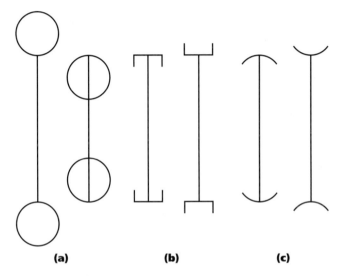

(a)   **(b)**   **(c)**

Figure 22.3   The Müller–Lyer illusion with the depth cues removed (after Delboeuf, 1892)

In a variation of the original Müller–Lyer illusion, Morgan (1969) placed a dot mid-way along the arrow.

Figure 22.4   Morgan's (1969) modified Müller–Lyer illusion

The dot appears to be nearer the left-hand end, and the only way this can be explained by Gregory is to claim that the fins make the arrow appear to slope away from us, providing a rather odd perspective interpretation of the figure. According to Gregory (1972), such a slope can be demonstrated, although this claim has been disputed (Eysenck & Keane, 1995).

In the Müller–Lyer illusion, we *know* the arrows are the same length, yet we still experience the illusion. Our

knowledge *should* enable us to modify our hypotheses in an adaptive way. Whilst some illusions can be explained in terms of the same unconscious processes occurring (an example being size constancy), not all illusions are amenable to explanation in the way Gregory proposes (Robinson, 1972).

GREGORY'S THEORY AND 'PERCEPTUAL SET'

Perceptual set is also directly relevant to Gregory's view that perception is an active process involving selection, inference and interpretation. Allport (1955) describes perceptual set as:

> 'a perceptual bias or predisposition or readiness to perceive particular features of a stimulus'.

It refers to the tendency to perceive or notice some aspects of available sense data and ignore others. According to Vernon (1955), set acts as a *selector* (whereby the perceiver has certain expectations which help focus attention on particular aspects of the incoming sensory information), and as an *interpreter* (whereby the perceiver knows how to deal with the selected data, how to classify, understand and name them, and what inferences to draw from them).

Several factors can influence or induce set, most of them being *perceiver* (or *organismic*) *variables*, but some relating to the nature of the stimulus or the conditions under which it is perceived (*stimulus* or *situational variables*). Both types of variable influence perception *indirectly*, through directly influencing set which, as such, is a perceiver variable or characteristic.

Box 22.2   Some findings relating to perceptual set

Motivation: People with some particular need (such as hunger) are more likely to perceive vague or ambiguous pictures as relating to that need (Sanford, 1937; McClelland & Atkinson, 1948).

Values: Lambert *et al.* (1949) found that when children were taught to value something more highly than they had previously done, they perceived the valued thing as being larger (*perceptual accentuation*).

Beliefs: The beliefs we hold about the world can affect our interpretation of ambiguous sensory signals. A person who believes in UFOs is likely to perceive an ambiguous object in the sky differently from a person who does not share that belief (Wade & Tavris, 1993).

Cognitive style: The way we deal with our environment appears to affect our perception of it. Some people perceive the environment as a whole and do not clearly differentiate the shape, colour and so on, of individual items. Others perceive the elements of the environment as separate and distinct from one another (Witkin *et al.*, 1962).

Cultural background: The Mbuti pygmies of Zaire, who seldom leave their forest environment and rarely encounter objects more than a few feet away, use perceptual cues differently from people with different cultural backgrounds (Turnbull, 1961: see also Chapter 24, pages 205–208).

Context and expectations: The interaction between context and expectations was demonstrated by Bruner & Postman (1949) and Bruner *et al.* (1952). When participants are asked to copy a briefly presented stimulus such as:

PARIS IN THE

THE SPRING

it is typically copied as PARIS IN THE SPRING (Lachman, 1984). One reason why eyewitness testimony (see Chapter 31) is so unreliable is that our general expectation of people is that they will be of 'average height and weight' and this is what almost all eyewitness accounts describe people as being (Loftus, 1980).

AN EVALUATION OF GREGORY'S THEORY OF PERCEPTION

According to Gregory (1996), even a minimal amount of 'bottom-up' data (sensory signals) can produce detailed hypotheses. He cites Johansson's (1975) study which showed that in darkness, just a few lights attached to a moving person evoke clear perceptions of people walking or dancing. Gregory has also drawn on research indicating that vision 'works' by many physiologically distinct 'channels' which are produced by their own 'modules'. A rotating spiral, for example, does not actually change size but appears to expand or contract. Because size and motion are signalled by different 'channels', disagreement between them leads to a *physiological paradox* being experienced (see Chapter 10, page 85).

Gregory's theory raises many important questions which have yet to be answered satisfactorily (Gordon, 1989). For example, if perception is essentially constructive, then we need to know how it gets started and why there is such commonality among the perceptions of different people, all of whom have had to construct their own idiosyncratic worlds. Also, given that perception is typically accurate (and our hypotheses are usually correct), it seems unlikely that our retinal images are really as ambiguous and lacking in detail as Gregory suggests.

Gregory has been much more successful in explaining at least some types of illusion than in explaining perception as a whole (Eysenck & Keane, 1995). His theory may be more relevant to explaining perception in artificial situations than perception as it takes place in the ordinary world. In Gordon's (1989) view, constructivist theories have underestimated the richness of sensory evidence in the real world. For Gordon:

'it is possible that we perceive constructively only at certain times and in certain situations. Whenever we move under our own power on the surface of the natural world and in good light, the necessary perceptions of size, texture, distance, continuity, motion and so on, may all occur directly and reflexively'.

Gibson's theory of 'direct perception'

Constructivists use the retinal image as their starting point for explaining perception. According to Gibson (1966), this approach mistakenly describes the input for a perceiver in the same terms as that for a single *photoreceptor*, namely a stream of photons. For Gibson, it is better to begin by considering the input as a pattern of light extended over time and space (an *optical array* containing all the visual information from the environment striking the eye). The optical array provides unambiguous, invariant information about the layout of objects in space and this information takes three main forms: *optic flow patterns*, *texture gradient* and *affordances*. Perception essentially involves 'picking up' the rich information provided by the optic array in a direct way which involves little or no (unconscious) information processing, computations or internal representations.

Optic flow patterns

During World War II, Gibson prepared training films describing the problems pilots experience when taking off and landing. He called the information available to pilots *optic flow patterns* (OFPs). As shown in Figure 22.5, the point to which a pilot moves appears motionless, with the rest of the visual environment apparently moving away from that point. Thus, all around the point there is an apparent radial expansion of textures flowing around the pilot's head.

The lack of apparent movement of the point towards which the pilot moves is an invariant, unchanging feature of the optic array. Such OFPs provide unambiguous information about direction, speed and altitude.

Figure 22.5   The optic flow patterns as a pilot approaches the landing strip (from Gibson, 1950)

Texture gradients

Textures expand as we approach them and contract as they pass beyond our head. This happens whenever we move toward something, so that over and above the behaviour of each texture element there is a 'higher-order' pattern or structure available as a source of information about the environment (and so the flow of the texture is *invariant*). *Texture gradients* (or *gradients of texture density*) are an important depth cue perceived directly without the need for any inferences. The depth cues identified in Box 21.3 are all examples of directly perceived, invariant, higher-order features of the optic array. For Gibson, then, the third dimension (depth) is available to the senses as directly as the other two dimensions, automatically processed by the sense receptors, and automatically producing the perceptual experience of depth.

Affordances

Affordances are directly perceivable, potential uses of objects (a ladder, for example, 'affords' climbing) and are closely linked with *ecological optics*. To understand an animal's perceptual system, we need to consider the environment in which it has evolved, particularly the patterns of light (the optical array) which reaches the eye (ecological optics). When an object moves further away from the eye, its image gets smaller (relative size) and most objects are bounded by texture surfaces and texture gradient gets finer as an object recedes. In other words, objects are not judged in complete isolation, and the optic array commonly contains far more information than that associated with a single stimulus array (often overlooked by the use of classical optics and laboratory experiments: Gordon, 1989).

AN EVALUATION OF GIBSON'S THEORY

According to Marr (1982), Gibson's concern with the problem of how we obtain constant perception in everyday life on the basis of continually changing sensations indicated that he correctly regarded the problem of perception as that of recovering from sensory information 'valid properties of the external world'. However, as Marr (1982) points out, Gibson failed to recognise two equally critical things:

> 'First, the detection of physical invariants, like image surfaces, is exactly and precisely an information-processing problem … Second, he vastly underrated the sheer difficulty of such detection'.

Gibson's concept of affordances is part of his attempt to show that all the information needed to make sense of the visual environment is directly available in the visual input (a purely 'bottom-up' approach to perception). Bruce & Green (1990) argue that this concept is most powerful and useful in the context of *visually guided behaviour*, as in insects. Here, it makes sense to speak of an organism detecting information available in the light needed to organise its activities, and the idea of it needing to have a conceptual representation of its environment seems redundant.

However, humans act in a *cultural* as well as physical environment. It seems unlikely that no *knowledge* of writing or the postal system is needed in order to detect that a pen affords writing or a postbox affords posting a letter, and that these are directly perceived invariants. People see objects and events as what they are in terms of a culturally given conceptual representation of the world, Gibson's theory says much more about 'seeing' than about 'seeing as'.

'SEEING' AND 'SEEING AS'

Fodor & Pylyshyn (1981) distinguish between 'seeing' and 'seeing as'. For them:

> 'What you see when you see a thing depends upon what the thing you see is. But what you see the thing as depends upon what you know about what you are seeing'.

This view of perception as 'seeing as' is the fundamental principle of *transactionalism*. Transactionalists (such as Ames, cited in Ittelson, 1952) argue that because sensory input is always ambiguous, the interpretation selected is the one most likely to be true given what has been perceived in the past.

In the Ames *distorted room* (see Figure 22.6 on page 188), the perceiver has to choose between two different beliefs about the world built up through past experience. The first is that rooms are rectangular, consist of right angles,

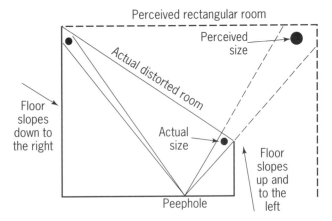

Figure 22.6   The Ames room and a schematic representation of its 'secret'. The room is constructed in such a way that, when viewed with one eye through a peephole, a person at one end may appear very small and the person at the other end very tall, When they cross the room, they appear to change size. The room itself appears perfectly normal and regular to an observer

A possible synthesis of Gregory's and Gibson's theories

Despite the important differences between Gibson's and Gregory's theories, they also agree on certain points.

Box 22.3   The main similarities and differences between Gibson and Gregory

Similarities

- Visual perception is mediated by light reflected from surfaces and objects.

- Some kind of physiological system is needed to perceive.

- Perception is an active process. (In Gibson's, 1966, view, 'a perceiving organism is more like a map-reader than a camera'.)

- Perceptual experience can be influenced by learning.

Differences

- Gregory believes that meaningless sensory cues must be supplemented by memory, habit, experience and so on in order to construct a meaningful world. Gibson argues that the environment (initially the optic array) provides us with *all* the information we need for living in the world. Perceptual learning consists not in 'gluing' together sensory 'atoms', but in coming to differentiate and discriminate between the features of the environment as presented in the optic array.

- To the extent that Gibson acknowledges the role of learning (albeit a different kind of learning from Gregory), he may be considered an *empirist* (see Chapter 23), together with his emphasis on what is provided by the physical world. In other respects, though, Gibson can be considered a *nativist* (see Chapter 23). He was very much influenced by the Gestalt psychologists (see Chapter 21), stressing the organised quality of perception. However, whilst for Gibson the organised quality of perception is part of the physical structure of the light impinging on the observer's eye, for Gestaltists it is a function of how the brain is organised.

---

and so on. The second is that people are usually of 'average' height. Most observers choose the first and so judge the people to be an odd size (although a woman who saw her husband in the room and judged the room to be odd shows that particularly salient past experiences can override more generalised beliefs about the world).

The Ames room is another example of a visual illusion, and the inability of Gibson's theory to explain mistaken perception is perhaps its greatest single weakness. Gibson argues that most 'mistaken perceptions' occur in situations very different from those which prevail in the natural environment. However, to suggest that illusions are nothing but laboratory tricks designed to baffle ordinary people is mistaken, since at least some produce effects that are similar to those found in normal perception. A striking example is the 'hollow mask' illusion described on page 184 (Bruce & Green, 1990).

Eysenck & Keane (1995) argue that the relative importance of bottom-up and top-down processes is affected by several factors. When viewing conditions are good, bottom-up processing may be crucial. However, with brief and/or ambiguous stimuli, top-down processing becomes increasingly important. Gibson seems to have been more concerned with *optimal* viewing conditions, whilst Gregory and other constructivists have tended to concentrate on *sub-optimal* conditions (Eysenck, 1993). In most circumstances, both bottom-up and top-down processes are probably needed, as claimed by Neisser (1976).

Box 22.4   Neisser's (1976) analysis-by-synthesis model

Neisser assumes the existence of a *perceptual cycle* involving *schemata, perceptual exploration* and *stimulus environment*. Schemata contain collections of knowledge based on past experience (see Chapter 29), and these direct perceptual exploration towards relevant environmental stimulation. Such exploration often involves moving around the environment leading the perceiver to actively sample the available stimulus information. If this fails to match that in the relevant schema, then the hypothesis is modified accordingly.

An initial *analysis* of the sensory cues/features (a bottom-up process) might suggest the hypothesis that the object being viewed is, say, a chair. This initiates a search for the expected features (such as four legs and a back), which is based on our schema of a chair (and this *synthesis* is a top-down process). However, if the environmental features disconfirm the original hypothesis (the 'chair' has only three legs and no back), then a new hypothesis must be generated and tested (it might be a stool) and the appropriate schema activated.

Neisser argues that perception never occurs in a vacuum, since our sampling of sensory features of the environment is always guided by our knowledge and past experience. Perception is an *interactive process*, involving both bottom-up feature analysis and top-down expectations.

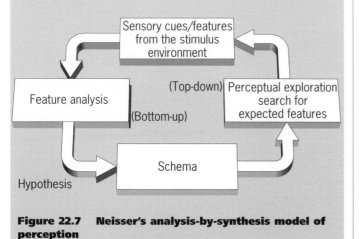

Figure 22.7   Neisser's analysis-by-synthesis model of perception

Marr's computational theory of vision

According to Marr (1982), the central 'problem' of perception is identifying the precise *mechanisms* and *computations* by which useful information about a scene is extracted from that scene ('useful information' being what will guide the thoughts or actions of the total system of which the visual system is part). Marr's theory begins by asking 'what is the visual system for?', because only by answering this can we understand how it works.

For Marr, there are three levels at which any process must be understood. The *computational theory level* is a theoretical analysis of the tasks performed by a system (in this case, the visual system) and the methods needed to perform them. The *algorithmic level* is concerned with identifying the actual operations by which perceptual tasks (processes and representations) are achieved. The *hardware* or *implementation level* is concerned with the mechanisms underlying the system's operation. In the case of a biological visual system, these are neuronal or nervous system structures.

Marr argues that vision's main 'job' is deriving a representation of *shape*, and that the first question to answer is how the visual system is able to derive reliable information regarding the shapes of objects in the real world from information contained in the retinal image. His answer was that visual representation is organised as an information processing system consisting of four successive stages which represent individual visual *modules* of progressive complexity (Eysenck, 1993).

Each stage or module takes as its input the information it receives from the previous stage and makes it into a more complex description or representation of the input. By taking the image as the starting point (the result of light rays from objects or scenes in the real world being focused onto a light-sensitive surface, either a screen or the retina), Marr's approach is strictly bottom-up (Roth, 1995). However, there are also top-down aspects to his theory (see below).

3-D MODEL REPRESENTATION AND OBJECT RECOGNITION

Since the 3-D model representation involves top-down processes (drawing on stored knowledge of what objects look like), Marr argued that in many cases 3-D structures can be derived from the 2½-D sketch using only general principles of the kind used in the earlier stages. This view rests on the observation that stick-figure representations (especially of animals and plants) are easy to recognise (Garnham, 1991). The brain automatically transposes the contours derived from the 2½-D sketch onto axes of symmetry which resemble stick figures composed of pipe cleaners. The 3-D model consists of a unique description of any object a person can distinguish – the same object should always produce the same unique description no matter what the angle of viewing.

Box 22.5   The four stages or modules of Marr's computational theory of vision

The image (or grey-level description): This represents the intensity of light at each point in the retinal image, so as to discover regions in the image and their boundaries. Regions and boundaries are parts of images, not parts of things in the world, so this represents the starting point of seeing.

The primal sketch: Useful attributes of a 3-D scene (such as surface markings, object boundaries and shadows) can be recovered from the image by locating and describing the places where the image intensity changes relatively abruptly from place to place. The function of the *raw primal sketch* is to describe potentially significant regions (those which may correspond in the real world to the boundaries between overlapping objects, their edges and texture). The *full primal sketch* provides information about how these regions 'go together' to form structures (it provides a functional explanation for the Gestalt grouping principles: see pages 172–173). Grouping is necessary, since in complex scenes, for example, the images of different objects may occlude each other. Overall, it provides a more useful and less cluttered description of the image, hence the term 'sketch'.

2½-D sketch: The primal sketch helps the formation of the 2½-D sketch. The function of this is to make explicit the orientation and depth of visible structures, as if a 'picture' of the world is beginning to emerge. It is no longer an image because it contains information about things in the world which provide the image. However, it describes only the visible part of the scene and so is not fully three-dimensional. Object recognition requires that the input representation of the object is mapped against a representation stored in memory, so that non-visible parts are taken into account and this is essentially what perceptual constancy (see pages 175–176) involves. Also, the sketch changes with the observer's viewpoint (it is *viewpoint dependent*) and so descriptions at this stage are not invariant.

3-D model representation: The function of the 3-D sketch is to make shapes and their spatial organisation explicit as belonging to particular 3-D objects, independently of any particular position or orientation on the retina (they are *viewpoint independent*). The observer now has a model of the external world and knowledge about the nature and construction of the object is utilised (top-down processing). The 3-D model representation corresponds to object recognition.

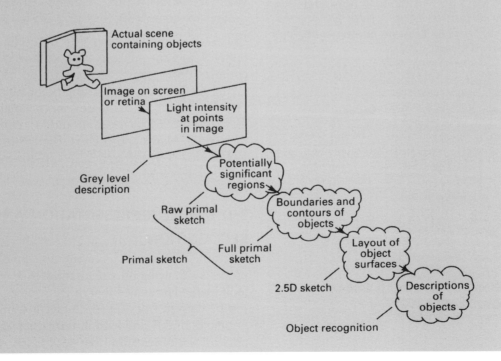

Marr & Nishihara (1978) argued that the parts of the body can be represented as jointed or generalised cylinders which change their size along their length (see Figure 22.8). They then showed that the cylinders which compose an object can be computed from the 2½-D sketch (the lines running down the centre of these cylinders – important in the recognition process – make up the stick figures). Once a generalised cylinder representation of objects in a scene has been computed, it can be compared with stored representations of objects in a catalogue of 3-D models where objects are represented in 'standard' orientations (Garnham, 1991).

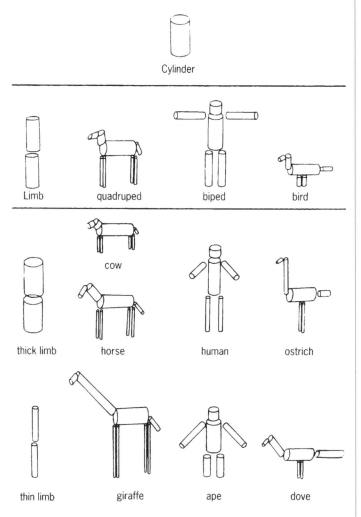

Figure 22.8   Combinations of cylinders can be used to represent the shapes of various objects or parts of objects

AN EVALUATION OF MARR'S THEORY

According to Harris & Humphreys (1995), Marr's framework remains the widest-ranging computational account of visual object recognition. Marr & Hildreth (1980) have

shown that Marr's model does generate a symbolic representation which corresponds to the significant components of the input. This does not mean that biological systems necessarily work in the same way (Roth, 1995), although the research conducted by Hubel and Wiesel (see Chapter 21, page 180) is relevant to Marr's theory (as are other findings from neurophysiology: Ono *et al.*, 1993).

The least well supported stage in Marr's theory is the 3-D model, since the early stages make only very general assumptions about the structure of the external world and do not require knowledge of specific objects. Although a bottom-up approach is not an inevitable consequence of the computational approach, it has dominated research. In part, this is because it is easier to derive computational theories from the early stages of perception, where the relationships between the stimulus and the world are much easier to specify (Harris & Humphreys, 1995).

Gardner (1985), too, has argued that most of Marr's theory focuses on the steps prior to the recognition of real objects in the real world ('the most central part of perception') and that:

'the procedures [Marr] outlined for object recognition may prove applicable chiefly to the perception of figures of a certain sort, for example, the mammalian body, which lends itself to decomposition in terms of generalised cylindrical forms'.

Researchers are beginning to reconsider whether top-down, domain-specific knowledge might be used, encouraged by *connectionist models of visual perception* and Biederman's (1987) *recognition-by-components theory* which proposes that stored object knowledge may be contacted directly from 2-D information in the image, without the elaboration of 2½-D and 3-D descriptions (see Chapter 21). Nevertheless, Marr's general approach to perception and his particular argument for computational theories is, in Harris & Humphreys' (1995) terms:

'likely to remain as one of the most important contributions of research in artificial intelligence to psychological theory. Such theories are able to guide empirical and theoretical research, even if the detailed models specified at any one time later turn out to be wrong'.

Conclusions

The various theories of visual perception considered in this chapter are all supported to some degree by experimental evidence. At present, however, no one theory seems to be sufficiently well-supported by evidence to be accepted as the 'best' explanation of visual perception.

Summary

■ Some psychologists are concerned with how **physical energy** received by the sense organs (sensation) forms the basis of **perceptual experience**. According to **top-down (conceptually-driven) perceptual processing theorists**, perception is the end result of an indirect process that involves making **inferences** about the world, based on knowledge and expectations. **Bottom-up (data-driven) perceptual processing theorists** argue that perception is a direct process, basically determined by the information presented to the sensory receptors.

■ According to Gregory's **constructivist theory**, perception sometimes involves selecting from all the available sensory stimulation, but often we go beyond the immediately given evidence of the senses by supplementing it with **unconscious inferences**.

■ The experience of illusions involves making a **perceptual hypothesis** which is not confirmed by the data. Our normal ways of construing the world turn out to be inappropriate when applied to particular stimulus figures.

■ Gregory's **misapplied size constancy theory** claims that in the Müller–Lyer illusion we interpret the ingoing and outgoing fins of the arrows as providing perspective cues to distance. However, removal of the perspective cues does not remove the illusion.

■ **Perceptual set** acts as a **selector** and **interpreter** and can be induced by **perceiver/organismic** and **stimulus/situational variables**. Perceiver variables include **expectations** which often interact with context.

■ Gregory's theory fails to explain how perception gets started and why there is such agreement among different people's perceptual experience. Gregory's theory may be more capable of explaining illusions than perception as a whole, and, hence, be more relevant to perception in artificial situations than in everyday life.

■ According to Gibson, the correct starting point for explaining perception is the **optical array**, which provides unambiguous/invariant information about the layout of objects in space. Little or no (unconscious) information processing, computations or internal representations are needed.

■ **Optic flow patterns**, **texture gradients/gradients of texture density** and **affordances** are all **invariant**, unchanging and 'higher-order' features of the optic array. Texture gradients are an important cue to depth, which is directly available to the senses and automatically processed by the sense receptors.

■ **Affordances** are closely linked with **ecological optics**. Objects are not judged in isolation, and the optic array usually contains far more information than is provided by any single stimulus.

■ Humans act in a **cultural** as well as a physical environment, and Gibson seems to have overlooked the role of **knowledge** in perception. He also failed to distinguish between seeing and seeing as, the latter forming the basic principle of **transactionalism** as demonstrated by the Ames **distorted room** illusion.

■ Gibson's theory seems incapable of explaining mistaken perception, like the hollow mask illusion, which is not a mere laboratory trick.

■ Both Gibson and Gregory agree that perception is an active process influenced by learning (making them **empirists**), although different kinds of learning are proposed in the two theories. Gibson is also a **nativist** in certain respects and was influenced by the Gestalt psychologists.

■ Bottom-up processing (Gibson) may be crucial under **optimal** viewing conditions, but under **sub-optimal** conditions, top-down processing (Gregory) becomes increasingly important.

■ According to Neisser's **analysis-by-synthesis model**, perception is an **interactive process** involving both bottom-up feature analysis and top-down expectations (appearing at different stages of a perceptual cycle).

■ Marr's **computational theory of vision** is concerned with what the visual system is for. For Marr, its main task is to derive a representation of object shape from information contained in the retinal image. This is achieved by a series of four increasingly complex stages or **modules**: the **image/grey-level description**, the **primal sketch**, the **2½-D sketch** (which is **viewpoint dependent**) and the **3-D model representation/object recognition** (which is **viewpoint independent**).

■ By taking the image as the starting point, Marr's approach is bottom-up, but the 3-D model representation involves top-down processes. Often, 3-D structures are derived from the 2½-D sketch using stick-figure representations which are composed of the lines running down the centre of jointed or generalised cylinders.

■ The 3-D model representation is the least well supported stage in the theory. It is easier to derive computational theories from the early (bottom-up) stages of perception.

■ **Connectionist models** of visual perception and Biederman's **recognition-by-components theory** have encouraged a reconsideration of the possible role of top-down, domain-specific knowledge.

192

23

STUDYING THE DEVELOPMENT OF VISUAL PERCEPTUAL ABILITIES 1: HUMAN NEONATE AND INFANT STUDIES

Introduction and overview

Chapter 21 showed that visual perception is a complex set of interconnected and overlapping abilities. Whether these are present at birth or develop through experience has been one of psychology's most enduring concerns. This and Chapter 24 examine the evidence concerning the development of visual perception.

This chapter concentrates on studies involving human neonates (new-born babies) and infants. Theoretically, the study of neonates is the most direct way of assessing which perceptual abilities are present at birth and which develop through experience. Unfortunately, neonates cannot *tell* us about their visual experiences, and so researchers have had to devise ingenious ways to allow them to *infer* what the new-born baby can perceive (but we can never be certain that such inferences are correct!). As well as the findings, some of the methods used in this area will also be considered.

The 'nature' and 'nurture' of visual perception

According to Mehler & Dupoux (1994):

'In certain cultures different from our own, the baby was thought of as a repository of a soul that had already lived before, and therefore possessed of all faculties utilised by adults. Closer to us, generations of parents believed, on the contrary, that their children were born deaf and blind and that they remained in this condition for weeks, even months. The notion that the new-born was about as competent as a potted plant and that it had to learn to see, hear, memorise and categorise, was extremely influential in Western thought'.

Philosophers and psychologists have long debated whether visual perceptual (and other) abilities are *innate* (or *inborn*) or the product of *experience* and *learning*. *Nativists* (or *innate theorists*) argue that we are born with certain capacities and abilities to perceive the world in particular ways. Whilst such abilities might be immature

or incomplete at birth, they develop gradually thereafter, proceeding through a genetically determined process of maturation in which experience plays only a minor (if any) role. The Gestalt psychologists (see Chapter 21) illustrate this perspective.

Those who believe that our capacities and abilities develop through experience are called *empirists* (and can be distinguished from *empiricists*, who follow a methodological prescription which says that we should rely on observation, experience and measurement to obtain reliable knowledge: Wertheimer, 1970). For Locke (1690), the mind at birth is a *blank slate* (or *tabula rasa*) on which experience 'writes' and, in the case of visual perception, the world can only be understood through learning and experience (see Chapter 83). Locke's belief was supported by James (1890), according to whom:

'the baby, assailed by eyes, ears, nose, skin and entrails at once, feels it all as one great booming, buzzing confusion'.

Studying neonate and infant visual perception

If visual perception is innate, then it should be possible to demonstrate perceptual abilities in human neonates. If visual perception is dependent on experience, such attempts should be doomed to failure. Before looking at the perceptual world of the human neonate, we need to be familiar with some of the methods that have been used in this area.

> **Box 23.1   Some methods used in studying neonate and infant perception**
>
> **Spontaneous visual preference technique (or *preferential looking*):** Two stimuli are presented simultaneously to the neonate. If more time is spent looking at one, it can reasonably be assumed that (a) the difference between the stimuli can be perceived, and (b) the stimulus which is looked at longer is preferred.

Sucking rate: In this, a dummy or pacifier is used and the sucking rate in response to different stimuli is measured. First, a *baseline sucking rate* is established and then a stimulus introduced. The stimulus may produce an increase or decrease in sucking rate but, eventually, *habituation* will occur, and the baby will stop responding. If the stimulus is changed and another increase or decrease in sucking rate occurs, it can be inferred that the baby has responded to the change as a novel stimulus and hence can tell the difference between the two stimuli.

Habituation: As well as being used as described above, habituation has been used as a method in its own right. If an external stimulus and a baby's representation of it match, then the baby presumably knows the stimulus. This will be reflected by the baby ignoring it. Mismatches will maintain the baby's attention, so that a novel (and discriminable) stimulus presented after habituation to a familiar stimulus re-excites attention.

Conditioned head rotation: In this, the infant is operantly conditioned (see Chapter 32) to turn its head in response to a stimulus. The stimulus can then be presented in, for example, a different orientation, and the presence or absence of the conditioned response noted. This method has been used to test for shape constancy (see page 175) and in auditory perception to study basic abilities such as frequency, localisation and complexity (Bornstein, 1988).

Physiological measures: Two of the most important physiological measures are heart rate and breathing rate. If a physiological change occurs when a new stimulus is presented, it can be inferred that the infant can discriminate between the old and new stimuli.

Measures of electrical activity in the brain: By using electrodes attached to the scalp, researchers can look for *visually evoked potentials* (VEPs) occurring in response to particular stimuli. If different stimuli produce different VEPs, the infant can presumably distinguish between those stimuli.

The perceptual equipment of babies

At birth, the whole nervous system is immature. The optic nerve is thinner and shorter than in adults and myelin sheath will not be fully developed until about four months. As a result, visual information is transmitted less effectively to the immature cortex. Also, at birth a baby's eye is about half the size and weight of an adult's, and the eyeball is shorter. This reduces the distance between the retina and lens which makes vision less efficient. So, although the new-born's eyeball is anatomically identical to an adult's, the relationship between the parts is different, and they do not develop at the same rate (see Chapter 10, pages 82–83).

Box 23.2   What can babies see?

Colour perception: The retina, rods and cones are reasonably well developed at birth. Using habituation, Bornstein (1976) found that in the absence of brightness cues, three-month-olds could discriminate blue-green from white, and yellow from green (tests which are typically failed by those who are red-green colour blind). Most babies possess largely normal colour vision at two months and some as early as one month (Bornstein, 1988).

Brightness: The fovea is also reasonably well developed at birth. The developing foetus reacts to bright light, and the *pupillary reflex* is present even in premature babies, with the *blink reflex* present at birth. These findings suggest that a baby's sensitivity to brightness is reasonably similar to an adult's. The ability to discriminate between lights of varying intensities improves with time and reaches adult levels within one year (Adams & Maurer, 1984).

Movement: The *optokinetic reflex* (or *optic nystagmus*), which enables us to follow a moving object, is present within two days of birth. Whilst it is less efficient than an adult's, it improves rapidly in the first three months. Horizontal movement is better tracked than vertical movement, but is still 'jerky'. This may be because *convergence* (essential for fixation and depth perception) is absent at birth, although fully developed by two to three months. *Accommodation* to the distance of objects is equivalent to that of an adult by about four months, and, like at least some of the above, is probably due to maturation (see Chapter 21, page 174).

Visual acuity: Gwiazda *et al.* (1980) used the preference method to show that the *threshold of visual acuity* (the ability to discriminate fine detail) is about 30 times poorer than in adults and, at birth, everything beyond 20 centimetres is seen as a blur. However, babies aged one to three months will learn to suck on a nipple connected to the focus on a projector to bring a blurred picture into focus (Kalnins & Bruner, 1973). Also, when electrodes are attached to a baby's scalp above its visual cortex, VEPs occur in response to visual stimuli, suggesting some degree of acuity at birth. Between six and 12 months, visual acuity comes within adult ranges, although it may not reach 20/20 vision until the age of ten or 11 (Adams, 1987).

The perceptual abilities of babies

PATTERN OR FORM PERCEPTION

Using the preferential looking technique, Fantz (1961) presented one- to 15-week-old babies with pairs of stimuli. The stimuli were presented at weekly intervals, and Fantz measured how long the babies spent looking at each. There was a distinct preference for more *complex stimuli*, that is, stimuli which contain more information and in which there is more 'going on'.

developed at birth). The babies tested at weekly intervals could discriminate between stimuli with progressively narrower stripes (cf. visual acuity in Box 23.2). Later, Fantz showed that two- to four-month-old babies prefer patterns to colour or brightness. In that experiment, six test objects were used. These were flat discs six inches in diameter. Three were patterned (a face, a bull's-eye and a patch of printed matter) and three were plain (a red disc, a fluorescent yellow disc and a white disc). The discs were presented one at a time against a blue background, and the time spent looking at each was recorded. The face was preferred over both the printed matter and the bull's-eye, and all of these were preferred to the plain discs.

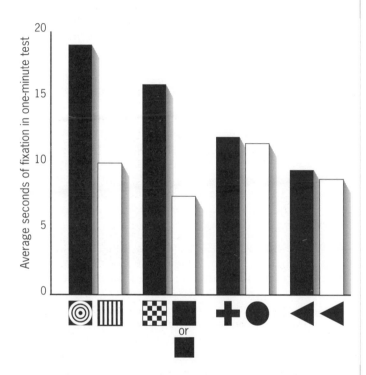

Figure 23.1   Average time spent looking at various pairs of stimulus patterns in babies aged one to 15 weeks (from Fantz, 1961)

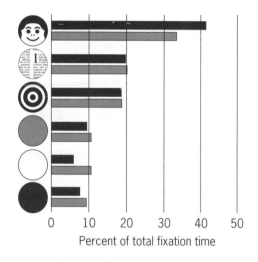

Figure 23.2   Preference for complex stimuli over simple stimuli as demonstrated by Fantz (1961). The black bars show the percentage of fixation time for two-to three-month-olds. The grey bars show the percentage of fixation time for four-month-olds (From Fantz, 1961)

According to Fantz:

> 'the relative attractiveness of the two members of a pair depended on the presence of a pattern difference. There were strong preferences between stripes and bull's-eyes and between checkerboard and square. Neither the cross and circle nor the two triangles aroused a significant differential interest. The differential response to pattern was shown at all ages tested, indicating that it was not the result of a learning process'.

Fantz also found that preference for complexity is apparently a function of age (reflecting the fact that the eye, the visual nerve pathways and the visual cortex are poorly

The preference for increasing complexity suggests that the baby's capacity for differentiation steadily improves. Possibly, this is because its ability to scan becomes more efficient and thorough. Support for this comes from studies showing that very young infants confine their scanning to one corner of a triangle, suggesting a preference for areas of greatest contrast (Salapatek, 1975). Only later does the baby begin to explore all around the stimulus and inside it, and attend to the whole pattern and not just specific parts. Before two months of age, neonates probably discriminate between shapes on the basis of lower-order variables such as orientation and contrast (Slater & Morison, 1985). After two months, however, 'true form perception' begins (Slater, 1989), and they respond to higher-order variables (such as configurational invariance and form categories).

THE PERCEPTION OF HUMAN FACES

The most interesting and attractive stimulus experienced by a baby is the human face. It is three-dimensional, contains high contrast information (especially the eyes, mouth and hairline), constantly moves (the eyes, mouth and head), is a source of auditory information (the voice) and regulates its behaviour according to the baby's own activities. Thus, the human face combines complexity, pattern and movement, all of which babies appear innately to prefer. Whether this preference occurs because of this combination of factors or whether there is an innate perceptual knowledge of a face *as a face* was also addressed by Fantz (1961).

Fantz presented babies aged between four days and six months with all possible pairs of the three stimuli shown in Figure 23.3. The stimuli were coloured black, presented against a pink background, and of the approximate shape and size of an adult's head.

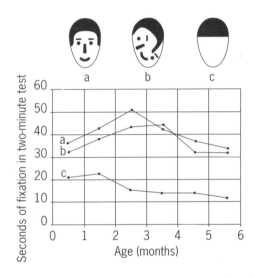

Figure 23.3   Looking times for each of the stimuli used in Fantz's study of the perception of faces (From Fantz, 1961)

Irrespective of age, the babies preferred to look at the schematic representation of a face (a) more than the 'scrambled' face (b). The control stimulus (c) was largely ignored. Even though the difference between (a) and (b) was small, Fantz concluded that 'there is an unlearned, primitive meaning in the form perception of infants', and that babies have an innate preference for 'facedness'.

Hershenson *et al.* (1965) pointed out that (a) and (b) were more *complex* than (c) and this might account for Fantz's findings, rather than a preference for looking at human faces. They controlled for complexity, and neonates were presented with all possible pairs of three equally complex

stimuli. These were: (1) a real female face, (2) a distorted picture which retained the outline of head and hair but altered the position of the other features, and (3) a scrambled face (stimulus (b) in Fantz's experiment). They found *no* preference for any of the three stimuli and concluded that a preference for real faces is not innate. In their view, such a preference does not appear until about four months of age.

Several researchers have argued that rather than babies innately preferring the human face, they actually develop a selective responsiveness to it and things that resemble it. According to Rheingold (1961), this is because the human face embodies all the stimulus dimensions which neonates seem innately to prefer, and these are 'packaged' in an attractive and stimulating form. For Rheingold, the human face is a *supernormal stimulus*.

Box 23.3   The perception of 'facedness'

Some researchers (e.g. Melhuish, 1982; Kleiner, 1987) have obtained findings which are inconsistent with Fantz's claims, whilst others (e.g. Bushnell & Sai, 1987) have shown that babies as young as two days and five hours old display a clear preference for their mother's face over the face of a female stranger when variables such as the overall brightness of the face and hair colour are controlled for.

Given the human face's complexity, it is hardly surprising that babies fail to make subtle distinctions about faces (such as distinguishing male from female) until mid- to late-infancy (Slater, 1994). Meltzoff & Moore (1992) have found that babies will, only minutes after birth, imitate a range of facial expressions they see an adult produce. For Slater (1994), this indicates that neonates can match what they see to some inbuilt knowledge of their own face, and can use this to produce a facial gesture which, in the case of furrowing the forehead, for example, they cannot see. The evidence indicates that:

'some knowledge about faces is present at birth, suggesting that babies come into the world with some innate, genetically determined knowledge about faces' (Slater, 1994).

DEPTH PERCEPTION IN BABIES

Perhaps the most famous way of investigating infants' depth perception is Gibson & Walk's (1960) *visual cliff apparatus* (see Figure 23.4). This consists of a central platform on the *shallow* side of which is a sheet of plexiglass. Immediately below this is a black and white checkerboard pattern. On the other *deep* side is another sheet of plexiglass, this time with the checkerboard pattern placed on the floor, at a distance of about four feet. This gives the appearance of a 'drop' or 'cliff'. The baby is placed on the central platform and its mother calls and beckons to it, first from one side and then the other.

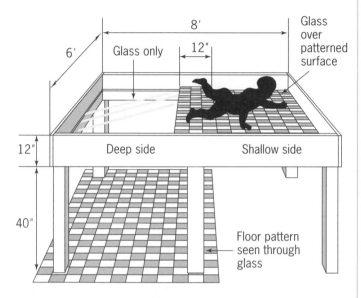

Figure 23.4   Gibson and Walk's 'visual cliff' apparatus

Gibson and Walk found that most babies aged between six and 14 months would not crawl onto the 'deep' side when beckoned by their mothers. This was interpreted as indicating that neonates have the innate ability to perceive depth. Those babies who did venture onto the deep side did so 'accidentally', either by backing onto it or resting on it. It is likely that their poor motor control was responsible for this rather than their inability to perceive depth.

The very nature of the visual cliff apparatus, however, required the researchers to use babies who could *crawl*, the youngest being six months old. An alternative explanation of Gibson and Walk's findings would be that the babies had *learned* to perceive depth during their first six months. Gibson and Walk subsequently tested a number of members of *precocial species* (capable of moving about independently at or shortly after birth). Chicks less than one day old never crossed onto the deep side, nor did goat kids and lambs. Rats would, if they could feel the glass with their very sensitive whiskers. However, when their whiskers were removed and they had to rely on vision, they too did not venture onto the deep side. If forcibly placed on the deep side, the various non-humans would 'freeze'.

Depth perception has also been studied by looking at how neonates react when an object approaches their face from a distance. For example, if a large box is moved towards a 20-day-old neonate's face, it shows an *integrated avoidance response*, that is, it throws back its head, shields its face with its hands, and even cries (Bower *et al.*, 1970). This suggests that the baby understands that the box is getting closer and, because it is potentially harmful, some sort of protective reaction is needed. Interestingly, the integrated avoidance response occurs even with one eye closed, but does not occur when equivalent pictures are shown on a screen. This indicates that *motion parallax* (see Chapter 21, page 175) is the critical cue for distance.

Bornstein (1988) has proposed that the roles of innate and experiential factors are both important and inseparable. For him:

'no matter how early in life depth perception can be demonstrated, no matter how late its emergence, it can never be proved that only experience has mattered'.

THE PERCEPTION OF 3-D OBJECTS

Bower *et al.*'s (1970) discovery of the integrated avoidance response suggests that as well as perceiving depth, neonates see boxes as solid, 3-D objects. To explore this, Bower (1979) devised a piece of apparatus that creates illusions of 3-D objects. Babies aged 16 to 24 weeks were put in front of a screen. A plastic, translucent object was suspended between lights and the screen so that it cast a double shadow on the back. When the screen is viewed from the front and the baby wears polarising goggles, the double shadows merge to form the image of a solid 3-D object.

Bower found that none of the babies showed any surprise when they grasped a real and solid object, but when they reached for the apparent object, and discovered there was nothing solid to get hold of, they all expressed surprise and some were even distressed. This indicates that they expected to be able to touch what they could 'see', an ability Bower believes to be innate.

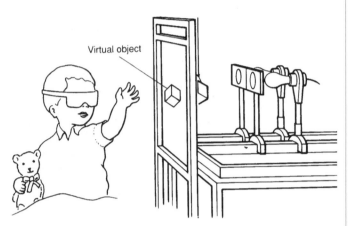

Figure 23.5   Trying to grasp a 'virtual object' produces surprise in a 4–6-month-old baby

PERCEPTUAL ORGANISATION: CONSTANCIES AND GESTALT PRINCIPLES

Size constancy

Perceptual constancy is a major form of perceptual organisation and seems to be a prerequisite for many other types of organisation (see Chapter 21). According to empirists, constancy is learned, and so neonates are likely to be 'tricked' by the appearance of things. For example, if something looks smaller (it projects a smaller retinal image), then it *is* smaller. Nativists, however, would argue that neonates are innately able to judge the size of an object regardless of retinal image.

Box 23.5   Bower's (1966) study of size constancy

To assess nativist and empirist claims, Bower (1966) initially conditioned two-month-olds to turn their heads whenever they saw a 30-centimetre cube at a distance of one metre (an adult popping up in front of the baby whenever it performed the desired behaviour served as a powerful reinforcer). Once the response was conditioned, the cube was replaced by one of three different cubes. The first was a 30-centimetre cube presented at a distance of three metres (producing a retinal image

---

one-third the size of the original). The second was a 90-centimetre cube presented at a distance of one metre (producing a retinal image three times the size of the original). The third was a 90-centimetre cube presented at a distance of three metres (producing exactly the same-sized retinal image as the conditioned stimulus).

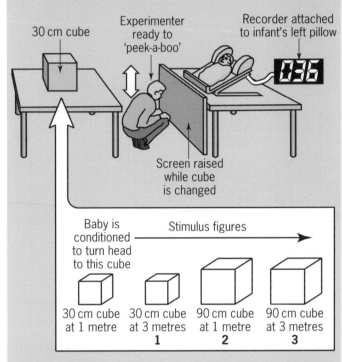

Figure 23.6   The experimental set-up in Bower's study of size constancy

Bower recorded the number of times each stimulus produced the conditioned response (CR), and used this as a measure of how similar the neonate considered the stimulus to be to the original. The original stimulus produced a total of 98 CRs, whilst the first produced 58, the second 54, and the third 22. The finding that most CRs occurred in response to the first stimulus indicates that the baby was responding to the actual size of the cube irrespective of its distance. This suggests the presence of size constancy and supports the nativist view that this constancy is inbuilt.

The nativist position is further strengthened by the finding that fewest CRs occurred in response to the third stimulus. If size constancy was absent, as predicted by empirists, neonates would 'compare' retinal images and base their perception of similarity on these regardless of distance. Empirists, then, would have expected the third stimulus to produce the most CRs. Bower's findings have been replicated with two-day-olds by Slater *et al.* (1990: cited in Slater, 1994).

Shape constancy

According to Slater (1989), new-borns are able to extract the constant real shape of an object that is rotated in the third dimension, that is, they are capable of recognising an object's form independently of (transformations in) its spatial orientation. For example, Bower (1966) found that if a two-month-old infant was conditioned to turn its head to look at a rectangle, it would continue to make the CR when the rectangle was turned slightly to produce a trapezoid retinal image. For Bornstein (1988), the evidence concerning shape constancy indicates that 'babies still only in their first year of life can perceive form *qua* form'.

Feature, identity and existence constancy

Feature constancy is the ability to recognise the invariant features of a stimulus despite some detectable but irrelevant transformation. If a new-born has been habituated to a moving stimulus, it will display a *novelty preference* when shown the same stimulus paired with a novel shape, both of which are stationary. This indicates that the new-born perceives the familiar stationary stimulus as the same stimulus when it was moving, and that feature constancy is present at birth.

Feature constancy is a prerequisite for *identity constancy* (the ability to recognise a particular object as being exactly the same object despite some transformation made to it). Distinguishing between feature and identity constancy is extremely difficult. In Bower's (1971) study, babies younger or older than 20 weeks were seated in front of mirrors which could produce several images of the mother. Babies younger than 20 weeks smiled, cooed and waved their arms to *each* of the 'multiple mothers', whereas older babies became upset at seeing more than one mother. What this suggests is that only the older babies, who are aware that they have just one mother, possess identity constancy.

Existence constancy refers to the belief that objects continue to exist even when they are no longer available to the senses (which Piaget calls *object permanence*: see Chapter 41). Together, existence and identity constancy comprise the *object concept*, which typically appears around six months of age. Both existence and identity constancy are more sophisticated than shape, size and feature constancies, and it is possible that the object concept arises from the less sophisticated constancies.

Gestalt principles

Bower has also looked at how neonate perception is organised in terms of certain Gestalt principles (see Chapter 21). Bower wanted to discover if *closure* (or *occlusion*) is, as Gestalt psychologists claim, an inborn characteristic.

Box 23.6   Bower's study of closure

Two-month-olds were conditioned to respond to a black wire triangle with a black iron bar across it (Figure 23.7 top). Then, various stimuli (Figure 23.7 bottom), were presented. Bower found that the CR was generalised to the complete triangle (A), suggesting that the babies perceived an unbroken triangle to lie behind the black iron bar. Given that they were unlikely to have encountered many triangles, Bower concluded that closure is almost certainly an inborn feature of neonate perceptual ability.

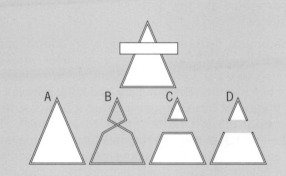

Figure 23.7   The stimulus figures used in Bower's study of closure

---

Conclusions

The earlier a perceptual ability appears, the less opportunity there has been for learning to have occurred, and the more likely it is that the ability has a biological basis. According to Slater (1994), the findings of many research studies into human neonate visual perception suggest that the new-born infant:

'comes into the world with a remarkable range of visual abilities ... Some rudimentary knowledge and understanding of important stimuli such as objects and faces is present at birth, and experience builds on this'.

Chapter 24 looks at other evidence bearing on the development of visual perception.

Summary

■ Studying neonates is the most direct way of assessing which perceptual abilities are **innate/inborn** and which develop through **experience** and **learning**, although researchers must make **inferences** about neonates' experiences. Methods used to study neonate perception include **spontaneous visual preference/ preferential looking, sucking rate, habituation, conditioned head rotation, physiological measures** (in particular heart rate and breathing rate) and **measures of electrical brain activity**, such as **visually evoked potentials** (VEPs).

■ **Nativists/innate theorists** argue that we are born with capacities and abilities to perceive the world in particular ways. If absent at birth, these abilities develop through maturation involving little or no learning.

■ **Empirists** (as distinct from **empiricists**) see the mind at birth as a **blank slate** (or **tabula rasa**) and argue that our perceptual abilities develop through learning and experience.

■ Anatomical differences between an adult's and a neonate's eyeball, optic nerve and cortex, make a neonate's vision less efficient. **Colour vision** appears by about two months. The **pupillary** and **blink reflexes** are both present at birth, suggesting that a baby's sensitivity to **brightness** is quite similar to an adult's. The **optokinetic reflex/optic nystagmus** appears soon after birth and quickly improves. **Convergence** and **accommodation** only reach adult levels by three to four months.

■ The new-born's **threshold of visual acuity** is much poorer than an adult's, but improves during the first six to 12 months. One- to three-month-olds will learn to suck on a nipple in order to bring a blurred picture into focus, and VEPs can be produced in new-borns.

■ Fantz found a preference for more **complex stimuli** among one-to 15-week-old babies, suggesting that this is innate. However, this preference is a function of age and reflects the maturation of the visual system. The preference for increasing complexity may be related to the increasingly efficient ability to scan the whole stimulus. Before two months, babies discriminate between shapes on the basis of lower-order variables, after which they respond to higher-order variables.

■ The **human face** combines complexity, pattern and movement, all of which babies innately prefer, in an attractive and stimulating form. Fantz claimed that babies innately know a face **as a face**. However, he failed to control adequately for complexity of the face-stimuli presented. Babies fail to make subtle distinctions about faces until mid- to late-infancy, but they can imitate a range of facial expressions minutes after birth. This suggests that neonates can match what they see to some inbuilt knowledge of their own face.

■ Using the **visual cliff apparatus**, Gibson and Walk concluded that neonates can innately perceive **depth**. However, the youngest babies studied were old enough to have **learned** depth perception, although members of **precocial species** avoid the cliff's deep side shortly after birth/hatching. Measuring changes in heart-rate on the visual cliff suggests that depth perception is probably innate, while avoidance behaviour is probably learnt.

■ Twenty-day-old babies display an **integrated avoidance response** to an approaching object, with **motion parallax** as the critical cue for distance. This, and babies' expectations that they can touch what they can see, suggests that neonates possess **3-D perception**.

■ Bower's experiment using cubes of different sizes presented from various distances provides support for the nativist view, at least as regards **size constancy** (neonates are able to judge the size of an object regardless of the retinal image it produces). Bower also found evidence of **shape constancy** in two-month-olds.

■ New-borns are apparently capable of recognising an object's form independently of (transformations in) its orientation in space. **Feature constancy** also seems to be innate and is a prerequisite for **identity constancy**, which is displayed by babies over 20 weeks old. Identity constancy together with **existence constancy** comprise the **object concept**, which normally appears at about six months.

■ Bower has shown that two-month-olds display the Gestalt principle of **closure**, strongly suggesting that this is an inborn ability.

STUDYING THE DEVELOPMENT OF VISUAL PERCEPTUAL ABILITIES 2: OTHER APPROACHES

Introduction and overview

Chapter 23 looked at what human neonate and infant research has told us about the development of visual perception. There are four other approaches to studying the development of visual perception. One involves studying people who, through a physical defect occurring early in life, have been deprived of normal visual experiences, but have later had their sight restored. A second approach, using non-humans, looks at the effects of early sensory restriction on visual perceptual development. A third studies non-humans' and humans' abilities to adapt to gross distortions in their visual worlds. The greater the degree of adaptation an organism can make, the greater the scope for learning in the development of visual perception. A fourth looks at the visual perceptual abilities of members of different cultures. If consistent differences between cultural groups exist, then, unless we have good independent reasons for believing that these are biologically based, they must be attributable to environmental factors.

This chapter examines the bearing these other approaches have on our understanding of visual perceptual development.

Studies of human cataract patients

Writing to Locke in 1688, Molyneux asked whether:

> 'a man *born* blind, and now adult, *taught* by touch to distinguish between a cube and sphere could, if his sight was restored, distinguish between those objects without touching them' (Locke, 1690).

Not surprisingly, Locke's reply to *Molyneux's question* (see page 193) was 'no' because the man would never have *learned* to see.

Von Senden (1932) summarised 65 cases of people who had undergone cataract removal surgery taking place

between 1700 and 1928. A cataract is a film over the eyes which allows only diffuse light to be perceived. Cataracts can be present at birth or develop any time afterwards and their surgical removal 'restores' vision.

Typically, patients who have undergone surgery are initially bewildered by the visual world. Hebb (1949) analysed von Senden's cases in terms of *figural unity* (the ability to detect the presence of a figure or stimulus, including scanning objects, distinguishing figure from ground, and following moving objects with the eyes) and *figural identity* (being able to name or in some other way identify an already familiar stimulus without touching it or, in the case of geometric figures, counting the corners).

Hebb concluded that the simpler figural unity was available shortly after surgery and so may not depend on prior visual experience. However, the more complex figural identity depended on learning. For Hebb, this is how these two aspects of perception *normally* develop. The evidence also indicated the absence of *perceptual constancy* (see Chapter 21, pages 175–176). For example, a sugar lump could be identified by sight alone when seen at a close distance in a person's hand, but it often could not be recognised when seen suspended from a piece of string at a distance. This is contradicted by evidence from research into human neonates suggesting that size and shape constancy *are* innate (see pages 198–199).

Gregory & Wallace (1963) described the case of S.B., a man blind since the age of six months whose sight was restored by means of a corneal graft at the age of 52. S.B. showed good judgement of size and distance, provided he was familiar with an object. Also, he could recognise objects visually *if* he was already familiar with them through touch while blind (he showed good *cross-modal transfer*). However, he found it impossible to judge distances by sight alone, and when he looked out of a window 40 feet above the ground (a view he had never experienced), he believed he would 'be able to touch the ground below the window with his feet if he lowered himself by his hands'. S.B. also never learned to interpret facial expressions of emotion, although he could interpret emotional states from the sound of a person's voice.

Box 24.1   Some cautions concerning the interpretation of data from human cataract patients

- Apart from vision, adults' sense modalities are better developed than neonates', so adult cataract patients are *not* the same as neonates. Patients might have to 'unlearn' previous (non-visual) experience in order to use vision. S.B., for example, preferred to use a sense modality he was *familiar* with (touch), and it is possible that figural identity is poorer for this reason rather than for any reason proposed by Hebb (1949).

- Many cataract patients are confused and distressed by their new 'visual world'. In some cases (including S.B.), they commit suicide. Their severe emotional distress might distort the findings concerning their perceptual abilities.

- The absence of figural identity could, as Hebb suggested, be due to the lack of visual experience. However, it could also be due to some sort of physical damage or deterioration of the visual system during the years of blindness.

- It is doubtful if all of the cases reported by von Senden were studied as rigorously as S.B. Also, there was great variability in the ages of the patients when they underwent surgery and when their cataracts first appeared. Consequently, they differed in terms of their visual experiences *prior* to the cataract developing.

Studies of sensory restriction using non-humans

Because of the limitations of human cataract patient data, researchers have sought other ways of addressing Molyneux's question. Methodologically, research using non-humans is useful because researchers are able to manipulate environments in ways not permissible with humans (see Chapter 85). Typically investigators have *deprived* non-humans of normal sensory and perceptual stimulation and recorded the effects of this on their sensory and perceptual abilities.

Riesen (1947) reared chimpanzees in total darkness (except for several 45-second periods of exposure to light during feeding) for the first 16 months of life. Compared with normally reared chimpanzees, they showed marked perceptual deficits, such as failing to blink in response to threatening movements made towards their faces, and only noticing objects if they were touched or bumped into.

These data suggest that perceptual abilities depend on visual experiences. However, Weiskrantz (1956) argued that the visual deficiencies observed by Riesen were caused by the chimpanzees' retinas failing to develop normally in the absence of light stimulation, and the likely degeneration of the visual cortex. All the 1947 study showed was that a certain amount of light is necessary to maintain the visual system and allow it to mature normally.

Riesen (1965) conducted further experiments involving three chimpanzees. Lad was reared under normal lighting conditions. Debi was reared in complete darkness. Kova spent an hour and a half per day wearing special goggles which allowed her to see *diffuse* or *unpatterned light* of different colours and brightnesses. The rest of Kova's time was spent in darkness.

At seven months, Kova had not suffered retinal damage, but her perceptual development was noticeably retarded compared with Lad. However, her *receptive fields* (see Chapter 10, page 83) failed to develop normally. Debi, raised in complete darkness, suffered the same retinal damage as Riesen's (1947) chimpanzees. In other studies, Riesen fitted translucent goggles to chimpanzees, monkeys and kittens for the first three months of their lives. Whilst simple perceptual abilities (such as differentiating colour, size and brightness) remained intact, more complex abilities (such as following a moving object) did not.

Overall, Riesen's findings suggest at least two things. First, light is necessary for the visual system's normal physical development (at least in the species he studied). Second, patterned light is also necessary for the development of some complex visual abilities (in those species). Early experience, in the form of certain kinds of visual stimulation, then, appears to be essential for normal perceptual development. If perceptual abilities are wholly innate, then environmental factors (over and above those which can either harm the organism or prevent maturation) should have no effects on perceptual development.

Other researchers have looked at the extent to which exposure to visual stimulation *and* motor activity affects the ability of non-humans to guide their movements.

Box 24.2   Held & Hein's (1963) kitten carousel experiment

Held & Hein (1963) kept kittens in darkness for the first eight weeks after birth. The kittens were then allowed three hours per day in a *kitten carousel*, the remainder of the time being spent in darkness.

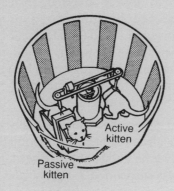

Figure 24.1   The 'kitten carousel' apparatus

The 'active' kitten could move itself around and, via a series of pulleys, its movement caused the 'passive' kitten (whose legs were not free to move) to move in the same direction and at the same speed. Since the visual environment was constant, both kittens had identical visual experiences. When *paw–eye coordination* was tested several weeks later, the 'passive' kittens were markedly inferior to the 'active' kittens, and showed no evidence of depth perception. However, after normal visual experiences, the 'passive' kittens did display depth perception, suggesting that rather than having failed to learn this ability, they had failed to learn the correct motor responses associated with it. This indicates that it is necessary to distinguish between perception and *sensory-motor coordination* (see perceptual distortion and readjustment studies on pages 204–205).

Blakemore & Cooper (1970) raised kittens in chambers (see Figure 24.2) which had either vertical or horizontal stripes painted on the inside, and a glass floor so as not to interrupt the pattern of stripes. The kittens wore special collars to prevent them from seeing their own bodies and the stripes were the only visual stimuli they saw. After five months, their vision was tested. Those raised in the 'vertical world' were insensitive to horizontal lines. For example, when a rod was shaken in front of them in the horizontal plane, they made no attempt to reach for it. However, they would do so when it was shaken vertically. The kittens raised in the 'horizontal world' responded when the rod was shaken horizontally but not when it was shaken vertically.

Figure 24.2   The 'vertical world' used in Blakemore & Cooper's (1970) experiment

The kittens were found to be both behaviourally and physiologically blind to horizontal (or vertical) stimuli. So, when the neural activity from their visual cortices was recorded using micro-electrodes, cells were sensitive to the types of stimuli which corresponded to the visual environment in which they were raised, but insensitive to other stimuli. Similarly, Wiesel (1982) gave kittens and infant monkeys simulated cataracts by sewing their eyelids closed. After infancy, when the eyelids were unstitched, the kittens and monkeys displayed perceptual limitations much like those of human cataract patients. When only the left (or right) eyelid was surgically closed from birth until 18 months, the *ocular dominance columns* (groups of cells in the cortex that respond to visual input from the eyes: see Chapter 10, page 84) were expanded for the seeing eye and dramatically shrunk for the non-seeing eye.

Blakemore and Cooper's study does not demonstrate conclusively that the environment determines the perception of lines in different orientations. It could be that cells receptive to *all* kinds of stimuli are present at birth, and they functionally reorganise themselves in the absence of relevant stimuli. However, it seems that the environment does play a role in the development of perception in at least some non-humans, although, like babies, non-humans cannot tell researchers about their abilities. We don't *know* that non-humans cannot perceive particular stimuli, only that they do not *behave* as if they can.

Of course, we must be cautious in generalising findings from non-humans to humans. However, the effects of early visual experience on *humans* has been investigated by studying people with an *astigmatism* early in life. Due to a distortion in the eye's shape, the astigmatism produces an image which is out of focus in either the horizontal or vertical dimension. Even when the astigmatism is corrected, people still see horizontal (or vertical) lines as blurs. As with Blakemore and Cooper's kittens, then, early visual experience has a permanent effect on the brain and perceptual ability (Mitchell & Wilkinson, 1974).

Perceptual distortion and readjustment studies

Another way of looking at the effects of experience on perception is to see how well an organism can adjust to new perceptual situations. The greater the degree of adaptation, the greater the role of learning. Neither salamanders (Sperry, 1943) nor chickens (Hess, 1956; Rossi, 1968) show any evidence of being able to readjust to distortions in their perceptual world, and so it is likely that for these species, genetic factors exert considerable control over perceptual abilities.

Stratton (1896, 1897) was the first to experiment with special lenses that distort the human visual world. He constructed a lens worn over one eye whilst keeping the other eye covered. The lens reversed his visual world so that objects in the top of the visual field appeared to be at the bottom and objects on the right appeared to be on the left. For the first three days, Stratton was extremely disoriented and he had difficulty even with simple behaviours, such as eating and drinking. After just one day, he reported that he felt nauseous, depressed and tired, and avoided activity as much as possible.

After three days, however, Stratton began to adapt and imagined unseen parts of his visual field as also being inverted. By the fifth day, he found that he could walk around without bumping into things and that the simple behaviours were now easy to accomplish. By the eighth and final day, everything seemed 'harmonious', although Stratton's adaptation was not, as he reported, complete:

'I often hesitated which hand was the appropriate one for grasping some object in view, began the movement with the wrong hand and then corrected the mistake'.

When the lens was removed, Stratton immediately recognised his visual environment as the one that existed prior to wearing the lens. He found it surprisingly bewildering, although definitely not inverted. This absence of an inverted after-effect is important, and shows that Stratton had not actually learnt to see the world as being inverted. If he had, removal of the lens would have caused the now 'normal' world to appear inverted! Instead, Stratton's adaptation involved learning the appropriate *motor responses* in an inverted world (cf. Held and Hein's kittens described on page 203). However, he did experience an after-effect which caused things before him to 'swing and sweep' as he moved his eyes, indicating that location constancy had been disrupted.

Stratton also made goggles which visually displaced his body so that he always appeared horizontally in front of himself. Wherever he walked, he 'followed' his own body image, which was suspended at right angles to his actual body. When he lay down, his body would appear above him, vertically and at right angles to him. After three days, Stratton found that he could adapt to this grossly distorted visual world, and was even able to go out for a walk on his own!

Box 24.3 Other studies of perceptual adaptation in humans

- Snyder & Pronko (1952) reported adaptation to reversal and inversion of the visual world in participants who wore special lenses for 30 days. Interestingly, when participants were re-tested two years later, they took less time to adapt than first-time participants, indicating that motor adaptations are resistant to forgetting.

- Held & Bossom (1961) showed that the opportunity for activity is an important factor in perceptual adaptation. Participants who were allowed to walk about freely adjusted quickly and showed after-effects. Those taken about the same environment in wheelchairs adjusted, but showed no evidence of after-effects.

- Kohler (1962) found that inversion of the visual world produced an inverted after-effect in *some* of his participants when the apparatus was removed. However, this lasted only a few minutes, suggesting that any purely perceptual learning was not substantial.

- Gilling & Brightwell (1982) studied a single participant, Susannah Fienues, who wore an inverted lens for several days. She gradually adapted and reverted to normal vision within a few minutes following removal of her special goggles.

What these (and Stratton's) studies show is that experience does influence our perception of the world, and that our visual system is flexible enough to adjust to distorted conditions. A system which was innate would not allow adaptation to take place. However, it is unlikely that *perceptual adaptation* takes place. Instead, *motor adaptation*, in which we learn to successfully negotiate a different-looking environment, occurs. The fact that humans are capable of learning a new set of body movements does not allow us to conclude that perceptual 'habits' are learned in the first place.

Finally, all the participants in perceptual adjustment studies are *adults*, who have already undergone a great deal of learning and in whom maturation has occurred. It is difficult to generalise from adults to babies, and so we cannot conclude that babies *have* to learn to perceive the world just because adults *can* learn to perceive the world differently.

Cross-cultural studies

Cross-cultural studies involve a comparison of how people from very different cultures perceive the same things. If we find consistent differences between different cultural groups, then unless there are good independent reasons for believing that those differences are biologically based, we must attribute them to environmental factors (such as social, ecological, linguistic, or some combination of these). Theoretically, then, cross-cultural studies enable us to discover the extent to which perception is structured by the nervous system (and so common to all humans) and by experience.

STUDIES USING VISUAL ILLUSIONS

There is a long history of cross-cultural research into perceptual development using visual illusions.

Box 24.4   Some early research into cross-cultural differences using visual illusions

- Rivers (1901) compared English adults and children with adult and child Murray Islanders (people from a group of islands between New Guinea and Australia) using the Müller–Lyer illusion and the horizontal–vertical illusion. The Murray Islanders were *less* susceptible to the Müller–Lyer illusion than their English counterparts, but *more* susceptible to the horizontal–vertical illusion.

- Allport & Pettigrew (1957) used the *rotating trapezoid* illusion. This is a trapezoid which has horizontal and vertical bars attached to it.

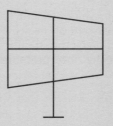

When attached to a motor and revolved in a circle, the trapezoid gives those from Western cultures the impression of being a window, and when rotated through 360°, most Western observers report seeing a rectangle that oscillates to and fro rather than a trapezoid rotating through 360° (which it actually is). Allport and Pettigrew reasoned that for people unfamiliar with windows (at least as people from Western cultures know them), expectations of rectangularity would be absent and the illusion not perceived. Using Zulus, who live in a rather 'circular environment', they found that when the trapezoid was viewed with both eyes and from a short distance, the Zulus were less likely than either urban Zulus or Europeans to perceive an oscillating rectangle and more likely to perceive a rotating trapezoid.

- Segall *et al.* (1963) used the Müller–Lyer illusion with members of African and Filipino cultures. As compared with South Africans of European descent and Americans from Illinois, the Africans and Filipinos were much less susceptible to the illusion. However, on the horizontal–vertical illusion, members of two African cultures (the Batoro and the Bayankole) were most susceptible. People of these cultures live in high, open country where visibility without 'interference' is possible. In such an environment, vertical objects are important focal points and are used to estimate distances. The Bete, who live in a dense jungle environment, were least likely of all groups tested to see the illusion. The South Africans of European descent and Americans fell between the extremes of the three African cultures.

- Stewart (1973) used the Ames distorted room (see page 188) with rural and urban Tongan children. The rural children were less likely to see the illusion than those living in urban environments and European children. This was also true for other illusions, including the Müller–Lyer.

ACCOUNTING FOR DIFFERENTIAL SUSCEPTIBILITY TO VISUAL ILLUSIONS

According to Segall *et al.*'s (1963) *carpentered world hypothesis*, people in Western cultures:

> 'live in a culture in which straight lines abound and in which perhaps 90 per cent of the acute and obtuse angles formed on [the] retina by the straight lines of [the] visual field are realistically interpretable as right angles extended in space'.

Segall *et al.*, therefore, believe that we tend to interpret illusions, which are 2-D drawings, in terms of our past experiences. In the 'carpentered world' of Western societies, we add a third dimension (depth) which is not actually present in the drawing, and this leads to the illusion experience (cf. Gregory's account of visual illusions: see Chapter 22, pages 183–185).

Annis & Frost (1973) looked at the perceptual acuity of Canadian Cree Indians who live in a non-carpentered environment consisting of summer tents and winter lodges with lines in all orientations. The task involved judging whether two lines were parallel or not, and pairs of lines in different orientations were used. The Crees had no difficulty in judging the lines no matter what angle they were presented at. However, whilst a comparison group of Crees who had moved away from their original environment were good at judging lines that were horizontal or vertical, they were less good with lines at an angle.

Whilst Annis and Frost's data are consistent with Segall *et al.*'s hypothesis, other studies are inconsistent with it. For example, Mundy-Castle & Nelson (1962) studied the Knysma forest dwellers, a group of isolated, white, illiterate South Africans. Despite the rectangularity of their environment, they were unable to give 3-D responses to 2-D symbols on a standard test and, on the Müller–Lyer illusion, their responses were not significantly different from non-Europeans, although they were significantly different from literate white adults.

STUDIES USING OTHER PERCEPTUAL PHENOMENA

In various African cultures, children and adults find it difficult to perceive depth in both pictorial material *and* the real world. Turnbull (1961), for example, studied the Bambuti pygmies who live in the dense rainforests of the Congo, a closed-in world without open spaces. When a Bambuti man was taken to a vast plain and shown a herd of buffalo grazing in the distance, he claimed he had never seen such *insects* before. When informed that the 'insects' were buffalo, the pygmy was offended. Turnbull and the

pygmy then rode in a jeep towards the buffalo. The sight of the buffalo in the distance was so far removed from the pygmy's experience that he was convinced Turnbull was using magic to deceive him. What this study shows is that the pygmy lacked *size constancy* (see Chapter 21, page 175), which is an important cue in 'reading' pictures.

In Hudson's (1960) study, people from various African cultures were shown a series of pictures depicting hunting scenes (see Figure 24.3). The participants saw each picture on its own and were asked to name all the objects in the scene to determine whether or not the elements were correctly recognised. Then they were asked about the *relationship* between the objects, such as 'Which is closer to the man?' If the 'correct' interpretation was made, and depth cues were taken into account, respondents were classified as having 3-D vision. If such cues were ignored, they were classified as having 2-D vision. Hudson reported that both children and adults found it difficult to perceive depth in the pictorial material, and whilst this difficulty varied in extent, it appeared to persist through most educational and social levels (Deregowski, 1972).

Figure 24.3   Hudson (1960) found that when shown the top picture and asked which animal the hunter is trying to spear, members of some cultures reply 'the elephant'. This shows that some cultures do not use cues to depth (such as overlap and known size of objects). The second picture shows the hunter, elephant and antelope in true size ratios when all are the same distance from the observer

Deregowski refers to a description given of an African woman slowly discovering that a picture she was looking at portrayed a human head in profile:

> 'She discovered in turn the nose, the mouth, the eye, but where was the other eye? I tried turning my profile to explain why she could see only one eye, but she hopped round to my other side to point out that I possessed a second eye which the other lacked'.

The woman treated the picture as an object rather than a 2-D representation of an object, that is, she did not 'infer' depth in the picture. What she believed to be an 'object' turned out to have only two dimensions, and this is what the woman found bewildering. However, when familiar pictorial stimulus material is used, recognition tends to be better (Serpell, 1976). Thus, some (but not all) of the Me'en of Ethiopia found it much easier to recognise material when it was presented in the form of pictures painted on cloth (which is both familiar to them and free of distracting cues such as a border) than line drawings on paper (Deregowski, 1972).

Evidence also indicates that the drawings in some of the studies emphasise certain depth cues whilst ignoring others putting non-Western observers at a 'double disadvantage'. For example, in Hudson's (1960) pictures (see Figure 24.3), two depth cues were used (namely relative size and overlap or superimposition). However, cues like texture gradient, binocular disparity and motion parallax were absent from all of Hudson's pictures. When they were redrawn so as to show texture gradients (by, for example, adding grass to open terrain), more Zambian children gave 3-D answers than in Hudson's original study (Kingsley *et al.*, cited in Serpell, 1976). Research summarised by Berry *et al.* (1992) indicates that the absence of certain depth cues in pictorial material makes the perception of depth difficult for non-Western peoples.

Finally, much research in this area implies that the Western style of pictorial art represents the real world in an *objectively* correct way. 'Artistic excellence' is not identical with 'photographic accuracy' (Gombrich, 1960) and so it might be that people of non-Western cultures 'reject' Western art forms simply on *aesthetic grounds*. As a result, research may have mistakenly described *stylistic preference* as a difference in perception (Serpell, 1976).

Certainly, unfolded 'split', 'developed' or 'chain-type' drawings as shown in Figure 24.4 (left) were originally preferred by African children and adults to the 'orthogonal' or perspective drawings as shown in Figure 24.4 (right), often because the drawing lacked important features (legs in the case of Figure 24.4).

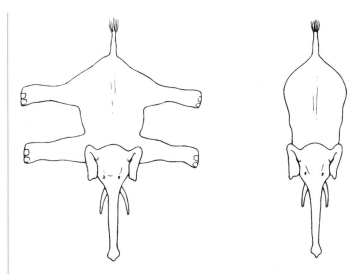

Figure 24.4   Members of certain African cultures generally prefer the 'split elephant' drawing shown on the left to the top-view perspective drawing shown on the right

(From J. Deregowski, 'Pictorial perception and culture'. Copyright © (1972) by Scientific American, Inc. All rights reserved.)

Also, the small lines used by cartoonists to imply motion were the least understood of all the pictorial conventions shown to rural African children (Duncan *et al.*, 1973). When shown a picture in which the artist had drawn a head in three different positions above the same trunk to indicate that the head was turning round, half the children thought the character depicted was deformed (see Figure 24.5 (a)). Likewise, Western observers require guidance from an anthropologist to understand the art forms of American Indians (see Figure 24.5 (b)).

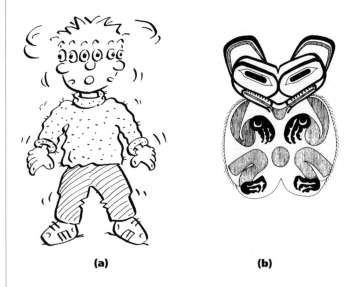

(a)   **(b)**

Figure 24.5   Is the work of an artist from one particular culture (a) always understandable to a viewer from a different culture (b)?

Whilst some psychologists believe that the physical environment (or ecology) is closely linked with perceptual experiences, others believe that ecology actually *determines* perceptual experience. However, they cannot agree about the key features of such cultural experiences, and so neither of the beliefs can be strongly supported.

Conclusions

Whilst evidence from studies of humans suggests that some visual perceptual abilities are probably innate (see Chapter 23), evidence from the four approaches considered in this chapter suggests that experience plays a vital role. Rather than seeing themselves as nativists or empirists, most psychologists see a *transactional perspective* as being the most profitable one to adopt as far as visual perception is concerned. Whilst we may be born with capacities to perceive the world in certain ways, stimulation and environmental influences in general are crucial in determining how, and even whether, these capacities actually develop.

Summary

■ Hebb re-analysed the 65 cases of people who had undergone **cataract removal** surgery (reported originally by von Senden) in terms of **figural unity** and **figural identity**. While figural unity is not dependent on visual experience, figural identity and **perceptual constancy** seem to depend on learning. Hebb believes this is how these two aspects of perception **normally** develop.

■ Unlike neonates, adults who undergo cataract surgery may have to unlearn previous perceptual experience involving their other sense modalities. The acquisition of vision can be emotionally distressing, and the visual system may have deteriorated during the years of blindness.

■ S.B. showed good **cross-modal transfer** but found it impossible to judge distances by sight alone and never learned to interpret facial expressions of emotion.

■ Another approach involves **depriving** non-humans of normal sensory and perceptual stimulation to see its effects on their sensory and perceptual abilities. Riesen's experiment with chimpanzees was flawed because of the possibility that the animals reared in total darkness may have suffered retinal damage. He later exposed one chimp to **diffuse/unpatterned light** which prevented retinal damage but produced retarded perceptual development compared with a normally reared chimp. Although simple perceptual abilities were unaffected, patterned light appears to be necessary for the development of more complex abilities.

■ Held and Hein's **kitten carousel** experiment showed that passive kittens fail to learn the correct motor responses rather than depth perception itself, implying a distinction between perception and **sensory-motor coordination**.

■ Blakemore and Cooper's kittens became both 'behaviourally and physiologically blind' to either vertical or horizontal stimuli. Although this suggests that the environment determines the perception of horizontal and vertical lines, it is possible that cells receptive to **all** kinds of stimuli are present at birth but functionally reorganise themselves if relevant stimuli are absent. All we can be sure of is that non-humans sometimes fail to behave as if they can perceive particular stimuli.

■ **Perceptual distortion and readjustment studies** assume that the greater the degree of adaptation in distorted perceptual situations, the greater the role of learning. Unlike salamanders and chickens, humans seem capable of considerable adjustment.

■ Stratton's studies involved wearing a lens over one eye that turned the visual world upside down. When he removed the lens, there was no inverted after-image or after-effect, indicating that adaptation had involved learning appropriate **motor responses**. However, location constancy had been disrupted.

■ What this and other readjustment studies demonstrate is **motor adaptation** (rather than **perceptual** adaptation), which by itself does not allow us to conclude that perception is originally learned. The adult participants have already undergone extensive learning, and it is difficult to generalise from what they **can** learn to what babies **must** learn.

■ **Cross-cultural studies** compare the perceptions of members of very different cultural groups, often using **visual illusions**. Consistent differences between different groups must be attributed to social, ecological or linguistic factors, unless there is good independent reason to attribute them to biological factors.

■ According to Segall *et al.*'s **carpentered world hypothesis**, members of Western cultures tend to interpret illusion figures by adding depth that is not actually in them. While Annis and Frost's study of Canadian Cree Indians supports the carpentered world hypothesis, several other studies are inconsistent with it.

■ Turnbull's study of the Bambuti pygmies demonstrated lack of **size constancy**, which is an important cue in interpreting pictures. Hudson's studies using pictures depicting hunting scenes found that both children and adults from a variety of African cultures, and regardless of educational or social levels, had difficulty perceiving depth.

■ However, Hudson's drawings only used relative size and overlap/superimposition, omitting other depth cues and making the task more difficult for non-Western peoples. When they were redrawn so as to include other depth cues, the number of 3-D responses increased.

■ People from non-Western cultures might be 'rejecting' Western art forms, expressing a **stylistic preference**, rather than showing an inability to perceive depth in pictures. Just as rural African children are unfamiliar with artistic conventions as used in Western cartoons, so Western observers need guidance to understand the art forms of American Indians.

■ Most psychologists adopt a **transactional perspective**, according to which stimulation and environmental influences are crucial in determining how and whether inborn perceptual capacities actually develop.

25

FOCUSED ATTENTION

Introduction and overview

According to Titchener (1903), a student of Wundt:

> 'the doctrine of attention is the nerve of the whole psychological system'.

However, because of their belief that a stimulus array's properties were sufficient to predict the perceptual response to it, *Gestalt* psychologists (see Chapter 21) believed the concept of attention was unnecessary, whilst *behaviourists* argued that since 'attention' was unobservable, it was not worthy of experimental study (see Chapters 1 and 83).

Interest in the study of attention re-emerged following the publication of Broadbent's (1958) *Perception and Communication*. Broadbent argued that the world is composed of many more sensations than can be handled by the perceptual and cognitive capabilities of the human observer. To cope with the flood of available information, humans must *selectively attend* to only some information and somehow 'tune out' the rest. To understand our ability to selectively attend to things, researchers study focused attention. This chapter considers some of the theory and research concerned with focused auditory and visual attention.

Focused auditory attention

CHERRY'S DICHOTIC LISTENING AND SHADOWING RESEARCH

Broadbent's (1958) book was partly an attempt to account for the *cocktail-party phenomenon* (Cherry, 1953); the ability to focus attention on one conversation whilst ignoring other conversations going on around us. In his initial experiments, Cherry's participants wore headphones through which pairs of spoken prose 'messages' were presented to both ears simultaneously (*binaural listening*). Cherry found that various physical differences affected the ability to select one of the messages to attend to, in particular voice intensity, the speaker's location and the speaker's sex. He also found that when these differences were controlled for in the two messages (so that each message was, say, spoken in an equally intense female voice), their meaning was extremely difficult to separate.

In later experiments, participants were presented with one message to the right ear and, simultaneously, a *different* message to the left ear (*dichotic listening*) instead of two messages through both ears. Participants were required to repeat out loud *one* of the messages, a procedure known as *shadowing*. Its purpose is to ensure that one of the messages is being attended to. Whilst participants were able to carry out the shadowing requirement, little of the non-shadowed message was remembered.

Box 25.1 Some other research using shadowing

Little of the non-shadowed message was remembered even when the same word was presented 35 times to the non-shadowed ear (Moray, 1959). Also, if the message was spoken in a foreign language or changed from English to a different language, participants did not notice this. Whilst speech played backwards was reported as having 'something queer about it', most participants believed it to be normal speech. However, a pure tone of 400 cycles per second was nearly always noticed, as was a change of voice from male to female or female to male (Cherry & Taylor, 1954). These data suggested that whilst the physical properties of the message in the non-shadowed ear were 'heard', semantic content (its meaning) was completely lost. People quickly gave up Cherry's original question about how we can attend to one conversation and began asking why so little seemed to be remembered about the other conversations (Hampson & Morris, 1996).

BROADBENT'S SPLIT-SPAN STUDIES

Broadbent (1954) reported the results of a series of studies using the *split-span procedure*. In this, three digits (such as 8, 2 and 1) are presented via headphones to one ear at the rate of one every half a second. Simultaneously, three different digits (such as 7, 3 and 4) are presented to the other ear. The task is to listen to the two sets of numbers and then write down as much as can be remembered.

The digits can be recalled either (a) according to the ear of presentation (*ear-by-ear recall*; thus, the numbers above could be recalled as either 8,2,1,7,3,4 or 7,3,4,8,2,1), or (b) according to their chronological order of presentation (*pair-by-pair recall*). Since the digits have been presented in pairs, this would involve recalling the first pair (8,7 or

7,8), followed by the second pair (2,3 or 3,2) and finally the third pair (1,4 or 4,1).

When people are simply given a list of six digits at a rate of one every half a second, serial recall is typically 95 per cent accurate. However, Broadbent found that the split-span procedure produced accurate recall only 65 per cent of the time. Moreover, pair-by-pair recall was considerably *poorer* than ear-by-ear recall. If given a choice, people preferred ear-by-ear recall.

Single-channel theories of focused auditory attention

Single-channel theories propose that somewhere in information processing there is a 'bottleneck' or *filter* which allows some information to be passed on for further analysis, either discarding or processing only to a limited degree the other information. The three theories that have been proposed essentially differ over whether the filtering takes place early or late in information processing, and hence they differ in terms of the nature of and extent to which processing of the non-attended material occurs.

BROADBENT'S EARLY SELECTION FILTER THEORY

Broadbent's (1958) theory was the first systematic attempt to explain both Cherry's findings and those of split-span experiments. Broadbent assumes that our ability to process information is capacity limited. Information from the senses passes 'in parallel' to a *short-term store*, a temporary 'buffer system' which holds information until it can be processed further and, effectively, extends the duration of a stimulus (see Chapter 27, page 233). The various types of information (such as two or more voices) are then passed, preserved in their original form, to a *selective filter*. This operates on the information's *physical characteristics* presented, selecting one source for further analysis and rejecting all others.

Information allowed through the filter reaches a *limited capacity channel* (and the filter is necessary precisely because the channel is capacity limited). This corresponds to the 'span of consciousness' (James, 1890) or what we experience as happening now. The information allowed through the filter is analysed in that it is recognised, possibly rehearsed, and then transferred to the motor effectors (muscles) and an appropriate response initiated.

Because Broadbent considered the short-term store to be capable of holding information for a period of time before it decayed away, two simultaneous stimuli *can* be processed provided that the processor can get back to the store before the information in it has decayed away. So, attending to one thing does not necessarily mean that everything else is lost. However, Broadbent believed that switching attention between channels took a substantial period of time, and so processing information from two channels would always take longer and be less efficient than processing the same information from one channel.

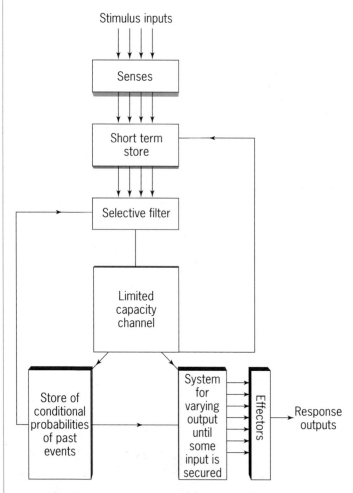

Figure 25.1   Broadbent's theory of the flow of information between stimulus and response

Tests of Broadbent's theory

Broadbent's theory could explain Cherry's findings concerning the fate of the non-shadowed message because the non-shadowed message is not permitted to pass through the filter. It also explained the data from split-span experiments by proposing that the input to the relevant ear is the physical property on which the information is selected. However, the theory assumes that because the non-shadowed message is filtered out according to its physical characteristics, its *meaning* should not be subject to any sort of higher-level analysis.

However, when we are at a party, our attention sometimes switches from the speaker to whom we are listening to another part of the room if we hear our name mentioned. This was demonstrated experimentally by Moray (1959), who found that when the participant's name was presented to the non-attended ear, attention switched to that ear about one-third of the time.

Box 25.2   Some experimental studies producing data inconsistent with Broadbent's theory

- Gray & Wedderburn (1960) showed that if participants were presented with 'Dear 2 Jane' in one ear and '3 Aunt 8' in the other, they were able to process the information alternately according to the ears, since they typically reported 'Dear Aunt Jane'. This indicates that the ears do not always function as different information channels, and that switching between channels is fairly easy to do.

- Treisman (1960) found that if meaningful material presented to the attended ear was switched in mid-sentence to the non-attended ear, participants would occasionally change the focus of their attention to the non-attended ear and shadow the material presented to it before changing back to the attended ear.

- Treisman (1964) discovered that if a French translation of the shadowed material was presented as non-shadowed material, some *bilingual* participants realised that the shadowed and non-shadowed material had the same meaning.

- Corteen & Wood (1972) conditioned participants to produce a *galvanic skin response* (or GSR, a minute increase in the electrical conductivity of the skin) whenever they heard a particular target word. A small electric shock was delivered immediately after the target word was heard. The target word produced a GSR when presented to the non-attended ear, and *synonyms* of it did as well. These findings were replicated by von Wright *et al.* (1975) using Finnish participants. However, in both experiments, GSRs did not occur on all the trials on which the conditioned words were presented.

- Mackay (1973) found that after the word 'bank' had been presented in a sentence and participants subsequently had to recognise the sentence they had heard, recognition was influenced by whether the word 'river' or 'money' had been presented to the non-attended ear.

The studies summarised in Box 25.2 suggest that the meaning of the input to the non-attended ear is processed at least sometimes. Further, Underwood's (1974) finding that participants *trained* at shadowing can detect two-thirds of the material presented to the non-attended ear casts doubt on Broadbent's claim that the non-shadowed message is always rejected at an *early* stage of processing. Additionally, when material used is sufficiently different, such as one being auditory and the other visual, memory for the non-shadowed message is good, indicating that it must have been processed at a higher level than proposed by Broadbent (Allport *et al.*, 1972).

TREISMAN'S ATTENUATION OR STIMULUS-ANALYSIS SYSTEM THEORY

According to Treisman (1960, 1964), competing information is analysed for things other than its physical properties, including sounds, syllable patterns, grammatical structure and the information's meaning (Hampson & Morris, 1996). Treisman suggested that the non-shadowed message was not filtered out early on but that the selective filter *attenuated* it. Thus, a message not selected on the basis of its physical properties would not be rejected completely, but would be diminished in intensity (or 'turned down').

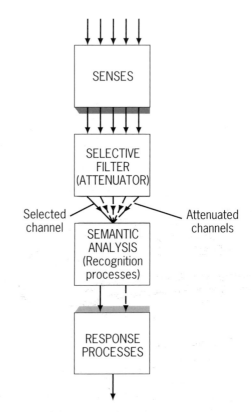

Figure 25.2   Treisman's theory of the processes by which information is selectively attended to

Both non-attenuated and attenuated information undergo the further analyses mentioned above. These may result in an attenuated message being attended to, depending on its features. Treisman suggested biologically relevant and emotionally important stimuli may be 'presets' to which attention is switched irrespective of the attenuated message's content. This accounts for our ability to switch attention to a different conversation when our name is mentioned. Since Treisman argues that it is the *features* of a stimulus which determine whether or not it is attended to, the concept of *probabilistic filtering* is perhaps a better way of appreciating Treisman's theory than that of attenuation (Massaro, 1989).

THE DEUTSCH–NORMAN LATE SELECTION FILTER THEORY

Deutsch & Deutsch (1963) and Norman (1968, 1976) completely rejected Broadbent's claim that information is filtered out early on. According to the Deutsch–Norman theory, filtering or selection only occurs after *all inputs* have been analysed at a high level, for example, after each word has been recognised by the memory system and *analysed for meaning*.

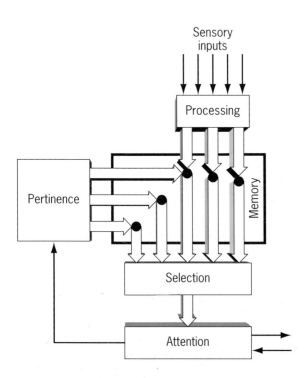

Figure 25.3   The Deutsch–Norman theory of focused attention. All sensory inputs receive perceptual processing and are recognised in the sense that they excite their representations (the black circle) in memory. The information selected is that which has the greatest pertinence (Norman, 1968)

Their filter is placed nearer the *response* end of the processing system, and hence it is a 'late' selection filter. Because processing will have already been undertaken on the information that has been presented before, some information will have been established as *pertinent* (most relevant) and have activated particular memory representations (hence the theory is sometimes called pertinence theory). When one memory representation is selected for further processing, attention becomes selective. The theory implies that we perceive everything we encounter, but are only consciously aware of some of it (Hampson & Morris, 1996).

Tests of Treisman's and the Deutsch–Norman theories

Both Treisman's and the Deutsch–Norman theories can account for the evident processing of non-shadowed material (which cannot be explained by Broadbent's theory). If the Deutsch–Norman theory is correct, then participants should be able to identify as many target words in the non-shadowed message as in the shadowed message, since the theory claims that both are completely analysed for meaning. Treisman & Geffen (1967), however, found that target words were much better detected in the shadowed message (87 per cent) than in the non-shadowed message (eight per cent), an outcome consistent with Treisman's view that the non-shadowed message is attenuated.

Treisman and Geffen's findings assume that the shadowed and non-shadowed messages are *equally important*. Deutsch & Deutsch (1967) argued that this assumption was not met, because the requirement to shadow one message made the target words in that message more important. Treisman & Riley (1969) overcame this problem by requiring participants to *stop* shadowing whenever a target word was heard in either the attended or non-attended ear. Under such circumstances, performance was still better for the shadowed message (76 per cent) than for the non-shadowed message (33 per cent).

This finding is consistent with Treisman's theory, but inconsistent with the Deutsch–Norman claim that performance should not differ given that the targets were equally pertinent irrespective of the ear they were presented to. However, the detection rate for the non-attended ear in Treisman and Riley's study (33 per cent) was much higher than that in the Treisman and Geffen study (eight per cent), a finding which provides some support for the Deutsch–Norman theory.

The theory predicts that participants asked immediately afterwards should be able to repeat back the words presented to the non-shadowed ear. However, the non-shadowed message gets into short-term memory for only a brief period and is then forgotten very quickly.

Norman (1969) found that participants *could* remember the last couple of words presented to the non-attended ear only if tested *immediately* rather than after a short continuation of the shadowing task, a finding replicated by Glucksberg & Cowan (1970). This relates to Neisser's (1967) *echoic memory* (see Chapter 27, page 230). The Deutsch–Norman theory is also supported by the studies summarised in Box 25.2.

The Deutsch–Norman theory's major problem is its claim that *every* input's meaning is subjected to higher-level analysis, because this makes information processing rigid and inflexible. The data indicate that whilst not as much is known about information presented in the non-attended ear as predicted by the Deutsch–Norman model, more is known about such information than predicted by either Broadbent's or Treisman's theories! (Wilding, 1982).

ALTERNATIVES TO SINGLE-CHANNEL THEORIES OF FOCUSED AUDITORY ATTENTION

The major criticism of single-channel theories is their lack of *flexibility* and several more 'flexible' theories have been advanced. According to Johnston & Heinz (1978), attentional selectivity can occur at several different stages of processing, depending upon the demands made by the experimental task. To minimise demands on capacity, selection is made as early as possible.

Johnston & Heinz (1979) and Johnston & Wilson (1980) have presented findings consistent with their view that processing is more flexible than predicted by single-channel theories. For example, Johnston and Wilson showed that participants processed words presented to *both* ears when they did not know to which ear particular target words would be presented, but did not do this when they knew which ear the target words would be presented to. These data suggest that non-target words are processed only to the extent necessary to perform a task. Similarly, other alternative theories (such as Kahneman, 1973; Norman & Bobrow, 1975) can also be applied to the phenomenon of *divided attention* (see Chapter 26).

Focused visual attention

According to Driver (1996):

'The cluttered scenes of everyday life present more objects than we can respond towards simultaneously, and often more than we can perceive fully at any one time. Accordingly, mechanisms of attention are required to select objects of interest for further processing. In the case of vision, one such mechanism is provided by eye movements, which allow us to fixate particular regions so that they benefit from the greater acuity of the fovea'.

The fovea (a very small area of the retina containing very sensitive *cone* cells: see Chapter 10, page 82) provides maximum acuity for visual stimuli. So, when we fixate on an object, maximum visual processing is given to the object that projects its image onto the fovea, whilst the resources given to the other part of the visual field are 'attenuated' (Anderson, 1995a).

Posner *et al.* (1978, 1980) found that when people are told to fixate on one part of the visual field, it is still possible to attend to stimuli seven or so degrees either side of the fixation point, and that attention can be shifted more quickly when a stimulus is presented in an 'expected' rather than an 'unexpected' location. Thus, visual attention is *not* identical to the part of the visual field which is processed by the fovea, but can be shifted without corresponding changes in eye movements. Indeed, such shifts in attention frequently *precede* the corresponding eye movement (Anderson, 1995a). Posner (1980) calls this phenomenon *covert attention*.

THE INTERNAL MENTAL SPOTLIGHT AND THE ZOOM LENS

Posner likened covert attention to an internal spotlight that 'illuminates' any stimulus in the attended region so that it is perceived in greater detail. It essentially duplicates the functions of eye movements internally, by allowing a particular region of space to be perceptually enhanced (Driver, 1996).

LaBerge (1983) required participants to judge whether the middle letter of five letters (such as LACIE) came from the beginning or end of the alphabet. On some occasions, however, a stimulus such as +7+++ was presented, and the task was to determine whether the 7 was one of two letters (T or Z). LaBerge found that the speed of judgement was a function of the distance from the centre of attention. Thus, reaction times were fastest for items at the centre of the stimulus and slower at its periphery, even though all items were within the fovea's region.

LaBerge concluded that visual attention is most concentrated at the centre of the internal spotlight and least at its periphery. When material beyond its centre needs to be processed, the spotlight must be shifted to ensure maximal processing. Because this takes time, participants in Posner *et al.*'s experiments took longer to judge a stimulus when it appeared in an 'unexpected' location (Eriksen & Yeh, 1987).

LaBerge also found that when participants were required to attend to the whole five-letter word string, the 'width' of the spotlight's 'beam' increased as indicated by the lack of difference in reaction times for items at the centre and periphery. These findings led Eriksen (1990) to propose the *zoom-lens model of visual attention* which accepts the existence of an internal mental spotlight but suggests that it has a beam which may be very narrow (in the case of LaBerge's letter task) or broad (in the case of LaBerge's word task).

While there is evidence that, consistent with the spotlight model, little or no processing occurs beyond the spotlight (Johnston & Dark, 1986), both the spotlight and zoom-lens models have been contradicted in several studies.

Box 25.4   Neisser & Becklen's (1975) study of selective visual attention

Visual selective attention was studied by superimposing a film of three people playing a ball game on a film which showed two people's hands clapping (see Figure 25.4).

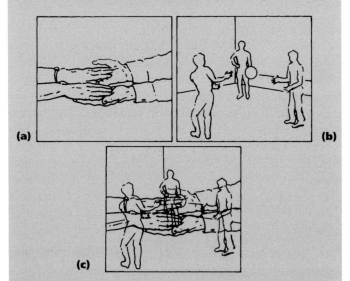

(a) (b) (c)

Figure 25.4   A film of two people clapping hands (a) and three people playing a ball game (b) which have been superimposed (c)

The task was to follow one of the films and press a key to indicate that a 'critical event', such as the ball being thrown, had occurred. Whilst adults found it difficult to

---

follow both events simultaneously, they were able to attend selectively to one or other of the films easily. This is difficult for the zoom-lens model to explain, since it proposes that the focus of attention is a given *area* in visual space rather than objects within that area (Eysenck & Keane, 1995). Using Neisser and Becklen's methodology, it has been shown that infants as young as four months can selectively follow one of the two episodes and, as a result, that selective visual attention is innate rather than learned (Bahrick *et al.*, 1981: see Chapter 23).

THE FATE OF UNATTENDED VISUAL STIMULI

For Johnston & Dark (1986), stimuli beyond the focus of visual attention are subject to no or virtually no semantic processing. Any such processing is limited to mainly simple physical features. However, Driver (1996) disagrees. For example, when a picture is shown as the unattended stimulus on one trial, it slows the processing of an attended word with an identical or similar meaning on the next trial, a phenomenon called *negative priming*. The fact that processing of the attended stimulus is lessened suggests that the meaning of the unattended stimulus must have been subject to some sort of processing (Tipper & Driver, 1988).

TREISMAN'S FEATURE-INTEGRATION THEORY

Treisman's (1988) theory was developed on the basis of findings using the *visual search procedure*. In this, participants are presented with an array of visual material in which a target item is embedded on some trials but absent on others, and the 'distractor' items can be varied so that they are similar to the target letter or different. The participant's task is to decide if the target is present or absent.

```
X  P  T  L  A  B  N  T

A  R  H  N  J  I  F  R

E  W  R  N  P  A  Z  X

A  H  Y  5  Y  T  E  S

A  N  H  C  E  S  T  I

G  D  T  K  D  Y  U  I
```

Figure 25.5   A visual search array. The task is to find the number five in amongst the letters

Neisser (1967) argued that when people perform a visual search task, they process many items simultaneously without being fully 'aware' of the exact nature of the distractor items. However, visual information processing might occur *pre-attentively* as a result of the nature of the stimuli presented (such as whether they have angular or curved features when the task is to detect a particular letter).

According to Treisman, attention must be focused on a stimulus before its features can be synthesised into a pattern. In one of Treisman & Gelade's (1980) experiments, participants were required to detect the presence of the letter T in amongst an array of I's and Y's. Because the horizontal bar at the top of a T distinguishes it from an I and a Y, this could be done fairly easily just by looking for the horizontal bar. Participants took around 800 milliseconds to detect the T and the detection time was not affected by the *size* of the array (that is, the number of I's and Y's).

In another experiment, the T was embedded in an array of I's and Z's. Here, looking for a horizontal bar on its own does not aid detection since the letter Z also has a horizontal bar on top of it. To detect a T, participants need to look for the *conjunction* of a horizontal and vertical line. They took around 1200 milliseconds to detect the T, that is, took *longer* to recognise the conjunction of features compared with just a single feature. Moreover, detection time was *longer* when the size of the array was increased. On the basis of these (and other) findings, Treisman proposed her *feature-integration theory*.

Box 25.5 Treisman's feature-integration theory

According to Treisman, it is possible to distinguish between *objects* (such as a strawberry) and the *features* of those objects (such as being red, possessing curves, and being of a particular size). In the *first stage of visual processing*, we process the features of stimuli in the visual environment and do so rapidly and in parallel without attention being required.

Next, the features of a stimulus are combined to form objects (such as a small, red strawberry). This *second stage of processing* is a slow and serial process (features are combined one after another). Processing is slower in this stage because several stimuli must be processed.

Focusing attention on an object's location provides the 'glue' which allows unitary features to be formed into their various objects, although features can also be combined on the basis of knowledge stored in memory (such as the knowledge that strawberries are typically red). When relevant stored knowledge is not available or

focused attention absent, feature combination occurs in a random way. This can produce *illusory conjunctions* (for example, a blue banana) or odd combinations of features.

(Based on Anderson, 1995a, and Eysenck & Keane, 1995)

Criticisms of Treisman's theory and alternatives to it

Duncan & Humphreys (1992) have argued that the time taken to detect a target depends on the target's *similarity* to the distractors and the distractors' *similarity to one another*. According to their *attentional-engagement theory*, all of the visual items in a display are initially segmented and analysed in parallel. After this, selective attention occurs in which items that are well matched to the description of the target item enter short-term visual memory (see Chapter 27, page 231).

Distractors which are similar to the target will *slow* the search process (because they are likely to be selected for short-term visual memory) as will non-targets that are dissimilar to each other but similar to the target (because items which are perceptually grouped will either be selected or rejected together for short-term visual memory). Since dissimilar distractors cannot be rejected together, the search process is slowed (Eysenck & Keane, 1995).

Treisman has claimed evidence for the occurrence of *illusory conjunctions* (see Box 25.5) in her visual search experiments. Treisman & Schmidt (1982), for example, required participants to identify two black digits flashed in one part of the visual field. In another part, letters in various colours were presented (such as a blue T or a red S). After reporting the digits, participants were asked what letters they had seen and their colour. Most reported seeing illusory conjunctions (such as a blue S) almost as frequently as correct conjunctions. This supports the view that accurate perception only occurs when attention is focused on an object. When it is not, the features of objects are processed but not always combined accurately.

Treisman & Sato (1990) have acknowledged that the degree of similarity between the target and the distractors is important, and the distance between Treisman's theory and Duncan and Humphreys' is narrowing, although the role of conjoining features and the importance of the similarity between non-targets remain important points of difference (Eysenck & Keane, 1995). Also, results from experiments in which moving items are intermingled with static items challenge Treisman's theory.

Box 25.6   McLeod *et al.*'s (1991) moving target experiment

Participants were asked to search for the presence or absence of a single moving X amongst static Xs and moving Os.

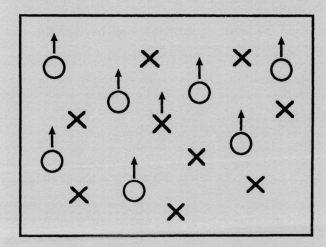

Figure 25.6   A schematic representation of the display used by McLeod *et al.* (1991). The arrows indicate motion, and the task is to search for a single moving X amongst moving Os and intermingled static Xs

The target is defined only by its specific conjunction of form and movement, since its shape is shared with the static Xs and its movement with the Os. Treisman's theory would predict that serial attention was necessary for each item when searching the target, and hence that decision times would increase with an increasing number of distractors. In fact, the target was found easily regardless of the display's size. This implies a parallel process, and in other experiments McLeod *et al.* showed that the parallel search arose because attention could be restricted to just the group of items with common motion to the exclusion of the static items. Because the target has a unique shape, it can be detected in parallel.

VISUAL ATTENTION AND BRAIN DAMAGE

Many researchers are interested in the brain regions involved in attention (e.g. Muller & Maxwell, 1994; Halligan, 1995; Driver, 1996). People who have suffered a right-hemisphere stroke involving the parietal cortex may completely ignore stimuli occuring on the opposite side to the affected hemisphere. For example, in right-hemisphere damage, they may fail to eat food from the left side of their plate and be unaware of their body on that side. The fascinating thing about this *unilateral neglect* is that these effects occur even though the pathways from the receptors to the central nervous system for the neglected information remain intact (see Chapter 7, page 63).

Conclusions

Research into focused auditory and visual attention indicates that we can attend selectively to certain information, and several theories have been advanced to explain how this is done. Some degree of processing of unattended material takes place in both the auditory and visual modalities, although the exact mechanisms by which this occurs have yet to be determined.

Summary

■ While Titchener saw attention as of central importance to psychology, **Gestalt psychologists** thought it an unnecessary concept, and **behaviourists** rejected it as unworthy of experimental study.

■ According to Broadbent, who was trying to account for Cherry's **cocktail-party phenomenon**, humans must **selectively attend** to some information and 'tune out' the rest.

■ Using **binaural listening**, Cherry identified several physical differences affecting selective attention to one of two messages. When these differences were controlled for, it was very difficult to separate the meaning of the two messages.

■ Cherry also used **dichotic listening**, in which participants had to **shadow** one of the messages. Although they could do this, they remembered little, if anything, of the non-shadowed message. Also, whilst the physical properties of the non-attended message were 'heard', its meaning was completely lost.

■ In Broadbent's **split-span studies**, each ear was presented with different information. **Pair by pair** recall was considerably **poorer** than **ear-by-ear recall**.

■ Three **single-channel theories** share the belief in a 'bottleneck' or **filter** which allows some information to be passed on for further processing, either discarding the rest or processing it only to a limited degree. They differ mainly in terms of how early or late the filtering takes place, and hence the nature and extent of the processing of the non-shadowed material.

■ According to Broadbent's **early selection filter theory**, sensory information passes 'in parallel' to a **short-term store**, then onto a **selective filter**. This operates on the **physical characteristics** of the selected source, rejecting all the others.

■ Broadbent's theory accounts for Cherry's findings and the split-span data. It also assumes that the **meaning** of the non-shadowed message will not be subjected to any higher-level analysis. However, Moray's demonstration that people sometimes switch attention to the non-attended ear when their name is spoken challenges this.

■ Also inconsistent with Broadbent's theory is Treisman's finding that participants could sometimes switch attention to the non-attended ear if meaningful material was transferred, mid-sentence, from the attended ear.

■ According to Treisman's **stimulus-analysis system theory**, competing information is analysed for its physical properties, **and** for sounds, syllable patterns, grammatical structures and meaning. The selective filter **attenuates** the non-shadowed message. If this includes biologically and emotionally relevant stimuli ('pre-sets'), our attention will switch to the non-shadowed message.

■ The **Deutsch–Norman late selection filter theory/pertinence theory** completely rejects Broadbent's claim that information is filtered out early on. Instead, selection only occurs after **all inputs** have been analysed at a high level. The filter is nearer the **response** end of the processing system (a late-selection filter). Since the presented information will have already been processed, some will have been established as **pertinent**: when it is selected for further processing, attention becomes selective.

■ The Deutsch–Norman theory predicts that as many target words will be identified in the non-shadowed as the shadowed message. Also, participants should be able to repeat back the words presented to the non-attended ear if asked to do so **immediately**, otherwise they will be lost rapidly from short-term memory.

■ Despite some experimental support, the Deutsch–Norman theory is an inflexible theory, since it claims that every input is analysed at a higher level. Although more processing of the non-shadowed message takes place than is claimed by either Broadbent or Treisman, it falls short of what is predicted by Deutsch and Norman.

■ Alternatives to single-channel models include Johnston and Heinz's proposal that attentional selectivity can occur at several different processing stages depending on the experimental task's demands.

■ Mechanisms involved in **focused visual attention** include eye movements that allow us to fixate specific regions of the visual field which can be projected on to the **fovea**.

■ Visual attention is **not** identical to the part of the visual field processed by the fovea, as demonstrated by **covert attention** which is like an **internal mental spotlight**, duplicating the functions of eye movements internally.

■ When we must process material beyond the spotlight's centre, the spotlight is shifted to ensure maximal processing. According to Eriksen's **zoom-lens model of visual attention**, the internal spotlight has a beam which may be very narrow or very broad.

■ Despite evidence that little or no processing occurs beyond the spotlight, findings from studies like Neisser and Becklen's are difficult for the zoom-lens model to explain. The focus of attention is supposedly a given **area** in visual space, rather than objects within that area.

■ According to Treisman's **feature-integration theory**, we can distinguish between **objects** and their **features**. The first stage processes the features of environmental stimuli, rapidly and in parallel, without attention being required. We then combine the features to form objects, which is done slowly and serially.

■ Focusing attention on their location allows unitary features to be formed into their various objects, although these can also be combined on the basis of stored knowledge. **Illusory conjunctions** can arise in the absence of relevant stored knowledge or focused attention.

■ According to Duncan and Humphreys' **attentional-engagement theory**, detection time depends on the **similarity** between the target and distractors and on their **similarity to one another**.

■ Treisman has claimed evidence for **illusory conjunctions**, supporting the view that accurate perception requires focused attention on an object (accurate combination of features).

■ Despite signs of convergence between Treisman and Duncan & Humphreys' theories, they still disagree over the role of combining features and of similarity between distractors. Evidence from studies of attention to moving displays is also inconsistent with Treisman's theory.

■ In **unilateral neglect**, stroke victims ignore stimuli occurring on the opposite side to the affected hemisphere, even though the pathways from the receptors to the central nervous system remain intact.

26

DIVIDED ATTENTION

Introduction and overview

Chapter 25 looked at studies requiring people to process the information from one of two stimulus inputs. Researchers interested in *divided attention* also typically present people with two stimulus inputs, but require responses to be made to *both* of them. Sometimes, we are able to do two things at once easily. Indeed, even though simultaneously attending to two conversations is difficult, it is not impossible (Underwood, 1974). Sometimes, though, it is extremely difficult to perform two tasks simultaneously (see Chapter 25).

This chapter looks first at research findings into divided attention, including factors affecting *dual-task performance*. It then looks at theories explaining how our attention can be divided between two tasks. Some theorists have argued that, with sufficient practice, many processes become *automatic* and make no demands on attention. This chapter reviews the evidence concerning automatic processing and considers how this can help us understand *'action slips'* (performing behaviours that were not intended).

Some demonstrations of dual-task performance

Allport *et al.* (1972) showed that skilled pianists were able to successfully read music whilst shadowing speech. Later, Shaffer (1975) reported the case of an expert typist who could accurately type from sight whilst shadowing speech. However, perhaps the most striking example of dual-task performance comes from Spelke *et al.* (1976), who had two students spend five hours a week training at performing two tasks simultaneously. Initially, the students were required to read short stories whilst writing down dictated words.

At first, they found this difficult, and both their comprehension and writing suffered. After six weeks of training, however, they could read as quickly and comprehend as much of what they read as when reading without dictation. Interestingly, though, they could remember very little of what they had written down, even though thousands of words had been dictated to them over the course of the experiment.

At this point, the task was altered and the students had to write down the category a word belonged to, a task which required more processing of the words, whilst simultaneously reading the short stories. Again, the task was initially difficult, but the students eventually performed it without any loss in their story comprehension.

Factors affecting dual-task performance

According to Hampson (1989), factors which make one task easier also tend to make the other easier because:

'anything which minimises interference between processes or keeps them "further apart" will allow them to be dealt with more readily either selectively or together'.

Eysenck & Keane (1995) identify three factors which affect our ability to perform two tasks at once. These are *difficulty*, *practice* and *similarity*.

> **Box 26.1   The effects of difficulty, practice and similarity on dual-task performance**
>
> **Difficulty:** Generally, the more difficult tasks are, the less successful dual-task performance is. However, it is hard to define task difficulty objectively, since a task that is difficult for one person might not be for another (and this relates to practice: see below). Also, the demands made by two tasks individually are not necessarily the same when they are performed concurrently. Thus, performing two tasks together may introduce fresh demands and require interference to be avoided.
>
> **Practice:** As has been seen, practice improves dual-task performance. This could be because people develop new strategies for performing each task, minimising interference between them. Another possibility is that practice reduces a task's attentional demands. Finally, practice may produce a more economical way of functioning using fewer resources (see pages 222–224).
>
> **Similarity:** As was seen in both this and Chapter 25, Allport *et al.* (1972) showed that when people are required to shadow one message and learn pictorial information, both tasks can be performed successfully, presumably because they do not involve the same stimulus modality.

Two tasks also disrupt performance when both rely on related memory codes (such as visual memory), make use of the same stages of processing (such as the input stage) or require similar responses to be made.

(Based on Eysenck & Keane, 1995)

A brief introduction to theories of divided attention

The theories of selective attention described in Chapter 25 assume the existence of a limited capacity filter which is capable of dealing with one channel of information at a time. As Hampson & Morris (1996) have observed, these theories:

'imply a series of stages of processing, starting with superficial, physical analysis, and working "upwards" towards the "higher" cognitive analyses for meaning'.

In Hampson and Morris's view, these processes are better thought of as an integrated mechanism with the high and low levels interacting and combining in the recognition of stimuli, and that as a result it is better to look at the system's *overall processing*.

Limited capacity theories

KAHNEMAN'S THEORY

According to Kahneman (1973), humans have a limited amount of processing capacity, and whether tasks can be performed successfully depends on how much demand they make on the limited capacity processor. Some tasks require little processing capacity and leave plenty available for performing another task simultaneously. Others require much more and leave little 'spare' processing capacity.

Kahneman calls the process of determining how much capacity is available 'effort', and effort is involved in the allocation of that capacity. How much capacity a task requires depends on things like its difficulty and a person's experience of it. How capacity is allocated depends on *enduring dispositions*, *momentary intentions* and the *evaluation of the attentional demands* (see Figure 26.1). The central processor is responsible for the allocation policy and constantly evaluates the level of demand. When demand is too high, the central processor must decide how available attention should be allocated.

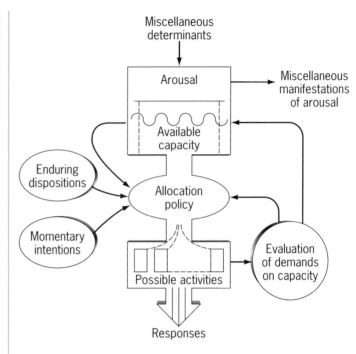

Figure 26.1 Kahneman's theory of attention. Enduring dispositions are the rules for allocating capacity which are outside voluntary control. These include allocating capacity to novel stimuli and hearing one's own name used in a different conversation. Momentary intentions are voluntary shifts in attention such as listening to a message in a dichotic listening task. Evaluation of demands on capacity include rules for overload on the system such as deciding to complete one task rather than failing to complete two

Kahneman sees *arousal* as playing an important part in determining how much capacity is available. Generally, more attentional resources are available when we are aroused and alert than when we are tired and lethargic. Attention can be divided between tasks as long as the total available capacity is not exceeded. This explains the findings from the dichotic listening tasks discussed in Chapter 25 by assuming that shadowing is a task which requires almost all of the capacity available, leaving the non-shadowed message insufficient capacity. Kahneman's theory also predicts that as skill on a task increases, so less capacity is needed for it and more becomes available for other tasks. Thus, in Underwood's (1974) study (see page 212), when people are *trained* at shadowing they become able to shadow *and* attend to the non-shadowed message.

Kahneman's theory suggests that attention is a much more flexible and dynamic system than suggested by the theories of focused attention described in Chapter 25. However, it does not address the issue of *how* decisions are made to channel attention, and the difficulty in defining the general limits of capacity has led some researchers to suggest that the concept of a limited capacity should be abandoned (Hampson & Morris, 1996).

NORMAN AND BOBROW'S THEORY

Following on from Kahneman, Norman & Bobrow (1975) have offered a *central capacity interference* account of attentional phenomena.

Box 26.2   Norman & Bobrow's (1975) central capacity interference theory

This theory's central feature is its distinction between *resource-limited* and *data-limited* processes. On a complex task, performance is related to the amount of resources devoted to it. As more resources are allocated, so task performance improves up to some point. Performance is thus *resource-limited*. On some tasks, though, applying more resources does not lead to improved performance because of external influences (as when participants are required to identify a quiet tone amongst loud, masking 'white' noise). This sort of task is *data-limited* because performance can only be improved by altering the stimuli (such as by making the tone louder and/or the masking noise quieter).

This distinction between resource- and data-limited processes can explain findings from both focused and divided attention research. For example, Treisman & Geffen (1967: see page 213) found that participants shadowing words in one ear had difficulty recognising target words presented simultaneously to the other ear. Lawson (1966), however, found that under similar conditions, participants were able to detect target tones presented in the non-attended ear. This finding can be explained by proposing that the tone-detection process becomes data-limited much sooner than the word-recognition process.

Norman and Bobrow's theory can explain the results of various attention studies simply by talking about tasks in terms of their being data-limited or resource-limited. However, its inability to predict beforehand the results an experiment is likely to produce is its biggest weakness. Additionally, because the theory allows for differential allocation of resources to tasks, an experimenter can never know the level of resources allocated to a particular task. Any results can therefore be interpreted in a way consistent with the theory, and no results can ever be taken as negative evidence.

Multi-channel theories

Supporters of limited-capacity models defend their approach by pointing out that the attentional system breaks down as more and more is demanded from it, and that if data from divided-attention studies are considered carefully it is *not* true that two tasks can be performed together with no disruption at all (Broadbent, 1982). Nevertheless, several researchers have rejected the concept of a general purpose, limited-capacity processor completely. For Allport (1980, 1989, 1993), the concept of attention is often used synonymously with 'consciousness', with no specification of how it operates, and this has done little to increase our understanding of the very problems it is meant to explain.

MODULES AND MULTIPLE RESOURCES

According to Allport, it is difficult to see how the neurology of the brain could produce a system of processing capacity that was completely open to any of the tasks that might be presented (Hampson & Morris, 1996). It is much more profitable to view the data in terms of tasks competing for the same specialised processing mechanisms or *modules*, each of which has a limited capacity but none of which is uniquely 'central'.

When two tasks are highly similar, they compete for the same modules, and this leads to performance impairments. However, because dissimilar tasks use different modules, both can be performed simultaneously. A virtually identical theoretical account has been proposed by Navon & Gopher (1979) and Wickens (1992) in their *multiple-resource theory*. Certainly, the findings of dual-task studies (e.g. Allport *et al.*, 1972) are consistent with the idea of different processing mechanisms handling the requirements of different tasks.

Given the variation in the amount of interference that two tasks can produce for each other, it is plausible to propose that modules or multiple resources exist. However, this approach is also non-falsifiable, since any pattern of data can be explained by proposing the existence of a particular pattern of modules (Navon, 1984). Additionally, the *number* of modules has yet to be specified, and no attempt has been made to explain how people evaluate and integrate multiple sources of information. Lastly, if multiple resources operate in parallel, they must do so in a highly integrated way, given that our behaviour is typically coherent (Eysenck & Keane, 1995).

Attempts at synthesising capacity and module accounts

According to Eysenck (1982, 1984, 1997a) and Baddeley (1986), a much better way of accommodating the data from divided-attention studies is to see capacity and module accounts as being complementary rather than competitive. *Synthesis models* propose the existence of a modality-free central capacity processor, which is involved in the coordination and control of behaviour, and specific processing systems. In Baddeley's (1986) model, for example, two independently operating and specific systems, an *articulatory loop* and a *visuo-spatial scratchpad* are proposed. These systems can explain why overt repetition of an overlearned sequence of digits does not interfere with verbal reasoning, since the former uses an *articulatory loop* and the latter a *central processor* (see Chapter 28, page 239).

Automatic processing

As has been seen, both laboratory evidence and everyday experience indicates that we can learn to perform two tasks simultaneously and highly efficiently. For some researchers, this is because many processes become *automatic* (in the sense that they make no attentional demands) if they are used (or practised) frequently enough. Two important theoretical contributions are those of Schneider & Shiffrin (1977) and Norman & Shallice (1986).

SCHNEIDER AND SHIFFRIN'S MODEL

According to Schneider & Shiffrin (1977; Shiffrin & Schneider, 1977), it is possible to distinguish between *controlled* and *automatic* attentional processing. They argue that controlled processing makes heavy demands on attentional resources, is slow, capacity limited, and involves consciously directing attention towards a task. Automatic processing, by contrast, makes no demands on attentional resources, is fast, unaffected by capacity limitations, unavoidable and difficult to modify (in the sense that it always occurs in the presence of an appropriate stimulus) and is not subject to conscious awareness.

The results of several studies (e.g. Gleitman & Jonides, 1978; Schneider & Fisk, 1982) are consistent with Schneider and Shiffrin's view, showing that if people are given practice at a task, they are able to perform it quickly and accurately, but their performance is resistant to change. An example of apparent automaticity in real life occurs when we learn to drive a car. At first, focused attention is required for each component of driving, and any distraction can

disrupt performance. Once we have learned to drive, and as we become more experienced, our ability to simultaneously attend to other things increases. Logan (1988) suggests that automaticity develops through practice, because automatic responses involve an almost effortless retrieval of an appropriate and well-learned response from memory. This does not involve conscious memory because no thought processes intervene between the presentation of a stimulus and the production of an appropriate response. In Logan's view, then, automaticity occurs when stored information about the sequence of responses necessary to perform a task can be accessed and retrieved rapidly.

Figure 26.2   A learner driver exhibits controlled processing to begin with; this will become automatic processing as his/her competence as a driver increases

Despite its intuitive appeal, serious criticisms have been made of Schneider and Shiffrin's model (Eysenck & Keane, 1995). For example, it is unclear whether automaticity results from a speeding up of the processes involved in a task or a *change* in the nature of the processes themselves. Also, the view that automatic processing makes *no* demands on attention has been challenged by findings indicating that allegedly automatic tasks *do* influence the performance of simultaneously performed tasks (e.g. Hampson, 1989). Additional problems occur with the *Stroop effect*.

> **Box 26.3   The Stroop effect**
>
> Stroop (1935) showed that if a colour word (such as 'blue') is presented in a colour with which the word conflicts (such as 'blue' being presented in red), participants find it difficult to name the *colour* the word has been

presented in. Presumably, because reading is such a well learned, unavoidable and automatic activity, the word interferes with the requirement to name the colour.

An analogue of the Stroop effect can be tried here. The task is to say as quickly as you can the *number* of characters in each of the following rows:

```
                5   5   5
            1   1   1   1
                    2
        3   3   3   3   3
                4   4
            5   5   5
    4   4   4   4   4
        5   5   5   5
                3
            4   4   4
    2   2   2   2
            3   3
        4   4   4
    1   1   1   1
                3
        2   2   2
```

Flowers *et al.* (1979) found that people have difficulty resisting saying the numbers that make up each row rather than counting the numbers because number recognition is much more automated relative to number counting. Kahneman & Henrik (1979) found that the Stroop effect is greater when the conflicting colour word is in the same location as the colour that has to be named than when it is in an adjacent location within the central fixation area. This suggests that automatic responses are *not* always unavoidable (Eysenck, 1993).

The application of Schneider and Shiffrin's theory beyond the cognitive psychological domain has also met with limited success. One example is in social facilitation and impairment research. For over 100 years, social psychologists have tried to explain why people perform some tasks better (a facilitation effect) and others more poorly (an impairment effect) when people watch their performance (Guerin, 1993).

According to Manstead & Semin (1980), 'simple' tasks are under what Adams (1976) calls *open-loop control* (equivalent to automatic processing). With such tasks, sequences

of responses are run off without being monitored continuously. Abrams & Manstead (1981) propose that when we perform simple tasks, performance is sub-optimal because not enough attention is paid to relevant feedback. When someone watches us perform a simple task, our attention is focused sharply on the performance, which causes feedback to be monitored more closely and performance to be improved (facilitated). According to this account, social facilitation effects only occur when a task is so well learned that continuous monitoring is not ordinarily required.

Manstead and Semin propose that 'complex' tasks are under what Adams calls *closed-loop control* (equivalent to controlled processing). Here, the performer is continuously monitoring feedback concerning performance and modifying it in the light of such feedback. The set-backs which inevitably occur during the learning of complex tasks distract the performer's attention away from the immediate requirement of monitoring a subsequent stage of the task. This interrupts the steady progression of learning, leading to increased errors. When performance is observed, the observer acts as an additional source of distraction (especially when set-backs occur), presumably because of the performer's concern about being evaluated by those observers. This places further demands on an already-stretched attentional system and results in an increase in errors.

Thus, the effects of being watched will only occur at or near the extremes of what Abrams & Manstead (1981) call a *task mastery continuum*. For them:

> 'the presence of a critical audience should improve the driving of a highly experienced driver, but impair that of a novice driver, since the latter would suffer from attentional overload whereas the former has spare attentional capacity which can be devoted to considering the audience's reaction to the task performance'.

Unfortunately, data exist which indicate that 'simple' task performance can be impaired by the presence of others whilst 'complex' task performance can be improved in their presence. Defining task difficulty objectively is not easy (see Box 26.1). However, unless it is assumed that the 'simple' tasks in such experiments were actually 'complex' and 'complex' tasks actually 'simple', the application of automatic and controlled processing to social facilitation and impairment is not strongly supported by evidence.

NORMAN AND SHALLICE'S MODEL

To overcome what Eysenck (1993) calls the 'unavoidability criterion', Norman & Shallice (1986) have proposed that processing involves *two* separate control systems, which they call *contention scheduling* and the *supervisory attentional system*. They accept that some behaviours involve *fully automatic processing* and that this occurs with little conscious awareness of the processes involved, since it is controlled by schemas (or organised plans for behaviour: see also pages 250–252).

However, such processes are capable of disrupting behaviour, and so contention scheduling occurs as a way of resolving conflicts among schemas. This produces *partially automatic processing* which generally involves more conscious awareness than fully automatic processing, but occurs without deliberate direction or conscious control. *Deliberate control* involves the supervisory attentional system and is involved in decision-making and troubleshooting, allowing flexible responding to occur in novel situations.

According to Eysenck & Keane (1995), Norman and Shallice's model is superior to Schneider and Shiffrin's because it:

'provides a more natural explanation for the fact that some processes are fully automatic whereas others are only partially automatic'.

Triesman's feature-integration theory (see Chapter 25) can be seen as an attempt to identify processing which is completely free from capacity limitations.

Action slips

These have been defined as the performance of actions that were not intended, and have been extensively researched by Reason (1979, 1992). Reason originally asked 35 participants to keep a diary record of the action slips they made over a two-week period. The participants recorded 433 action slips between them. Reason was able to place 94 per cent of these into one of five categories.

Box 26.4   Reason's five categories of action slips

1 **Storage failures:** These were the most common and accounted for 40 per cent of those recorded. They involve performing again an action that has already been completed. An example would be pouring a second kettle of boiling water into a tea pot of freshly made tea without any recognition of having made the tea already.

2 **Test failures:** These involve forgetting the goal of a particular sequence of actions and switching to a different goal. An example would be intending to turn on the radio but walking past it and picking up the telephone instead. These accounted for 20 per cent of those recorded and presumably occur because a planned sequence of actions is not monitored sufficiently at some crucial point in the sequence.

3 **Sub-routine failures:** Accounting for 18 per cent of the action slips recorded, these involve either omitting or re-ordering the stages in a sequence of behaviour. An example would be making a pot of tea but failing to put any tea bags in it.

4 **Discrimination failures:** These involve failing to discriminate between two objects involved in different actions. An example would be mistaking toothpaste for shaving cream. These accounted for 11 per cent of the total recorded.

5 **Programme assembly failures:** This was the smallest category, accounting for five per cent of the total recorded. They involve incorrectly combining actions as in unwrapping a sweet, putting the paper in your mouth, and throwing the sweet in the waste-paper bin.

(Based on Reason, 1992, and Eysenck, 1997b)

Paradoxically, action slips seem to occur with highly practised and over-learned actions (which should, therefore, be least subject to errors). Reason (1992) proposes that when we first learn to perform a behaviour, our actions are subject to *closed-loop control* (see page 223). In this, a central processor or attentional system guides and controls behaviour from start to finish. When we are skilled at a behaviour, it is under *open-loop control* (see page 223) and controlled by motor programs or other automatic processes.

Closed-loop control is slow and effortful, whereas open-loop control is fast and allows attentional resources to be given over to other activities. However, closed-loop control is less prone to error and responds more flexibly to environmental demands than open-loop control. As a result, action slips occur because of an over-reliance on open-loop control when closed-loop control (selectively attending to the task) should be occurring.

As seen in studies of focused attention (see Chapter 25) material not attended to is typically poorly remembered because it does not get stored in long-term memory. The most common type of action slip, storage failures, can thus be explained in terms of open-loop induced attentional failures leading to a failure to store (and hence recall) previous actions. As a result, an action may be repeated. Other slips also seem amenable to explanation in terms of open-loop control (Eysenck, 1997b).

"Damn! I keep forgetting it's AD not BC now..."

Figure 26.3   What kind of action slip do you think this is?

An alternative theoretical account has been advanced by Norman (1981) and elaborated by Sellen & Norman (1992). Their theory is based on the concept of the *schema*, first proposed by Bartlett (1932). Briefly, a schema is an organised mental representation of everything we understand by a given object, concept or event, based on past experience (see Chapter 27, page 228 and Chapter 29).

Box 26.5   Sellen & Norman's (1992) schema theory of action slips

This distinguishes between *parent* and *child* schemas. Parent schemas are the highest-level schemas and correspond to an overall intention or goal (such as going to a football match). At a lower level are child schemas, which correspond to the actions involved in accomplishing the overall intention or goal (such as driving the car to the football ground, buying a ticket and so on). Each schema has a particular activation level, and a behaviour occurs when the activation level is reached (which depends on the current situation and current intentions) and appropriate 'triggering' conditions exist.

If (a) there is an error in the formation of an intention, (b) an incorrect schema is activated, (c) activation of the correct schema is lost, or (d) there is faulty triggering of an active schema, then an action slip occurs. Thus, a regular beer drinker may decide, because he or she is driving, not to drink alcohol on a visit to the pub with friends. However, without realising it, the drinker finds he or she has ordered a pint of beer in the pub as a result of faulty triggering.

Reason & Mycielska (1982) believe that a thorough understanding of the nature of action slips is necessary to avoid potential disaster occurring in the real world (see, for example, Box 36.8, page 315). Eysenck (1994) maintains that action slips would be eliminated if we were to use closed-loop control for all behaviours. However, this would be a waste of valuable attentional resources! The frequency of action slips reported by Reason's (1979) participants (an average of about one per day) suggests that people alternate between closed-loop and open-loop control as the circumstances dictate. For Eysenck (1994):

> 'the very occasional action slip is a price which is generally worth paying in order to free the attentional system from the task of constant monitoring of our habitual actions'.

Each type of action slip might require its own explanation, because whilst the mechanisms underlying them may *appear* similar, they might *actually* be very different (Eysenck & Keane, 1995). Additionally, any theoretical account depends on the validity of the data it attempts to explain. The diary method employed by Reason may supply weak data because participants might not have detected some of their action slips or remembered to record them when they did (Eysenck, 1997b). As a result, the percentages reported by Reason may be inaccurate. Finally, in Eysenck & Keane's (1995) words:

> '... the number of occurrences of any particular kind of action slip is meaningful only when we know the number of occasions on which the slip might have occurred but did not. Thus, the small number of discrimination failures [reported by Reason] may reflect either good discrimination or a relative lack of situations requiring anything approaching a fine discrimination'.

Conclusions

It is sometimes possible to divide attention between two different tasks, although how this is achieved has not yet been satisfactorily explained. The idea that many processes become automatic and make no demands on attention has some support and helps explain why we sometimes perform behaviours we did not intend.

Summary

■ Researchers interested in divided attention typically present people with two stimulus inputs, and require them to respond to both (**dual-task performance**). Three factors affecting dual-task performance are **task difficulty**, **practice** and **similarity**.

■ Generally, difficult tasks produce unsuccessful dual-task performance. However, difficulty is hard to define objectively, and performing two tasks simultaneously may introduce interference not present when they are performed separately.

■ Practice might improve dual-task performance either through minimising interference, by reducing a task's attentional demands, or producing a more economical way of functioning.

■ Two tasks disrupt performance when they both involve the same stimulus modality, rely on related memory codes, make use of the same processing stages, or require similar responses to be made.

■ Theories of selective attention assume the existence of a limited capacity filter, capable of dealing with only one information channel at a time. Instead of a series of processing stages, we should consider the system's **overall processing**.

■ According to Kahneman, humans have only a limited processing capacity. Different tasks require different amounts of processing capacity, leaving more or less available for performing other tasks. The **central processor** controls the allocation policy and constantly evaluates demand level. **Arousal** is important for determining the amount of available capacity, and the more skilled we are at a particular task, the less capacity is needed.

■ Despite the greater flexibility of the attentional system in Kahneman's theory, it fails to address the issue of how decisions are made to channel attention.

■ Norman and Bobrow's **central capacity interference** theory distinguishes between **resource-limited** and **data-limited** performance. This can explain findings from both focused and divided-attention studies but cannot predict **beforehand** whether an experiment is likely to produce data-limited or resource-limited data.

■ Several researchers have rejected the concept of a general purpose, limited-capacity processor. They argue that the most useful way of interpreting the data is in terms of tasks competing for the same **modules**, each of which has a limited capacity but none of which is uniquely 'central'.

■ Two highly similar tasks compete for the same modules, leading to performance deficits, whilst dissimilar tasks use different modules and thus do not compete. This view is also taken by **multiple-resource theory**.

■ Eysenck and Baddeley believe that capacity and module accounts are complementary. **Synthesis models** propose the existence of a modality-free central capacity processor, which coordinates and controls behaviour, plus specific independent processing systems, such as Baddeley's **articulatory loop** and **visuo-spatial scratchpad**.

■ Schneider and Shiffrin distinguish between **controlled** and **automatic processing**. Practice makes performance fast and accurate, but resistant to change. According to Logan, practice leads to automaticity through effortless retrieval from memory of an appropriate and well-learned response, with no intervening conscious thought processes. The 'Stroop effect' shows that well-learned, unavoidable and automatic skills (such as reading) can interfere with other tasks (such as naming the colour of a written word).

■ Schneider and Shiffrin's model has been applied to social facilitation and impairment. According to Manstead and Semin, 'simple' tasks are under **open-loop control** (equivalent to automatic processing), whilst 'complex' tasks are under **closed-loop control** (controlled processing). However, some research findings dispute this claim.

■ **Contention scheduling** is used to resolve conflicts among **schemas** which control **fully automatic processing** and produces **partially automatic processing**. The **supervisory attentional system** is involved in **deliberate control**, which allows flexible responses in novel situations.

■ The most common type of **action slips** are **storage failures**. Other categories include **test, sub-routine, discrimination** and **programme assembly failures**.

■ Paradoxically, action slips seem to involve actions that are highly practised or over-learned. Performance of new behaviours is subject to **closed-loop control**, whilst skilled performance is under **open-loop control**. Action slips reflect an over-reliance on open-loop control when focused attention is needed. They are the price for freeing the attentional system from constantly having to monitor our actions.

■ Different types of action slip may require their own explanations. Also, Reason's participants might not have detected some of their action slips or remembered to record them. We also need to know when a particular slip did **not** happen and not just how many times it **did**.

PART 2

Memory

THE NATURE OF MEMORY AND AN INTRODUCTION TO THE MULTI-STORE MODEL OF MEMORY

Introduction and overview

Reber (1985) identifies three meanings of the word 'memory'. First, it is the mental function of retaining information about events, images, ideas and so on after the original stimuli are no longer present. Second, memory is a hypothesised 'storage system' that holds such information. Third, it is the actual information that has been retained. Whatever meaning we consider, memory clearly plays a central role in all cognitive processes.

Learning is a relatively permanent change in behaviour as a result of experience, and clearly without memory we could not benefit from such experience (see Chapter 32). The uses we have for memory and the amount of information we can store almost defies belief, and it is astonishing to think that an average brain weighing around three pounds can store more information than the world's most advanced supercomputers (Baron, 1989). Yet, memory can also be frustratingly fallible. According to Blakemore (1988):

> 'Without the capacity to remember and learn, it is difficult to imagine what life would be like, whether we could call it living at all. Without memory we would be servants of the moment, with nothing but our innate reflexes to help us deal with the world. There could be no language, no art, no science, no culture. Civilization itself is the distillation of human memory'.

This chapter examines the nature of memory and considers the *multi-store model of memory*, one of the most influential models attempting to describe memory's structure. It begins by looking at some 'traditions' and 'approaches' to the study of memory, the ways in which memory can be measured, and the concept of memory as 'information processing'.

'Traditions' and 'approaches' to the study of memory

THE EBBINGHAUS 'TRADITION'

The systematic, scientific investigation of memory began with Ebbinghaus (1885). To study memory in its 'purest' form, Ebbinghaus invented material which he considered to be meaningless, varied and simple. This consisted of three-letter *nonsense syllables* (a consonant followed by a vowel followed by another consonant, such as XUT and JEQ). Ebbinghaus spent several years using only himself as the subject of his research. He read lists of nonsense syllables out loud and when he felt that he had recited a list sufficiently to retain it, he tested himself.

If Ebbinghaus achieved two consecutively correct repetitions of a list, he considered it to be learnt. After recording the time taken to learn a list, he then began another one. After specific periods of time, Ebbinghaus would return to a particular list and attempt to memorise it again. The amount he had forgotten could be expressed in terms of the number of attempts (or *trials*) it took him to relearn the list, as a percentage of the number of trials it had originally taken to learn it. If this figure is subtracted from 100 per cent, an indication of the amount 'saved' (*savings score*) is obtained. He found that memory declines sharply at first, but then levels off, a finding which has been subsequently replicated numerous times.

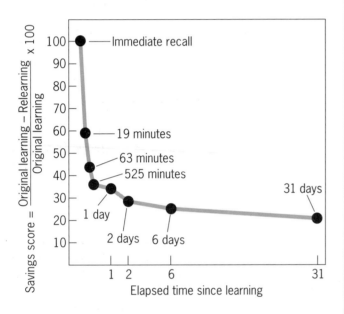

Figure 27.1   The forgetting curve obtained by Ebbinghaus. The savings score declined very rapidly on the first day, but then levelled off

Ebbinghaus carried out many experiments of this sort, and his experimental rigour showed that memory could be scientifically investigated under carefully controlled conditions. He suspected, for example, that memory may not be the same at different times of the day (confirmed by contemporary researchers: see Chapter 11, page 90). In studies conducted between 1883 and 1884, Ebbinghaus *always* tested himself between 1 p.m. and 3 p.m.

THE BARTLETT 'APPROACH'

The Ebbinghaus 'tradition' (Baddeley, 1976) remains popular with today's memory researchers. Some, though, were critical of Ebbinghaus's methodology. Bartlett (1932) argued that Ebbinghaus excluded 'all that is most central to human memory', and that the study of 'repetition habits' had very little to do with memory in everyday life. If anything, research should examine people's active search for meaning rather than their passive

responses to meaningless stimuli presented by an experimenter.

Although he accepted that meaningful material is more complex than meaningless material, Bartlett's 'approach' (Baddeley, 1976) argued that it too could be studied experimentally. In one series of experiments, participants were asked to recall an American Indian folktale (*War of the Ghosts*) they had heard after various periods of time. Participants tended to modify the tale in such a way as to make it more consistent with their own frames of reference (Clifford, 1980).

Bartlett proposed that the learning of new things is based on already-existing knowledge (or *schemata*) of the world. He saw both learning and remembering as an *active process* involving 'effort after meaning' (Baddeley, 1976). When existing schemata conflict with new information, distortions occur, as happened with the participants' recall of the folk tale. Whereas Bartlett believed schemata distort the reconstruction of material during its retrieval, Eysenck (1993) thinks it is far more likely that they influence the understanding of material at the time of learning (see Chapter 29).

Baddeley (1976) has noted that memory research has been torn between Ebbinghaus's insistence on simplification (with its danger of trivialisation) and Bartlett's emphasis on memory's complexities (with its danger of being difficult to work with). However, in common with other memory researchers, Baddeley sees the conflict as a healthy one. Neither methodological approach is uniquely correct and both are useful, depending on what aspect of memory is being studied.

The measurement of memory

As noted above, Ebbinghaus's major method of measuring memory involved *relearning*, that is, recording the number of repetitions needed to learn some material compared with the number of repetitions needed to relearn it. Another technique is *recognition*, which involves deciding whether or not a particular piece of information has been encountered before.

In *recall* tasks, participants recall items either in the order in which they were presented (*serial recall*) or in any order they like (*free recall*). One version of serial recall is the *memory-span procedure*. In this, a person is given a number of unrelated digits or letters and then required to immediately repeat them back in the order they were heard. The number of items on the list is successively increased until recall error is made. The maximum number of items that can be consistently recalled correctly is a measure of *immediate memory span*.

In *paired-associates* recall tasks, participants are required to learn a list of paired items (such as 'chair' and 'elephant'). When one of the words (e.g. 'chair') is re-presented, the participant must recall the word it was paired with.

Memory as information processing

The concept of information processing derives partly from computer science and its related fields (Baron, 1989: see Chapter 3 and Box 83.3). For some researchers, memory can best be understood in terms of the three basic operations involved in the processing of information by modern computers: *registration* (or *encoding*), *storage* and *retrieval*. Advocates of an information-processing approach do not believe that memory operates in *exactly* the same way as a computer. Rather, the approach is a helpful way of conceptualising an extremely complex phenomenon.

Box 27.1   The three basic information-processing operations involved in memory

- **Registration** (or **encoding**) involves the transformation of sensory input (such as a sound or visual image) into a form which allows it to be entered into (or registered in) memory. With a computer, for example, information can only be encoded if it is presented in a format recognisable to the computer.

- **Storage** is the operation of holding or retaining information in memory. Computer data are stored by means of changes in the system's electrical circuitry. With people, the changes occurring in the brain allow information to be stored, though exactly what these changes involve is unclear.

- **Retrieval** is the process by which the information that has been stored is extracted from memory.

Another process is *forgetting*, which is the inability to recall accurately what has been presented. This can occur at the encoding, storage or retrieval stage (see Chapter 30).

Registration can be thought of as a *necessary* condition for storage to take place. However, it is not *sufficient* (since not everything which registers on the sensors is stored). Similarly, storage can be seen as a necessary but not sufficient condition for retrieval. Thus, we can only recover

information that has been stored, but the fact that something has been stored is no guarantee that it will be remembered on any particular occasion. This suggests a distinction between *availability* (whether or not the information is actually stored) and *accessibility* (whether or not it can be retrieved). This distinction is especially relevant to theories of forgetting (see Chapter 30, page 255).

The nature of memory

James (1890) observed that whilst some information seems to be stored in memory for a lifetime, other information is lost very quickly. He distinguished between two structures or types of memory which he called *primary* and *secondary memory*. These relate to the psychological *present* and *past* respectively (Eysenck, 1993). Today, what James called primary memory is referred to as *short-term memory*, whilst secondary memory is referred to as *long-term memory*. To these two types of memory, a third can be added. This is *sensory memory*.

SENSORY MEMORY

Sights, sounds and so on are constantly stimulating our senses but not all of this information is important, and an efficient memory system would be one which retained only information which was 'significant' in some way. The function of sensory memory (the *sensory register*) is apparently to retain information for a period of time long enough to enable us to decide whether it is worthy of further processing. The encoding of information in sensory memory is related to the process of *transduction*. This is the transformation of sensory information from the environment into neural impulses that can be processed by our sensory systems and the brain. In the case of the eye, the excitation on the retina lasts for a few tenths of a second after the stimulus has gone.

Mostly, we are unaware of sensory memory. However, if you watch someone wave a lighted cigarette in a darkened room, a streak rather than a series of points will be seen (Woodworth, 1938), indicating the persistence of an image when the stimulus has disappeared. Since humans have several sensory systems, it is likely that a sensory memory exists for all sense modalities. Most research, though, has concentrated on visual and auditory sensory memories.

Visual sensory memory

Much of what is known about visual sensory memory (or *iconic memory*) comes from experiments conducted by Sperling (1960). Sperling used a *tachistoscope* to flash visual displays to participants for very brief periods of time (around 50 to 100 milliseconds). In the *whole-report procedure*, participants had to identify as many of nine letters (arranged in three rows of three) as they could. Participants could typically identify a maximum of four or five correctly. They claimed, however, that they could actually remember more than that, but that after naming four or five, the image of them had faded completely.

To test these claims, Sperling used the *partial-report procedure*. In this, the three rows of three letters were again presented tachistoscopically, but were immediately followed by a high-, medium- or low-pitched tone. The tone was the signal for the participant to recall the top, middle or bottom row of letters respectively. When the tone *preceded* the presentation of the visual display, recall was (not unexpectedly) almost faultless. When the tone *followed* the display's presentation, recall was almost as good, even though participants had to retrieve the information from the sensory register. Sperling concluded that the capacity of sensory memory is large, and may even be large enough to hold brief representations of virtually everything that impinges on the visual sensory system (Reeves & Sperling, 1986).

In other experiments, Sperling delayed sounding the tone after the visual display had been presented. With a half a second delay, recall was only 63 per cent accurate, and after one second very little was recalled, suggesting that visual sensory memory is like a 'rapidly decaying mental photograph' (Hassett & White, 1989). Because information decays so rapidly, then, it is hardly surprising that participants in the whole-report procedure were unable to recall more items than they did.

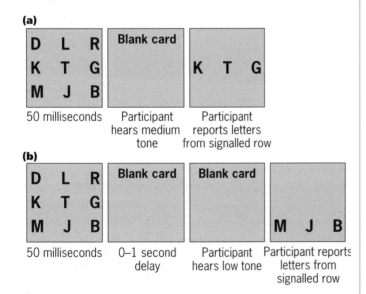

Figure 27.2   (a) shows Sperling's partial-report method, and (b) shows the partial-report method with a delay

Auditory sensory memory

Auditory sensory memory (*echoic memory*, or what Morton, 1970, calls the *pre-categorical acoustic store*) is very similar, if not identical to Broadbent's *sensory buffer store* (see Chapter 25; page 211). Echoic memory enables us to hear a sound after it has stopped. Since we cannot identify a word until we have heard all the sounds that make it up, echoic memory is necessary to hold a representation of an initial sound until the whole word has been heard. Only then can the sound be put into context (Baddeley, 1995). Probably for this reason, echoic memory persists for longer than iconic memory. It can last as long as ten seconds, depending on the method of measurement used (Cowan, 1984) but an upper limit of around four seconds is more realistic (Darwin *et al.*, 1972).

As noted earlier, sensory registration is a *necessary* but not sufficient condition for information storage. Something must be done with the information very quickly if the material is to be passed on for further processing (see Box 27.2). Also, it is likely that there is a sensory memory for all sense modalities (sensory memory is *modality specific*).

Box 27.2   The 'attentional gate'

Reeves & Sperling (1986) asked participants to watch a stream of letters appearing in their left visual field. Participants were instructed to shift their attention to their right visual field whenever a target (the letters C, U or a square) appeared in their left visual field. A stream of numbers was already being presented in the right visual field, and participants had to report the first four numbers they saw.

The time between the occurrence of a target and the reporting of a number was taken as a measure of how quickly attention could be shifted, and the researchers assumed that this interval would indicate how long an 'attentional gate' between sensory memory and short-term memory (STM) remained open.

The gate remained open for around 0.4 seconds, and participants could not report the numbers they saw in the correct order, even though they thought they could, suggesting a loss of information during the transfer from sensory memory to STM.

SHORT-TERM MEMORY

Probably less than one-hundredth of all the sensory information that impinges every second on the human senses reaches consciousness, and of this, only about five per cent achieves anything like stable storage (Lloyd *et al.*, 1984). Clearly, if we possessed only sensory memory, our capacity for retaining information would be extremely limited. Information that has not been lost from the sensory register is passed on to a second storage system called *short-term memory* (STM).

The capacity of STM

Miller (1956) showed that most people could store only about seven *independent* items (numbers, letters, words). He used the word *chunk* to refer to a discrete piece of information. So, when people attempt to remember an *unrelated* string of letters, each constitutes one chunk of information. However, STM's capacity could be enlarged if separate pieces of information were *combined* into a larger piece of information.

For example, the sequence 246813579 can be 'chunked' by applying a rule concerning odd and even numbers. The amount that can be held in STM, then, depends on the *rules* which are used to organise the information. For Miller, the capacity of STM is seven plus or minus two chunks rather than individual pieces of information.

Box 27.3   Miller and the concept of 'chunking'

Miller argues that chunking is a *linguistic recoding* which is 'the very lifeblood of the thought process'. In his view, chunking is not a surprising phenomenon given how lexical information is normally processed. Thus, our capacity to read and understand is largely based on the chunking of letters into words, words into phrases, and phrases into sentences. So, STM's ability to deal with a vast amount of information is facilitated by the chunking of information. However, we cannot do this until certain information in *long-term memory* (LTM) has been activated and a match made between incoming information and its representation in LTM.

Miller & Selfridge (1950) gave participants 'sentences' of varying lengths which approximated true English (to different degrees), and asked them to recall the words in their correct order. The closer a 'sentence' approximated true English, the better immediate recall of it was. This suggests that knowledge of semantic and grammatical structure (presumably stored in LTM) is used to facilitate recall from STM.

In a conceptually similar study, Bower & Springston (1970) presented some participants with a letter sequence in which the letters were presented in a way that formed a well-known group (e.g. fbi, phd, twa, ibm). Others were presented with the same letters but in a way that did not form a well-known group (e.g. fb, iph, dtw, aib, m). The former recalled many more letters than the latter, the material to the former being clustered in acronyms familiar to most American college students. In effect, the pause after 'fbi' and so on allowed participants to 'look up' the material in their mental lexicon and so encode the letters in one chunk.

Coding in STM

Conrad (1964) presented participants with a list of six consonants (such as BKSJLR), each of which was *seen* for about three-quarters of a second. Participants were then instructed to write down what they had seen. The errors they made tended to be linked to a letter's *sound*. For example, there were 62 instances of B being mistaken for P, 83 instances of V being mistaken for P, but only two instances of S being mistaken for P. These *acoustic confusion errors* suggested to Conrad that STM must code information according to its sound. When information is presented visually, it must somehow be *transformed* into its acoustic code.

However, STM also codes information in other ways. For example, Shulman (1970) visually presented participants with lists of ten words. They were then tested for their recognition of them using a visually presented 'probe word'. The probe word was a *homonym* of one of the words on the list (such as 'bawl' instead of 'ball'), a *synonym* (such as 'talk' instead of 'speak') or was identical to it. Shulman found that homonym and synonym probes produced similar error rates, implying that some *semantic coding* (or coding for meaning) had taken place in STM, since if an error was made on a synonym probe, some matching for meaning must have taken place. Other research indicates that visual images (such as abstract pictures, which would be hard to store in the form of an acoustic code) can be maintained in STM, if only briefly.

The duration of STM

A way of studying 'pure' STM was devised by Brown (1958) and Peterson & Peterson (1959) and is called the Brown–Peterson technique. By repeating something that has to be remembered (*maintenance rehearsal*), information can be held in STM almost indefinitely.

Box 27.4   The Brown–Peterson technique

The *Brown–Peterson technique* involves participants hearing various *trigrams* (such as XPJ). Immediately afterwards, they are instructed to recall what they heard or to count backwards in threes from some specified number for a pre-determined period of time (the *retention interval*). The function of this *distractor* task is to prevent rehearsal. At the end of the time period, the trigram must be recalled.

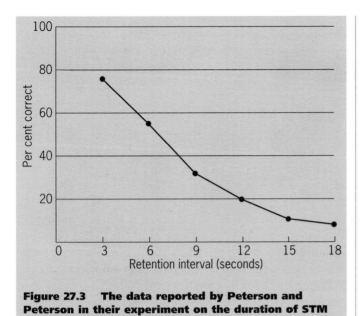

Figure 27.3   The data reported by Peterson and Peterson in their experiment on the duration of STM

Peterson and Peterson found that the average percentage of correctly recalled trigrams was high with short delays, but decreased as the delay interval lengthened, dropping to a mere six per cent after only 18 seconds. In the absence of rehearsal, then, STM's duration is very short, and it can be made even shorter if a more difficult distractor task is used (Reitman, 1974).

LONG-TERM MEMORY

Long-term memory (LTM) has been conceptualised as a vast storehouse of information in which memories are stored in a relatively permanent way. Exactly how much information can be stored in LTM is not known, but most psychologists agree that there is no evidence for any limit to LTM's capacity. In contrast with STM, then, the *capacity* of LTM is far greater and its duration is also considerably longer.

With verbal material, *coding* in LTM appears to be primarily according to its *meaning* (semantic coding). For example, Baddeley (1966) presented participants with words which were acoustically similar (such as 'mad', 'man' and 'mat'), semantically similar ('big', 'broad' and 'long'), acoustically dissimilar ('foul', 'old' and 'deep') or semantically dissimilar ('pen', 'day' and 'ring'). When recall from STM was tested, acoustically similar words were recalled less well than acoustically dissimilar words (supporting the claim that acoustic coding occurs in STM). Semantically similar words were significantly less well recalled than semantically dissimilar words, although this difference was very small (64 per cent compared with 71 per cent), a finding which suggests that whilst some semantic coding occurs in STM, it is not the dominant method.

When an equivalent study was conducted on LTM, semantically similar material impaired long-term recall, but acoustically similar material had no effect. Such findings do *not* imply that LTM only codes material semantically (Baddeley, 1976). The fact that we can conjure up the image of a place we visited on holiday indicates that at least some information is stored or coded in *visual* form. Also, some types of information are coded *acoustically* in LTM (such as songs). Smells and tastes are also stored in LTM, suggesting that as well as being large and long-lasting, it is also a very flexible system (see Chapter 28).

The multi-store model

Atkinson & Shiffrin's (1968, 1971) multi-store model of memory (sometimes called the *dual-memory model* because of its emphasis on STM and LTM) was an attempt to explain the flow of information from one system to another. The model sees sensory memory, STM and LTM as *permanent structural components* of the memory system and intrinsic features of the human information-processing system (see Figure 27.4). In addition to these structural components, the memory system comprises relatively transient *control processes*.

One important transient process is *rehearsal*, which has two functions. First, it acts as a buffer between sensory memory and LTM by maintaining incoming information within STM. Second, it enables information to be transferred to LTM. Although Atkinson and Shiffrin saw rehearsal as the most common method of transfer, they accepted that there were other ways in which material could be transferred. Indeed, they suggested that it was even possible for information to bypass STM and enter LTM directly from the sensory register, a point which some of their critics tend to ignore (see below).

Two lines of evidence supporting Atkinson and Shiffrin's view that STM and LTM may be considered to be separate and distinct storage systems come from *experimental studies of STM and LTM* and *clinical studies of amnesics*.

EXPERIMENTAL STUDIES OF STM AND LTM

Murdock (1962) presented participants with a list of words at a rate of about one per second. They were required to free-recall as many of these as they could. The words were not equally likely to be recalled, and those at the beginning and the end of the list were much more likely to be recalled than those in the middle. Murdock called this the *serial position effect*.

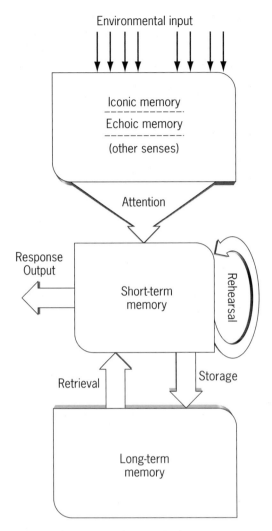

Figure 27.4   The multi-store/dual-memory model of memory proposed by Atkinson and Shiffrin

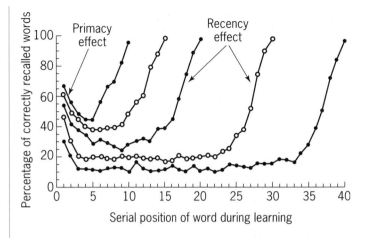

Figure 27.5   Serial position curves for word lists of different lengths

In a variation of Murdock's study, Glanzer & Cunitz (1966) showed that delaying recall of a list of words for 30 seconds and preventing rehearsal (by using Peterson and Peterson's counting task) resulted in the recency effect disappearing, but the primacy effect remaining (see Figure 27.6). Presumably, the earlier words had been transferred to LTM (from where they were recalled), whilst the most recent words were 'vulnerable' to the counting task (Eysenck, 1993). Other research (e.g. Murdock & Walker, 1969) has shown that under certain conditions, the recency effect can be left intact, but the primacy effect massively depressed.

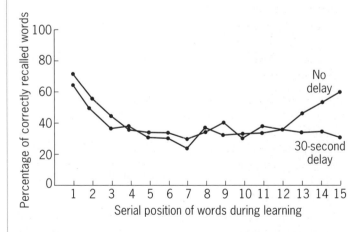

Figure 27.6   Data from Glanzer and Cunitz's study showing serial position curves after no delay and a delay of 30 seconds

The superior recall of the items that appeared at the beginning of the list is called the *primacy effect*, whilst the superior recall of those at the end is called the *recency effect*. The primacy effect occurs because the items at the beginning of the list have presumably been rehearsed and transferred to LTM from where they are recalled. To test the idea that items are transferred through rehearsal, Rundus & Atkinson (1970) asked participants performing a Murdock-type task to rehearse out loud the list they were presented with. Tape recordings indicated that words from the beginning of the list were more likely to be rehearsed than later ones. The recency effect can be explained in terms of items currently held in STM being recalled from that system. Because STM's capacity is limited and can only hold items for a brief period of time, words in the middle of the list are thought to be either lost from the system completely or otherwise unavailable for recall.

CLINICAL STUDIES OF AMNESICS

Amnesics are people who suffer memory loss, usually as a result brain damage. If STM and LTM are distinct and separate storage systems, then certain types of damage affecting only one of the systems should leave the other intact, which would be reflected in the person's ability to remember. In *Korsakoff's syndrome*, found in chronic alcoholics, STM appears to be intact, it is possible to carry on a normal conversation with them, and they are capable of reading a newspaper. However, the transfer of information to LTM is seriously impaired, and they may have no memory of a conversation taking place or of a paper having been read.

Shallice & Warrington (1970) reported the case of K.F., a man who had suffered brain damage as a result of a motorbike accident. His STM was severely impaired, and he could often recall no more than one or two digits on a digit span test. However, his LTM for events occurring after the accident was normal. This also supports the view that STM and LTM are separate and distinct, and suggests that information can find its way into LTM even if STM is severely impaired (see page 232).

Other research, using PET and MRI scanning devices, suggests the existence of multiple memory systems. Periani *et al.* (1993), for example, reported differential changes in brain structure metabolism according to the type of amnesia a person was experiencing with the hippocampus, thalamus and cingulate gyrus being important structures (see Chapter 4, pages 39–40).

Box 27.5   A case of amnesia caused by hippocampal damage

In March 1985, Clive Wearing, former chorus master of the London Sinfonietta, suffered a brain infection caused by the herpes simplex (cold sore) virus. As well as damaging parts of his cortex, the virus destroyed his hippocampus. The consequence of this is that Wearing appears to be unable to transfer new information from STM to LTM, and as a result lives in a 'snapshot' of time constantly believing that he has just awoken from years of unconsciousness. Thus, he reacts to people as if they had been parted for years, even though those people might have paid him a visit minutes earlier.

Wearing can still speak and walk, as well as play the organ and conduct, and his musical ability is remarkably well preserved. He can learn some new skills, and these appear to be stored in LTM. However, whenever he is asked to perform the skill, he reacts as though he has never attempted to learn it before. His memory of his early life is patchy, and his ability to recall details of his life extremely poor.

When shown pictures of Cambridge, where he had studied, he recognised King's College chapel (the most well known and distinctive building in Cambridge) but did not recognise his own college. He could not remember who wrote *Romeo and Juliet*, and identified the Queen and the Duke of Edinburgh as singers he had known from a Catholic church.

Wearing's lack of conscious recollection is, in his own words, 'Hell on earth – it's like being dead – all the bloody time'.

(Adapted from Blakemore, 1988; Baddeley, 1990)

Other cases involving effects similar to those seen in Clive Wearing include three children who had suffered hippocampal damage early in life. All were unable to remember everyday events, such as where their belongings were located or what day it was. Incredibly, though, they all attended mainstream schools and learned to read and write with average competency (Highfield, 1997a).

SOME CHALLENGES TO THE MULTI-STORE MODEL

Despite the continuing influence of the multi-store model in memory research, it has been argued that there is no real need to make a distinction between the various storage systems and that it is far more profitable to view them as being different phases of a continuous process. Moreover, Atkinson and Shiffrin's 'compartmentalisation' of memory into units from which information flows has also been challenged.

Box 27.6   The two-way flow of information between STM and LTM

Certainly, studies suggest that it is highly unlikely that STM contains only *new* information. What seems more likely is that information is retrieved from LTM for use in STM. For example, the string of numbers 18561939 may appear to be independent. However, they can be 'chunked' into one unit according to the rule 'the years in which Sigmund Freud was born and died'. If we can impose meaning on a string of digits, we must have learned this meaning *previously*, the previously learned rule presumably being stored in LTM. In this case, information has flowed not only from STM to LTM but also in the opposite direction.

A vivid example of this comes from studies of people who are experts in some particular domain. De Groot (1966), for example, showed that expert chess players had a phenomenal STM for the position of chess pieces

---

on a board *provided* they were organised according to the rules of chess. When the pieces were randomly arranged, experts' recall was no better than that of non-chess players. With chess experts, information from LTM about the rules of chess were used to aid recall from STM.

Other researchers have challenged the role of rehearsal in the multi-store model. Craik & Watkins (1973) asked participants to remember only certain 'critical' words (those beginning with a particular letter) from lists presented either rapidly or slowly. The position of the critical words relative to the others determined the amount of time a particular word spent in STM and the number of potential rehearsals it could receive. Retention over long periods was unrelated to either the amount of time a word had spent in STM or the number of explicit or implicit rehearsals.

Based on this and other findings (e.g., Glanzer & Meinzer, 1967), Craik and Watkins have distinguished between *maintenance rehearsal* (see page 237), in which material is rehearsed in the form in which it was presented ('rote'), and *elaborative rehearsal* (or *elaboration of encoding*) which *elaborates* the material in some way (such as by giving it a meaning or linking it with pre-existing knowledge). It is the *kind* of rehearsal or processing that is important rather than the *amount* of rehearsal (Craik & Lockhart, 1972). The evidence for this distinction is considered in Chapter 28.

Conclusions

This chapter has discussed some of the findings relating to the nature of memory and considered the multi-store model as a way of conceptualising how various storage systems are linked. Although influential, and supported by evidence, the multi-store model has been the subject of criticism and alternatives to it have been advanced.

Summary

- Memory was first studied systematically by Ebbinghaus, using **nonsense syllables** to study it in its 'purest' form, and himself as the sole subject. He found that memory declines rapidly at first before levelling off, a finding subsequently replicated many times.

- Bartlett criticised Ebbinghaus's approach for being largely irrelevant to memory in everyday life. Research

should examine people's active search for meaning rather than passive 'repetition habits'. Learning new material is based on already-existing **schemata**.

- Ebbinghaus assessed memory using **relearning**. Other methods include **recognition**, **serial** or **free recall** and **paired associates** recall tasks.

- The **information-processing approach** sees registration (**encoding**) as necessary for **storage**, the retention of the information in memory. Not everything that is registered on the senses is stored, and not everything that is stored can be **retrieved**.

- James distinguished between **primary** (referred to today as **short-term**) and **secondary** (**long-term**) **memory**, relating to the psychological **present** and **past** respectively.

- **Sensory memory** (or the **sensory register**) retains information just long enough for us to decide whether or not it is worthy of further processing. The image of a stimulus must persist for a brief time after the stimulus has been removed, otherwise we would be unable to respond to it. Sensory memory is **modality-specific** and research has concentrated on the visual (**iconic**) and auditory (**echoic**) modalities.

- Sperling's **whole-report** and **partial-report procedures** suggest that sensory memory has a large capacity and that information decays very rapidly.

- **Echoic memory** (the **pre-categorical acoustic store**) enables us to hear a sound after it has stopped. This is necessary for identifying spoken words.

- Only a fraction of all the information that reaches the senses at any one time is actually stored. If memory were limited to sensory memory, our capacity for retaining information would be extremely restricted.

- According to Miller, STM's capacity is seven plus or minus two **chunks** of information. If unrelated or independent items of information are **combined** ('chunked'), STM's capacity can be increased.

- **Acoustic confusion errors** indicate that STM **codes** information **acoustically**. There is also evidence of **semantic coding**, and visual images can be briefly maintained in STM.

- The **Brown–Peterson technique** shows that by using a **distractor** task to prevent rehearsal, almost no information is recalled after an 18-second **retention interval**.

- LTM's **capacity** is apparently limitless. Its **duration** is also considerably longer than STM's, with information probably being stored permanently. The **coding** of verbal material in LTM is primarily **semantic**, but other information is coded **visually** and **acoustically**. LTM is a very flexible system.

■ According to Atkinson and Shiffrin's **multi-store/dual-memory model**, sensory memory, STM and LTM are **permanent structural components** of the memory system, with STM and LTM being distinct storage systems. **Rehearsal** is a transient **control process**.

■ Rehearsal acts as a buffer between sensory memory and LTM and also aids the transfer of information to LTM. But information can enter LTM directly from the sensory register.

■ According to Murdock's **serial position effect**, free recall of a list of words produces better recall at the **beginning** and **end** of the list (the **primacy** and **recency effect** respectively). The primacy effect is taken to reflect recall from LTM, whilst the recency effect reflects recall from STM.

■ **Clinical studies of amnesics** also support the STM/LTM distinction. In people with **Korsakoff's amnesia**, STM appears to be intact, but the transfer of information to LTM is seriously impaired.

■ Studies using PET and MRI also support the idea of multiple memory systems, with the hippocampus, thalamus and cingulate gyrus all apparently playing important roles.

■ Although the multi-store model continues to be influential, it may be unnecessary to distinguish between the various storage systems. Rather than seeing STM as containing only **new** information, it is likely that information is retrieved from LTM for use in STM, as in chunking.

■ The kind of rehearsal proposed by the multi-store model is what Craik and Watkins call **maintenance rehearsal**, which they distinguish from **elaborative rehearsal (elaboration of encoding)**. What matters is the **kind** of rehearsal or processing, rather than the **amount**.

28

SOME ALTERNATIVES TO THE MULTI-STORE MODEL OF MEMORY

Introduction and overview

As noted in Chapter 27, the multi-store model of memory has attracted both support and criticism. This chapter considers three major efforts to revise Atkinson and Shiffrin's model. Craik and Lockhart argue against its claim that memory can be 'compartmentalised', Baddeley reconceptualises the nature of STM, and Tulving challenges the claim that LTM is unitary. Whilst all these alternatives are critical of the multi-store model, none is an outright rejection of it. Rather, they all see the multi-store model as an oversimplified account of our highly complex memory.

The levels-of-processing model

Although Craik & Lockhart (1972) accepted that the multi-store model accommodated research findings reasonably well, they argued that there was also evidence directly contradicting it. As noted in Chapter 27 (see page 235), their distinction between maintenance and elaborative rehearsal allowed them to argue that the amount of rehearsal *per se* was less important in determining the transfer of information than the *type* of rehearsal (as supported by Craik & Watkins', 1973, study).

It was also seen that the multi-store model distinguishes between the *structural components* of memory (sensory memory, STM and LTM) and *control processes* (such as rehearsal and coding), with the latter being tied to the former. It emphasises the sequence of processing stages that information goes through as it passes from one structural component to another. Craik and Lockhart, however, began with the hypothesised processes and then formulated a memory system (the structural components) in terms of these operations.

They saw memory as a by-product of perceptual analysis. A crucial concept is the *central processor*, capable of analysing data on various levels and of finite capacity and therefore incapable of dealing with all aspects of a stimulus. The surface features of a stimulus (such as whether a word is in lower or upper case letters) are analysed superficially (processed at a *shallow level*). The semantic features (such as a word's meaning) are analysed more extensively (processed at a *deep level*). Lying between these two extremes, a verbal stimulus can also be analysed according to its sound (processed at a *phonemic* or *phonetic* level).

The level used depends on both the nature of the stimulus and the processing time available. The more deeply information is processed, the more likely it is to be retained.

Box 28.1 Craik & Tulving's (1975) experiment

Craik & Tulving (1975) presented participants with a list of words via a tachistoscope. Following each word, participants were asked one of four questions to which they had to respond 'yes' or 'no'. The four questions were:

1 Is the word (e.g. TABLE/table) in capital letters?

2 Does the word (e.g. hate/chicken) rhyme with 'wait'?

3 Is the word (e.g. cheese/steel) a type of food?

4 Would the word (e.g. ball/rain) fit in the sentence 'He kicked the … into the tree'?

Question (1) corresponds to structural processing, (2) to phonetic processing, and (3) and (4) to semantic processing. Later, participants were unexpectedly given a test in which the words they had seen appeared amongst words they had not seen. The task was to identify which words had been presented earlier. There was significantly better recognition of words that had been processed at the deepest (semantic) level. Additionally, recognition was superior when the answer to the question was 'yes' rather than 'no'.

It has also been found that *elaboration* (the *amount* of processing of a particular kind at a particular level) is important in determining whether material is stored or not. For example, Craik & Tulving (1975) asked participants to decide if a particular word would be appropriate in simple sentences such as 'She cooked the …' or complex sentences such as 'The great bird swooped down and carried off the struggling …'. When participants were later given a *cued recall* test, in which the original sentences were again presented but without the particular words, recall was much better for those compatible with the complex sentences. Since the same depth of (semantic) processing occurred in both cases, some additional factor (elaboration) must also be involved.

Bransford *et al.* (1979) showed that the *nature* of the elaboration is more important than the amount of elaboration. Minimally elaborated sentences such as 'A mosquito is like a doctor because they both draw blood' were better remembered than multiply elaborated similies like 'A mosquito is like a racoon because they both have hands, legs and jaws'. Possibly, this is because material which is *distinctive* in some way is more likely to be remembered. This is another way of conceptualising 'depth' – it may be the non-distinctiveness of shallow encodings (as opposed to their shallowness *per se*) which leads to their poor retention (Eysenck & Keane, 1995).

It is often difficult to choose between level of processing, elaboration and distinctiveness because they can occur together (Eysenck, 1993). Retention cannot be predicted solely on the basis of processing level because more elaborate or distinctive semantic encodings are usually better remembered than non-elaborate or non-distinctive ones. Thus, Eysenck & Eysenck (1980) found that a shallow level of processing could result in remembering that was almost as good as a deep level, as long as it was also distinctive. Quite possibly, all three make separate contributions to remembering, but distinctiveness, which relates to the nature of processing and takes account of relationships between encodings, is probably more important than elaboration, which is only a measure of the amount of processing (Eysenck, 1986).

EVALUATION OF THE LEVELS-OF-PROCESSING MODEL

The model was proposed as a new way of interpreting existing data and to provide a conceptual framework for memory research. It is generally accepted that it contains some truth, and that perception, attention and memory are interdependent. Prior to 1972, few studies had compared the effects on memory of different kinds of processing, because it was implicitly assumed that any particular stimulus would typically be processed in a very similar way by all participants on all occasions. For Parkin (1987), the model has led to general acceptance of the idea that *processing strategies* may provide at least the basis for understanding memory.

However, many researchers see the model as rather simplistic and predominantly descriptive rather than explanatory (Eysenck & Keane, 1995). For example, it fails to address the question of *why* deeper processing leads to better recall. Another problem concerns the difficulty of defining or measuring depth *independently* of a person's actual retention score. So, if 'depth' is defined as 'the number of words remembered', and 'the number of words remembered' is taken as a measure of 'depth', the model's logic is *circular*. Although attempts have been made to provide an independent measure of depth (e.g. Hyde & Jenkins, 1973), there is no *generally accepted* way of independently assessing depth. This 'places major limits on the power of the levels-of-processing approach' (Baddeley, 1990).

Finally, some studies have directly contradicted the model. For example, Morris (1977) showed that rhyming recognition tests produce better recall when they are processed at the 'shallow' than the 'deep' level. Apparently, the *relevance* of the processing is influential. If material is usually processed at a shallow level, recall is better at that level. According to Parkin (1993), the different instructions participants are given vary in terms of the extent to which they require them to treat the stimulus as a word (compare, for example, 'Is a "tiger" a mammal?' with 'Does "tiger" have two syllables?'), yet retention tests *always* require participants to remember words. Since semantic tasks, by definition, require attention to be paid to stimuli as words, their superior retention could reflect the bias of the retention test towards the type of information being encoded.

Reconceptualising short-term memory: the working-memory model

Baddeley & Hitch (1974) criticised the multi-store model's concept of a *unitary* STM. Whilst not rejecting the multi-store model's view of STM as rehearsing incoming information for transfer to LTM, they argued that it was much more complex and versatile than a mere 'stopping-off station' for information. For example, information can flow from LTM to STM as well as in the other direction. Whenever we begin a sentence, we think about what we are going to say (which must be based on information stored in LTM) as well as what we have just said.

Baddeley and Hitch's concept of STM as a *working-memory store* emphasises that it is an active store used to hold information which is being manipulated. For Cohen (1990), working memory is:

'the focus of consciousness – it holds the information you are consciously thinking about now'.

The original model has been modified and elaborated by Baddeley and his colleagues (e.g. Baddeley, 1981, 1986; Salame & Baddeley, 1982). In its present form, it consists of a system in 'overall charge' (the *central executive*) and a number of sub-systems or *slave systems* whose activities are directed by the central executive. These are the *articulatory loop*, *visuo-spatial scratch pad* (or *sketch pad*), and *primary acoustic store*.

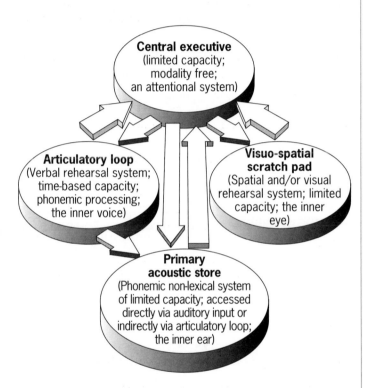

Figure 28.1   The working-memory model

The central executive

This is used whenever we deal with a task which makes cognitive demands. Although capacity limited, it is very flexible and can process information in any sense modality (it is *modality free*) in various ways. The central executive approximates to a *pure attentional system* (Baddeley, 1981).

The articulatory (or phonological) loop

This can be regarded as a verbal rehearsal loop used when, for example, we try to remember a telephone number for a few seconds by saying it to ourselves. It is also used to hold words we are preparing to speak aloud. Because it uses an *articulatory/phonological code*, in which information is represented as it would be spoken, it has been called the *inner voice*.

The visuo-spatial scratch pad

This can also rehearse information, but deals with visual and/or spatial information as, for example, when we drive along a familiar road, approach a bend, and think about the road's spatial layout beyond the bend (Eysenck, 1986: see Figure 28.2). Because it uses a *visual code*, representing information in the form of its visual features such as size, shape and colour, it has been called the *inner eye*. Baddeley (1986) describes the visuo-spatial scratch pad as:

'a system especially well adapted to the storage of spatial information, much as a pad of paper might be used by someone trying, for example, to work out a geometric puzzle'.

Figure 28.2   The visuo-spatial scratchpad is where we store information about familiar roads, so we know what is round the bend

The primary acoustic store

This receives auditory input directly, but visual input can only enter it indirectly, after it has been processed by the articulatory loop and *converted* to a phonological form. Because it uses an *acoustic/phonemic code*, representing information in the form of auditory features such as pitch and loudness, it is called the *inner ear*.

Box 28.2   Working memory in action

One way of understanding how working memory operates can be gained from trying to determine the number of windows you have in your house (Baddeley, 1995). Most of us attempt to do this by forming a visual image and then either 'looking' at the house from the outside or taking a 'mental journey' through its various rooms. To set up and manipulate the image, we need the visuo-spatial scratch pad, and to sub-vocally count the number of windows we need the articulatory loop. The whole operation is organised and run by the central executive.

Research into working memory has often used the *concurrent* or *interference-* (or *dual-*) *task method* (similar to the studies on divided attention described in Chapter 26). Assuming that each slave system's capacity is limited, then with two tasks making use of the same component(s), performance on one or both should be worse when they are performed together than when they are performed separately (Baddeley *et al.*, 1975). If two tasks require different slave systems, it should be possible to perform them as well together as separately. Some researchers have used *articulatory suppression*, in which the participant rapidly repeats out loud something meaningless (such as 'hi-ya' or 'the'). This uses up the articulatory loop's resources, so it cannot be used for anything else. If articulatory suppression produces poorer performance on another task being performed simultaneously, then we can infer that this task also uses the articulatory loop (Eysenck & Keane, 1995).

AN EVALUATION OF THE WORKING MEMORY MODEL

It is generally accepted that STM is better seen as a number of relatively independent processing mechanisms than as the multi-store model's single unitary store. It is also generally accepted that attentional processes and STM are part of the *same* system, mainly because they are probably used together much of the time in everyday life. The idea that any one component of working memory (such as the articulatory loop) may be involved in the performance of apparently very different tasks (such as memory span, mental arithmetic, verbal reasoning and reading) is also a valuable insight. The working-memory model also has practical applications which extend beyond its theoretical importance (Gilhooly, 1996).

Box 28.3   Working memory and learning to read

The articulatory loop is 'not just a way of linking together a number of laboratory phenomena' (Baddeley, 1990). Rather it (or some similar system) plays an important part in learning to read. One of the most striking features of children with specific problems in learning to read (despite being of normal intelligence and having a supportive family background) is that they have an impaired memory span (Gathercole & Baddeley, 1990). They also tend to do rather poorly on tasks which do not directly test memory, such as judging whether words rhyme. Such children might experience some form of phonological deficit (detectable before the child has even begun to read) that seems to prevent them from learning to read. This deficit might be related to the phonological loop system's development, although not enough is yet known to draw any firm conclusions (Baddeley, 1990).

One weakness of the model is that we know *least* about the component that is *most* important, namely the central executive (Hampson & Morris, 1996). It can apparently carry out an enormous variety of processing activities in different conditions. This makes it difficult to describe its *precise* function, and the idea of a single central executive might be as inappropriate as that of a unitary STM (Eysenck, 1986).

Reconceptualising long-term memory

Box 27.5 (page 234) noted that whilst Clive Wearing was severely impaired as a result of his brain damage, he was still able to use many skills and capable of learning some new ones (even though he did not know he had learnt them). These findings suggest that certain parts of his LTM were still intact, whilst others were not. This is difficult for the multi-store model to explain, since it regards LTM as a *unitary* entity.

Squire (1987) proposes a distinction between two basic types of LTM, *declarative memory* and *procedural memory*. Declarative memory has been called 'fact' memory, since it stores knowledge of specific information, for example, *knowing that* we first learned to ride a bicycle when we were three and that bicycles have two wheels. Procedural memory, by contrast, has been called 'skill' memory, since it stores our knowledge of *how to*, for example, ride a bicycle.

DECLARATIVE MEMORY

Declarative memory can be divided into *episodic memory* (EM) and *semantic memory* (SM: Tulving, 1972, 1985).

Episodic memory

EM is an autobiographical memory system responsible for storing a record of the events, people, objects and so on which we have personally encountered. This typically includes details about times and places in which things were experienced (so knowing that we learned to ride a bicycle at the age of three is an example of EM). Although EMs have a subjective or 'self-focused' reality, most of them (such as knowing what we had for breakfast) can, at least in theory, be verified by others.

Semantic memory

SM is our store of general factual knowledge about the world, including concepts, rules and language. Tulving (1972) describes it as:

'a mental thesaurus, organised knowledge a person possesses about words and other verbal symbols, their meanings and referents'.

SM can be used without reference to where and when the knowledge was originally acquired. Most people, for example, do not remember 'learning to speak'. Rather we 'just know' our native language. SM can, however, also store information about ourselves, such as the number of sisters and brothers we have, and with memories like this we do not have to remember specific past experiences to retrieve this information. Similarly, much of our SM is built up through past experiences. For example, a 'general knowledge' about word processors is built up from past experiences with particular word processors through abstraction and generalisation (and such experiences are, of course, examples of EMs).

Originally, Tulving conceived of EM and SM as being distinct systems within LTM. However, a 'general knowledge' of word processors built up from past experiences with particular word processors suggests that a better way to view SM is as a collection of EMs (Baddeley, 1995). Also, Tulving saw EM as synonymous with *autobiographical memory* (AM), that is, our *involvement* in an event that is stored in memory. He also suggested that when we try to recall a word list as part of an experiment, EM is being assessed (since our exposure to the words was an episode in our life). However, this is not what most people understand by the term 'autobiographical' memory (Cohen, 1993). In Cohen's view, AM is a special kind of EM concerned with specific life events that have personal significance (*autobiographical EM*) as distinct from *experimental EM* which is assessed when we take part in experiments that require us to learn word lists.

Flashbulb memories

Brown & Kulik (1977) coined the termed *flashbulb memory* to refer to a special kind of EM in which we can supply a vivid and detailed recollection of where we were and what we were doing when we heard about or saw some major public event.

Box 28.4   Flashbulb memories

Brown & Kulik (1977) asked participants about their memories of various actual or attempted assassinations which had occurred in the previous 15 years, including those of John F. Kennedy, Martin Luther King and Robert Kennedy. They were also asked if they had flashbulb memories for more personal shocking events.

Of 80 participants, 73 reported a flashbulb memory associated with a personal shock, commonly the sudden death of a relative. John F. Kennedy's assassination was recalled most vividly, although other successful or unsuccessful assassinations also produced detailed memories. Brown and Kulik also found that flashbulb memories were more likely if an event was unexpected and personally consequential. This was shown in memories of the death of Martin Luther King. Whilst 75 per cent of black participants reported a flashbulb memory for his assassination, only 33 per cent of white participants did so. Similar findings have been obtained by Palmer *et al.* (1991) concerning memories for earthquakes amongst those living in or well away from the affected area.

The flashbulb memory phenomenon is so called because it is as though the brain has recorded an event like the scene caught in the glare of a camera's flashlight. Indeed, Brown & Kulik (1982) have argued for the existence of a special neural mechanism triggered by events that are emotionally arousing, unexpected or extremely important, resulting in the whole scene becoming 'printed' on the memory.

According to an evolutionary explanation, in prehistoric times an unexpected and consequential event threatening survival would need to be retained in memory to decrease the chance of harm from recurrence of that event. Thus, a special memory for storing events of physical significance would benefit an organism that possessed it, and this system was expanded to incorporate survival-threatening events that the organism only witnessed (Brown & Kulik, 1982).

Box 28.5   Some important findings relating to flashbulb memories

The durability of flashbulb memories stems from their frequent rehearsal and reconsideration after the event, and the detail of people's memories and their vividness are not necessarily signs of their accuracy (Neisser, 1982). For example, Neisser & Harsch (1992) asked college students to report how they learned about the explosion of the space shuttle *Challenger* the day after it occurred. When the students were asked about the explosion three years later, none produced an entirely accurate report, and over one-third produced a *completely* inaccurate report even though they believed it to be completely accurate.

Similar findings have been obtained in a study of recall of the 1989 Hillsborough football disaster when 95 spectators were crushed to death at a soccer match. Wright (1993) found that five months later participants could remember little and, with the passage of time, they were more likely to say they were watching television when the event occurred. According to Wright, people reconstruct events *post hoc* with recall altering over time, and such memories may not require a 'special' flashbulb mechanism.

Conway *et al.* (1994) have argued that in studies failing to find evidence of flashbulb memories, it is not entirely clear whether the events had personal consequences for the participants (a key characteristic of flashbulb memories). Since, for most British people, the resignation in 1990 of the then prime minister Margaret Thatcher was of some personal consequence, a flashbulb memory for this event might be expected. This was the case with 86 per cent of British participants having a flashbulb memory after 11 months. Significantly, only 29 per cent of participants from other countries had a flashbulb memory after the same period of time.

Box 28.6   The case of H.M.

H.M. had suffered epileptic fits since the age of 16. Because they became so devastating, he underwent surgery at the age of 27 to try to cure them. The surgery, which involved removal of the hippocampus on both sides of the brain, was successful in treating the epilepsy, but left H.M. with severe amnesia. Although he had a near-normal memory for things he had learned prior to the operation, his ability to store memories of events after the surgery was very poor. Although H.M.'s STM was generally normal, he either could not transfer information into LTM or, if he could, he could not retrieve it. Thus, he had almost no knowledge of current affairs because he forgot the news shortly after having read it in a newspaper. Unless he looked at his clock, he had no idea what time of day it was.

Whilst H.M. could recognise his friends, state their names and relate stories about them, he could do so only if he knew them before his operation. Those he met afterwards remained, in effect, total strangers, and H.M. had to 'get to know them' afresh each time they came to his house. Although H.M. could learn and remember perceptual and motor skills, he had to be reminded each day just what skills he possessed. As Blakemore (1988) has remarked:

'new events, faces, phone numbers, places, now settle in his mind for just a few seconds or minutes before they slip, like water through a sieve, and are lost from his consciousness'.

When Gabrieli *et al.* (1988) gave H.M. extensive training every day for ten days in the meaning of unfamiliar words which had come into popular use since his operation, he made little progress. This failure to update SM is characteristic of amnesics (Eysenck & Keane, 1995). When new learning does occur, amnesics typically *deny* having encountered the task before, despite (as with Clive Wearing) simultaneously displaying it. Hence, the amnesic is able to demonstrate learning without the need for conscious awareness of the learning process.

Declarative memory involves conscious recollection of the past, and its adequate functioning seems to be disrupted by damage to a number of cortical and sub-cortical areas (including the temporal lobes, hippocampus, thalamus and mamillary bodies: Baddeley, 1995). N.A., a young man who suffered damage to the left side of his thalami as a result of a fencing accident, has been unable to read a book or follow a television programme, which require declarative knowledge, but has learned to ride a horse, swing a golf club and swim, which

PROCEDURAL MEMORY

As noted on page 241, PM stores our knowledge of *how to*, for example, ride a bicycle. Unlike EM and AM, PM cannot be inspected consciously and its contents described to another person. When we initially learn something, it is learned and encoded declaratively, but with practice it becomes compiled into a procedural form of knowledge (Anderson, 1983). This corresponds to the distinction between controlled/automatic processing and focused/divided attention made in Chapter 26.

In Clive Wearing's case (see page 234), most aspects of his PM were intact, but his EM and SM were impaired. Another amnesic patient similarly affected was H.M.

require procedural knowledge (Kaushall *et al.*, 1981). This suggests that 'fact' and 'skill' knowledge must be stored in different parts of the brain. PET studies have lent considerable support to the view that different clusters of cerebral areas are associated with primary components of memory function (Periani *et al.*, 1993: see Chapter 27).

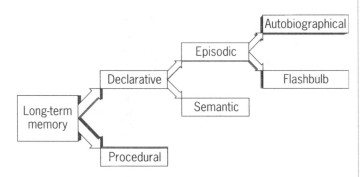

Figure 28.3   A summary of the different kinds of LTM

Conclusions

This chapter has considered some major alternatives to the multi-store model of memory. Whilst the levels-of-processing model sees memory as a by-product of control processes (reversing the multi-store model's view), the working memory model challenges the view of STM as unitary. Similarly, the distinction between declarative and procedural LTM accounts for cases of amnesic patients much better than the multi-store model's unitary LTM.

Summary

■ Using the distinction between **maintenance** and **elaborative rehearsal**, Craik has argued that **amount** of rehearsal is less important than **type** of rehearsal.

■ The multi-store model stresses the sequence of stages that information goes through as it passes from one **structural component** to another, driven by rehearsal and other **control processes**. Craik and Lockhart's **levels-of-processing model** sees memory as a by-product of these processes, specifically of perceptual analysis.

■ A finite-capacity **central processor** can analyse data at either a **structural/shallow level**, a **phonemic/phonetic level** or a **semantic/deep level**. The more deeply information is processed, the better it is retained.

■ **Elaboration** (the **amount** of processing) is an important determinant of retention, but the **nature** of the

elaboration is more important. **Distinctive** material may be more easily remembered.

■ Level of processing, elaboration and distinctiveness often co-occur, making it difficult to choose between them. However, distinctiveness is probably more important than elaboration, which is only a measure of 'how much'.

■ The levels-of-processing model sees perception, attention and memory as interdependent, and challenges the assumption that any stimulus is typically processed similarly by all participants on all occasions. It is now generally accepted that **processing strategies** may help in understanding memory.

■ However, the model fails to explain **why** deeper processing is more effective and **how** depth should be defined or measured independently of actual retention scores. The **relevance** of the processing is influential and the superior retention produced by semantic tasks could reflect the bias of retention tests towards the type of information being processed (words in both cases).

■ Baddeley and Hitch criticised the multi-store model's view of STM as **unitary**. Their **working memory model** sees STM as an active store, holding information which is being manipulated. It is the 'focus of consciousness'. Working memory (WM) consists of a **central executive**, with overall control of the activities of several **slave systems**, namely the articulatory/phonological loop (inner voice), visuo-spatial scratch pad/sketch pad (inner eye) and primary acoustic store (inner ear). The limited-capacity central executive is very flexible and **modality free**, resembling a **pure attentional system**.

■ It is widely accepted that attentional processes and STM are part of the **same** system, and seeing any one component as involved in apparently different tasks is a valuable insight. An important practical application of the model is in helping to explain why children have specific problems in learning to read.

■ The multi-store model's view of a **unitary** LTM has difficulty explaining cases like that of Clive Wearing, whose LTM appeared to be intact in some respects but not others.

■ Squire distinguishes between **declarative** ('fact') **memory**, concerned with **knowing that**, and **procedural** ('skill') **memory**, concerned with **knowing how**. Tulving distinguishes two kinds of declarative memory: **episodic memory (EM)** and **semantic memory (SM)**. Rather than these being distinct systems within LTM, SM is better viewed as a collection of EMs, as when we build up general knowledge through particular past experiences.

■ Tulving believed that EM is synonymous with **autobiographical memory (AM)**, denoting our **involvement** in the event that is stored. However, Cohen sees AM as a special kind of EM, concerned with personally significant life events distinct from **experimental EM**.

■ **Flashbulb memory** is another kind of EM, involving vivid and detailed recollection of the circumstances in which we learned of some major public event. Such memories are more likely if the event is unexpected and personally consequential.

■ Brown and Kulik argue for a special neural mechanism triggered by emotionally arousing, unexpected or especially important events. This makes sense from an evolutionary perspective.

■ Unlike EM and SM, **procedural memory** (PM) cannot be inspected consciously. Anderson believes that learning is initially declarative (controlled processing/focused attention), but with practice becomes compiled into a procedural form of knowledge (automatic processing/divided attention).

■ Both Clive Wearing and H.M. showed a largely intact PM, whilst EM and SM were impaired. Their inability to update SM is typical of amnesics. When amnesics do learn psychomotor skills, they typically **deny** having encountered them before.

■ Declarative memory involves conscious recollection of the past and is disrupted by damage to several cortical and sub-cortical areas. PET studies show that different clusters of cerebral areas are associated with primary components of memory function.

29

THE ORGANISATION OF INFORMATION IN MEMORY

Introduction and overview

Chapter 27 discussed the limited capacity of STM and noted that 'chunking' can apparently increase its capacity by imposing meaning on the information presented. 'Chunking' involves integrating and relating incoming information to knowledge already in LTM, *organising* it and giving it a structure it does not otherwise have. For Baddeley (1995), the secret of a good memory is, like a library, organisation, and:

> 'good learning typically goes with the systematic encoding of incoming material, integrating and relating it to what is already known'.

Support for the view that memory is highly organised comes from a case study reported by Hart *et al.* (1985). Two years after suffering a stroke, M.D. appeared to have made a complete recovery, the only problem being his inability to remember the names of fruits or vegetables or sort their pictures into proper categories. His ability to identify and sort types of food or vehicles into categories suggests that related information in memory is stored together, and may even be stored in specific cortical areas. This chapter looks at organisation in memory and considers models of how information is represented in semantic memory.

Some experimental studies of organisation in memory

Bousfield (1953) asked participants to learn 60 words, comprised of four categories (animals, people's names, professions and vegetables) with 15 examples of each, all mixed up. When participants free-recalled the list, they tended to cluster items from particular categories. For example, 'onion' was very likely to be recalled with other vegetables. This tendency to recall words in clusters suggested that participants had tried to organise the material (*categorical clustering*). In a more naturalistic setting, students asked to recall staff members' names tended to do so by department (Rubin & Olson, 1980).

Instructions to organise material will facilitate learning, even when participants are not trying to remember it. Mandler (1967) used a pack of 100 cards, each with a word printed on it. Participants were told to arrange the cards into categories that 'went together'. Half were told to try to remember the words, but the other half were not. Participants continued the sorting task until the cards they put into each category were 95 per cent the same from one trial to the next. When asked to remember as many words as possible, they tended to display categorical clustering. Also, those instructed just to sort the cards into categories recalled *as many* as those instructed to try and remember them, suggesting that once we become involved in working with material, we tend to organise it.

Box 29.1 Subjective and experimenter organisation

People will tend to create their own categories when material they are presented with does not obviously fall into categories. Tulving (1968) calls this *subjective organisation* (SO) and distinguishes it from *experimenter organisation* (EO) in which organisation is imposed by the experimenter. Bower *et al.* (1969) asked participants to learn a list of words arranged into conceptual hierarchies (Figure 29.1, page 246). For one group, the words were organised in a hierarchical form. The other group were presented with the same words, arranged randomly. The first group recalled an average of 65 per cent of words correctly, compared with an average of only 19 per cent for the other group.

Imagery as a form of organisation

Imagery is the basis of many kinds of *mnemonic devices* (memory aids: see Chapter 31). Verbal material is better remembered if it can be associated in some way with a visual image. This is true for both initial learning (how the material is encoded) and retrieval. The use of imagery can be traced to the writing of Cicero, who tells the story of the Greek poet Simonides who lived around 500 BC.

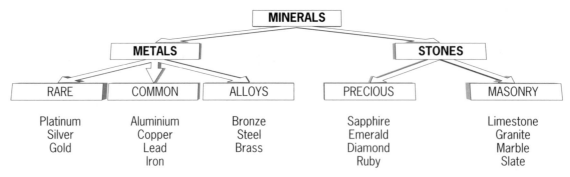

Figure 29.1   A conceptual hierarchy as used by Bower *et al.* (1969)

Simonides' *method of loci* ('loci' is the Greek for 'places') is still used today. One variation is the *narrative story method*. The items to be remembered are incorporated into a meaningful story which is then retold in order to remember them (Bower & Clark, 1969). A famous user of this method was a Russian journalist called Sheresheveski ('S') studied by Luria (1968). S's memory appeared to be limitless and included the ability to recall lists of more than a 100 digits and elaborate scientific formulae, even though he was not a scientist.

Bower (1972) presented participants with 100 different cards one at a time, each having two unrelated words printed on it (such as 'cat' and 'brick'). Participants in one group were instructed to form mental images to *link* the unconnected words, the more vivid the image the better, whilst those in another group were simply instructed to memorise the words. Each participant was then shown a card with the first word of each pair, and asked to recall the second word. Those who used imagery recalled 80 per cent of the words, compared with only 45 per cent by the non-imagers.

Bizarre, interacting and *vivid* images are most effective (Anderson, 1995b), possibly because they tend to be more distinctive or novel and take more time to form. According to Paivio's (1986) *dual-code* model of memory, memories are stored in either *sensory codes* (as visual images or sounds) or *verbal codes* (as words). Within the latter, each known word is represented by a *logogen* and within the former by *imagens*. The two systems are connected by means of *referential links* which allow a word to be associated with its relevant image (and vice versa). This can explain why it is easier to form images of *concrete* words (such as 'apple') than *abstract* words (such as 'nourishment'). Whilst abstract words may be represented in the verbal system only, concrete words may be represented in both systems (Parkin, 1993).

Eidetic imagery is a special type of mental imagery involving a persistent and clear image of some visual scene enabling it to be recalled in astonishing detail. Eidetic imagery is more common in children than adults, but only about five per cent of children display it (Haber, 1969). The ability declines with age, and has largely disappeared by early adulthood. *Eidetikers* perform no better than non-eidetic classmates on other tests of memory, and eidetic imagery appears to be an essentially perceptual phenomenon in which the coding of information is not a factor (Haber, 1980).

Semantic-network models

Semantic-network models attempt to account for the *kind* of organisation that occurs in memory. Different models share a concern with how meaningful material (rather than meaningless material, such as nonsense syllables) is organised, and they all assume that semantic organisation is best thought of in terms of multiple, interconnected associations, relationships or pathways. The models assume that information is embedded in an organised, structured

network composed of semantic units and their functional relationships to one another (Houston *et al.*, 1991).

HIERARCHICAL-NETWORK MODELS

Collins and Quillian's model

Collins & Quillian's (1969, 1972) *teacher language comprehender* is primarily concerned with *lexical memory* (memory for particular words rather than grammar or sentences).

Box 29.4   The hierarchical network model of semantic memory

Collins and Quillian see SM as organised in the form of a hierarchical network. Major concepts are represented as *nodes*, each node having several properties or features associated with it. Each node is also associated with other concepts elsewhere in the hierarchy.

In Figure 29.2, the concept 'animal' and the properties or features associated with animals appear at the top of the hierarchy. The concept 'animal' is also associated with the concepts of 'bird' and 'fish' which appear at the next level in the hierarchy. In turn, these concepts are associated with yet other concepts lower down in

---

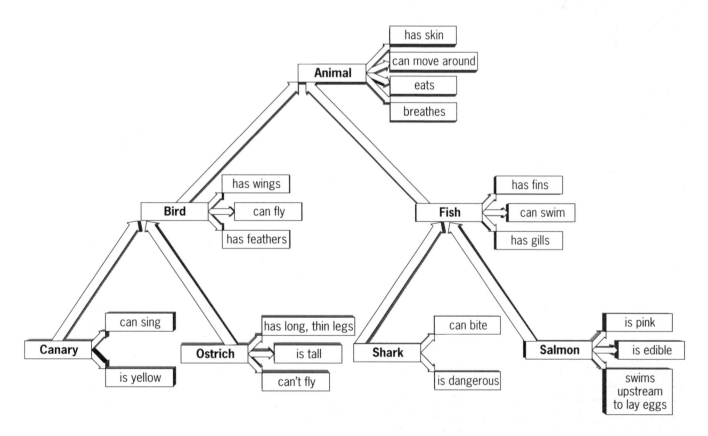

Figure 29.2   An example of a hierarchical network (based on Collins & Quillian, 1969, 1972)

the hierarchy. Thus, the 'bird' concept is associated with 'canary' and 'ostrich' whilst the 'fish' concept is associated with 'shark' and 'salmon'. Since almost all birds have wings, feathers and can fly, it is not necessary for these features to appear lower down the hierarchy as properties of canaries and ostriches. This hierarchical arrangement means that large amounts of information can be stored very economically.

Experimental tests of the model typically involve *sentence verification tasks*. In these, participants are given a sentence such as 'A canary can sing' or 'A canary can fly' and asked to verify whether the sentence is true or not. The time taken to verify each sentence is recorded. The model predicts that with a sentence like 'A canary can sing', reaction time should be shorter than with the sentence 'A canary can fly'. This is because the property 'can sing' is associated with the concept 'canary', whilst 'can fly' is associated with the concept 'bird', one level further up the hierarchy. A sentence like 'A canary breathes' should take even longer to verify, since this involves crossing two levels of the hierarchy.

Consistent with their model, Collins and Quillian found that the time taken to decide whether a statement was true increased as a function of the number of levels of the hierarchy that had to be crossed to verify it.

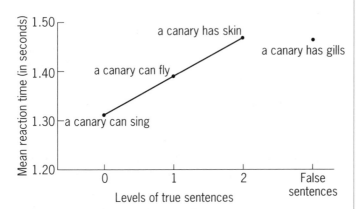

Figure 29.3   Data from Collins and Quillian's sentence verification tasks

---

Box 29.5   Alternative explanations of Collins and Quillian's data

- It might take longer to verify 'A canary is an animal' because there are more animals than birds. In other words, their findings could be explained in terms of the *category size* and reaction time relationship.

- The sentence 'A canary is a bird' (in which the canary is a *typical* instance) is verified *more* quickly than 'An ostrich is a bird' (an *atypical* instance). Since both sentences involve crossing the same number of levels, Collins and Quillian's model would predict no difference in verification time for the two sentences (Baddeley, 1990).

- Conrad (1972) found that response time may reflect the *relative frequency* with which certain attributes are commonly associated with a particular concept. When frequency was controlled for, there was no evidence for longer response times to categories supposedly stored at a higher level. This suggests that 'semantic relatedness' (the attributes commonly associated with particular concepts) could account for the original findings. Conrad's data suggest that not all attributes of a concept are *equally important* or salient.

- Rips *et al.* (1973) found that it takes longer to verify 'A bear is a mammal' than 'A bear is an animal'. Since 'animal' is higher up in the hierarchy than 'mammal', this is the *opposite* of what Collins and Quillian's model predicts.

According to Bower & Hilgard (1981):

'a realistic memory, of course, contains thousands of ... concepts, each with very many connections, so that the actual topographical representation would look like a huge "wiring diagram"'.

In Lindsay & Norman's (1977) model, just a fragment of information enables many questions to be answered. For example, if the system was asked to compare the similarities and differences between beer and wine, it could do this (see Gross & McIlveen, 1997).

MATRIX MODELS

Broadbent *et al.* (1978) gave participants a list of 16 words to remember. For the control group, the words were presented randomly, whilst for one experimental group, they were organised hierarchically. A second experimental group was presented with the words in the form of a matrix (see Figure 29.4).

The two experimental groups' participants remembered significantly more words than those in the control group. However, the experimental groups did not differ from one another, suggesting that both hierarchical and matrix organisations are equally helpful in remembering.

FEATURE MODELS

Smith *et al.*'s (1974) *feature approach* is concerned with our ability to decide whether certain nouns belong to certain

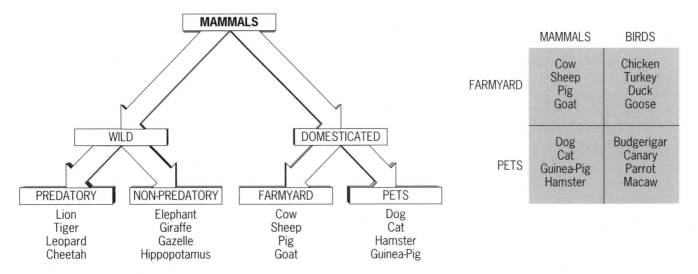

Figure 29.4   The hierarchical organisation of words in Broadbent *et al.*'s experiment (a), and the same words presented in matrix form (b)

categories (see Rips *et al.*'s 1973 study in Box 29.5). For example, suppose we are asked to verify 'A cat is an animal'. For Smith *et al.*, the crucial factor is not the spatial relationship between the two concepts, but the number of *features* they have in common. A cat and an animal have a large number of shared features and as a result, it should not take long to verify the sentence. The same would be true of 'A cat is sand', since these two concepts have nothing in common.

Sometimes, though, the number of common attributes is *intermediate*. In 'A mould is a plant', the two concepts share some features, but it is difficult to generate enough to enable a quick decision to be reached. In such circumstances we look at *defining features* (a necessary and sufficient condition for reaching a decision) and *characteristic features* (a typical attribute of an item belonging to a category, but not itself sufficient to determine whether something belongs to a category). For example, any animal that has feathers is a bird, since there are no featherless birds and no non-birds that have feathers. However, whilst birds characteristically fly, not all do, and some things that do fly are not birds. When the number of common attributes belonging to a category is intermediate, and a decision is difficult to reach, we consider *only* defining features, which inevitably slows down the decision process (Hampton, 1979). This feature approach to SM can, therefore, explain some of the data that are difficult for Collins and Quillian's model.

SPREADING-ACTIVATION MODELS

Collins & Loftus (1975) proposed a revised network model, intended to address the criticisms made of Collins and Quillian's hierarchical model.

> **Box 29.6   Differences between the spreading activation model and Collins and Quillian's hierarchical network model**
>
> - The network is not limited to hierarchical relationships between concepts.
>
> - The *semantic distance* between concepts varies. The greater the distance, the weaker the relationship between the concepts. Thus, highly related concepts are located close together.
>
> - When a particular item is processed, activation spreads out along the pathways from a concept in all directions. An activated item can be more easily processed (retrieved, judged, recognised or evaluated) than an unactivated one.
>
> (See Figure 29.5, page 250)

Several studies have provided data consistent with the model (e.g. Jones & Anderson, 1987). In *lexical-decision experiments*, participants are first shown a *prime*, such as the word 'dog'. Then, a *target* word is shown for a very brief period of time. This may be related to the prime word (e.g. 'dalmatian'), unrelated (e.g. 'banana') or even a nonsense word (e.g. 'grilf'). Participants have to judge whether the target word actually is a word or whether it belongs to a certain category. The speed with which a decision is reached is increased the closer the relationship between the target and prime. In terms of the spreading-activation model, this is because the prime activates material in the semantic network, and the closer the prime is to the target, the more activated and more easily processed it is.

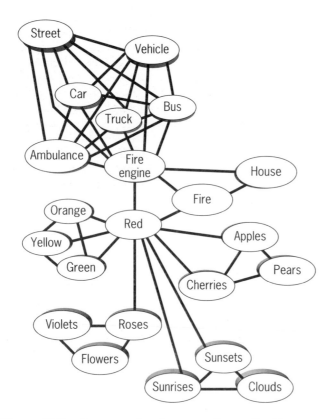

Figure 29.5   An example of a spreading-activation model. The length of each line (or link) represents the degree of association between particular concepts (based on Collins & Loftus, 1975)

However, Johnson-Laird *et al.* (1984) observe that there are many examples where the interpretation offered by the network will tend, in actual discourse, to be overridden by the constraints of real-world knowledge. Consider, for example, the sentence 'The ham sandwich was eaten by the soup'. Whilst this may seem nonsensical, for waiters and waitresses (who often label customers according to their orders) the sentence is quite understandable. This 'failure to escape from the maze of symbols into the world' is called the *symbolic fallacy*: a person has to know the relationship between symbols and what they refer to (see also Chapter 37).

Schemas

Clearly, SM must contain structures much larger than the simple concepts considered by the models so far discussed. This 'larger unit' is the *schema*, a term introduced to memory research by Bartlett (see Chapter 27, page 228). Bartlett was the first to recognise that memory is a *reconstructive* process in which information already stored

affects the remembering of other events. He found that people frequently add or delete details to make new information more consistent with their conception of the world. So, for Bartlett memory is not like a computer, with output matching input, but an 'imaginative reconstruction' of experience.

Schemas provide us with preconceived expectations, operating in a 'top-down' way to help interpret the 'bottom-up' flow of information reaching the senses. Schemas help to make the world more predictable. They can, however, also lead to significant distortions in memory processes, because they have a powerful effect on the way in which memories for events are encoded (Crooks & Stein, 1991). For example, Allport & Postman (1947) showed white participants a picture of two men evidently engaged in an argument.

Figure 29.6   The stimulus material used by Allport & Postman (1947). The two men are engaged in an argument. The better-dressed man is black, and the white man has a cut throat razor in his left hand

After briefly looking at the picture, participants were asked to describe the scene to someone who had not seen it. This person was then required to pass the information on to another person, and so on. As the information was passed, so features of it changed, the most important being that the knife was reported as being in the black man's hand.

Neisser (1981) studied the testimony given by John Dean, a key figure in the Watergate conspiracy. Dean testified to

250

a committee (that was trying to determine whether President Nixon had been involved in a plan to 'bug' the Democratic National Committee headquarters) about an event that had occurred nine months earlier.

Box 29.7   Neisser's (1981) analysis of John Dean's testimony

According to Dean:

'When I arrived at the Oval Office, I found Haldeman and the President. The President asked me to sit down. Both men appeared to be in very good spirits, and my reception was warm and cordial. The President then told me that Bob [Haldeman] had kept him posted on my handling of the Watergate case. The President told me that I had done a good job and he appreciated how difficult a task it had been and the President was pleased that the case had stopped with Liddy'.

A comparison of this statement with transcripts of the tape-recording Nixon *secretly* made of the meeting revealed the following discrepancies:

- Nixon did not ask Dean to sit down.

- Nixon did not say that Haldeman had 'kept him posted'.

- No compliment was paid by Nixon on the job Dean had done.

- Nixon did not say that he 'appreciated how difficult a task it had been'.

- There was no reference made to Liddy and the case by Nixon.

Neisser suggests that Dean's specific recollection might have come from the schema that describes what generally happens when people enter a room (viz., the host greets the guest, and the guest is invited to sit down).

Schemas can also powerfully enhance memory, as shown by Bransford & Johnson (1972), whose participants were asked to read the passage below.

Box 29.8   The passage read by participants in Bransford & Johnson's (1972) experiment

The procedure is actually quite simple. First you arrange items into several different groups. Of course, one pile might be sufficient, depending on how much there is to do. If you have to go somewhere else due to lack of facilities, that is the next step; otherwise you are pretty well set. It is important not to overdo things. That is, it

is better to do a few things at once than too many. In the short run, this may not seem important but complications can easily arise. A mistake can be expensive as well. At first, the whole procedure will seem complicated. Soon, however, it will become just another fact of life. It is difficult to see any end to the necessity of this task in the immediate future, but then one can never tell. After the procedure is completed, one arranges the material into different groups again. They then can be put into their appropriate places. Eventually, they will be used once more and the whole cycle will have to be repeated. However, that is part of life.

Participants found the passage difficult to understand and later recalled only a few of its 18 distinct ideas. This was because they could not relate the material to what they already knew (they lacked an appropriate schema). However, when another group of participants were told in advance that the passage was about *washing clothes*, they found it more understandable and recalled twice as many ideas as the first group.

SCHEMA THEORIES

Schema theory is one of the most influential approaches to understanding the complex pattern of remembering and forgetting (Cohen, 1993). Several schema theories have been advanced (e.g. Rumelhart, 1975; Schank, 1975; Schank & Abelson, 1977), and there is considerable overlap between them.

Box 29.9   Similarities between schema theories

- Schemas are viewed as 'packets of information' consisting of a fixed compulsory value and a variable (or optional) value. Our schema for buying things has fixed slots for the exchange of money and goods, and variable slots for the amount of money and nature of the goods. In some cases, a slot may be left unspecified and can often be filled with a 'default value, or 'best guess' given the available information.

- Schemas are not mutually exclusive but can combine to form systems. A schema for a picnic, for example, might be part of a larger system of schemas including 'meals' and 'outings'.

- Schemas can relate to *abstract* ideologies and concepts (such as 'justice') and *concrete* objects (such as the appearance of a face).

- Schemas represent knowledge and experience of the world rather than definitions and rules about the world.

- Schemas are active recognition devices which enable us to make sense of ambiguous and unfamiliar information in terms of our existing knowledge and understanding.

Schank and Abelson argue that we develop schemas (or *scripts*) which represent the sequence of actions when carrying out commonly experienced social events, such as going to a restaurant and the objects and people likely to be encountered. These scripts enable us to fill in much of the detail which might not be specified in a piece of information. Consider, for example, the sentences 'We had a tandoori chicken at the Taj Mahal last night. The service was slow, and we almost missed the start of the play.' This can only be interpreted by bringing in additional information (Baddeley, 1990). We need schemas to predict what would happen next and to fill in those aspects of the event which are left implicit. Such scripts are essential ways of summarising common cultural assumptions. This helps us understand text and discourse, and enables us to predict future events and behave appropriately in given social situations.

Schank & Abelson (1977) built their scripts into a computer program called *SAM*. The program, whose 'restaurant script' is shown in Table 29.1, can evidently 'answer' questions and 'understand' stories about restaurants.

Table 29.1   A simplified version of Schank and Abelson's schematic representation of activities involved in going to a restaurant

Name	Restaurant
Props	Tables, menu, food, bill, money, tip
Entry conditions	Customer is hungry Customer has money
Roles	Customer, waiter, cook, cashier, owner
Results	Customer has less money Owner has more money Customer is not hungry
Scene 1	Entering Customer enters restaurant Customer looks for table Customer decides where to sit Customer goes to table Customer sits down
Scene 2	Ordering Customer picks up menu Customer looks at menu Customer decides on food Customer signals waiter Waiter comes to table Customer orders food Waiter goes to cook Waiter gives food order to cook Cook prepares food
Scene 3	Eating Waiter gives food to customer Customer eats food
Scene 4	Exiting Waiter prepares bill Waiter goes over to customer Waiter gives bill to customer Customer gives tip to waiter Customer goes to cashier Customer gives money to cashier Customer leaves restaurant

(Based on Bower *et al.*, 1979)

There are certain actions and events that form part of people's knowledge about what is involved in going into a restaurant, and these broadly agree with Schank and Abelson's restaurant script (Bower *et al.*, 1979). Also, when people are asked to recall a passage of text concerning 'restaurant behaviour', they falsely recall aspects which were not explicitly included but which are consistent with a 'restaurant script', *and* change the order of events so as to make them consistent with such a script (exactly as Bartlett would have predicted).

An evaluation of schema theories

According to Cohen (1993), the whole idea of a schema appears to be so vague as to be of little practical use. Also, schema theories tend to emphasise the inaccuracies of memory and overlook the fact that complex events are sometimes remembered very accurately (especially their unexpected and unusual aspects). Finally, theories have little to say about the acquisition of schemas. Without schemas, we are unable to interpret new experiences, and we need new experiences in order to build up schemas (Cohen, 1993).

Schank's (1982) *dynamic-memory theory* attempts to take account of the dynamic aspects of memory and is a more elaborate and flexible version of his original theory. It tries to clarify the relationship between general knowledge schemas and memories for specific episodes, based on a hierarchical arrangement of memory representations. At the bottom of the hierarchy are *memory organisation packets* (MOPs) which store specific details about specific events. At higher levels, the representations become more and more general and schema-like. MOPs are not usually stored for very long, and become 'absorbed' into the 'event schemas' that store those features common to repeated experiences. Details of unusual or atypical events, however, are retained (Cohen, 1993).

According to Alba & Hasher (1983) and Bahrick (1984), whilst there is some evidence for schema theories, schemas themselves are unlikely to be involved in the retrieval of general knowledge, such as remembering one's name, facts and rules. Bahrick's own research concerns memory which closely resembles the original content (*replicative memory*: Bahrick, 1984). Even people who studied a particular language (Spanish) 50 years earlier, and have never used it since, remembered 'large portions of the originally acquired information'. This suggests that at least some types of information can be stored for very long periods of time and recalled in their *original* form.

Conclusions

Evidence supports the view that memory is highly organised. The organisation of information can be achieved by a variety of methods, and several models have been proposed to explain the kind of organisation that occurs in memory, although no one model is completely supported by research.

Summary

■ Chunking is a way of **organising** information by giving it a structure it does not otherwise have. Organisation is the secret of a good memory.

■ Bousfield found that participants free-recalled randomly presented words in clusters (**categorical clustering**), despite not being told of the categories into which they fell. This suggested that they had tried to organise the words.

■ Mandler showed that instructions to organise material will facilitate learning, even when participants are not trying to remember it. Not only did categorical clustering occur, but participants instructed just to sort the cards into categories remembered as many as those instructed to remember them.

■ Tulving distinguishes between **subjective organisation** (SO), and **experimenter organisation** (EO). Bower

et al. showed that when words were presented in the form of conceptual **hierarchies**, they were recalled significantly better than when they are presented randomly.

■ **Imagery** represents a form of organisation and is the basis of many kinds of **mnemonic devices**. The use of imagery can be traced to the ancient Greek poet Simonides, who used the **method of loci**, a modern form of which is the **narrative story method**.

■ Bower found that participants instructed **to link** pairs of unrelated words through visual images performed much better on a recall test than those simply instructed to memorise the words. **Bizarre**, **interacting** and **vivid** images are most effective, possibly because they are more distinctive.

■ According to Paivio, imagery's effectiveness can be explained in terms of a **dual-code model of memory** (with memories being stored as **imagens** or **logogens**). The two systems are connected by **referential links**, which explains why it is easier to form images of **concrete** than **abstract** words.

■ **Semantic-network models** attempt to identify the kind of organisation that occurs in memory. They assume that information is embedded in an organised structural network composed of semantic units and their functional relationships to one another.

■ Collins and Quillian's **teachable language comprehender** is mainly concerned with the **nature of lexical memory**. SM is organised as a **hierarchical** network, with major concepts represented as **nodes**, each having several properties or features associated with it and linked with concepts at a lower level in the hierarchy. These, in turn, are linked with concepts lower down in the hierarchy.

■ Using **sentence verification tasks**, Collins and Quillian confirmed the model's prediction that the more levels that have to be crossed, the longer it takes to verify a sentence's truth or falsity. However, this could be explained in terms of the relationship between **category size** and reaction time, and some members of a category are much more **typical** than others. Response time may also reflect 'semantic relatedness'. Different attributes of a particular concept may not be equally important.

■ Broadbent *et al.* found that participants presented with words in either a hierarchical or matrix form remembered significantly more of them than participants presented with the words in a random order. However, the first two groups did equally well, suggesting that SM may be organised in the form of **matrices**.

253

■ According to Smith *et al.'s* **feature model**, the crucial factor in deciding whether a sentence is true is the number of features the concepts have in common. When the number of common features is **intermediate**, the task becomes more difficult.

■ The network in Collins and Loftus's **spreading-activation model** is not limited to hierarchical relationships between concepts. The **semantic distance** between concepts varies, and when a particular item is processed, activation spreads out along the pathways from a concept in all directions.

■ SM must contain structures considerably larger than the simple concepts proposed by the various semantic network models. **Schemas** represent this larger unit providing preconceived expectations and making the world more predictable. However, they may also distort our memories.

■ **Schema theories** share a common view of schemas as interrelated 'packets of information ' comprising both a fixed compulsory value and a variable or optional value. They can refer to both abstract concepts and concrete objects and are active recognition devices which help make sense of ambiguous or unfamiliar information.

■ Schank and Abelson believe that we develop **scripts** regarding the sequence of actions involved in commonly experienced social events. Scripts help us to fill in missing details by allowing us to predict what would happen next, as well as enabling us to behave appropriately in given social situations.

■ Schema theories tend to emphasise the limitations of memory and overlook the sometimes accurate recall of complex events. Schank's **dynamic-memory theory** identifies the relationship between general knowledge schemas and memories for specific episodes.

30

THEORIES OF FORGETTING

Introduction and overview

Forgetting can occur at the encoding, storage or retrieval stage. A crucial distinction in forgetting is between *availability* and *accessibility*. Availability refers to whether or not the material has been stored in the first place, whereas accessibility refers to being able to retrieve what has been stored. In terms of the multi-store model of memory, since information must be transferred from STM to LTM for permanent storage, availability mainly concerns STM and the transfer of information from it into LTM. Accessibility, by contrast, mainly concerns LTM. Forgetting may be caused by many factors, including physical trauma and drug abuse which cause actual brain damage (Clifford, 1991). This chapter reviews the various *psychological* explanations of forgetting and their related evidence.

Motivated-forgetting theory

According to Freud, forgetting is a motivated process rather than a failure of learning or other processes. *Repression* refers to an unconscious process in which certain memories are made inaccessible. Those memories likely to elicit guilt, embarrassment, shame or anxiety are repressed from consciousness as a form of *defence mechanism* (see Chapter 66).

Box 30.1   A case of repression

Freud (1901) reported the case of a man who continually forgot the line that followed 'with a white sheet' even though he was familiar with the poem from which it came. Freud found that the man associated 'white sheet' with the linen sheet that is placed over a corpse. An overweight friend of the man's had recently died from a heart attack, and the man was worried that because he was a little overweight, and his grandfather had died of heart disease, the same fate would befall him. For Freud, the apparently innocent forgetting of a line from a poem involved the repression of unconscious conflicts over a fear of death.

There is little doubt that traumatic experiences can produce memory disturbances, but there is greater doubt as to whether a Freudian explanation best accounts for them (Anderson, 1995b). Clinical evidence exists which is consistent with Freud's theory, an example being *psychogenic amnesia* (amnesia which does *not* have a physiological cause). One common form of this is loss of memory for events occurring over some particular time frame (*event-specific* amnesia). Psychogenic amnesia is linked to stressful events, and may last for hours or years, although it may disappear as suddenly as it appeared, which is difficult for motivated-forgetting theory to explain.

According to Parkin (1993), repressive mechanisms may play a beneficial role in enabling people experiencing *post-traumatic stress disorder* (see Chapter 70) to adjust. For example, Kaminer & Lavie (1991) found that Holocaust survivors judged to be better adjusted to their experiences were less able to recall their dreams when woken from REM sleep than those judged to be less well adjusted. However, when the term 'repression' is used, it does not necessarily imply a strict Freudian interpretation. Instead, Parkin sees the use of the word as:

'simply acknowledging that memory has the ability to render part of its contents inaccessible as a means of coping with distressing experiences [and that] the mechanism by which memory achieves this ... is an elusive one'.

Box 30.2   Recovered memories and false memory syndrome

One difficulty with accepting *recovered memories* as literal interpretations of past events (such as child sexual abuse) is that they might (supposedly) have happened at a very early age, when experience is not verbalised as it is later on in life (British Psychological Society/BPS, 1995). Child sexual abuse which occurs before the age of four and doesn't continue beyond that age might not be retrievable in a narrative form (describable in words). Very early memories are implicit rather than explicit and are reflected in behaviour outside conscious awareness. This means that we don't need repression to explain the 'forgetting' of childhood experiences, but it also implies that some recovered memories could be either false or inaccurate.

The BPS's survey of 810 chartered psychologists indicated that 90 per cent believed recovered memories to

---

be sometimes or 'essentially' correct, a very small percentage believed that they are always correct, about 66 per cent believed that they are possible, and 14 per cent believed that one of their own clients has experienced false memories.

According to Loftus (1997), false memories can be constructed by combining actual memories with the content of suggestions from others. This may result in *source confusion*, in which the content and the source become dissociated. However:

'... although experimental work on the creation of false memories may raise doubt about the validity of long-buried memories, such as repeated trauma, it in no way disproves them ...' (Loftus, 1997).

Distortion and decay theories

THE GESTALT THEORY

The Gestalt theory of forgetting (also known as *systematic distortion of the memory trace*) is closely related to the Gestalt theory of perception (see Chapter 21). Gestalt theorists claim that memories undergo *qualitative changes* over time rather than being lost completely, and become distorted towards a 'better', more regular, symmetrical form. Several studies have claimed to support this theory, mainly using participants' reproduction by drawings of material seen earlier (e.g. Wulf, 1922; Irwin & Seidenfeld, 1937; James, 1958). Such studies claim that genuine changes in memory occur with the passage of time.

However, several researchers (e.g. Baddeley, 1968) have found that such results can be explained in terms of experimental artefacts and biases (such as a limitation in participants' abilities to accurately draw the figures they had seen). The Gestalt theory of forgetting, then, has proved to be 'both experimentally and theoretically sterile' (Baddeley, 1976).

DECAY THEORY

Decay (or *trace decay*) theory attempts to explain why forgetting increases with time. Clearly, memories must be stored somewhere, the most obvious location being the brain. Presumably, some sort of structural change (the *engram*) occurs when learning takes place. According to decay theory, metabolic processes occur over time which degrade the engram (unless it is maintained by repetition and rehearsal), resulting in the memory contained within it becoming unavailable.

Hebb (1949) argued that whilst learning is taking place, the engram which will eventually be formed is very delicate

and liable to disruption (the *active trace*). With learning, it grows stronger until a permanent engram is formed (the *structural trace*) through neurochemical and neuroanatomical changes. The active trace corresponds roughly to STM, and according to decay theory forgetting from STM is due to the disruption of the active trace. Although Hebb did not apply the idea of decay to LTM, other researchers have argued that it can explain such forgetting if it is assumed that decay occurs through *disuse*. So, if certain knowledge or skills are not used or practised for long time periods, the engram corresponding to them will eventually decay away (Loftus & Loftus, 1980).

However, even if they are not practised, certain motor skills (such as driving a car or playing the piano) are not lost (as shown by Bahrick, 1984: see page 253). Also, even if people haven't used something like algebra for years, it can be remembered *if* they follow a 'refresher' course at college (Bahrick & Hall, 1991). The ability of a delirious person to remember a foreign language not spoken since childhood also testifies against a simple 'decay through disuse' explanation of forgetting.

Peterson & Peterson's (1959) study (see Chapter 27, page 232) is often taken as evidence for the role of decay in STM forgetting. If such decay did occur, then we would expect poorer recall of information with the passage of time, which is exactly what the Petersons reported. However, the difficulty with the Petersons' study in particular, and decay theory in general, is that other possible effects need to be excluded before an account based on decay can be accepted.

The ideal way to study decay's role in forgetting would be to have people receive information and then do *nothing* physical or mental for a period of time. If recall was poorer with the passage of time, it would be reasonable to suggest that decay had occurred. Such an experiment is, of course, impossible. However, Jenkins & Dallenbach (1924) were the first to attempt to *approximate* it.

Box 30.3 Jenkins & Dallenbach's (1924) experiment

Participants learnt a list of ten nonsense syllables. In one condition, they then went to sleep immediately, approximating to the ideal 'do nothing' state. Others continued with their normal activities. After intervals of one, two, four or eight hours, participants were tested for their recall of the syllables.

The period spent asleep did not result in greater forgetting, which led Jenkins and Dallenbach to conclude that:

'forgetting is not so much a matter of decay of old impressions and associations as it is a matter of interference, inhibition or obliteration of the old by the new'.

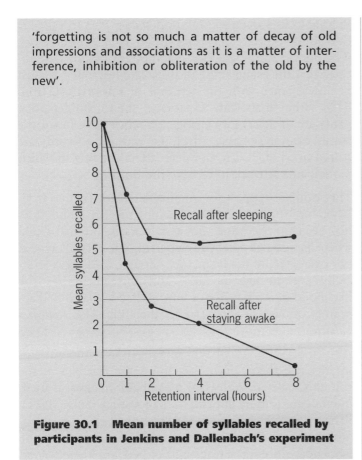

Figure 30.1   Mean number of syllables recalled by participants in Jenkins and Dallenbach's experiment

Although some data indicate that neurological breakdown occurs with age and disease (such as Alzheimer's disease), it is generally accepted that neurological decay is *not* the major cause of forgetting from LTM (Solso, 1995).

Interference theory

According to interference theory, forgetting is influenced more by what we do before or after learning than by the passage of time. In *retroactive interference* (or *retroactive inhibition*), later learning interferes with the recall of earlier learning. Suppose a person originally learned to drive in a manual car, then learned to drive an automatic car. When returning to a manual car, the person might try to drive it as though it was an automatic.

In *proactive interference* (or *proactive inhibition*), earlier learning interferes with the recall of later learning. Suppose a person learned to drive a car in which the indicator lights are turned on using the stalk on the left of the steering wheel, and the windscreen wipers by the stalk on the right. After passing the driving test, the person then buys a car in which this arrangement is reversed. Proactive interference would be shown by the windscreen

wipers being activated just before the person signalled his or her intention to turn left or right!

Interference theory has been extensively studied in the laboratory using *paired-associates lists*, and the usual procedure for studying interference effects is shown in Figure 30.2.

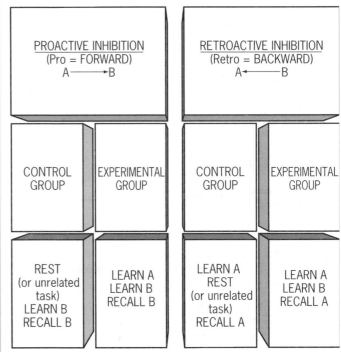

Figure 30.2   Experimental procedures for investigating retroactive and proactive interference

Usually, the first member of each pair in list A is the same as in list B, but the second member of each pair is different in the two lists. In retroactive interference (RI), the learning of the second list interferes with recall of the original list (working *backwards* in time). In proactive interference (PI), the learning of the original list interferes with recall of the later learned second list (working *forwards* in time).

Interference offers an alternative explanation of Peterson & Peterson's (1959) data (see page 232). Having noted that the Petersons administered two *practice trials* before their test, Keppel & Underwood (1962) looked at what happened after these trials in the actual experiment. They found that the first two trials did have an effect on those that followed, in that there was no evidence of forgetting on the first trial, some on the second and yet more on the third. Whilst other researchers (e.g. Baddeley & Scott, 1971) have shown that forgetting *can* occur on the first trial (supporting decay theory), Keppel and Underwood's finding that performance did not decline until the second trial suggests the occurrence of proactive interference in the Petersons' experiment.

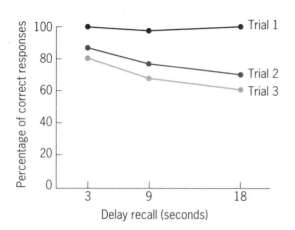

Figure 30.3   Mean percentage of items correctly recalled on trials 1, 2 and 3 for various delay times (Based on Keppel & Underwood, 1962)

Probably the most important cause of proactive interference is interference with *retrieval*. Like Keppel and Underwood, Wickens (1972) found that participants became increasingly poor at retaining information in STM on successive trials. However, when the *category* of information was changed, participants performed as well as on the first list. So, performance with lists of numbers was increasingly poor over trials, but if the task was changed to lists of letters, it improved. This is called *release from proactive inhibition*.

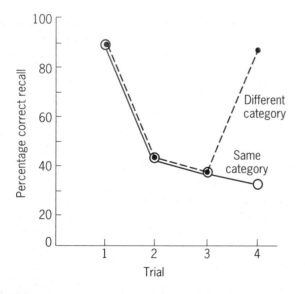

Figure 30.4   The effect on recall of being presented with a list of stimuli from a different category

Release from proactive inhibition occurs when people are told about a change of category *either before or after it occurs* (Gardiner *et al.*, 1972). This is important because it indicates that the major cause of proactive interference must be interference with the retrieval of information from STM rather than with its storage, since telling participants about a category change *after* they have heard the words cannot possibly affect the way those words are stored in STM. It can, however, affect the way in which participants attempt to retrieve the words.

The strongest support for interference theory comes from laboratory studies. However, learning in such studies does not occur in the same way as it does in the real world where learning of potentially interfering material is spaced out over time. In the laboratory, though, learning is artificially compressed in time, and this maximises the likelihood of interference occurring (Baddeley, 1990). Laboratory studies of interference, therefore, lack *ecological validity*.

Also, most laboratory-based investigations supportive of interference theory have used nonsense syllables as the stimulus material, and when meaningful material is used, interference is more difficult to demonstrate (Solso, 1995). When people have to learn the response 'bell' to the stimulus 'woj', the word 'bell' is not actually learned in the laboratory since it is already part of people's *semantic memory* (SM). Rather, what has to be learned is that 'bell' is the response word to 'woj', and this is stored in *episodic memory*, since the learning is taking place in a specific laboratory situation. Experimental studies of interference are largely based on episodic memory and hence interference effects apply only to that type of LTM. Since SM is much more stable and structured, it is also much more resistant to the effects of interference (Solso, 1995).

However, there is some evidence of interference outside the laboratory. For example, Gunter *et al.* (1980) found that if participants viewed successive television news broadcasts, they experienced retroactive interference, whilst Chandler (1989) showed that if students have to study more than one subject in the same time frame, subjects that are as dissimilar as possible should be chosen to minimise the possibility of interference occurring (see Chapter 31, page 268).

Displacement theory

In a *limited capacity* STM system, forgetting might occur through displacement. When the system is 'full', the oldest material in it would be displaced ('pushed out') by incoming new material. This possibility was explored by Waugh & Norman (1965) using the *serial probe task*. Participants were presented with 16 digits at the rate of either one or four per second. One of the digits (the 'probe') was then repeated and participants had to say which digit *followed* the probe.

Presumably, if the probe was one of the digits at the beginning of the list, the probability of recalling the digit that followed would be small, because later digits would have displaced earlier ones from the system. However, if the probe was presented towards the end of the list, the probability of recalling the digit that followed it would be high, since the last digits to be presented would still be available in STM.

When the number of digits following the probe was small, recall was good, but when it was large, recall was poor. This is consistent with the idea that the earlier digits are displaced by later ones. Waugh and Norman also found that recall was generally better with the faster (four-per-second) presentation rate, which is consistent with decay theory. Since less time had elapsed between presentation of the digits and the probe in the four-per-second condition, there would be less opportunity for those digits to have decayed away.

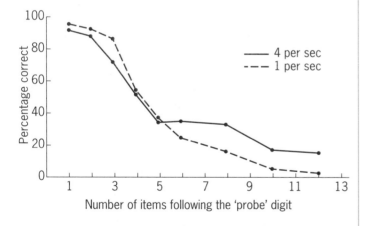

Figure 30.5   Data from Waugh and Norman's serial probe experiment

Waugh and Norman's findings were confirmed by Shallice (1967), although Shallice found that elapsed time was *less* important than the number of subsequent items. Despite such evidence, it is unclear that displacement is a process distinct from either decay or interference or, indeed, some combination of the two.

Retrieval-failure theory

According to retrieval-failure theory, memories cannot be recalled because the correct *retrieval cues* are not being used. The role of retrieval cues is demonstrated by the *tip-of-the-tongue phenomenon*, in which we know that we know something but cannot retrieve it at that particular point in time (Brown & McNeill, 1966).

Brown and McNeill gave participants dictionary definitions of unfamiliar words and asked them to provide the words themselves. Most participants either knew the word or knew that they did not know it. Some, however, were sure they knew the word but could not recall it (it was on the tip of their tongue). About half could give the word's first letter and the number of syllables, and often offered words which sounded like the word or had a similar meaning. This suggests that the required words were in memory, but the absence of a correct retrieval cue prevented them from being recalled.

Box 30.4   An example of a tip-of-the-tongue test

For each of the six examples below, try to identify the word that fits each definition. You may find that you cannot think of the word, yet you know that it is on the verge of coming to you. When a word is on the tip-of-your-tongue, see if you can prompt its retrieval by writing down (1) the number of syllables, (2) the initial letter, (3) words which sound similar, and (4) words of similar meaning.

1 A small boat used in the harbours and rivers of Japan and China, rowed with a scull from the stern, and often having a sail.

2 A navigational instrument used to measure angular distances at sea, especially the altitude of the sun, moon and stars.

3 Favouritism, especially governmental patronage extended to relatives.

4 The common cavity into which the various ducts of the body open in certain fishes, reptiles, birds and mammals.

5 An opaque, greyish, waxy secretion from the intestines of the sperm whale, sometimes found floating on the ocean or lying on the shore, and used in making perfumes.

6 An extending portion of a building, usually semicircular with half a dome; especially the part of a church where the altar is located.

(Based on Brown & McNeill, 1966, and adapted from Carlson, 1987. The answers are given on page 261)

Tulving & Pearlstone (1966) read participants lists of varying numbers of words (12, 24 or 48) containing categories of one, two or four exemplars per list along with the category name. Participants were instructed only to try to remember the exemplars (such as category name = animal, exemplar = dog). Half the participants free-recalled the words and wrote these down on a blank piece of paper. The other half were provided with the category names. Those participants given the category names recalled significantly more words, and the difference was most pronounced on the 48-item list. However, when the category names were provided for those who had written their responses on the blank sheet of paper, their recall improved, indicating that the category names helped to make information that was available for recall accessible.

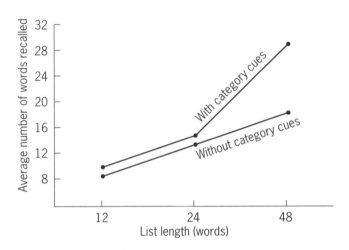

Figure 30.6   Average number of words recalled with and without category cues in Tulving & Pearlstone's (1966) experiment.

Tulving (1968) has also shown that retrieval failure offers a better account of forgetting from LTM than either decay or interference theory.

Box 30.5   Tulving's (1968) experiment

Participants were shown a list of words and then asked to write down as many as they could remember in any order they liked. Later, and without being presented with the list again or seeing the words they had written down previously, participants were asked for a second time to recall as many of the words as possible. Even later, they were asked to recall for a third time the words on the original list.

Table 30.1   Hypothetical results

Trial 1	Trial 2	Trial 3
Table	Table	Table
Driver	Escalator	Driver
Escalator	Apple	Escalator
Apple	Railway	Apple
Railway	Pen	Pen
Pen		Fountain

As Table 30.1 shows, the same words were *not* recalled across the three trials. This finding is difficult for decay theory to explain, because it would not predict the recall of a word on trial 3 if it was not recalled on either trial 1 or 2. The fact that some words were recalled on the second and third trials, but not on the first, is difficult for interference theory to explain because it would have to be assumed that what had been unlearned on trial 1 was learned on trial 2 and/or trial 3 (Clifford, 1991). Retrieval-failure theory, however, can explain these findings by arguing that different retrieval cues were in operation across the three trials. Unfortunately, the precise way in which retrieval cues act is not known (Hampson & Morris, 1996).

According to Tulving & Thomson's (1973) *encoding specificity principle*, recall improves if the same cues are present during recall as during the original learning. Tulving (1974) used the term *cue-dependent forgetting* to refer jointly to *context-dependent* and *state-dependent* forgetting. Forgetting is, therefore, a failure of retrieval cues to match the encoded nature of items in memory (Solso, 1995). Environmental or contextual variables represent *external cues*, whilst psychological or physiological *states* represent *internal cues*.

Abernathy (1940) asked one group of participants to learn and then recall material in the same room, whilst a second group learned material in one room but recalled it in another. Recall was better in the first than second group. Similarly, Godden & Baddeley (1975) had divers learn word lists either on land or 15 feet under water and then tested their recall in either the same or a different context. The results showed a 30 per cent decrement when recall was tested in a different context. They also found that cue-dependent forgetting applies to recall, but not to recognition.

According to Baddeley (1995), large effects of context on memory are only found when the contexts in which encoding and retrieval occur are very different. Although less marked changes can produce some effects, studies (other than Abernathy's) looking at the effects of context on examination performance have *tended* to show few effects. This may be because when we are learning, our surroundings are not a particularly *salient* feature of the situation. However, our internal state is more salient, and can have a powerful effect on recall. Clark *et al.* (1987) have argued that victims' inabilities to recall details of a violent crime may be due at least in part to the fact that recall occurs in a less emotionally aroused state (see Box 31.4), whilst McCormick & Mayer (1991) have suggested that the important link is between mood and the sort of material being remembered. Thus, we are more likely to remember happy events when we are feeling happy rather than sad.

THE PERMANENCE OF MEMORY

In studies conducted in the 1940s and 50s, Penfield electrically stimulated the cerebral cortex of conscious and alert patients about to undergo brain surgery (see Chapter 6). Stimulation of certain cortical areas seemed to produce a 'memory' in these patients. Although these 'released memories' were not perfectly detailed, Penfield (1969) concluded that 'each succeeding state of consciousness leaves its permanent imprint on the brain'. Loftus & Loftus (1980) found that 84 per cent of psychologists they surveyed believed that memories were permanently stored, as did 69 per cent of non-psychologists.

However, the evidence from Penfield's studies is not particularly convincing (Eysenck, 1993). For example, of the 520 patients he studied, only 40 reported the recovery of an apparently long-forgotten memory, and those memories that were recovered were typically neither vivid nor detailed.

Conclusions

This chapter has considered several psychological explanations of forgetting. Some of these are better supported by evidence than others. Of those that have survived experimental investigation, some are better applied to forgetting from STM and others to LTM forgetting.

Answers to the tip-of-the-tongue test presented in Box 30.4

1 sampan
2 sextant
3 nepotism
4 cloaca
5 ambergris
6 apse

Summary

■ In terms of the multi-store model, **availability** mainly concerns STM and the transfer of information from STM into LTM, whilst **accessibility** mainly concerns LTM.

■ According to **motivated-forgetting theory**, memories likely to elicit guilt, embarrassment, shame or anxiety are made inaccessible through the defence mechanism of **repression**.

■ Traumatic experiences can produce memory disturbances (as in **psychogenic amnesia**). However Freud's theory has difficulty explaining why psychogenic amnesia sometimes disappears as suddenly as it appeared. Repression may help people experiencing **post-traumatic stress disorder** to cope, but 'repression' does not necessarily imply a strict **Freudian** interpretation.

■ **Recovered memories** of child sexual abuse cannot be taken literally because they may relate to pre-verbal early experiences. Repression is not needed to explain 'forgotten' childhood experiences. Similarly, there is experimental evidence for **false memory syndrome**.

■ According to the **Gestalt theory of forgetting**, memories become distorted over time in the direction of 'good form'. Apparent empirical support can often be explained in terms of experimental artefacts and biases, and the theory is of little value.

■ **Decay/trace decay theory** tries to explain why forgetting increases over time. Some sort of structural change occurs in the brain when learning first occurs (the **engram**) and, unless this is maintained by rehearsal, the memory contained within it will cease to be available.

■ Hebb distinguished between an **active trace** (corresponding roughly to STM) and the **structural trace**. Forgetting is caused by disruption of the engram.

■ Decay can also explain LTM forgetting, on the assumption that decay occurs through **disuse**. However, certain motor – and other – skills are not lost, even if they are not practised for long periods of time. Neurological decay is **not** the major cause of LTM forgetting.

■ Peterson and Peterson's findings that poorer recall of information occurs with the passage of time appears to support the view that decay occurs in STM. Jenkins and Dallenbach concluded that interference rather than decay is the major cause of LTM forgetting.

■ According to **interference theory**, forgetting is influenced more by what we do before or after learning than by the passage of time. In **retroactive interference/inhibition** (RI), later learning prevents the recall of earlier learning (working **backwards**). In **proactive interference/inhibition** (PI), earlier learning prevents recall of later learning (working **forwards**).

■ The most important cause of PI may be interference with **retrieval**, as shown by Wickens' participants who became increasingly poor at retaining information in STM on successive trials. But when the **category** of information was changed, participants displayed **release from PI**. This also occurs when people are told about a change of category **either before or after it occurs**, indicating that interference with retrieval rather than storage is the crucial factor.

■ Laboratory studies of interference lack **ecological validity**. They tend to use nonsense syllables rather than meaningful material, which is more resistant to interference. Learning to pair words (already part of SM) with nonsense syllables is stored in **episodic memory** (EM), and so interference effects apply mainly to EM. SM is more resistant to interference.

■ According to **displacement theory**, in a **limited-capacity** STM system the oldest material is pushed out by incoming new material. Using the **serial-probe task**, Waugh and Norman produced findings consistent with both displacement and decay theories. However, it is unclear whether displacement is distinct from either decay or interference, and may be a combination of the two.

■ According to **retrieval-failure theory**, memories cannot be recalled because the correct **retrieval cues** are not being used (as in the **tip-of-the-tongue phenomenon**).

■ Tulving's finding that participants free-recalled **different** words on three separate recall trials is better explained by retrieval-failure theory than either decay or interference theories.

■ According to the **encoding specificity principle**, recall improves if the same cues are present during recall as during the original learning. **Cue-dependent forgetting** refers jointly to **context-** and **state-dependent** forgetting (relating to environmental/contextual variables and psychological/physiological **states** respectively).

■ Large context effects are only found when the encoding and retrieval contexts are very different. During learning, our internal state may be much more **salient**, which might also explain why victims often fail to recall details of a violent crime.

■ Penfield's discovery of 'released memories' when electrically stimulating the cortex led him to conclude that memories are permanently stored. However, his evidence is far from convincing and there is no compelling evidence to support the permanent-memory hypothesis.

31

SOME PRACTICAL APPLICATIONS OF RESEARCH INTO MEMORY

Introduction and overview

As interesting as laboratory studies of memory are, they tend to 'minimise many of the features that may be central to our memory in everyday life' (Hampson & Morris, 1996). 'Everyday' things that have been researched include the 'mental maps' of the world we develop through our experiences (e.g. Smith *et al.*, 1994), our memory for medical information (e.g. Ley, 1988), 'prospective memory' (memory for things we *have* to do rather than things we have done: e.g. Morris, 1992), memories across our lifetimes (e.g. Schuman & Rieger, 1992) and our memory for familiar objects such as coins and postage stamps (e.g. Richardson, 1993).

Other areas of interest include eyewitness testimony (e.g. Loftus, 1974), strategies for improving memory (e.g. Higbee, 1996) and memory expertise (e.g. Valentine & Wilding, 1994). This chapter examines research findings concerning these three areas.

Eyewitness testimony

In 1973, the Devlin Committee was established to look at legal cases in England and Wales that had involved an identification parade. Of those people prosecuted after being picked out from an identification parade, 82 per cent were convicted. Of the 347 cases in which prosecution occurred when eyewitness testimony was the *only* evidence against the defendant, 74 per cent were convicted (Devlin, 1976). Although eyewitness testimony is regarded as important evidence in legal cases, the reconstructive nature of memory has led some researchers to question its usefulness (e.g. Fruzzetti *et al.*, 1992; Wells, 1993). Even law-abiding psychologists have been the victims of misidentification.

Box 31.1 The dangers of being a psychologist interested in eyewitness testimony

A psychologist in Australia who had appeared in a TV discussion on eyewitness testimony was arrested some time later, picked out in an identity parade by a very distraught woman and told he was being charged with rape. It became clear that the rape had been committed at the time he was taking part in the TV discussion. When the psychologist told the police that he had many witnesses including an Assistant Commissioner of Police, the policeman taking the statement replied: 'Yes, and I suppose you've also got Jesus Christ and the Queen of England too'. It turned out that the woman had been watching the TV programme when the rape occurred and had correctly recognised the face, but not the circumstances.

As noted in Chapter 30, memory may involve fiction as well as fact, due to our tendency to 'fill in the gaps' in our knowledge, or to modify memories so as to match existing schemas. Loftus, the leading researcher in the area of eyewitness testimony, has posed questions like 'Is eyewitness testimony influenced by people's tendency to reconstruct their memories of events to fit their schemas?', 'Can subtle differences in the wording of a question cause witnesses to remember an event differently?' and 'Can witnesses be misled into remembering things that did not actually occur?' Based on numerous studies, Loftus has argued that the evidence given by witnesses in court cases is very unreliable.

Figure 31.1 Eyewitness testimony may not be useful as we would like

THE IMPORTANCE OF EYEWITNESS TESTIMONY, EVEN WITH A DISCREDITED WITNESS

Using a fictitious case, Loftus (1974) asked students to judge the guilt or innocence of a man accused of robbing a grocer's and murdering the owner and his five-year-old granddaughter. On the evidence presented, only nine of the 50 students considered the man to be guilty. Other students were presented with the same case, but were also told that an assistant in the store had testified that the accused was the man who had committed the crimes. This resulted in 36 of the 50 students judging him to be guilty, suggesting that eyewitness testimony does influence juror decisions.

A third group of students was presented with the original evidence and the assistant's eyewitness testimony. However, this group was told that the eyewitness had been *discredited* by the defence lawyer, who had shown that the shortsighted eyewitness was not wearing his glasses when the crime occurred, and could not possibly have seen the face of the accused from his position in the store. Loftus reasoned that if the students were totally fair in their decisions, about the same number would consider the accused to be guilty as occurred in the first group. In fact, 34 of the 50 students judged him to be guilty, suggesting that a mistaken eyewitness is 'better' than no eyewitness at all.

FACTORS INFLUENCING EYEWITNESS TESTIMONY

Wells (1993) has reviewed research indicating that several factors concerning suspects are particularly important in influencing the accuracy of eyewitness testimony.

Box 31.2 Two important factors influencing the accuracy of eyewitnesses

Race: Errors are more likely to occur when the suspect's race differs from that of the witness (Brigham & Malpass, 1985). Luce (1974), for example, found that African American, white American and Chinese American participants recognised members of their own race extremely well. However, participants of *all* races were significantly poorer at recognising faces of people of other races. This is reflected in the comment that 'They all look the same to me' when referring to members of different races (the *illusion of outgroup homogeneity*: see Box 53.6).

Clothing: According to Sanders (1984), witnesses pay more attention to a suspect's clothing than to more stable characteristics such as height and facial features. In Sanders' experiment, participants saw a video

---

of a crime in which the criminal wore glasses and a T-shirt. Afterwards, they were asked to select the criminal in an identification parade and were more likely to select a person wearing glasses and a T-shirt. Evidently, criminals are aware of this, since they change their appearance prior to an identity parade (Brigham & Malpass, 1985).

THE EFFECTS OF 'LEADING QUESTIONS' ON EYEWITNESS TESTIMONY

According to Loftus, it is the form of questions that witnesses are asked which mainly influences how they 'remember' what they 'witnessed'. 'Leading questions' are interesting because they can introduce new information which may alter a witness's memory of an event. By either their *form* or *content*, such questions can suggest to a witness the answer that *should* be given. Lawyers are skilled at deliberately asking such questions, and the police may also use such questioning when interrogating suspects and witnesses to a crime.

Loftus & Palmer (1974) tested the effect of changing a single word in certain critical questions on the judgement of speed. Participants were shown a 30-second videotape of two cars colliding, and were then asked several questions about the collision. One group was asked 'About how fast were the cars going when they *hit?*'. For others, the word 'hit' was replaced by *smashed, collided, bumped* or *contacted*. These words have very different connotations regarding the speed and force of impact, and this was reflected in the judgements given. Those who heard the word 'hit' produced an average speed estimate of 34.0 mph. For 'smashed', 'collided', 'bumped' and 'contacted', the average estimates were 40.8 mph, 39.3 mph, 38.1 mph, and 31.8 mph respectively.

Figure 31.2   Assessments of speed of crashing vehicles can be influenced by the verb used to describe the impact. While (a) represents 'two cars hitting', (b) represents 'two cars smashing'. Which word is used in a question about speed can influence people's estimates of how fast the cars were travelling at the time of impact

Loftus and Palmer wanted to know if memory itself undergoes change as a result of misleading questions or whether the existing memorial representation of the accident is merely being supplemented by misleading questions. *Memory as reconstruction* implies that memory itself is transformed at the time of retrieval, that is, what was originally encoded changes when it is recalled.

This was tested in a follow-up experiment in which those participants who had heard the words 'smashed' and 'hit' returned to the laboratory one week later. Without seeing the film again, the participants were asked questions, one of which was whether they remembered seeing *any broken glass* (even though there was none in the film). If 'smashed' really had influenced participants' memories of the accident as being more serious than it was, then they might also 'remember' details they did not actually see, but which are consistent with an accident occurring at high speed (such as broken glass).

Of the 50 participants asked about the 'smashing' cars, 16 (32 per cent) reported that they had seen broken glass. Only seven (14 per cent) of the 50 asked about the 'hitting' cars reported seeing broken glass. This suggests that the answer to the question about the glass was determined by the earlier question about speed, which had changed what was originally encoded when seeing the film.

Box 31.3   The effects on memory of 'after-the-fact' information (Loftus, 1975)

Participants witnessed a short videotape of a car travelling through the countryside. Half were asked 'How fast was the white sports car going while travelling along the country road?' The other half were asked 'How fast was the car going when it passed the barn while travelling along the country road?' The second question, of course, *presupposes* that the car actually passed a barn. In fact, it didn't. A week later, participants were again questioned about what they had seen. Of those who had previously answered the question presupposing there was a barn on the videotape, 17.3 per cent answered 'yes' to the question 'Did you see a barn?'. Only 2.7 per cent of the other participants claimed to have seen one.

Loftus argues that leading questions not only produce biased answers, but actually distort memory. Loftus & Zanni (1975) showed participants a short film depicting a car accident, after which each participant answered questions about what they had witnessed. Some were asked whether they had seen *a* broken headlight, whilst others were asked whether they had seen *the* broken headlight. The results showed that those asked about *the* headlight were far more likely to report having seen one than those asked about *a* headlight.

The same effect has been obtained in non-laboratory settings. For example, Loftus (1979) staged a fake crime at a busy train station. Two of Loftus's female students left a large bag unattended on a bench, and while they were gone, a male student reached inside the bag, pretended to pull out an object and place it under his coat before walking away. When the women returned, one cried out: 'Oh my God, my tape recorder is missing!'. They then began to talk to potential eyewitnesses, most of whom agreed to give them their phone number in case their testimony was needed.

A week later, a student posing as an 'insurance agent' phoned the witnesses and asked them to recall details about the incident. The questioning ended with the witness being asked 'Did you see the tape recorder?'. Although there was no tape recorder, more than half of the eyewitnesses 'remembered' seeing it, and most were able to give 'details' about it such as its colour, shape and even the height of the aerial. Most also claimed that they would be able to recognise the thief again.

Using a staged event with five- and seven-year-old children, Memon & Vartoukian (1996) found that recall improved on repeated questioning using open questions. However, accuracy tended to deteriorate upon repetition of closed questions (requiring a 'yes' or 'no' answer). The use of repeated, closed questions may lead witnesses to conclude, incorrectly, that their initial response was incorrect, which may have an adverse effect on accuracy.

Loftus believes that her findings are disturbing, particularly when viewed in the light of what often happens to eyewitnesses questioned by the police, who may introduce incorrect information by asking leading questions. The answer to the question 'are eyewitnesses reliable?' is, therefore, 'sometimes' at best, and 'no' at worst (Loftus, 1979).

An evaluation of Loftus's research

According to Tversky and Tuchin (1989):

> 'there is now substantial support for the view that misleading information affects memory for the original information'.

However, Bekerian & Bowers (1983) have argued that if witnesses are asked questions that follow the order of events in strict sequence, rather than being asked in Loftus's relatively unstructured way, they are *not* influenced by the bias introduced by subsequent questions. For Baddeley (1995), the 'Loftus effect' is *not* due to the destruction of the memory trace. Rather, it is due to interfering with its *retrieval*.

McCloskey & Zaragoza (1985) have challenged the claim that eyewitnesses are mainly unreliable. Loftus herself has acknowledged that when misleading information is 'blatantly incorrect', it has no effects on a witness's memory. For example, Loftus (1979) showed participants colour slides of a man stealing a red purse from a woman's bag. Ninety-eight per cent of those who saw the slides correctly identified the purse's colour, and when they read a description of the event which referred to a 'brown purse', all but two continued to remember it as red.

This suggests that our memory for obviously important information accurately perceived at the time is not easily distorted, a finding confirmed in studies where people have witnessed a real (and violent) crime (Yuille & Cutshall, 1986). People are more likely to be misled if the false information they are given concerns *insignificant* details peripheral to the main event, if the false information is given after a delay (when the memory of the event has had time to fade), and if they have no reason to distrust it (Cohen, 1993).

COGNITIVE INTERVIEWS

To elicit accurate and detailed information from eyewitnesses, an increasing number of police forces are using the *cognitive interview technique* (Geiselman, 1988). This draws on Tulving's research concerning the relationship between encoding and retrieval (see Chapter 30, page 260).

Box 31.4   The four procedures of the cognitive interview technique

1 **Reinstating the context:** This involves the interviewer and interviewee attempting to recreate the context (the surrounding environment, such as the temperature and the witness's own state) in which the incident occurred before any attempt is made to recall what happened.

2 **Reporting the event:** Once the context has been recreated, the witness is required to report any information he or she can remember, even if it is not considered important.

3 **Recalling the event in a different order:** The third step is for the witness to try to recall the events in, say, the reverse order or by starting from whatever was most memorable about the event.

4 **Changing perspectives:** Finally, the witness is asked to try to recall the event from, say, the perspective of a prominent figure in the event (such as the cashier in the case of a bank robbery), and to think about what the cashier must have seen.

(Adapted from Hampson & Morris, 1996)

Geiselman has shown that the cognitive interview technique produces significantly better recall than the usual interview techniques used by the police, a finding also obtained by other researchers (e.g. Roy, 1991).

Despite continued debate about eyewitness testimony, there is little doubt that Loftus and others have shown that our knowledge of the processes involved in memory can be usefully applied in the 'real world'. The Devlin Committee's report (see page 263), for example, recommended that the trial judge be required to instruct the jury that it is not safe to convict on a single eyewitness testimony alone, unless (a) the circumstances are exceptional (such as the witness being a close friend or relative), or (b) when there is substantial corroborative evidence. The Devlin Committee's safeguards are much stronger than those of the US supreme court, but similar to those of American legal experts.

Improving memory

MNEMONICS

Techniques for aiding recall, which most people consider unusual and artificial, are called *mnemonics*. According to Belezza (1981), mnemonics have two fundamental characteristics. First, they are not inherently connected to the material that has to be learned but impose meaning and structure on material that is otherwise not very meaningful and structured. Second, they typically involve adding something to the material to create meaningful associations between what is to be learned and what is already stored in LTM.

Rather than simplifying information, mnemonic devices make it more elaborate, resulting in *more*, rather than less, information being stored in memory. However, the additional information makes the material easier to recall, organising it into a cohesive whole so that retrieval of part of the information ensures retrieval of the rest.

Snowman *et al.* (1980) taught college students on a 'study skills' course to use the *method of loci* (see page 246) to remember the central concepts from a 2200-word passage of prose. Compared with students taught more traditional study skills, the group that used the loci method recalled significantly more ideas from the passage. The method of loci has also been used successfully by special populations such as the blind, brain damaged and elderly (Yesavage & Rose, 1984).

In the seventeenth century, Herdson used a device which involves imagining numbers as objects (Hunter, 1957). For example, 1 might be imagined as a pencil, 2 as a swan and so on. The items to be remembered are then imagined interacting with their relevant number. For example, if the first item to be remembered were 'clock', an image of a clock with a pencil for the minute hand might be formed.

Higbee (1996) has distinguished between visual mnemonic *systems* (using imagery) and verbal mnemonic *techniques*, which make associations with words. Verbal mnemonics include *rhymes* ('In fourteen hundred and ninety-two, Columbus sailed the ocean blue'), *acrostics* (a verse in which the first letters correspond with the material that needs to be remembered, as in 'Richard Of York Gave Battle In Vain' for the colours of the rainbow), *acronyms* (such as HOMES for the five great lakes: Huron, Ontario, Michigan, Erie and Superior) and *association* ('my PAL the princiPAL', to distinguish its spelling from 'principLE as a ruLE').

Other mnemonic *methods* (neither 'systems' nor 'techniques') consist of both a verbal and a visual process, such as the *key-* or *peg-word system* introduced to England in the late nineteenth century by Sambrook (Paivio, 1979). In this, a rhyme such as 'one is a bun, two is a shoe, three is a tree' and so on is used to associate an object (the key or peg word) with each number in the rhyme. The items to be remembered are then individually paired with a key word by means of a mental image. For example, if the first word to be remembered is 'clock', an image of a bun with a clock face might be formed. For each of the items, the rhyme is recited and the mental image previously formed is 'triggered', resulting in the item's recall.

Figure 31.3   An example of the link-word method being used to remember the word skooleekee, the Greek for 'worm'

The link-word method is highly effective for foreign language learning (Young, 1971), and has also been successfully used by medical students. Bower (1973) gives an example of a method by which the twelve cranial nerves can be stored:

'At the oil factory (*olfactory nerve*), the optician (*optic*) looked for the occupant (*oculomotor*) of the truck (*trochlear*). He was searching because three gems (*trigeminal*) had been abducted (*abducens*) by a man who was hiding his face (*facial*) and ears (*auditory*). A glossy photograph (*glossopharyngeal*) had been taken of him, but it was too vague (*vagus*) to use. He also appeared to be spineless (*spinal accessory*) and hypocritical (*hypoglossal*)'.

Box 31.5   The link-word method

A variation on the key- or peg-word method is the *link-word method*. First systematically studied by Atkinson (1975), it has been used extensively in the teaching of foreign languages (e.g. Gruneberg, 1992). It involves initially constructing a concrete link word or words to represent the foreign word to be learned. For example, the Greek word for 'worm' is 'skooleekee'. This could be represented by two words which sound similar to 'skooleekee', namely 'school' and 'leaky'. Next, a verbal image is formed connecting the link word or words with its English meaning. For example, the learner could picture his or her school leaky and worms falling through the roof. Once the image has been formed, which involves the learner thinking very hard about it for at least ten seconds, the meaning of the Greek word can be obtained by retrieving the link words 'school' and 'leaky' and then the stored image that links these words to 'worm'.

OTHER APPROACHES TO MEMORY IMPROVEMENT

Several studies have shown that it is easier to recall an event or experience if we are in the same location or *context* in which the information was first encoded (Estes, 1972: see Chapter 30). This suggests that if we learn material in a particular place, the best way of trying to recall it would be to go to the same place (revising in the examination hall in roughly the position you would expect to be sitting in the examination, perhaps?). Consistent with Abernathy's (1940) results (see page 260), students appear to perform better if tested in the room in which they were taught (Wingfield, 1979), and it may even be helpful to *imagine* that we are in that place when we try to recall information (Smith, 1979).

As seen in Chapter 30, our *internal state* (emotions or physiological condition) can act as a context which influences recall. For example, some studies have shown that when people encode material under the influence of drugs like alcohol and marijuana, recall is better when the intoxicated state is re-created compared with recall in a non-intoxicated state. Similarly, some studies have shown that people remember things better when they are in the same mood or emotional state as when the information was encoded (e.g. Eich & Metcalf, 1989), although others have found little evidence of this (e.g. Bower & Mayer, 1985).

STUDY SKILLS

Many textbooks (including this one) offer an introduction and overview to each chapter and a summary of the material. Reder & Anderson (1980) found that of two groups of students who spent the same amount of time studying, those who read only the summary remembered more than those who read the whole text. This was true when questions were taken directly from the text or required the combination of material and the drawing of inferences! Moreover, the difference was maintained even when the main points to be remembered were underlined for the students reading the whole text. Clearly, we would not wish to advocate reading only the summaries of each chapter in this book, but Reder and Anderson's findings suggest that summaries can be useful as revision aids.

Study guides designed to help the reader retain as much information as possible from a book include Thomas & Robinson's (1972) *PQ4R method*. In this, the reader begins by **p**reviewing the material to familiarise him/herself with the range of topics a chapter covers. Next, the reader prepares **q**uestions that focus on key concepts and issues. With these questions in mind, the chapter is then **r**ead, with time being taken to **r**eflect on the meaning of the information and its relation to what is already known. Once the chapter has been read, the reader **r**ecites what has been read, using the questions as reminders (with those parts that are difficult being re-read). Finally, the entire material is **r**eviewed in the reader's mind, again using questions to structure this task.

Box 31.6   Practical strategies for maximising learning

- **Reduce the material to a manageable amount:** It is unlikely that every single point in a chapter is important. Therefore, try to reduce the material to its salient points.

- **Impose meaning on the material:** *Elaborative rehearsal* is much more effective than maintenance rehearsal in producing retention (see Chapter 28). An example would be making something you have read about relevant to your own experiences.

- **Learn the whole:** Recall tends to be better if material is reviewed as a whole rather than being broken into smaller parts. Only when material is particularly long and complicated is breaking it up effective.

- **Use periodic retrieval:** Instead of passively reading and re-reading material, engage in periodic retrieval to determine if the material has been effectively encoded. If it has not, review the material again.

- **Engage in overlearning:** Ebbinghaus (see Chapter 27, page 227) found that he could improve his retention of material by repeatedly reviewing it after he had reached 100 per cent accuracy. Once something has been mastered, it should be reviewed at least once or twice.

- **Use study breaks and rewards:** We can only function so long at maximum efficiency before our concentration begins to wane. Taking a break every so often, and doing something rewarding in between, allows us to return to work refreshed.

- **Space study sessions:** Two three-hour or three two-hour study sessions usually result in better retention than a single six-hour session.

- **Avoid interference:** Competing material produces interference effects. If you have to work on two or more subjects in the same time frame, try to make them as dissimilar as possible to reduce proactive and retroactive interference (see Chapter 30, pages 257–258). Planning study sessions to avoid this possibility is obviously helpful.

- **Use time effectively:** Try to develop a time management schedule (incorporating spaced study sessions) in which certain times are devoted to study and certain others to leisure. Once the schedule has been constructed, stick to it!

(Based on Crooks & Stein, 1991)

Understanding memory expertise

People with 'supernormal' memories have long been of interest to both the general public and professional psychologists. Wilding & Valentine (1994) have made a special study of memory expertise, drawing on (amongst other sources) the World Memory Championships (or 'Memoriad'), first staged in 1991. The feats of some of the competitors are truly astonishing. For example, Hideaki Tomoyori recited 40,000 digits of pi in 17 hours and 21 minutes (including 255 minutes for breaks!), whilst the 1993 winner could recall the correct order of 416 playing cards (or eight complete packs).

Valentine & Wilding (1994) have shown that outstanding performers can be divided into *strategists*, who use particular methods to store information (such as the mnemonic techniques described above) and *naturals*, who do not (and appear to have a yet-to-be-understood 'natural ability'). The former tend to perform better on 'strategic' tasks, such as face recognition and word recall, whilst the latter tend to perform better on 'non-strategic' tasks, such as recognising snow crystals and the temporal order of pictures.

Whilst Valentine and Wilding have also found that some people appear to have a superior memory across a wide range of tasks, other research indicates that in some 'strategists' performance is confined to tasks for which their methods are best suited (Biederman *et al.*, 1992). Valentine and Wilding believe that the principles employed by strategic memorisers are those on which normal memory processes are based, namely *semanticisation* (making the meaningless meaningful), *imagery* and *association*. Strategists, however, use these methods in a conscious and intentional way.

Whilst the study of naturally good memory is very recent, Valentine and Wilding believe that progress can be made by looking at the development of natural memory and the possibility of a critical period for its development, the relationship between memory and cognitive abilities such as intelligence, and the neurophysiological and biochemical bases of natural memory.

Conclusions

This chapter has looked at some of the ways in which our knowledge of human memory has been applied practically, and has identified important insights into 'everyday' memory. Although such research has been criticised for using methodologies which fall short of those employed in laboratory studies of memory (e.g. Banaji & Crowder, 1989), a 'balance sheet' on the advantages and disadvantages of research into the practical applications of memory research seems to show it to be very much in the black (Eysenck & Keane, 1995).

Summary

■ Three aspects of everyday memory which have been researched are eyewitness testimony, strategies for improving memory and memory expertise.

■ The Devlin Committee found that even when identification parades were the **only** evidence against the defendant, conviction rates were very high. This is worrying given memory's reconstructive nature and known miscarriages of justice resulting from eyewitness testimony.

■ According to Loftus, the evidence given by witnesses in court cases can be highly unreliable. A **discredited** eyewitness may influence jurors to almost the same extent as a non-discredited witness.

■ The accuracy of eyewitness testimony is influenced by the suspect's **race** (reflecting the **illusion of outgroup homogeneity**) and **clothing** (which is more influential than height or facial features).

■ Loftus believes that **leading questions** are especially important because they can introduce new information which can alter memory of the event. **Memory as reconstruction** implies that memory, at the time of retrieval, undergoes change as a result of misleading questions. 'After-the-fact' information can also change memory for an event.

■ The 'Loftus effect' may be due to interference with the retrieval of the memory trace, not to its destruction. If witnesses are asked questions that follow the sequence of events, rather than in Loftus's unstructured way, they are **not** influenced by the bias introduced by subsequent questions.

■ Loftus herself has demonstrated that memory for obviously **significant** details which are accurately perceived at the time is not easily distorted. People are more likely to be misled if the false information concerns insignificant details, is delayed, and if they have no reason to believe they are being misinformed.

■ Increasingly, police forces are using Geiselman's **cognitive interview technique**, which involves **reinstating the context, reporting the event, recalling the event in a different order** and **changing perspectives**. This technique produces significantly better recall than traditional police interviews.

■ **Mnemonics** are not inherently connected to the material that has to be learned, but impose meaning and structure on relatively meaningless or unstructured material. They also involve adding something to the material by way of meaningful associations with what is already stored in LTM.

■ Visual mnemonic **systems** use imagery, whilst verbal mnemonic **techniques** (such as **rhymes**, **acrostics**, **acronyms** and **association**) use word associations. Other methods combine verbal and visual components, such as the **key-** or **peg-word system** and the related **link-word method** (widely used in foreign language teaching and by medical students).

■ It is easier to recall something in the same **context** in which it was originally encoded. **Internal state**, such as being under the influence of drugs, can act as a context influencing recall, but the evidence is inconclusive, as it is in relation to mood or emotional state.

■ Many textbooks include an introduction and overview to each chapter, plus a summary of the chapter content, as aids to learning. Reder and Anderson found that reading just the chapter summaries can be more useful than reading the whole text.

■ A popular form of study guide is the **PQ4R method**. Other practical strategies for maximising learning include: reducing the material to a manageable amount, imposing meaning on the material (elaborative rehearsal); learning the whole, periodic retrieval, overlearning, using study breaks and rewards, spacing study sessions, avoiding interference, and using time effectively.

■ Valentine and Wilding have studied the feats of people with supernormal memories. They divide outstanding performers into **strategists** and **naturals**. The former use **semanticisation**, **imagery** and **association**, the basic principles of normal memory processes. Less is known about the strategies used by naturals.

32

LABORATORY STUDIES OF CONDITIONING AND OTHER FORMS OF LEARNING

Introduction and overview

As was seen in Chapter 1, the *behaviourist* approach has been a major influence in psychology. In view of its emphasis on learning, it is not surprising that learning should itself be one of psychology's most researched and discussed topics. There are several different theories of what learning involves. Watson (1913), whose behaviourist approach was discussed in Chapter 1, based his explanation of human learning on *classical conditioning* (see pages 272–274). Another theory was proposed by Thorndike, and extended by Skinner, for whom *operant conditioning* is the crucial form of all human and non-human learning.

This chapter considers some of the important similarities and differences between these two forms of conditioning, together with their limitations. It also considers how conditioning has been interpreted in *cognitive* terms, as well as major alternatives to it, in particular Tolman's *cognitive behaviourism* and *social learning theory*.

How do psychologists define learning?

Learning is a *hypothetical construct* (it cannot be directly observed but only *inferred* from observable behaviour), and it normally implies a fairly *permanent* change in a person's behavioural performance. Because temporary fluctuations in behaviour can occur as a result of fatigue, drugs, temperature changes, and so on, this is another reason for taking *permanence* as a minimum requirement for saying that learning has occurred. However, permanent behaviour changes can also result from things that have nothing to do with learning, as when brain damage and changes associated with puberty and other maturational processes alter behaviour. So, if behaviour change is to be counted as learning, the change must be linked to some kind of *past experience*. A fairly representative definition of learning is:

'... the process by which relatively permanent changes occur in behavioural potential as a result of experience' (Anderson, 1995a).

This definition implies a fundamental distinction between *learning* (behavioural potential) and *performance* (actual behaviour) (see below).

Box 32.1   Learning and other abilities

According to Howe (1980), learning is:

'... a biological device that functions to protect the human individual and to extend his capacities'.

In this context, learning is neither independent of, nor entirely separate from, several other abilities, including memory and perception. Indeed, learning and memory may be regarded as two sides of the same coin (see Chapter 27).

Also, most instances of learning take the form of *adaptive changes* whereby we increase our effectiveness in dealing with the environment, which has undoubted survival value (Howe, 1980). Similarly, Anderson (1995a) describes learning as:

'... the mechanism by which organisms can adapt to a changing and nonpredictable environment'.

SOME BASIC QUESTIONS ABOUT LEARNING

Whilst psychologists generally agree that learning is relatively permanent and due to past experience, there is much less agreement about exactly *what* changes when learning occurs, and what *kinds* of past experience are involved. Psychologists differ as to how much they focus on the *overt, behavioural changes* as opposed to the *covert, cognitive changes*. Whilst Watson and Skinner emphasise the former to the exclusion of the latter, cognitive psychologists are more interested in the latter as they are reflected in the former.

Behaviourist approaches: learning theory (classical and operant conditioning)

The major figures in the behaviourist (learning theory) tradition are shown in Figure 32.1 (page 272). Skinner appears at the top because of his distinction between *respondents* (or respondent behaviour), which are triggered automatically by particular environmental stimuli, and *operants* (or operant behaviour) which are essentially voluntary.

Related to Skinner's distinction is that between *classical* (Pavlovian) *conditioning* and *operant* (instrumental or Skinnerian) *conditioning*. Although both represent the behaviourist approach to learning, there are important differences between them, hence Skinner's distinction (see Box 32.6). Neither Hull nor Tolman fits easily into either type of conditioning, which is why they are placed between the others (Hull's drive reduction theory was discussed in Chapter 17).

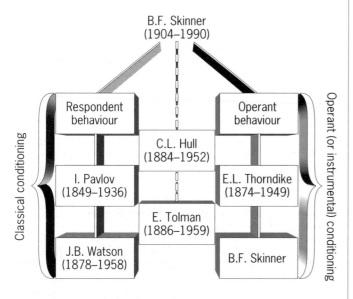

Figure 32.1   Major figures in the behaviourist (learning theory) tradition

CLASSICAL CONDITIONING

Pavlov was a physiologist interested in the process of digestion in dogs. He developed a surgical technique for collecting a dog's salivary secretions which incorporated a tube attached to the outside of its cheek so the drops of saliva could be easily measured.

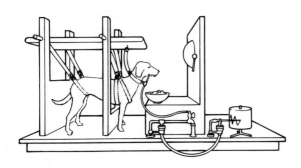

Figure 32.2   The apparatus used by Pavlov in his experiments on conditioned reflexes

Pavlov (1927) noticed that the dogs would often start salivating *before* any food was given to them, such as when they looked at the food, saw the feeding bucket or even heard the footsteps of the laboratory assistant about to feed them. These observations led to the study of what is now called *classical* (or Pavlovian) *conditioning*, whereby a stimulus (such as a bell) which would not normally produce a particular response (such as salivation) will eventually do so by being paired repeatedly with another stimulus (such as food) which *does* normally produce the response.

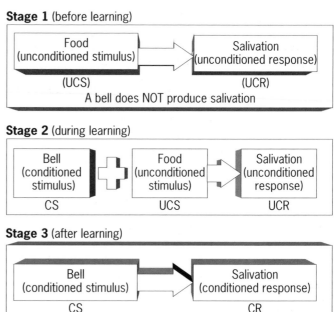

Figure 32.3   The basic procedure involved in classical conditioning

Before conditioning, the taste of food will naturally, and automatically, make the dog salivate, but the sound of a bell will not. The food is an *unconditioned stimulus* (UCS) and salivation an *unconditioned response* (UCR), which is automatic, reflexive and biologically built-in. During conditioning, the bell is paired with the food. Because the bell does not naturally produce salivation it is called a *conditioned stimulus* (CS), because its production of salivation is *conditional* upon it being paired with the UCS. The terms used by Pavlov were, in fact, 'conditional' and 'unconditional' but these were mistranslated from the Russian as 'conditioned'/'unconditioned' and have 'stuck'. The CS is also *neutral* with regard to salivation prior to conditioning.

If the bell and food are paired a sufficient number of times, salivation will occur whenever the dog hears the bell and before the food is presented. When this occurs, conditioning has taken place and the salivation is now a *conditioned response* (CR) because it is produced by a conditioned stimulus (CS) – the bell.

This basic procedure can be used with a variety of conditioned stimuli, such as buzzers, metronomes, lights, geometric figures and so on. The exact relationship between the CS and the UCS can also be varied to give different kinds of conditioning.

Table 32.1 Four types of classical conditioning based on different CS–UCS relationships

1	Delayed or forward	The CS is presented before the UCS and remains 'on' while the UCS is presented and until the UCR appears. Conditioning has occurred when the CR appears before the UCS is presented. A half-second interval produces the strongest learning. As the interval increases, learning becomes poorer. This type of conditioning is typically used in the laboratory, especially with non-humans.
2	Backward	The CS is presented after the UCS. Generally this produces very little, if any, learning in laboratory animals. However, much advertising uses backward conditioning (e.g. the idyllic tropical scene is set and then the coconut bar is introduced: see Chapter 82, page 704).
3	Simultaneous	The CS and UCS are presented together. Conditioning has occurred when the CS on its own produces the CR. This type of conditioning occurs often in real-life situations (e.g. the sound of the dentist's drill accompanies the contact of the drill with your tooth).
4	Trace	The CS is presented and removed before the UCS is presented, so that only a 'memory trace' of the CS remains to be conditioned. The CR is usually weaker than in delayed or simultaneous conditioning.

Generalisation and discrimination

In *generalisation*, the CR transfers spontaneously to stimuli similar to, but different from, the original CS. For example, if a dog is conditioned using a bell of a particular pitch, and is then presented with a bell a little higher or lower in pitch, it will still salivate. However, if the dog

is presented with bells that are increasingly different from the original, the CR will gradually weaken and eventually stop altogether, that is, the dog is showing *discrimination*.

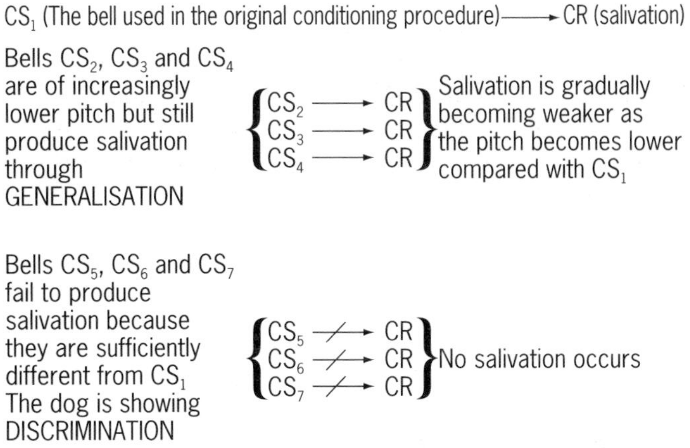

Figure 32.4   An example of discrimination occurring spontaneously as a result of generalisation stopping

---

Box 32.2   Discrimination training and experimental neurosis

Pavlov *trained* dogs to discriminate in the original conditioning procedure. For example, if a high-pitched bell is paired with food but a low-pitched bell is not, the dog will start salivating in response to the former but not to the latter (*discrimination training*).

Related to discrimination is what Pavlov called *experimental neurosis*. He trained dogs to salivate to a circle but not to an ellipse, and then gradually changed the shape of the ellipse until it became almost circular. When this happened, the dogs started behaving in 'neurotic' ways, whining, trembling, urinating and defecating, refusing to eat and so on. It was as if they did not know how to respond: was the stimulus a circle (in which case, through generalisation, they 'should' salivate) or was it an ellipse (in which case, through discrimination, they 'should not' salivate)?

Extinction and spontaneous recovery

If dogs have been conditioned to salivate to a bell, and the bell is then repeatedly presented *without* food, the CR of salivation gradually becomes weaker and eventually stops altogether (*extinction*). However, if a dog that has undergone extinction is removed from the experimental situation, and then put back a couple of hours or so later, and the bell re-presented, it will start salivating again. Although no further pairing of the bell and food has occurred, the CR of salivation reappears in response to the bell (*spontaneous recovery*). This shows that extinction does not involve an 'erasing' of the original learning but rather a learning to *inhibit* or *suppress* the CR when the CS is continually presented without a UCS.

Classical conditioning and human behaviour

There have been many laboratory demonstrations of classical conditioning in humans, and the basic procedure is a useful way of thinking about how certain fairly automatic responses may be acquired in real life. The impact of conditioning principles (both classical and operant) within *clinical psychology* has been considerable (see Chapter 74).

Box 32.3   Some general issues relating to conditioning and human behaviour

It is relatively easy to classically condition and extinguish CRs, such as the eye-blink and galvanic skin response (GSR). But what relevance does this have for understanding human learning and memory, let alone thinking, reasoning or problem-solving? In normal adults, the conditioning process can apparently be over-ridden by instructions: simply *telling* participants that the UCS will not occur again causes instant loss of a CR which would otherwise extinguish only slowly (Davey, 1983). Most participants in a conditioning experiment are aware of the experimenter's contingencies (the relationship between stimuli and responses), and in the absence of such awareness often fail to show evidence of conditioning (Brewer, 1974).

There are also important differences between very young children or those with severe learning difficulties and older children and adults regarding their behaviour in a variety of *operant* conditioning and discrimination learning experiments. These seem largely attributable to language development (Dugdale & Lowe, 1990).

All this suggests that people have rather more efficient, language- (or rule-) based forms of learning at their disposal than the laborious formation of associations between a CS and UCS. Even behaviour therapy, one of the apparently more successful applications of conditioning principles to human behaviour (see Chapter 74) has given way to *cognitive behaviour therapies* (see Chapter 75).

(Based on Mackintosh, 1995)

OPERANT CONDITIONING

Whilst not rejecting Pavlov's and Watson's discoveries, Skinner (1938) argued that most behaviour (human and non-human) is not elicited by specific stimuli. He saw learning as a much more *active* process, in which animals *operate* on their environment, and this is *instrumental* in bringing about certain *consequences* which then determine the probability of that behaviour being repeated.

Thorndike's law of effect

Skinner's study of operant conditioning derived from Thorndike's (1898) *law of effect*. Thorndike built puzzle-boxes in which cats had to learn to operate a latch that automatically caused the door to spring open. When they managed to escape, they were rewarded with a piece of fish visible from inside the puzzle-box. The cats were deprived of food for a considerable time before the experiments began and so were highly motivated. Each time, after eating the fish, they were put straight back in and the whole procedure repeated.

At first the cats behaved in a purely random fashion, and it was only by chance that they escaped. However, each time they were returned to the puzzle-box, it took them less time to escape. For instance, with one of the boxes, the average time for the first escape was five minutes, but after 10–20 trials it was about five seconds.

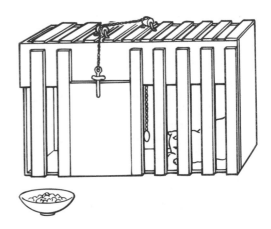

Figure 32.5   Thorndike's puzzle box

Thorndike explained this by claiming that the learning was essentially random or *trial-and-error*. There was no sudden flash of insight into how the releasing mechanism worked, but rather a gradual reduction in the number of errors made and hence escape time (see Chapter 35). What was being learned was a connection between the stimulus (the manipulative components of the box) and the response (the behaviour which allowed the cat to escape). Further, the stimulus–response connection is 'stamped in when pleasure results from the act, and stamped out when it doesn't' (the law of effect).

Skinner's 'analysis of behaviour'

Skinner used a form of puzzle-box known as a *Skinner box* intended to automate Thorndike's research and designed for a rat or pigeon to do things in rather than escape from (see Chapter 1, page 11). The box has a lever (in the case of rats) or illuminated discs (in the case of pigeons), under which is a food tray, and the experimenter decides exactly what the relationship will be between pressing the lever/pecking the disc and the delivery of a food pellet, giving the experimenter total *control* of the animal's environment.

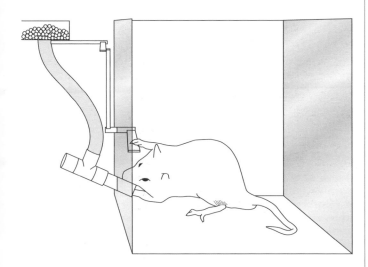

Figure 32.6   A rat in a Skinner box

Skinner used the term *strengthen* in place of Thorndike's 'stamping in' and *weaken* in place of 'stamping out', because he regarded Thorndike's terms as too mentalistic and his own as more objective and descriptive.

Box 32.4   Skinner's analysis of behaviour (or the ABC of operant conditioning)

The *analysis of behaviour* requires an accurate but neutral representation of the relationship (or *contingencies*) between:

- *Antecedents* (the stimulus conditions, such as the lever, the click of the food dispenser, a light that may go on when the lever is pressed);

- *Behaviours* (or *operants*, such as pressing the lever);

- *Consequences* (what happens as a result of the operant behaviour, that is, reinforcement or punishment).

This is the ABC of operant conditioning.

According to Skinner's version of the law of effect, 'behaviour is shaped and maintained by its consequences'. The consequences of operants can be *positive reinforcement*, *negative reinforcement*, or *punishment*.

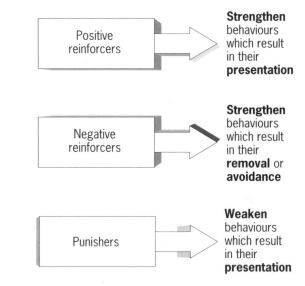

Figure 32.7   The consequences of behaviour and their effects

Whilst positive and negative reinforcement both *strengthen* behaviour (making it more probable), each works in a different way. *Positive reinforcement* involves presenting something pleasurable (such as food), whilst *negative reinforcement* involves the removal or avoidance of some 'aversive' (literally 'painful') state of affairs (such as electric shock). *Punishment* has the effect of *weakening* behaviour (making it less probable) through the presentation of an aversive stimulus).

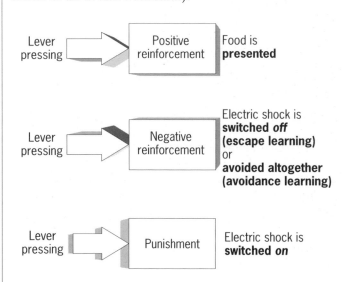

Figure 32.8   Three possible consequences of lever pressing in a Skinner box

Reinforcement and reinforcers

Whilst food itself is a *reinforcer*, the presentation of food as a result of lever-pressing is (positive) *reinforcement*. Similarly, an electric shock is a *punisher*, and the presentation of electric shock is called *punishment*.

According to Skinner, whether something is a reinforcer or punisher is a *retrospective* decision, that is, after food or shock has been made contingent on, say, lever-pressing on several occasions. So, if a behaviour is strengthened when followed by food, the food is a reinforcer. However, if shock weakens a behaviour, the shock is a punisher. Reinforcers and punishers cannot be defined independently of the effects they have on behaviour.

Skinner believes that this is a more scientific approach, since the intended and actual effect may not always coincide. For example, if children who feel deprived of their parents' attention find that their parents respond when they are naughty, they are more likely to continue being naughty, even if the parents' response is to shout or smack (at least they get some attention this way!). Similarly, a positive reinforcement can only loosely be called a reward as 'reward' implies that the rewarder *expects* to strengthen behaviour, whereas 'positive reinforcement' refers to what has been *shown* to strengthen behaviour.

Primary and secondary reinforcers

Primary reinforcers such as food, water, sex are natural reinforcers (reinforcing in themselves). *Secondary* (or *conditioned*) *reinforcers* acquire their reinforcing properties through association with primary reinforcers, that is, we have to *learn* (through classical conditioning) to find them reinforcing. Examples of human secondary reinforcers are money, cheques and tokens (see Chapter 74, pages 640–641). In a Skinner box, if a click accompanies the presentation of each food pellet, rats will eventually find the click reinforcing on its own, such that the click can be used as a reinforcer for getting rats to learn some new response. Secondary reinforcers often 'bridge the gap' between a response and a primary reinforcer which may not be immediately forthcoming.

Schedules of reinforcement

Another important aspect of Skinner's work is the effects on behaviour of how frequently and regularly (or predictably) reinforcements are presented. Ferster & Skinner (1957) identified five major schedules of reinforcement, each of which produces a characteristic pattern of responding.

Rats and pigeons (and probably most mammals and birds) typically 'work harder' (press the lever/peck the disc at a faster rate) for scant reward. When reinforcements are

relatively infrequent and irregular or unpredictable, they will go on working long after the reinforcement has actually been withdrawn. So, each schedule can be analysed in terms of *pattern and rate of response* and *resistance to extinction* (see Table 32.2, page 277).

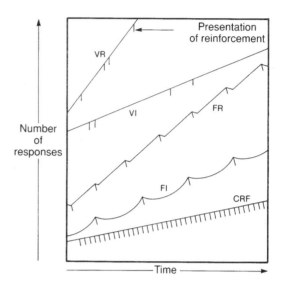

Figure 32.9   Typical cumulative records for a response (such as lever pressing) reinforced using five schedules of reinforcement. VR = variable ratio; VI = variable interval; FR = fixed ratio; FI = fixed interval; CRF = continuous reinforcement

A *continuous* schedule is usually used only when some new response is being learned. Once emitted regularly and reliably, it can be maintained by using one of the four *partial* or *intermittent* schedules. However, this change must be gradual. Skinner (1938) originally used an interval schedule because a reinforcer is guaranteed, sooner or later, so long as one response is made during the interval.

Shaping: the reinforcement of successive approximations

Reinforcement can be used to build up relatively complex behaviour (not part of an animal's natural repertoire) by reinforcing closer and closer approximations to the desired behaviour. First, the behaviour must be broken down into a number of small steps, each of which is reinforced in sequence, so that gradually what the learner can do is much more like what the experimenter is trying to teach it. This is the method used by animal trainers and by Skinner to teach pigeons to play ping-pong. Most human skills are learned in this step-by-step manner.

Table 32.2 Common reinforcement schedules and associated patterns of response and resistance to extinction

Reinforcement schedule	Example	Pattern and rate of responding	Resistance to extinction	Example of human behaviour
1 Continuous reinforcement (CRF)	Every single response is reinforced	Response rate is low but steady	Very low – the quickest way to bring about extinction	1 Receiving a high grade for every assignment 2 Receiving a tip for every customer served
2 Fixed interval (FI)	A reinforcement is given every 30 seconds (FI 30), provided the response occurs at least once during that time	Response rate speeds up as the next reinforcement becomes available; a pause after each reinforcement. Overall response rate fairly low	Fairly low – extinction occurs quite quickly	1 Being paid regularly (every week or month). 2 Giving yourself a 15-minute break for every hour's studying done
3 Variable interval (VI)	A reinforcement is given on average every 30 seconds, but the interval varies from trial to trial. So, the interval on any one occasion is unpredictable	Response rate is very stable over long periods of time. Still some tendency to increase response rate as time elapses since the last reinforcement	Very high – extinction occurs very slowly and gradually	Many self-employed people receive payment irregularly (depending on when the customer pays for the product or service)
4 Fixed ratio (FR)	A reinforcement is given for a fixed number of responses, however long this may take, e.g. one reinforcement every 10 responses (FR 10)	There is a pronounced pause after each reinforcement and then a very high rate of responding leading up to the next reinforcement	As F1	1 Piece work (the more work done, the more money earned) 2 Commission (extra money for so many goods made or sales completed)
5 Variable ratio (VR)	A reinforcement is given on average every 10 responses (VR 10) but the number varies from trial to trial. So the number of responses required on any one occasion is unpredictable	Very high response rate – and very steady	Very high – the most resistant of all the schedules	Gambling

Shaping also provides an important foundation for *behaviour modification*, which is used to teach children and adults with learning difficulties to use the toilet, feed and dress themselves and other social skills. It has also been used to develop speech in autistic children and adult schizophrenics (see Chapter 74).

Negative reinforcement: escape and avoidance learning

Escape and avoidance learning are the two major ways in which negative reinforcement has been studied in the laboratory. *Escape learning* is relatively simple. For example, rats can learn to press a lever to turn off electric shock. *Avoidance learning* is more complex and more relevant to certain aspects of human behaviour, especially the persistence of phobias (see Chapters 70 and 74).

Punishment

Skinner maintained that with both non-humans and humans, positive (and, to a lesser extent, negative) reinforcement is a much more potent influence on behaviour than punishment, largely because punishment can only make certain responses less likely. Nothing *new* can be taught by punishment alone.

However, Campbell & Church (1969) argue that punishments are, if anything, a *stronger* influence on behaviour than the incentive effects of reinforcements (at least with laboratory animals). The problem, however, is the unpleasant side-effects of stress, anxiety, withdrawal, aggression and so on.

Estes (1970) concluded that punishment merely *suppressed* rats' lever pressing in the short term, but did not weaken it. Others have shown that the strength and duration of the suppression effect depend on the *intensity* of the punishment and the degree of deprivation. However, the response is still suppressed rather than unlearned.

When alternative ways of obtaining reinforcers are available, punishment has a more powerful suppressive effect on the punished behaviour (Howe, 1980). For example, Azrin & Holz (1966) combined punishment and reinforcement so that response A was punished whilst response B, incompatible with A, was positively reinforced. This is something that Skinner advocates with humans.

The antecedents of behaviour: stimulus control

In operant conditioning, the stimulus indicates the likely consequence of emitting a particular response: the operant behaviour is more likely to occur in the presence of some stimuli than others (see Box 32.6). If a rat has been reinforced for lever pressing, it is more likely to go on doing so as the lever becomes associated both with reinforcement and the action of pressing. Technically, lever pressing is now under the *stimulus control* of the lever, but there is still no inevitability about pressing it, only an increased probability.

Similarly, drivers' behaviour is brought under the stimulus control of traffic signals, road signs, other vehicles, pedestrians and so on. Much of our everyday behaviour can be seen in this way. Sitting on chairs, answering the telephone, turning on the television and so on, are all operants which are more likely to occur in the presence of those stimuli because of the past consequences of doing so.

A special case of stimulus control is a *discriminative stimulus*. If a rat in a Skinner box is reinforced for lever pressing *only* when a light is on, the light soon becomes a discriminative stimulus (the rat only presses the lever when the light is on).

operant involves the strengthening or weakening of response tendencies already present in the animal's behavioural repertoire.

- In classical conditioning, the reinforcer (the UCS) is presented *regardless* of what the animal does and is presented *before* the response. In operant conditioning, the reinforcer is only presented if the animal emits some specified, pre-selected behaviour and is presented *after* the behaviour.

- In classical conditioning, the *strength* of conditioning is typically measured in terms of response magnitude (e.g. how many drops of saliva) and/or latency (how quickly a response is produced by a stimulus). In operant, conditioning strength is measured mainly as *response rate* (see Chapter 1, page 11).

Does conditioning work in the same way for all species?

The fact that many experiments involving a variety of species can all be described as classical conditioning, does *not* in itself mean that there is only one mechanism involved, or only one explanation which applies, equally, to all species and all cases (Walker, 1984). Although *conditionability* seems to be an almost universal property of nervous systems, many psychologists have argued that there can be no general laws of learning (Seligman, 1970).

If such laws do exist, one of them is likely to be the *law of contiguity*: events (or stimuli) which occur close together in time and space are likely to become associated with each other. Most of the examples of conditioning considered so far appear to 'obey' the law of contiguity.

Box 32.7   Taste aversion studies

These represent an important exception to the 'law' of contiguity (e.g. Garcia & Koelling, 1966; Garcia *et al.*, 1966). In Garcia *et al.*'s study, rats were given a novel-tasting solution, such as saccharine-flavoured water (the CS), prior to a drug, apomorphine (the UCS), which has a *delayed* action, inducing severe intestinal illness (the UCR).

In two separate experiments, the precise time-lapse between tasting the solution and the onset of the drug-induced nausea was either (a) 5, 6, 7, 8, 9, 10, 11, 12, 15, 16, 17, 18, 19, 20, 21 and 22 minutes, or (b) 30, 45, 75, 120 and 180 minutes. In (a), the rats received just four treatments (one every third day) and in (b) five were given (one every third day). In all cases, a conditioned aversive response to the solution was acquired, that is,

intestinal illness became a CR (a response to the solution alone). In some replications, just a single treatment has been needed.

Whilst rats can also be conditioned to novel smells, auditory, visual and tactile stimuli are not so readily associated with internal illness. It is impossible to deter pigeons from water and for other species, taste aversions are very difficult to establish even if the animal is made very ill. Thus, there seem to be definite biological limitations on the likelihood of animals developing conditioned aversions.

Similarly, rats typically learn very quickly to avoid shock in a shuttlebox and to press a lever for food. However, they do not learn very readily to press a lever to avoid shock. Pigeons can be trained quickly to fly from one perch to another in order to avoid shock, but it is almost impossible to train them to peck a disc to avoid shock.

This has led Bolles (1980) and others to conclude that we cannot regard the basic principles of learning as applying equally to all species in all situations. We must take into account the evolutionary history of the species as well as the individual organism's learning history.

Box 32.8   Seligman's concept of preparedness

According to Seligman (1970), animals are biologically prepared to learn actions that are closely related to the survival of their species (such as learned water or food aversions) and these *prepared* behaviours are learned with very little training. Equally, *contra-prepared* behaviours are contrary to an animal's natural tendencies and so are learned with great difficulty, if at all. Most of the behaviour studied in the laboratory falls somewhere in between these two extremes.

Oakley (1983) believes that *preparedness* in classical and operant conditioning is an inherited characteristic. If in a species' history, individuals have often been exposed to certain biologically significant kinds of association, then the ability to learn rapidly about such associations becomes genetically transmitted.

Much of the relevant human data relates to how easily certain conditioned fear responses can be induced in the laboratory or how common certain phobias are compared with others (See Chapter 70, pages 605–607). Most human phobias tend to be of non-humans or dangerous places. Most common of all are the fears of snakes, spiders, the dark, high and closed-in places, and often there is no previous evidence for the fear actually having been conditioned (Seligman, 1972).

The role of cognition

According to Mackintosh (1978, 1995), conditioning is *not* reducible to the strengthening of stimulus–response connections through an automatic process called reinforcement. It is more appropriate to think of it as involving the detection and learning of *relations between events* in the environment, whereby animals typically discover what signals food, water, danger or safety.

Instead of treating salivation or lever-pressing as what is learned, we could regard it simply as a convenient *index* of what has been learned, namely that certain relationships exist in the environment. Indeed, Pavlov himself described the CS as a '*signal*' for the UCS, the relationship between CS and the UCS as one of '*stimulus substitution*', and the CR as an '*anticipatory*' response (or '*psychic secretions*'), suggesting that his dogs were *expecting* the food to follow the bell.

To support this interpretation, Rescorla (1968) presented two groups of rats with the same number of CS–UCS pairings, but the second group also received additional presentations of the UCS on its own without the CS. The first group showed much stronger conditioning than the second, indicating that the most important factor (in classical conditioning anyway) is how *predictably* the UCS follows the CS, *not* how often they are paired.

Pavlov's discovery of *higher-order conditioning* also suggests a more complex process than the basic procedure described earlier (see pages 272–273).

Box 32.9   Higher order conditioning

Pavlov (1927) demonstrated that a strong CS could be used in place of food to produce salivation in response to a new stimulus which had never been paired with food. For example, if the CS is a buzzer, it can be paired with, say, a black square in such a way that after ten pairings (using delayed conditioning), the dog will salivate a small but significant amount at the sight of the black square before the buzzer is sounded. It is as if the CS were functioning as a UCS.

The buzzer and food pairing is referred to as *first order conditioning* and the black square and buzzer pairing as *second order conditioning*. Pavlov found that learning could not go beyond third or fourth order conditioning.

Cognitive approaches

Cognitive alternatives to conditioning sometimes come in the form of *extensions* of conditioning theory, such as social learning theory (see below), and sometimes in the form of accounts of learning stemming from a theoretical approach which is diametrically opposed to the S–R approach. A good example of the latter is *insight learning* (see Chapter 36) as proposed by the *Gestalt psychologists* (see Chapter 21).

TOLMAN'S COGNITIVE BEHAVIOURISM: LATENT LEARNING AND COGNITIVE MAPS

One of the earliest challenges to Skinner's view that learning cannot take place in the absence of reinforcement came from Tolman (1948). Although studying rats within the behaviourist tradition in the 1920s, 1930s and 1940s, Tolman would today be regarded as a cognitive psychologist, because he explained rats' learning in terms of inferred cognitive processes, in particular *cognitive or mental maps*.

Box 32.10   Tolman & Honzik's (1930) demonstration of latent learning

Group 1 rats were reinforced every time they found their way through a maze to the food box. *Group 2 rats* were never reinforced, and *Group 3* rats received no reinforcement for the first ten days of the experiment but did so from day 11.

Not surprisingly, Group 1 learned the maze quickly and made fewer and fewer mistakes, whilst Group 2 never reduced the time it took to find the food and moved around aimlessly much of the time. Group 3, however, having apparently made no progress during the first ten days, showed a sudden decrease in the time it took to reach the goal-box on day 11 when they received their first reinforcement and caught up almost immediately with Group 1.

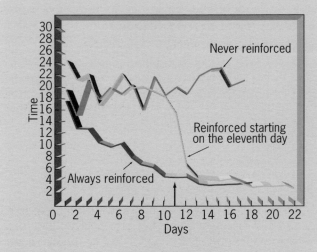

Figure 32.10   The results of Tolman and Honzik's study of latent learning in rats

Clearly, Group 3 rats had been learning their way through the maze during the first ten days but the learning was *latent* ('behaviourally silent'), that is, it did not show up in their actual behaviour (performance) until they received the incentive of the reinforcement on day 11.

Tolman and Honzik concluded that reinforcement may be important in relation to *performance* of learned behaviour, but it is *not necessary* for the learning itself.

Tolman's (1948) *place-learning* (or *sign-learning*) theory maintains that rats learn expectations as to which part of the maze will be followed by which other part. Tolman called these expectations *cognitive maps* and they represent a primitive kind of perceptual map of the maze or understanding of its spatial relationships.

Although a cognitive map can only be inferred from behaviour, it is difficult to know how else to explain the finding that rats will take short-cuts to the food box if the old path is blocked, or how, if the maze were rotated, they can find the usual food location from several different starting points (Tolman *et al.*, 1946). Similarly, Restle (1957) flooded a maze immediately after a group of rats had learnt to run it, and they were able to swim to the goal-box with no more errors than when they had walked. This clearly supports Tolman's interpretation.

SOCIAL LEARNING THEORY AND OBSERVATIONAL LEARNING

Social learning theory (SLT) originated in the USA in the 1940s and 1950s as an attempt to re-interpret certain aspects of Freud's psychoanalytic theory in terms of conditioning theory. This was carried on in the 1960s and 1970s, notably by Bandura, who tried to make Freud's concept of identification more objective by studying it in the laboratory in the form of *imitation* (see Chapters 44 and 45)

Box 32.11   Some important similarities and differences between SLT and orthodox learning theory

- Whilst SL theorists agree that all behaviour is learned according to the same learning principles, they are interested specifically in *human learning*, especially social and moral behaviour.

- Although SL theorists agree that we should observe what is observable, they also believe that there are important *cognitive* or *mediating variables* which intervene between stimulus and response and without which we cannot adequately explain behaviour.

- SL theorists emphasise *observational learning* (learning through watching the behaviour of others, called *models*), which takes place spontaneously, with no deliberate effort on the learner's part or any intention to teach on the model's part.

- Observational learning, as such, takes place without any reinforcement (Bandura, 1965): mere exposure to the model is sufficient for learning to occur. However, whether the model's behaviour is imitated depends partly on the *consequences* of the behaviour, both for the model and the learner (Bandura *et al.*, 1963). Like Tolman, SL theorists see reinforcement as important only in so far as it affects *performance* (not the learning itself).

Reinforcement as information about the future

Bandura (1977) challenged Skinner's claim that reinforcements and punishments *automatically* strengthen and weaken behaviour. For Bandura:

'Reinforcement serves principally as an informative and motivational operation rather than as a mechanical response strengthener'.

Reinforcement provides the learner with *information* about the likely consequences (reinforcement or punishment) of certain behaviour under certain conditions, that is, it improves our prediction of whether a given action will lead to pleasant or unpleasant outcomes in the future. It also *motivates* us by causing us to anticipate *future* outcomes. Our present behaviours are largely governed by the outcomes we expect them to have, and we are more likely to try to learn the modelled behaviour if we value the consequences related to that behaviour.

The role of cognitive factors in observational learning

The learning process is much more complex for Bandura than it is for Skinner. In Bandura's (1974) view:

' ... contrary to mechanistic metaphors, outcomes change behaviour in humans through the intervening influence of thought'.

Box 32.12   The five major functions involved in observational learning (Bandura, 1974)

- The learner must *pay attention* to the pertinent clues in the stimulus situation and ignore those aspects of the model and the environment that are incidental and irrelevant.

- A *visual image* or *semantic code* for the modelled behaviour is recorded in memory. Without an adequate coding system, the learner fails to store what has been seen or heard (see Chapter 27). Whereas infants are largely confined to immediate imitation, the older child can defer imitation because of its superior use of symbols (see Chapter 41).

- *Memory permanence* refers to devices such as rehearsal and use of multiple codes to help retain the stored information over long periods.

- *Reproducing the observed motor activities* accurately usually requires a number of trials to get the *muscular feel* of the behaviour (through feedback). Older children enjoy greater muscular strength and control.

- *Motivation* relates to the role of reinforcement (see text above).

Conclusions

This chapter has considered some of the major similarities and differences between classical and operant conditioning. Whilst behaviourist psychologists have explained conditioning in stimulus–response terms, it can also be interpreted in terms of cognitive factors. Important alternatives to conditioning, including Tolman's cognitive behaviourism, and social learning theory, have also been discussed. Both these alternatives see cognitive factors as playing a crucial part in the learning process.

Summary

■ Learning is one of psychology's central areas of research and has played a major part in its development as a scientific discipline.

■ **Theories of learning** differ regarding the nature of the processes involved, especially the role of cognitive factors. However, all agree that learning involves a relatively permanent behaviour change due to past experience. An important distinction is that between **learning** and **performance**, referring to **potential** and **actual** behaviour respectively. Also, learning is **adaptive** and closely related to other abilities, particularly memory.

■ Skinner distinguished between **respondent** and **operant behaviours**, which correspond to **classical** (or Pavlovian) and **operant** (or instrumental) **conditioning** respectively.

■ In **classical** conditioning, the pairing of a conditioned (CS) and an unconditioned stimulus (UCS) results in the former eliciting a response that previously was only produced by the latter. **Delayed** (or **forward**), **backward**, **simultaneous**, and **trace** conditioning differ according to the relationship between the conditioned and unconditioned stimuli.

■ **Generalisation, discrimination, extinction** and **spontaneous recovery** apply to both classical and operant conditioning. Spontaneous recovery demonstrates that extinction involves a learning to inhibit or suppress the CR, not an erasing of it.

■ Compared with classical conditioning, **operant** conditioning sees learning as much more **active**. Skinner was interested in how animals **operate** on their environment and how their activity is **instrumental** in producing certain **consequences**.

■ In classical conditioning, a response is **elicited** by a stimulus and is involuntary, whilst operant responses are **emitted** by the learner and are voluntary. Also, in classical conditioning, the reinforcer is presented regardless of what the learner does, **before** the response, whilst in operant conditioning, the reinforcement is contingent upon a specified response being emitted and is presented **after** the response.

■ Skinner's work was based on Thorndike's **law of effect**. Skinner designed a form of puzzle-box (a **Skinner box**) and called the consequences of behaviour **positive reinforcement, negative reinforcement** and **punishment**. Reinforcement (both positive and negative) **strengthens** behaviour, whilst punishment **weakens** it.

■ **Primary reinforcers** are naturally reinforcing, whilst **secondary** (or **conditioned**) **reinforcers** come to be reinforcing through association with primary reinforcers. **Shaping** involves the reinforcement of **successive approximations** to the desired behaviour.

■ Different **schedules of reinforcement** can be analysed in terms of **pattern/rate of response** and **resistance to extinction**. **Variable** schedules involve high, steady rates of response and high resistance to extinction compared with **fixed** and **continuous** schedules.

■ **Escape** and **avoidance learning** have been explained by the **two-factor theory**, according to which both classical and operant conditioning are involved. The persistence of human phobias can be understood in terms of avoidance learning.

■ **Punishment** seems to involve a **suppression** of behaviour and is most effective when combined with the reinforcement of an incompatible response.

■ In operant conditioning, the stimulus makes certain behaviour **more likely** to occur, but this is not inevitable as it is in classical conditioning. This is called **stimulus control**.

■ **Taste aversion** experiments contribute to the view that the basic principles of conditioning do not apply equally to all species in all situations. **Preparedness** helps to explain experimental findings showing that different species acquire certain conditioned responses more or less easily, and why certain human phobias are more common than others.

■ Rather than a simple strengthening of stimulus–response associations, conditioning can be thought of as the learning about **relations between events**.

■ Tolman's theory of **latent learning** explains how learning can take place in the absence of reinforcement. Rats learn a **cognitive map** of the maze, not the individual movements of walking or running that take them to the food box.

■ **Social learning** theorists are primarily concerned with explaining human learning, and stress the role of **cognitive** variables. The key learning process is **observational learning**, and, like Tolman, SL theorists distinguish between learning and performance.

■ Bandura stresses the **informational** and **motivational** aspects of reinforcement, as well as fundamental cognitive processes such as attention and memory.

PART 3

Language and thought

33

DESCRIBING LANGUAGE DEVELOPMENT

Introduction and overview

Until recently, the study of language was largely the domain of *linguistics*, which is concerned primarily with language's *structure*, the sounds that compose it, their relation to words and sentences, and the rules governing such relations. Fairly recently, though, psychologists have become interested in language from the perspective of how it develops, whether it is unique to humans, and how it is related to learning, memory and thought.

The 'marriage' between psychology and linguistics is called *psycholinguistics*, which studies the perception, understanding and production of language, together with the development of these activities. This, and Chapters 34 and 37, look at some of the major issues concerning language. This chapter describes the course of language development in humans but begins by looking at what language is and its major components.

What is language?

According to Brown (1965), language is an arbitrary set of symbols:

'which, taken together, make it possible for a creature with limited powers of discrimination and a limited memory to transmit and understand an infinite variety of messages and to do this in spite of noise and distraction'.

Whilst other species are able to *communicate* with each other, they can do so only in limited ways, and it is perhaps the 'infinite variety of messages' part of Brown's definition that sets humans apart from non-humans. For example, wild chimpanzees use over 30 different vocalisations to convey a large number of meanings, and repeat sounds in order to intensify their meaning. However, they do not string these sounds together to make new 'words' (Calvin, 1994). The claim that chimpanzees are capable of using language are based largely, and until recently, on *deliberate training*. Human language is mastered spontaneously and quite easily within the first five years of life.

Brown (1973) pointed out that humans do not simply learn a repertoire of sentences but:

'acquire a rule system that makes it possible to generate a literally infinite variety of sentences, most of them never heard from anyone else'.

This rule system is called *grammar* (or *mental grammar*). However, for psycholinguists, grammar is much more than the parts of speech we learn about in school. It is concerned with the description of language, the rules which determine how a language 'works', and what governs patterns of speech (Jackendoff, 1993).

The major components of grammar

Grammar consists of *phonology*, *semantics* and *syntax* (see Figure 32.1, page 285).

PHONOLOGY

Phonologists are concerned with a language's sound system, what counts as a sound and what constitutes an acceptable sequence of sounds. Basic speech sounds are called *phones* or *phonetic segments* and are represented by enclosing symbols inside square brackets. For example, [p] is the initial phone in the word 'pin'. Some languages have as few as 15 distinguishable sounds and others as many as 85. The English language has some 46 phones (Solso, 1995).

Although all phones are different, only those which affect the meaning of what is being said matter. For example, the [p] phone can be pronounced slightly differently each time without changing the perception of the 'p' in 'pin'. However, the difference between [p] and [d] does matter because it can lead to two words with different meanings (such as 'pin' and 'din'). Because [p] and [d] cannot be interchanged without altering a word's meaning, they belong to different functional classes of phones called *phonemes*.

Phonemes or *phonological segments* are a language's functionally important classes of phones. The phones [p] and [d] belong to the different phonemes /p/ and /d/. Languages differ in their number of phonemes. For example, [l] and [r] belong to different phonemes in English, but not in Japanese. *Phonological rules* constrain the permitted sequence of phonemes. For example, 'port' is an *actual* sequence of phonemes, 'plort' is a *possible* sequence, but 'pbort' is a *prohibited* sequence in English.

In themselves, phonemes have no meaning. They are just sounds and correspond roughly to the vowels and consonants of a language's alphabet. However, languages (including English) can have more phonemes than letters in the alphabet (see above). This is because some letters, such as 'o', can be pronounced differently (as in 'hop' and 'hope'). The development of speech sounds continues for several years after birth (see page 286) and most children *recognise* sounds in adult speech before they can *produce* them. So, in response to the instruction: 'I am going to say a word two times and you tell me which time I say it right and which time I say it wrong: *rabbit, wabbit*', a child might reply: '*Wabbit* is *wight* and *wabbit* is *wong*', indicating that the 'r' sound can be recognised but not yet produced (Dale, 1976).

SEMANTICS

Semantics is the study of the *meaning* of language, and can be analysed at the level of *morphemes* and *sentences*. Morphemes are a language's basic units of meaning and consist mainly of *words*. Other morphemes are *prefixes* (letters attached to the beginning of a word, such as 'pre' and 're') and *suffixes* (word-endings, such as 's' to make a plural). Some morphemes, such as the plural 's', are 'bound' (they only take on meaning when attached to

other morphemes), but most morphemes are 'free' (they have meaning when they stand alone, as most words have). Single words, however, have only a limited meaning and are usually combined into longer strings of phrases and sentences, the other level of semantic analysis.

SYNTAX

Syntax refers to the rules for combining words into phrases and sentences. One example of a *syntactic rule* is word order. This is crucial for understanding language development. Clearly, the sentences 'The dog bit the postman' and 'The postman bit the dog' have very different meanings, as a competent language user will recognise.

Another example of a syntactic rule occurs in the sentence 'The dog chased the …'. In English, only a noun can complete this sentence. Some sentences may be syntactically correct but have no semanticity. For example, 'The player scored a goal' and 'The goal post scored a banana' are both syntactically correct, but one has much more meaning than the other. A sentence like 'Breakfast English full enjoy I a' breaks syntactic rules and is also meaningless. These examples show that syntax and semantics are closely related, but distinct. Also, whilst sentences have sounds and meanings, syntax refers to the *structures* which relate the two.

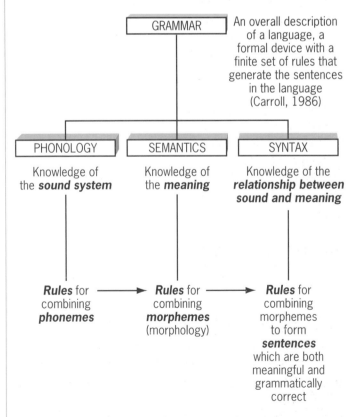

Figure 33.1   The major components of grammar (Adapted from Gross, 1996)

Stages in language development

For many psychologists, language development follows a universal timetable, that is, regardless of their language or culture, all children pass through the same sequence of stages at approximately the same ages (although children may vary with respect to their rate of development). Whilst this belief implies the role of *maturation*, environmental factors are also necessary in that children can only come to speak a language if they are exposed to it. The claim that children are *programmed* to develop language if exposed to it is one of the competing theoretical views examined in Chapter 34.

It is generally agreed that there are three major stages in language development. These are the *pre-linguistic stage* (0–12 months), the *one-word stage* (12–18 months) and the *stage of two-word sentences*. This third stage is divided into two sub-stages: *Stage 1 grammar* (18–30 months) and *Stage 2 grammar* (30 months and beyond).

THE PRE-LINGUISTIC STAGE (0–12 MONTHS)

In their first year, babies are essentially pre-linguistic. They make various sounds with their vocal organs (including crying) long before they can talk. Crying tends to dominate in the first month, with parents gradually learning to discriminate between the various cries (Gustafson & Harris, 1990). By one month, babies are able to distinguish between phonemes (such as 'ba' and 'pa') and other sounds, even though these may be physically and acoustically almost identical (Aslin *et al.*, 1983). Quite possibly, this perceptual ability (*categorical speech perception*) is innate (see Chapter 34).

At about six weeks, *cooing* begins. This is associated with pleasurable states and does not occur when babies are hungry, tired or in pain. Although vowel sounds may be produced at this age, they are different from those that will be made later and from which the first words will be formed. This is because the baby's oral cavity and nervous system are not sufficiently mature to enable it to produce the sounds necessary for speech.

Box 33.1   The development of babbling

This is the major development in the first year of life and usually begins between six and nine months. Phonemes are produced and take the form of combinations of consonants and vowels (such as *ma* and *da*). These may be repeated to produce *reduplicated monosyllables* (such as *mama* and *dada*). Although these are very different from the earlier cooing sounds, they have no meaning (despite the claim of parents that their child is trying to communicate some message).

Babbling and pre-babbling vocalisations differ in two main ways. First, babies spend more time making noises, especially when *alone* in their cots (*spontaneous babbling*), and they seem to enjoy exercising their voices for the sake of it. For Tartter (1986), they:

'appear to be playing with the sounds, enjoying the tactile and auditory feel of vocalisation'.

Second, babbling has intonational patterns, just like speech, with rising inflections and speech-like rhythms. By one year, syllables are often produced over and over again (as in *dadadada*), a phenomenon called *echolalia*.

Because babbling occurs at around the same age in all babies, regardless of culture or whether the baby is deaf and its parents deaf-mute, its onset is probably based on maturation. However, since smiling, soft sounds and pats on the abdomen can all increase the frequency of babbling, experience can play a role in modifying it (Rheingold *et al.*, 1959).

Babies initially produce only a few phonemes, but within a short period almost every available phoneme is produced, whether or not it belongs in what will become the baby's native language. The onset of this *phonemic expansion* is probably maturational. At around nine or ten months, *phonemic contraction* begins, and phoneme production is restricted to those used in the baby's native language, probably based on the baby's sampling of phonemes used in its 'linguistic environment'. Thus, babies whose native languages will be different can be distinguished by the sounds they produce. Additionally, deaf babies usually *stop* babbling at around nine or ten months, presumably because of the lack of feedback from their own voice (see Chapter 79).

Phonemic contraction does not mean that *all* phonemes have been mastered. By two and a half years of age, only about 60 per cent of the phonemes used in English are mastered, and complete mastery will not be achieved until around age seven.

ONE-WORD STAGE

Typically, children produce their first word at around one year, although there is considerable variability in this (Rice, 1989). Babies do not, of course, suddenly switch from babbling to the production of words, and non-words (*jargon*) continue to be produced for up to another six months. The baby's first words (or articulate sounds) are often invented, and not like 'adult words' at all. Scollon (1976) has defined a word as 'a systematic matching of form and meaning'. On this definition, 'da' is a word if it is consistently used to refer to a doll, since the same sound is being used to label the same thing or kind of thing, and there is a clear intention to communicate.

However, an infant's earliest words are usually *context-bound*, produced only in very limited and specific situations or contexts in which particular actions or events occur (Barrett, 1989). For example, one infant, at least initially, only produced the word 'duck' whilst hitting a toy duck off the edge of a bath. The word was never used in any other context (Barrett, 1989).

Barrett has argued that an infant's first words often do not serve a communicative purpose as such. Rather, because they typically occur as accompaniments to particular actions or events (as in the case above) they function as 'performatives'. Some words may be more like the performance of a ritualised action than the expression of a lexical meaning to another person. However, words seem to have either an *expressive function*, in that they communicate internal states (such as pleasure and surprise) to others, or a *directive function*, in which the behaviour of others is directed (by, for example, requesting or obtaining and directing attention).

Box 33.2   Holophrases: making a sentence out of a word

The one-word stage is also characterised by the use of *holophrases*. In holophrastic speech, a single word (such as 'milk') is used to convey a much more complex message (such as 'I want some more milk' or 'I have spilt my milk'). Because holophrases are accompanied by gestures and tone of voice to add full meaning to an individual word, they may be seen as precursors of later, more complex sentences (Greenfield & Smith, 1976). They are, however, dependent upon the recipient of the holophrase making the 'correct' interpretation.

Nelson (1973) identified six categories of words and calculated the percentage of children's first 50 words (typically acquired by 19 to 20 months) that fell into each category (see Table 33.1).

Nelson argued that it is not just the amount of exposure to objects and words that is important in word acquisition. Rather, given that specific and general nominals and action words make up the vast majority of those produced (78 per cent), it is the child's active involvement with its environment that determines many of its first words.

Table 33.1   Nelson's six categories and the percentage of children's first 50 words falling into each of them

1 *Specific nominals*. Names for unique objects, people or animals (14 per cent).

2 *General nominals*. Names for classes of objects, people or animals, e.g. 'ball', 'car', 'milk', 'doggie', 'girl', 'he', 'that' (51 per cent).

3 *Action words*. Describe or accompany actions or express or demand attention, e.g. 'bye-bye', 'up', 'look', 'hi' (13 per cent).

4 *Modifiers*. Refer to properties or qualities of things, e.g. 'big', 'red', 'pretty', 'hot', 'all gone', 'there', 'mine' (9 per cent).

5 *Personal-social words*. Say something about a child's feelings or social relationships, e.g. 'ouch', 'please', 'no', 'yes', 'want' (8 per cent).

6 *Function words*. Have only grammatical function, e.g. 'what', 'is', 'to', 'for' (4 per cent).

(Taken from Gross, 1996)

Children *understand* more words than they can produce. For example, a child who uses 'bow-wow' to refer to all small animals will nonetheless pick a picture of a dog rather than any other animal when asked to select a 'bow-wow' (Gruendel, 1977). The child's *receptive vocabulary* (the words it can understand) is therefore much bigger than its *expressive vocabulary* (the words it uses in speech).

Even before age two, children begin acquiring words at the rate of about 20 per day (Miller, 1978). Whilst some of these are context-bound, they gradually become decontextualised as the one-word stage progresses. Other words are used from the start in a decontextualised way (Barrett, 1989). As the one-word stage progresses, so the child becomes able to ask and answer questions and provide comments on people and objects in the immediate environment. These abilities enable the child to participate in very simple conversations with other people.

STAGE OF TWO-WORD SENTENCES

Like the one-word stage, this stage is universal (although individual differences become more marked) and, like the transition from babbling to the one-word stage, the transition to the two-word stage is also gradual (Slobin, 1979). As well as continued vocabulary development, the understanding of grammar grows, and Bee & Mitchell (1980) divide this stage into *Stage 1 grammar* (18 to 30 months) and *Stage 2 grammar* (after 30 months).

Stage 1 grammar (18–30 months)

Here, the child's speech is essentially *telegraphic* (Brown, 1965), that is, only those words which convey the most information (*contentives*) are used. Purely grammatical terms (*functors*), such as the verb 'to be', plurals and possessives, are left out. For example, children will say 'There cow' to convey the underlying message 'There is a cow'. It seems that irrespective of their culture, children express basic facts about their environment (Brown, 1973).

Significantly, there is a *rigid word order*, which seems to preserve a sentence's meaning. For example, if asked 'Does John want some milk?', the child might reply 'John milk' (or, later on, 'John want milk'). Adult speech, by contrast, does not rely exclusively on word order to preserve meaning, as in the passive form of a sentence. So, 'John drank the milk' and 'The milk was drunk by John' both convey the same meaning, even though the two sentences' word order is different.

Children's imitations of adult sentences are also simple and retain the original sentence's word order. For example, 'John is playing with the dog' is imitated as 'Play dog', a phenomenon Brown (1965) calls *imitation by reduction*. Complementary to this is *imitation with expansion*, which is the adult's imitation of the child's utterances. Here, adults insert the 'missing' functors so that the child's production of 'John milk' becomes 'John would like some milk'. The rigid order of the child's utterances makes it easier to interpret their meaning, but gestures and context still provide important clues (as with the one-word stage).

Compared with talking to one another, adults talking to children tend to use much shorter sentences and simpler syntax, raise the pitch of their voice for emphasis, and repeat or paraphrase much of what the child says. This *motherese* or *baby-talk register* helps to achieve a mutual understanding with children who have not yet mastered the full complexity of language. Sensitivity to the child's vocabulary and its intellectual and social knowledge is an example of a *pragmatic rule* for ensuring a degree of shared understanding (Greene, 1990) and also supports a social interaction approach to language acquisition (see Chapter 34).

Children's two-word utterances are not just random word combinations, but systematic expressions of specific semantic relations (see Table 33.2). Brown (1970) has distinguished between two main types of semantic relations: those expressed by combining a single constant term or pivot word (such as 'more') with another word which refers to an object, action or attribute (such as 'milk'), and those that do not involve the use of constant or pivot

Table 33.2   The eight most common semantic relationships produced by children in the two-word stage

Semantic relationships	Examples
agent + action	mommy give, daddy sit
action + object	give money, open door
agent + object	mommy car, Angel bone
action + location	sit there, fall floor
entity + location	plane rug, phone table
possessor + possession	my mommy, baby bed
entity + attribute	truck red, house pretty
demonstrative + entity	dat tree, dis mop

(From Brown, 1973)

words. The appearance of two-word utterances can therefore be attributed to the child's acquisition of two different types of combinatorial rule, namely *pivotal* and *categorical rules*. There is considerable individual variation in the type of two-word utterances which different children produce. Some rely largely on pivotal rules, whereas others rely primarily on categorical rules (Barrett, 1989).

Box 33.3   Cromer's cognition hypothesis

Word order in two-word utterances seems to reflect the child's pre-linguistic knowledge. According to Cromer's (1974) *cognition hypothesis*, language structures can only be used correctly when permitted by our cognitive structures. Children form schemata to understand the world and then talk about it. A good example is object permanence, which is a prerequisite for understanding that words can represent things. If a child did not already understand the relationships between objects, people and events in the real world, its first words would be like random unconnected lists. These are important concepts in Piaget's developmental theory (see Chapter 41) and are consistent with his view of language development reflecting the child's stage of cognitive development (see Chapter 34).

Stage 2 grammar (from about 30 months)

This lasts until around age four or five, and whilst it may be different for different languages, the rule-governed behaviour in language development is universal. The child's vocabulary grows rapidly and sentences become longer and more complex. *Mean length of utterance* (MLU) is the number of words in a sentence divided by the total number of sentences produced. So, a child who produced 100 sentences with 300 words would have a MLU of 3.00.

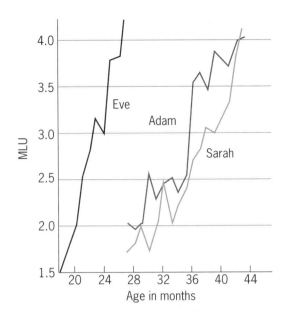

Figure 33.2   Mean length of utterance (MLU) plotted against age in months for three children (Based on Brown, 1973)

The increase in MLU shown above is due largely to the inclusion of the functors that are omitted from the telegraphic speech of Stage 1 grammar. For example, 'Daddy hat' may become 'Daddy wear hat' and finally 'Daddy is wearing a hat'. Sentences also become longer because conjunctions (such as 'and' and 'so') are used to form compound sentences like 'You play with the doll and I play with the ball'. Stage 2 grammar, then, really begins with the first use of purely grammatical words. There does not appear to be a 'three-word' stage.

Brown (1973) has found a distinct regularity among English-speaking children in terms of the order in the addition of grammatical complexities. Similarly, de Villiers & de Villiers (1979) have found that, irrespective of culture, children acquire functional words in the same general order but at different rates. Each function word corresponds to a syntactic rule. Several studies show that when children begin to apply these rules (such as the rule for forming plurals), they are not just imitating others.

Box 33.4   Berko's (1958) study of rule formation in children

Berko showed children a picture of a fictitious creature called a wug and told them 'This is a wug'.

They were then shown a second picture in which there were two of the creatures and told 'Now there is another one. There are two of them.'

The children were asked to complete the sentence 'There are two ...'. Three- and four-year-olds answered 'wugs" despite never having seen a 'wug' before. Although the children could not have been imitating anybody else's speech, and had not been told about the rule for forming plurals, they were able to apply this rule. Significantly, they were not consciously aware of having acquired the rule for forming a plural and could not say what the rule was.

The rule-governed nature of language is also shown in children's grammatical mistakes. For example, whilst the rule 'add an "s" to a word to form a plural' usually works, there are exceptions to it (such as 'sheep' rather than 'sheeps' and 'geese' rather than 'gooses'). Similarly, the rule 'add "ed" to form the past tense' usually works but not in the case of 'cost' and 'go'. The observation that children use words like 'costed' and 'goed', without ever having heard others use them, suggests that they are applying a rule rather than using imitation. In these cases, however, the rule is being *overgeneralised* or the language *over-regularised*.

Box 33.5   An example of how the misapplication of a rule is greater than any desire to imitate (Gleason, 1967)

The following is a transcript of an interaction between a mother and her child:

CHILD: My teacher holded the baby rabbits and we patted them.

MOTHER: Did you say your teacher held the baby rabbits?

CHILD: Yes.

MOTHER: What did you say she did?

CHILD: She holded the baby rabbits and we patted them.

MOTHER: Did you say she held them tightly?

CHILD: No, she holded them loosely.

By age four or five, basic grammatical rules have been acquired, and by five or six, children have acquired most of what they need to know about phoneme construction. For example, if four-year-olds are asked to say which of two made-up speech sounds would be a better name for a toy, and one of the names is consistent with the rules for combining phonemes in the English language (such as 'Klek') and the other is not (such as 'Lkel'), most will choose the former. However, a typical five-year-old will have difficulty understanding passive sentences. For example, if asked to act out the sentence 'The horse is kissed by the cow', most five-year-olds will reverse the meaning and make the horse do the kissing. There are also many irregular words still to be learned, and this aspect of grammatical development will take several more years.

By age 13, most English-speaking children have a vocabulary of 20,000 words, and by age 20, this will have risen to 50,000 or more (Aitchison, 1996), a vocabulary which is acquired at an *average rate* of nine words per day (Templin, 1957). Not surprisingly, language development and brain development are closely related.

Conclusions

This chapter has described the course of language development. As many psychologists contend, there appears to be a 'timetable' for language development amongst speakers of English and other languages. Thus, at particular ages, children have particular linguistic capabilities. The importance of this is explored in Chapter 34.

Summary

■ **Psycholinguistics** is the study of the perception, understanding and production of language and their development.

■ Whilst non-humans can **communicate** with each other only in a limited way, humans are capable of transmitting and understanding an infinite variety of messages. Language is mastered spontaneously early in life, without the need for **deliberate training**.

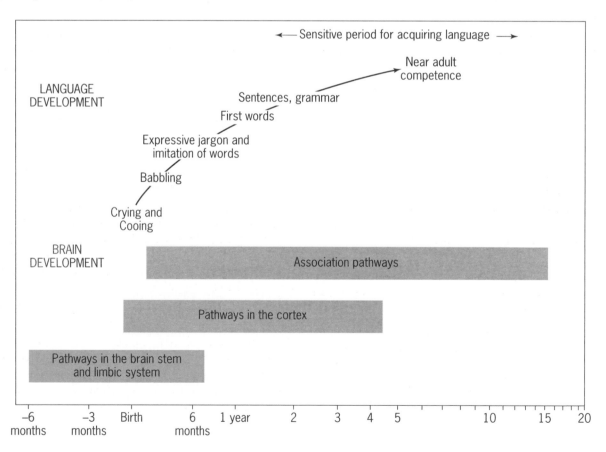

Figure 33.3   The relationship between language development and brain development. Early speech is associated with development of pathways in the cortex, but more complex speech depends on the development of association pathways in the cortex (Fischer & Lazerson, 1984)

■ Language involves the acquistion of a rule system (**grammar/mental grammar**) which consists of phonology, semantics and syntax.

■ **Phonology** is a language's sound system. Different languages have different numbers and combinations of **phones/phonetic segments** and **phonemes/phonological segments**, the functionally important classes of phones. Phonemes themselves are meaningless sounds but important for meaning. Most children **recognise** sounds in adult speech before they can **produce** them themselves.

■ **Semantics** is a language's meaning. **Morphemes** are the basic unit of meaning, consisting mainly of **words** but also including **prefixes** and **suffixes**.

■ **Syntax** refers to the rules for combining words into phrases and sentences. Word order is an example of a **syntactic rule** important for understanding language development.

■ Although language development follows a universal timetable, reflecting the role of **maturation**, exposure to language (an environmental influence) is also necessary.

■ During the **pre-linguistic stage** (0–12 months), babies make various non-speech sounds including crying and **cooing**. **Babbling** (starting at six to nine months), however, involves the production of phonemes, although these still lack meaning.

■ **Phonemic expansion** is replaced at around nine or ten months by **phonemic contraction**. This reflects the baby's sampling of phonemes used in its 'linguistic environment'. It will still take another six years or so for **all** phonemes in the child's native language to be mastered.

■ There is a gradual transition from babbling to the **one-word stage**. The child's first words are often invented and **context bound**, denoting specific actions, events or objects. They perform less of a communicative function and more of a performative function.

■ The one-word stage is also characterised by **holophrases**, whose full meaning is provided by accompanying gestures and tones of voice. They can be thought of as precursors of later, more complex sentences.

■ **Specific nominals**, **general nominals**, and **action words** account for most of a child's first 50 words, implying the child's active involvement in its environment.

■ The child's **receptive vocabulary** outstrips its **expressive vocabulary**, but the latter increases rapidly before

age two. Words become more decontextualised and the child becomes increasingly capable of participating in simple conversations.

■ The **two-word stage** is universal and can be divided into **Stage 1 grammar** (18–30 months) and **Stage 2 grammar** (30 months and beyond).

■ Language in Stage 1 grammar is **telegraphic**, consisting of **contentives** but no **functors**. Telegraphic speech involves a **rigid word order**, helping adults to interpret a sentence's meaning. This is also true of **imitation by reduction**, which is complemented by the adult's **imitation with expansion**.

■ **Motherese/baby-talk register** involves sensitivity to the child's immature vocabulary and knowledge, and represents a **pragmatic rule** for ensuring mutual understanding. It also supports a social-interaction approach to language acquisition.

■ **Two-word utterances** represent systematic expressions of specific semantic relations. Two main types of semantic relations are **pivotal rules** and **categorical rules**. These are combinatorial rules, and children show considerable individual variation in which type they use for forming two-word utterances.

■ Word order seems to reflect the child's pre-linguistic knowledge, as claimed by Cromer's **cognition hypothesis**. Similarly, Piaget believes that language development reflects the child's stage of cognitive development.

■ The rule-governed nature of **Stage 2 grammar** is universal. There is rapid growth of vocabulary, with sentences becoming longer and more complex, as measured by the **mean length of utterance (MLU)**. MLU increase is due largely to the inclusion of functors missing from Stage 1 telegraphic speech.

■ There appears to be a universal developmental sequence of grammatical complexities/functional words, although the rates may differ. Each functor corresponds to a syntactic rule and is not simply an imitation of others' speech. The rule-governed nature of language is also illustrated in children's grammatical mistakes, which often involve the **overgeneralised/over-regularised** application of a rule.

■ By age four or five, basic grammatical rules have been acquired. Later development involves understanding the difference between active and passive sentences, learning many irregular words, and continuing expansion of vocabulary.

34

THEORIES OF LANGUAGE DEVELOPMENT

Introduction and overview

Chapter 33 looked at the major milestones in language development. This chapter considers some of the theories of the mechanisms by which children develop their native language. According to one account, associated with Skinner and Bandura, language development can be attributed primarily to environmental input and learning.

Another position argues that whilst the environment may supply the *content* of language (such as the specific words children use), the *structure* of language (its *grammar*) is an inherent, biologically determined capacity of human beings. According to Chomsky, Lenneberg and McNeill, the process of language development is essentially one of *acquistion* (as distinct from *learning*).

This chapter considers the evidence for and against the learning theory and biological approaches as well as some alternative approaches. Significant amongst these are approaches which stress the relationship between language and children's cognitive development, and children's interactions with other language users.

Learning theory

CLASSICAL CONDITIONING

The earliest theory implicating learning principles suggested that much of language is developed through *classical conditioning* (Houston *et al.*, 1991). Consider, for example, the development of the sound 'mama'. If this initially neutral sound (which will eventually become a *conditioned stimulus*) is repeatedly paired with the *unconditioned stimulus* of the mother, then the baby's responses to her become classically conditioned to 'mama'. Equally, words like 'hot' may acquire their meaning through repeated pairings with a certain class of unconditioned stimuli such as fires, radiators and so on (Houston *et al.*, 1991: see Chapter 32).

OPERANT CONDITIONING

According to Skinner (1985):

'verbal behaviour evidently came into existence when, through a critical step in the evolution of the human species, the vocal musculature became susceptible to operant conditioning'.

Skinner (1957) first applied operant conditioning principles to explain language development when he argued that:

'a child acquires verbal behaviour when relatively unplanned vocalisations, selectively reinforced, assume forms which produce appropriate consequences in a given verbal community'.

Whilst Skinner accepted that pre-linguistic vocalisations, such as cooing and babbling were probably inborn (see Chapter 33, page 286), he argued that adults *shape* the baby's sounds into words by *reinforcing* those which approximate the form of real words. Through selective reinforcement, words are shaped into sentences with correct grammar being reinforced and incorrect grammar ignored.

One form of positive reinforcement is the child getting what it asks for. For example, 'May I have some water?' produces a drink that reinforces that form of words (Skinner called these requests *mands*). Reinforcement may also be given by parents becoming excited and poking, touching, patting and feeding children when they vocalise. Evidence suggests that babbling increases when it results in adult smiles, strokes and so on (see Chapter 33, page 286). The mother's delight on hearing her child's first real word is exciting for the child, and so acquiring language becomes reinforcing in itself.

Skinner also believed that *imitation* plays an important role. When children imitate, or produce *echoic responses* of verbal labels (*tacts*), they receive immediate reinforcement in the form of parental approval to the extent that the imitations resemble correct words. As children continue to learn new words and phrases through imitation, so their language becomes progressively more like that of adults (Moerk & Moerk, 1979).

An evaluation of Skinner's theory

Brodbeck & Irwin (1946) found that, compared with institutionalised children who received less attention, children whose parents reinforced their early attempts at meaningful sounds tended to vocalise more. Parents often reinforce children when they imitate adult language, and using *behaviour modification* Lovaas (1987) has shown that selective reinforcement can be used successfully to teach language to emotionally disturbed or developmentally delayed children (see Chapters 74 and

80). However, Skinner's views have been challenged by a number of researchers.

Box 34.1   Does selective reinforcement have any influence on children's grammar?

- Mothers respond to the 'truth value' or presumed meaning of their children's language rather than to its grammatical correctness or complexity. Mothers extract meaning from, and interpret, their children's incomplete and sometimes primitive sentences (Brown *et al.*, 1969).

- Tizard *et al.* (1972) argue that attempts to correct grammatical mistakes or teach grammar have very little effect (see also Chapter 33, page 289). Indeed, vocabulary develops more slowly in children of mothers who systematically correct poor word pronunciation and reward good pronunciation (Nelson, 1973).

- Slobin (1975) found that children learn grammatical rules *despite* their parents, who usually pay little attention to the grammatical structure of their children's speech and, often reinforce *incorrect* grammar. According to Slobin:

  'a mother is too engaged in interacting with her child to pay attention to the linguistic form of [its] utterances'.

These studies suggest that whilst parents usually respond to (or reinforce) true statements and criticise or correct false ones, they pay little regard to grammatical correctness. Even if they do, this has little effect on language development.

Imitation's role in language development has also been criticised. Whilst imitation must be involved in the learning of accent and vocabulary, its role in complex aspects of language (syntax and semantics) is less obvious. As was seen in Chapter 33 (see page 288), when children do imitate adult sentences, they tend to reduce or convert them to their own currently operating grammar. So, between 18 and 30 months, the child's imitations are as telegraphic as its own spontaneous speech. Furthermore, since at least some adult language is ungrammatical, imitation alone cannot explain how children ever learn 'correct language'. Even if we do not always speak grammatically ourselves, we still know the difference between good and bad grammar.

In response to these criticisms, Bandura (1977) has broadened the concept of imitation. He accepts that the *exact* imitation of particular sentences plays a relatively minor role in language development, but argues that children may imitate the *general* form of sentences, and fill in these general forms with various words. *Deferred imitations* are those word sequences and language structures stored in a child's memory for long periods before being used (and are often used in the same situation in which they were first heard). *Expanded imitations* are repetitions of sentences or phrases not present in the original form (Snow, 1983). Children's language production sometimes exceeds their competence in that they imitate forms of language they do not understand. By storing examples of adult language in memory, children have a sort of 'delayed replay' facility that enables them to produce language forms after they have been acquired.

Box 34.2   Some reasons for disputing learning theory's explanation of language development

There are at least four reasons for disputing the value of attempts to explain language development in learning theory terms.

- If language is established through reinforcement, we would expect that all children living under widely varying social conditions would acquire language in different ways. The existence of a culturally universal and invariant sequence in the stages of language development, which occurs under highly variable conditions, contradicts this. Indeed, even children born to, and raised by, deaf parents apparently acquire language in the same sequence as other children (Slobin, 1986).

- Learning theory cannot explain the *creativity of language*, that is, native speakers' ability to produce and understand an infinitely large number of sentences never heard or produced before by anyone. As Chomsky (1968) states:

  'the normal use of language is innovative, in the sense that much of what we say in the course of normal language use is entirely new [and] not a repetition of anything that we have heard before'.

- Learning theory has difficulty explaining children's spontaneous use of grammatical rules which they have never heard or been taught. These rules are often overgeneralised and incorrectly used, and (as noted in Box 34.1) children are largely impervious to parental attempts to correct grammatical errors.

- Learning theory cannot account for children's ability to understand sentence as opposed to word meaning. A sentence's meaning is not simply the sum of the meanings of the individual words. The structure of language is comparable to the structure of perception as described by the Gestalt psychologists (Neisser, 1967: see Chapter 21). Learning theory might account for how children learn the meaning of individual nouns and verbs since these have an obvious reference. It cannot, however, explain acquisition of the meaning of grammatical terms.

Chomsky's LAD and the biological approach

Although language cannot develop without some form of environmental input, Chomsky (1957, 1965, 1968), Lenneberg (1967) and McNeill (1970) believe that environmental factors could never explain language development adequately. According to Chomsky, children are born already programmed to formulate and understand all types of sentences even though they have never heard them before.

Chomsky proposed the existence of an innate *language acquisition device* (LAD). According to Whitehurst (1982), the LAD provides children with an 'internal street map' of language and enables them, for example, to distinguish between verbs (what things do) and nouns (the things themselves).

Chomsky (1957) argues that language is much more complex and much less predictable than Skinner believed. Central to his theory of *transformational grammar* (TG) are *phrase-structure rules*, which specify what are and are not acceptable utterances in a speaker's native language. When applied systematically, these rules generate sentences in English (or any other language: see Figure 34.1).

Whilst phrase-structure rules specify *some* important aspects of language, they do not specify them all (Chomsky, 1957). Some sentences (such as 'A small boy helped the girl') share the *same* meaning as other sentences (such as 'The girl was helped by a small boy') but have *different* phrase structures. Also, two sentences (such as 'Performing fleas can be amusing' and 'Playing tiddlywinks can be amusing') may have the *same* superficial structure but *different* meanings. In the first example, 'performing' describes the fleas, whereas in the second, 'playing' is a verb. As a result, the word 'are' can replace 'can be' in the first example but not in the second. The reverse is true for the word 'is'. Finally, certain sentences (such as 'The missionary was ready to eat') can have ambiguous meanings.

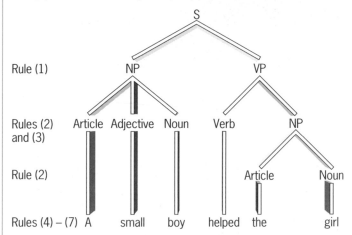

Rule (1) An S (sentence) consists of (or can be broken down into) NP (noun phrase) and VP (verb phrase)

Rule (2) NP ——→ Article + (Adjective) + Noun

(The brackets denote 'optional')

Rule (3) VP ——→ Verb + NP

Rule (4) Article ——→ a(n), the

Rule (5) Adjective ——→ big, small, red, etc.

Rule (6) Noun ——→ boy, girl, stone, etc.

Rule (7) Verb ——→ hit, threw, helped, etc.

} These are *Lexical Rewrite Rules*.

The commas imply that only *one* word should be selected from the list

Figure 34.1   Some of Chomsky's phrase-structure rules and an example of a sentence produced by using them

Box 34.3   Deep structure and surface structure, and transformational grammar

Chomsky distinguished between a sentence's *deep structure* and its *surface structure*. A sentence's surface structure is its grammatical structure (the actual words or phrases used). Its deep structure more or less corresponds to the sentence's meaning. Chomsky argued that when we hear a spoken sentence, we do not 'process' or retain its surface structure but transform it into its deep structure. Chomsky called the understanding or knowledge of how to transform a sentence's meaning into the words that make it up (and vice versa), *transformational grammar* (TG). This understanding or knowledge is an innate *language acquisition device* and is what enables us to produce an infinite number of meaningful sentences.

A single surface structure may have more than one deep structure, as in the sentence 'The missionary was ready to eat'. In one representation it is the missionary who is ready to consume a meal, whilst in another the missionary has been made ready for consumption by others. Conversely, different surface structures can have the same deep structure (as in the sentences 'A small boy helped the girl' and 'The girl was helped by a small boy').

Figure 34.2 As 'New Labour' took over from 'Old Labour', two veteran socialists (Arthur Scargill and Tony Benn) contemplated the party's future. Scargill's question has two deep structures and, given all the 'Old Labour' policies that have, along with Scargill and Benn, been put in the dustbin, we might expect Benn's reply simply to be 'No'. Benn's reply to the alternative deep structure is out of context and hence the cartoon is funny

For Chomsky, children are equipped with the ability to learn the rules for transforming deep structure into various surface structures, and they do this by looking for certain kinds of linguistic features common to all languages, such as the use of consonants and vowels, syllables, modifiers and so on. Collectively, these linguistic features provide the deep structure.

Chomsky calls these features *linguistic universals*. They must be universal because all children can learn with equal ease any language to which they are exposed. So, a child born in England of English parents who went to live in China soon after birth would learn Chinese if brought up by a Chinese-speaking family just as easily as a native-born Chinese child. Chomsky argues that only some kind of LAD can account for children's learning and knowledge of grammatical rules in view of the often ungrammatical and incomplete samples of speech they hear.

Chomsky did not suggest that we go through the procedures of phrase structure and TG each time we prepare to speak a sentence (Hampson & Morris, 1996). For Chomsky, a language's grammar is an idealised description of the *linguistic competence* of its native speakers. Any model of how this competence is applied in actual *performance* must acknowledge certain psychologically relevant factors such as memory, attention, the workings of the nervous system and so on (Lyons, 1970).

Box 34.4 Some evidence supporting Chomsky's theory

- The human vocal organs, breathing apparatus, auditory system and brain are all specialised for spoken communication.

- Babies as young as two days old can discriminate between 'ba' and 'pa' sounds (Eimas, 1975). According to Chomsky, these phonetic discriminations can be thought of as the first linguistic universals the baby discovers.

- All adult languages appear to have certain linguistic universals and TG is acquired in some form by all people (unless brain damaged or reared in isolation) irrespective of their culture and despite enormous variations in the ability to learn other skills (Lenneberg, 1967). The fact that a person with an IQ of 50 may have difficulty in learning simple tasks but still learns to talk, indicates that language develops independently of factors that affect the learning of those tasks. For Lenneberg, this shows that language acquisition must be controlled by genetic factors that are (at least partially) independent of those controlling general intelligence.

- Some twin studies have revealed the existence of a 'private language', intelligible only to the twins (Malmstrom & Silva, 1986). Likewise, studies of some deaf children in Nicaragua have revealed a parallel phenomenon with sign language (Gerrard, 1997). These languages are apparently not a variation of ordinary language, but have the characteristics of ordinary languages (such as verbs, nouns and syntax). This supports the view that knowledge of syntax is innate.

- Studies of congenitally deaf children have shown the emergence of 'gestural language' even though the children received no encouragement or training from their parents (Goldin-Meadow & Feldman, 1977). This suggests that language is very difficult to suppress even in adverse environmental circumstances, provided the individual has someone with whom to communicate.

Lenneberg has argued that the years leading to puberty constitute a *critical period* for language development, based on the still-developing brain's relative lack of specialisation. Children born brain damaged and who lose their language abilities can relearn at least some of them because other, non-damaged, parts of the brain seem to take over. However, adolescents or adults who experience an equivalent amount of damage are unable to regain abilities corresponding to the site of the injury because the brain is now specialised (or 'committed') and no longer 'plastic' (see Chapter 8, page 72). Evidence exists, however, which suggests that the first ten years or so may not necessarily be the critical period Lenneberg has argued for.

Box 34.5   The case of Genie (Curtiss, 1977)

Genie was an American child raised in conditions of extreme (de)privation until her discovery at the age of 13 years and seven months. Amongst other appalling treatment, Genie was beaten if she made any noise, and had learned to suppress almost all vocalisations except for a whimper. According to Curtiss, 'Genie was unsocialised, primitive, hardly human'.

Genie could understand a handful of words (including 'rattle', 'bunny' and 'red') but always responded to them in the same way. Essentially, then, she had to learn language at the age of nearly 14. She never developed normal language skills, and by age 18 could produce only short sentences which lacked important aspects of grammar (such as the use of pronouns).

Her vocabulary expanded and she could hold a conversation, but her use of intonation was poor and only those who knew her well could understand much of what she said. Genie herself had great difficulty in understanding complex syntax. Nonetheless, the fact that she was capable of learning any language at all weakens Lenneberg's claim for a critical period. However, her obvious linguistic retardation is consistent with the existence of a *sensitive period* for language development.

AN EVALUATION OF CHOMSKY'S THEORY

If phrase structure and TG do describe language, it is not unreasonable to investigate whether the actual processes involved in preparing to speak actually follow the same steps. In general, investigations have failed to find strong evidence for the application of Chomsky's rules when people speak and listen (Hampson & Morris, 1996).

Aitchison (1983) agrees with Chomsky's claim that children are 'wired' with the knowledge that language is rule-governed, and that they make a succession of hypotheses about the rules underlying speech. However, she disputes the claim that the LAD also consists of TG (what she calls 'Content Cuthbert'). Aitchison prefers a process approach in which children are seen as having inbuilt puzzle-solving equipment which enables them to process linguistic data along with other sorts of data ('Process Peggy').

By contrast, Chomsky (1979) argues that an innate language ability exists *independently* of other innate abilities, because the mind is constructed of 'mental organs' which are:

> 'just as specialised and differentiated as those of the body ... and ... language is a system easy to isolate among the various mental faculties'.

Some alternatives to learning theory and biological approaches

Recently, there has been a growing acceptance that neither learning theory nor nativist approaches offers a complete account of language development. Instead, an integrated view maintains that children cannot acquire language until an appropriate maturational level has been reached, but that language development is more closely related to environmental input and cognitive development than Chomsky proposes. Maratsos (1983) has identified several assumptions made by *integrative theorists*.

Box 34.6   Some assumptions made by integrative theorists

- Children are highly motivated to communicate and therefore are *active* rather than *passive* language learners.

- Children can learn the major aspects of grammar because they have already acquired important concepts on which grammar is based (namely that events involve agents, actions, objects of actions and so on). For this reason, learning a grammar does not require much information processing.

- Other aspects of language can be explained by the language parents use to talk to children.

- Those grammatical rules that do not fit in with children's natural cognitive processes, and are not conveyed adequately through parental input, are unnatural and difficult for the child. They are also acquired very late (such as the passive voice in English).

THE LANGUAGE AND SOCIAL-INTERACTION APPROACH

One alternative explanation of the rule-bound nature of children's speech, which represents a departure from the grammatical competence approach inspired by Chomsky, is that it arises from the child's *pre-linguistic knowledge*. During the 1970s, psychologists began to look at language development in the first 12 to 18 months of life because the basic skills acquired then contribute substantially to the syntactic skills characteristic of adult language.

A purely syntactic analysis of language cannot explain how children 'discover' their language, that is, how they learn that there is such a thing as language which can be used for communicating, categorising, problem-solving and so on. However, Smith & Cowie's (1991) *language and social-interaction approach* sees language as being used to communicate needs and intentions and as an enjoyable means of entering into a community.

Several studies have indicated how babies initially master a social world onto which they later 'map' language. Snow (1977), for example, notes that adults tend to attach meaning to a baby's sounds and utterances. As a result, burps, grunts, giggles and so on are interpreted as expressions of intent and feeling, as are non-verbal communications (such as smiling and eye contact). Snow sees this as a kind of primitive conversation (or *proto-conversation*) which has a rather one-sided quality in that it requires a 'generous' adult attributing some kind of intended meaning to the baby's sounds and non-verbal behaviours. From this perspective, the infant is an inadequate conversational partner.

Box 34.7 Visual co-orientation and formats: two-way interaction

Much more two-way exchanges are *visual co-orientation* (or joint attention) and *formats* (Collis & Schaffer, 1975). Visual co-orientation involves two individuals coming to focus on some common object. This puts an infant's environmental explorations into a social context, so that an infant-object situation is converted into an infant-object-mother situation (Schaffer, 1989). The joint attention this entails provides opportunities for learning how to do things. So, as parents and children develop their mutual patterns of interaction and share attention to objects, some activities recur, as happens in joint picture-book reading.

Bruner (1975, 1978) uses Collis and Schaffer's term 'formats' to refer to rule-bound activity routines in which the infant has many opportunities to relate language to familiar play (as when the mother inserts name labels into a game or activity), initially in *indicating* formats and later in *requesting* them. These ritualised exchanges stress the need for *turn-taking* and so help the baby to discover the social function of communication. As a result, the infant can learn about the structures and demands of social interaction, and prepare and rehearse the skills that will eventually become essential to successful interchanges such as conversation.

LASS: THE ACTIVE ADULT

According to Bruner (1983), formats comprise the *language acquisition support system* (LASS). He is concerned with the pragmatics and functions of language (what language is used for). In Bruner's view:

> 'entry into language is entry into discourse that requires both members of a dialogue pair to interpret a communication and its intent. Learning a language ... consists of learning not only the grammar of a particular language, but also learning how to realise one's intentions by the appropriate use of that grammar'.

The emphasis on intent requires a far more active role on the adult's part in helping a child's language acquisition than just being a 'model' or providing the input for the child's LAD. According to Moerk (1989), 'the LAD was a lady', that is, the lady who does most of the talking to the child (namely its mother). Mothers simplify linguistic input and break it down into helpful, illustrative segments for the child to practise and build on. This view sees language development as a very sophisticated extension of the processes of meaningful interaction that the caregiver and child have constructed over several months (Durkin, 1995).

THE ACTIVE CHILD

Another way of looking at the 'partnership' between adults and infants is to see the infant (rather than the adult) as being the more 'active' partner in their relationship. The view of language as a *cause–effect analytic device* has been summarised by Gauker (1990), according to whom:

'the fundamental function of words is to bring about changes in the speaker's environment ... Linguistic understanding consists of a grasp of these causal relations'.

Box 34.8   The emergence of communicative intentionality

According to Gauker (1990), language comprises a set of symbols whose use results in a change of behaviour in the listener. The use of words as communicative tools is shown in the *emergence of communicative intentionality*. During the pre-linguistic stage, children have no awareness that they can gain a desired effect indirectly by changing somebody else's behaviour. So, they may cry and reach for something but not direct the cry towards the caregiver or look back at the caregiver. The cry merely expresses frustration and is not a communicative signal designed to affect the other's behaviour. This 'analysis' of means–ends relationships (what causes what) solely as a product of one's own actions, is called *first-order causality*.

The emergence of communicative intentionality involves *second-order causality*, the awareness that it *is* possible to bring about a desired goal by using another person as a tool. Pointing gestures and glances now rapidly proliferate as a means of asking others to look at or act upon an object. According to Savage-Rumbaugh (1990), the child is beginning to understand in a general sense:

'that it is possible to "cause" others to engage in desired actions through the mechanism of communication about those actions'.

(Based on Gauker, 1990)

This use of animate tools (other people) parallels the use of inanimate tools (physical objects), and this is an important feature of what Piaget (1952) calls *sensorimotor intelligence* (see Chapter 41). Some kind of *instrumental understanding* (what leads to what) seems to underlie both activities.

It is, however, more difficult to analyse language *comprehension* in terms of a cause–effect analysis than it is to analyse *language production*, since what do we cause to happen when we understand things that have been said to us? Based on her work with chimpanzees, Savage-Rumbaugh (1990) concludes that language comprehension is clearly the driving force underlying the language acquisition process, and that under normal circumstances, language production is just one outcome of the development of language comprehension.

PIAGET AND LANGUAGE DEVELOPMENT

According to Piaget (1952), the growth of language can be predicted from an understanding of children's cognitive skills. He believed that children must first understand concepts before they can use words that describe them. Piaget's views are an important contribution to the debate concerning the language and thought relationship (see Chapter 37).

Conclusions

Explanations of language development range from accounts based on conditioning to the view that language is biologically determined. The evidence suggests that conditioning accounts are unlikely to be true. However, whilst biologically based accounts are probably closer to the truth, it is unlikely that they offer a complete account of language development.

Summary

■ In **classical conditioning** accounts, certain sounds (words) become **conditioned stimuli** through repeatedly being paired with particular **unconditioned stimuli**, such as the mother's actions or physical objects.

■ According to Skinner, verbal behaviour is acquired through **operant conditioning**. Whilst cooing and babbling are probably inborn, adults **shape** these into words by **reinforcing** sounds which approximate real words. Selective reinforcement shapes words into grammatically correct sentences.

■ Children whose parents reinforce their early attempts at meaningful sounds tend to vocalise more, compared with institutionalised children. Also, Lovaas has used **behaviour modification** to teach language to emotionally disturbed or developmentally delayed children.

■ However, mothers respond to the 'truth value' of their children's language rather than to its grammatical correctness or complexity, and children learn grammatical rules **despite** their parents, who often reinforce incorrect grammar. Attempts to correct grammatical mistakes have little effect and may even slow down vocabulary development.

■ Whilst **imitation** is necessary for the learning of accent and vocabulary, it cannot explain the development of syntax and semantics, and imitation of adult speech reflects the child's currently operating grammar. However, children may imitate the **general** forms of sentences and then fill these in with various words. Snow distinguishes between **deferred** and **expanded imitations**.

■ Learning theory cannot explain the culturally universal and invariant sequence in the stages of language development. It also fails to explain the **creativity of language**, children's spontaneous use of grammatical rules never heard or taught, and their ability to understand the meaning of sentences.

■ Chomsky, Lenneberg and McNeill argue that environmental input is an inadequate explanation of language development. According to Chomsky, children are innately equipped with a **language acquisition device** (LAD) which consists essentially of **transformational grammar** (TG).

■ Central to TG are **phrase-structure rules**. However, these cannot specify **all** aspects of languages and Chomsky distinguishes between a sentence's **surface** and **deep structure**. TG enables us to transform one into the other.

■ LAD is used to look for **linguistic universals**, such as consonants and vowels, syllables, and modifiers. Collectively, these provide the deep structure. Linguistic universals must exist because children can learn any language to which they are exposed with equal ease and a LAD is needed to account for children's learning of grammatical rules despite exposure to limited and often ungrammatical speech.

■ All adult languages have certain linguistic universals, and TG is acquired by everyone, including those with very low IQs. Language acquisition is probably controlled by genetic factors distinct from those controlling general intelligence.

■ Deaf twins' 'private language' supports the claim that humans are born with some knowledge of syntax. Studies of 'gestural language' in congenitally deaf children suggest that language is very difficult to suppress, even in adverse environmental conditions.

■ Lenneberg's proposed **critical period** is based on the finding that only in adolescents and adults does brain damage cause permanent loss of the corresponding abilities, since the brain is now specialised, unlike the child's 'plastic' brain. However, the case of Genie suggests that the idea of a **sensitive period** might be more valid.

■ Aitchison disputes Chomsky's claim that LAD comprises **both** a hypothesis-making device **and** TG ('Content Cuthbert'). She prefers 'Process Peggy', according to which linguistic data are just one kind of data to which inbuilt puzzle-solving equipment is applied. Chomsky believes that innate language ability represents an **independent** 'mental organ', distinct from other innate abilities.

■ According to **integrative theorists**, children are **active** learners of language whose learning of grammar is based on important concepts already acquired. The **language and social-interaction approach** represents an alternative to Chomsky's views and emphasises children's **pre-linguistic knowledge**. Language is used to communicate needs and intentions and is an enjoyable means of entering into a community.

■ Babies initially master a social world onto which they later 'map' language, as demonstrated by **proto-conversations**. More two-way exchanges include **visual co-orientation** and **formats**, the latter comprising the **language acquisition support system (LASS)**, which reflects how we use appropriate grammar in order to realise our intentions.

■ Seeing language as a **cause–effect analytic device** depicts the child as a more 'active' partner, using words as a tool for bringing about a change in the listener's behaviour. The **emergence of communicative intentionality** involves **second-order causality** (the use of other people as tools). It parallels the use of physical objects, an important feature of Piaget's **sensorimotor intelligence**. Children must first understand concepts before they can use words that describe them.

299

35

SOME ASPECTS OF READING AND WRITING

Introduction and overview

According to Massaro (1989), a literate person faced with a written word is captured by it and seems to have no choice but to read it. One experimental demonstration of this was provided by Stroop (1935) who showed that when the name of a colour is written in a different colour, it is difficult to name the colour but ignore the word (see Box 26.3, page 222). This indicates that reading is such an overlearned skill that it is not easily 'put on hold' (Massaro, 1989). The first part of this chapter considers some of the research into the processes involved in reading.

Complementary to the cognitive skill of reading is writing. Writing is the production and organisation of connected discourse and, like reading, is almost always meaningful (Gagné, 1985). The second part of this chapter focuses on the cognitive processes involved in writing.

Some basic findings in reading research

Reading is 'a meaningful interpretation of written or printed verbal symbols' (Harris & Sipey, 1983). Research into how this meaningful interpretation is made began in the 1870s with the invention of the *tachistoscope* (see Chapter 27, page 229), and the discovery of *saccadic eye movements*. Prior to this, it had been assumed that the eye moved smoothly and continuously across the page, identifying each letter as it appeared. However, the eye makes a series of start-stop jumps across a line of print (*saccades)* and *fixations* (the periods of time in which the eyes are at rest: see Box 35.1).

PHONOLOGICAL MEDIATION

When we are reading, we sometimes hear an 'inner voice', which speaks the words written on a page. One of the oldest questions in reading research is whether printed language must be translated into some form of speech *before* meaning can be accessed (*phonological mediation*). The view that reading could be dependent on cognitive processes, which interpret the words we hear, is supported by the 'inner voice' experience and by the finding

---

Box 35.1   Saccades and fixations

Although there are several methods for investigating reading, the study of eye movements during the silent reading of words is generally accepted as being the best currently available.

Each saccade takes only a few milliseconds and covers about seven to nine characters on a line (Just & Carpenter, 1984). The eye is essentially 'blind' during a saccade, and the most important information is processed during fixations.

Fixations last about 250 milliseconds (equivalent to about eight letters or spaces) and take up more than 90 per cent of total reading time. For a typical line of print, about five or six fixations are made (Rayner & Sereno, 1994). Although our *perceptual span* (or 'effective field of view': Eysenck & Keane, 1995) can be limited by factors such as print size, the maximal span is around three or four letters to the left of the fixation and in the region of 15 letters to the right. This is reversed in people whose language reads from right to left (Pollatsek *et al.*, 1981).

Whilst most of our eye movements are forward towards new words, some are backward to earlier words (*regression*).

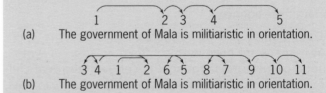

(a)   The government of Mala is militiaristic in orientation.

(b)   The government of Mala is militiaristic in orientation.

Figure 35.1   Regressions occur in about ten to 20 per cent of eye movements in skilled readers. In poor readers, regressions occur much more frequently. The figure shows the sequence of fixations for a skilled reader (a) and an unskilled reader (b)

---

that we can use phonological mediation for reading unfamiliar words (such as 'the kurnel sailed his yott': Hampson & Morris, 1996). However, our ability to use phonological mediation does not necessarily mean that it is the basis of all reading. It may, however, be a useful way of tackling unfamiliar words (Hampson & Morris, 1996).

Models of word recognition

Several studies have investigated whether or not the recognition of a word first involves identifying the letters that compose it. Whilst research (e.g. Cosky, 1976; Reicher, 1969) suggests that this is not necessary, theories of word recognition assume that letter recognition is involved in the process of identifying words.

Word identification is a generally automatic process, taking about 50 milliseconds (Rayner & Sereno, 1994). As well as involving recognition of letters, word identification may also involve *spelling* (or *orthographic*) *regularities*, a word's *shape, familiarity* and, in unskilled readers or poorly presented text, *context* (Ellis, 1993; Hampson & Morris, 1996). As seen above, evidence also suggests that some information about word sound is available during reading, and that such phonological information can play a role in identifying rare as opposed to common words.

Several models try to explain how word identification occurs, all assuming the existence of some form of representation of words known by us, and that this representation must be activated for identification to occur (Hampson & Morris, 1996).

THE LOGOGEN MODEL

According to Morton's (1964, 1969) *logogen model of word recognition*, each word a person knows has a representation (or logogen) in LTM (see Chapter 29, page 246). A logogen for a given word has a *resting level of activity* which can be increased by stimulus events (such as hearing or seeing the word). When the activity level exceeds a logogen's threshold, the logogen fires and the word is recognised. Because high-frequency words are recognised more quickly than low-frequency words (Frederikson & Kroll, 1976), high-frequency words either have a lower threshold of activation or their meaning can be checked more quickly once the logogen has fired (Morton, 1979).

THE COHORT MODEL

An influential approach to the recognition of spoken words, which has also been applied to reading, is the *cohort model* (Marslen-Wilson, 1984). Words are recognised letter by letter in a left-right manner, and word recognition occurs by means of the elimination of alternative word candidates (or cohorts). Thus, the recognition of the first letter in the word eliminates all words that do not have that letter in their initial position. Recognition of the second letter eliminates the remaining cohorts that do not have the second letter in the second position and so on, until only one word remains. This is the point at which word recognition occurs.

THE INTERACTIVE-ACTIVATION MODEL

Rumelhart & McClelland's (1982) *interactive-activation model* proposes the existence of three types of recognition unit. The first detects the various features of letters such as vertical and horizontal lines. The second detects the letter represented by the combination of letter features. When a letter is recognised as appearing in a particular position in a word, the recognition units for all words which have that letter in a particular position are activated, whilst all other word units are inhibited. Following the activation of the word units which have all of the letters making up a particular word and which appear in a particular position, integration occurs in which 'only one word wins and stays active' (Hampson & Morris, 1996).

Comparing the models

Available evidence does not yet generally favour one model over another, and all can claim some experimental support. However, much of the evidence concerning the information used in word recognition comes from studies in which one word is read at a time, and such information may not be necessary to normal reading (Hampson & Morris, 1996). Thus, the processes involved in reading clearly printed continuous text, at the reader's own pace, may differ from those used when one word is flashed briefly via a tachistoscope or on a computer screen.

Comprehension

Whilst models of word recognition are important, they tell us little about the comprehension of written language. As Massaro (1989) has noted:

> 'the leap from recognition [a *bottom-up process*: see Chapter 21] to comprehension [a *top-down process*: see Chapter 21] requires certain cognitive prerequisites on the part of the reader. The text must be capable of activating the appropriate knowledge to effect understanding of the message'.

When we read, we draw *inferences* to help our understanding, and use our knowledge and expectations to 'fill in the gaps' (Schank & Abelson, 1977: see Chapter 29).

Bransford & Johnson (1972) found that a particular prose passage (see Box 29.8) was rated as incomprehensible by participants given the passage in isolation, and that their subsequent recall of it was poor. However, if the theme 'washing clothes' was provided, it was rated as being more comprehensible and was better recalled. Text comprehension, then, depends on activating appropriate knowledge sources. Consider, for example, the passage shown in Box 35.2 which was presented to participants by Bransford (1979).

Box 35.2   The passage used in Bransford's (1979) experiment

The man was worried. His car came to a halt and he was all alone. It was extremely dark and cold. The man took off his overcoat, rolled down the window and got out of the car as quickly as possible. Then he used all his strength to move as fast as he could. He was relieved when he finally saw the lights of the city, even though they were far away.

You will probably agree that the passage makes sense, but can you explain *why* the man took off his overcoat or rolled down the window? The actions only make sense if the car is submerged in water. So, whilst we may feel we know something's meaning, we may actually know only a little or nothing!

Towards a theory of reading

According to Just & Carpenter's (1980, 1992) model, the reader encounters new information through reading and, after extracting a word's physical features, assigns preliminary meaning to it instead of storing it for later processing. The word is then integrated with the material that has previously been read and if the sentence is ended, its meaning is assimilated.

Both LTM and working memory (WM: see Chapter 27) contribute to the reading process, although the main activities of reading (like other cognitive processes) occur in WM. Thus, our schemata affect both the information we take in and how we take it in (the way in which we read). Also, our existing knowledge is modified and transformed by the new content. Like other cognitive processes, then, reading is a *dynamic* process, and the meaning obtained is influenced by the content, prior knowledge, goals and context.

The claim that the processes required to understand each word and its relationship to other words are carried out as soon as a word is encountered is called the *immediacy*

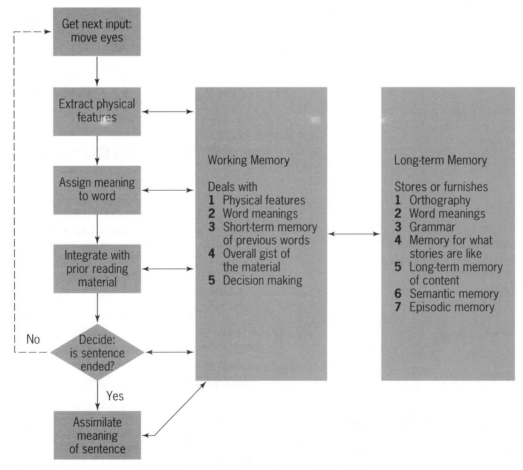

Figure 35.2   Just and Carpenter's model of the cognitive processes in reading

assumption, and is held to occur because of WM's limited capacity. According to Just and Carpenter, individual differences in WM capacity influence how well language is comprehended. Whilst the finding that readers sometimes move their eyes *back* to an earlier part of the text and sometimes *fixate* the same word more than once, casts doubt on the immediacy assumption, the assumption about WM is better supported.

Box 35.3   Reading span

One measure of WM capacity is *reading span*, defined as the largest number of sentences for which a person can recall all of the final words more than 50 per cent of the time. Just and Carpenter have found that reading span correlates highly with the ability to comprehend written material, and that people with large reading spans read difficult text faster than those with small reading spans. This suggests that people with more processing resources available can carry out forms of processing that those with fewer resources are unable to do (Eysenck & Keane, 1995).

Unfortunately, other differences in comprehension ability which do not depend solely on WM capacity (such as the ability to reject inappropriate information), and the model's emphasis on WM capacity at the expense of more specific processes involved in comprehension, limit its explanatory power (Eysenck & Keane, 1995).

The model also has little to say about the eye movements that occur during reading. Alternative models of reading (such as the *interactive model* proposed by Rayner & Pollatsek, 1989) do incorporate such findings. However, Rayner and Pollatsek's model says little about other processes in reading, such as drawing inferences. It seems, then, that we are some way from a complete explanation of the cognitive processes involved in reading.

Learning to read

READING READINESS

Harris & Sipey (1983) have argued that learning to read occurs in several stages, beginning with 'reading readiness' and culminating in the refinement of reading skills in school and adulthood.

Box 35.4   When should reading begin?

For Spache (1981), reading readiness consists of a large group of characteristics which include visual skills, auditory factors and 'general coordination'. For Butler *et al.* (1985), it can be defined more narrowly in terms of *critical pre-reading skills,* which include attending to letter order and matching and blending sounds.

There has been much debate about the optimum age at which reading instruction should begin (Chall, 1983). For a long time, Morphett & Washburne's (1931) view that it is best to postpone reading instruction until children reach a mental age of six years and six months was widely held. However, Coltheart (1979) has shown that this 'critical stage of reading readiness' viewpoint is unlikely to be true.

Marsh *et al.* (1981) have identified four stages in learning to read found in British and American schoolchildren. These are *glance and guess, sophisticated guessing, simple grapheme–phoneme correspondence* and *skilled reading*. Frith (1985) has re-described the stages as three skills. The first two correspond to *logographic skills*, which involve the direct recognition of words as wholes. The third stage corresponds to *alphabetic skills*, which involve using the visual correspondence between particular letters and their sounds. The fourth stage corresponds to *orthographic skills*, which involve the use of regularities in the structure of words to obtain their pronunciation.

TEACHING READING

One approach to teaching reading is called the *phonics method*, which emphasises symbol–sound relationships (such as how to pronounce 'sp', 'st' and 'br'). The *whole-word method*, encourages the recognition of words by sight. Chall (1967) analysed 67 studies comparing different approaches to reading and concluded that there was nothing to choose between them.

The debate about which strategy produces a better basis for teaching reading continues (Goswami, 1993), although the balance appears to have tipped in favour of phonic methods. Whilst it is difficult to obtain unambiguous evidence concerning the effectiveness of teaching methods:

'it does appear that teaching phonic methods can benefit rather than harm the new reader' (Hampson & Morris, 1996).

Writing

The evolution of written language is a relatively recent phenomenon. Some psychologists have approached the processes involved in writing by focusing on individual words, the similarities and differences between written languages, and (by studying brain-damaged individuals) the processes involved in spelling (Ellis & Young, 1988). Others have studied writing from a broader perspective. The most influential model of the processes involved in writing is that developed by Hayes & Flower (1980, 1983).

HAYES AND FLOWER'S MODEL OF WRITING

Hayes and Flower's information-processing model of writing emphasises the role of WM, in which three major processes occur: *planning*, *translating* and *reviewing*.

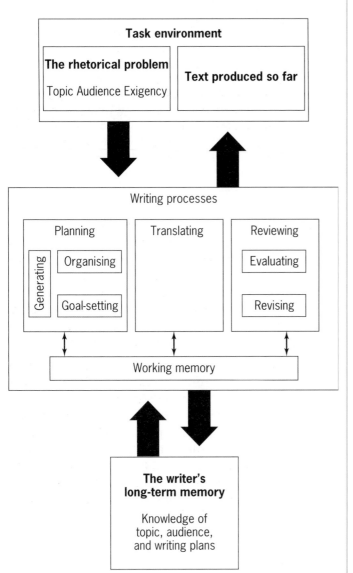

Figure 35.3   Hayes and Flower's model of writing

Planning

This involves setting goals and organising ideas based on information from the *task environment* and LTM. Examples of task environments include an essay set by a

teacher (such as 'Describe and evaluate any two theories of forgetting'), receiving feedback from a teacher (such as 'Your essay lacks evaluation of the theories you describe') and knowledge about the intended audience (such as an examiner or a group of fellow students). The particular task environment will, of course, influence the planning of the writing.

LTM is used in several ways in the planning process. For example, we may use our knowledge of different writing forms to begin an essay with a question or a bold statement. Our knowledge of the audience can also influence planning. We may know that a particular teacher likes to see lots of references to experimental research whilst another likes the use of analogies. Finally, information from LTM may incorporate factual information such as the inclusion of certain procedures which, in the case of an essay on theories of forgetting, have been used to study the phenomenon. Knowledge about writing in general, the particular form that needs to be presented for a given task, the intended audience and specific knowledge about the task, can all influence the quality of planning that occurs (Glover & Bruning, 1987).

Whilst *knowledge* about a particular task influences the plan that is produced (Voss *et al.*, 1980), Figure 35.3 shows three sub-processes that are also involved in planning, namely *generating*, *organising* and *goal-setting*.

Generating refers to obtaining information from LTM relevant to the task in question (such as the names of two theories of forgetting) and the task environment (this essay has to be no longer than 1500 words). *Organising* involves the selection and organisation of information into a writing plan, which can be achieved through the use of *outlines* (Beach & Bridwell, 1984). Thus, an essay on theories of forgetting might begin with an introductory paragraph, a description of one theory, an evaluation of it, a description of a second theory, an evaluation of it, and a concluding paragraph. *Goal-setting* involves evaluating the relevance of available information (an example might be deciding whether to include a lengthy description of a particular study or a summary of its main findings). These three sub-processes are clearly both interactive and interdependent. For example, without being able to generate information, it is unlikely that a goal can be met, and when a goal has been set, this will influence what new information is generated and how it is organised (Glover & Bruning, 1987).

According to Hayes and Flower, skilled and unskilled writers differ in their abilities to plan a written product in terms of the types of goals they set, how they generate ideas and how well these ideas are organised.

Box 35.5   Some individual differences in planning

Setting goals: Skilled writers set themselves the goal of communicating meaning. They also produce more goals and sub-goals than unskilled writers (Hayes & Flower, 1986). The goal of unskilled and immature writers is 'associative writing' or putting down everything in memory that is relevant to a task (Scardamalia & Bereiter, 1987) or avoiding errors (Birnbaum, 1982).

Generating ideas: Skilled writers can think of many ideas relating to what they are writing about (Raphael & Kirschner, 1985). This is not necessarily because unskilled writers run out of ideas, but because they have no 'internal cues' to keep the ideas going (Scardamalia *et al.*, 1982).

Organisation: Organisation is important in communicating meaning. Skilled writers plan the meaning they are going to communicate, whereas unskilled writers focus their planning on the mechanics (Geisler *et al.*, 1985). Skilled writers use *cohesive ties*, that is, linguistic devices for linking one idea to the next (Halliday & Hasan, 1976). Unskilled writers have difficulty in writing cohesively and, in particular, assume that the reader knows what is being referred to even if the referent has never been specified (King & Rentel, 1981). Coherent ties enable sentence organisation. *Coherent structures* enable an *entire* piece of writing to fit together in an organised way (McCutchen & Perfetti, 1982).

Translating

Typically, the plan constructed during the planning process is much shorter than the final product (Hayes & Flower, 1986). Translating (or *sentence generation*) is the process of transforming the writing plan into the actual writing of phrases, either written on paper or stored on computer disk. The starting point for translating is the first part of the writer's plan (such as a definition of the topic in question), which is then transformed into phrases or a sentence. The completion of a sentence is often followed by self-questioning about the next part of the writing plan and how this should be expressed. After the next phrase or sentence has been written, the plan is returned to and, following self-questioning, the process continues in cyclical fashion until the task has been completed.

Translating can stretch WM to its limits, because the writer is trying to keep many things active in memory at once (Gagné, 1985). Unskilled writers need to read what they have just written in order to maintain cohesion whilst skilled writers do not. This may be because skilled writers have cohesive plans (see Box 35.5) or because

more WM is available to 'hold' what has just been written. More WM may be available because skilled writers spell and punctuate automatically. In unskilled writers, the need to constantly check spelling and sentence construction results in the representation of what has just been written being lost.

Box 35.6   Atwell's (1981) study of cohesion during translating

Skilled and unskilled writers were asked to write an essay on a personal topic. For the first half of the writing session, the writers were able to see what they had written. However, for the second half they used *inkless pens*. Their writing was recorded by means of carbon paper, but since the pens contained no ink, the writers could not see what they had written. Writing 'blind' caused a loss of cohesion in the unskilled writers but had little effect on the skilled writers. To maintain cohesion, then, unskilled writers need to read what they have written.

As most students and textbook writers will know, 'getting going' and 'keeping going' are barriers to translating. This *writer's block* has several causes, one of which is the need for more knowledge about the task (a problem with a straightforward solution). Another is the application of *rigid rules*, such as sticking to the original writing plan. However, if the plan is inadequate, the writing process is bound to grind to a halt (Eysenck & Keane, 1995).

Similarly, following certain rules that one has been told to apply may also produce writer's block. Examples include 'always grab the reader's attention immediately', 'begin with a humorous but relevant comment' and 'make at least five evaluative points'. When a task does not lend itself to such rules, it is hardly surprising that writer's block occurs (Rose, 1980). Much more effective are rules which facilitate writing and are not stated in absolute terms, such as '*try to* produce evaluative points in your essay' (Gagné, 1985).

Reviewing

This involves evaluating what has been written to determine how well it meets the set goals. Clearly, the writer's knowledge of writing, especially its mechanical aspects, is an important part of the revision process (and hence reviewing interacts with planning). Those parts considered unsatisfactory are then improved in quality by *reading* and *editing*. Reading involves being sensitive to ideas from the plan that have been omitted, possible superfluous information, and mechanical errors (such as spelling mistakes). In editing, the writer rewrites material, moves it from one place to another and changes writing (hence reviewing also interacts with translating).

Skilled writers are more likely to recognise and overcome coherence and structure-related problems when they review the material than are unskilled writers. They are also more likely to make meaning-related revisions. As a result, they tend to spend *longer* revising material (Hayes *et al.*, 1985). Unskilled writers focus on mechanical errors rather than errors in meaning (Bridwell, 1980) and tend not to make revisions which alter the entire structure of what has been written (Faigley & Witte, 1981).

Hayes and Flower's model proposes that the component skills of planning, translating and reviewing are guided by the *rhetorical problem*, the text that has been produced so far and the writer's LTM. The rhetorical problem is the writer's interpretation of the task and the achievement of the goals that have been set. If the written text does not match the goals, then revision is likely. If, however, the match is a close one then not much revision will be undertaken.

Box 35.7   Some practical applications deriving from Hayes and Flower's model

Setting goals: Effective writing is more likely if clear goals are established. This can be achieved by writing a summary of ideas against which the final product can be compared to assess the extent to which the goals have been met.

Outlining for planning: Given that outlining improves the quality of writing and aids in reviewing the final product, writers should outline what is to be written before writing takes place. Outlining also helps the revision process.

Generating ideas: Since skilled writers can think of many ideas related to a particular task, writers should be encouraged to generate ideas.

Communicating meaning: Writers should be encouraged to plan the meaning of what is to be communicated, rather than concentrate on the mechanics (although these are, of course, important).

Revision: For skilled writers, revision is an important part of the writing process. Revision is particularly useful if a goal has been set and an outline developed, since the criteria set may then be checked (see above).

Correcting and rewriting: Feedback about writing can improve performance if the writer re-submits a piece of work, since this focuses attention on feedback given about the writing and provides practice in writing correctly.

Peer-editing: Revision can also be aided by having colleagues edit the final product for both coherence and mechanics, and by editing the colleagues' work.

Of course, the success of the processes outlined above depends on other factors, such as *resources*, the provision of extensive practice in writing (e.g. regular essay setting) and encouraging writing.

(Adapted from Applebee, 1984, and Glover & Bruning, 1987)

Evaluating Hayes and Flower's model

As the writers of this book are only too painfully aware, writing does not proceed smoothly from planning to translating to reviewing. For example, a brief period of pre-planning may be followed by a writing phase in which the skills of planning, translating and reviewing are employed. Indeed, reviewing may occur *before* writing begins (as when a potential idea is modified) and *during* writing (as when evaluating a point that has been made) as well as at the end of writing. Some researchers dispute whether the three processes identified by Hayes and Flower can *ever* be completely separated from one another.

Eysenck & Keane (1995) have also criticised the model because of its reliance on *protocol analysis* (or *verbal protocols*) as a way of obtaining data. In this, the writer verbalises his or her thoughts as writing takes place. However, this method provides information only about those processes of which there is conscious awareness. Eysenck and Keane argue that there is probably little or no conscious awareness of many (or even most) of the processes involved in writing. Nevertheless, there is general agreement that Hayes and Flower's model has helped our understanding of the writing process.

Conclusions

Both reading and writing are complex skills which are taken for granted. This chapter has reviewed some of the research concerned with understanding the processes involved in those skills. Although much data have been accumulated and several theories advanced to explain them, the complete understanding of the processes involved is still some distance away.

Summary

■ During reading, the eye makes a series of start-stop jumps (**saccades**). The intervals during which the eyes are at rest are called **fixations**. Each saccade takes a few milliseconds, during which the eye is essentially 'blind'.

■ The most important information is processed during fixations, comprising over 90 per cent of total reading time. Whilst most eye movements are forward towards new words, some **regressions** occur, especially in poor readers.

■ The inner-voice experience implies we use **phonological mediation** for reading unfamiliar words. However, it may not be the basis of all reading.

■ Not all letters of a word need to be identified for whole word recognition, but theories of word recognition assume that letter recognition plays some part in word identification. This appears to be automatic, involving letter recognition and **spelling/orthographic regularities**, a word's **shape** and **familiarity**, and, for unskilled readers or poorly presented text, the **context**.

■ Models of word identification all assume that some form of word representation must be activated for identification to occur. These include the **logogen model of word recognition**, the **cohort model** and the **interactive-activation model**. No one model is supported better by evidence than the others, and they tell us little about the **comprehension** of written language. Reading involves drawing **inferences** to aid our understanding.

■ According to Just and Carpenter's model, both LTM and WM contribute to reading, but the main cognitive processes involved occur in WM. Our schemata affect the way we read, and existing knowledge is modified by the new content, making reading a dynamic process. The **immediacy assumption** reflects WM's limited capacity, although backward eye movements and fixations make the assumption doubtful.

■ One measure of WM is **reading span**, which is correlated with the ability to comprehend written material. However, not all differences in comprehension ability can be explained in terms of WM capacity. Also, Just and Carpenter's model says little about eye movements, unlike Rayner and Pollatsek's **interactive model**, although this says little about other processes, such as drawing inferences.

■ 'Reading readiness' has been defined broadly as comprising a large group of visual skills, auditory factors and 'general coordination', and more narrowly in terms of **critical pre-reading skills**.

■ According to Marsh *et al.*, there are four stages in learning to read, namely **glance and guess**, **sophisticated guessing**, **simple grapheme–phoneme correspondence** and **skilled reading**. These have been re-described by Frith as **logographic**, **alphabetic** and **orthographic skills**. On balance, the evidence seems to favour **phonic methods** of teaching reading over the **whole-word method**.

■ Hayes and Flower's **information-processing model** of writing stresses the role of WM in which **planning**, **translating** and **reviewing** take place. These component skills are guided by the **rhetorical problem**, the **text** produced so far and the writer's **LTM**.

■ **Planning** involves setting goals and organising ideas on information from the **task environment** and **LTM**. Quality of planning is affected by several factors and the interacting and interdependent sub-process of **generating**, **organising** and **goal-setting**.

■ Skilled writers set themselves the goal of communicating meaning and produce more goals and sub-goals. Unskilled/immature writers produce 'associative writing' and try to avoid errors. Skilled writers plan the meaning of what they are going to write, using **cohesive ties** and **coherent structures**.

■ **Translating/sentence generation** involves transforming the (shorter) writing plan into the (longer) actual writing. There is a continuous process of writing followed by referral back to the plan until the task is completed. Translating can stretch WM to its limits, especially in unskilled writers.

■ **Reviewing/revision** involves evaluating what has been written in terms of the goals set. There is interaction between revision and planning, and improvements are made based on **reading** and **editing**. Skilled writers are more likely to make meaning-related revisions, whilst unskilled writers focus on mechanical errors.

■ Writing does not proceed from planning to translating to reviewing, as the model predicts, and it may not be possible to completely separate these processes. Also the model relies on **protocol analysis/verbal protocols**, which can only tap processes of which the writer is consciously aware.

36

PROBLEM-SOLVING AND DECISION-MAKING

Introduction and overview

The basic cognitive processes considered in the previous chapters are all aspects of 'thought'. However, there is more to thinking than perception, attention, memory and language. Two closely related aspects of thinking of interest to cognitive psychologists are problem-solving and decision-making. This chapter considers research into the processes involved in solving problems and making decisions.

The nature of problems

STAGES IN PROBLEM-SOLVING (PS)

A problem is a situation in which there is a discrepancy between a present state and some goal state, with no obvious way of reducing it. PS is an attempt to reduce the discrepancy and achieve the goal state, and progresses through a series of logical stages (Bourne *et al.*, 1979). These are *defining or representing the problem, generating possible solutions* and *evaluating possible solutions*. Some researchers have claimed that there is an *incubation stage* (in which no attempt is made to solve the problem) occurring between the generating and evaluating stages. Others suggest that incubation typically occurs after preparation (Wallas, 1926).

REPRESENTING AND DEFINING PROBLEMS

How problems are represented (such as in verbal, visual or mathematical form), their form of presentation and our ability to 'weed out' unimportant information can all influence the understanding of a problem (Duncker, 1945; Simon & Hayes, 1976). Ill-defined problems are more difficult to solve than well-defined ones, and complex problems are more difficult to solve than simple ones (Matlin, 1989).

Once we understand a problem, we can *generate possible solutions*. Sometimes, finding a solution is straightforward, and simply involves retrieving information from LTM. On other occasions, certain tendencies and biases operate which lead us to overlook potential solutions and so we 'get stuck'. This is why generating lots of possible solutions can be useful in some contexts.

Once possible solutions have been generated, they can be *evaluated*. As with generating solutions, the evaluation of solutions is sometimes straightforward, especially when the problem is clearly defined or represented. With unclear or poorly defined problems, though, the generated solutions are typically difficult to evaluate. Also, the various stages in PS do not necessarily occur in a fixed order, and we may move between stages or go back to the defining or representing stage.

TYPES OF PROBLEMS

Garnham (1988) distinguishes between two broad classes of problem, *adversary* and *non-adversary*. Adversary problems are those in which two or more people compete for success, as in chess. In non-adversary problems, other people are involved only as problem setters for the problem solver.

PS: from behaviourism to information-processing

According to behaviourists, PS is essentially a matter of *trial-and-error* and *accidental success* (Thorndike, 1911: see Chapter 32). Behaviourists argued that as acquired habits are learned, so PS (essentially a chain of stimulus–response associations) improves. Whilst trial-and-error can be effective in solving some problems, the behaviourist approach was challenged by *Gestalt psychologists*. They maintained that our perceptions are organised according to the laws of proximity, closure, similarity and so on (see Chapter 21).

The Gestalt approach to PS was to look at how we impose *structure* on a problem by understanding how its elements are related to one another. Thus, rather than being 'senseless drill and arbitrary associations' (as Katona, 1940, argued was the case with the behaviourist approach), PS is held to occur through *meaningful apprehension of relations*.

Gestalt psychologists distinguished between *reproductive thinking* and *productive thinking* (Maier, 1931). In reproductive thinking, past solutions are applied to new problems. Whilst past experience can lead to success, it can also hinder PS (see below). In productive thinking, problems are solved by the principle of *reorganisation*, or solving a problem by perceiving new relationships among its elements.

Consider, for example, trying to arrange six matchsticks into four equilateral triangles with each side equal to one stick. If you try to arrange the matchsticks by pushing them around on a table, the problem cannot be solved. Through reorganisation, though, and realisation that the matchsticks do not *have* to be arranged in two dimensions, the problem can be solved (as shown in Figure 36.4 on page 315). The principle of reorganisation is similar to what Köhler (1925) called *insight* in his studies of PS in chimpanzees.

Box 36.1   Köhler's studies of PS in chimpanzees

Köhler suspended an out-of-reach bunch of bananas from the ceiling of the cage of a chimpanzee called Sultan. In the cage were several items that could be used to reach the bananas (such as different length sticks), although none on its own was sufficient. Eventually, Sultan solved the problem by placing empty boxes beneath the bananas and climbing on the boxes.

Later, Köhler allowed Sultan to see a box being placed in the corridor leading to his cage. Sultan was then taken to his cage where, again, bananas were suspended from the ceiling. Sultan's first strategy was to remove a long bolt from the open cage's door. Quite suddenly, though, he stopped, ran down the corridor, and returned with the box which was again used to retrieve the bananas.

For Köhler, Sultan's behaviour was a result of sudden perceptual reorganisation or *insight*, which was different from trial-and-error learning. Other experiments showed that Sultan's perceptual reorganisation was maintained as a plan of action. So, when the bananas were placed *outside* the cage, Sultan still built several boxes. Experience can sometimes be an obstacle to PS!

Whilst Gestalt psychologists made a significant contribution to our understanding of the processes involved in solving certain types of problem, they did not develop a theory that applies to all aspects of PS. Additionally, whilst the concepts of 'insight' and 'restructuring' are attractive because they are easily understood (especially when accompanied by perceptual demonstrations), they are radically understated as theoretical constructs (Eysenck & Keane, 1995). Thus, it is very unclear under what conditions they will occur and exactly what insight involves.

Information-processing approaches analyse cognitive processes in terms of a series of separate stages. In the case of PS, the stages are those mentioned earlier, that is, representing the problem, generating possible solutions and evaluating those solutions.

Generating possible solutions: algorithms and heuristics

ALGORITHMS

An *algorithm* is a systematic exploration of every possible solution until the correct one is found. For example, to solve the anagram YABB, we could list *all* the possible combinations of letters, checking each time to see if the result is a word. Thus, we might generate BBAY (non-word), BYAB (non-word) and so on, until we eventually arrive at BABY. Algorithms *guarantee* a solution to a problem, and are effective when the number of possible solutions is small (as in the above example). However, when the number of possible solutions is large, algorithms are *time consuming* (unless we are fortunate enough to find the solution early).

HEURISTICS

Heuristics are 'rules of thumb' which, whilst not guaranteeing a solution to a problem, can result in solutions being reached more quickly (Newell *et al.*, 1958). These 'fuzzy' procedures are based on intuition, past experience and any other relevant information. With solving anagrams, for example, a heuristic approach would involve looking for letter combinations that are and are not permitted in the English language. BB is not a permitted combination of letters at the beginning of a word, and so this would immediately exclude BBAY as a solution to the example above. Although unlikely with four-letter anagrams, heuristic devices applied to longer anagrams might not be successful, and we might miss a solution based on a lack of intuition, past experience and other relevant factors.

Heuristic devices include *analogies* and *means–end analysis* (Newell & Simon, 1972). Analogies involve recognising that a particular problem is similar to one encountered before. In means–end analysis (or *working backwards*), the search for a solution begins at the goal (or end) and works backwards to the original state (the means being the steps that must be taken to get from the present state – the problem – to the goal of solving the problem).

In one version of the game of 'Nim', 15 matchsticks are placed in front of two players. Each player is allowed to remove at least one matchstick but not more than five on each turn. Players take turns in removing matchsticks until one takes the last matchstick and so wins the game. In order to win, then, a player must reach his or her turn with one to five matchsticks left. By working backwards, we can see that if an opponent is left with six or 12 matchsticks, then it doesn't matter what he or she does because we will always win. The optimum strategy is therefore to remove enough matchsticks so as to leave the opponent with six or 12 of them.

Because it is often not possible to achieve the main goal in one step, working backwards can involve breaking down the main goal into a series of *sub-goals* or *sub-problems*, each of which must be solved before the main goal can be reached (*problem-reduction representation*). As each of the sub-problems is solved, so the distance between the original state and the goal state lessens (Newell & Simon, 1972). A good example is the 'hobbit and orcs' problem (Thomas, 1974). In this, the goal is to get three hobbits and three orcs across a river in a boat that can carry a maximum of two creatures at a time. To take the boat back across the river, at least one hobbit or one orc must be on it. Moreover, the orcs must never outnumber the hobbits on either side of the river (because the orcs will eat the hobbits).

Leaving aside the main goal of getting everybody across the river, we might begin, as shown in Figure 36.1, by sending two orcs across. Since there is no constraint on the same orc going back to the other side, we might have one make a return trip, pick up another orc, send one orc back, and then allow two hobbits to cross the river (see Steps 1–5). By working on this particular sub-goal, we can eventually get all the hobbits and orcs across to the other side in 11 moves.

Unfortunately, measuring progress in this problem is difficult. Computers can be programmed to work out a sequence of all possible moves and then plot the quickest path to a solution (using a *check-every-move algorithm*). People, however, cannot hold this amount of information in a limited-capacity WM. Also, in working backwards we sometimes have to move *further away* from the goal to achieve it. One reason why the 'hobbits and orcs' problem is so difficult is that at one point (Step 6), it becomes necessary to take a hobbit *and* an orc *back* to the side they started from, which apparently increases the distance from the final goal (Greene, 1987).

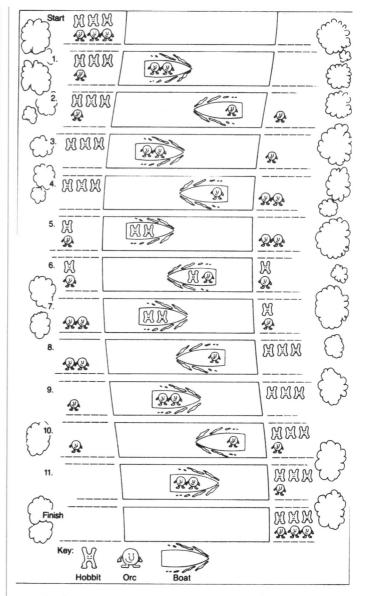

Figure 36.1   The 'hobbits and orcs' problem
(From *Psychology: An Introduction 6/E.* by Morris, © 1988. Reprinted by permission of Prentice-Hall, Inc., Upper Saddle River, NJ.)

Evaluating potential solutions to a problem is the final PS stage. Where the problem and goal have been stated precisely, as in the 'hobbits and orcs' problem, evaluation is relatively simple. With poorly defined problems, it is much more difficult.

Problems in solving problems

Earlier on it was mentioned that certain tendencies and biases can hinder the ability to solve particular problems. Two circumstances in which past experience hinders rather than helps were identified by Gestalt psychologists. These are *mental set* (or *rigidity*) and *functional fixedness*. A third obstacle to PS is the *confirmation bias*.

MENTAL SET

This is the tendency to continue using a previously successful strategy to solve new problems, even when more efficient strategies exist. Luchins (1942) and Luchins & Luchins (1959) asked people to imagine they had three different containers each of a different size. The task was to use the containers to obtain a specific amount of liquid. Once this problem had been solved, the task was repeated, but participants had to imagine a different set of three containers.

Table 36.1   The water container problems used by Luchins & Luchins (1959)

Problem No.	Containers with capacity in fluid ounces			Obtain exactly these amounts of water
	Container A	Container B	Container C	
1	21	127	3	100
2	14	163	25	99
3	18	43	10	5
4	9	42	6	21
5	20	59	4	31
6	23	49	3	20
7	10	36	7	3

The first five problems can be solved using the formula B–2C–A (that is, fill container B, pour its contents into container C twice and then pour what remains in container B into container A to leave the desired amount in container B). Whilst the sixth problem can also be solved using this formula, there is a more direct solution, namely A–C. The seventh problem *cannot* be solved using the formula B–2C–A, but can be solved using the formula A–C.

Once people discovered a solution to the first problem, they continued to use it even when (in the case of the sixth problem) it was less efficient or (in the case of the seventh problem) did not apply. In Gestalt terms, mental set produces reproductive thinking when a problem calls for productive thinking (Scheerer, 1963).

FUNCTIONAL FIXEDNESS

Functional fixedness (or 'fixity') is a type of mental set in which we fail to see that an object may have functions (or uses) other than its normal ones. Duncker (1945) gave

participants a box of drawing pins and a candle and instructed them to attach the candle to a wall so it would stay upright and burn properly.

Whilst participants devised several inelegant solutions to the problem, they failed to empty the box, pin it to the wall and place the candle in it. However, when people are shown an *empty* box and the drawing pins are scattered on a table, the box is much more likely to be used as a candle holder (Glucksberg & Weisberg, 1966).

Box 36.3   Confirmation bias

This is the tendency to search for information that confirms our ideas and simultaneously overlook contradictory information. Wason (1960) gave participants the three-number sequence 2–4–6 and asked them to discover the rule that he had in his head which applied to the sequence. Participants were allowed to generate their own three-number sequences and ask if it conformed to the rule that applied to 2–4–6.

Wason's rule was actually very simple, namely 'any three ascending numbers'. However, 80 per cent of participants failed to discover it, despite being extremely confident that they had. Most formed a wrong idea about the rule (such as 'counting in twos') and then searched only for confirming evidence (such as 1–3–5 or 42–44–46) which also conformed to Wason's rule. What participants did not do was look for evidence that would *disconfirm* their hypotheses. Thus, 4–6–9 would disconfirm the counting-in-twos rule, but since it conforms to Wason's rule, it would have allowed thinking to shift.

Decision-making

Decision-making (DM) is a special case of PS in which we already know the possible solutions (or choices). Some decisions we have to make are relatively trivial. Others are more important, such as a married couple deciding whether or not to have children, or a student deciding which university to study at. In DM, then, we are faced with various alternative choices from which one must be selected and the others rejected.

COMPENSATORY AND NON-COMPENSATORY MODELS OF DM

Compensatory models

If we were completely logical in our DM, we would evaluate how all of the desirable potential outcomes of a particular decision might *compensate* for the undesirable potential outcomes. According to the *additive compensatory model*, we start the DM process by listing common features of various alternatives and assigning arbitrary weights that reflect their value to us. The weights are then added up to arrive at a separate score for each alternative. Provided that the criteria have been properly weighted and each criterion has been correctly rated, the alternative with the highest score is the most rational choice given the available information.

Another compensatory model is the *utility-probability model*, which proposes that important decisions are made by weighting the desirability of each potential outcome according to its *utility* and *probability*. Utility is the value placed on potential positive or negative outcomes. Probability is the likelihood that the choice will actually produce the potential outcome.

Table 36.2   Using the utility-probability model for the decision about whether to get married whilst still at college

Potential outcome	Utility (on a scale of −10 to +10)	Probability (0 to 1.0)	Expected utility (utility × probability)
Choice:			
Get married			
Happy	+10	.7	+7
Good study habits	+5	.8	+4
Ample alone time (personal space needs)	+6	.2	+1.2
Financial difficulties	−8	.8	−6.4
Friendships limited	−4	.7	−2.8
Lowered motivation to stay trim	−3	.4	−1.2
			+1.8
Choice:			
Do not get married			
Happy	+10	.2	+2
Good study habits	+5	.3	+1.5
Ample alone time (personal space needs)	+6	.9	+5.4
Financial difficulties	−8	.1	−.8
Friendships limited	−4	.1	−.4
Lowered motivation to stay trim	−3	0	0
			+7.7

Note: Each potential outcome is assigned a utility value (which may be positive or negative) and a probability value indicating the likelihood that the potential outcome will occur. Expected utilities are calculated by multiplying utility and probability. The total expected utility is the sum of the expected utilities. In this example, the decision not to get married has the greatest expected utility and so should be the decision made.

(From Crooks & Stein, 1991)

Figure 36.2   One of life's major decisions: to have children or not? Harry Enfield as 'Kevin the Teenager' would probably swing the balance heavily towards not having children

Non-compensatory models

Evidence suggests that we actually use various, and less precise, *non-compensatory models*. In these, not all features of each alternative may be considered and features do not compensate for each other. There are at least four such models.

Box 36.4   Some non-compensatory DM models

Elimination by aspects: When faced with complex decisions, we eliminate various options if they do not meet particular criteria irrespective of their quality on other criteria (Tversky, 1972). This assumes that we begin with a maximum criterion and use it to test the various options. If, after applying this criterion, more than one alternative remains, the second most important criterion is used. The procedure continues until just one option remains. This is the chosen option.

Maximax strategy: After comparing the various options according to their best features, we then select the one with the strongest best feature.

Minimax strategy: After considering the weakest feature of each option, we select the option whose weakest feature is most highly rated.

Conjunctive strategy: This involves setting a 'minimum' acceptable value on each option. Any option which does not meet or exceed this value as the criteria are considered from most to least important is discarded. The chosen option is that which does meet or exceed the minimum acceptable value on each criterion.

HEURISTICS IN DM

Clearly, important decisions should be approached systematically. However, it is not always easy to make rational decisions, even in important matters, because of the absence of information about the various alternatives. Moreover, with all the decisions we have to make daily, there is not time to engage in the rational processes described above. As a result, we often rely on heuristics. Two of these are the *availability heuristic* and the *representativeness heuristic* (Tversky & Kahneman, 1973).

Availability heuristic

Sometimes, decisions must be made on the basis of whatever information is most readily available in LTM. The availability heuristic is based on the assumption that an event's probability is directly related to the frequency with which it has occurred in the past, and that more frequent events are usually easier to remember than less frequent events.

For example, if asked whether the letter 'K' appears more often as the first letter of words or as the third letter, you would probably say the former. In fact, 'K' is three times more likely to appear as the third letter, but because words beginning with 'K' come to mind more easily, we presume that they are more commonplace (Hastie & Park, 1986).

The availability heuristic also plays a role in our tendency to overestimate the chances of being a victim of a violent crime or a plane crash (Tyler & Cook, 1984). This is because the extensive media coverage of these actually very rare events brings vivid examples of them to mind very readily.

Representativeness heuristic

Tversky & Kahneman (1973) gave participants the following information about a person called 'Steve':

> 'Steve is very shy and withdrawn, invariably helpful, but with little interest in people, or in the world of reality. A meek and tidy soul, he has a need for order and structure, and a passion for detail'.

The participants were asked to decide how likely it was that Steve was involved in one of a number of occupations including musician, pilot, physician, salesman and librarian. Most guessed he was a librarian, presumably because his personality characteristics matched certain stereotypes about librarians (see Chapter 52, pages 454–457).

Whenever we judge the likelihood of something by intuitively comparing it with our preconceived ideas of a few characteristics that we believe represent a category, we are using the representative heuristic.

Box 36.5   The gambler's fallacy

Consider the following possible outcomes of tossing a coin six times: HHHHHH, TTTHHH and HTTHTH. Most people believe the first outcome to be the least likely of the three and the third to be the most likely. In fact, the probability of the three sequences is *identical*. Our assumption that coin tossing produces a random sequence of heads and tails leads us to decide that the third is the most likely. Indeed, if people observe five consecutive heads and are asked to estimate the probability of the next toss being a head, they tend to suggest that a tail is the more likely outcome, even though the probability of either is actually 0.5. This tendency is called the *gambler's fallacy*.

The representativeness heuristic can also cause us to overlook important information about *base rates*, that is, the relative frequency of different objects/events in the world. For example, Tversky & Kahneman (1973) asked participants to decide whether a student who could be described as 'neat and tidy', 'dull and mechanical' and 'a poor writer' was a computer-science student or a humanities student. Over 95 per cent decided the student studied computing. Even after they were told that over 80 per cent of students at their school were studying humanities, their estimates remained virtually unchanged. So, even when we know the relative frequency of two things, we tend to ignore this information and base a decision on how well something matches our stereotype, that is, how representative it is.

Box 36.6   Some other influences on DM

Belief perseverance: This is the tendency to cling to a belief even in the face of contrary evidence (Lord *et al.*, 1979). It can be overcome by *considering the opposite*. However, some false beliefs are difficult to remove even when information exists which clearly discredits them. Examples include stereotyped beliefs.

Entrapment: When we make costly investments in something (such as a relationship) that goes wrong, we may come to feel that we have no choice but to continue, because withdrawal cannot justify the costs already incurred (Brockner & Rubin, 1985). For example, industrial disputes often continue beyond the stage where either side can hope to achieve any gains (Baron, 1989).

Over-confidence: This is the tendency to overestimate the accuracy of our current knowledge. This can occur because it is generally easier for us to remember successful decisions or judgements than unsuccessful ones. So, using the availability heuristic, we overestimate our

---

success at particular tasks. Over-confidence can be overcome by providing feedback about the accuracy of decisions and judgements.

Loss aversion and costs against losses: Typically, we tend to reject riskier, though potentially more rewarding, decisions in favour of a certain gain *unless* taking a risk is a way to avoid loss (Tversky & Kahneman, 1986). We also tend to see losses as being more acceptable if we label them as 'costs' rather than 'losses' (although the evaluation of a cost depends on the context: Kahneman & Tversky, 1984).

Expectations: Expectations can affect both our perception of the world (see Chapter 22, page 186) and what is done with the perceived information. For example, the shooting down of an ascending Iranian airliner by an American warship occurred as a result of initial, but later corrected, computer information that the plane was a descending F14 fighter jet. The expectation of an attack led the ship's captain to pay more attention to his crew's reports of an emergency than to the new computer information (Wade & Tavris, 1993).

Hindsight: *Hindsight bias* refers to our tendency to overestimate the probability that something would have happened after it has happened, as if we knew this all along (Hawkins & Hastie, 1990).

Framing: When the same issue is presented (or *framed*) in two different but equivalent ways, we tend to make different judgements about it. For example, people respond more positively to ground beef if it is described as '75 per cent lean' rather than '25 per cent fat'. Also, medical treatments are seen as being more successful if framed as having a '50 per cent success rate' rather than a '50 per cent failure rate' (Levin & Gaeth, 1988).

Computers, PS and DM

At the heart of the information-processing approach lies the *computer analogy*, the view that human cognition can be understood by comparing it with the functioning of digital computers (see Chapter 27 and 83). Newell *et al.*'s (1958) *general problem solver* (GPS) was an ambitious attempt to simulate the entire range of PS and was the first computational model of a psychological phenomenon. The GPS was based on *verbal protocols* (see Chapter 35, page 306) given by people as they attempted to solve particular problems, and employed the working-backwards heuristic (see page 309).

Tests of the GPS (e.g. Atwood & Polson, 1976) involved giving it and a person the same problem and comparing the performance of both in terms of the number and types of steps gone through and the solution arrived at. Results indicated that the GPS and people do use similar strategies for solving particular problems, although measuring the 'goodness of fit' between verbal protocols (which are themselves suspect: see page 306) and the 'traces' of a computer program is difficult (Garnham, 1988; Hampson & Morris, 1996).

Research has also looked at computer simulations of adversary problems (especially chess) where substantial *domain-specific knowledge* is required. Studies of experts and novices have revealed many important differences between them (see Chapter 31). These do not necessarily occur because experts are faster thinkers, have better memories or are cleverer than non-experts (Hampson & Morris, 1996: see Box 27.6, page 234). Thus, the gain from being an expert would seem to be that it places less strain on WM. Since PS strategies depend on knowledge which is already available, 'the more you know, the less you have to think' (Greene, 1987).

Figure 36.3   Chess experts are only better at remembering the position of chess pieces when they are positioned as they might be during a game. If the pieces are placed randomly, the experts are no better than non-experts at memorising their positions (de Groot, 1966)

Box 36.7   Expert systems

Expert systems (ESs or *intelligent knowledge-based systems*) are computer programs that apply knowledge in a specific area, enabling a computer to function as effectively as a human expert. ESs include MYCIN (Shortliffe, 1976), which helps doctors diagnose and treat infectious diseases, and PROSPECTOR (Feigenbaum

& McCorduck, 1983) which helps geologists explore for minerals. ESs obtain their 'knowledge' from human experts. However, experts cannot always formulate explicitly the knowledge they use in solving particular problems, nor can they say how they combine different items of information to reach a decision about a particular case. As a result, ES production is both difficult and time consuming.

Whilst ESs have been shown to be useful, they are much less flexible than their human counterparts. In Boden's (1987) view:

'In almost every case, their 'explanations' are merely recapitulations of the previous firing of if-then rules … for they still have no higher-level representations of the knowledge domain, their own problem-solving activity or the knowledge of their human user'.

Whether ESs can be provided with causal reasoning, so that they can reach a conclusion *and* explain the reason for it, is currently the focus of much research interest. A detailed discussion of ESs and the scope of *artificial intelligence* can be found in Gross (1996).

Naturalistic DM

Unlike traditional research into DM which typically studies decisions made by naïve participants in laboratory experiments, *naturalistic decision-making* (NDM) has emerged as a paradigm shift in applied DM research (Skriver, 1996). NDM researchers argue that only by studying experienced people can they gain insight into the way decision-makers utilise both their domain knowledge and contextual information, and how the contextual factors affect DM processes.

Areas of NDM research interest include military command and control, firefighting incident command, offshore installation emergency response, and medical DM (Heller *et al.*, 1992). How real decision-makers arrive at difficult, dynamic decisions in often ill-structured and changing environments is NDM's major concern.

Box 36.8   Some 'disastrous decisions'

- In 1902, Mount Pelée erupted on the Caribbean island of Martinique. Despite numerous warning signs that it was about to erupt, the authorities decided to do nothing. Indeed, the Governor posted troops to prevent an exodus by the inhabitants of the city of St Pierre. Over 26,000 people died in the blast, and all but two of the 18 ships in the city's harbour were sunk.

- In 1974, a DC10 crashed shortly after leaving Orly Airport, killing 345 people. The plane's cargo door had not been secured properly by a baggage handler. The authorities had earlier decided not to provide adequate instructions in appropriate languages on how to check and lock the door. The baggage handler's error occurred because he did not understand the language the instructions were written in.

- In Riyadh, the 301 passengers and crew of a Lockheed Tristar died of asphyxiation because the aircraft's captain decided not to evacuate the smoke-filled plane.

- In 1989, the port engine of a Boeing 737 caught fire. The pilot turned off the perfectly good starboard engine and the plane crashed at Kegworth.

(Adapted from Dixon, 1994)

Conclusions

Psychological research has revealed much about the cognitive processes underlying successful and unsuccessful PS and DM. Whilst we might think that our approaches to PS and DM are always rational and unbiased, the evidence indicates that this is not so, and that various factors influence the solutions we arrive at and the decisions we make.

Figure 36.4   Solution to the problem presented on page 310

Summary

■ According to an **information-processing approach**, problem-solving progresses through a series of logical stages: **defining/representing the problem**, **generating possible solutions** and **evaluating possible solutions**. However, they may not always occur in this sequence.

■ Ill-defined and complex problems are more difficult to solve than well-defined, simple ones. Generating possible solutions might simply involve retrieving information from LTM.

■ The **behaviourist** view of PS as **trial-and-error** and **accidental success** was challenged by the **Gestalt** psychologists, who looked at how we impose **structure** on a problem through **meaningful apprehension of relations**. Maier distinguished between **reproductive** and **productive thinking**, the latter involving **reorganisation** (similar to **insight**). Whilst these concepts are easy to understand, they are more difficult to define.

■ **Algorithms** and **heuristics** are two ways of **generating possible solutions** to a problem. Algorithms **guarantee** a solution, but are **time-consuming** (and hence ineffective), when the number of possible solutions is large. Heuristics do not guarantee a solution, but can help produce solutions more quickly. Examples include **analogies** and **means–end analysis**.

■ Means–end analysis involves **working backwards** from the goal or end (the solution) to the original state (the problem). The means are the steps required to get from one to the other. The main goal may have to be broken down into **sub-goals/sub-problems** through a process of **problem-reduction representation**.

■ Computers can be programmed with a **check-every-move algorithm**, but human WM is unable to hold this amount of information. Also, we sometimes have to move **further away** from the goal in order to achieve it.

■ **Mental set/rigidity, functional fixedness/fixity** and the **confirmation bias** are ways in which past experience can hinder PS. In mental set, people continue to use a solution to past problems (reproductive thinking) even when the current problem requires productive thinking. Functional fixedness is a type of mental set in which we fail to see that an object may have functions or uses other than its normal ones.

■ **Decision-making** (DM) is a special case of PS in which we already know the possible solutions or choices. According to a **compensatory model,** we evaluate how all desirable potential outcomes might **compensate** for undesirable ones. Two examples are the **additive compensatory model** and the **utility-probability model**.

■ **Non-compensatory models** are less precise but more commonly used approaches, in which not all features of each alternative are considered, and features do not compensate for each other. Examples include **elimination by aspects, maximax, minimax** and **conjunctive strategies**.

■ Rational decisions cannot always be made because of the absence of information and time. So we often resort to the availability and representativeness heuristics.

■ The **availability heuristic** assumes that an event's probability is directly related to its past frequency: more frequent events are easier to retrieve from LTM. The **representativeness heuristic** involves judging the likelihood of something by intuitively comparing it with preconceived ideas of a few characteristics believed to represent a category.

■ Central to the information-processing approach is the **computer analogy**. Newell *et al.*'s **general problem solver** (GPS) attempted to simulate the entire range of PS and was the first computational model of a psychological phenomenon. The GPS was based on **verbal protocols** using means–end analysis. When the GPS and a person are given the same problem to solve, they tend to use similar strategies.

■ Compared with non-experts, experts are not necessarily faster, cleverer thinkers, with better memories. Chess experts are only better at remembering board positions that could appear in an actual game, as opposed to random positions. Expertise reduces the strain on WM by enabling the expert to draw on already available knowledge.

■ **Expert systems** (ESs) are computer programs that apply knowledge in a specific area (such as medical diagnosis), enabling a computer to function as effectively as a human expert. However, human experts cannot always say explicitly how they solve particular problems or make particular decisions. This makes writing ESs difficult and time-consuming.

■ ESs are much less flexible than human experts, lacking higher-level representations of the knowledge domain or their own PS activity. This prevents them from explaining how they reach a decision.

■ **Naturalistic decision-making** (NDM) is a new paradigm in applied DM research. NDM's major concern is how real decision-makers reach difficult, dynamic decisions in often ill-structured and changing environments, such as military command and control, firefighting incident command and medical DM. Such research may help prevent 'disastrous decisions'.

37

THE RELATIONSHIP BETWEEN LANGUAGE AND THOUGHT

Introduction and overview

Knowing what we want to say but being unable to 'put it into words', is one of several examples of thought taking place without language (Weiskrantz, 1988). However, the exact relationship between language and thought has been the subject of much debate amongst philosophers and psychologists. For some, thought is dependent on, or caused by, language. Others believe that language is dependent on, and reflects, thought or an individual's level of cognitive development. Yet others maintain that thought and language are initially quite separate activities which come together and interact at a certain point in development.

This chapter reviews the evidence relating to each of these major theoretical perspectives concerning language and thought's relationship. It begins by briefly examining the view that language and thought are the same.

Language and thought are the same

WATSON'S 'PERIPHERALIST' APPROACH

The earliest psychological theory of language and thought's relationship was advanced by the behaviourist Watson (1913). In his view, thought processes are really no more than the sensations produced by tiny movements of the speech organs too small to produce audible sounds. Essentially, thought is talking to oneself very quietly. Part of Watson's rejection of 'mind' was his denial of mentalistic concepts such as 'thought', and hence his reduction of it to 'silent speech' (see Chapter 1, page 10, and Chapter 81).

Watson's theory is called *peripheralism* because it sees 'thinking' occurring peripherally in the larynx, rather than centrally in the brain. Movements of the larynx do occur when 'thought' is taking place. However, this only indicates that such movements may *accompany* thinking, not that the movements *are* thoughts or that they are *necessary* for thinking to occur.

Smith *et al.* (1947) attempted to test Watson's theory by injecting Smith himself with *curare*, a drug that causes total paralysis of the skeletal muscles without affecting consciousness. The muscles of the speech organs and the respiratory system are paralysed, and so Smith had to be kept breathing artificially. When the drug's effects had worn off, Smith was able to report on his thoughts and perceptions during the paralysis.

Additionally, Furth (1966) has shown that people born deaf and mute, and who do not learn sign language, can also think in much the same way as hearing and speaking people. For Watson, deaf and mute individuals should be incapable of thought because of the absence of movement in the speech organs.

Thought is dependent on, or caused by, language

Several theorists believe that thought is dependent on, and reflects, language. Bruner (1983), for example, has argued that language is essential if thought and knowledge are not to be limited to what can be learned through our actions (the *enactive mode of representation*) or images (the *iconic mode*). If the *symbolic mode* (going beyond the immediate context) is to develop, then language is crucial (see Chapter 42, pages 367–369).

Social constructionists (e.g. Gergen, 1973) have argued that our ways of understanding the world derive from other people (past and present) rather than from objective reality. We are born into a world where the conceptual frameworks and categories used by people in our culture already exist. Indeed, these frameworks and categories are an essential part of our culture, since they provide meaning, a way of structuring experience of both ourselves and the world of other people. This view has much in common with the 'strong' version of the *linguistic relativity hypothesis*, the most extensively researched of the theories arguing that thought is dependent on, or caused by, language.

THE LINGUISTIC RELATIVITY HYPOTHESIS

According to Wittgenstein (1921), 'The limits of my language mean the limits of my world'. By this, he meant that people can only think about and understand the world through language, and that if a particular language does not possess certain ideas or concepts, these could not exist for its native speakers. The view that language determines *how* we think about objects and events, or even determines *what* we think (our ideas, thoughts and perceptions), can be traced to the writings of Sapir (1929), a linguist and anthropologist, and Whorf (1956), a linguist and student of Sapir. Their perspective is often called the *Sapir–Whorf linguistic relativity hypothesis*, and is sometimes referred to as the *Whorfian hypothesis* in acknowledgement of the greater contribution made by Whorf. For Whorf (1956):

> 'We dissect nature along the lines laid down by our native languages. The categories and types that we isolate from the world of phenomena we do not find there because they stare every observer in the face; on the contrary, the world is presented in a kaleidoscopic flux of impressions that has to be organised by our minds – and this means largely by the linguistic systems in our minds. We cut nature up, organise it into concepts and ascribe significance as we do, largely because we are parties to an agreement to organise it this way – an agreement that holds throughout our speech community and is codified in patterns of our language'.

According to Whorf's *linguistic determinism*, language determines our concepts, and we can only think through the use of concepts. So, acquiring a language involves acquiring a 'world view' (or *Weltanschauung*). People who speak different languages have different world views (hence linguistic 'relativity').

Box 37.1 Some vocabulary differences consistent with the Sapir–Whorf linguistic relativity hypothesis

Whorf claimed that the Inuit Eskimos have over 20 words for snow (including 'fluffy snow', 'drifting snow' and 'packed snow'), whereas Standard Average European languages (such as English) have only one. Similarly, the Hanuxoo people of the Philippines use 92 words for 'rice' depending on whether it is husked or unhusked and its mode of preparation. The Shona people (Zimbabwe) have only three words for colour, and the Dani (New Guinea) just two. 'Mola' is used for bright, warm hues, whereas 'mili' is used for dark, cold hues. The Hopi Indians (whose language Whorf studied for several years) have two words for flying objects. One applies to birds and the other to anything else that travels through the air (Rathus, 1990).

Whorf also saw a language's *grammar* as determining an individual's thought and perception. In the Hopi language, for example, no distinction is made between past, present and future which, compared with English, makes it a 'timeless language'. In European languages, 'time' is treated as an *objective* entity, with a clear demarcation between past, present and future. Although the Hopi language recognises duration, Hopis talk about time only as it appears *subjectively* to the observer. For example, rather than saying 'I stayed for ten days', Hopis say 'I stayed until the tenth day' or 'I left on the tenth day'.

In English nouns denote objects and events, and verbs denote actions. In the Hopi language, 'lightning', for example, is a verb, since events of necessarily brief duration must be verbs. As a result, a Hopi would say 'it lightninged'.

Figure 37.1   At least as far as British politicians are concerned, the relationship between language and thought is (in the eyes of the media) a clear-cut one!

Testing the linguistic relativity hypothesis (LRH)

Miller & McNeill (1969) distinguish between *three* different versions of the LRH, all of which are consistent with it but vary in the *strength* of claim they make. The *strong* version claims that *language determines thought*. The *weak* version claims that *language affects perception*, and the *weakest* version claims that *language influences memory*, such that information which is more easily described in a particular language will be better remembered than information more difficult to describe.

Attempts at testing the 'weak' and 'weakest' versions of the LRH have typically involved the perception and memory of *colour*. Since language users such as the Jalé (New Guinea) only have terms for black and white, whilst those of the Ibibio culture (Nigeria) have terms for black, white, red and green, tests of colour perception and memory should be more difficult for the Jalé than the Ibibio. Since the Ibibio word for green encompasses the English green, blue and yellow, the Ibibio should find colour perception and memory tasks more difficult than English speakers.

Early tests appeared to support the two weaker versions of the LRH. For example, Brown & Lenneberg (1954) found that Zuni Indians, who have a single word to describe yellows and oranges, did make more mistakes

than English speakers in recognising these colours. However, the results (and those of other researchers using a similar methodology) were challenged by Berlin & Kay (1969). They found that whilst cultures may differ in the number of basic colour terms they use, all cultures draw their basic (or *focal*) terms from only 11 colours. These are black, white, red, green, yellow, blue, brown, purple, pink, orange and grey. Moreover, the colour terms emerge in a particular sequence in the history of languages.

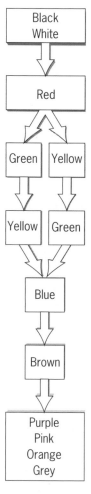

Figure 37.2   The sequence in which focal colours emerge (Berlin & Kay, 1969)

So, for cultures with only two colours, these will always be black and white, whereas in cultures with three colours, these will always be black, white and red (Newstead, 1995). As Newstead has observed:

'This, then, gives a rather different perspective on the use of colour terms. It had been assumed that verbal labels were chosen more or less arbitrarily, and that those chosen influenced the way in which colour was perceived.

Berlin and Kay's findings suggest that there are certain focal colours which will always be labelled if colour terms are used at all. This suggests an alternative explanation for Brown and Lenneberg's findings: that the colours which participants in their study had found easier to learn were the focal colours and these were easy to remember not because they had verbal labels but because they were the most basic colours'.

A study which supports Berlin and Kay's findings and the alternative explanation for Brown and Lenneberg's is that conducted by Heider & Oliver (1972).

Box 37.3 Heider & Oliver's (1972) study of colour naming

As noted, the Dani have only two words for colours, whereas native English speakers have words for 11 basic colours. Heider and Oliver gave both Dani and English-speaking participants a coloured chip which they were allowed to look at for five seconds. After a 30-second delay, participants were asked to pick out a chip of the same colour among a set of 40 different coloured chips. On the weakest version of the LRH, the Dani's colour vocabulary should have influenced their memory for colours, and on the weak version they should have had difficulty in discriminating similar colours of a slightly different hue that they had labelled with the same name.

The results showed that whilst the Dani-speaking and English-speaking participants made many mistakes, there were no significant differences between them in their rate of confusion of similar colours, despite the differences in their colour vocabularies. In other research, Heider showed that both Dani and English speakers were better at recognising focal colours than non-focal colours, and that the Dani found it much easier to learn labels for focal than non-focal colours.

Heider (1972) concluded that:

'far from being a domain well suited to the study of the effects of language on thought, the colour-space would seem a prime example of the influence of underlying perceptual-cognitive factors on the formation and reference of linguistic categories'.

By this, Heider means that her data are better explained in terms of *physiological factors* underlying colour vision, rather than linguistic factors. Thus, people are sensitive to focal colours because the human visual system processes reality in a certain way (Lakoff, 1987).

Indeed, evidence suggests that focal colours can be discriminated *before* any verbal labels for them have been learned. Bornstein (1988), for example, has argued that pre-verbal infants categorise the visible spectrum in a similar way to adults, in that categorisation occurs on the basis of the relatively discrete hues of blue, green, yellow and red (see Chapter 23, page 194).

AN EVALUATION OF THE LRH

According to Sapir and Whorf, the differences between language speakers determine differences in how the world is perceived, thought about and remembered. The world *is* different depending on what language we speak (or 'think in'). However, Berry *et al.* (1992) and Jackendoff (1993) have argued that Whorf's evidence was anecdotal rather than empirical, and that he exaggerated the differences between Hopi and other languages. Moreover, far from having 'over 20' words for 'snow', the Inuit Eskimos have relatively few such words (Newstead, 1995).

Even if the criticisms about vocabulary and grammar are ignored, Whorf did not actually *show* that the Inuit Eskimos *perceive* more varieties of snow than English speakers, or that the Hopi Indians cannot discriminate between past, present and future. Greene (1975) has argued that if we conduct a Whorfian analysis of English from the perspective of a Hopi Indian, it is unlikely that a Hopi would really believe that we hold the 'primitive' beliefs that cars are female ('she's a fine motor') or that 'a car', 'a hard bargain' and 'a golf ball' are all things that can be 'driven'. This is because we distinguish between a language's grammar and our perceptual experience. The fact that Hopi can be translated into English (and vice versa) implies that there is a universally shared knowledge of the world that is independent of the particular language in which it is expressed.

Whorf also appears to have overlooked *why* Inuit Eskimos have more than one word for snow. One possibility is that the more significant an experience or environmental feature is for us, the larger the number of ways in which it can be expressed. So, instead of language determining our perceptions, our perceptions (which reflect what is important for us) might influence our language. As Solso (1995) says:

'The development of specific language codes ... is dependent on cultural needs; the learning of these codes by members of a language group also involves the learning of significant values of the culture, some of which must be related to survival'.

Solso's view is supported by the fact that English-speaking skiers *do* learn to discriminate between varied snow conditions and *invent* a vocabulary to describe these differences. Such terms include 'sticky snow', 'powder', 'corn' and 'boilerplate' (or ice: Crooks & Stein, 1991).

It is now widely accepted that Whorf overestimated the importance of language differences. As Berry *et al.* (1992) have observed:

'language as an instrument for thinking has many cross-culturally variant properties. As humans, we may not all be sharing the same thoughts, but our respective languages do not seem to predestine us to different kinds of thinking'.

What language may do, though, is to affect the ease of information processing. Newstead (1995), for example, describes research conducted by Hunt & Agnoli (1991) which supports this view. The English word 'seven' has two syllables whereas the equivalent French word ('sept') has only one. The English word 'eleven' has three syllables whereas the French word 'onze' has one. Hunt and Agnoli argue that when a name is shorter, information is processed more quickly, and so French speakers would have an advantage over English speakers when performing mental arithmetic involving these numbers, at least in processing terms.

THE LRH, SOCIAL CLASS AND RACE

Social-class differences in language and thought

Bernstein (1961) was interested in language's role as a social (rather than individual) phenomenon, especially its relation to cultural deprivation. He showed that whilst there were generally no differences between the verbal and non-verbal intelligence test performances of boys from public schools, boys from lower working class homes often showed considerable differences, with non-verbal performance sometimes being as much as 26 points better than verbal performance. Bernstein argued that working and middle class children speak two different kinds (or codes) of language which he called *restricted code* and *elaborated code* respectively.

Because Bernstein saw the relationship between potential and actual intelligence as being mediated through language, he argued that the lack of an elaborated code would prevent working class children from developing their full intellectual potential. The different language codes underlie the whole pattern of relationships (to objects and people) experienced by members of different classes, as well as the patterns of learning which their children bring with them to school (see Table 37.1).

Supportive of Bernstein's views is Hess & Shipman's (1965) finding that social-class differences influence children's intellectual development. In particular, there was a lack of *meaning* in the mother–child communication system for low-status families. Language was used much less to convey meaning (to describe, explain, express and so

Table 37.1   Characteristics of restricted and elaborated codes (Bernstein, 1961)

Restricted code

1   Grammatically crude, repetitive, rigid, limited use of adjectives and adverbs, uses more pronouns than nouns. Sentences often short, grammatically simple and incomplete.

2   Context-bound: the meaning not made explicit but assumes listener's familiarity with the situation being described, e.g. 'He gave me it'; listener cannot be expected to know what 'he' or 'it' refers to.

3   'I' rarely used, and much of the meaning conveyed non-verbally.

4   Frequent use of uninformative but emotionally reinforcing phrases such as 'you know', 'don't I'.

5   Tends to stress the present, the here-and-now.

6   Doesn't allow expression or abstract or hypothetical thought.

Elaborated code

1   Grammatically more complex, flexible. Uses a range of subordinate clauses, conjunctions, prepositions, adjectives, adverbs. More nouns than pronouns. Sentences longer and more complex.

2   Context-independent: the meaning is made explicit, e.g. 'John gave me this book'.

3   'I' often used, making clear the speaker's intentions, as well as emphasising the precise description of experiences and feelings.

4   Relatively little use of emotionally reinforcing phrases.

5   Tends to stress past and future, rather than the present.

6   Allows expression of abstract or hypothetical thought.

(From Gross, 1996)

on) and much more to give orders and commands to the child. A discussion of the implications that Bernstein's theory has for education can be found in Gross (1996).

However, instead of seeing 'restricted' and 'elaborated' as distinct types of language code, they are better thought of as two ends of a continuum. Also, the terms 'restricted' and 'elaborated' imply a value judgement of middle class speech as being superior to working class speech (closer to 'standard' or 'the Queen's' English). The lack of objectivity makes this judgement difficult to defend.

Black English

A version of English spoken by segments of the American black community is called 'Black English'. For example, when asked to repeat the sentence 'I asked him if he did it, and he said he didn't do it', one five-year-old girl repeated the sentence like this: 'I asks him if he did it, and he says he didn't did it, but I knows he did' (Labov, 1973). Bernstein argued that Black English is a restricted code and that this makes the thinking of Black English speakers less logical than that of their white elaborated-code counterparts.

One major difference between Black and Standard English relates to the use of verbs (Rebok, 1987). In particular, Black English speakers often omit the present tense copula (the verb 'to be'). So, 'he be gone' indicates Standard English 'he has been gone for a long time' and 'he gone' signifies that 'he has gone right now'. Black English is often termed *sub-standard* and regarded as illogical rather than *non-standard* (Bereiter & Engelman, 1966). According to Labov (1970), Black English is just one dialect of English and speakers of both dialects are expressing the same ideas and understand each other equally well.

Whilst the grammatical rules of Black English differ from those of Standard English, Black English possesses consistent rules which allow the expression of thoughts as complex as those permitted by Standard English (Labov, 1973). Several other languages, such as Russian and Arabic, also omit the present-tense verb 'to be' and yet we do not call them 'illogical'. This suggests that black dialects are considered sub-standard as a matter of convention or prejudice, and not because they are poorer vehicles for expressing meaning and thinking logically. However, because the structure of Black English does differ in important ways from Standard English, and since intelligence tests are written in Standard English, Black English speakers do have a linguistic handicap (as, indeed, do white working class children: see Chapters 82 and 84).

Labov also showed that the social situation can be a powerful determinant of verbal behaviour. A young boy called Leon was shown a toy by a white interviewer and asked to tell him everything he could about it. Leon said very little and was silent for much of the time, even when a black interviewer took over. However, when Leon sat on the floor and shared a packet of crisps with his best friend and with the same black interviewer introducing topics in a local black dialect, Leon became a lively conversationalist. Had he been assessed with the white or black interviewers on their own, Leon would have been labelled 'non-verbal' or 'linguistically retarded'.

Black children may actually be *bilingual*. In their home environment, the school playground and their neighbourhoods, they speak the accepted vernacular. In the classroom, however, and when talking to any one in authority, they must adopt Standard English with which they are unfamiliar. This results in short sentences, simple grammar and strange intonation. Out of school, however, their natural language is easy, fluent, creative and often gifted. So, whilst Black English is certainly *non-standard*, it is another language with its own grammar which is certainly not sub-standard.

Box 37.4 'Ebonics': an ongoing debate

Ebonics is a fusion of the words 'ebony' and 'phonics' and was coined in 1975 as an alternative to the term 'Black English'. In 1996, Ebonics was officially recognised by the Oakland public school board in California, and schools were ordered to teach 28,000 black children in their own 'tongue'. The board claimed that Ebonics was a separate language, genetically rooted in the West-African and Niger–Congo language system, rather than a dialect of standard American English (Hiscock, 1996; Whittell, 1996).

In early 1997, the school board edited its statement so that the word 'genetically' referred to linguists' use of the word for the roots of a language rather than to a gene pool. They also indicated that it was not the intent to teach in Ebonics, but rather to have teachers use the vernacular to understand their children (Zinberg, 1997). Both conservatives and liberals in America claim that the decision to require Ebonics to be taught would be 'political correctness run amok' (Cornwell, 1997). Educationalists such as Zinberg disagree. In her view, many students are:

'bewildered, then angered and finally alienated from the schools where their language and self-esteem are belittled by a seemingly insensitive system'.

Language is dependent on, and reflects, thought

According to Piaget (1950), children begin life with some understanding of the world and try to find linguistic ways of expressing their knowledge. As language develops, it 'maps' onto previously acquired cognitive structures, and so language is dependent upon thought (Piaget & Inhelder, 1969).

According to Piaget's concept of object permanence (the realisation that objects continue to exist even when they cannot be seen: see Chapter 41, pages 356–357), a child should begin talking about objects that are not present in its immediate surroundings only after object permanence had developed (see Chapter 33, page 288 and Chapter 34, page 298).

Corrigan (1978) showed that children were able to talk about absent objects only after they had demonstrated an advanced level on an object permanence test. Similarly, children who had the ability to conserve liquid quantity (to recognise that different-shaped containers can hold the same amount of liquid: see Chapter 41) understood the meaning of phrases and words such as 'as much as', 'bigger' and 'more'. However, children who could not conserve did not improve their performance of the correct use of these words after having been given linguistic training (Sinclair-de-Zwart, 1969).

In Piaget's view, children can be taught words but they will not *understand* them until they have mastered certain intellectual skills during the process of cognitive growth. So, language can exist without thought, but only in the sense that a parrot can 'speak'. Thought, then, is a necessary forerunner to language if language is to be used properly.

Contrary to Piaget's view that thought structures language, Luria & Yudovich (1971) suggest that language does play a central role in cognitive development. However, it is probably much more reasonable to conclude that language reflects, to an extent, our understanding of the world.

Box 37.5   Luria & Yudovich's (1971) study

Luria and Yurovich studied five-year-old twin boys whose home environment was unstimulating. They played almost exclusively together and had only a very primitive level of speech. The boys received little encouragement to speak from adults and made little progress towards the symbolic use of words. Essentially, their speech was *synpraxic*, a primitive form in which words cannot be detached from the action or object they denote.

The twins hardly ever used speech to describe objects or events or to help them plan their actions. They could not understand other people's speech, and their own constituted a kind of signalling rather than symbolic system. Although they never played with other children and played with each other in a primitive and monotonous way, they were otherwise normal.

After being separated, one twin was given special remedial treatment for his language deficiency but the other was not. The former made rapid progress and, ten months later, was ahead of his brother. However, both made progress, and their synpraxic speech died away. For Luria and Yudovich:

'The whole structure of the mental life of both twins was simultaneously and sharply changed. Once they acquired an objective language system, [they] were able to formulate the aims of their activity verbally, and after only three months we observed the beginnings of meaningful play'.

Thought and language are initially separate activities which interact at a certain point of development

According to Vygotsky (1962), language and thought begin as separate and independent activities. Early on, thinking occurs without language (consisting primarily of images) and language occurs without thought (as when babies cry or make other sounds to express feelings, attract attention or fulfil some other social aim). Around age two, however, *pre-linguistic thought* and *pre-intellectual language*:

'meet and join to initiate a new kind of behaviour [in which] thought becomes verbal and speech rational' (Vygotsky, 1962).

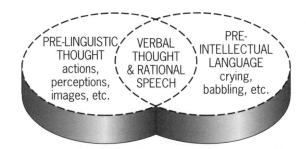

Figure 37.3   A diagrammatic representation of Vygotsky's views on the relationship between language and thought

Vygotsky believed that between ages two and seven, language performs two functions. The first is an *internal* function, which enables internal thought to be monitored and directed. The second is an *external* function, which enables the results of thinking to be communicated to others. However, children cannot yet distinguish between the two functions and, as a result, their speech is *egocentric*. Thus, they talk out loud about their plans and actions and can neither think privately nor communicate publicly to others. Instead, they are caught somewhere between the two and cannot distinguish between 'speech for self' (what Piaget calls *autistic speech*) and 'speech for others' (*socialised speech*).

Vygotsky believed that around age seven (when children typically enter Piaget's *concrete operational* stage of intellectual development: see Chapter 41, pages 357–359), overt language begins to be restricted to communication whilst the thought function of language becomes internalised as internal speech or verbal thought. Piaget saw egocentric speech as a kind of 'running commentary' on the child's behaviour and believed that around age seven it was replaced by socialised (or communicative) speech.

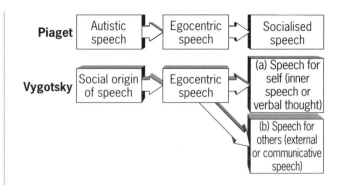

Figure 37.4   The difference between Piaget and Vygotsky with respect to egocentric speech

---

Box 37.6   The function of egocentric speech

Vygotsky (1962) showed that when six- or seven-year-olds are trying to solve a problem and a mishap occurs (such as a pencil breaking) which requires them to revise their thinking, they often *revert* to overt verbalisation. Adults sometimes do the same in similar situations, especially when they believe that no one can hear them. For example, we will often re-trace our steps out loud (such as 'Now, I know I didn't have it when I went in the room, so what did I do before that?'). Vygotsky concluded that the function of egocentric speech was similar to that of inner speech. It does not merely accompany the child's activity but:

'serves mental orientation, conscious understanding; it helps in overcoming difficulties, it is speech for oneself, intimately and usefully connected with the child's thinking. In the end it becomes inner speech' (see Figure 37.4).

Eventually, Piaget accepted Vygotsky's view concerning the function and fate of inner speech. Both inner speech and egocentric speech differ from speech for others in that they do not have to satisfy grammatical conventions. Thus, both are abbreviated, incomplete and concerned more with the essential meaning rather than how it is expressed. For Vygotsky, inner speech is a 'dynamic, shifting and unstable thing which "flutters" between word and thought' (see Figure 37.4).

Overt speech can sometimes resemble inner speech in its abbreviated nature long after egocentric speech has been replaced. For example, people who know each other well may talk in an abbreviated form that would not be used with strangers. Understanding occurs because the more familiar we are with others, and the more shared experiences we have in common, the less explicit our speech has to be. 'Beer?', for example, asked with a rising inflection and in a particular context, would be interpreted as

'Would you like another beer?' in a similar way to how adults interpret the holophrastic speech of young children (see Chapter 33, page 287). In Bernstein's terms, we use restricted code when talking in familiar surroundings to familiar others, whose view of the world we assume to be similar to ours.

Conclusions

Whilst there are many examples indicating that thought can occur without language, the exact language and thought relationship remains to be determined. Of several theoretical perspectives, all can claim some support from the experimental literature.

Summary

■ According to Watson's **peripheralism**, thought is no more than sensations produced by tiny movements of the larynx which are too small to produce audible sounds. Whilst these movements accompany thought, they are not necessary for thinking to occur. Thinking can occur despite complete paralysis and people born deaf and mute are also capable of thinking.

■ Bruner argues that language is essential for thought and knowledge to progress beyond the **enactive** and **iconic modes of representation** to the **symbolic mode**. **Social constructionists** claim that conceptual frameworks and categories provide meaning within a culture, a way of structuring our experience of ourselves and the world.

■ According to the **Sapir–Whorf linguistic relativity hypothesis** (LRH), language determines **how** we think about objects and events, and even **what** we think. This is related to **linguistic determinism**. Both the vocabulary and grammar of a language help to determine a world view.

■ Miller and McNeill distinguish between the **'strong'**, **'weak'** and **'weakest'** versions of the LRH. The 'weak' and 'weakest' versions have typically been tested through perception and memory of **colour**. The fewer colour words there are in a language, the more difficult native speakers should find tests of colour perception and memory.

■ Early studies seemed to support these two versions. However, according to Berlin and Kay, whilst cultures may differ in the number of basic colour terms they use, all cultures draw their basic or **focal** terms from only 11 colours, which emerge in a particular sequence in the history of languages.

■ Berlin and Kay's findings are supported by Heider and Oliver's comparison of Dani-speaking and English-speaking participants' rate of confusion of similar colours. Heider also found that the Dani learnt labels for focal colours much more easily than for non-focal colours. She argues that her data are better explained in terms of **physiological factors** underlying colour vision than linguistic factors.

■ Whorf's evidence was anecdotal rather than empirical, and he exaggerated the differences between Hopi and other languages. Also, we distinguish between a language's grammar and our perceptual experience, and translation between languages implies a universally shared knowledge of the world independent of any particular language. However, language does affect how easily information is processed.

■ Bernstein argued that working class children speak a **restricted code** and middle class children an **elaborated code**. The relationship between actual and potential intelligence is mediated through language, so working class children are prevented from developing their full intellectual potential.

■ Language codes underlie the patterns of learning children bring with them to school. However, identifying two basic types of code is an oversimplification, and the terms 'restricted' and 'elaborated' imply a value judgement.

■ Differences between Standard and **Black English**, which Bernstein sees as a restricted code, have resulted in the latter being called **sub-standard**, rather than **non-standard**. According to Labov, this is an expression of prejudice, and the fact that intelligence tests are written in Standard English puts Black English speakers at a real disadvantage.

■ Black children may be **bilingual**, using the accepted register fluently and creatively at home and with their peers, but adopting unfamiliar standard English in the classroom. **Ebonics** was officially recognised by the Oakland public school board in California in 1996 as a separate language and not a dialect of standard (American) English.

■ According to Piaget, language 'maps' onto previously acquired cognitive structures, so that language is dependent on thought. One example is **object permanence**. Similarly, children who cannot yet **conserve** will not benefit from linguistic training on the use of conservation-related terms. Words can only be understood if certain intellectual skills have already been mastered. So, thought **structures** language.

■ According to Vygotsky, language and thought are initially separate and independent activities. At around age two, **pre-linguistic thought** and **pre-intellectual language** begin to interact to form verbal thought and rational speech.

■ Between the ages of two and seven, language performs both an **internal** and **external** function. The child's failure to distinguish between them results in **egocentric speech**, which largely disappears around age seven. For Vygotsky, this indicates the separation of the two functions. The function of egocentric speech is similar to that of inner speech, which is what it eventually becomes.

UNIT 4
Developmental Psychology

PART 1

Early socialisation

38

EARLY SOCIAL DEVELOPMENT

Introduction and overview

One important challenge faced by human beings is learning to relate to other people. Normally, the first people with whom the new-born interacts are its parents. In early childhood, relationships are formed with brothers and/or sisters, and other children beyond the immediate family. As development continues, so the child's network of relationships increases, with teachers, classmates, neighbours and so on becoming an important part of social development.

This chapter looks at theories and research relating to the process of social development in the first years of life. It concentrates on the processes of *sociability* and *attachment*, beginning with what sociability and attachment are, how attachments develop, and the factors affecting the quality of attachment between a caregiver and infant. However, the focus will be on the theories that have been advanced to explain the attachment process.

What is sociability?

Sociability refers to one of three dimensions of temperament (the others being emotionality and activity), which are taken to be present at birth and inherited (Buss & Plomin, 1984). Specifically, sociability is seeking and being especially gratified by rewards from social interaction, preferring to be with others, sharing activities, and being responsive to and seeking responsiveness *from* others. Whilst babies differ in their degree of sociability, it is a general human tendency to want and seek the company of others. As such, it can be regarded as a prerequisite for attachment development and corresponds to the pre-attachment and indiscriminate attachment phases of the attachment process (see below).

What is attachment?

Kagan *et al.* (1978) have defined attachment as:

'an intense emotional relationship that is specific to two people, that endures over time, and in which prolonged separation from the partner is accompanied by stress and sorrow'.

Whilst this definition applies to attachment formation at any point in the life cycle, our first attachment is crucial for healthy development since it acts as a *prototype* for all later relationships.

Attachment, then, is a close emotional bond that will last for many years. Although affectionate relationships may be established with any consistent caregiver, the most intense relationship that usually occurs in development's early stages is between mother and child, and most research interest has focused on that particular attachment.

STUDYING THE DEVELOPMENT OF ATTACHMENTS

A way of studying attachment in the laboratory is the *Strange Situation,* devised by Ainsworth *et al.* (1971, 1978).

Box 38.1   The Strange Situation

In this, an infant and its mother (and/or sometimes its father) are taken to an unfamiliar room and the infant is free to explore whilst the mother sits passively. After three minutes, a female adult stranger enters the room. Following one minute of silence, the stranger speaks to the mother for one minute, and then approaches the infant.

At this point, the mother leaves, and the stranger and infant are left alone for three minutes. The mother then returns and the stranger leaves. After the mother has tried to resettle the baby, she leaves again and the baby is left alone in the room. After about three minutes, the stranger returns and begins to interact with the baby.

When a further three minutes (or less) have elapsed, the mother returns and the stranger leaves unobtrusively. In all, there are eight increasingly stressful episodes. These may be curtailed (if the baby is unduly distressed) or prolonged (if more time is needed for the baby to become reinvolved in play).

Phases in the development of attachments

The attachment process can be divided into several *phases*. The first (*pre-attachment phase*) lasts until about three months of age. From about six weeks, babies develop an attraction to other human beings in preference to inanimate environmental features. At about six weeks, they engage in behaviours such as nestling, gurgling and smiling which are directed to just about anyone (indeed, for this reason, smiling is referred to as the *social smile*).

At about three months, infants begin to distinguish between people and can discriminate between familiar and unfamiliar people (Maurer & Salapatek, 1976). Although the social smile disappears, infants will allow strangers to handle and look after them without becoming noticeably distressed, provided the stranger gives adequate care. This *indiscriminate attachment phase* (what Ainsworth, 1985, calls the *attachment-in-the-making phase*) lasts until around seven months.

From this time, infants begin to develop specific attachments and actively seek the proximity of certain people (particularly the mother). They become distressed when separated (*separation anxiety*). This *discriminate attachment phase* occurs when infants can reliably distinguish the mother from other people and have developed *object permanence* (the awareness that things continue to exist even when they cannot be seen: see Chapter 41, page 356). At around seven or eight months, infants avoid proximity with unfamiliar people and some, though not all, display the *fear of strangers response* (Schaffer, 1966), which

includes crying and/or trying to move away. The fear response is not elicited by the simple physical presence of strangers. Typically, it will be elicited only by direct contact with a stranger.

From about nine months onwards, infants become increasingly independent of the caregiver. This is called the *multiple attachments phase*, and strong additional bonds are formed with other major caregivers (such as the father, grandparents and siblings) and with peers. Although the fear of strangers response typically diminishes, the strongest attachment continues to be with the discriminate attachment figure of the previous phase.

The quality of attachment

Using the Strange Situation, Ainsworth *et al.* (1978) discovered that infants form one of three basic attachments to the mother. The crucial feature determining the quality of attachment is the mother's *sensitivity* (how she responds to her baby's needs). The sensitive mother sees things from her baby's perspective, correctly interprets its signals, responds to its needs, and is accepting, cooperative and accessible. By contrast, the insensitive mother interacts almost exclusively in terms of her own wishes, moods and activities. Ainsworth *et al.*'s research indicated that sensitive mothers have babies that are *securely attached*, whereas insensitive mothers have *insecurely attached* babies. The insecurely attached babies were either *anxious-avoidant* (or *detached*) or *anxious-resistant* (or *ambivalent,* as shown in Table 38.1.)

An evaluation of the Strange Situation

Vaughn *et al.* (1980) showed that attachment type may change depending on variations in the family's circumstances, suggesting that attachment types are not necessarily permanent characteristics. Others have proposed that *innate differences* between babies could explain differences in attachment quality. Asher (1987), for example, has proposed that some human (and non-human) infants are more intense and anxious than others. Such differences in *temperament* apparently persist into young adulthood at least (Larsen & Diener, 1987). Although accounting for such temperamental differences is difficult, a *reactive sympathetic nervous system* might be responsible (Kagan, 1989).

There may also be other attachment types. Main (1991), for example, has proposed the existence of an *insecure-disorganised/disoriented* attachment type (type D). This refers to a baby that acts as if the attachment figure (as well as the environment) is fear-inducing. To increase attachment behaviour, the baby must seek closer proximity to one of its sources of fear (namely, the attachment figure).

Table 38.1 Behaviour associated with three types of attachment in one-year-olds using the 'Strange Situation'

Category	Name	Sample (%)
Type A	**Anxious-avoidant**	15

Typical behaviour: Baby largely ignores mother, because of indifference towards her. Play is little affected by whether she is present or absent. No or few signs of distress when mother leaves, and actively ignores or avoids her on her return. Distress is caused by being alone, rather than being left by the mother. Can be as easily comforted by the stranger as by the mother. In fact, both adults are treated in a very similar way.

Category	Name	Sample (%)
Type B	**Securely attached**	70

Typical behaviour: Baby plays happily while the mother is present, whether the stranger is present or not. Mother is largely 'ignored' because she can be trusted to be there if needed. Clearly distressed when mother leaves and play is considerably reduced. Seeks immediate contact with mother on her return, is quickly calmed down in her arms and resumes play. The distress is caused by the mother's absence, not being alone. Although the stranger can provide some comfort, she and the mother are treated very differently.

Category	Name	Sample (%)
Type C	**Anxious-resistant**	15

Typical behaviour: Baby is fussy and wary while the mother is present. Cries a lot more and explores much less than types A and B and has difficulty using mother as a safe base. Very distressed when mother leaves, seeks contact with her on her return, but simultaneously shows anger and resists contact (may approach her and reach out to be picked up, but then struggles to get down again). This demonstrates the baby's ambivalence towards her. Doesn't return readily to play. Actively resists stranger's efforts to make contact.

(Based on Ainsworth *et al.*, 1978, taken from Gross, 1996)

This produces a conflict between seeking and avoiding proximity which are incompatible.

Cross-cultural research indicates that there are marked differences in the distributions of Ainsworth *et al.*'s three types of attachment (Takahashi, 1990). Although type B appears to be universally the most common, type A is relatively more common in Western European countries, whereas type C is more common in Israel and Japan.

Despite various empirical, methodological and ethical criticisms (Durkin, 1995), the Strange Situation is generally considered to be a useful procedure for studying socioemotional development in infancy (Lamb *et al.*, 1985). Indeed, secure attachment appears to *predict* future social competence. For example, securely attached infants at 12 to 18 months functioned more confidently at age two to five, in that they were enthusiastic and persistent when given challenging tasks (Sroufe *et al.*, 1983). They

were also more outgoing and responsive with other children, suggesting that they had developed a sense of *basic trust* (Erikson, 1963: see Chapter 47, page 413). Additionally, three- to five-year-old children with insecure attachments found it difficult to get on with other children in nursery school and were often hostile, isolated and socially inept (Bretherton, 1985).

THEORIES OF THE ATTACHMENT PROCESS
'Cupboard love' theories

According to *psychoanalytic* accounts, infants become attached to their caregivers (usually the mother) because of the caregiver's ability to satisfy *instinctual needs*. For Freud (1926):

'the reason why the infant in arms wants to perceive the presence of its mother is only because it already knows by experience that she satisfies all its needs without delay'.

Freud believed that healthy attachments are formed when feeding practices satisfy the infant's needs for food, security and oral sexual gratification (see Chapter 66, page 570). Unhealthy attachments occur when infants are *deprived* of food and oral pleasure, or are *overindulged*. Thus, psychoanalytic accounts emphasise the significance of feeding practices, especially breast-feeding, and the importance of the *maternal figure* whose status Freud saw as being:

'unique, without parallel, [and] established unilaterally for a whole lifetime as the first and strongest love-object ... the prototype of all later love-reactions'.

The *behaviourist* view of attachment also sees infants as becoming attached to those who satisfy their need for nourishment and tend to their other physiological needs (a very rare example of agreement between the psychoanalytic and behaviourist perspectives: see Chapter 1). Infants associate their caregivers (who act as *conditioned reinforcers*) with gratification, and they learn to approach them to have their needs satisfied. This eventually *generalises* into a feeling of security whenever the caregiver is present (see Chapter 32).

However, neither behaviourist nor psychoanalytic accounts of attachment as 'cupboard love' are likely to be true, as was demonstrated by Harlow and his associates (e.g. Harlow, 1959; Harlow & Zimmerman, 1959). Harlow was actually interested in learning in rhesus monkeys and, to control for experience and prevent the spread of disease, he separated new-born monkeys from their mothers and raised them in individual cages. Each cage contained a 'baby blanket', and the monkeys became intensely attached to them, showing great distress when they were taken away to be laundered. This apparent attachment to their blankets, and the display of behaviours comparable to those of infant monkeys actually separated from their mothers, seemed to contradict the view that attachment comes from an association with nourishment.

Figure 38.2   Infant monkeys frightened by a novel stimulus (in this case a toy teddy bear banging a drum) retreat to the terry cloth-covered 'mother' rather than to the wire 'mother'

Box 38.2   The need for contact comfort in rhesus monkeys

To determine whether food or the close comfort of a blanket was more important, Harlow placed infant rhesus monkeys in cages with two 'surrogate mothers'. In one experiment, one of the surrogate mothers was made from wire and had a baby bottle attached to 'her'. The other was made from soft and cuddly terry cloth but did not have a bottle attached. The infants spent most of their time clinging to the cloth mother, even though she provided no nourishment. Harlow concluded from this that monkeys (at least) have an unlearned need for *contact comfort* which is as basic as the need for food.

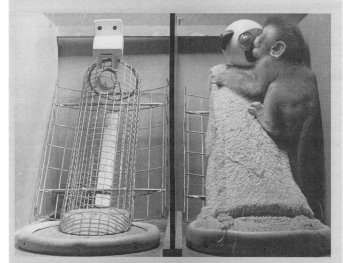

Figure 38.1   Even when the wire monkey is the sole source of nourishment, infant monkeys showed a marked preference for the terry-cloth 'mother'

The cloth surrogate mother also served as a 'secure base' from which the infants could explore their environment. When novel stimuli were placed in the cage, the infants would gradually move away from the 'mother' for initial exploration, often returning to 'her' before exploring further. When 'fear stimuli', such as an oversized wooden insect or a toy bear loudly beating a drum, were placed in the cage, the infants would cling to the cloth mother for security before exploring the stimuli. However, when the infants were alone or were with the wire surrogate mother, they would either 'freeze' and cower in fear or run aimlessly around the cage.

Later research showed that when the cloth 'mother' had other qualities, such as rocking, being warm and feeding, the attachment was even stronger (Harlow & Suomi, 1970). There are clear parallels between Harlow's experimental manipulations and what often happens when human infants have contact with warm-bodied parents who rock, cuddle and feed them.

Although attachment clearly does not depend on feeding alone, the rhesus monkeys reared exclusively with their cloth 'mothers' did *not* develop normally. They became extremely aggressive adults, rarely interacting with other monkeys, made inappropriate sexual responses, and were difficult (if not impossible) to breed. So, in monkeys, at least, normal development seems to depend on factors other than food. Harlow & Suomi's (1970) research indicates that one of these is interaction with other members of the species during the first six months of life.

Research on attachment in humans also casts doubt on 'cupboard love' theories. Schaffer & Emerson's (1964) longitudinal study found that infants *do* become attached to people who do not perform caregiving activities. For Schaffer (1971), 'cupboard love' theories of attachment see infants as passive recipients of nutrition rather than active seekers of stimulation. In Schaffer's view, babies do not 'live to eat', but rather they 'eat to live'.

Ethological theories

The term attachment was actually introduced to psychology by *ethologists*. Lorenz (1935) showed that some non-humans form a strong bond with the first moving object they encounter (which is usually, but not always, the mother). In *precocial species* (in which the new-born is capable of locomotion and possesses well-developed sense organs), the mobile young animal needs to learn rapidly to recognise its caregivers and to stay close to them. Lorenz called this *imprinting* and, since it occurs through mere exposure without any feeding taking place, it too casts doubt on the plausibility of 'cupboard love' theories of attachment, at least in non-humans.

Box 38.3   Some characteristics of imprinting

The response of following a moving object indicates that a bond has been formed between the infant and the individual or object on which it has been imprinted. Ethologists see imprinting as an example of a *fixed-action pattern* which occurs in the presence of a species-specific releasing stimulus (or *sign stimulus*). Lorenz saw imprinting as unique because he believed that it only occurred during a brief *critical period* of life and, once it had occurred, was irreversible.

This is supported by the finding that when animals imprinted on members of other species reach sexual maturity, they may show a sexual preference for members of that species.

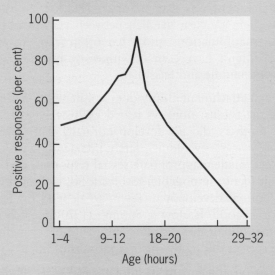

Figure 38.3   The graph represents the relationship between imprinting and the age (hours after hatching) at which a duckling was exposed to a moving model of a male duck. Imprinting was measured in terms of the percentage of trials on which the duckling followed the model on a later test. Imprinting reached a peak at between 12 and 17 hours after hatching (Adapted from Hess, 1958)

A *critical period* is a restricted time period during which certain events must take place if correct development is to occur (Bornstein, 1989). Lorenz saw imprinting as being genetically 'switched on' and then 'switched off' at the end of the critical period, and in some species the critical period appears to be bounded by the age at which they are first able to move and the age at which they develop a fear of strangers. However, the view that the critical period is under genetic control has been disputed by studies showing that the period of imprintability can be extended (e.g. Sluckin, 1965).

This has led researchers to propose the existence of a *sensitive period*, in which learning is most likely to happen, and will happen most easily, but which is not absolutely critical. Also, imprinting *can* be reversed (at least in the laboratory). Imprinting of the sort that occurs in geese, for example, clearly does not occur in humans, since new-born children separated from their mothers will not attach to a mannikin. Moreover, and as noted on page 329, not all children develop a fear of strangers and, when they do, it appears *before* they are capable of independent movement.

Bowlby's theory

The most comprehensive theory of human attachment formation is that of Bowlby (1953, 1969, 1973, 1980). Bowlby was influenced by ethological theory in general and Lorenz's concept of imprinting in particular. Bowlby argued that because new-born human infants are entirely helpless, they are *genetically programmed* to behave towards their mothers in ways that ensure their survival.

Box 38.4   Species-specific behaviours used by infants to shape and control their caregivers' behaviour

Sucking: Whilst sucking is important for nourishment, not all sucking is nutritive (Piaget, 1952). Non-nutritive sucking, also seen in non-humans, appears to be an innate tendency which inhibits a new-born's distress. In Western societies, babies are often given 'dummies' to pacify them when they are distressed.

Cuddling: Human infants adjust their posture to mould themselves to the contour of the parent's body. The reflexive response that encourages front-to-front contact with the mother plays an important part in reinforcing the caregiver's behaviour (see Harlow's experiments on page 331).

Looking: When parents do not respond to an infant's eye contact, it usually shows signs of distress (Tronick *et* *al.*, 1978). An infant's looking behaviour thus acts as an invitation for the mother to respond. If she does not, the infant is disturbed and avoids further visual contact. Mutual gazing, by contrast, is rewarding for the infant (Stern, 1977).

Smiling: This appears to be an innate behaviour, since babies can produce smiles shortly after birth. Adults view the smiling infant as a 'real person' which they find very rewarding.

Crying: Young infants usually cry only when they are hungry, cold or in pain, and crying is most effectively ended by picking up and cuddling them. Caregivers who respond quickly during the first three months tend to have babies that cry *less* during the last four months of their first year than infants with unresponsive caregivers (Bell & Ainsworth, 1972). Thus, babies with responsive caregivers learn to cry only when they need attention. Moreover, such infants learn to communicate effectively by means of behaviour other than crying (e.g. gestures and pre-speech sounds).

(Adapted from Carlson, 1988)

Bowlby argued that the mother also inherits a genetic blueprint which programmes her to respond to the baby. There is a critical period during which the *synchrony* of action between mother and infant produces an attachment. In Bowlby's (1951) view, mothering is useless for all children if delayed until after two-and-a-half to three years and for most children if delayed until after 12 months. Once the mother and baby attachment has been formed, it activates an internal system that regulates how far away from the mother the child will move and the amount of fear the child will show towards strangers (Krebs & Blackman, 1988). For Bowlby (1969):

> 'No form of behaviour is accompanied by stronger feelings than is attachment behaviour. Infants greet those with whom they are attached with joy, and become anxious, angry and sorrowful when they leave or threaten to leave'.

Infants display a strong innate tendency to become attached to one particular individual (*monotropy*), an attachment that is *qualitatively* different from any subsequent attachments. For Bowlby (1951):

> 'mother love in infancy is as important for mental health as are vitamins and proteins for physical health'.

Bowlby's view that there is a critical period for the development of attachment is, however, almost certainly untrue (see Chapter 39).

Box 38.5   Is there a maternal-sensitive period for bonding?

Related to Bowlby's belief in a critical period for a baby's attachment to the mother is his belief in the existence of a *maternal-sensitive* period, during which mother–child bonding is most likely to occur. According to Klaus & Kennell (1976), if the infant was taken away from the mother during the maternal-sensitive period (which they believed might be governed by the release of maternal hormones), bonding between the mother and infant would not occur.

Klaus and Kennell's *extended contact hypothesis* proposed that mothers who had large amounts of contact with their new-borns were more likely to cuddle, soothe and enjoy their babies than mothers who had only brief periods of contact. Although there were several methodological flaws in Klaus and Kennell's research, their views were influential in changing hospital practices: prior to the findings' publication, most hospitals tended to separate new-borns from their mothers after delivery.

'Bonding' can, however, take place if mothers see their babies one day or even several months after birth (Durkin, 1995). Moreover, the father's caregiving can be just as effective as the mother's (Lamb, 1976), and there seems to be little difference in how children form attachments to their mothers and fathers despite the father's lack of 'bonding hormones' (Parke & Swain, 1980: see also Box 38.6).

Bowlby's views on monotropy have also been criticised. For example, several indicators of attachment can be shown for a variety of attachment figures other than the mother (Rutter, 1981). Although Bowlby did not dispute the formation of *multiple attachments*, he saw attachment to the mother as being unique in that it is the first to appear and the strongest of all. However, Schaffer & Emerson (1964) showed that whilst not all the child's attachments are of equal strength, multiple attachments seem to be the rule rather than the exception, and that the mother is not always or necessarily the main attachment figure.

For Bowlby, the father is of no direct emotional significance to the young infant, but only of indirect value as an emotional and economic support for the mother. Whilst, as contemporary sociobiology suggests, mothers may have a greater *parental investment* in their offspring and hence are better prepared for child rearing and attachment (Kenrick, 1994), Bowlby's views on fathers as attachment figures are disputed by the findings of several studies, including that conducted by Lamb (see above).

Box 38.6 The father–child bond

- Many fathers form close bonds with their offspring shortly after birth (Greenberg & Morris, 1974).

- Some 12-month-old (or older) infants are equally or more attached to the father than the mother (Kotelchuck, 1976).

- Although fathers tend to spend less time with their children than mothers, the time they do spend is typically related to play rather than to care (Easterbrooks & Goldberg, 1984).

- When fathers become primary caregivers, they interact with their infants in the nurturing, gentle fashion which is more typical of mothers (Field, 1978).

- In general, whilst there may be differences in the style of interaction, there are no differences in the quantity or even quality of mothers' and fathers' caregiving (Yogman *et al.*, 1977).

(Adapted from Crooks & Stein, 1991)

Figure 38.4   According to Bowlby, the father is of no direct emotional significance to the infant/young child. But the evidence suggests that fathers are capable of caregiving which is comparable to that of mothers – both in quantity and quality

According to Parke (1981):

'both mother and father are important attachment objects for their infants, but the circumstances that lead to selecting mum or dad may differ'.

As Box 38.6 shows, rather than being a poor substitute for a mother, the father makes his own unique contribution to the care and development of infants and young children.

Cognitive–developmental accounts

Instead of looking at attachment in terms of the emotional bonds it involves, cognitive–developmental theorists emphasise the *cognitive* relationships between parents and offspring. Cognitive–developmental theory focuses on the infant's ability to distinguish between itself and others (Krebs & Blackman, 1988). Once that ability has been acquired, the infant begins to distinguish between strangers and primary caregivers. Cognitive–developmental theorists are also interested in the ways in which caregivers stimulate the infant's *growth of knowledge*.

Schaffer's (1971) research is fundamentally cognitive-developmental in nature, since it shows that infants only become attached to a specific individual when they are able to distinguish that person from others. For cognitive–developmental theorists, infants become attached to their caregivers because they provide the most interesting, informative and cognitively challenging events in their lives. The satisfaction infants derive from securing an attachment can thus be explained in terms of their growing sense of competence and mastery as well as the

effective mutual stimulation of caregiver and infant. Rather than being due to the satisfaction of instinctual needs, then, cognitive–developmental theorists see attachment as coming from the development of an increasingly organised and integrated conception of the social world.

Conclusions

This chapter has looked at theories and research relating to the process of social development in the first years of life, particularly attachment and theories which seek to explain it. Each theory focuses on a particular aspect of attachment, with some emphasising innate factors and others emphasising learning. No one theory is correct, and all the factors identified by the various theories are implicated in the attachment process.

Summary

■ **Sociability** and **attachment** are two major aspects of social development. **Sociability** is the general human tendency to want/seek the company of other humans and is a prerequisite for the development of attachments.

■ An **attachment** is an intense, lasting, emotional relationship, disruption to which causes stress and sorrow. The child's most intense early attachment is usually with its mother. The **Strange Situation** is a method for studying attachment in the laboratory.

■ The attachment process can be divided into the **pre-attachment** (six weeks to three months), **indiscriminate attachment** (three to seven months), and **discriminate attachment** (seven to nine months) **phases**. During the latter, infants begin to develop specific attachments and actively seek proximity with attachment figures.

■ Whilst all babies display **separation anxiety**, only some display the **fear of strangers response**. This is typically only triggered by direct contact with a stranger. During the **multiple attachments phase** (nine months onwards), the child becomes increasingly independent of its caregiver and forms strong additional attachments.

■ Ainsworth *et al.* found differences in the **quality of attachment** of infants to their mother, with the mother's **sensitivity** being the determining factor. Sensitive mothers tend to have **securely attached** (type B) babies, whilst those with insensitive mothers tend to be either **anxious-avoidant/detached** (type A), or **anxious-resistant/ambivalent** (type C).

■ Securely attached babies use the mother as a safe base and are distressed by her absence, whilst anxious-avoidant babies are distressed by being alone. Anxious-resistant babies have difficulty using the mother as a safe base and explore much less than the other types.

■ Attachment types are not necessarily fixed characteristics, and Main has found evidence of an **insecure-disorganised/disoriented** (type D) attachment type. Cross-cultural research suggests that whilst type B is universally the most common, type A is relatively more common in Western European countries, and type C is more common in Israel and Japan.

■ According to Freud, infants become attached to their mother because she satisfies their **instinctual needs**. Similarly, **behaviourists** see caregivers as **conditioned reinforcers** who become associated with gratification; this **generalises** into a feeling of security whenever the caregiver is present.

■ Harlow exposed the limitations of the **cupboard-love approach** by showing that rhesus monkeys have an unlearnt need for **contact comfort**, which is as basic as the need for food. The cloth mother also served as a secure base from which the infants could explore their environment. However, interaction with other monkeys during the first six months appears to be necessary for normal development.

■ Lorenz showed that the young of **precocial species** form a strong bond with the first moving object they encounter (usually the mother), through **imprinting**. This is a **fixed-action pattern** which occurs in response to a species-specific **sign stimulus**. It was believed to be irreversible and confined to a brief **critical period**. However, imprinting probably involves a **sensitive period**.

■ According to Bowlby, babies are **genetically programmed** to shape/control their caregivers' behaviour in **species-specific** ways that ensure survival. The mother also inherits a genetic blueprint which programmes her to respond to the baby. Once the attachment has been formed, it activates an internal system that regulates proximity to the mother and fear of strangers.

■ Infants display a strong innate tendency to become attached to one particular person (**monotropy**), and the attachment to the mother is **qualitatively** different from any subsequent attachments. However, there is little difference in how children form attachments to mothers and fathers, despite the latters' lack of 'bonding hormones'.

■ Although the child's attachments vary in strength, **multiple attachments** seem to be the rule, and the mother is not always/necessarily the main attachment figure.

■ Whilst sociobiology sees the mother as having greater **parental investment** in her offspring, the findings of several studies suggest that the father is an important attachment figure in his own right.

■ **Cognitive–developmental** theories emphasise the **cognitive** relationships between parents and offspring, such as infants' ability to distinguish between themselves and others, and between strangers and primary caregivers. These theories are also interested in how caregivers stimulate the infant's growth of knowledge. Attachments stem from the satisfaction derived from a growing sense of competence/mastery/understanding of the social world.

39

THE EFFECTS OF EARLY DEPRIVATION

Introduction and overview

Chapter 38 described Harlow's research on infant rhesus monkeys which explored 'cupboard love' theories' claims that nutritional provision is a crucial element in attachment formation. As well as dispelling those theories, Harlow's research also provided insights into the effects on infant rhesus monkeys of being raised without a real mother. For example, when the females reached maturity, most of them rejected the advances of males and only four of 18 females conceived through natural insemination. Those producing offspring either rejected their young, by pushing them away, or behaved 'indifferently' towards them.

What are the effects on *humans* of being deprived of nurturing caregivers and, if any effects do occur, are they permanent? This chapter critically considers research into the effects and permanence of certain types of deprivation in human children.

Bowlby's maternal deprivation hypothesis

As was seen in Chapter 38, Bowlby argued for the existence of a critical period in attachment formation. This, along with his theory of monotropy, led him to claim that mother–infant attachment could not be broken in the first few years of life without serious and permanent damage to social, emotional and intellectual development. For Bowlby (1951):

'an infant and young child should experience a warm, intimate and continuous relationship with his mother (or permanent mother figure) in which both find satisfaction and enjoyment'.

Bowlby's *maternal deprivation hypothesis* was based largely on studies conducted in the 1930s and 1940s of children brought up in residential nurseries and other large institutions (such as orphanages).

Box 39.1 Some early research findings on the effects of institutionalisation

Goldfarb (1943): Fifteen children raised in institutions from about six months until three and a half years of age were matched (according to genetic factors and mothers' education and occupational status) with 15 children who had gone straight from their mothers to a foster home. The institutionalised children lived in almost complete social isolation during the first year of life.

At age three, the institutionalised group were behind the fostered group on measures of abstract thinking, social maturity, rule-following and sociability. Between ten and 14, the institutionalised group continued to perform more poorly on the various tests, and their average IQs were 72 and 95 respectively. Despite their non-random assignment to the institutionalised and fostered 'conditions' (so that important individual differences between the children might have determined how they were assigned), Goldfarb concluded that *all* the institutionalised children's poorer abilities could be attributed to the time spent in the institutions.

Spitz (1945, 1946) and Spitz & Wolf (1946): Focusing on the *emotional* effects of institutionalisation, Spitz found that in some very poor South American orphanages, children received only minimal attention from the staff. The orphans were apathetic and displayed *anaclitic depression*, which involves such symptoms as a poor appetite and morbidity. After three months of unbroken deprivation, recovery was rarely, if ever, complete. *Hospitalism*, which involves physical and mental deterioration, is caused by separation from the mother as a result of long-term hospitalisation. In their study of 91 orphanage infants in the United States and Canada, Spitz and Wolf found that over one third died before their first birthday, despite good nutrition and medical care.

Unfortunately, Bowlby, Goldfarb, Spitz and Wolf all failed to recognise that the *understimulating nature* of the institutional environment, as well as (or instead of) the absence of maternal care, could be responsible for the effects they observed. To implicate *maternal deprivation* in developmental retardation, it is necessary to disentangle the different *types* of deprivation and the different kinds of retardation they produce (Rutter, 1981).

Rutter also pointed out that Bowlby's use of the term 'deprivation' failed to distinguish between the effects of being separated from an attachment figure and the effects of never having formed an attachment at all. *Deprivation* (de-privation) is properly used to describe the *loss* through separation of the maternal attachment, and Bowlby's theory and research were mainly concerned with this. By contrast, *privation* is properly used to refer to the *absence* of an attachment figure. The effects of both deprivation and privation will be considered in the remainder of this chapter.

Deprivation (or separation)

SHORT-TERM EFFECTS

One example of short-term deprivation (days or weeks rather than months) is when a child goes into a nursery whilst its mother goes into hospital. Another is when the child itself goes into hospital (cf. Spitz's research described in Box 39.1). Bowlby showed that when young children go into hospital, they display *distress*, a response which is characterised by three important components or stages.

Box 39.2   The components or stages of distress

Protest: The initial, immediate, reaction takes the form of crying, screaming, kicking and generally struggling to escape, or clinging to the mother to prevent her leaving. This is an outward and direct expression of the child's anger, fear, bitterness, bewilderment and so on.

Despair: The struggling and protest eventually give way to calmer behaviour. The child may appear apathetic, but internally still feels all the anger and fear previously displayed. It keeps such feelings 'locked-up' and wants nothing to do with other people. The child may no longer anticipate the mother's return and barely reacts to others' offers of comfort, preferring to comfort itself by rocking, thumb sucking and so on.

Detachment: If the separation continues, the child begins to respond to people again, but tends to treat everybody alike and rather superficially. However, if reunited with the mother at this stage, the child may well have to 'relearn' the relationship with her and may even 'reject' her (as she 'rejected' her child).

Factors influencing distress

Evidence suggests that not all children go through the stages of distress, and that they differ in terms of how much distress they experience. Separation is likely to be most distressing between the age of seven to eight months (when the infant has just formed an attachment: see Chapter 38, page 329) and three years, with the period between 12 and 18 months being associated with maximum distress (Maccoby, 1980). The child's ability to

hold a mental image of the absent mother is one of the variables associated with age, as is its limited understanding of language. Thus, because young children do not understand the meaning of phrases like 'in a few days' time' or 'next week', it is difficult to explain to them that the separation is only temporary. Children might believe they have been abandoned completely, that their mother no longer loves them, and that they are in some way to blame for what has happened ('Mummy is going away because I've been naughty').

Although there are wide differences *within* the genders, boys are generally more distressed and vulnerable than girls. Additionally, and irrespective of gender, any behaviour problems, such as aggressiveness, that existed before the separation are likely to be accentuated. Children appear to cope best if their relationship with the mother is stable and relaxed, but not too close. An extremely close and protective relationship, in which the child and mother are rarely apart and the child is unused to meeting new people, may produce extreme distress simply because the child has not experienced anything like it before.

Figure 39.1   John (17 months) experienced extreme distress while spending 9 days in a residential nursery when his mother was in hospital having a second baby. According to Bowlby, he was grieving for the absent mother. Robertson & Robertson (1969) (who made a series of films called *Young Children in Brief Separation*) found that the extreme distress was caused by a combination of factors: loss of the mother, strange environment and routines, multiple caretakers and lack of a mother substitute

---

Box 39.3   The benefits of separation

'Good' previous separations can help the child cope with subsequent separations and become more independent

---

and self-sufficient generally. Stacey *et al.* (1970) studied four-year-olds who had gone into hospital to have their tonsils removed. They were in hospital for four days, and their parents were not allowed to stay overnight. Those children who coped best had experienced separations before, such as staying overnight with their grandparents.

The existence of *multiple attachments* has also been shown to make separation less stressful. For example, when the father is also actively involved as a caregiver, children in the Strange Situation (see Chapter 38, page 329) are more comfortable than when only the mother acts as the main caregiver (Kotelchuck, 1976). The quality of the substitute care is also influential and even institutions can provide high-quality care, as in Burlingham & Freud's (1944) Hampstead nursery where stability, affection and active involvement were encouraged.

Unfortunately, many institutions are run in such a way that it is extremely difficult for substitute attachments to develop. High staff turnover, a large number of children competing for the attention of a small number of staff, and the sometimes deliberate policy of no special relationships being formed in order to avoid claims of favouritism and consequent jealousy, can all act against the development of high-quality substitute attachment (Tizard & Rees, 1974).

The evidence concerning *day care* seems to indicate that, contrary to Bowlby's views, the consequences are not necessarily detrimental to the child (Kagan *et al.*, 1980). It is the *quality* and *stability* of the substitute care that seem to matter. When a centre is well staffed and well equipped, there are very few negative effects. A poor centre, however, can have harmful effects. This also seems to be the case with day nurseries (Garland & White, 1980) and child-minders (Mayall & Petrie, 1983). Mayall and Petrie found that the quality of British child-minding was variable, with some minders being highly competent and others failing to provide a stimulating environment.

Box 39.4   To work or not to work?

In a review of 40 years' research, Mooney and Munton (cited in Judd, 1997) conclude that there is no evidence that working mothers stunt their children's emotional or social development. Even poor childcare may make no difference to a child from a stable family, whilst good quality care may provide positive benefits. Instead of debating the rights and wrongs of working mothers, we should focus on how to provide enough good childcare.

British families have changed fundamentally in the past 25 years. In more than 70 per cent of two-parent families with dependent children, both parents work, and the proportion of children living in single-parent families has risen from eight to 21 per cent.

What is needed is a national strategy for childcare which ensures that all employees are properly trained and paid.

(Based on Judd, 1997)

However, according to Varin (cited in Cooper, 1996a), babies who spend long periods in day-care nurseries are more likely to behave uncooperatively than those who stay at home with their mothers and are less likely to make friends. Varin argues that:

'these results suggest that at least for some children an early and extended group experience does not ... foster socio-moral development, even if the quality of group care is "good enough"'.

In Varin's view, governments should introduce measures promoting more flexible employment patterns so that children could be cared for at home by their parents in the early stages of life, 'a unique type of care which cannot be substituted for by any education'.

LONG-TERM EFFECTS

Long-term deprivation includes the permanent separation resulting from parental *death* and the increasingly common separation caused by *divorce*. Possibly the most common effect of long-term deprivation is what Bowlby calls *separation anxiety* (the fear that separation will occur again in the future).

Box 39.5   Characteristics associated with separation anxiety

- Increased aggressive behaviour and greater demands towards the mother.

- Clinging behaviour: the child will not let the mother out of its sight. This may generalise to other relationships, so that a man who experienced 'bad' childhood separations may be very dependent on, and demanding of, his wife.

- Detachment: the child becomes apparently self-sufficient because it cannot afford to be let down again.

- Some fluctuation between clinging and detachment.

- Psychosomatic (psychophysiological) reactions.

According to Bowlby, *school phobia/refusal* is an expression of separation anxiety. The child fears that something dreadful will happen to its mother whilst it is at school, so it stays at home in order to prevent this.

The effects of divorce

According to Schaffer (1996a), nearly all children (especially boys), regardless of their age, are adversely affected by parental divorce, at least in the short-term. However, the nature, severity and duration of the effects vary greatly between children. Many children gradually adjust after two to three years following the divorce, although this is influenced by many factors, including continuity of contact with the non-custodial parent, the financial status/lifestyle of the single-parent family, and whether the custodial parent remarries and a congenial step-family is formed.

Box 39.6   Some of the major effects on children of parental divorce

Compared with children of similar social backgrounds whose parents remain married, those whose parents divorce show consistent but small differences throughout childhood. They also have different life courses as they move into adulthood. The differences include:

- Lower levels of academic achievement and self-esteem.

- Higher incidence of conduct and other problems of psychological adjustment during childhood.

- Earlier social maturity with some transitions to adulthood (such as leaving home, beginning sexual relationships, entering cohabitation or marriage, and childbearing) typically occurring at earlier ages.

- A tendency in young adulthood to more changes of job, lower socioeconomic status, and indications of a higher frequency of depression and lower scores on measures of psychological well-being.

- More distant relationships in adulthood with parents and other kin.

These differences refer to *average* scores for children of divorced and non-divorced parents. The variation is wide, particularly for those whose parents have divorced.

(Based on Richards, 1995)

The findings summarised by Richards (1995) are *correlational*, and divorce may not be the only factor producing the differences described in Box 39.6. For example, *divorce-prone couples* (those most likely to divorce) might

have particular child-rearing styles which account for the differences. This hypothesis is supported by the finding that some of the effects associated with divorce can be seen *before* couples separate (Elliott & Richards, 1991). However, this hypothesis cannot account for all the effects seen *later* (Booth & Amato, 1994).

Another hypothesis implicates the amount of contact and parenting styles after separation. For example, children reared in a single-parent household with a same-sex parent do less well than other children (Downey & Powell, 1996). Although growing up in a single-parent household may not necessarily be disadvantageous, the *change* from two parents to a single residential parent might be significant (Richards, 1987).

According to Schaffer (1996a), *inter-parental conflict* before, during and after the separation/formal divorce, is the single most damaging factor. Amato (1993), for example, has shown that conflict between parents who live together is associated with low self-esteem in children, and low self-esteem may lead to other difficulties including lower school achievement and difficulties in forming relationships. Other hypotheses concern *economic factors*, *life changes*, *relationships with wider kin* and *relationship patterns*. Richards (1995) argues that we need to test these hypotheses, since all have implications for social policy.

Figure 39.2   It is not divorce as such that makes children whose parents split up more likely to become maladjusted, but inter-parental conflict, especially when the child becomes the focus of the conflict, as in *Kramer vs Kramer*, starring Dustin Hoffman and Meryl Streep

Some evidence suggests that divorce can actually *benefit* both parents and children by increasing self-reliance and giving them control over their lives. Woollett and Fuller's research (cited in Laurance, 1996) does *not* indicate that divorce is a 'good thing'. However, their data suggest that children experience a sense of stability as a result of a feeling of love being focused on them (see Chapter 49).

Box 39.7   The effects of parental death

Parental death is a special kind of separation because, unlike divorce, it is unlikely that there was a history of discord, although in some cases the period prior to death may have been difficult (Flanagan, 1996). At least one study (Bifulco *et al.*, 1992) has shown that children who experience their mother's death have higher rates of anxiety and depression in adulthood compared with children whose mother separated from them for longer than a year. As with divorce, several factors can modify the effect of parental death, including the degree of subsequent substitute care and the effect the death has on other family members (Flanagan, 1996).

Privation

As noted earlier (see page 337), *privation* is the failure to develop an attachment to any individual. In humans, it is usually (but not necessarily) associated with children reared in institutions, either from or shortly after birth. Given the obvious importance of the child's first relationship, the failure to develop an attachment of any kind is likely to adversely affect all subsequent relationships.

Harlow's research (see page 331) showed that monkeys brought up with only surrogate mothers were very disturbed in their later sexual behaviour and had to be artificially inseminated because they would not mate naturally. Also, the unmothered females became very inadequate mothers. In humans, privation has been shown to have a variety of physical, intellectual and social effects.

Affectionless psychopathy

According to Bowlby, separation experiences in early childhood cause *affectionless psychopathy* (the inability to have deep feelings for other people and the consequent lack of meaningful interpersonal relationships).

Box 39.8   Bowlby's (1946) study of 44 juvenile thieves

Of 44 juvenile thieves, 14 showed many affectionless characteristics (such as an inability to experience guilt). By contrast, none in a control group of emotionally disturbed juveniles not guilty of a crime showed such characteristics. Seven of the thieves had suffered complete and prolonged separation from their mothers, or established foster mothers, for six months during their first five years of life. A further two had spent nine months in hospital, unvisited, during their second year (which is when attachments are normally being consolidated: see Chapter 38). Only three of the 30 other non-affectionless thieves had suffered comparable separations.

Bowlby interpreted his findings in terms of deprivation, but it is more likely that *privation* was the major cause of the affectionless character. The general picture is of multiple changes of mother-figure and home during the children's early years, making the *establishment* of attachments very difficult (Rutter, 1981). Additionally, the study itself has methodological problems. For example, it was a *retrospective* study in which the children and their mothers had to remember past events, and they may have done this less than accurately. Also, Bowlby did not offer any explanation for the remainder of the children (in fact the majority) who had *not* suffered complete and prolonged separations.

Later, Bowlby *et al.* (1956) studied 60 children aged seven to 13 who had spent between five months and two years in a tuberculosis sanitorium (in which no substitute mothering was provided) at various ages up to four. About half had been separated from their parents before they were two years old. There were few significant differences in terms of IQ scores or teachers' ratings when these children were compared with a group of non-separated 'control' children from the same school classes. Although the separated children were more prone to 'daydreaming', showed less initiative, were over-excited, rougher in play, less able to concentrate and less competitive, the *overall* picture was that the two groups were more similar than different. They did not differ as far as affectionless psychopathy was concerned, regardless of whether the separation had occurred before or after age two.

Referring to the common occurrence of illness and death in the sanitorium children's families (10 per cent of the mothers had died by the time of follow-up), Bowlby *et al.* were forced to conclude that 'part of the emotional disturbance can be attributed to factors other than separation'. The claimed link between affectionless psychopathy and *separation* (or bond disruption) is, therefore, largely unsubstantiated. Unwittingly, however, Bowlby may have provided evidence to support the view that *privation* is associated with the affectionless character. This is certainly Rutter's (1981) view, who suggests that a failure to form bonds in early childhood is likely to lead to:

'an initial phase of clinging, dependent behaviour, followed by attention-seeking, uninhibited, indiscriminate friendliness and finally a personality characterised by lack of guilt, an inability to keep rules and an inability to form lasting relationships'.

Developmental retardation

According to Dennis (1960), there is a *critical period* for intellectual development before age two. Dennis's claim was based on his study of Iranian orphanages, in which children adopted after the age of two appeared incapable of closing the gap between themselves and average children, unlike those adopted before age two. However, the *reversal* of privation's effects on intellectual functioning *after* age two (as well as the long-term effects of early privation in the absence of any intervention) were dramatically shown by Skeels & Dye (1939) and followed up by Skeels (1966).

Figure 39.3   Children raised in large institutions are not only denied the opportunity of forming an attachment with a mother-figure but also experience poor, unstimulating environments that are associated with learning difficulties and retarded linguistic development

---

Box 39.9   Reversing the effects of early intellectual privation (Skeels & Dye, 1939; Skeels, 1966)

The original study looked at 25 children raised until the age of two in an American orphanage which offered a minimum of social interaction and stimulation. At age two, 13 children (average IQ 64.3) were transferred to a school for the mentally retarded, where older girls provided individual care. These children also enjoyed superior play facilities, intellectual stimulation, staff–child ratios and so on. The other 12 children (average IQ 86.7) remained in the orphanage.

At about three and a half, those who had been transferred (the 'experimental' group) either returned to the orphanage or were adopted. Whilst their average IQ had risen from 64.3 to 92.8, the average IQ of the other children (the 'control' group) had fallen from 86.7 to 60.5. At age seven, the average gain for the experimental group was 36 points, whereas the average loss for the control group was 21 points.

Skeels followed up the children into adulthood. All those in the experimental group had finished high school, and about one third had gone to college, married, had children of normal intelligence, and been self-supporting through their adult lives. The control group members had mostly remained in institutions, were unable to earn enough to be self-supporting, and were still mentally retarded.

Skeels and Dye's findings suggest that a crucial variable in intellectual development is the amount of *intellectual stimulation* a child receives, rather than the amount of mothering (as claimed by Spitz, Goldfarb and Bowlby). In general, poor, unstimulating environments are associated with learning difficulties and retarded linguistic development, the latter being crucial for intellectual development generally.

ARE THE EFFECTS OF LONG-TERM PRIVATION REVERSIBLE?

The permanence of privation's effects has been questioned. For example, Harlow found that the effects of early environmental impoverishment in rhesus monkeys *could* be reversed, or at least moderated, by providing them with extensive contact with 'therapist monkeys' (Novak & Harlow, 1975; Suomi & Harlow, 1977; Novak, 1979). In humans, too, research indicates that babies deprived of early bonding can recover from such deprivation. For example, Kagan & Klein (1973) studied a Guatemalan Indian society in which babies routinely spend the first year of their lives confined to small, windowless huts because of the parental belief that sunlight and fresh air are harmful. As judged by standards of normal development, these babies, who are rarely cuddled, played with or talked to by their parents, are listless, unresponsive and intellectually retarded. However, after their first birthdays, they are allowed out of the huts and rapidly become involved in play and exploration, forming attachments just like children who have not been similarly deprived.

Clarke & Clarke (1976) claimed that the effects of early privation are much more easily reversible than studies such as Dennis's (1960) suggest. For example, Tizard (1977) and Tizard & Hodges (1978) looked at children who, on leaving care, were either adopted or returned to their own families. Although the institutions provided good physical care and appeared to provide reasonably adequately for their cognitive development, staff turnover was high, and they operated a policy against allowing too strong an attachment to develop between the staff and children (see page 338). As a result, the children had little opportunity to form close, continuous relationships with an adult. Indeed, by age two, they had been looked after for at least a week by an average of 24 different caregivers. By age four, this had risen to 50. The children's attachment behaviour was very unusual and, in general, their first opportunity to form a long-term attachment came when they left the institutions and were placed in families. This occurred between the ages of two and seven.

The adoptive parents very much wanted a child, and Tizard & Hodges (1978) found that by age eight, the majority of adopted children had formed close attachments to their parents, despite their lack of early attachments in the institutions. At the same age, however, only *some* of those children returned to their own families had formed close attachments. In contrast to the adoptive parents, the biological parents were ambivalent about having the child, and often had other children and material difficulties competing for their attention. As reported by their parents, the ex-institutional children as a whole did not display more problems than a comparison group who had never been in care. According to their teachers, however, they tended to display attention-seeking behaviour, restlessness, disobedience and poor peer relationships.

Box 39.10 Ex-institution children at age 16 (Hodges & Tizard, 1989)

At age 16, the family relationships of most of the adopted children seemed satisfactory, both for them and their parents, and differed little from a non-adopted comparison group who had never been in care. Thus, early institutional care had not necessarily led to a later inability to form a close attachment to parents and become as much a part of the family as any other child. However, those children returned to their families still suffered difficulties and poor family relationships. These included mutual difficulty in showing affection, and the parents reported feeling closer to siblings than to the returned child.

Outside the family, however, both the adopted and returned children showed similar relationships with peers and adults. They were still more often oriented towards adult affection and approval than a comparison group. They were also still more likely to have difficulties in peer relations, less likely to have a special friend or to see peers as sources of emotional support, and more likely to be friendly to any peer rather than choosing their friends.

Hodges and Tizard's research indicates that children deprived of close and lasting relationships with adults in the first years of life *can* make such attachments later. However, these do not arise automatically if the child is placed in a family. Rather, they depend on the adults concerned and how they nurture such attachments. Also, these children experience difficulties in their relationships with peers and adults outside the family, which seem to originate in their early institutional experience. These may have implications for future adult relationships (see Gross, 1994).

Other adoption studies have also shown that the outcome for the adoptees is much better than might have been expected based on their early history of neglect, multiple changes of foster parents, and late ages of adoption (e.g. Kadushin, 1970; Triseliotis, 1980). Triseliotis, for example, interviewed 40 people born in 1956 or 1957 who had experienced long-term fostering (between seven and 15 years in a single foster home before age 16). Triseliotis concluded that, if the quality and quantity of care and relationships are adequate, the effects of earlier disruptions and suffering can be reversed and normal development achieved.

Another way of studying privation's long-term effects is to examine the context in which it is embedded. This means following up the children closely in order to trace the steps leading from early experience to outcome in maturity (Schaffer, 1996b). This approach was used by Quinton & Rutter (1988) to determine whether children deprived of parental care in turn become depriving parents. They observed women, brought up in care, interacting with their own children. Compared with non-institutionalised women, these mothers were, as a group, less sensitive, supportive and warm towards their children.

According to Quinton and Rutter, this difference can be explained in terms of various subsequent experiences the women had as a result of being brought up in care (such as teenage pregnancy, marrying an unsupportive spouse, and marital breakdown) as well as in terms of their deprived childhoods. However, there was also considerable variability *within* the group brought up in care, and by no means all of them exhibited deficient parenting skills.

One way of explaining this variability is in terms of *developmental pathways*. For example, some of the women had more positive school experiences than others, making them three times more likely as adolescents or young adults to make proper career and marriage partner choices. Consequently, they were 12 times more likely to marry for positive reasons, which in turn increased by five times the chances of their marital relationship being supportive. This itself increased their chance of good social functioning (including being a caring parent) by a factor of three (Rutter, 1989). This represents a route for escaping early adversity. Similar adverse childhood experiences can give rise to *multiple* outcomes (Schaffer, 1996b).

Positive school experience

3×

Planning for work and marriage

12×

Marriage for positive reasons

5×

Marital support

3×

Good social functioning and good parenting

Figure 39.4   A simplified adaptive chain of circumstances in institution-reared women (Based on Quinton & Rutter, 1988; Rutter, 1989)

THE REVERSIBILITY OF EXTREME EARLY PRIVATION

Several studies have looked at the long-term effects of *extreme* early privation in which children have endured years of isolation. Such studies include those of Anna (Davis, 1940), Isabelle (Mason, 1942), survivors of concentration camps (Freud & Dann, 1951), P.M. and J.M. (Koluchova, 1972), L.H. (Koluchova, 1976), Genie (Curtiss, 1977) and Mary and Louise (Skuse, 1984).

Box 39.11   The case of P.M. and J.M. (Koluchova, 1972)

Identical twin boys in the former Czechoslovakia were cruelly treated by their stepmother. They were found in 1967 aged seven. They had grown up in a small, unheated closet, had often been locked in the cellar, and suffered harsh beatings. Following their discovery, the boys spent time in a children's home and a school for the mentally retarded. In 1969, they were fostered.

At first, they were terrified of many aspects of their new environment, communicated largely by gestures, and had little spontaneous speech. However, they gradually made progress, both socially and intellectually. When followed up seven years after their discovery (aged 14), the twins showed no psychopathological symptoms or unusual behaviour. By age 20, they had completed a quite demanding apprenticeship and were of above average intelligence. They still had very good relationships with their foster mother, her relatives, and their adopted sisters. They had also both recently experienced their first heterosexual love affairs.

As with other similar studies, this highlights the importance of having somebody (not necessarily a mother-figure) with whom it is possible to form an emotional bond. The effects of long-term extreme privation *can* be reversed.

According to Skuse (1984), victims of extreme privation show a characteristic clinical picture when first discovered. This involves motor retardation, absent or very rudimentary vocal and symbolic language, grossly retarded perceptuomotor skills, poor emotional expression, lack of attachment behaviour, and social withdrawal. The early combination of profound language deficit (the most vulnerable cognitive faculty), and apathy/withdrawal from social contact, leads to special difficulties in developing a normal range and quality of relationships later on.

However, the various studies of extreme early privation suggest the inadequacy of the view that early experience is of overriding importance for later growth (cf. Clarke & Clarke, 1976). Whilst adverse early life experiences may have serious lasting effects on development in some circumstances, this is not inevitable. For Schaffer (1996a):

'Early experiences ... do not necessarily produce irreversible effects just because they are early'.

If recovery of normal ability in a particular faculty is going to occur, rapid progress is the rule. However, further progress can be made several years after discovery, even when obstacles to success were thought to be genetic/congenital, as in Skuse's (1984) study of Mary and Louise.

After their discovery, both Mary and Louise received speech therapy, but Mary's was later abandoned because of poor progress. Four years later, however, Mary's poor social communication and language (which were reminiscent of autism) had improved dramatically (aided by consistent, intensive speech therapy, despite many changes of children's homes). In the absence of genetic or congenital abnormalities, victims of extreme privation have an excellent prognosis (Skuse, 1984).

Conclusions

This chapter has reviewed research into the effects of early deprivation on children. Although short- and long-term deprivation and privation can have detrimental effects, these are not irreversible, and recovery from both deprivation and privation is possible.

Summary

■ Bowlby's **maternal deprivation hypothesis** claims that attachment between mother and infant cannot be broken in the first few years of life without causing serious/permanent developmental damage. This combines the concept of a critical period for attachment formation and his theory of monotropy.

■ The maternal deprivation hypothesis was based largely on studies of children raised in institutions. Goldfarb's study assessed the **intellectual** impact of institutionalisation. Spitz and Wolf focused on the **emotional** effects, such as **anaclitic depression** and **hospitalism**. Both failed to recognise the **understimulating nature** of the institutions. Different types of deprivation, and the different kinds of developmental retardation they produce, need to be distinguished.

■ Bowlby's use of 'deprivation' confuses loss through separation (de-privation) with **privation**. Bowlby was mainly concerned with **short-term deprivation/separation** such as children going into a residential nursery. A typical response by the child is **distress**, comprising **protest**, **despair** and **detachment**.

■ There are important individual differences regarding the degree of distress experienced. These are associated with age, gender, behaviour problems prior to separation, prior relationships with the mother, and the nature of previous separations. The quality of substitute care also influences the degree of distress children experience, with **multiple attachments** helping to reduce it.

■ Contrary to Bowlby's views, **day care** is not necessarily detrimental to the child. What matters are the **quality** and **stability** of the substitute care. However, babies who spend long periods in day-care nurseries are more likely to behave badly and less likely to make friends than those who stay at home with their mothers.

■ **Long-term deprivation/separation** includes parental **death** and **divorce**. Perhaps the most common effect is **separation anxiety**, which manifests itself in various ways, including **school phobia/refusal**.

■ **Divorce** has serious effects on children. How quickly they adjust is influenced by several factors, including continuity of contact with the non-custodial parent and the custodial parent's re-marriage. Children whose parents divorce have, on average, lower levels of academic achievement and self-esteem, and higher incidence of psychological adjustment problems during childhood and young adulthood, compared with those of similar social backgrounds whose parents remain married.

■ Divorce may not be the only factor producing these differences. Another possibility is that **divorce-prone couples** have particular child-rearing styles. The harmful effects of divorce may also be associated with several other factors, but **inter-parental conflict** is probably the single most damaging.

■ Unlike divorce, **parental death** is not usually preceded by discord. However, children who experience their mother's death have higher adult anxiety and depression rates compared with children whose mother separated from them for more than a year.

■ According to Bowlby, separation experiences in early childhood cause **affectionless psychopathy**. Rutter sees **privation** as the more likely cause of the affectionless character, with the **establishment** of attachments having been the major difficulty.

■ According to Dennis, there is a **critical period** for intellectual development before the age of two. However, Skeels and Dye's and Skeels' studies indicate that early privation's effects can be reversed after age two, as well as showing the long-term effects of privation. The effects of early privation are much more easily reversible than is often claimed.

■ Hodges and Tizard's study of 16-year-olds raised in care found that the family relationships of most adopted children seemed good, whilst those of the children returned to their biological families were still poor. However, **outside** the family, both groups were more often oriented towards adult approval and still more likely to have difficulties in peer relationships.

■ Other adoption studies show that the outcome for late-adopted children is better than might be expected given their early history of neglect and multiple changes of foster parents.

■ In Quinton and Rutter's study, the women raised in care were less sensitive, supportive and warm mothers. However, there was also considerable variability **within** this group. This could be explained by examining the **developmental pathways** that led individual mothers from childhood experience to adult behaviour. Similar adverse experience in childhood can give rise to **multiple** outcomes.

■ Studies of **extreme** early privation show that its effects **can** be reversed. According to Skuse, victims of extreme privation initially display a typical clinical picture, including absent or very basic vocal and symbolic language, lack of attachment behaviour and social withdrawal. Language is the most vulnerable cognitive faculty.

■ If recovery of normal ability is going to happen, rapid progress is the rule. However, further progress can be made several years after discovery. In the absence of genetic or congenital abnormalities, victims of extreme privation have an excellent prognosis.

40

CHILD-REARING

Introduction and overview

Perhaps the first psychologist to offer advice on raising children was Watson (1928). He adopted a no-nonsense approach to child-rearing because he believed that giving children too much love would make them 'totally unable to cope with the world in which they must live'. For Watson:

> 'Treat [children] as though they were young adults. Dress them, bathe them with care and circumspection. Let your behaviour always be objective and kindly firm. Never hug and kiss them, never let them sit on your lap. If you must, kiss them once on the forehead when they say good night.'

Perhaps the most famous subsequent parenting guide was Spock's (1946) *Baby and Child Care*. The book began with the words: 'Trust yourself. You know more than you think you do.' Spock advised parents to feed their babies on demand and avoid physically punishing their children. Twenty years after his book was published, Spock was publicly blamed for the 'permissive society' of the 'swinging sixties' (Wilson, 1996).

This chapter looks at some of the social and cultural variations in child-rearing, including the major parenting styles and their effects on children's development. It also considers research into culturally specific aspects of child-rearing, and examines cross-cultural studies of child-rearing styles.

Dimensions of child-rearing

It is generally agreed that parental approaches to child-rearing can be classified on two main dimensions. These are *emotional responsiveness* and *control/demandingness*. Emotional responsiveness ranges from responding to children with warmth, love and affection, to cold and rejecting responses. 'Warm' parents behave in ways which communicate their happiness at having children and their enjoyment of being with them (Sears *et al.*, 1957). They show great affection by hugging and kissing their children and frequently smiling at them. 'Cold' parents have few affectionate feelings towards their children and tend not to enjoy being with them. They are likely to complain about their behaviour, and attribute it to 'naughtiness' or the child having 'a mind of its own'. Warm parents' children

differ from those of cold parents on several important measures. For example, they display fewer behavioural problems and are more likely to develop values similar to their parents' (Martin, 1975).

The control/demandingness dimension describes the extent to which parents restrict their children's behaviour. Parents who are extremely restrictive (showing *authoritarian power restriction*) impose many rules on their children's behaviour and watch them very closely (Sears *et al.*, 1957). Extremely permissive parents impose few, if any, rules and supervise their children less closely. As a group, extremely permissive parents show little concern over their children's cleanliness (*indifferent* and *neglecting*). The two dimensions are *independent* of one another. This means that parents who are warm may be restrictive *or* permissive, as can parents who are cold.

Figure 40.1   The cover of what is, arguably, the most famous and influential guide to parenting ever written

BAUMRIND'S MODEL OF CHILD-REARING

By observing how parents interacted with their three- and four-year-old children, and by interviewing these parents, Baumrind (1967, 1991) identified three child-rearing styles called *permissive*, *authoritarian* and *authoritative*.

Box 40.1 Baumrind's three styles of child-rearing

Baumrind (1967) originally identified four dimensions of child-rearing (cf. the dimensions identified earlier). *Control* refers to parental attempts to shape and modify children's expressions of dependent, aggressive and playful behaviour. *Demands for maturity* refers to parental pressures on their children to perform up to their ability. *Clarity of communication* is the seeking out of children's opinions and using reason when demanding compliance. *Nurturance* refers to the expressions of warmth towards children and pride in their accomplishments.

The permissive style: These parents make few demands on their children and are reluctant to punish inappropriate behaviour. There is little attempt to 'control' them and a 'hands-off' policy is adopted. Permissiveness may stem from parents' indifference or preoccupation with other functions. However, they hope that giving children freedom will encourage the development of self-reliance and initiative.

The authoritarian style: These parents rely on strictly enforced rules to make children adhere to their standards. Authoritarian parents tend to be autocratic and leave little room to discuss alternative points of view. Punishment is often used to ensure compliance. They show minimal warmth, nurturance or communication towards their children.

The authoritative style: These parents also have definite standards/rules that their children are expected to meet. However, the children are usually asked for their opinions during discussion and rule-making sessions. Children are encouraged to think independently and acquire a sense that their views are valuable, although at the same time they are made aware of the parents' expected standards.

(Adapted from Crooks & Stein, 1991)

Baumrind found that children of permissive, authoritarian and authoritative parents differed in terms of *instrumental competence*. This consists of 'social responsibility', 'independence', 'achievement orientation' and 'vitality'. Children of authoritative parents scored highest on all four of these measures (Baumrind, 1971). Thus,

they tended to be cooperative, friendly, successful, achievement-oriented, independent and self-assertive in their dealings with peers and teachers. Children of authoritarian parents, by contrast, tended to be withdrawn, low in vitality, shy, dependent and tense around their peers. Children of permissive parents were quite confident and self-reliant compared with children of authoritarian parents. On other measures of instrumental competence, however, their scores tended to be low. Baumrind also found sex differences in parenting style and instrumental competence.

Box 40.2 Child-rearing styles, instrumental competence and sex differences

The permissive style: Both boys and girls show low social competencies. However, whilst girls' cognitive competencies are low, they are *very* low in boys.

The authoritarian style: Both boys and girls show average social competencies. However, boys' cognitive competencies are *low* whereas girls' are *average*.

The authoritative style: Boys show high, but girls *very* high, cognitive and social competencies.

(Adapted from Shaffer, 1985)

Baumrind (1975) later assessed the children in the original study when they were adolescents, and confirmed her original findings. Thus, parents who use an authoritative style have socially competent and mature children. Based on Baumrind's research, it is widely accepted that whilst the authoritarian and permissive styles are almost opposite to one another, neither is helpful in developing children's social and emotional competence. This may be because neither style enables children to develop *internal standards*. With authoritarian parents' children, this may be due to the parents' excessive control. With permissive parents, the failure to hold children responsible for the consequences of their actions may be at fault.

MACCOBY AND MARTIN'S MODEL OF CHILD-REARING

Baumrind's original categories were subsequently modified by Maccoby & Martin (1983), who devised a two-dimensional classification of child-rearing styles which provides a way of distinguishing the different contexts parents can create for their children's development (Moshman *et al.*, 1987: see Table 40.1).

Table 40.1 Maccoby & Martin's (1983) classification of child-rearing styles

	Parent-centred	Child-centred
Demanding	AUTHORITARIAN–AUTOCRATIC	AUTHORITATIVE–RECIPROCAL
Undemanding	INDIFFERENT–UNINVOLVED	INDULGENT–PERMISSIVE

(From Moshman *et al.*, 1987)

The *authoritarian–autocratic* and *authoritative–reciprocal* categories correspond to Baumrind's authoritarian and authoritative styles respectively. The undemanding dimension corresponds to Baumrind's permissive style. As Table 40.1 shows, Maccoby and Martin identify two permissive styles, the *indifferent–uninvolved* and the *indulgent–permissive*. In the former, parents minimise the amount of contact they have with their children, and there are few or no behavioural rules. Their children tend to feel unloved and engage in behaviours designed to get others to pay attention to them. In extreme cases, parental neglect can lead to malnutrition, illness or even death (Patterson, 1982). In general, children of indifferent–uninvolved parents are considerably less achievement-oriented than other children.

Like the indifferent–uninvolved style, the indulgent–permissive style is characterised by a lack of rules, and few restrictions are placed on children. However, rather than being parent-centred, this style is child-centred. Indulgent–permissive parents are responsive to their children, tolerant, and reinforce desirable behaviour but rarely use punishment. Few demands are made for mature behaviour, and the children are allowed to make their own decisions wherever possible.

The benefits of the authoritative style

Exactly why the authoritative style is the most beneficial is unclear, but by looking at this style in more detail, it may be possible to suggest some reasons.

Box 40.3   A more detailed look at the key elements of the authoritative style of child-rearing

Expectations for mature behaviour: Authoritative parents set their children clear standards and do not reinforce immature behaviour.

Encouragement of individuality: The parents see the child's individuality as being positive and they support it.

Respect for children's rights: Authoritative parents recognise that their children have rights, and these (along with their own) are respected.

Firm enforcement of rules: Having established clear expectations for mature behaviour, authoritative parents use commands to action and enforce sanctions wherever necessary.

Two-way communication: Communication occurs from child to parent as well as from parent to child. Authoritative parents encourage verbal 'give-and-take' and are receptive to communication.

(Based on Baumrind, 1971)

One of the advantages of the authoritative style is that it gives children *control* over their lives (Baumrind, 1983). Established rules have been negotiated rather than merely imposed. Because authoritative parents tend to enforce rules with consistent, predictable discipline, their children are more likely to acquire a sense of control over the consequences of their actions. As well as control, authoritative parenting also promotes the development of self-esteem, a sense of autonomy, and nurtures skills in interpersonal relations (Durkin, 1995). Elements of the authoritative style can be *taught* to parents, and as parents learn these elements, their children develop more positive social skills (Patterson, 1982).

Box 40.4   Child-rearing styles and the media

Durkin (1995) has observed that the media can also be influential in promoting an authoritative style of child-rearing, and research (e.g. Burman, 1994) indicates that parents are influenced by scientific theories of child development as presented in the media. As Durkin (1995) has remarked:

'Look at the noticeboard the next time you visit your general practitioner. Most likely you will see posters from parents' associations advising that "A child needs love. A child needs respect. A child needs choice. A child needs responsibility". You will not find the Authoritarian Aunties' proclamation "A child needs a good hiding" (and the Permissive Parents never get around to producing a poster at all)'.

Of course, no parents fit perfectly into any of these parenting styles, and most show some characteristics of all of them at one time or another (Moshman *et al.*, 1987). Several factors have been shown to have important effects on parenting style. A child's biological organisation has much to do with the sort of parenting it receives (Scarr, 1984). Thus, 'hot-headed' children are more likely to prompt parental aggression than 'level-headed' children (Olweus, 1980). Marital discord and parental personality may also be influential (Durkin, 1995). In Bronfenbrenner's (1979) view, the most critical factor may be the child's *perception* of the parenting style used. If children understand that their parents love them and are genuinely concerned about them, then even an extreme authoritarian style may not be completely negative.

The vast majority of research into child-rearing styles is *correlational*. Although it is tempting to conclude that a particular parenting style *produces* a particular type of child, correlational studies do not allow cause-and-effect relationships to be inferred (see Chapter 2, page 25). Whilst an authoritative style may cause children to be socially, emotionally and cognitively competent, other causal mechanisms might be responsible or operate simultaneously. For example, children who are socially and emotionally well adjusted may *elicit* an authoritative style from their parents (Lewis, 1981).

According to Darling & Steinberg's (1993) *contextual model of parenting style*, it is necessary to distinguish parental *styles* from parental *practices*. Parental practices are things like helping with homework and can *directly* affect children's behaviour. Parental styles create a particular *emotional climate* and affect children *indirectly* by making practices more or less effective, influencing children's receptiveness to those practices. In turn, children's receptiveness influences parental practices (Tavris & Wade, 1995).

Box 40.5   Parental temperament and the 'terrible twos'

According to Belsky (cited in Matthews, 1996b), toddlers' temper tantrums are caused by their parents' 'failure to show respect for the emerging autonomy of the child'. Belsky found that children's temperaments at a very early age were *not* correlated with the likelihood of them turning into a 'terrible two'. Rather, their parents' temperament and attitude to discipline were much more important predictors.

Parents who reported financial difficulties and high levels of occupational stress were much more likely to have children experiencing the 'terrible twos', and these parents tended to use an authoritarian style. Parents who adopted what Belsky calls a *control-with-guidance* approach showed respect for their children's emerging autonomy and recognised them as individuals with their own wills, desires and needs.

Belsky also suggests that once the 'terrible two' emerges, the child is likely to become a 'terrible' three, four and five and that:

'those children having more difficulty at three are much more likely to have such problems as they get into elementary school as well'.

(Adapted from Matthews, 1996b)

ENFORCING RESTRICTIONS

Three methods of parental discipline are *induction*, *love-withdrawal* and *power assertion*. Of these, inductive methods are the most effective (Staub, 1979). They involve trying to give children knowledge enabling them to behave appropriately in other situations. The most widely used inductive technique is 'reasoning' with the child (explaining why one behaviour is good and appropriate, whilst another is bad and inappropriate).

Love-withdrawal uses the explicit or implicit message that 'if you don't behave in this way, I won't love you any more'. Parents sometimes ignore or isolate their children when they have misbehaved. On other occasions, they express great disappointment in them.

Power assertion involves coercing children to behave in the desired way by overpowering and intimidating them. Parents who use power assertion believe strongly in the use of tangible rewards and punishments, and tend to yell at their children rather than reason with them.

Box 40.6   Rewards and punishments

Rewarding children for behaving appropriately is generally more effective than punishing them for behaving inappropriately. Unlike induction, which can foster the development of *empathy*, punishment cannot. Krebs & Blackman (1988) identify four general problems with the use of punishment:

- The punishing agent (the parent) presents an aggressive model to the child.

- The negative feelings elicited by the punishment become associated with the surrounding cues. This makes it less likely that the child will turn to the parent in times of conflict or doubt.

- Punishing a child may teach it what *not* to do, but it does not teach positive alternatives.

- Frequent punishment may make the child insecure and erode its sense of autonomy and self-esteem.

Leach (1993) points out that in many countries (including Britain), physical punishment is banned in educational and other care institutions. In certain other countries (including Sweden, Denmark and Austria), physical punishment by parents has also been outlawed. Under current British law, parents are allowed to use 'reasonable chastisement' to discipline a child.

Leach argues that 'popular ideas' about psychology and punishment are usually seriously mistaken. The 'pseudo-scientific' approach used in many popular books and magazines:

'lends credence to "common-sense" parental statements such as "If he gets a slap every time he does it, he'll soon learn not to"'.

Evidence suggests, however, that punishment *can* be effective, at least in the situation in which it is applied (see also Chapter 63). To be effective in *suppressing* behaviour, it must be emphatic and adminstered immediately after the inappropriate behaviour (Aronfreed, 1976). Also, punishment is effective when the child perceives it to be judiciously applied, and when the punisher is seen as warm and loving (Martin, 1975). Despite this, Leach (1993) argues that physical punishment is unlikely to be effective in helping parents to shape their children's behaviour as they themselves wish, or in building the self-discipline society requires of all socialised citizens.

For Leach, the use of physical punishment:

'frequently provokes or exacerbates behaviours parents and others wish to minimise, may be harmful to children in a number of ways, and increases their vulnerability to physical abuse. Literature from psychology and related professions provides clear evidence, and suggests some explanations, for the inter-generational continuance of physical punishment. It suggests that, despite evidence of the greater effectiveness of non-punitive disciplinary methods, the use – and abuse – of parental physical punishment is unlikely to end without external intervention such as legal change'.

In 1996, an unnamed 11-year-old boy launched a case in the European Court of Human Rights against the British Government. The boy's claim is that the Government failed in its duty to protect him from 'inhuman and degrading treatment' at the hands of his stepfather, who punished his misdemeanours by hitting him with a garden cane (McCartney, 1996). The case could result in the European Court laying down parameters for the circumstances in which corporal punishment would be permitted (Dyer, 1996).

Although any such ruling would not be directly enforceable in Britain, the Government would be expected to bring the law into line to comply with its obligations under Article 3 of the European Human Rights Convention, which prohibits inhuman or degrading treatment or punishment.

'There, that's the midwife who smacked me'

Figure 40.2   Children are asserting their rights at an increasingly early age!
(The Telegraph Group Limited)

PARENTING STYLES AND THE DEVELOPMENT OF CHILDREN'S INTELLIGENCE

As was seen in Chapter 39, babies are sometimes reared in unresponsive and unstimulating environments. In the worst of these, nothing children do has any effect on what happens to them. Many babies reared in such environments are generally passive and apathetic because they stop trying to affect anything in their environments. In responsive environments, by contrast, the individual learns that events are contingent on behaviour.

Research indicates that early home environments and parenting styles can affect measured intelligence (IQ). For example, high levels of maternal restrictiveness and punishment at age two are correlated with lower IQ scores later on in life (Rathus, 1990). Good parent–child relationships and maternal encouragement of independence, however, have been shown to correlate positively with later IQ scores (McGowan & Johnson, 1984).

Stimulating child-rearing styles are clearly tied to the development of measured intelligence. The lower IQs of some children have been explained in terms of thwarted curiosity, an under-developed attention span, and a general mistrust of adults (Morris, 1988). However, Whitehurst *et al.* (1988) have shown that the parenting skills beneficial to children can be taught and produce significant gains, at least as far as language and vocabulary skills are concerned (see Chapter 43).

Cross-cultural studies

Berry *et al.* (1992) have identified two main approaches to the cross-cultural study of child-rearing practices. These are *archival studies* and *field studies*. A large number of archival studies have drawn on *ethnographic reports* (reports of studies in which the investigators have become members of the societies being investigated). These are contained in the *Human Relations Area Files* (or HRAF).

ARCHIVAL STUDIES

The HRAF are based on Murdock's (1975) *Outline of World Cultures* and Murdock *et al.*'s (1971) *Outline of Cultural Material*. The former identifies many societies, data about which can be used to look for similarities and differences between them. The latter identifies 79 categories considered to be a universal set of concepts found in all cultural groups. Barry (1980) has arranged the original 79 categories into eight broader categories. For researchers interested in child-rearing, two of these (*individual and family activities* and *sex and the lifecycle*) are particularly important.

The HRAF have been used *holoculturally* (to find correlations between cultural variables across cultures). With child-rearing, the HRAF have been used to identify the major dimensions of *variation* in such practices as used in different cultures. As Berry *et al.* (1992) have noted:

> 'this archival approach allows us to examine child-rearing practices ... in the context of other variables ... that have also been included in the archives; we are thus able to examine how child-rearing fits into ... other features of the group's circumstances'.

In an early study using the HRAF, Whiting & Child (1953) argued that child-rearing is identical the world over 'in that it is found always to be concerned with certain universal problems of behaviour'. However, they also argued that in other respects, child-rearing practices differ from one society to another. According to Barry *et al.* (1959), there are six central dimensions of child-rearing which are common to all societies.

Barry *et al.* argued that the six dimensions could be essentially reduced to a single dimension which had *pressure towards compliance* (combining training for responsibility and obedience) at one end, and *pressure towards assertion* (combining training for achievement, self-reliance and independence) at the other. Different societies could be placed at different positions along this dimension. Barry *et al.* also claimed that across *all* societies, girls were more socialised for 'compliance' and boys for 'assertion', and that the size of these differences is linked to a society's *economic mode of subsistence*.

Pastoral or agricultural ('high food accumulating') societies showed greater 'pressure towards compliance' than hunter-and-gatherer ('low food accumulating') societies. However, Barry *et al.*'s claims have been disputed. In a re-analysis of the HRAF data, Hendrix (1985) claimed that there are no differences in societies' socialisation of males and females, and that whilst attempts to correlate socialisation with economic mode of subsistence are 'more-or-less accurate', Barry *et al.*'s conclusions 'were oversimplified [and] somewhat misleading'.

However, according to Berry *et al.* (1992), Hendrix is almost certainly wrong. The data actually show males to be more assertive, achievement oriented and dominant. Females tend to be socially responsive, passive and submissive, although Berry *et al.* acknowledge that their interpretation 'risks oversimplification'.

FIELD STUDIES

Field studies of child-rearing began with Whiting's (1963) 'six cultures' project. The cultural groups studied were the Ilocos (Philippines), Guisii (Kenya), Mixtecan (Mexico), Rajput (India), Taira (Japan) and Orchard Town (United States). Using data derived from interviews with mothers in each of these cultural groups, Minturn & Lambert (1964) found that generally there was greater variation in child-rearing practices *within* cultures than *between* cultures. Some subsequent research has supported Minturn and Lambert's findings. In Lambert *et al.*'s (1979) study of 11 national populations, there were variations in child-rearing practices. However, these were due more to individual and class differences than to cultural differences.

This is clearly different from Barry *et al.*'s finding that cultures could be placed at different points on a single dimension of child-rearing. For Berry *et al.* (1992):

'There is thus a major inconsistency in the literature: the studies employing ratings from archives have revealed a great deal of variation across cultures in child-rearing, while those using direct field observations ... tend to find little. Since the archival indices of child-rearing fit into a plausible pattern of relationship with other cultural and ecological variables, it is difficult to dismiss them as invalid. Similarly, the field studies provide compelling evidence that also needs to be taken seriously. This discrepancy clearly sets the stage for future research on these topics'.

Conclusions

There are several child-rearing styles used by parents. Those using too much or too little power do not seem to be as effective as that which exercises neither too much nor too little power. Some research in non-Western cultures has shown that there are variations in child-rearing practices. Other research has failed to find such variations and indicates that there are greater differences within cultures than between them.

Summary

■ Psychologists generally agree that child-rearing can be classified in terms of two **independent** dimensions, **emotional responsiveness** and **control/demandingness**.

■ Emotional responsiveness ranges from warmth, love and affection to coldness and rejection. 'Warm' parents' children display fewer behavioural problems and their values become more similar to their parents' compared with 'cold' parents' children.

■ Control/demandingness ranges from extremely restrictive (**authoritarian power restriction**) to extremely permissive (**indifferent and neglecting**).

■ Baumrind identified four dimensions of child-rearing (**control, demands for maturity, clarity of communication** and **nurturance**) and three child-rearing styles: **permissive, authoritarian** and **authoritative**.

■ **Permissive** parents make few demands on their children and are reluctant to punish them for inappropriate behavior. **Authoritarian** parents rely on strictly enforced rules to make children adhere to their standards. **Authoritative** parents have definite standards and rules that they expect their children to meet. However, children are consulted and encouraged to think independently and acquire a sense that their views are valued.

■ Children of authoritative parents score highest on all four measures of **instrumental competence**, those of authoritarian parents tend to score lowest, whilst those of permissive parents are quite confident and self-reliant but score low on other measures.

■ Baumrind also found sex differences in instrumental competence related to different styles. Neither the permissive nor the authoritarian styles helps children to develop social or emotional competence. This may be because neither style enables children to develop **internal standards**.

■ Maccoby and Martin modified Baumrind's original categories to produce a two-dimensional classification of child-rearing styles. The two dimensions are **demanding/**

undemanding and **parent-centred/child-centred**. They identify two permissive styles, **indifferent–uninvolved** and **indulgent–permissive**.

■ The authoritative style is the most beneficial to children because of parental expectations for mature behaviour, the encouragement of individuality, respect for children's rights, the firm enforcement of rules and the encouragement of two-way communication. It also gives children control over their lives and aids development of interpersonal skills.

■ Most parents show some characteristics of all styles at one time or another. Parenting style is influenced by the child's biological organisation, marital discord and parental personality. Perhaps the most crucial factor is the child's **perception** of the parenting style.

■ Most relevant evidence is **correlational**, so we cannot be sure that a particular style produces a particular type of child. Also, according to Darling and Steinberg's **contextual model of parenting style**, we should distinguish between parental **styles** and **practices**. These have an indirect and direct influence on children respectively.

■ **Induction, love-withdrawal** and **power assertion** are three methods used by parents to **enforce restrictions**. Most effective are inductive methods. Rewarding children for appropriate behaviour is generally more effective than punishing inappropriate behaviour. Punishment can effectively suppress inappropriate behaviour, but it cannot teach children about appropriate behaviour and may erode a sense of autonomy, self-esteem and security.

■ Physical punishment can be harmful to children, making them more vulnerable to physical abuse. Punishment tends to persist across generations, and is unlikely to end without legal intervention.

■ Babies brought up in extremely unresponsive and unstimulating environments are generally passive and apathetic. High levels of maternal restrictiveness and punishment at age two are correlated with subsequent lower IQ scores, whilst having an emotionally and verbally responsive mother is correlated with higher IQ scores.

■ **Archival** and **field studies** are used in **cross-cultural studies** of child-rearing. According to Barry *et al.*, there are six central dimensions of child-rearing common to all societies. These can be reduced to a single dimension with **pressure towards compliance** at one end and **pressure towards assertion** at the other. Different societies can be placed at different positions along this dimension.

■ Field studies of child-rearing began with Whiting's 'six cultures' project. Based on interviews with mothers, Minturn and Lambert found that generally there was greater variation **within** than **between** cultures. Subsequent research has supported this conclusion. Differences that are found may be due more to individual and class differences than culture.

PART 2

Cognitive development

41

PIAGET'S THEORY OF COGNITIVE DEVELOPMENT

Introduction and overview

According to Meadows (1993, 1995), cognitive development is concerned with the study of 'the child as thinker'. *Information-processing theorists* see children as symbol manipulators. Vygotsky, by contrast, saw children as participants in an interactive process by which socially and culturally determined knowledge becomes individualised. A third approach is that of Bruner (e.g. 1963), who is often referred to as an *interventionist*, because of his belief that cognitive development could be accelerated by 'challenging' children to reach as high a level of academic performance as possible (Sutherland, 1992). However, the theory of cognitive development which has received most attention is that of Jean Piaget, for whom children's behaviour represents *adaptation to the environment*.

This chapter describes and evaluates Piaget's theory. Although once regarded as the major framework for understanding cognitive development, Piaget's theory has been criticised. Nevertheless, it continues to be influential and inspirational within both psychology and education. Chapter 42 considers the theory's application to education, together with Vygotsky's and Bruner's theories, the information-processing approach and their educational applications.

Piaget's theory

Piaget's theory focuses on the organisation of intelligence and how it changes as children grow. Piaget founded *genetic epistemology*, the study of the development of knowledge. Based originally on observations of his own three children, Piaget concluded that younger children's intelligence is *qualitatively* as well as *quantitatively* different from older children's.

Cognitive development occurs through the interaction between innate capacities and environmental events, and progresses through a series of *hierarchical stages*. All children pass through the stages in the same sequence without skipping any or, except in the case of brain damage, regressing to earlier ones (they are *invariant*). The stages are also the same for everyone irrespective of culture (they are *universal*). Underlying the changes are certain *functional invariants*, fundamental aspects of the developmental process which remain the same and work in the same way through the various stages. The most important of these are *assimilation*, *accommodation* and *equilibration*. The two principal *cognitive structures* subject to change are *schemas* (or *schemata*) and *concepts*.

SCHEMAS (OR SCHEMATA) AND CONCEPTS

A *schema* (or *scheme*) is the basic building block or unit of intelligent behaviour (see Chapter 29). Piaget saw schemas as mental structures which organise past experiences and provide a way of understanding future experiences. Life begins with simple schemas which are largely confined to inbuilt reflexes (such as sucking and grasping). These operate independently of other reflexes and are activated only when certain objects are present. As we grow, so our schemas become increasingly complex. Piaget sees the acquisition of knowledge of the environment as occurring through the development of *concepts*, or rules that describe the properties of events and their relationships with other concepts (Carlson, 1988).

ASSIMILATION, ACCOMMODATION AND EQUILIBRATION

Assimilation is the process by which we incorporate new information into existing schemas. For example, babies will reflexively suck a nipple and other objects such as a finger. To suck from a bottle or drink from a cup, the initial sucking reflex must be *modified* through *accommodation*. When a child can deal with most, if not all, new experiences by assimilating them, it is in a state of *equilibrium*. This is brought about by *equilibration* or the process of seeking 'mental balance'. However, if existing schemas are inadequate to cope with new situations, *cognitive disequilibrium* occurs. To restore equilibrium, the existing schema must be 'stretched' in order to take in (or 'accommodate') new information. The necessary and complementary processes of assimilation and accommodation constitute the fundamental process of *adaptation*.

PIAGET'S FOUR STAGES OF COGNITIVE DEVELOPMENT

Each represents a stage in the development of intelligence (hence *sensorimotor intelligence*, *pre-operational intelligence* and so on), and is a way of summarising the various schemas a child has at a particular time. The ages shown in Table 41.1 are approximate, because children move through the stages at different rates due to differences in both the environment and their biological maturation. Children pass through *transitional periods* in which their thinking is a mixture of two stages.

Table 41.1   Piaget's four stages of cognitive development

Stage	Approximate age
Sensorimotor	Birth to two years
Pre-operational	Two to seven years
Concrete operational	Seven to 11 years
Formal operational	11 years onwards

The concept of developmental 'stages' is often taken to mean that development is *discontinuous*. However, for Piaget, development is a gradual and *continuous* process of change, although later stages build on earlier ones (which is why the sequence is invariant). The passage from one stage to the next occurs through *cognitive disequilibrium*. To achieve equilibrium, the child is 'forced' to higher levels of intellectual understanding (Krebs & Blackman, 1988).

The sensorimotor stage

This lasts for approximately the first two years of life. Infants learn about the world primarily through their senses ('sensori-') and by doing ('motor'). Based on observations of his own children, Piaget (1952) divided the sensorimotor stage into six sub-stages.

Box 41.1   The six sub-stages of the sensorimotor stage

Sub-stage 1 (Exercising reflexes; birth to one month): Reflexes are practised until they function smoothly. Infants have no intentionality and no understanding of an object.

Sub-stage 2 (Primary circular reactions; one to four months): Reflexes are extended to new objects and infants coordinate simple schemas (such as grasping and looking). Behaviours causing specific events are repeated. Infants look at where a disappearing object was last seen (for a few moments).

Sub-stage 3 (Secondary circular reactions; four to ten months): Fluid coordination of all senses is achieved as is the ability to anticipate events and results of actions. A partially hidden object can be found and, in the last months of this sub-stage, infants achieve *object permanence* (but see main text).

Sub-stage 4 (The coordination of secondary circular reactions; ten to 12 months): Infants represent objects in their minds and demonstrate the beginning of symbolic behaviour and memory. A goal can be decided and then acted on. A completely hidden object can be found.

Sub-stage 5 (Tertiary circular reactions; 12 to 18 months): Infants search for environmental novelty and use several interchangeable schemas to achieve goals. Experiments are conducted to see what will happen. An object hidden under one of several covers can be found.

Sub-stage 6 (Invention of new means through mental combinations; 18 to 24 months): Infants think about a problem before acting, and thoughts begin to dominate actions. Objects can be mentally manipulated to reach goals. An object placed in a container and then hidden can be found.

(Based on Tomlinson-Keasey, 1985)

Object permanence

Frequent interaction with objects ultimately leads to the development of *object permanence*. As Box 41.1 shows, in sub-stage 2, an infant will look where an object disappears for a few moments, but will not search for it. If the object does not reappear the infant apparently loses interest. Piaget called this *passive exploration*, because the infant expects the object to reappear but does not actively search for it ('out of sight' is 'out of mind').

Figure 41.1   If an object is made to disappear from an infant's sight, the infant seems to lose interest in it and does not actively search for it

Figure 41.2   Whilst a six-month-old child will not search for an object that has been removed from its sight, an eight-month-old child will, because it has developed some degree of object permanence

In sub-stage 3, an infant will reach for a partially hidden object, suggesting that it realises that the rest of it is attached to the visible part. However, if the object is *completely hidden*, infants make no attempt to retrieve it. In sub-stage 4, a hidden object will be searched for ('out of sight' is no longer 'out of mind'). Although the infant will retrieve a hidden object, it will persist in looking for it where it was last hidden, even when it is hidden somewhere else.

Whilst this no longer occurs in sub-stage 5, object permanence is not yet fully developed. For example, suppose an infant sees an object placed in a matchbox, which is then put under a pillow. When the infant isn't looking, the object is removed from the matchbox and left under the pillow.

If the matchbox is given to the infant, it will open it expecting to find the object. On not finding it, the infant will *not* look under the pillow. This is because it cannot take into account the possibility that something it has not actually seen might have happened (*failure to infer invisible displacements*). Once the infant can infer invisible displacements (in sub-stage 6), the development of object permanence is complete.

Object permanence's emergence occurs simultaneously with the emergence of a *fear of strangers* (see Chapter 38). By eight months, the infant probably has schemas for familiar faces, and faces that cannot be assimilated into these schemas cause distress (Kagan, 1984).

Box 41.2   The general symbolic function

Other cognitive structures that have developed by the end of the sensorimotor stage include *self-recognition* (the ability to name the self correctly in a mirror: Bertenthal & Fischer, 1978), and *symbolic thought*. This is the capacity to construct a mental representation of an object (a symbol) and deal with it as though it were the object (Crider *et al.*, 1989). *Language* is one example of symbolic thought.

Schemas are now 'interiorised'. For example, to open a door, an infant might need to put a cup down. After looking at the door and then the cup, the infant 'realises', through a mental image of the door opening, that the cup is in the way. So, the infant moves the cup to a safer place before opening the door.

Two other manifestations of the *general symbolic function* are *deferred imitation* and *representational* (or *make-believe*) *play*. Deferred imitation is the ability to imitate or reproduce something that has been perceived but is no longer present (Meltzoff & Moore, 1983). Representational play involves using one object as though it were another. Like deferred imitation, this ability depends on the infant's growing ability to form mental images of things and people in their absence (to *remember*).

The pre-operational stage

Probably the main difference between this and the sensorimotor stage is the continued development and use of internal images, symbols and language, especially important for the child's developing sense of self-awareness. However, the child tends to be influenced by how things *look* rather than by logical principles or operations (hence the term 'pre-operational'). Piaget subdivided the stage into the *pre-conceptual sub-stage* (two to four) and the *intuitive sub-stage* (four to seven). The absolute nature of the pre-conceptual child's thinking makes relative terms such as 'bigger' or 'stronger' difficult to understand (things tend

to be 'biggest' or just 'big'). The intuitive child can use relative terms, but its ability to think logically is still limited.

Seriation and artificialism

In *seriation*, the pre-conceptual child has difficulty arranging objects on the basis of a particular dimension, such as increasing height (Piaget & Szeminska, 1952). *Artificialism* is the belief that natural features have been designed and constructed by people. For example, the question 'Why is the sky blue?' might produce the answer 'Somebody painted it'.

Transductive reasoning and animism

Transductive reasoning involves drawing an inference about the relationship between two things based on a single shared attribute. If both cats and dogs have four legs, then cats must be dogs. This sort of reasoning can lead to *animism*, the belief that inanimate objects are alive. So, because the sun appears to follow us when we walk, it must be alive, just like people (Piaget, 1973).

Centration

This involves focusing on only a single perceptual quality at a time. A pre-conceptual child asked to divide apples into those that are 'big and red' and those that are 'small and green' will either put all the red (or green) apples together irrespective of their size, or all the big (or small) apples together irrespective of their colour. Until the child can *decentre*, it will be unable to classify things logically or systematically. Centration is also illustrated by *syncretic thought*, the tendency to link neighbouring objects or events on the basis of what *individual instances* have in common. By age five, however, most children can select examples of things and say what they have in common. Centration is also associated with the inability to conserve (see page 358).

Egocentrism

According to Piaget, pre-operational children are *egocentric*, that is, they see the world from their own standpoint and cannot appreciate that other people might see things differently. They cannot put themselves 'in other people's shoes' to realise that other people do not know or perceive everything they themselves do. Consider the following example (Phillips, 1969) of a conversation between the experimenter and a four-year-old boy:

Experimenter: 'Do you have a brother?'
Child: 'Yes.'
Experimenter: 'What's his name?'
Child: 'Jim.'
Experimenter: 'Does Jim have a brother?'
Child: 'No.'

357

Box 41.3 The 'Swiss mountain scene' test of egocentrism (Piaget & Inhelder, 1956)

The three papier-mâché model mountains (see Figure 41.3) are of different colours. One has snow on the top, one a house, and one a red cross. The child walks round and explores the model and then sits on one side whilst a doll is placed at some *different* location. The child is shown ten pictures of different views of the model and asked to choose the one that represents how the doll sees it.

Four-year-olds were completely unaware of perspectives different from their own and always chose a picture which matched their view of the model. Six-year-olds showed some awareness, but often chose the wrong picture. Only seven- and eight-year-olds consistently chose the picture that represented the doll's view. According to Piaget, children below the age of seven are bound by the *egocentric illusion*. They fail to understand that what they see is relative to their own position and instead take it to represent 'the world as it really is'.

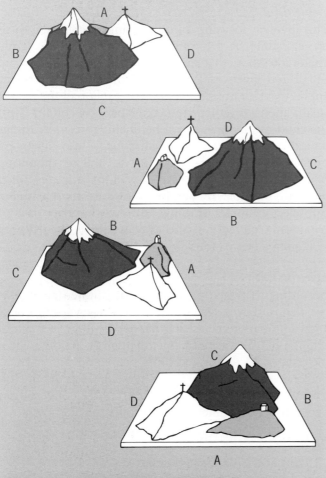

Figure 41.3 Piaget and Inhelder's three-mountain scene, seen from four different sides (From Gross, 1996, and based on Smith & Cowie, 1991)

Conservation

Conservation is the understanding that any quantity (such as number, liquid quantity, length and substance) remains the same despite physical changes in objects' arrangement. Piaget believed that pre-operational children could not conserve because their thinking is dominated by objects' perceptual appearance.

The inability to conserve is another example of *centration*. With liquid quantity, for example, the child centres on just one dimension of the beaker, usually its height, and fails to take width into account. Only in the concrete operational stage do children understand that 'getting taller' and 'getting narrower' tend to cancel each other out (*compensation*). If the contents of the taller beaker are poured back into the shorter one, the child will again say that the two shorter beakers contain the same amount. However, it cannot perform this operation mentally and so lacks *reversibility* (understanding that what can be done can be undone *without any gain or loss*).

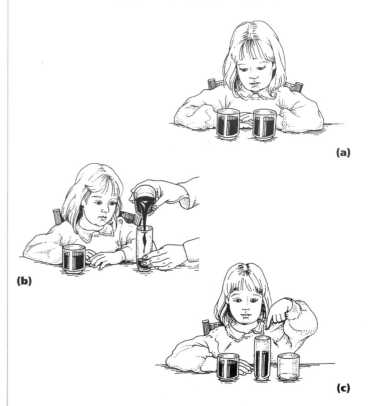

Figure 41.4 Piaget's test for the conservation of liquid quantity The child is shown two identical beakers and agrees that they contain the same amount of liquid (a). The contents of one of the beakers is then poured into another beaker which is taller but narrower (b). Although the child has seen the liquid being poured and agrees that none has been added or spilled in the process (Piaget calls this 'identity'), when asked if one beaker contains more or if the two have identical quantities, the pre-operational child typically says that the taller beaker contains more (c)

Box 41.4   Tests for the conservation of number, length and substance or quantity

Conservation of number: Two rows of counters are placed in one-to-one correspondence. The child agrees that the two rows contain an equal number.

One row is then extended (or contracted). The child is asked whether each row still has the same number of counters.

Conservation of length: Two sticks are aligned and the child agrees that they are both the same length.

One of the sticks is moved to the right (or left). The child is asked whether they are still the same length.

Conservation of substance or quantity: Two identical Plasticine balls are presented. The child agrees that there is the same amount in each.

The shape of one ball is changed, and the child is asked whether there is still the same amount in each.

(Based on LeFrancois, 1986)

Concrete operational stage

The child is now capable of performing logical operations, but only in the presence of actual objects. He or she can conserve and shows reversibility and more logical classification.

Further examples of the child's ability to *decentre* include its appreciation that objects can belong to more than one class (as in the case of Andrew being Bob's brother *and* Charlie's best friend). There is also a significant decline in egocentrism (and the growing relativism of the child's viewpoint), and the onset of seriation and reciprocity of relationships (such as knowing that adding one to three produces the same amount as taking one from five).

One remaining problem for the concrete operational child is *transitivity* tasks. For example, if told that 'Alan is taller than Bob, and Bob is taller than Charlie' and asked whether Alan or Charlie is taller, children under 11 cannot solve this problem entirely in their heads. They can usually only solve it using real (or concrete) objects (such as dolls). Nevertheless, concrete operational children enjoy jokes that enable them to utilise abilities such as conservation, as in the following: Mr Jones went into a restaurant and ordered a whole pizza for his dinner. When the waiter asked if he wanted it cut into six or eight pieces, Mr Jones said 'Oh, you'd better make it six, I could never eat eight pieces!' (McGhee, 1976).

Box 41.5   Horizontal and vertical décalage

Some types of conservation are mastered before others, and their order tends to be invariant. Liquid quantity is mastered by age six to seven, substance/quantity and length by seven to eight, weight by eight to ten, and volume by 11 to 12. This step-by-step acquisition of new operations is called *décalage* (displacement or 'slips in level of performance'). In conservation, décalage is *horizontal* because there are inconsistencies *within* the same kind of ability or operation (a seven-year-old child can conserve number but not weight, for example). *Vertical* décalage refers to inconsistencies *between* different abilities or operations (a child may have mastered all kinds of classification, but not all kinds of conservation).

The formal operational stage

Whilst the concrete operational child is still concerned with manipulating *things* (even if this is done mentally), the formal operational thinker can manipulate *ideas or propositions* and can reason solely on the basis of verbal statements ('first order' and 'second order' operations respectively). 'Formal' refers to the ability to follow the form of an argument without reference to its particular content. In transitivity problems, for example, 'If A is taller than B, and B is taller than C, then A is taller than C' is a form of argument whose conclusion is logically true, regardless of what A, B and C might refer to.

Formal operational thinkers can also think *hypothetically*, that is, they can think about what *could* be as well as what actually *is*. For example, asked what it would be like if people had tails, they might say 'Dogs would know when you were happy' or 'Lovers could hold their tails in secret under the table'. Concrete operational thinkers might tell you 'not to be so silly' or say where on the body the tail might be, showing their dependence on what has actually been seen (Dworetzky, 1981). The ability to imagine and discuss things that have never been encountered is evidence of the continued decentration that occurs beyond concrete operations: formal operational thinkers display *hypothetico-deductive reasoning*.

Box 41.6   A demonstration of formal operational thinking

Inhelder & Piaget (1958) gave adolescents five containers filled with clear liquid. Four were 'test chemicals' and one an 'indicator'. When the proper combination of one or more test chemicals was added to the indicator, it turned yellow. The problem was to find this proper combination. Pre-operational children simply mixed the chemicals randomly, and concrete operational children, although more systematic, generally failed to test all possible combinations. Only formal operational thinkers considered all alternatives and systematically varied one factor at a time. Also, they often wrote down all the results and tried to draw general conclusions about each chemical.

AN EVALUATION OF PIAGET'S THEORY

Piaget's theory has had an enormous impact on our understanding of cognitive development. However, as Flavell (1982) has remarked:

> 'Like all theories of great reach and significance … it has problems that gradually come to light as years and years of thinking and research get done on it. Thus, some of us now think that the theory may in varying degrees be unclear, incorrect and incomplete'.

Object permanence

Piaget's claims about the sensorimotor stage have been criticised in both general and specific terms. Bower & Wishart (1972), for example, found that how an object is made to disappear influences the infant's response. If the infant is looking at an object and reaching for it and the lights are turned off, it will continue to search for up to one and a half minutes (as filmed with special cameras). This suggests that it *does* remember the object is there (so, 'out of sight' is not 'out of mind': see page 356). Baillargeon (1987) has shown that object permanence can occur as early as three and a half months and that it is *not* necessary for a baby younger than six months to see the whole object in order to respond to it.

Centration

One way to study centration (and classification) is through *class inclusion tasks*. If a pre-operational child is presented with several wooden beads, mostly brown but a few white, and asked 'Are they all wooden?', the child will respond correctly. If asked 'Are there more brown or more

white beads?', the child will again respond correctly. However, if asked 'Are there more brown beads or more beads?', the child will say there are more brown beads. According to Piaget, the child fails to understand the relationship between the whole (the class of wooden beads) and the parts (the classes of brown and white beads). These are the *superordinate* and *subordinate* classes respectively. The brown beads are more numerous than the white and can be perceived in a more immediate and direct way than the wooden beads as a whole (despite the first question being answered correctly).

Piaget argued that this was another example of the inability to decentre. However, Donaldson (1978) has asked if the difficulty the child experiences is to do with what is expected of it and how the task is presented.

Box 41.7   Alternatives to Piaget's class-inclusion task

Donaldson describes a study with six-year-olds using four toy cows, three black and one white. The cows were laid on their sides and the children told they were 'sleeping'. Of those asked 'Are there more black cows or more cows?', 25 per cent answered correctly. However, of those asked 'Are there more black cows or more *sleeping* cows?', 48 per cent answered correctly.

Similarly, the word 'more' has a different meaning for children and adults (Gelman, 1978). Adults use 'more' to mean 'containing a greater number'. For children, however, 'more' refers to the general concept of larger, longer, occupying more space and so on.

Hodkin (1981) showed children two rows of sweets.

When asked if there were more Smarties or more sweets, the children replied 'more Smarties'. However, when asked if there were 'more Smarties or more *of all of the sweets*', children replied that there were more of all of the sweets, showing that they could understand class inclusion.

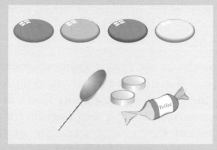

Top row = Smarties
Bottom row = Other kinds of sweets

Figure 41.5   Stimuli used in Hodkin's (1981) experiment

Egocentrism

Gelman (1979) has shown that four-year-olds adjust their explanations of things to make them clearer to a blind-fold listener. If the children were entirely egocentric, such a finding would be unlikely. Nor would we expect four-year-olds to use simpler forms of speech when talking to two-year-olds, yet this is what they do (Gelman, 1979). We would, however, expect egocentric children to choose toys *they* liked for their mothers' birthday. However, at least some four-year-olds choose presents appropriate for their mothers (Marvin, 1975).

Critics of the 'Swiss mountain scene' test (see Box 41.3) see it as an unusually difficult way of presenting a problem to a young child. Borke (1975) and Hughes (cited in Donaldson, 1978) have shown that when the task is presented in a meaningful context (making what Donaldson calls 'human sense'), even three and a half-year-olds can appreciate the world as another person sees it.

Conservation

The ability to conserve also seems to occur earlier than Piaget believed. Rose & Blank (1974) showed that when the *pre-transformation* question (the question asked before the contents of one beaker, say, are poured into another) was dropped, six-year-olds often succeeded on the conservation of number task. Importantly, they made fewer errors on the standard version of the task when tested a week later. These findings were replicated by Samuel & Bryant (1984) using conservation of number, liquid quantity and substance. The standard version of the task unwittingly 'forces' children to produce the wrong answer against their better judgement by the mere fact that the same question is asked twice, before *and* after the transformation (Donaldson, 1978). Hence, children believe they are expected to give a *different* answer on the second question. On this explanation, contextual cues may override purely linguistic ones.

According to Piaget, it should not matter *who*, in the case of number conservation, rearranges the counters/Smarties or *how* this happens. Yet when 'Naughty Teddy', a glove puppet, causes the transformation 'accidentally', pre-operational children can conserve number and length (McGarrigle & Donaldson, 1974; Light *et al.*, 1979). This also applies when the transformation is made by a *person* other than the experimenter (Hargreaves *et al.*, 1982; Light, 1986). Whilst Piaget's original procedure might convey the implicit message 'take note of the transformation because it is relevant', studies using accidental transformations might convey the message 'ignore the transformation, it makes no difference'. It follows that if some change actually takes place, the implicit message to ignore the transformation would make children give an incorrect answer. The standard Piagetian task involves an *irrelevant perceptual change* (nothing is added or taken away), but where some *actual change* occurs, children tested under the accidental/incidental transformation condition should do *worse* than those tested in the standard way. This outcome has been obtained in several studies (Light & Gilmour, 1983; Moore & Frye, 1986).

As noted on page 360, children's understanding of 'more' and 'less' may differ from adults' in a way that can mislead us about their true abilities. For example, in the conservation of liquid quantity task, since some children use the words 'more' or 'less' when referring to height and length, in their own terms they might be quite correct in saying that the taller beaker has 'more' in it (Bruner *et al.*, 1966). When a child asks for 'more milk', it observes the level in the glass rise (Dworetszky, 1981).

Piaget believed that the attainment of a new stage arises from a major reorganisation of mental operations rather than the acquisition of new skills. Hence, attempts to teach children to conserve should be unsuccessful. Smedslund (1961) showed that whilst children *could* be taught to behave as though they could conserve, they did not actually understand what conservation means. However, when non-conservers are placed with a group of conservers and listen to the conservers' reasoning about their responses, understanding can occur (Botvin & Murray, 1975).

In general, special training techniques may speed children's understanding of conservation, but only if they have reached the necessary stage of development. Such training appears at most:

> 'to move children through a period of formation and into the period of attainment more quickly than they would otherwise progress' (Krebs & Blackman, 1988).

Methodological criticisms

Piaget's observation of individual children, often his own, falls short of the controlled methodology characteristic of experimental psychology (see Chapter 2). His use of particular observations to demonstrate general points is also unscientific (Brainerd, 1978). However, both Ginsberg (1981) and Dasen (1994) see Piaget's methods as a superior way of exploring the subtleties of a child's abilities, since they are tailored to an individual child's requirements.

The ambiguity of concepts

According to Yussen and Santrock (1982):

> 'the most interesting concepts in the theory – assimilation, accommodation and equilibration – which are used

to explain how progress is made in development are tricky to pin down operationally, despite their theoretical glitter. Despite work over the years to flesh out these concepts and anchor them in concrete procedures, not much progress has been made'.

For Yussen and Santrock (and others), Piagetian concepts are too loosely defined to be of any practical use.

The validity of stages

Children *can* reach later stages without having gone through earlier ones (Horn, 1976), as when some children walk without ever having crawled. Whether the concept of 'stages' is valid or not is hotly disputed and has both its supporters (e.g. Flavell, 1971) and opponents (e.g. Sternberg, 1990).

The cultural universality of the stages

Although some researchers have accepted the validity of the stages, they have suggested that there are cultural differences in the rates of development in the various cognitive domains. Development of the cerebral hemispheres apparently overlaps with the timing of Piaget's stages (Thatcher *et al.*, 1978). For Dasen (1994):

'the *deep* structures, the basic cognitive processes, are indeed universal, while at the *surface* level, the way these basic processes are brought to bear on specific contents, in specific contexts, is influenced by culture. Universality and cultural diversity are not opposites, but are complementary aspects of all human behaviour and development'.

The role of social factors in cognitive development

According to Meadows (1995), Piaget implicitly saw children as largely independent and isolated in their construction of knowledge and understanding of the world. This excluded the contribution of other people to children's cognitive development. The *social* nature of knowledge and thought has been investigated by Bruner and Vygotsky (see Chapter 42).

The permanence of conservation and the attainment of formal operational thought

Children appear to master and then lose the ability to conserve weight (Bower, 1976). This is illustrated by the concrete operational thinker's failure to realise that a pound of lead weighs the same as a pound of feathers. According to Bower, a stable understanding of this concept is not reached until age 13.

Some researchers (e.g. White & Ferstenberg, 1978; Dasen, 1994) have argued that only one third of adolescents and adults actually attain formal operations, and that in some cultures, it is not the typical mode of thought. Conversely,

others (e.g. Riegel, 1976; Labouvie-Vief, 1980) have argued that some people reach stages *beyond* the formal operational stage.

Conclusions

Despite criticism, Piaget's theory of cognitive development continues to attract much interest. For Campbell (1996):

'the treatment of Piaget's work in Britain has been disgraceful. Convenient opinions of that work are casually constructed from reading a page of one Piaget book, or worse, from second-hand accounts. These opinions lead to crude experiments to refute them, and complaisant editors publish yet another paper proving a toy version of 'Piaget's theory' wrong'.

We hope our coverage of Piaget's theory has been balanced and fair.

Summary

■ Piaget sees behaviour as **adaptation to the environment**. Although criticised from several perspectives, his theory continues to be influential, within both psychology and education.

■ Piaget's theory focuses on the organisation of intelligence and how it changes as children grow (**genetic epistemology**). Younger children's intelligence is both **quantitatively** and **qualitatively** different from that of older children.

■ Cognitive development occurs through the interaction between innate capacities and environmental events, and progresses through a series of **hierarchical stages** which are **invariant** and **universal**. Underlying the changes are **functional invariants**, the most important being **assimilation**, **accommodation** (which together constitute **adaptation**) and **equilibration**. The two major cognitive structures that change are schemas/schemata and concepts.

■ A **schema/scheme** is the basic building-block of intelligent behaviour. Our first schemas are mainly inborn reflexes which operate independently of each other and become increasingly complex. Knowledge of the environment occurs through development of **concepts** (or rules describing the properties of events and their relationships to other concepts).

■ **Assimilation** involves incorporating new information into existing schemas. **Accommodation** occurs when schemas are **modified** to deal with new experiences. When a child can deal with most or all new experiences through assimilation, it is in a state of **equilibrium**. When this is not the case, **cognitive disequilibrium** occurs, making accommodation necessary to restore equilibrium.

■ Piaget's four stages of cognitive development are **sensorimotor**, **pre-operational**, **concrete operational** and **formal operational**. Children move through the stages at different rates, and all pass through transitional periods. Piaget saw development as a gradual or **continuous** process of change, although later stages build on earlier ones.

■ During the **sensorimotor stage**, frequent interaction with objects ultimately leads to **object permanence**, which is fully developed when the child can **infer invisible displacements**.

■ By the end of the sensorimotor stage, **self-recognition** and **symbolic thought** have emerged. Schemas are now 'interiorised'. **Deferred imitation** indicates an important advance in the capacity to **remember**, and **representational/make-believe play**, like deferred imitation, reflects the **general symbolic function**.

■ During the **pre-operational stage**, things are very much as they **seem**, with logical principles and operations having little influence. This is more pronounced in the **pre-conceptual** than the **intuitive sub-stage**.

■ Pre-operational children have difficulty in **seriation** tasks and also display **artificialism**, **transductive reasoning** and **animism**. **Centration** involves focusing on a single perceptual quality to the exclusion of others. To be able to classify things logically or systematically, the child must be able to **decentre**.

■ Centration is also illustrated by **syncretic thought** and the **inability to conserve**. This occurs because of an inability to understand **compensation** and a lack of **reversibility**.

■ Pre-operational children are also **egocentric** and cannot understand that others may not know or perceive everything they themselves know or perceive. Using the 'Swiss mountain scene' test, Piaget and Inhelder found that children under seven are bound by the **egocentric illusion**.

■ During the **concrete operational stage**, logical operations can only be performed in the presence of actual or observable objects. There is a significant decline in egocentrism, together with the onset of seriation and reciprocity of relationships. Some types of conservation appear before others (**horizontal décalage**). A child who has mastered all kinds of classification but not all kinds of conservation is displaying **vertical décalage**.

■ **Formal operational** thinkers can manipulate ideas and propositions, can reason solely on the basis of verbal statements ('second order' operations) and think **hypothetically**.

■ The **way** an object is made to disappear influences the infant's response, so that 'out of sight' does not always mean 'out of mind'. Object permanence can occur as early as three and a half months.

■ Using **class inclusion tasks**, Piaget claimed that the pre-operational child fails to understand the relationship between wholes (the **superordinate class**) and the parts (**subordinate classes**). However, the child may have difficulty knowing what is expected of it.

■ The word 'more' has different meanings for children and adults, which can explain pre-operational children's failure on Piaget's class inclusion tasks. It is also relevant to understanding performance on **conservation** tasks.

■ The 'Swiss mountain scene' may be too difficult for a young child. Even three and a half-year-olds can take another person's viewpoint if the task makes 'human sense'.

■ When the **pre-transformation** question is dropped in **conservation** tasks, children under seven often succeed who would fail the standard form of the task. The standard version may unwittingly make children give the wrong answer against their better judgement. Whilst for Piaget it is irrelevant **who** makes the transformation or how it happens, the 'Naughty Teddy' experimental procedure shows that it does matter.

■ Piaget's observation of individual children falls short of experimental psychology's controlled methodology, but his methods are designed to explore the subtleties of children's thinking. However, the concepts of assimilation, accommodation and equilibration are difficult to measure.

■ Whilst **deep** structures (the basic cognitive processes) may be universal, how these are brought to bear on specific contents (at the **surface** level) is influenced by culture and so is **culturally diverse**. Only a third of adolescents and adults actually attain formal operations and, in some cultures, it is not the typical mode of thought.

■ Piaget excluded other people's contribution to children's cognitive development, seeing them as largely independent and isolated in their construction of knowledge of the physical world.

42

SOME ALTERNATIVE THEORIES OF COGNITIVE DEVELOPMENT AND THEIR APPLICATION TO EDUCATION

Introduction and overview

According to Dasen (1994) and Durkin (1995), the challenges to Piaget's theory of cognitive development have been so strong that there are few 'orthodox' Piagetians left, and even fewer who subscribe to 'stage' theories of cognitive development. This chapter considers the alternatives to Piaget's theory proposed by Vygotsky, Bruner and the information-processing theorists, and looks at how they have been applied to education. It begins, however, by briefly considering the application of Piaget's theory to education.

Applying Piaget's theory to education

Piaget did not actually advocate a 'theory of instruction' (Ginsberg, 1981). However, his theory has three main implications for education (Brainerd, 1983). These are the concept of *readiness*, the *curriculum* (what should be taught), and *teaching methods* (how the curriculum should be taught).

Much of what was said in Chapter 41 about limits set on learning by children's current stage of development relates to the concept of readiness. The apparent success of some attempts to train certain concepts (such as conservation: see page 361) suggests that readiness is not a particularly helpful concept. Regarding the curriculum, appropriate content would include logic (such as transitive inference), maths (numbers), science (conservation) and space (Euclidean geometry). Teaching materials should consist of concrete objects that children can easily manipulate.

However, Ginsberg (1981) has argued that attempting to base a curriculum on the teaching of Piagetian stages is a misapplication of his theory. It would be more useful to *modify* the curriculum in line with what is known about the various Piagetian stages, without allowing them to limit teaching methods. Piaget's theory seems to suggest

that there are definite sequences in which concepts should be taught. For example, different types of conservation appear at different times (see Chapter 41, page 359). However, many traditional schools do *not* base their teaching on this or other developmental sequences (Elkind, 1976).

Central to a Piagetian perspective is the view that children learn from actions rather than from passive observation (*active self-discovery/discovery learning*). Regarding *teaching methods*, teachers must recognise that each child needs to construct knowledge for itself, and that deeper understanding is the product of active learning (Smith & Cowie, 1991).

Box 42.1   The role of the teacher in the Piagetian classroom

- It is essential for teachers to assess very carefully each individual child's current stage of cognitive development (this relates to the concept of readiness). The child can then be set tasks tailored to its needs which become *intrinsically motivating*.

- Teachers must provide children with learning opportunities that enable them to advance to the next developmental step. This is achieved by creating *disequilibrium* (see page 355). Rather than providing the appropriate materials and allowing children to 'get on with it', teachers should create a proper balance between actively guiding and directing children's thinking patterns and providing opportunities for them to explore by themselves (Thomas, 1985).

- Teachers should be concerned with the learning process rather than its end product. This involves encouraging children to ask questions, experiment and explore. Teachers should look for the reasoning behind children's answers, particularly when they make mistakes.

- Teachers should encourage children to learn from each other. Hearing other (and often conflicting) views can help to break down egocentrism (see pages 357–358).

Peer interaction has both a *cognitive* and a *social value*. As a result, small-group activity is as important as individual work.

- Teachers are the guides in children's process of discovery, and the curriculum should be adapted to each child's individual needs and intellectual level (Smith & Cowie, 1991).

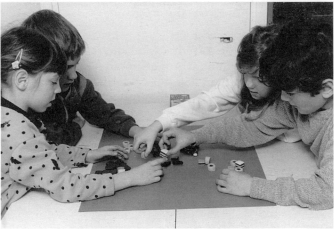

Figure 42.1   In the traditional classroom (top), the teacher is at the centre of the learning process, imparting ready-made ('academic/school') knowledge. By contrast, in the Piagetian classroom the child actively discovers knowledge for itself, often through interaction with other children in small groups (bottom)

Vygotsky's theory

Vygotsky outlined a major alternative to Piaget's theory which was published in the former Soviet Union in the 1920s and 30s, but not translated into English until the early 1960s (Vygotsky, 1962).

INTERNALISATION AND THE SOCIAL NATURE OF THINKING

Vygotsky believed that a child's cognitive development does not occur in a social vacuum. The ability to think and reason by and for ourselves (*inner speech* or *verbal thought*) is the result of a fundamentally *social* process. At birth, we are social beings capable of interacting with others, but able to do little either practically or intellectually by or for ourselves. Gradually, however, we move towards self-sufficiency and independence, and by participating in social activities, our abilities become transformed. For Vygotsky, cognitive development involves an active *internalisation* of problem-solving processes that takes place as a result of mutual interaction between children and those with whom they have regular social contact (initially the parents, but later friends and classmates).

This is the reverse of how Piaget (at least initially) saw things. Piaget's idea of 'the child as a *scientist*' is replaced by the idea of 'the child as an *apprentice*', who acquires the culture's knowledge and skills through graded collaboration with those who already possess them (Rogoff, 1990). According to Vygotsky (1981):

'Any function in the child's cultural development appears twice, or on two planes. First it appears on the social plane, and then on the psychological plane'.

Box 42.2   Pointing: an example of cultural development from the social to the psychological

Initially, a baby's pointing is simply an unsuccessful attempt to grasp something beyond its reach. When the mother sees her baby pointing, she takes it as an 'indicatory gesture' that the baby wants something, and so helps it, probably making the gesture herself. Gradually, the baby comes to use the gesture deliberately. The 'reaching' becomes reduced to movements which could not themselves achieve the desired object even if it were in reach, and is accompanied by cries, looks at the mother and eventually words. The gesture is now directed towards the mother (it has become a gesture 'for others') rather than toward the object (it is no longer a gesture 'in itself': Meadows, 1995).

SCAFFOLDING AND THE ZONE OF PROXIMAL DEVELOPMENT

Scaffolding refers to the role played by parents, teachers and others by which children acquire their knowledge and skills (Wood *et al.*, 1976). As a task becomes more familiar to the child and more within its competence, so those who provide the scaffold leave more and more for the child to do until it can perform the task successfully. In this way, the developing thinker does not have to create cognition 'from scratch' because there are others available who have already 'served' their own apprenticeship.

The internalised cognitive skills remain social in two senses. First, as mature learners we can 'scaffold' ourselves through difficult tasks (self-instruction), as others once scaffolded our earlier attempts. Second, the only skills practised to a high level of competence for most people are those offered by their culture: cognitive potential may be universal, but cognitive expertise is culturally determined (Meadows, 1995).

Since the 1980s, research has stressed the role of social interaction in language development, especially the facilitating effects of the use of child-contingent language by adults talking with children (Meadows, 1995: see Chapter 34, page 297). This 'fit' between adult and child language closely resembles the concept of 'scaffolding'.

Box 42.3 Scaffolding (Wood *et al.*, 1976)

Wood *et al.* (1976) found that on a construction task with four- and five-year-olds, different mothers used instructional strategies of varying levels of specificity. These ranged from general verbal encouragement to direct demonstration of a relevant action. No single strategy guaranteed learning, but the most efficient maternal instructors were those who combined general and specific interventions according to the child's progress.

The most useful help is that which adapts itself to the learner's successes and failures (Bruner, 1983). An example would be initially using a general instruction until the child runs into difficulties. At this point, a more specific instruction or demonstration is given. This style allows the child considerable autonomy, but also provides carefully planned guidance at the boundaries of its abilities (Vygotsky's *zone of proximal development*).

The zone of proximal development (or ZPD) defines those functions that have not yet matured but are in the process of maturing (Vygotsky, 1978). These could be called the 'buds' or 'flowers' rather than the 'fruits' of development. The actual developmental level characterises mental development *retrospectively*, whilst the ZPD characterises mental development *prospectively*.

APPLYING VYGOTSKY'S THEORY TO EDUCATION

Vygotsky defines intelligence as the capacity to learn from instruction. Rather than teachers playing an enabling role, Vygotsky believes that teachers should *guide* pupils in paying attention, concentrating and learning effectively (a *didactic* role: Sutherland, 1992). By doing this, teachers *scaffold* children to competence.

The introduction of the National Curriculum and national testing at various ages has returned Britain to the 'teacher-centred' or 'traditional' approach to young children's education. Whilst this approach was dominant up to the 1960s, it was 'revolutionised' by the Piagetian-influenced 'child-centred' or 'progressive' approach. However, Vygotsky did not:

> 'advocate mechanical formal teaching where children go through the motions of sitting at desks and passing exams that are meaningless to them … On the contrary, Vygotsky stressed intellectual development rather than procedural learning' (Sutherland, 1992).

Vygotsky rejected any approach advocating that teachers have rigid control over children's learning. Rather, as with Piaget, teachers' control over children's activities is what counts. Teachers extend and challenge children to go beyond where they would otherwise have been.

Box 42.4 Applying the concept of the ZPD to education

Suppose a child is currently functioning at level 'x' in terms of attainment. Through innate/environmental means, the child has the potential to reach level 'x + 1'.

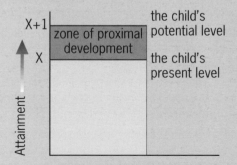

The area between 'x' and 'x + 1' is the child's ZPD. The ZPD may be different for individual children, and children with large ZPDs will have a greater capacity to be

---

helped than those with small ZPDs. Irrespective of the ZPD's size, Vygotsky saw the teacher as being responsible for giving children the cues they need or taking them through a series of steps towards the solution of a problem.

(Based on Sutherland, 1992)

Vygotsky also believed in *collaborative learning*. As well as being helped by teachers, more advanced children are important in helping less advanced children. As Foot & Cheyne (1995) have observed:

'The child takes on or 'internalises' the communicative procedures that he or she experiences when interacting with a peer, and in the process enriches his or her own intellectual capacity'.

Using the peer group for teaching was for a long time the basis of Marxist education in the former Soviet Union. According to Sutherland (1992):

'The socialist rationale was one of all children working for the general good rather than the capitalist one of each child trying to get out of school as much benefit as [she or he] can without putting anything back into it. The brighter child is helping society by helping the less able one since the latter … will be more of an asset to society as a literate than as an illiterate adult'.

This approach is supported by several other perspectives such as 'constructivism', especially with mixed-ability groups in which the more able pupil can act as a 'substitute teacher' (Sutherland, 1992). Whilst much of the research into collaborative learning has been undertaken with young children, there is evidence that group work and collaborative learning can also be effective in adult and higher education (Foot, 1994).

For Vygotsky, then, there is much educational value in direct teaching, but with the child as an active learner. Using techniques derived from Vygotsky's work, Shayer (cited in Sylva, 1996) has shown that specially designed material for science teaching can increase 'learning ability' (gains on tests of psychological functioning) as well as educational test scores and standardised attainment tests (SATs). Moreover, such improvement also appears to generalise to performance in English and mathematics (see also the work of Adey *et al.*, 1989, described on page 369).

Bruner's theory

Like Vygotsky, Bruner was an early critic of Piaget and was strongly influenced by Vygotsky (as reflected in the concept of 'scaffolding'). However, Bruner also shares some of Piaget's basic beliefs, such as children being born with a biological organisation helping them to understand their world. Their underlying cognitive structures mature over time, enabling them to think about and organise the world in increasingly complex ways. Also, children are actively curious and explorative, capable of adapting to their environment through interacting with it. Abstract knowledge grows out of action, and competence in any knowledge area is rooted in active experience and concrete mental operations.

Bruner's main disagreements with Piaget derive from certain shared beliefs with Vygotsky. In particular, Bruner stressed the role of language and interpersonal communication, and the need for active involvement by expert adults (or more knowledgeable peers) in helping the child to develop as a thinker and problem-solver. As well as language playing a crucial part in the scaffolding process, instruction is seen as important in both natural and educational settings.

MODES OF REPRESENTATION

Unlike Piaget's theory, Bruner's (1966) is not about stages of development as such. Rather, it is about ways or *modes* of representing the world (forms that knowledge and understanding can take). Bruner's theory is, therefore, concerned with knowledge in general, as well as cognitive growth. The three modes of representation Bruner describes are the *enactive, iconic* and *symbolic*, which develop in this order.

The enactive mode

This corresponds to Piaget's sensorimotor stage. Initially, babies represent the world through actions, and any knowledge they have is based on what they have experienced through their own behaviour. Past events are represented through appropriate motor responses. Many motor schemas, such as those for riding a bicycle and tying knots, are represented 'in our muscles' ('motor memories').

Even when we can use language, it is often extremely difficult to describe in words only how we carry out certain behaviours. Through repeated encounters with recurrent events and conditions, we build up virtually automatic patterns of motor activity which are 'run off' as units in the appropriate situation. Like Piaget, Bruner sees the onset of object permanence (see page 356) as a major qualitative change in young children's cognitive development.

The iconic mode

This involves building up mental images of things we have experienced (an icon is an image). Such images are normally composed of many past encounters with similar objects or situations. This corresponds to the last six months of the sensorimotor stage (where schemas become interiorised) and the whole of the pre-operational stage, where things are as they look.

The symbolic mode

Bruner's main interest was in the transition from the iconic to the symbolic mode. Like Piaget, Bruner agrees that a very important cognitive change occurs around age six or seven. Whereas Piaget sees this is the start of logical operations, Bruner sees it as the appearance of the symbolic mode, with language coming into its own as an influence on thought. For Bruner (1957), the child is now freed from the immediate context and begins to 'go beyond the information given'.

Box 42.5   The transition from the iconic to symbolic modes. Bruner & Kenney's (1966) experiment

Nine plastic glasses were arranged on a 3 × 3 matrix as shown in (a) below:

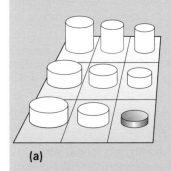 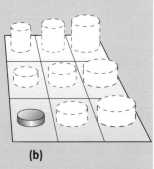

(a)   (b)

Three- to seven-year-olds familiar with the way in which the glasses were arranged were given a *reproduction task* and a *transposition task*. On the reproduction task, the glasses were 'scrambled' and the children were asked to put them back the way they had seen them before. On the transposition task, the glasses were removed from the matrix and the glass which had been in the bottom right-hand square was placed in the bottom left-hand square, and so on, until the glasses appeared as shown in (b). The task was to rebuild the matrix in the transposed manner.

Children could generally reproduce the matrix earlier than they could transpose it. The reproduction task involves the iconic mode, and 60 per cent of five-year-olds, 72 per cent of six-year-olds and 80 per cent of seven-year-olds were successful. The transposition task involves the symbolic mode, and none of the five-year-

olds, 27 per cent of six-year-olds and 79 per cent of seven-year-olds were successful.

These findings indicate that the five-year-olds were dominated by the visual image of the original matrix, whilst the six- and seven-year-olds were able to translate their visual information into the symbolic mode. They relied upon verbal rules to guide them, such as 'It gets fatter going one way and taller going another'. Thus, a child using images but not symbols can reproduce but not restructure.

LANGUAGE AND COGNITIVE DEVELOPMENT

The major difference between Bruner and Piaget concerns the role of language in cognitive development. Bruner believes that the leap from the iconic to symbolic mode is due to the development of language. For Piaget, by contrast, the development of logical thought is due to the acquisition of operations: language is not the cause of cognitive development, but is a tool to be used for operational thinking. For Bruner, language and logical thinking are inseparable, and without language human thought would be limited to what could be learned through actions or images. For Piaget, language merely reflects and builds on cognitive structures which have already developed through interaction with the environment.

One implication of Bruner's belief is that it should be possible to speed up cognitive development by training children in symbol use. For Piaget, such training should have no effect.

Box 42.6   Training children to use symbols

Bruner *et al.* (1966) gave four- to seven-year-olds the standard Piagetian test for the conservation of liquid quantity. Nearly all the four- to five-year-olds failed to conserve, as did about half of the six- to seven-year-olds.

The children were then shown two standard beakers and a third much wider beaker. The beakers were then screened, so that when the contents of one was poured into the wider beaker, only the tops of the beakers (but not the level of liquid) could be seen. When asked which contained the most liquid, almost all five- to seven-year-olds answered correctly, as did about half the four-year-olds. However, when the screen was removed, all the four-year-olds reverted to their pre-screening answers.

The other children, however, stuck to the answer they had given when the screen was in place.

The children were then given the standard Piagetian test of conservation using two beakers and a third taller one. The four-year-olds were unaffected by having seen the beakers screened and failed to show conservation. However, the five-year-olds' success rate at conserving rose from 20 to 70 per cent. For the six to seven-year-olds, the success rate rose from 50 to 90 per cent.

Bruner *et al.* argued that activating the children's speech (symbolic mode), by having them 'say' their judgement when the screen was covering the liquid levels, prevented those aged five and over (who normally fail the standard Piagetian task) from being dominated by the iconic mode. The four-year-olds, however, were clearly not ready to benefit from the symbolic training and, to a degree, this supports Piaget's view that mental structures must have already developed before training can help. Nonetheless, the fact that the five-year-olds benefited is contrary to what Piaget would predict, and so Bruner too is supported to some extent by the data.

Sinclair-de-Zwart (1969) has also shown that unless children understand the concept of conservation, teaching them relevant words like 'as much as' and 'the same' has little effect on their conservation ability (see Chapter 37, page 323). Regarding formal operational thought, Piaget claims that whilst language may be necessary, it is not sufficient. Indeed, for Piaget, the formal operational thinker's language does not differ significantly from what it was earlier.

APPLYING BRUNER'S THEORY TO EDUCATION

Bruner's view that cognitive development can be significantly speeded up, underlies his belief that teachers should try to find ways of stimulating children (particularly those from deprived backgrounds). As Sutherland (1992) has observed:

'Bruner's case for acceleration seems worth examining, particularly at a time when there is a special concern for below-average pupils. One reason for the introduction of the National Curriculum is to improve standards of attainment among the bottom 40 per cent of the school population. How can teachers reach the targets set by the government without some form of acceleration of the slow learner? Are the most able pupils being fully stretched in comprehensive schools, particularly in mixed-ability classes? Should they be accelerated on to the next stage?'

Box 42.7 A CASE of accelerating development

Adey *et al.* (1989) established experimental and control groups in various comprehensive schools. The experimental groups were taught CASE (Cognitive Acceleration Science Education) material. This involves practical problems requiring the use of formal operational schemas for their solution. For example, children are given tubes of different lengths and told to blow across them. The task is to determine which variable affects the note produced. The knowledge acquired should then transfer to other tasks. The control group was taught by the same teachers but received only standard science material.

Using the onset of formal operational thinking as the criterion for cognitive understanding, the researchers found that after three years, the boys (but not the girls) did significantly better on the tests than the boys and girls in the control group. However, this effect was confined to those in Year 8. Year 7 pupils did not appear to benefit from CASE material. These data suggest that specially designed material may produce accelerated learning at least with some children (those who are 'ready' to be accelerated) in at least one subject (science: cf. Shayer's research described on page 367).

Another relevant concept is the *spiral curriculum*, according to which a subject's principles come to be understood at increasingly more complex levels of difficulty. Like Vygotsky, Bruner was unhappy with Piaget's concept of 'readiness' and proposed a much more active policy of intervention, based on his belief that:

'any subject can be taught effectively in some intellectually honest form to any child at any stage of development' (Bruner, 1963).

Educators should provide learners with the means of grasping a discipline's structure (the underlying principles and concepts), rather than just mastering factual information. This enables learners to go beyond the information they have been given and develop their own ideas. Teachers also need to encourage learners to make links and understand the relationships within and between subjects (Smith & Cowie, 1991).

Box 42.8 Applying the spiral curriculum to the topic of volume

The baby: Volume can be introduced at the sensorimotor stage by providing the baby with the opportunity to play with water in buckets (e.g. at the beach).

The pre-schooler: The topic can be re-introduced in the pre-operational stage by giving the child buckets of water to play with. At the same time, words like 'bucket' and 'more' can be introduced, and intuitive concepts like 'more water' (when water is poured into the bucket) and 'less water' (when it is poured out) encouraged. This enables the child to develop pre-concepts and then intuitive concepts.

The junior schooler: The child can be re-exposed to the topic in a variety of settings. Specific use of the word 'volume' is introduced and, through the use of planned activities and spontaneous behaviour by the child, conservation should be achieved along with a concrete operational understanding of 'volume'.

The secondary schooler: The child at Piaget's formal operational stage is taught in abstract and symbolic terms, with formulae concerning volume being required to be learnt without 'concrete props'.

(Adapted from Sutherland, 1992)

Box 42.9   Task analysis

To understand why children cannot solve problems that adults can, we need to understand a particular task's component steps (Oakhill, 1984). For example, five elements are necessary to solve the following problem: 'If Ann is not as bad as Betty, and Betty is not as bad as Carol, who is the best?'. First, the child must perceive and encode the important premises of the question which involves attending to it. Second, the premises must be stored in working memory (WM). Third, they must be combined in memory to form an integrated representation. Fourth, the question must be encoded. Fifth, the representation of the premises must be scanned to answer the question or formulate a conclusion about it.

In Bruner's (and Vygotsky's) view, teachers should be 'interventionists', obliged 'to make demands on their pupils' (Sutherland, 1992). Cultural tools are also seen as vitally important, ranging from pencils to computers. Unlike Vygotsky, whose approach is essentially teacher-centred with direct instruction, Bruner favours a child-centred approach.

Information-processing theories

Information-processing (IP) theories focus on the cognitive process and kinds of information children can acquire from the environment and what they are capable of doing with it (Krebs & Blackman, 1988). IP theorists (e.g. Sternberg, 1990) share Piaget's view that there are psychological structures in people's minds that explain their behaviour, and which are essentially independent of the individual's social relationships, social practices and cultural environment (Meadows, 1995).

The central metaphor underlying the IP approach is the computer (see Chapters 27 and 84). Like computers, children receive information ('input') from the environment, store, retrieve and manipulate it, and then respond behaviourally ('output'). To study how children's 'mental programs' and strategies for processing information develop, IP theorists use *task analysis*.

IP theorists argue that children fail to correctly solve such problems because of errors in encoding the problem, being unable to hold information in memory for long enough, or because holding it in memory may interfere with other task performance (Trabasso, 1977). For example, Maccoby & Hagen (1965) showed children aged six to 12 pictures of various objects and told them to remember only the colour of the picture's background, the picture itself being immaterial.

The ability to perform this task increased with age, 12-year-olds being able to accurately recall twice as many background colours as six-year-olds. However, when the children were later asked to remember the objects in the pictures (and ignore the background colour), the six-year-olds were more successful. This shows how *selective attention* (see Chapter 25) develops through childhood and how it is necessary for solving problems. Presumably, the six-year-olds performed better on the object recognition task because they were able to focus their attention according to the *original* task demands (Rathus, 1990).

One neo-Piagetian approach couched in IP terms is that of Pascual-Leone (1980) and Case (1985). Children do not use just one cognitive strategy in solving Piagetian tasks (as Piaget believed), but several, the number required being correlated with a problem's difficulty. Like Oakhill (1984), Pascual-Leone and Case also see WM as storing the information necessary to solve problems (see Chapter 28). The amount of memory space necessary is also correlated with the problem's complexity and, as the child develops, so available memory space increases. Pascual-Leone and Case also believe that certain strategies become *automatic* with practice and so require less space in memory (see Chapter 26). An adult, for example, would instantly 'see' that $(10 + 6) - (10 + 6)$ equals zero. A child, however, would require time to solve this problem, since each component must be stored in memory before a solution can be reached.

APPLYING IP THEORIES TO EDUCATION

One strength of the IP approach is its emphasis on memory's role and young children's limited capacity to process information. As well as memory's importance in the child's ability to operate effectively, knowledge also has a considerable influence on learning, and the more children know about a situation, the more successful they will be at dealing with it. As Sutherland (1992) has noted:

> 'Since knowledge is generally contained within language, the skill of storing knowledge in some valid linguistic form (whether this be oral memory or written) is a vital prerequisite of successful IP performance. One of the teacher's main roles is to help children find strategies for reducing their memory load – for instance to write down a list of the facts they need to solve a maths problem'.

Whilst young children can add numbers together when two digits are involved (e.g. 22 + 56), they make errors when three digits are used (Van Lehn, 1983). For example, faced with the problem:

$$231 + \\ \underline{42}$$

young children tend to either ignore the third column and arrive at 73 as the answer, or muddle up the hundreds and tens columns to produce 673. Van Lehn uses the term *repair* to refer to the process by which addition involving three digits can be successfully achieved. This process implies a teacher-led approach to teaching mathematics. However, IP theories also see *metacognition* (making children aware of their own learning) as playing a vital role. As well as having greater IP capabilities, older children have greater *insight* into how they process information (Kail & Nippold, 1984). Children should be encouraged to (a) test hypotheses by, in the case of mathematics, checking their answers, and (b) use visual imagery to apply these answers to real-life situations.

Conclusions

This chapter has looked at some alternatives to Piaget's theory of cognitive development and explored their application to education. Theories of cognitive development clearly have a role to play in education but, as Berveridge (cited in Sylva, 1996) has pointed out:

> 'Policy makers are moving quickly towards ... the "commodification of education". This is the process by which "goods" called school learning are "produced" by teachers and others in such a way as to maximise their value to society and minimise the cost to taxpayers. Politicians and some practitioners are turning away from subtle theories of school learning and teaching in favour of a brutish instrumentalism centred on narrow educational attainment (grades) and records of school discipline'.

Summary

■ Although Piaget did not actually advocate a 'theory of instruction', his theory of cognitive development has three main implications for education: **the concept of readiness**, **the curriculum** and **teaching methods**.

■ Central to Piagetian views of the educational process is **active self-discovery/discovery learning**. Teachers assess each individual child's current stage of cognitive development to set **intrinsically motivating** tasks and provide learning opportunities that create **disequilibrium**.

■ Teachers should also encourage children to ask questions, experiment and explore, looking for the reasoning behind children's answers (especially their mistakes). Small-group activity can help break down egocentrism and has a **social value**.

■ Vygotsky sees the ability to think and reason by and for ourselves as the result of a fundamentally **social** process. The initially helpless baby actively internalises problem-solving processes through interaction with parents.

■ Whilst Piaget saw the child as a **scientist**, Vygotsky's child **apprentice** acquires cultural knowledge and skills through graded collaboration with those who already possess them (**scaffolding**). As children become more familiar and competent with a task, so adults and teachers can leave more for them to do alone.

■ The most useful assistance mothers can give their child's task performance is to initially use general instruction until the child experiences difficulties, then give more specific instruction or demonstration. This relates to Vygotsky's **zone of proximal development** (ZPD). Children with a larger ZPD have a greater capacity to be helped.

■ For Vygotsky, intelligence is the capacity to learn from instruction. Teachers occupy a **didactic role**, guiding pupils in paying attention, concentrating and learning effectively. In this way, children are **scaffolded**. Vygotsky also believed in **collaborative learning**, whereby more advanced children ('substitute teachers') help other, less advanced ones.

■ Bruner shared many of Piaget's beliefs about cognitive development. However, like Vygotsky, but unlike Piaget, Bruner stressed the role of language and interpersonal communication, and the need for active involvement by expert adults and more advanced peers in helping children develop thinking and problem-solving.

■ Bruner's theory of cognitive development is not a stage theory, but identifies three **modes of representation**. The **enactive mode** involves representing the world through actions and motor responses ('motor memories'). The **iconic mode** involves building up mental images of things we have experienced. The **symbolic mode** involves language coming into its own as an influence on thought.

■ This frees the child from the immediate context and allows it to 'go beyond the information given'. Without language, human thought would be limited to what could be learned through actions or images. By contrast, Piaget believes that language is merely a tool used in operational thinking.

■ Bruner's position implies that cognitive development can be speeded up by training children to use symbols. For Piaget, this should not be possible. Evidence supports both Bruner and Piaget.

■ Teachers should try to find ways of stimulating children, especially those from deprived backgrounds. This is a current concern in Britain for below-average pupils, and the National Curriculum was introduced partly to improve standards of attainment among the school population's bottom 40 per cent.

■ According to Bruner's **spiral curriculum**, a subject's principles come to be understood at increasingly complex levels of difficulty. Educators should help learners grasp a discipline's underlying principles and concepts. Whilst both Bruner and Vygotsky see the teacher as an 'interventionist', Bruner's is more child-centred.

■ **Information-processing** (IP) **theories** focus on cognitive processes. **Task analysis** is used to study how children's 'mental programs' and strategies for processing information develop.

■ According to Pascual-Leone and Case, children use several cognitive strategies in solving Piagetian tasks. WM stores the information necessary for problem-solving, the amount of space needed depending on the problem's difficulty. Available memory space increases as the child develops. With practice, certain strategies become **automatic**, so requiring less memory space.

■ Emphasis on memory's role and young children's limited IP capacity can explain why they are poorer at tasks involving memorising and reading. Storing knowledge linguistically is a vital prerequisite of successful IP performance. Teachers have a crucial role to play in helping children to find strategies for reducing memory load.

■ IP theorists see **metacognition** as playing a vital role. Older children have greater IP abilities and greater **insight** into how they process information. Children should be encouraged to test hypotheses by checking their answers and using visual imagery to apply these answers to real-life situations.

43

THE DEVELOPMENT OF MEASURED
INTELLIGENCE

Introduction and overview

Both biological (or genetic) and environmental factors, occurring before or after birth, can influence the development of measured intelligence. Pre-natal influences affect *potential* intelligence by affecting brain development. Genetic influences may be *hereditary* (as in the inherited metabolic disorder *phenylketonuria*) or *non-hereditary* (as in *Down's syndrome*: see Chapter 78) Many pre-natal environmental factors are known to have harmful effects on development. These include maternal malnourishment, diseases (such as *maternal rubella*), toxic agents (such as lead and mercury), drugs (such as cigarettes, alcohol), irradiation (X-rays), maternal stress during pregnancy and maternal age.

This chapter considers claims about the influence of genetic and environmental factors on the development of measured intelligence. It begins by looking at evidence for the view that differences between people in measured intelligence are largely determined by genetic factors. Then, it looks at evidence concerning the influence of post-natal environmental factors. Finally, it examines the interaction between genetic and environmental factors.

Genetic influences

Tryon (1940) attempted to show that rats' ability to learn mazes could be in-bred. Rats were divided into two groups: those who were good at finding their way through mazes (*maze-bright*) and those who were not (*maze-dull*). They were placed in separate but identical pens (to control for environmental effects) and left free to breed. Within a few generations, the 'maze-dull' offspring made many more mistakes in maze learning than their 'maze-bright' counterparts. Although Tryon could not explain *how* maze-learning ability was transmitted, his study demonstrated that a specific ability can apparently be passed down from one generation of rats to another (Morris, 1988).

Clearly, there are dangers in generalising findings concerning rats' maze-learning abilities to complex human cognitive abilities, and the influence of genetic factors on

the development of measured intelligence in humans cannot (for ethical, legal and practical reasons) be studied in the laboratory through selective breeding (Rathus, 1990). However, heredity's influence on the development of intelligence as measured by IQ tests can be investigated.

STUDIES OF IQ STABILITY

Since people's genetic inheritance is a constant, if measured intelligence (an IQ test score) is largely determined by genetic factors, there should be a high degree of continuity in IQ throughout a person's life-span (McGurk, 1975). IQ is not normally used as a measure of intelligence below age two. Instead, a *developmental quotient* (DQ) is used. This assesses a child's developmental rate compared with the 'average' child of the same age (Bayley, 1969). The younger a child is when given a developmental test, the lower the correlation between its DQ and later IQ. Once IQ is measurable, it becomes a better predictor of adult IQ.

Whilst many studies have shown little fluctuation in IQ over time, there are many short-term fluctuations which are often related to disturbing factors in an individual's life. Although the *stability coefficients* reported by some researchers (e.g. Honzik *et al.*, 1948) are impressive, they are based on large numbers of people and tend to obscure individual differences.

Others have reported unimpressive stability coefficients. For example, McCall *et al.* (1973) found that in 140 middle class children, the average IQ change between the ages of two-and-a-half and 17 was 28 points. The most 'stable' children changed an average of ten points, whilst 15 per cent shifted 50 points or more in either direction. One child's IQ increased by 74 points!

Even in studies where the correlation between IQ at different ages is *statistically significant* (see Chapter 2, page 19), the stability coefficients are low and suggest greater fluctuation in scores than a simple genetic theory predicts. There is, therefore, a large amount of convincing evidence that a person's intelligence level can alter, sometimes very substantially (Howe, 1997).

FAMILY RESEMBLANCE STUDIES

These examine the correlation in intelligence test scores among people who vary in genetic similarity. If genetic factors influence IQ, then the closer the genetic relationship between two people, the greater should be the correspondence (or *concordance*) between their IQs.

Monozygotic (MZ) or identical twins are unique in having exactly the same genetic inheritance, since they develop from the same single fertilised egg. *Dizygotic* (DZ) or non-identical twins, by contrast, develop from two eggs and are no more alike than ordinary siblings (they share about 50 per cent of their genes). If genes have any influence on the development of measured intelligence, then MZs should show the *greatest* correspondence in terms of their intelligence test performance. Any difference between them would have to be attributed to environmental or experiential influences. Many studies (e.g. Erlenmeyer-Kimling & Jarvik, 1963; Bouchard & McGue, 1981; Wilson, 1983) have shown that the closer people's genetic similarity, the more strongly correlated are their IQs. Table 43.1 presents a summary of Bouchard and McGue's world-wide review of 111 studies reporting IQ correlations between people of varying genetic similarity.

As Table 43.1 shows, the closer the genetic relationship between two individuals, the stronger the correlation between their IQ scores. So, the correlation between cousins (who share roughly 12.5 per cent of their genes) is weaker than that for parents and their offspring (who share roughly 50 per cent). The strongest correlation of all, however, is for MZs. At first sight, these data suggest that heredity is a major influence on IQ test performance. However, as the genetic similarity between people increases, so does the similarity of their environments: parents and offspring usually live in the same household, whereas unrelated people do not.

Studies of separated twins

One way of overcoming this problem is to compare the IQs of MZs *reared together* in the same environment with those raised *separately* in different environments. As Table 43.1 shows, MZs reared together show a greater similarity in IQ scores than those reared separately. However, the fact that MZs reared separately are still more similar than same-sex DZs reared together suggests a strong genetic influence (Bouchard *et al.*, 1990). The data obtained from studies of separated MZs have, however, been criticised.

Box 43.1   Criticisms of twin studies

- 'Separated' twins often turn out not to have been reared separately at all. In Shields' (1962) and Juel-Nielsen's (1965) studies, some of the twins were

Table 43.1   Familial correlations for IQ. The vertical bar on each distribution indicates the median correlation. The arrow indicates the correlation predicted by a simple polygenic model (i.e. the view that many pairs of genes are involved in the inheritance of intelligence) (From Gross, 1996, and based on Bouchard & McGue, 1981)

	No. of correlations	No. of pairings	Median correlation	Weighted average
Monozygotic twins reared together	34	4672	0.85	0.86
Monozygotic twins reared apart	3	65	0.67	0.72
Midparent–midoffspring reared together	3	410	0.73	0.72
Midparent–offspring reared together	8	992	0.475	0.50
Dizygotic twins reared together	41	5546	0.58	0.60
Siblings reared together	69	26 473	0.45	0.47
Siblings reared apart	2	203	0.24	0.24
Single parent–offspring reared together	32	8433	0.385	0.42
Single parent–offspring reared apart	4	814	0.22	0.22
Half-siblings	2	200	0.35	0.31
Cousins	4	1176	0.145	0.15
Non-biological sibling pairs (adopted/natural pairings)	5	345	0.29	0.29
Non-biological sibling pairs (adopted/adopted pairings)	6	369	0.31	0.34
Adopting midparent–offspring	6	758	0.19	0.24
Adopting parent–offspring	6	1397	0.18	0.19
Assortative mating	16	3817	0.365	0.33

raised in related branches of the parents' families, attended the same school and/or played together (Farber, 1981; Horgan, 1993). When these are excluded from analysis in Shields' study, for example, the correlation decreases from 0.77 to 0.51. Moreover, even if the twins are separated at birth, they have shared the same environment of the mother's womb for nine months. Their identical *pre-natal* experiences may account for the observed similarities in IQ (Howe, 1997).

- When twins have to be separated, the agencies responsible for placing them will try to match the respective families as closely as possible. When the environments are substantially different, there are marked IQ differences between the twins (Newman *et al.*, 1937).

- Experimenter and participant bias may also play an important role. In Newman *et al.*'s and Shields' studies, the experimenters *knew* which twins were identical and which had been separated. Participants in Bouchard *et al.*'s (1990) study were recruited by means of media appeals and 'self-referrals'. Kaprio (cited in Horgan, 1993) claims that Bouchard *et al.*'s study has tended to attract people who enjoy publicity, and therefore constitute an atypical sample.

- Different studies have used different IQ tests, making comparisons between them difficult. Moreover, some of the tests used were inappropriate and/or not standardised on certain groups.

- The most widely cited and best-known studies of MZs are those reported by Burt (e.g. 1966) who found high correlations between the IQs of 53 pairs of twins supposedly reared in very different environments. After noticing several peculiarities in Burt's procedures and data, Kamin (1974) and Gillie (1976) questioned the genuineness of Burt's research. Even Burt's most loyal supporters have conceded that at least some of his data were fabricated (e.g. Hearnshaw, 1979).

The various problems with twin studies undoubtedly led to an *overestimation* of genetic influences. However, methodological improvements have produced correlations that are still impressive and which, for Plomin & DeFries (1980):

'implicate genes as the major systematic force influencing the development of individual differences in IQ'.

A major ongoing study is that directed by Bouchard at the University of Minnesota. Separated and non-separated twins are given comprehensive psychological and medical tests and answer some 15,000 questions! For some abilities (such as verbal ability), the correlations

Figure 43.1   Barbara Herbert and Daphne Goodship, one of the pairs of (English) separated identical twins reunited through their participation in the Minnesota twin study

between MZs reared apart are very high, suggesting a strong genetic influence. However, for others (such as memory), the correlations are low or, as with spatial ability, inconsistent (Thompson *et al.*, 1991).

Adoption studies

Adopted children share half their genes but none of their environment with their biological parents, and they share at least some of their environment but none of their genes with their adoptive parents. One research methodology involves comparing the IQs of children adopted in infancy with those of their adoptive and biological parents. Support for the influence of genetic factors would be obtained if the correlation between the adopted children's IQ scores and their biological parents was stronger than that between the adopted children and their adoptive parents.

This is exactly what some studies have shown. Munsinger (1975) found that the average correlation between adopted children and their biological parents was 0.48, compared with 0.19 for adopted children and their adoptive parents. Also, by the end of adolescence, adopted children's IQs are correlated only weakly with their adoptive siblings who share the same environment but are biologically unrelated (Plomin, 1988).

One problem with adoption studies is the difficulty in assessing the amount of similarity between the biological and adoptive parents' environments. When the environments are very different (as when the children of poor, under-educated parents are adopted into families of high socio-economic status), substantial increases in IQ scores are observed.

Box 43.2 Adoption studies involving very different natural and adoptive parental environments

Scarr & Weinberg (1976) carried out a 'transracial' study of 101 white families, above average in intelligence, income and social class, who adopted black children. If genetics were the only factor influencing the development of measured intelligence, then the average IQ of the adopted children would have been expected to be more or less what it was before they were adopted. In fact, their average IQ was 106 following adoption, compared with an average of 90 before adoption.

This finding has been replicated in other studies. For example, Schiff *et al.* (1978) studied a group of economically deprived French mothers who had given up one baby for adoption whilst retaining at least one other child. The average IQ of the children adopted into middle class homes was 110, whilst that of the siblings who remained with the biological mother was 95. Similarly, adoptees raised by parents of high socio-economic status were around 12 IQ points higher than adoptees raised by parents of low socio-economic status, irrespective of their biological background (Capron & Dayme, 1989).

Scarr & Weinberg's (1976) data also indicated that children adopted early in life (within their first year) have higher IQs than those adopted later. So, when adoptive homes provide a superior intellectual climate, they can have a substantial effect on the development of measured intelligence. However, when the economic status of the biological and adoptive parents is roughly equal, the IQs of adopted children tend to be much more similar to those of the biological parents than the adoptive parents (Scarr & Weinberg, 1978).

Environmental influences

Those who believe that the environment influences the development of measured intelligence do not deny that genetic factors play a role. However, they believe that measured intelligence can be strongly influenced by a whole range of (pre- and post-natal) environmental factors.

DATA FROM STUDIES OF NON-HUMANS

Cooper & Zubek (1958) mixed groups of 'bright' and 'dull' rats in either absolutely plain or stimulating environments (the latter containing, toys, activity wheels and a ladder). There were no differences between the 'bright' and 'dull' rats raised in the plain environment, indicating that the inherited abilities of the 'bright' rats had failed

to develop. For those raised in the stimulating environments, there were also no differences between 'dull' and 'bright', suggesting that the genetically dull rats had 'made up' (through experience) the differences they lacked in heredity compared with their 'bright' counterparts. Moreover, the rats raised in the stimulating environment had heavier brains than those raised in the plain environment, irrespective of whether they were 'maze dull' or 'maze bright'.

Others have shown that rats raised in enriched conditions develop more regions for synaptic connections, and thicker and heavier cortexes than rats raised in deprived conditions (Wallace, 1974; Greenough & Black, 1992). All these findings suggest that (at least in rats) the environment can have a direct impact on the brain, which is, of course, the biological basis of intelligence.

DATA FROM STUDIES OF HUMANS

Stock & Smythe (1963) found that infants who suffered *extreme malnutrition* during infancy averaged 20 IQ points lower than similar children with adequate diets. Many other post-natal environmental influences have been shown to affect intellectual development.

Box 43.3 Some post-natal environmental influences on the development of measured intelligence

Environmental 'insults', illness and disease: Lead from lead-based paint chips peeling from walls is just one environmental toxin associated with reduced IQ (Needleman *et al.*, 1990). Anoxia (lack of oxygen) at birth, head trauma and various childhood illnesses (such as encephalitis) can cause brain damage and lower potential intelligence. In later life, brain damage from strokes, metabolic disturbances, brain infections, and diseases (e.g. Alzheimer's) can all adversely affect measured intelligence.

Family size and birth order: According to Zajonc & Markus (1975):

'Intelligence declines with family size; the fewer children in your family, the smarter you are likely to be. Intelligence also declines with birth order; the fewer older brothers or sisters you have, the brighter you are likely to be'.

A study of 200,000 children from large Israeli families (Davis *et al.*, 1977) supports Zajonc and Markus's claim at least up to the seventh child. At this point, the trend reverses itself, so that the tenth-born child has a higher IQ than the ninth-born, who in turn has a higher IQ than the eighth-born. One possible explanation is that each new-born that enters a family lowers the 'intellectual environment' because the parents' intellectual capacity needs to be spread among a larger number of children. Alternatively, the mother's uterus might be less conducive to optimal pre-natal growth for later than earlier pregnancies, and this affects IQ (Crooks & Stein, 1991). However, neither explanation can account for the trend reported by Davis after the seventh child.

Coaching: This involves specific instruction and practice in taking intelligence tests to promote higher scores. Whilst short-term coaching may increase IQ score, the increase is seldom great. Additionally, the higher IQ scores produced by coaching do not seem to produce any improvement in underlying mental abilities (Linn, 1982).

Stressful family circumstances: Sameroff & Seifer's (1989) *Rochester longitudinal study* indicates that intellectual competence and general adjustment are correlated with a variety of 'family risk factors' including low parental work skills and a father who does not live with the family. Children with no risk factors score more than 30 IQ points higher than children with seven or eight risk factors.

Child-rearing styles: How parents interact with their children and the stimulation they provide are correlated with the development of measured intelligence (see Chapter 40).

(Based on Morris, 1988; Wade & Tavris, 1993; Zimbardo & Weber, 1994)

ENVIRONMENTAL ENRICHMENT STUDIES

As was seen in Chapter 39, Skeels (1966) followed up a group of children removed from orphanages into more stimulating environments 20 years earlier (Skeels & Dye, 1939). Most of those raised by foster mothers showed significant improvements in their measured intelligence, whereas those raised in the orphanage had dropped out of high school, or were still institutionalised or not self-supporting.

Other studies of children raised in orphanages have also shown that environmental enrichment can have beneficial effects. For example, Hunt (1982) studied 11 children living in an Iranian orphanage. The typical child could not sit up unassisted at age two or walk at age four. The children were emotionally retarded, passive and unresponsive to the environment. Hunt began a programme of 'tutored human enrichment' in which, for example, the caregivers were trained to play vocal games with the infants. All 11 showed a marked acceleration in language acquisition and generally began to behave in ways typical of children raised in a natural home environment.

Hunt (1961) and Bloom (1964) argued that intelligence was not a fixed attribute but depended on, and could be increased by, experience. This led to the United States government initiating a number of *intervention programmes* based on the assumption that intelligence could be increased through special training.

Box 43.4   Operation Headstart

In 1965, *Operation Headstart* began. It was an ambitious compensatory programme designed to give culturally disadvantaged pre-school children enriched opportunities in early life. Operation Headstart started as an eight-week summer programme and shortly afterwards became a full year's pre-school project. In 1967, two additional *Follow Through* programmes were initiated, in an attempt to involve parents and members of the wider community. Early findings indicated that there were significant short-term gains for the children, and this generated much optimism. However, when IQ gains did occur, they disappeared within a couple of years, and the children's educational improvement was minimal.

Similar to Operation Headstart was the *Milwaukee Project*. Heber & Garber (1975) worked with 40 poor, mostly black families, whose average IQ score was 75. Twenty of the women were given job training and sent to school (the 'experimental group'). The other twenty (the 'control group') received no job training or special education. The findings initially showed that the children of the 'experimental group' parents had an average IQ score of 126, 51 points higher than the average obtained by their mothers. The average score of the 'control group' children was 94, also higher than their mothers' average score.

As with Headstart, however, the IQ gains diminished over time. Moreover, the children's academic gains were very modest, in that whilst the experimental group did have better reading scores than the controls, there was little difference between them in mathematics, in which both groups performed poorly. Like Headstart, the Milwaukee project showed that vigorous and relatively prolonged intervention can make a difference to severely disadvantaged children's cognitive performances. However, much of the gain is lost in the years following the end of the programme, at the time of starting school (Rutter & Rutter, 1992). Figure 43.2 illustrates this.

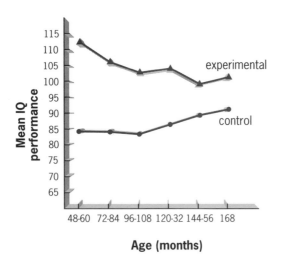

Figure 43.2   IQ performance with increasing age of severely disadvantaged children participating in a broad-ranging intensive intervention programme in the preschool years. (Data from Garber, 1988 and taken from Rutter & Rutter, 1992)

Headstart in particular has been subject to several criticisms. Hunt (1969), for example, has claimed that it was inappropriate to the children's needs and did not provide them with the skills they had failed to develop at home during their first four years, and which are developed by most middle class children. Also, it emphasised IQ changes as an outcome measure in evaluating its effectiveness. Critics have argued that measures which reflect social competence, adaptability and emotional health are much better criteria of success (Weinberg, 1989).

However, the criticisms were apparently premature, and several reviews looking at Headstart's long-term effects have concluded that the programme has brought about *lasting* changes in children's cognitive abilities (Brown & Grotberg, 1981), with the greatest gains being shown by children with the lowest initial IQ. Additionally, there is a *sleeper effect* at work, in that the impact of intervention programmes is cumulative (Collins, 1983).

Box 43.5   Collins' conclusions about intervention programmes

Compared with non-participants, participants in intervention programmes:

- tend to score higher on tests of reading, language and maths, and this 'achievement gap' tends to widen between the ages of six and 14;

- are more likely to meet the school's basic requirements, that is, are less likely to be assigned to special education/remedial classes, to repeat a year in the same grade or to drop out of high school;

- are more likely to want to succeed academically;

- have mothers who are more satisfied with their children's school performance and hold higher occupational aspirations for them.

The IQ gains, which lasted for up to four years after the programme ended, were *not* sustained, and by age 11 to 12 there were no differences between those who had participated and those who had not. However, the *academic benefits* were long lasting. Garber (1988) reports the reverse result in the Milwaukee programme, although as Figure 43.2 shows, the IQ gains declined over time.

Other intervention studies (Schweinhart & Weikart, 1980) also indicate that cognitive abilities can be enhanced through extensive training. However, researchers argue that there has been an overemphasis on the early childhood period. In their view, intervention can be effective *at any time* during the life-span, particularly as regards problem-solving skills and abstract thinking (Barber, 1996).

Although there have been methodological criticisms of intervention and enrichment studies, they can apparently have beneficial effects. This indicates that the environment has an important influence on the development of measured intelligence, at least in those children subjected to poor environmental conditions. Such programmes have less impact on children raised in 'normal' environments (Scarr, 1984).

HOTHOUSING

According to Scarr (1984):

'Parents who are very concerned about providing special educational lessons for their babies are wasting their time'.

Whether it is possible and, indeed, desirable to accelerate children's development is currently the subject of much debate. For some psychologists (including Scarr), development is largely a matter of maturation. Others believe that whilst accelerated progress can occur in some areas, other skills (such as language) are essentially pre-programmed and not much affected by early experience (Howe, 1995). Howe (1990) and Howe & Griffey (1994) have reviewed the evidence concerning early acceleration. In their view, efforts to help babies gain basic skills (such as running and jumping) earlier than usual can be beneficial. Even language development can be accelerated such that at 24 months of age, children given special graduated language programmes were as linguistically capable as typical 32-month-olds. Specific benefits have been found in pronoun and plural use and, in general, children given special programmes are well ahead of those not given them (Howe, 1995).

However, researchers have cautioned against generalising about the effects of providing children with enriched environments. White (1971), for example, showed that infants in enriched visual surroundings (a highly colourful mobile suspended over their cribs) were advanced in some respects, but *delayed* in others. Similarly, studies of perceptual and motor development indicate that acceleration in one area of development can have a 'blunting' effect on development in other areas (Cratty, 1970).

Parents determined to make their child into a genius or prodigy can pressurise it with their high expectations and by sending it to an organisation established to serve 'gifted children'. However, there is no convincing evidence that such organisations are actually effective (Llewellyn-Smith, 1996). Also, children who experience intensive *hothousing regimes* may miss other experiences which, whilst not necessarily 'educational', are important for healthy development (Howe, 1995). A child who successfully completes a mathematics degree before the age of 14 clearly has developed a useful skill. But he or she might not have developed important social skills (such as the ability to make friends) because of an inability to join in 'normal' children's conversations.

Howe & Griffey (1994) have suggested ways that children can be encouraged to learn which avoid the potential problems described above.

Box 43.6 Encouraging learning

- Learning should be informal and take place in the context of game or play activities.

- Parents should never persist in encouraging learning when the child demonstrates a lack of interest or reluctance.

- Children's efforts should never be criticised or the child made aware that parents are disappointed with the progress being made.

- Parents should make sure that there are times when the child has their full attention.

- Children should share in their parents' everyday activities and be included in their daily life as much as is reasonably possible.

- Children should be talked to, not talked at. Parents should create opportunities when they and their children can respond to one another.

- Parents should try to see things from the child's perspective, acting as 'guides' rather than 'teachers'.

- Parents should be serious about directing their child towards experiences that provide opportunities for learning and discovering.

(Adapted from Howe, 1995)

The interaction between genetic and environmental factors

Clearly, both genetic and environmental factors can influence the development of measured intelligence. For most psychologists, measured intelligence can be attributed to an *interaction* between genetic and environmental factors. As Weinberg (1989) has noted:

'Genes do not fix behaviour. Rather, they establish a range of possible reactions to the range of possible experiences that environments can provide. Environments can also affect whether the full range of gene reactivity is expressed. Thus, how people behave, or what their measured IQs turn out to be or how quickly they learn, depends on the nature of their environments and on their genetic endowments bestowed at conception'.

Researchers have attempted to determine the *relative* contributions made by genetic and environmental factors. The term *heritability* is used by behaviour geneticists to refer to the mathematical estimate of how much variability in a particular trait is a result of genetic variability (Carlson, 1988). Eye colour, for example, is affected almost entirely by heredity and little, if at all, by environmental factors. As a result, the heritability of eye colour is close to 100 per cent.

Early heritability estimates for IQ of 80 per cent (Jensen, 1969) have been revised down more recently to around 50 to 60 per cent (Bouchard & Segal, 1988). However, to say that the heritability of measured intelligence is 50 to 60 per cent does *not* mean that 50 to 60 per cent of measured intelligence is determined by genetic factors. This is because heritability estimates apply only to a particular *population* or group of people and not to a single individual. So, of the variation in intelligence test scores *within a group of people*, about 50 to 60 per cent (if Bouchard and Segal's estimate is correct) can be attributed to genetic factors. However, this statement must be qualified, because the heritability of any trait depends on the *context* in which it is being studied. Thus, a trait that is highly heritable is not necessarily fixed at birth and impossible to change.

Box 43.7   Why between-group differences cannot be inferred from within-group differences

Lewontin (1976) asks us to consider ten tomato plants grown in poor soil. Their different heights are the result of genetic factors. If the same ten plants were grown in fertile soil, differences in height would again be due to genetic factors. However, the difference in the average height of the plants grown in poor and fertile soil is due to the environmental differences of the soils. So, even when the heritability of a trait is high *within* a particular group, differences in that trait *between* groups may have environmental causes (Myers, 1990).

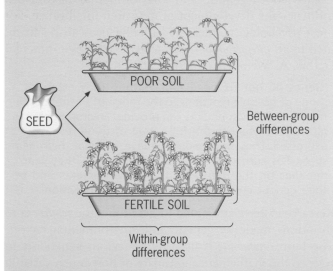

Figure 43.3   Although we can account for within-group differences in terms of genetic factors, between-group differences may be caused by environmental factors (i.e. poor/fertile soil)

Genetic and environmental factors, then, can never be isolated from one another. For this reason, it is logically absurd to ask how much of an individual's measured intelligence is *determined* by genetic factors and how much by environmental factors, since the answer will depend on the group that is studied and the environment in which they were raised.

Conclusions

Both genetic and environmental factors can influence the development of measured intelligence. These factors are intertwined, not separate. For measured intelligence to develop to its full potential, people should be provided with an optimal environment, whatever their heredity may be.

Summary

■ Genetic influences may be **hereditary** or **non-hereditary.** Pre-natal environmental factors having harmful effects on development include maternal malnourishment, stress, diseases, toxic agents, drugs, irradiation and maternal age.

■ One way of investigating heredity's influence on measured intelligence is to study the **stability of IQ**. If IQ is largely determined by genetic factors, then it should remain stable throughout the life-span. Although several studies show high **stability coefficients**, these obscure sometimes very large individual differences and there are many short-term fluctuations.

■ **Family resemblance studies** involve examining the correlations in IQ among people who vary in genetic similarity. If genetic factors influence IQ test performance, then the closer the genetic relationship between two people, the greater the correspondence (**concordance**) between their IQ scores. **MZ**s should show the **greatest** correspondence: any difference between them is attributable to environmental influences.

■ Although there is evidence supporting this prediction, as people's genetic similarities increase so do the similarities of their environments. This can be overcome by comparing the IQs of MZs **reared together** with those raised **separately**. MZs reared separately are still more similar than same-sex **DZ**s reared together, suggesting a strong genetic influence.

■ Studies of separated MZs have been criticised on several important grounds. However, the Minnesota twin study indicates that for verbal ability the correlations among separated MZs are very high, although for memory they are low and for spatial ability inconsistent.

■ Further support for the influence of genetic factors comes from **adoption studies**. When the economic status of the biological and adoptive parents is roughly equal, biological factors seem to be more influential. However, when children from disadvantaged parents are adopted into high socio-economic families, substantial gains in IQ can occur, as in 'transracial' studies. Also, children adopted within their first year have higher IQs than those adopted later.

■ While not denying the role of genetic factors, environmentalists argue that the development of measured intelligence can be strongly influenced by **environmental factors**. This is supported by studies of rats raised in enriched environments.

■ Human infants suffering **extreme malnutrition** have much lower IQs than similar children with adequate diets. **Environmental 'insults', illness** and **disease** can all cause brain damage and lower potential intelligence. **Family size** and **birth order** are also related to intelligence, as are **stressful family circumstances** and **child-rearing styles**. IQ can also be affected by **coaching**.

■ **Intervention programmes** started with **Operation Headstart**. Early findings indicated significant short-term IQ gains, but these were short-lived and the educational improvement was minimal. Similar results were reported for the **Milwaukee Project**.

■ Headstart was criticised for not providing the skills the disadvantaged children had failed to develop at home. It also overemphasised IQ as a measure of effectiveness, at the expense of social competence, adaptability and emotional health.

■ Studies of the long-term effects have concluded that Headstart has lasting cognitive benefits, especially for those whose IQ scores are initially the lowest. There is also a **sleeper effect**. Other intervention studies have also shown that cognitive abilities can be enhanced.

■ Whether **hothousing** accelerates development is debatable. Acceleration in one area of development can have a 'blunting' or **delaying** effect on others. Children exposed to **hothousing regimes** may miss out on other experiences important for healthy development.

■ For most psychologists, the development of measured intelligence is due to an **interaction** between genetic and environmental factors. Genes establish a range of possible reactions to environmental experiences.

■ **Heritability** refers to how much of the variability in a particular trait is due to genetic variability **within a particular population or group of people** (not within a single individual). Even when a trait's heritability is high **within** a particular group, differences in that trait **between** groups may have environmental causes.

PART 3

Social behaviour and diversity in development

THEORIES OF MORAL DEVELOPMENT

Introduction and overview

At birth, humans are *amoral* and do not possess any system of personal values and judgements about what is right or wrong. By adulthood, though, most of us possess *morality*. Psychologists are not interested in morality as such, but in the *process* by which it is acquired. Explanations of moral development include Freud's (1924) psychoanalytic theory, accounts based on learning (Eysenck, 1964) and social learning theories (Aronfreed, 1976).

This chapter critically considers some of these theories but emphasises the cognitive–developmental theories of Piaget (1932) and Kohlberg (1963).

Freud's psychoanalytic theory

 Freud saw life as an ongoing conflict between sexual and aggressive instincts and society's constraints on behaviour (see Chapter 1). The *ego* develops to negotiate compromises between such instincts and constraints. However, it is concerned with *practical* rather than moral compromises, so a person with a particularly 'strong' ego might still behave immorally, if he or she felt that such behaviour would go undetected.

For Freud, morality is rooted in the *superego*, the part of personality that punishes us (in the form of *guilt*) when society's standards are violated, and rewards us (in the form of enhanced *self-esteem*) when these standards are

upheld. The terms *conscience* and *ego-ideal* are used to describe the punishing and rewarding aspects of the superego respectively, which Freud believed are acquired by age five or six.

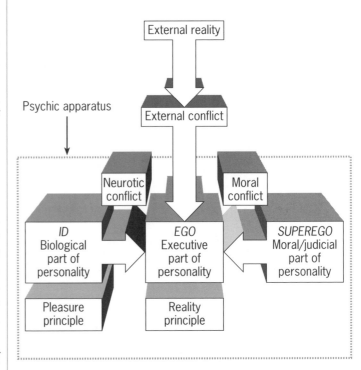

Figure 44.1   The relationship between the id, ego and superego

382

Also, children today are exposed to moral influences which extend much more beyond the family, in particular, television and other mass media (see Chapter 64), than was true when Freud formulated his theory. The family's influence was probably much greater than it is now.

A social learning theory account

Orthodox learning theorists argue that moral behaviours are acquired through classical and operant conditioning (see Chapters 1 and 32). We resist temptation because we have been *reinforced* for so doing and *punished* for transgressions (Aronfreed, 1963). Whilst social learning (SL) theorists recognise the role of conditioning, they emphasise the importance of *modelling* (or *observational learning*) and see the *cognitive factors* intervening between a stimulus and a response as being of crucial importance (see Chapter 32).

The stronger the motive, the stronger (or more complete) the identification. Freud maintained that boys' *identification with the aggressor* results in a much stronger superego than in girls, whose superegos develop through *anaclitic identification* (fear of loss of the mother's love). There is, however, little evidence that males are morally superior to females. Indeed, in a review of relevant research, Hoffman (1975) concluded that there are no overall gender differences in at least some aspects of morality, and where there are (as in the case of resisting temptation), females behave with *greater* morality.

AN EVALUATION OF FREUD'S THEORY

Kohlberg (1969) and others (e.g. Hoffman, 1976) have argued that moral development is a *gradual* process which begins in childhood and extends into adulthood, rather than something which comes into existence at around age five or six.

Freud's view of an internalised conscience implies that moral behaviour should be consistent across *different situations*. If moral behaviour is determined by an unchanging part of personality, it should not depend on the details of the moral situation. However, evidence does not support such an inference (Hartshorne & May, 1930).

Figure 44.2 This father is modelling behaviour which his daughters are learning spontaneously, i.e. observing his behaviour is the crucial factor, rather than being directly reinforced for 'doing the dishes'

The development of self-control is strongly influenced by *models* (Bandura, 1977: see Chapter 63, pages 546–547). Self-control is also influenced by patterns of direct reinforcement children encounter, that is, adults' disciplinary measures. Whilst it is not necessary for us to know models personally, there are several aspects of their specific behaviour that make them more likely to be imitated.

Box 44.2   Factors influencing the likelihood of a model being imitated

- **Appropriateness:** The more appropriate or fitting a behaviour is seen as being, the more likely it is to be imitated. Bandura *et al.* (1961), for example, showed that children were more likely to imitate aggressive males than aggressive females, because in our culture at least, aggression is more acceptable in men than women.

- **Relevance and similarity:** The more relevance a behaviour has, the more likely it is to be imitated. In Bandura *et al.*'s (1961) experiment, boys were more likely to imitate an aggressive male than were girls. The greater relevance to the boys lies in their perception of similarity between themselves and the model. Perception of similarity is based on gender identity (see Chapter 45).

- **Consistency:** One of the most consistent characteristics of human behaviour is its inconsistency! Children tend to imitate adults in a rather 'literal' way. If adults behave in a way which is inconsistent with how they say they'll behave, children typically imitate the inconsistency.

According to Mischel (1973), people develop *self-regulatory systems and plans*. These are self-imposed standards or rules used to regulate behaviour. Rather than seeing reinforcement and punishment as always being *external* (as when children are directly rewarded or punished), SL theorists argue for *internal* sources of reinforcement. Children eventually no longer need an external agency (parents and other adults) to administer rewards and punishments, but can reward themselves through feelings of pride (a *rewarding reaction*) and punish themselves through guilt (a *punishing reaction*) by thoughts of doing wrong or the intention to do wrong.

Self-reinforcement and self-punishment (SL theory's equivalent of the superego) are acquired through observation and imitation of the parents' rewards and punishments. Behaviour which was previously rewarded or punished by parents can be reinforced or punished by the child's own *imitative self-approval* or *disapproval*. Children who model an adult's behaviour construct an *internal image* of that behaviour, which then serves as a guide for performing it in the future.

AN EVALUATION OF SL THEORY

Hoffman (1970) showed that excessive parental use of power-assertive techniques (such as physical punishment, withdrawal of privileges, or the threat of either) was associated with low levels of moral development. Reasoning or explaining, by contrast, was correlated with high levels. Parents who explain why particular behaviours are wrong induce children to understand the principles of moral behaviour, rather than learning how to avoid punishment or maximise reward (see Chapter 40, page 349).

Although these findings are consistent with SL theory, critics argue that it says nothing about *moral progress*. Rather than developmental changes being *qualitative* (with children changing in similar ways as they get older), SL theorists view such changes as merely *quantitative* (they learn more as they get older). This particular weakness is addressed by the cognitive–developmental theories of Piaget and Kohlberg.

Cognitive–developmental theories

PIAGET'S THEORY

According to cognitive–developmental theorists, it is the reasons that *underlie* a behaviour, rather than the behaviour itself, which make it right or wrong. Piaget (1932) argued that morality develops gradually during childhood and adolescence, with children passing through *qualitatively* different *stages* of moral development. To discover how moral knowledge and understanding change with age, Piaget began by looking at children's ideas about the rules of the game of marbles, believing that the essence of morality lies in rules and that marbles is a game in which children create and enforce their own rules free from adult influence. Piaget felt that in this way he could discover how children's moral knowledge in general develops. As he noted:

> 'Children's games constitute the most admirable social institutions. The game of marbles, for instance, as played by boys, contains an extremely complex system of rules, that is to say, a code of laws, a jurisprudence of its own … All morality consists in a system of rules, and the essence of all morality is to be sought after in the respect which the individual acquires for these rules.'

By pretending he did not know the rules, Piaget asked children to explain them to him and, during the course of a game, to tell him who made the rules, where they came from, and whether they could be changed. He found that children aged between five and nine or ten tended to believe that the rules had always existed in their present form, and that they had been created by older children, adults or even God. The rules were sacred and could not be changed in any way (an *external law*). Nevertheless, children unashamedly broke them to suit themselves and saw nothing contradictory in the idea of both players winning the game.

Children aged ten and above understood that the rules were invented by children themselves and could be changed, but only if all players agreed, the function of rules being to prevent quarrelling and ensure fair play. They adhered rigidly to the rules and discussed the finer points and implications of any changes. Piaget called this moral orientation towards cooperation with peers *mutual respect*, to distinguish it from the *unilateral respect* shown by younger children who are oriented towards adult authority.

Figure 44.3   According to Piaget, the rules of marbles could be used to study morality, since all morality consists of a system of rules

Piaget also told children pairs of stories about (hypothetical) children who had told lies, stolen or broken something.

Box 44.3   Examples of pairs of stories used by Piaget

Example 1a: A little boy called John was in his room. He was called to dinner and went into the dining room. Behind the door there was a chair and on the chair there was a tray with 15 cups on it. John couldn't have known that the chair was behind the door, and as he entered the dining room, the door knocked against the tray and the tray fell on the floor, breaking all of the cups.

Example 1b: One day, a little boy called Henry tried to get some jam out of a cupboard when his mother was out. He climbed onto a chair and stretched out his arm. The jam was too high up, and he couldn't reach it. But while he was trying to get it, he knocked over a cup. The cup fell down and broke.

Example 2a: A little girl called Marie wanted to give her mother a nice surprise and so she cut out a piece of sewing for her. But she didn't know how to use the scissors properly and she cut a big hole in her dress.

Example 2b: A little girl called Margaret went and took her mother's scissors one day when her mother was out. She played with them for a bit and then, as she didn't know how to use them properly, she made a hole in her dress.

Piaget asked children who they believed was the naughtier and should be punished more. He was more interested in the *reasons* the children gave for their answers than the answers themselves. Whilst five- to nine- or ten-year-olds could distinguish an intentional act from an unintentional one, they tended to base their judgement on the severity of the outcome or the sheer amount of damage done. So, John and Marie (see Box 44.3) were typically judged to be naughtier (*objective* or *external responsibility*).

By contrast, children aged ten or above judged Henry and Margaret to be naughtier, because they were both doing something they shouldn't have been. Although the damage they caused was not deliberate, older children saw the motive or intention behind an act as being important in determining naughtiness (*internal responsibility*).

Regarding punishment, younger children believed that naughty people should pay for their crimes and, generally, the greater the suffering the better, even though the form of punishment might be quite arbitrary. Such *expiatory* ('paying the penalty for') *punishment* is seen as decreed by authority and accepted as just because of its source (*moral realism*). Thus, when a child in a class does not admit to a misdeed and the rest of the class do not identify the offender, young children see *collective punishment* (punishment for all) as being acceptable.

Younger children also often construed a misfortune which befalls a person who has behaved naughtily as a punishment for the misdeed (*immanent justice*). For example, a child who lied but was not found out and later fell and broke its arm was seen as being punished for the lie. Younger children believed that God (or an equivalent force) is in league with those in authority to ensure that 'the guilty will always be caught in the end'.

Older children saw punishment as bringing home to the offender the nature of the offence and as a deterrent to behaving wrongly in the future. They also believed that punishing innocent people for the misdeeds of only one was immoral, and that 'the punishment should fit the crime'. So, if one child stole another's sweets, the *principle of reciprocity* should apply, and the offender must be deprived of his or her own sweets or punished in some other appropriate way. *Community service* applies the principle of reciprocity, as when a footballer who assaults a spectator, say, is required to spend time working with young footballers. Older children display *moral relativism* in which justice is no longer tied to authority, there is less belief in immanent justice, and collective punishment is seen as wrong.

Figure 44.4 Eric Cantona, whose infamous attack on a Crystal Palace supporter resulted in punishment by both the football authorities and the police. His community service took the form of working with young footballers in and around Manchester

---

Box 44.4   Heteronomous and autonomous morality

Piaget called the morality of younger children *heteronomous* ('being subject to another's laws or rules'). Older children have *autonomous morality* (the *morality of cooperation*), and see rules as the product of social agreements rather than sacred and unchangeable laws. Piaget believed that the change from heteronomous to autonomous morality occurred because of the shift at about seven from egocentric to operational thought (see Chapter 41). This suggests that cognitive development is necessary for moral development, but since the latter lags at least two years behind the former, it cannot be sufficient. Another important factor is the change from *unilateral respect* (the child's unconditional obedience of parents and other adults) to *mutual respect* within the peer group (where disagreements between equals have to be negotiated and resolved).

An evaluation of Piaget's theory

Piaget's theory has been supported by several other researchers, and by cross-cultural studies which suggest that the shift from heteronomous to autonomous morality occurs around the age of nine or ten (Kruger, 1992). However, whilst his theory is intended to explain how *practical morality* develops (how we conceive those situations in which we are actively involved and which demand a moral response or decision), Piaget's evidence was derived from samples of children's *theoretical morality* (how their own and others' real and hypothetical moral problems are thought about when they are not immediately or directly involved: Wright, 1971).

For Piaget, theoretical morality is the *conscious realisation* of the moral principles on which we actually operate. In other words, we can already do things by the time we come to think about and reflect on them. So, there will always be a delay before developmental change at the practical level is registered at the theoretical level, which implies that theoretical morality is shaped by practical morality rather than the other way round. Therefore, adult theorising (tuition) will not affect the child's practical morality, although it might help theoretical morality catch up with it.

Piaget believed that popular girls' games (such as hopscotch) were so simple compared with boys' most popular game (marbles) that they did not warrant investigation. Whilst girls *eventually* achieve similar moral levels to boys, Piaget saw them as being less concerned with *legal elaborations*. This apparent gender bias is also evident in Kohlberg's theory (see below).

Children's understanding of *intention* is much more complex than Piaget believed, and children are able to bring this understanding to bear on moral decision-making. The pre-school child is *not* amoral (Durkin, 1995).

Box 44.5   Some experimental challenges to Piaget's theory of moral development

• Six-, eight- and ten-year-old children read stories about a boy who emptied his box of toys onto the floor, so that he could either sort them out (good motive/intention) or make a mess (bad motive/intention). When his mother, who was unaware of his intentions, entered the room, she either approved or disapproved of his behaviour (a measure of his action's consequences). Consistent with Piaget, only six-year-olds judged him as being naughty, regardless of his actual intentions, when his mother *disapproved*. However, when she approved, the older children *and* the six-year-olds were just as likely to judge him according to his intentions (Constanzo *et al.*, 1973). The fact that the youngest children's judgement was no different from that of the older children is difficult for Piaget to explain.

• Piaget's stories make a behaviour's consequences explicit rather than the intentions behind it (Nelson, 1980). When three-year-olds see people bringing about negative consequences, they assume that the intentions are negative. However, when information about intentions is made explicit, even three-year-olds can make judgements about those intentions, regardless of the behaviour's consequences. This suggests that three-year-olds are *less proficient* than older children at discriminating intentions from consequences, and in using these separate pieces of information to make moral judgements.

• Depending on the extent and nature of the damage described to them, six-year-olds are capable of judging that a small amount of deliberate damage is naughtier than a large amount of accidental damage (Armsby, 1971). In Armsby's study, 60 per cent of six-year-olds (compared with 90 per cent of ten-year-olds) judged the deliberate breaking of a cup more deserving of punishment than accidental damage to a television set. This suggests that at least some six-year-olds are capable of understanding intention in the sense of 'deliberate naughtiness'.

• Information-processing theorists (e.g. Gelman & Baillargeon, 1983) argue that aspects of development which Piaget believed to be a result of the increasing complexity and quality of thought, are actually a result of an increasing capacity for the storage and retrieval of information. Most five-year-olds say that

John is naughtier because he broke more cups than Henry (see Box 44.3). For Piaget, this is because five-year-olds focus on the amount of damage done instead of the wrongdoer's intentions. However, Gelman and Baillargeon argue that children make such judgements because, although they can remember who broke more cups, they *cannot remember all the other details of the stories*. When an effort is made to ensure that all details of the stories are remembered, five-year-olds frequently do consider intentions as well as the amount of damage.

KOHLBERG'S THEORY

Kohlberg has had the greatest impact on the study of moral development. He argued that the only way to find underlying consistencies and developmental trends in people's behaviour was by studying the philosophy, logic or reasoning behind their thinking (Piaget's theoretical morality) and behaviour (Piaget's practical morality). Like Piaget, Kohlberg believed that morality develops gradually during childhood and adolescence, and that children pass through stages of moral development.

Kohlberg (1963) created ten *moral dilemmas* that typically involved a choice between two alternatives, both of which would be considered socially unacceptable. One of the most famous of these dilemmas concerns Heinz.

Box 44.6   An example of a moral dilemma

In Europe, a woman was near death from a special kind of cancer. There was one drug that the doctors thought might save her. It was a form of radium that a druggist in the same town had recently discovered. The drug was expensive to make, but the druggist was charging ten times what the drug cost him to make. He paid $400 for the radium and charged $4000 for a small dose of the drug. The sick woman's husband, Heinz, went to everyone he knew to borrow the money, but he could only get together about $2000, which is half of what the drug cost. He told the druggist that his wife was dying and asked him to sell it cheaper or let him pay later. But the druggist said, 'No, I discovered the drug and I'm going to make money from it.' So Heinz gets desperate and considers breaking into the man's store to steal the drug for his wife.

1 Should Heinz steal the drug?

   a) Why or why not?

2 If Heinz doesn't love his wife, should he steal the drug for her?

   a) Why or why not?

---

3 Suppose the person dying is not his wife but a stranger. Should Heinz steal the drug for the stranger?

a) Why or why not?

4 (If you favour stealing the drug for a stranger.) Suppose it's a pet animal he loves. Should Heinz steal to save the pet animal?

a) Why or why not?

5 Is it important for people to do everything they can to save another's life?

a) Why or why not?

6 Is it against the law for Heinz to steal? Does that make it morally wrong?

a) Why or why not?

7 Should people try to do everything they can to obey the law?

a) Why or why not?

b) How does this apply to what Heinz should do?

(From Kohlberg, 1984)

Like Piaget, Kohlberg was more interested in how thinking about right and wrong changes with age. For example, irrespective of age, most of us would say that it is wrong to break society's laws. Our *reasons* for upholding the law, however, as well as our views about whether there are circumstances in which breaking the law can be justified, might change as we develop. In Heinz's case, then, Kohlberg was interested in why people believed Heinz should or should not steal the drug.

Kohlberg (1963) presented his moral dilemmas to 58 males aged between seven and 17. Based on the reasoning offered by his sample, Kohlberg identified six qualitatively different ways of viewing moral issues. Because these types of moral reasoning differed in complexity, with more complex types being used by older children, Kohlberg argued that they could be seen as *stages* in the development of morality. The six stages span three basic levels of moral reasoning.

At the *pre-conventional level*, we do not have a personal code of morality. Instead, it is shaped by the standards of adults and the consequences of following or breaking their rules. At the *conventional level*, we begin to internalise the moral standards of valued adult role models. People who are capable of formal operational thought (see Chapter 41, page 359) may progress to the level of *post-conventional morality*. Stage 5 affirms the values society agrees on such as individual rights, the need for

democratically determined rules, and *reciprocity* (or *mutual action*). In stage 6, people are guided by *universal ethical principles*, in which they do what they believe to be right as a matter of conscience, even if such behaviour conflicts with society's rules.

Box 44.7 Kohlberg's three levels and six stages of moral development and their application to the Heinz dilemma

LEVEL 1: PRE-CONVENTIONAL MORALITY

Stage 1 (punishment and obedience orientation): What is right and wrong is determined by what is punishable and what is not. If stealing is wrong, it is because authority figures say so and will punish such behaviour. Moral behaviour is essentially the avoidance of punishment.

- Heinz *should* steal the drug because if he lets his wife die, he would get into trouble.

- Heinz *should not* steal the drug because he would get caught and sent to jail.

Stage 2 (instrumental relativist orientation): What is right and wrong is determined by what brings rewards and what people want. Other people's needs and wants are important, but only in a reciprocal sense ('if you scratch my back, I'll scratch yours').

- Heinz *should* steal the drug because his wife needs it to live and he needs her companionship.

- Heinz *should not* steal the drug because he might get caught and his wife would probably die before he got out of prison, so it wouldn't do much good.

LEVEL 2: CONVENTIONAL MORALITY

Stage 3 (interpersonal concordance or 'good boy–nice girl' orientation): Moral behaviour is whatever pleases and helps others and doing what they approve of. Being moral is 'being a good person in your own eyes and the eyes of others'. What the majority thinks is right by definition.

- Heinz *should* steal the drug because society expects a loving husband to help his wife regardless of the consequences.

- Heinz *should not* steal the drug because he will bring dishonour on his family and they will be ashamed of him.

Stage 4 (maintaining the social order orientation): Being good means doing one's duty – showing respect for authority and maintaining the social order for its own sake. Concern for the common good goes beyond the stage 3 concern for one's family: society protects the rights of individuals, so society must be protected by the individual. Laws are unquestionably accepted and obeyed.

- Heinz *should* steal the drug because if people like the druggist are allowed to get away with being greedy and selfish, society would eventually break down.

- Heinz *should not* steal the drug because if people are allowed to take the law into their own hands, regardless of how justified an act might be, the social order would soon break down.

LEVEL 3: POST-CONVENTIONAL MORALITY

Stage 5 (social contract–legalistic orientation): Since laws are established by mutual agreement, they can be changed by the same democratic process. Although laws and rules should be respected, since they protect individual rights as well as those of society as a whole, individual rights can sometimes supersede these laws if they become destructive or restrictive. Life is more 'sacred' than any legal principle, and so the law should not be obeyed at all costs.

- Heinz *should* steal the drug because the law is not set up to deal with circumstances in which obeying it would cost a human life.

- Heinz *should not* steal the drug because even though he couldn't be blamed if he did steal it, even such extreme circumstances do not justify a person taking the law into his own hands. The ends do not always justify the means.

Stage 6 (universal ethical principles orientation): The ultimate judge of what is moral is a person's own conscience operating in accordance with certain universal principles. Society's rules are arbitrary and they may be broken when they conflict with universal moral principles.

- Heinz *should* steal the drug because when a choice must be made between disobeying a law and saving a life, one must act in accordance with the higher principle of preserving and respecting life.

- Heinz *should not* steal the drug because he must consider other people who need it just as much as his wife. By stealing the drug he would be acting in accordance with his own particular feelings with utter disregard for the values of all the lives involved.

(Based on Rest, 1983; Crooks & Stein, 1991; Gross, 1996)

Both Piaget and Kohlberg see cognitive development as necessary but not sufficient for moral development, that is, cognitive development sets a limit on the maturity of moral reasoning, with the latter usually lagging behind the former. Furthermore, just because a person is capable of formal operational thought and conventional and post-conventional moral reasoning, there is no *guarantee* that he or she will behave more morally, even though the evidence suggests this tends to be the case (Lerner & Shea, 1982). Because formal operational thought is achieved by a comparatively small proportion of people, it is hardly surprising that the percentage of people attaining the highest level of moral reasoning is only 15 per cent (Colby *et al.*, 1983: see also Table 44.1, page 391).

An evaluation of Kohlberg's theory

Kohlberg followed up his original sample to see if those who were initially at a low stage had advanced to a higher one. Since the original study, Kohlberg's sample has been tested every two to five years. Based on findings reported by Colby *et al.* (1983), which suggest that 'moral progression' does occur, Kohlberg argued that the first five stages of moral reasoning are *universal* and that they occur in an *invariant sequence*.

When factors like education and social class are controlled for, juvenile delinquents are more likely to show lower levels of moral reasoning than non-delinquents of the same ages (Smetana, 1990). Stage 2 reasoning is also characteristic of adults who engage in robbery and other 'instrumental' crimes (Thornton & Reid, 1982). A 20-year longitudinal study conducted by Rest (1983) of men from adolescence to their mid-30s has shown that stages of moral development seem to occur in the order described by Kohlberg, although such change is *gradual* with the sample changing, on average, less than two stages. From 45 studies conducted in 27 different cultures, Snarey (1987) has concluded that the data 'provide striking support for the universality of Kohlberg's first four stages'.

Figure 44.5   Mahatma Gandhi was a moral leader who defied his countrys' traditional moral and legal standards, in pursuit of humanistic causes. He seems to have been guided by universal ethical principles (Kohlberg's stage 6)

Figure 44.6 Mother Theresa of Calcutta: another moral leader who, like Gandhi, pursued humanistic causes and was guided by universal ethical principles

Box 44.8 Some concerns about Kohlberg's theory of moral development

Not surprisingly, several major theoretical, methodological and empirical issues have been raised about Kohlberg's theory.

- Although some of Kohlberg's stages may be universal, his theory can be seen as biased towards *Western* cultures. As noted, stage 6 reasoning is based on supposedly 'universal' ethical principles. Whilst the principles of justice, equality, integrity and reverence for life may be relevant to a culture that idealises them, they are *not* universally held (Shweder, 1991; Eckensberger, 1994). Moreover, some societies have developed moral principles not covered by Kohlberg's theory. Amongst Papua New Guineans, for example, a *principle of collective moral responsibility* exists (Snarey, 1987). Accordingly, Heinz should steal the drug because all resources should be available to the community at large.

- Gilligan (1982) has argued that because Kohlberg's theory was based on his study of males, the stages are based on a male definition of morality (see Chapter 84). Whilst men's morality is based on abstract principles of law and justice, women's is based on principles of compassion and care. Consequently, women are rated as being at the conventional level, whilst men are at the post-conventional level. Rather than one type of moral reasoning being *better* than another, the woman's social perspective is a different

view which *complements* male notions of morality. However, when the domain of moral reasoning is restricted to one of *common interest*, men and women produce very similar types of moral reasoning. Gender differences in moral reasoning are due to *situational differences* rather than stable gender differences, and women and men are likely to use similar forms of reasoning when faced with similar moral problems (Clopton & Sorrell, 1993).

- Kohlberg has been almost exclusively concerned with moral *thinking*, and his dilemmas assess only 'storybook morality' (how people reason about relatively unusual hypothetical dilemmas). However, moral reasoning and behaviour do not necessarily go together (Gibbs & Schnell, 1985). Whilst moral reasoning may determine moral talk, 'talk is cheap' (Blasi, 1980), and what we say and what we do when faced with a moral dilemma often differ, particularly under strong social pressure. Moral development research should really look at what people do rather than what they say they would do (Mischel & Mischel, 1976).

- Kohlberg's study began in the 1950s in the USA. The original participants have lived through the civil rights movement, Vietnam, Watergate and the women's movement. Their judgements are unlikely to be the same as those who grew up with the depression, World War II and the Cold War. Nor are they likely to be the same as those who grow up in the next 20 to 30 years.

- Kohlberg's dilemmas are unfamiliar to most people asked to consider them, and more mature reasoning might be shown if the dilemmas were about relevant, real-life, day-to-day experiences (Sobesky, 1983). They are also hypothetical and do not involve any serious personal consequences. Sobesky gave people Heinz's dilemma with the consequence of him being sent to prison because he would definitely be caught. When asked to imagine themselves in Heinz's position, people were less likely to advocate stealing *and* their levels of moral reasoning were lower.

- The higher stages in Kohlberg's theory are associated with education and verbal ability (Shweder *et al.*, 1987). Evidence suggests that 'college-educated' people give higher level and more mature explanations of moral decisions than those not college educated. The former may not be more moral than the latter, but might be more verbally sophisticated. Additionally, post-conventional morality may not necessarily be preferable to conventional morality (Shweder, 1991). Even Kohlberg (1978) acknowledges that there may not be a separate sixth stage.

Table 44.1   The relationship between Kohlberg's and Piaget's stages of moral development and Piaget's stages of cognitive development

Kohlberg's levels of moral development	Age group included within Kohlberg's developmental levels	Corresponding stage of moral development (Piaget)	Corresponding stage of cognitive development (Piaget)
1 Pre-conventional (Stages 1 and 2)	Most nine-year-olds and below. Some over nine	Heteronomous (five to nine or ten)	Pre-operational (two to seven)
2 Conventional (Stages 3 and 4)	Most adolescents and adults	Heteronomous (e.g. respect for the law and authority figures) plus autonomous (e.g. taking intentions into account)	Concrete operational (seven to 11)
3 Post-conventional (Stages 5 and 6)	10–15% of adults, not before mid-30s	Autonomous (ten and above)	Formal operational (11 and above)

(Taken from Gross, 1996)

Conclusions

Several theories of moral development have been proposed. Psychoanalytic and SL theories see morality as being imposed on people by parents and other socialising agents. Cognitive–developmental theories concentrate on the structures of reasoning that underlie behaviour and assume that moral reasoning develops through qualitatively different stages.

Summary

■ According to Freud, morality is rooted in the **super-ego**, acquired by age five or six. It comprises **conscience** and **ego-ideal**.

■ The **Oedipus complex** is resolved through **identification** with the same-sex parent. The child **introjects** that parent's image into its ego, forming the superego, which takes over the parental role of punisher within the child's psyche.

■ **Fear of castration** is a very powerful motive for boys identifying with their fathers, but is missing in girls, making identification with their mothers weaker and giving them weaker superegos. However, there is little evidence that males are morally superior.

■ Although **social learning theorists** accept the role of classical and operant conditioning, they emphasise **modelling** or **observational learning** and see the **cognitive factors** intervening between stimulus and response as crucial.

■ Models are more likely to be imitated the more **appropriate** and **relevant** their behaviour, based on perceived similarity. **Consistency** is another model characteristic influencing the likelihood of imitation.

■ **Self-regulatory systems and plans** represent **internal** sources of reinforcement. Children eventually no longer need an **external** agent of reinforcement or punishment, but can reward or punish themselves. These are acquired through observation and imitation of the parents' rewards (imitative self-approval) and punishments (imitative self-disapproval).

■ SL theory's major limitation is its failure to deal with **moral progress**. This is addressed by **cognitive–developmental theorists** who see the reasons **underlying** behaviour as what make it right or wrong.

■ Piaget called five- to nine-year-olds' morality **heteronomous**. It is associated with **unilateral respect**, **objective/external responsibility**, **moral realism**, and belief in **expiatory punishment** and **immanent justice**. The morality of children over ten is **autonomous**, which is associated with **mutual respect**, **internal responsibility**, the **principle of reciprocity** and **moral relativism**.

■ The change from heteronomous to autonomous occurs due to the shift from egocentric to operational thought, and freedom from unilateral respect and adult constraint to mutual respect within the peer group.

■ Whilst Piaget's theory is meant to explain the development of **practical morality**, his evidence was derived from samples of children's **theoretical morality**. Also, children's understanding of **intention** is much more complex than Piaget believed. The pre-schooler is **not** amoral and may simply be **less proficient** than older children at discriminating between intentions and consequences.

■ Like Piaget, **Kohlberg** was interested in how moral thinking changes with age. He identified six qualitatively different **stages** in moral development, spanning three basic **levels** of moral reasoning: **pre-conventional**, **conventional** and **post-conventional morality**.

■ Despite considerable empirical support for the sequence and universality of the (first four) stages, Kohlberg's theory is biased towards **Western** cultures. Ethical principles such as justice, equality, integrity and reverence for life are **not** universally held. Conversely, some societies have developed moral principles not covered by Kohlberg's theory.

■ Gilligan regards the stages as based on a **male** definition of morality. Consequently, women are rated as being at the conventional level, whilst men are at the post-conventional level.

■ Kohlberg's original participants lived through particular social changes, such as the Vietnam War and the women's movement. Their moral judgements are unlikely to be the same as those of either earlier or later generations.

■ Kohlberg's dilemmas are unfamiliar to most participants. More mature reasoning might be shown if the dilemmas dealt with relevant, real-life, everyday experiences.

45

THE DEVELOPMENT OF GENDER

Introduction and overview

Every known culture distinguishes between male and female, a distinction which is accompanied by widely held beliefs (*stereotypes*: see Chapter 52) about their psychological make-up and behaviours. The study of psychological sex differences is really an attempt to see how accurate these stereotypes are.

Feminist interpretations of sex differences share the belief that social, political, economic and cultural factors determine *gender*, our awareness and understanding of the differences that distinguish males from females. This view is directly opposed to those of sociobiologists and evolutionary psychologists, who argue that sex differences are 'natural', having evolved as a part of the more general adaptation of the human species to its environment.

Several other theoretical accounts of gender and gender differences have been advanced, including biological approaches, biosocial theory, psychoanalytic theory, social learning theory, cognitive–developmental theory and gender schema theory. This chapter considers these various accounts, but begins by defining some of the basic terms needed to evaluate the different theories.

The 'vocabulary' of sex and gender

Feminist psychologists (e.g. Unger, 1979) distinguish between *sex* and *gender*. Sex refers to some biological fact about us, such as a particular genetic make-up, reproductive anatomy and functioning, and is usually referred to by the terms 'male' and 'female'. Gender, by contrast, is what culture makes out of the 'raw material' of biological sex. It is, therefore, the social equivalent or social interpretation of sex.

Sexual identity is an alternative way of referring to our biological status as male or female. Corresponding to gender is *gender identity*, our classification of ourselves (and others) as male or female, boy or girl, and so on. Sexual and gender identities correspond for most of us, but not in *transsexualism*. Whilst being anatomically male or female, transexuals firmly believe that they belong to the opposite sex. As a result, their biological sexual identities are fundamentally inconsistent with their gender identities.

Gender role (or *sex role*) refers to the behaviours, attitudes, values, beliefs and so on which a particular society either expects from, or considers appropriate to, males and females on the basis of their biological sex. To be *masculine* (or *feminine*), then, requires males (or females) to conform to their respective gender roles.

All societies have carefully defined gender roles, although they differ in men and women's prescribed roles (see below). *Gender* (or sex) *stereotypes* are widely held beliefs about psychological differences between males and females which often reflect gender roles (see below).

Figure 45.1   Renee Richards, formerly known as Richard Raskin, one of the world's best-known transsexuals. Born male, Richard had his sex reassigned through surgery and continued her tennis career as a woman

Sex typing refers to our acquisition of a sex or gender identity and learning the appropriate behaviours (adopting an appropriate *sex role*). Sex typing begins early in Western culture, with parents often dressing their new-born baby boy or girl in blue or pink. Even in infancy's earliest days, our gender influences how people react to us (Condry & Ross, 1985). Indeed, the first question asked by friends and relatives of parents with a new-born baby is 'Boy or girl?' (Intons-Peterson & Reddel, 1984). By age three or four, most children have some knowledge about their gender. They know, for example, that boys become men and girls become women, and that some games are played by boys and others by girls. A permanent gender identity is usually acquired by age five, and children know that a girl is a girl even if she can climb a tree (Zimbardo & Weber, 1994: see pages 399–400).

Biology and sexual identity

Biologically, sex is not a unidimensional variable, and attempts to identify the biological factors influencing gender identity have yielded at least five categories.

Box 45.1   Five categories of biological sex

Chromosomal sex: Normal females inherit two X chromosomes, one from each parent (XX). Normal males inherit one X chromosome from the mother and one Y chromosome from the father (XY). Two chromosomes are needed for the complete development of both internal and external female structures, and the Y chromosome must be present for the complete development of male internal and external structures (Page *et al.*, 1987). If the Y chromosome is absent, female external genitals develop. A gene on the Y chromosome called TDF (*testis-determining factor*) appears to be responsible for testis formation and male development (Hodgkin, 1988).

Gonadal sex: This refers to the sexual or reproductive organs (ovaries in females and testes in males). *H-Y antigen*, controlled by genes on the Y chromosome, causes embryonic gonads to be transformed to testes. If H-Y antigen is not present, gonadal tissue develops into ovaries (Amice *et al.*, 1989).

Hormonal sex: When the gonads are transformed to testes or ovaries, genetic influences cease and biological sex determination is controlled by *sex hormones*. The male sex hormones are called *androgens*, the most important being *testosterone* (secreted by the testes). The ovaries secrete two distinct types of female hormone, *estrogen* and *progesterone* (see Chapter 5, page 47). Both males and females produce androgens and estrogens, but males usually produce more androgens and females more estrogens.

Sex of the internal reproductive structures: The Wolffian ducts in males and the Mullerian ducts in females are the embryonic forerunners of the internal reproductive structures. In males, these are the prostate gland, sperm ducts, seminal vesicles and testes. In females, they are the fallopian tubes, womb and ovaries.

Sex of the external genitals: In males, the external genitalia are the penis and scrotum. In females, they are the outer lips of the vagina (*labia majora*). In the absence of testosterone (which influences both the internal and external structures of chromosomal males), female structures develop (see text).

The categories identified in Box 45.1 are usually highly correlated, such that a person tends to be male (or female) in all respects. The categories also tend to be correlated with non-biological aspects of sex, including the sex the baby is assigned to at birth, how it is brought up, gender identity, gender-role identity and so on. Either pre- or post-natally, however, disorders can occur leading to an inconsistency or low correlation between the categories. These disorders can tell us a great deal about the development of gender identity, gender role and gender-role identity.

People with such disorders are called hermaphrodites. *True hermaphrodites* have either simultaneously or sequentially functioning organs of both sexes. They are very rare and their external organs are often a mixture of male and female structures. *Pseudohermaphrodites* are more common. Although they too possess ambiguous internal and external reproductive structures, they are born with *gonads* that match their chromosomal sex (unlike true hermaphrodites).

Box 45.2   Three major types of pseudohermaphroditism

- In *androgen insensitivity syndrome* (AIS) (or *testicular feminising syndrome*), pre-natal development in a chromosomally normal (XY) male is *feminised*. The internal reproductive structures of either sex fail to develop, and the external genitals fail to differentiate into a penis and scrotum. Normal-looking female external genitals and a shallow vagina are present at birth. At puberty, breast development occurs but the individual fails to menstruate. Because of the presence of a very shallow (or 'blind') vagina, little or no surgery is needed for the adoption of a female appearance.

- In *adrenogenital syndrome* (AGS), a chromosomally normal (XX) female is exposed to an excessive amount of androgens during the critical period of pre-natal sexual differentiation (see Chapter 5, page 47). Whilst the internal reproductive structures are unaffected, the external structures resemble those of a male infant. For example, an enlarged clitoris appears to be a penis (see Figure 45.2). These individuals are usually raised as females (see Box 5.7, page 48).

---

though they were female (Dorner, 1976). However, evidence from human studies tends not to support this claim. For example, Daphne Went, although chromosomally male, has a female external appearance, is married, and leads an active and successful life as a woman (Goldwyn, 1979).

However, there is some evidence of sex differences in *hemispheric specialisation*. For example, when males perform spatial tasks, there is greater electrical activity in the right hemisphere (Bryden & Saxby, 1985). In women, both hemispheres are activated. According to McGlone (1980), the right hemisphere is generally the dominant one in men, whilst the left is generally dominant in women (see Box 45.3).

Despite evidence that the corpus callosum is larger overall in women and longer towards the back of the brain (an example of a 'dimorphic' characteristic), Kimura (1992) has cautioned against accepting this evidence uncritically. It has not been clearly established that the number of fibres is the crucial male-female difference (as has been assumed), and sex differences in cognitive functioning have yet to be related to the size of the corpus callosum (see Chapter 4, page 40).

Gender stereotypes and gender differences

There appears to be a high degree of agreement across 30 countries regarding the characteristics associated with each gender group (Williams & Best, 1994). For example, male-associated terms included 'aggressive', 'determined' and 'sharp-witted' whilst female-associated terms included 'cautious', 'emotional' and 'warm'. However, as far as *actual* differences are concerned, many stereotypes about males and females have little empirical support.

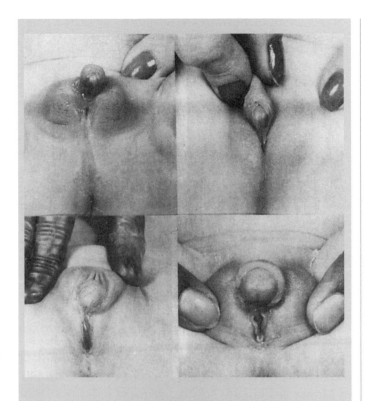

- In *DHT-deficient males*, a genetic disorder prevents the normal pre-natal conversion of testosterone into *dihydrotestosterone* (DHT). This hormone is necessary for the normal development of male external genitals. These males are usually incorrectly identified as females and raised as girls.

Figure 45.2 Ambiguous appearance at birth of the genitalia of individuals with the adrenogenital syndrome (XX, but with excessive androgen during pre-natal differentiation) (From Money & Ehrhardt, 1972)

Supporters of a biological approach argue that males and females are *biologically programmed* for certain kinds of activities compatible with male and female roles. For example, of 18 DHT-deficient males, all but two responded to the dramatic biological changes at puberty (the clitoris-like organ enlarges and becomes a penis and the testes descend) by adopting a male gender-role, despite being raised as females (Imperato-McGinley *et al.*, 1979). Of the two that did not, one acknowledged that he was a male but continued to dress as a female, whilst the other maintained a female gender-identity, married and underwent a sex-change operation. This suggests that their testosterone had pre-programmed masculinity into their brains. Several researchers have argued that male and female brains are structurally different. For example, destruction of small parts of rats' hypothalami resulted in new-born males behaving as

Box 45.3 Some findings relating to gender differences

Aggression: According to Maccoby & Jacklin (1974) and Weisfeld (1994), boys are more verbally and physically aggressive than girls, a difference which appears as soon as social play begins (around two and a half years). Whilst both sexes become less aggressive with age, boys and men remain more aggressive throughout development. However, some studies have shown that women score higher for certain kinds of indirect non-physical aggression (Durkin, 1995), whilst others have found no sex differences at all (e.g. Campbell & Muncer, 1994).

Verbal ability: From pre-school to adolescence, the sexes are very similar with respect to verbal ability. At age 11, however, females become superior and this increases during adolescence and possibly beyond (Maccoby & Jacklin, 1974). Again, though, evidence suggests that any such differences are so small as to be negligible (Hyde & Linn, 1988).

Spatial ability: Males' ability to perceive figures or objects in space and their relationship to each other is consistently better than that of females in adolescence and adulthood (Maccoby & Jacklin, 1974). However, whilst there is male superiority on some spatial tasks, *within-sex* variability is large. Moreover, when between-sex differences are found, they are usually small (Durkin, 1995).

Mathematical ability: Mathematical skills increase faster in boys, beginning around age 12 or 13 (Maccoby & Jacklin, 1974). However, whilst there are significant sex differences, these are in the *reverse* direction to the stereotype (Hyde *et al.*, 1990).

(Adapted from Durkin, 1995)

Durkin (1995) suggests that:

'The overwhelming conclusion to be drawn from the literature on sex differences is that it is highly controversial'.

A statistically significant difference does not imply a large behavioural difference. Rather, what determines a significant result is the *consistency* of the differences between groups, such that if, for example, all the girls in a school scored 0.5 per cent higher than all the boys on the same test, a small but highly significant result would be produced (Edley & Wetherell, 1995).

Eagly (1983), however, has argued that in at least some cases a significant difference does reflect a substantial sex difference. By combining the results of different but comparable studies (*meta-analysis*: see Chapter 77), substantial sex differences emerge on some measures. According to Eagly, research has actually tended to *conceal* rather than *reveal* sex differences. However, the differences *within* each gender are, as noted earlier, at least as great as the differences between them (Maccoby, 1980).

Biosocial theory

According to Edley & Wetherell (1995), to ask 'What is the biological basis of masculinity (or femininity)?' is to pose a false question. In their view:

'It requires us to separate what cannot be separated: men [and women] are the product of a complex system of factors and forces which combine in a variety of ways to produce a whole range of different masculinities [and femininities]'.

Biosocial theory takes social factors into account in relation to biological ones. It sees the *interaction* between biological and social factors as important, rather than biology's direct influence. Adults prefer to spend time with babies who respond to them in 'rewarding' ways, and 'demanding' babies tend to receive more attention than 'passive' babies.

As far as other people are concerned, the baby's sex is just as important as its temperament. For example, the 'baby X' experiments (Smith & Lloyd, 1978) involved dressing babies in unisex snowsuits and giving them names which were sometimes in line with their true gender and sometimes not. When adults played with them, they treated the babies according to the gender they believed them to be. This indicates that a person's (perceived) biological make-up becomes part of his or her social environment through the process of others' reactions to it. According to Money & Ehrhardt (1972), 'anatomy is destiny': how an infant is labelled sexually determines how it is raised or socialised. In turn, this determines the child's gender identity, and from this follow its gender role, gender-role identity and sexual orientation.

Box 45.4   Pseudohermaphrodites and gender identity

Money & Ehrhardt (1972) studied girls with AGS who were raised as boys and, before age three, had their genitals surgically corrected and raised as girls. Money and Ehrhardt claim that it is possible to change the sex of rearing without any undue psychological harm being done, provided this occurs within a 'critical' or 'sensitive period' of about two and a half to three years. However, after this, reassignment to the opposite sex can cause extreme psychological disturbance. Money and Ehrhardt's study of ten people with testicular feminising syndrome showed there was a strong preference for the female role, which also supports the view that sex of rearing is more important than biological sex.

Just because some people appear to be flexible in their psychosexual identities does not in itself disprove that 'built-in biases' still have to be overcome (Diamond, 1978). Money and Ehrhardt's participants are clearly an atypical sample, and there is no evidence that people in general are as flexible in their psychosexual orientation and identity.

Box 45.5   The case of the penectomised twin

Money (1974) has reported a case in which, as a result of an accident during a circumcision, one of a pair of twins lost his penis. This penectomised boy was raised as a girl and, at 17 months, 'he' was castrated, estrogen was given, and a vaginal canal constructed. At age four, the child preferred dresses to trousers, took pride in 'his' long hair, and was cleaner than 'his' brother. At age nine, although 'he' had been the dominant twin since birth, 'he' expressed this by being a 'fussy little mother' to 'his' brother. This finding seems to support the view that gender identity (and gender role) is *learned*.

The reversal of original sexual assignment is possible if it takes place early enough and is consistent in all respects, which includes the external genitalia conforming well enough to the new sex. However, castration and the use of estrogen clearly contributed to the ease of reassignment and probably also account for the unaffected twin being taller. Significantly, when the 'girl' had reached her teens she was an unhappy adolescent, with few friends, uncertain about 'her' gender, and maintaining that boys 'had a better life'. She also looked rather masculine. For Diamond (1982), these findings indicated that biology had ultimately proven irrepressible.

Sociobiological theory

Sociobiologists (evolutionary theorists) argue that gender has gradually evolved over the course of human development as part of our broader adaptation to the environment (Lumsden & Wilson, 1983). Males and females have developed different roles as a function of their respective contributions to reproduction and domestic labour (Wilson, 1978; Hoyenga & Hoyenga, 1979). The relatively greater physical strength, lung capacity and so on of males make them better suited to hunting and defending territory and family. The child-bearing and milk-producing capacities of females, however, make them ideally suited to childcare and other nurturant roles.

According to *parental investment theory* (Kenrick, 1994), females invest considerably more in reproduction than do males. Society came to be organised in sexually exclusive domestic partnerships as a way of meeting the female's needs for protection and the male's need for preventing his mate from mating with other males. The consequence of this was the evolution of different courtship displays and roles (such as 'playing hard to get')

which are still evident in many Western and other cultures. According to Buss (1994), what females universally find attractive in males are the characteristics associated with the provision of resources. Men, by contrast, see physical beauty as being of most importance (see Chapter 56, page 489).

The sociobiological approach has been criticised on several grounds. For example, dominance patterns are not, as sociobiological approaches assume, equated with greater aggression. In humans, at least, dominance often relates to status seeking, which implies the role of culturally determined values (Sayers, 1982). Sociobiological approaches to sex differences are also difficult to test. We have only incomplete knowledge about the ways in which our ancestors adapted to their environments, and so our hunches about which characteristics were adaptive and why differences between the sexes evolved are 'educated guesses' at best (Krebs & Blackman, 1988).

Freud's psychoanalytic theory

Freud's theory is related to his explanation of moral development (see Chapter 44). Up until the resolution of the Oedipus complex, gender identity is assumed to be flexible. Resolution of the Oedipus complex occurs through *identification* with the same-sex parent, and results in the acquisition of both a superego and gender identity. As well as a weaker conscience, Freud also saw the development of gender identity as being weaker in girls than boys.

There are at least three reasons for doubting a Freudian interpretation of gender identity's development. First, children of a particular age do *not* appear to acquire gender identity in 'one fell swoop' (Krebs & Blackman, 1988). Second, children who grow up in 'atypical' families (e.g. single-parent or lesbian couples) are not necessarily adversely affected in terms of their gender identity (Golombok *et al.*, 1983). Indeed, there is evidence of more secure attachments amongst children reared in fatherless families (whether lesbian or heterosexual: Golombok *et al.*, 1997). Also, whilst identification might promote gender identity, children are aware of gender roles well before the age at which Freud believed their complexes are resolved. For example, boys prefer stereotypically masculine toys (such as trucks) and girls stereotypically feminine toys (such as dolls) *in infancy* (O'Brien *et al.*, 1983).

Social learning theory

According to social learning theory (SLT), one reason girls and boys learn to behave differently is that they are *treated differently* by their parents and others. As was seen in the 'baby X' study (see page 396), when informed of a child's biological sex, parents and others often react to it according to their *gender-role expectations*. Thus, girls and boys are often given different toys, have their rooms decorated differently, and are even spoken about in different terms (Rubin *et al.*, 1974). When girls play with soft toys and dolls, parents tend to react positively, whilst they tend to react negatively to boys playing with them (Fagot, 1978). The response from fathers to boys playing with such 'feminine' toys is more aggressive than from mothers (Lansky *et al.*, 1961).

Figure 45.3   Playing with dolls and displaying nurturant behaviour, and playing with guns and displaying assertive, even aggressive, behaviour, conform to female and male gender role expectations/stereotypes respectively. According to social learning theory, children receive parental reinforcement for displaying such gender-appropriate behaviours

SLT also emphasises *observational learning* and *reinforcement's* roles. By observing others behaving in particular ways and then imitating that behaviour, children receive reinforcement from 'significant others' for behaviours considered to be sex-appropriate (Bandura, 1977). Parents tend to positively reinforce boys more for behaviours reflecting independence, self-reliance and emotional control. Girls, however, tend to be reinforced for compliance, dependence, nurturance, empathy and emotional expression (Block, 1979).

Box 45.6   Findings supporting SLT

- Sears *et al.* (1957) found that parents allowed sons to be more aggressive in their relationships with other children, and towards their parents, than daughters. For some mothers, 'being a boy' meant being aggressive, and boys were often encouraged to fight back. Although parents believe they respond in the same way to aggressive acts committed by boys and girls, they actually intervene much more frequently and quickly when girls behave aggressively (Huston, 1983).

- Boys were more likely to imitate aggressive male models than were girls (Bandura *et al.*, 1961, 1963: see Box 44.2, page 384) Children are also more likely to imitate a same-sex model than an opposite-sex model, even if the behaviour is 'sex-inappropriate'.

- Although parents are important models, SL theorists are also interested in media portrayals of males and females. A large body of evidence suggests that *gender-role stereotypes* are portrayed by the media, as well as by parents and teachers (Wober *et al.*, 1987). Moreover, children categorised as 'heavy' viewers of television hold stronger stereotyped beliefs than 'lighter' viewers (Gunter, 1986: see also Chapter 64).

SL theorists see the reinforcement of sex-typed behaviours as continuing throughout life rather than being confined to childhood. For example, parents of adolescents endorsed different statements concerning the ways their sons and daughters are treated. 'I encourage my child always to do his/her best' tended to be endorsed for boys, whereas 'I encourage my child to keep control of his/her feelings at all times' tended to be endorsed for girls (Block, 1978).

Although social reinforcement plays a role in young children's sex typing, the evidence concerning modelling is less impressive. Thus, whilst modelling plays an important role in children's socialisation, there is no consistent preference for the same-sex parent's behaviour (Hetherington, 1967). Instead, children prefer to model the behaviour of those with whom they have most contact (usually the mother). Also, there is no significant correlation between the extent to which parents engage in sex-typed behaviours and the strength of sex-typing in their children (Smith & Daglish, 1977).

Box 45.7   Findings not supporting SLT

- According to Maccoby & Jacklin (1974), there are no consistent differences in the extent to which boys and girls are reinforced for aggressiveness or autonomy. Rather, there appears to be remarkable uniformity in the sexes' socialisation. This is supported by Lytton & Romney (1991), who found very few sex differences in terms of parental warmth, overall amount of interaction, encouragement of achievement or dependency, restrictiveness and discipline, or clarity of communication.

- Although Bandura *et al.*'s research is often cited, the evidence concerning imitation and modelling is actually inconclusive, and at least some studies have failed to find that children are more likely to imitate same-sex models than opposite-sex models. Indeed, children have been shown to prefer imitating behaviour that is 'appropriate' to their own sex *regardless* of the model's (Maccoby & Jacklin, 1974).

- The view that television can impact upon a passively receptive child audience with messages about sex-role stereotyping, and mould young children's conceptions of gender is oversimplistic (see Chapter 64). For Gunter & McAleer (1990), children respond selectively to particular characters and events, and their perceptions, memories and understanding of what they have seen may often be mediated by the dispositions they bring with them to the viewing situation. Whilst 'heavy' viewers of television might hold stronger stereotyped beliefs than other children, no precise measures were taken of the programmes they actually watched.

Cognitive–developmental and gender-schematic processing theories

COGNITIVE–DEVELOPMENTAL THEORY

The cognitive–developmental approach (Kohlberg, 1969; Kohlberg & Ullian, 1974) emphasises the child's participation in developing both an understanding of gender and gender-appropriate behaviour. Children's discovery that they are male or female *causes* them to identify with members of their own sex (not the other way round, as psychoanalytic and SL theories suggest). Whilst rewards and punishments influence children's choices of toys and activities, these do not mechanically strengthen stimulus–response connections, but provide children with *information* about when they are behaving in ways that other people deem appropriate (see Chapter 32, page 281).

According to cognitive–developmental theorists, young children acquire an understanding of the concepts *male* and *female* in three stages.

Box 45.8   Stages in the development of gender identity

Stage 1 (Gender labelling or basic gender identity): This occurs somewhere around age three (Ruble, 1984) and refers to the child's recognition that it is male or female. According to Kohlberg, knowing one's gender is an achievement that allows us to understand and categorise the world. However, this knowledge is fragile, and children do not yet realise that boys invariably become men and girls always become women.

Stage 2 (Gender stability): By age four or five, most children recognise that people retain their gender for a lifetime. However, there are still limitations, in that children rely on superficial signs (such as the length of a person's hair) to determine their gender (Marcus & Overton, 1978).

Stage 3 (Gender constancy or consistency): At around age six or seven, children realise that gender is *immutable*. So, even if a woman has her hair cut very short, her gender remains constant. Gender constancy represents a kind of *conservation* (see Chapter 41) and, significantly, appears shortly after the child has mastered the conservation of quantity (Marcus & Overton, 1978).

Once children acquire gender constancy, they come to value the behaviours and attitudes associated with their sex. Only at this point do they identify with the adult figures who possess the qualities they see as being most central to their concepts of themselves as male or female (Perry & Bussey, 1979).

Evidence suggests that the concepts of gender identity, stability and constancy do occur in that order across many cultures (Munroe *et al.*, 1984). Slaby & Frey (1975) divided two- to five-year-olds into 'high' and 'low' gender constancy. The children were then shown a silent film of adults simultaneously performing a series of simple activities. The screen was 'split', with males performing activities on one side and females performing activities on the other. Children rated as 'high' in gender constancy showed a marked same-sex bias, as measured by the amount of visual attention they gave to each side of the screen. This supports Kohlberg's belief that gender constancy is a *cause* of the imitation of same-sex models rather than an effect. Children actively construct their gender-role knowledge through purposeful monitoring of the social environment.

A major problem for cognitive–developmental theory is that it predicts there should be little or no gender-appropriate behaviour *before* gender constancy is achieved. However, even in infancy, both sexes show a marked preference for stereotypical male and female toys (Huston, 1983: see page 397). Whilst such children might have developed a sense of gender identity, they are, as far as cognitive–developmental theory is concerned, some years away from achieving gender stability and constancy (Fagot, 1985).

GENDER-SCHEMATIC PROCESSING THEORY

This addresses the possibility that gender identity *alone* can provide children with sufficient motivation to assume sex-typed behaviour patterns (e.g. Bem, 1985; Martin, 1991). Like SLT, this approach suggests that children learn 'appropriate' patterns of behaviour by observation. However, consistent with cognitive–developmental theory, children's active cognitive processing of information also contributes to their sex-typing.

Children learn that strength is linked to the male sex-role stereotype and weakness to the female stereotype, and that some dimensions (including strength–weakness) are more relevant to one gender (males) than the other (Rathus, 1990). So, a boy learns that the strength he displays in wrestling (say) affects others' perceptions of him. Unless competing in some sporting activity, most girls do not see this dimension as being important. However, whilst boys are expected to compete in sports, girls are not, and so a girl is likely to find that her gentleness and neatness are more important in the eyes of others than her strength (Rathus, 1990).

According to gender-schematic processing theory, then, children learn to judge themselves according to the traits considered to be relevant to their genders. Consequently, the self-concept (see Chapter 46) becomes mixed with the gender schemas of a particular culture which provides standards for comparison. The theory sees gender identity as being sufficient to produce 'sex-appropriate' behaviour. The labels 'boy' and 'girl', once understood, give children the basis for mixing their self-concepts with their society's gender schemas. Children with gender identity will actively seek information about gender schemas, and their self-esteem will soon become influenced by how they 'measure up' to their gender schema (Rathus, 1990).

Conclusions

This chapter has considered various theories of gender development and psychological sex differences. Whilst every known culture distinguishes between male and female (reflected in stereotypes regarding typical male/female characteristics and behaviour), the evidence for the truth of such stereotypes is not conclusive. No single theory adequately explains the complex process by which a person acquires his or her gender role, yet all those discussed in this chapter have contributed to our understanding of that process.

Summary

■ Every known society distinguishes between male and female. The study of psychological sex differences attempts to test the accuracy of sex **stereotypes**.

■ Feminist psychologists distinguish between **sex** or **sexual identity** (some aspect of our biological make-up as 'male' or 'female'), and **gender**. **Gender identity** is how we classify ourselves and others as male or female.

■ There is little empirical support for **actual** gender differences in terms of either **aggression**, **verbal**, **spatial** or **mathematical ability**.

■ A statistically significant difference does not imply a large behavioural difference, although **meta-analysis** sometimes produces large differences on some measures. However, **within**-gender differences are at least as great as **between**-gender differences.

■ **Biologically**, sex refers to five main categories: **chromosomal sex**, **gonadal sex**, **hormonal sex**, **sex of the internal reproductive structures** and **sex of the external genitalia**. These are usually highly correlated with each other, as well as with non-biological factors such as sexual assignment at birth, sex of rearing and gender identity. In **hermaphroditism** and **pseudohermaphroditism**, pre- and post-natal disorders produce an inconsistency between these categories.

■ Major types of pseudohermaphroditism are **androgen insensitivity syndrome** (AIS)/**testicular feminising** syndrome, **adrenogenital syndrome (AGS)** and **dihydrotestosterone (DHT)-deficient males**.

■ According to the biological approach, males and females are biologically programmed for certain activities compatible with gender roles. The 18 DHT-deficient males studied by Imperato-McGinley *et al.* appear to have masculinity pre-programmed into their brains by testosterone.

■ Claims that male and female brains are structurally different are largely based on studies of rats, and are unsupported by human evidence. Whilst studies of **hemispheric specialisation** are consistent with some of the claimed male–female differences in cognitive abilities, evidence that the corpus callosum is sexually dimorphic is far from conclusive.

■ **Biosocial theory** stresses the **interaction** of social and biological factors. A person's (perceived) biological make-up (such as sex) becomes part of his or her social environment through others' reactions to it.

■ Money and Ehrhardt claim that there is a 'critical' or 'sensitive' period for the development of gender identity. However, their participants were clearly atypical. Nevertheless, the case of the penectomised twin boy raised as a girl is consistent with the claim that gender identity and gender role are **learned**.

■ According to **sociobiologists**, gender has evolved as part of human beings' broader adaptation to the environment. **Parental investment theory** claims that sexually exclusive domestic partnerships meet the female's need for protection and the male's need for preventing his mate from mating with other males.

■ **Psychoanalytic theory** sees gender identity as being related to moral development. Gender identity is acquired through **identification** with the same-sex parent which ends the Oedipus complex. Girls do not resolve their Oedipus complex as effectively as boys, resulting in a weaker conscience and gender identity.

■ However, gender identity develops much more gradually than Freud claimed. Also, studies of children who grow up in 'atypical' families show that their gender identity is not adversely affected.

■ According to **social learning theory** (SLT), girls and boys learn to behave differently through being **treated differently** by parents and others. SLT also stresses the role of **observational learning** and **reinforcement** for imitating sex-appropriate behaviours.

■ Whilst there is some evidence that boys and girls are treated differently by their parents, some researchers claim that socialisation of the sexes is highly uniform.

■ Evidence is inconclusive regarding the importance for imitation of the sex-appropriateness of a model's behaviour and the model's sex. There is no consistent preference for the same-sex parent's behaviour, but rather for the parent the child spends most time with.

■ According to the **cognitive–developmental approach**, children's discovery that they are male or female **causes** them to identify with and imitate same-sex models. Rewards and punishments provide children with **information** about when they are behaving in appropriate ways.

■ Three stages in the development of gender identity are **gender labelling (basic gender identity)**, **gender stability** and **gender constancy** (or **consistency**). Cross-cultural evidence supports this sequence. The claim that children actively construct their gender role knowledge through monitoring their social environment has received experimental support.

■ **Gender-schematic processing theory** maintains that gender identity alone can provide a child with sufficient motivation to assume sex-typed behaviour. Children learn to judge themselves according to the traits seen as relevant to their genders, resulting in a self-concept that is mixed with the gender schemas of a particular culture.

46

THE DEVELOPMENT OF THE SELF

Introduction and overview

When you look in a mirror, you are both the person being looked at and the person doing the looking. When you think of the kind of person you are, you are both the person being thought about and the person doing the thinking. You use the personal pronoun 'me' to refer to yourself as the *object* (what is being looked at or thought about) and 'I' to refer to yourself as the *subject* (the person doing the looking or thinking).

Although non-humans have consciousness (sensations of hunger, thirst, pain and so on), only humans have *self-consciousness* (our same self can be both the subject and the object). This chapter looks at the development of the self-concept (our perception of our own personality). After examining the various components of the self-concept, the chapter considers some of the theoretical approaches to the development of the self and the evidence on which they are based.

Components of the self-concept

According to Murphy (1947), the self is 'the individual as known to the individual'. The self-concept has three components: *self-image*, *self-esteem* (or *self-regard*) and the *ideal-self*.

SELF-IMAGE

This is how we describe ourselves (the sort of person we think we are). One way of assessing self-image is to ask people to answer the question 'Who am I?' 20 times. This typically produces two main categories of answer relating to *social roles* and *personality traits* (Kuhn & McPartland, 1954).

Social roles are objective aspects of our self-image (such as being a son, daughter, student and so on) which can be verified by others. Personality traits are more a matter of opinion and judgement, and what we think we are like may be different from how others see us. However, how others behave towards us has an important influence on our self-perception (see page 403).

> **Box 46.1   The development of social roles**
>
> Social roles are important in the development of the self-concept (Argyle, 1983). Kuhn (1960) asked seven-year-olds and undergraduates to give 20 different answers to the question 'Who am I?' (cf. Kuhn & McPartland, 1954). On average, the children gave five answers relating to social roles, whereas the under-graduates gave ten. As we get older, we incorporate more and more roles into our self-image. This is not unexpected since, as we get older, we assume an increasing number and variety of roles. The number and range of a pre-schooler's roles are limited compared with the older child or adult. As we grow up, our duties, responsibilities and choices involve us in all kinds of roles and relationships with others.

Self-image also includes *body image* (*bodily self* or *bodily me*). This refers to our physical characteristics, such as being tall, short, brown-haired and so on. Our 'bodily me' also includes bodily sensations (usually temporary states), such as pain, cold and hunger.

As part of the normal process of maturation, we all experience 'growth spurts', changes in height, weight and the general appearance and 'feel' of our bodies. Each time this happens, we have to make an adjustment to the body image. One fundamental aspect of body image relates to biological sex. *Gender* is the social interpretation of sex (see Chapter 44). Other fundamental aspects of body image are the bodily changes involved in *puberty* which marks the onset of *adolescence* (see Chapter 47).

SELF-ESTEEM

Whilst self-image is essentially *descriptive*, self-esteem (self-regard) is essentially *evaluative*. Coopersmith (1967) has defined self-esteem as:

> 'a personal judgement of worthiness that is expressed in the attitudes the individual holds towards himself'.

It is, therefore, the extent to which we like or approve of ourselves, and how worthwhile we think we are. This can take the form of an overall judgement or relate to specific aspects of our lives. For example, we might have a generally high opinion of ourselves, yet not like certain attributes (such as if we lacked assertiveness but wanted to be assertive). Alternatively, it might be very difficult to have high overall self-esteem if we are very badly disfigured or desperately shy. Clearly, certain abilities (such as being good at sport) and characteristics (such as being attractive) have a greater value in society generally, and these are likely to influence self-esteem accordingly. The value attached to abilities and characteristics will also depend on culture, gender, age, and social background.

Box 46.2   The reaction of others and self-esteem

Guthrie (1938) tells of a dull and unattractive female student whose classmates decided to play a trick on her by pretending she was the most desirable girl in the college. Her classmates drew lots to decide who would take her out first, second and so on. By the fifth or sixth date, she was no longer regarded as dull and unattractive. By being treated as attractive she had, in a sense, *become* attractive (perhaps by wearing different clothes or smiling more), and her self-image had clearly changed. For the boys who dated her later, it was no longer a chore! Within a year, she had developed an easy manner and a confident assumption that she was popular (Guthrie, 1938).

The *reaction of others* (another factor identified by Argyle as influencing the development of the self) is stressed by James and Cooley (see page 406).

Comparison with others

Certain parts of self-image and self-esteem are affected by how we compare with others. Indeed, there are certain parts of self-image which only become significant *through* comparison with others. For example, 'tall' and 'fat' are not *absolute* characteristics (like, say, blue-eyed), and we are only tall or fat *in comparison* with people who are taller or shorter or fatter or thinner than ourselves. This is true of many other characteristics, including intelligence. Parents and other adults often react to children by comparing them with their siblings or other children.

If a child is told repeatedly that it is 'less clever' than its big sister, it will come to incorporate this as part of its self-image, probably producing lower self-esteem. This could adversely affect academic performance so that the child does not achieve in line with its true abilities. A child of above average intelligence who has grown up in the shadow of a brilliant brother or sister may be less successful academically than an average or even below-average child who has not had to face these unfavourable comparisons. Adolescents with the highest self-esteem tend to be of higher social class, have done better at school and been leaders in their clubs, all of which represent the basis for a favourable comparison between the self and others (Rosenberg, 1965).

IDEAL-SELF

Self-esteem is also partly determined by how much our self-image differs from our ideal-self, the self-concept's third component. Ideal-self (*ego-ideal* or *idealised self-image*) is the kind of person you would *like* to be. This can vary in both extent and degree. So, you might want to be different in certain respects or you may want to be a totally different person (perhaps even wish you were someone else). In general, the greater the gap between self-image and ideal-self, the lower self-esteem (see Rogers', 1951, theory of self: Chapters 1, 66 and 76).

SELF-SCHEMATA

We not only represent and store information about other people, but also about ourselves, although in a more complex and varied way. This information constitutes the self-concept. We tend to have very clear self-schemata on some dimensions (including those that are important to us), but not on others. For example, if you think of yourself as being athletic and being athletic is important to you, then you would be *self-schematic* on that dimension. Being athletic, then, would be part of your self-concept (Hogg & Vaughn, 1995).

Most people have a complex self-concept with many self-schemata. These include an array of 'possible selves', or future-oriented schemata of what we would like to be (our ideal-self). Visions of future possible selves may influence some of the decisions we make, such as career choice. The idea of multiple selves raises the question of whether any one self is actually more real or authentic than any other. Personality theorists typically assume that a person has a single, unitary self (and so the instructions on a personality questionnaire do not specify which self should be described: Hampson, 1995). Social psychologists, however, recognise the possibility that the self refers to a complex set of perceptions, composed of a number of schemata relating both to what we *are* like and what we *could* be like.

How does the self-concept develop?

Achieving identity, in the sense of acquiring a *self-schema* (set of beliefs about the self) is one of the central developmental tasks of a social being (Lewis & Brooks-Gunn, 1979). Identity development progresses through several levels of complexity and continues throughout the life-span. Many psychologists (including Piaget, see Chapter 41) believe that new-born babies have no self-concept and cannot distinguish between 'me' and 'not me'. For Piaget (1952):

'When a baby discovers his own body – his fingers, feet, arms – he looks at them no differently than he regards other objects, without any idea that he himself is the one responsible for moving the particular objects that he is admiring ... To begin with, a baby has no sense of self at all'.

During its first few months, the baby gradually distinguishes itself from its environment and from other people, related to which is a sense of continuity through time (the *existential* self). The baby's discovery that it can control things other than its hands and feet (for example, its mother) contributes to this development, as does its discovery that some things (such as its limbs) are always there whereas other things (such as its mother) are not. However, the infant's self-knowledge is comparable to that of other species (such as monkeys). What makes our self-knowledge distinctive is becoming aware that we have it: we are conscious of our existence and uniqueness (Gross, 1996).

Box 46.3 Learning to distinguish ourselves from others

According to Maccoby (1980), there are at least two counts on which babies are able to distinguish between themselves and others. First, their own fingers hurt when they are bitten, but these sensations do not occur when they bite their rattles or mothers. Second, and probably quite early in life, they begin to associate the feelings of their own body movements with the sight of their own limbs and the sounds of their own cries. These sense-impressions are bound together into a cluster that defines the bodily self, and so this is likely to be the first aspect of the self-concept to develop.

Other aspects of the self-concept develop by degrees, (rather than clearly defined *stages*). Whilst young children may know their own names and understand the limits of their own bodies, they may not yet be able to think about themselves as coherent entities. *Self-awareness* or *self-consciousness*, then, develops very gradually. For Piaget, self-awareness comes through the gradual process of adaptation to the environment (see Chapter 41). As the child explores objects and *accommodates* to them (resulting in new sensorimotor schemas), it simultaneously discovers aspects of itself. Trying to put a large block into the mouth and finding it will not fit, for example, is a lesson in selfhood as well as a lesson about certain objects.

SELF-RECOGNITION

One way of studying the bodily self's development is through *self-recognition*. This involves more than just a simple discrimination of bodily features. For example, to determine that the person in a photograph, video-recording or mirror reflection is yourself, you need to have a basic knowledge of yourself as continuous through time (in the case of photographs or video recordings) and space (in the case of mirrors). You must also know what you look like (your particular features). Other kinds of recognition, such as of our voices or feelings, are also possible, but only visual recognition has been studied extensively in both humans and non-humans.

At around six months, a baby makes deliberate repetitive movements in front of a mirror, apparently to explore the mirror's possibilities. It also looks behind the mirror (Krebs & Blackman, 1988). Many non-humans (such as fish, birds and monkeys) react to their mirror images as though they were *other animals*, and they do not seem to recognise their own reflection at all. In the higher primates (chimpanzees and other great apes), however, self-recognition has been found.

Box 46.4 Self-recognition in chimpanzees

When Gallup (1977) placed a full-length mirror on the cage wall of several pre-adolescent, wild-born chimps, they acted as if their reflections were other chimps. Although they initially threatened, vocalised or made conciliatory gestures, these behaviours almost disappeared after three days. Then, the chimps used the reflections to explore themselves. For example, they would pick up pieces of food and place it on their faces, which could not be seen without the mirror.

After ten days with the mirror, the chimps were anaesthetised. Using odourless and non-irritating dye, a bright red spot was painted on the uppermost part of one eyebrow ridge and a second spot on the top of the opposite ear. After recovering from the anaesthetic, the chimps were returned to their cages. The mirror had been removed and Gallup observed how often they touched the painted parts of their bodies. When the mirror was put back in the cage, they explored the red spots 25 times more often than had been done without the mirror's presence.

The procedure was repeated with chimps who had *never* seen themselves in a mirror. They reacted to their mirror images as if they were other chimps, and did not touch the red spots. This suggests that the first group had learned to recognise themselves. Lower primates (monkeys, gibbons and baboons), however, are unable to recognise their mirror image whether they are raised in isolation or normally.

A version of Gallup's technique has been used with six- to 24-month-old humans. Whilst pretending to wipe the baby's face, its mother carefully applies a dot of rouge to its nose. After observing how many times the baby touches its nose, it is then placed in front of a mirror. Touching did not occur before 15 months (Lewis & Brooks-Gunn, 1979). However, between 15 and 18 months, five to 25 per cent of infants touched their noses, rising to 75 per cent between 18 and 20 months. To use the mirror image to touch the dot, a baby must have built up a schema of how its face should look in the mirror before it can notice the discrepancy caused by the dot. Since this does not appear to develop before about 18 months (when *object permanence* is completed: see Chapter 41, page 356), object permanence is probably *necessary* for the development of self-recognition.

Figure 46.1   Self-recognition appears quite early in the development of self-awareness/self-consciousness. Humans share this ability with chimpanzees and other great apes

SELF-DEFINITION

Language plays an important role in consolidating the early development of self-awareness by providing labels permitting distinctions to be made between self and non-self (such as 'I', 'you', 'me' and 'it'). These can then be used by infants to communicate notions of selfhood to others. An important label is a *name*. Parents choose names they like and sometimes name a child after a relative or famous person. Names are not neutral labels in terms of people's responses to them and what they associate with them. Names can be used as one basis for *social stereotyping* (see Chapter 52, pages 454–457).

Box 46.5   Names and the self-fulfilling prophecy

The Ashanti people of West Africa name children according to the day of the week on which they are born because they believe they have different personalities (Jahoda, 1958). Police records indicated that a very high proportion of juvenile delinquents were born on a Wednesday (the day of the 'naturally aggressive' personality), whilst a very low proportion were born on a Monday (the day of the 'quiet and calm' personality). If Ashanti boys are treated in a way consistent with their names, they may consequently 'become' what their names indicate they are 'really' like (a *self-fulfilling prophecy*). In English-speaking countries, certain days of the week (such as Tuesday) and months (such as April) are used as names, and they have associations which may influence others' reactions (as in the rhyme 'Monday's child is fair of face, Tuesday's child is full of grace ...').

When children refer to themselves as 'I' or 'me' and others as 'you', they are reversing the labels that are normally used to refer to them by others. Also, of course, they hear others refer to themselves as 'I' and not as 'you', 'he' or 'she'. This is a problem of *shifting reference*. Despite this, most children do not invert 'I' and 'you', but two interesting exceptions are *autistic* and *blind* children, who often use 'I' for others and 'you' for the self (see Chapter 80).

THE PSYCHOLOGICAL SELF

What exactly do children mean when they refer to themselves as 'I' or 'me'? Are they referring to anything more than a physical entity enclosed by an envelope of skin? Young children are aware that whilst people and dolls are alike in some ways (such as having hands and legs), they are different in others (dolls cannot think). When asked to identify the part of themselves that knows their name and thinks about things, some children gave a fairly clear localisation for the thinking self (namely 'in the head'). When looked directly in the eye and asked 'Can I see you thinking in there?', most children thought not (Flavell *et al.*, 1978).

These findings suggest that by age three-and-a-half to four, children have a basic concept of a private thinking self that is not visible, even to someone looking directly into their eyes, and which can be distinguished from the bodily self, which they know is visible to others. This constitutes the beginnings of a *theory of mind* an awareness that they and other people have mental processes (Shatz, 1994: see Chapter 80).

THE CATEGORICAL SELF

Parts of the central core of self-image are *age* and *gender*, which are also used to perceive and interpret others' behaviour. Age is the first social category to be acquired and occurs even before a concept of number develops. For example, six- to 12-month-old infants can distinguish between photographs, slides and papier-mâché heads of adults and babies. By 12 months, they prefer interacting with strange babies to strange adults and, as soon as they have acquired labels like 'mummy' and 'daddy', they almost never make age-related mistakes (Lewis & Brooks-Gunn, 1979).

Before age seven, children tend to define the self in physical terms, such as height and favourite activities. Their inner psychological experiences and characteristics are not described as being distinct from overt behaviour and external, physical characteristics. Although there are important cultural differences in how the self-concept develops, between middle childhood and adolescence self-descriptions do include many more references to internal, psychological characteristics such as competencies, knowledge, emotions, values and personal traits (Damon & Hart, 1988).

Theories of the self

JAMES' AND COOLEY'S THEORIES

James (1890) was the first to make the distinction between the *self-as-subject or knower* ('I') and the *self-as-known or object* ('me'). The 'I' represents the principal form of the self and lies at the centre of our state (or 'stream') of consciousness. However, the self is *multifaceted*: we have as many selves as we have social relationships. This is consistent with the widely shared view that we modify our behaviour to some extent depending on whom we are with: different others bring out different aspects of our personality (Hampson, 1995).

James's view of the self as multifaceted is also consistent with *self-presentation* (the creation and maintenance of a public self: Goffman, 1959). Using the theatre as an analogy, Goffman argues that each participant in a social interaction is engaged in a 'performance' designed as much for its effect on the 'audience' as for honest and open self-expression. Indeed, according to this *dramaturgical approach*, personality is equated with the various roles a person plays in life. However, James's idea of multiple selves goes much further than this by suggesting that different personalities are constructed in the context of every relationship a person has (Hampson, 1995).

Box 46.6   The looking-glass self (Cooley, 1902)

This holds that the self is reflected in the reactions of other people, who are the 'looking-glass' for oneself. For Cooley (1902), to understand what we are like, we need to see how others see us, and this is how children gradually build up an impression of what they are like. What is reflected back to us are judgements and evaluations of our behaviour and appearance which produce some form of self-feeling (such as pride or shame). Consistent with James's idea of multiple selves, Cooley claims that the looking-glass is not a 'mere technical reflection' because it will differ depending on whose view we take. The individual and society are opposite sides of the same coin (Denzin, 1995).

MEAD AND SYMBOLIC INTERACTIONISM

Influenced by James and Cooley, Mead (1934) argued that people act towards things in terms of their *meanings*. As well as existing in a physical environment, we exist in a symbolic environment, such that the importance of social interaction is derived from the meaning it holds for the participants. The 'interaction' refers specifically to the fact that people communicate with each other, and this provides opportunities for meanings to be learned. Because we share a common language and have the ability for symbolic thought, we can, at least in principle, look at the world from other perceivers' points of view and take their roles. For Mead, this is essentially the process by which the self develops.

Children initially think about their conduct as good or bad only as they react to their own acts in the remembered words of their parents. At this stage, 'me' is a combination of the child's memory of its own actions and the kind of reaction they received. Later, in 'pretend play', children *role-take* and play 'mummies and daddies', 'doctors and nurses' and so on. This helps them to understand and incorporate adult attitudes and behaviour. The child is not merely imitating, but also 'calls out in himself the same response as he calls out in the other' (Mead, 1934), that is, the child is being both him or herself *and* the parent. As the 'parent', the child is responding to him- or herself as the child. So, when playing with a doll, the child 'responds in tone of voice and attitude as [its] parents respond to [its] cries and chortles' (Mead, 1934). For Mead, play can be distinguished from games, which involve rules:

'The child must not only take the role of the other, as [it] does in play, but must assume the various roles of all the participants in the game accordingly'.

Through role-taking, children acquire various social viewpoints or 'perspectives' (mother, father, nurse, doctor and so on) which are then used to accompany, direct and evaluate their own behaviour. This is how the socialised part of the self (Mead's 'me') expands and develops. At first, these viewpoints are based upon those of specific adults. Over time, the child comes to react to itself and its behaviour from the viewpoint of a 'typical mother', a 'typical nurse' or 'people in general' (the 'perspectives of the generalised other'). The incorporation of the *generalised other* marks the final qualitative change in the 'me' and provides the child with a self. Our 'me' is an image of the self seen from the perspective of a judgemental, non-participant observer. By its very nature, 'me' is social because it grows out of this role-playing whereby the child is being the other person.

Mead's theory turns those of James and Cooley on their heads. Mead does not see the self as mentalistic or something privately going on inside a person. Rather, like mind, the self is a cognitive process lodged in the ongoing social world. However, Mead did accept Cooley's view that the self and society are two terms in a reciprocal process of interaction (Denzin, 1995). Our knowledge of self and others develops simultaneously, both being dependent on social interaction. The self and society represent a common whole, with neither able to exist without the other.

Mead sees people as organisms with selves and this converts us into special kinds of actors, transforms our relations to the world, and gives our actions unique characters. People are objects to themselves: we can perceive ourselves, have conceptions about ourselves, communicate with ourselves and so on. We are capable of interacting with ourselves, and this *self-interaction* is a great influence on our transactions with the world in general, and other people in particular. Self-interaction is a *reflexive* process, and is Mead's way of making the 'I'/'me' distinction. The experiencing 'I' cannot be an object and cannot itself be experienced, because it is the very act of experiencing. What we experience and interact with is our 'me'.

Language and the self

Mead has influenced many sociologists and psychologists who see language as fundamental to the construction and maintenance of the self. What we say about ourselves often depends on who is listening, and in selecting what to say and not to say, we are actively constructing a self in relation to the other person and constantly 'making a self'. The self is not a static, internal entity, but a process that is constantly changing (Petkova, 1995).

Our understanding and experience of ourselves as human beings (our subjective experience of selfhood) are laid down by the beliefs about a person implicit in our language (Harré, 1985, 1989). The structure of our language implies certain assumptions and beliefs about human nature, which we live out in our daily social interactions. For example, the words 'I' and 'me' mislead us into believing that each of us is represented by a coherent, unified self which operates mechanisms and processes responsible for our actions. However, 'self', 'ego', 'mind' and so on do not refer to anything that exists *objectively* in the world. Rather, they are *hypothetical constructs* which perform the important function of helping us organise and structure our world (Burr, 1995).

Similarly, the very experience of being a person, the kind of mental life one can have and perhaps even how we experience sensory information, are dependent on the particular ways of accounting for and talking about ourselves available to us in our culture (Potter & Wetherell, 1987). These 'stories' or accounts, whose meaning is shared by members of a culture, are called *discourses*. Since these differ from culture to culture, it follows that members of different cultures will experience being 'selves' in different ways.

In Maori culture, a person is invested with a particular kind of power (*mana*), given by the gods in accordance with family status and birth circumstances. This enables a person to be effective, whether in battle or everyday dealings with others. However, this power is not a stable resource but can be increased or decreased by the person's day-to-day conduct. A person who forgot a ritual observance or committed some misdemeanour would have his or her power decreased. A person's social standing, successes and failures, and so on are seen as dependent on external sources rather than internal states (such as personality or motivation). Indeed, *mana* is only one of the external forces which inhabit a person.

Instead of representing themselves as the centre and origin of their actions (crucial to the Western concept of the self), the individual Maori does not own experiences such as fear, anger, love and grief. Rather:

'they are visitations governed by the unseen world of powers and forces' (Potter & Wetherell, 1987).

According to Moscovici (1985), 'the individual' is the greatest invention of modern times. Only recently has the idea of the autonomous, self-regulating and free-standing individual become dominant. We need to distinguish between the *independent* and the *interdependent* self (Smith & Bond, 1993). The former is what is stressed in Western, individualist cultures and the latter by non-Western, collectivist cultures (see Chapter 84).

Conclusions

The self-concept comprises self-image, self-esteem and ideal-self. The bodily self develops in early infancy, gradually followed by self-recognition, self-definition, the psychological self and the categorical self. Most major self-theories stress the influence of interaction with others, and Mead and Cooley see self and society as two sides of the same coin. The nature of the self is also shaped by culture, with language playing a crucial role.

Summary

■ The self-concept consists of the **self-image**, **self-esteem (self-regard)** and **ideal-self (ego-ideal** or **idealised self-image)**.

■ Self-image comprises **social roles, personality traits**, and **body image (bodily self** or **bodily me)**. Biological sex is a fundamental aspect of body image. **Gender** is the social interpretation of sex.

■ Self-esteem is essentially **evaluative**, and refers to how much we like and approve of ourselves and how worthwhile we think we are. Certain abilities and characteristics have a greater social value generally and a correspondingly greater influence on our self-esteem.

■ Self-esteem is influenced by the **reaction of others** and **comparison with others**. It is also partly determined by how much our self-image differs from our ideal-self. The greater the discrepancy, the lower our self-esteem.

■ We represent and store information about ourselves as **self-schemata**, which constitute our self-concept. Whilst personality theorists assume a single, unitary self, social psychologists recognise that the self refers to a complex set of schemata relating to both what we **are** like and what we **could** be like.

■ Achieving identity and a **self-schema** is one of the central developmental tasks of a social being. Many psychologists see the new-born baby as unable to distinguish between 'me'/'not me'. Related to this is development of the **existential self**. The bodily self is the

first aspect of the self-concept to develop. **Self-awareness** and **self-consciousness** develop very gradually.

■ The bodily self has been studied through visual **self-recognition**, which requires a basic knowledge of ourself as continuous through time and space. Chimps and other great apes, although not lower primates, have self-recognition.

■ Most 18–20-month-old babies use their mirror reflection to touch a dot of rouge on the nose. The baby must have already built up a schema of how its face should look in the mirror before it is able to notice the discrepancy caused by the dot. This seems to require **object permanence** to have developed.

■ Language provides labels which permit distinctions to be made between self and non-self, which can then be used by infants for **self-definition**. **Names** are important labels, which can form the basis of **social stereotyping**.

■ By three-and-a-half or four, children have a basic concept of a private thinking self or **psychological self**, distinct from the bodily self which they know others can see. This constitutes the beginning of a **theory of mind**. **Age** and **gender** form part of the central core of the self-concept (**categorical self**).

■ James first distinguished between **self-as-subject/ knower** ('I') and **self-as-known/object** ('me'). The self is **multifaceted**, with as many selves as we have social relationships. This is consistent with Goffman's account of **self-presentation**. According to the **dramaturgical approach**, personality comprises the various roles a person plays.

■ According to Cooley's **looking-glass self** theory, the self is reflected in others' reactions. Children gradually build up an impression of what they are like by seeing how others react to them. The looking-glass differs depending on whose view we take. The individual and society are two sides of the same coin.

■ According to Mead's **symbolic interactionism**, we exist in a symbolic as well as physical environment. Communication involved in social interactions provides opportunities for the learning of meanings. The self develops through sharing a common language, being able to see the world from others' points of view, and role-taking.

■ Through pretend play, children acquire a variety of social viewpoints which are then used to accompany, direct and evaluate its own behaviour, expanding the 'me'. At first, these are based on specific adults but are gradually replaced by 'the perspectives of the generalised other'. This marks the final qualitative change in the 'me'.

■ For Mead, the self is a cognitive process located in the ongoing social world. Our knowledge of self and society develops simultaneously, and both depend on social interaction.

■ Our understanding of ourselves as human beings with subjective experiences of selfhood is based in the beliefs about a person implicit in our language. The very experience of being a person depends on **discourses**, whose meaning is shared by members of a culture. Discourses differ between cultures, making the self-concept a **cultural phenomenon**.

PART 4

Adolescence, adulthood and old age

47

PERSONALITY CHANGE AND SOCIAL DEVELOPMENT IN ADOLESCENCE

Introduction and overview

The word 'adolescence' comes from the Latin *adolescere* meaning 'to grow into maturity'. As well as being a time of enormous physiological change, adolescence is also marked by changes in behaviour and expectations. Traditionally, adolescence has been regarded as a prelude to and preparation for adulthood, a transitional period of life between immaturity and maturity. Although there is no single initiation rite in our society that signals the passage into adulthood, there are a number of important 'marker' events, such as leaving school or college, obtaining a job, or moving out of the family home.

In Western societies, adolescence typically spans the ages 12 to 20 which, by other cultures' standards, is unusually long. Indeed, in some non-industrialised societies, adolescence is either virtually non-existent or simply a period of rapid physical changes leading to maturity.

This chapter examines several theories and associated research into personality change and social development in adolescence. Emphasis will be given to the theories of Hall, Erikson, Marcia and Coleman, and sociological (or social psychological) approaches. It begins by looking at the concept of adolescence.

The concept of adolescence

Adolescence is usually taken to begin at *puberty*, the period when sexual maturation begins. Puberty typically begins about two years later for boys than for girls (Chumlea, 1982). However, whilst ten and 12 are the ages by which most girls and boys respectively have entered puberty, there are considerable individual differences. There are also *secular growth trends* (differences between *cultures* in the age at which puberty begins). In some cultures, the age at which puberty begins has been *declining* (Hamburg & Takanishi, 1989). Improvements in nourishment and health care are at least partly responsible for the observed secular growth trends.

> **Box 47.1   Major changes in puberty**
>
> Physiologically, puberty begins when the seminal vesicles and prostate gland enlarge in the male, and the ovaries enlarge in the female. Both males and females experience the *adolescent growth spurt*. Male *secondary sex characteristics* include growth of pubic and then chest and facial hair, and sperm production. In females, breast size increases, pubic hair grows, and menstruation begins (see Figure 47.1, page 411).

Given the considerable variation in the timing of these physical changes, it is difficult to define adolescence in terms of *chronological age* (such as 'the teenage years').

410

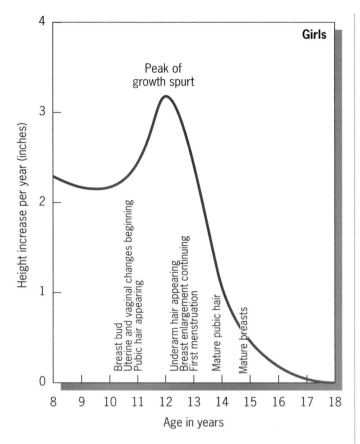

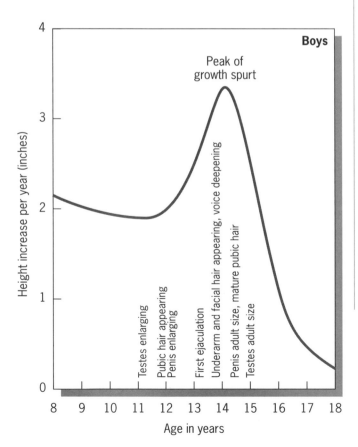

Figure 47.1 The development of secondary sex characteristics. The curved lines represent the average increase in height from eight to 18 years of age. The characteristics shown may occur earlier or later in a person's development but usually occur in the order shown (Based on Tanner, 1978, and Tanner & Whitehouse, 1976)

Indeed, some researchers maintain that adolescence is difficult to define because it has been *artificially created* by Western culture and is a recent 'invention' of Western capitalist society. For example, it has been argued that the concept of the 'rebellious teenager' is a relatively recent phenomenon, popularised in the 1950s through films like *Rebel Without A Cause*. However, the 2000-year-old writings of the ancient Greek philosopher Plato illustrate how the young were seen as being the most likely to challenge the existing social order (Coleman, 1995). Furthermore, Montemayor's (1983) analysis of parent–adolescent relationships from the 1920s to the 1980s, shows that both the issues over which disagreement occurred and the overall levels of conflict were extremely similar.

Figure 47.2 1950s films such as *Rebel Without A Cause*, starring James Dean, have been seen as helping to create the concept of the 'rebellious teenager'. However, Plato was writing about youth's challenge to the existing social order more than 2000 years ago

Montemayor's research indicates that adolescence has changed very little in the twentieth century, despite enormous social and economic changes. Although the term 'teenager' came into existence only in 1953, adolescence has been in existence for very much longer and has probably manifested itself differently according to culture and

411

historical context. However, *some* form of transitional change is common to most societies, suggesting that adolescence is *not* an invention of Western capitalist society (Coleman, 1995).

The 'classical' view of adolescence proposes three main components: *storm and stress*, *identity crisis* and the *generation gap*. Several theories have, in various ways, contributed to this classical view.

Hall's theory

This is probably the earliest formal theory of adolescence. Influenced by Darwin's evolutionary theory, Hall (1904) believed that each person's psychological development *recapitulates* (or recaptures) both the biological and cultural evolution of the human species. He saw adolescence as a time of 'storm and stress' (or *Sturm und Drang*), which mirrored the volatile history of the human race over the last 2000 years.

Some evidence suggests that reactions are more *intense* during adolescence than any other period of life, and that adolescence can be a 'difficult' phase, at least for parents. The National Children's Bureau study, for example, looked at over 14,000 16-year-olds born in a single week in 1958 in England, Scotland and Wales (Fogelman, 1976). Parents most often described their adolescent children as solitary, irritable ('quick to fly off the handle') or 'fussy and overparticular'.

Box 47.2   Csikszentmihalyi & Larson's (1984) study of adolescent reactions

Seventy-five Chicago-area high-school students from diverse social and racial backgrounds were asked to wear electronic pagers for a week. Every two hours, the pager signalled to the students who were instructed to write a description of what they were doing and how they felt about it. After a week, the students filled out questionnaires about both their general moods and their specific mood during particular activities. About 40 per cent of waking time was spent pursuing leisure activities, such as socialising with friends, playing sport or just 'thinking'. The other 60 per cent was spent roughly equally in 'maintenance activities' (such as commuting and eating) and 'productive activities' (such as studying and working).

Particularly revealing were the extreme mood swings. Csikszentmihalyi and Larson found that the students swung from extreme happiness to deep sadness (and vice versa) in less than an hour. For adults, such mood swings usually require several hours to reach the same emotional peaks and troughs.

Although adolescence can be a difficult time of life, little evidence supports Hall's contention that it is a period of storm and stress, and much rejects it. For example, amongst families of middle class American adolescents, adolescence is no more stressful than childhood or adulthood (Bandura & Walters, 1959). British research has reached the same conclusion. Rutter *et al.* (1976) found only small differences between the number of ten-year-olds (10.9 per cent), 14-year-olds (12.5 per cent) and adults (11.9 per cent) judged as having mental disorders. Moreover, a large proportion of 14-year-olds with disorders had had them since childhood. When difficulties did first appear during adolescence, they were mainly associated with stressful situations such as parents' marital discord.

Likewise, Siddique & D'Arcy (1984) found that over a third of adolescents reported no symptoms of psychological distress, and around 40 per cent reported only mild levels. So, whilst adolescence may be a period of stress and turmoil for some, the vast majority adjust well to this transitional phase. For Offer (1969), the vast majority of adolescents possess egos strong enough to withstand the pressures of that phase of life. Because they are in touch with their feelings and develop meaningful relationships with significant others, they do not experience the turmoil of the disturbed adolescent.

Erikson's theory

Along with Adler (1927), Erikson (1963) was one of the first to challenge the view that personality development stops in childhood (see Chapter 1, Box 1.10). Erikson believed that there is a fixed and pre-determined sequence of stages in human development. His *epigenetic principle* maintains that the entire pattern of social and psychological growth is governed by a genetic structure common to all humans, in which genes dictate a timetable for development. It is human nature to pass through a genetically determined sequence of *psychosocial stages*.

Erikson saw the sequence of stages as being *universal*. However, he also saw the sociocultural environment as having a significant influence on our dominant modes of acting and thinking. Based on observations of patients in his psychoanalytic practice, Erikson proposed eight psychosocial stages, each of which centres around a crisis involving a struggle between two conflicting personality outcomes. One of these outcomes is positive (or *adaptive*) whilst the other is negative (or *maladaptive*). Erikson did not, however, see these as either/or alternatives. Rather, every personality is a mixture of the two: healthy development involves the adaptive outweighing the maladaptive (see Table 47.1).

The major challenges of adolescence represent the fifth of Erikson's eight psychosocial stages, in which the individual must face the crisis of establishing a strong sense of personal identity. The dramatic onset of puberty, combined with more sophisticated intellectual abilities (see Chapter 41), results in adolescents becoming particularly concerned with finding their own personal place in adult society. It also results in a lengthy and sometimes painful process of assessing particular strengths and weaknesses so that realistic goals can be set.

Western societies, at least, see adolescence as a *moratorium*, an authorised delay of adulthood, which frees adolescents from most responsibilities and helps them make the difficult transition from childhood to adulthood. Although this can be helpful, it can also be extremely unhelpful. For example, although adolescents may still be dependent on adults, they are expected to behave in an independent and adult way. Thus, the question 'When do I become an adult?' elicits a response from a teacher which is different from a doctor's, parent's or police officer's (Coleman, 1995).

As well as having to deal with the question 'Who am I?', the adolescent must also deal with the question 'Who will I be?'. Erikson saw the creation of an adult personality as accomplished mainly through choosing and developing a commitment to an occupation or role in life. The development of *ego identity* (a firm sense of who one is and what one stands for) is positive, and can carry people through difficult times. For some, however, the need to achieve their potential and create the best possible life is contrasted with the concern to remain true to their ideals. When working with psychiatrically disturbed soldiers in World War II, Erikson coined the term *identity crisis* to describe the loss of personal identity which the stress of combat seemed to have caused. Some years later, he extended the use of the term to include:

> 'severely conflicted young people whose sense of confusion is due ... to a war within themselves'.

Failure to integrate perceptions of the self into a coherent whole, results in *role confusion*. According to Erikson, role confusion can take several forms. Sometimes it is shown in an aimless drifting through a series of social and occupational roles. However, the consequences can be more severe, leading the adolescent into abnormal or delinquent behaviour (such as drug taking and even suicide). Erikson calls this type of role confusion *negative identity*, the choice of adolescents who, because they cannot resolve their identity crises, adopt extreme positions that set them aside from the crowd. For someone with negative identity, the extreme position is preferable to the loneliness and isolation that come with failing to achieve a distinct and more functional role in life.

Table 47.1   Erikson's eight psychosocial stages of development

Stage	Personal and social relationships	Crisis or conflict	Possible outcome
Birth to 1 year	Mother	Trust vs. mistrust	Trust and faith in others or a mistrust of people
2 years	Parents	Autonomy vs. shame and doubt	Self-control and mastery or self-doubt and fearfulness
3 to 5 years	Family	Initiative vs. guilt	Purpose and direction or a loss of self-esteem
6 to 11 years	Neighbourhood and school	Industry vs. inferiority	Competence in social and intellectual pursuits or a failure to thrive and develop
Adolescence	Peer groups and outgroups; models of leadership	Identity vs. role confusion	A sense of 'who one is' or prolonged uncertainty about one's role in life
Early adulthood	Partners in friendship, sex, competition, co-operation	Intimacy vs. isolation	Formation of deep personal relationships or the failure to love others
Middle age	Divided labour and shared household	Generativity vs. stagnation	Expansion of interests and caring for others or a turning inward toward one's own problems
Old age	'Mankind', 'My kind'	Integrity vs. despair	Satisfaction with the triumphs and disappointments of life or a sense of unfulfilment and a fear of death

(After Erikson, 1963)

Tests of Erikson's theory have typically used measures of the self-concept (especially self-esteem: see Chapter 46) as indicators of crisis. Simmons & Rosenberg (1975) have shown that, especially in girls, low self-esteem is more common during early adolescence than in either late childhood or later adolescence. However, in general, there is no increase in the disturbance of the self-image during early adolescence (Offer *et al.*, 1988). For Coleman & Hendry (1990), such disturbance is more likely in early than late adolescence (especially around puberty), but only a very small proportion of the total adolescent population is likely to have a negative self-image or very low self-esteem.

Erikson's theory has also been criticised on the grounds that it is based on observations of a restricted group of people (largely middle class, white males). Gilligan (1982) has argued that Erikson's theory is applicable only to males (see Chapter 84). Whilst it might be true that male adolescents want to forge a separate identity, Gilligan argues that females are more interested in developing warm and nurturing relationships and less interested in the idea of separateness. For Gilligan, Erikson is guilty of taking the male experience as the standard (*androcentrism*) and applying this to both men and women.

Marcia's theory

In an extension of Erikson's work, Marcia (1980) defines identity as:

'A self structure – an internal, self-constructed, dynamic organisation of drive, abilities, beliefs and individual history. The better developed this structure is, the more aware individuals appear to be of their own uniqueness and similarity to others and of their strengths and weaknesses in making their way in the world.'

Marcia identified four *statuses* of adolescent identity formation which characterise the search for identity. A mature identity can be achieved if an individual experiences several *crises* in exploring and choosing between life's alternatives, finally arriving at a *commitment* or investment of the self in those choices.

According to Marcia, identity moratorium is a prerequisite for identity achievement. Beyond that, however, he does not see the four statuses as being sequential, which means that they are not Erikson-type stages. However, evidence suggests that, amongst 12- to 24-year-old men, the statuses *are* broadly age-related. Meilman (1979), for example, has reported that younger men (aged 12 to 18) were more likely to experience diffusion or foreclosure, whereas older men were increasingly likely to be identity achievers. However, irrespective of age, relatively few men were achieving moratorium. Since Marcia sees moratorium as the peak of crisis, Meilman's data cast doubt on the validity of the four statuses. Meilman's study, though, is cross-sectional. Several *longitudinal* studies have indicated clear patterns of movement from foreclosure and diffusion to moratorium and achievement statuses (Kroger, 1996). However, when applied to females, even Marcia (1980) accepts that his statuses work 'only more or less'. This is another example of androcentrism (see Chapter 83).

A sociological (or social psychological) theory

Sociologists see *role change* as an integral feature of adolescent development (Coleman, 1995). Changing school or college, leaving home and beginning a job, all involve a new set of relationships, producing different and often greater expectations. These expectations themselves demand a substantial reassessment of the self-concept and *speed up* the socialisation process. Some adolescents find this problematic because of the wide variety of competing socialisation agencies (such as the family, mass media and peer group) which often represent *conflicting* values and demands.

Sociologists also see socialisation as being dependent more on the adolescent's *own generation* than on the family or other social institutions (*auto-socialisation*: Marsland, 1987). As Marsland has observed:

> 'The crucial meaning of youth is withdrawal from adult control and influence compared with childhood. Peer groups are the milieu into which young people withdraw ... this withdrawal ... is, within limits, legitimated by the adult world'.

Marsland is describing *the generation gap*. However, there is considerable evidence of good relationships between the vast majority of parents and their adolescent children.

Of course, it is almost inevitable that there should be conflict between parents and their adolescent children. Adolescents could not grow into adults unless they were able to test out the boundaries of authority, and they could not discover their beliefs unless given the opportunity to push hard against other people's (Coleman, 1995). However, little evidence supports the extreme view that whatever generation gap exists leads to a 'war'

between the generations or the formation of an adolescent sub-culture. For example, Offer *et al.* (1988) found that over 91 per cent of adolescents in nine different cultures (including Bangladesh, Turkey and Taiwan) denied holding grudges against their parents. A similar percentage rejected the idea that their parents were ashamed of them or would be disappointed in them in the future.

Box 47.5   Is there a generation gap?

- Bandura & Walters (1959) found that the typical American adolescent tended to accept most parental values quite freely and associated with other adolescents who shared such values.

- In the National Children's Bureau study (Fogelman, 1976), parents were given a list of issues on which it is commonly believed that they and their 16-year-old adolescent children disagree. As Tables 47.2 and 47.3 illustrate, parents saw their relationships with their adolescent children as being harmonious, a view confirmed by their children. The only major disagreements concerned appearance and evening activities.

- Other research (e.g. Noller & Callan, 1990) indicates that music, fashion and sexual behaviour tend to be the issues on which a sizeable 'generation gap' appears.

Table 47.2   Percentage of parents reporting disagreement with their adolescent children (N = 11,521)

	Often (%)	Sometimes (%)	Never or hardly ever (%)
Choice of same-sex friends	3	16	81
Choice of opposite-sex friends	2	9	89
Dress or hairstyle	11	35	54
Time of coming in at night or going to bed	8	26	66
Places visited in own time	2	9	89
Doing homework	6	18	76
Smoking	6	9	85
Drinking	1	5	94

(From the National Children's Bureau study, Fogelman, 1976)

Table 47.3   Reports by adolescents concerning their parents (N = 11,045)

	Very true (%)	True (%)	Uncertain (%)	Untrue (%)	Very untrue (%)
I get on well with my mother	41	45	8	4	1
I get on well with my father	35	45	13	5	2
I often quarrel with a sister or brother	23	43	10	19	5
My parents have strong views about my appearance	15	33	19	27	6
My parents want to know where I go in the evening	27	51	8	11	3
My parents disapprove of some of my male friends	9	19	18	37	16
My parents disapprove of some of my female friends	5	15	18	40	22

(From the National Children's Bureau study, Fogelman, 1976)

Coleman's focal theory

According to Coleman & Hendry (1990), the theories above are relevant and provide a foundation for an understanding of young people with serious problems and those who belong to minority or deviant groups. However, adolescence requires a theory of *normality* rather than *abnormality*. The transition from childhood to adolescence requires substantial psychological and social adjustment. Whilst adolescence is a difficult time for some, for the majority it appears to be a period of relative stability with which most young people cope without undue stress. Coleman's (1980) *focal theory* is an attempt to explain how this is achieved.

The theory is based on a study of 800 six-, 11-, 13-, 15- and 17-year-old boys and girls. Coleman found that on various tests dealing with self-image, being alone, heterosexual and parental relationships, and friendships and large-group situations, attitudes to all of these changed as a function of age. More important, though, was the finding

that concerns about different issues reached a peak at different ages for both sexes.

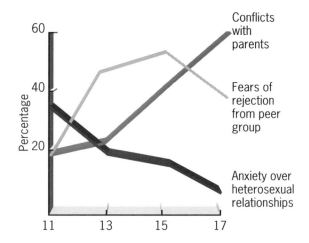

Figure 47.3   Peak ages of the expression of different themes. These data are for boys only (From Coleman & Hendry, 1980)

Particular sorts of relationship patterns come into *focus* (are most prominent) at different ages. However, no pattern is specific to one age. The patterns overlap and there are wide individual differences with respect to them, but just because an issue is not the predominant feature of an age does not mean it will not be critical for some adolescents. Coleman believes that adolescents are able to cope with the potentially stressful change with relative stability by dealing with one issue at a time.

Thus, adolescents spread the process of adaptation over a span of years, attempting to resolve one issue first before addressing the next. Because different problems and relationships come into focus and are dealt with at different stages, the stresses resulting from the need to adapt are rarely concentrated so that all must be dealt with at once. Adolescents who, for whatever reason, must deal with more than one problem at a time are those most likely to experience difficulties (Coleman & Hendry, 1990).

Box 47.6   How valid is Coleman's theory?

Coleman's original findings concerning patterns of development have been successfully replicated by Kroger (1985) with large North American and New Zealand samples. Others (e.g. Simmons & Blyth, 1987) have successfully tested hypotheses deriving from Coleman's theory. Simmons and Blyth proposed that those who adjust less well during adolescence would be more likely to be those facing more than one interpersonal issue at a time. Their results strongly supported the prediction. So, if change occurred at too young an age (causing the individual to be 'off-time' in development), was marked by sharp discontinuity, or involved an accumulation of significant and temporally close changes, adjustment was much poorer. Whilst Coleman's theory needs further testing, it is widely accepted as an important contribution to the understanding of adolescence.

Conclusions

This chapter has looked at several theoretical accounts of personality change and social development in adolescence. Although adolescence is 'classically' seen as a period of 'storm and stress' in which an adolescent experiences an 'identity crisis', and the 'generation gap' is at its widest, evidence does not favour such a view. The theories that have contributed to this classical view are probably furthest away from capturing the essence of adolescence.

Summary

■ 'Adolescence' means 'to grow into maturity'. It spans the ages 12 to 20 and involves enormous changes in physiology, behaviour and expectations, a transitional period between immaturity and maturity. However, in some non-industrialised societies, adolescence either does not exist or simply denotes a period of rapid physical changes.

■ Adolescence is usually taken to begin at **puberty**. Both sexes experience the **adolescent growth spurt** and the development of **secondary sex characteristics**. Girls typically begin puberty earlier than boys, but there are large individual differences within each sex. There are also **secular growth trends**.

■ Some researchers see adolescence as a recent and **artificially created** stage in human development within Western capitalist society. However, adolescence has changed very little for much of the twentieth century, despite enormous social and economic changes. Some transitional period is found in most societies.

■ Several theories have contributed to the 'classical' view of adolescence, which comprises **'storm and stress'**, **'identity crisis'** and the **'generation gap'**.

■ According to Hall, each person's psychological development **recapitulates** both the biological and cultural evolution of humans. Adolescence is a time of 'storm and stress' ('Sturm und Drang'), mirroring the human race's volatile history over the last 2000 years.

■ Emotional reactions are more **intense** during adolescence compared with other periods of life, making it a 'difficult' time, at least for parents. Nevertheless, evidence suggests that adolescence is no more stressful than childhood or adulthood, and the rate of mental disorder is no greater for adolescents.

■ According to Erikson's **epigenetic principle**, there is a fixed, pre-determined sequence of social and psychological development. It is human nature to pass through a genetically determined sequence of **psychosocial stages**.

■ During adolescence, the individual faces a crisis centred on establishing a strong sense of personal identity (**identity** vs. **role confusion**). In Western societies, adolescence is a **moratorium**, designed to help individuals make the difficult transition from childhood to adulthood. This can be confusing, because 'adult' is defined differently by different social institutions.

■ The creation of an adult personality (**ego-identity**) is achieved mainly through commitment to an occupational role. **Role confusion** can take the form of aimless drifting through a series of social and occupational roles. Alternatively, an adolescent may adopt a **negative identity**, as in delinquent behaviour. Three other forms of role confusion relate to **intimacy**, **time perspective** and **industry**.

■ Although low self-esteem (a measure of **identity crisis**) may be more common in early adolescence (especially in girls), only a very small proportion of all adolescents has a disturbed self-image. Erikson's theory is also based largely on observations of white, middle class males, making it androcentric.

■ Marcia identifies four **statuses** of adolescent identity formation: **identity diffusion**, **identity foreclosure**, **identity moratorium** and **identity achievement**. A mature identity can only be achieved if an individual experiences several **crises** before arriving at a **commitment** to certain choices.

■ Whilst identity moratorium is a prerequisite for identity achievement, Marcia's four statuses are not sequential stages. Supporting evidence is based on male samples and the four statuses apply only loosely to females.

■ For sociologists, adolescent development involves **role change**, requiring a substantial reassessment of the self-concept and **speeding up** of the socialisation process. Some adolescents find this difficult because a wide range of socialisation agencies often present **conflicting** values and demands.

■ Sociologists also stress **auto-socialisation**. However, most evidence shows adolescents sharing their parents' values, attitudes and beliefs, and the existence of harmonious family relationships.

■ Some degree of conflict between parents and their adolescent children is necessary for adolescents to grow into adults. However, this is very different from claiming that there is a **generation gap** or that a separate adolescent sub-culture exists.

■ Coleman's **focal theory** attempts to explain the **normality** of adolescents. Concerns about different issues reach a peak at different ages for both sexes. Adolescents cope with change by dealing with one issue at a time, spreading the process of adaptation over several years. Those who must deal with more than one issue at once are most likely to experience difficulties.

48

PERSONALITY CHANGE IN EARLY AND MIDDLE ADULTHOOD

Introduction and overview

Assuming we enjoy a normal life-span, the longest phase of the life-cycle will be spent in adulthood. Until recently, however, personality changes in adulthood attracted little psychological research interest. Indeed, as Levinson *et al.* (1978) have observed, adulthood is:

'one of the best-kept secrets in our society and probably in human history generally'.

This chapter attempts to reveal some of these secrets by examining what theory and research have told us about personality change in adulthood. Many theorists believe that adult concerns and involvements are patterned in such a way that we can speak about *stages* of adult development. Early (or young) adulthood covers the two decades from 20 to 40, and middle adulthood spans the years from 40 to 60 or 65. These are both discussed in this chapter. Later adulthood (or 'old age') is discussed in Chapter 50.

Erikson's theory

Chapter 47 described Erikson's views on adolescence and his theory that human development occurs through a sequence of psychosocial stages. As far as early and middle adulthood are concerned, Erikson described two primary developmental crises (the sixth and seventh of his psychosocial stages: see Table 47.1, page 413).

The first is the establishment of *intimacy* which is a criterion of having attained the psychosocial state of adulthood. By intimacy, Erikson means the ability to form close, meaningful relationships with others without 'the fear of losing oneself in the process' (Elkind, 1970). Erikson believed that a prerequisite for intimacy was the attainment of *identity* (the reconciliation of all our various roles into one enduring and stable personality: see page 413). Identity is necessary because we cannot know what it means to love someone and seek to share our life with them until we know who we are and what we want to do with our lives. Thus, genuine intimacy requires us to give up some of our sense of separateness, and we must each have a firm identity to do this.

Intimacy need not involve sexuality. Since intimacy refers to the essential ability to relate our deepest hopes and fears to another person, and in turn to accept another's need for intimacy, it describes the relationship between friends just as much as that between sexual partners (Dacey, 1982). By sharing ourselves with others, our personal identities become fully realised and consolidated. Erikson believed that if a sense of identity were not established with friends or a partner, then *isolation* (a sense of being alone without anyone to share with or care for) would result. We normally achieve intimacy in *young adulthood* (our 20s and 30s), after which we enter *middle age* (our 40s and 50s). This involves the attainment of *generativity*, the second developmental crisis.

Box 48.1 Generativity

The central task of the middle years of adulthood is to determine life's purpose or goal, and to focus on achieving aims and contributing to the well-being of others (particularly children). Generativity means being concerned with others beyond the immediate family, such as future generations and the nature of the society and world in which those future generations will live. As well as being displayed by parents, generativity is shown by anyone actively concerned with the welfare of young people and in making the world a better place for them to live and work. People who successfully resolve this developmental crisis establish clear guidelines for their lives and are generally productive and happy within this *directive framework*. Failure to attain generativity leads to *stagnation*, in which people become preoccupied with their personal needs and comforts.

EVALUATION OF ERIKSON'S THEORY

The sequence from identity to intimacy may not accurately reflect present-day realities. In recent years, the trend has been for adults to live together before marrying, so they tend to marry later in life than people did in the past (see Chapter 49, page 430). Many people struggle with identity issues (such as career choice) *at the same time* as dealing with intimacy issues.

Additionally, some evidence suggests that females achieve intimacy *before* 'occupational identity'. The typical life course of women involves passing directly into a stage of intimacy without having achieved personal identity. Sangiuliano (1978) argues that most women submerge their identities into those of their partners, and only in mid-life do they emerge from this and search for separate identities and full independence. Sangiuliano's research appears, however, not to have taken into account the possibility that *social class* interacts with gender. For example, amongst working class men, early marriage is seen as a 'good' life pattern. They see early adulthood as a time for 'settling down', having a family and maintaining a steady job. Middle class men and women, by contrast, see early adulthood as a time for exploration, in which different occupations are tried. Marriage tends to occur after this, and 'settling down' does not usually take place before 30 (Neugarten, 1975).

Hodgson & Fischer (1979) discovered sex differences in the relationship between identity and intimacy. Ninety per cent of female university students rated as identity achievers were also rated as showing intimacy in their relationships. However, 52 per cent of those *not* rated as identity achievers were also rated as showing intimacy. Amongst male students, very few showed intimacy without identity.

Erikson's psychosocial stages were meant to be *universal*, applying to both sexes in all cultures. However, he acknowledged that the sequence of stages is different for a woman, who suspends her identity as she prepares to attract the man who will marry her. Men achieve identity before achieving intimacy with a sexual partner, whereas for women, Erikson's developmental crises appear to be fused (see Chapter 84). As Gilligan (1982) has observed:

'the female comes to know herself as she is known, through relationships with others'.

Neugarten's (1975) findings indicate that as well as describing developmental patterns separately for gender, it is also necessary to do this for social class. This suggests that it is almost certainly impossible to describe *universal* stages for adults. Moreover, there is evidence of a growing prolongation of adolescence.

Box 48.2 Perpetual adolescence

According to Sheehy (1996), whilst childhood is ending earlier, adults are prolonging adolescence into their 30s. Indeed, many people are not acknowledging maturity until they reach 40. Sheehy suggests that:

'Adolescence is now prolonged for the middle classes until the end of their 20s, and for blue-collar men and women until their mid-20s, as more young adults live at home longer. True adulthood does not begin until 30. Most Baby Boomers, born after World War II, do not feel fully 'grown up' until they are in their 40s, and even then they resist'.

Beaumont (1996) argues that we have evolved into a generation of 'Peter Pans', perpetually stuck in adolescence:

'You see them in Hyde Park – 30- and 40-somethings on rollerblades and skateboards, hanging out at Glastonbury or discussing the merits of Oasis versus Blur at dinner parties'.

The fictional models of this 'new generation' are Gary and Tony from the BBC television programme *Men Behaving Badly*, and Patsie and Eddy from *Absolutely Fabulous*. Real-life examples of 'Peter Pans' include Mick Jagger, Cliff Richard and Richard Branson.

Figure 48.1   Gary and Tony, the 'perpetual adolescents' in BBC TV's *Men Behaving Badly*

According to Orbach (cited in Beaumont, 1996), one problem created by adults who refuse to grow up is their own parenting. Unable to look up to figures of authority themselves, they feel a sense of loss and look to their own children for emotional sustenance in a curious role reversal.

Levinson *et al.*'s '*Seasons of a Man's Life*'

Perhaps the most systematic study of personality and life changes in adulthood began in 1969, when Levinson *et al.* interviewed 40 men aged 35 to 45 from a variety of occupational backgrounds. Transcripts were made of the five to ten tape-recorded interviews that each participant gave over several months. Levinson *et al.* looked at how adulthood is actually *experienced*.

In *The Seasons of a Man's Life*, Levinson *et al.* (1978) advanced a *life structure theory*, defining life structure as the underlying pattern or design of a person's life at any given time. Life structure allows us to 'see how the self is in the world and how the world is in the self', and evolves through a series of *phases* or *periods* which give overall shape to the course of adult development. Adult development comprises a sequence of *eras* which overlap in the form of *cross-era transitions*. These last about five years, terminating the outgoing era and initiating the incoming one. The four eras are pre-adulthood (age 0–22), early adulthood (17–45), middle adulthood (40–65) and late adulthood (60 onwards).

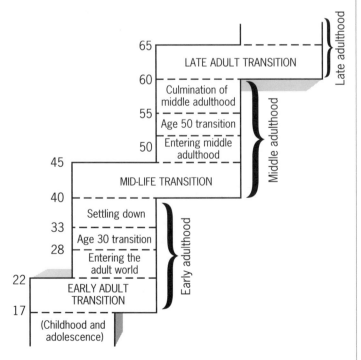

Figure 48.2   Levinson *et al.*'s theory of adult development. The life-cycle is divided into four major eras that overlap in the form of cross-era transitions (From Gross, 1996)

The phases or periods alternate between those that are *stable* (or *structure-building*) and *transitional* (or *structure-changing*). Although each phase involves biological, psychological and social adjustments, family and work roles are seen as central to the life structure at any time, and individual development is interwoven with changes in these roles.

THE ERA OF EARLY ADULTHOOD

Early adult transition (17–22) is a developmental 'bridge' between adolescence and adulthood.

> **Box 48.3   Separation and attachment**
>
> Two key themes of the early adult transition are *separation* and the formation of *attachments* to the adult world. *External* separation involves moving out of the family home, increasing financial independence, and entering more independent and responsible roles and living arrangements. *Internal* separation involves greater psychological distance from the family, less emotional dependence on the parents, and greater differentiation between the self and family. Although we separate from our parents, Levinson *et al.* argue that we never complete the process which continues throughout life. Attachment involves exploring the world's possibilities, imagining ourselves as parts of it, and identifying and establishing changes for living in the world before we become 'full members' of it.

Between ages 22 and 28, we *enter the adult world*. This is the first *structure-building* (rather than *structure-changing*) phase and hence is referred to as the *entry life structure for early adulthood*. In it, we try to fashion:

> 'a provisional structure that provides a workable link between the valued self and adult society'.

In the *novice phase*, we try to define ourselves as adults and live with the initial choices we make concerning jobs, relationships, lifestyles and values. However, we need to create a balance between 'keeping our options open' (which allows us to explore possibilities without being committed to a given course) and 'putting down roots' (or creating stable life structures).

Our decisions are made in the context of our *dreams* (the 'vague sense' we have of ourselves in the adult world and what we want to do with our lives). We must overcome disappointments and setbacks, and learn to accept and profit from successes, so that the dream's 'thread' does not get lost in the course of 'moving up the ladder' and revising the life structure. To help us in our efforts at self-definition, we look to *mentors*, older and more experienced others, for guidance and direction. Mentors can take a *formal* role in guiding, teaching and helping novices to define their dreams. Alternatively, a mentor's role may be *informal*, providing an advisory and emotionally supportive function (as a parent does).

The *age-30 transition* (28–33) provides an opportunity to work on the flaws and limitations of the first life structure, and to create the basis for a more satisfactory structure that will complete the era of young adulthood. Most of Levinson *et al.*'s participants experienced *age-30 crises* which involved stress, self-doubt, feelings that life was losing its 'provisional quality' and becoming more serious, and time pressure. Thus, the participants saw this as being the time for change, if change was needed. However, for a minority the age-30 transition was crisis-free.

Box 48.4   Settling down

The *settling down* (or *culminating life structure for early adulthood*: 33–40) phase represents consolidation of the second life structure. This involves a shift away from tentative choices regarding family and career towards a strong sense of commitment to a personal, familial and occupational future. Paths for success in work and husband and father roles are mapped out and, instead of just beginning to find out what is important and what our opinions are, we see ourselves as responsible adults.

The settling down phase comprises two sub-stages: *early settling down* (33–36) and *becoming one's own man* or *BOOM* (36–40). In the latter, we strive to advance and succeed in building better lives, improve and use our skills, be creative, and in general contribute to society. We want recognition and affirmation from society, but we also want to be self-sufficient and free of social pressure and control. Although a 'boy-man' conflict may be produced, this can represent a step forward. This sub-stage may also see us assume a *mentor role* for someone younger (see above).

THE ERA OF MIDDLE ADULTHOOD

The *mid-life transition* (40–45) involves terminating one life structure, initiating another, and continuing the process of individuation started during the *BOOM* sub-stage. This is a time of soul-searching, questioning and assessing the real meaning of the life structure's achievement. It is sometimes referred to as the *mid-life crisis*, although Levinson *et al.* did not actually use this term. For some people, the change is gradual and fairly painless. For others, however, it is full of uncertainties.

The age-50 mid-life crisis stems from unconscious tensions between attachment and separation, the resurfacing of the need to be creative (which is often repressed in order to achieve a career), and retrospective comparisons between 'dreams' and life's reality.

Most participants in Levinson *et al.*'s study had not reached age 45. Following interviews two years after the study was concluded, some were chosen for more extensive study. However, the evidence for the remaining phases is much less detailed than for the earlier ones.

In entering *middle adulthood* (or *early life structure for middle adulthood*: 45–50), we have resolved (more-or-less satisfactorily) whether what we have committed ourselves to really is worthwhile, and it is again necessary to make choices regarding a new life structure. Sometimes, these choices are defined by *marker events* such as divorce, illness, occupational change, or the death of a loved one. However, the choices may also be influenced by less obvious but significant changes, such as shifts in the enthusiasm for work or in the quality of marriage. As before, the resulting life structure varies in how satisfying it is and how connected it is to the self. It may not be intrinsically happy and fulfilling. The restructuring consists of many steps and there may be setbacks in which options have to be abandoned ('back to the drawing board').

The validity of the 'mid-life crisis'

Just as the 'identity crisis' is part of the popular stereotype of adolescence (see page 413), Levinson *et al.* have helped to make the 'mid-life crisis' part of the common-sense understanding of adult development. Like Erikson, Levinson *et al.* see crisis as *inevitable*. As they note:

'It is not possible to get through middle adulthood without having at least a moderate crisis in either the mid-life transition or the age-50 transition'.

They also see crisis as *necessary*. If we do not engage in soul searching, we will:

'pay the price in a later developmental crisis or in a progressive withering of the self and a life structure minimally connected to the self'.

The view that crisis is both inevitable and necessary (or *normative* to use Erikson's term) is controversial. People of all ages suffer occasional depression, self-doubt, sexual uncertainty and concerns about the future. Indeed, there appears to be an increasingly wide age range (and a growing number) of people who decide to make radical changes in their life-style, both earlier and later than predicted by Levinson *et al.*'s theory (see Box 48.5).

Figure 48.3   The image of an older man's attraction to younger women is part of the popular concept of the 'mid-life crisis'. It is portrayed here by Woody Allen and Juliette Lewis in *Husbands and Wives*

Box 48.5   'Downshifting'

According to Tredre (1996), the concept of a mid-life crisis is too narrow in that traditionally, or stereotypically, it refers to someone in his or her late 40s, with grown-up children, who gives up a secure and well-paid 'respectable' career, and moves to a small market town or village in order to enjoy a less stressful, more peaceful and generally better quality of life. We need to spread the net wider nowadays and think in terms of early-, mid- and late-life crises: people of all age groups and walks of life are 'feeling the itch'.

Downshifting refers to voluntarily opting out of a pressurised career and interminably long hours in the office, and often involves giving up an exceptionally well-paid job in a high-profile industry in the pursuit of a more fulfilling way of life. Tredre identifies a number of possible reasons for downshifting, including anti-urbanism (fuelled by concerns over urban pollution), crime, violence, and increasing job insecurity.

Durkin (1995) notes that a large proportion of middle-aged people actually feel *more* positive about this phase of life than earlier ones, with only ten per cent reporting feeling as though they had experienced a crisis. For Durkin, the mid-life crisis is not as universal as Levinson *et al.* suggest, and the time and extent to which we experience uncomfortable self-assessments vary as a function of several factors (such as personality). Although the evidence is sparse, going through middle age in a relatively peaceful and untroubled way is actually a *favourable* indicator of future development, that is, a *lack* of emotional

disturbance predicts *better* rather than poorer functioning in later life (Rutter & Rutter, 1992).

Two other components of the mid-life crisis are much less contentious. The first is a wide range of adaptations in the life pattern. Some of these stem from role changes that produce fairly drastic consequences, such as divorce, remarriage, a major occupational change, redundancy or serious illness. Others are more subtle, and include the ageing and likely death of parents, the new role of grandparent, and the sense of loss which sometimes occurs when children have all moved away from the family home (*empty-nest distress*). The impact of some of these life or marker events is discussed in Chapter 49.

The second non-controversial component is the significant change in the *internal* aspects of life structures, which occurs regardless of external events. This involves reappraising achievements and remaining ambitions, especially those to do with work and the relationship with our sexual partner. A fundamental development at this time is the realisation that the final authority for life rests with us. (This relates to Gould's, 1978, 1980, theory: see page 425.) Sheehy (1976) has suggested that men in their 40s begin to explore and develop their more 'feminine' selves (by becoming more nurturant, affiliative and intimate). Women, by contrast, discover their more 'masculine' selves (by becoming more action-oriented, assertive, and ambitious). The passing-by in *opposite directions* produces the pain and distress which is the 'mid-life crisis'.

However, it has been argued that the mid-life crisis is not a stage through which everyone *must* pass. For example, it can stem from several sources, including ineffective adjustment to the normal stresses of growth and transition in middle-age and the reaction of a particularly vulnerable person to these stresses (Hopson & Scally, 1980). The diversity of adult experience makes terms like 'stages' and 'seasons' inappropriate. *Themes*, perhaps, is a better term.

Many stressful biological, social and psychological life changes are likely to occur together in any particular society (Bee & Mitchell, 1980). As a result, most people will experience transitions or crises at roughly the same time in their life-cycles. People will differ regarding how much stress they can tolerate before a 'crisis' is experienced, and in how they respond to it when it does occur. Personal growth may be one response, and changing the major 'external' aspects of our lives (by, for example, changing jobs or, getting divorced) another.

The seasons of a woman's life

Levinson *et al.*'s research was carried out on men, and no women were included in the sample. Similar research investigating women has found similarities with Levinson *et al.*'s findings. However, men and women have been shown to differ in terms of their *dreams*.

Box 48.6   Women's dreams and 'gender splitting'

Levinson (1986) argues that a 'gender-splitting' phenomenon occurs in adult development.

Men have fairly unified visions of their futures which tend to be focused on their careers. Women, however, have 'dreams' which are more likely to be split between a career and marriage. This was certainly true of academics and business women, although the former were less ambitious and more likely to forego a career, whereas the latter wanted to maintain their careers but at a reduced level. Only the *homemakers* had unified dreams (to be full-time wives and mothers, as their own mothers had been).

Roberts & Newton (1987) saw the family as playing a 'supportive' role for men. Women's dreams were constructed around their relationship with the husband and family, which subordinated their personal needs. So, part of *her* dream is *his* success. For Durkin (1995), this difference in women's and men's priorities may put women at greater risk:

'of disappointment and developmental tension as their investment in others' goals conflict with their personal needs'.

Women who give marriage and motherhood top priority in their 20s tend to develop more individualistic goals for their 30s. However, those who are career-oriented early on in adulthood tend to focus on marriage and family concerns later. Generally, the transitory instability of the early 30s lasts *longer* for women than for men, and 'settling down' is much less clear cut. Trying to integrate career and marriage/family responsibilities is very difficult for most women, who experience greater conflicts than their husbands are likely to.

The validity of stage theories of adult development

Erikson's and Levinson's theories of adult development emphasise a 'ladder-like' progression through an inevitable and universal series of stages. The view that adult development is 'stage-like' has, however, been criticised (Rutter & Rutter, 1992) on the grounds that it underestimates the degree of *individual variability*. Many members of the mainstream working class population do *not* grow or

change in systematic ways. Instead, they show many rapid fluctuations, depending on things like relationships, work demands and other life stresses that are taking place (Craig, 1992).

Stage theories also imply a *discontinuity* of development. However, many psychologists maintain there is also considerable *continuity* of personality during adult life. The popular stereotype sees middle adulthood as the time when a person is responsible, settled, contented and at the peak of achievement. People who find that they do not conform to this stereotype tend to blame themselves rather than seeing the stereotype as being wrong (Hopson & Scally, 1980). Schlossberg *et al.* (1978) have suggested that we use some sort of *social clock* to judge whether we are 'on time' with respect to particular life events (such as getting married). If we are 'off time', either early or late, we are *age deviant*. Like other types of deviancy, this can result in social penalties, such as amusement, pity or rejection.

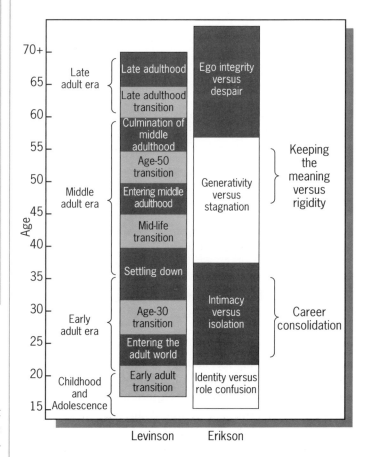

Figure 48.4   A comparison of Levinson *et al.*'s and Erikson's adult stages. Note how the former's are defined primarily by age and the latter's by crisis (From Santrock, 1986)

Craig (1992) sees changes in adult thought, behaviour and personality as being less a result of chronological age or specific biological changes, and more a result of personal, social and cultural events or forces. Because of the sheer diversity of experiences in an adult's life, Craig does not believe it is possible to describe major 'milestones' that will apply to nearly everyone.

Gould's theory of the evolution of adult consciousness

Whereas Levinson *et al.* discussed adult development in terms of evolving life structures, Gould (1978, 1980) prefers to talk about the evolution of adult consciousness which occurs when:

> 'we release ourselves from the constraints and ties of childhood consciousness'.

Gould sees the thrust of adult development as being towards the realisation and acceptance of ourselves as creators of our own lives, and away from the assumption that the rules and standards of childhood determine our destiny. His theory is an extension of the Freudian idea of *separation anxiety*. According to Gould, we have to free ourselves of the *illusion of absolute safety*, an illusion which dominated childhood. This involves *transformations*, giving up the security of the past to form our own ideas. We have to replace the concept of parental dependency with a sense of *autonomy*, or owning ourselves. This, however, is difficult because dependency on parents is a normal feature of childhood. Indeed, without it, childhood would be very difficult. As well as shedding childhood consciousness, Gould believes that our *sense of time* also changes.

Box 48.7　Our changing sense of time

Up until age 18 or so, we feel both protected and constrained by our parents, and never quite believe that we will escape the 'family world'. This is like being in a timeless capsule in which 'the future is a fantasy space that may possibly not exist'. However, we begin to glimpse an endless future and see an infinite amount of time ahead of us.

In our 20s, we become confident about being separated from the family. However, we have not yet formed early-adult life structures. Gould (1980) puts it like this:

> 'Because of all the new decisions and novel experiences that come with setting up new adult enterprises, our time sense, when we're being successful, is one of movement along a chosen path that leads linearly to some obscure prize decades in the future. There is plenty of time, but we're still in a hurry once we've developed a clearer, often stereotyped, picture of where we want to be by then'.

At the end of our 20s, our sense of time incorporates our adult past as well as future. The future is neither infinite nor linear, and we must choose between different options because there isn't time to take them all. From our mid-30s to mid-40s, we develop a sense of urgency that time is running out. We also become aware of our own mortality and, once attained, is never far from our consciousness. How we spend our time becomes a matter of great importance. Additionally, we begin to question whether our 'prize' (freedom from restrictions by those who have formed us – our parents) either exists or, if it does, whether it has been worth it (cf. Levinson *et al.*'s 'dream').

Conclusions

This chapter has considered several theories of personality change in early and middle adulthood. The stage theory approach has been popular, although critics argue that development does not occur in predictable and ordered ways. Whether personality development in adulthood is characterised by stability or change has yet to be resolved.

Summary

■ Adulthood is the longest phase of the life-cycle. Early and young adulthood covers the years 20 to 40, whilst middle adulthood spans the years 40 to 60 or 65.

■ In Erikson's psychosocial theory, young adulthood involves the establishment of **intimacy**. This can be achieved through friendship as well as through a sexual relationship. Failure to achieve intimacy results in a sense of **isolation**. The central task of middle adulthood is the attainment of **generativity**. Failure to achieve generativity results in **stagnation**.

■ The sequence from identity to intimacy may no longer accurately reflect relationship patterns. Many people struggle with issues of identity and intimacy **at the same time**, especially women. Women tend to achieve intimacy **before** 'occupational identity', submerging their identity into their partners'. There are also important social class differences in the timing of marriage and 'settling down'.

■ According to Sheehy, whilst childhood is ending earlier, people, especially those from middle class backgrounds, are prolonging adolescence into their 30s.

■ Levinson *et al.* were concerned with how adulthood is actually **experienced**. Their **life structure theory** identifies **phases** or **periods** which give overall shape to the course of adult development. These are either **stable** (**structure-building**) or **transitional** (**structure-changing**). A sequence of **eras** overlaps in the form of **cross-era transitions**.

■ **Early adult transition** (17–22) is a developmental bridge between adolescence and adulthood. It involves both internal and external **separation** from parents and **attachment** to the adult world.

■ **Entry life structure for early adulthood** (22–28) is the first **structure-building** phase. In the novice phase, we make choices in the context of our **dreams**. We look to **mentors** to help us in the task of self-definition and defining our dreams.

■ The **age-30 transition** (28–33) provides an opportunity to create the basis for a more satisfactory life structure that will complete the era of young adulthood. An **age-30 crisis** is commonly experienced.

■ The **culminating life structure for early adulthood/settling down** phase (33–40) involves two sub-stages, **early settling down** (33–36) and **becoming one's own man** (BOOM) (36–40), which may involve the assumption of a **mentor role** for some younger adult.

■ The **mid-life transition** (40–45) is a time of soul-searching and assessing the meaning of the life-structure achievement (**mid-life crisis**).

■ In **early life structure for middle adulthood/entering middle adulthood** (45–50), we must again make choices regarding new life structures. These choices are sometimes defined by **marker events**.

■ Levinson *et al.* have helped to make the 'mid-life crisis' part of our common-sense understanding of adult development. They see crisis as both **inevitable** and **necessary** (**normative**).

■ People of all ages suffer crises, and a growing number of people are deciding to make radical changes in their life-style (**downshifting**), both earlier and later than predicted by Levinson *et al.*

■ A large proportion of middle-aged people actually feel **more** positive about their lives than earlier, and the mid-life crisis is not as universal as Levinson *et al.* suggest.

■ Research involving women has found similarities with Levinson *et al.*'s findings based on their all-male sample. However, there is a 'gender splitting' that occurs in relation to men's and women's **dreams**. Whilst men have fairly unified, career-focused visions of the future, women's dreams are split between career and marriage/family responsibilities.

■ The age-30 transition generally lasts longer for women than for men, and 'settling down' is much less clear cut. Trying to integrate career and marriage and family responsibilities is very difficult for most women.

■ The view that adult development is 'stage-like' has been criticised on the grounds that it underestimates **individual variability**. Stage theories also imply a **discontinuity** of development, whilst many psychologists stress the **continuity** of adult personality. The sheer diversity of adult experience makes it impossible to describe major 'milestones' that apply to everyone.

■ According to Gould, the thrust of adult development is towards the realisation and acceptance of ourselves as creators of our own lives (adult consciousness) and freeing ourselves of the **illusion of absolute safety**.

■ Gould also believes that adult development involves a change in the **sense of time**. By the end of our 20s, the future is seen as neither infinite nor linear, and we must make choices. From our mid-30s to mid-40s, we sense that time is running out and are aware of our mortality.

49

THE IMPACT OF LIFE EVENTS IN ADULTHOOD

Introduction and overview

As Chapter 48 showed (see page 424), evidence concerning the predictability of changes in adult life (or what Levinson, 1986, calls *psychobiosocial transitions*) is conflicting. Three kinds of influence can affect the way we develop in adulthood (Hetherington & Baltes, 1988). *Normative age-graded influences* are biological (such as the menopause) and social (such as marriage and retirement) changes that normally occur at fairly predictable ages. *Normative history-graded influences* are historical events that affect whole generations or cohorts at about the same time (examples include wars, recessions and epidemics). *Non-normative influences* are idiosyncratic transitions such as divorce, unemployment and illness.

Levinson (1986) uses the term *marker events* to refer to the age-graded and non-normative influences. Others prefer the term *critical life events* to describe such influences (although it is perhaps more accurate to describe them as *processes*). Some tend to happen early in adulthood (such as marriage and parenthood). Others occur much later (such as retirement, which marks entry into late adulthood). Yet others (such as bereavement and unemployment) can occur at any age. Studying the impact of events such as these is another way of looking at how we adjust to adulthood. This chapter examines research findings concerning the impact of some of these life events.

Unemployment

Unemployment produces both psychological and physical effects which take time to emerge, rather than occurring immediately after an individual has been made unemployed (Argyle, 1989). One psychological effect is *depression*. As well as being more prevalent amongst the unemployed, depression's severity is strongly correlated with the *length* of unemployment. In the long-term unemployed, a sense of *learned helplessness* (Seligman, 1975) develops (see Chapter 69), in which they see themselves as being the main cause of their unemployment and believe that nothing can be done to change the state of affairs. Along with other factors associated with unemployment, such as poverty and reduced social support, depression is one that contributes to *suicide*. Suicide is much more common among the unemployed than the employed.

Unemployment is also associated with a *loss of self-esteem* through ceasing to be the bread-winner and becoming a recipient of government benefits. The material hardships of low income bring a financial strain which is greatest when there are dependent children. Not surprisingly, financial problems are themselves a major source of emotional distress.

> **Box 49.1 Some major sources of distress among the unemployed**
>
> **Length of unemployment:** The initial response to unemployment is *shock*, *anger* and *incomprehension*. This is followed by *optimism*, a feeling of being between jobs (a kind of 'holiday'), coupled with active job searching. As job searching fails, optimism is replaced by *pessimism*, which gives way to *fatalism*. Hopelessness and apathy set in and job hunting is sometimes abandoned completely.
>
> **Commitment:** Those who are most committed to their jobs are most distressed by unemployment. This might explain why unemployment has a greater negative effect on middle-aged men than young people or married women (Warr, 1987).
>
> **Social support:** The complex set of relationships enjoyed at work conveys identity and status which are both lost in unemployment. The unemployed typically withdraw from friendships, partly because they cannot afford to pay for drinks, entertainment and so on. Because the unemployed is a group to which most people do not wish to belong, the bonds between the unemployed are weak. Social support, especially from the family, can 'buffer' these effects.
>
> **Activity level:** Those unemployed who have a structured or organised pattern of life (achieved by unpaid work, pursuing a hobby or keeping active in other ways) experience less distress than those who adapt by staying in bed, watching a lot of television and 'killing time'.
>
> **Perceived cause of unemployment:** During periods of full employment, to be out of work might be seen as a sign of failure. However, because unemployment is widespread and includes people from all sections of society, many unemployed feel less responsible for their plight and more accepting of it. For example, satisfaction with

the self is greater among unemployed people when the local level of unemployment is high (Warr, 1984).

(Based on Argyle, 1989)

As well as depression and loss of self-esteem, other mental states associated with unemployment include anxiety, negative affect, self-reported cognitive difficulties, worry about the future, demoralisation and resignation (Dooley & Prause, 1995).

Box 49.2   Some effects of unemployment

- Unemployment *causes*, rather than results from, poor psychological health.

- The risk of a person's mental health deteriorating in at least some ways increases compared with an otherwise similar person who does not become unemployed.

- Unemployment puts at risk the mental health of unemployed people and their spouses, children and members of the extended family.

- The implicit assumption that the transition from unemployment to re-employment is symmetrical to that from employment to unemployment is not fully warranted, since some effects of unemployment may persist into the period of re-employment.

- The anticipation of unemployment is at least as distressing as its actual experience.

- Job insecurity is associated with experienced powerlessness and impaired mental health.

- Indicators of psychological stress are associated with measures of both subjective and objective financial stress.

(Based on Fryer, 1992; 1995)

Although unemployment is clearly associated with impaired mental health, Argyle's claim that physical health suffers as a result of unemployment is not as strongly supported. For example, Warr (1984) found that whilst 27 per cent of unemployed men said that their physical health had deteriorated, 11 per cent reported that it had *improved* (due to less work strain and more relaxation and exercise). However, in a ten-year census study of British men who had lost their jobs in 1971, Moser *et al.* (1984) showed that the death rate was 36 per cent higher than for the whole population of males aged between 15 and 64. When social class and age were taken into account, the figure was 21 per cent.

The data also indicated that unemployed men's wives were 20 per cent more likely to die prematurely, a risk that was greater in the second half of the decade in which the study was conducted.

Retirement

Unlike unemployment, which is a sudden and generally unanticipated loss of work, retirement is anticipated and many people experience it without undue psychological upheaval (Raphael, 1984). It is, then, both inevitable and often acceptable. However, it may be unacceptable to people when, for example, they see themselves as being 'too young' to stop work.

One consequence of retirement is the loss of everyday, ritualised, patterns of behaviour which contribute to the very fabric of our existence. Whilst the early weeks of retirement may be celebrated, emptiness is experienced for a time following retirement. As the months go by, frustration and a sense of 'uselessness' can set in, and this may produce an angry and irritable response to the world.

Figure 49.1   Victor Meldrew (star of BBC TV's *One Foot in the Grave*) seems to personify the sense of frustration and uselessness that often sets in, especially for men, after the 'honeymoon period' of retirement

Retirement also leads to change. For example, many couples find themselves spending an increased amount of time together. Some people compound the negative aspects of retirement by moving to a new house, which involves loss of familiar surroundings, friendships and neighbourhood networks. The transition from an economically productive to an unproductive role can also be stressful. All of these factors mean that psychological adjustment to retirement is necessary, and those who are able to develop lifestyles that retain continuity with the past, and meet their long-term needs, adjust well.

Retirement is a *process* and *social role* which unfolds through a series of six phases, each of which requires an adjustment to be made (Atchley, 1982, 1985). The phases do not correspond with any particular chronological ages, occur in no fixed order, and not all of them are necessarily experienced by everyone.

Box 49.3   The six phases in the process of retirement

1 **Pre-retirement phase:** (i) In the *remote* sub-phase, retirement is seen as being in a reasonably distant future; (ii) the *near* sub-phase may be initiated by the retirement of older friends and colleagues and there may be much anxiety about lifestyle changes, especially financial ones.

2 **Honeymoon phase (immediate post-retirement):** This phase typically involves euphoria, partly due to new-found freedom, and is often a busy period (which may be long or short).

3 **Disenchantment phase:** This involves a slowing down after the honeymoon phase, with feelings of being let down and even depression. The degree of disenchantment is related to declining health and finances. Eagerly anticipated post-retirement activities (e.g. travel) may have lost their original appeal. Disenchantment may be produced by unrealistic pre-retirement fantasies or inadequate preparation for retirement.

4 **Reorientation phase:** This is a time to develop a more realistic view of life alternatives, and may involve exploring new avenues of involvement, sometimes with the help of community groups (e.g. special voluntary or paid jobs for the retired). This helps to decrease feelings of role loss and is a means of achieving self-actualisation (see Chapters 1 and 17).

5 **Stability phase:** This involves the establishment of criteria for making choices, allowing people to deal with life in a fairly comfortable and orderly way. They know what's expected of them, what their strengths and weaknesses are, allowing mastery of the retirement role.

6 **Termination phase:** Illness and disability usually make housework and self-care difficult or impossible, leading to the assumption of a sick or disabled (as opposed to retirement) role.

(From Gross, 1996, and based on Atchley, 1982, and Atchley & Robinson, 1982)

People who retire *voluntarily* seem to have little or no difficulty in adjusting. However, those who retire because they have reached a compulsory age tend to be dissatisfied at first, although eventually they adapt. The least satisfied are those whose health is poor when they retire (which may have caused their retirement), although health often improves following retirement.

Bromley (1988) believes that it is the *transition* between employment and retirement that causes adjustment problems. Those who are most satisfied in retirement tend to be scientists, writers and other academics, who simply carry on working with little loss of continuity from very satisfying jobs. Those who discover satisfying leisure activities, with at least some of the characteristics of work, also adjust well.

Some people decide to retire before their job requires them to. This means that retirement cannot be seen as a necessarily sudden and enforced dislocation of a working life, inevitably causing feelings of rejection and leading to physical and psychological ill health. Even after 60 or 65, many people do not actively seek paid work, although the lower level of income in retirement constitutes a strong incentive to work. A woman not only has to adjust to her own retirement, but may also have to adjust to her husband's retirement or to widowhood. However, since home and family still occupy a major part of a working woman's time, she is likely to see retirement as less of a lifestyle change than are men.

Clearly, retirement and unemployment are similar in some respects and different in others. According to Campbell (1981), retirement is an accepted and 'honourable' social status, whereas unemployment is not. Moreover, retirement is seen as a proper reward for a hard life's work, whilst unemployment has the implication of failure, being unwanted, and a 'scrounger' who is 'living on state charity'. Most men might see retirement as a rather benign condition of life, but being unemployed is a disturbing and often degrading experience.

Marriage and divorce

Since over 90 per cent of adults marry at least once, marriage is an example of a normative age-graded influence (see page 427). Marriage is an important transition for many young adults, because it involves a lasting personal commitment to another person, financial responsibilities and, perhaps, family responsibilities. However, it cannot be the *same* type of transition for everyone. In some cultures, for example, people have little choice as to who their partners will be (as is the case in *arranged marriages*: see Chapter 55).

Marriage and preparation for marriage can be very stressful. Davies (1956) identified mental disorders occurring for the first time in those who were engaged to be married. Typically, these were anxiety and depression, which usually began in connection with an event that hinged on the marriage date (such as booking the reception). Since the disorders improved when the engagement was broken off or the marriage took place, Davies concluded that it was the *decision* to make the commitment that was important rather than the act of getting married itself.

Box 49.4   Cohabitation

Apparently, couples who live together (or *cohabit*) before marriage are actually *more* likely to divorce later, and be less satisfied with their marriages, than those who marry without having cohabited. Also, about 40 per cent of couples who cohabit do not marry. Whilst this suggests that cohabitation may prevent some divorces, cohabitees who do marry are more likely to divorce. Bee (1994) argues that this is because people who choose to cohabit are *different* from those who choose not to. As a group, cohabitees seem to be more willing to flout tradition in many ways (such as being less religious and disagreeing that one should stay with a marriage partner no matter what). Those who do not cohabit include a large proportion of 'more traditional' people.

It has long been recognised that mortality is affected by marital status. Married people tend to live longer than unmarried people, are happier, healthier and have lower rates of various mental disorders than the single, widowed or divorced (see Chapter 57, page 491). The excessive mortality of the unmarried relative to the married has generally been increasing over the past two to three decades, and it seems that divorced (and widowed) people in their 20s and 30s have particularly high risks of dying compared with people of the same age (Cramer, 1995). Measures of marital adjustment indicate that agreement between partners on various issues (a measure of marital compatibility) is positively correlated with other components of relationship adjustment, such as satisfaction, affection and doing various activities together (Eysenck & Wakefield, 1981: and see Box 57.2 for a discussion of the factors that contribute to marital unhappiness and divorce).

Bee (1994) has argued that the greatest beneficiaries of marriage are men, partly because they are less likely than women to have close confidants outside marriage, and partly because wives provide more emotional warmth and support for husbands than husbands do for wives. Marriage is less obviously psychologically protective for women, not because a confiding and harmonious relationship is any less important for them (indeed, if anything it is more important), but because (a) many marriages do not provide such a relationship and (b) other consequences of marriage differ between the sexes. Although our attitudes towards education and women's careers have changed, Rutter & Rutter (1992), echoing the idea of 'gender-splitting' (see Chapter 48, page 424), have proposed that:

> 'the potential benefits of a harmonious relationship may, for a woman, be counterbalanced by the stresses involved in giving up a job or in being handicapped in a career progression or promotion through having to combine a career and parenthood'.

According to Turnbull (1995), divorce rates are highest during the first five years of marriage and then peak again after couples have been married for 15–25 years. Divorce is a stressor for both men and women, since it involves the loss of one's major attachment figure and source of emotional support. However, men appear to experience more stress than women. Also, divorce can have serious effects on the psychological adjustment of children whose parents are separating (for example, Richards, 1995: see Chapter 39).

According to Woollett & Fuller (cited in Cooper, 1996b), mothers who have been through a divorce often report experiencing a sense of achievement in their day-to-day activities and a feeling of 'a job well done'. This is because they use their experiences of divorce in a positive way to 'galvanise' them into taking charge of their lives. According to Woollett:

> 'when the marriage breaks down, the mother is thrown into all sorts of things that are unfamiliar. There are new areas, new decisions, and she is forced to cope'.

However, Lewis (cited in Cooper, 1996b) argues that:

> 'we must be careful about thinking about the positive changes [divorced women report] because we are always comparing a positive change against the negative feeling that went before. The positive is only relative'.

430

Parenthood

For most people, parenthood and child-rearing represent key transitions. According to Bee (1994), 90 per cent of adults will become parents, mostly in their 20s and 30s. Parenthood, however, varies in meaning and impact more than any other life transition. It may occur at any time from adolescence to middle age, and for some men, may even occur in late adulthood! Parenthood may also be planned or unplanned, wanted or unwanted, and there are many motives for having children.

Box 49.5   The variety of parenthood

Traditionally, parenthood is the domain of the married couple. However, it may involve a single woman, a homosexual couple, a cohabiting couple or couples who adopt or foster children. Since the 1950s, there has been a greater acceptability of sexuality among young people, and this has been accompanied by a marked rise in the number of teenage pregnancies. Equally, though, the increasing importance of work careers for women has also led to more and more couples *postponing* starting a family so that the woman can become better established in her career (see Chapter 48, page 424). As a result of this, there is a new class of middle-aged parents with young children (Turnbull, 1995).

Parenthood brings with it several psychological adaptations. For example, many women worry that their babies may be abnormal, and about the changes in their bodies and how they will cope with parenthood. Another concern is how the relationship with the husband or partner will be affected. Certainly, pregnancy brings many couples closer together, but most men take longer than women to become emotionally involved in the pregnancy, and some men feel left out. This feeling of exclusion may continue after the baby is born, as the mother becomes preoccupied with it.

Marital satisfaction tends to be highest before children arrive. It then drops and remains relatively low as long as there are dependent children in the home. Finally, it rises again during the 'post-parental' and retirement stages (see Chapter 57, pages 492–493). For new parents, the roles of parent and spouse are at least partially incompatible. New parents report having less time for each other, whether it be conversing, having sex, being affectionate or carrying out routine chores that used to be done together (Bee, 1994).

Parents are, of course, attachment figures for their dependent children. Unlike the relationship with a partner, the relationship with a child is *asymmetrical*. This new form of

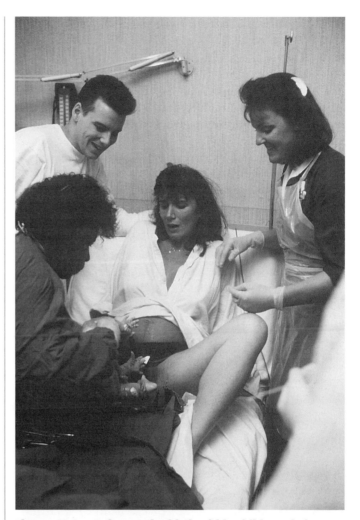

Figure 49.2   Being at the birth of his child can help to counteract a father's feelings of being excluded during the pregnancy – and afterwards. It can also help him to form an emotional bond with the baby

responsibility can be very stressful and has implications for how parents adapt to these new role demands and the quality of their interactions with the child (Durkin, 1995). Unhappy couples sometimes stay together not 'just for the kids' sake', but because the parental role has sufficient meaning and value for each partner to outweigh the dissatisfaction with their marriage (Levinson *et al.*, 1978).

Regarding *empty-nest distress* (see Chapter 48, page 423), most parents do not find their children's departure from home a distressing time (Durkin, 1995). Indeed, many report that the end of child-rearing responsibilities is a 'liberating experience', and they welcome new opportunities for a closer relationship with their partner, personal fulfilment through work, a return to education and so on. The extent to which women report empty-nest distress may be cohort-related, that is, it may be more typical of women who reached maturity during historical periods when traditional roles were stressed (Durkin, 1995). The *crowded nest* (Datan *et al.*, 1987) can, however, be a source of stress. This occurs when grown-up children opt *not* to leave home, which defies the demands of the 'social clock' established by preceding generations. Parents find it difficult to adjust to 'adult children' living at home, especially if the parents themselves are still doing much of the material providing.

Bereavement

The older we become, the more likely it is that we will suffer the loss, through death, of loved ones, parents, husbands or wives, siblings, friends and even our children. We refer to such losses as *bereavement*. The psychological and bodily reactions that occur in people who suffer bereavement are called *grief*. The 'observable expression of grief' (Parkes & Weiss, 1983) is called *mourning*, although mourning is often used to refer to the social conventions surrounding death such as funerals, and wearing dark clothes.

Box 49.6   The three phases of 'griefwork'

Engel (1962) sees *griefwork* (the process of mourning through which a bereaved person adjusts to a loss) as comprising three stages or phases.

- **Disbelief and shock:** This can last for a few days and involves the refusal to accept the truth of what has happened.

- **Developing awareness:** This is the gradual realisation and acknowledgement of what has happened. It is often accompanied by feelings of guilt, apathy, exhaustion and anger.

- **Resolution:** The bereaved individual views the situation realistically, begins to cope without the deceased, establishes a new identity and comes to accept fully what has happened. This phase marks the completion of 'griefwork'.

(Based on Engel, 1962)

Although researchers differ over the details of the stages or phases of the grieving process, it is widely agreed that grief follows some sort of natural progression which must be experienced if healthy adjustment to the loss is to be achieved. However, instead of stages or phases, some researchers prefer to talk about the *components* of grief. Ramsay & de Groot (1977), for example, have identified nine components, some of which occur early and some late in the grieving process.

Box 49.7   Ramsay and de Groot's nine components of grief

1 **Shock:** Usually the first response, most often described as a feeling of 'numbness', and can also include pain, calm, apathy, depersonalisation and derealisation. It is as if the feelings are so strong that they are 'turned off'. This can last from a few seconds to several weeks.

2 **Disorganisation:** The inability to do the simplest thing or, alternatively, might involve organising the entire funeral and then collapsing.

3 **Denial:** Behaving as if the deceased were still alive, a defence against feeling too much pain. It is usually an early feature of grief but one that can recur at any time. A common form of denial is searching behaviour (e.g. waiting for the deceased to come home, or having hallucinations of them).

4 **Depression:** Emerges as the denial breaks down but can occur, usually less frequently and intensely, at any point during the grieving process. It can consist of either 'desolate pining' (a yearning and longing, an emptiness 'interspersed with waves of intense psychic pain') or 'despair' (feelings of helplessness, the blackness of the realisation of powerlessness to bring back the dead).

5 **Guilt:** Can be both real and imagined, for actual neglect of the deceased when they were alive, or for angry thoughts and feelings.

6 **Anxiety:** Can involve fear of losing control of one's feelings, of going mad or more general apprehension about the future (changed roles, increased responsibilities, financial worries, and so on).

7 **Aggression:** Can take the form of irritability towards family and friends, outbursts of anger towards God or fate, doctors and nurses, the clergy or even the person who has died.

8 **Resolution:** An emerging acceptance of the death, a 'taking leave of the dead and acceptance that life must go on'.

9 **Reintegration:** Putting acceptance into practice by reorganising one's life in which the deceased has no place. However, pining and despair may reappear on anniversaries, birthdays, and so on.

(Based on Gross, 1996)

Whether everyone experiences all the components identified by Ramsay and de Groot is questionable, and there are wide individual differences in grieving patterns. Grief is not a simple, universal process through which we all go (Stroebe *et al.*, 1993).

Normal and abnormal grieving

Distinguishing normal from pathological grief is difficult. Parkes & Weiss (1983) identify prolonged, incapacitating grief (*chronic* grief) as the most common variant of the usual pattern of grieving. Hinton (1975) identifies three other abnormal patterns. The first is an exaggeration of the *numbness* associated with the shock of the loss. The second is the 'shading' of some of the more immediate responses into *neurotic forms of emotional distress*. These include fears of being alone, enclosed spaces, of one's own death, and feelings of depersonalisation (a sense of being unreal or unfamiliar to oneself: see Chapter 68). The third pattern is the appearance of *physical symptoms*. Sometimes these accompany, and sometimes overshadow, the emotional disturbance. Such symptoms include fatigue, insomnia, loss of appetite and weight, headaches and palpitations.

According to Stroebe *et al.* (1993), both widows and widowers have a greater risk of suffering illness and dying following the death of a spouse than married people of a similar age. Parkes *et al.* (1969) see this risk as being largely confined to the first six months after the bereavement and identify *self-neglect*, *suicide* and *cardiac disease* (a 'broken heart') as the important factors. In widowers, death sometimes occurs through a disease similar to that experienced by the wife.

Box 49.8   Recovery from bereavement or adaptation to it?

Lieberman (1993) has criticised traditional bereavement research for its underlying assumption that bereavement is a stressor that upsets a person's equilibrium and requires a return to a normal and balanced state. Recovery is not a simple 'return to baseline' level of functioning (Weiss, 1993). Both Lieberman and Weiss see 'adaptation' to bereavement as being a better term than 'recovery' from bereavement. Whilst the majority of bereaved people stop grieving intensely after a year or two, a minority continue to do so for longer, and aspects of grief may never end for some otherwise normally adjusted and bereaved individuals. For Stroebe *et al.* (1993):

'if there has been a strong attachment to a lost loved one, emotional involvement is likely to continue, even for a lifetime'.

Adjustment is more difficult when a death is 'off time', as is the case in sudden accidents (Lopata, 1988).

Coming to terms with death

Most adolescents and young adults rarely think about their own deaths, since death is an event far removed in time. Some people even engage in an *illusion of immortality*, and completely avoid confronting the fact that their own days are numbered (Barrow & Smith, 1979). As people age, however, so their thoughts become increasingly preoccupied with death. Our attitude towards death is ambivalent: sometimes we shut it out and deny it, and sometimes we desperately want to talk about it and share our fears of the unknown. Kübler-Ross (1969) uses the term *anticipatory grief* to describe how the terminally ill come to terms with their own imminent death. One common feature of this is *reminiscing*. This may be a valuable way of 'sorting out' the past and present (Butler, 1963). The recognition of impending death allows us to re-examine old conflicts, consider how we have treated others, and come to some conclusion about our lives. This *life review* may result in a new sense of accomplishment, satisfaction and peace (and corresponds to Erikson's *ego-integrity*: see Chapter 50, page 441).

Figure 49.3   Looking through old photographs represents a form of reminiscing, part of the life review in which the elderly person tries to come to terms with his/her death

Coming to terms with our own deaths is a crucial *task* of life which Peck (1968) calls *ego-transcendence* versus *ego-preoccupation*. We may review our lives privately (or internally), or we may share our memories and reflections with others. By helping us to organise a final perspective on our lives for ourselves, and leaving records that will live on with others after we have died, sharing serves a double purpose.

Conclusions

Several critical life (or marker) events or processes have been identified. These include unemployment, retirement, marriage, divorce, parenthood and bereavement. Psychological research has told us much about their effects and how they help us understand adjustment to adulthood.

Summary

■ Whilst marriage and parenting, and retirement, tend to occur in early and late adulthood respectively (**normative, age-graded influences**), bereavement and unemployment can occur at any age (**non-normative influences**). These are also called **marker events** or **critical life events**.

■ **Unemployment** produces both physical and psychological effects including depression. The long-term unemployed seem to develop a sense of **learned helplessness**. This contributes to **suicide**, which is far more common among the unemployed.

■ Unemployment is also associated with a **loss of self-esteem**. Distress is increased amongst those most committed to their jobs, who lack social support, whose level of activity is low and who perceive the cause of unemployment as personal incompetence.

■ Unemployment can cause anxiety, negative affect, self-reported cognitive difficulties, worry about the future, demoralisation, resignation and powerlessness. Evidence regarding physical health is more mixed than that for mental health.

■ **Retirement** is an inevitable, often acceptable, anticipated loss of work. It is a **process** and **social role** which proceeds through six phases, each requiring a different adjustment.

■ People who retire **voluntarily** have little or no difficulty in adjusting, compared with those who retire because they have reached retirement age or whose health is poor. It is the **transition** between employment and retirement that causes adjustment problems.

■ **Married people** tend to live longer, and are happier, healthier and have lower rates of mental disorder than unmarried people. Men benefit most from marriage, partly because they are less likely than women to have close confidants outside marriage, and partly because wives provide more emotional warmth and support for their husbands than vice versa. The potential benefits of marriage for women may be counterbalanced by the stresses involved in having to combine parenthood with a career.

■ Couples who **cohabit** before marriage are more likely to divorce later or be dissatisfied with their marriages than those who don't cohabit.

■ **Parenthood** has greater variability in meaning and impact than any other life transition. Whilst pregnancy can bring couples closer together, men can feel excluded, especially after their babies are born, thus pulling the parents further apart.

■ Marital satisfaction tends to peak before children arrive, then drops and remains relatively low until the 'post-parental' and retirement stages, when it rises again. There is little support for **empty-nest distress**. The **crowded nest** is likely to be more stressful.

■ As we grow older, we are more likely to suffer **bereavement**. Griefwork comprises three stages: disbelief and shock, developing awareness and resolution. Ramsay and de Groot prefer to talk about the **components** of grief, which do not occur in a fixed order and which are not necessarily experienced by everyone. There are wide individual differences in grieving patterns.

■ Perhaps the commonest form of pathological grief is **chronic grief**. Others include an exaggeration of the **numbness** associated with the shock of the loss, **neurotic forms of emotional distress** and **physical symptoms**. Both widows and widowers are more likely to suffer illness and die compared with married people of a similar age.

■ A common feature of **anticipatory grief** is reminiscing, a valuable way of sorting out our lives and relationships. This **life review** may produce a new sense of achievement, satisfaction and peace (corresponding to Erikson's **ego-integrity**).

50

ADJUSTMENT TO LATE ADULTHOOD

Introduction and overview

'Growing up' is normally taken to be something desirable and almost an end in itself. By contrast, 'growing old' has traditionally had negative connotations. The negative view of ageing is based on the *decrement model*, which sees ageing as a process of decay or decline in physical and mental health, intellectual abilities and social relationships.

An alternative to the decrement model is the *personal growth model*, which stresses the potential advantages of late adulthood or 'old age', and this much more positive attitude is how ageing has been studied within the lifespan approach. Kalish (1982), for example, emphasises the increase in leisure time, the reduction in many day-to-day responsibilities, and the ability to pay attention only to matters of high priority among the elderly. Older people respond to the reality of a limited and finite future by ignoring many of life's inconsequential details, and instead channel their energies into what is really important.

This chapter considers some of the theories and research concerned with the adjustment to late adulthood or old age. It begins by looking at what is meant by the term 'old' and at some of the physical and psychological changes that occur in late adulthood.

The meaning of 'old'

People today are living longer and retaining their health better than any previous generation (Baltes & Baltes, 1993). The proportion of older people in the British population has increased dramatically in recent years. In 1961, two per cent of the population (one million people) were aged 80 or over. In 1991, this figure had risen to four per cent (2.2 million). The number of centenarians has risen from 271 (in 1951), to 1185 (1971), to 4400 (1991). In 1997, the number stood at 8000 with projections of 12,000 (2001) and 30,000 (2030) (McCrystal, 1997). Because of this *demographic imperative* (Swensen, 1983), developmental psychologists have become increasingly interested in our older years. But what do we mean by 'old'? Kastenbaum's (1979) 'The ages of me' questionnaire assesses how people see themselves at the present moment in relation to their age.

Box 50.1   Kastenbaum's 'Ages of me' questionnaire

- My *chronological* age is my actual or official age, dated from my time of birth. My chronological age is ...

- My *biological* age refers to the state of my face and body. In other people's eyes, I *look* as though I am about ... years of age. In my own eyes, I judge my body to be like that of a person of about ... years of age.

- My *subjective* age is indicated by how I feel. Deep down inside, I really feel like a person of about ... years of age.

- My *functional* age, which is closely related to my *social* age, refers to the kind of life I lead, what I am able to do, the status I believe I have, whether I work, have dependent children and live in my own home. My thoughts and interests are like those of a person of about ... years of age, and my position in society is like that of a person of about ... years of age.

(Adapted from Kastenbaum, 1979)

(a)   (b)   (c)

Figure 50.1   Whilst (c) might depict someone's chronological age, (a) might correspond to his biological age and (b) might represent his subjective age

Few people, irrespective of their chronological age, describe themselves *consistently*. Thus, we often give different responses to the ages identified by Kastenbaum. For example, people in their 20s and above usually describe themselves as feeling younger than their chronological ages, and this is also true for many people in their 70s and 80s. People also prefer to 'be younger', that is, we generally consider ourselves to be *too* old. Very few people over 20 say they want to be older.

It seems, then, that knowing a person's chronological age isn't particularly helpful in allowing us to say anything meaningful about the sort of life that person leads. However, one of the dangerous aspects of *ageism* is that chronological age assumed to be an accurate indicator of all the other ages. We tend to infer that people over 60 have certain characteristics which, taken together, make up the decrement model (illustrated by expressions like 'past it' and 'over the hill'). Stereotypes of the elderly are more deeply entrenched than (mis)conceptions of gender differences. It is therefore not surprising that people are overwhelmingly unenthusiastic about becoming 'old' (Stuart-Hamilton, 1997). By recognising the different 'ages of me', the idea of ageing as decay should be dispelled and lead to a more analytical and positive approach to old age (cf. Kalish, 1982).

Box 50.2   A decade-by-decade description of 'the elderly'

The young old (60–69): This period marks a major transition. Most adults must adapt to new role structures in an effort to cope with the losses and gains of the decade. Income is reduced due to retirement. Friends and colleagues start to disappear. Although physical strength wanes somewhat, a great many 'young old' have surplus energy and seek out new and different activities.

The middle-aged old (70–79): This is often marked by loss or illness. Friends and family may die. The middle-aged old must also cope with reduced participation in formal organisations which can lead to restlessness and irritability. Their own health problems become more severe. The major developmental task is to maintain the personality re-integration achieved in the previous decade.

The old old (80–89): The old old show increased difficulty in adapting to and interacting with their surroundings. They need help in maintaining social and cultural contacts.

The very old old (90–99): Although health problems become more acute, the very old old can successfully alter their activities to make the most of what they have. The major advantage of old age is freedom from responsibilities. If previous crises have been resolved

satisfactorily, this decade may be joyful, serene and fulfilling.

(Based on Burnside *et al.*, 1979, and Craig, 1992)

The aged are not one cohesive group (Craig, 1992). Rather, they are a collection of sub-groups, each of which has unique problems and capabilities, but all of whom share to some degree the age-related difficulties of reduced income, failing health and the loss of loved ones. For Craig, however:

'having a problem is not the same as being a problem, and the all-too-popular view of those over age 65 as needy, non-productive, and unhappy needs revision'.

Similarly, Dietch (1995) has commented that:

'life's final stage is surrounded by more myths, stereotypes and misinformation than any other developmental phase'.

Exactly why there is an upper limit for how long humans can live is not known. According to *genetic clock* or *programmed theory*, ageing is built into every organism through a genetic code that informs cells when to stop working. This is supported by the finding that rare human conditions involving accelerated ageing are the result of defective genes, and also by the observation that identical twins have very similar life-spans. *Accumulated damages theory*, by contrast, sees ageing as a consequence of damage resulting from the wear-and-tear of living. Like a machine, a body eventually wears out as a result of accumulated damage from continued, non-stop use. As we grow older, our cells lose the ability to replace or repair damaged components and eventually cease to function.

Physical and psychological changes in old age

PHYSICAL CHANGES
Bee & Mitchell (1980) have summarised the major physical changes that occur in old age.

Box 50.3   Physical changes in old age

Smaller: Connective tissues holding the long bones together become compressed and flattened. As a result, height tends to decrease. Changes in calcium metabolism lead to a smaller total body weight than in younger people. Muscle mass is reduced, and some organs (e.g. the bladder) get smaller.

Slower: Since nerve impulses travel more slowly to and from the brain, reaction time is slower. Older people

---

recover more slowly under stressful conditions since the immune system functions less effectively. Fractures take longer to heal, and the renewal of liver and skin cells also slows down.

Weaker: Because of gradual changes in calcium metabolism, bones become brittle and break more easily. Muscles also become weaker. In general, the senses become less efficient.

Lesser: The gradual lessening of elastic tissue in the skin causes wrinkling and sagging. The ear drum and lens of the eye lose some elasticity, producing problems in hearing and seeing. Blood vessels also become less elastic which can give rise to circulatory problems.

Fewer: Body hair becomes more sparse, and the number of teeth and taste buds is reduced (hence food does not taste as good to older people).

(Adapted from Bee & Mitchell, 1980)

Many of the declines that occur in old age can be compensated for. Moreover, regular exercise can significantly reduce the deterioration of many bodily functions, since tissue *disuse* accounts for about half the functional decline between the ages of 30 and 70.

PSYCHOLOGICAL CHANGES

It is commonly believed that old age is associated with a decrease in cognitive abilities. Until recently, it was thought that intellectual capacity peaked in the late-teens or early 20s, levelled off, and then began to decline fairly steadily during middle age and more rapidly in old age. The evidence on which this claim was based came from *cross-sectional studies* (studying *different* age groups at the *same* time). However, we cannot draw firm conclusions from such studies, because the age groups compared represent different cohorts who have had different *experiences* (the *cohort effect*). Unless we know how 60-year-olds, say, performed when they were 40 and 20, it is impossible to say whether or not intelligence declines with age.

An alternative methodology is the *longitudinal study* (the *same* people are tested and re-tested at *various* times during their lives). Several studies have produced data contradicting the results of cross-sectional studies, indicating that at least some people retain their intellect well into middle age and beyond (Holahan & Sears, 1995). However, the evidence suggests that there are some age-related changes in different *kinds* of intelligence and *aspects* of memory.

Changes in intelligence

Although psychologists have always disagreed about the definition of intelligence, there is general acceptance that it is *multi-dimensional* (composed of a number of different abilities). *Crystallised intelligence* results from accumulated knowledge, including a knowledge of how to reason, language skills and an understanding of technology. This type of intelligence is linked to education, experience and cultural background, and is measured by tests of general information. *Fluid intelligence* refers to the ability to solve novel and unusual problems (those not previously encountered). It allows us to perceive and draw inferences about relationships among patterns of stimuli and to conceptualise abstract information, which aids problem-solving. Fluid intelligence is measured by tests using novel and unusual problems not based on specific knowledge or any particular previous learning.

Crystallised intelligence *increases* with age, and people tend to continue improving their performance until near the end of their lives (Horn, 1982). Using the *cross-longitudinal* method (in which different groups of people of different ages are followed up over a long period of time), Schaie & Hertzog (1983) reported that fluid intelligence declines for all age groups over time, having peaked between the ages of 20 and 30. The decline of fluid intelligence with age, but the relative constancy (and improvement) of crystallised intelligence is difficult to explain. The tendency to continue to add to our knowledge as we grow older could account for the constancy of crystallised intelligence. The decline in fluid intelligence may be an inevitable part of the ageing process related to the reduced efficiency of neurological functioning. Alternatively, we might be more likely to maintain our crystallised abilities because we exercise them on a regular basis (Denney & Palmer, 1981). In old age, however, we may be less frequently challenged to use our fluid abilities (Cavanaugh, 1995).

Changes in memory

Some aspects of memory appear to decline with age, possibly because we become less effective at processing information (which may underlie cognitive changes in general: Stuart-Hamilton, 1994). On recall tests, older adults *generally* perform more poorly than younger adults. However, the reverse is sometimes true, as shown by Maylor's (1994) study of the performance of older contestants' performance on *Mastermind*. On recognition tests, the differences between younger and older people are less apparent and may even disappear. As far as *everyday memory* is concerned, the evidence indicates that the elderly do have trouble recalling events from their youth and early life (for example, Miller & Morris, 1993).

WOMEN BECOME FORGETFUL WHILE MEN GET GRUMPIER (REPORT ON AGEING)

Figure 50.2   Former Conservative Prime Ministers, Margaret Thatcher and Edward Heath, are well known for their political disagreements. If recent reports on ageing are to be believed, Thatcher will have difficulty remembering them, whilst Heath will remember them with irritation

Significant memory deficits are one feature of *dementia*, the most common form of which is *Alzheimer's disease*. However, over 90 per cent of people above 65 show *little* deterioration (Diamond, 1978). The loss of cortical neurons is minimal in most humans until very late in life, and even in old age, such neurons seem capable of responding to enriched conditions by forming additional functional connections with other neurons. Support for this comes from Rogers *et al.*'s (1990) finding that those who keep mentally active are those who maintain their cognitive abilities. The view that decline is wired into the nervous system has also been challenged by those who believe that *negative cultural stereotypes* of ageing actually *cause* memory decline in the elderly.

Box 50.4   The influence of stereotypes on memory

Levy & Langer (1994) investigated the memory capabilities of hearing Americans, members of the American deaf community and people from mainland China. It was assumed that members of the deaf community were less likely to have been exposed to negative cultural stereotypes. People from mainland China were chosen because of the high esteem in which Chinese society holds its aged members. The older American deaf participants and the Chinese participants performed much better on memory tasks than the older American hearing participants.

Also, younger hearing Americans held less positive views of ageing than any of the other groups. Amongst the older participants, attitudes towards ageing and memory performance were positively correlated. Levy and Langer believe that negative stereotypes about ageing may become *self-fulfilling prophecies*, in which low expectations mean that people are less likely to engage in activities that will help them maintain their memory abilities.

The subliminal (below conscious awareness) presentation of negative self-stereotypes (e.g. 'Because of my age I am forgetful') tended to worsen memory performance, whilst positive self-stereotypes (e.g. 'Because of my age I have acquired wisdom) tended to improve it (Levy, 1996). Levy found no such effect with young participants, for whom stereotypes of ageing are less salient.

Social changes in old age

SOCIAL DISENGAGEMENT THEORY

Cumming & Henry (1961) attempted to describe what happens to us socially when we grow old. *Social disengagement theory* was based on a five-year study of 275 50–90-year-olds in Kansas City, USA. Bromley (1988) has defined disengagement as:

'a systematic reduction in certain kinds of social interaction. In its simplest and crudest form, the theory of disengagement states that diminishing psychological and biological capacities of people in later life necessitates a severance of the relationships they have with younger people in the central activities of society, and the replacement of these older individuals by younger people. In this way, society renews itself and the elderly are free to die'.

According to Cumming (1975), social disengagement is the withdrawal of society from the individual (through compulsory retirement, children growing up and leaving home, the death of a spouse and so on) and the withdrawal from society of the individual (through reduced social activities and a more solitary life). Hence, the withdrawal is mutual.

Cumming sees disengagement as having three aspects. *Shrinkage of life space* refers to the fact that as we age, we tend to interact with fewer others, and begin to occupy fewer roles. *Increased individuality* means that in the roles that remain, older people are much less governed by strict rules and expectations. Finally, the healthy, older adult actively disengages from roles and relationships and turns increasingly inward and away from interactions with others, as if preparing for death (*acceptance – even embrace – of these changes*). Withdrawal is seen as the most appropriate and successful way to age.

An evaluation of social disengagement theory

Bee (1994) sees Cumming's first two aspects as being beyond dispute. However, the third is more controversial because of its view of disengagement as a natural and *inevitable* process rather than an imposed one, and because it may not accurately describe and account for what happens. Bromley (1988) has offered three main criticisms of social disengagement theory. First, such a view of ageing encourages a policy of segregation, even indifference, to the elderly, and the very destructive belief that old age has no value (the *practical* criticism). Second, disengagement is not a true theory, but more a *proto-theory* (a collection of loosely related assumptions and arguments: the *theoretical* criticism). The most serious criticism is *empirical* and concerns whether *everyone* actually does disengage.

Box 50.5   Do the elderly disengage?

Although retirement brings losses in social relationships (as when children leave home or a spouse dies), relationships with others (in particular grandchildren, neighbours and friends) go some way to replacing them. In later life, the *quality* of activities and relationships may become more important than their *quantity*. As a result, older people are more likely to seek engagement and activity.

Evidence supporting this came from Havighurst *et al.*'s (1968) follow-up of about half the sample originally studied by Cumming & Henry (1961). Although increasing age was accompanied by increasing disengagement, at least some of those studied remained active and engaged. Amongst the active and engaged, there were high levels of contentment, and the most active were the happiest. The fact that those who disengage the least are the happiest, have the highest morale and live the longest, contradicts social disengagement theory's view that the tendency to withdraw from mainstream society is natural and an inherent part of the ageing process (Bee, 1994). Whilst some people do choose to lead socially isolated lives and find contentment in them, such disengagement does not appear to be necessary for overall mental health in old age.

Bromley (1988) believes that it is generally more accurate to speak of 'industrial' (rather than 'social') disengagement and increased socio-economic dependence. In this way, the origins and circumstances of retirement are kept in focus. For example, many of the past social conditions forcing adults into restricted environments have changed (Turner & Helms, 1989). Improved health care, earlier retirement age and higher educational levels have opened up new areas of pursuit for the elderly and made more active life-styles possible. In Kermis' (1984) view:

'disengagement represents only one of many possible paths of ageing. It has no blanket application to all people'.

Disengagement may also be *cohort specific*, that is, it may have been adaptive to withdraw from an ageist society in the 1950s, but not in a more enlightened culture. Moreover, an individual rarely disengages from *all* roles to the same degree. Psychological disengagement may not, therefore, coincide with disengagement from social roles. The disposition to disengage is a *personality dimension* as well as a characteristic of ageing (Bromley, 1988). Havighurst *et al.*'s (1968) follow-up study identified several different personality types. These included *reorganisers*, who were involved in a wide range of activities and reorganised their lives to substitute for lost activities, and the *disengaged*, who voluntarily moved away from role commitments. Consistent with disengagement theory, the disengaged reported low levels of activity but high 'life satisfaction'.

ACTIVITY (OR RE-ENGAGEMENT) THEORY

The major alternative to disengagement theory is *activity (or re-engagement) theory* (Havighurst, 1964; Maddox, 1964). Activity theory says that except for inevitable changes in biology and health, older people are the same as middle-aged people, with essentially the same psychological and social needs. Decreased social interaction in old age is the result of the withdrawal by society from the ageing person and happens against the wishes of most elderly people. The withdrawal is *not* mutual.

Optimal ageing involves staying active and managing to resist the 'shrinkage' of the social world. This can be achieved by maintaining the activities of middle age for as long as possible, and then finding substitutes for work or retirement and for spouses and friends upon their death. It is important for older adults to maintain their *role counts* (to ensure they always have several different roles to play).

An evaluation of activity theory

There are many exceptions to the 'rule' that the greater the level of activity, the greater the level of satisfaction. Some elderly people seem satisfied with disengagement (see above). This suggests that activity theory *alone* cannot explain successful ageing. People will select a style of ageing best suited to their personality and past experience or lifestyle, and there is no single way to age successfully (Neugarten & Neugarten, 1987). Some people may develop new interests or pursue in earnest those they did not have time enough for during their working lives. Others will be developing relationships with grandchildren or even great-grandchildren, remarrying or perhaps getting married for the first time. Yet others will go on working part time or in a voluntary capacity in their local community.

As a counterbalance to disengagement theory, activity theory sees the natural tendency of most elderly people as associating with others, particularly in group and community affairs, although this is often blocked by present-day retirement practices. Whilst disengagement enables or obliges older people to relinquish certain roles (namely those they cannot adequately fulfil), activity or re-engagement prevents the consequences of disengagement from going too far in the direction of isolation, apathy and inaction.

Figure 50.3   The elderly couple above seem to fit the stereotype of the withdrawn, isolated, 'disengaged' person, whilst the couple below illustrate an alternative, but less common, stereotype, of the person who remains as active in old age as when he/she was middle-aged

An evaluation of theories of ageing

Both disengagement and activity theories refer to a legitimate process through which some people come to terms with the many changes that accompany ageing (they are *options*: Hayslip & Panek, 1989). Just as disengagement

may be involuntary (as in the case of poor health), so we may face involuntarily high levels of activity (as in looking after grandchildren). Both disengagement and activity may, therefore, be equally maladaptive. Quite possibly, disengagement theory actually *under*estimates, and activity theory *over*estimates, the degree of control people have over the 'reconstruction' of their lives. Additionally, both theories see ageing as essentially the same for all people. For Turner & Helms (1989), however:

'personality is the pivotal factor in determining whether an individual will age successfully, and activity and disengagement theories alone are inadequate to explain successful ageing'.

Increasingly, theorists see development as a lifespan phenomenon, and therefore adjustments to old age or late adulthood are an extension of personality styles (Baltes, 1987). Theoretical emphasis is therefore placed on the *continuity* between earlier and later phases of life. Satisfaction, morale and adaptations in later life generally appear to be closely related to a person's life-long personality style and general way of dealing with stress and change (Reedy, 1983). As Reedy notes:

'In this sense, the past is the prologue to the future. While the personality changes somewhat in response to various life events and changes, it generally remains stable throughout all of adult life'.

SOCIAL EXCHANGE THEORY

Activity theory oversimplifies the issues involved in adjusting to late adulthood and has received little empirical support. As has been seen, activity can decline without seriously affecting morale. Indeed, a more leisurely lifestyle, with fewer responsibilities, can be regarded as one of the *rewards* of old age. This view is at the centre of *social exchange theory*. According to Dyson (1980), both disengagement and activity theories fail to take sufficient account of the physical and economic factors which might limit people's choices about how they age. Rather than accounting for how most people do age, both theories tell us what the elderly *should* be doing and are therefore *prescriptive*. Disengagement and activity theories also involve *value judgements* about what it is to age successfully (Hayslip & Panek, 1989).

For Dyson, a more useful approach is to see the process of adjusting to ageing in general, and retirement in particular, as a sort of *contract* between the individual and society. We give up our roles as economically active members of society when we retire, but in *exchange* we receive increased leisure time, take on fewer responsibilities and so on (Dowd, 1975). Although the contract is largely unwritten and not enforceable, most people will probably conform to the expectations about being elderly which are built into social institutions and stereotypes.

PSYCHOSOCIAL THEORY

Another alternative to disengagement and activity theories is Erikson's *psychosocial theory* (see Chapter 48). A more valid and useful way of looking at what all elderly people have in common might be to examine the importance of old age as a stage of development, albeit the last (which is where its importance lies). This brings us back to the personal growth model (see page 435), which stresses the advantages and positive aspects of ageing.

In old age, there is a conflict between *ego-integrity* (the positive force) and *despair* (the negative force). The task is to end this stage, and hence life, with greater ego-integrity than despair. This achievement represents successful ageing. However, as with the other psychosocial stages, we cannot avoid the conflict which occurs as a result of inevitable biological, psychological and social forces. For Erikson, the important thing is how successfully this is resolved. Therefore, the task of ageing is to take stock of one's life, to look back over it, and assess and evaluate how worthwhile and fulfilling it has been.

Box 50.6   The characteristics of ego-integrity

* Life does have a purpose and makes sense.

* Within the context of our lives as a whole, what happened was somehow inevitable and could only have happened when and how it did.

* A belief that all of life's experiences offer something of value. We can learn from everything that happens to us. Looking back, we can see how we have grown psychologically as a result of life's ups and downs, triumphs and failures, calms and crises.

* Seeing our parents in a new light and being able to understand them better because we have lived through our own adulthood and have probably raised children of our own.

* Seeing that what we share with other humans, past, present and future, is the inevitable cycle of birth and death. Whatever the differences (be they historic, cultural, economic and so on), all of us have this much in common. In the light of this, death 'loses its sting'.

Lack or loss of ego-integrity is signified by a fear of death, which is the most conspicuous symptom of despair. In despair, we express the feeling that it is too late to undo the past and put the clock back in order to right wrongs or do what hasn't been done. Life is not a 'rehearsal' and this is the only chance we get.

Conclusions

Several theories concerned with adjustment to late adulthood have been advanced. Of these, social disengagement theory and activity (or re-engagement) theory have attracted a great deal of research interest. Whilst there is some evidence consistent with both theories, neither is a completely satisfactory account, and several factors not considered by the theories appear to contribute to 'successful ageing'.

Summary

■ Whilst 'growing up' has positive connotations, 'growing old' has negative ones, reflecting the **decrement model**. An alternative, more positive view, is the **personal growth model**.

■ The proportion of older people in the British population has increased dramatically and is expected to go on increasing. This **demographic imperative** has made developmental psychologists much more interested in late adulthood.

■ Age can be defined in different ways, specifically **chronological**, **biological**, **subjective** and **functional** (closely related to **social**). Few people, regardless of chronological age, describe themselves **consistently**.

■ Although chronological age tells us little about a person's life-style, one feature of **ageism** is the assumption that chronological age is an accurate indicator of biological, subjective, functional and social ages.

■ Burnside *et al.*'s decade-by-decade description is a way of seeing the aged as a collection of sub-groups, each with its own problems and capabilities. We need to change our stereotypes of the elderly as being needy, non-productive and unhappy.

■ According to **genetic clock/programmed theory**, ageing is genetically built into every organism, whereas **accumulated damages theory** sees ageing as the result of damage due to wear-and-tear of the body during a person's lifetime. Regular exercise can significantly reduce the deterioration of many bodily functions.

■ The claim that intelligence declines fairly rapidly in old age is based on **cross-sectional studies**, which face the problem of the **cohort effect**. **Longitudinal studies** indicate that some changes in different **kinds** of intelligence appear to be age-related.

■ Whilst **crystallised intelligence** increases with age, **fluid intelligence** declines for all age groups over time. This may reflect the inevitable reduction in the efficiency of neurological functioning, although we may be less often challenged to use these abilities in old age.

■ Some aspects of **memory** decline with age, perhaps due to less effective information processing. Older adults **generally** perform more poorly than younger adults on recall tests, but the differences are reduced or may even disappear when recognition tests are used. Loss of cortical neurons is minimal in most humans until very late in life.

■ **Negative cultural stereotypes** of ageing actually **cause** memory decline in the elderly and may become **self-fulfilling prophecies**.

■ **Social disengagement theory** refers to the mutual withdrawal of society and the individual. Its most controversial feature is its claim that the elderly accept and even welcome disengagement and that this is a natural and **inevitable** process.

■ Although there are losses in certain relationships, these are replaced to some extent by new ones. Not only is disengagement just one of many possible ways of ageing, but individuals rarely disengage from **all** roles to the same degree.

■ According to **activity** or **re-engagement theory**, older people are psychologically and socially essentially the same as middle-aged people. The withdrawal of society and the individual is **not** mutual, and optimal ageing involves maintaining the activities of middle age for as long as possible.

■ However, people select a style of ageing that is best suited to their **personality**, past experiences and life-style. Adjustment to old age is increasingly being seen as **continuous** with earlier phases of life.

■ According to **social exchange theory**, there is a mainly unwritten and unenforceable **contract** between the individual and society. This involves giving up our roles as economically active members of society in **exchange** for increased leisure time and fewer responsibilities.

■ Erikson's psychosocial theory is an example of the personal growth model. Old age involves a conflict between **ego-integrity** and **despair**. The task of ageing is to assess and evaluate life's value and meaning. Despair is characterised by a fear of death and a feeling that it is too late to undo the past and right the wrongs.

UNIT 5

Social Psychology

PART 1

Social cognition

THEORIES OF ATTRIBUTION AND BIASES IN THE ATTRIBUTION PROCESS

Introduction and overview

How do we explain our own and other people's behaviour? *Attribution theory* deals with the general principles governing our selection and use of information to arrive at *causal explanations* for behaviour in a variety of situations (or *domains*). *Theories of attribution* draw on attribution theory's principles and predict how people will respond in particular situations (or *life domains*: Fiske & Taylor, 1991).

Rather than being a single body of ideas and research, attribution theory is a collection of diverse theoretical and empirical contributions sharing several common concerns. Six different traditions form attribution theory's backbone (Fiske & Taylor, 1991). These are: Heider's (1958) *'commonsense' psychology*, Jones & Davis's (1965) *correspondent inference theory*, Kelley's (1967, 1972, 1983) *covariation and configuration models*, Schachter's (1964) *cognitive labelling theory*, Bem's (1967, 1972) *self-perception theory*, and Weiner's (1986, 1992) *motivational theory of attribution*.

This chapter critically considers the contributions to this area made by Heider, Jones and Davis, and Kelley. Their models and theories view people as being logical and systematic in their explanations of behaviour. In practice, however, people tend to make attributions quickly, use much less information than the theories and models suggest, and show clear tendencies to offer certain sorts of explanations for certain behaviours (Hewstone & Fincham, 1996). This chapter also examines some of the *biases* in the attribution process and why they occur.

Heider's 'commonsense' psychology

Heider (1958) argued that the starting point for studying how we understand our social world is the 'ordinary' person. Heider posed questions like 'How do people usually think about and infer meaning from what goes on around them?' and 'How do they make sense of their own and other people's behaviours?' These questions relate to what he called *commonsense psychology*. In Heider's view, the 'ordinary' person is a *naïve scientist* who links observable behaviour to unobservable *causes*, and these causes (rather than the behaviour itself) provide the meaning of what people do.

What interested Heider was the fact that members of a culture share certain basic assumptions about behaviour. These assumptions belong to the belief system that forms part of the culture as a whole and distinguishes one culture from another. As Bennett (1993) has observed:

'it is important that we *do* subscribe to a common psychology, since doing this provides an orienting context in which we can understand, and be understood by, others. Imagine a world in which your version of everyday psychology was fundamentally at odds with that of your friends – without a shared 'code' for making sense of behaviour, social life would hardly be possible'.

Heider pointed out that in our culture at least, we explain people's behaviour in terms of *personal* (or *dispositional/internal*) factors (such as ability or effort), and *situational* (or *environmental/external*) factors (such as circumstances or luck). When we observe somebody's behaviour, we are inclined to attribute its cause to one or other of these two general sources.

Although Heider did not formulate his own theory of attribution, he inspired other psychologists to pursue his original ideas. As well as his insight relating to personal and situational factors as causes of behaviour, three other ideas have been particularly influential (Ross & Fletcher, 1985). First, Heider suggested that when we observe others we tend to search for enduring, unchanging, and dispositional characteristics. Second, we distinguish between intentional and unintentional behaviours. Third, we are inclined to attribute behaviours to events (causes) that are present when the outcome is present and absent when the outcome is absent.

Jones and Davis's correspondent inference theory

Suppose you are on a bus and see someone give up his or her seat to an elderly person. If, from this behaviour, you think 'what a kind and unselfish person', you are making what Jones & Davis (1965) call a *correspondent inference*. This is because the disposition you attributed to the person ('kind and unselfish') corresponds to the behaviour itself (giving up a seat for another person is 'kind and unselfish'). However, we do not always attribute behaviour to people's dispositions, and sometimes explain their behaviour by reference to the circumstances or situation in which it occurred. So why do we make correspondent inferences about dispositions in some cases but not others?

Box 51.1   Intentionality

Jones and Davis argue that a precondition for a correspondent inference is the attribution of *intentionality*: the behaviour is deliberate rather than accidental. Two conditions are seen as being necessary for this. First, we have to be confident that the person *knew* the behaviour would have the effects it did, and second that the person had the *ability* to perform that behaviour. Only if we are confident that a behaviour was not accidental can we proceed to try to explain its occurrence in dispositional terms.

Once a behaviour has been judged to be intentional, we then look for a disposition that could have caused it. One way we do this is through the *analysis of non-common effects*. Suppose there are several places you could visit for your holiday. All will be hot and have bars and discos, and all *except one* has hotels offering full board. If you were to choose the place that offers self-catering, it could be inferred that you had a strong preference for being independent and did not wish to be tied to regular meal times.

According to Jones and Davis, the smaller the number of differences between the chosen course of action and those that are not, the more confidently a dispositional attribution can be made. We can be even more confident about the importance of a behaviour's distinctive consequence the more *negative* elements there are involved in the chosen action. For example, if self-catering means having to walk to restaurants and meals are more expensive than at a hotel, your desire for independence would assume even greater importance to someone explaining your behaviour.

Box 51.2   Other factors influencing the likelihood of a dispositional attribution

Free choice: If we know that a person freely chose to behave in a particular way, we usually assume that the behaviour reflects an underlying disposition. However, if we know that a person was pressed to act in that way, behaviour is more likely to be attributed to external causes.

Expectedness and social desirability: Some behaviours are so expected and socially acceptable that they tell us little about a person's dispositions (such as when a politician shakes hands with people and kisses babies). However, unexpected and socially undesirable behaviour is much more informative (Jones *et al.*, 1961). This is largely because when we behave unexpectedly or in a socially undesirable way (such as making jokes and laughing at a funeral), we are more likely to be shunned, ostracised or disapproved of.

Prior expectations: The better we know people, the better placed we are to decide whether their behaviour on a particular occasion is 'typical'. If it is 'atypical' ('she doesn't normally react like that'), we are more likely to dismiss it, play down its significance, or explain it in terms of situational factors.

Whilst there are data consistent with Jones and Davis's theory, several weaknesses in it have been identified. For example, Eiser (1983) has argued that intentions are *not* a precondition for correspondent inferences (see Box 51.1).

For example, when someone is called 'clumsy', that dispositional attribution does not imply that the behaviour was intentional. In Eiser's view, behaviours which are unintended or accidental are beyond the scope of Jones and Davis's theory. Also, whilst behaviour which disconfirms expectations is informative, so sometimes is behaviour which confirms expectations, a good example being behaviour that confirms a stereotype (Hewstone & Fincham, 1996).

Kelley's covariation and configuration models

Jones and Davis's theory continues to attract interest. However, most of the studies supporting it did not measure *causal* attributions (Gilbert, 1995). Inferring a disposition is not the same as inferring a cause and each appears to reflect different underlying processes (Hewstone & Fincham, 1996). Both of Kelley's (1967, 1972, 1983) models are concerned with the processes that determine whether an *internal* or *external* attribution is made for a behaviour's cause.

THE COVARIATION MODEL

This tries to account for the attributions made when we have some degree of knowledge about how a person whose behaviour we want to explain (the 'actor') usually behaves in various situations, and how other people behave in the same situation. According to the *principle of covariation*:

'an effect is attributed to one of its possible causes with which, over time, it covaries'.

This means that if two events repeatedly co-occur, we are more likely to infer that they are causally related than if they rarely co-occur. According to Kelley, an attribution about some effect (or behaviour) depends on the extent to which it covaries with *consensus*, *consistency*, and *distinctiveness* information.

Box 51.3 Consensus, consistency and distinctiveness information

Consensus refers to the extent to which other people behave in the same way towards the same stimulus. For example, if one person is laughing at a particular comedian and other people are as well, consensus is *high*. However, if nobody else is laughing, consensus is *low*.

Consistency refers to the stability of behaviour, that is, the extent to which a person has reacted in the same

---

way to the same stimulus on other occasions. If, for example, a person is laughing at a comedian now, and has laughed at this comedian before, consistency is *high*. However, if the person has not laughed at this comedian before, consistency is *low*.

Distinctiveness refers to the extent to which a person reacts in the same way towards other similar stimuli or entities. For example, if a person is laughing at a comedian and laughs at other comedians, distinctiveness is *low* (there is nothing about the behaviour that makes it distinctive). However, if the person does not find other comedians funny, distinctiveness is *high* (laughing at this comedian *is* a distinctive behaviour).

Kelley proposed that how these three types of information covary determines the type of attribution made. Consider, for example, explaining the behaviour of Peter, who is late for a psychology tutorial. As can be seen in Figure 51.1 (see page 447), Kelley's model predicts that Peter's behaviour will be explained differently when the information about him and other students covaries in certain ways.

Several studies have shown that when people are asked to explain a behaviour (such as Peter being late for his tutorial) and are given information which covaries in the ways shown above, attributions tend to be made in the ways Kelley predicted (McArthur, 1972; Harvey & Weary, 1984). However, just because people make attributions as if they are using covariation 'rules', does not *necessarily* mean that they are (Hewstone & Fincham, 1996). Several researchers have attempted to look at exactly how people make causal attributions, the most promising of these being Hilton & Slugoski's (1986) *abnormal conditions focus model*.

Box 51.4 The abnormal conditions focus model

According to Hilton and Slugoski, Kelley's three types of information are useful to the extent that the behaviour requiring information contrasts with the information given. Thus, with low consensus information, the person is abnormal, whereas with low consistency information the circumstances are abnormal. With high distinctiveness information, the stimulus is abnormal. The model proposes that we attribute as a cause the necessary condition that is abnormal when compared with the background of the target event (Hewstone & Fincham, 1996). This model may explain certain findings that Kelley's model has difficulty with, one of these being that the three types of information do not appear to be used to the same extent (Nisbett & Borgida, 1975; Wells & Harvey, 1977; Major, 1980).

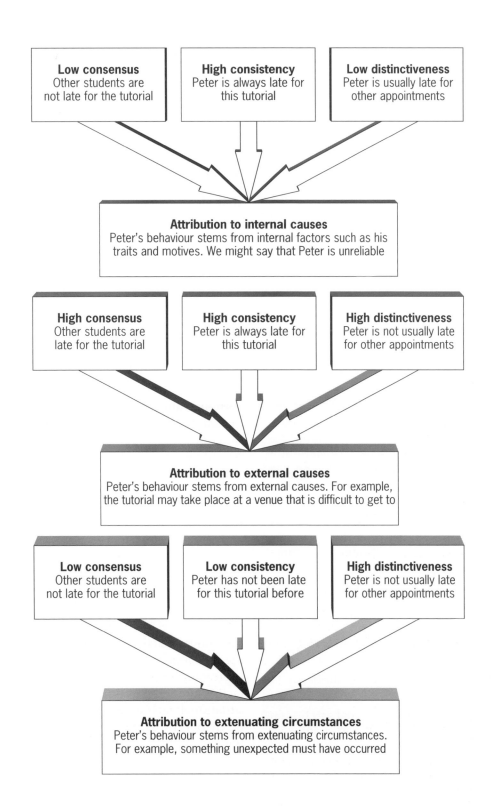

Figure 51.1   Predictions made by Kelley's covariation model given different types of consensus, consistency and distinctiveness information

THE CONFIGURATION MODEL

Kelley recognised that in many situations (most notably when we do not know the actor) we will not have access to any or all of the covariation model's three types of information. Yet we can still offer explanations for behaviour. The configuration model was Kelley's attempt to account for attributions about behaviour given a single occurrence of it by a particular individual.

When we make 'single event attributions' we do so using *causal schemata* (Kelley, 1972). These are general ideas (or ready-made beliefs, preconceptions, and even theories: Hewstone & Fincham, 1996) about how certain kinds of causes interact to produce a specific kind of effect.

Causal schemata are a 'causal shorthand' (Fiske & Taylor, 1991) for explaining behaviour quickly and easily. We develop causal schemata through experience, and the two most extensively researched are *multiple sufficient causes* and *multiple necessary causes*.

Box 51.5   Multiple sufficient causes and multiple necessary causes

Multiple sufficient causes: With some behaviours, any number of causes are *sufficient* to explain their occurrence. For example, a footballer who advertises aftershave may do so because he genuinely believes it is a good product or because he is being paid a large sum of money to advertise it – either of these is a sufficient cause. In these circumstances, we follow the *discounting principle* (Kelley, 1983), according to which:

'given that different causes can produce the same effect, the role of a given cause is discounted if other plausible causes are present'.

With the footballer advertising aftershave, it is more reasonable to assume that money explains the behaviour and so we discount the other possible cause.

Multiple sufficient causes are also associated with the *augmenting principle* (Kelley, 1983). According to this:

'the role of a given cause is augmented or increased if the effect occurs in the presence of an inhibitory factor'.

So, we are more likely to make an internal attribution (to effort and ability) when a student passes an exam after (say) suffering the death of a relative than would be the case for a student who had passed without having suffered such a loss.

Multiple necessary causes: Experience tells us that to stand any chance of winning a marathon, for example, a person must be fit, highly motivated, have trained hard for several months, wear the right sort of running shoes, and so on. Even if all these conditions are met,

success is not guaranteed. However, the *absence* of any one of them is likely to produce failure. Thus, there are many causes needed to produce certain behaviours (typically those which are unusual or extreme).

Biases in the attribution process

Kelley's is a *normative model* of the attribution process (it tells us how people *should* make causal attributions). As has been seen, however, people are far less logical and systematic (less 'scientific') than the model requires. A more accurate account of how causal attributions are made may come from an analysis of the systematic errors and biases that occur in the attribution process. A bias is:

'the tendency to favour one cause over another when explaining some effect. Such favouritism may result in causal attributions that deviate from predictions derived from rational attributional principles like covariation' (Zebrowitz, 1990).

Although almost all behaviour is the product of *both* the person and the situation, we tend to emphasise one or other of these when making attributions. Perhaps this is because we want to be seen as competent interpreters of behaviour and so we naïvely assume that simple explanations are better than complex ones (Jones & Nisbett, 1971). Our tendency to act as 'cognitive misers' means that we do not analyse the interactions between personal and situational factors even if a lot of information is available. Three important attributional biases are the *fundamental attribution error*, the *actor–observer effect*, and the *self-serving bias*.

THE FUNDAMENTAL ATTRIBUTION ERROR

The fundamental attribution error (FAE) – also known as the *correspondence bias* (Gilbert, 1995) – is the tendency to overestimate the importance of personal or dispositional factors and underestimate the importance of external or situational factors as explanations for other people's behaviours (Ross, 1977). The FAE, then, is a failure to use the discounting principle (see Box 51.5) and has been demonstrated in numerous studies.

Box 51.6   An experimental demonstration of the FAE

Napolitan & Goethals (1979) had students talk, one at a time, with a young woman who acted in either an aloof and critical, or warm and friendly manner. Before the experiment began, half the students were told that the woman's behaviour would be spontaneous. The other half were told that, for the purposes of the experiment, she had been *instructed* to act in an unfriendly (or friendly) way.

Even though the students had been told the woman was behaving in a particular way for the purposes of the experiment, they disregarded that information. So, if she acted in a friendly (or unfriendly) way towards them, they inferred that she really was a warm (or cold) person. Only if the students interacted with the woman twice, and saw her act in a friendly way on one occasion and in an unfriendly way on the other, did they consider the situational reasons for her behaviour.

Jones & Nisbett (1971) have proposed two explanations for the FAE. First, we have a different *focus of attention* when we view ourselves, and when we behave we see the world around us more clearly than we see our own behaviour. However, when we observe somebody else behaving, we focus attention on what seems most salient and relevant, namely their behaviour, and not on the person's situation. Second, *different types of information* are available to us about our own and other people's behaviour. We, for example, have more consistency information available because we are likely to be able to remember how we acted on previous occasions in the same circumstances, and also have a better notion of the stimuli to which we are attending.

By explaining behaviour in personal or dispositional ways, other people seem more predictable, enhancing our sense of control over the environment (Ross, 1977). Gilbert (1995) sees the FAE as an efficient and automatic process of inferring dispositions from behaviour which, on average, produces accurate perceptions by perceivers who are too 'cognitively busy' to make conscious corrections based on situational causes.

In some circumstances, however, we *overestimate* the importance of situational factors as causes for other people's behaviour. For example, Quattrone (1982) showed that when people are alerted to the possibility that behaviour may be influenced by environmental constraints, there is a tendency to perceive these constraints as causes. This occurs even though such behaviour can be explained in terms of the actor's dispositions. For this reason, Zebrowitz (1990) prefers the term 'bias' to 'error' in this respect (see above).

In Zebrowitz's view,

'this bias may be limited to adults in Western societies and it is most pronounced when they are constrained to attribute behaviour to a single cause'.

Certainly, the FAE is by no means universal (Fletcher & Ward, 1988). In our society, we tend to believe that people are responsible for their own actions. In India, however, people are more embedded in their family and caste networks and are more likely to recognise situational constraints on behaviour. As a result, situational attributions are more likely for other people's behaviour (Miller, 1984).

In Western culture, the likelihood of the FAE being made depends on the *importance of the consequences* (Walster, 1966). The more serious a behaviour's consequences, the more likely the actor is to be judged responsible for it. Walster gave participants an account of a car accident in which a young man's car had been left at the top of a hill and rolled down backwards. Participants told that the car had crashed into a shop, injuring the shopkeeper and a small child, rated the young man as being more 'guilty' than those told that the car had crashed into and damaged another vehicle. Participants told that very little damage was done to the car, and that no other vehicle was involved, rated him least 'guilty' of all. Similarly, Chaikin & Darley (1973) found that the FAE was more likely when a person was described as having spilt ink over a large and expensive book than over a newspaper.

Box 51.7   Two other factors influencing the likelihood of the FAE occurring

Intentionality: Darley & Huff (1990) found that participants' judgements of the damage caused by an action depended on intentionality. Three groups of participants read the same description of some damage that had been done. However, one was told that the damage had been done intentionally, one that it was a result of negligence, and one that it had occurred naturally. Estimations of the damage done were inflated by those told that it had been done intentionally.

Personal relevance: The greater the personal (or *hedonic*) relevance an action has (the more it affects us personally), the more likely the FAE is. So, if the large and expensive book used as stimulus material in Chaikin and Darley's study (see text) had been described as belonging to us, the FAE would be more likely than if it was described as belonging to someone else.

THE ACTOR-OBSERVER EFFECT

The actor-observer effect (AOE) refers to the tendency to make different attributions about behaviour depending on whether we are performing ('acting') it or observing it. Actors usually see behaviour as a response to the situation, whereas observers attribute the same behaviour to the actor's intentions and dispositions (that is, observers make the FAE).

Figure 51.2   An illustration of the actor-observer effect: Actors look for situational causes of their behaviour whilst observers look for dispositional causes

(Copyright House of Viz/John Brown Publishing Ltd)

There are several explanations for the AOE. One of these proposes that because we do not like to be pigeon-holed, we tend not to explain our own behaviour in terms of trait labels. However, we have no such reservations about pigeon-holing others. Because we like to see ourselves as being flexible and adaptive, and others as understandable and predictable, we explain the same behaviour differently depending on whose behaviour it is (Sande *et al.*, 1988).

A second explanation is based on the amount of information actors and observers have at their disposal. Actors know they have behaved differently in other situations, and would behave differently in this one if conditions were changed. Unless they know the actor well, observers have no such information and so assume that actors have behaved similarly in the past (and consequently make a dispositional attribution).

A third possible explanation suggests that people do not usually look at or perceive themselves (unless in a mirror). When explaining their own behaviour, they attend to things they can see or are most conspicuous, namely the external situation or environment. As observers, though, other people are attended to because they are the most interesting thing in the environment, and a dispositional attribution becomes more likely. Storms (1973), for example, found that when people are induced to view *themselves* as observers (by means of a videotape of themselves from the perspective of an observer) they do make internal attributions (see Figure 51.3). Additionally, when people

are induced to view others from the same perspective they view themselves (by, for example, empathising with them), external attributions for their behaviours tend to be made (Regan & Totten, 1975)

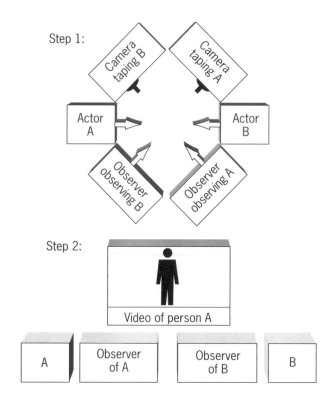

Figure 51.3   Diagram depicting the arrangement in Storms' (1973) experiment

THE SELF-SERVING BIAS

From what has just been said about the AOE, it might be thought that actors *always* explain their own behaviour in external terms. Everyday experience, though, indicates that this is not so. Certainly, people who fail an examination often explain this in terms of poor teaching or a very hard paper, and not in terms of a lack of intelligence. When people pass an examination, however, they don't usually explain their success in terms of 'an easy examination paper' or 'soft marking'. Most people explain success in terms of dispositional factors like 'effort', 'ability', 'high intelligence' and so on.

The tendency for us to 'take credit' when things go right and 'deny responsibility' when they go wrong is called the self-serving bias (SSB) (Miller & Ross, 1975). It has been demonstrated in a variety of settings.

> **Box 51.8   Some illustrations of the self-serving bias**
>
> - Lau & Russell (1980) found that American football players and coaches tended to credit their wins to internal causes (such as determination) but blame their defeats on external causes (such as bad luck or injuries).
>
> - Gilovich (1983) showed that gamblers at sports events attribute winning bets to the greater ability of the winning team. Losing bets are explained in terms of 'flukes', such as refereeing errors or unforeseen factors.
>
> - Students who taught boys whose performance in maths was rigged to 'improve', explained the improvement in terms of their teaching skills. Those who taught boys whose performance did not 'improve' explained performance in terms of the boys' poor motivation or intelligence (Johnson *et al.*, 1964).
>
> - Students tend to regard exams in which they do well as good indicators of their abilities, and exams in which they do badly as poor indicators. When students do well, teachers are more likely to assume responsibility for their performance than when they do badly (Arkin *et al.*, 1980).
>
> - When politicians are victorious in elections, they tend to attribute their success to internal factors such as their personal service to constituents. When they are defeated, this is usually attributed to external factors such as national trends (Kingdon, 1967).

Two broad types of explanation for the SSB have been advanced. One proposes that it can best be explained in *motivational* or '*need-serving*' terms, such as the need to enhance or protect self-esteem (Greenberg *et al.*, 1982). If a person explains success in terms of dispositional factors, self-esteem is enhanced (a *self-enhancing bias*). If failure is explained in terms of external factors, self-esteem is protected (a *self-protecting bias*). Alternatively, the SSB could reflect a motivation to appear in a favourable light to other people (Weary & Arkin, 1981).

The second position explains the SSB in *cognitive* or *information-processing* terms. Miller & Ross (1975) and Feather & Simon (1971) argue that we typically intend and expect to succeed at a task, although there are, of course, occasions on which we expect to be unsuccessful. Intended and expected successful outcomes tend to be attributed internally to factors, such as trying hard. Unintended and unexpected outcomes tend to be attributed to external factors, such as bad luck. Disentangling the role played by motivational and cognitive factors in the SSB is difficult,

but evidence suggests that both are involved (Tetlock & Levi, 1982).

> **Box 51.9   Attributions and depression**
>
> An interesting exception to the SSB comes from observations of the attributions made by clinically depressed people. They tend to explain failures in terms of their own inadequacies, and successes in terms of external factors such as luck or chance (Abramson *et al.*, 1978). This *attributional style* has also been observed in non-depressed women. According to Davison & Neale (1994), women are more likely to cope with stress by blaming themselves for their plight and to attribute their achievements to external factors (see Chapter 69). Although these differences in attributional style can help to explain why married people differ in their degree of happiness (see Chapter 57), the exact reasons for different attributional styles remain to be discovered.

Conclusions

This chapter has looked at some theories of attribution and biases in the attribution process. Theories of attribution are helpful in understanding how we arrive at explanations for people's behaviours but, because of various biases, they cannot tell the whole story. As normative theories of the attribution process, theories of attribution tell us how we *should* make causal attributions for behaviour rather than how we actually *do* make them.

Summary

- **Attribution theory** deals with the general principles governing causal explanations in a variety of situations. **Theories of attribution** draw on these principles to predict how people will respond in particular situations/**life domains**. Attribution theory is a collection of diverse theoretical and empirical contributions. Important contributors include Heider, Jones and Davis, and Kelley.

- **Heider's 'commonsense' psychology** sees people as naïve scientists, inferring unobservable causes (or meaning) from observable behaviour. Members of a culture share basic assumptions about behaviour. In western culture, behaviour is explained in terms of both **personal** (dispositional/internal) and **situational** (environmental/external) factors.

- **Jones and Davis** were concerned with explaining why we make **correspondent inferences** about people's dispositions. A precondition for correspondent inferences is the attribution of **intentionality**. This, in turn, depends on the belief that people know behaviours have the effects they do and have the abilities to perform them.

■ One way of looking for dispositions that could have caused behaviour is through the **analysis of non-common effects**. The likelihood of dispositional attributions is influenced by **free choice, expectedness and social desirability** and **prior expectations**.

■ Intentions do not, however, appear to be a precondition for correspondent inferences, and unintended/accidental behaviours are beyond correspondent inference theory's scope. Also, behaviour that confirms expectations can be informative.

■ Kelley was concerned with the processes by which internal and external attributions are made for the causes of behaviour. In his **covariation model**, the principle of covariation says that we are more likely to infer that two events are causally related if they repeatedly co-occur. Attributions about some effect/behaviour depend on the extent of its covariation with information regarding **consensus, consistency** and **distinctiveness**. How these types of information vary determine the attribution made.

■ Although Kelley's model is supported by evidence, this does not necessarily mean that people do use covariation 'rules'. The **abnormal conditions focus model** sees the three types of information as being useful to the extent that they contrast with the behaviour being explained.

■ Kelley's **configuration model** tries to account for 'single event attributions' in terms of multiple sufficient and multiple necessary **causal schemata**. The former are associated with the **augmenting principle**, and we choose between two or more possible causes by using the **discounting principle**.

■ People are less rational and scientific than Kelley's **normative** model requires. A more accurate account of the attribution process involves looking at the **systematic biases**. Although most behaviour is the product of both personal factors and the situation, we tend to emphasise one of these.

■ The **fundamental attribution error** (FAE) is the tendency to exaggerate the importance of internal/dispositional factors relative to external/situational factors. It may be limited to adults in Western culture, where people are seen as being more responsible for their actions. Its likelihood depends on the importance of a behaviour's consequence and personal/hedonic relevance.

■ In the **actor–observer effect** (AOE), actors see their behaviours as responses to situational factors, whereas observers explain the same behaviours in dispositional terms. The effect may occur because actors have more information than observers about their own behaviours or because of perceptual differences.

■ People do not, as the AOE implies, always explain their own behaviour in external terms. Whilst failures are often explained in this way, successes tend to be explained in dispositional ways. This is the **self-serving bias** (SSB), which may occur because of a need to enhance or protect self-esteem. Alternatively, a cognitive/information processing explanation proposes that we attribute intended/expected outcomes internally and unintended/unexpected outcomes externally.

■ The SSB is reversed in clinically depressed people, who explain their successes in situational terms and their failures in dispositional terms. The reasons for this attributional style, also displayed by some non-depressed women, is unclear.

SOCIAL AND CULTURAL INFLUENCES ON PERCEPTION: STEREOTYPES AND SOCIAL REPRESENTATIONS

Introduction and overview

The concept of a 'stereotype' was introduced to psychology by Lippmann (1922). The word derives from its use in printing, where it refers to a printing mould or plate which, when cast, is difficult to change (Reber, 1985). Research into stereotyping has a long history. This chapter examines research relating to the origins and maintenance of cultural and social stereotypes.

Related to stereotypes are social representations. These are shared beliefs and expectations held by the society in which we live or the group to which we belong (Moscovici, 1961, 1976). This chapter also reviews some of the research relating to social representations and considers its contribution to our knowledge of how we share, transmit, and reflect upon our understanding of the world.

Implicit personality theory and illusory correlations

In his study of the processes involved in interpersonal perception, Asch (1946) showed that when people are presented with characteristics describing a person, they often go beyond the information given and assume that the person also possesses certain other characteristics. For example, when people were presented with a list containing the words 'intelligent', 'skilful', 'industrious', 'warm', 'determined', 'practical' and 'cautious', they also inferred that the person was 'serious' rather than 'frivolous' and 'persistent' rather than 'unstable'. Asch also found that certain words (*central traits*) had more impact on the inferences made than others (*peripheral traits*). Thus, 'warm' and 'cold' had a greater effect than 'polite' and 'blunt'.

Box 52.1 The halo effect

Asch's finding that including 'warm' in a list of traits produces a more positive impression of a person compared with the same list including 'cold' demonstrates the *halo effect*. If told that a person has a particularly favourable characteristic (such as being 'warm'), we tend to attribute other favourable characteristics to them (a *positive* halo). If told that a person has a particularly unfavourable characteristic (such as being 'cold'), we attribute other unfavourable characteristics to them (a *negative* halo).

According to Bruner & Tagiuri (1954), our perception of others is not based on what they are 'really' like, but on our own general 'theory' or expectations about them. Everyone has ideas about which personality traits go with, or are consistent with, others, and use these to 'fill in the gaps' in their representations of other people. Bruner and Tagiuri coined the term *implicit personality theory* (IPT) to describe the unconscious inference processes that enable us to form impressions of others based on very little evidence.

Bruner and Tagiuri propose that IPTs are shared by everyone and are consistent within a culture. This explains why, for example, many people think that intellectuals have larger than average skulls, and thick lips mean gluttony (Leyens & Codol, 1988). Indeed, so entrenched are such beliefs, despite evidence to the contrary, that the term *illusory correlation* (see also page 455) has been used to describe them (Chapman & Chapman, 1969).

Although IPT is at least partly derived from our background culture, individual experiences of interacting with, and making judgements about, people also provide us with a set of assumptions and inferences. These may not be shared with others. For example, one student in a class who hears that a new member is 'vivacious' might feel differently from another, depending on their personal experiences (Abrahams & Stanley, 1992).

Moreover, since certain languages, such as Eskimo and Maori, embody very different theories about people from those embodied in English (Harré, 1983), the resulting perception of others is likely to be very different: they begin with a very different set of basic categorisations. As Abrahams & Stanley (1992) note, we share a basic theory of others through our language, but we develop personal variations through particular social experience.

Stereotypes and stereotyping

IPT has been demonstrated using different experimental techniques, and manifests itself in several ways (Gahagan, 1980). One of these is the phenomenon of *stereotyping*. In IPT, a single item of information about a person generates inferences about other aspects of that person's character. In stereotyping, information is limited to some highly visible aspect of a person such as sex, race, nationality, and so on. This information generates judgements about what any person belonging to a given group is like (an *individual stereotype*), and that all people belonging to a given group possess the same characteristics (a *group stereotype*). Social stereotypes, then, can be defined as grossly oversimplified and generalised abstractions that people share about their own or another group (Oakes *et al.*, 1994; Hogg & Vaughan, 1995).

Figure 52.1   Millie Tant is the embodiment of the stereotype of feminists as held by non-feminists

(Copyright House of Viz/John Brown Publishing Ltd)

Early research examined how different ethnic groups were stereotyped and whether people actually hold traditional social stereotypes as portrayed in newspapers and magazines. Katz & Braly (1933) asked Princeton University students to indicate which five or six of a list of 84 words describing personality were most closely associated with each of ten ethnic groups (including Germans, Negroes, Jews and Turks). Katz and Braly used agreement across students as the criterion for a stereotype's existence. Thus, if 75 per cent or more of students assigned the trait of, say, 'obedience' to a given ethnic group, that was taken as evidence of the existence of a stereotype.

There was substantial agreement amongst the students with the traditional social stereotypes, especially derogatory traits. For example, Negroes were stereotyped as 'lazy' and 'ignorant', whilst Jews were stereotyped as 'shrewd', 'mercenary' and 'grasping'. Disturbingly, these stereotypes were held despite the fact that most of the students had not actually had any personal contact with members of most of the ethnic groups. Presumably, the students had absorbed the images of these groups as portrayed by the media. The results were also used to compare the favourability of different ethnic groups. In 1933, Americans had the 'best' stereotype, and Turks the 'worst'.

Box 52.2   Changes in stereotypes over time

Using Katz and Braly's methodology, other researchers examined how stereotypes changed over time. For example, Gilbert's (1951) study of Princeton students showed that the stereotypes reported by Katz and Braly had become significantly weaker. Thus, only 41 per cent thought Negroes were 'superstitious' (compared with 84 per cent reported by Katz and Braly), 47 per cent thought Jews were 'shrewd' (70 per cent), and 62 per cent thought Germans were 'scientifically minded' (78 per cent).

Karlins *et al.*, (1969) found that whilst Americans were seen as 'industrious', 'intelligent', but not particularly 'materialistic' in 1933, they were seen as 'materialistic' but not particularly 'industrious' or 'intelligent' in 1967. This research also revealed changes in the favourability of ethnic groups. By 1969, for example, Turks had improved markedly, whilst Americans had lost their position slightly. Interestingly, in both Gilbert's and Karlins *et al.*'s studies, the student participants expressed great irritation at being asked to make generalisations.

One criticism of research in this area is that it forces judgements and is subject to the artefacts of *social desirability responding* (Gahagan, 1991). As noted in Box 52.2, in studies that followed Katz and Braly's, students were markedly less willing to engage in the exercise. Since negative stereotypes have become less acceptable, people would be less likely to offer them even if they were held.

One way of overcoming social desirability responding was devised by Razran (1950). Participants were led to believe they would be rating pictures of girls according to various psychological qualities. Later, they were shown the same pictures but each girl was identified with an Irish, Italian or Jewish-sounding name. Razran used changes in the ratings previously given as evidence of ethnic stereotyping. Girls with Jewish-sounding names were rated higher in terms of 'intelligence' and 'ambition', but lower on 'niceness'. Razran argued that since the participants did not know they were involved in a study on stereotyping, their responses were free from social desirability responding.

EXPLAINING STEREOTYPING: THE 'GRAIN OF TRUTH' HYPOTHESIS

One important question is where stereotypes come from. According to Campbell (1967), stereotypes originate from two major sources – a person's experience with another person or group of people, and the communication of those experiences to others. For example, if the stereotypical view of the Scots is that they are extremely thrifty, someone at some time *must* have experienced a thrifty Scot. Equally, if Germans are stereotyped as 'getting up at dawn to reserve a sunbed', somebody at some time must have observed this.

At some time, then, the stereotypical characteristic attributed to a given group must have been an attribute of at least one member of that group. Later on, the process of communication would establish the stereotype as a truism in people's minds. Stereotypes therefore originate in someone's experience and consequently must contain at least a 'grain of truth' (Allport, 1954). The fact that people do make inferences corresponding with their experiences was shown by Wegner *et al*. (1976).

Box 52.3   Inferences and experience

Wegner *et al*. (1976) gave one group of participants a series of personality traits designed to cultivate the inference that the traits of 'persuasiveness' and 'realism' were positively correlated. A second group was read similar descriptions, but the descriptions were designed to cultivate the inference that 'persuasiveness' and 'realism' were negatively correlated.

Afterwards, both groups were asked to read other descriptions that made no reference to 'persuasiveness' or 'realism'. However, each participant was asked to rate how 'persuasive' and 'realistic' the individual described appeared to be. Participants given positive correlation descriptions between the traits perceived a more positive correlation than those given descriptions suggesting a negative correlation. Thus, experiences can change expectations about behaviour.

The 'grain of truth' hypothesis assumes that a person, who was at one time in a particular situation, made a perfectly logical inference (the person's expectancies and inferences matched his or her experiences *exactly*). However, people sometimes see two variables as being related when in fact they are not (*illusory correlation*).

In connection with stereotypes, people perceive differences between two or more social groups in terms of the strength of correlation between membership in one group and certain characteristics, even when such differences do not exist (Baron, 1989). For example, Sanbonmatsu *et al*. (1987) found that their participants saw people of Cuban descent as being more violent than people of European descent, even though being Cuban or European is equally unrelated to this characteristic.

EXPLAINING ILLUSORY CORRELATIONS

Illusory correlations may occur because expectations about certain events distort the ways in which we process information.

Box 52.4   The distorting effects of expectations on information processing

Hamilton & Gifford (1976) asked participants to read two short statements about various people. Two-thirds of those they read about were identified as members of 'Group A'. The other one-third were identified as members of 'Group B'. Statements about the people were either 'desirable' ('John, a member of Group A [Group B] visited a sick friend in hospital') or 'undesirable' ('Roy, a member of Group B [Group A] always talks about himself and his problems').

Within each group, the majority (two-thirds) were described by 'desirable' qualities. However, even though there were twice as many Group A members as Group B members, neither group had a higher *proportion* of 'desirable' or 'undesirable' members. Although there was no relationship between membership of either

---

455

group and 'desirability', participants thought that there was, since when they read about all the people and then reported their impressions of the 'typical' member of each group, the Group B member was rated as less desirable than the Group A member.

Wegner & Vallacher (1976) have argued that illusory correlation is similar to the fundamental attribution error (see Chapter 51, page 448). Just as other people's behaviours tend to be explained in terms of personal rather than situational factors, 'odd' behaviour can be explained by attributing it to a person's membership in an unusual group of people. When two distinctive events co-occur one or more times, we tend to conclude that they are causally related (Mullen & Johnson, 1990). According to Wegner and Vallacher, although people's inference systems are built from their transactions with reality, our perceptions sometimes go awry, and we make inferences about relationships that were never there at all.

Moreover, once an illusory correlation is made, we tend to seek out, notice, and remember information that supports the belief. This is called the *confirmation bias* (see Chapter 36, page 310). As a result, the belief in non-existent correlations grows stronger. Such illusory correlations can give rise to serious inferential errors (Gahagan, 1991). For example, an employer who believes that being blonde and having fun are causally linked, may conclude that blondes are a poor choice for responsible jobs since they are too busy having fun (Baron & Byrne, 1984).

STEREOTYPING: A NORMAL OR ABNORMAL COGNITIVE PROCESS?

Many North American psychologists (e.g. Katz & Braly, 1933) have condemned stereotypes for being both false and illogical, and users of stereotypes have been seen as prejudiced and even pathological. According to Taylor & Porter (1994), there are compelling reasons why Americans should condemn stereotyping and wish to rid society of this evil. One is political ideology, according to which everyone who lives in America is first and foremost 'American', regardless of their country of origin or their ethnic/cultural background. This has been called the 'melting pot', in which differences between people are 'boiled away', leaving just one culture.

Some European social psychologists, however, were brought up in contexts in which it is normal to categorise people into groups, where society is expected to be culturally diverse, and where people are proud of their identity. A good example is Tajfel (1969). Drawing on his own experiences, Tajfel challenged the American view of stereotyping. For Tajfel, stereotyping can be reconceptualised as the product of quite normal cognitive processes common to all (non-prejudiced) people.

Box 52.5   Stereotyping and categorisation

Tajfel sees stereotyping as a special case of *categorisation* (see Chapter 53, page 465), which involves an exaggeration of similarities within groups and of differences between groups (the accentuation principle). According to Oakes *et al.* (1994), Tajfel's contribution is widely seen as having been revolutionary, one effect of his ideas being to move researchers away from studying the *content* of stereotypes and towards the study of the *process* of stereotyping in its own right.

Brislin (1993) has argued that stereotypes should not be viewed as a sign of abnormality. In his view:

'they reflect people's need to organise, remember, and retrieve information that might be useful to them as they attempt to achieve their goals and to meet life's demands'.

Like Allport (1954), Brislin sees stereotypes as 'categories about people', and categories (in general) and stereotypes (in particular) are shortcuts to thinking. From a cognitive perspective, there is nothing unique about stereotypes: they are universal and inevitable and 'an intrinsic, essential and primitive aspect of cognition' (Brown, 1986).

As noted earlier, though, stereotypes have been defined as oversimplified and generalised abstractions (or *exceptionless generalisations*), so that, for example, *every* skinhead is assumed to be aggressive and *every* American materialistic. However, it is doubtful that stereotypes are factually true, because no group is completely homogeneous and individual differences are the norm. Yet in Katz & Braly's (1933) study, the instruction to list traits typical of each ethnic/national group was thought to have been understood by the participants as an instruction to list the traits *true of all members* of each group (Brown, 1986).

However, early studies like Katz and Braly's never actually found out exactly what was understood by the word 'typical'. As noted in Box 52.2, in the follow-up studies, some students objected to doing what was asked of them. In fact, a substantial number actually refused to take part in the study, sensing that characterising ethnic groups at all would be interpreted as ignorant or even morally wrong.

Box 52.6 What does 'typical' mean?

That 'typical' does not appear to mean an exceptionless generalisation was shown by McCauley & Stitt (1978). They had students answer questions requiring them to estimate things like the percentage of American cars that are Chevrolets. Interspersed with these questions were 'critical' questions about the percentage of Germans that are efficient, extremely nationalistic, scientifically minded, pleasure-loving, and superstitious. There were also questions about the percentage of people in the world who possessed these characteristics.

McCauley and Stitt found that none of the estimates given about Germans was close to 100 per cent, so clearly 'typical' is not an exceptionless generalisation, and does not seem to mean 'true of all'. What 'typical' apparently means is 'true of a higher percentage of the group in question than people in general', or *characteristic* (Brown, 1986).

The view of stereotyping as a normal cognitive process has led to interesting developments in research, particularly with respect to prejudice and discrimination (Taylor & Porter, 1994). Some of the findings that have emerged are considered in Chapter 53 (see Box 53.5). What can be said here is that relying on stereotypes to form impressions of strangers (*category-driven processing*) is:

'the least effortful cognitive route we can take, whereas relying on the unique characteristics of the target person [*attribute-driven processing*] is the most effortful route' (Fiske & Neuberg, 1990).

Perhaps stereotypes are resistant to change because they represent a way of simplifying our complex social world.

Social representations

Whilst stereotypes illustrate the shared nature of cognition, we do not all share the same knowledge constructs or form precisely the same opinions about other people. However,

'It is apparent ... that a great deal of information, and hence meaning, is collectively shared by sets of individuals, groups or societies. This is a natural consequence of the social life we lead, which involves a plethora of communication and sources of information ... Our perception is determined by the ecological context in which we exist. Our religious beliefs, political and social ideologies, ideas about right and wrong, and even scientific theories are for the most part defined by the social contexts in which they occur' (Leyens & Dardenne, 1996).

As mentioned at the beginning of this chapter, Moscovici (1961, 1976) coined the term *social representations* (SRs) to refer to the shared beliefs and explanations held by the society in which we live or the group to which we belong. Specifically, Moscovici (1981) defines SRs as:

'a set of concepts, statements and explanations originating in daily life in the course of inter-individual communications'.

In his view, SRs in our society are equivalent to the myths and belief systems that exist in traditional societies, and are 'the contemporary version of common sense'. Such representations explain how 'the strange and the unfamiliar become, in time, the familiar' (Farr & Moscovici, 1984).

A group or society's SRs provide the framework within which its members can share, transmit, and reflect upon their understanding of the world. To that extent, SRs are 'the essence of *social* cognition' (Moscovici, 1981) because they help us master and make sense of the world, and enhance our communication about it with others. Two main processes used to realise the functions of SRs are *anchoring* and *objectifying*. *Anchors* are established concepts within a pre-existing system to which new experiences can be related. *Objectifying* involves making abstract things concrete in a way that most people can understand so that they become generally accepted as 'knowledge'.

Objectification can be achieved by means of *personification* and *figuration*. For example, Moscovici (1961) showed that people have simplified (and often mistaken) ideas about psychoanalytic theory, but know the name Sigmund Freud. Similarly, there are few of us who have much understanding about the origins of the universe or evolutionary theory, but most of us have heard the names Stephen Hawking and Charles Darwin. These are all examples of the *personification* of complex ideas, that is, linking an idea with a particular person's name that represents those ideas.

Complex ideas can also be converted into images and metaphors that represent the concept in question. This is *figuration*. When British general elections occur, for example, the concept of a 'swing' to one political party as a result of people's voting behaviours is depicted in the form of a pendulum that shows the effect a change in voting behaviour would produce on the national balance of power. In Freud's psychodynamic model, the impulsive (or id) side of a person's personality is often portrayed as a devil, whilst the moralistic (or superego) side is portrayed as an angel. Both of these images stand on the shoulders of the person him or herself (the ego: see Chapter 66, page 569).

Perhaps the best example of figuration is the formula $E = mc^2$, where E = energy, m = mass, and c^2 = the speed of light squared, a formula derived from the theory of relativity personified by Albert Einstein. As Leyens & Dardenne (1996) have observed:

'even this trivial amount of knowledge is sufficient to maintain conversation at a party, which is good evidence that cognitions can be socially shared'.

Box 52.7   Social representations of 'split-brain' research

In the 'split-brain operation', the nerve fibres connecting the two cerebral hemispheres are severed (see Chapter 9, page 74). The purpose of this is to control the severity of epileptic seizures by confining abnormally amplified brain activity to one cerebral hemisphere. As a result of studying patients who had undergone this operation, Sperry and his colleagues discovered that, as a *broad generalisation*, the two cerebral hemispheres are specialised for different kinds of mental activity, with the left showing superior linguistic and mathematical skills and the right superior skills on spatial tasks.

Moscovici & Hewstone (1983) have argued that Sperry and his colleagues' findings have been transformed in the public mind to the belief that people are 'logically left-brained' or 'intuitively right-brained' depending on how they behave. What was a tentative description of how the brain is organised has become a general statement about the social and economic differences between people and societies (Hayes, 1994).

SOCIAL REPRESENTATIONS IN CHILDHOOD

Durkin (1995) has reviewed evidence relating to SRs in childhood and of development itself. Drawing on Emler *et al.*'s (1990) and Corsaro's (1993) research, Durkin argues that children attempt to transform the puzzling and ambiguous features of the adult world (such as the rules that adults impose on them) by incorporating them into their own collective practices, so making 'the unfamiliar familiar'.

Box 52.8   SRs in childhood

Teachers in an Italian nursery prohibited the children from bringing personal objects to school. From a four-year-old's perspective, this presumptuous constraint makes little sense (the whole point of having personal objects is that they are fun to play with), but the children know that grown-ups set the rules. So, the sensible thing

to do is smuggle small playthings in, concealed in one's pockets. Of course, having got around the system it is essential to share the achievement with one's peers, who can appreciate the risks undertaken and the delights of the illicit goods. This calls for discretion, and all disclosures have to be made out of sight of the agents of repression. But through these defiant arrangements, the rules themselves are given meaning and transformed into a basis for social organisation.

According to Corsaro, the children are trying to make sense of the adult rule by anchoring it in the collective security of their own culture. As they begin to incorporate the rule, and find ways of working around it, so they themselves lend it a form of objectivity: it influences how they organise their shared activities. By avoiding someone's authority and persuading your peers to avoid it, the authority is confirmed. In this way, through working jointly within the rules that adults impose, children begin to reconstruct jointly a SR of how the world (or their fragment of it) is regulated.

(From Durkin, 1995)

Durkin argues that development itself is something about which any society has SRs. As he says:

'a society has a belief system, a set of expectations and explanations, concerning what children should be like and what should be done with them. These social representations influence the context in which the young are raised'.

One such SR is *intelligence*, a construct that eludes a definition that everyone agrees with, but is widely believed in our society to be a useful 'thing' to have. Our beliefs about what determines intelligence influence how we behave towards others. For example, teachers who believe that intelligence is a genetically determined and inherited 'thing' are likely to teach children differently from teachers who see intelligence as something acquired through experience (Selleri *et al.*, 1995; Hayes, 1997).

OTHER RESEARCH INTO SOCIAL REPRESENTATIONS

Although SRs have been discussed as shared beliefs, different groups within a single society may have different SRs and this can lead to differences between them. Di Giacomo (1980) studied Belgian university students staging a protest movement about changes to student grants. The representations held by the student leaders and those of the main student body were different. Principally, the concept of 'student–worker solidarity' was held by the student leaders, but not by the main student body. As a result, when the leaders called for action there was very little student support for it.

Box 52.9   The central figurative nucleus

The stability of SRs has also attracted research interest. Whilst particular SRs may be held by individuals and societies, they are not completely unchanging and may be altered by a variety of sources, one being the mass media. Moscovici (1984) explains the durable but open-to-change nature of SRs in terms of a *central figurative nucleus*. This is linked to a number of peripheral elements that provide additional detail about something. Changes in SRs occur when major changes in the peripheral elements break the link between them and the central core.

SR theory's major weakness concerns its abstract or 'fuzzy' nature (Jahoda, 1988). As a result, critics argue that it does not suggest many hypotheses that can be experimentally investigated and that it is non-falsifiable: any data obtained can be interpreted in a way consistent with the theory. The first criticism is refuted by the various studies described in this section. However, the second criticism is more difficult to defend, and a major task of SR theorists is to address the theory's 'fuzziness'.

Conclusions

This chapter has reviewed some of the theory and research relating to stereotyping and SRs. Stereotypes are not exceptionless generalisations, and may even be an example of a normal rather than abnormal cognitive process. Research into social representations reveals information about how we share, transmit, and reflect upon our understanding of the world. However, its critics have challenged the theory's 'fuzzy' nature and non-falsifiability.

Summary

- When forming impressions of people, we tend to go beyond the information given about them and assume they also possess other characteristics. People's **central traits** (e.g. 'warm' and 'cold') have more impact on inferences than **peripheral traits** (e.g. 'polite' and 'blunt'). Inferring other favourable (unfavourable) characteristics on the basis of a positive (negative) characteristic is called a **positive (negative) halo effect**.

- **Implicit personality theories** (IPTs) are beliefs about which personality traits belong together. We use IPTs to 'fill in the gaps' when we have little information about people. IPTs are shared by everyone and consistent within a culture. Some are so entrenched they illustrate **illusory correlation**, the tendency to see variables as being related when they are not. Social experiences and language also contribute to impression formation.

- IPT manifests itself in **stereotyping**, in which impressions about someone are built around something highly visible, such as sex or race. There are both individual and group stereotypes.

- The existence of stereotypes can be explained by the 'grain of truth' hypothesis which says that at some time the stereotypical characteristic attributed to a given group must have been displayed by at least one member of that group. This characteristic is then communicated to others, establishing the stereotype as a truism in people's minds.

- The 'grain of truth' hypothesis assumes that people's expectancies and inferences match their experiences exactly. However, illusory correlations contradict this. These may occur because expectations about certain events distort how we process information. When an illusory correlation is made, belief in it grows stronger through the **confirmation bias**.

- Stereotyping is traditionally viewed as an abnormal cognitive process. However, it may be the product of normal cognitive processes, specifically as a special case of categorisation involving the **accentuation principle**. Stereotypes are not exceptionless generalisations. Research indicates that 'typical' does not mean 'true of all members'. Rather, it seems to mean characteristic of the group in question.

- Relying on stereotypes to form impressions of strangers (**category-driven processing**) is less cognitively demanding than relying on the unique characteristics of a person (**attribute-driven processing**). Stereotypes may be resistant to change because they are a way of simplifying our complex social world.

- **Social representations** (SRs) are shared beliefs and explanations held by the societies in which we live or the groups to which we belong. They are equivalent to the myths and belief systems of traditional societies and 'the contemporary version of common sense'. SRs explain how the strange and familiar become, in time, the familiar.

- Two major processes involved in SRs are **anchoring** and **objectifying**. The latter can be achieved through **personification** (linking complex ideas with a particular person's name) and **figuration** (converting complex ideas into images and metaphors).

■ Children attempt to transform the puzzling and ambiguous features of the adult world by incorporating them into their own collective practices, thereby making the unfamiliar familiar. All societies have SRs about development itself, a set of expectations concerning what children should be like and how they should be treated. Different groups within a particular society may have different SRs.

■ SRs are subject to change, one major source being the mass media. The **central figurative nucleus** is linked to several peripheral elements. When this link is broken, the SR changes. SR theory's major weakness is its abstract or 'fuzzy' nature, making it difficult to test experimentally. It may also be non-falsifiable.

SOME THEORIES OF PREJUDICE AND DISCRIMINATION

Introduction and overview

Social psychologists have long been interested in the causes of prejudice and discrimination. Age (e.g. Levy & Langer, 1994: see Chapter 50), sex (e.g. Tavris, 1993: see Chapter 84), sexuality (e.g. Rose & Platzer, 1993: see Chapter 84), and race (e.g. Coolican, 1997: see Chapter 84) have all been investigated in this respect, although prejudice and discrimination based on *race* has attracted most attention. This chapter looks at some of the theories that try to explain the occurrence and maintenance of racial prejudice and discrimination. These theories focus on the role of *individual* factors, *external* factors, and the impact of *group membership*.

Defining prejudice and discrimination

Literally, 'prejudice' means to pre-judge, and we are all prejudiced towards and against certain things. In everyday language, 'prejudice' and 'discrimination' are typically used synonymously. For social psychologists, however, the two words have subtly different meanings. Prejudice is a special type of *attitude* (a psychological tendency that is expressed by evaluation of a particular entity: Hewstone *et al.*, 1996). As an example of an extreme type of attitude, prejudice comprises three components (the *cognitive*, *affective* and *behavioural*) common to all attitudes.

The cognitive component is the beliefs and preconceived expectations (or *stereotypes*: see Chapter 52) a person has about a particular group or its individual members. These may be positive, but are generally negative. The affective component of prejudice is the feelings or emotions (which may be positive, but are mostly negative) that a particular group or its members incite in us. The behavioural component is the way a person acts towards a group or its members. This component constitutes *discrimination* and ranges from anti-locution (such as the telling of racist jokes) to the genocide (or extermination) of an entire group (Allport, 1954; Hirsch, 1995). Discrimination, then, is *not* the same thing as prejudice. Rather, it is the behavioural component of prejudice.

The prejudiced personality

Sartre (1948) asked whether:

> 'a man may be a good father and a good husband, a conscientious citizen, highly cultured, philanthropic, *and* in addition detest the Jews'.

Sartre did not think so. In his view, anti-semitism, and hostility to other groups, was a symptom of the 'fear of the human condition'. Sartre believed that ethnic prejudice was not a personality characteristic that resided in an otherwise normal personality, but a 'symptom' of a broader style or type of personality (Brigham, 1986).

The most famous attempt to establish a link between personality and prejudice, is that of Adorno *et al.* (1950). They reported the results of a research programme aimed at understanding the anti-semitism and *ethnocentrism* (or 'general prejudice') that had emerged in Nazi Germany in the 1930s. Adorno *et al.* hypothesised that a person's political and social attitudes formed a coherent pattern that was 'an expression of deep-lying trends in personality'.

Box 53.1   Prejudice and early experience

Adopting a Freudian perspective, Adorno *et al.* argued that personality development was shaped by a child's parents. In normal development, parents strike a balance between disciplining a child and the child's self-expression. If, however, parents adopted an excessively harsh disciplinary regime which did not allow self-expression, the child would displace aggression against the parents on to some alternative target (because the consequences of displacing aggression towards the parents would elicit too much fear).

Adorno *et al.* reasoned that likely targets for displaced aggression would be those perceived as being weaker or inferior, such as members of ethnic or deviant groups who could not fight back, and who possessed the hostility towards authority repressed in the child itself. Adorno *et al.* devised several personality inventories which measured anti-semitism (*AS scale*), ethnocentrism (*E scale*), political–economic conservatism (*PEC scale*), and potentiality for fascism (*F scale*).

The AS scale measured 'stereotyped negative opinions' describing the Jews as threatening, immoral, and categorically different from non-Jews, (and) hostile attitudes urging various forms of restriction, exclusion, and suppression as a means of solving the 'Jewish problem' (Brown, 1965). The E scale measured:

'a view of things in which one's own group is the centre of everything, and all others are scaled and rated with reference to it ... Each group ... boasts itself superior ... and looks with contempt on outsiders (and each) thinks its own folkways the only right one ...' (Sumner, 1906).

The PEC scale measured attachment to things as they are and a resistance to social change. The F scale measured implicit authoritarian and anti-democratic trends in personality, which make someone with such a personality susceptible to explicit fascist propaganda.

Box 53.2   Some items appearing on the F scale

For each statement, respondents are asked to decide whether they strongly agree, moderately agree, slightly agree, slightly disagree, moderately disagree or strongly disagree. The scale is arranged so that higher scorers strongly agree with the statements and low scorers strongly disagree with them.

1 Obedience and respect for authority are the most important virtues children should learn.

2 Young people sometimes get rebellious ideas, but as they grow up they ought to get over them and settle down.

3 Sex crimes, such as rapes and attacks on children, deserve more than mere imprisonment. Such criminals ought to be publicly whipped or worse.

4 When a person has a problem or worry, it is best for him not to think about it, but to keep busy with more cheerful things.

5 Some day it will probably be shown that astrology can explain a lot of things.

6 People can be divided into two distinct classes: the weak and the strong.

7 Human nature being what it is, there will always be war and conflict.

8 Nowadays, when so many different kinds of people move around and mix together so much, a person has to protect himself especially carefully against catching an infection or disease from them.

9 The wild sex life of the old Greeks and Romans was tame compared to some of the goings-on in this country, even in places where people might least expect it.

AN EVALUATION OF ADORNO *ET AL.*'S RESEARCH

Adorno *et al.* found that high scorers on the F scale (*authoritarian personalities*) also tended to score highly on the other scales and were more likely to have had the sort of childhood described earlier in Box 53.1. However, although it is tempting to conclude that childhood experiences lead to the formation of a prejudiced personality, many criticisms have been made of Adorno *et al.*'s research.

The F scale (and, indeed, the other scales) can be criticised on methodological grounds. It was constructed so that agreement with a statement *always* indicated authoritarianism (see Box 53.2). Constructing a scale like this often leads to *acquiescent response sets*, that is, the tendency to agree with the remainder of a questionnaire's items (irrespective of their content) when the first few have been agreed with. Other methodological criticisms include the biased nature of the original sample (white, middle class, non-Jewish, Americans), the use of retrospective questions (about childhood) and experimenter effects (the interviewers *knew* the interviewee's scores on the F scale).

Box 53.3   Dogmatism and toughmindedness

Adorno *et al.* also only identified people on the political *right*. According to Rokeach (1948, 1960), dogmatism (a rigid outlook on life and intolerance of those with opposing beliefs regardless of one's own social and political position) is a major characteristic of prejudice. Similarly, prejudice may arise from a personality dimension Eysenck (1954) calls *toughmindedness*. The toughminded individual is attracted to extreme left-wing *or* right-wing political ideologies.

Empirically, predictions derived from the theory have sometimes been unsupported. For example, Pettigrew (1958) found that F scale scores were no higher among Southerners in the USA than among Northerners, even though anti-black attitudes were more common in the south than the north of the USA when Pettigrew conducted his research.

An approach based on personality is reductionist (see Chapter 81), simplistic and ignores sociocultural and demographic factors. Indeed, personality factors are *weaker* predictors of prejudice than age, education, socioeconomic status, and the region of a country in which a person lives (Maykovich, 1975). The *social* nature of prejudice and discrimination requires a social explanation.

462

Figure 53.1   According to the frustration–aggresssion hypothesis, prejudice is the displacement of frustration-induced aggression onto a socially approved scapegoat

The frustration–aggression approach

According to Dollard *et al.*'s (1939) frustration–aggression hypothesis, frustration always gives rise to aggression and aggression is always caused by frustration (see also Chapter 63). Frustration (being blocked from achieving a desirable goal) has many sources. Sometimes, *direct aggression* against the source of the frustration may be possible, and sometimes not. Drawing on Freudian theory, Dollard *et al.* proposed that when we are prevented from being aggressive towards the source of frustration, we *displace* it on to a substitute, or '*scapegoat*'.

The choice of a scapegoat is not usually random. In England during the 1930s and 1940s, the scapegoat was predominantly the Jews. In the 1950s and 1960s, it was West Indians, and since the 1970s it has mainly been Asians from Pakistan. In one retrospective correlational study, Hovland & Sears (1940) found that the number of lynchings of blacks in America from 1880 to 1930 was correlated with the price of cotton: as cotton's price dropped the number of lynchings increased. Presumably, the economic situation created frustration in the white cotton farmers who, unable to confront those responsible for it (the government), displaced their aggression on to blacks.

Although Hovland and Sears' interpretation of their data has been challenged (Hepworth & West, 1988), other research (e.g. Doty *et al.*, 1991) has confirmed that prejudice rises significantly in times of social and economic threat (a point explored further below). Whilst these findings are consistent with the concept of displaced aggression, the fact that some rather than other minority groups are chosen as scapegoats suggests that there are usually socially approved (or legitimised) groups that serve as targets for frustration-induced aggression. As the prominent Nazi Hermann Rausching observed: 'If the Jew did not exist, we should have to invent him' (cited in Koltz, 1983).

Conflict approaches

RELATIVE DEPRIVATION THEORY

According to relative deprivation theory, the discrepancy between our *expectations* (the things we feel entitled to) and *actual attainments* produces frustration (Davis, 1959; Davies, 1969). When attainments fall short of rising expectations, relative deprivation is particularly acute and results in collective unrest. A good example of this is the 1992 Los Angeles riots. Their immediate cause was an all-white jury's acquittal of four police officers accused of beating a black motorist, Rodney King. Against a background of rising unemployment and deepening disadvantage, this was seen by blacks as symbolic of their low value in the eyes of the white majority (Hogg & Vaughan, 1995). The great sense of injustice at the acquittal seemed to demonstrate acutely the injustice which is an inherent feature of both discrimination and relative deprivation.

Figure 53.2   The 1992 Los Angeles riots were triggered by an all-white jury's aquittal of four Los Angeles police officers accused of beating a black motorist, Rodney King

The Los Angeles riots are an example of *fraternalistic relative deprivation*, based on a comparison either with dissimilar others or with other groups (Runciman, 1966). This is contrasted with *egoistic relative deprivation*, based on comparison with other similar individuals. For example, Vanneman & Pettigrew (1972) found that whites who expressed the greatest anti-black attitudes were those who felt most strongly that whites *as a group* are badly off relative to blacks. Since, in objective terms, whites are actually better off, this shows the subjective nature of relative deprivation.

According to Vivian & Brown (1995), the most militant blacks appear to be those with higher socioeconomic and educational status. They probably have higher expectations, both for themselves and for their group, than non-militant blacks. Consequently, they experience relative deprivation more acutely.

REALISTIC CONFLICT THEORY

Data obtained from many nations and historical periods show that the greater the competition for scarce resources, the greater the hostility between various ethnic groups. For example, competition for land between European settlers and native Americans during America's development led to prejudice and discrimination against the minority native Americans (Brigham & Weissbach, 1972).

Sherif's (1966) *realistic conflict theory* proposes that intergroup conflict arises when interests conflict. When two distinct groups want to achieve the same goal but only one can, hostility is produced between them. Indeed, for Sherif, conflict of interest (or *competition*) is a *sufficient* condition for the occurrence of hostility or conflict. This claim is based on a field study conducted by Sherif *et al.* (1961).

> **Box 53.6 The 'Robber's Cave' field experiment**
>
> Sherif *et al.*'s (1961) experiment involved 22 eleven- and twelve-year-old white, middle class, well-adjusted American boys who were attending a summer camp at Robber's Cave State Park in Oklahoma. The boys were divided in advance into two groups of 11 and housed separately, out of each other's sight.
>
> As a result of their shared activities, such as pitching tents and making meals, the two groups quickly developed strong feelings of attachment for their own members. Indeed, a distinct set of norms for each group emerged, defining their identity. One group called themselves the 'Rattlers' and the other the 'Eagles'. A week later, the groups were brought together, and a series of competitive events (for which trophies, medals and prizes would be awarded) was organised.
>
> The two groups quickly came to view one another in highly negative ways, manifesting itself in behaviours such as fighting, raids on dormitories, and refusing to eat together. The competition threatened an unfair distribution of rewards (the trophy, medals, and prizes), and the losing group saw the winners as undeserving.

The view that competition is sufficient for intergroup conflict has, however, been challenged. For example, Tyerman & Spencer (1983) studied boy scouts at their annual camp. The boys already knew each other well and much of what they did was similar to what Sherif's boys had done. The scouts were divided into four 'patrols' which competed in situations familiar to them from previous camps, but the friendship ties which existed between them prior to their arrival at the camp were maintained across the patrols. Under these conditions, competition remained friendly and there was no increase in ingroup solidarity.

In Tyerman and Spencer's view, the four groups continued to see themselves as part of the whole group (a view deliberately encouraged by the scout leader) and therefore Sherif *et al.*'s results reflect the *transitory* nature of the experimental groups. The fact that the scouts knew each other beforehand, had established friendships, were familiar with camp life, and had a leader who encouraged co-operation, were all important contextual and situational influences on their behaviour. So, whilst conflict *can* lead to hostility, it is not sufficient for it and this weakens the explanatory power of Sherif's theory.

Social categorisation and social identity approaches

Whether conflict is a *necessary* condition for prejudice and discrimination (whether hostility can arise in the absence of conflicting interests), has been addressed by several researchers. According to Tajfel *et al.* (1971), merely being in a group and being aware of the existence of another group are sufficient for prejudice and discrimination to develop.

Evidence for this comes from Tajfel *et al.*'s study of 14- and 15-year-old Bristol schoolboys. Each boy was told that he would be assigned to one of two groups, which would be decided according to some purely arbitrary criterion (such as the toss of a coin). They were also told that other boys would be assigned in the same way to either their group or the other group. However, none of the boys knew who these others were, and did not interact with them during the study.

Box 53.7 The task used in Tajfel *et al.*'s (1971) minimal group experiment

Each boy worked alone in a cubicle on a task that required various matrices to be studied (see Figure 53.3) and a decision to be made about how to allocate points to a member of the boy's own group (but not himself) and a member of the other group. The boys were also told that the points could be converted to money after the study. The top line in the figure represents the points that can be allocated to the boy's own group, and the

---

bottom line the points to the other group. For example, if 18 points are allocated to the boy's own group, then 5 are allocated to the other group. If 12 are allocated to the boy's own group, 11 are allocated to the other group.

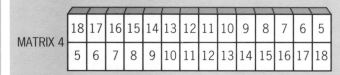

Figure 53.3 One of the matrices used by Tajfel *et al.* (1971)

At the end of the study, Tajfel *et al.* scored the boys' allocations to see if they chose for fairness, maximum gain to their own group, or maximum difference in favour of their own group. Although the matrices were arranged so that both groups would benefit from a cooperative strategy, the boys allocated points to the advantage of their own group and to the disadvantage of the other group.

SOCIAL CATEGORISATION THEORY

Several other studies using Tajfel *et al.*'s method (called the *minimal group paradigm*), have found that people favour their own group over others (Tajfel & Billig, 1974; Brewer & Kramer, 1985). According to *social categorisation theory* (Hewstone & Jaspars, 1982), this is because people tend to divide the social world into two categories, 'us' (the *ingroup*) and 'them' (the *outgroup*). In Tajfel's view, discrimination cannot occur until this division has been made (categorisation being a *necessary* condition for discrimination), but when it is made it produces conflict and discrimination (categorisation is a *sufficient* condition as well). Amongst the criteria used for categorisation are race, nationality, religion and sex.

Research into ingroups and outgroups shows that ingroup members see themselves in highly favourable terms, as possessing desirable characteristics, and being strongly liked. Linville *et al.* (1989) call the ingroup's tendency to see all kinds of differences among themselves the *ingroup differentiation hypothesis*. The opposite perceptions apply to outgroup members (Wilder, 1984). Additionally, outgroup members are evaluated less favourably and the ingroup sees them as being more alike in attitudes, behaviour and even facial appearance (Judd & Park, 1988). The view that 'they all look the same to me' is called the *illusion of outgroup homogeneity* (Quattrone, 1986), and may be a natural cognitive process. The illusion of outgroup homogeneity effect has clear social implications, especially as far as the legal justice system is concerned (Brigham & Malpass, 1985: see Box 53.6).

Figure 53.4 How the 'ingroup' and 'outgroup' are defined can change depending on the circumstances. Here, the ingroup (England supporters) incorporates a large number of what are usually outgroups (supporters of other clubs)

Box 53.8 The illusion of outgroup homogeneity

JUDGE DENIES 'ASIAN' REMARK WAS RACIST

A judge who told an all-white jury that Asians 'all look the same' to him has refused to apologise. The judge made the comments during the trial of a young Asian man accused of robbery. After viewing photographs of a dozen Asians, he told the jury: 'I have in front of me photographs of 12 Asian men, all of whom look exactly the same, which I'm sure you'll appreciate.'

He insisted his remark had been misinterpreted. 'I want to make it clear that (my) observation, far from being an accidental affront to any section of the community, was merely intended to indicate that on examination of the photographs, the appearance of those people depicted was similar. The comment – which perhaps should not have been made – was, if anything, directed by implication to warn the jury that there was nothing singularly striking about any of the persons depicted in the photographs, in so far as identification is an issue in this case. That comment has been taken as carrying with it some sort of insult. I'm appalled that anybody could suppose that such an inference was fairly to be drawn.'

(Adapted from *The Daily Telegraph*, 22 February, 1995)

There has, however, been disagreement with the view that intergroup conflict is an *inevitable* consequence of ingroup and outgroup formation. For example, Wetherell (1982) studied white and Polynesian children in New Zealand and found the latter to be much more generous towards the outgroup, reflecting cultural norms which emphasised co-operation. Also, the minimal group paradigm itself has been criticised on several grounds, most notably its artificiality (Schiffman & Wicklund, 1992; Gross, 1994).

SOCIAL IDENTITY THEORY

Exactly why people tend to divide the social world into 'us' and 'them' is not completely clear. However, Tajfel (1978) and Tajfel & Turner (1986) propose that group membership provides people with a *positive self-image* and a sense of 'belonging' in the social world. According to *social identity theory* (SIT), people strive to achieve or maintain a positive self-image. There are two components of a positive self-image: *personal identity* (our personal characteristics and attributes which make us unique) and *social identity* (a sense of what we are like, derived from the groups to which we belong).

Box 53.9 Social identities, comparison and competition

Each of us actually has several social identities which correspond to the number of different groups we identify with. In relation to each one, the more positive the group's image, the more positive social identity and hence self-image will be. To enhance self-esteem, group members make *social comparisons* with other groups. To the extent that the group sees itself in favourable terms as compared with others, self-esteem is increased. However, since every group is similarly trying to enhance self-esteem, a clash of perceptions occurs, and prejudice and discrimination arise through what Tajfel calls *social competition*.

SIT has been applied beyond the laboratory (see Brown, 1988, for a review of applications to wage differentials, ethnolinguistic groups, and occupational groups). The theory also helps us understand how prejudice is maintained. Phenomena like the *confirmatory bias* (the tendency to prefer evidence which confirms our beliefs: see Chapter 36), *self-fulfilling prophecies* (in which our expectations about certain groups determine their behaviour) and the promotion of our own group's identity, can all be understood when viewed in terms of SIT.

Whilst there is considerable empirical support for SIT, much of this comes from the minimal group paradigm which, as noted, has been criticised. More importantly, the available evidence shows only a positive ingroup bias and not derogatory attitudes or behaviour towards the outgroup, which is what we normally understand by 'prejudice'. So, although there is abundant evidence of intergroup discrimination, this apparently stems from raising the evaluation of the ingroup rather than denigrating the outgroup (Vivian & Brown, 1995).

Conclusions

Several theories of prejudice and discrimination have been advanced. Some see prejudice as stemming from individual factors, some concentrate on the role of external factors, and some emphasise the impact of group membership. Whilst all have some support, none is yet accepted as a definitive theory of prejudice.

Summary

■ Prejudice is an **extreme attitude** comprising the three components common to all attitudes. These are **cognitive** (mainly stereotyped beliefs and pre-conceived expectations), **affective** (mostly negative feelings/emotions) and **behavioural** (**discrimination**, ranging from anti-locution to extermination).

■ Based on Freudian theory, Adorno *et al.* argued that prejudiced people were subjected to an excessively harsh disciplinary regime as children, which prevented self-expression. Aggression towards their parents would be displaced onto targets seen as weaker or inferior, such as members of ethnic or deviant groups.

■ Adorno *et al.* constructed several personality inventories. The F scale was designed to measure authoritarian/anti-democratic tendencies (**authoritarian personalities**). High F scale scorers tended to score highly on measures of anti-semitism, ethnocentrism, and political–economic conservatism. They were also likely to have had the punitive upbringing that prevented direct expression of hostility towards their parents.

■ Adorno *et al.*'s research and their conclusions have been extensively criticised. Methodological criticisms include acquiescent response sets on the various scales, a biased sample, and experimenter effects. Also, they only identified people on the political right. Rokeach argues that **dogmatism** is a major factor in prejudice, regardless of a person's right- or left-wing political views.

■ Experimental evidence does not support Adorno *et al.*'s theory, and it fails to explain prejudice in entire societies or sub-groups and the rise and decline of prejudice in societies. **Conformity to social norms** is a better explaination of these observations, although this does not explain the origins of prejudice or its continuation following changes in social norms.

■ Since prejudice is a social phenomenon, it requires social explanations. According to the **frustration–aggression hypothesis**, frustration always results in aggression and aggression always stems from frustration. When aggression cannot be expressed directly against the frustration's source, it can be displaced onto a substitute or **scapegoat**.

■ According to **relative deprivation theory**, the discrepancy between expectations and actual attainments produces frustration, especially when attainments fall short of rising expectations. **Fraternalistic relative deprivation** is based on comparisons with either dissimilar others or with other groups. **Egoistic relative deprivation** is based on comparisons with other similar individuals.

■ Sherif's **realistic conflict theory** proposes that intergroup conflict arises when interests conflict. Conflict of interest (or competition) is a sufficient condition for hostility. This claim is based on the Robber's Cave experiment. However, competition does not inevitably produce intergroup conflict, and contextual and situational factors influence the effects of competition.

■ Tajfel *et al.* argue that conflict may not even be necessary for prejudice and discrimination. Based on studies using the **minimal group paradigm**, they argue that merely belonging to a particular group and being aware of another group's existence is sufficient. **Social categorisation theory** explains this in terms of the division of the world into 'us' (the **ingroup**) and 'them' (the **outgroup**). This division is both necessary and sufficient for discrimination.

■ As well as evaluating outgroup members less favourably, the ingroup sees them as being more alike in attitudes, behaviour and even facial appearance (the **illusion of outgroup homogeneity**). However, it is unlikely that ingroup/outgroup formation inevitably results in intergroup conflict.

■ **Social identity theory** (SIT) sees group membership as providing individuals with a positive self-image, consisting of personal identity and social identity. The more positive the image of a group to which one belongs, the more positive is one's social identity and hence self-image. The more favourable social comparisons are with other groups, the higher members' self esteem will be. This results in social competition, since every group is similarly trying to enhance self-esteem.

■ SIT explains the maintenance of prejudice through phenomena like the **confirmatory bias, self-fulfilling prophecies** and the promotion of one's group identity. However, much of the theory's support comes from the minimal group paradigm, which has been criticised for its artificiality. Also, the evidence tends to show a positive ingroup bias, rather than negative attitudes/behaviour towards the outgroup, which is what prejudice and discrimination normally imply.

THE REDUCTION OF PREJUDICE AND DISCRIMINATION

Introduction and overview

Chapter 53 looked at some of the theories concerning the origins and maintenance of prejudice and discrimination. This chapter looks at some approaches to their reduction and the effectiveness of these. As Hirsch (1995) has noted, 50 years after the Nazi extermination and concentration camps were liberated, extreme discriminatory behaviour (in the form of genocide):

'continues unabated, neither punished nor prevented. In what used to be [Yugoslavia], torture, murder, rape and starvation are everyday occurrences'.

Given their continued existence, the reduction of prejudice and discrimination is a very important issue indeed.

Prejudice reduction based on theories of its causes

One approach to reducing prejudice and discrimination is to look at the implications of the theories of them discussed in Chapter 53.

Box 54.1 How can theories of prejudice and discrimination contribute to their reduction?

The prejudiced personality: Evidence suggests that the authoritarian personality is *self-perpetuating*. Authoritarian parents tend to produce authoritarian children, and there is a strong correlation between parents and their offspring's F scale scores (Cherry & Byrne, 1976). However, level of education is also correlated with authoritarianism. Presumably, the provision of, and access to, education would go some way to reducing prejudice (Pennington, 1986). Additionally, changing patterns of child rearing (which Adorno *et al.* saw as being crucially important) might reduce prejudice. By allowing children to express hostility, the need to displace it on to ethnic and other groups would not arise.

Frustration–aggression and relative deprivation: According to these theories, preventing frustration, lowering people's expectations, and providing them

with less anti-social ways of venting their frustration should result in a reduction of prejudice and discrimination. However, the practical problems of putting back the 'historical clock' or changing social conditions in quite fundamental ways are immense.

Conflict approaches: These make it clear that removing competition and replacing it with goals requiring co-operation (*superordinate goals*) will remove or prevent hostility.

Social categorisation and social identity approaches: These imply that if intergroup stereotypes can become less negative and automatic, and if the boundaries that exist between groups can be made less distinct or more flexible, then group membership may become a less central part of the self-concept. Consequently, positive evaluation of the ingroup might no longer be inevitable.

Socialisation

One theory of prejudice not explored in Chapter 53 derives from *social learning theory* (see Chapter 32). According to this, children acquire negative attitudes towards various social groups as a result of 'significant others' (such as parents, peers and teachers) exposing them to such views or rewarding them for expressing such attitudes (Stephan & Rosenfield, 1978). For example, Ashmore & Del Boca (1976) found that children's racial attitudes are often closely aligned with those of their parents, and children might internalise the prejudices they observe in them.

Another 'significant other' is the mass media (Coolican, 1997). If some groups are portrayed by the mass media in demeaning or comic roles, then it is hardly surprising that children acquire the belief that these groups are inferior to others (Worchel *et al.*, 1988). The mass media which have the greatest, and most immediate impact, and to which children are most exposed, are television and films (see Chapter 64). However, others include newspapers, magazines and textbooks.

Box 54.2   Racism and textbooks

Proctor (cited in Birch, 1985) gives numerous examples to support the argument that many textbooks, particularly history textbooks, are sometimes actively racist, both in intention and effect. Proctor gives as one example Manhattan Island being bought from American Indians for only a few dollars. The island's current value has been used as evidence of the Indians' 'stupidity'. Yet as Proctor points out:

'To the Indians, the notion of a person *owning* land was ridiculous. The land cannot belong to one person, and why should one want to own it? The sale of Manhattan Island was a joke in Indian eyes. Somebody gave them four dollars to buy what cannot be possessed. It was like buying the sun to a European'.

Owusu-Bempah & Howitt (1994) have pointed out that in some leading *psychology* textbooks and elsewhere, black nations are still described in derogatory and deprecatory terms such as 'primitive', 'tribal', 'underdeveloped' and 'undeveloped'. In their view:

'Each and every psychologist needs to be able to question their "broadmindedness" … There is little point in railing against the overt racists in psychology while at the same time ignoring matters closer to home'.

If children's attitudes are shaped by their observations of 'significant others', then, presumably, discouraging those others from expressing prejudiced views and discriminatory behaviour should help to prevent prejudice and discrimination from developing. Whilst psychologists cannot interfere in parent–child relationships, they can alert parents to the prejudiced views they are expressing and the important costs attached to them (Baron & Byrne, 1994).

Parents could also encourage *self-examination* in their children (Rathus, 1990). For example, some of the things we say or do reflect our prejudices without us being aware of this. Rathus gives the example of a Catholic referring to an individual as 'that damned Jew'. It is extremely unlikely that a Catholic would say 'that damned Catholic'. Parents could, therefore, stress to their children the importance of remembering to attribute behaviour to people as *individuals* rather than *group representatives* (Hogg & Vaughan, 1995).

Several researchers have looked at the extent to which directly experiencing prejudice and discrimination may help children to understand them and, as a result, reduce their occurrence. McGuire (1969) showed that providing children with counter-arguments to attitudes and behaviours they might experience as adults lessens prejudice and discrimination. A well-documented example of this

approach was taken by Jane Elliott, an American school-teacher (Elliott, 1977).

As a way of helping her nine-year-old pupils understand the effects that prejudice and discrimination can have, she divided them into two groups on the basis of their eye colours. Elliott told her pupils that brown-eyed people are more intelligent and 'better' than blue eyed people. Brown-eyed students, though in the minority, would therefore be the 'ruling class' over the inferior blue-eyed children and would be given extra privileges. The blue-eyed students were told that they would be 'kept in their place' by restrictions such as being last in line, seated at the back of the class, and being given less break time. They were also told that they would have to wear special collars as a sign of their low status.

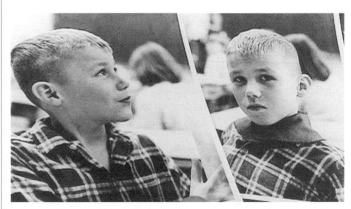

Figure 54.1   Still from the film of Elliott's classroom experiment in which wearing collars as an overt sign of low status was part of the discrimination sanctioned by the teacher

Within a short time, the blue-eyed children began to do more poorly in their schoolwork, became depressed and angry, and described themselves in negative ways. The brown-eyed group became mean, oppressed the others, and made derogatory statements about them. The next day, Elliott told her pupils that she had made a mistake and that it was really blue-eyed people who were superior. With the situation reversed, the pattern of prejudice and discrimination quickly switched from the blue-eyed children to the brown-eyed children as victims.

At the end of her demonstration, Elliott debriefed her pupils. She told them that its purpose was to provide them with an opportunity to experience the evils of prejudice and discrimination in a protected environment. Interestingly, the consequences of the demonstration were not short-lived. In a follow-up study of the pupils when they were 18, Elliott (1990) found that they reported themselves as being more tolerant of differences between groups and actively opposed to prejudice.

Box 54.3   Weiner & Wright's (1973) study

The implications of Elliott's informal demonstration were investigated by Weiner & Wright (1973). They randomly assigned white nine-year-olds to either a 'green' or an 'orange' group, group membership being indicated by an appropriately coloured armband. First, the 'green' pupils were labelled inferior and denied social privileges. After a few days, the labelling was reversed. Children in a second class were not treated in this way and served as a control group.

Once the children had experienced being in the 'green' and 'orange' conditions, they and the control group children were asked if they wanted to go on a picnic with black children from another school. Ninety-six per cent of children from the 'green–orange' group expressed a desire to go compared with only 62 per cent of the control group. The experience of prejudice and discrimination evidently led the 'green–orange' children to think that discrimination on the basis of colour is wrong. This suggests that experience of being discriminated against can make children more aware of the sensitivities and feelings of outgroup members.

The 'contact hypothesis'

People who are separated, segregated, and unaware of one another have no way of checking whether an interpretation of another group's behaviour is accurate. Because any interpretation is likely to be consistent with a (negative) stereotype held about that group, the stereotype will be strengthened. Equally, if we do not know why members of a particular group behave the way they do, we are likely to see them as being more dissimilar from ourselves than is actually the case.

Figure 54.2   The 'us' and 'them' mentality is a feature of the mirror-image phenomenon and autistic hostility

Related to this *autistic hostility* is what Bronfenbrenner (1960) calls the *mirror-image phenomenon*. In this, enemies come to see themselves as being in the right (each has 'God on its side') and the other in the wrong. In the same way, each attributes to the other the same negative characteristics (the 'assumed dissimilarity of beliefs').

Box 54.4   Why does enhanced contact reduce prejudice and discrimination?

By enhancing or increasing contact between separated and segregated groups, prejudice and discrimination may be reduced for at least four reasons.

- Increased contact might be effective because it leads people to realise that their attitudes are actually more similar than they assumed. The recognition of similarity between people leads to increased liking and attraction (see Chapter 55, page 478).

- Increased contact may have benefits through the *mere exposure effect* (according to which, the more we come into contact with certain stimuli, the more familiar and liked they become: Zajonc, 1968).

- Favourable contact between two groups may lead to an opportunity to disconfirm the negative stereotypes held about them.

- Increased contact may lead to a reduction in *outgroup homogeneity* (see Chapter 53, page 466), because the outgroup members lose their strangeness and become more differentiated. As a result, they are seen as a collection of unique individuals rather than interchangeable 'units'.

It is generally agreed, however, that increased contact by itself is not sufficient to reduce prejudice, and may even have the opposite effect. Despite evidence that we prefer people who are familiar, if contact is between people of consistently *unequal* status, then 'familiarity may breed contempt'. Many whites in the United States have always had a great deal of contact with blacks, but with blacks in the role of dishwashers, toilet attendants, domestic servants, and so on. Contacts under these conditions may simply reinforce the stereotypes held by whites of blacks as inferior (Aronson, 1980).

Similarly, Amir (1994) has argued that the central issues to address are those concerning the important conditions under which increased intergroup contact has an effect, who is affected by it, and with respect to what particular outcomes. Some of these issues were addressed by Allport (1954). According to his *contact hypothesis*:

'Prejudice (unless deeply rooted in the character structure of the individual) may be reduced by equal status contact between majority and minority groups in the pursuit of common goals. The effect is greatly enhanced if this contact is sanctioned by institutional supports (i.e. by law, custom or local atmosphere) and provided it is of a sort that leads to the perception of common interests and common humanity between members of the two groups'.

Most programmes aimed at promoting harmonious relations between groups that were previously in conflict have adopted Allport's view, and stressed the importance of *equal status contact* and the *pursuit of common* (or *superordinate) goals*.

EQUAL STATUS CONTACT

One early study of equal status contact was conducted by Deutsch & Collins (1951). They compared two kinds of housing project, one of which was thoroughly integrated (blacks and whites were assigned houses regardless of their race) and the other segregated. Residents of both were intensively interviewed, and it was found that both casual and neighbourly contacts were greater in the integrated housing and that there was a corresponding decrease in prejudice among whites towards blacks. Wilner *et al.* (1955) showed that prejudice is particularly reduced in the case of next-door neighbours, illustrating the effect of *proximity* (see Chapter 55, page 477).

Related to these studies are the findings reported by Minard (1952), Stouffer *et al.* (1949), and Amir (1969). As mentioned in Chapter 53 (see page 463), Minard studied white coalminers in the USA and found that whilst 80 per cent of his sample were friendly towards blacks *underground*, only 20 per cent were friendly *above ground*. This suggests that prejudice was reduced by the equal status contact between the two groups when they were working together, but that the *social norms* which operated above ground at that time did not permit equality of status. Likewise, Stouffer *et al.* (1949) and Amir (1969) found that inter-racial attitudes improved markedly when blacks and whites served together as soldiers in battle and on ships, but that their relationships were less good when they were at base camp.

Desegregation and equal educational opportunities

In the USA, much research has been conducted into the effects of desegregation in schools. The decision to desegregate schools was taken in 1954, at least partly as a result of research conducted by Clark & Clark (1947: see Box 54.8). Whether integration is the best means for ensuring equal educational opportunities for children, and whether

it actually reduces racial tension, have both been hotly disputed.

Box 54.5   Desegregation in America's schools

According to some researchers, the continued academic underachievement of black students, and inter-racial hostility between black and white students on many school campuses, show that integration has failed to bring about equal educational opportunities and a lessening of racial tension. Supporters of integration, however, argue that this is because a reduction in racial tension and prejudice and an improvement in black achievement can occur *only* when school desegregation has been planned to promote equal status for majority and minority groups, and has been implemented with the outspoken support of all authority figures involved. When these conditions are not met, as seems to be true in many cases, an increase in tension and prejudice are not surprising (Cook, 1984).

However, evidence suggests that desegregation may be working better than even contact hypothesis supporters believe. According to Braddock (1985), the literature on school desegregation suggests that the effects may actually be far-reaching and include lifelong social integration and occupational attainment for blacks (Crooks & Stein, 1991).

From the evidence considered, it would seem that if intergroup contact does reduce prejudice, it is not because it encourages interpersonal friendship (as Deutsch and Collins would claim), but rather because of changes in the nature and structure of *intergroup relationships*. Brown & Turner (1981) and Hewstone & Brown (1986) argue that if the contact between individual groups is *interpersonal* (people are seen as individuals and group memberships are largely insignificant), any change of attitude may not generalise to other members of the respective group. So, and at the very least, people must be seen as typical members of their group if generalisation is to occur (Vivian *et al.*, 1994). The problem here is that if, in practice, 'typical' means 'stereotypical' and the stereotype is negative, reinforcement of it is likely to occur. Thus, any encounter with a 'typical' group member should be a pleasant experience (Wilder, 1984).

PURSUIT OF COMMON GOALS

As noted in Chapter 53 (see page 464), Sherif *et al.* (1961) produced conflict in two groups of children by creating competition between them. The researchers initially attempted to resolve the conflict by having the children watch movies, attend a party, and eat meals together.

However, this was unsuccessful and none of the situations, either individually or collectively, did anything to reduce friction. Indeed, the situations actually resulted in increased hostility between the groups.

Box 54.6   Co-operation and superordinate goals

Another approach used by Sherif *et al.* was more successful. This involved creating situations in which the problems both groups faced could only be solved through *co-operation* between them (Deaux *et al.*, 1993). For example, the researchers arranged for the camp's drinking water supply to be cut off, with the only way of restoring it requiring both groups to work together. Similarly, on a trip to an overnight camp, one of the trucks carrying the boys got 'stuck', and the only way in which it could resume the journey was if all the boys pulled together on a large rope.

The researchers found that by creating these *superordinate goals* (goals that can only be achieved through co-operation), the group divisions gradually disappeared. Indeed, at the end of the experimental period, the boys actually suggested travelling home together on one bus. Sixty-five per cent of friendship choices were made from members of the *other* group, and the stereotypes previously held became much more favourable.

Sherif *et al.*'s findings have subsequently been replicated in other similar studies (e.g. Clore *et al.*, 1978) in a variety of contexts (such as inter-racial sports teams: Slavin & Madden, 1979). However, imposing superordinate goals is not always effective and may sometimes *increase* antagonism towards the outgroup if the co-operation fails to achieve its aims (Brown, 1996). It may also be important for groups engaged in cooperative ventures to have distinctive and complementary roles to play, so that each group's contributions are clearly defined. When this does not happen, liking for the other group may actually decrease, perhaps because group members are concerned with the ingroup's integrity (Brown, 1996).

The pursuit of common goals has also been investigated in studies of cooperative learning in the classroom. Aronson (1992) was originally approached by the superintendent of schools in Austin, Texas, to give advice about how inter-racial prejudice could be reduced. Aronson *et al.* (1978) devised an approach to learning that involved mutual interdependence among the members of a class.

Box 54.7   The jigsaw classroom technique

In Aronson *et al.*'s *jigsaw classroom technique*, students (regardless of their race) are placed in a situation in which they are given material that represents one piece of a lesson to be learned. Each child must learn his or her part and then communicate it to the rest of the group. At the end of the lesson, all children are tested on the whole lesson and given an individual score. Thus, the children must learn the full lesson and there is complete *mutual interdependence* because each is dependent on the others for parts of the lesson that can only be learned from them.

Aronson originally studied white, black and hispanic students, who met for three days a week for a total of six weeks. At the end of this period, the students showed increased self-esteem, academic performance, liking for their classmates, and some inter-racial perceptions, compared with a control group given six weeks of traditional teaching. Aronson's method has been used in many classrooms with thousands of students, and the results consistently show a reduction in prejudice (Singh, 1991).

Importantly, though, whilst the children who had actually worked together came to like each other better as individuals, this research has not been longitudinal and so the consequences of cooperative learning have only shown *short-term* benefits. Whether the changes last, and whether they *generalise* to other social situations, is unclear. However, at least in the short term, the pursuit of common goals can be effective, especially with young children in whom prejudiced attitudes have not yet become deeply ingrained.

Figure 54.3   Pursuit of common goals: multiracial children in harmony

Racism and childhood identity

Earlier in this chapter, socialisation and the reduction of prejudice were considered. According to Milner (1996, 1997), the development of children's racial attitudes has been seen as an essentially *passive* process in which parents and others provide behaviours which children then absorb and reproduce. Racial attitude development is seen as being the result of irresistible social and cultural factors which impinge on the child from a variety of sources, with the child's only active participation being an attempt to make 'cognitive sense' of the messages he or she receives.

Whilst Milner accepts that a variety of sources provide the *content* of children's racist attitudes, he argues that:

> 'there has been a tendency to make a rather facile equation between, on the one hand, children's racial attitudes, and culturally mediated racism on the other. It is as though we have said a) "children have rather hostile racial attitudes", and b) "our cultural products contain many instances of implicit or explicit racism", and therefore a) must be caused by b)'.

Milner does not see sources such as children's books as containing enough 'raw material' in themselves to account for the development of their racial attitudes. In his view, children play an *active* role in the development of their racial awareness and rudimentary attitudes. Rather than solely absorbing adults' attitudes in 'junior form' or seeking to construct a cognitively well-ordered world, they are motivated by *needs* to locate themselves and their groups within that social world 'in ways which establish and sustain positive self- and social-regard or identity'. This is consistent with social identity theory (see Chapter 53, page 466).

The principal need in a society with a competitive ethos (such as our own) is to understand the complexity of the social world and locate oneself at an acceptable station within it. Aligning oneself with a particular category might lead to social acceptance or to marginality or ostracism. Identification with a particular childhood category membership, then, has a positive aspect whose value is much sought after, and negative racial attitudes *may* fulfil this function for the majority-group child in a multi-racial society. As Milner points out, though, negative racial attitudes cannot (by definition) fulfil the same function for the minority group. This can be seen in the phenomenon of *misidentification*.

Box 54.8   Misidentification

Clark & Clark (1947) asked black and white children aged between three and seven to choose a black or white doll to play with. Regardless of their own colour, the children consistently chose the white dolls, saying that they were prettier and nicer. These findings were replicated by other researchers, and it was also shown that the 'doll tests' are a valid measure of self-concept related to ethnic identification (Ward & Braun, 1972).

Morland (1970) found that when the level of actual discrimination increases, so self-contempt increases. Thus, more black children from Southern states in America chose a white child as a preferred playmate than was the case for black children from the Northern states. As Rowan (1978) has remarked:

'What this means is that when whites are taught to hate blacks, blacks themselves come to hate blacks – that is, themselves. When whites are taught that blacks are inferior, blacks themselves comes to see themselves as inferior. In order to cease to be inferior, they have (it sometimes seems to them) to cease to be black'.

The *self-denigration* by minority groups was addressed by civil rights and black politico-cultural movements that encouraged a positive connotation about blackness with slogans like 'Black is Beautiful'. As a result of these movements, the misidentification phenomenon all but disappeared, even among young children who might not be expected to be attuned to the relevant cultural and political messages (Milner, 1997). But what about the majority group? As Milner notes:

> 'If it is true that majority-group children may actively seek, or be drawn to, a set of racial attitudes partly because the superior/inferior group relations they portray satisfies the developing need for a positive social identity, then this might seem to underscore both the inevitability and ineradicability of racism, among the majority group.'

However, Milner argues that many other things can serve the purpose of satisfying the need for a positive social identity (supporting a winning soccer team, for example), and far from embedding racism deeper in the child's 'psychological economy', this notion actually undercuts the significance of childhood racism. For Milner, racist ideas may have more to do with the developing identity needs of children than with the objects of those attitudes, and may be rapidly superseded by other sources of status and self-esteem.

This would account for Pushkin & Veness's (1973) finding that racial attitudes peak in hostility around the age of six to seven and decline subsequently. Moreover, if racial attitudes were central in a child's identity, they would endure into adulthood, but (with a few exceptions) this does not seem to happen. That hostile racial attitudes may be transient phenomena 'would be encouraging for multiracial education and for the wider society' (Milner, 1997).

Conclusions

This chapter has examined a variety of approaches to the reduction of prejudice and discrimination. As the previous chapter showed, prejudice and discrimination cannot be explained in a simple and straightforward way. As a result, we should not be surprised that the reduction of these phenomena is also not straightforward.

Summary

■ All theories of the origins and maintenance of prejudice and discrimination have something to say about their reduction. **Social learning theory**, for example, proposes that children acquire negative attitudes towards particular social groups as a result of significant others (such as parents) exposing them to such views or reinforcing them for expressing such attitudes. The mass media are another significant other. Some textbooks are actively racist.

■ By discouraging parents from expressing prejudiced views and discriminatory behaviour, these should be prevented from developing in children. Providing children with the opportunity to directly experience prejudice and discrimination in a protected environment may help their reduction by increasing children's understanding. This was demonstrated in Elliot's 'brown-eyes–blue-eyes' experiment and Weiner and Wright's 'green–orange' study.

■ When segregated and ignorant of others, we rely on our (negative) stereotypes to interpret their behaviours, and tend to see them as being more dissimilar from ourselves than they really are (**autistic hostility**). Related to this is the **mirror-image phenomenon** and the 'assumed dissimilarity of beliefs'.

■ Increasing contact between segregated groups can help people realise that their attitudes are actually more similar than they assumed, which can increase attraction. This can also happen through the **mere exposure effect**. Favourable contact may also present opportunities for disconfirming negative stereotypes and reducing outgroup homogeneity.

■ Increased contact by itself is not, however, sufficient and may even increase prejudice and discrimination. If contact is between people of consistently **unequal status**

(for example, due to particular social norms) then stereotypical beliefs may be reinforced.

■ The **contact hypothesis** proposes that there must be **equal status contact** and the **pursuit of common goals**. The benefits of the former have been shown in studies of racially integrated housing projects. However, if contact does reduce prejudice, this probably occurs because of changes in the nature and structure of **intergroup relationships** rather than the encouragement of **interpersonal friendship**.

■ In the USA, there has been much debate about the effects of **desegregation** in schools. Supporters of integration argue that continued underachievement of black students will continue unless desegregation has been planned to promote equal status for majority and minority groups, and has the outspoken support of all the authority figures involved.

■ The pursuit of common goals is only effective when **superordinate goals**, which can only be achieved through **co-operation**, are created. However, if co-operation fails to achieve its goals, antagonism towards the outgroup may increase. It is important that each group's contributions are clearly defined.

■ Cooperative learning in the classroom has been studied using the **jigsaw technique**, which creates **mutual interdependence** between students. The technique can produce increases in self-esteem, academic performance, liking for classmates, and some inter-racial perceptions. However, little is known about the **long-term** benefits and whether they **generalise** to other situations.

■ Children do not passively absorb and reproduce parents' and others' behaviours. Although the **content** of racial attitudes is provided by a variety of social/cultural sources, children play more active roles in the development of their racial awareness and attitudes.

■ Children are motivated by **needs** to locate themselves and their groups within their social world in ways that promote positive self- and social-identities. Adopting negative racial attitudes **may** help achieve acceptance for the majority-group child in a multi-racial, competitive society. Negative racial attitudes cannot fulfil this function for minority group children, as seen in **misidentification**.

■ Minority groups' self-denigration was addressed by civil rights and black politico-cultural movements, which led to the near disappearance of misidentification, even among young children. Racist attitudes may be more to do with children's developing identity needs than with the objects of those attitudes. This would account for racial hostility peaking at ages six to seven.

PART 2

Social relationships

THE FORMATION OF ADULT RELATIONSHIPS

Introduction and overview

According to Duck (1995), the study of interpersonal relationships is one of the most fertile and all-embracing aspects of social scientific research. This, and the two chapters that follow, provide an introduction to the study of social relationships and examine how and why such relationships are formed, maintained and sometimes dissolved. These chapters look at theories of adult interpersonal relationships, the components and effects of such relationships, and individual, social and cultural variations in them.

This chapter considers the formation of adult relationships, that is, how these relationships 'get started'. Much of the research in this area originates from North America, and both its quality and validity have been questioned. However, before looking at the research, and critiques of it, affiliation as a precondition for relationship formation will be briefly considered.

Affiliation

Affiliation is a basic need for the company of others. According to Duck (1988), we are more affiliative and inclined to seek other people's company in some circumstances than others. These include moving to a new neighbourhood, and terminating a close relationship. One of the most powerful factors influencing affiliation, however, is *anxiety*.

Box 55.1   The effects of anxiety on affiliation

In one of Schachter's (1959) experiments, female students were led to believe that they would receive electric shocks. Half were told that the shocks would be extremely painful (high anxiety condition) and half that they would not be at all painful (low anxiety condition). The students were then told that there would be a delay whilst the equipment was being set up, and that they could wait on their own or with another participant. Two-thirds of those in the high anxiety condition chose to wait with another participant, whilst only one-third in the low anxiety condition chose this option.

In another experiment, Schachter told all participants that the shocks would be extremely painful. This time, though, the members of one group were given the option of waiting alone or with another participant who would be receiving the shocks. Members of a second group were given the option of waiting alone or with a student waiting to see her teacher. Those in the first group preferred to sit with another participant, whilst those in the second group preferred to be alone. This suggests that if we have something to worry about, we prefer to be with others in the same situation as us.

Anxiety's role in affiliation has also been demonstrated in other studies. For example, Kulik & Mahler (1989) found that most patients awaiting coronary bypass surgery preferred to share a room with someone who had already undergone that operation, rather than with someone who was waiting to undergo it. The main motive for this preference seemed to be the need for *information* in order to reduce the stress caused by the forthcoming operation (Buunk, 1996).

Forming relationships: interpersonal attraction

According to Clore & Byrne (1974), we are attracted to people whose presence is *rewarding* for us. These rewards may be direct (and provided by the other person) or indirect (the other person takes on the emotional tone of the surrounding situation). The more rewards someone provides for us, the more we should be attracted to them. Although rewards are not the same for everyone, several factors are important in influencing the initial attraction between people through their reward value. These include proximity, exposure, familiarity, similarity, physical attractiveness, reciprocal liking, complementarity and competence.

PROXIMITY

Proximity means geographical closeness, and is a minimum requirement for attraction because the further apart two people live, the less likely it is that they will have the chance to meet, become friends or marry each other. Festinger *et al.* (1950) found that students living in campus accommodation were most friendly with their next-door neighbours and least friendly with those at the end of the corridor. Students separated by four flats hardly ever became friends and, in two-storey flats, residents tended to interact mainly with people who lived on the same floor. On any one floor, people who lived near stairways had more friends than those living at the end of the corridor.

Festinger *et al.*'s findings have been replicated in numerous studies. For example, home owners are more likely to become friendly with their next-door neighbours, especially when they share a drive (Whyte, 1956), and apartment dwellers tend to form relationships with those on the same floor (Nahemow & Lawton, 1975). At school, students are more likely to develop relationships with those they sit next to (Segal, 1974).

> **Box 55.2   Physical proximity and personal space**
>
> There are, however, 'rules' governing physical proximity. Sommer (1969) and Felipe & Sommer (1966) showed that when a stranger sits next to or close to someone, that person experiences an unpleasant increase in arousal. This is because his or her *personal space* (Hall, 1959: a sort of 'invisible bubble' around a person in which it is unpleasant for others to be) has been invaded.
>
> In Hall's view, we learn *proxemic rules*. These prescribe the physical distance that is appropriate between people in daily situations, and the kinds of situation in which closeness or distance is proper. These rules are not the same in all cultures (Collett, 1993), and there are individual differences with regard to them, even within the same culture (violent criminals, for example, are more sensitive to physical closeness than non-violent criminals). Successful relationships may require an initial establishment of 'boundary understandings', that is, strangers must be *invited* into our personal space rather than 'invade' it.

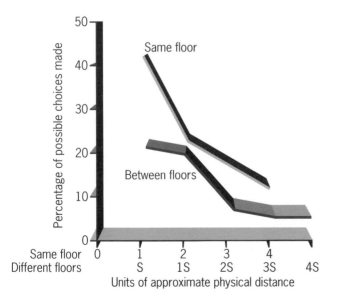

Figure 55.1   Data from Festinger *et al.*'s (1950) investigation. The 'units of approximate physical distance' refer to how many doors apart people lived. For example, 3S means three doors and a stairway apart

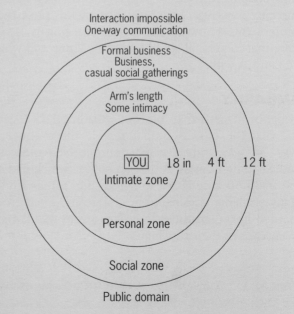

Figure 55.2   Hall's four zones of personal space (From Nicholson, 1977)

EXPOSURE AND FAMILIARITY

Proximity provides increased opportunity for interaction (*exposure*) which, in turn, increases how familiar others become to us (*familiarity*). Far from breeding *contempt*, familiarity apparently breeds *contentment* unless we initially dislike something, in which case we tend to dislike it even more (Rubin, 1973; Grush, 1976). This is what Zajonc (1968) calls the *mere exposure effect*, and several studies have found a positive correlation between frequency of exposure to stimuli and liking for them (e.g. Moreland & Zajonc, 1982; Nuttin, 1987; Brooks & Watkins, 1989). Argyle (1983) has argued that increased exposure to, and familiarity with, others causes an increased polarisation of attitudes towards each other. Usually, this is in the direction of greater liking, but only if the interaction is as equals.

The impact of familiarity on attraction was demonstrated by Newcomb (1961). He found that whilst similarity of beliefs, attitudes and values (see below) was important in determining liking, the key factor was familiarity. So, even when students were paired according to the similarity or dissimilarity of their beliefs, attitudes and values, room-mates became friends far more often than would be expected on the basis of their characteristics.

Other research has shown that our preference for what is familiar even extends to our own facial appearance. For example, Mita *et al.* (1977) showed people pictures of themselves as they appear to others and mirror-images (how we appear to ourselves when we look in a mirror). Most people preferred the latter – this is how we are used to seeing ourselves. However, their friends preferred the former – this is how others are used to seeing us. It seems, then, that in general we like what we know and what we are familiar with.

SIMILARITY

Evidence suggests that 'birds of a feather flock together', and that the critical similarities are those concerning *beliefs*, *attitudes*, and *values*. For example, Newcomb (1943) studied students at an American college which had a liberal tradition among teaching staff and senior students. Many students coming from conservative backgrounds adopted liberal attitudes in order to gain the liking and acceptance of their classmates.

Box 55.3   Some other research findings relating to similarity and attraction

- We are more strongly attracted to people who share our attitudes. Moreover, the greater the proportion of shared attitudes, the greater the attraction.
- The more dogmatic we are, the more likely we are to reject people who disagree with us.
- When we believe that politicians share our attitudes, we may fail to remember statements they made that *conflict* with our attitudes.
- Some attitudinal factors are more important than others. One of the most important is religion

(Based on Howard *et al.*, 1987)

According to Rubin (1973), similarity is rewarding for at least five reasons. First, agreement may provide a basis for engaging in joint activities. Second, a person who agrees with us helps to increase our confidence in our own opinions which enhances self-esteem. In Duck's (1992) view, the validation that friends give us is experienced as evidence of the accuracy of our personal construction of the world. Third, most of us are vain enough to believe that anyone who shares our views must be a sensitive and praiseworthy person. Fourth, people who agree about things that matter to them generally find it easier to communicate. Fifth, we may assume that people with similar attitudes to ourselves will like us, and so we like them in turn (*reciprocal liking*: see page 481).

According to *balance theory* (Heider, 1946; Newcomb, 1953), people like to have a clear, ordered and consistent view of the world so that all the parts 'fit together'. If we agree with our friends and disagree with our enemies, then we are in a state of balance (Jellison & Oliver, 1983). As Figure 55.3 shows, the theory predicts that two people (A and B) will like each other if their opinions about something (X) are the same. If A and B's opinions about X are different, however, they will not like each other. This imbalance can be resolved either by A or B changing his or her opinion, or by A and B disliking each other.

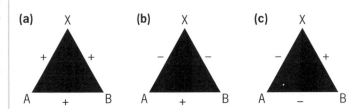

Figure 55.3   Balance theory predicts that two people, A and B, will like each other (+) if their opinions about something (X) are both favourable, as shown in (a), or unfavourable, as shown in (b). A and B will dislike each other if their opinions about X are different, as shown in (c). (After Heider, 1946, and Newcomb, 1953)

A slightly different approach to understanding similarity's importance is provided by Rosenbaum's (1986) *repulsion hypothesis*. Rosenbaum argues that whilst other people's agreement with our attitudes provides balance, this psychological state is not especially arousing. However, when people disagree with our attitudes, we experience arousal and discomfort as a result of the imbalance. So, disagreement has more effect than agreement (Crider *et al.*, 1989). Whilst similarity is important, then, the role of dissimilarity in attraction should not be ignored.

PHYSICAL ATTRACTIVENESS

A large body of evidence supports the general view that physical attractiveness influences the impression we form of the people we meet. For example, attractive-looking people are believed to have attractive personalities, such as being sexually warm and responsive, kind, strong, outgoing, nurturant, interesting, and so on (Dion *et al.*, 1972).

Box 55.4   Some research findings relating to attractiveness

Compared with unattractive people, attractive people are:

- more popular and sought after;

- assumed to be higher in positive traits such as intelligence;

- more likely to be employed even when their physical attractiveness is not a prerequisite for a job;

- perceived as happier, more sensitive, more successful, and more socially skilled

(Based on Solomon, 1987)

Given the importance of *stereotypes* in influencing first impressions (see Chapter 52), it seems that attractive people have a 'head start' in this early phase of relationship development (Solomon, 1987). Interestingly, though, it is not always in our best interests to be seen as being highly attractive. For example, Dermer & Thiel (1975) found that female participants judged extremely attractive women to be egoistic, vain, materialistic, snobbish, and less likely to be successfully married.

Furthermore, although mock jury experiments and observational studies have shown that attractive people are more likely to be found *innocent* of crimes (Michelini & Snodgrass, 1980), there are exceptions to this. For example, if a woman is standing on trial for fraud, accused of having charmed a man into giving her money

for some non-existent cause, she is *more* likely to be found guilty if she is very attractive. In terms of attribution theory, her good looks may result in the jury being more likely to make a *correspondent inference* (see Chapter 51, page 445).

Albeit unconsciously, adults may treat children differently according to their physical appeal and may expect attractive children to be better behaved than less attractive ones (Stephan & Langlois, 1984). When the former behave badly, their behaviour is more likely to be explained by adults in situational ('it wasn't really their fault') rather than dispositional (something about them made them behave that way) terms (Dion, 1972). According to Dion & Dion (1995), stereotyping based on facial attractiveness appears at least as early as six.

Interestingly, data exist suggesting that even infants as young as two months have a marked preference for attractive faces over unattractive ones. For example, Langlois *et al.* (1990) showed that when infants are presented with pairs of colour slides of adult faces rated by adults as being unattractive and attractive, they spend longer looking at the attractive face. According to Langlois *et al.* (1987), such a finding:

'challenges the commonly held assumption that standards of attractiveness are learned through gradual exposure to the cultural standard of beauty and are merely "in the eye of the beholder"'.

Box 55.5   Who is attractive? The role of culture and gender

Different cultures have different criteria concerning physical beauty. For example, chipped teeth, body scars, artificially elongated heads and bound feet have all been regarded as being attractive (Ford & Beach, 1951). In Western culture, definitions of beauty change over time, a particularly good instance of this being the 'ideal' figure for women. Traditionally, facial beauty has been generally regarded as more important in women than men. For men, stature (particularly height), a muscular body, and (at least at present) firm, rounded buttocks, influence how attractive they are judged to be (Jensen-Campbell *et al.*, 1995).

The above examples apparently show that 'attractive' cannot be defined objectively. However, 'average', (not too big or too small), may be one way of moving away from a purely subjective definition. For example, Langlois & Roggman (1994) digitised the faces of a number of college students and used a computer to average them. Students judged the composite faces as more appealing than 96 per cent of the individual faces.

Brehm (1992) has argued that in the context of personal advertisements and commercial dating services, the primary 'resource' (or reward) offered by females seeking a male partner is still physical attractiveness, which matches what men actually seek from a female partner. However, Buss (1989) has argued that this is a universal phenomenon rather than one confined to Western culture (see Chapter 56, page 489).

What makes a pretty face?

Bruce *et al.* (1994) examined the relationship between facial distinctiveness and attractiveness. They found that the variables were not correlated, and that 'distinctiveness' can be accounted for in terms of a physical deviation from the norm. Exactly what the 'norm' is was addressed by Perrett *et al.* (1994). They asked white male and female undergraduates to rate each of 60 young adult white female faces for attractiveness.

After this, an 'average' composite was constructed from the photographs using Langlois and Roggman's computer averaging method (see Box 55.5). An attractive composite was made from the 15 faces rated as being most attractive, and a highly attractive composite by exaggerating the shape of the attractive composite by 50 per cent. The composites were then rated by female and male students. Both sexes preferred the attractive composite to the average one and the highly attractive composite to the attractive one.

Gender transformed   Original image   Aged

Figure 55.4   Computers can be used in a variety of ways to study facial attractiveness. (From Perrett et al., 1994)

Perrett *et al.* then attempted to replicate their findings cross-culturally. Young female Japanese adult faces were rated by Japanese and white raters. The results did not differ from those in the original study. The most attractive face generally had higher cheek bones, a thinner jaw and larger eyes relative to facial size. There was also a shorter distance between the mouth and chin and the nose and mouth. These findings suggest there is a systematic differ-

ence between an 'average' and 'attractive' face, but cast doubt on the view that attractiveness is averageness (see also Bruce & Young, 1998).

Box 55.6   The psychological effects of hair loss

Interestingly, evidence indicates that certain factors associated with physical attractiveness can cause psychological distress in those who do not possess them. Research into impression formation indicates that bald and balding men are generally rated less favourably in terms of physical and social attractiveness, self-assertiveness, personal likeability and life success.

Wells *et al.* (1995) wanted to know if men with hair loss suffer the kinds of psychological distress that might accompany such unfavourable impressions. They studied 182 men of a variety of ages and whose hair loss ranged from none to severe.

The participants were asked to complete a personality questionnaire which revealed that, irrespective of their age, the greater their hair loss, the more likely they were to report low self-esteem, feelings of depression and unattractiveness, and signs of neuroticism and psychoticism. These effects tended to be larger amongst the younger men.

The matching hypothesis

According to *social exchange theory* (Thibaut & Kelley, 1959; Blau, 1964; Homans, 1974; Berscheid & Walster, 1978), people are more likely to become romantically involved if they are fairly closely matched in their ability to reward one another. Ideally, we would all like to have the 'perfect partner' because, the theory says, we are all selfish. However, since this is impossible we try to find a compromise solution. The best general bargain that can be struck is a *value-match* (a subjective belief that our partner is the most rewarding we could realistically hope to find).

Several studies have attempted to test the matching hypothesis (Walster *et al.*, 1966; Dion & Berscheid, 1974; Berscheid *et al.*, 1971; Silverman, 1971; Murstein, 1972; Berscheid & Walster, 1974). These show that people rated as being of high, low or average attractiveness tend to choose partners of a corresponding level of attractiveness. Indeed, according to Price & Vandenberg (1979):

'the matching phenomenon (of physical attraction between marriage partners) is stable within and across generations'.

The findings from the various matching hypothesis studies imply that the kind of partner we would be satisfied with is one we feel will not reject us, rather than one we positively desire. Brown (1986), however, maintains that the matching phenomenon results from a well-learned sense of what is 'fitting', rather than a fear of being rebuffed. For Brown, then, we learn to adjust our expectations of rewards in line with what we believe we have to offer others.

Box 55.7 'Mate selection' in twins

The term 'mate selection' refers to choosing someone we hope will be our lifetime partner. Because identical twins share the same genes and, typically, the same environment, their choice of a mate might be expected to be similar. However, using 738 sets of identical twins, Lykken & Tellegren (1993) found that this was not the case, and the spouses of an identical twin-pair were hardly more likely to be similar than were spouses of random pairs of same-sex adults. When the researchers asked the twins how they felt about their co-twin's choice of mate, less than half (of both sexes) reported that they were attracted to their co-twin's choice. Indeed, just as many reported negative attitudes.

Lykken and Tellegren argue that if people adopt reasonably discriminating criteria to guide mate selection, then those of identical co-twins should be more similar (even though these criteria will differ from person to person). The evidence, though, suggests that whilst we do tend to choose from among people like ourselves, identical twins are not likely to be drawn to the same choice. According to Lowe (1994), this suggests that:

'although most human choice behaviour is fairly rational, the most important choice of all – that of a mate – seems to be an exception'.

RECIPROCAL LIKING

In *How to Win Friends and Influence People*, Carnegie (1937) advised people to greet others with enthusiasm and 'praise' if we wanted them to like us. It is certainly a very pleasant experience when someone compliments and generally seems to like us. Indeed, we often respond by saying 'flattery will get you everywhere'. When we are the recipients of compliments and liking, we tend to respond in kind, or *reciprocate* (Byrne & Murnen, 1988). This often influences those to whom we respond to like us even more (Curtis & Miller, 1988).

According to Aronson's (1980) *reward–cost principle*, we are most attracted to a person who makes entirely positive comments about us over a number of occasions, and least attracted to one who makes entirely negative comments. This is, however, not particularly surprising or interesting. More interesting is Aronson & Linder's

(1965) *gain–loss theory*. According to this, someone who starts off by disliking us and then comes to like us will be more liked than someone who likes us from the start. Equally, someone who begins by liking us and then adopts a negative attitude towards us, will be disliked more than someone who dislikes us from the start.

COMPLEMENTARITY

As noted in the section on similarity, 'birds of a feather flock together'. But do 'opposites attract'? There is a little evidence to support the view that some relationships are based on *complementarity* rather than similarity. For example, Winch (1958) found a tendency for each partner in a marriage to possess needs or traits that the other lacked (which he called *complementarity of needs*: see Chapter 56, page 488). In Winch's study, women who displayed a need to be nurturant were often married to men who needed to be nurtured.

If complementarity does occur in relationship formation, this is probably because opposing traits reinforce each other and benefit both individuals. However, apart from Winch's research, the evidence for complementarity is weak (Nias, 1979), and it is more likely that complementarity develops during a relationship (Rubin, 1973). There is, though, stronger evidence for complementarity of *resources* (see Chapter 56, page 489).

COMPETENCE

Whilst we are generally more attracted to competent than incompetent people, there are exceptions to this. For example, when a highly talented male makes an embarrassing error, we come to like him *more* (Aronson et al., 1966). Presumably, this is because the error indicates that, like the rest of us, he is 'only human'. Additionally, Aronson et al. found that when a person of average ability makes an error, he is liked less, and his error is seen as being just another example of his incompetence. These findings seem to be confined to men (Deaux, 1972), possibly because men are more competitive and like other competent people better when they show a weakness.

Duck's critique of the research

As noted in this chapter's introduction, the quality and validity of the data in this research area have been questioned. One of the strongest critics has been Duck (1995), who argues that much research is:

'typically based on scrutiny of the point of interaction at which the partners were, at best, strangers to each other. The studies (use) college students, for the most part, and [focus] only on immediate judgements of attractiveness or expressions of desire to see the other person again – [and are] rarely followed up or checked for correspondence to later realities of actual interaction or second meetings'.

Duck has called for appropriate caution to be taken about such data, and for the scope of research to be broadened beyond studies of 'initial attraction'. He cites commuter marriages (Rohlfing, 1995), relationships conducted across electronic mail (Lea & Spears, 1995), and relationships among the elderly (Blieszner & Adams, 1992) as areas attracting interest.

Duck's review of the ever-growing literature in this area indicates that the study of social relationships has recovered from what he describes as:

'the [biased] discussions … that used to make up the bulk of … our social psychology textbooks'.

Whilst a general text such as this cannot possibly even briefly review *all* of the areas currently under investigation, the following two chapters at least begin to look at the wider concerns of social relationships research.

Conclusions

This chapter has looked at social psychological research into the formation of adult relationships. Many factors have been shown to influence initial attraction between people, although the research conducted in this area has been subjected to criticism.

Summary

■ **Affiliation** is a precondition for relationship formation and is the basic need for other people's company. When anxious, people prefer the company of others in the same situation. One motive for this is the need for stress-reducing information.

■ We are attracted to people who **reward** us, either directly or indirectly. The greater the rewards, the greater the attraction. Several factors influence initial attraction through their reward values.

■ **Proximity** is a minimum requirement for attraction. Numerous studies show that proximity increases the likelihood of relationship formation. However, there are 'rules' governing physical proximity which differ between and within cultures. When these rules are broken, an unpleasant arousal state occurs. Successful relationships may require initial 'boundary understandings'.

■ Proximity increases opportunity for **exposure** to others. This increases **familiarity** through the **mere exposure effect** and/or increased polarisation of attitudes. Familiarity appears to breed **contentment** rather than contempt. The preference for what is familiar even extends to our own facial appearance.

■ **Similarity** is rewarding for several reasons. For example, we are likely to see people who agree with us as sensitive and praiseworthy, as well as easier to communicate with. Through **reciprocal liking**, we like people who share our attitudes because we assume they will like us.

■ **Balance theory** proposes that we like to have an ordered and consistent world view. Two people will like each other if their opinions about something are both favourable or unfavourable. They will dislike each other if their opinions differ. However, the **repulsion hypothesis** says that the imbalance produced by disagreement is more arousing. As important as similarity is, dissimilarity is also important.

■ **Physical attractiveness** also influences impression formation. Compared with unattractive people, attractive people are (in general) seen as having attractive personalities, and being of higher intelligence, happier, more sensitive, successful and socially skilled, and are more popular and sought after.

■ Standards of attractiveness are evidently culturally determined, and different cultures have different criteria concerning physical beauty. In Western cultures at least, these change over time.

■ Although 'attractive' cannot be objectively defined, the use of digitised 'average' faces is one alternative to a purely subjective definition. Attractiveness is not correlated with facial distinctiveness, but distinctiveness can be accounted for in terms of a physical deviation from the norm. This norm is best defined in terms of an exaggeration of averageness.

■ According to **social exchange theory**, people are more likely to become romantically involved the more closely they are matched in their abilities to reward each other. In the absence of a perfect partner, we settle for a **value-match** (the **matching hypothesis**). People rated as being of high, low or average attractiveness tend to choose partners of a corresponding attractiveness level. In married couples, the matching phenomenon is apparently stable within and across generations. Matching does not just reflect a fear of rejection. Instead, we learn to adjust our expectations of reward in line with what we believe we have to offer others.

■ **Reciprocal liking** tends to occur when others pay us compliments and show they like us. **Gain–loss** theory claims that someone who begins by disliking us and then comes to like us will be more liked than someone who likes us from the start. The reverse is true for someone who likes us initially, then comes to dislike us.

■ Relationships can be based on **complementarity of needs** rather than similarity. However, complementarity develops during a relationship and, rather than personality traits, it involves resources, such as physical beauty and money.

■ Duck argues that most research into relationship formation focuses on first meetings and judgements of initial attraction, and fails to follow up relationship development. More interesting research goes beyond 'initial attraction'.

56

THE MAINTENANCE OF ADULT RELATIONSHIPS

Introduction and overview

Chapter 55 looked at some of the factors that influence initial attraction to others and hence the likelihood that we will try to form relationships with them. This chapter looks at how relationships are *maintained*.

Some of the factors discussed in the previous chapter apply here as well. For example, the greater the similarity between two people, the more likely it is that a relationship endures (Byrne, 1971). Byrne found that this is true for a variety of groups from school children to adult alcoholics! Before looking at theory and research into the maintenance of relationships, however, the liking and loving distinction, and cross-cultural conceptions of love, will be briefly considered.

Liking and loving

According to Rubin (1973), liking and loving are not the same. Liking is the positive evaluation of another and consists of respect and affection. Rubin sees loving as being more than an intense liking. In his view, loving is qualitatively different and composed of *attachment, caring* and *intimacy*. Attachment is the need for the physical presence and support of the loved one. Caring is a feeling of concern and responsibility for the loved one. Intimacy is the desire for close and confidential contact, and wanting to share certain thoughts and feelings with the loved one more fully than with anyone else. Rubin's idea of caring corresponds to Fromm's (1962) definition of love as 'the active concern for the life and growth of that which we love'.

Much of the support for Rubin's distinction between liking and loving comes from people's responses on scales devised by him to measure them. Amongst other things, Rubin found that lovers tend to give similar but not identical positive responses to items on both scales. So, we tend to like the people we love, but the relationship is not perfect. Also, high-scorers on the love scale are more likely to say that they expect to marry their partners. This means that love is correlated with an anticipated permanent relationship.

The love scale can also be applied to same-sex friends. Here, Rubin found that females reported loving their friends more than men did. Other research has shown that

Table 56.1 Some items from Rubin's (1973) liking scale and love scale

Respondents are asked to indicate if a particular statement reflects accurately their perception about another person.

Liking scale
1 I think that _____ is unusually well adjusted.
2 I have great confidence in _____'s good judgement.
3 _____ is the sort of person whom I myself would like to be.

Love scale
1 If _____ were feeling bad, my first duty would be to cheer him/her up.
2 I feel that I can confide in _____ about virtually everything.
3 If I could never be with _____ I would feel miserable.

women's friendships tend to be more intimate than men's, and that spontaneous joint activities and exchange of confidences occur more in women. For men, loving may be channelled into single, sexual relationships whilst women may be better able to experience attachment, caring and intimacy in a wider range and variety of relationships (Rubin & McNeil, 1983).

It has been argued that a concept like love cannot be measured at all, let alone by using pencil-and-paper devices. Rubin, though, has shown that partners high on the love scale engage in more eye contact than dating couples who are lower on it. For Rubin (1973), this is good evidence that the love scale has at least some validity.

TYPES OF LOVE

For some researchers, love is a label that we learn to attach to our own state of physiological arousal. However, for most of the time love does not involve intense physical 'symptoms', and it is perhaps better to view it as a sort of attitude that one person has towards another (Rubin & McNeil, 1983). It seems likely that the sort of love a couple married for 50 years experiences is different from that of a couple 'going steady' at college.

Berscheid & Walster (1978) distinguish between *romantic* love and *companionate* love. Romantic love (or *passionate* love) is characterised by intense feelings of tenderness, elation, anxiety, and sexual desire. It is also associated with increased activity in the sympathetic branch of the ANS (see Chapter 5). According to Hatfield & Rapson (1987):

'passionate love is like any other form of excitement. By its very nature, excitement involves a continuous interplay between elation and despair, thrills and terror ... Sometimes men and women become entangled in love affairs where the delight is brief, and pain, uncertainty, jealousy, misery, anxiety, and despair are abundant. Often, passionate love seems to be fuelled by a sprinkling of hope and a large dollop of loneliness, mourning, jealousy, and terror'.

Romantic love usually occurs early in a relationship but does not last very long. Companionate love (sometimes called *true* or *conjugal* love) is the affection that remains after the passion of romantic love has subsided, and is essential if a relationship is to be maintained. Companionate love is less intense than romantic love and involves thoughtful appreciation of one's partner. It is also characterised by a tolerance for weaknesses and a desire to solve conflicts and difficulties in a relationship (Rubenstein, 1983).

According to Sternberg (1986b, 1988), love has three basic components, *intimacy*, *passion* and *decision/commitment*. The presence or absence of these produces different types of love.

Box 56.1   Sternberg's triangular theory of love

Intimacy is the emotionally based part of love, and refers to feelings of closeness, connectedness and bondedness in loving relationships.

Passion is the motivational component of love. It refers to the drives that lead to romance, physical attraction and sexual consummation.

Decision/commitment is the cognitive 'controller' in a loving relationship. The short-term decision involves acceptance of such a relationship. The long-term aspect involves the commitment to maintain the relationship.

Table 56.2   Types of love and their components

Kind of love	Component		
	Intimacy	Passion	Decision/ commitment
Non-love	Absent	Absent	Absent
Liking	Present	Absent	Absent
Infatuated love	Absent	Present	Absent
Empty love	Absent	Absent	Present
Romantic love	Present	Present	Absent
Companionate love	Present	Absent	Present
Fatuous love	Absent	Present	Present
Consummate love	Present	Present	Present

Consider, for example, *infatuated love*. This includes those relationships which we describe as being 'love at first sight'. The love is aroused by passion, but there is no intimacy or decision/commitment. Such relationships can arise almost instantaneously and end just as quickly.

Sternberg's three dimensions help us to understand various relationships. However, most loving relationships fit between the categories because the various components of love are expressed along dimensions, not discretely (Houston *et al.*, 1991). Also, alternatives to Sternberg's theory exist, most notably the six basic love styles identified by Hendrick *et al.* (1986), which recognise that 'love' means different things to different people, even the partners themselves (Bellur, 1995).

LOVE ACROSS CULTURES

According to Moghaddam *et al.* (1993), much of the theory and research relating to social relationships is a reflection of the dominant values of North America, from where many theories and an even larger number of studies originate (see Chapter 84).

Box 56.2   The importance of cross-cultural analyses

Goodwin (1995) has argued that cross-cultural analyses of relationships are important for at least three reasons.

- They allow competing theories to be compared and assessed according to whether they are universal or the products of particular cultural or historical conditions.

- Contact between people from different cultural backgrounds is increasing in both frequency and intensity. As people acculturate to a new society, their relationships with those around them are important in determining their psychological well-being.

- Increasing business and leisure contacts raise important issues about cross-cultural communications, and understanding the rules of commerce in different cultures is an important part of a business person's armoury.

One of the main dimensions on which cultures differ is *individualism–collectivism* (see Chapter 84). Individualism places greatest emphasis on personal achievement and self-reliance. Collectivism, by contrast, places priority on the welfare and unity of the group (Bellur, 1995). Although this division is somewhat simplified (because some cultures seem to be highly individualist in some settings and more collectivist in others), it is useful in helping to summarise some of the cross-cultural variations in personal relationships (Goodwin, 1995).

Goodwin argues that love, 'at least in its passionate stomach churning Hollywood manifestation', is largely a Western and individualistic phenomenon and that in

Western cultures, marriage is seen as the culmination of a 'loving' relationship. In cultures where 'arranged marriages' occur, the relationship between love and marriage is the other way around, and marriage is seen as the basis on which to explore a loving relationship (Bellur, 1995). As Bellur notes, the cultural background in which people have learned about love is important in shaping their concept of it.

The fact that love is seen as something that will develop in the arranged marriage does not necessarily mean that such a marriage will be unhappy. Indeed, evidence suggests that these marriages may produce more happiness than 'love' marriages. For example, Gupta & Singh (1992) found that couples in India who married out of love reported diminished feelings of love if they had been married for more than five years. By contrast, those who had undertaken arranged marriages reported more love if they were not newly-weds.

These findings reveal that passionate love 'cools' over time and that there is scope for love to flourish within an arranged marriage. In the case of those cultures in which arranged marriages occur, then, courtship is accepted to a certain degree, but love is left to be defined and discovered after marriage (Bellur, 1995).

Stage theories of relationships

As we all know and expect, relationships develop and change over time. Indeed, relationships which stagnate, especially if sexual/romantic in nature, may well be doomed to failure (Duck, 1988: see Chapter 57). Several theories charting the course of relationships have been proposed. These typically cover both sexual and non-sexual relationships, although they sometimes make specific mention of marriage/marriage partners.

KERCKHOFF AND DAVIS'S 'FILTER' THEORY

According to Kerckhoff & Davis (1962), relationships pass through a series of 'filters'. They base this claim on a comparison between 'short-term couples' (less than 18 months) and 'long-term couples' (more than 18 months). Initially, similarity of *sociological* (or *demographic*) variables (such as ethnic, racial, religious, and social class groups) determines the likelihood of people meeting in the first place. To some extent, our choice of friends and partners is made for us because, to use Kerckhoff's (1974) term, 'the field of availables' (the range of people who are realistically, as opposed to theoretically, available for us to meet) is reduced by social circumstances.

The next 'filter' involves people's *psychological* characteristics and, specifically, agreement on basic values. Kerckhoff and Davis found this was the best predictor of a relationship becoming more stable and permanent. Thus, those who had been together for less than 18 months tended to have stronger relationships when the partners' values coincided. With couples of longer standing, though, similarity was not the most important factor. In fact, *complementarity of emotional needs* was the best predictor of a longer term commitment, and this constitutes the third 'filter'.

MURSTEIN'S STIMULUS–VALUE–ROLE (SVR) THEORY

Murstein (1976, 1987) sees intimate relationships proceeding from a *stimulus* stage, in which attraction is based on external attributes (such as physical appearance), to a *value* stage, in which similarity of values and beliefs becomes more important. Then comes a *role* stage, which involves a commitment based on successful performance of relationship roles, such as husband and wife. Although all these factors have some influence throughout a relationship, each one assumes its greatest significance during one particular stage.

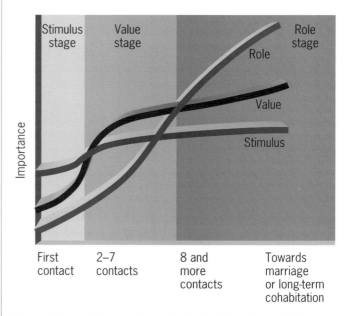

Figure 56.1   States of courtship in Murstein's SVR theory (From Gross, 1996)

LEVINGER'S THEORY

For Levinger (1980), relationships pass through five stages rather than the three proposed by Murstein. These are: acquaintance or initial attraction, building up the relationship, consolidation or continuation, deterioration and decline, and ending. At each stage, there are positive factors that promote the relationship's development and corresponding negative factors that prevent its development or cause its failure.

For example, and as seen in Chapter 55, repeated interaction with someone makes initial attraction more likely, whilst infrequent contact makes it less likely. Similarity of attitudes and other characteristics helps a relationship to build, whilst dissimilarity makes building difficult (Levinger's second stage), and so on. However, the major limitation of Levinger's theory and, indeed, other stage theories, is that there is only weak evidence for a fixed sequence of stages in interpersonal relationships (Brehm, 1992). As a result, Brehm suggests that it is better to talk about 'phases' that take place at different times for different couples.

What keeps people together?

If we consider what our important relationships have in common, we would find that all are rewarding for us and yet all can at times be complex, demanding, and even painful. If relationships involve both positive and negative aspects, then what determines our continued involvement in them?

SOCIAL EXCHANGE THEORY

Social exchange theory was mentioned briefly in Chapter 55 (see page 480). It provides a general framework for analysing all kinds of relationship, both intimate and non-intimate, and is really an extension of reward theory (also discussed briefly in Chapter 55: see page 477).

According to Homans (1974), we view our feelings for others in terms of profits (the amount of reward obtained from a relationship minus the cost). The greater the reward and lower the cost, the greater the profits and hence the attraction. Blau (1964) argues that interactions are 'expensive' in the sense that they take time, energy and commitment, and may involve unpleasant emotions and experiences. Because of this, what we get out of a relationship must be more than what we put in.

Similarly, Berscheid & Walster (1978) have argued that in any social interaction there is an exchange of rewards (such as affection, information and status) and that the degree of attraction or liking will reflect how people evaluate the rewards they receive relative to those they give. However, whether or not it is appropriate to think of relationships in this economic, and even capitalistic, way has been hotly debated.

Figure 56.2   According to social exchange theory, we stay in relationships which are 'profitable' for us. Different individuals will define the costs and rewards involved in different ways

> **Box 56.3   Are relationships really seen in economic terms?**
>
> Social exchange theory sees people as fundamentally selfish and views human relationships as based primarily on self-interest. Like many theories in psychology, social exchange theory offers us a *metaphor* for human relationships and should not be taken too literally. However, although we like to believe that the joy of giving is as important as the desire to receive, it is true that our attitudes towards other people are determined to a large extent by our assessments of the rewards they hold for us (Rubin, 1973).
>
> Equally, though, Rubin (1973) does not believe that social exchange theory provides a complete, or even adequate, account of human relationships. In his view:
>
> > 'Human beings are sometimes altruistic in the fullest sense of the word. They make sacrifices for the sake of others without any consideration of the rewards they will obtain from them in return'.
>
> Altruism is most often and most clearly seen in close interpersonal relationships (and is discussed further in Chapter 62).
>
> Consistent with Rubin's view, Brown (1986) distinguishes between 'true' love and friendship (which are altruistic) and less admirable forms which are based on

considerations of exchange. For example, Fromm (1962) defines true love as giving, as opposed to the false love of the 'marketing character' which depends upon expecting to have favours returned.

Support for this distinction comes from Mills & Clark (1980), who identify two kinds of intimate relationship. In the *communal couple*, each partner gives out of concern for the other. In the *exchange couple*, by contrast, each keeps mental records of who is 'ahead' in the relationship and who is 'behind'.

EQUITY THEORY

Social exchange theory is really a special case of a more general account of human relationships called equity theory. The extra component in equity theory that is added to reward, cost and profit is *investment*. For Brown (1986):

'a person's investments are not just financial; they are anything at all that is believed to entitle him (or her) to his (or her) rewards, costs, and profits. An investment is any factor to be weighed in determining fair profits or losses'.

Equity means a constant ratio of rewards to costs or profit to investment. So, it is concerned with *fairness* rather than equality. Equity theory does not see the initial ratio as being important. Rather, it is *changes* in the ratio of what is put into a relationship and what is got out of it that cause us to feel differently about the relationship. For example, we might feel that it is fair and just that we should give more than we get, but if we start giving very much more than we did and receiving very much less, we are likely to become dissatisfied with the relationship.

Some versions of social exchange theory do actually take account of factors other than the simple and crude profit motives of social interactors. One of these was introduced by Thibaut & Kelley (1959).

Box 56.4   The concepts of comparison level and comparison level for alternatives (Thibaut & Kelley (1959)

Comparison level (CL) is essentially the average level of rewards and costs a person is used to in relationships, and is the basic level expected in any future relationship. So, if a person's reward:cost ratio falls below his or her CL, the relationship will be unsatisfying. If it is above the CL, the relationship will be satisfying.

Comparison level for alternatives (CL alt.) is essentially a person's expectation about the reward:cost ratio which

could be obtained in other relationships. If the ratio in a relationship exceeds the CL alt., then a person is doing better in it than he or she could do elsewhere. As a result, the relationship should be satisfying and likely to continue. If the CL alt. exceeds the reward:cost ratio, then a person is doing worse than he or she could do elsewhere. As a result, the relationship should be unsatisfying and unlikely to continue.

The concept of CL alt. implies that the endurance of a relationship (as far as one partner is concerned) could be due to the qualities of the other partner and the relationship, *or* to the negative and unattractive features of the perceived alternatives, *or* to the perceived costs of leaving. This, however, still portrays people as being fundamentally selfish, and many researchers (e.g. Duck, 1988) prefer to see relationships as being maintained by an equitable distribution of rewards and costs for both partners. In this approach, people are seen as being concerned with the equity of outcomes both for themselves and their partners.

Murstein *et al.* (1977) argue that concern with either exchange or equity is negatively correlated with marital adjustment. According to Argyle (1988), people in close relationships do not think in terms of rewards and costs at all until they start to feel dissatisfied. Murstein & MacDonald (1983) have argued that the principles of exchange and equity do play a significant role in intimate relationships. However, they believe that a conscious concern with 'getting a fair deal', especially in the short term, makes compatibility (see page 489) very hard to achieve, and that this is true for friendship and, especially, marriage (see Box 56.3 and Mills and Clark's *exchange couple*).

THE ROLE OF COMPLEMENTARITY

Complementarity refers to the reinforcement of opposing traits to the mutual benefit of both individuals in a relationship (see Chapter 55, page 481). According to Winch (1958), happy marriages are often based on each partner's ability to fulfil the needs of the other (*complementarity of emotional needs*) and Winch obtained limited support for this.

The evidence for *complementarity in resources* is, however, stronger (Brehm, 1992). As noted elsewhere (see Box 55.4), men seem to give a universally higher priority to 'good looks' in their female partners than women do in their male partners. In the case of being a 'good financial prospect' and having a 'good earning capacity', however, the situation is reversed.

Sociobiological theory

According to Buss (1988, 1989), these differences between the sexes 'appear to be deeply rooted in the evolutionary history of our species'. Buss bases this claim on a study of 37 cultures involving over 10,000 people. In Buss's view, the chances of reproductive success should be increased for men who mate with younger, 'healthy' adult females as opposed to older, 'unhealthy' ones. Fertility is a function of a female's age and health, which affects pregnancy and her ability to care for her child.

Since reproductive success is crucial to the survival of a species, natural selection should favour those mating patterns that promote the offspring's survival. Men often have to rely on a woman's physical appearance to estimate her age and health, with younger, healthier women being perceived as more attractive. For women, mate selection depends on their need for a provider to take care of them during pregnancy and nursing. Men who are seen as powerful and as controlling resources that contribute to the mother and child's welfare, will be seen as especially attractive.

There are, however, a number of drawbacks to sociobiological theory in this regard. For example, it seems to take male–female relationships out of any cultural or historical context (captured by the use of the term 'mate selection'). It is equally plausible to argue that women have been forced to obtain desirable resources through men because they have been denied direct access to political and economic power. Sigall & Landy (1983) argue that, traditionally, a woman has been regarded as a man's property, wherein her beauty increases his status and respect in the eyes of others.

Importantly, Buss ignores the fact that in his cross-cultural study, 'kind' and 'intelligent' were universally ranked *above* 'physically attractive' and 'good earning power' by both men *and* women. Finally, Buss's argument fails to account for homosexual relationships (Kitzinger & Coyle, 1995). Such relationships clearly do not contribute to the species' survival, despite being subject to many of the same sociopsychological influences as heterosexual relationships (Brehm, 1992).

THE ROLE OF COMPATIBILITY IN MAINTAINING RELATIONSHIPS

As far as it exists, complementarity can be taken to be a component of *compatibility*. However, as seen in Chapter 55 (page 478), the evidence for similarity's importance in relationship formation is much greater. It also suggests that similarity plays a much greater role in *maintaining* relationships.

Figure 56.3   Sociobiologists argue that men's desire for attractive female partners, and women's desire for good providers, represents a universal sex difference rooted in human evolutionary history

Box 56.5   The role of similarity in relationship maintenance

Hill *et al.* (1976) studied 231 steadily dating couples over a two-year period. At the end of this period, 103 (45 per cent) had broken up, and when interviewed often mentioned differences in interests, background, sexual attitudes, and ideas about marriage as being responsible. By contrast, those who were still together tended to be more alike in terms of age, intelligence, educational and career plans, as well as physical attractiveness.

Hill *et al.* found that the maintenance or dissolution of the relationship in the couples they studied could be predicted from initial questionnaire data collected about them. For example, about 80 per cent of those who stayed together described themselves as being 'in love', compared with 56 per cent of those who did not stay together.

Of couples in which both members initially reported being equally involved in the relationship, only 23 per cent broke up. However, where one member was much more involved than the other, 54 per cent broke up. The latter type of couple is a highly unstable one in which the person who is more involved (putting more in but getting less out) may feel dependent and exploited. The one who is less involved (putting less in but getting more in return) may feel restless and guilty (implying some sense of fairness).

Other research has confirmed the general rule that the more similar two people in a relationship see themselves as being, the more likely it is that the relationship will be maintained. Thus, individuals who have similar needs (Meyer & Pepper, 1977), attitudes, likes and dislikes (Newcomb, 1978), and are similar in attractiveness (White, 1980), are more likely to remain in a relationship than dissimilar individuals.

Another way of looking at compatibility is *marital satisfaction*. In a review of studies looking at marital satisfaction and communication, Duck (1992) found that happy couples give more positive and consistent non-verbal cues than unhappy couples, express more agreement and approval for the other's ideas and suggestions, talk more about their relationship, and are more willing to compromise on difficult decisions.

The importance of positive interactions was shown by Spanier & Lewis (1980). They propose that there are three main components in relationships that last. These are 'rewards from spousal interaction', 'satisfaction with lifestyle', and 'sufficient social and personal resources'. These rewards include positive regard for one's partner and emotional gratification. When these elements are positive, spouses or partners are more likely to report satisfaction with their relationship, and it is more likely to endure (Houston *et al.*, 1991).

Conclusions

The maintenance of relationships has been addressed by many researchers, and several theories of relationship maintenance have been advanced, all of which can claim some degree of support. Complementarity and compatibility also play important roles in maintaining relationships.

Summary

■ Some of the factors involved in relationship formation also apply to relationship maintenance, one of them being similarity.

■ Rubin sees liking and loving as **qualitatively** different. Loving involves **attachment**, **caring** and **intimacy**. Berscheid and Walster distinguish between **romantic (passionate) love** and **companionate (true/conjugal)** love. For Sternberg, the basic components of love are **intimacy**, **passion** and **decision/commitment**. The presence or absence of these components produces several different types of love, including infatuated, romantic, companionate, fatuous and consummate.

■ **Cross-cultural studies** of love suggest that passionate love is largely a Western and individualistic phenomenon, and marriage is the culmination of a loving relationship. The reverse is true in cultures which favour arranged marriages, where marriage is seen as the basis for love to develop. Arranged marriages may produce more happiness than 'love' marriages, because love is left to be defined and discovered after marriage.

■ Relationships change and develop over time, and their stagnation may be a major cause of their failure. Several stage theories have tried to chart the courses of both sexual and non-sexual relationships.

■ **Filter theory** proposes that similarity of sociological/demographic variables determines whether people will meet in the first place, and this is the first filter. The second filter involves people's psychological characteristics, specifically agreement about basic values. The best predictor of a longer term commitment among long-term couples is complementarity of emotional needs.

■ **Stimulus–value–role theory** proposes that intimate relationships pass from a stimulus stage (external attributes being important), to a value stage (similarity of values and attitudes are important) to a role stage (a commitment based on successful performance of relationship roles).

■ In Levinger's theory, acquaintance/initial attraction is followed by a relationship's build-up. After this, consolidation/continuation occurs, followed by deterioration/decline and ending. At each stage, there are both positive and negative factors, either promoting or preventing the relationship's development.

■ All stage theories suffer from the limitation of there being weak evidence for a fixed sequence of stages. It may be better to talk about phases which occur at different times for different people.

■ **Social exchange theory** is an extension of reward theory. It is a framework for analysing all kinds of relationship. Different versions of exchange theory see social interactions as involving an exchange of rewards: the degree of liking/attraction reflects how highly we value rewards we have received relative to those we have given.

■ Variations on social exchange theories see people as being fundamentally selfish. However, Rubin and others argue that we are capable of genuine altruism, and this is most clearly seen in close interpersonal relationships. The concepts of comparison level and comparison level for alternatives are important in this respect.

■ Social exchange theory is really a special case of **equity theory**, which adds the concept of investment to those of reward, cost and profit. Fairness in relation to the reward:cost/profit:investment ratio is more important than equality. Changes in this ratio, rather than the initial ratio, determine how we feel about a relationship.

■ Whilst evidence for complementarity of needs is weak, it is stronger for **complementarity in resources**. Sociobiologists claim that the universal preference of men for physical beauty in females and women's preference for males as good financial prospects are rooted in human evolutionary history. However, sociobiological theory takes male–female relationships out of any cultural and historical context and is also unsupported by evidence.

■ Similarity plays a greater role than complementarity in **compatibility** and the maintenance of relationships. Happily married couples give more positive and consistent non-verbal cues than unhappy couples, express more agreement with their partners' ideas, talk more about their relationship, and are more willing to compromise on difficult decisions.

■ There appear to be three main components in relationships that last. These are rewards from spousal interaction, satisfaction with lifestyle, and sufficient personal and social resources.

57

THE DISSOLUTION OF ADULT RELATIONSHIPS

Introduction and overview

The previous two chapters have considered the formation and maintenance of adult relationships. There are many *positive* effects of being in a relationship and this chapter begins by looking at these. However, its main concerns are with the negative effects that follow the dissolution (break-up) of a relationship and why some relationships are dissolved.

Some positive effects of relationships

In 1885, William Farr, then Superintendent of the Statistical Department of the Registrar General's Office for England, proposed that mortality is affected by mental status (Cramer, 1995). After studying mortality rates for single women, married women and widows, Farr concluded that marriage:

'is a healthy state. The single individual is more likely to be wrecked on his voyage than the lives joined together in matrimony' (cited in Humphreys, 1975).

Farr also found that the difference between the single and married state was more striking for men than women, and contemporary research has generally confirmed his conclusions. For example, Hu & Goldman (1990) found that married people tend to live longer than the unmarried, whilst Cramer's (1994) research indicates that married people are happier, healthier and have lower rates of various mental disorders than the single, widowed or divorced (see Chapter 49, page 430).

Also, Cochrane (1996) has shown that age for age, the data for England indicate that a person is 22 per cent more likely to die in a given year if he or she is single rather than married, and 30 per cent more likely if divorced.

Box 57.1 Explaining the beneficial effects of marriage

A number of explanations for the data presented above have been advanced. Kessler & Essex (1982), for example, found that married people in their sample were significantly higher in self-esteem, and it could be that marriage provides some sort of 'protection' from mental ill-health in the same way that a healthy diet protects against physical illness (Cochrane, 1996). Such protection may come from the intimacy and security provided by a relationship, home-building, sexual satisfaction, and so on. Marriage may also contribute to psychological well-being and the *prevention* of stress, rather than its cause, by, for example, providing social support (see page 494).

The explanations presented in Box 57.1 assume that marital status *causes* variations in mental health status. An alternative approach, the *selection for marriage hypothesis*, suggests that mental health status *causes* marital status. According to this hypothesis, a predisposition to illness reduces the likelihood of a person marrying, either because an unwell person is not motivated to marry and/or because he or she is an unattractive proposition to potential spouses. Whichever explanation is accepted, on the basis of the findings concerning marriage and physical and mental health, we might expect people to continue in a relationship for as long as possible! So how and why do relationships go wrong?

Marital unhappiness and divorce

Duck (1988, 1992) has identified several factors which make it more likely that a marriage will either be unhappy or end in divorce.

Box 57.2 Factors contributing to marital unhappiness and divorce

• Marriages in which the partners are younger than average tend to be more unstable. This can be related to Erikson's concept of intimacy (see Chapter 47), whereby teenage marriages, for example, involve individuals who have not yet fully established their sense of identity and so are not ready for a commitment to one particular person. Additionally, there seems to be a connection between the rising divorce rate and early parenthood, which gives young couples little time to adjust to their new relationships and marital responsibilities. The arrival of a baby brings added financial and housing problems (Pringle, 1986).

- Marriages between couples from lower socioeconomic groups and educational levels tend to be more unstable. These are also the couples who tend to have children very early on in their marriage.

- Marriages between partners from different demographic backgrounds (race, religion, and so on) also tend to be more unstable. This finding can be related to Kerckhoff and Davis's 'filter' theory, considered in Chapter 56 (see page 486).

- Marriages also tend to be more unstable between people who have experienced parental divorce as children or who have had a greater number of sexual partners than average before marriage.

Relationships are, of course, highly complex, and the factors identified in Box 57.2 cannot on their own adequately explain why marriage break-ups occur (Duck, 1995). For example, only a proportion of marriages involving the young, those from lower socioeconomic groups, or different demographic backgrounds, actually end in divorce. Equally, many divorces occur between couples who do not fit these descriptions. There is a link between *communication strategies* employed early on in married life and subsequent marital unhappiness, with manipulative and coercive styles being good predictors of the dissatisfaction experienced by wives but *not* by husbands (McGhee, 1996).

Brehm (1992) identifies two broad types of cause for marital unhappiness and divorce, these being *structural* (including gender, duration of the relationship, the presence of children, and role-strain created by competing demands of work and family) and *conflict resolution*.

GENDER DIFFERENCES

Men and women appear to differ in their perceptions of their relationship problems. In general, women report more problems, and evidence suggests that the degree of female dissatisfaction is a better predictor than male unhappiness of whether the relationship will end. This could mean that women are more sensitive to relationship problems than men. Alternatively, it could be that men and women enter into relationships with different expectations and hopes, with men's generally being fulfilled to a greater extent than women's.

Consistent with this possibility is evidence of gender differences in the specific *types* of relationship problems that

are reported. For example, whilst men and women who are divorcing are equally likely to cite communication problems as a cause for the dissolution of their relationships, women stress basic unhappiness and incompatibility more than men do. Again, men seem to be particularly upset if there is 'sexual withholding' by female partners, whilst women are distressed by their male partners' aggression.

DURATION OF RELATIONSHIPS AND THE PASSAGE OF TIME

The longer partners have known each other before they marry, the more likely they are to be satisfied in their marriages and the less likely divorce is. However, couples who have cohabited before marriage report fewer barriers to ending the marriage, and the longer a relationship lasts the more likely it is that people will blame their partners for negative events.

Two major views of changes in marital satisfaction are Pineo's (1961) *linear model* and Burr's (1970) *curvilinear model*. According to the linear model, there is an inevitable fading of the romantic 'high' of courtship before marriage. The model also proposes that people marry because they have achieved a 'good fit' with their partners, and that any changes occurring in either partner will reduce their compatibility. For example, if one partner becomes more self-confident (which, ironically, may occur through the support gained from the relationship), there may be increased conflict between two equals who now compete for 'superiority' in the relationship. The linear model is supported by at least some evidence (Blood & Wolfe, 1969).

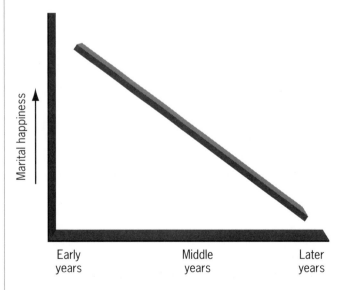

Figure 57.1   The linear model of marital satisfaction (From Gross, 1996)

The curvilinear model of martial satisfaction proposes that marital happiness is greatest in the earliest years of marriage, reaches a low in the middle years, and then begins to rise again in the later years. The middle years of marriage are often associated with the arrival and departure of children. The model proposes that marital happiness declines when children are born and during their growing up, but increases as they mature and leave home. However, whilst it is generally agreed that a decline in marital happiness begins in the early years, whether happiness ever does increase or merely 'levels off' is debatable.

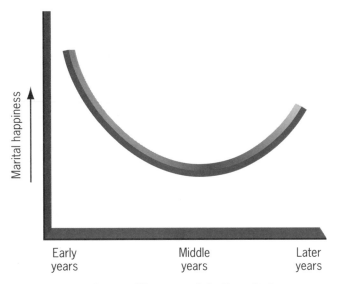

Figure 57.2   The curvilinear model of marital satisfaction (From Gross, 1996)

Gilford & Bengston (1979) argue that it is an oversimplification to talk about marital 'satisfaction' or 'happiness'. In their view, it is much more productive to look at the *pattern of positive rewards* and the *pattern of negative costs* that occur in a marriage. The early years of marriage are associated with very high rewards and very high costs. In the middle years, there is a decline in both, whilst in the later years there is a continuing decline in costs and an increase in rewards.

CONFLICT RESOLUTION

According to Duck (1988), some kind and degree of conflict is inevitable in all kinds of relationship. However, the process of resolving conflicts can often be a positive one that promotes the relationship's growth (Wood & Duck, 1995). The important question is not whether there is conflict, but *how* this conflict can best be dealt with. Unfortunately, the recurrence of conflicts, indicating a lack of agreement and an inability to resolve the

conflict's underlying source, may lead the partners to doubt each other as 'reasonable persons'. This might produce a 'digging in of the heels', a disaffection with each other, and, ultimately, a 'strong falling out'.

> **Box 57.3   Attributional patterns and conflict resolution**
>
> Bradbury & Fincham (1990) have argued that happy and unhappy couples resolve their conflicts in typically different ways, and that these can be understood as different *attributional patterns* (see Chapter 51). Happy couples use a *relationship-enhancing* attributional pattern in which a partner's negative behaviour is explained in terms of situational and other variable causes. By contrast, unhappy couples use a *distress-maintaining* attributional pattern in which a partner's negative behaviour is explained in terms of underlying and unchanging personality dispositions.
>
>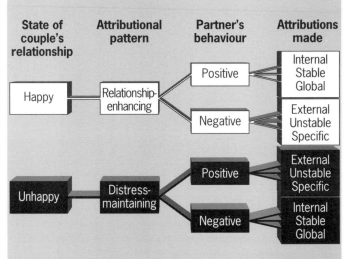
>
> **Figure 57.3   Attributions made by happy and unhappy couples according to Bradbury & Fincham (1990) (From Brehm, 1992)**

RULE-BREAKING AND DECEPTION

Argyle & Henderson (1984) have conducted many studies looking at the *rules* people use in different types of relationship. By rules, they mean shared opinions or beliefs about what should and should not be done. According to Argyle and Henderson, the two major functions of rules are to regulate behaviour in order to minimise potential sources of conflict, and to check on the exchange of rewards which motivate people to stay in relationships. Their research has uncovered rules which are thought to apply to all or most types of relationship, such as 'respecting other people's privacy', 'not discussing what has been said in confidence' and 'being emotionally supportive'.

Additional rules apply in particular types of relationship. Argyle and Henderson's findings indicate that relationships fall into clusters, with similar rules applying within a particular cluster. One such cluster includes spouse, sibling and close friends, whilst another includes doctor, teacher and boss. *Deception* is probably the most important rule that should not be broken. However, what counts as deception will depend on the nature of the relationship: if we cannot trust a friend or a partner, then the relationship is almost certainly doomed.

Some effects of relationship dissolution

In his review of relevant studies, Duck (1992) found that people in disrupted relationships are more susceptible than others of the same sex and age group to coronary heart disease, alcoholism, drug dependency, and sleep disturbances. The relationship between marital status and vulnerability to mental disorders has been extensively investigated by Cochrane (1983, 1996), who has found that marital status is one of the strongest correlates of risk of mental health hospital admissions.

> **Box 57.4   Marital status and mental health**
>
> Allowing for age differences, Cochrane's data indicate that the divorced are five-and-a-half times more likely than the married to be admitted to a mental hospital in any one year. Stress could account for this, since the relationship between stress and illness is strongly supported by evidence (see Chapter 20, page 162). Additionally, a loss of the 'protective' factors mentioned on page 491 could also be important. Even the 'selection for marriage' hypothesis might have something to contribute given that, with about 40 per cent of British marriages ending in divorce, divorce is becoming 'normal'.

There may, however, be an important gender difference regarding the effects of divorce, depending on the point of the dissolution process being considered. Whilst much has been made of the detrimental effects of divorce on men, as opposed to women, these usually occur *after* the relationship has ended. Men discover that they miss the emotional support that marriage can provide, and that on their own they have very little opportunity to express feelings to friends around them. With women, it is the stage *before* divorce, during marital stress, when they are far more likely than men to become depressed. That is

the point when marriage is probably worse for female mental stability than divorce itself.

In a survey involving over a 100 couples, Fincham (1997) compared levels of marital discord and symptoms of depression in men and women. According to Fincham:

> 'Our result suggests something pretty clear and robust and raises all sorts of interesting questions. It is widely believed that marriage protects men from mental health problems but if you look at women you find the opposite' (cited in Cook, 1997).

The situation for men (depression predicted marital stress) is the mirror-image of what happens for women, for whom marital stress predicted depressive symptoms. Women seem to value relationships more than men, and when the marital relationship is not working, this can cause depression. According to Fincham, women may feel greater responsibility for making the relationship work, so that when it does not, they blame themselves and this makes them more susceptible to depression (see Chapter 51).

There is, however, much evidence to suggest that the social support given to people following the dissolution of a relationship can *reduce* the probability of psychological distress and ill-health (McGhee, 1996). For example, Buehler & Legge (1993) found that companionship and other reassurance to self-esteem improved the level of psychological well-being in a sample of 144 women with children. If women are better at confiding in others (especially other women: see Chapter 56), they are more likely to receive social and emotional support following divorce, whereas men are more likely to be socially and emotionally isolated.

The process of relationship dissolution

As noted above, relationships are highly complex, and this is as true of relationship dissolution as it is of relationship formation and maintenance. The complexity of relationship dissolution is evident not just in the case of marriage, but in all sorts of relationships such as friendships and sexual relationships. The complexity is even greater if the relationship is a long-term one that has embraced many parts of a person's emotional, communicative, leisure and everyday life (Duck, 1988).

One way of looking at the break-up of a relationship is to regard it as a *process*, rather than an event, which takes place over a period of time. For Duck (1988):

'breaking up is not only hard to do, but also involves a lot of separate elements that make up the whole rotten process'.

Several models of the stages through which relationships pass as they dissolve have been proposed. If there are aspects that characterise many, if not all, dissolving relationships, it might be possible to identify the kinds of counselling or other 'repair work' that may work best for dissatisfied couples who want to avoid dissolving their relationships. Such models are, therefore, of more than theoretical importance (McGhee, 1996).

LEE'S MODEL

Lee (1984) has proposed that there are five stages in *pre-marital* romantic break-ups. First of all, *dissatisfaction* (D) is discovered. This dissatisfaction is then *exposed* (E). Some sort of *negotiation* (N) about the dissatisfaction occurs, and attempts are made to *resolve* (R) the problem. Finally, the relationship is *terminated* (T). Lea surveyed 112 premarital break-ups and found that (E) and (N) tended to be experienced as the most intense, dramatic, exhausting and negative aspects of the whole experience.

Those who skipped these stages (by just walking out of the relationship) reported feeling less intimate with their ex-partners, even when the relationship had been progressing smoothly. Lee also found that in those cases where the passage from (D) to (T) was particularly prolonged, people reported feeling more attracted to their ex-partners and experienced the greatest loneliness and fear during the break-up.

DUCK'S MODEL

Duck's (1982, 1988) model of relationship dissolution consists of four phases, each of which is initiated when a threshold is broken. The first, *intrapsychic phase*, begins when one partner sees him- or herself as being unable to stand the relationship any more. This initiates a focus on the other's behaviour, and an assessment of how adequate the partner's role performance is. Also, the individual begins to assess the negative aspects of being in the relationship, considers the costs of withdrawal, and assesses the positive aspects of being in an alternative relationship. Duck uses the term 'intrapsychic' because the processes are occurring only in the individual's mind and have not yet shown themselves in actual behaviour.

The next threshold is when the individual considers him- or herself as being justified in withdrawing from the relationship. This leads to the *dyadic phase*, and involves the other partner. Here, the dissatisfied individual must decide whether to confront or avoid the partner. When this decision is made, negotiations occur about, for example, whether the relationship can be repaired and the joint costs of withdrawal or reduced intimacy.

If the negotiations in this phase are unsuccessful, the next threshold is when the dissatisfied partner determines that he or she means the relationship to end. This leads to the *social phase*, so-called because it involves consideration of the social implications of the relationship's dissolution. This state of the relationship is made public, at least within the individual's own social network, and publicly negotiable face-saving/blame-placing stories and accounts of the relationship's breakdown may be given. 'Intervention teams', such as family or very close friends, may be called in to try to bring about a reconciliation.

Unless the 'intervention teams' are successful, the next threshold is when the relationship's dissolution becomes inevitable. This leads to the final *grave-dressing phase*. In this, the partners attempt to 'get over' the relationship's dissolution and engage in their own 'post-mortem' about why the relationship dissolved, a version of events which is then given to friends and family. Each partner needs to emerge from the relationship with an intact reputation for relationship reliability.

'Dressing the grave' involves 'erecting a tablet' which provides a credible and socially acceptable account of the relationship's life and death. Whilst helping to save face, it also serves to keep alive some memories and to 'justify' the original commitment to the ex-partner. For Duck (1988):

'Such stories are an integral and important part of the psychology of ending relationships ... By helping the person get over the break-up, they are immensely significant in preparing the person for future relationships as well as helping them out of old ones'.

Table 57.1   A summary of the phases involved in Duck's (1982, 1988) model of relationship disolution

Breakdown–dissatisfaction with relationship
Threshold: *'I can't stand this any more'*
INTRAPSYCHIC PHASE Personal focus on partner's behaviour Assess adequacy of partner's role performance Depict and evaluate negative aspects of being in the relationship Consider costs of withdrawal Assess positive aspects of alternative relationships Face 'express/repress dilemma'

Threshold: *'I'd be justified in withdrawing'*

DYADIC PHASE
Face 'confrontation/avoidance dilemma'
Confront partner
Negotiate in 'Our Relationship Talks'
Attempt repair and reconciliation?
Assess joint costs of withdrawal or reduced intimacy

Threshold: *'I mean it'*

SOCIAL PHASE
Negotiate post-dissolution state with partner
Initiate gossip/discussion in social network
Create publicly negotiable face-saving/blame-placing stories and accounts
Consider and face up to implied social network effect, if any
Call in intervention team

Threshold: *'It's now inevitable'*

GRAVE-DRESSING PHASE
'Getting over' activity
Retrospective; reformative post-mortem attribution
Public distribution of own version of break-up story

(From Gross, 1996)

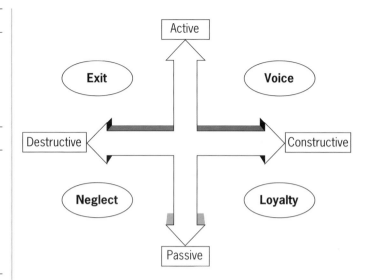

Figure 57.4   Rusbult's exit–voice–loyalty–neglect model

Marital reconciliation

We have looked in detail at the process of relationship breakdown. Other research has attempted to identify the factors involved in marital reconciliation which might predict successful reconciliation.

As well as Lee and Duck's models, several others have been advanced to explain the process of relationship dissolution. These include Rusbult's (1987) *exit–voice–loyalty–neglect model* which proposes four basic responses to relationship dissatisfaction. These are *exit* (leaving the relationship), *neglect* (ignoring the relationship), *voice* (articulating concerns), and *loyalty* (staying in the relationship and accepting the situation and the other's behaviour).

The two active strategies in the face of dissatisfaction are exit and voice, whilst the two 'passive' strategies are neglect and loyalty. Exit and neglect are 'destructive', whereas voice and loyalty are 'constructive'. According to McGhee (1996), the usefulness of this model, and the accuracy of its predictions about which type of couple will engage in which type of strategy, have been supported by studies conducted in both Britain (Goodwin, 1991) and America (Rusbult, 1987: see Figure 57.4).

Felmlee (1995) has proposed the *fatal attraction model of relationship breakdown*. Felmlee argues that the perceived characteristics in a person that initially attract someone to him or her are the very characteristics that lead to the breakdown of a relationship. So, a characteristic that initially makes a person appear 'exciting', say, to another, later on makes that person 'unpredictable', and the relationship breaks down because of this perceived unpredictability.

> **Box 57.5   Wineberg's (1994) study of marital reconciliation**
>
> Wineberg studied 506 white women who had attempted reconciliations in their first marriages. Women who had made 'successful' reconciliations, and were still married a year later, were compared with those who had made 'unsuccessful' reconciliations and were separated/divorced within a year of the attempted reconciliation. Wineberg found that, overall, 30 per cent of reconciliations were successful, and that important factors linked with the reconciliation included:
>
> - both partners being of the same religion (especially if one partner had changed religion in connection with the marriage);
>
> - cohabitation with a partner before marriage;
>
> - marriage with a partner of the same age.
>
> Different factors were associated with marital dissolution, including age at separation, duration of marriage, and education. Wineberg argues that although these factors may be reflected in the decision to separate, there are other factors that may have a bearing on whether an attempted reconciliation is successful. Amongst these are social and religious ties, advice from family and friends, and life after separation.

Conclusions

The breakdown and dissolution of relationships have been the subject of extensive research and theorising. However, much remains to be investigated. For example, this chapter has concentrated on the breakdown of heterosexual relationships. Whether homosexual relationship dissolution involves the same processes has yet to be discovered. As McGhee (1996) has noted:

'We know much, much more now about how relationships become unsatisfactory and break down than we did even 10 years ago, and yet like so many areas in social psychology, what we do know now is but an infinitesimal fraction of what remains to be known'.

Summary

- Married people live longer and are happier, healthier and have lower rates of various mental disorders than the single, widowed or divorced. Explanations of marriage's beneficial effects assume that mental status causes variations in mental health. However, the **selection for marriage hypothesis** reverses this, saying that a predisposition to illness may reduce the likelihood of a person marrying.

- Several factors make it more likely that a marriage will end in divorce. These include age, socioeconomic status, educational level, demographic factors, the experience of parental divorce, and number of pre-marital sexual partners. However, these factors on their own cannot completely explain marital breakdown.

- **Communicative strategies** employed early on in married life are linked with subsequent marital happiness. Manipulative and coercive styles predict dissatisfaction experienced by wives, but not by husbands. **Structural causes** and **conflict resolution** are also linked to marital unhappiness and divorce.

- Women report relationship problems more than men. Female dissatisfaction is a better predictor of relationship dissolution than male dissatisfaction. Women also stress basic unhappiness and incompatibility more than men do as reasons for relationship dissolution.

- Two models of changes in marital satisfaction are Pineo's **linear model** and Burr's **curvilinear model**. The former proposes an inevitable decline in romantic love over time and that any changes in a partner reduce compatibility. The latter sees marital happiness as being greatest in the early years, lowest in the middle years, and rising again in the later years. This is linked to children's arrival, growing up, and leaving home.

- **Conflict resolution** can often be a positive process promoting a relationship's growth. However, recurring conflicts suggest failure to resolve the underlying cause. This may lead partners to doubt each other as reasonable people.

- Happy and unhappy couples display different **attributional patterns** when resolving their conflicts. This is **relationship-enhancing** with happy couples and **distress-maintaining** with unhappy couples.

- The main functions of relationship **rules** are to regulate behaviour in order to minimise conflict and check on the exchange of rewards. Many rules apply to most or all relationships, but others apply to particular types or clusters of relationships.

- People in disrupted relationships are more likely to suffer certain diseases, alcoholism, drug dependence and sleep disturbances, than others of the same age and sex. Marital status is a strong correlate of the risk of mental health admission.

- In men, most of the harmful effects occur **following** relationship dissolution. In women, they are more likely to occur **before** relationship dissolution (during marital stress). However, women's ability to confide in others means they are more likely to receive social and emotional support, which can reduce the probability of mental ill-health.

- Dissolution is best thought of as a **process** rather than an event. Several models try to identify the stages or phases relationships pass through as they dissolve. These include Lee's **five stage model** and Duck's **four phase model**. Other approaches include Rusbult's **exit–voice–loyalty–neglect model** and Felmlee's **fatal attraction model of relationship breakdown**.

- Successful **marital reconciliation** is linked to several factors. These include the partners being of the same religion and age, and cohabitation with the partner before marriage. Unsuccessful reconciliation is associated with age at separation, duration of marriage, and education.

PART 3

Social influence

58

CONFORMITY

Introduction and overview

Conformity has been defined in a number of ways. For Crutchfield (1955), it is 'yielding to group pressure', whilst Mann (1969) argues that whereas this is its essence, 'it may take different forms and be based on motives other than group pressure'. Zimbardo & Leippe (1991) see conformity as:

'a change in belief or behaviour in response to real or imagined group pressure when there is no direct request to comply with the group nor any reason to justify the behaviour change'.

What the definitions above have in common is that they all make reference to *group pressure*, although none of them specifies particular groups with particular beliefs or practices. Rather, it is the pressure exerted by *any* group which is important to a person at a given time that is influential. These may be composed of 'significant others' such as family or peers (*membership groups*), or groups whose values a person admires or aspires to, but is not actually a member of (*reference groups*). Conformity, then,

does not imply adhering to any particular set of attitudes or values. Instead, it involves yielding to the real or imagined pressures of *any* group regardless of its majority or minority status (van Avermaet, 1996).

Experimental research into conformity began in the early 1930s, and the phenomenon continues to attract research interest today. This chapter reviews what is known about conformity to real or imagined pressure from others.

Experimental studies of conformity

Sherif (1935) had participants make estimates of the amount by which a spot of light in an otherwise darkened room appeared to move (the *autokinetic effect*: see Chapter 21, page 179). In one experiment, participants first made their estimates privately and then as members of a group. Sherif found that participants' individual estimates converged, and became more alike. Thus, a *group norm* developed which represented the average of the individual estimates (see Figure 58.2, page 500).

Whilst Sherif believed that his study demonstrated conformity, Asch (1951) disagreed. According to Asch, the fact that Sherif's task was ambiguous, in that there was no right or wrong answer, made it difficult to draw conclusions about conformity in group situations. In Asch's view, the best way to measure conformity was in terms of a person's tendency to agree with other people who unanimously give the *wrong answer* on a task with an

Figure 58.1   A humorous look at conformity

499

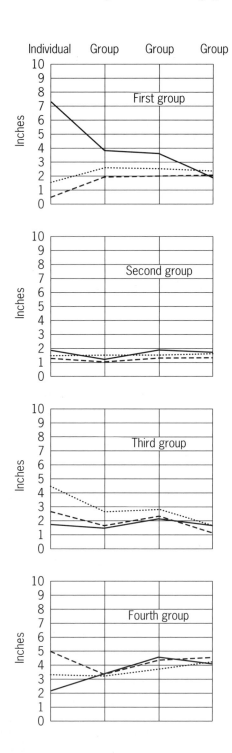

Figure 58.2   Median judgements of the apparent movement of a stationary point of light given by participants in Sherif's (1935) experiment. In the data shown, participants first made their estimates alone ('individual') and then in groups of three on three occasions ('group'). The figure shows the estimates given by four groups. Sherif also found that when the procedure was reversed, that is, participants made three estimates in groups followed by an estimate alone, the 'individual' estimates did not deviate from one another (From Sherif, 1936)

obvious and unambiguous solution. Asch devised a simple perceptual task that involved participants deciding which of three comparison lines of varying length matched a standard line.

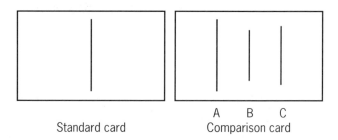

Figure 58.3   An example of the line-judgement task devised by Asch

In a pilot study, Asch tested 36 participants individually on 20 slightly different versions of the task shown in Figure 58.3. Since they made a total of only three mistakes in the 720 trials (an error rate of 0.42 per cent), Asch concluded that the tasks were simple and their answers obvious and unambiguous. Asch's procedure for studying conformity was ingenious and, because the basic set-up can be adapted to investigate the effects of different variables on conformity, it is known as the *Asch paradigm*.

Box 58.1   The Asch paradigm

Some of the participants who had taken part in Asch's pilot study (see text) were requested to act as 'stooges' (or confederates). The stooges were told that they would be doing the tasks again, but this time in a *group* rather than individually. They were also told that the group would contain one person who was completely ignorant that they were stooges.

On certain *critical* trials, which Asch would indicate by means of a secret signal, all the stooges were required to say *out loud* the same *wrong answer*. In Asch's original experiment, the stooges (usually seven to nine of them) and the naïve participant were seated either in a straight line or round a table (see Figure 58.4) The situation was rigged so that the naïve participant was always the last or last but one to say the answer out loud.

On the first two trials, all the stooges gave the correct answers. However, on the third trial they unanimously gave a wrong answer. In all, this happened a further 11 times in the experiment, with four additional 'neutral' trials (in which all stooges responded with the correct answers) between the critical trials.

Figure 58.4   A naïve participant (number 6), having heard five stooges give the same incorrect answer, offers his own judgement as to which of three comparison lines matches a stimulus line

Table 58.1 The findings from Asch's original experiment

No. of conforming responses made	No. of people making those responses
0	13
1	4
2	5
3	6
4	3
5	4
6	1
7	2
8	5
9	3
10	3
11	1
12	0

The important measurement in the Asch paradigm is whether the naïve participant conforms and gives the same wrong answer as the stooges have unanimously done, or is independent and gives the obviously correct answer.

Asch found a *mean* conformity rate of 32 per cent, that is, participants agreed with the incorrect majority answer on about one third of the critical trials. If the *median* is used as the measure of central tendency, the conformity rate is 25 per cent. However, and as Table 58.1 shows, there are wide individual differences. Thus, no one conformed on all the critical trials, and 13 of the 50 participants tested (26 per cent) never conformed at all. However, one person

conformed on 11 of the 12 critical trials and about three-quarters conformed at least once. Given that the task was simple and unambiguous, such findings indicate a high level of conformity. As van Avermaet (1996) has remarked:

> 'the results reveal the tremendous impact of an "obviously" incorrect but unanimous majority on the judgements of a lone individual'.

How did the naïve participants explain their behaviour?

After the experiment, participants were interviewed about their behaviour. The interviews revealed a number of specific reasons for the occurrence of conformity. For example, some participants claimed that they wanted to act in accordance with what they imagined were the experimenter's wishes, and convey a favourable impression of themselves by 'not upsetting the experiment' (which they believed they would have done by disagreeing with the majority: see Chapter 83).

Others, who had no reason to believe that there was anything wrong with their eyesight, claimed they genuinely doubted the validity of their own judgements by wondering if they were suffering from eye strain, or if the chairs had been moved so that they could not see the task material properly. Yet others denied being aware of having given incorrect answers – they had unwittingly used the stooges as 'marker posts' (Smith, 1995). Some participants said that they 'didn't want to appear different', or 'didn't want to be made to look a fool' or 'inferior'. For them, there was clearly a discrepancy between the answer they gave in the group and what they *privately believed*. Whilst they knew the answer they were giving was wrong, they nonetheless went along with the views of the group (see page 504).

That participants were justified in fearing potential ridicule by group members was shown in an experiment in which 16 naïve participants and a *single stooge* were tested (van Avermaet, 1996). When the stooge gave a wrong answer on the critical trials, the naïve participants reacted with sarcasm and laughter. In other experiments, Asch (1952) showed that when the stooges gave their answers out loud, but the naïve participant *wrote down* the answers, conformity was significantly reduced. This indicates that it must have been *group pressure*, rather than anything else, that produced conformity.

There is evidence to suggest that participants in Asch-type experiments experience some degree of *stress*. For example, Bogdonoff *et al.* (1961) showed that plasma-free fatty acid levels (a measure of arousal) increased in naïve participants as they heard the stooges giving wrong answers. When the naïve participant responded, the levels decreased if a conforming response was made, but continued to increase if a non-conforming response was given.

FACTORS AFFECTING CONFORMITY

Using the Asch paradigm, researchers have, as noted earlier, manipulated particular variables in order to see if they increase or decrease the amount of conformity reported in Asch's original experiment.

Box 58.2   Some factors affecting conformity

Group size: With one stooge and the naïve participant, conformity is very low (3 per cent), presumably because it is a simple case of the participant's 'word' against the stooge's. With two stooges, conformity rises to 14 per cent. With three stooges, it reaches the 32 per cent which Asch originally reported. Thereafter, however, further increases in group size do not lead to increases in conformity. With very large groups, conformity may drop dramatically (Asch, 1955), one reason being that participants begin (quite rightly) to suspect *collusion* (Wilder, 1977).

Unanimity: Conformity is most likely to occur when the stooges are unanimous in their answers. When one stooge does not go along with the majority judgement, conformity decreases (Asch, 1956). The stooge need not even share the naïve participant's judgement (the stooge may, for example, appear to have a visual impairment as evidenced by the wearing of thick glasses). Thus, just breaking the unanimity of the majority is sufficient to reduce conformity (Allen & Levine, 1971). For Asch, unanimity is a more important factor than group size:

'a unanimous majority of three is, under given conditions, far more effective (in producing conformity) than a majority of eight containing one dissenter' (Asch, 1951).

Additionally, when a stooge begins by giving the correct answer but then conforms to the majority incorrect answer, conformity is increased.

Task difficulty, ambiguity, and familiarity with task demands: With difficult tasks, as when the comparison lines are all similar to the stimulus line, conformity increases (Asch, 1956). Ambiguous tasks, such as making judgements about the number of clicks produced by a fast metronome, also produce increased conformity (Shaw *et al.*, 1957). The more familiar we are with a task's demands, the less likely we are to conform. For example, women are more likely to conform to group pressure on tasks involving the identification of tools (such as wrenches), whereas men are more likely to conform on tasks involving the identification of cooking utensils (Sistrunk & McDavid, 1971).

Gender and other individual differences: It has been reported that women conform more than men (Cooper, 1979), although this claim has been disputed. For example, Eagly & Steffen (1984) found that men conform to group opinions as frequently as women do when their conformity or independence will be kept private. However, when conformity or independence will be made known to the group, men conform less than women, presumably because non-conformity is consistent with the masculine stereotype of independence. Conformity has also been found to be higher amongst those who:

- have low self-esteem (Santee & Maslach, 1982);

- are especially concerned about social relationships (Mullen, 1983);

- have a strong need for social approval (Sears *et al.*, 1991);

- are attracted towards other group members (Wyer, 1966).

EVALUATING ASCH'S CONTRIBUTION TO THE STUDY OF CONFORMITY

One of the earliest criticisms of Asch's work was that the Asch paradigm was both time consuming (in terms of setting up the situation) and uneconomical (in the sense that only one naïve participant at a time can be investigated). Crutchfield (1954) attempted to overcome both of these problems.

Box 58.3   Crutchfield's procedure

In Crutchfield's procedure, participants are seated in a cubicle which has a panel with an array of lights and switches (the *Crutchfield device*). Questions can be projected on to a wall and, by pressing switches, the participant can answer them. The participant is told that the lights on the panel represent the responses given by other participants. In fact, this is not true, and the lights are controlled by an experimenter who has a 'master panel' in another cubicle.

Of course, the participant does not know this, and the arrangement removes the need for stooges. It also allows several participants in different cubicles to be tested at once. Crutchfield tested over 600 people.

Amongst many findings were those indicating that college students agreed with statements which, in other

---

circumstances, they would probably not agree with. These included statements like 'The life expectancy of American males is only 25 years', 'Americans sleep four to five hours per night and eat six meals a day' and 'Free speech being a privilege rather than a right, it is only proper for a society to suspend free speech when it feels itself threatened'.

Asch's original findings have stimulated much research. Twenty or so years after they were published, Larsen (1974) found significantly lower rates of conformity among American students. Larsen explained the discrepancy in terms of a change in climate of opinion in America:

'away from the stupefying effects of McCarthyism in the 1950s [towards] a more sceptical and independent individual'.

Five years later, however, Larsen *et al.* (1979) found conformity rates similar to those reported by Asch, possibly suggesting a move *away* from independence and criticism in American students.

In Britain, Perrin & Spencer (1981) found very low rates of conformity among university students. However, when they tested young offenders on probation, with probation officers as stooges, very similar rates of conformity to those reported by Asch were obtained. According to Perrin and Spencer, the rate of conformity obtained in studies is a useful indicator of the cultural expectations people bring to the experiment from their contemporary world, a view with which Asch agreed (Perrin & Spencer, 1980). However, as well as participants' expectations influencing the amount of conformity obtained, it is possible that *experimenters* exert an influence too. As Brown (1986) has noted, experimenters may also have changed over time. Perhaps their expectations of the amount of conformity that will occur in an experiment are unwittingly conveyed to the participants, who respond accordingly.

MAJORITY OR MINORITY INFLUENCE IN ASCH-TYPE EXPERIMENTS?

In reviewing the findings from Asch's studies, Turner (1991) observed that most concern has centred around:

'the weakness of the individual in face of the group and the strength of spontaneous pressures for conformity inherent in the group context'.

However, and as Table 58.1 shows (see page 501), most participants remained independent either most or all of the time, and so conformity was actually the *exception* to the rule.

Typically, the stooges in an Asch-type experiment are thought of as the majority and, numerically, they are. However, Moscovici & Faucheux (1972) have argued that it is more profitable to think of the naïve participant as the majority (in that he or she embodies the 'conventional', self-evident opinion of most of us) and the stooges as the minority (who reflect an unorthodox, unconventional, eccentric and even outrageous viewpoint). In Asch's experiments, this minority influenced the majority 32 per cent of the time, and it is those participants remaining independent who are actually the conformists!

Asch-type experiments, viewed from this perspective, offer evidence related to the question of how new ideas come to be accepted, rather than about the processes that operate to maintain the *status quo* (Tanford & Penrod, 1984). In Moscovici's (1976) view, a *conformity bias* exists in this area of research, such that all social influence serves the need to adapt to the *status quo* for the sake of uniformity and stability. However, change is sometimes needed to adapt to changing circumstances, and this is very difficult to explain given the presence of a conformity bias. What is needed is an understanding of the dynamics of *active minorities*. If such minorities did not exert influence in any arena of human social and scientific activity, innovations would simply never happen (van Avermaet, 1996).

How do minorities exert an influence?

If the data from Asch's original experiments are reanalysed, conformity or non-conformity can be shown to be related to the *consistency* of the stooge's judgements (Moscovici, 1976). Moscovici and his colleagues were able to show that by giving consistent responses, minorities can change the majority's views. In one experiment, Moscovici & Lage (1976) instructed a stooge minority of two to consistently describe a blue-green colour as green. The majority's views changed to that of the minority and this effect persisted when further judgements were asked for after the minority had withdrawn from the experiment.

> **Box 58.4   Why are consistency and other factors important in minority influence?**
>
> According to Hogg & Vaughan (1995), consistency has five main effects:
>
> 1 It disrupts the majority norm, and produces uncertainty and doubt.
>
> 2 It draws attention to itself as an entity.
>
> 3 It conveys the existence of an alternative, coherent point of view.

4 It demonstrates certainty and an unshakeable commitment to a particular point of view.

5 It shows that the only solution to the current conflict is the minority viewpoint.

Minorities are also more effective if they are seen to have made significant personal/material sacrifices (*investment*), are perceived as acting out of principle rather than ulterior motives (*autonomy*), and display a balance between being 'dogmatic' (*rigidity*) and 'inconsistent' (*flexibility*) (Nemeth & Wachtler, 1973; Papastamou, 1979; Wood *et al.*, 1994; Hogg & Vaughan, 1995). Minorities also have more influence if they are seen as being similar to the majority in terms of age, gender and social category (Clark & Maass, 1988), and particularly if minority members are categorised as part of the ingroup (see Chapter 53, page 465).

Why do people conform?

As Abrams *et al.* (1990) have noted:

'we know groups constrain and direct the actions of their members, but there is considerable controversy as to how, and under what conditions, various forms of influence operate'.

One attempt to account for conformity was provided by Deutsch & Gerard (1955). They argued that in order to explain group influence it was necessary to distinguish between *informational social influence* (ISI) and *normative social influence* (NSI).

INFORMATIONAL SOCIAL INFLUENCE

Festinger's (1954) *social comparison theory* states that people have a basic need to evaluate ideas and attitudes and, in turn, to confirm that these are correct. This can provide a reassuring sense of control over the world and a satisfying sense of competence. In situations which are novel or ambiguous, social reality is defined by the thoughts and behaviours of others. For example, if we are in a restaurant and not clear about which piece of cutlery to use with a particular course, we look to others for 'guidance' and then conform to their behaviours. This is ISI.

The less we can rely on our own direct perceptions and behavioural contacts with the physical world, the more susceptible we should be to influences from other people (Turner, 1991). As mentioned earlier (see page 501), some participants in Asch's experiment claimed that they believed the majority opinion to be correct and that their own perceptions were incorrect. Taken at face value, this would suggest that ISI occurs even in unambiguous

situations (Insko *et al.*, 1983). However, such explanations may actually be *defensive* (or perhaps *self-serving*) *attributions* (see Chapter 51, page 451) given by participants to justify submission to the influence of the majority (Berkowitz, 1986).

NORMATIVE SOCIAL INFLUENCE

Underlying NSI is the need to be accepted by others and to make a favourable impression on them. We may conform in order to gain social approval and avoid rejection, and we may agree with others because of their power to reward, punish, accept, or reject us. As noted previously, in both Asch's and Crutchfield's experiments, most participants were quite clear as to the correct answer. However, in making their own judgements they risked rejection by the majority, and so for at least some participants conformity probably occurred because of NSI.

Box 58.5   The costs of non-conformity

Schachter (1951) provided evidence that the fear that others will reject, dislike or mistreat us for holding different opinions is justified.

Groups of male university students read and discussed the case of a delinquent youth called 'Johnny Rocco'. Johnny was described as having grown up in an urban slum, experiencing a difficult childhood, and having often been in trouble. Participants were asked to recommend that Johnny receive a great deal of love and affection, harsh discipline and punishment, or some combination of the two.

Johnny's case notes were written sympathetically, and participants made lenient recommendations. Included in each group, however, was a stooge who sometimes agreed with the genuine participants and sometimes recommended that Johnny be given harsh discipline and punishment. When the stooge adopted the deviant opinion, he maintained and defended it as best he could.

Schachter found that participants immediately directed their comments to the stooge in an effort to get him to agree with their lenient recommendations. When the stooge failed to do this, communication dropped off sharply and he was largely ignored. After the discussion, participants were asked to assign group members to various tasks and recommend who should be included in the group. When the stooge's opinion deviated from the group majority, he was rejected. However, in groups where he took the majority opinion, he was viewed positively and not rejected.

So, holding an unpopular opinion, even in a short group discussion, can lead to an individual being ostracised, and it seems reasonable to suggest that under at least some circumstances, a fear of rejection for failing to conform is justified.

Internalisation and compliance

Related to NSI and ISI are two major *kinds* of conformity. *Internalisation* occurs when a private belief or opinion becomes consistent with a public belief or opinion. In internalisation, then, we say what we believe and believe what we say. Mann (1969) calls this *true conformity*, and it can be thought of as a conversion to other people's points of view. This probably explains the behaviour of participants in Sherif's experiment (see page 499). In Asch-type conformity experiments, however, people face conflicts and reach compromises in the form of *compliance*, in which the answers given publicly are *not* those that are privately believed. In compliance, then, we say what we do not believe and what we believe we do not say.

Conformity and group belongingness

The distinction between NSI and ISI has been called the *dual process dependency model of social influence*. However, this model underestimates the role of group 'belongingness'. One important feature of conformity is that we are influenced by a group because, psychologically, we feel we belong to it. This is why a group's norms are relevant standards for our own attitudes and behaviour. The dual process dependency model emphasises the *interpersonal* aspects of conformity experiments, which could just as easily occur between individuals as group members.

Box 58.6 Referential social influence

Abrams *et al.* (1990) argue that we only experience uncertainty when we disagree with those with whom we expect to agree. This is especially likely when we regard those others as members of the same category or group as ourselves in respect to judgements made in a shared stimulus situation. Social influence occurs, then, when we see ourselves as belonging to a group and possessing the same characteristics and reactions as other group members. Turner (1991) calls this self-categorisation in which group membership is salient *referent informational influence*.

Abrams *et al.*'s approach suggests that in Sherif's (1935) experiment, for example, participants were influenced by the assumption that the autokinetic effect is actually real, and their expectations of agreement between themselves.

In support of this, it has been shown that when participants discover that the autokinetic effect is an illusion, mutual influence and convergence cease because the need to agree at all is removed (Sperling, 1946).

If, however, we believe that there *is* a correct answer, and we are uncertain what it is, *only* those whom we categorise as belonging to 'our' group will influence our judgements. As Brown (1988) has remarked:

'there is more to conformity than simply "defining social reality": it all depends on who is doing the defining'.

According to this self-categorisation approach, people conform because they are group members, and evidence indicates that conformity on Asch-type experiments is higher when participants see themselves as ingroup members (Abrams *et al.*, 1990). This implies that it is not the validation of physical reality or the avoidance of social disapproval that is important. Rather, it is the upholding of a group norm that is important, and *people* are the source of information about the appropriate ingroup norm.

Conformity: good or bad?

Sometimes, *dissent* is just an expression of disagreement, a refusal to 'go along with the crowd'. On other occasions, it is more creative, as when someone suggests a better solution to a problem (Maslach *et al.*, 1985). A refusal to 'go along with the crowd' may be an attempt to remain independent as a matter of principle (which Willis, 1963, calls *anticonformity*) and may betray a basic fear of a loss of personal identity. Constructive dissent and independence, by contrast, are positive qualities.

In most circumstances, conformity serves a valuable social purpose in that it:

'lubricates the machinery of social interaction [and] enables us to structure our social behaviour and predict the reactions of others' (Zimbardo & Leippe, 1991).

For most people, though, the word 'conformity' has a negative connotation and is often used to convey undesirable behaviour. In laboratory research, conformity has most often been studied in terms of 'the conspiratorial group' who 'limit, constrain, and distort the individual's response' (Milgram, 1965).

As a result, it has been implicitly assumed that independence is 'good' and conformity is 'bad', a value judgement made explicit by Asch (1952). However, conformity can be highly functional, helping us satisfy social and non-social needs, as well as being necessary (at least to a degree) for social life to proceed at all. Moreover, because each of us has a limited (and often biased) store of information on which to make our decisions, why shouldn't we consider information from others, especially those with more expertise than us? A conforming response, then, may be a *rational judgement* by a person who does not have sufficient information on which to make a decision, and so relies on others for assistance. However, whilst dissent can create unpleasantness, and conformity can help preserve harmony:

'there are obvious dangers to conformity. Failure to speak our minds against dangerous trends or attitudes (for example, racism) can easily be interpreted as support' (Krebs & Blackman, 1988).

Conclusions

There are some circumstances in which we conform as a result of either real or imagined pressure from others. Exactly why we sometimes conform and sometimes show independent behaviour has been the subject of much research, and many factors influencing conformity have been identified. Whilst conformity is usually viewed as the influence of a majority over a minority, minorities can, under certain circumstances, exert influence over majorities.

Summary

■ The essence of conformity is yielding to real or imagined **group (membership** or **reference) pressure** in the absence of any direct request to comply with the group. Conformity does not imply adhering to particular attitudes or values, and the group may have majority or minority status.

■ The **Asch paradigm** enables conformity to be studied experimentally. In this, a naïve participant is led to believe that other participants ('stooges') are genuine when in fact they are not. The 'stooges' sometimes unanimously give incorrect answers on a task which has an obviously correct answer. The crucial measurement is whether the naïve participant gives the same wrong answer as the 'stooges' on critical trials.

■ Asch found a mean conformity rate of 32 per cent (or 25 per cent if the median is used). No participant conformed all the time, but all conformed at least once in Asch's original experiment. Participants explained their behaviour in several ways. Some wondered if their eyesight was reliable, or said they conformed because they did not want to look foolish. Others denied being aware they had given incorrect answers.

■ When naïve participants are allowed to write down their answers, conformity disappears, indicating that **group pressure** is the critical factor. Increases in participants' physiological arousal indicates that the Asch paradigm is a stressful experience.

■ Several factors influence the amount of conformity observed when the Asch paradigm is used. These include **group size, unanimity, task difficulty, ambiguity,** and **familiarity. Gender** and other individual differences can also influence how much conformity occurs.

■ A less time-consuming and more economical way of studying conformity is provided by the **Crutchfield device.** This produced similar amounts of conformity to those originally reported by Asch.

■ The amount of conformity observed in American students has not remained constant over time. In Britain, low rates of conformity have been reported in university students, but high rates in young offenders on probation. Conformity rates apparently reflect the cultural expectations of participants and those of the experimenters.

■ The 'stooges' in Asch-type experiments are usually seen as the majority. However, it may be more useful to see the naïve participant as embodying the 'conventional', self-evident, majority, whilst the 'stooges' reflect an unorthodox, unconventional, minority opinion. From this perspective, the minority influenced the majority 32 per cent of the time, and it is those participants who remained independent who are actually the conformists. This perspective is relevant to understanding how new ideas come to be accepted.

■ A consistent minority can change the majority's view by drawing attention to itself as an entity, conveying the existence of an alternative, coherent point of view, and demonstrating certainty and a commitment to a particular point of view which represents the only solution to a current conflict.

■ Minorities are also more effective if they display **investment, autonomy,** and a balance between **rigidity** and **flexibility.** They also have more influence if they are perceived as similar to the majority in terms of age, gender and social category.

■ Both **informational social influence** (ISI) and **normative social influence** (NSI) operate in Asch-type experiments and other settings. Related to ISI is **internalisation** or **true conformity,** in which we say what we believe and believe what we say. Related to NSI is **compliance,** in which we say what we do not believe and do not believe what we say.

■ The distinction between ISI and NSI has been called the **dual process dependency model of social influence.**

However, this emphasises the **interpersonal** aspect of conformity experiments and underestimates the role of **group belongingness**. We may only experience uncertainty when we disagree with those with whom we expect to agree, especially those regarded as belonging to the same category/group and sharing certain characteristics and reactions (**referential informational influence**).

■ Dissent may represent an attempt to remain independent as a matter of principle (**anticonformity**). Alternatively, it can be constructive and creative. Conformity may be a **rational judgement** by someone who does not have sufficient information on which to make a decision and so relies on others with greater expertise. However, failure to speak one's mind can be (mis)interpreted as support for something.

59

OBEDIENCE

Introduction and overview

When people in authority tell us to do something, we tend to comply with their orders. For example, Cohen & Davis (1981, cited in Carlson, 1987) describe a case in which a physician prescribed ear drops for a patient with an ear infection and left instructions that the nurse should 'place drops in R ear'. However, the physician evidently did not leave a suitably big gap between the 'R' (for right) and the word 'ear'. Neither the nurse nor the patient questioned a treatment for earache in which the medication was delivered rectally.

The more serious *social* problems that obedience can cause have been described by Milgram (1974):

'From 1933 to 1945 millions of innocent persons were systematically slaughtered on command. Gas chambers were built, death camps were guarded, daily quotas of corpses were produced with the same efficiency as the manufacture of appliances. These inhuman policies may have originated in the mind of a single person, but they could only be carried out on a massive scale if a very large number of persons obeyed orders'.

This chapter looks at research into obedience, much of it conducted by Milgram, and considers what such research can tell us about why we are sometimes blindly obedient to others and how we might behave more independently.

Distinguishing between conformity and obedience

According to Milgram (1992), conformity and obedience are similar in that both involve the abdication of individual judgement in the face of some external pressure. However, there are at least three important differences between them. First, in conformity there is no *explicit* requirement to act in a certain way, whereas in obedience we are *ordered* or *instructed* to do something. Second, those who influence us when we conform are our *peers* (or *equals*) and people's behaviours become more alike because they are affected by *example*. In obedience, there is a difference in status from the outset and, rather than mutual influence, obedience is affected by *direction*, with somebody in *higher authority* influencing behaviour.

Third, conformity has to do with the psychological 'need' for acceptance by others and involves going along with one's peers in a group situation (see Chapter 58, page 504). Obedience, by contrast, has to do with the social power and status of an authority figure in a hierarchical situation. Although we typically deny that we are conformist (because it detracts from a sense of individuality), we usually deny *responsibility* for our behaviour in the case of obedience. As a result, behaviours occur because 'I was only following orders' (an explanation given by Adolf Eichmann, Director of the Nazi deportation of Jews to concentration camps) or because 'if the Commander in Chief tells this lieutenant colonel to go and stand in the corner and sit on his head, I will do so' (a response given by Oliver North in the Iran–Contra hearings of 1987).

Experimental studies: Milgram's research

The original purpose of Milgram's (1963, 1964, 1974) research was to test 'the "Germans are different" hypothesis'. This has been used by historians to explain the systematic destruction of millions of Jews, Poles and others by the Nazis during the 1930s and 1940s (see above and also Chapter 53, page 461). The hypothesis maintains that Hitler could not have put his evil plans into operation without the co-operation of thousands of others, and that the Germans have a basic character defect (namely, a readiness to obey authority without question, regardless of the acts demanded by the authority figure) which provided Hitler with the co-operation he needed. After piloting his research in America, Milgram planned to continue it in Germany to test for the existence of this hypothesised character defect. As will be seen, though, his results indicated that this was not necessary.

MILGRAM'S PARTICIPANTS

Originally, Milgram advertised for volunteers to take part in a study of learning to be conducted at Yale University. The experiment would last about an hour and participants would be paid $4.50 for their involvement. The first participants to be studied were 20–50-year-old men from all walks of life.

Public Announcement

WE WILL PAY YOU $4.00 FOR ONE HOUR OF YOUR TIME

Persons Needed for a Study of Memory

*We will pay five hundred New Haven men to help us complete a scientific study of memory and learning. The study is being done at Yale University.

*Each person who participates will be paid $4.00 (plus 50c carfare) for approximately 1 hour's time. We need you for only one hour: there are no further obligations. You may choose the time you would like to come (evenings, weekdays, or weekends).

*No special training, education, or experience is needed. We want:

Factory workers	Businessmen	Construction workers
City employees	Clerks	Salespeople
Laborers	Professional people	White-collar workers
Barbers	Telephone workers	Others

All persons must be between the ages of 20 and 50. High school and college students cannot be used.

*If you meet these qualifications, fill out the coupon below and mail it now to Professor Stanley Milgram, Department of Psychology, Yale University, New Haven. You will be notified later of the specific time and place of the study. We reserve the right to decline any application.

*You will be paid $4.00 (plus 50c carfare) as soon as you arrive at the laboratory.

- -

TO:
PROF. STANLEY MILGRAM, DEPARTMENT OF PSYCHOLOGY, YALE UNIVERSITY, NEW HAVEN, CONN. I want to take part in this study of memory and learning. I am between the ages of 20 and 50. I will be paid $4.00 (plus 50c carfare) if I participate.

NAME (Please Print)..........................

ADDRESS..........................

TELEPHONE NO............... Best time to call you.......

AGE........OCCUPATION..................SEX......
CAN YOU COME:

WEEKDAYS....... EVENINGS......WEEKENDS.........

Figure 59.1   The advertisement used by Milgram to recruit participants for his study (From Milgram, 1974)

THE BASIC PROCEDURE

When participants arrived at Yale University's psychology department, they were met by a young, crew-cut man in a grey laboratory coat who introduced himself as Jack Williams, the experimenter. Also present was a Mr Wallace, a mild and harmless looking accountant in his late fifties. In fact, neither the experimenter nor Mr Wallace was genuine, and everything else that followed in the procedure (apart from the naïve participants' behaviour) was carefully pre-planned, staged and scripted.

The participant and Mr Wallace were told that the experiment was concerned with the effects of punishment on learning, and that one of them would be the 'teacher' and the other the 'learner'. Their roles were determined by each drawing a piece of paper from a hat. In fact, both pieces of paper had 'teacher' written on them. Mr Wallace drew out the first and called out 'learner'. As a result, the real participant was always the 'teacher'. All three then went to an adjoining room where the learner was strapped into a chair with his arms attached to electrodes that would supposedly deliver an electric shock from a generator in the adjacent room.

The teacher and experimenter then went into the adjacent room. The teacher was shown the generator, which had a number of switches on it, each clearly marked with voltage levels and verbal descriptions. The shocks began at 15 volts and went up in 15-volt increments to 450 volts. The teacher was then given a 45-volt shock to convince him that the generator was real. However, and unknown to the teacher, this would be the only *actual* electric shock delivered during the whole experiment.

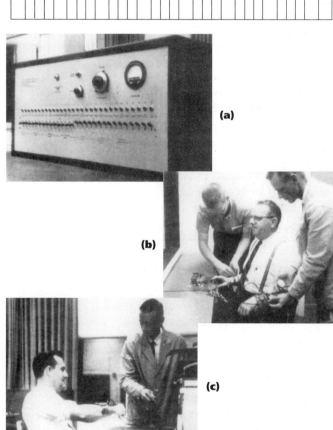

Figure 59.2   (a) The 'electric shock generator' used by Milgram (left) and a schematic representation of its front panel showing the voltages and verbal labels (top). In (b), the 'learner' is strapped into his chair, and in (c), the 'teacher' receives a shock of 45 volts (From Milgram, 1974)

The task involved the teacher reading out a list of word pairs (such as 'blue–girl' and 'fat–neck'). After this, the first word of a pair was read out followed by a number of other words, one of which was the word it had been paired with. The learner had to choose the correct word by pressing one of four switches which turned on a light on a panel in the teacher's room. Each time the learner made a mistake, the teacher had to deliver a shock, with each successive mistake being punished by a shock 15 volts higher than the previous one.

In Milgram's first experiment (the *remote victim* variation), the learner was scripted to pound loudly on the wall at 300 volts and, after 315 volts, to stop pounding on the wall *and* give no further answers. In the second experiment (the *voice feedback* variation), the teacher heard a tape-recorded series of verbal responses that were Mr Wallace's 'spontaneous reactions' to the increasing shock levels.

Box 59.1   Mr Wallace's 'spontaneous reactions' to increasing shock levels administered by the teacher

75, 90 and 105 volts: Makes a little grunt.

120 volts: Tells the experimenter that the shocks are becoming painful.

150 volts: Cries out 'Experimenter, get me out of here! I won't be in the experiment any more! I refuse to go on!'

180 volts: Shouts out 'I can't stand the pain!'

270 volts: Lets out an agonised scream and continues to insist on being released.

300 volts: Desperately shouts out that he will no longer provide answers.

315 volts: Lets out a violent scream and reaffirms vehemently that he will no longer provide answers.

330 volts: There is an ominous silence.

The scripted behaviours were, of course, dependent upon any participant actually continuing with the experiment up to that shock level. When Milgram asked his students what they thought would happen in the experiment, a few thought that some people would continue all the way to 450 volts, but that most would stop early or in the middle of the shock range. Psychiatrists asked to predict the teachers' behaviour suggested that less than one per cent would administer the highest voltage, and that most would stop around 120 volts (Milgram, 1974).

The teacher had been instructed to treat a non-response from Mr Wallace (which, as Box 59.1 shows, occurred at 330 volts) as an incorrect response, so that shocks could continue to be given. Milgram's participants showed reluctance to administer the shocks and, whenever this happened, the experimenter gave a series of scripted 'verbal prods'. These were 'please continue' (or 'please go on'), 'the experiment requires that you continue', 'it is absolutely essential that you continue' and, finally, 'you have no other choice, you *must* go on'. The experimenter was also scripted to say 'although the shocks may be painful, there is no permanent tissue damage' in order to reassure the teacher that no permanent harm was being done to the learner. The experiment was terminated either when the participant refused to continue or when the maximum 450-volt shock had been administered four times.

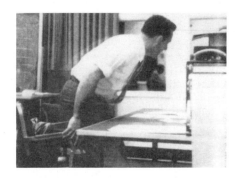

Figure 59.3   A participant refuses to continue any further with the experiment (From Milgram, 1974)

MILGRAM'S RESULTS

The participants displayed great anguish, verbally attacked the experimenter, twitched nervously, or broke out into nervous laughter. Many were observed to:

> 'sweat, stutter, tremble, groan, bite their lips and dig their nails into their flesh. Full-blown, uncontrollable seizures were observed for three [participants]' (Milgram, 1974).

Indeed, one experiment had to be stopped because the participant had a violent seizure. It is quite astonishing, then, that in the remote victim variation every teacher administered at least 300 volts and 65 per cent administered 450 volts. In the voice feedback variation, 62.5 per cent continued all the way up to 450 volts.

To determine why the obedience level was so high in these two studies, Milgram conducted a number of variations using the voice feedback condition as his baseline measure of obedience. In all, a further 16 variations were conducted.

Box 59.2 Some variations on Milgram's basic procedure

Institutional context (variation 10): In post-experimental interviews, many participants said they continued administering shocks because the experiment was being conducted at Yale University, a highly prestigious institution. However, when Milgram transferred the experiment to a rundown office in downtown Bridgeport, the 450 volt obedience rate was 47.5 per cent. This suggests that whilst the institutional context played a role, it was not a crucial factor.

Proximity and touch proximity (variations 3 and 4): In the original variation, the teacher and learner were in adjacent rooms and could not see one another. However, when they were in the same room (about 1.5 feet/46 cm apart), the 450 volt obedience rate dropped to 40 per cent (variation 3). When the teacher was required to force the learner's hand down onto a shock plate (variation 4), the 450 volt obedience rate dropped to 30 per cent. Whilst seeing the effects of the shock on the participant reduces obedience, the figures observed are still very high.

Remote authority (variation 7): When the experimenter left the room (having given the essential instructions), and gave subsequent instructions by telephone, 450 volt obedience dropped to 20.5 per cent. Indeed, participants often pretended to administer a shock or administered a shock lower than they were supposed to. This suggests they were trying to compromise between their conscience and the experimenter's instructions. In his absence, it was easier to follow their conscience.

Two peers rebel (variation 17): In this variation, the teacher was paired with two other (actor) teachers. The teachers read out the list of word-pairs and informed the learner if the response was correct. The real participant administered the shocks. At 150 volts, the first teacher refused to continue and moved to another part of the room. At 210 volts, the second teacher did likewise. The experimenter ordered the real teacher to continue. Only ten per cent of participants continued to 450 volts. Most stopped obeying when the first or second teacher refused to continue. According to Milgram (1965):

> 'the effects of peer rebellion are most impressive in undercutting the experimenter's authority'.

A peer administers the shocks (variation 18): When the teacher was paired with another teacher (an actor) and had only to read out the word-pairs rather than administer the shock, obedience rose to 92.5 per cent. This shows that it is easier for participants to shift responsibility from themselves to the other teacher.

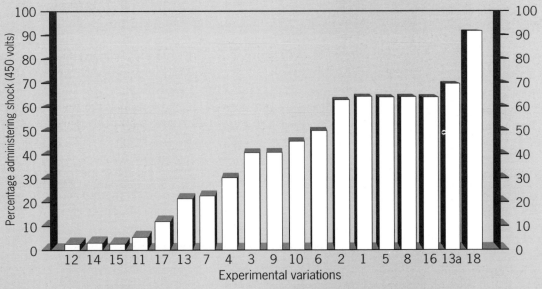

1	Remote victim		personnel	11 Subjects free to	14 Authority as victim	16 Two authorities –
2	Voice feedback	7	Remote authority	choose shock level	– an ordinary man	one as victim
3	Proximity	8	Women as subjects	12 Learner demands to	commanding	17 Two peers rebel
4	Touch proximity	9	The victim's limited	be shocked	15 Two authorities –	18 A peer administers
5	New baseline		contract	13 An ordinary man	contradictory	shock
6	Change of	10	Institutional context	gives orders	commands	

Figure 59.4   The percentage of participants administering 450-volt shocks across the 18 variations of Milgram's original experiment. Note that one experiment has two variations (13 and 13a) (From Zimbardo & Weber, 1994)

EXPLAINING MILGRAM'S RESULTS

According to Milgram (1974):

'the most fundamental lesson of our study is that ordinary people, simply doing their jobs, and without any particular hostility on their part, can become agents in a terrible destructive process'.

A number of explanations as to why people obey have been proposed.

The set-up's credibility

Participants might not have believed the experimental set-up they found themselves in, and knew the learner was not really being given electric shocks. Sheridan & King's (1972) study appears to exclude this possibility. They had students train a puppy to learn a discrimination task by punishing it with increasingly severe and *real* electric shocks each time it made an error. Although the puppy received only a small shock, it could be seen and its squeals heard by the participants.

After a time, an odourless anaesthetic was released into the puppy's cage causing it to fall asleep. Although participants complained about the procedure (and some even cried), they were reminded that failure to respond was a punishable error and that shocks should continue to be given. Seventy-five per cent of participants delivered the maximum shock possible. Clearly, then, it is unlikely that Milgram's procedure leads participants to believe that the learner is not really being harmed, and so the experiment has *experimental realism* (Orne & Holland, 1968).

Demand characteristics

Another possibility is that cues in the experimental setting influenced the participants' perceptions of what was required of them. Obedience might, then, simply have been a response to the demands of the unusual experimental setting (Zimbardo & Weber, 1994: see Chapter 83). Naturalistic studies of obedience, however, dispute this and indicate that Milgram's research also has *mundane realism* (Orne & Holland, 1968), in that its results extend beyond the laboratory setting. For example, Hofling *et al.* (1966) showed that when nurses were instructed by telephone to administer twice the maximum dosage of a drug (actually a harmless tablet) to a patient, 21 out of 22 did so. Even when there are good reasons to defy authority, then, it is hard to resist it (Zimbardo & Weber, 1994).

Personal responsibility

Many participants raised the issue of responsibility should harm befall the learner. Although the experimenter did not always discuss this, when he did say 'I'm responsible for what goes on here', participants showed visible relief.

Indeed, when participants are told that *they* are responsible for what happens, obedience is sharply reduced (Hamilton, 1978). Milgram saw this *diffusion of responsibility* (see also Chapter 62, pages 534–535) as being crucial to understanding the Nazi atrocities of people like Eichmann, and his defence that he was 'just carrying out orders'. It can also explain the behaviour of William Calley, an American soldier who was court-martialed for the 1968 massacre by troops under his command of several hundred Vietnam civilians at My Lai (Opton, 1973).

The perception of legitimate authority

As mentioned earlier (see page 510), many participants showed signs of distress and conflict in Milgram's experiments, and so the diffusion of responsibility explanation cannot tell the whole story. Perhaps, then, the experimenter was seen as a legitimate authority by participants, at least up until the point when he said 'you have no other choice, you *must* go on'. The most common mental adjustment in the obedient participant is to see him/herself as an agent of external authority (the *agentic state*). This state (the opposite of an *autonomous state*) is what allows us to function in an organised and hierarchical social system. For a group to function as a whole, individuals must give up responsibility and defer to others of higher status in the social hierarchy. Legitimate authority thus replaces a person's own self-regulation (Turner, 1991).

Authority figures often possess highly visible symbols of their power or status that make it difficult to refuse their commands. In Milgram's experiments, the experimenter always wore a grey laboratory coat to indicate his position as an authority figure. The impact of such 'visible symbols' has been demonstrated by Bickman (1974), who showed that when people are told by a person in a guard's uniform to pick up a paper bag or give a coin to a stranger, obedience is higher (80 per cent) than when the instruction is given by somebody in civilian clothes (40 per cent). For Milgram:

'a substantial proportion of people do what they are told to do, irrespective of the content of the act and without limitations of conscience, so long as they perceive that the command comes from a legitimate authority'.

Box 59.3   The prison simulation experiment

Zimbardo *et al.* (1973) recruited participants through newspaper advertisements asking for student volunteers for a two-week study of prison life. After potential participants had been given clinical interviews, 25 of over 100 who volunteered were selected. They were all judged to be emotionally stable, physically healthy, 'normal to average' on the basis of personality tests, and also law abiding.

Participants were told that they would be randomly assigned to the role of either 'prisoner' or 'guard' (although all had stated a preference for being a prisoner). At the beginning of the study, then, there were no differences between those selected to be prisoners and guards. They were a relatively homogeneous group of white, middle class college students from all over America and Canada.

Zimbardo *et al.* converted the basement of the Stanford University psychology department into a 'mock prison'. It was made as much like a real prison as possible in an attempt to simulate functionally some of the significant features of the psychological state of imprisonment. The experiment began one Sunday morning, when those allocated to the 'prisoner' role were unexpectedly arrested by the local police. They were charged with a felony, read their rights, searched, handcuffed, and taken to the police station to be 'booked'. After being fingerprinted, and having forms prepared for their central information file, each prisoner was taken blindfold to the 'prison'.

Upon arrival, the prisoners were stripped naked, skin-searched, deloused, and issued a uniform and bedding. They wore a loose-fitting smock with an identification number on the front and back, plus a chain bolted around one ankle. They also wore nylon stockings to cover their hair (in a real prison, their hair would have been shaved off). The prisoners were referred to by their numbers and housed in 639-foot (191.7-metre) cells, three to a cell. The guards wore military-style khaki uniforms, silver reflector sunglasses (making eye contact with them impossible) and carried clubs, whistles, handcuffs and keys to the cells and main gate. The guards were on duty 24 hours a day, in eight-hour shifts, and had complete control over the prisoners. The prisoners were imprisoned around the clock, and allowed out of their cells only for meals, exercise, toilet privileges, head counts and work.

After an initial 'rebellion' had been crushed, the prisoners began to react passively as the guards stepped up their aggression each day (by, for example, having a roll call in the middle of the night simply to disrupt the prisoners' sleep). This made the prisoners feel helpless, and no longer in control of their lives.

The guards began to enjoy their power. As one said, 'Acting authoritatively can be great fun. Power can be a great pleasure'. After less than 36 hours, one prisoner had to be released because of uncontrolled crying, fits of rage,

disorganised thinking and severe depression. Three others developed the same symptoms and had to be released on successive days. Another prisoner developed a rash over his whole body, which was triggered when his attempt to get 'parole' was rejected. Prisoners became demoralised and apathetic, and even began to refer to themselves and others by their prison numbers.

The whole experiment, planned to run for two weeks, was stopped after *six days* because of the pathological reactions of the prisoners who had originally been selected for their emotional stability. An outside observer, who had a long history of being incarcerated, reported that the mock prison and both the guards' and prisoners' behaviours were strikingly similar to real life. One conclusion which can be drawn from this study is that the distinction between *role-playing* and *role enactment* is a very fine one.

The 'foot in the door' and not knowing how to disobey

According to Gilbert (1981), participants in Milgram's experiments may have been 'sucked in' by the series of graduated demands, which began with seemingly innocuous orders that gradually escalated. It is possible that having begun the experiment, participants found it difficult to extricate themselves from it. They may even not have known *how* to disobey, since nothing they said had any effect on the experimenter (at least until they refused the final verbal 'prod' in which they were told they had no choice but to continue).

Socialisation

Despite our expressed ideal of independence, obedience is something we are socialised into from a very early age by significant others (including our parents and teachers). Obedience may be an *ingrained habit* (Brown, 1986) that is difficult to resist.

AN EVALUATION OF MILGRAM'S RESEARCH

Not surprisingly, Milgram's results caused much interest when they were published. Critics have largely focused on three main areas, namely *methodological issues*, *issues of generalisation*, and *ethical issues*.

Methodological issues

One criticism made of Milgram's research was that his sample was *unrepresentative*. However, Milgram studied a total of 636 participants in his experiments, representing a cross-section of New Haven's population, thought to be a fairly typical small American town. However, Milgram did concede that those participants who continued administering shocks up to 450 volts were more likely to see the learner as being responsible for what happened to him rather than themselves. These participants seemed to have a stronger authoritarian character (see Chapter 53, page 462) and a less advanced level of moral development, although this was a matter of degree only. Indeed, people who volunteer for experiments (as, of course, Milgram's participants did) tend to be considerably *less* authoritarian than those who do not (Rosenthal & Rosnow, 1966).

Milgram was also criticised for using mainly male participants. However, of the 40 females who did serve as participants (in variation 8), 65 per cent continued administering shocks up to 450 volts, a figure comparable to the obedience shown by their male counterparts. A further methodological criticism concerns the cross-cultural replicability of Milgram's findings. Studies conducted in many countries have produced various obedience rates ranging from 16 per cent (Kilham & Mann, 1974, using female Australian students) to 92 per cent (Meeus & Raaijmakers, 1986, using members of the general Dutch population).

Issues of generalisation

Several researchers have argued that whilst Milgram's experiments had high *internal validity*, his results would not prevail in other circumstances. The charge here is that Milgram's findings lack *external* or *ecological validity* (or *mundane realism*: see page 512). According to Milgram, though, the essential process in complying with the demands of an authority figure is the same whether the setting is the artificial one of the psychological laboratory or a naturally occurring one outside it, a point accepted by many researchers (e.g. Colman, 1987).

There are, of course, differences between laboratory studies of obedience and the obedience observed in Nazi Germany. However, as Milgram (1974) has remarked in this context:

'yet differences in scale, numbers and political context may turn out to be relatively unimportant as long as certain essential features are retained. The essence of obedience consists in the fact that a person comes to view himself as the instrument for carrying out another person's wishes, and he, therefore, no longer regards himself as responsible for his actions. Once this critical shift of viewpoint has occurred in the person, all the essential features of obedience follow'.

Hofling *et al.*'s (1966) study, which showed that 95 per cent of nurses studied complied with an instruction that involved them infringing both hospital regulations and medical ethics (see page 512), indicates that obedience is not a phenomenon that is confined to the setting of Milgram's laboratory.

Unfortunately, the available data are not particularly helpful in allowing us to comment on cross-cultural similarities or differences in obedience. One reason is that the replications undertaken have only been *partial*, and have not completely duplicated Milgram's procedures. For example, in Kilham & Mann's (1974) study, the female participants were required to administer the electric shocks to another *female*. In Milgram's experiments, however, the learner was always a *male* (Smith & Bond, 1993). Humphreys (1994) identifies other differences in cross-cultural studies of obedience. These include the use of a maximum shock value of 330 volts rather than 450 volts (Ancona & Pareyson, 1968), and the use of a long-haired student as the learner rather than a 'Mr Wallace'-type character (Kilham & Mann, 1974).

Ethical issues

One of Milgram's strongest critics was Baumrind (1964), who argued that the rights and feelings of Milgram's participants had been abused and that inadequate measures were taken to protect participants from stress and emotional conflict. Whilst accepting that participants did experience stress and conflict in his experiment, Milgram countered that Baumrind's criticism presupposes that the experiment's outcome was *expected*, which, of course, it was not (at least not by those students and psychiatrists asked to anticipate what might happen: see page 510).

Inducing stress was not an intended and deliberate effect of the experimental procedure. As Milgram (1974) noted:

'understanding grows because we examine situations in which the end is unknown. An investigator unwilling to accept this degree of risk must give up the idea of scientific enquiry'.

An experimenter cannot, then, know what the results are going to be before the experiment begins.

Box 59.4   Deception

A further ethical issue concerns *deception*. According to Vitelli (1988), more than one third of social psychological studies (and virtually all of those that investigate conformity and obedience) deceive participants over the research's purpose, the accuracy of the information they are given, and/or the true identity of a person they believe to be another genuine participant (or experimenter).

In his defence, Milgram pointed out that, after learning about the deception when they were extensively

---

debriefed, 84 per cent of participants said they were glad or very glad to have participated, whereas fewer than two per cent said they were sorry or very sorry to have participated. Moreover, 80 per cent said they felt *more* experiments of this kind should be conducted, and 74 per cent felt that they had learned something of personal importance after being a participant.

Other researchers have defended Milgram's use of deception on the grounds that if he had not used it, he would have found results which simply do not reflect how people behave when they are led to believe they are in real situations (Aronson, 1988). In some circumstances, then, deception may be the best (and perhaps the only) way to get useful information about how people behave in complex and important situations (see Chapter 85).

WHAT DO MILGRAM'S STUDIES TELL US ABOUT OURSELVES?

Perhaps one of the reasons Milgram's research was criticised is that it paints an unacceptable picture of humans. Thus, it is far easier for us to accept that a war criminal like Adolf Eichmann was an inhuman impostor than that 'ordinary people' can be destructively obedient. Yet atrocities, such as those committed in Rwanda and the former Yugoslavia, continue to occur. Perhaps, like the 51 per cent of those people questioned following the trial and conviction of William Calley (see page 512) who said they would behave in the same way if commanded, 'we do as we are told'. Such actions may be seen as:

'normal, even desirable because [people like Calley] performed them in obedience to legitimate authority' (Kelman & Lawrence, 1972).

Box 59.5   Genocide

Hirsch (1995) has noted that many of the greatest crimes against humanity are committed in the name of obedience. *Genocide*, a term coined in 1944, tends to occur under conditions created by three social processes. The first of these, *authorisation*, relates to the 'agentic state' (see page 512), that is, obeying orders because of where they come from. The second, *routinisation*, refers to massacre becoming a matter of routine, or a mechanical and highly programmed operation. The third is *dehumanisation*, in which the victims are reduced to something less than human which allows us to suspend our usual moral prohibition on killing (see Humphreys, 1994).

The ingredients of genocide were personified by Eichmann who, at his trial after the Second World War, denied ever killing anybody, but took great pride in the way he transported millions to their death 'with great zeal and meticulous care' (Arendt, 1965). The comments of an East German judge in 1992, when sentencing a former East German border guard for having shot a man trying (three years earlier) to escape to the West, echo the spirit of the Nuremberg Accords which followed the Nazi war crimes trials:

'Not everything that is legal is right ... At the end of the twentieth century, no one has the right to turn off his conscience when it comes to killing people on the orders of authorities' (cited in Berkowitz, 1993).

As noted, it is difficult to disobey authority. However, we are most likely to rebel when we feel that social pressure is so strong that our *freedom* is in danger of being lost. In one demonstration of this, Gamson *et al.* (1982) invited the citizens of a midwestern town to a hotel conference centre in order to discuss community standards. The researchers explained that a local petrol station manager had publicly opposed high petrol prices and that the petrol company was taking legal action against him.

The participants were led to believe that an oil company was videotaping the group discussion, and were asked to speak out against the petrol station manager and to allow their taped discussions to be used in court. The researchers then left the participants. The participants reacted strongly to this threat to their freedom (even citing Milgram's research to justify their behaviour!). They strongly defended the station manager and refused to give in to the oil company's demands. Some participants even made plans to report the company whilst others decided to tell their story to the newspapers.

Milgram himself felt that by *educating* people about the dangers of blind obedience, encouraging them to *question authority*, and exposing them to the actions of *disobedient models*, obedience would be reduced. Other researchers have emphasised the importance of *reactance*. According to Brehm (1966), we need to believe that we have freedom of choice. When we believe that this is not the case and when we believe we are *entitled* to freedom, we experience *reactance*, an unpleasant emotional state (see Chapter 17, page 136). To reduce this state, and restore the sense of freedom, disobedience occurs.

Conclusions

As is apparent in this chapter, there are circumstances in which we can become what Milgram calls 'agents in a terrible destructive process'. However, we are not *always* blindly obedient. Social psychology's task is to continue uncovering those situations in which such destructive obedience occurs and to look at how it can be prevented.

Summary

■ Conformity and obedience are similar in some important respects but different in others. In obedience, we are ordered or instructed to do something by somebody higher in authority. Typically, we **deny responsibility** for our behaviours when we are obedient.

■ Important research into obedience was conducted by Milgram, who originally intended to test the 'Germans are different' hypothesis. In Milgram's basic procedure, participants are led to believe that they will be delivering increasingly severe electric shocks to another person in a learning experiment. In fact, no shocks are actually given, and neither the learner nor the experimenter in charge is genuine.

■ In Milgram's **remote victim variation**, 65 per cent of participants administered the maximum 450-volt shock. In the **voice feedback condition**, the figure was 62.5 per cent. These results were unexpected. When Milgram asked psychiatrists and students to predict participants' behaviour, few believed anyone would administer the maximum shock.

■ Participants were given pre-determined 'verbal prods' by the experimenter when they showed a reluctance to continue. Despite being reassured that no permanent harm was being done to the learner, participants showed great anguish and experienced considerable stress. One experiment had to be stopped due to a participant's violent seizure.

■ Milgram conducted 16 further variations of the two original studies to determine the factors influencing obedience. **Proximity, touch proximity, remote authority, peer rebellion** and changing the **institutional context** all reduced obedience to various degrees. Having a **peer administer shocks**, however, increased obedience.

■ It is unlikely that Milgram's procedure led participants to believe that the learner was not really being harmed, and so the experiment has **experimental realism**. It is unlikely that **demand characteristics** account for the findings, since obedience has been observed in naturalistic settings. So, Milgram's research has **mundane realism**.

■ When participants are told **they** are responsible for what happens to the learner, obedience is sharply reduced. Milgram saw **diffusion of responsibility** as crucial to understanding destructive obedience. The perception of the experimenter as a **legitimate authority**, which induces an **agentic state**, also contributes to obedient behaviour.

■ People's tendency to obey those perceived as legitimate authorities was dramatically shown in Zimbardo *et al.*'s 'prison simulation' experiment. Since obedience is an **ingrained habit** acquired through early **socialisation**, Milgram's participants might not have known how to disobey.

■ Milgram's research has been criticised on **methodological grounds**, although none of the criticisms destroys its credibility. Whilst it has high **internal validity**, critics contend that the research lacks **external/ecological validity**. Although there are obvious differences between obedience observed in laboratory experiments and natural settings, Milgram believes that the **essential features** are the same for both.

■ The most serious objections to Milgram's research have been **ethical**. Charges of failing to protect participants from harm can be dismissed, because distress could not have been anticipated.

■ Milgram defended his use of **deception** by pointing out that participants were extensively debriefed. Eighty-four per cent said they were glad/very glad to have participated, and only two per cent said they were sorry/very sorry. Deception may be unavoidable if we are to obtain information about how people behave in complex and important situations.

■ Milgram's studies indicate that ordinary people can be destructively obedient. Many of the greatest crimes have been committed in the name of obedience. **Genocide** tends to occur under conditions created by **authorisation, routinisation** and **dehumanisation**.

■ Whilst it is difficult to disobey authority, we are most likely to rebel when we feel our **freedom** is being threatened. Disobedience can occur when we try to reduce **reactance** and restore the sense of freedom.

■ Milgram believed that obedience can be reduced by **educating** people about the dangers of blind obedience, encouraging them to **question authority**, and exposing them to **disobedient models**.

60

SOCIAL POWER: LEADERS AND LEADERSHIP

Introduction and overview

Hollander (1985) defines a *leader* as the person who exercises the most influence in a group, and *leadership* as the exercise of influence or power over others. The earliest research in this area attempted to identify the individual qualities that result in some people rising to positions of power and authority. Thus, the concern was with whether leaders are born or made and what it is about leaders, compared with followers, that makes them leaders. This focus on 'the leader' is often referred to as the *trait approach*.

Later research concentrated on identifying the conditions which influence the effectiveness of those who are appointed to a formal leadership role, and was typically carried out in large organisations (such as businesses). This is often referred to as the *situational approach*, since it acknowledges that leadership is a complex social process in which the leader depends on the group and *vice versa*. This chapter reviews theory and research relating to the emergence of leaders, and the factors affecting their leadership once they have assumed a position of power and authority.

Leaders: traits, situations and transactions

TRAITS AND LEADER EMERGENCE

For many years, theorising on the emergence of leaders was dominated by the 'great person' or *trait theory*. According to this, leaders are extraordinary people who naturally rise to positions of power and authority because they possess certain personality traits which suit them for 'life at the top'. For Huczynski & Buchanan (1991):

'the fate of societies ... is in the hands of key, powerful, idiosyncratic individuals who by the force of their personalities reach positions of influence from which they can direct and dominate the lives of others. Such men are simply born great and emerge to take power in any situation regardless of the social or historical context'.

In a review of the research, Stogdill (1974) looked at leadership in various contexts, including the military, nursery schools, and political parties. Stogdill concluded that leaders tend to be slightly more intelligent, sociable, achievement oriented, experienced, older and taller than their followers. Other studies have shown that people who emerge as leaders tend to score higher on measures of self-confidence and dominance (Costantini & Craik, 1980) and combine orientations towards success and affiliating with other people (Sorrentino & Field, 1986).

Evidence of particular traits in leaders has, however, been mixed and, in general, leaders have *not* been shown to be consistently different from non-leaders in terms of their personality traits (Turner, 1991). Whilst claims continue to be made about the characteristics that separate leaders from non-leaders (e.g. Kirkpatrick & Locke, 1991), it is generally agreed that the trait approach to leadership is limited, and that the kinds of traits a leader needs will vary from group to group and problem to problem.

SITUATIONS AND LEADER EMERGENCE

The view that different kinds of traits are needed in different situations was examined by Bales (1950), who stressed the *functional demands* of the situation. According to this perspective, the person most likely to emerge as a leader is the one who is best equipped to help the group fulfil its objectives in a particular context. Thus, the leader will be the one whose *skills* and *competence* are most useful to the group in a given situation. At another time, and in another situation, someone else may be more suited for the leader's role. A good example of this comes from Sherif *et al.*'s (1961) Robber's Cave field experiment (see Chapter 53, page 464) in which, when competition between two groups of boys was increased, one of the groups replaced its leader with a physically much stronger boy.

Whilst there is evidence consistent with the view that the situation determines who will emerge as a leader, this approach assumes that under the appropriate conditions *anyone* can become a leader. However, the evidence does not support this, and whilst personality factors may not be as crucial as the trait approach proposes, it seems that some people adopt the role of a leader more readily than others (Nydegger, 1975). Also, people seem to be fairly well aware of their relative abilities to assume positions of power and authority.

TRANSACTIONS AND LEADER EMERGENCE

In recent years, *transactional theory* (Shaw, 1981) has been applied to both the trait and situational approaches to leader emergence. According to this, both the characteristics of people *and* the demands of the situation determine who will become a leader. This approach to leaders is looked at more closely in the section on *leader effectiveness*.

Leadership style and behaviour

AUTOCRATIC, DEMOCRATIC AND LAISSEZ-FAIRE STYLES

An early study of leadership style was conducted by Lewin *et al.* (1939). They wanted to investigate the effects of three different kinds of adult behaviour on a group of ten-year-old boys attending after-school clubs. The clubs, which were concerned with model making, were led by adults who acted *autocratically*, *democratically* or in a *laissez-faire* manner.

> **Box 60.1   The behaviour of the adults in Lewin *et al.*'s study**
>
> **Autocratic leaders** told the boys what sort of models they would make and with whom they would work. They sometimes praised or blamed the boys for their work but did not explain their comments and, although friendly, were also aloof and impersonal.
>
> **Democratic leaders** discussed various possible projects with the boys, and allowed them to choose whom they would work with and to make their own decisions. The leaders explained their comments and joined in with the group activities.
>
> **Laissez-faire leaders** left the boys very much to their own devices, and only offered help when asked for it (which was not very often) and gave neither praise nor blame.

The boys with an *autocratic leader* became aggressive towards each other when things went wrong and were submissive in their approaches to the leader (and these approaches were often attention seeking). If the leader left the room, the boys stopped working and became either disruptive or apathetic. However, the models they made were comparable, in terms of both quantity and quality, to those produced by the boys with the democratic leader.

Whilst the boys with the *democratic leader* actually produced slightly less work than those with the autocratic leader, they got on much better and seemed to like each other much more than did the boys with the autocratic leader. Any approaches made to the leader tended to be task related, and when the leader left the room, the boys carried on working and showed greater independence. They also co-operated when things went wrong.

Like the boys with the autocratic leader, those with the *laissez-faire leader* were aggressive towards each other (although slightly less than the former). The boys also got very little work done, whether the leader was present or not, and were easily discouraged from finding solutions when things did not go exactly right for them.

The leader was changed every seven weeks and adopted one of the other kinds of leadership style. Thus, each group of boys was exposed to the same leadership style which was enacted by three different leaders. This was meant to ensure that the boys' behaviour could be attributed to leadership style rather than the leader's personality traits. Interestingly, when two of the most aggressive boys from the autocratic group were switched to the democratic group, they quickly became cooperative and involved in the tasks.

Lewin *et al.*'s findings suggest that it is leadership style (which is not necessarily a fixed characteristic) that is important, rather than the leader's personality (which is). However, people, their groups and leaders, can only really be understood in the context of the wider society of which they form a part (Brown, 1985). The democratic style is, implicitly, the most favourable and acceptable one of the three studied by Lewin *et al.*, because that style was the prevalent one in American society during the 1930s.

The results of many experimental and survey studies looking at the effects of these leadership styles in industrial settings were reviewed by Sayles (1966). No one style was consistently superior to any other in experimental studies of supervisors, but survey studies showed the democratic style to be associated with greater productivity and more acceptable than an autocratic style. However, Sayles argued that the tasks used in the experimental studies were so boring and limited that people did not really get involved in them. As a result, differences in leadership style were not really given the opportunity to show up. Sayles also pointed out that democratic supervisors probably differ from autocratic supervisors in ways other than leadership style (such as level of intelligence).

INITIATING STRUCTURE AND SHOWING CONSIDERATION

One of the largest-ever leadership studies was conducted by Halpin & Winer (1952). They asked people in many different kinds of groups what they felt were the most important behaviours a leader should exhibit. Two major categories emerged. The first was called *initiating structure*, which means that a leader should define the goals of the group, plan how those goals should be achieved, indicate how each member of the group will be involved, and generally direct the action of the whole group. The second was called *showing consideration*. This involves communicating with individual members of the group, explaining why certain actions have been taken, and demonstrating positive regard for group members.

Initiating structure involves giving orders, telling people what to do, getting the task underway and, perhaps, ruffling a few feathers. Showing consideration involves listening and explaining to group members, making people feel better and, perhaps, smoothing feathers. These two behaviours can be difficult, though not impossible, for one person to show. This incompatibility, coupled with the finding that leaders have somewhat different traits in different situations, led researchers to try to identify leaders according to whether they primarily initiate structure or show consideration.

TASK SPECIALISTS AND SOCIOEMOTIONAL SPECIALISTS

Research into the leadership patterns that emerge in small, unstructured groups was undertaken by Bales & Slater (1955). They studied a group of college students who spent about five hours per day discussing and trying to come up with solutions for a number of labour-management conflicts. At the end of each day, the students were required to indicate which person in the group had come up with the best ideas, which had most effectively guided the group discussion, and how much they liked each group member.

Box 60.2 The results of Bales and Slater's study

Bales and Slater found that at the end of the first day, the person who was most liked was also the person rated as having the best ideas and making the greatest contribution to moving group discussion towards a successful task solution. However, after the first day, the tendency for the best-liked person also to be the one rated as having the best ideas diminished rapidly. What apparently happened on the following days was that two leaders emerged. One of these, the *task specialist*, made suggestions, provided information and expressed opinions. The other, the *socioemotional specialist*, helped other group members express themselves, cracked jokes, released tension, and expressed positive feelings for others.

Bales and Slater's task specialist style corresponds to the 'initiating structure' behaviour identified by Halpin and Winer. The socioemotional style corresponds to the 'showing consideration' behaviour. Bales and Slater believed that these styles were *inversely related* and that no one person could display both of them simultaneously. However, the results from the Ohio State Leadership studies (e.g. Stogdill, 1974) suggested that the two styles are *independent dimensions* and that the most effective leaders are those who score above average on both. Later studies have tended to confirm this. For example, Sorrentino & Field (1986) carried out detailed observations of 12 problem-solving groups over a five-week period. Those members who scored high on both of Bales and Slater's styles were subsequently elected leaders by the group members.

Another interesting finding concerns the relationship enjoyed by the two types of leader. Whilst there is rivalry between them, they get along well and co-operate extensively (Crider *et al.*, 1989). However, and as Crider *et al.* note, the general tendency to split leadership in unstructured groups has one qualification. According to Bales and Slater, the split happens only *after* the task specialist is identified and agreed upon. Once it has been decided who will lead the group in pursuit of its goal, the group can afford the luxury of a socioemotional leader.

Fiedler's contingency model of leader effectiveness

In his review of research concerning leadership effectiveness, Shaw (1981) claimed that both autocratic (or task specialist) leaders and democratic (or socioemotional specialist) leaders can be effective. In terms of group dynamics, followers are clearly happier in groups with socioemotional leaders. In terms of productivity, however, task specialist leaders are, on average, more successful.

However, Shaw made some important qualifications to this. For example, the productivity of groups with socioemotional leaders is highly variable, and both the most and the least productive groups can have socioemotional leaders. Because evidence suggests that both task specialist and socioemotional leaders are more effective, researchers have looked at the possibility that each style may be more advantageous in different situations.

The *contingency model of leader effectiveness*, first proposed by Fiedler (1964, 1981; Fiedler & Chemers, 1984), is mainly concerned with the fit or match between a leader's personal qualities (or leadership style) and the requirements of the situation in which the group must operate. Fiedler began by measuring the extent to which leaders distinguished between their most and least preferred co-workers (LPC). Fiedler then developed a scale to produce a LPC score.

Box 60.3 Fiedler's LPC scale

A leader is asked to think of all those people (or subordinates) who have ever worked under him or her, and to select the one that was the most difficult to work with. This person is then rated on 18 bipolar scales including 'pleasant' – 'unpleasant', 'trustworthy' – 'untrustworthy', and 'friendly' – 'unfriendly'. The sum of the values on the 18 scales gives a LPC score.

The LPC scale is arranged so that leaders with a high LPC score still see their least preferred co-workers in a relatively favourable light. Leaders with a low LPC score have a very negative attitude towards their least preferred co-workers. Those with high LPC scores tend to be more accepting, permissive, considerate and person oriented in their relationships with group members (*relationship-oriented leaders*). Those with low LPC scores tend to be directive, controlling and dominant in relationships with group members (*task-oriented leaders*).

Fiedler then investigated the fit between the two leadership styles identified in Box 60.3 and the situation in which the group must operate. His basic hypothesis was that a leader's effectiveness is *contingent* upon the fit between the leader's style and the degree of 'favourableness' of the situation (the extent to which the situation allows the leader to exert influence). The degree of favourableness of the situation is determined by three situational variables, each of which can have a high or low value. These are *quality of leader–member relationships*, *task structure*, and *position-power*. Fiedler sees the first of these as being most important, and the third as least.

Box 60.4 The three situational variables that influence a situation's degree of favourableness

Quality of leader–member relationships: This is the extent to which the leader has the loyalty and confidence of group members and the group's general psychological atmosphere.

Task structure: This is the clarity and complexity of the task and the number of possible solutions. The more unstructured the task is, the more the leader must motivate and inspire members to find solutions.

Position-power: This is the power inherent in the leader's role, such as the rewards and punishments at his or her disposal, and the organisational support from superiors.

How combinations of these factors (according to whether they are high or low) covary to produce conditions which are favourable or unfavourable to the leader is shown in Figure 60.1. Fiedler hypothesised that task-oriented leaders will be most effective in situations which are either highly favourable (the values of the three situational variables are high) or highly unfavourable (the values are low). Relationship-oriented leaders will be more effective when the degree of favourableness is neither very high nor very low.

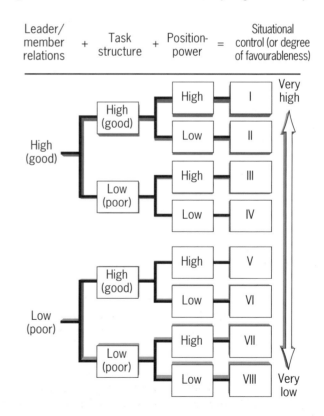

Figure 60.1 The covariation of factors producing varying degrees of favourability for a leader (From Gross, 1996)

The rationale for these hypotheses is that when the situation is very favourable, task-oriented leaders do not have to waste any time worrying about the group members' morale, and an emphasis on interpersonal relations is not only unnecessary but may even irritate the group. In highly unfavourable situations, a task-oriented style is necessary since, without an emphasis on production, the group may fall apart. When conditions are moderately favourable or unfavourable, a relationship-oriented style may be able to smooth over differences of opinion in the group and improve co-operation enough to compensate for an ill-defined task and a lack of authority (Brown, 1988).

AN EVALUATION OF FIEDLER'S MODEL

According to Fiedler (1967):

> 'except perhaps for the unusual case, it is simply not meaningful to speak of an effective or an ineffective leader; we can only speak of a leader who tends to be effective in one situation and ineffective in another'.

Fiedler has studied leadership in a wide range of groups including store managers, research chemists, basketball players, furnace workers, and bomber crews, and reported data consistent with his model's predictions. Other researchers, too, agree that there is considerable empirical support for the model (e.g. Greenberg & Baron, 1995), although this is stronger from laboratory than field studies.

Perhaps one reason the data have not always offered strong support for the model concerns some of the assumptions it makes. For example, Fiedler claims that leadership style is a relatively fixed characteristic of the leader (part of the leader's personality). As a result, leaders would be expected to find it difficult to modify their leadership styles. However, the test–retest reliability of LPC scores has been found to be low (Rice, 1978), suggesting that leadership style can change.

Another criticism concerns Fiedler's assumption that the most important of the three situational variables is the quality of the leader–follower relationship, and the least important the leader's legitimate power (see Box 60.6). It is not clear on what basis this assumption has been made, and the relative importance of the three situational variables could be a function of contextual factors (Hogg & Vaughan, 1995).

Hogg and Vaughan also argue that the contingency model ignores the group processes responsible for the rise and fall of leaders and the situational complexity of leadership. Despite these criticisms, though, there is little doubt that Fiedler's model has been useful in helping us begin to understand leadership effectiveness. As additional leadership qualities (such as intelligence and prior experience) are incorporated into the model, so a more complete picture will emerge (Smith, 1995).

Leadership as a process

Leadership involves leaders *and* followers in various role relationships, and there are several paths to becoming *validated* as a leader. The issue of validation concerns how a leader comes to occupy the role (how he or she achieves *legitimacy* as a leader). In a formal group structure, the leader is assigned by an external authority and is imposed on the group. Such a person is an *appointed leader*. In an informal group, however, the leader achieves authority from the group members (who may withdraw their support just as they gave it). A person who achieves authority in this way is called an *emergent leader*. Note, though, that even in formal groups there are emergent (or 'informal') leaders who exert influence among their peers by virtue of their personal qualities, especially how verbal they are.

Even with appointed leaders, leadership is a complex social process involving an exchange (or *transaction*) between group members. The leader is dependent on the group members for liking and approval, and their attitudes towards the leader will influence the leadership process. It is easy to overlook the fact that leaders are actually members of the groups they lead. At one and the same time, they represent and embody the group's norms and also act as agents of change, steering the group in new directions. A leader, then, is both a *conformist* (because he or she embodies the group's norms) and a *deviant* (because he or she can change prevailing norms).

However, the right to bring about change must be 'earned' by building up what Hollander (1958) calls *idiosyncrasy credit*. This can be earned by initially conforming closely to established norms, showing the necessary competence to fulfil the group's objectives, identifying with the group's ideals and aspirations, and so on. In one study supportive of this, Merei (1949) brought older children who had previously shown evidence of leadership potential into small groups of younger children in a Hungarian nursery. Merei found that the most successful leaders were those who initially conformed to the existing group practices and gradually introduced minor changes.

Whilst the 'leadership as a process' approach is a dynamic one, like Fiedler's it neglects two features of the leader's interactions with others.

- The focus of leadership research has been on the links between leaders and their immediate subordinates. In practice, though, leaders devote substantial time to their own superiors, relevant colleagues, and many others inside (and sometimes outside) the organisations in which they work. According to Likert (1961), leaders play crucial roles as 'linking pins' between various groups within large institutions. This idea has been developed in theories which have reformulated the concept of leadership to emphasise how leader effectiveness can be thought of as the successful management of the conflicting needs and demands of the leader's *role set* (those that make demands on the occupant of a particular role: Smith & Peterson, 1988). Taking this broader view of a leader's interactions implies that the leader uses different leadership styles, or forms of influence, with different members of the role set (Smith, 1995).

- Leaders not only lead their groups but, in varying ways, lead them against other groups. This is illustrated well by the familiar tactic of political leaders who are unpopular at home pursuing aggressive foreign policies. Examples would be Margaret Thatcher's policy in the Falklands conflict (1982) and George Bush's in the Gulf War (1991). This *intergroup dimension* of leadership is usually overlooked in theory and research (Hogg & Vaughan, 1995).

Leadership and power

Clearly, leadership and power are closely related concepts. However, just as there are different kinds of leader (such as appointed and emergent), so there are different kinds of power. One classification of the different types of power was proposed by French & Raven (1959).

Box 60.6   The five kinds of power identified by French & Raven (1959)

Legitimate power is the formal power invested in a particular role regardless of the role occupant's personality. Examples of people holding legitimate power include the Prime Minister and a school head teacher.

Reward power refers to control over valued resources (or 'rewards') such as money, food, love, respect and co-operation. Holders of this sort of power include employers, store owners, parents, friends and work colleagues.

Coercive power is the control over feared consequences ('punishments'). Such consequences include the withdrawal of rewards, demotion, loss of love and so on. In both coercive and reward power, power is largely inherent in the role itself, although personality can play some part.

Expert power is the possession of special knowledge, skills and expertise. Holders of this sort of power include doctors, teachers and car mechanics. This is related to *informational power*, which is to do with access to important sources of information such as the Internet.

Referent power consists of personal qualities, such as charm and the ability to persuade and 'win' people over. The *charismatic leader* (Greenberg & Baron, 1995) has great referent power which often exceeds his or her legitimate power. However, parents, teachers, and so on may also have referent power in addition to their other forms of power.

Possibly, one characteristic consistently displayed by every leader is the *lust after power*. If we accept Adler's claim that each of us has a 'will to power' (a tendency to overcome our fundamental feelings of inferiority: see Chapter 1, page 13), then perhaps leadership is how leaders satisfy the 'will to power'. According to Gergen & Gergen (1981), however, whilst leadership does imply power, it would be wrong to assume that everybody who possesses power is highly motivated to achieve it. In their view, many political leaders, for example, are recruited and encouraged by others who promote them to powerful positions. If anything, the need for affiliation may be far stronger than the need for power in such people.

Figure 60.2   Hitler can be regarded as embodying the 'will to power'. His lust for control of Germany's fate influenced the course of world history

Conclusions

This chapter has reviewed theories concerning the emergence of leaders and the factors that influence leadership effectiveness once a position of power has been attained. Several theoretical positions exist with respect to both leader emergence and leader effectiveness, although the complexity of this area rules out the uncritical acceptance of any one position over any other.

Summary

■ A **leader** is the person who exerts most influence in a group. **Leadership** is the exercise of influence or power over others. The **trait approach** to leadership is concerned with whether leaders are born or made. The **situational approach** is concerned with **leader effectiveness**.

■ The 'great person' or **trait theory** of leader emergence sees leaders as possessing personality traits which make them suitable for positions of power and authority. However, in general, leaders are not consistently different from non-leaders in terms of their personality traits.

■ Another theory stresses the situation's **functional demands**. According to this, the person most likely to emerge as leader is the one whose **skills** and **competence** are most useful to a group in a given setting. This approach assumes that anyone can become a leader in appropriate conditions, although the evidence disputes this.

■ Different types of **leadership style** exist. Lewin *et al.* identified **autocratic**, **democratic**, and **laissez-faire styles**, the most favoured being the democratic. **Initiating structure** and **showing consideration** are important behaviours for leaders to exhibit. Other leadership styles are the **task specialist** and **socioemotional specialist**. The most effective leaders display both of these styles.

■ Fiedler's **contingency model of leader effectiveness** is mainly concerned with the match between a leader's personal qualities/leadership style and the requirements of the situation in which the group must operate. Fiedler identified **relationship-oriented** and **task-oriented leaders**.

■ Fiedler's model proposes that leader effectiveness is contingent upon the fit between the leader's style and

a situation's 'favourableness' to the leader. This is determined by the quality of **leader–member relations**, **task structure**, and **position-power**, each of which can have a high or low value.

■ The model predicts that a task-oriented leader will be most effective when the situation is either highly favourable or highly unfavourable. A relationship-oriented leader will be more effective when the situation is neither very favourable nor unfavourable.

■ Fiedler's predictions have been more strongly supported in laboratory studies than field studies. The model's assumption that leadership style is part of a leader's personality is not, however, supported by evidence. Also, the assumptions regarding the relative importance of the three situational variables is unclear and may be a function of contextual factors.

■ **Validation** refers to how a leader achieves **legitimacy** as a leader. In a formal group structure, the leader is **appointed** by an external authority and is imposed on the group. In an informal group, the leader achieves authority from the group members themselves and is an **emergent** leader.

■ Even with appointed leaders, leadership is a complex social process involving a **transaction** between group members. Leaders are also members of the group they lead, and will be influenced by the group. Leaders are simultaneously both conformists (embodying the group's norms) and deviants (capable of changing these norms). Leaders must earn **idiosyncrasy credit** if they are to bring about change.

■ This, and Fiedler's approach, overlook the leader's interactions with their own superiors and other relevant colleagues. The view of leaders as 'linking pins' between various groups within large institutions has been adopted by theories which see leader effectiveness in terms of successful management of the leader's **role set**. This broader view implies that the leader adopts different styles with different members of the role set.

■ Five kinds of **power** are **legitimate, reward, coercive, expert** (related to **informational power**) and **referent** (as displayed by the **charismatic leader**). All leaders may share a 'lust after power'. This could be a way of overcoming a fundamental feeling of inferiority we all experience. However, whilst leadership implies power, not everyone who possesses it is highly motivated to achieve it. Many political leaders have greater needs for affiliation than for power itself.

61

COLLECTIVE BEHAVIOUR

Introduction and overview

Milgram & Toch (1969) define collective behaviour as:

'behaviour which originates spontaneously, is relatively unorganised, fairly unpredictable and planless in its course of development, and which depends upon inter-stimulation among participants'.

Several phenomena can be identified as examples of collective behaviour, all of which could be included in this chapter. However, the two types that will be the focus of attention here are *crowds* and *mobs*. This chapter considers explanations and research evidence into these forms of collective behaviour.

Types of collective behaviour

On Milgram and Toch's definition (see above), many phenomena can be identified as examples of collective behaviour.

Box 61.1   Some examples of collective behaviour

Panic: Panic is a form of action in which a crowd, excited by a belief in some imminent threat, may engage in uncontrolled, and therefore dangerous, collective flight. The action of the panicky crowd is not wholly irrational. Each individual acts to escape a perceived threat. However, the uncoordinated and uncontrolled action, and the response based on emotional contagion (see page 526), give panic an irrational character.

Fad: A fad is a trivial, short-lived variation in speech, decoration or behaviour. One example of a fad was that for 'streaking', which first emerged in the mid-1970s during the summer months, but died out as winter approached.

Fashion: This is similar to a fad, but is less trivial and changes less rapidly. Long hair in men has been in and out of fashion several times, as have different lengths of women's dresses.

Craze: Whereas a panic is a rush away from a perceived threat, a craze is a rush towards some satisfaction. Crazes differ from fads in that they become obsessions for their followers.

Propaganda: Propaganda includes all efforts to persuade people to a point of view upon an issue. The distinction between education and propaganda is that the former cultivates the ability to make discriminating judgements, whereas the latter seeks to persuade people to the undiscriminating acceptance of a ready-made judgement (see Chapter 82).

Public opinion: Public opinion can be defined as (1) an opinion held by a substantial number of people, or (2) the dominant opinion among a population. The first use allows for many public opinions, whereas the second refers to public consensus on some issue.

Social movement: A social movement is a 'collectivity' acting with some continuity to promote or resist a change in the society or group of which it is a part.

Revolution: A revolution is a sudden, usually violent, and relatively complete change in a social system.

(Based on Turner & Killian, 1957; Smelser, 1963, and Horton & Hunt, 1976)

Crowds and mobs

Two examples of collective behaviour that could also have appeared in Box 61.1 are crowds and mobs. A *crowd* can be defined as a collection of people gathered around a centre or point of common attention (Young, 1946). Several types of crowd may be distinguished (Brown, 1965). A *casual crowd* is one whose members rarely know one another and whose forms of behaviour are mostly unstructured. In times of social unrest or tension, casual crowds may be transformed into *acting crowds* or *mobs*.

Broom & Selznick (1977) define a mob as:

'a crowd bent upon an aggressive act such as lynching, looting, or the destruction of property. The term refers to a crowd that is fairly unified and single-minded in its aggressive intent. Mob action is not usually randomly destructive but tends to be focused on a single target'.

Box 61.2   Mob behaviour

Colonel Charles Lynch provided a name for a particularly barbaric and unofficial method of dealing with crime. Lynch's unofficial courts against those who opposed the

---

revolutionary cause in America in the 1700s did not exact the death penalty. However, they 'filled a gap left by the inadequacies of the official courts' (Sprott, 1958). Two examples of what Cantril (1941) calls *proletariat lynchings*, in which the victim is in a minority and the object is persecution, are those of James Irwin and Arthur Stevens.

- Raper (1933) reports the case of James Irwin, a black man who was chained to a tree in front of around 1000 people. These people watched as members of the mob cut off his fingers and toes joint by joint, pulled out his teeth with wire pliers, castrated him, and 'hung his mangled but living body ... on a tree by the arms'. The mob then set fire to him, and shot him.

- Miller & Dollard (1941) describe the lynching in the southern states of America of a black man called Arthur Stevens. Stevens confessed to murdering his lover, who was white, when she told him she wanted to end their relationship. Because the arresting sheriff feared violence, Stevens was moved 200 miles during the night of his arrest. However, over 100 people stormed the gaol and returned Stevens to the scene of his crime. There, he was tortured, emasculated and murdered. After dragging his body through the town, the mob went on the rampage, chasing and beating other black people. Their behaviour was brought to an end only by the intervention of troops.

Figure 61.1   The Heysel Stadium footballer disaster: a casual crowd became an acting crowd or mob

Theoretical approaches to collective behaviour

Turner & Killian (1972) identify several broad theoretical approaches to collective behaviour which have been specifically applied to crowds and mobs. The three most important of these are *contagion theories*, *convergence theories*, and *emergent norm theories*.

CONTAGION THEORIES

According to Le Bon (1879):

> 'isolated, a man may be a cultured individual; in a crowd he is a barbarian. [Crowd behaviour is] an irrational and uncritical response to the psychological temptations of the crowd situation'.

In Le Bon's view, the question that needed answering was why crowds act in ways that are uncharacteristic of the individuals comprising them and in ways contrary to their everyday norms. Le Bon identified several situational determinants of behaviour which come into operation when a crowd is assembled, these being *suggestibility*, *social contagion*, *impersonality* and *anonymity*. The last of these has been the subject of most research.

Suggestibility

In the absence of a leader or recognised behaviour patterns for members of a crowd to carry out, a situation may be chaotic and confused. Suggestion, if made in an authoritative manner, may lead people to react readily and uncritically (Lang & Lang, 1961). Le Bon believed that, in such circumstances, what he called the 'conscious personality' vanished, and the 'racial unconscious' took over.

Whilst few psychologists today would agree with this view, Freud (1921) suggested that crowds permit the expression of behaviour that would otherwise be *repressed*. According to Freud, we possess a need, derived from our relationship with our father, to submit to more powerful forces, whether embodied in authorities or groups. Whilst some (e.g. Couch, 1968) believe that the role played by suggestibility has been overemphasised, heightened suggestibility does make *rumour* an important part of collective behaviour.

Box 61.3   Rumour

According to Shibutani (1966), heightened suggestibility makes rumour important in situations of collective excitement. A rumour is an unconfirmed, but not necessarily false, communication. Usually it is transmitted by word of mouth in a situation of anxiety or stress. Rumours occur in unstructured situations when information is needed but reliable channels do not exist.

Rumours tend to be passed rapidly from person to person and usually distort or falsify the facts. This is because they are often coloured by emotions. A rumour may begin as an inaccurate report because of the narrowing of perception that occurs in emotionally charged situations. It may become progressively more distorted because *all* oral communication is subject to distortion. Even in the absence of emotional elements, factual reports tend to become shorter and simpler as they are passed on. The distortion of details typically occurs in accordance with personal or cultural predispositions or 'sets'. This relates to Bartlett's theory of reconstructive memory (see Chapter 27).

(Adapted from Broom & Selznick, 1977)

Social contagion

Social contagion (or *interactional amplification*) is the process whereby the members of a crowd stimulate and respond to one another and thereby increase their emotional intensity and responsiveness (Horton & Hunt, 1976). When so aroused, a crowd needs emotional release, and it may act on the first suggested action which accords with its impulses (Lang & Lang, 1961). Thus, when an intended black victim of a lynching was protected by the town's mayor, the mob attempted to lynch the mayor and very nearly succeeded (Horton & Hunt, 1976).

Impersonality

Consider the account of a shooting reported by Lee & Humphrey (1943) described below.

Box 61.4   An impersonal attack

We drove around for a long time. We saw a lot of coloured people, but they were in bunches. We didn't want any of that. We wanted some guy all by himself. We saw one at Mack Avenue.

Aldo drove past him and then said 'Gimme that gun'. I handed it over to him and he turned around and came back. We were about 15 feet from the man when Aldo pulled up, almost stopped and shot. The man fell and we blew.

We didn't know him. He wasn't bothering us. But other people were fighting and killing and we felt like it, too.

(From Lee & Humphrey, 1943)

The description given above shows *impersonality*. In the case of a *riot* (see page 530), the impersonality of crowd behaviour is illustrated by treating one member of the 'enemy' as being as bad as another (which explains why innocent passersby are often the victims of a riot).

Anonymity

Le Bon believed that the more anonymous the crowd, the greater was its potential for extreme action, because anonymity removes the sense of *individuality* from members. When a person does not feel that he or she is being singled out as an individual, and when attention is not paid to others as individuals, restraints on behaviour are removed and a person is 'free' to indulge in behaviour that would ordinarily be controlled. The reason for this is that moral responsibility for behaviour has been shifted from the individual person to the group of which he or she is a member.

As mentioned earlier (see page 525), Le Bon wanted to know why people in crowds act in uncharacteristic ways and contrary to their everyday norms. Fromm (1941), however, was more concerned with the *motives* that lead some people to hide their individuality in crowds. Le Bon and Fromm's concerns were combined by Festinger *et al.* (1952) who proposed the concept of *deindividuation*, defining it as:

'a state of affairs in a group where members do not pay attention to other individuals *qua* individuals and, correspondingly, the members do not feel they are being singled out by others'.

According to Festinger *et al.*, membership of a group not only provides us with a sense of identity and *belongingness* (see Chapter 53, page 466), but allows us to merge with the group, forego our individualities, and become anonymous. This may lead to a reduction of inner constraints and inhibitions. A field experiment demonstrating the effects of anonymity was reported by Zimbardo (1969). Zimbardo reasoned that a big city is a more anonymous place than a small town because people are more likely to know one another in a small town. For the big city, the Bronx area of New York was chosen. The little town was the Stanford area of Palo Alto, California.

In each location, a similar car was parked in a street adjoining a university campus. The car's number plates were removed and its bonnet raised in order to make it appear that it had been abandoned. Research assistants photographed the car and filmed people's behaviour from hidden locations. In New York, the car's battery and radiator were removed within ten minutes of it being parked. Within a day, just about everything else that could be removed was. Within three days, there was little left of the car, a result of 23 incidents of 'destructive contact'. These were nearly always observed by a passerby, who occasionally stopped to chat with the perpetrator. Moreover, the incidents were carried out in daylight by well-dressed, clean-cut whites who, argued Zimbardo, were the very people who would protest against such behaviour and demand a greater police presence! By contrast, the car left in Palo Alto was left alone for seven days. Indeed, on the day it rained, a passer-by lowered the car's bonnet in order to protect its engine!

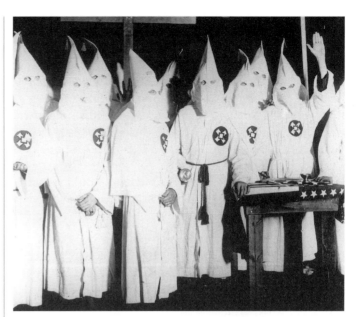

Figure 61.2   The Ku Klux Klan: deindividuated individuals but an easily identifiable group

---

Box 61.5   Some research showing the effects of deindividuation

- Defining deindividuation as 'a subjective state in which people lose their sense of self-consciousness', Singer *et al.* (1965) found that reduced individuality within a group was associated with a greater liking for the group and a larger number of obscene comments being made in a discussion of pornography. In a follow-up study, Singer *et al.* found that although deindividuated participants liked their group more, they conformed to it less.

- In one of several studies conducted by Zimbardo (1969), female undergraduates were required to deliver electric shocks to another student as 'an aid to learning'. Half the participants wore bulky laboratory coats and hoods that hid their faces. These participants were spoken to in groups of four and never referred to by name. The other half wore their normal clothes, were given large name tags to wear, and introduced to each other by name. They could also see each other dimly whilst giving the shocks.

  Both sets of participants could see the student supposedly receiving the shocks, who pretended to be in extreme discomfort. The hooded participants gave twice as much shock as the other group. Moreover, the amount of shock given by the hooded participants, unlike that given by the other group, did not depend on whether they were told that the student receiving the shocks was 'honest, sincere and warm' or 'conceited and critical'.

- Watson (1973) investigated 23 different cultures. Those warriors who depersonalised themselves with face paints or masks were significantly more likely than those with exposed faces to kill, torture or mutilate captured enemies.

- Diener *et al.* (1976) observed 1300 'trick-or-treating' American children one Halloween night. When the children were anonymous, as a result of wearing costumes which prevented them from being recognised, and went from house to house in large groups, they were more likely to steal money and candy.

Diener's theory of deindividuation

According to Diener (1980):

> 'a deindividuated person is prevented by situational factors in a group from becoming *self-aware*. Deindividuated persons are blocked from an awareness of themselves as separate individuals and from monitoring their own behaviour'.

Diener argues that in everyday life we are frequently unaware of our individual identities or of ourselves as separate persons. Indeed, when we perform well-learned behaviours, express well-thought-out cognitions, or enact culturally scripted behaviour, we are not consciously aware. In some circumstances, such as when we are evaluated by others or when a behaviour does not produce an expected outcome, self-awareness and behavioural self-regulation are initiated. In other circumstances, such as when we are immersed in a group, self-awareness and individual self-conception are blocked, and it is this which Diener believes leads to deindividuation. When deindividuation occurs, certain self-regulatory capacities are lost. These include a weakening of normal restraints against impulsive behaviour, a lack of concern about what others will think of our behaviour, and a reduced capability to engage in rational thinking.

Prentice-Dunn and Rogers' theory of deindividuation

Prentice-Dunn & Rogers (1982, 1983) argue that it is possible to distinguish between two types of self-awareness. *Public self-awareness* refers to a concern about the impression we are giving others who will hold us accountable for our behaviour. *Private self-awareness* refers to the attention we pay our own thoughts and feelings.

Public self-awareness can be reduced by three factors. For example, we would be difficult to identify in a crowd and this would make us feel *anonymous*. If other members were behaving anti-socially, a *diffusion of responsibility* (see Chapter 62, page 535) would also occur because one person alone could not be blamed for the group's actions. Finally, other group members' behaviours would set some sort of standard or *norm* for behaviour and supply models to *imitate* (see also emergent norm theory: page 530).

Private self-awareness can also be reduced by several factors. For example, in a crowd attending a rock concert, our attention would be directed outward, and we might become so engrossed in what was going on (singing, dancing, and/or drinking alcohol, for example) that we would 'forget' who we are. Prentice-Dunn and Rogers argue that deviant behaviour can occur through a loss of either of these forms of self-awareness, although this occurs through different routes.

When we are publicly self-aware, we engage in rational calculations about the likelihood of being punished for deviant behaviour. A deindividuated state, however, is an *irrational state of altered consciousness*. As Figure 61.3 illustrates, Prentice-Dunn and Rogers' theory does not see reductions in public or private self-awareness by themselves as causing deviant behaviour. Rather, both factors make us susceptible to *behavioural cues*, one being other people's behaviour in a crowd.

The data presented in Box 61.5 (page 527) are consistent with both theories described above. These theories may also explain other phenomena such as the 'baiting crowd' in cases of threatened suicide. For example, in an analysis of 21 incidents of potential suicides threatening to jump from buildings, Mann (1981) found that in ten cases, people were more likely to shout 'Jump!' when they were part of a large crowd, when it was dark, and when the victim and crowd were distant from one another (as is the case when the victim threatens to jump from a tall building). Baiting was also linked to other behavioural cues (see above) such as high temperatures and how long the episode lasted.

An evaluation of deindividuation research

Although there is much experimental support for the concept of deindividuation, several cautions should be exercised. First, participants in Zimbardo's (1969) study outlined in Box 61.5 wore clothing resembling that worn by the Ku Klux Klan, an American racist group (see Figure

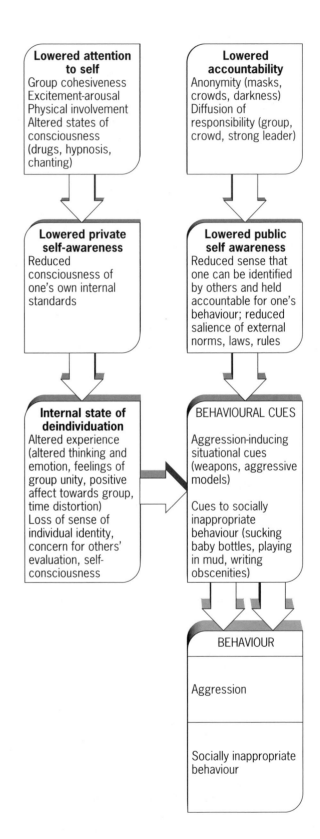

Figure 61.3   Prentice-Dunn and Roger's theory sees deviant behaviour as occurring through two different paths, namely lowered attention to self and lowered accountability (From Prentice-Dunn & Rogers, 1983)

528

61.2). This uniform may have acted as a *demand characteristic* (see Chapters 2 and 83), in that it might have led American participants to believe that more extreme behaviour was expected of them (Johnson & Downing, 1979). In support of this, Johnson and Downing found that when participants wore surgical masks and gowns, they delivered significantly *less* electric shock than those participants whose names and identities were emphasised. This suggests that the participants' clothing, rather than deindividuation, may have led to differences in behaviour.

Similarly, Brown (1985) has pointed out that in another of Zimbardo's (1969) studies, the participants were Belgian soldiers rather than the female undergraduates investigated in the study described in Box 61.5. When these soldiers wore the hoods, they did *not* behave more aggressively. Instead, they became self-conscious, suspicious and anxious. Their apparently *individuated* counterparts, who wore army-issue uniform, retained their 'normal' level of deindividuation resulting from their status as *uniformed soldiers*. One of the functions of uniforms in the 'real world' is to *reduce* individuality and hence, at least indirectly, to increase deindividuation (Brown, 1985). Indeed, dispossessing someone of the clothes they normally wear is a major technique of depersonalising them in 'total institutions' such as prisons and psychiatric hospitals (Goffman, 1968, 1971).

Also, whilst the anonymity produced by wearing, say, police or military uniform may increase the likelihood of deindividuated behaviour, such anonymity may make the wearers of these uniforms appear less human and affect the perceptions and attitudes of others (Brown, 1985).

Box 61.6   Do crowds resent the anonymity of their opponents?

In a disturbance in the Notting Hill area of London in 1982, 100 police officers were sent to the scene wearing special flameproof suits. According to *The Times* newspaper:

(The) uniform, combined with a hard helmet and visor, does not include a police serial number, making it difficult for anyone who wishes to identify and complain against an individual officer to pursue a grievance. A middle-aged West Indian, who was in a restaurant when it was raided, said yesterday: 'When they came through the door they looked like zombies, dressed in full black with headgear. All they had was one white stripe saying 'police' on it. We could not know in the world who they were, their faces were covered and they had helmets.'

(Taken from Brown, 1985)

Finally, deindividuation does not necessarily produce anti-social behaviour. Gergen *et al.* (1973) showed that in some circumstances when people cannot be identified, more *affiliative* behaviours can occur. In their study, groups of six men and six women were placed in either a normally lit room (control group) or a completely dark room (experimental group). The participants, who had never met one another, were told that there was nothing special the experimenters wanted them to do. The experimenters left the participants for one hour, tape recorded what they said and, when the experiment was over, asked them what had happened.

During the first 15 minutes, the experimental group participants mainly explored the room and chatted idly to one another. In the following 30 minutes, the conversation turned to more serious matters. In the final 15 minutes, the participants began to get physical in that half of them hugged one another. Some of them became quite intimate, and 80 per cent reported feeling sexually aroused! It seems that we can become uninhibited in the dark where the norms of intimacy no longer prevail. We feel less accountable for our behaviour in such situations, but this state of deindividuation can be to the mutual benefit of all (Gergen & Gergen, 1981).

CONVERGENCE THEORY

Convergence theory (e.g. Shellow & Roemer, 1966) argues that crowd behaviour arises from the gathering together of people who share the same needs, impulses, dislikes and purposes. According to Durkheim (1898), 'controlled emotional contagion' (as occurs in a peaceful crowd) can serve a useful social function. For example, it may allow people to release emotions and tensions they cannot ordinarily express (consider, for instance, the behaviour of some types of spectators at wrestling bouts) and stimulate feelings that enhance group solidarity.

Organised gatherings of many kinds (such as mass meetings and religious services) provide settings that integrate crowd behaviour into the social structure (Broom & Selznick, 1977). For example, Benewick & Holton (1987) interviewed members of the 80,000-strong crowd that gathered at Wembley Stadium for an open air-mass given by the Pope during his visit to Britain in 1982. Interviewees reported that they found the event powerful and meaningful, and experienced strong feelings of unity with the others present.

EMERGENT NORM THEORY

One weakness of contagion theory is that it does not explain why a crowd takes one course of action rather than another (Turner & Killian, 1957; Turner, 1964). According to emergent norm theorists, contagion theorists are guilty of exaggerating the irrational and purposeless components of crowd behaviour. In support of this, consider social psychological analyses of certain *riots*.

Smelser (1963) defines a riot as a form of civil disorder marked by violent mob action, a 'hostile outburst' of resentment or rebelliousness. Prior to the 1960s, the dominant view of riots was the *riffraff theory*. As applied to race riots, this says that the small percentage of people who take part in riots are criminals, drug addicts, drifters, leaders of youth gangs, and welfare cheaters, and that a riot is an isolated event which receives little or no support from the community (Sears & McConahay, 1969).

Analyses conducted in the 1960s, however, showed that there was little if any truth in riffraff theory. For example, Orum (1972) found that participants in American race riots were relatively representative cross-sections of the categories of people involved. Moreover, they were motivated by genuine group grievances rather than personal instabilities.

Orum found that the burning and looting which accompanied race riots was *not* indiscriminate. Whilst stores and offices perceived as exploitative were looted and burned, private homes, public buildings, and agencies serving the needs of the people were usually spared. Of course, not all riots are alike, but according to emergent norm theory the perceptions and grievances of a group, fed by the contagion process, lead to the emergence of a norm which justifies and sets limits to the behaviour of the crowd (Horton & Hunt, 1976).

An analysis of why 'ordinary people' can turn into looters and rioters was attempted by Brown (1954). According to Brown, there are varying *thresholds for participation* in physical action.

Box 61.7   Brown's thresholds for participation

1 **The lawless:** These are impulsive people, usually men and often with criminal records, who need little provocation before they try to retaliate. The lawless have little understanding of or concern for the consequences of their actions.

2 **The suggestible:** These are people who are easily influenced by an impulsive leader. They only need 'a little push' to follow an example, although it is unlikely that they would initiate action on their own.

3 **The cautious:** These are people with strong interests in the kinds of action initiated by others, but who would not act because of a fear of the law. If this

constraint is lifted, they take action in pursuit of their own interests.

4 **The yielders:** These are people who are easily persuaded that everybody is engaged in a particular behaviour. Yielders act when a sufficient number of people are acting because they do not want to be left out, and see an action is right because others are engaged in it.

5 **The supportive:** Whilst the supportive cannot be 'stampeded' into action, they do not actively oppose it. They may watch or shout encouragement. They are not violent, but they do not stand out against violence in others.

6 **The resisters:** These are people whose values are opposed to mob action, and who will not support it even passively. Because of this, they are in danger of their lives if they speak up at the wrong time.

(Based on Brown, 1954)

In an extension of emergent norm theory, Reicher (1984) has proposed a model of collective behaviour based on *social identity* (see Chapter 53, page 466). Reicher argues that a crowd is:

'a form of social group in the sense of a set of individuals who perceive themselves as members of a common social category, or, to put it another way, adopt a common *social* identification'.

Reicher analysed the riots that occurred in the St Paul's area of Bristol in 1980. Following a tip-off about illegal drinking, police raided a cafe and arrested two men. However, as they tried to leave, bricks were thrown at them. Police reinforcements subsequently arrived, and were attacked by a crowd of several thousand who overturned cars and set them alight.

Reicher's analysis showed that the crowd did not behave in a random and unpredictable manner. For example, they did not damage any vehicles other than police cars and those suspected of being unmarked police cars, and did minimal damage to property. The crowd also confined their behaviour to the St Paul's district and prevented any other forms of violence from taking place. In Reicher's view, the crowd saw the police as an illegitimate presence. The community members (the *ingroup*) behaved in a way they perceived as being legitimate given the police's presence.

Unfortunately, Reicher's analysis is weakened by the finding that crowds do not always behave in a like-minded way. During the riot that took place in the Watts district of Los Angeles, looting and burning occurred at different times and in different areas. Whether these actions, occurring in different locations and at varying times, are the expression of common social identity is difficult to answer without considerable first-hand experience of riots (Brown, 1985).

Conclusions

This chapter has reviewed explanations and evidence concerning crowds and mobs, two important examples of collective behaviour. Several theoretical accounts have been advanced to explain their behaviour. However, whilst supported to some extent by evidence, none offers a completely adequate account of such behaviour.

Summary

■ Two extensively researched examples of collective behaviour are **crowds** and **mobs**. A crowd is a collection of people gathered around some point of common attention. **Casual crowds** can be transformed into **acting crowds** or **mobs** at times of social unrest. A mob is a crowd bent upon an aggressive act such as lynching, looting, or the destruction of property. A mob is fairly unified and single-minded in its aggressive intent, and tends to be focused on a single target (as in **proletariat lynchings**).

■ The three most important theoretical approaches to collective behaviour which apply specifically to crowds and mobs are **contagion**, **convergence** and **emergent norm theories**.

■ Le Bon's version of contagion theory tried to explain why crowds behave in ways uncharacteristic of the individuals composing them and contrary to everyday norms. He identified several situational influences on crowd behaviour, namely **suggestibility** (and **rumour**), **social contagion** (**interactional amplification**), **impersonality**, and **anonymity**.

■ The more anonymous the crowd, the greater its potential for extreme action, since members lose their sense of **individuality**. This, combined with a failure to perceive others as individuals, removes restraints on behaviour, freeing the person to indulge in behaviour that is ordinarily controlled. Moral responsibility is shifted from the individual to the group.

■ Through the concept of **deindividuation**, Festinger *et al.* combined Fromm's concerns with people's motives for hiding individuality with Le Bon's concern for people's

uncharacteristic behaviours in crowds. Groups provide us with a sense of identity and belongingness and an opportunity to merge in with them, thus foregoing our individuality and becoming anonymous. This may reduce our inner constraints and inhibitions.

■ According to Diener, **deindividuated** people are prevented from an awareness of themselves as separate individuals and from monitoring their own behaviours. This occurs when immersed in a group, resulting in certain self-regulatory capacities being lost.

■ Prentice-Dunn and Rogers distinguish between **public** and **private self-awareness**, both of which can be reduced by being in a crowd. Deviant behaviour can occur through a loss of either type of self-awareness. However, this happens indirectly, either through inducing an internal state of deindividuation (an **irrational state of altered consciousness**) in the case of reduced private self-awareness, or making us more susceptible to **behavioural cues** (such as other people's behaviour in a crowd) in the case of reduced public self-awareness.

■ There is considerable experimental support for the concept of deindividuation, although some findings are open to alternative explanations. Additionally, under some circumstances, deindividuation can increase **affiliative** behaviours.

■ According to **convergence theory**, crowd behaviour is the result of the gathering of people sharing the same needs, impulses, dislikes and goals. 'Controlled emotional contagion' can be socially useful, as when people release tension at a sporting event, or when group solidarity is increased. Many organised gatherings provide settings that integrate crowd behaviour into the social structure.

■ **Emergent norm theory** argues that contagion theories overemphasise the irrational and purposeless components of crowd behaviour. In **riots**, for example, people are motivated by genuine group grievances. Whilst not all riots are alike, emergent norm theory claims that a group's perceptions and grievances, fed by contagion, lead to the emergence of a norm which justifies and sets limits to the crowd's behaviour.

■ In Reicher's extension of emergent norm theory, a crowd is seen as a set of individuals who adopt a common **social identity**. The crowd involved in the St Paul's riots in Bristol did not behave randomly and unpredictably but in a way they perceived as legitimate. However, Reicher's view is weakened by those riots in which looting and burning occur at different locations at varying times.

PART 4

Pro- and anti-social behaviour

BYSTANDER BEHAVIOUR AND ALTRUISM

Introduction and overview

In April, 1994, under the heading 'Violent Britain', *The Sun* newspaper published the photograph shown in Figure 62.1. The journalist wrote:

> 'These are the appalling injuries six thugs inflicted on brave cop Gary Boughen as 30 people just stood and watched. The sergeant was battered senseless after he asked the drunken teenagers to stop swearing outside a village chip shop at 11.30 p.m. … Det. Sgt. John Hope said "What's so worrying is that the officer approached the men politely and simply asked them to go home. It was a routine situation – yet these men resorted to dreadful violence. He could have died. Thirty people saw the attack. One woman comforted the officer afterwards but it seems the others did nothing. None of them have come forward to give us assistance and I would ask them to contact us"' (Sharpe, 1994).

Contrast the above with a newspaper report in which a book-dealer on a business trip from Bristol to London, was taken 194 miles to York after he helped to carry a woman's luggage on to her train and was trapped when the doors locked automatically. As the passenger remarked:

> 'Nobody was helping this poor woman, so I gave her a hand. I couldn't believe my eyes when the automatic doors closed and a few seconds later the train started moving … I only stopped at the station for a cup of coffee and I ended up at the other end of the country' (reported in O'Neill, 1996).

These two accounts are probably the tip of an iceberg of incidents that actually find their way into our national newspapers. We may be appalled at the behaviour of people in the first incident and admire the person's behaviour in the second. The conditions under which

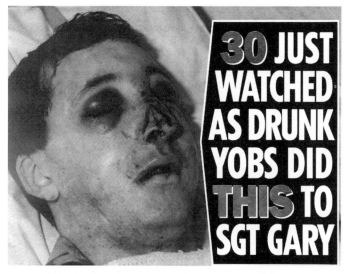

Figure 62.1   One of the consequences of bystander apathy

bystanders behave or do not behave *pro-socially* or *altruistically* have been the subject of much social psychological research. This chapter reviews that research.

The tragic case of Kitty Genovese

At 3.20 a.m., 23 March 1964, 28-year-old Kitty Genovese was fatally wounded by a knife-wielding stalker close to her apartment in the Queens district of New York. Miss Genovese's screams of 'Oh, my God, he stabbed me!' and 'Please help me!' woke up 38 of her neighbours in the apartment block. Their lights went on, and they opened their windows to see what was going on. One neighbour even turned *out* his light and pulled a chair to the window to get a better view of the disturbance. As Miss Genovese lay dying, her attacker fled, only to return to sexually assault her and stab her again. Despite her shouts for help, it was not until 3.50 a.m., half an hour after the attack had begun, that the police were made aware as a result of a neighbour's telephone call. When police later questioned the witnesses, they were unable to explain their inaction.

Explaining 'bystander apathy': the decision model of bystander intervention

According to Milgram (cited in Dowd, 1984) Kitty Genovese's murder:

> 'touched on a fundamental issue of the human social condition. If we need help, will those around us stand around and let us be destroyed, or will they come to our aid?'.

The first researchers to investigate systematically the circumstances in which bystanders are and are not likely to intervene to help others were Latané & Darley (1968).

At the time of Miss Genovese's murder, America's commentators attributed her neighbours' indifference to a cold and apathetic (urban) society:

> 'It can be assumed … that their apathy was indeed one of the big-city variety. It is almost a matter of psychological survival, if one is surrounded and pressed by millions of people, to prevent them from constantly impinging on you, and the only way to do this is to ignore them as often as possible. Indifference to one's neighbour and his troubles is a conditioned reflex in New York as it is in other big cities' (Rosenthal, 1964).

Latané & Darley (1968) were the first to show that the reasons for Miss Genovese's neighbours' apathy were *not* quite as straightforward as this. As a result of their research, they proposed a five-step decision model of bystander intervention.

The model proposes that before a person helps a stranger, five decisions must be made. First, a situation requiring help must be *noticed*. If a situation has not been noticed, then intervention cannot occur. Second, the event that has been noticed must be *defined* as a situation in which help is needed. If the decision that help is needed is made, then, in the third step, the potential helper must *assume personal responsibility* for helping. If this is assumed,

the potential helper must then *select a way to help*. If this decision is successfully made, the potential helper must decide whether to *implement* the selected way.

The decision model represents a logical sequence of steps, such that a negative decision at any step results in the bystander not intervening, with help only being given when a positive decision has been reached in all five steps.

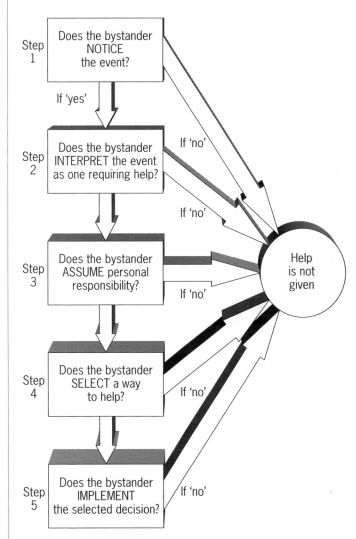

Figure 62.2   Latané and Darley's five-step decision model of bystander intervention and non-intervention (Based on Schroeder *et al.*, 1995)

DEFINING THE SITUATION AS ONE WHERE HELP IS NEEDED

Latané and Darley have shown that we are less likely to define a situation as being dangerous if other people are present, a phenomenon they called *pluralistic ignorance*.

Latané & Darley (1968): Participants were taken to a room to fill out a questionnaire either alone or with others. After a while, steam, which resembled smoke, began to pour out through a wall vent. Participants reacted most quickly when they were alone. With others present, they often failed to react, even though the steam was so thick it was difficult to see the questionnaire! In Latané and Darley's words, the participants:

> 'continued doggedly working on the questionnaire and waving the fumes away from their faces. They coughed, rubbed their eyes, and opened the window – but they did not report the smoke'.

Latané & Rodin (1969): Participants sitting in a room waiting to be called for an experiment heard a voice from an adjoining room (actually the voice of a female experimenter) cry out and moan for nearly a minute. Participants were significantly slower to respond and offer help when they were with other people than when they were alone.

Clark & Word (1974): In a similar experiment to Latané and Rodin's, a 'workman' carried a ladder and venetian blinds past a room in which participants were sitting. Shortly afterwards, a loud crash was heard. Again, the more people there were in the room, the less likely help was to be given, *unless* the workman made it clear what had happened.

Interviews conducted with participants after the experiments described in Box 62.1 indicated that one reason for people's failure to help was *social influence*. Many participants indicated that they had looked at, and tended to follow, the reactions of others. Since these others were trying (and evidently succeeding) to appear calm, participants defined the situation as 'safe'. Thus, each participant influenced others into thinking there was no cause for alarm.

Another reason for failing to help is the potential *embarrassment* of incorrectly defining a situation. One person snatching money from another *might* be a potential 'mugging', but it may also be the result of a harmless bet between two friends. The fear of making a social blunder and being subject to ridicule if a situation is ambiguous also deters people from helping (Shotland & Straw, 1976; Pantin & Carver, 1982).

Interestingly, Latané & Rodin (1969) found that when two friends were placed in an ambiguous situation, their response to a potential emergency was just as quick as when either was alone, and much quicker than when two strangers were together or when a naïve participant was with a 'stooge' instructed *not* to respond. Presumably, with people we do not expect to see again, we are deterred from acting because we will not have the opportunity to explain ourselves if our interpretations are incorrect (Shotland & Heinold, 1985).

There is, however, evidence indicating that when an emergency *clearly* requires bystander intervention, help is much more likely to be given, even when a large number of people witness the emergency (see below). For example, Clark & Word (1974) staged a realistic 'accident' (in which a 'technician' supposedly received a severe electric shock) in a room next to one in which individual participants or participants in groups of two or five were answering a questionnaire. All participants responded and went to the 'technician's' assistance.

ASSUMING PERSONAL RESPONSIBILITY OR DIFFUSING RESPONSIBILITY?

Whilst some witnesses to Kitty Genovese's murder claimed they believed the attack to be a 'lover's tiff', it is doubtful if pluralistic ignorance was operating, since her screams when the attacker returned would have made the situation unambiguous (if, after the first attack, it was not already).

In a laboratory simulation of an emergency, Darley & Latané (1968) led students, who were in separate cubicles, to believe they were participating in a group discussion of the problems of living in a high-pressure urban environment. To avoid any embarrassment and preserve anonymity, the students were told that the discussion would take place over an intercom system, and that only the person whose microphone was switched on could be heard. The students were also told that each would talk for two minutes and then comment on what the others had said.

Some students were told that there were five others in the discussion group, some that there were two others, and some that there was only one other. In actual fact, the other 'participants' were pre-recorded tapes played through the intercom system. Early on in the 'discussion', one of the 'participants' hesitantly admitted that he had epilepsy and that the anxiety and stress of urban living made him prone to seizures. Later on, the 'participant' had a 'seizure', began to speak incoherently, and stammered out a request for help before lapsing into silence (see Figure 62.3).

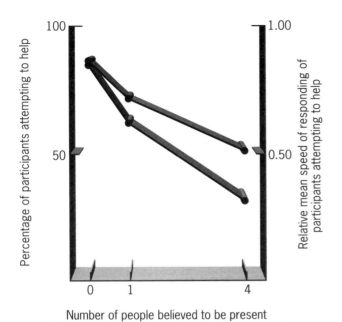

Figure 62.3   Percentage of participants attempting to help (by leaving their room to look for the 'victim' within five minutes) as a function of the number of others believed to be present, and the relative mean speed of responding of participants attempting to help (Adapted from Darley & Latané, 1968)

As Figure 62.3 shows, almost all (85 per cent) participants left the room to offer help when they believed themselves to be the only other person. However, when they believed there were witnesses other than themselves, they were much less likely to leave the room, and the likelihood of helping lessened the more witnesses there were. Also, participants responded more quickly when they believed themselves to be the only other person present.

> **Box 62.2   Diffusion of responsibility and the inverse law of helping behaviour**
>
> Darley & Latané (1968) called the phenomenon they observed in their experiment *diffusion of responsibility*, suggesting that, as probably happened in the Kitty Genovese murder, people reason that somebody else should, and probably will, offer assistance. The consequence of no one feeling responsible is that the victim is not helped, and the more people present, the less likely it is that any one of them will give assistance (the *inverse law of helping behaviour*).

When participants in Darley & Latané's (1968) experiment were interviewed about their behaviour, they were actually *not* indifferent, callous or apathetic to the student's plight. Indeed, Darley and Latané reported that:

'if anything they seemed more emotionally aroused than the (participants) who reported the emergency',

and they typically asked the experimenter who entered the room whether the victim was being taken care of. Darley and Latané's explanation for the participants' behaviour was that they were caught in a *conflict* between a fear of making fools of themselves and ruining the experiment by over-reacting (the anonymous nature of the experiment had previously been stressed as important by the experimenter), and their own guilt and shame at doing nothing.

Piliavin *et al.* (1981) have pointed out that Darley and Latané's experiment actually shows a *dissolution* rather than a *diffusion* of responsibility. In Darley and Latané's experiment, participants could not observe other people's behaviours and 'reasoned' that someone must have intervened. In other situations, responsibility is *accepted* by the participant but *shared* by all witnesses. The term diffusion best applies in these circumstances, whilst dissolution is a better descriptor for what happened in Darley and Latané's experiment.

Whether this distinction is important or not is debatable. What is important is the reliability with which the inhibitory effects of the presence of others on helping behaviour occurs. Latané *et al.* (1981) reviewed over 50 studies, conducted in both the laboratory and the natural environment, in which a variety of 'emergencies' were staged. In almost all of them (but see below), the *bystander effect* was observed.

CHOOSING A WAY TO HELP: THE ROLE OF COMPETENCE

Related to diffusion of responsibility, and something which may interact with it, is a bystander's *competence* to intervene and offer help (Huston & Korte, 1976). When bystanders have the *necessary skills* (such as a knowledge of first aid: 'Let me through, I'm a doctor.'), helping is more likely. However, in the presence of others, one or more of whom we believe to be better equipped to help, diffusion of responsibility is increased (Huston *et al.*, 1981). Thus, the inhibitory effects of other people may not necessarily indicate bystander apathy – non-helpers may sincerely believe that someone else is more likely, or better qualified in some way, to help (Schroeder *et al.*, 1995).

> **Box 62.3   Proximity and competence**
>
> Bickman (1971) replicated Darley & Latané's (1968) 'seizure' experiment (see page 534), but manipulated the participants' beliefs about the victim's proximity. Those who believed that another person was as close to

the victim as they were (in the same building), and equally capable of helping, showed diffusion of responsibility and were less likely to help than those who believed they were alone. However, when participants believed that the other person was in another building, and therefore less able to help, they helped as much as those who believed they were alone.

AN EVALUATION OF THE DECISION MODEL

Schroeder *et al.* (1995) argue that Latané and Darley's model provides a valuable framework for understanding why bystander non-intervention occurs. Moreover, whilst the model was originally designed to explain intervention in emergency situations, it has been successfully applied in other situations ranging from preventing someone from drinking and driving to deciding whether to donate a kidney to a relative. However, the model does not tell us *why* 'no' decisions are taken at any of the five steps, particularly once the situation has been defined as an emergency. Additionally, it focuses on why people *don't* help and pays much less attention to why they *do*.

Also, whilst the presence of others is a powerful and well-established factor influencing bystander behaviour, other factors have been shown to increase or decrease helping behaviour. In Piliavin *et al.*'s (1969) study, a stooge pretended to collapse in a subway carriage. Sometimes the stooge carried a cane, and sometimes a bottle in a brown paper bag (and wore a jacket which smelled strongly of alcohol). Help was much more likely to be given to the 'victim' with the cane (helped 90 per cent of the time within 70 seconds, compared with 20 per cent for the other victim).

In one of Piliavin & Piliavin's (1972) experiments, the 'victim' who 'collapsed' bit off a capsule of red dye resembling blood and let it run down his chin. This reduced the helping rate to 60 per cent, with those who witnessed the event being likely to enlist the help of others whom they believed to be more competent. In another experiment, Piliavin and Piliavin looked at the effect of the victim having an ugly facial birthmark. They found that helping dropped from 86 per cent when the victim was not disfigured to 61 per cent when he was.

Box 62.4 Some situational and individual differences in bystander behaviour

According to Amato (1983), help is less likely to be given in *urban* than *rural* environments. This is because the conditions that discourage bystander intervention (such as the situation's ambiguity) are more likely to be met in cities than rural areas. Amato studied 55 cities and towns in Australia selected on the basis of size and geographical isolation. Using a variety of measures of helping behaviour, Amato found that city size was negatively correlated with all but one measure of helping. A population of about 20,000 was the point at which helping behaviour was inhibited. If the findings from these Australian cities and towns generalise to Britain, then helping behaviour would be expected to be an infrequently occurring phenomenon even in some smaller towns.

People are more likely to help when put in a *good mood* than when mood is neutral or negative (Brown & Smart, 1991). In Europe and America, *husband and wife disputes* are considered to be private affairs. In Mediterranean and Latin cultures, however, anyone can intervene in a dispute between *any* two people (Wade & Tavris, 1993). People who feel a *moral obligation* to a victim, have deeply held *moral values* or personal feelings for the victim, and/or *empathy* with the victim, are more likely to act as helpers (Dovidio *et al.*, 1990). People with a *high need for approval* from others are more likely to help than people low on this need (Deutsch & Lamberti, 1986). People who score high on measures of *fear of being embarrassed* in social situations are less likely to offer help (McGovern, 1976).

Women are more likely than men to *receive* help (Eagly & Crowley, 1986), and victims who are similar in appearance to the potential helper are more likely to receive help than victims dissimilar in appearance (Hensley, 1981). Interestingly, most victims themselves do not actually like to ask for help and feel they will be viewed as being less competent if they accept it (De Paulo & Fisher, 1981). In a *reverse bystander effect*, victims are generally less likely to seek help as the number of potential helpers increases (Williams & Williams, 1983).

Piliavin *et al.*'s research is also interesting in terms of the operation of a diffusion of responsibility. Earlier (see page 535) it was noted that in *almost* all studies looking at the effects of the presence of others on helping behaviour, an inhibitory effect has been found. However, Piliavin *et al.* (1969) found that help was just as likely to be given on a crowded subway as on a relatively empty one. To explain this, Piliavin offered an alternative model of the conditions under which help is and is not likely to be given.

Arousal: cost–reward model

Although originally proposed as an explanation for the results obtained in their 'subway studies', Piliavin *et al.* (1981) and Dovidio *et al.* (1991) subsequently revised and expanded this model to cover both emergency *and* non-emergency helping behaviour.

The model emphasises the interaction between two sets of factors. The first are situational, bystander and victim characteristics, along with what Piliavin and his colleagues call 'we-ness'. The second are cognitive and affective reactions. Situational characteristics include things like a victim asking for help rather than not asking for help. Bystander characteristics include both *trait* factors (such as the potential helper being an empathic person) and *state* factors (such as the potential helper being in a positive or negative mood). Victim characteristics include things like the victim's appearance and other factors identified in Box 62.4. 'We-ness' refers to what Piliavin *et al.* call:

'a sense of connectedness or the categorisation of another person as a member of one's own group'.

The various characteristics produce certain *levels of arousal*. Whether or not helping behaviour occurs depends on *how* the arousal is interpreted or *attributed*. For example, if it can be attributed to the victim's distress rather than to other factors, helping is more likely to occur because the arousal is unpleasant and the bystander is motivated to reduce it (Batson & Coke, 1981). However, the exact way in which arousal is reduced depends upon the *rewards and costs* involved in helping and not helping. Piliavin *et al.*

suggest that bystanders weigh the costs and benefits of intervening, and the result of this *hedonic calculus* determines whether or not they help.

In the case of helping, rewards include enhanced self-esteem, praise from others, and even financial reward. In the case of not helping, rewards include time and the freedom to go about our normal business (Darley & Batson, 1973; Bierhoff & Klein, 1988). Costs of helping include lost time, effort, physical danger, embarrassment, the disruption of ongoing activities, and psychological aversion (as in the case of a victim who is bleeding or drunk). The costs of not helping include guilt, others' disapproval, and cognitive and/or emotional discomfort associated with knowing that a person is suffering.

When the costs of helping are low and the costs of not helping are low, the likelihood of intervention will be fairly high, although bystanders' behaviours will vary according to individual differences and the norms operating in a particular situation.

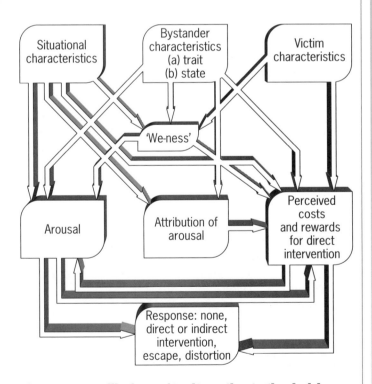

Figure 62.4   Piliavin *et al.*'s alternative to the decision model proposed by Latané and Darley. The model emphasises the interaction between the potential helper, the situation and the victim, and the cognitive and affective reactions of the potential helper (From Piliavin *et al.*, 1981)

Box 62.5   The application of Piliavin *et al.*'s model to some of the data reported by Piliavin *et al.* (1969) and Piliavin & Piliavin (1972)

1 Circumstances: The costs of helping are low (e.g. there is little danger to the self) and the costs of not helping are high (e.g. one may receive criticism for not helping).

Prediction: Direct intervention and helping are very likely.

Finding: A person carrying a cane who collapses is helped 90 per cent of the time within 70 seconds.

2 Circumstances: The costs of helping are high (e.g. the situation is dangerous or the person seems very strange) and the costs of not helping are high (something needs to be done).

Prediction: Indirect helping, such as calling for an ambulance, will be fairly likely to occur.

Finding: People are more likely to get somebody else to help when they see a person who collapses with 'blood' running down his chin.

3 Circumstances: The costs of helping are high (e.g. the person could be violent) and the costs of not helping are low ('who would blame me if I didn't help?').

Prediction: The likelihood of helping is very low.

Finding: People are less likely to help a 'victim' who collapses smelling of alcohol and carrying a bottle in a brown paper bag.

Whilst arousal and helping are often only correlated, the model clearly sees the former as *causing* the latter. According to Dovidio *et al.* (1991), evidence indicates that emotional reactions to other people's distress play an important role in motivating helping. The model proposes that bystanders will choose the response that most rapidly and completely reduces the arousal, incurring as few costs as possible. So, the emotional component provides the motivation to do *something*, whilst the cognitive component determines what the most effective response will be. As far as costs are concerned, what is high cost for one person might be low cost for another, and costs may even differ for the same person from one situation to another or from one occasion to another.

Piliavin *et al.*'s original model was subsequently elaborated to take account of the role played by other factors, such as bystander personality and mood, the clarity of the situation, characteristics of the victim, the relationships between the victim and potential helpers, and attributions made by potential helpers of the victim's deservingness. Not surprisingly, many of these variables interact, and contribute to how aroused the bystander is and the perceived costs and rewards for direct intervention.

'PERSONAL COSTS' VERSUS 'EMPATHY COSTS'

Two costs associated with not helping are *personal costs* (such as self-blame and public disapproval) and *empathy costs* (such as knowing that the victim is continuing to suffer). According to Dovidio *et al.* (1991),

'in general ... costs for *not* helping affect intervention primarily when the costs for helping are low'.

Although *indirect helping* becomes more likely as the costs for helping increase (as in serious emergencies), indirect helping is relatively infrequent, possibly because it is difficult for bystanders to 'pull away' from such situations in order to seek other people to assist (Schroeder *et al.*, 1995).

Box 62.6 Cognitive reinterpretation and bystander behaviour

The most common (and positively effective) way of resolving the high-cost-for-helping/high-cost-for-not-helping dilemma (as shown in (2) in Box 62.5) is *cognitive reinterpretation*. This can take one of three forms, namely, redefining the situation as one *not* requiring help, diffusing responsibility, or denigrating (blaming) the victim. Each of these has the effect of reducing the perceived costs of not helping. However, cognitive reinterpretation does *not* mean that bystanders are

uncaring. Rather, it is the fact that they do care that creates the dilemma in the first place (Schroeder *et al.*, 1995).

IMPULSIVE HELPING

Piliavin *et al.*'s model suggests that help is least likely to be given in high-cost (life-threatening) situations. In some situations, however, people act in almost reflexive ways, irrespective of the personal consequences and the number of others present (Anderson, 1974). Such examples of *impulsive helping* appear to occur in (but are not limited to) situations which are clear and realistic and in which the potential helper has some sort of prior involvement with the victim.

As Piliavin *et al.* (1981) have noted:

'not coincidentally, [these] factors ... have also been demonstrated to be related to greater levels of bystander arousal'.

Piliavin *et al.* argue that when people encounter emergency situations they cannot avoid, they become 'flooded' with intense arousal and this produces a narrowing of attention which is directed towards the victim's plight. In their view, cost considerations become peripheral and not attended to and, more speculatively,

'there may be an evolutionary basis for ... impulsive helping'.

Figure 62.5 When Hurricane Hortense hit Puerto Rico in 1996, at least eight people were killed in flash floods and mudslides. Here, José Louis de Leon and Miguel Rodriguez brave the flood to attach a rope to the home of the Gomez family and bring one-year-old Cassandra, her three brothers and sisters and father to the safety of dry land

Bystander behaviour: universal egoism or empathy–altruism?

One conclusion that might be drawn from studies on bystander behaviour is that we are an essentially selfish species, motivated to minimise costs and behave in ways that cause us least displeasure. An *altruistic act* is one performed to benefit others and which has no expectation of benefit or gain for the benefactor (and may even involve some degree of cost). So, is a responsive bystander's behaviour ever motivated by a *genuine* wish to benefit others?

UNIVERSAL EGOISM

Universal egoism is the view that people are fundamentally selfish, a dominant view in the social sciences which sees altruism as an impossibility (Dovidio, 1995). There are many examples of apparently altruistic behaviour in non-humans. For example, in certain songbirds an individual which detects a predator signals this by making a vocal 'alarm call', which causes those in the immediate vicinity to form a flock (for other examples of such apparent altruism see Clamp & Russell, 1998).

Box 62.7   The paradox of altruism

From a Darwinian perspective, altruistic behaviour is *not adaptive*, because it reduces the likelihood of an individual who raises an alarm surviving (the predator is likely to be attracted to the signal's source). According to sociobiologists, this 'paradox of altruism' can be resolved if apparently altruistic behaviour is viewed as *selfish* behaviour 'in disguise'.

Sociobiologists argue that an individual animal should be seen as a *set of genes* rather than a separate 'bounded organism', and that these 'selfish genes' (Dawkins, 1976) aim to secure their own survival. For a detailed account of how this can be achieved – notable examples include Hamilton's, 1964, *kin selection theory* and Trivers', 1971, *delayed reciprocal altruism theory* – see Clamp & Russell, 1998.

Theories that explain the apparently altruistic behaviour of non-humans can, at least for sociobiologists, be applied to humans (Wilson, 1978). Piliavin *et al.*'s model is clearly one form of universal egoism, in that it sees the decision making relating to probable rewards and costs as ultimately being concerned with arriving at a course of action that is really directed towards *self-benefit*.

EMPATHY–ALTRUISM

The *empathy–altruism hypothesis* accepts that much of what we do is egoistic, including much that we do for others. However, this hypothesis argues that in some circumstances we feel *empathic concern* when people are in difficulty, and we help in order to relieve the distress of *others* rather than our own emotional distress. The emotions associated with empathic concern include sympathy, compassion, and tenderness, and can be distinguished from the more self-oriented emotions of discomfort, anxiety and upset (which corresponds to the distinction between personal and empathic costs for not helping: see page 538). Whilst personal distress produces an egoistic desire to reduce our own distress, empathic concern produces an altruistic desire to reduce others' distress, and these are *qualitatively* different.

According to Darley (1991), who is clearly a universal (or at least a Western capitalist) egoist:

'In the United States and perhaps in all advanced capitalistic societies, it is generally accepted that the true and basic motive for human action is self-interest. It is the primary motivation, and is the one from which other motives derive. Thus it is the only 'real' motivation, a fact that some bemoan but most accept ... To suggest that human actions could arise for other purposes is to court accusations of naïvety or insufficiently deep or realistic analysis'.

Biological and psychological altruism

Whilst there is some plausibility in sociobiological accounts of altruism, sociobiologists have failed to make the distinction between *biological* (or what Sober, 1992, calls *evolutionary*) altruism and *psychological* (or *vernacular*) altruism. Biological altruism is the kind displayed by, for example, birds and rabbits when they give alarm signals. We would not normally attribute their behaviours to altruistic 'motives' or 'intentions' (it would be *anthropomorphic* to do so). Rather, such behaviour is better seen as part of the animal's biologically determined behavioural repertoire.

Psychological altruism is displayed by the higher mammals, in particular primates and especially humans. Whether humans are capable of biological altruism has been the subject of much debate. For Brown (1988):

'human altruism goes beyond the confines of Darwinism because human evolution is not only biological in nature but also cultural and, indeed, in recent times primarily cultural'.

However, biological altruism *may* be triggered under very specific conditions. With impulsive helping (see page 538), people react in a rapid and almost reflexive way in certain conditions (an example being a natural disaster such as an earthquake or a flood).

Impulsive helping is generally unaffected by social context or the potential costs of intervention (Piliavin *et al.*, 1981). In clear and realistic situations, especially those involving friends, relatives or acquaintances, the bystander is (as noted previously) most concerned with the costs for the victim of not receiving help. This is very close to Sober's definition of evolutionary altruism. Our ability to carry out sophisticated reasoning (as in psychological altruism) along with more primitive, non-cognitive, biological mechanisms, may permit us to perform a range of altruistic behaviours well beyond those of other species (Schroeder *et al.*, 1995).

Conclusions

Research into bystander behaviour and altruism has told us much about the conditions under which we are likely to behave (or not behave) pro-socially towards others. Thirty years after the brutal murder of Kitty Genovese, we seem to be closer to understanding bystander intervention and apathy.

Summary

■ Latané and Darley were the first to systematically investigate the circumstances under which bystanders are/are not likely to intervene to help others. Their interest was stimulated by the murder of Kitty Genovese in front of 38 witnesses, none of whom did anything to help her.

■ Latané and Darley proposed a five-step **decision model** of bystander intervention. According to this, a situation must first be **noticed** before it can be **defined** as one requiring help. The potential helper must then **assume personal responsibility** and **select a way to help** before **implementing it**. This is a logical sequence of steps, such that a negative decision at any time leads to non-intervention.

■ In other people's presence, we are less likely to define a situation as dangerous and hence less likely to act (**pluralistic ignorance**). Potential **embarrassment** and fear of **ridicule** for making a social blunder in an ambiguous situation also deter people from helping. However, when an emergency **clearly** requires bystander intervention, help is much more likely to be given even when many witnesses are present.

■ In the presence of others, however, people often believe that another person will act. As a result of this **diffusion of responsibility**, help is not given. The more people that are present, the less likely any one of them is to offer assistance (the **inverse law of helping behaviour**). Helping also depends on **competence**. When bystanders have the necessary skills, they are likely to respond.

■ The decision model has also been successfully applied to non-emergency situations. However, it fails to say why 'no' decisions are taken, and concentrates on why people **don't** help rather than why they do. Also, factors other than the presence of others influence helping behaviour. **Situational factors** include type of environment (urban versus rural) whilst **individual factors** include mood.

■ Piliavin *et al.*'s **arousal: cost–reward model** emphasises the interaction between (a) situational, bystander and victim characteristics, plus 'we-ness', and (b) cognitive and affective reactions. These characteristics produce **arousal**. How this arousal is attributed determines whether or not helping occurs. Exactly how arousal is reduced depends on the **hedonic calculus** of the rewards and costs for helping or not helping.

■ **Rewards for helping** include enhanced self-esteem and praise from others. **Not helping** brings rewards such as being free to carry on with one's normal behaviour. **Costs of helping** include lost time and physical danger. **Costs of not helping** include guilt, others' disapproval and the discomfort of knowing someone is suffering.

■ The model predicts the likelihood and nature of helping, depending on the combination of costs for helping and not helping. When the costs are low in both cases, intervention is quite likely, although there will be individual differences between potential helpers. When the costs are high in both cases, indirect helping is quite likely.

■ Two costs associated with not helping are **personal** and **empathy costs**. These become relevant when the costs of helping are low. As the costs increase, so **indirect helping** becomes more likely but remains relatively infrequent.

■ The high-cost-for-helping/high-cost-for-not-helping dilemma can be resolved through **cognitive reinterpretation**. This can take the form of redefining the situation as one not requiring help, diffusing responsibility, or blaming the victim. All of these reduce the costs of not helping.

■ The model predicts that helping is least likely in high cost (life-threatening) situations. However, **impulsive helping** sometimes occurs regardless of personal consequences and the presence of others. Unavoidable emergencies induce intense arousal in those who witness them, narrowing attention towards the victims' plights. Considerations of cost become peripheral.

■ **Universal egoism** sees people as being fundamentally selfish and unable to perform truly **altruistic acts**. According to sociobiologists, all apparently altruistic behaviour is really **selfish** behaviour in disguise.

■ Piliavin *et al.*'s model is a form of universal egoism, since the cost/reward analysis is ultimately concerned with **self-benefit**. By contrast, the **empathy–altruism hypothesis** acknowledges that we sometimes feel **empathic concern** for others' distress.

■ Sociobiology fails to distinguish between **biological/evolutionary altruism** and **psychological/vernacular altruism**. The former is seen in various non-humans and is part of their biologically determined behavioural repertoires. The latter is displayed by higher mammals, in particular primates and especially humans.

63

THEORIES OF AGGRESSION AND THE REDUCTION AND CONTROL OF AGGRESSIVE BEHAVIOUR

Introduction and overview

Baron & Richardson (1994) define anti-social behaviours as those 'which show a lack of feeling and concern for the welfare of others'. One anti-social behaviour is aggression. Used as a noun, 'aggression' usually refers to some behaviour intended to harm or destroy another person who is motivated to avoid such treatment. Penrod (1983) calls this *anti-social aggression* to distinguish it from those instances when, for example, a person defends him- or herself from attack (*sanctioned aggression*) or when, for example, an aircraft hijacker is shot and killed by security agents (*pro-social aggression*). When used as an adjective, 'aggressive' sometimes conveys an action carried out with energy and persistence, and may even be regarded as socially desirable (*Lloyd et al.*, 1984).

Moyer (1976) and Berkowitz (1993) see aggression as always involving behaviour, either physical or symbolic, performed with the intention of harming someone. They reserve the word *violence* to describe an extreme form of aggression in which a deliberate attempt is made to inflict serious physical injury on another person or damage property. One long-standing issue in social psychology concerns the causes of interpersonal aggression. For many years, debate has centred around the nature versus nurture controversy, that is, whether aggression, as a characteristic of human beings, is biologically determined (nature) or the product of learning and various environmental influences (nurture) (see Chapter 83).

This chapter reviews the claims made by theories of interpersonal aggression and considers evidence relating to them. It also looks at some of the ways in which aggressive behaviour can be reduced and controlled.

'Instinct' theories

According to Hobbes (1651), people are naturally competitive and hostile, interested only in their own power and gaining advantage over others. Hobbes argued that to prevent conflict and mutual destruction, people needed government. Two theories which share Hobbes's pessimistic views about people's nature are those proposed by Freud and Lorenz.

FREUD'S PSYCHOANALYTIC APPROACH

According to Freud, the purpose of all instincts is to reduce tension or excitation to a minimum and, ultimately, to totally eliminate them. Freud's early writing emphasised what he called *Eros*, the human drive for pleasure and self-preservation. After the great loss of lives in the First World War, however, Freud (1920, 1923) proposed the existence of *Thanatos*, a drive directed towards self-destruction, death and the return to an inanimate, lifeless state (which Freud saw as the only way of achieving the idyllic state we enjoyed in the womb and at the mother's breast: see Chapter 82).

Freud thought that because these two instincts conflicted, the self-directed aggression of Thanatos was satisfied by being turned *outward*, and that some other thing or person must be destroyed if we are not to destroy ourselves. So, unless a more acceptable way to express Thanatos could be achieved (through some sort of *cathartic activity* such as sport), people would act aggressively from time to time to dissipate or discharge their built-up aggressive energy. For Freud, then, just as we need to eat, drink and express our sexual needs periodically, so we need to express our hostile and destructive impulses periodically.

LORENZ'S ETHOLOGICAL APPROACH

Although Freud's and Lorenz's views are, in most respects, very different, Lorenz also saw aggression as being instinctive, with aggressive energy needing to be released periodically if it is not to build up to dangerously high levels. Lorenz (1966) argued that aggression is instinctive in all species because it is *adaptive*, that is, it allows animals to adapt to their environment, survive in it, and successfully reproduce. Lorenz defined aggression as:

'the fighting instinct in beast and man which is directed *against* members of the same species'.

Box 63.1   Ritualisation and appeasement rituals

Most animals have what Lorenz called 'built-in safety devices' which prevent them from killing members of their own species when they fight for territory or dominance. One device is *ritualisation*, a way of discharging aggression in a fixed, stereotyped pattern in which fights between members of the same species result in relatively little harm to either but allow a victor to emerge. For example, a fight between two wolves will end with the loser exposing its jugular vein to indicate submission and end the conflict (see Figure 63.1).

Alternatively, a conflict may be avoided by means of an *appeasement ritual*, in which a particular gesture will prevent an attack even when one animal is on the verge of attacking another. Thus, in one species of jackdaw, the nape section of the bottom of the head is clearly marked off from the rest of the body by its plumage and colouring. A conflict is avoided when one bird 'offers' its nape to a potential attacker.

Figure 63.1   Unlike non-humans, human aggression is no longer under the control of rituals

Lorenz felt that humans are biologically weaker, 'basically harmless', and lacking the strong compensating devices seen in non-humans. Whilst aggression is basically adaptive, for humans it is no longer under the control of rituals. This is not to say that human appeasement gestures are not effective, because behaviours like cowering, cringing, and begging for mercy clearly are. However, Lorenz argued that once we acquired the ability to kill each other through our *weapons technology*, in which aggression can take place without eye contact (as with intercontinental ballistic missiles), our appeasement rituals became ineffective. As Lea (1984) has noted:

'we have developed a technology which enables our intentions to override our instincts'.

An evaluation of instinct theories

Support for instinct theories has been claimed by Megargee (1966) in his study of people who had committed brutally aggressive crimes. Megargee found that such crimes were often committed by *overcontrolled individuals*. These people repress their anger and, over a period of time, the pressure to be aggressive builds up. Often, a seemingly trivial event provokes an aggressive outburst and, when the aggression has been released, the aggressor returns to a passive state in which he or she is seemingly incapable of violence (Megargee & Mendelsohn, 1962).

There are, however, many problems with instinct theories of aggression. Freud's theory, for example, is difficult to test empirically (see Chapter 1, pages 13–14). As Mummendey (1996) has noted:

'the essential concepts such as that of destructive energy are so global and inexact that one can derive no precise predictions or hypotheses that can then be tested. The psychoanalytic approach is really only able to attempt an explanation of events or behaviour that have already taken place'.

There is a large body of evidence to dispute Lorenz's claims. For example, Lea (1984) cites several examples of non-human aggression resulting in the loser's death, and he believes Lorenz's claim that aggression always stops before one of the animals is killed to be little more than a myth. Lorenz has also been criticised for failing to take account of how the *goals* of behaviour influence the degree of ritual. For example, whilst antelopes are more likely to engage in ritualised aggression when fighting over territory, they are less likely to do this when competing for a sexual partner. Finally, Lorenz's view of aggression as being spontaneous rather than reactive has also been questioned.

Like Freud, Lorenz believed that aggression does not occur in response to environmental stimuli, but spontaneously when aggressive energy builds up (the *hydraulic model*). Lorenz's evidence for this is actually very sparse, amounting to the male cichlid fish (which attacks its female mate) and an anecdote about his maiden aunt! (Siann, 1985). The view that aggression is inevitable because aggressive energy builds up, and is unrelated to external events, has been attacked by many biologists and ethologists (e.g. Hinde, 1974). In their view, aggression in non-humans is reactive and modifiable by a variety of internal and external conditions.

The frustration–aggression hypothesis

Freud's ideas on aggression had little impact until the publication of *Frustration and Aggression* by Dollard *et al.* (1939). Intended partly to 'translate' Freudian psychoanalytic concepts into learning theory terms, the frustration–aggression hypothesis proposes that:

'aggression is always a consequence of frustration and, contrariwise … the existence of frustration always leads to some form of aggression'.

In everyday language, 'frustration' refers to an unpleasant feeling produced by an unfulfilled desire. Dollard *et al.*, however, defined frustration as:

'an interference with the occurrence of an instigated goal-response at its proper time in the behaviour sequence'.

Put differently, frustration prevents an *expected reinforcer's* occurrence.

Whilst Dollard *et al.* agreed that aggression was an innate response, they argued that it would only be elicited in specific situations. Thus, whenever an important need was thwarted, the resulting frustration would produce an aggressive response. This does not mean that aggression is always directed towards the object of the frustration. Aggression may be delayed, disguised or displaced from its most obvious source to a more accessible target. One example of such displacement behaviour is *scapegoating* which, as was seen in Chapter 53 (see page 465), is one theory of prejudice and discrimination.

Evidence consistent with Dollard *et al.*'s hypothesis was reported by Barker *et al.* (1941). Young children were shown an attractive set of toys but prevented from playing with them. When the children were eventually allowed access to the toys, they threw them, stomped on them, and smashed them. These behaviours did not occur in a comparison group of children who were not frustrated. Despite this support, however, the original version of the frustration–aggression hypothesis has attracted much criticism.

Box 63.2   Some criticisms of the original frustration–aggression hypothesis

According to Miller (1941), frustration is an instigator of aggression, but situational factors (such as learned inhibition or the fear of retaliation) may prevent actual aggression from occurring. So, whilst frustration may make aggression more likely, it is far from being a *sufficient* cause of aggressive behaviour. Miller also suggested that frustration can produce several possible responses, of which aggression is only one. These include withdrawal, apathy, hopelessness, depression, and sometimes an increased effort to achieve the goal.

Frustration can produce different responses in different people in different situations (Kulik & Brown, 1979). Miell (1990) and Berkowitz (1993) have suggested that aggression is most likely when a person is close to achieving a goal, or the frustrator is perceived as being arbitrary or illegitimate. So, we are not usually bothered by a failure to reach a goal unless we believe that the frustrator intentionally or improperly interfered with our efforts.

This *attribution of intention* perspective (Brown & Kulik, 1979) is consistent with the definition of aggression as the (perceived) intention to harm another person. If there are mitigating circumstances, the attribution made by the victim may change (Weiner, 1992; see also page 548). Interestingly, research indicates that children who display chronic aggression have a strong attributional bias towards seeing others as acting against them with hostile intent, especially in ambiguous situations. These biased attributions often lead to retaliatory aggression (Taylor *et al.*, 1994).

Berkowitz's cue–arousal (or aggressive cue) theory

Whilst frustration and aggression are related, frustration does not always lead to aggression (see Box 63.2). Berkowitz (e.g. 1966, 1978, 1989) was the first to point out that aggression, like any other behaviour, can be reinforced. For example, a hired assassin kills for *money*, and frustration does not play a causal role in an assassin's behaviour. Moreover, things other than frustration can produce aggressive behaviour. For example, if two non-humans are placed in a cage and receive electric shocks to their feet, they are likely to fight (Carlson, 1987).

Berkowitz proposed that frustration produces *anger* rather than aggression. However, frustration is psychologically painful, and anything that is psychologically (or, indeed, physically) painful can produce aggression. According to Berkowitz, two conditions act together to produce aggression when frustration occurs. The first is a *readiness* to act aggressively. The second is the presence of *environmental cues* associated either with aggressive behaviour or with the frustrating person or object. For Berkowitz, then, whilst we might become angry as a response to frustration, aggressive behaviour will be elicited only when certain environmental cues are present.

Box 63.3   Three tests of Berkowitz's cue–arousal theory

- Geen & Berkowitz (1966) had a stooge, who was introduced as either Kirk Anderson or Bob Anderson, insult and berate participants for failing to solve a jigsaw puzzle. Participants then watched a film in which the actor Kirk Douglas was brutally beaten. Afterwards, participants were given the opportunity to administer supposed electric shocks to the stooge. Participants gave higher intensity 'shocks' to the stooge called Kirk. Geen and Berkowitz argued that because of its association with brutality in the film, 'Kirk' served as a cue to aggressive behaviour.

- Berkowitz & Geen (1966) introduced the stooge as Bob Kelly, Bob Dunne or Bob Riley. Dunne was the name of the victorious character in the film in which Kirk Douglas was brutally beaten. Douglas's character was called Kelly. The stooge received 'shocks' of greater intensity when he was called Kelly. Presumably, the character called Kelly was associated with an instance of successful aggression and this made it more likely that anger would be converted into aggression (Berkowitz, 1993).

- Berkowitz & LePage (1967) had participants perform a task which was then evaluated by a stooge. The evaluation involved the stooge delivering electric shocks to the participant. The number of shocks produced different levels of anger in participants. Later, participants were required to evaluate the stooge, also by delivering electric shocks. Participants were taken to a 'control room' and shown the shock apparatus. For some, a shotgun and revolver had been placed on a nearby table. Sometimes, participants were told that these belonged to the stooge, and sometimes they were given no explanation for their presence. In two other conditions, there were either badminton rackets and shuttlecocks on the table or no objects at all.

Angry participants delivered most shocks when the weapons were associated with the stooge, and only

slightly fewer shocks when they were present but not associated with the stooge. The no objects and badminton rackets conditions led to significantly fewer shocks being delivered. Berkowitz (1968) called this *the weapons effect*. In his view:

> 'guns not only permit violence, they can stimulate it as well. The finger pulls the trigger, but the trigger may also be pulling the finger'.

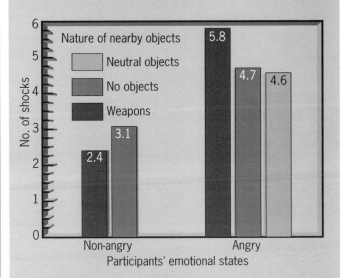

Figure 63.2   Mean number of shocks given as a function of presence of weapons (From Gross, 1996, and based on Berkowitz & Le Page, 1967)

Whilst several researchers have failed to replicate the weapons effect (Mummendey, 1996), Berkowitz (1995) cites several examples of successful replications in a number of countries. Indeed, in Sweden, Frodi (1975) reported the weapons effect among high-school boys even when they had not been angered by means of receiving electric shocks.

The results of Berkowitz's own experiments and those of other researchers suggest that frustration and pain are *aversive stimuli*. Other aversive stimuli include noise (Donnerstein & Wilson, 1976), uncomfortably high temperature (Bell & Baron, 1974) and foul odours such as cigarette smoke (Berkowitz, 1983).

Zillman's excitation-transfer theory

According to Zillman (1982), arousal from one source can be transferred to, and energise, some other response. This is because arousal takes time to dissipate. When we are aroused, aggression may be heightened provided that the aroused person has some disposition to react aggressively, and provided that the arousal is incorrectly attributed to the aggression-provoking event rather than to the correct source.

In one test of this, Zillman & Bryant (1974) created a state of arousal in participants by requiring them to ride bicycles. For some, a high level of arousal was induced, whilst for others a low level was induced. Then, participants played a game during which they were verbally insulted by a stooge. When participants were later given the opportunity to deliver a harsh noise in headphones worn by the stooge, significantly more noise was delivered by highly aroused participants.

> **Box 63.4 Excitation transfer and sexual arousal**
>
> Excitation-transfer theorists have been particularly interested in the relationship between sexual arousal and aggression (Zillman & Bryant, 1984). Unfortunately, the data have been inconsistent. 'Soft' pornography apparently either decreases or has no effect on aggression, whereas 'hard core' pornography can lead to an increase in aggressive behaviour (Donnerstein et al., 1987). Also, sexual excitement, combined with aggressive behaviour in the sexually arousing material, has been shown to produce an increase in aggression (Donnerstein & Berkowitz, 1981). The effects of observing aggressive behaviour are considered briefly in the following section, and in greater detail in Chapter 64.

Excitation-transfer theory sees the relationship between arousal and aggression as a *sequence*, in which arousal is generated and then, depending on its perceived causes, labelled, producing a specific emotion such as anger (Mummendey, 1996). Berkowitz (1990), however, disputes the existence of 'unspecific' or 'neutral' arousal. According to his *cognitive–neoassociationistic approach*, anger and aggression are *parallel* rather than sequential processes, because aversive events automatically lead to the instigation of aggression, depending on what situational cues are present (Mummendey, 1996).

Social learning theory

According to social learning theory (SLT), aggressive behaviours are learned through the *reinforcement* and *imitation* of aggressive 'models' (Bandura, 1965, 1973, 1994: see Chapter 32). Reinforcement of aggressive behaviour can occur in a number of ways. For example, a child who behaves aggressively in order to play with attractive toys will quickly learn to repeat the behaviour in the future. Non-tangible reinforcement, such as praise for 'being tough', can also increase the tendency to behave aggressively.

Imitation is the reproduction of learning through observation (*observational learning*), and involves observing other people who serve as models for behaviour. Bandura *et al.* (1961, 1963) demonstrated how a child's aggressive tendencies can be strengthened through *vicarious reinforcement* (seeing others being rewarded for behaving aggressively).

> **Box 63.5 Bandura *et al.*'s research into the effects of observing aggressive behaviour**
>
> Bandura's procedure involved 3-, 4- and 5-year-old children observing an adult model behaving aggressively towards an inflated plastic 'Bobo' doll. Later, the children were allowed to play with the doll themselves. Those who saw the adult model being reinforced for displaying aggressive behaviour performed significantly more imitative aggressive acts than those who saw the model's behaviour being neither reinforced nor punished. Those who saw the model being punished for behaving aggressively made fewest imitative responses of all.

Figure 63.3 Spontaneous imitation of an aggressive model

However, Bandura *et al.* pointed out the important distinction between *learning* and *performance*. The fact that a child does not perform an imitative behaviour does not necessarily mean that it has not been learned. In other experiments, Bandura (1965) showed that when children who had seen the model being punished for his behaviour were themselves offered rewards for behaving aggressively, they showed they had learned (or acquired) the model's behaviours just as well as those who saw the behaviours being reinforced.

Whilst there are methodological concerns with Bandura *et al.*'s research which make it difficult to generalise their findings to the 'real world', SLT has received support from a number of quarters (Hollin & Howells, 1997). For example, children who are raised by aggressive and physically abusive parents often behave in the same way (Kaufman & Zigler, 1987). Indeed, for Straus *et al.* (1980), 'each generation learns to be violent by being a participant in a violent family'. SLT has also contributed to our understanding of the role played by the media in both pro-social and anti-social behaviour. This contribution is considered in Chapter 64.

The social constructionist approach

The most recent theoretical approach to understanding aggression comes from social constructionists. Mummendey (1996) has proposed that whether or not a behaviour is aggressive or non-aggressive depends on whether the behaviour (or, in the case of failing to help someone, the non-behaviour) is *judged* to be aggressive either by an observer or by the performer. In Mummendey's view, the appraisal of a behaviour as aggressive involves going beyond a description to an *evaluation* of it. For Mummendey:

'when asking about the causes of aggression, more is of interest than simply the conditions for the occurrence of that behaviour. Of even greater importance are the conditions for judging the individual behaviour as "aggressive"'.

Mummendey's own research (Mummendey & Otten, 1989) and that of others (e.g. Mikula, 1994) suggests that the intention to harm, actual harm, and norm violation are the main criteria people use to label behaviour as aggressive. In looking for the cause of aggressive behaviour, then:

'we should not concentrate on the conditions that energise individual drives or reduce the rational control of

behaviour. Rather, we should look for the conditions (at least from the actor's point of view) which make intentionally harming another person seem both situationally appropriate and justified' (Mummendey, 1996).

The reduction and control of aggressive behaviour

CATHARSIS
Both the Freudian and ethological approaches to aggression propose that the most effective way of reducing it is through *catharsis*. The view that giving people the opportunity to 'let off steam' through arousing but non-harmful actions is not, however, strongly supported by experimental evidence. Thus, watching scenes of filmed or television violence (Williams, 1986: and see also Chapter 64) does not appear to be effective in reducing aggression, nor does attacking inanimate objects (Mallick & McCandless, 1966) or attending sporting events (Arms *et al.*, 1980). Indeed, aggression may actually be *increased* by such conditions (Baron & Byrne, 1994).

Similarly, acting out aggression has been shown to lead to even more aggression (Geen *et al.*, 1975). Possibly, the reduction of unpleasant feelings creates the conditions for *negative reinforcement*, which is achieved through the termination of an aversive stimulus. So, when a person behaves cathartically and feels better afterwards, the experience tends to increase rather than decrease the likelihood of aggressive behaviour occurring (Carlson, 1987).

PUNISHMENT
Punishment can be effective in deterring aggressive behaviour provided that it is prompt, of sufficient magnitude to be aversive, and highly probable following the aggressive behaviour (Bower & Hilgard, 1981: see Chapter 40, pages 349–350). However, punishment does not tend to be used in this way, at least in some societies including our own. In Britain, many crimes (even those involving aggression) are not reported to the police and the 'clear up' rate for the most frequent categories of anti-social behaviour (theft and robbery) is very low (Holdaway, 1988).

The weak association between committing an anti-social act and the probability of being caught and punished for it, means that most criminals hardly think about incarceration at all when contemplating and committing anti-social acts (Giddens, 1993). The delay between committing an anti-social act and being punished for it can

547

be very long and, when punishment is administered, it can vary greatly. Additionally, being punished for behaving anti-socially does not teach new, positive behaviours (as, perhaps, is indicated by the fact that 60 per cent of offenders reoffend and return to prison within four years: Giddens, 1993).

Whilst common sense suggests that punishment is an effective way of deterring anti-social behaviour, psychological research suggests a more cautious view. Punishment may also be ineffective because the recipient sees it as being unjustified (particularly if it is not applied in the same way to others). Indeed, when this is the case, anti-social behaviour may be *more* likely to occur because of the recipient's desire for *revenge* (Baron & Byrne, 1994).

EXPOSURE TO NON-AGGRESSIVE MODELS

A further reason why punishment may not be effective in reducing anti-social behaviour is that those who deliver it are seen as *aggressive models* by those who receive it. Similarly, in Bandura's (1965) study, children who observed an adult being punished for behaving aggressively still behaved more aggressively than children who did not witness any aggression at all. As shown in Chapter 64, exposure to aggressive behaviour as portrayed by the media can produce heightened aggression amongst at least some of those who observe it.

Box 63.6 Setting a non-aggressive example

It is impossible to eliminate all aggressive models from society (Deaux *et al.*, 1993). However, it may be possible to reduce aggression by adding more non-aggressive models to the environment. A number of studies have shown that seeing other people behaving non-aggressively, even in the face of extreme provocation, can reduce aggression (e.g. Donnerstein & Donnerstein, 1976).

Given that children raised by aggressive and physically abusive parents often behave in the same way, parents and other significant role models could reduce aggression by not engaging in those behaviours, either with their own children or with other adults. For Patterson (1986), encouraging children (by means of positive reinforcement) to develop socially positive traits such as nurturance and sensitivity, and at the same time discouraging inappropriate aggression (using, for example, consistent but non-physical punishment), can strengthen pro-social behaviours.

SOCIAL SKILLS TRAINING, COGNITIVE INTERVENTIONS, AND INCOMPATIBLE RESPONSES

Baron & Byrne (1994) suggest three other approaches that might be effective in reducing aggression. These are social skills training, cognitive interventions, and incompatible responses.

Social skill training

People who lack the ability to communicate their wishes to others often suffer repeated frustration, and this can lead them to behave aggressively (Hollin & Howells, 1997). Those lacking essential *social skills* evidently account for a high proportion of the violence occurring in any given society (Toch, 1980). Toch's solution, therefore, is to train people in the essential social skills. Several studies (e.g. Goldstein *et al.*, 1981; Schneider, 1991) suggest that such training can be effective in reducing the likelihood of a person being either the source or a target of aggressive behaviour.

Cognitive interventions

If, as seems likely, our attributions for a person's behaviour determine the likelihood of us behaving aggressively, it seems reasonable to propose that changing our attributions for a particular behaviour might be effective in reducing aggression. Several studies (e.g. Kremer & Stephens, 1983) have found that when people are made aware of the *mitigating circumstances* for a person's potentially aggression-inducing behaviour, they are less likely to behave aggressively, provided that the information about the mitigating circumstances is given early enough and is believable.

Incompatible responses

According to the principle of *reciprocal inhibition* (Wolpe, 1958: see Chapter 74), it is impossible to experience two incompatible emotional responses simultaneously. Several researchers (e.g. Baron, 1983) have applied this principle to the reduction of aggressive behaviour, and shown that when emotional states incompatible with anger or actual aggression are induced in people, the tendency to react aggressively is reduced.

CLINICAL APPROACHES TO THE REDUCTION OF AGGRESSION

With those people convicted of violent offences and referred by a probation officer to the forensic services, a variety of techniques drawn from mainstream clinical psychology may be used (Hollin & Howells, 1997).

Box 63.7 Using a multi-faceted intervention programme with an aggressive adult offender

John, aged 23 was described by his probation officer as:

'a violent man who seems incapable of controlling his temper … he displays his anger verbally and physically …he describes himself as like a "fuse" ready to explode … he is very disturbed by his behaviour and … fears that he may hurt someone seriously'.

The four techniques used with John were:

- **desensitisation**, in which he imagined provoking stimuli and then used relaxation to bring about self-control over his angry thoughts and arousal (see Chapter 74);

- **active challenging** of his thoughts and the development of more realistic views of other people;

- **environmental control**, in which he was encouraged to remove himself from risky environments, such as nightclubs;

- **rehearsal and practice** of alternative ways of dealing with the escalating verbal exchanges that preceded violent incidents.

The success of the *anger management* interventions with John suggest that a knowledge of the individual person, the situations in which he or she behaves aggressively, and the complex interactions between cognition, emotion and behaviour can all be useful in reducing aggressive behaviour.

(Taken from Hollin & Howells, 1997).

Conclusions

The occurrence of aggressive behaviour has been explained in a variety of ways. Several approaches to the reduction and control of aggressive behaviour have also been advanced. As with theories of aggression, research findings support the effectiveness of some approaches more than others.

Summary

- There are different types of aggression including **anti-social**, **sanctioned** and **pro-social**. Aggression always involves some behaviour, either physical or symbolic, intended to harm another person. **Violence** is an extreme form of aggression involving an attempt to inflict serious physical injury or damage to property.

- Both Freud and Lorenz explained aggression in terms of **instincts**. However, Freud's theory is difficult to test experimentally, and a large body of evidence disputes Lorenz's. Freud and Lorenz believed that aggression occurs spontaneously when aggressive energy builds up (the **hydraulic model**). There is little support for this, and many biologists and ethologists see aggression in non-humans as being reactive and modifiable by internal and external conditions.

- Dollard *et al.*'s **frustration–aggression hypothesis** was intended to translate Freudian concepts into learning theory terms. Whilst agreeing that aggression is an innate response, they argued that it would only be triggered in specific situations. The original version of the hypothesis has been modified in various ways. For example, frustration may make aggression more likely, but it is **not** sufficient to cause aggressive behaviour.

- According to Berkowitz's **cue–arousal theory**, frustration produces **anger**. However, this only results in aggression if there is a **readiness** to act aggressively and there are **environmental cues** associated with aggressive behaviour or the frustrating person/object. Experimental tests of the theory measure aggressive responses when participants are frustrated in the presence/absence of aggressive cues, such as guns (the **weapons effect**).

- Zillman's **excitation-transfer theory** proposes that arousal from one source can be transferred to, and energise, some other response. Because arousal takes time to dissipate, aggression may be heightened if an aroused person is disposed to act aggressively and the arousal is incorrectly attributed to the aggression-provoking event.

- Excitation-transfer theory sees the arousal-aggression relationship as a **sequence**. However, Berkowitz rejects the existence of 'unspecific'/'neutral' arousal. His **cognitive–neoassociationistic approach** sees anger and aggression as parallel processes.

- **Social learning theory** sees aggressive behaviours as being learned through **reinforcement** and **imitation** (closely related to **observational learning**). Bandura *et al.* showed that children's aggressive tendencies can be strengthened by **vicarious reinforcement**, and drew an important distinction between the **learning** and **performance** of aggressive behaviours.

- According to the **social constructionist approach**, behaviour is aggressive or non-aggressive as **judged** to be so, either by an observer or actor. Calling behaviour 'aggressive' involves an evaluation of it. The main criteria used to label behaviour as aggressive are the intention to harm, actual harm, and norm violation.

- There is little support for **catharsis** as a way of reducing aggression. If anything, aggression may be increased through cathartic activity, possibly because of the **negative reinforcement** of aggressive behaviour through the reduction of unpleasant feelings.

■ Under certain circumstances, **punishment** can be effective in deterring aggressive behaviour. However, it fails to teach new, positive behaviours and the punished individual may see it as unjustified, prompting a desire for **revenge**. The punisher is also an **aggressive model**.

■ Increasing the number of **non-aggressive models** in society may reduce aggression. Pro-social behaviours can be increased by combining positive reinforcement for socially positive traits with punishment for inappropriate aggression.

■ **Social skills training** can be effective in reducing aggression as can **cognitive interventions**. The latter involves changing people's attributions for particular behaviours, such as making them aware of **mitigating circumstances**.

■ Based on **reciprocal inhibition**, the tendency to react aggressively can be reduced by inducing emotional states incompatible with anger or actual aggression. **Clinical approaches** to treating violent offenders include **desensitisation**, **active challenging**, **environmental control**, and **rehearsal and practice**. Successful **anger management** involves a knowledge of the aggressive individual, the situations in which s/he behaves aggressively, and the complex interactions between cognition, emotion and behaviour.

64

MEDIA INFLUENCES ON PRO-SOCIAL AND ANTI-SOCIAL BEHAVIOUR

Introduction and overview

Chapters 62 and 63 looked at theory and research relating to pro- and anti-social behaviour. This chapter examines the influence of the *media* on these two types of social behaviour. The media are:

'the methods and organisations used by specialist groups to convey messages to large, socially mixed and widely dispersed audiences' (Trowler, 1988).

Most research has looked at media's (in particular television's) influence on anti-social behaviour. However, there has been a growing interest in the relationship between the media and pro-social behaviour. This chapter looks first at the media and anti-social behaviour and then turns its attention to pro-social behaviour.

How much aggressive behaviour is shown on television?

The basic method of quantifying the amount of violence shown on television involves simple counting techniques. Researchers define violence objectively, and then code samples of television programmes for incidents which match those definitions.

Box 64.1   Gerbner's studies of violence on American television (Gerbner, 1972; Gerbner & Gross, 1976; Gerbner *et al.*, 1980, 1986)

Defining violence as:

'the overt expression of physical force against others or self, or the compelling of an action against one's will on pain of being hurt or killed',

Gerbner's team have found that since 1967 the percentage of television shows containing violent episodes has remained about the same, but the number of violent episodes per show has gradually increased. In 1986, there was an average of around five violent acts per hour on prime-time television. On children's weekend shows, mostly consisting of cartoons, about 20 violent acts per hour occurred.

Gerbner's analysis provided the framework for British research initiated by Halloran & Croll (1972) and the BBC's Audience Research Department. Both studies found that violence was a common feature of programming, although it was not as prevalent on British as on American television. Cumberbatch (1987), commissioned by the BBC, analysed all programmes broadcast on the (then) four terrestrial channels in four separate weeks between May and September 1986.

Box 64.2   The main findings from Cumberbatch's (1987) study

Cumberbatch found that 30 per cent of programmes contained some violence, the overall frequency being 1.14 violent acts per programme and 1.68 violent acts per hour. Each act lasted around 25 seconds, so violence occupied just over 1 per cent of total television time. These figures were lower if boxing and wrestling were excluded, but higher (at 1.96 violent acts per hour) if verbal threats were included.

Death resulted from violent acts in 26 per cent of cases, but in 61 per cent of acts no injuries were shown and the victim was portrayed as being in pain or stunned. In 83 per cent of cases, no blood was shown as a result of a violent act, and considerable blood and gore occurred in only 0.2 per cent of cases. Perpetrators of violent acts were much more likely to be portrayed as 'baddies' than 'goodies', and violence occurred twice as frequently in law-breaking than in law-upholding contexts.

Cumberbatch argued that whilst violence and concerns about it had increased in society in the decade up to 1987, this was not reflected by a proportional increase on television, even in news broadcasts. He concluded that:

'while broadcasters may take some comfort from our data on trends in television violence, they must expect to be continually reminded of their responsibilities in this area and be obliged to acknowledge that a significant minority of people will remain concerned about what's on the box'.

More recently, the BBC and ITV commissioned Gunter & Harrison (1995) to look at the frequency of violence on terrestrial and satellite channels (Armstrong, 1997).

Box 64.3 Some findings from Gunter & Harrison's (1995) analysis of violence on British television

The researchers monitored 2084 programmes on eight channels over four weeks in October 1994 and January/February 1995. The findings include:

- On BBC 1 and 2, ITV and Channel 4, 28 per cent of programmes contained violent acts, compared with 52 per cent on Sky One, UK Gold, Sky Movies and the Movie Channel.

- Violence occupied 0.61 per cent of time on the terrestrial channels and 1.53 per cent on the satellite stations.

- The greatest proportion of violent acts (70 per cent) occurred in dramas and films; 19 per cent occurred in children's programmes.

- Most violent acts occurred in contemporary settings in inner-city locations. The majority of perpetrators were young, white males.

- One per cent of programmes contained 19 per cent of all violent acts. *Double Impact*, shown on the Movie Channel, for example, contained 105 violent acts, as against an average of 9.7.

- The United States was the most common location for violence (47 per cent), followed by the United Kingdom (12 per cent). The third most likely location was a cartoon setting (7 per cent) and then science fiction locations (4 per cent).

(Taken from Frean, 1995, and Armstrong, 1997)

On the basis of the finding that violent acts account for one per cent of programme content on terrestrial channels and less than two per cent on some satellite stations, and the fact that one per cent of programmes contained 19 per cent of all violent acts, Gunter and Harrison concluded that:

'The picture that emerges is not one of a television system permeated by violence, but rather one in which violence represents only a tiny part of the output and where it tends to be concentrated principally in a relatively small number of programmes' (cited in Frean, 1995).

An almost identical conclusion was reached by the US National Television Violence Study (1996).

As well as television, violent behaviour can also be seen at the *cinema* or on *video* (and what is shown may or may not be subsequently screened on television). Evidence indicates that a large percentage of 9–11-year-olds have watched 18-rated videos, including the particularly violent *Nightmare on Elm Street*, *The Silence of the Lambs*, and *Pulp Fiction* (Ball & Nuki, 1996; Wark & Ball, 1996).

Figure 64.1 Jean-Claude van Damme performs another aggressive act in *Double Impact*

The effects of television on children's behaviour

Research into the effects of television on children's behaviour began in America in the 1960s, following the publication of the results of Bandura *et al.*'s 'Bobo doll experiments' (see Chapter 63, page 546). These 'first generation' (or 'phase one': Baron, 1977) studies involved filmed (or symbolic) models. Essentially, Bandura *et al.* showed that children can acquire new aggressive responses not previously in their behavioural repertoire merely through exposure to a filmed or televised model.

If children could learn new ways of harming others through such experiences, then the implication was that media portrayals of violence might be contributing to increased levels of violence in society (Baron, 1977). However, Bandura (1965) warned against such an interpretation in the light of his finding that the learning of aggressive responses does not necessarily mean that they will be displayed in a child's behaviour (see Chapter 63, page 547). Nevertheless, the *possibility* that such effects could occur was sufficient to focus considerable public attention on Bandura *et al.*'s research.

HOW MUCH TELEVISION DO PEOPLE WATCH?

American research conducted since 1965 suggests that the time people in a typical household spend in front of the television has, in general, been steadily increasing (Burger, 1982; Liebert & Sprafkin, 1988). However, these data are typically derived from paper-and-pen surveys concerning viewing habits and may not be reliable.

Anderson *et al.* (1986) installed automated time-lapse video recording equipment in the homes of 99 families consisting of 462 people aged between one and 62. The recordings began when the television was switched on and stopped when it was switched off. One camera used a wide-angled lens to record people's behaviour in the room where the television was, whilst a second focused on the television screen itself.

> **Box 64.4   The main findings from Anderson et al.'s (1986) study**
>
> - No one actually watches the television for more than 75 per cent of the time it is on.
>
> - Children spend an average of 12.8 hours per week with the television on and 9.14 hours looking at it. Adults spend an average of 11.5 hours per week with the television on, and 7.56 hours looking at it.
>
> - Adult females pay significantly less attention to television than do children. Adult males look at the television more than females but watch it less than school-aged children.
>
> - The number of hours spent looking at television increases up to the age of ten, after which it decreases, levels off at about age 17, and continues around the same level (ten hours per week) into adulthood.

Exactly why people have the television on but do not watch it is an interesting question in its own right! However, Anderson *et al.*'s findings suggest that data about how much television people *watch* should be treated with caution.

Figure 64.2   The fact that the television is on does not necessarily mean that anyone is watching it

HOW DO VIEWERS PERCEIVE VIOLENCE?

Much of the concern over television's effects has centred on children. Cumberbatch (1987) found that whilst violence was more likely after 9 p.m., and whilst violence in children's programmes was rare, a notable exception was *cartoons*. Whether children perceive cartoons as representing 'reality' is debatable.

According to Gunter & McAleer (1990), viewers can be highly discriminating when it comes to portrayals of violence, and do not invariably read into television content the same meanings researchers do. Thus, merely knowing how often certain pre-defined incidents occur in programmes does not tell us how significant these features are for viewers.

Viewers' perceptions of how violent television content is, then, may not agree with objective counts of violence in programmes. However, *realism* appears to be an important element in viewers' perceptions of violence, since real-life incidents in news and documentary programmes are generally rated as being more violent than those in fictional settings. Children are very similar to adults as far as their judgements of the *amounts* of violence are concerned. However, their *ratings* of violence differ and, with cartoons, an objectively high number of violent acts may be subjectively perceived as hardly containing any. Subjective assessment of violence should, therefore, be incorporated into assessments of the amount of violence shown on television (Gunter & McAleer, 1990).

METHODS USED TO STUDY TELEVISION VIOLENCE

What Baron (1977) calls 'phase two' research (research into the effects of media violence) has been conducted using various methodological approaches. *Correlational studies* typically involve asking people which programmes they like best and which they watch most often. These data are then correlated with measures of aggression given by parents, teachers, self-reports, peers, and so on. Evidence from such studies has generally been inconsistent, but one finding is that the overall amount of viewing is related to self-reports of aggressive behaviour. Of course, it is possible that those who watch violent television are *different* in some way from those who do not, and the inability to infer cause and effect in correlational studies weakens this methodology (Freedman, 1984: see Chapter 2).

Laboratory studies are designed to enable the causal link between watching violent television and behaving aggressively to be established (if it exists). Liebert & Baron (1972) randomly assigned children to two groups. One watched *The Untouchables*, a violent television programme, whilst the other watched an equally engaging and arousing, but non-violent, sports competition. Afterwards, the children were allowed to play. Those who had watched the violent programme behaved more aggressively than the others.

The problem with laboratory studies is that most use small and unrepresentative samples who are exposed to the independent variable under highly contrived and unnatural viewing conditions. The measures of television viewing and aggression tend to be so far removed from normal everyday behaviour that it is doubtful whether such studies have any relevance to the real world (Gunter & McAleer, 1990). Much more ecologically valid are *field experiments* (see Chapter 2). In these, children or teenagers are assigned to view violent or non-violent programmes for a period of a few days or weeks.

Measures of aggressive behaviour, fantasy, attitude and so on are taken before, during and after the period of controlled viewing. To ensure control over actual viewing, children in group or institutional settings are studied, mostly from nursery schools, residential schools, or institutions for adolescent boys. In general, the results show that children who watch violent television are more aggressive than those who do not (Parke *et al.*, 1977).

The weakness of the field experiment, however, is that the setting cannot be as well controlled as that of the laboratory experiment. As a result, we cannot be certain that the *only* difference between the children is who watches violent and non-violent television, especially when par-

ticipants are not assigned randomly to conditions. In Parke *et al.*'s study, for example, 'cottages' (or pre-existing *groups*), rather than individuals, were assigned to the viewing conditions. Also, and by definition, such participants (juvenile delinquent males in Parke *et al.*'s study) are not representative of children or adolescents in general.

Box 64.5 Longitudinal panel studies

Like experiments, but unlike correlational studies, *longitudinal panel studies* can say something about cause and effect *and* normally use representative samples. Their aim is to discover relationships that may exist or develop over time between television viewing and behaviour. These studies, then, look at television's *cumulative* influence and whether or not attitudes and behaviour are linked with watching it.

American (e.g. Lefkowitz *et al.*, 1972; Eron & Huesmann, 1985; Phillips, 1986) and British research (e.g. Sims & Gray, 1993; Bailey, 1993) shows that such a link exists. Sims and Gray, for example, reviewed an extensive body of literature linking heavy exposure to media violence and subsequent aggressive behaviour. Similarly, Bailey's study of 40 adolescent murderers and 200 young sex offenders showed repeated viewing of violent and pornographic videos to be 'a significant causal factor'. This was particularly important in adolescents who abused while they were babysitting, where videos provided 'a potential source of immediate arousal for the subsequent act', including imitating violent images.

However, at least some studies have failed to find such a link. Milavsky *et al.* (1982) found only small associations between exposure to violent programmes and verbal and physical aggression amongst 3200 elementary school children and adolescents. Variables such as family background, social environment, and school performance were actually much better predictors of aggressiveness, if not crime (Ford, 1998).

One of the most useful kinds of study is the *natural experiment*, in which the researcher does not manipulate an independent variable, but takes advantage of a fortuitous and naturally occurring division (see Chapter 2). Williams (1986) studied a community ('Notel') where television had only been recently introduced. This community was compared with one in which there was a single television channel and another with several channels. Verbal and physical aggression in both male and female 6–11-year-olds increased over a two-year period following the introduction of television to 'Notel', but no such increase occurred in the communities that already had television.

In July 1994, a study began to look at the effects of the introduction of television to St Helena. This remote island in the south-east Atlantic has fewer than 6000 inhabitants, none of whom had ever seen live television. Of its 9–12-year-olds, only 3.4 per cent have behavioural problems, compared with 14 per cent of children in London. Of the 3–4-year-olds, less than 7 per cent have behavioural problems, compared with 12 per cent in London. The figure of 3.4 per cent for the 9–12-year-olds is the lowest ever recorded for any age range anywhere in the world.

Prior to several 24-hour channels (including BBC World Television, MNET [a South African commercial service] and the American satellite channel, CNN) being introduced, the only access the islanders had to news was on short-wave radio from the BBC World Service. Whilst the island has three video libraries, it does not have a cinema.

The study's leader, Tony Charlton, is looking at the effects of the introduction of television on 59 pre-school children, who will be monitored until they are 13, and all 800 children on the island who are of first and middle-school age. According to Charlton:

'the children on the island represent a unique control group – it is extraordinarily difficult to find a group that doesn't have television'.

Prior to the study beginning, Charlton noted that:

'it could be that excessive viewing interferes with the development of social skills and mental capacities which children need to acquire. But there could be enormous educational benefits'.

In the fourth year of the seven-year study, *pro-social behaviour* (defined as helping others and playing amicably) has not only been maintained since television's introduction, but has actually *improved* slightly.

(Based on Cooper, 1994, McIlroy, 1994, Frean, 1994, Lee, 1996, and Midgley , 1998)

Despite the findings described above, on the basis of the studies that have been carried out, involving at least 100,000 participants (Hearold, 1986), many researchers believe that there is a link between television and aggressive behaviour in children and adolescents (Singer, 1989). Indeed, the American National Institute of Mental Health's (1982) review of 2500 studies led it to conclude that:

'the consensus amongst most of the research community is that violence on television does lead to aggressive behaviour by children and teenagers who watch the programmes. This conclusion is based on laboratory experiments and field studies. Not all children become aggressive, of course, but the correlations between violence and aggression are positive. In magnitude, television violence is as strongly correlated with aggressive behaviour as any other behavioural variable that has been measured'.

HOW DOES TELEVISION EXERT ITS EFFECTS?

Four specific effects of television violence have been investigated. These are *arousal*, *disinhibition*, *imitation* and *desensitisation*.

Arousal: Arousal is a non-specific, physiological response, whose 'meaning' will be defined by the viewer in terms of the type of programme being watched (Zillman, 1978). It has been claimed that watching violence on television increases a viewer's overall level of emotional arousal and excitement (Berkowitz, 1993). However, there does not seem to be any strong overall relationship between perceiving a programme as violent and verbal or physiological reports of emotional arousal (Gadow & Sprafkin, 1993; Bryant & Zillman, 1994), although the more *realistic* the violence is perceived as being, the greater the reported arousal and involvement are likely to be.

Disinhibition: Disinhibition is the reduction of inhibitions about behaving aggressively oneself or coming to believe that aggression is a permitted or legitimate way of solving problems or attaining goals. Berkowitz's cue–arousal (aggressive cue) theory, discussed in Chapter 63, is relevant here.

Imitation: Perhaps the most direct link between watching television and the viewer's own behaviour is imitation. This, of course, is directly related to Bandura *et al.*'s studies of imitative aggression (see page 546). However, SL theorists acknowledge the role of cognitive factors as mediating between stimulus and response (Bandura, 1994), and so how television violence is perceived and interpreted, and the issue of realism, are clearly important intervening variables for both children and adults.

Desensitisation: Desensitisation is the reduction in emotional response to television violence (and an increased acceptance of violence in real life) as a result of repeatedly viewing it. As with drug tolerance, increasingly violent programmes may be required to produce an emotional response (Gadow & Sprafkin, 1989). In one study implicating desensitisation, Drabman & Thomas (1974) showed eight-year-olds a violent or non-violent programme before witnessing a 'real' (but actually staged) fight between two other children. Those who saw the violent programme were much less likely than those who saw the non-violent programme to tell an adult that a fight was occurring.

RECONSIDERING MEDIA VIOLENCE

The debate about media violence and aggression's relationship is far from being resolved (Barker & Petley, 1997; Harrower, 1998). In Britain, the link between the two was brought back into the spotlight following two-year-old James Bulger's murder by two teenage boys in February, 1993. At their trial, Mr Justice Moreland said:

'It is not for me to pass judgement on their upbringing, but I suspect that exposure to violent video films may, in part, be an explanation' (cited in Cumberbatch, 1997).

The call for legislation controlling the supply of videos to children was supported by many psychologists, including Newson (1994), whose report (*Video Violence and the Protection of Children*) was also endorsed by many psychiatrists and paediatricians.

Cumberbatch (1997), however, has questioned the validity of the evidence on which Newson's report was based. He notes that whilst it might be true that the father of one of the murderers of James Bulger had rented the video *Child's Play 3* some weeks before the murder occurred (as one British tabloid claimed), his son was not living with him at that time, disliked horror films, and was upset by violence in videos. Similarly, it was claimed that the massacre of 16 people in Hungerford in 1987 was inspired by the murderer seeing the character 'Rambo' in the film *First Blood*. In fact, there is no evidence to support this claim (Cumberbatch, 1997).

Cumberbatch has also criticised Comstock & Paik's (1991) conclusion that, based on Huesmann & Eron's (1986) cross-national survey in six countries (Holland, Australia, USA, Israel, Poland and Finland), viewing television violence at an early age is a predictor of later aggression.

Box 64.8 Cumberbatch's criticisms of the claim that viewing television violence at an early age is a predictor of later aggression

- The Dutch researchers concluded that their results showed no effects of television and refused to allow their findings to be included in Huesmann and Eron's edited book of the research study.
- The Australian research showed no significant correlations between early television violence viewing and later aggression.

- The American study found that when initial aggression was controlled for, the correlation between early television viewing and later aggression was significant only in girls.
- Israeli researchers found significant effects in the city samples but not in the Kibbutz samples.
- In Poland, the researchers agreed that a greater preference for violent viewing was predictive of later aggression, but that 'the effects are not large and must be treated cautiously'.
- The Finnish researchers appeared to misunderstand their own data. Rather than there being a positive correlation between viewing violent television and aggressive behaviour, the correlation is actually *negative*, indicating that the more television is watched, the *less* aggressive children were later.

(Adapted from Cumberbatch, 1997)

Cumberbatch (1997) cites several other studies (e.g. Hagell & Newburn, 1994) which cast doubt on claims about the connection between media violence and aggression in children. In his view:

'it is all too easy to scaremonger. However, we should remember that Britain is still a safe, highly regulated country. UK television has roughly half the amount of violence as most countries studied. It is ironic that the media seem largely to blame for the particularly British moral panic about our behaviour'.

The media and pro-social behaviour

According to Gunter & McAleer (1990):

'concern about the possible anti-social influences of television far outweighs the consideration given to any other area of children's involvement with television ... Television programmes contain many examples of good behaviour, of people acting kindly and with generosity. It is equally logical to assume that these portrayals provide models for children to copy'.

TELEVISION VIOLENCE AND CATHARSIS

One positive effect of television might be that witnessing others behaving aggressively helps viewers to get their aggressive feelings 'out of their systems' and hence be less likely to behave aggressively. The claim that television can act as a form of *vicarious catharsis* is based partly on the theories of aggression advanced by Freud and Lorenz (see Chapter 63, pages 542–543).

The evidence does not, however, support the view that television is cathartic for everybody. If a discharge of hostile feelings can occur at all, it is probably restricted to people of a particular personality type or those who score high on cognitive measures of fantasy, daydreaming and imagination (Singer, 1989). For only some people, then, does television violence have positive effects and provide a means of reducing aggressive feelings (Gunter & McAleer, 1990).

TELEVISION AND PRO-SOCIAL BEHAVIOUR

If television can have harmful effects as a result of watching anti-social behaviour then, presumably, it can have beneficial effects by promoting pro-social behaviour. According to Gunter & McAleer (1990), the evidence for the pro-social effects of television can be grouped into four types.

Box 64.9   The evidence for the pro-social effects of television

- **Laboratory studies with prepared television or filmed material:** Specially prepared materials have been shown to influence courage, the delay of gratification, adherence to rules, charitable behaviour, friendliness, and affectionate behaviour.

- **Laboratory studies using broadcast materials specially produced for social skills teaching purposes:** Television productions designed to enhance the social maturity and responsibility of young viewers include *Sesame Street* and *Mister Rogers' Neighborhood*. Children who watch these programmes are able to identify and remember the cooperative and helping behaviours emphasised in certain segments of them. Some programmes are better at encouraging pro-social behaviour in children than others, but the reasons for this are unclear.

- **Laboratory studies with programme materials from popular television series:** Specially manufactured television programmes or film clips influence children's pro-social tendencies, at least when the pro-social behaviour portrayed is very similar to that requested of the child. However, only some evidence indicates that ordinary broadcast material can enhance a wide range of helping behaviours.

- **Field studies relating amount of viewing of pro-social television content to strength of pro-social behaviour tendencies:** Children who watch little television, but watch a lot of programmes with high levels of pro-social content, are more likely than others to behave pro-socially. However, the correlations between viewing habits and pro-social behaviour are

lower than those between viewing habits and anti-social behaviour.

In part, this may be because pro-social behaviours are verbally mediated and often subtle, whereas anti-social behaviours are blatant and physical. Children learn better from simple, direct and active presentation, and so aggressive behaviours may be more readily learned. Also, the characters who display pro-social behaviour (typically female and non-white) and anti-social behaviour (typically male and white) may confound the relative influence of pro-social and anti-social behaviours with the types of character that portray them.

(Taken from Gunter & McAleer, 1990)

On the basis of their review of the literature, Gunter and McAleer concluded that:

> 'televised examples of good behaviour can encourage children to behave in friendlier and more thoughtful ways to others'.

An alternative approach to what Greenfield (1984) has called *television literacy* involves teaching children to be 'informed consumers' of television. This includes distinguishing between social reality and the (at least sometimes) make-believe world of television, understanding the nature and purpose of advertisements, and interpreting and assessing sex-role and minority-group stereotyping.

Huesmann *et al.* (1983) allocated young children known to be 'heavy' watchers of television to a control or experimental group. The experimental group received three training sessions designed to reduce the modelling of aggressive behaviour seen on television. They were taught that television does not portray the world as it really is, that camera techniques and special effects give the illusion that characters are performing their highly aggressive and unrealistic feats, and that most people use other methods to solve the problems encountered by characters in television programmes. Compared with the control group, the experimental group showed less overall aggressive behaviour and lowered identification with televised characters. These effects had persisted when the participants were followed up two years later.

COMPUTER GAMES AND PRO-SOCIAL BEHAVIOUR

According to Griffiths (1997), little is known about the long-term effects of playing violent computer games, but great concern has been voiced that such games may have a more adverse effect on children than television because of the child's *active involvement*. Griffiths's review of research indicates that the effects of long-term exposure to computer games on subsequent aggressive behaviour are 'at best speculative'. As regards pro-social behaviour, computer games have received support from a number of researchers (e.g. Loftus & Loftus, 1983; Silvern, 1986).

Box 64.10   The positive effects of computer games

- Computer games have become an integral part of modern language teaching in America because they are seen:

    'as a motivating device, a means for providing comprehensible input and a catalyst for communicative practice and the negotiation of meaning' (Hubbard, 1991).

    However, whether a game is perceived as educational depends on factors such as the player's age, gender, proficiency level and educational background.

- Computer games give children access to 'state of the art' technology, a sense of confidence, and equip them with computer-related skills for the future (Surrey, 1982).

- Computer games may also promote social interaction. In a study on the impact of computers on family life, Mitchell (1983, cited in Griffiths, 1993) found that families generally viewed computer games as promoting interaction in a beneficial way through co-operation and competition.

- The aggressive content of some computer games may be cathartic (see page 556) in that it allows players to release their stress and aggression in a non-destructive way, and has the effect of relaxing the players (Kestenbaum & Weinstein, 1984). Other benefits include the enhancement of cognitive skills, a sense of mastery, control and accomplishment, and a reduction in other youth problems due to 'addictive interest' (!) in video games (Anderson & Ford, 1986).

(Adapted from Griffiths, 1993)

According to Griffiths (1997), there appear to be some genuine applied aspects of computer game playing, although he notes that many of the assertions made in Box 64.10 were subjectively formulated and not based on empirical research findings.

And finally ...

In a lecture given in 1994, the BBC newsreader Martyn Lewis claimed that television producers were failing to reflect the true state of the world through their tendencies to ignore positive news (Lewis & Rowe, 1994). BBC managers attacked Lewis's views, charging that he was calling for news to be trivialised in order to make it more palatable, a charge Lewis vigorously denied.

Johnson and Davey (cited in Matthews, 1997b) conducted a study in which three groups of participants were shown news bulletins with positive, negative or neutral blends of stories. After the bulletins, those shown the negative blend of stories were considerably more worried and depressed about their own lives (rather than the issues they had seen in the bulletin).

According to Davey:

'television producers need to think very carefully about the emotional impact news might have on their viewers'.

Davey sees slots like 'And finally ... ' on ITN's *News at Ten* as being beneficial:

'Having a light piece at the end is no bad thing. The trouble is [the broadcast] then gives a quick summary of all the news at the end, so it's not as effective as it could be'.

Reporting on solutions as well as problems, then, may be beneficial for all of us.

Conclusions

There has been much research into media influences on pro- and anti-social behaviour. The evidence reviewed in this chapter suggests that the media can exert an influence on the expression of both anti-social and pro-social behaviours, although it is dangerous to talk about this in simple cause-and-effect terms.

Summary

■ American research has shown an increase in the amount of violence depicted on television since 1967. In Britain, television violence is not as prevalent, and represents only a very small proportion of the total output. Intererestingly, whilst the television might be switched on for longer in households than was the case in the 1960s, people are not always attentive to it.

■ Bandura *et al.* exposed children to filmed (symbolic) models. They found that children can acquire new aggressive responses merely through exposure to a filmed or televised model. These findings implied that media portrayals of violence might contribute to violence in society.

■ Cartoons contain a great deal of violence, and yet are aimed mainly at children. However, viewers' **perceptions** of violent television content may not correspond with objective counts of violent incidents. Real-life incidents in news and documentaries are generally rated as more violent than those in fictional settings.

■ **Correlational studies** indicate that the overall amount of television watched is related to self-reports of aggressive behaviour. However, cause and effect cannot be inferred from such studies, and those who watch violent programmes may **differ** in some way from those who do not.

■ **Laboratory experiments** are designed to detect causal links between watching television and behaviour. However, most use small, unrepresentative samples, and their measures are far removed from everyday behaviour.

■ **Field experiments** are more ecologically valid. They involve controlled viewing over an extended time period. Data consistently indicate that children who watch violent television are more aggressive than those who do not. However, they lack control and often use unrepresentative samples.

■ **Longitudinal panel studies** say something about cause and effect **and** use representative samples. They look at the **cumulative influence** of television. Some studies have shown a link between heavy exposure to media violence and aggression, but others have not.

■ **Natural experiments** look at communities/societies before and after the introduction of television. Some studies have shown increases in aggressive behaviour following the introduction of television whilst others have not.

■ The four specific effects of television that have been investigated are **arousal, disinhibition, imitation** and **desensitisation.** All of these have been shown to increase following exposure to media violence.

■ Some researchers believe the link between media violence and aggressive behaviour to be over-stated. They believe that it is difficult to justify the overall conclusion that viewing television at an early age predicts later aggression.

■ As well as being a potential influence on anti-social behaviour, television may influence **pro-social behaviour.** The evidence that television may exert a pro-social effect comes from **laboratory studies** using **prepared television/filmed material,** broadcast material specially produced for **teaching social skills,** or programme materials from **popular TV series.**

■ **Field studies** also indicate that the amount of pro-social content viewed is related to the strength of pro-social behaviour. However, this relationship is weaker than that between viewing habits and anti-social behaviour. This may be because anti-social behaviours (which are blatant and physical) are learnt more easily than verbal and subtle pro-social behaviours.

■ Little is known about the long-term effects of playing **violent computer games,** but the child's **active involvement** makes them potentially more harmful than television. There is some evidence for the pro-social effects of such games, but much of this has not been gathered in carefully controlled ways.

■ The benefits of computer games include providing motivation, a sense of confidence, mastery, control, and computer-related skills for the future. They also provide an opportunity for releasing stress and aggression in a non-destructive way.

■ News bulletins can induce anxiety and depression in viewers. Producers of news programmes should think carefully about the emotional impact news might have on their audiences.

UNIT 6

Abnormal Psychology

PART 1

Conceptions and models of abnormality

WHAT IS ABNORMALITY?

Introduction and overview

Whilst much of psychology is concerned with normal psychological processes and development, some psychologists are interested in abnormal psychological processes and atypical development. This Unit looks at the definition and classification of abnormality, the causes of certain types of abnormal behaviour, and how abnormality can be treated. The last three chapters consider some aspects of atypical development.

The themes of the following twelve chapters assume that it is both possible and meaningful to draw the line between normal and abnormal. This chapter looks at some of the ways in which abnormality has been defined and examines some of the practical and ethical issues arising from these definitions. As will be seen, apparently reasonable definitions are actually very limited.

Abnormality as a 'deviation from statistical norms'

By definition, abnormality means 'deviating from the norm or average'. Perhaps the most obvious way to define abnormality is in terms of *statistically infrequent* characteristics or behaviours. This definition is intuitively appealing. For example, if the average height of a given population of adults is 5' 8", we would probably describe someone who was 7' or 3' as being 'abnormally' tall or short respectively. When someone behaves in ways that the vast majority do not, or does not behave in ways that the vast majority do, we often label him or her 'abnormal'.

Unfortunately, there are drawbacks to using a purely statistical approach to defining abnormality. One is that it does not take into account the *desirability* of a behaviour or characteristic. Some behaviours are both statistically infrequent *and* probably undesirable. But what about having a Biology degree at age 13 and, at 17, being the youngest doctor in the world? Balamurali Ambati, who completed a six-year medical course in less than four years and can now operate on life and limb, has abilities we can only marvel at. But he would still be defined as 'abnormal' according to the statistical definition (as indeed would Mozart, who performed his own concerto at age three).

Figure 65.1   Balamurali Ambati: a graduate in Biology at the age of 13, a doctor at 17, but abnormal by the deviation-from-statistical-norms definition of abnormality

Another limitation is that there are people involved in a range of undesirable behaviours in all cultures. According to Hassett & White (1989):

'Americans are involved in a wide variety of socially undesirable behaviour patterns from mild depression to child abuse, (and) if it were possible to add up all the numbers, it would become clear that as many as one out of every two people would fall into at least one of these categories'.

These behaviour patterns, which characterise half the American population, would be 'normal' in a statistical sense, but they are also regarded as constituting mental disorders (see Chapter 67). Moreover, just how *far* from the average must a person deviate before being considered 'abnormal'? If a population's average height is 5' 8", exactly *when* does a person become abnormally tall or short? Any chosen cut-off point is necessarily *arbitrary* (Miller & Morley, 1986).

It is clearly not sufficient to define abnormality *solely* in terms of a deviation from statistical norms. However, it can sometimes be a helpful way of looking at abnormality. Western cultures consider people who see or hear things that are not there to be 'abnormal', and *most* people in those cultures do not experience such hallucinations. Nonetheless, a useful definition of abnormality needs to take more into account than just the statistical frequency of behaviours.

Abnormality as a 'deviation from ideal mental health'

A second approach is to identify the characteristics and abilities (which may or may not be statistically frequent) that people *should* possess in order to be considered 'normal' (Parker *et al.*, 1995). Abnormality is then defined as deviating from these characteristics either by not possessing them or by possessing characteristics that should not be possessed. Several 'ideals' have been proposed. Jahoda (1958), for example, identified *individual choice, resistance to stress, an accurate perception of reality* and *self-actualisation* as some characteristics of ideal mental health.

This approach is also appealing, since the ideals identified above have at least some sort of validity. However, they are so demanding that almost everybody would be considered abnormal to some degree, depending on how many of them they failed to satisfy. According to Maslow (1968), only a few people achieve *self-actualisation* (see Chapters 1 and 17). As a result, most of us would be considered abnormal on this definition (and if most of us are abnormal and therefore in the majority, then by the statistical definition being abnormal is normal).

> **Box 65.1   Value judgements and mental health**
>
> Lists of ideals defining mental health are *value judgements*, reflecting the beliefs of those who construct them. Someone who hears voices when nobody is there may well be unhealthy as far as some people are concerned. But the person who hears the voices, and welcomes them, would define him- or herself as being perfectly healthy and normal. A culture that emphasised *group co-operation* would reject Jahoda's view that *individual choice* is part of *ideal mental health*. This problem does not arise when judgements are made about *physical health*, since such judgements are neither moral nor philosophical. What (physical) health is can be stated in anatomical and physical terms (Szasz, 1960). If there are no abnormalities present, then a person is considered to be in 'ideal' health.

Another reason for questioning this definition is that it is *bound by culture*. Whilst different cultures have some shared ideals about what constitutes mental health, some ideals are not shared. In the Sambia of New Guinea, for example, male youths are taught that females are poison, and the males engage in prescribed unlimited fellatio. Such behaviour is considered healthy and, indeed, desirable. Again, soccer is popular on the island of Java, although not in quite the same way as in Britain. The Javan game is a necessarily quick-passing one, since the ball is first soaked in petrol and then set alight. Provided that the game is played near water and the legs are shaved, Javans consider playing soccer like this to be 'healthy'. It is unlikely that this view would be shared in Britain.

Figure 65.2   Soccer the Javan way: mentally healthy behaviour or not?

However, those who define abnormality in this way would argue that there ought to be some sort of *universal standard* to which we should all aspire, irrespective of culture. As Chance (1984) has observed:

'Would it really make sense to say that murder and cannibalism are healthy just because some cultures believed them to be, and if it does, then why not apply the same standards to communities within a society? Murder is a popular activity among Baltimore youth. Shall we say that, in that city, murder is healthy?'.

Even if we accept Chance's observation, the deviation from the ideal mental health definition also changes over time *within* a particular culture (it is *era-dependent*). Seeing visions was a sign of healthy religious fervour in thirteenth-century Europe, but in twentieth-century Europe, seeing such visions might be a sign of *schizophrenia* (Wade & Tavris, 1993: see Chapter 68).

A final problem with this approach is that it is limited by the *context* in which a behaviour occurs. For example, it is 'healthy' to walk around wearing a steel helmet if one works on a building site, but it is probably less healthy if one is a waiter in a restaurant. Faced with the choice between a plate of highly nutritious salad and a full English breakfast, the former would be a healthier choice. In the absence of an alternative, however, a full English breakfast might be better than nothing at all.

Defining abnormality as a deviation from ideal mental health can sometimes be helpful. On its own, however, it is less than satisfactory.

Abnormality as a 'failure to function adequately'

According to this way of defining abnormality (which overlaps with the definition just discussed), every human being should achieve some sense of personal well-being and make some contribution to a larger social group. Any individual who fails to function adequately in this respect is seen as being 'abnormal'. Sue *et al.* (1994) use the terms *practical* or *clinical criteria* to describe the ways in which people fail to function adequately, since they are often the basis on which people come to the attention of psychologists or other professionals (Buss, 1966).

PERSONAL DISTRESS

One way in which people can come to a professional's attention is if they are experiencing *personal distress* or *discomfort*. Echoing Buss (1966), Miller & Morley (1986) have remarked that:

'People do not come to clinics because they have some abstract definition of abnormality. For the most part, they come because their feelings or behaviours cause them distress'.

Such feelings or behaviours might not be obvious to other people, but may take the form of intense anxiety and depression, and a loss of appetite.

Unfortunately, whilst such psychological states might cause personal distress, we could not use personal distress by itself as a definition of abnormality, since certain states causing personal distress might be *appropriate responses* in particular circumstances. Examples here include experiencing anxiety in response to the presence of a real threat and depression as a response to the death of a loved one. We would not consider such responses to be abnormal unless they persisted long after their source was removed or after most people had adjusted to them.

Moreover, some major forms of mental disorder are not necessarily accompanied by personal distress. *Dissocial personality disorder*, for example, involves repeated acts of crime and violence *without* experiencing guilt or remorse. With *substance-related disorders*, the consequences of excessive use of, say, alcohol, may be strenuously denied by the user.

OTHERS' DISTRESS

Although certain psychological states might not cause personal distress, they may be *distressing to others*. For example, a person who tried to assassinate the Prime Minister might not experience any personal distress at all. However, the fact that such a person is a threat to others also constitutes a failure to function adequately.

MALADAPTIVENESS

Even someone who does not experience personal distress, or is not distressing to others, would be failing to function adequately if the behaviour was *maladaptive*, either for the individual concerned or society. Maladaptive means preventing the person from efficiently satisfying social and occupational roles. Some mental disorders, such as the substance-related disorders mentioned earlier, are defined in terms of how the (ab)use of the substance produces social and occupational difficulties, such as marital problems and poor work performance.

UNEXPECTED BEHAVIOUR

We could also include *unexpected behaviour* as a failure to function adequately (Davison & Neale, 1994). This involves reacting to a situation or event in ways that could not be predicted or reasonably expected from what is known about human behaviour. If a person behaves in a way which is 'out of all proportion to the situation', then we might say that he or she was failing to function adequately. An example would be a person who reacted to the relegation of a favourite soccer team by attempting to commit suicide.

BIZARRENESS

Finally, we could also include a behaviour's *bizarreness* as an example of a failure to function adequately. Unless it actually is true that the Martians, in collusion with the CIA, *are* trying to extract information from someone, it would be hard to deny that a person making such claims was behaving bizarrely (and, hence failing to function adequately).

For some psychologists, and other professionals, the failure to function adequately definition is the most useful single approach and closest to 'common sense'. However, as with the other definitions, there are problems with defining abnormality in this way. Using the distress of others as a failure to function adequately is a double-edged sword. In some cases, it can be a 'blessing' in that one person's distress as a result of another's behaviour can, on occasion, literally be a 'life saver' (as when someone lacks insight into his or her own self-destructive behaviour). In other cases, it can be a curse, as when, say,

a father experiences distress over his son's homosexuality, whilst the son feels perfectly comfortable with it (Gross, 1995).

We could also question the meaning of the phrase *out of all proportion to the situation*, which was used when unexpected behaviour was described as a failure to function adequately. Davison & Neale (1994) appear to view unexpected behaviours as those involving an *over-reaction*. However, a behaviour which is out of all proportion can equally refer to an *under-reaction* as well.

Finally, we can question what the term *bizarreness* means. There are certain behaviours which *in general* would be considered bizarre, but which have occurred under conditions and in contexts such that the perpetrators could justify them in terms of survival, political or religious meanings (Houston *et al.*, 1991). Whether or not we agree with the justifications, we must accept that, in some contexts, seemingly bizarre behaviours might not be described as 'abnormal' because they allow an individual to function adequately. Dressing up in clothes of the opposite sex, for example, may, depending on the context, be entertaining for others and profitable for the person engaging in the behaviour.

Abnormality as a 'deviation from social norms'

All societies have standards or *norms* for appropriate behaviours and beliefs (expectations about how people should behave as well as what they should think). It is useful to think of these in terms of a *continuum of normative behaviour* ranging from behaviours which are *unacceptable, tolerable, acceptable/permissible, desirable*, and finally those that are *required/obligatory* (Gross, 1995). A fourth way to define abnormality is in terms of breaking society's standards or norms.

Figure 65.3 Homosexuality is judged by many to be abnormal, because it deviates from heterosexuality, which is defined as the norm

It is certainly sometimes true that behaviour which deviates from social norms is also statistically infrequent. However, some behaviours which are considered to be socially unacceptable in our culture are actually statistically *frequent*. Various studies (e.g. Gibson, 1967) have shown high 'confession rates' amongst people asked if they had engaged in a prosecutable offence without actually being convicted for it. As far as the deviation from social norms definition is concerned, most people would be defined as 'abnormal' (and as far as the deviation from statistical norms definition is concerned, criminal behaviour, at least that found in various studies, would be considered 'normal'!).

Like the deviation from ideal mental health definition, the deviation from social norms definition is also bound by culture. In Western culture, we consider anyone who assumes that a stranger will try to take advantage of us, and be hostile towards us, to be overly suspicious. We might even call such a person *paranoid*. However, when Mead (1935) studied the Mundugumor people, she found that perpetual suspicion was the norm, since strangers (and even male members of the same household) actually *were* hostile.

Box 65.4 Social norms in the Trobriand islanders

In Western cultures, the sons of a deceased father are not expected to clean his bones and distribute them to relatives to wear as ornaments. Amongst the Trobriand islanders studied by Malinowski (1929), however, such behaviour was expected and hence 'normal'. Indeed, a widow who did not wear her former husband's jawbone on a necklace was failing to behave in accordance with her culture's expectations and was considered abnormal.

The deviation from social norms definition is further weakened by the fact that it, too, is era-dependent. As values change, so particular behaviours move from being considered abnormal to normal to abnormal again and so on. Some behaviours today tend to be viewed as differences in lifestyle rather than signs of abnormality, the smoking of marijuana being, perhaps, one such example (Atkinson *et al.*, 1993).

As with the other definitions of abnormality, it can be helpful to use the idea of violating societal norms or expectations as an approach to defining abnormality. By itself, however, it cannot serve as a complete and acceptable definition.

Conclusions

All the definitions of abnormality discussed have strengths and weaknesses. All are helpful as ways of conceptualising abnormality, but none on its own is a sufficient definition. As will be seen elsewhere in this Unit, not all the characteristics of the definitions of abnormality are necessarily evident in those behaviours which are *classified* as mental disorders. Indeed, any of the behaviours classified as being mental disorders may reflect only one, or a combination, of the characteristics.

Different definitions carry different implications, and there is certainly no consensus on a 'best definition' (Sue *et al.*, 1994). Sue *et al.* have suggested that a *multiple perspectives* (or *multiple definitions*) view is one way of approaching the very difficult task of defining abnormality. A truly adequate understanding of abnormality can probably only be achieved through a comprehensive evaluation of all points of view.

Summary

■ One way of defining abnormality is in terms of characteristics/behaviours that are **statistically infrequent** (the **deviation-from-statistical-norms** definition). However, this does not take into account the desirability of a characteristic or behaviour.

■ The definition also fails to recognise that in all cultures up to half the population may engage in behaviours that constitute mental disorders. A further problem is in how far a person must deviate before being considered 'abnormal'. Any cut-off point is necessarily **arbitrary**.

■ The **deviation-from-ideal-mental-health** definition proposes that abnormal people possess characteristics that mentally healthy people do not possess, or do not possess those that mentally healthy people do. This definition relies on **value judgements** about what constitutes ideal mental health. It is also **bound by culture**, is **era-dependent**, and limited by the **context** in which a behaviour occurs.

■ Abnormality has also been defined as a **failure to function adequately** (achieving some sense of personal well-being and making some contribution to a larger social group). Experiencing **personal distress/discomfort**, causing **distress to others** and behaving **maladaptively, unexpectedly,** or **bizarrely** are often the grounds on which people come to the attention of psychologists and other professionals.

■ Many consider the failure to function adequately definition as being the most useful single approach, and the one closest to common sense. However, none of the above experiences on its own constitutes an adequate definition of abnormality since bizarre behaviour, for example, might actually allow a person to function adequately in a particular context.

■ Another way of defining abnormality is in terms of a **deviation from social norms**. According to this, abnormal people behave in ways society disapproves of or do not behave in ways it approves of. Like other definitions, this is **bound by culture** and **era-dependent**. Also, since most of us have behaved in ways society disapproves of, most of us would be defined as 'abnormal'.

■ No one definition of abnormality on its own is adequate. Behaviours that are **classified** as mental disorders do not necessarily reflect all these various definitions. A truly adequate definition of abnormality can probably only be achieved through a **multiple perspectives/multiple definitions** approach.

AN INTRODUCTION TO MODELS IN ABNORMAL PSYCHOLOGY

Introduction and overview

Chapter 65 looked at definitions of abnormality, and noted that no single definition satisfies everyone. Similarly, psychologists do not agree on what *causes* abnormality (whatever it is) and how it can best be *treated*. Five models (or *paradigms*) in abnormal psychology place distinct interpretations on abnormality's causes, the focus or goals of therapy, and the methods used to treat disturbed people. This chapter outlines the assumptions made by the *medical*, *psychodynamic*, *behavioural*, *cognitive* and *humanistic* models of abnormality, and their implications for treatment. Before this, however, it looks briefly at historical models of abnormality.

A brief history of models of abnormality

Throughout much of human history, abnormality was regarded as a sign of 'possession' by demons or evil spirits. Skeletons from the Stone Age, for example, have been discovered with egg-shaped holes in the skull. Although we cannot be certain, these holes were possibly drilled into the skull (*trephining*) to 'release' the spirits presumably responsible for a person's abnormal behaviour. Whether trephining was effective is debatable. However, because the skulls of some skeletons show evidence of the holes growing over, the 'operations' did not inevitably lead to immediate death.

This '*demonological*' model of abnormality was especially popular in the Middle Ages. Thousands of people (mostly women) were convicted of being 'witches' and executed for their 'crimes'. A birthmark, scar or mole on a woman's skin was interpreted as indicating that she had signed a pact with the devil. To establish whether they were possessed, those accused underwent various tests. Based on the fact that pure metals sink to the bottom of a melting pot whereas impurities float to the surface, it was 'reasoned' that pure people would sink to the bottom when placed in water whilst impure people (who were in league with the devil) would be able to keep their heads above water. 'Pure' people would, of course, die by

drowning, and 'impure' people would suffer some other fate (such as being burned at the stake).

Figure 66.1   Etching of a witch ducking stool, one of the tests used in the Middle Ages to establish whether someone was a witch. A 'pure' person would sink to the bottom (and drown), whilst an 'impure' person would be able to keep her head above water

The medical model

Although some physicians in the Middle Ages called for a more rational approach to abnormality, it was not until the eighteenth century (the *age of enlightenment*) that the demonological model began to lose its appeal, and a different model or perspective emerged. Pinel, in Europe, and Dix, in America, were the pioneers of change. Rather than seeing abnormal behaviour as supernatural possession, they argued that it should be seen as a kind of *illness* which could be treated with appropriate *medical* techniques.

Although different, this viewpoint was not new. The ancient Greek physician Hippocrates proposed that in what is now called *epilepsy*:

'If you cut open the head, you will find the brain humid, full of sweat and smelling badly. And in this way you may see that it is not a god which injured the body, but disease' (cited in Zilboorg & Henry, 1941).

Box 66.1   The rise of the medical model

In the eighteenth century, the view that mental disorders are illnesses based on an organ's pathology (the brain) was emphasised by von Haller. He believed that the brain played a central role in 'psychic functions' and that understanding could be gained by studying the brains of the 'insane' through post-mortem dissection. Nearly 100 years later, Griesinger insisted that *all* forms of mental disorder could be explained in terms of brain pathology. The discovery that *general paresis of the insane*, characterised by a deterioration in thought processes and memory, was caused by a micro-organism (the *syphilis spirochete*), coupled with findings relating to the adverse effects exerted by toxins, infections and so on, gave the medical model immense prestige.

The medical (or *biomedical*) model's early successes were largely based on showing that mental disorders could be linked to gross destruction of brain tissue. More recently, the medical model has looked at the role played by *genetics* and *neurotransmitters* in the development of mental disorders, whilst retaining its interest in brain damage's role in such disorders. *Biochemical theories* explain the development of mental disorders in terms of an *imbalance* in the concentration of neurotransmitters. *Genetic theories* derive from the observation that at least some mental disorders have a tendency to run in families. By means of DNA (the material that contains genetic codes), some disorders may be transmitted from generation to generation. The methodology involved in studying the role of genetic factors is explored in detail in Chapter 68 (see pages 591–592).

Because the medical model sees mental disorders as having physical causes, the therapeutic approaches it favours are *physical* and are known collectively as *somatic therapy*.

Box 66.2   An overview of somatic approaches

Three somatic approaches are *chemotherapy* (drugs), *electroconvulsive therapy* (electricity) and *psychosurgery* (surgical procedures). As Chapter 72 shows, these therapies have been successful in treating various disorders. However, they have also been extensively criticised. For example, the drugs used in chemotherapy all have unpleasant, and sometimes permanent, side-effects. Moreover, they do not offer a 'cure' for disorders, but merely *alleviate* their symptoms for as long as they remain active in the nervous system.

More disturbingly, *biological directives* (Kovel, 1978) have been used as *agents of social control*. Critics see the zombie-like state that some *psychotherapeutic* drugs produce as 'pharmacological strait-jackets', exerting the same effects as the actual strait-jackets they were intended to replace. Electroconvulsive therapy and psychosurgery lack a convincing scientific rationale to explain their effects. For some critics, this is reason enough for their use to be discontinued.

The psychodynamic model

The view that mental disorders have physical origins was challenged in the late nineteenth century by Freud. Whilst Freud believed that mental disorders were caused by internal factors, he saw these as being psychological rather than physical in nature (see Chapter 1). He first made this claim as a way of explaining *hysteria*, in which physical symptoms (such as deafness) are experienced, but there are no underlying physical causes. Freud, a qualified physician, astonished his medical colleagues by proposing that hysteria's cause stemmed from unresolved and unconscious *conflicts* originating in childhood.

The psychodynamic perspective has been both influential and controversial. As was seen in Chapter 44, Freud believed that personality is comprised of three interacting structures. The *id* is present at birth, and is the impulsive, subjective and pleasure-seeking part of personality. The id operates on the *pleasure principle* (the immediate gratification of instinctual needs without regard for how this is achieved). The *ego* develops from the id to help us cope with the external world, which is necessary for survival. It operates on the *reality principle* (the gratification of the id's needs in socially acceptable ways). The *superego* is the last to develop and is concerned with moral judgements and feelings. It comprises *conscience* (the source of guilt when we engage in immoral or unethical behaviours) and the *ego-ideal* (which rewards moral or ethical behaviour with feelings of pride).

When these structures are 'in balance', psychological normality is maintained. However, Freud saw conflict between them as always present to some degree and when conflict cannot be managed, disorders arise. Freud viewed early childhood experiences as shaping both normal and abnormal behaviour. As noted earlier, he believed hysteria stemmed from unresolved and unconscious sexual conflicts originating in childhood. He also believed that all mental disorders could be explained in this way.

Box 66.3   Psychosexual stages of development

Freud saw human development as passing through a series of *psychosexual stages*.

The oral stage (0–1 year): The principal sexually sensitive zone is the mouth, and the infant's greatest source of gratification is sucking.

The anal stage (1–3): The membranes of the anal region provide the major source of pleasurable stimulation.

The phallic stage (3–5/6): Self-manipulation of the genitals provides the major source of pleasurable sensation.

The latency stage (5/6–12): The child's sexual motivations recede in importance as a preoccupation with developing skills and other activities occurs.

The genital stage: After puberty, the deepest feelings of pleasure come from heterosexual relations.

The nature of the conflicts and how they are expressed reflect the stage of development the child was in when the conflict occurred. To avoid the pain caused by the conflict, Freud proposed the existence of *defence mechanisms* as a way of preventing anxiety-arousing impulses and thoughts from reaching consciousness. All of these unconsciously operating mechanisms serve to protect us by distorting reality.

Box 66.4   Some defence mechanisms

Repression: Unacceptable thoughts or impulses are 'forgotten' by being pushed from consciousness into unconsciousness (see Chapter 29).

Reaction formation: The opposite of an unacceptable wish or impulse is expressed. For example, a person strongly drawn to gambling may express the view that gambling is repulsive.

Rationalisation: Socially acceptable reasons are given for thoughts or actions based on unacceptable motives. An example would be eating an entire chocolate cake because we 'didn't want it to spoil in the summer heat'.

Displacement: An emotional response is redirected from a dangerous object to a safe one. For example, anger towards one's boss might be redirected towards the family dog.

Projection: Unacceptable motives or impulses are transferred to others. For example, a man who is sexually attracted to a neighbour perceives the neighbour as being sexually attracted to him.

Regression: Responding to a threatening situation in a way appropriate to an earlier age or level of development. For example, an adult has a 'temper tantrum' when he or she does not get his or her own way.

To treat mental disorders, Freud developed *psychoanalysis*. As Chapter 73 shows, the first aim of therapy is to *make the unconscious conscious*. Through a *therapeutic regression* (Winnicott, 1958), the person receiving psychoanalysis is directed to re-experience *repressed* (or deeply buried) unconscious feelings and wishes frustrated in childhood. This takes place in the 'safe' context of the psychoanalyst's consulting room, and the person is encouraged to experience the feelings and wishes in a more appropriate way with *a new ending* (Alexander, 1946). Providing disturbed people with *insight* (self-knowledge and self-understanding) enables them to adjust successfully to their deep-rooted conflicts, and deal with them in a 'more mature' way.

The psychodynamic model's assumptions and the therapies deriving from it have been subject to much criticism. Despite the model's claims to have explanatory power, experimental support for it is weak (see Chapter 73). Freud's lack of scientific rigour in developing the model (most notably his dependence on inference rather than objective evidence), has also attracted criticism. His model was based on data derived largely from treatment of upper-middle class Viennese women aged between 20 and 44. Despite this restricted sample, Freud developed a model of personality development in children! Even though the women studied by Freud had serious emotional problems, he was still able to develop a theory of normal psychological development. Although the women lived in a time and place when all forms of sexual expression were universally frowned upon, Freud concluded that their sexual preoccupations were typical of all people.

Box 66.5   The psychodynamic model, reductionism and determinism

The psychodynamic model has also been criticised for its *reductionist* interpretation of life (see Chapter 81). In its purest form, the model sees people as being driven by 'animal instincts' which are beyond their control. Because 'the die is cast early in life' (Bootzin & Acocella, 1984), we are seen as being helpless to change ourselves (so the model is also *deterministic*). Although weaker versions of Freud's original theory have attempted to overcome these criticisms, Freud (1915) seemed unmoved by at least some of them:

'One can only characterise as simple-minded, the fear that … all the highest goods of humanity, as they are called – research, art, love, ethical and social sense – will lose their dignity because [the psychodynamic model] is in a position to demonstrate their origins in elementary and animal instinctual impulses'.

The behavioural model

Both the medical and psychodynamic models explain mental disorders in terms of *internal* factors, their difference being that the former sees disorders as having an underlying physical cause whilst the latter sees their cause as being psychological. By contrast, the behavioural model sees disorders as *maladaptive behaviours* which are learned and maintained in the same way as adaptive behaviours. According to this model, the best way of explaining mental disorders is to look at the *environmental conditions* in which a particular behaviour is displayed.

CLASSICAL AND OPERANT CONDITIONING

The principles of classical and operant conditioning were described in Chapter 32. Classical conditioning's role in human learning was taken up by Watson (see Chapter 1, page 10), who is credited with recognising its importance as a potential explanation of how mental disorders develop.

Box 66.6   Classically conditioning a fear response

In one of psychology's most famous (or infamous) experiments, Watson & Rayner (1920) classically conditioned a fear response in a young child called Albert. According to Jones (1925):

'Albert, eleven months of age, was an infant with a phlegmatic disposition, afraid of nothing "under the sun" except a loud noise made by striking a steel bar. This made him cry. By striking the bar at the same time that Albert touched a white rat, the fear was transferred to the white rat. After seven combined stimulations, rat and sound, Albert not only became greatly disturbed at the sight of a rat, but this fear had spread to include a white rabbit, cotton wool, a fur coat and the experimenter's (white) hair. It did not transfer to wooden blocks and other objects very dissimilar to the rat'.

Figure 66.2   A very rare photograph of John Watson and Rosalie Rayner during the conditioning of Little Albert

---

Watson and Rayner showed that a *phobia* could be acquired through classical conditioning and for some psychologists, classical conditioning explains the acquisition of *all* abnormal fears. For Wolpe & Rachman (1960):

'any neutral stimulus, simple or complex, that happens to make an impact on an individual at about the same time a fear reaction is evoked, acquires the ability to evoke fear subsequently ... there will be generalisation of fear reactions to stimuli resembling the conditioned stimulus'.

According to the behavioural model, a fear of something results in it being avoided, which reduces the fear. This, says the model, is how certain abnormal behaviours are *maintained* (see Chapter 70). As Chapters 68–71 and 74 illustrate, the principles of both classical and operant conditioning can be used to explain the development and maintenance of some mental disorders and to treat them.

As Chapter 74 illustrates, therapeutic approaches based on the behavioural model have been extremely influential. All of them have at least three things in common. First, they focus on maladaptive behaviours and, rather than speculating about their cause and the historical reasons for their development, *behaviour* itself is seen as being the problem. Consequently, the therapies attempt to change behaviour by systematically applying learning principles. Second, a treatment's success or failure is based on specific and observable changes in behaviour. Third, all behaviourally oriented therapists are committed to the idea that the value claimed for any treatment must be documented by evidence from controlled experimental studies (see Chapters 77 and 85).

The cognitive model

Both classical and operant conditioning require that people actually perform behaviours for them to be learned. However, whilst accepting conditioning's principles, *social learning theorists* point out that certain behaviours can be acquired simply by watching them being performed. Bandura (1969) calls this *observational learning*, and his approach to understanding and treating mental disorders represents a link between the behavioural and cognitive models of abnormality (see Chapter 32).

Like the psychodynamic model, the cognitive model is concerned with internal processes. However, instead of emphasising the role of unconscious conflicts, the cognitive model focuses on internal events such as thoughts, expectations and attitudes accompanying and, in some cases, causing mental disorders. The cognitive model developed partly from dissatisfaction with the behavioural model's concentration on overt behaviours, to the neglect of thoughts and interpretations.

Instead of literal environmental contingencies, the cognitive model proposes that *mediating processes*, such as thoughts, interpretations and perceptions of ourselves, others and the environment, are important in causing mental disorders. The cognitive model became influential in the 1950s, but recognition of the importance of cognitive factors in mental disorders is not new. For example, Shakespeare's Hamlet expresses a similar point when he says 'there is nothing either good or bad but thinking makes it so'.

Box 66.7   Information processing and mental disorders

One cognitive approach to understanding behaviour sees people as *information processors* (see Chapter 1, page 3, and Chapter 27, page 229). The information-processing approach likens the mind to a computer. As with computers, information (based on our perceptions) is put into the system, stored, manipulated and later retrieved from it. According to this view, disorders occur when the input–output sequence is disturbed in some way. For example, the faulty storage or manipulation of information may lead to distorted output or a lack of output.

An alternative approach sees some mental disorders as stemming from irrational and maladaptive assumptions and thoughts (Ellis, 1962). Beck (1967) calls these *cognitive errors*, whilst Meichenbaum (1976) uses the term *counter-productive self-statements*. Since the cognitive model sees mental disorders arising from 'faulty thinking' and since, to a large degree, our behaviour is controlled by the way we think, the most logical and effective way to change maladaptive behaviour is to change the maladaptive thinking underlying it.

Wessler (1986) defines cognitively-based therapies as a set of treatment interventions in which human cognitions are assigned a central role. Beck & Weishaar (1989) summarise cognitive approaches to therapy in the following way:

'Cognitive therapy consists of highly specific learning experiences designed to teach patients (1) to monitor their negative, automatic thoughts (cognitions); (2) to recognise the connection between cognition, affect and behaviour; (3) to examine the evidence for and against distorted automatic thoughts; (4) to substitute more reality-oriented interpretations for these biased cognitions; and (5) to learn to identify and alter the beliefs that predispose them to distort their experiences'.

Several types of cognitive therapy are considered in Chapter 75. One of the most important contributors has been Beck (1974). Beck argues that disorders like depression are often 'rooted' in the maladaptive ways people think about themselves and the world. Depressed people characteristically think in a negative way and are likely to view minor (or even neutral) events as self-devaluing or hopeless. Beck believes that illogical thoughts deepen the depression and lower a person's motivation to take constructive action.

Box 66.8   Some examples of illogical thinking contributing to depression (after Beck, 1974)

Magnification and minimisation: Some people magnify difficulties and failures whilst minimising their accomplishments and successes. For example, a student who gets a low grade on one essay might magnify that and minimise his or her high-grade achievements on previous essays.

Selective abstraction: People sometimes arrive at conclusions based on only one rather than several factors that could have made a contribution. For example, the goalkeeper of a beaten football team may blame himself, despite the fact that other team members also played badly.

Arbitrary inference: A person arrives at a conclusion about him- or herself, despite the absence of any supporting evidence. For example, a student who misses a lecture might see him- or herself as incompetent, despite the fact that the bus to college was late.

Overgeneralisation: A person arrives at a sweeping conclusion based on a single and sometimes trivial event. For example, a student might conclude that he or she is unworthy of a place at university because an application form contained a minor mistake.

Beck's therapy aims to alter the way depressed people think about their situations and challenge beliefs about their worthlessness, inadequacy and inability to change their circumstances. This *cognitive restructuring* approach is characteristic of all therapeutic approaches based on the cognitive model.

By attempting to identify maladaptive thoughts and beliefs that occur in many different situations and with many different disorders, the cognitive model and its therapeutic approaches are less mechanical and more 'in tune' with people's conscious experiences than approaches based on the behavioural model. Not surprisingly, supporters of the behavioural model have been the most critical of the cognitive model. Skinner (1990), for example, saw it as a return to *unscientific mentalism* and warned that, because cognitive phenomena are not observable, they cannot possibly form the foundations of empiricism (Sue *et al.*, 1994). Arguing from a humanistic perspective (see below), Corey (1991) proposes that human behaviour is more than thoughts and beliefs and that, in a sense, the cognitive model is as mechanistic as the behavioural model in reducing human beings to 'the sum of their cognitive parts'.

Despite these reservations, psychology's current emphasis on the role of cognition suggests that the cognitive model will continue to be influential as a way of both explaining and treating mental disorders.

The humanistic model

As noted earlier (see page 570), one criticism of the psychodynamic model is that it is both deterministic and pessimistic in seeing people as being inevitably bound in a struggle against the selfish desires of the id. Rather than emphasising the unconscious sexual and aggressive impulses of 'sick' people, humanistic psychologists take a very different view of human nature and assume that people are *sets of potentials* who are basically good and strive for growth, dignity and self-determination.

Instead of the behavioural model's mechanistic approach which, in its strictest form, reduces subjective experiences to a chain of conditioned responses, humanistic psychologists see the whole of personality (including our experiences of sorrow and joy, frustration and fulfilment, and alienation and intimacy) as worthy of study. This emphasis on positive human potential and seeing the world through a person's rather than an experimenter's eyes has been championed by Maslow and Rogers (see Chapter 1, pages 14–16).

Box 66.9 Blocks to personal growth

For humanistic psychologists, what makes us different from non-humans is our possession of *free will* (see Chapter 81) and our desire to achieve *self-actualisation*. These make each of us unique, free, rational and self-determining. Humanistic psychologists see psychological normality as the ability to accept ourselves, realise our potential, achieve intimacy with others and find meaning in life.

The humanistic model sees mental disorders as arising because external factors somehow block personal growth. For example, instead of providing us with *unconditional positive regard* (the assurance that we

will be loved and accepted despite our shortcomings: Rogers, 1951), acceptance by others is often *conditional* on us acting in certain ways or meeting specific standards. Some people hide their emotions behind a 'social mask', and pay little or no attention to the emotions we are experiencing. This results in a *distorted self-concept*, a view of the self that does not match our feelings or experiences. This causes us to deny our true feelings, narrows awareness of our own uniqueness, and blocks potential for growth.

Humanistic therapies evolved relatively recently and, although they peaked in popularity in the 1960s and 1970s, they continue to be influential. Humanistic therapy's goals are to remove blocks to self-development, put people in touch with their true selves, and promote continued growth rather than allowing external factors to determine behaviour. People undergoing humanistic therapy are called *clients* rather than *patients*, and are treated as *partners* in the therapeutic endeavour. Indeed, responsibility for the therapy's success is placed more with the client than the therapist (or *facilitator*).

Therapy takes place in special, supportive environments that allow clients to achieve self-awareness, self-acceptance, personal fulfilment and self-actualisation. Rather than making the past the focus of attention, humanistic therapies *tend* to focus on the present or the 'here and now' and on conscious thoughts and feelings rather than repressed conflicts. Additionally, the therapist consciously avoids giving advice or assuming the role of an 'expert', since this would serve to impose the therapist's own views on the client.

Many different forms of humanistic therapy exist. Some are considered to be on the 'fringe', but others have been influential. The best known and most widely practised are *client-centred therapy* and *Gestalt therapy*. The procedures used in these therapies, along with several others, are discussed in Chapter 76.

Conclusions

This chapter has outlined several models which attempt to explain the causes of abnormal behaviour and identify methods by which it can be treated. In their different ways, each model has made a significant contribution to the understanding and treatment of abnormal behaviour.

Summary

■ Psychologists disagree about abnormality's **causes** and the best way to **treat** it. Five major models are the **medical**, **psychodynamic**, **behavioural**, **cognitive**, and **humanistic**.

■ The **medical model** sees abnormality as having an underlying physical cause, a kind of **illness** which can be treated **medically**. An early success for it came from the discovery that 'general paresis of the insane' was caused by syphilis. More recently, the model has turned to **genetics** and imbalances in **neurotransmitters** as causes of mental disorders.

■ The therapeutic approaches favoured by the medical model are collectively known as **somatic therapy**. Three somatic approaches currently used are **chemotherapy**, **electroconvulsive therapy** and **psychosurgery**. Although useful in treating some disorders, they have also been subjected to much criticism.

■ Freud's **psychodynamic model** sees mental disorders as being caused by internal, psychological factors, namely unresolved, unconscious, childhood conflicts. **Psychoanalysis** involves re-experiencing repressed childhood feelings and wishes. The disturbed person is provided with **insight**, which provides a more mature way of coping with deep-rooted conflicts.

■ Freud's model has been criticised for its lack of scientific rigour and experimental evidence. His theory of normal psychological development was based on an unrepresentative sample of adults, and his emphasis on 'animal instincts' as the source of all behaviour is **reductionist** and **deterministic**.

■ According to the **behavioural model**, disorders are **learned maladaptive behaviours**. The learning processes involved are classical and operant conditioning. Watson was the first to suggest that mental disorders (such as phobias) can be explained in conditioning terms, as demonstrated in the study of 'Little Albert'.

■ Therapies based on the learning model focus on maladaptive behaviours, and try to change them without establishing their causes and history. Success is measured in terms of changes in specific and observable behaviours, and any therapy's value can be documented through controlled experimental studies.

■ According to **social learning theorists**, some behaviours can be acquired simply through **observational learning**. This approach stresses the role of thoughts, interpretations and other cognitions as **mediating processes** between the individual and environmental contingencies.

■ Social learning theory is a link between the behavioural and **cognitive model** of abnormality. The **information-processing** approach compares the mind to a computer. Disorders occur when the 'input–output' sequence is disturbed in some way.

■ Other cognitive approaches see mental disorders as stemming from 'irrational assumptions' (Ellis), 'cognitive errors' (Beck) or 'counter-productive self-statements' (Meichenbaum). The cognitive model sees the changing of 'faulty thinking' underlying maladaptive behaviour as the most logical and effective approach to treatment. All therapies involve **cognitive restructuring**.

■ According to the **humanistic model**, people are basically good, and strive for growth, dignity and self-determination. The whole range of human experience is worthy of study, and what makes us distinctive as a species is our **free will** and the desire to achieve **self-actualisation**. Mental disorders are seen as arising because external events prevent personal growth. For example, instead of receiving **unconditional positive regard**, acceptance by others may be **conditional**, or they may ignore our emotions. The result is a **distorted self-concept**.

■ The goal of humanistic therapy is to remove the blocks to personal growth. The 'client' is given greater responsibility for the therapy's success than the therapist/facilitator. The focus is on present conscious thoughts and feelings within a supportive environment.

CLASSIFYING ABNORMAL BEHAVIOUR

Introduction and overview

Of all the models presented in Chapter 66, the most influential has been the medical model. An integral part of this model is the *diagnosis* of mental disorders through the use of *classificatory systems*. The two currently used classificatory systems both derive from the work of Kraepelin (1913). In Britain and most other parts of the world, the classificatory system used is ICD-10. The system currently used in North America is DSM-IV. This chapter describes these classificatory systems and examines some of the issues surrounding their use. It begins, however, by briefly looking at the history of attempts to classify abnormal behaviour.

A brief history of classificatory systems

Sorting people into categories in order to predict their behaviour is not new. The first attempt at a unified classification of abnormal mental states was made by the Ancient Greek physician Hippocrates. Hippocrates identified three categories of abnormal behaviour: *mania* (abnormal excitement), *melancholia* (abnormal dejection) and *phrenitis* (brain fever). Later, the Greek physician Asclepiades described differences between hallucinations, delusions and illusions, and explained how each could be used as a diagnostic sign. Attempts at beginning a classificatory system were made by Pinel, who grouped disorders he believed were psychological or mental in nature into a category called *neurosis* (functional diseases of the nervous system) which was divided into several types.

The first comprehensive attempt to classify abnormal behaviours was developed by Kraepelin (1913), who published a classificatory system that brought together earlier systems and at the same time elaborated on them in important ways. After carefully observing hospitalised patients and examining their records, Kraepelin proposed 18 distinct types of mental disorder, each with a characteristic pattern of *symptoms* (a *syndrome*), a distinct developmental course, particular underlying physical causes and a characteristic outcome. Kraepelin's work was important in the development of two classificatory systems introduced after the Second World War.

Both ICD and DSM have undergone several revisions since their introduction. The most recent revision of the ICD is the tenth (ICD-10). The *Clinical Descriptions and Diagnostic Guidelines of the ICD-10 Classification of Mental and Behavioural Disorders* (CDDG) was published in 1992 and the *Diagnostic Criteria for Research* (DCR) in 1993. The version of DSM currently in use is *DSM-IV*, published in 1994 by the American Psychiatric Association.

Kraepelin's system is also embodied in the 1983 Mental Health Act (England and Wales), which identifies three categories of *mental disturbance* or *mental disorder*. These are *mental illness* (neurosis, organic psychosis and functional psychosis), *personality disorder* and *mental impairment*.

ICD-10 and DSM-IV

ICD-10 identifies 11 major categories of mental disorder. These are detailed in Box 67.2, together with examples of *some* of the disorders included in these categories.

Box 67.2   Major categories in ICD-10 and some specific examples of disorders included in those categories

1   **Organic, including symptomatic, mental disorders:** dementia in Alzheimer's disease; personality and behavioural disorders due to brain disease, damage and dysfunction

2   **Mental and behavioural disorders due to psychoactive substance use:** substances include alcohol, cannabinoids, cocaine and hallucinogens

3 **Schizophrenia, schizotypal and delusional disorders:** schizophrenia (paranoid, hebephrenic, catatonic, undifferentiated, residual, simple, other and unspecified types); schizotypal disorder

4 **Mood (affective) disorders:** manic episode (including hypomania); bipolar affective disorder; depressive episode; recurrent depressive disorder; persistent mood (affective) disorders (including cyclothymia and dysthymia)

5 **Neurotic, stress-related and somatoform disorders:** phobic anxiety disorders (including agoraphobia, social phobias and specific (isolated) phobias); anxiety disorders (including panic disorder, generalised anxiety disorder); obsessive–compulsive disorder; reaction to severe stress and adjustment disorders (including post-traumatic stress disorder); dissociative (conversion) disorders (including dissociative amnesia, fugue and multiple personality disorder); somatoform disorders (including hypochondriacal disorders)

6 **Behavioural syndromes associated with physiological disturbances and physical factors:** eating disorders (including anorexia nervosa and bulimia nervosa); non-organic sleep disorders (including sleep-walking, night terrors); sexual dysfunction not caused by organic disorder or disease

7 **Disorders of adult personality and behaviour:** specific personality disorders (including paranoid, schizoid, dissocial, emotionally unstable, anxious or avoidant, and dependent); habit and impulse disorders (including pathological gambling, fire-setting and stealing); gender and identity disorders (including transsexualism); disorders of sexual preference (including fetishism, voyeurism and paedophilia)

8 **Mental retardation:** mental retardation which is mild, moderate, severe or profound

9 **Disorders of psychological development:** specific disorders of speech and language (including expressive, specific speech articulation and receptive language disorders); specific developmental disorders of scholastic skills (including disorders of reading, spelling, arithmetic); pervasive developmental disorder (including childhood autism, atypical autism, Rett's syndrome, Asperger's syndrome)

10 **Behavioural and emotional disorders with onset usually occurring in childhood and adolescence:** hyperkinetic disorder (including disorders of activity and attention, hyperkinetic conduct disorder); conduct disorders; mixed disorders of conduct and emotion

11 **Unspecified mental disorder:** mental disorder not otherwise specified.

Box 67.3 identifies the major categories and *some* specific examples of disorders recognised in DSM-IV.

Box 67.3   Major categories in DSM-IV and some specific examples of disorders included in those categories

1 **Delirium, dementia, amnestic and other cognitive disorders:** dementias (e.g. of Alzheimer's type); amnestic disorders

2 **Schizophrenic and other psychotic disorders:** schizophrenia (paranoid, disorganised, catatonic, undifferentiated and residual types); schizophreniform disorder; schizoaffective disorder

3 **Substance-related disorders:** alcohol-use disorders; hallucinogen-use disorders; opioid-use disorders; sedative, hypnotic or anxiolytic substance-use disorders

4 **Mood disorders:** depressive disorders (e.g. major depressive disorder); bipolar disorders (e.g. bipolar I disorder, such as single manic episode, and bipolar II disorder, i.e. recurrent major depressive episodes with hypomania); cyclothymic disorder

5 **Anxiety disorders:** panic disorder (with or without agoraphobia); agoraphobia; specific or simple phobia; social phobia; obsessive–compulsive disorder; post-traumatic stress disorder

6 **Somatoform disorders:** somatisation disorder; conversion disorder; hypochondriasis

7 **Dissociative disorders:** dissociative disorder; dissociative fugue; dissociative identity disorder or multiple personality disorder; depersonalisation disorder

8 **Adjustment disorders:** adjustment disorder (with anxiety, depressed mood, disturbance of conduct, mixed disturbance of emotions and conduct, or mixed anxiety and depressed mood)

9 **Disorders first diagnosed in infancy, childhood or adolescence:** mental retardation (mild, moderate, severe, profound); learning disorders (reading disorder, mathematic disorder, disorder of written expression); disruption-behaviour and attention deficit disorders (attention deficit/hyperactivity disorder)

10 **Personality disorders:** paranoid; schizoid; schizotypal; antisocial; borderline; histrionic; narcissistic; avoidant; dependent; obsessive–compulsive

11 Sexual and gender identity disorders: sexual desire disorders; sexual arousal disorders; paraphilias (e.g. exhibitionism, fetishism, voyeurism); gender identity disorders (in children or in adolescents and adults)

12 Impulse control disorders not elsewhere classified: intermittent explosive disorder; kleptomania; pyromania; pathological gambling

13 Factitious disorders: factitious disorder with predominantly psychological or physical signs and symptoms

14 Sleep disorders: dyssomnias (e.g. primary insomnia, narcolepsy); parasomnias (e.g. sleep terror disorder, sleepwalking disorder)

15 Eating disorders: anorexia nervosa; bulimia nervosa

16 Mental disorders due to a general medical condition not elsewehere classified: catatonic disorder due to a general medical condition; personality change due to a general medical condition

17 Other conditions that may be a focus of clinical attention: relational problems (e.g. partner or sibling relational problem); problems related to abuse or neglect (e.g. physical and/or sexual abuse of child); additional conditions that may be a focus of clinical attention (e.g. bereavement, occupational problem, phase of life problem).

COMPARING ICD-10 AND DSM-IV

ICD-10 and DSM-IV overlap extensively and, for many categories, they are virtually identical (Cooper, 1995). For example, what ICD-10 calls *mental and behavioural disorders due to psychoactive substance use* are referred to as *substance-related disorders* in DSM-IV.

From Boxes 67.2 and 67.3 it is also clear, however, that each system uses a different number of major categories, and that differences arise because of the larger number of discrete categories used in DSM-IV to classify disorders that appear under a smaller number of more general categories in ICD. For example, *neurotic, stress-related* and *somatoform* disorders appear as a single category in ICD-10 and include those appearing under four headings in DSM-IV (*anxiety disorders, somatoform disorders, dissociative disorders* and *adjustment disorders*). Similarly, what ICD-10 calls *disorders of adult personality and behaviour* appears in DSM under four headings (*personality disorders, sexual and gender identity disorders, impulse control disorders not elsewhere classified* and *factitious disorders*). Additionally, a general DSM-IV category can incorporate more than one ICD-10 category. For example, what DSM-IV calls

disorders usually first diagnosed in infancy, childhood or adolescence is categorised by ICD-10 as *behavioural and emotional disorders with onset usually occurring in childhood or adolescence, disorders of psychological development* and *mental retardation*.

PSYCHOSIS AND NEUROSIS

One of abnormal psychology's oldest distinctions has been between *psychosis* and *neurosis*. As a psychiatrist's joke has it, the psychotic believes that $2 + 2 = 5$, whilst the neurotic knows that $2 + 2 = 4$ but is really bothered by the fact. Of course, the distinction is much more complex than the joke would suggest.

> **Box 67.4   The traditional distinctions made between neurosis and psychosis**
>
> **Effects on personality:** Only a part of personality is affected in neurosis. In psychosis, the whole of personality is affected.
>
> **Contact with reality:** The neurotic maintains contact with reality, whereas the psychotic loses contact. Hallucinations and delusions, for example, represent the inability to distinguish between subjective experience and external reality.
>
> **Insight:** The neurotic has insight, and recognises a problem exists. The psychotic lacks this insight.
>
> **Relationship of disorder with 'normal' behaviour:** Neurotic behaviours are an exaggeration of normal behaviour. Psychotic behaviours are *discontinuous* with normal behaviour.
>
> **Relationship of disorder with pre-morbid personality:** Neurotic disturbances are related to the individual's personality prior to the disorder (the pre-morbid personality). Psychotic disorders are not related to the pre-morbid personality.

Although the traditional distinction between psychosis and neurosis has been dropped in present classificatory systems, ICD-10 still uses the term *neurotic* and DSM-IV the term *psychotic*. Gelder *et al.* (1989) identify four reasons for abolishing the distinction. First, disorders that were included under the broad categories of neurosis and psychosis actually had little in common. Thus, diverse conditions were grouped together under these broad headings. Second, it is less informative to classify a disorder as neurotic or psychotic than to classify it as a disorder *within* those very broad categories. For example, the label *schizophrenic* is much more informative than the label *psychotic*. Third, the criteria used to distinguish neurosis and psychosis are all liable to exceptions. Finally, the neuroses were grouped because of the view that they shared common origins (a view strongly influenced by the psychodynamic model), rather than on the basis of observable commonalities between them.

Despite moves to abolish the distinction between psychosis and neurosis, the terms are still used in everyday psychiatric practice, as they are convenient terms for disorders that cannot be given more precise diagnoses. They are also still in general use as, for example, is the case with the term *antipsychotic drugs* to describe drugs used to treat schizophrenia (see Chapter 72, page 620).

Classificatory systems and the concept of mental illness

Although neither DSM-IV nor ICD-10 uses the term *mental illness*, much of abnormal psychology's vocabulary comes from medicine. For example, abnormal behaviour is referred to as *psychopathology* and is classified on the basis of its *symptoms*, the classification being called a *diagnosis*. *Therapy* refers to methods used to change behaviour, and therapies are often conducted in *mental hospitals*. Indeed, the individual is usually referred to as a *patient* and considered *cured* when the abnormal behaviour is no longer displayed.

The tendency to think about abnormal behaviour as indicative of some underlying illness has been defended by Blaney (1975), on the grounds that it is more *humane* to regard the disturbed individual as *ill* or *mad* rather than simply *bad*. However, critics argue that the label *mentally ill* removes *responsibility* for behaviour, and a person so described is seen as being a 'victim' to whom something has happened and who needs 'care'. However, the label *mentally ill* may be more stigmatising than the label *bad* or *morally defective*, since illness is something a person has no control over, whilst 'being bad' implies an element of choice.

Box 67.5   Labelling

Szasz (1974, 1994) argues that stigmatising labels are used for political purposes by those in power to exclude people who have upset the social order. Of course, behaviours that society does not approve of can result in imprisonment. The imprisoned person is, however, still seen as being responsible for his or her behaviour. Yet in the former Soviet Union, for example, political

dissidents were diagnosed as schizophrenic for expressing views that only a person whom the authorities saw as 'not being in their right mind' would express. Since those views were expressed, dissidents were obviously not 'in their right minds'.

Labelling has many other negative consequences. For example, people react to 'former mental patients' more negatively than to people with the same symptoms who are not so labelled (Farina, 1992). Labelling also denies people's uniqueness if they are pigeon-holed and stereotyped in terms of a diagnostic category. A label may even become *self-fulfilling*: a person might respond to being labelled by behaving in a way that is consistent with the label, thus *confirming* the label that was originally applied.

Szasz (1962) argued that psychiatry assumes that mental illness is caused by diseases or disorders of the nervous system, particularly the brain, and that these manifest themselves in terms of abnormal thinking and behaviour. If this is so, argues Szasz, then they should be called *diseases of the brain* or *neurophysiological disorders*. This would remove the confusion between disorders with a physical or organic basis and the 'problems in living' the person might have. The former, of course, must be seen in an anatomical and physiological context, whereas the latter must be seen in an ethical and social one.

Szasz argued that the vast majority of 'mental illnesses' are actually 'problems in living', and that it is the exception rather than the rule to come across an individual suffering from some organic brain disorder, who would be considered 'mentally ill'. This fact is recognised by those psychiatrists who distinguish between *organic psychoses* (which have an underlying physical cause) and *functional psychoses* (which either do not or have yet to be shown to have an underlying physical cause: Bailey, 1979, see below). Indeed, even if the functional psychoses could be shown to be organic, there would still be many disorders which even organic psychiatrists would accept cannot be conceived of as bodily diseases (Heather, 1976).

Furthermore, if an illness does not affect the brain, then how can something like the mind (a non-spatial, non-physical entity) be conceived of as suffering from a disorder of a physico-chemical nature? (see Chapter 81). Like Szasz, Bailey has argued that organic mental illnesses are not actually mental illnesses at all. Rather, they are *physical illnesses* in which mental symptoms are manifested, and these aid diagnosis and treatment. Additionally, functional mental illnesses are also not illnesses. Rather, they are disorders of *psychosocial or interpersonal functioning*

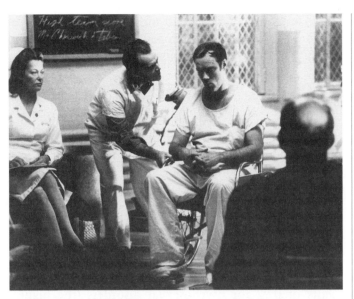

Figure 67.1   A still from *One Flew Over the Cuckoo's Nest* (1975). McMurphy (Jack Nicholson) is trying to persuade an unresponsive member of the ward therapy group to vote for a change in the ward routine at the state mental hospital where both are patients. McMurphy is an anti-conformist, a charming, but manipulative rebel, who gets involved in a power struggle with 'Big Nurse' Ratched (Louise Fletcher); she succeeds in preventing the desired change. Eventually, McMurphy is crushed by the system, which labels his rebellious behaviour 'mental illness' and 'treats' it, initially by ECT and finally by lobotomy. In this way, not only is his rebelliousness stopped, but his entire personality is destroyed

(Szasz's 'problems in living') in which mental symptoms are important in determining an appropriate form of therapy.

As a result of this debate, neither DSM-IV nor ICD-10 uses the term *mental illness*. Instead, *mental disorder* is used, which DSM-IV defines as:

> 'a clinically significant behaviour or psychological syndrome or pattern that occurs in a person and that is associated with present distress (a painful symptom), disability (impairment of one or more important areas of functioning), a significant increased risk of suffering death, pain, disability or an important loss of freedom. In addition, this syndrome or pattern must not be merely an expectable response to a particular event such as, for example, the death of a loved one'.

ICD-10 uses the term *mental disorder* to imply the existence of a clinically recognisable set of symptoms or behaviours associated in most cases with distress and interference with personal functions.

Box 67.6   The end of 'organic'?

DSM-IV has removed the category *organic mental disorders* and replaced it with *delirium, dementia, amnestic and other cognitive disorders*, because it implies that other disorders in the manual do not have an organic component. According to Henderson *et al.* (1994), because research has shown that biological factors influence a whole range of disorders, it is misleading to use the term *organic*. Consequently, the concept of psychological abnormality has become even more 'medicalised' than ever. Whilst ICD-10 retains a separate category for *organic* disorders, the use of the word organic has been challenged as 'a neuropsychiatrist's nightmare' (Lewis, 1994), although DSM-IV's preference for *cognitive* instead of *organic* may be seen as undervaluing the frequent behavioural component in many cognitive (or organic) disorders (Henderson *et al.*, 1994).

The goals of classification

Whatever their differences and similarities, both DSM-IV and ICD-10 have certain *goals*. The first is *to provide a common shorthand language*, that is, a common set of terms with agreed-on meanings. Diagnostic categories summarise large amounts of information about characteristic symptoms and a disorder's typical cause, along with its typical age of onset, predisposing factors, course, prevalence, sex ratio and associated problems. This allows effective communication between professionals, research on different aspects of disorders, and an evaluation of appropriate treatment (see below).

The second goal concerns *understanding the origins of disorders*. If disorders have different origins, these might be uncovered by grouping people according to behavioural similarities and then looking for other similarities. For example, a group of people displaying a particular behaviour might show, say, a certain structural brain abnormality or have had similar early experiences. Accurate diagnosis is necessary to enable research to be carried out into their origins. Any conclusions are likely to be biased if people have been assigned to the wrong grouping. Additionally, misdiagnoses produce inaccurate estimates about the *incidence* and *prevalence* of mental disorders, as well as misleading information about their causes and correlates. Fewer mistakes would be made if more was known about the causes and natural history of disorders.

The third goal concerns *treatment plans*. Since there is a wide variety of therapies (see Chapters 72 to 76), accurate diagnosis is necessary to match a disorder to a treatment and ensure maximum benefit for the individual. By treating everybody as new and unique, it is difficult to predict how to treat any one. Therefore, knowing that a person's symptoms are similar to those of another person whose progress followed a particular course, or who benefitted from a certain kind of treatment, can also be helpful.

SOME PROBLEMS WITH THE CLASSIFICATION OF MENTAL DISORDERS

The goals of classification can only be achieved if the classification of abnormal behaviour is both *reliable* and *valid*. In one of psychology's most famous investigations, Rosenhan (1973) reported what happened when eight psychiatrically normal people from various backgrounds presented themselves at the admissions offices of different American psychiatric hospitals, complaining of hearing bizarre and disembodied voices saying 'empty', 'hollow' and 'thud'.

Box 67.7   On being sane in insane places (Rosenhan, 1973)

All of the *pseudopatients* were admitted to the hospitals, most being diagnosed as schizophrenic. Once admitted, they behaved normally. However, their diagnoses seemed to bias the staff's interpretation of their behaviours. For example, pacing a corridor out of boredom was interpreted as 'anxiety' by the staff. When one pseudopatient began to make notes, it was recorded as 'patient engages in writing behaviour'.

Shortly after admission, the pseudopatients stopped claiming to hear voices, and all were eventually discharged with diagnoses of 'schizophrenia in remission' (a lessening in the degree of schizophrenic symptoms). The only people who were apparently suspicious of them were their 'fellow' patients, one of whom commented, 'You're not crazy, you're a journalist or a professor. You're checking up on the hospital'. It took between seven and 52 days (the average being 19) for staff to be convinced that the pseudopatients were 'well enough' to be discharged.

In a second investigation, members of a teaching hospital were told about Rosenhan's findings and informed that more pseudopatients would try to gain admission to the hospital during a particular three-month period. Each staff member was asked to rate every new patient as an impostor or not. During the period, 193 patients were admitted, of whom 41 were confidently alleged to be impostors by at least one member of staff. Twenty three were suspected by one psychiatrist, and a further 19 were suspected by one

psychiatrist *and* one other staff member. However, Rosenhan did not send *any* pseudopatients. All of those who presented themselves for admission were genuine.

The reliability of classificatory systems

In this context, *reliability* refers to the *consistency* of a diagnosis across repeated measurements. Clearly, no classificatory system is of value unless users can agree with one another when trying to reach a diagnosis. Zigler & Phillips (1961) reported a range of 54–84 per cent agreement in studies assessing reliability for broad categories of disorders. However, Kendell (1975) showed that when more differentiated categories were used (such as specific types of anxiety), reliability ranged from only 32–57 per cent.

Davison & Neale (1994) have reported reliability coefficients of 0.92 for psychosexual disorders (the highest agreement rate) and 0.54 for somatoform disorders (the lowest). Although agreement for some disorders is low, they are as good as those in some medical diagnoses. For example, an agreement rate of only 66 per cent has been reported for cause of death when death certificates were compared with post-mortem reports, and agreement between doctors regarding angina, emphysema and tonsillitis (diagnosed without a definitive laboratory test) was no better, and sometimes worse, than that for schizophrenia (Falek & Moser, 1975).

There have been several attempts to improve the reliability of diagnosis. The *US–UK diagnostic project* (Cooper *et al.*, 1972) arose from the observation that schizophrenia was much more likely to be diagnosed by American than British psychiatrists, whereas for manic depression the reverse was true. Cooper *et al.* found that when specific criteria for the two disorders were established and the clinicians trained in these, the agreement level rose significantly. Agreement can also be improved if psychiatrists use standardised interview schedules such as Wing *et al.*'s (1974) *present state examination* (e.g. Okasha *et al.*, 1993).

In DSM-III (1980), a system of *multiaxial classification* was introduced. DSM-II (1968) required only a 'diagnostic label' (such as schizophrenia) to be used. However, DSM-III and DSM-IV make use of five different axes which represent different areas of functioning.

Box 67.8   The five axes used in DSM-IV

Axis I: Clinical syndromes and other conditions that may be a focus of clinical attention: This lists all the mental

---

disorders (except personality disorders and mental retardation). A person with more than one disorder has all listed, with the principal disorder listed first. 'Other conditions' may include problems related to abuse or neglect, academic problems and 'phase of life' problems.

Axis II: Personality disorders: These are life-long, deeply ingrained, inflexible and maladaptive traits and behaviours which may occur quite independently of Axis I clinical disorders. They are likely to affect an individual's ability to be treated.

Axis III: General medical conditions: This lists any medical conditions that could potentially affect a person's mental state and hence would be relevant to understanding and treating a disorder.

Axis IV: Psychosocial and environmental problems: These are problems that might affect the diagnosis, treatment and prognosis of a diagnosed disorder. For example, a person may have experienced a stressful event such as divorce or the death of a loved one. Ratings are made from one to seven, with seven indicating a *catastrophic* event or events.

Axis V: Global assessment of functioning: On this, the clinician provides a rating of the person's psychological, social and occupational functioning. Using the *global assessment of functioning scale*, nought denotes *persistent danger* and 100 *superior functioning* with no symptoms.

Rather than being assigned to a single category, people are assessed more broadly, giving a more global and in-depth picture. Axes I, II and III are compulsory in terms of diagnosis, but Axes IV and V are optional. Although ICD-10 does not have the same separate axes, built into its groupings of disorders are broad types of aetiology or causes (such as organic causes, substance use and stress).

During ICD-10's construction, it was agreed that the incomplete and controversial state of knowledge about the causes of mental disorders meant that classification should be worked out on a *descriptive* basis. This implied that disorders should be grouped according to similarities and differences of symptoms and signs, so that a particular disorder should appear only in one diagnostic category. Unfortunately, this did not appeal to clinicians, who like to give prominence to aetiology (causation) wherever possible. As a result, ICD-10 includes broad types of aetiology within its various categories. Whilst ICD-10 is 'impure' from a classificatory view, it is much more likely to be used by clinicians (Cooper, 1995). DSM-IV, by contrast, makes no assumptions about causation when a diagnosis is made and is *atheoretical*.

Both DSM-IV and ICD-10 appear to be much more reliable than their predecessors, and ICD-10's clinical guidelines are suitable for widespread international use because of their high reliability (Sartorius *et al.*, 1993). Holmes (1994) reports that the use of *decision trees* (as shown in Figure 67.2), and *computer programs* to aid diagnosis, has also increased reliability. Even so, there is still room for subjective interpretation in the diagnostic process. For example, in *mania* (see Chapter 69, page 596), the elevated mood must be 'abnormally and persistently elevated', and the assessment on Axis V requires comparison between the individual 'and an average person', which begs the question of what an average person actually is (Davison & Neale, 1994).

The validity of classificatory systems

Validity refers to an estimation of a particular measure's accuracy. In this context, validity is the extent to which a diagnosis reflects an actual disorder. Clearly, reliability is a precondition for validity. If a disorder cannot be agreed upon, the different views expressed cannot all be correct. Because there is no absolute standard against which a diagnosis can be compared for most disorders, validity is much more difficult to assess and there is no guarantee that a person has received the 'correct' diagnosis (Holmes, 1994).

At least one purpose of making a diagnosis is to enable a suitable program of treatment to be chosen (the third goal of classification identified above). However, there is only a 50 per cent chance of correctly predicting what treatment people will receive on the basis of the diagnosis they are given (Heather, 1976). Indeed, in a 1000 cases studied by Bannister *et al.* (1964), there was no clear-cut relationship between diagnosis and treatment (one reason being that factors other than diagnosis may be equally important in deciding on a particular treatment).

Critics of classificatory systems argue that the diagnostic process cannot be valid if the label a person is given does not allow a clinician to make a judgement about the disorder's cause or a prediction about prognosis and likely response to treatment. As Mackay (1975) has observed:

'The notion of illness implies a relatively discrete disease entity with associated signs and symptoms, which has a specific cause, a certain probability of recovery and its own treatments. The various states of unhappiness, anxiety and confusion which we term "mental illness" fall far short of these criteria in most cases.'

Defenders of classificatory systems have countered their critics by comparing psychiatric diagnosis with medical diagnosis. As noted previously, medical diagnosis is not without its problems. Moreover, whilst Rosenhan's (1973) study is widely interpreted as a damning indictment of psychiatric diagnosis, his claims can be disputed.

Box 67.9   Some challenges to Rosenhan's (1973) study

As the clinicians in Rosenhan's study were not required to distinguish between normal and abnormal, the study tells us nothing about the accuracy of diagnosis *per se*. Rather, the study was really assessing whether people pretending to have mental disorders could be detected. Spitzer (1975) has made the following observations:

- On the basis of the clinician's data, no diagnoses other than those given were justified. Each pseudopatient *insisted* on admission, which itself is an important symptom of emotional disturbance. A person who swallowed a quart of blood and then went to hospital vomiting blood would probably be diagnosed as having a peptic ulcer. Just because the physician failed to notice the deception would not imply that diagnosis was impossible (Kety, 1974).

- The pseudopatients' behaviour after admission was *not* normal. Normal people would say, 'I'm not crazy, I just pretended to be. Now I want to be released'. At least, initially, however, the pseudopatients remained impassive.

- The label *in remission* (which the pseudopatients were released with) is very rarely used and implies that the psychiatrists knew there was something different about the pseudopatients. All the non-psychotic people observed by the psychiatrists were, by virtue of being given the label *in remission*, diagnosed as non-psychotic. This, of course, is a 100 per cent record of accuracy (Fleischman, 1973).

- The use of the word 'insane', whilst catchy, is inaccurate. Insane is not a psychiatric diagnostic category, but a legal term decided in a court of law. As such, Rosenhan used the term incorrectly.

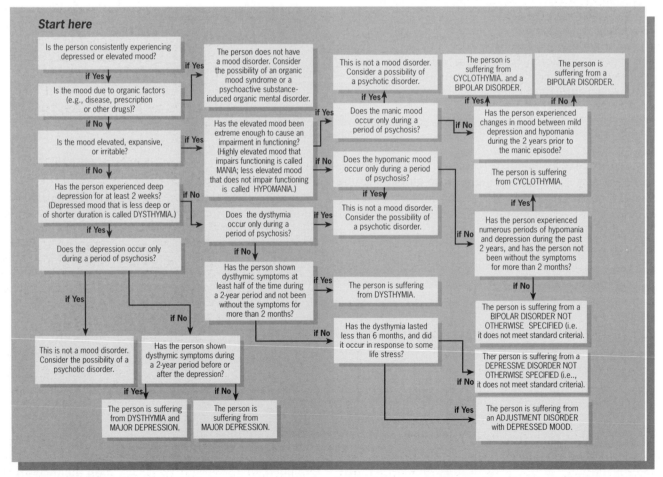

Figure 67.2   Decision tree for mood disorder. Note that cyclothymia (or cyclothymic disorder) is defined as numerous periods of hypomania and depression during the past two years but absent for more than two months. Dysthymia (or dysthymic disorder) refers to a depressed mood that is less severe or shorter lasting than major depression (From Holmes, 1994)

SOME OTHER ISSUES SURROUNDING CLASSIFICATORY SYSTEMS

When Kraepelin visited south-east Asia at the turn of the century, he noted that there were cultural variations in mental disorders. Despite this, he considered mental disorder to be universal. As he noted:

> 'Mental illness in Java showed broadly the same clinical picture as we see in our country ... The overall similarity far outweighed the deviant features' (cited in Dein, 1994).

Box 67.10   Transcultural psychiatry

Until quite recently, Western diagnostic categories were viewed as universal, and non-Western patterns of unusual or undesirable behaviour were seen as variants of these Western categories. According to Dein (1994), *transcultural psychiatry* was preoccupied with the pursuit of *culture-bound syndromes* and the systematic attempt to fit them into Western psychiatric categories. The view was taken that, whilst the expression of a disorder might be culturally variable, there was a *core* hidden within the disorder which is common to all cultures (Littlewood, 1992). Unfortunately, the difficulty with this is that the *biological core* remained elusive.

Transcultural psychiatry is 'now synonymous with the psychiatry of ethnic minorities' (Dein, 1994). Rather than looking at the pathological aspects of immigrant groups' cultures, emphasis has changed to a preoccupation with race and racism. In Britain, markedly increased rates of schizophrenia among Afro-Caribbean immigrants and overdoses among British Asian women have been the themes that have attracted most attention. Although black people account for only five per cent of the total British population, 25 per cent of patients on psychiatric wards are black (Banyard, 1996: see Figure 67.3). According to Littlewood & Lipsedge (1989), black patients in psychiatric hospitals are more likely than white patients to see a junior doctor, rather than a consultant or senior doctor, and are more likely to receive some types of therapy than others.

Several explanations have been advanced to explain the higher incidence of diagnosed schizophrenia in immigrant groups (Gaines, 1992). One of these concerns the misinterpretation by white, middle class psychiatrists of behaviour which is perfectly ordinary within Afro-Caribbean culture. For white people, dominoes is a quiet affair, the silence being broken only when a player 'knocks' to indicate a domino cannot be played. The way

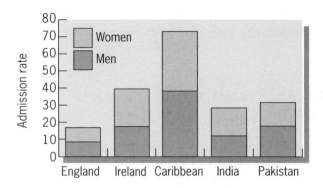

Figure 67.3   Country of birth and hospital admission for schizophrenia (From Banyard, 1996a)

Caribbean men play dominoes, however, could be seen as 'aggressive' and 'threatening' by a white observer, who might consider such behaviour to be indicative of a psychological problem (Banyard, 1996a).

Another explanation derives from the observation that of those people from Caribbean backgrounds diagnosed as schizophrenic, only 15 per cent showed the classic diagnostic indicators. The other 85 per cent had a distinctive pattern of symptoms which some psychiatrists refer to as *West Indian psychosis* (Littlewood & Lipsedge, 1989). Littlewood and Lipsedge have argued that mental illness in ethnic minorities is often an intelligible response to disadvantage and racism.

Box 67.11   The adaptive paranoid response

One of the major 'symptoms' displayed by members of ethnic minorities is the feeling of being persecuted (a *delusion of persecution*: see Chapter 68, page 587). Delusions are false beliefs. If a person believes that someone is 'out to get me', when this is not the case, he or she is deluded. But if someone really *is* being persecuted, the belief is an accurate perception of the world rather than a delusion. Grier & Cobbs (1968) use the term *adaptive paranoid response* to describe a mental disorder brought about by a hostile environment. In a society which is intolerant of minority groups, survival depends at least partly on a 'healthy' cultural paranoia, which is a demanding requirement.

Several other issues have also interested transcultural psychiatrists. Littlewood (1992), for example, has challenged the international validity of DSM-IV on the grounds that the assumptions Axis V (global assessment of functioning) makes about nuclear family life, occupation and education are *ethnocentric* (see Chapter 84). Scheper-Hughes (1991) discusses the political implications of psychiatric diagnosis and the way that psychiatric diagnoses may function as ideologies, which mystify reality, obscure relations of power and domination and prevent people from grasping their situations in the world. In Brazil, for example, hunger is medicalised into a diagnosis of *nervos* and treated by medication, an example of psychosocial stress being misidentified in biological terms.

Do we need ICD and DSM?

Since ICD-10 and DSM-IV are so similar, the need for both of them has been questioned. Cooper (1995) points out that from the perspective of the WHO, there is a statutory obligation to the member states of the United Nations Organisation to update the ICD at regular intervals (which, until recently, has been every ten years). The American Psychiatric Association has no such obligation, but Cooper believes that it would argue that national classifications are able to reflect national traditions and usage, and that national pride suggests there should be a worthy successor to DSM-IV.

Conclusions

This chapter has looked at classificatory systems currently used in the diagnosis of abnormal behaviour. Two classificatory systems are currently in use: ICD-10 and DSM-IV. Although generally accepted as being useful, there are important practical and other issues that surround their use.

Summary

- The medical model is the most influential model of abnormality. Central to it is the **classification** and **diagnosis** of mental disorders. Kraepelin's original system proposed 18 distinct disorders, each with its own characteristic pattern of **symptoms** (a **syndrome**), distinct course of development, underlying physical causes, and outcome.

- The **ICD** and **DSM** classificatory systems derive from Kraepelin's work. Their latest versions are **ICD-10** and **DSM-IV**. The former is used in Britain and most other parts of the world. The latter is used in North America.

- There is considerable overlap between the two systems. However, DSM-IV uses a larger number of categories to classify disorders that appear under a smaller number of more general ICD-10 categories. Conversely, a general DSM-IV category sometimes incorporates more than one ICD-10 category.

- Neither ICD-10 nor DSM-IV makes the traditional distinction between **neurosis** and **psychosis**, one reason being that there are exceptions to all the criteria used to make it. However, ICD-10 still uses the term 'neurotic' and DSM-IV the term 'psychotic'. Psychiatrists find it convenient to use them in everyday practice.

- Because of the debate about the meaning of 'mental illness', both DSM-IV and ICD-10 use the term **mental disorder** instead. DSM-IV has dropped the category 'organic mental disorders' because this misleadingly implies that other disorders are not influenced by biological factors. This makes the concept of abnormality more medical than it has ever been.

- Three main goals of classificatory systems are providing a common shorthand language concerning a disorder's relevant aspects, understanding a disorder's origins, and setting up treatment plans. These goals can only be achieved if classificatory systems are both **reliable** and **valid**.

- Reliability refers to the **consistency** with which different users reach the same diagnosis. The degree of agreement varies depending on how broad or specific the category is, and between different disorders. Overall, reliability is as good as in some medical diagnoses.

- DSM-IV uses **multi-axial classification**. This provides a more global and in-depth assessment than just applying a single diagnostic label. Whilst ICD-10 does not have separate axes, broader types of cause (such as organic, substance use and stress) are built into its groupings of disorders. This makes it less 'pure' than DSM-IV from a classificatory perspective, but it is more attractive to clinicians who prefer highlighting aetiology.

- **Validity** is the extent to which a diagnosis reflects an actual disorder. Whilst reliability is a precondition for validity, there is no absolute standard against which a diagnosis can be matched, making validity difficult to assess.

- Studies showing the low predictability of treatment based on patients' diagnoses suggest that classificatory systems have low validity. Similarly, validity requires that clinicians should be able to make judgements about the causes of a disorder and its prognosis.

- Rosenhan found that it was possible for 'pseudopatients' to gain admission into various American psychiatric hospitals, suggesting that clinicians cannot distinguish between the 'sane' and 'insane'. This, and the finding that the genuinely disturbed were sometimes suspected of being pseudopatients have been taken to indicate that psychiatric diagnosis is neither reliable nor valid. Rosenhan's research has, however, been criticised.

■ Until recently, Western diagnostic categories were seen as universal, with a biological 'core' of disorders sometimes hidden by cultural variations. **Transcultural psychiatry** is concerned with these variations or **culture-bound syndromes**. It no longer concentrates on the pathological aspects of immigrant groups' cultures, but looks at the incidence of different disorders among different cultural/ethnic groups, different hospitalisation rates, and issues of race and racism within psychiatry.

■ Axis V **on DSM-IV** (global assessment of functioning) has been accused of being **ethnocentric**. Psychiatric diagnoses may function as ideologies preventing people from appreciating the power relationships in their societies.

PART 2

Psychopathology

SCHIZOPHRENIA

Introduction and overview

Of all the disorders identified in ICD-10 and DSM-IV, schizophrenia is the most serious. Kraepelin (1913) called the disorder *dementia praecox* (*senility of youth*), believing that it occurred early in adult life and was characterised by a progressive deterioration or dementia. However, Bleuler (1911) observed that it often began in later life and was not always characterised by dementia. Bleuler coined the word *schizophrenia* to refer to a *splitting* of the mind's various functions in which the personality loses its unity.

This chapter examines schizophrenia's nature, its characteristics and sub-types and its course. Perhaps because of its nature, schizophrenia's causes have received more attention than any other mental disorder and many theories have been advanced to explain it. This chapter also examines the plausibility of these theories.

The characteristics of schizophrenia

As noted, schizophrenia is a disorder in which personality loses its unity. It should not be confused with *multiple personality disorder*, in which personality splits into two or more separate *identities*. The confusion probably arises because the word *schizophrenia* derives from the Greek words *schizein* (to split) and *phren* (the mind). As will be seen, schizophrenia is a 'splitting' between thoughts and feelings, the consequences being bizarre and maladaptive behaviour.

In Britain, schizophrenia's diagnosis relies on *first-rank symptoms* (Schneider, 1959). The presence of one or more of these, in the absence of brain disease, is likely to result in a diagnosis of schizophrenia. The three first rank symptoms are *passivity experiences and thought disturbances*, *hallucinations* and *primary delusions*.

PASSIVITY EXPERIENCES AND THOUGHT DISTURBANCES

These include *thought insertion* (the belief that thoughts are being inserted into the mind from outside, under the control of external forces), *thought withdrawal* (the belief that thoughts are being removed from the mind under the control of external forces), and *thought broadcasting* (the belief that thoughts are being broadcast or otherwise made known to others). External forces may include 'the Martians', 'the Communists' and 'the Government', and the mechanism by which thoughts are affected is often a 'special ray' or a radio transmitter. Thought broadcasting is also an example of a *delusion* (see below).

HALLUCINATIONS

Hallucinations are perceptions of stimuli not actually present. They may occur in any sense modality, but the most common are *auditory*. Typically, voices come from outside the individual's head and offer a 'running commentary' on behaviour in the third person (such as 'He is washing his hands. Now he'll go and dry them.'). Often, they will comment on the individual's character, usually insultingly, or give commands.

Somatosensory hallucinations involve changes in how the body feels. It may, for example, be described as 'burning' or 'numb'. *Depersonalisation*, in which the person reports feeling separated from the body, may also occur. Hallucinations are often distortions of real environmental perceptual cues, so that noises from (say) a heating system are heard as voices whispering (Frude, 1998).

Box 68.1   What causes auditory hallucinations?

Bick & Kinsbourne (1987) propose that at least some auditory hallucinations may be projections of the individual's *own* thoughts. Friston (cited in Highfield, 1995b) has shown that there is a breakdown in 'dialogue' between the frontal lobes (which deal with intentions) and the temporal lobes (which process language and register the consequences of actions). This results in a failure to integrate behaviour with the perception of its consequences. In auditory hallucinations, normal thoughts may progress via internal language into a form in which they can be articulated and, if desired, spoken. This involves a *feedback loop* which warns the next stage of the process what is happening, and tells us that the inner speech is our own. Auditory hallucinations may occur because the feedback loop is broken. According to Friston, schizophrenics talk to themselves without realising it.

PRIMARY DELUSIONS

Delusions are false beliefs which persist even in the presence of disconfirming evidence. A *delusion of grandeur* is the belief that one is somebody who is or was important or powerful (such as Jesus Christ or Napoleon). A *delusion of persecution* is the belief that one is being plotted or conspired against or being interfered with by certain people or organised groups. A *delusion of reference* is the belief that objects, events and so on have a (typically negative) personal significance. For example, a person may believe that the words of a song specifically refer to him or her. A *delusion of nihilism* is the belief that nothing really exists and that all things are simply shadows. The belief that one has been dead for years and is observing the world from afar is also common. All delusions are held with extraordinary conviction, and the deluded individual may be so convinced of their truth that they are acted on, even if this involves murder.

Box 68.2   Capgras syndrome

Sufferers of Capgras syndrome believe that family members and others are *imposters*. Ramachandran & Hirstein (cited in Johnston, 1997) report the case of D.S., who suffered damage to the right side of his brain following a traffic accident. D.S. shows no physiological response to people's faces or pictures of himself and is convinced that his parents are 'doubles'. Ramachandran and Hirstein believe that when we meet people, the brain creates memory 'files' about them. When we next meet them, our emotional responses cause their files to be retrieved rather than new ones opened. This does not happen in Capgras syndrome because the links between pattern recognition and emotion have been severed.

First rank symptoms are subjective experiences and can only be inferred on the basis of the individual's verbal reports. According to Slater & Roth (1969), hallucinations are the least important first rank symptom because they are not exclusive to schizophrenia (which is also true of delusions: see Chapter 69). Slater and Roth identify four different characteristics of schizophrenia directly observable from behaviour. These are *thought process disorder*, *disturbances of affect*, *psychomotor disorders* and *lack of volition*.

Figure 68.1   There is considerable similarity between the paintings produced by psychotic patients and this section of a picture of Hell, painted by the sixteenth-century Dutch painter Hieronymus Bosch

THOUGHT PROCESS DISORDER

Although constantly bombarded by sensory information, we are usually able to selectively attend to some and exclude the rest (see Chapter 25). This ability is impaired in schizophrenia and leads to overwhelming and unintegrated ideas and sensations, which affect concentration. Thus, schizophrenics are easily distracted. Their failure to maintain an attentional focus is reflected in the inability to maintain a focus of thought. In turn, this is reflected in the inability to maintain a focus in language.

The classic disturbance in the *form* of schizophrenic thought (as opposed to its *content*) involves *loose associations*. In these, the individual shifts from topic to topic as new associations arise, and fails to form coherent and logical thoughts. As a result, language is often rambling and disjointed. Often, one idea triggers an association with another. When associations become too loose, incoherence results (a *word salad*).

Box 68.3   Loose associations and word salad

I am the nun. If that's enough, you are still his. That is a brave cavalier, take him as your husband, Karoline, you well know, though you are my Lord, you were just a dream. If you are the dove-cote, Mrs K. is still beset by fear. Otherwise I am not so exact in eating. Handle the gravy carefully. Where is the paint brush? Where are you, Herman?

(From Bleuler, 1911)

A word's sound may also trigger an association with a similar sounding word (*clang association*) as in:

'The King of Spain feels no pain in the drain of the crane. I'm lame, you're tame: with fame, I'll be the same'.

Schizophrenic thought is also reflected in *neologisms*, the invention of new words (such as *glump* and *wooger*), or the combination of existing words in a unique fashion (such as 'belly bad luck and brutal and outrageous' to describe stomach ache). Other characteristics include *thought blocking*, *literal interpretation* and *poverty of content*.

DISTURBANCES OF AFFECT

In some cases, thought process disorder may be brief and intermittent. However, disturbances of affect (or *emotional disturbances*), and other characteristic disturbances tend to be fairly stable. The three main types of emotional disturbance are *blunting*, *flattened affect* and *inappropriate affect*.

Blunting

This is an apparent lack of emotional sensitivity in which the individual remains impassive in response to events that would ordinarily evoke a strong emotional reaction. For example, when told that a close relative had died, a schizophrenic might respond in a monotonic voice: 'Really? Is that so?'

Flattened affect

This is a more pervasive and general absence of emotional expression in which the person appears devoid of any sort of emotional tone. Flattened affect may reflect the schizophrenic's 'turning off' from stimuli they are incapable of dealing with for self-protection (Mednick, 1958).

Inappropriate affect

This is the display of an emotion which is incongruous with its context. For example, when asked if a meal was enjoyable or when offered a gift, a schizophrenic may become agitated and violent. However, the receipt of bad news may be followed by uncontrolled giggling.

PSYCHOMOTOR DISORDERS

In some schizophrenics, motor behaviour is affected. In *catatonia*, the individual assumes an unusual posture which is maintained for hours or even days. Attempts to alter the posture are usually met with resistance and sometimes violence. In *stereotypy*, the person engages in purposeless, repetitive movements, such as rocking back and forth or knitting an imaginary sweater. Instead of being mute and unmoving, the individual may be wild and excited, showing frenetically high levels of motor activity.

LACK OF VOLITION

This is the tendency to withdraw from interactions with other people. It sometimes involves living an asocial and secluded life, through loss of drive, interest in the environment, and so on. More disturbed individuals appear to be oblivious to others' presence and completely unresponsive when people like friends and relatives attempt contact.

Types of schizophrenia

Both ICD-10 and DSM-IV distinguish between different types of schizophrenia. This is because the disorder's characteristics are so variable.

HEBEPHRENIC SCHIZOPHRENIA

The most severe type of schizophrenia is *hebephrenic* (or *disorganised*) *schizophrenia* (*hebephrenic* means 'silly mind'). It is most often diagnosed in adolescence and young adulthood, and is usually progressive and irreversible. Its main characteristics are incoherence of language, disorganised behaviour, disorganised delusions, vivid hallucinations (often sexual or religious) and a loosening of associations. It is also characterised by flattened or inappropriate affect and by extreme social withdrawal and impairment.

SIMPLE SCHIZOPHRENIA

This usually appears during late adolescence and has a slow, gradual onset. Principally, the individual withdraws from reality, has difficulty in making or maintaining friends, is aimless and lacks drive, and shows a decline in academic or occupational performance. Males often become drifters or tramps, whilst females may become prostitutes. Simple schizophrenia is only recognised by ICD-10 which, whilst acknowledging that it is controversial, retains it because some countries still use it.

CATATONIC SCHIZOPHRENIA

The major characteristic of catatonic schizophrenia is a striking impairment of motor activity. Individuals may hold unusual and difficult positions until their limbs grow swollen, stiff and blue from lack of movement. A particularly striking feature is *waxy flexibility*, in which the individual maintains a position into which he or she has been manipulated by others.

Catatonic schizophrenics may engage in *agitated catatonia*, bouts of wild, excited movement, and may become dangerous and unpredictable. In *mutism*, the person is apparently totally unresponsive to external stimuli. However, catatonic schizophrenics often *are* aware of what others were saying or doing during the catatonic episode, as evidenced by their reports after the episode has subsided. Another characteristic is *negativism*, in which the individual sits either motionless and resistant to instructions or does the opposite of what has been requested.

PARANOID SCHIZOPHRENIA

This has the presence of well-organised, delusional thoughts as its dominant characteristic. Paranoid schizophrenics show the highest level of awareness and least impairment in the ability to carry out daily functions. Thus, language and behaviour appear relatively normal. However, the delusions are usually accompanied by hallucinations which are typically consistent with them. It tends to have a later onset than the other schizophrenias, and is the most homogenous type (paranoid schizophrenics are more alike than simple, catatonic and hebephrenic schizophrenics).

UNDIFFERENTIATED (OR ATYPICAL) SCHIZOPHRENIA

This is a 'catch-all' category for people who either fit the criteria for more than one type, or do not appear to be of any clear type. For example, disorders of thought, perception and emotion, without the features particular to the types described above, would result in the label undifferentiated being applied.

OTHER DISORDERS

These include *schizophreniform psychosis* (similar to schizophrenia, but lasting for less than 6 months), *schizotypal disorder* (eccentric behaviour and unusual thoughts and emotions resembling those of schizophrenia, but without characteristic schizophrenic abnormalities), and *schizoaffective disorder* (episodes in which both schizophrenic and affective characteristics are prominent, but which do not justify a diagnosis of either schizophrenia or an affective disorder).

The course of schizophrenia

The characteristics of schizophrenia rarely appear in 'full-blown' form. Typically, there are three phases in schizophrenia's development. The *prodromal phase* usually occurs in early adolescence (*process schizophrenia*), or in relatively well-adjusted people in early adulthood (*reactive schizophrenia*). The individual becomes less interested in work, school, leisure activities and so on. Typically, he/she becomes increasingly withdrawn, eccentric, emotionally flat, cares little for health and appearance, and shows lowered productivity at either work or school. This phase may last from a few weeks to years.

In the second or *active phase*, the major characteristics of schizophrenia appear. This phase varies in its duration. In some people, it lasts only a few months, whereas in others it lasts a lifetime. If and when this phase subsides (usually when therapy is given), the person enters the *residual phase*. This is characterised by a lessening of the major characteristics and a more-or-less return to the prodromal phase. Around 25 per cent of schizophrenics regain the capacity to function normally, ten per cent remain permanently in the active phase and 50–65 per cent alternate between the residual and active phases (Bleuler, 1978).

Explanations of schizophrenia

BEHAVIOURAL MODEL

According to the behavioural model, schizophrenia can be explained in terms of conditioning and observational learning. Ullman & Krasner (1969) argue that people show schizophrenic behaviour when it is more likely than normal behaviour to be reinforced. In psychiatric institutions, staff may unintentionally reinforce schizophrenic behaviour by paying more attention to those displaying it. Patients can 'acquire' the characteristics by observing others being reinforced for behaving bizarrely. Alternatively, schizophrenia may be acquired through the *absence* of reinforcement for attending to appropriate objects.

Certainly, schizophrenic behaviour can be modified through conditioning (see Chapter 74), although little evidence suggests that such techniques can affect the expression of thought disorders. Moreover, it is difficult to see how schizophrenic behaviour patterns can be *acquired* when people have had no opportunity to observe them. For these reasons at least, it is generally accepted that the behavioural model contributes little to understanding schizophrenia's *causes* (Frude, 1998).

PSYCHODYNAMIC MODEL

One psychodynamic explanation proposes that schizophrenia results from an ego which has difficulty in distinguishing between the self and the external world. Another account attributes it to a *regression* to an infantile stage of functioning. Freud believed that schizophrenia occurred when a person's ego either became overwhelmed by the demands of the id, or was besieged by unbearable guilt from the superego (see Chapter 66).

Rather than resolving the intense *intrapsychic conflict*, the ego retreats to the oral stage of psychosexual development, where the infant has not yet learned that it and the world are separate. Initially, *regressive symptoms* occur, and the individual may experience delusions of self-importance. Fantasies become confused with reality, which gives rise to hallucinations and delusions (Freud called these *restitutional symptoms*), as the ego attempts to regain reality.

The incoherent delusions and bizarre speech patterns displayed in schizophrenia *may* make sense when preceded by the phrase 'I dreamed …'. However, the fact that schizophrenic behaviour is not that similar to infantile behaviour, and the psychodynamic model's inability to predict schizophrenic outcome on the basis of theoretically predisposing early experiences, has resulted in it being given little credibility.

THE ROLE OF SOCIAL AND FAMILY RELATIONSHIPS

According to Bateson *et al.* (1956), parents predispose children to schizophrenia by communicating in ways that place them in 'no-win' situations. A father might, for example, complain about his daughter's lack of affection, whilst simultaneously telling her that she is too old to hug him when she tries to be affectionate. Bateson *et al.* used the term *double bind* to describe such contradictory multiple verbal and non-verbal messages. Children who experience double binds may lose their grip on reality and see their own feelings, perceptions, knowledge and so on as being unreliable indicators of it.

Similarly, *deviant communication* within families may lead to children doubting their own feelings and perceptions. Wynne *et al.* (1977) propose that some parents often refuse to recognise the meaning of words used by their children and instead substitute words of their own. This can be confusing if the children are young, and may play a role in schizophrenia's development.

The view that social and family interactions play a causal role in schizophrenia's development lacks empirical support, and has difficulty in explaining why abnormal patterns develop in some rather than all the children in a family. Klebanoff (1959) has suggested that the family patterns correlated with schizophrenia actually constitute a *reasonable* response to an unusual child. Thus, children who were brain-damaged and retarded tended to have mothers that were more possessive and controlling than mothers of non-disturbed children. Although family factors probably do not play a causal role in the development of schizophrenia, how the family reacts to offspring when the symptoms have appeared may play a role in influencing an individual's functioning. In support of this, Doane *et al.* (1985) found that the recurrence of schizophrenic symptoms was reduced when parents reduced their hostility, criticism and intrusiveness towards the offspring.

COGNITIVE MODEL

As noted previously, schizophrenia is characterised by disturbances in thought, perception, attention and language. The cognitive model views these as *causes* rather than *consequences* of the disorder. Maher (1968) sees the bizarre use of language as a result of faulty information processing. When words with multiple meanings to an individual (*vulnerable words*) are used, a person may respond in a personally relevant but semantically irrelevant or inappropriate way.

The cognitive model proposes that catatonic schizophrenia may be the result of a breakdown in auditory selective attention (see Chapter 25). Because our abilities to process information are limited, we need to purposefully select information to process. Impairment of the selective attention mechanism would result in the senses being bombarded with information. The catatonic schizophrenic's lack of interaction with the outside world may occur because it is the only way in which sensory stimulation can be kept to a manageable level (Pickering, 1981: see Box 68.7).

MEDICAL MODEL
Genetic influences

Schizophrenia has a tendency to run in families. The likelihood of a person developing it is about one in 100. However, with one schizophrenic parent, the likelihood increases to one in five. If both parents are schizophrenic, it increases to about one in two or one in three. These observations have led some researchers to propose that schizophrenia can be explained in *genetic* terms.

> ### Box 68.6   Concordance and discordance
>
> One method of studying the inheritance of characteristics involves comparing the *resemblance* of identical and non-identical twins (and, in very rare cases, quadruplets: see Rosenthal, 1963). With *continuous* characteristics (e.g. intelligence test scores), resemblance is defined in terms of *correlation*. However, schizophrenia is considered to be *discontinuous* (a person either is schizophrenic or is not) and resemblance is defined in terms of a *concordance rate*. If two twins are schizophrenic, they are *concordant* for schizophrenia. If one is schizophrenic and the other is not, they are *discordant*.

Gottesman & Shields (1972) looked at the history of 45,000 individuals treated at two London hospitals between 1948 and 1964. They identified 57 schizophrenics with twins who agreed to participate in their study. Using diagnosis and hospitalisation as the criteria for schizophrenia, the researchers reported a concordance rate of 42 per cent for identical (monozygotic or MZ) twins and nine per cent for non-identical (dizygotic or DZ) twins.

Other studies have consistently reported concordance rates which are higher for MZs than DZs (see Table 68.1, page 592). In *all* of them, though, the concordance rate is less than the theoretically expected 100 per cent. However, Heston (1970) found that if a MZ had a schizophrenic disorder, there was a 90 per cent chance that the other twin had *some sort* of mental disorder.

Of course, the *environment* may play an influential role, and given that twins tend to be raised in the same environment, it would be reckless to attribute Heston's (and others') findings exclusively to genetic factors. However, when MZs are separated at birth (and presumably raised in different environments), the concordance rate is as high as that obtained for MZs raised in the same environment (Gottesman, 1991).

Clearly, looking at MZs reared apart is one way round the problem of controlling environmental factors. Another is to study children of schizophrenic parents brought up in foster or adoptive homes. The usual method is to compare the incidence of schizophrenia in the biological and adoptive parents of adopted children with the disorder. Heston (1966) compared 47 children of schizophrenic mothers adopted before the age of one month, with 50 children raised in the home of their biological and non-schizophrenic mothers. Psychiatrists' 'blind' testing of the children revealed that ten per cent with schizophrenic mothers were diagnosed as schizophrenic, whereas no children of non-schizophrenic mothers were so diagnosed.

Table 68.1 Concordance rates for schizophrenia for identical (MZ) and non-identical (DZ) twins (Based on Rose *et al.*, 1984)

Study	'Narrow' concordance *		'Broad' concordance *	
	% MZs	% DZs	% MZs	% DZs
Rosanoff *et al.* (1934) USA (41 MZs, 53 DZs)	44	9	61	13
Kallmann (1946) USA (174 MZs, 296 DZs)	59	11	69	11–14
Slater (1953) England (37 MZs, 58 DZs)	65	14	65	14
Gottesman & Shields (1966) England (24 MZs, 33 DZs)	42	15	54	18
Kringlen (1968) Norway (55 MZs, 90 DZs)	25	7	38	10
Allen *et al.* (1972) USA (95 MZs, 125 DZs)	14	4	27	5
Fischer (1973) Denmark (21 MZs, 41 DZs)	24	10	48	20

(* 'Narrow' based on attempt to apply a relatively strict set of criteria when diagnosing schizophrenia. 'Broad' includes 'borderline schizophrenia', 'schizoaffective psychosis' and 'paranoid with schizophrenia-like features'.)

Also, children of schizophrenic mothers were more likely than children of non-schizophrenic mothers to be:

'morally defective, sociopathic, neurotic, criminal and to have been discharged from the armed forces on psychiatric grounds' (Heston, 1966).

Kety *et al.* (1968) examined Denmark's *Folkregister*, a lifelong record of Danish citizens. The researchers compiled lists of adopted children who either developed or did not develop schizophrenia. Its incidence in the adoptive families of those who developed the disorder (five per cent) was as low as in the adoptive families of those who did not develop it. However, in those who did develop schizophrenia its incidence in the biological families was far higher than expected (21 per cent). If the disposition towards schizophrenia is environmental, the incidence would be higher among adoptive relatives with whom the adopted child shared an environment. However, if

hereditary factors are important, the incidence would be higher in biological than in adoptive relatives (which is what the researchers found). Klaning *et al.* (1996) have looked at the incidence of schizophrenia in twins *as a population* and found that it is higher than in the general population. This might be due to twins' greater exposure to perinatal complications (such as low birth weight) which could lower the 'threshold' for developing schizophrenia. Alternatively, the psychological environment might be different for twins and provide a greater risk of developing the disorder.

From what has been said, genetic factors appear to play some (and perhaps a major) role in schizophrenia. However, attempts to identify the gene or genes *responsible* have not been successful. Claims have been made about genetic markers on chromosomes 5 and 22, and then quickly retracted in the light of subsequent research. As noted, even if genes are involved, genetic factors alone cannot be responsible.

Box 68.7 Chromosome 15 and the alpha-7 nicotinic receptor

Many schizophrenics are chain smokers. This may not be coincidental. Research indicates that a genetic defect on chromosome 15 is responsible for a site in the brain (the alpha-7 nicotinic receptor) that plays a role in filtering information and which can be stimulated by nicotine (Freedman *et al.*, cited in Highfield, 1997c). This is the first time that malfunctioning neurons have been implicated in schizophrenia, and chain-smoking may be an unwitting form of 'self-medication'.

Biochemical influences

One way in which genes may influence behaviour is through biochemical agents in the brain (see Chapter 66, page 569). According to the *inborn-error of metabolism hypothesis*, some people inherit a metabolic error which causes the body to break down naturally occurring chemicals into toxic ones which are responsible for schizophrenia's characteristics. Osmond & Smythies (1953) noted that there were similarities between the experiences of people who had taken hallucinogenic drugs and those of people diagnosed as schizophrenic. Some evidence supports the view that the brain produces its own *internal hallucinogens*. For example, Smythies (1976) found small amounts of hallucinogen-like chemicals in schizophrenics' cerebrospinal fluid, whilst Murray *et al.* (1979) reported that the hallucinogen *dimethyltryptamine* (DMT) was present in schizophrenics' urine. Moreover, when DMT levels decreased, schizophrenic symptoms also decreased. However, later research indicated that the characteristics of schizophrenia were *different* from those produced by hallucinogenic drugs, and researchers turned to other biochemicals.

Perhaps because hallucinogenic drugs are chemically similar to noradrenaline and dopamine (which occur naturally in the brain), these neurotransmitters became the focus of research, with dopamine receiving most attention. The earliest theory implicating dopamine proposed that schizophrenia was caused by its *excess* production, and post-mortem studies of diagnosed schizophrenics showed higher than normal concentrations of dopamine, especially in the limbic system (Iversen, 1979). However, rather than producing more dopamine *per se*, it is widely accepted that more dopamine is *utilised* as a result of overly sensitive post-synaptic receptors for it, or because of above normal reactivity to dopamine due to an increased number of receptor sites. For example, the density of one site (the D4 receptor) is six times greater in schizophrenic than non-schizophrenic brain tissue (Davis *et al.*, 1991).

Dopamine's role is supported by several lines of evidence. For example, in non-schizophrenics, cocaine and amphetamine produce delusions of persecution and hallucinations similar to those observed in some types of schizophrenia. Both drugs are known to cause the stimulation of dopamine receptors. Additionally, cocaine and amphetamine *exacerbate* schizophrenic symptoms (Davis, 1974). Research also indicates that drugs which treat schizophrenia (see Chapter 72) reduce the concentration of brain-dopamine by blocking dopamine receptors and preventing them from becoming stimulated (Kimble, 1988).

Box 68.8 The diathesis–stress and vulnerability–stress models

Genetic factors might create a predisposition towards schizophrenia which interacts with other factors to produce the disorder. Whilst most environments are conducive to normal development, some may trigger disorders like schizophrenia. The *diathesis–stress model* is one explanation of an interaction between genetic and biochemical factors, which accounts for the finding that not everybody who might be genetically predisposed to schizophrenia (by virtue of, say, having a schizophrenic parent) develops it.

The model proposes that schizophrenia occurs as a result of a biological vulnerability (*diathesis*) to a disorder interacting with personally significant environmental stressors. Genetic vulnerability puts a person at risk, but

environmental stressors (like leaving home or losing a job) must be present for the gene to be 'switched on'. The *vulnerability–stress model* (Nuechterlein & Dawson, 1984) is an extension of the diathesis–stress model and specifies the genetically determined traits that can make a person vulnerable. These include hyperactivity and information-processing deficits.

Although the evidence linking dopamine to schizophrenia is impressive, its causal role has been questioned. For example, dopamine's availability could be just *one* factor in the sequence of schizophrenia's development rather than the *only* factor. More importantly, drugs used to treat schizophrenia are not always effective (see Chapter 72).

Drugs are evidently only helpful in treating what Kraepelin called the *positive* (or *Type 1*) *symptoms* of schizophrenia (Crow *et al.*, 1982). These include the classic symptoms of delusions, hallucinations and thought disorder. The *negative* (or *Type 2*) *symptoms* of decreased speech, lack of drive, diminished social interaction and loss of emotional response, are little affected by drug treatment. This has led to the proposal that the positive symptoms have one cause (possibly related to dopamine), whereas the negative symptoms have some other cause.

Neurodevelopmental influences

One possible cause of the negative symptoms is *brain damage*. There is evidence of structural abnormalities in schizophrenics' brains, which is 'powerful evidence that schizophrenia is a brain disease' (Johnson, 1989). Stevens (1982) showed that many schizophrenics display symptoms clearly indicating neurological disease, especially with regard to eye movements. These included decreased rate of eye blink, staring, lack of blink reflex in response to a tap on the forehead, poor visual pursuit movements, and poor pupillary reactions to light. Post-mortems suggested a disease that had occurred earlier in life and had partially healed, or one that was slowly progressing at the time of death.

Some schizophrenics underwent difficult births and their brains might have suffered a lack of oxygen (Harrison, 1995). The apparent decline in the number of cases of schizophrenia might be related to improvements in maternity care. Research using imaging devices to compare schizophrenic and non-schizophrenic brains has been reviewed by Chua & McKenna (1995). Several kinds of structural abnormality have been discovered in the schizophrenic brain, including an unusually small corpus collosum, high densities of white matter in the right frontal and parietal lobes, a smaller volume of temporal lobe grey matter, and unusually large ventricles (the hollow spaces in the brain filled with cerebrospinal fluid), indicating the loss of brain tissue elsewhere. However, Chua and McKenna argue that the only well-established structural abnormality in schizophrenia is lateral ventricular enlargement, and even this is modest and shows considerable overlap with the non-schizophrenic population. Whilst schizophrenia is not characterised by any simple focal reduction in brain activity, Chua and McKenna believe that complex alterations in the normal reciprocal patterns of activation between anatomically related areas of the cerebral cortex might characterise the disorder.

Box 68.9   The viral theory of schizophrenia

If schizophrenia is the result of the brain's failure to develop normally for some reason (which would make it a *neurodevelopmental disorder*), it is important to know when this damage occurs. One theory suggests that the damage may be due to a *viral infection*. Seasonal variations in chickenpox and measles (both caused by viruses) are well known. The finding that significantly more people who develop schizophrenia are born in late winter and early spring than at other times of the year is not a statistical quirk (Torrey *et al.*, 1977).

Torrey (1988) believes that schizophrenia may be the result of a virus affecting pre-natal development, especially during the second trimester of pregnancy, when the developing brain is forming crucial interconnections. For example, in normal development, *pre-alpha cells* are formed in the middle of the brain and migrate towards the cortex. In schizophrenic brains, however, the cells get only 85 per cent of the way to their final destination. Support for a viral theory comes from longitudinal studies conducted by Barr *et al.* (1990) and O'Callaghan *et al.* (1991, 1993) who reported an increased risk for schizophrenia for those in the fifth month of foetal development during the 1957 *influenza pandemic*.

Bracha *et al.* (1991) have shown that one MZ twin who develops schizophrenia is significantly more likely to have various hand deformities compared with the other twin. Since the hands are formed during the second trimester of pregnancy, the same pre-natal trauma or virus which affects the brain may also affect the hands. To explain schizophrenia's tendency to run in families, Stevens (1982) has proposed that whatever causes the damage affects only people with an *inherited susceptibility* to schizophrenia and does not affect those with non-schizophrenic heredity.

At present, there is little agreement over the plausibility of viral theories. Some researchers, for example, have failed to find an association between births during the 1957 influenza epidemic and the later development of schizophrenia. It is ridiculous to suggest that the alleged schizophrenogenic effects of the epidemic were genuine and present in Finland, England, Wales and Edinburgh (as some studies have reported) but absent in the rest of Scotland and the United States (which other studies have found), since the virus that caused the epidemic could not have changed (Crow & Done, 1992).

Others have failed to find evidence of *any* significant associations between later schizophrenia and maternal exposure to a variety of infectious diseases other than influenza (O'Callaghan *et al.*, 1994). As Claridge (1987) has remarked, the season of birth effect has many equally plausible explanations, one being that it might reflect the cycles of sexual activity among the parents of future psychotics, a hypothesis which does not seem to have attracted much attention, despite its credibility as an explanation for the data.

What is likely, though, is that schizophrenia is *not* a result of a virus caught from domestic cats, a theory based on the observation that there is a higher incidence of the disorder in countries where cats are kept as pets (Bentall, 1996).

Conclusions

This chapter has looked at schizophrenia's characteristics and various explanations for the disorder. Some are more plausible than others and have received considerable support. However, an explanation which is accepted by all of those working in the area so far remains elusive.

Summary

■ Schizophrenia is the most serious of all the disorders identified in ICD-10 and DSM-IV. In Britain, its diagnosis is based on Schneider's **first rank symptoms (passivity experiences and thought disorder, hallucinations**, and **primary delusions**).

■ First rank symptoms can only be inferred from the individual's verbal reports. Four characteristics directly observable from behaviour are **thought process disorder, disturbances of affect/emotional disturbances, psychomotor disturbances** and **lack of volition**.

■ Both ICD-10 and DSM-IV distinguish between different types of schizophrenia. **Hebephrenic (disorganised)**, catatonic, **paranoid**, and **undifferentiated (or atypical)** schizophrenias are recognised by both systems. ICD-10 also recognises **simple** schizophrenia.

■ The course of schizophrenia is characterised by **prodromal, active,** and **residual phases.** The term **process schizophrenia** is used when the prodromal phase occurs in early adolescence. **Reactive schizophrenia** refers to the prodromal phase occurring in early adulthood. Around 25 per cent of schizophrenics regain the capacity to function normally, and ten per cent remain permanently in the active phase. Fifty to sixty-five per cent alternate between the residual and active phases.

■ The **behavioural model** can account for schizophrenia's maintenance, but has difficulty explaining its origins. The **psychodynamic model's** explanation is a poor predictor of a schizophrenic outcome. Neither model contributes much to understanding schizophrenia's causes.

■ Social and family relationships (**double bind, deviant communication,** and **marital schism/skew**) have also been implicated in schizophrenia. However, it is difficult to explain why only **some** children in a family develop schizophrenia, and family patterns may be a response to an unusual child rather than a cause of abnormality.

■ The observation that schizophrenia tends to run in families, and that schizophrenic parents have a greater chance of producing schizophrenic offspring, suggests that **genetic** factors may be involved in the disorder.

■ There are higher **concordance rates** for schizophrenia in MZ than DZ twins, and a higher incidence of schizophrenia in **adopted** children of schizophrenic parents. Whilst genetic factors appear to play at least some role in schizophrenia, attempts to identify the gene or genes responsible have been equivocal.

■ One way in which genes can influence behaviour is by altering **brain biochemistry.** The **inborn-error of metabolism hypothesis** claims that some people inherit metabolic errors. This causes their bodies to break down naturally occurring chemicals into toxic ones which produce schizophrenia's symptoms.

■ Another hypothesis proposes that the brain produces its own 'internal hallucinogens'. However, whilst early research found similarities between the effects of hallucinogenic drugs and the experiences of schizophrenics, it is generally accepted that this hypothesis is unlikely to be true.

■ Explanations implicating **dopamine** have received more support. Schizophrenia is not caused by an excess of dopamine, but by the manner of its utilisation. Schizophrenics apparently have more numerous or densely packed receptor sites for dopamine.

■ Cocaine and amphetamine stimulate dopamine receptors, producing schizophrenia-like symptoms in non-schizophrenics, and exacerbating the symptoms of diagnosed schizophrenics. Drugs which block dopamine receptors reduce schizophrenic symptoms.

■ The **diathesis–stress model** proposes that schizophrenia is the result of an interaction between biological vulnerability and personally significant environmental stressors. The **vulnerability–stress model** specifies the genetically determined traits that can make a person vulnerable, such as hyperactivity and faulty information-processing.

■ Schizophrenia's **positive (Type 1) symptoms** might have one cause (related to dopamine), whilst its **negative (Type 2)** symptoms might have some other cause (related to brain damage). Damage may be caused by oxygen deficits at birth. However, although there are several structural differences between schizophrenic and non-schizophrenic brains, these differences are modest with considerable overlap between the two populations.

■ Schizophrenia might be a **neurodevelopmental disorder** in which the brain fails to develop normally. One cause might be a **viral infection** occurring during the second trimester of pregnancy when the brain forms crucial interconnections. However, the evidence concerning viral theories is inconclusive and sometimes contradictory.

69

DEPRESSION

Introduction and overview

Mood (or *affective*) *disorders* involve a prolonged and fundamental disturbance of mood and emotions. Mood is a pervasive and sustained emotional state that colours perceptions, thoughts and behaviours. At one extreme is *manic disorder* (or *mania*), characterised by wild, exuberant and unrealistic activity, and a flight of ideas or distracting thoughts. At the other is *depressive disorder*. Mania usually occurs in conjunction with depression and in such cases is called *bipolar disorder*. However, when mania occurs alone, the term bipolar is also used, the term *unipolar* being reserved for the experience of depression only. The term *manic–depressive* refers to both the unipolar and bipolar forms of affective disorder.

This chapter describes depression's characteristics and looks at some of the explanations for 'the common cold' (Seligman, 1973) of psychological problems.

The characteristics of depression

By 'common cold', Seligman means that depression is the most common psychological problem people face. During the coming year, most of us will experience some symptoms of depression (Beck & Young, 1978). When a loved one dies or a relationship ends, depression is a normal reaction. Indeed, most psychologically healthy people occasionally 'get the blues' or 'feel down'. However, this usually passes fairly quickly. For a diagnosis of *clinical depression*, several characteristics need to have co-occurred for a period of time.

> **Box 69.1   The characteristics of clinical depression**
>
> Clinical depression is defined by persistent low mood for at least two weeks, plus at least five of the following:
>
> - poor appetite or weight loss or increased appetite or weight gain (a change of 0.5 kg per week over several weeks or 4.5 kg in a year when not dieting);
> - difficulty in sleeping (*insomnia*) or sleeping longer than usual (*hypersomnia*);

> - loss of energy or tiredness to the point of being unable to make even the simplest everyday decisions;
> - an observable slowing down or agitation. In an attempt to discharge feelings of restlessness, people will often wring their hands, pace about or complain (*agitated depression*);
> - a markedly diminished loss of interest or pleasure in activities that were once enjoyed;
> - feelings of self-reproach or excessive or inappropriate guilt over real or imagined misdeeds. These may develop into *delusions* (see Chapter 68, page 587);
> - complaints or evidence of diminished ability to think or concentrate;
> - recurrent thoughts of death (not just a fear of dying), suicide, suicidal thoughts without a specific plan, or a suicide attempt or a specific plan for committing suicide.
>
> (Adapted from Spitzer *et al.*, 1981)

Unipolar depression can occur at any age, and may appear gradually or suddenly. In the United States, around 15 per cent of adults aged between 18 and 74 will experience serious depression. In Britain, the estimated figure is five per cent (SANE, 1993a).

> **Box 69.2   A typical case of depression**
>
> A 55-year-old man has suffered from appetite loss and a 23 kg weight loss over the past six months. His appetite loss has been accompanied by a burning pain in his chest, back and abdomen, which he is convinced indicates a fatal abdominal cancer. He is withdrawn and isolated, unable to work, uninterested in friends and family, and unresponsive to their attempts to make him feel better. He awakes at 4 a.m. and is unable to fall back asleep. He claims to feel worse in the mornings and to improve slightly as the day wears on. He is markedly agitated and speaks of feelings of extreme unworthiness. He says that he would be better off dead and that he welcomes his impending demise from cancer.
>
> (Adapted from Spitzer *et al.*, 1981)

Deeply embedded within psychiatric thinking is the distinction between *endogenous* and *exogenous* (or *reactive*) depression. Endogenous ('coming from within') was used to describe depression arising from biochemical disturbances in the brain. Exogenous ('coming from the outside') was used to describe depression occurring as a reaction (hence *reactive*) to stressful life experiences. However, this distinction is controversial and endogenous is now used to describe a cluster of symptoms, rather than the origins of the depression (Williams & Hargreaves, 1995).

As stated earlier, bipolar disorder is characterised by alternating periods of mania and depression, which seem to be unrelated to external events. Their duration and frequency vary from person to person. In some cases, manic and depressive episodes may be separated by long periods of normal functioning. In others, the episodes quickly follow one another. These unending cycles can be destructive for the people affected, their families and friends.

Bipolar disorder generally appears in the early 20s. Unlike depression (which is more prevalent in women: see pages 601–602), bipolar disorder is equally prevalent in men and women, although the disorder itself is much less common than depression. Interestingly, there is a disproportionately higher incidence of bipolar disorder among creative people (Jamison, 1989). For example, of 47 award-winning British writers and artists, 38 per cent were treated for the disorder (see also Post, 1994). In the general population, this figure is about one per cent.

> **Box 69.3   A case of bipolar disorder**
>
> For four months, Mrs S. has spent most of her time lying in bed. She appears sad and deep in thought and often states, 'I'm no good to anyone; I'm going to be dead soon'. She expresses feelings of hopelessness and listlessness and has difficulty concentrating. Suddenly, one day, her mood seems to be remarkably better. She is pleasant, verbalises more and appears somewhat cheerful. The following day, however, the rate of her speech is increased, she moves rapidly, shows a flight of ideas, and intrudes into everyone's activities. Over a couple of days, this activity increases to the point where she is unable to control her actions and attempts to break the furniture.
>
> (Adapted from Spitzer *et al.*, 1981)

Explanations of depression

THE BEHAVIOURAL MODEL

Behavioural approaches to depression focus on the role played by *reinforcement*. Ferster (1965) proposed that depression is a result of a reduction in reinforcement. Lewisohn (1974) expanded Ferster's theory and proposed that certain events, such as the death of a loved one, induce depression, because they reduce positive reinforcement.

Depressed people may spend less time in social activities. At least initially, this leads to concern and attention being paid by their friends. Lewinsohn argues that concern and attention *reinforces* the depressed behaviour. However, after a while this concern and attention wanes. Thus, reinforcement is reduced and this exacerbates the depression. The result is that the depressed individual is caught in a cycle from which escape is difficult.

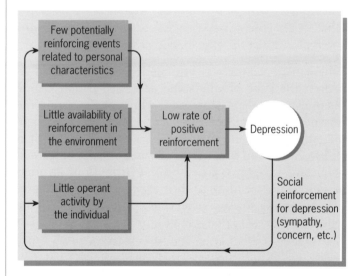

Figure 69.1   Lewinsohn's model of depression

Lewinsohn sees people lacking social skills as prime candidates for depression, because social ineptness is unlikely to bring reinforcement from others. Consequently, the socially unskilled individual may exhibit the form of passive behaviour characterising depression. MacPhillamy & Lewinsohn (1974) found that depressed people report having fewer pleasant experiences than non-depressed people, and that greater depression was correlated with fewer pleasant experiences. However, whilst depression might *follow* a reduction in pleasant experiences, it could *precede* a reduction in those experiences, implying that people who become depressed might lower their participation in reinforcing events.

COGNITIVE–BEHAVIOURAL MODEL

Seligman's research represents a link between behavioural and cognitive perspectives. Seligman & Maier (1967) conducted an experiment in which dogs were restrained so that they could not avoid electric shocks. The dogs appeared to become passively resigned to the receipt of the shocks. Later, when they were placed in a situation in which they *could* escape the shocks, they made no attempt to do so. Seligman called this phenomenon *learned helplessness*.

Box 69.4 Learned helplessness

Seligman argued that the dogs' behaviours (which included lethargy, sluggishness, and a loss of appetite) were similar to those exhibited by depressed humans. Depressed people (like dogs) learn from experience to develop an expectancy that their behaviours will be fruitless in bringing about an environmental change. When people feel helpless to influence their encounters with pleasurable and unpleasurable stimuli, they become depressed.

Seligman's account was criticised because it failed to address the issue of why some depressed people blame themselves for their depression, whilst others blame the external world, and the observation that depressed people tend to attribute their successes to luck rather than ability. Abramson *et al.*'s (1978) revised version of learned helplessness theory is based on the attributions or interpretations people make of their experiences (see Chapter 51). According to Abramson *et al.*, people who attribute failure to *internal* ('It's my fault'), *stable* ('It's going to last forever') and *global* ('It's going to affect everything I do') causes, and attribute successes to luck, are more likely to become depressed, because these factors lead to the perception that they are helpless to change things for the better. This *attributional style* (see Chapter 51, page 431) derives from learning histories, especially in the family and at school.

Questionnaires assessing how people interpret adversities in life predict (to some degree) their future susceptibility to depression. However, although cognitions of helplessness often accompany depressive episodes, the cognitive pattern changes once the depressive episode ends. According to Gotlib & Colby (1995), people who were formerly depressed are actually no different from people who have never been depressed in terms of their tendencies to view negative events with an attitude of helpless resignation. This suggests that an attitude of helplessness could be a *symptom* rather than a *cause* of depression.

Box 69.5 Beck's cognitive triad model

A similar account to Seligman's is Beck's (1974) cognitive model of emotional disorders which states that:

'an individual's emotional response to an event or experience is determined by the conscious meaning placed on it'.

Beck believes that depression is based in self-defeating *negative beliefs* and *negative cognitive sets* (or tendencies to think in certain ways) that develop as a result of experience. Certain childhood and adolescence experiences (such as the loss of a parent or criticism from teachers) leads to the development of a *cognitive triad* consisting of three interlocking negative beliefs. These concern the *self*, the *world* and the *future*, and cause people to have a distorted and constricted outlook on life. The beliefs lead people to magnify bad, and minimise good, experiences. The cognitive triad is maintained by several kinds of distorted and illogical interpretations of real events that contribute to depression (see Chapter 66, page 573).

Some depressed people do describe their world in the ways outlined by Beck (White *et al.*, 1985). However, correlations do not imply causality, and it could be that depressed feelings and logical errors of thought are both caused by a third factor (perhaps a biochemical imbalance: see below). Additionally, the perception and recall of information in more negative terms might be the *result* of depression rather than the *cause* of it (Hammen, 1985).

Other research has looked at the role of *depressogenic schemata* (cognitions which may precipitate depression, and remain latent until activated by *stress*). Haaga & Beck (1992) have specified several types of stressor that may activate dysfunctional beliefs in people. For example, *sociotropic* individuals may be stressed by negative interactions with, or rejections by, others, whereas *autonomous* individuals may be stressed by a failure to reach personal goals. According to Teasdale's (1988) *differential activation hypothesis*, the increased accessibility of negative thoughts after an initial shift in mood may explain why some people suffer persistent rather than transient depression (Scott, 1994).

PSYCHODYNAMIC MODEL

Psychodynamic approaches to mood disorders were first addressed by Abraham (1911). However, it was Freud (1917) who attempted to apply psychodynamic principles. He noted a similarity between the grieving that occurs when a loved one dies and the symptoms of depression. For Freud, depression was an excessive and irrational grief response to loss that evokes feelings associated with real or imagined loss of affection from the person on whom the individual was most dependent as a child.

Freud argued that both *actual losses* (such as the death of a loved one) and *symbolic losses* (such as the loss of a job or social prestige) lead us to re-experience parts of our childhood. Thus, depressed people become dependent and clinging or, in very extreme cases, regress to a child-like state. The greater the experience of loss in childhood, the greater the regression that occurred during adulthood. The evidence for Freud's account is, however, mixed. Some studies report that children who have lost a parent are particularly susceptible to depression later on (Roy, 1981). Others, however, have failed to find such a susceptibility (Lewinsohn & Hoberman, 1982).

Freud also argued that unresolved and repressed hostility towards one's parents was also important. When loss is experienced, anger is evoked and is turned *inward* on the self because the outward expression of anger is unacceptable to the superego. This self-directed hostility creates feelings of guilt, unworthiness and despair, which may be so intense as to motivate *suicide* (the ultimate form of inward-directed aggression). Freud further believed that grief was complicated by inevitable mixed feelings. As well as affection, mourners are likely to have had at least occasionally angry feelings towards the deceased. However, these unacceptable feelings are also redirected towards the self, leading to lowered self-esteem and feelings of guilt.

Psychodynamic theorists see the occurrence of bipolar disorder as the result of the alternating dominance of personality by the superego (in the depressive phase of the disorder), which floods the individual with exaggerated ideas of wrong-doing and associated feelings of guilt and worthlessness, and the ego (in the manic phase), which attempts to defend itself by rebounding and asserting supremacy. As a response to the ego's excessive display, the superego dominates, resulting in feelings of guilt which again plunges the individual into depression.

Box 69.6   Weaknesses of the psychodynamic model's account of depression

At least four reasons suggest that the psychodynamic model is inadequate in explaining mood disorders in general, and depression in particular. First, there is no direct evidence that depressed people interpret the death of a loved one as desertion or rejection of themselves (Davison & Neale, 1990). Second, if anger is turned inward, we would not expect depressed people to direct excessive amounts of hostility towards people

who are close to them. This does, however, occur (Weissman & Paykel, 1974). Third, there is little evidence for a direct connection between early loss and the risk of depression in adult life (Crook & Eliot, 1980). Finally, since symbolic loss cannot be observed, this aspect of the theory cannot be experimentally assessed.

MEDICAL MODEL
Genetic influences

Based on the observation that mood disorders tend to run in families, a *genetic* basis for them has been proposed. According to Weissman (1987), people with first-degree relatives (relatives with whom an individual shares 50 per cent of his or her genes – parents and siblings) who have a mood disorder are ten times more likely to develop one than people with unaffected first-degree relatives. Allen (1976) has reported a higher average concordance rate for bipolar disorder in MZs (72 per cent: the highest for *any* mental disorder) than in DZs (14 per cent).

For major depression, the average concordance rate for MZs is 40 per cent and only 11 per cent for DZs (Allen, 1976). The fact that concordance rates for bipolar disorder and major depression differ suggests that, if genetic factors *are* involved, they are different for the two disorders. As noted in Chapter 68, however, the data from families and twins is limited by the fact that they usually share the same environment. However, as with schizophrenia, this problem has been at least partially overcome by adoption studies. Adopted children who later develop a mood disorder appear to be much more likely to have a biological parent who has a mood disorder, becomes alcoholic or commits suicide, even though the adopted children are raised in very different environments (Wender *et al.*, 1986).

Box 69.7   DNA markers and mood disorders

DNA markers have been used to identify the gene or genes involved in mood disorders. This approach looks at the inheritance of mood disorders within high-risk families, and then searches for a DNA segment that is inherited along with a predisposition to develop the disorder. Egeland *et al.* (1987) studied 81 people from four high-risk families, all of whom were members of the Old Order Amish community in Pennsylvania. Fourteen were diagnosed as having a bipolar disorder, and all had specific genetic markers at the tip of chromosome 11. However, subsequent research has failed to replicate this finding in other populations in which bipolar disorder appears to be inherited.

Whilst these data do not invalidate those of Egeland *et al.*, other researchers have failed to support their findings when the analysis was extended to other Amish relatives (Kelsoe *et al.*, 1989). This suggests at least two possibilities: the gene for bipolar disorder may not actually be on chromosome 11, or several genes play a role, only one of which is on chromosome 11. The latter is supported by the observation that a gene on the X chromosome has also been implicated in bipolar disorder (Baron *et al.*, 1987).

Ogilvie *et al.* (1996) have shown that cells use a gene called SERT to make a serotonin transporter protein which plays an important role in the transmission of information between neurons. In most people, part of this gene (the *second intron*) contains ten or 12 repeating sections of DNA. However, in a significant number of people with depression, this part of the gene has only nine repeating sequences. The fact that serotonin is strongly implicated in depression (see below) and that newer anti-depressant drugs such as Prozac (see Chapter 72) interact with the serotonin transporter protein, offers one of the strongest hints yet that genes may be involved in depression.

Biochemical influences

As mentioned in Chapter 66, genes act by directing biochemical events. Researchers have looked at the *biochemical processes* which may play a causal role in affective disorders. Research has linked these disorders to chemical imbalances in *serotonin* and *noradrenaline*. Schildkraut (1965) argued that too much noradrenaline at certain sites caused mania, whereas too little caused depression. Later research suggested that serotonin played a similar role.

Certainly, some evidence supports these proposals. For example, non-humans given drugs that diminish noradrenaline production become sluggish and inactive, two symptoms of depression (Wender & Klein, 1981). Similar effects occur when humans are given *reserpine*, used to treat high blood pressure. Additionally, drugs which are effective in reducing depression (see Chapter 72, pages 621–622) increase brain levels of noradrenaline and/or serotonin (Lemonick, 1997). *Iproniazid* (used to treat tuberculosis) produces elation and euphoria and increases noradrenaline and serotonin levels. Lithium carbonate (a treatment for mania: see Chapter 72, page 622) decreases noradrenaline and serotonin levels.

Research also indicates that depressed people's urine contains lower than normal levels of compounds produced when noradrenaline and serotonin are broken down by enzymes (Teuting *et al.*, 1981), suggesting lower than normal activity of noradrenaline and serotonin-secreting neurones in the brain. Abnormally high levels of noradrenaline compounds have been found in the urine of manic people (Kety, 1975), and the level of these compounds fluctuates in people with bipolar disorder (Bunney *et al.*, 1972).

Box 69.8 The permissive amine theory of mood disorder

Schildkraut's theory was weakened by the finding that whilst noradrenaline *and* serotonin are lower in depression, lower levels of serotonin are also found in mania. Thus, it cannot be a simple case of an excess or deficiency of these neurotransmitters that causes mania and depression. An attempt to reconcile these observations is Kety's *permissive amine theory of mood disorder* (noradrenaline and serotonin are examples of *biogenic amines*, hence the theory's name). According to Kety, serotonin plays a role in limiting noradrenaline levels. When serotonin levels are normal, so are noradrenaline levels, and only normal highs and lows are experienced. However, when serotonin is deficient, it cannot play its limiting role and so noradrenaline levels fluctuate beyond normal high and low levels, leading to mania and depression.

Whilst drugs that alleviate depression increase noradrenaline and serotonin levels, they do so only in the period immediately after taking the drug. Within a few days, the levels return to baseline. The problem for Kety's theory is that antidepressant effects do *not* occur during the period when transmitter levels are elevated. All anti-depressants take some time before they alleviate depression (see Chapter 72, page 621). This suggests that depression cannot be explained simply in terms of a change in neurotransmitter levels. It is more likely that the drugs act to reduce depression by increasing the *sensitivity* of receiving neurons, thereby allowing them to utilise limited neurotransmitter supplies in a more effective way (Sulser, 1979).

Additionally, antidepressant drugs are not always effective in reducing depression, not everyone suffering from depression shows reduced neurotransmitter levels, and not everyone displaying mania shows increased noradrenaline levels. Whilst it is likely that neurotransmitters play a role in mood disorders, these findings demonstrate that their exact role remains to be determined (Fields, 1991).

Box 69.9   Structural differences in the brains of depressives

Part of the brain called the subgenual prefrontal cortex, which is located about 2½ inches (6 cm) behind the bridge of the nose, is known to play an important role in the control of emotion. In depressed people, it is eight per cent less active than in non-depressed people, and there is 40–50 per cent less tissue in the depressed. This deficit may result from a catastrophic loss of an as yet unknown subset of neurons by an also unknown cause (Gorman, 1997).

External factors and biochemical influences

Whilst the evidence suggests that affective disorders are heritable and that biochemical factors are involved, the exact cause-and-effect relationships remain to be established. If a gene is involved, its exact mode of transmission must be complex, given the variation in the severity and manner of the expression of mood disorders. Serotonin might act as the regulator, or serotonin and noradrenaline might play different roles in different types of mood disorders. Also, the possibility that neurotransmitter levels change as a result of the mood disorder rather than being its cause cannot be excluded. For example, environmental stimuli may cause depression which causes biochemical changes in the brain. Noradrenaline levels are lower in dogs in whom learned helplessness has been induced (Miller *et al.*, 1977). The dogs did not inherit such levels but acquired them as a result of their experiences.

Two sub-types of *seasonal affective disorder* of particular interest are *summer depression* (associated with loss of appetite, weight and sleep) and *winter depression* (associated with increased weight, sleep and appetite for carbohydrate foods). Wurtman & Wurtman (1989) have argued that summer depression is associated with deficiencies in serotonin levels, whilst winter depression is almost certainly caused by the desynchronisation of the rhythm of *melatonin* (see Box 11.8) as the result of decreasing natural light exposure in winter (Wehr & Rosenthal, 1989). In summer depression, a mechanism other than decreasing light exposure must play a role.

Laboratory studies of non-humans have shown that changes in magnetic field exposure, which alters the direction of the magnetic field, are correlated with decreased melatonin synthesis and serotonin production (Rudolph *et al.*, 1993). On the basis of these findings, Kay (1994) hypothesises that geomagnetic storms might partly account for the bimodal annual distribution of depression (that is, summer *and* winter depression). Kay reported a 36 per cent increase in male hospital admissions for depression in the second week following such storms, and believes that the effects of geomagnetic storms on melatonin synthesis and serotonin production are the same in humans and non-humans.

Bush (cited in Whittell, 1995) has investigated the high suicide rate in the remote Alaskan hinterland, where suicide levels among the state's 15–24 year olds are six times the USA average. Bush argues for a link between the *aurora borealis* (or Northern lights), a source of changes in geomagnetism, and electrical activity in the brain. Additionally, the British finding that new mothers and pregnant women are 60 per cent more likely to suffer depression if they live near high-voltage electricity cables than those who do not, coupled with clusters of suicides in people living close to such cables, suggests that electromagnetic fields *might* be involved this disorder (Westhead, 1996).

Whatever seasonal depression's causes, the anti-depressant drug *sertraline* is effective, at least in winter depression, and produces even better effects than phototherapy (see Chapter 11, pages 96–97) which is inconvenient, costly and associated with headaches and eye strain (Syal, 1997).

Sex differences in depression

According to Cochrane (1995), when all relevant factors are controlled for, depression contributes most highly to the overall rate of treatment for mental disorders in women, who are two to three times more likely than men to become clinically depressed (Williams & Hargreaves, 1995).

Several factors may account for the sex difference. These include hormonal fluctuations associated with the menstrual cycle, childbirth, the menopause, taking oral contraceptives, brain chemistry and diet.

Box 69.10   Brain biochemistry and diet

According to Diksic *et al.* (cited in Highfield, 1997d), serotonin is made by men's brain stems at a rate 52 per cent higher than in women. This could be due to the way men and women develop. One possibility is that dieting during the teenage years might alter brain biochemistry. Smith *et al.* (1997) found that women experienced symptoms of depression when *tryptophan*, a protein component, was removed from their diets. Tryptophan is an amino-acid precursor of serotonin, and even a standard 1000-calorie carbohydrate-restricted diet can lower blood plasma levels of it enough to alter serotonin function.

The evidence concerning hormonal and other factors is, however, weak. For example, although one in ten women who have just given birth are sufficiently depressed to need medical or psychological help, no specific causal hormonal abnormality has been identified. It is just as plausible to suggest that social factors (such as the adjustment to a new role) are as important as any proposed physical factors (Callaghan & O'Carroll, 1993; Murray, 1995).

Cochrane (1995) has summarised non-biological explanations of women's greater susceptibility to depression. For example, girls are very much more likely to be sexually abused than boys, and victims of abuse are at least twice as likely to experience clinical depression in adulthood, compared with non-abused individuals. Abuse alone, then, might explain the sex difference. An alternative account is based on the fact that the sex difference is greatest between the ages of 20 and 50, the years when marriage, child-bearing, motherhood and the *empty nest syndrome* (see Chapter 49) will be experienced by a majority of women.

Although women are increasingly becoming part of the labour force, being a full-time mother and wife, having no employment outside of the home, and lacking an intimate and confiding relationship, are increasingly being seen as risk factors for depression (Brown & Harris, 1978). The acceptance of a traditional female gender role may contribute to *learned helplessness* (see page 598), because the woman sees herself as having little control over her life.

Depression may be seen as a *coping strategy* that is available to women Cochrane (1983). Not only is it more acceptable for women to admit to psychological problems, but such problems may represent a means of changing an intolerable situation. As Callaghan & O'Carroll (1993) have observed:

'Unhappiness about their domestic, social, and political circumstances lies at the root of many women's concerns. This unhappiness must not be medicalised and regarded as a "female malady"'.

Conclusions

Like schizophrenia, depression is a serious mental disorder with many distinct characteristics. Several explanations have been advanced to explain the disorder. All have received support, although we are still some way from a single accepted explanation for depression.

Summary

■ At one extreme of **mood/affective disorder** is **manic disorder/mania**. At the other is **depressive disorder**. Mania on its own or, more usually, in conjunction with depression, is called **bipolar disorder**. **Unipolar disorder** refers to depression only. **Manic–depression** refers to both unipolar and bipolar disorders.

■ Depression is the most common mental disorder and can be a response to certain life events or just part of 'everyday life'. To be diagnosed as **clinically depressed**, a person must display persistent low mood for at least two weeks, plus at least five other symptoms identified in diagnostic criteria.

■ The traditional distinction between **endogenous** and **exogenous/reactive** depression is controversial. Endogenous no longer denotes depression's origins, but refers to a cluster of symptoms. Depression can occur at any age and is more common in women. Bipolar disorder generally appears in the early 20s and is equally prevalent in men and women.

■ **Behavioural** explanations of depression focus on the role played by a reduction in **positive reinforcement**. Cognitive–behavioural accounts use the concept of **learned helplessness** to explain depression. However, learned helplessness on its own cannot account for depressed peoples' **attributional styles**.

■ According to Beck's **cognitive model**, depression is based in self-defeating **negative beliefs** and **cognitive sets**. The **cognitive triad** leads people to exaggerate their bad experiences and minimise their good experiences.

■ **Depressogenic schemata** may be activated by rejections from others (in **sociotropic** individuals) or a failure to reach personal goals (in **autonomous** individuals). The **differential activation hypothesis** is an attempt to explain persistent and transient depression.

■ The **psychodynamic model** proposes that both **actual** and **symbolic losses** cause us to re-experience parts of childhood, and depression may involve a regression to a childlike dependency. However, the psychodynamic model is inadequate in explaining mood disorders in general and depression in particular.

■ Because mood disorders run in families, they might have a **genetic** basis. This is supported by the higher concordance rate in MZs than DZs. DNA markers have been used to identify the gene(s) involved, although the data are equivocal in this respect. The SERT gene offers the strongest evidence yet for a genetic basis to mood disorders.

■ Lower than normal levels of activity in **serotonin-** and **noradrenaline**-secreting neurons may be a causal factor in depression. Kety's **permissive amine theory** describes their interaction, but is inconsistent with some evidence. Whilst it is likely that neurotransmitters play a role in mood disorders, exactly what it is remains to be discovered.

■ Seasonal variations in the incidence of depression are well-established. **Winter depression** is almost certainly caused by the desynchronisation of **melatonin** as a result of decreasing natural light exposure in winter. **Summer depression** is more difficult to explain. Geomagnetic factors may be involved in both forms of depression, by influencing melatonin synthesis and serotonin production.

■ Sex differences in depression have been explained both in biological and psychological terms. Biological explanations implicate the menstrual cycle, childbirth, the menopause, oral contraceptives, and the influence of dieting on brain biochemistry. Psychological explanations implicate sexual abuse, the stress associated with marriage, childbearing, motherhood, and the 'empty nest syndrome'. Depression may even be a **coping strategy** for women.

70

ANXIETY DISORDERS

Introduction and overview

Researchers generally agree that some anxiety is *biologically adaptive* because it produces enhanced vigilance and a more realistic appraisal of a situation, allowing us to develop appropriate coping responses. Some people, however, experience anxiety that is so overwhelming it interferes with normal everyday functioning.

Anxiety disorders is a category in DSM-IV that is subsumed by the category *neurotic, stress-related and somatoform disorders* in ICD-10. DSM-IV recognises four types of anxiety disorder. These are *panic disorders and generalised anxiety disorder*, *phobic disorders* (which ICD-10 calls *phobic anxiety disorders*), *obsessive–compulsive disorder* and *post-traumatic stress disorder* (which ICD-10 includes under the heading *stress and adjustment disorders*). This chapter describes the characteristics associated with each of the four disorders identified by DSM-IV and examines explanations for their causes.

Panic disorder (PD) and Generalised anxiety disorder (GAD)

Anxiety is a general feeling of dread or apprehensiveness typically accompanied by various physiological reactions, including increased heart rate, rapid and shallow breathing, sweating, muscle tension and a dryness of the mouth. In both *panic disorder* (*PD*) and *generalised anxiety disorder* (*GAD*), the anxiety is 'free-floating', and occurs in the absence of any obvious anxiety-provoking object or situation. Thus, a person experiences anxiety but does not know why.

The physiological reactions accompanying unpredictable and repeated anxiety and panic attacks are similar to those that occur during a heart attack. Other reactions include chest pain and a tingling in the hands or feet, and it is common for people experiencing panic disorder to actually *believe* they are having a heart attack. Other symptoms include *derealisation* (the feeling that the world is not real) and *depersonalisation* (the loss of a sense of personal identity, manifested as a feeling of

detachment from the body). Panic attacks can last for a few minutes to several hours. Although they usually occur during wakefulness, they can occur during sleep (Dilsaver, 1989).

Box 70.1   A typical case of panic disorder

When this 38-year-old man experienced intense anxiety, it seemed as if he were having a heart seizure. He had chest pains and heart palpitations, numbness and shortness of breath, and felt a strong need to breathe in air. He reported that in the midst of this, he developed a tight feeling over his eyes and could only see objects directly in front of him. He also feared he would not be able to swallow.

The anxiety's intensity was very frightening, and on two occasions his wife had rushed him to hospital because he was in a state of panic, sure that his heart was going to stop beating. His symptoms were relieved after an injection of tranquilliser medication. He began to note where doctor's offices and hospitals were wherever he happened to be, and became extremely anxious if medical help were not close by.

(Adapted from Leon, 1990)

PD may be so terrifying that a person experiencing it can be driven to suicide. In many cases, it is accompanied by *agoraphobia*, a fear of finding oneself in a situation from which escape is difficult or where help is not available should a panic attack occur (see page 606). Because PD occurs without any apparent cause, sufferers also experience *anticipatory anxiety*, a worry about when the next attack will occur and the avoidance of situations in which it has occurred.

GAD is characterised by persistent high levels of anxiety and worry about things, accompanied by the physical sensations associated with PD. However, although GAD's physical sensations are more persistent than in PD, they are less intense. The physical, cognitive and emotional problems caused by GAD lead people experiencing it to become tired, irritable, socially inept and to have difficulty functioning effectively.

EXPLANATIONS OF PD AND GAD

As mentioned previously, some people develop anticipatory anxiety and actively avoid situations in which they believe PD will occur. The cues associated with situations in which anxiety is aroused can lead to it being experienced (Clark, 1993). This is *reinforced* by a reduction in the disorder's fear component. However, the *origins* of all cases of PD probably cannot be explained in conditioning terms, and it is likely that classical conditioning increases PD's severity rather than causes it (Sue *et al.*, 1994).

> ### Box 70.2   Catastrophising cognitions
>
> Certain cognitions can act as *internal triggers* for PD (Belfer & Glass, 1992). Clark (1993) proposes that the core disturbance in panic is an abnormality in thinking. When external or internal stressors cause increased physiological activity, this is noticed but interpreted in *catastrophic* ways (such as 'I am having a heart attack'). This leads to even more physiological activity, which only confirms the catastrophic thinking, and so a *positive feedback loop* between cognitions and bodily activity occurs. Although some evidence supports this proposal, sufferers often report being unaware of particular thoughts during a panic attack. It is also unclear why catastrophic thoughts *should* be characteristic of the disorder.

The psychodynamic model sees GAD as the result of unacceptable unconscious conflicts blocked by the ego. These are powerful enough to produce constant tension and apprehension, but since they are unconscious, the person is unaware of the anxiety's source. To defend ourselves, we try to repress the impulses, but our defences are occasionally weakened and PD occurs. Alternatively, PD could represent unresolved *separation anxiety*, which may be experienced later in life when a threat of separation is either perceived or actually occurs (see Chapter 39, page 338).

There might be a *genetic* component in PD and GAD. Around 40 per cent of first-degree relatives of PD sufferers have the disorder themselves (Balon *et al.*, 1989), and there is a higher concordance rate in MZs than in DZs (Slater & Shields, 1969). Although environmental factors cannot be ruled out, what might be inherited is a predisposition towards anxiety in the form of a highly reactive ANS (Eysenck, 1967). For example, some people with GAD demonstrate *autonomic lability*, that is, they are more easily aroused by environmental stimuli.

Lesch *et al.* (cited in Highfield, 1996e) have shown that neuroticism levels are correlated with two versions of a gene responsible for transporting serotonin. One of these leads to more serotonin and neuroticism and the other to less of these. However, the gene accounts for only about four per cent of the total variation in anxiety, so other factors clearly cannot be ruled out. Papp *et al.* (1993) argue that PD is triggered by a dysfunction in receptors that monitor oxygen levels in the blood. By incorrectly informing the brain that the levels are low, fear of suffocation and hyperventilation result. PD is accompanied by an elevated blood level of *lactic acid*, a by-product of muscular activity. In *biological challenge tests*, sodium lactate is given to people with PD and, in most of them, a panic attack occurs (George & Ballenger, 1992).

This may be because the *locus coeruleus*, a brain structure associated with anxiety, is overly sensitive to anything that is *anxiogenic* (anxiety-inducing). However, the results of biological challenge tests are influenced by *expectations*. People informed they will experience pleasant sensations report less anxiety than those informed they will experience unpleasant sensations. Even if biological factors do play a role, then, it is likely that cognitive factors can modify them (Sue *et al.*, 1994).

Phobic disorders

Being afraid of something that might objectively cause us harm is a normal reaction. However, some people show strong, persistent and *irrational* fears of, and desires to avoid, particular objects, activities or situations. When such behaviour interferes with normal everyday functioning, a person has a phobia. Encountering the phobic stimulus results in intense anxiety. Although a phobic usually acknowledges that the anxiety is out of proportion to the actual danger the phobic stimulus poses, this does little to reduce the fear, and he or she is highly motivated to avoid it.

> ### Box 70.3   Some varieties of phobias
>
> Acrophobia (high places)
> Ailurophobia (cats)
> Algophobia (pain)
> Anthropophobia (men)
> Aquaphobia (water)
> Arachnophobia (spiders)
> Astraphobia (storms, thunder, lightning)
> Belonophobia (needles)
> Cancerophobia (cancer)
> Claustrophobia (enclosed spaces)
> Cynophobia (dogs)
> Hematophobia (blood)
> Monophobia (being alone)
> Mysophobia (contamination or germs)

Nycotophobia (darkness)
Ochlophobia (crowds)
Ophidiophobia (snakes)
Pathophobia (disease)
Pyrophobia (fire)
Siderophobia (railways)
Taphophobia (being buried alive)
Thanatophobia (death)
Triskaidekaphobia (thirteen)
Xenophobia (strangers)
Zoophobia (animals or a specific animal)

Figure 70.1   Technophobia is a feeling of fear or frustration experienced by people unfamiliar with modern digital and computer technology

DSM-IV identifies three categories of phobia. These are *agoraphobia*, *social phobia* and *specific phobias*. *Agoraphobia* is a fear of open spaces but, as mentioned earlier (see page 604), it typically involves a fear of being in situations from which escape may be difficult or where help is unavailable. In extreme cases, agoraphobics become 'prisoners' trapped in their own homes and dependent on others. Agoraphobia accounts for around 10–50 per cent of all phobias, and most agoraphobics are women. The phobia typically occurs in early adulthood.

Social phobia was identified as an entity in the UK in 1970, but not included in DSM until 1980 (Menninger, 1995). It is an intense and excessive fear of being in a situation in which being scrutinised by others is a possibility. It is also characterised by the fear that, in a particular situation, one will act in a way humiliating or embarrassing for the self or others.

Box 70.4   Types of social phobia

Three types of social phobia can be distinguished. *Performance* social phobia is characterised by excessive

anxiety over activities like public speaking or being in a restaurant. In *limited interactional* social phobia, anxiety occurs only in specific situations, such as interacting with an authority figure. *Generalised* social phobia involves displaying anxiety in most social situations. Social phobia accounts for around ten per cent of all phobias and, like agoraphobia, most social phobics are women. Social phobia typically arises in adolescence.

Figure 70.2   Having to make a speech in front of any kind of audience is likely to induce some degree of anxiety in most people. As a social phobia, anxiety over public speaking is an intense and excessive fear of being exposed to scrutiny by other people; it is an example of performance social phobia

A *specific phobia* is an extreme fear of a specific object (such as spiders) or situation (such as being in an enclosed space). The phobias identified in Box 70.3 are all specific phobias. Taken together, specific phobias are the most common phobic disorders, but also the *least disruptive*. Phobias are the most common type of anxiety disorder, and whilst there are sex differences in the likelihood of developing agoraphobia or social phobia, there are no such differences for most of the specific phobias. Specific phobias usually develop in childhood, but can occur at any time. The *nosophobias* (or 'illness and injury' phobias, such as cancerophobia and thanatophobia) tend to occur in middle age.

Box 70.5   Popeye phobia

A three-year-old girl suddenly developed recurrent bronchitis which got worse when she attended nursery school. The trouble was traced to the slippers of a boy in the same class. Every time the girl saw them she began to retch, cough and become upset. The slippers sported a picture of Popeye, the cartoon character. Even the mention of his name provoked coughing. The girl had seen a cartoon of Popeye at her friend's house and became frightened of him. Following behaviour therapy (see Chapter 74), the girl recovered.

(Based on Murray, 1997)

EXPLANATIONS OF PHOBIC DISORDERS

The psychodynamic model sees phobias as the *surface* expression of a much deeper conflict between the id, ego and superego, which has its origins in childhood. Freud (1909) described the case of 'Little Hans', a five-year-old boy, whose phobia of horses prevented him from leaving his house. Freud believed that phobias were expressions of unacceptable wishes, fears and fantasies displaced from their original, internal source onto some external object or situation that can be easily avoided. Freud saw Hans's fear of horses as an expression of anxieties related to his Oedipal complex. Since Hans unconsciously feared and hated his father (whom he perceived to be a rival for his mother's affection), he displaced this fear onto horses, which could be avoided more easily than his father.

Freud's explanation was challenged by the behavioural model. Hans's phobic response *only* occurred in the presence of a large horse pulling a heavily loaded cart at high speed, and his phobia had developed *after* Hans had witnessed a terrible accident involving a horse pulling a cart at high speed. As noted in Chapter 66 (see page 571), phobias can be classically conditioned, and the behavioural model's interpretation of Hans's phobia is at least as plausible as Freud's.

Wolpe (1969) has argued that classical conditioning explains the development of *all* phobias. Certainly, the pairing of a neutral stimulus with a frightening experience is acknowledged by some phobics as marking their phobias' onset. Moreover, the *resilient* nature of some phobias (their *resistance to extinction*) can also be explained in conditioning terms.

Box 70.6   The two-process theory of phobias

According to Mowrer's (1947) *two-process* or *two-factor theory*, phobias are acquired through classical conditioning (factor 1) and maintained through operant conditioning (factor 2), because the avoidance of the phobic stimulus and the associated reduction in anxiety is *negatively reinforcing* (although Rachman's, 1984, *safety signal hypothesis* sees avoidance as being motivated by the *positive* feelings of safety).

However, the fact that some phobics cannot recall any traumatic experiences and that profound trauma does not inevitably lead to a phobia developing is difficult for the behavioural model to explain. Research also indicates that certain classes of stimuli (such as snakes) can more easily be made a conditioned stimulus than others (such as flowers).

Box 70.7   Preparedness

Rosenhan & Seligman (1984) propose an interaction between organic and conditioning factors that biologically predisposes us to acquire phobias towards certain classes of stimuli. According to the concept of *preparedness* or *prepared conditioning*, we are genetically prepared to fear things that were sources of danger in our evolutionary past (see Chapter 32, pages 279–280). Hugdahl & Öhman (1977) and Menzies (cited in Hunt, 1995) have shown that, in laboratory studies, people are more 'prepared' to acquire fear reactions to some stimuli than others. However, such studies do *not* demonstrate biological preparedness. Because we live in a society in which many people react negatively to certain animals, learning experiences rather than genetic factors might prepare us to fear these stimuli.

According to Rachman (1977), many phobias are acquired through information transmitted by *observation* and *instruction*. Although preparedness for direct conditioning does not seem to be relevant, a preparedness for observational and instructional learning is possible (Murray & Foote, 1979). Slater & Shields' (1969) observation of a 41 per cent concordance rate amongst MZs and only a four per cent rate amongst DZs is suggestive of a genetic role. However, without data relating to MZs reared *apart*, the role played by genetic factors is unclear. A relationship might also exist between a person's arousal level and the likelihood of a phobia developing, although the finding that high levels of physiological arousal are not associated with specific phobias casts doubt on such a proposal's generality (Tallis, 1994).

Obsessive–compulsive disorder

As its name suggests, in *obsessive–compulsive disorder* (OCD) the profound anxiety is reflected in obsessions and compulsions. *Obsessions* are recurrent thoughts or images that do not feel voluntarily controlled and are experienced as senseless or repugnant. *Compulsions* are irresistable urges to engage in repetitive behaviours performed according to rituals or rules as a way of reducing or preventing the discomfort associated with some future undesirable event.

All of us have thoughts and behaviour patterns that are repeated, but these would only be a problem if they caused personal distress or interfered with daily life. OCD has recently undergone a dramatic change in status (Tallis, 1994, 1995). Once regarded as a rare neurosis, it now occupies a central position in clinical psychology and contemporary psychiatry. In the United States, OCD is the fourth most common psychological problem. In Britain, an estimated one to one-and-a-half million people suffer from it. Females are slightly more likely to be OCD sufferers and the disorder usually begins in young adulthood, and sometimes childhood.

Box 70.8   Characteristics of obsessive thought

Frequently, obsessive thoughts take the form of violent images, such as killing oneself or others. However, they can take other forms. The four most common obsessional characteristics are *impaired control over mental processes* (such as repetitive thoughts of a loved one's death), *concern of losing control over motor behaviours* (such as killing someone), *contamination* (by, for example, germs) and *checking behaviours* (such as concern over whether a door has been locked). Whatever form they take, the thoughts cannot be resisted and are unpleasant for the sufferer (Sanavio, 1988).

Often, compulsions arise from obsessions. For example, a person persistently thinking about contamination by germs may develop complex rituals for avoiding contamination, which are repeated until the person is satisfied that cleanliness has been achieved (even if the hands become raw as a result of being washed over 500 times a day: Davison & Neale, 1990).

Shakespeare's character Lady Macbeth, who acquired a hand-washing compulsion after helping her husband murder the King of Scotland, is perhaps the most famous fictional OCD sufferer. The late billionaire Howard Hughes, who wore gloves all the time, walked on clean paper, bathed repeatedly and refused to see people for fear of being contaminated by them, is perhaps the most well-known non-fictional sufferer, along with Charles Darwin, Martin Luther and John Bunyan (Bennett, 1997). Compulsives recognise that their behaviours are senseless, yet if prevented from engaging in them, they experience intense anxiety which is reduced only when the compulsive ritual is carried out (Hodgson & Rachman, 1972).

Box 70.9   A case of obsessive thoughts leading to compulsive behaviour

Shirley K., a 23-year-old housewife, complained of frequent attacks of headaches and dizziness. During the preceding three months, she had been disturbed by recurring thoughts that she might harm her two-year-old son either by stabbing or choking him (the obsessive thought). She constantly had to go to his room, touch the boy and feel him breathe in order to reassure herself that he was still alive (the compulsive act), otherwise she became unbearably anxious. If she read a report in the daily paper of the murder of a child, she would become agitated, since this reinforced her fear that she, too, might act on her impulse.

(From Goldstein & Palmer, 1975)

EXPLANATIONS OF OCD

Comings & Comings' (1987) finding that people with OCD often have first-degree relatives with some sort of anxiety disorder suggests a genetic basis to OCD. However, the finding that in over half of the families of an OCD sufferer, members become actively involved in the rituals (Tallis, 1994), indicates the potential influence of *learning* (and supports the behavioural model). This might be particularly applicable to OCD's development in childhood: children with a parent who engages in ritualistic behaviour may see such behaviour as the norm (see below).

Evidence suggests that people with OCD show a different pattern of brain activity compared with non-OCD controls, in the form of increased metabolic activity in the left hemisphere's frontal lobe. When drugs are given which reduce this activity, the symptoms of OCD decline (McGuire *et al.*, 1994). However, whether OCD is a consequence of increased activity, a cause of it or merely a correlate is not yet known (Tallis, 1995). The fact that OCD can be treated using drugs which increase serotonin's availability indicates that a deficiency of that neurotransmitter might be implicated in it.

According to the psychodynamic model, obsessions are *defence mechanisms* (see Box 66.4, page 570) that serve to occupy the mind and displace more threatening thoughts. Laughlin (1967), for example, sees the intrusion of obsessive thoughts as preventing the arousal of anxiety:

'by serving as a more tolerable substitute for a subjectively less welcome thought or impulse'.

Certainly, something like this might be practised by athletes who 'psych themselves up' before a competitive event and, from a psychodynamic perspective (and indeed from a cognitive perspective: see Chapter 66), this might function to exclude self-defeating doubts and thoughts. However, it is hard to see what thoughts of killing someone (which, as noted in Box 70.8, is one of the more common obsessional thoughts) are a more tolerable substitute for.

The behavioural model sees OCD as a way of reducing anxiety. If a particular thought or behaviour reduces anxiety, then it should (because it is reinforcing) become more likely to occur. This *anxiety-reduction hypothesis* explains the maintenance of OCD, but does not explain the disorder's development. However, the *superstition hypothesis* does.

Box 70.10   The superstition hypothesis

Skinner (1948a) argued that what we call 'superstition' develops as a result of a chance association between a behaviour and a reinforcer. In Skinner's experiments, pigeons were given food at regular intervals irrespective of their behaviour. After a while, they displayed idiosyncratic movements, presumably because these were the movements they were making when the food was given (see Chapter 32, pages 275–278).

The superstition hypothesis can account for many compulsive rituals (O'Leary & Wilson, 1975). Amongst soccer players, for example, many superstitious behaviours exist. These include always being last onto the pitch and putting the left sock on before the right. Such behaviours may occur because, in the past, they were associated with success. If such rituals are not permitted, anxiety is aroused. However, whilst chance associations between behaviours and reinforcers might explain the persistence of some *behaviours*, the development of intrusive *thoughts* is much more difficult for the behavioural model to explain.

Post-traumatic stress disorder

During the First World War, many soldiers experienced *shell shock* (a shock-like state which followed the traumatic experiences of prolonged combat). Prior to being described as a clinical condition, it had been taken as a symptom of cowardice and sometimes resulted in summary trial and execution. In World War II, *combat exhaustion* was used to describe a similar reaction, characterised by terror, agitation or apathy, and insomnia.

Today, the term *post-traumatic stress disorder* (PTSD) is used to describe an anxiety disorder occurring in response to an extreme psychological or physical trauma outside the range of normal human experience (Thompson, 1997).

As well as war, such traumas include a physical threat to one's self or family, witnessing other people's deaths, and being involved in a natural or human-made disaster. In Britain, several disasters associated with PTSD have been extensively researched. These include the Piper Alpha oil rig disaster, the bombing of the PanAm airliner that crashed at Lockerbie, and the death of over 90 spectators at the Hillsborough football ground.

Box 70.11   Children and PTSD

The capsize of the cross-channel ferry *The Herald of Free Enterprise* in Zeebrugge has also been extensively researched. Studies of those who survived the disaster have shown that even very young children can be emotionally upset by such a trauma. Yule (1993), for example, reports that child survivors of recent disasters show PTSD's characteristic symptoms, including distressing recollections of the event, avoidance of reminders, and signs of increased physiological arousal, manifested as sleep disturbances and poor concentration.

Often, these children do not confide their distress to parents or teachers for fear of upsetting them. Consequently, their school work is affected and they are often thrown off their educational career course. However, when asked sympathetically and straightforwardly, they usually share their reactions. Other research has confirmed that children can experience PTSD. Pynoos *et al.* (1993) found a strong correlation between children's proximity to the epicentre of the 1988 Armenian earthquake and the overall severity of the core components of PTSD, with girls reporting more persistent anxiety than boys.

PTSD may occur immediately following a traumatic experience or weeks, months and even years later. In the Vietnam war, there were relatively few cases of shell shock or combat fatigue, probably because of the rapid turnover of soldiers in and out of the combat zone. However, on their return home, soldiers found it more difficult to adjust to civilian life than did those in the two World Wars.

As well as tiredness, apathy, depression, social withdrawal and nightmares, veterans reported *flashbacks* of events they had witnessed or participated in. They also showed *hyperalertness*, exaggerated startle reactions and felt guilty that they had survived but others had not. Like some people experiencing PTSD, they also reported using alcohol, drugs or violence to try to curb the disturbing symptoms (as have the survivors of *The Herald of Free Enterprise* disaster: Joseph *et al.*, 1993). Many veterans also cut themselves off from society to escape the sense of not being able to fit in as a result of their experiences.

One civilian disaster causing PTSD in those who survived it was the collision between two jumbo jets that killed 582 passengers in Tenerife in 1977. A combination of environmental and human factors led to a Dutch jumbo jet colliding with an American airliner. Many passengers were killed instantly, but some survived.

Box 70.12   A case of post-traumatic stress disorder

Martin lost his wife and blames himself for her death, because he sat stunned and motionless for some 25 seconds after the Dutch jumbo jet hit. He saw nothing but fire and smoke in the aisles, but roused himself and led his wife to a jagged hole above and behind his seat. Martin climbed out onto the wing and reached down and took hold of his wife's hand, but 'an explosion from within literally blew her out of my hands and pushed me back and down onto the wing'. He reached the runway, turned to go back after her, but the plane blew up seconds later.

Five months later, Martin was depressed and bored, had 'wild dreams', a short temper and became easily confused and irritated. 'What I saw there will terrify me forever,' he says. He told the psychologist who interviewed him that he avoided television and movies, because he couldn't know when a frightening scene would appear.

(Adapted from Perlberg, 1979)

Hunt (1997) has studied apparent PTSD amongst people in their 60s and 70s evidently disturbed by their experiences in World War II. This is hardly surprising if it is assumed that they have been bothered *continuously* since the war. However, this assumption appears to be false, as most survivors got on with their lives, raised families and so on (Bender, 1995). For some reason, the memories seem to be coming back to disturb them now that they have retired (see below).

EXPLANATIONS OF PTSD

Unlike other anxiety disorders, PTSD's origins can be explained largely, if not exclusively, in *environmental* terms. Whilst phobics or sufferers of OCD tend not to have common background factors, all PTSD sufferers share the experience of a profoundly traumatising event or events, even though these may be different from one another in other ways.

Classical conditioning is involved in PTSD (Kolb, 1987). Sufferers often show reactions to stimuli which were present at the time of the trauma. Hunt (1997), for example, interviewed veterans of the Normandy landings in World War II around the time of the fiftieth anniversary events in 1994. Many reported still being troubled by their memories of the war in general, but in particular were adversely affected by specific memories which had been revived by the anniversary commemorations.

As with phobias, however, classical conditioning cannot be the only mechanism involved, since not everyone who is exposed to a traumatic event develops PTSD. Green (1994) reports that PTSD develops in about 25 per cent of those who experience potentially traumatic events, although the range is quite large being about 12 per cent for accidents and 80 per cent for rape, with a *dose–effect* relationship between the stressor's severity and the degree of consequent psychological distress. Presumably, individual differences in how people perceive events as well as the *recovery environment* (such as support groups) also play an influential role.

Paton (1992), for example, found that relief workers at Lockerbie reported differences between what they expected to find and what they actually encountered, and that this was a source of stress. This was also reported by Dixon *et al.* (1993) in their study of PTSD amongst 'peripheral' victims of the *Herald of Free Enterprise* disaster. For relief workers, then, some way of increasing predictability (and hence control) that would minimise the differences between what is expected and what is observed, would be useful. Amongst the Normandy veterans, Hunt (1997) found that support systems, in the form of comradeship, were *still* important and were used by veterans as a means of coping with the traumatic memories (and often the physical consequences) of their war experiences.

Figure 70.3   Despite being trained to deal with emergency situations, members of the emergency services cannot be prepared for major disasters, such as the Lockerbie, Hillsborough and Herald of Free Enterprise disasters. Police involved in the 1989 Hillsborough disaster were awarded (in 1996) substantial financial compensation for the 'mental injury' they suffered (post-traumatic stress disorder) and can be considered peripheral victims of the disaster

The return of memories many years after a traumatic event suggests that keeping busy with socially valued life roles enables a person to *avoid* processing the traumatic memories. The unfortunate consequence of this, however, is that memories do not get integrated into a person's views about the world. To resolve the discrepancy, Bender (1995) suggests that people must process the traumatic experience and integrate it into their world views. In conditioning terms, thinking about the traumatic event would lead to *extinction* of the responses associated with it.

Although it is likely that social/psychological factors cause PTSD's onset, researchers are still interested in understanding the associated *biological processes*. The observation of similarities between PTSD and withdrawal from opioid drugs, and the finding that stress-induced analgesia can be reversed by *naloxone* (which reverses morphine's pharmacological action) in PTSD combat victims exposed to a combat movie, suggests that PTSD involves *disturbed opioid function* (van der Kolk *et al.*, 1989). Krystal *et al.* (1989) have proposed that the locus coeruleus acts as an 'alarm centre' and plays a pivotal role in PTSD's genesis. In support of this, drugs which are effective in treating PTSD also prevent the development of *learned helplessness* in non-humans exposed to inescapable shock (see Chapter 69, page 598) when these drugs are infused directly into the locus coeruleus (Davidson, 1992).

Conclusions

This chapter has examined the characteristics of anxiety disorders and explanations of them. Some explanations are more powerful than others, depending on the anxiety disorder. As with the disorders considered in Chapters 68 and 69, however, there is still much debate about how anxiety disorders can best be explained.

Summary

■ Mild/moderate anxiety is biologically adaptive. Sometimes, though, it is so intense that it interferes with normal functioning. Both **panic disorder** (PD) and **generalised anxiety disorder** (GAD) involve '**free-floating anxiety**' which is accompanied by various physiological and other reactions.

■ Classical conditioning might increase PD's severity, but cannot account for its origins. Certain cognitions might act as internal triggers for PD, and the core disturbance in panic might be an abnormality in thinking.

■ Stress-induced physiological activity may be interpreted in 'catastrophic' ways, establishing a positive feedback loop between cognitions and bodily activity. However, not everybody reports such cognitions, and it is not obvious why catastrophic thoughts should characterise the disorder.

■ PD and GAD have also been addressed by the psychodynamic and medical models. There is evidence for a genetic component in PD. However, if biological factors play a role, it is likely that cognitive factors can modify them.

■ It is the irrational nature of the fear involved, together with its interference with normal functioning, that makes a **phobia** a disorder. Three categories of phobias are **agoraphobia**, **social phobia**, and **specific phobias**.

■ Wolpe believes that all phobias can be explained in terms of classical conditioning. Their resilience/resistance to extinction can be explained in terms of both classical and operant conditioning as in the **two process/factor theory** and the **safety signal hypothesis**.

■ Some classes of stimuli can more easily become the objects of phobias than others. This has been explained in terms of **preparedness/prepared conditioning**, although studies claiming to demonstrate preparedness can be explained in terms of non-genetic factors. For example, phobias may be acquired through **observation** and **instruction**. There may be a preparedness for this rather than for direct conditioning.

■ In **obsessive–compulsive disorder** (OCD), profound anxiety is reflected in obsessions and compulsions. The four most common obsessional characteristics are **impaired control over mental processes**, **concern of losing control over motor behaviour**, **contamination**, and **checking behaviours**. Compulsions may arise from obsessions. Compulsives recognise their behaviours are senseless, but experience great anxiety if prevented from engaging in them.

■ Genetic and learning factors might be involved in OCD. The most promising neurological evidence involves differences between sufferers and non-sufferers in left frontal lobe metabolic activity. However, this might be a consequence or correlate of OCD rather than a cause of it.

■ The **anxiety-reduction hypothesis** explains OCD's maintenance but not its origins. The **superstition hypothesis** proposes that the compulsions arise through a chance association between a behaviour and a reinforcer. However, this does not explain the development of intrusive thoughts.

■ **Post-traumatic stress disorder** (PTSD) is a response to an extreme psychological/physical experience outside the range of normal human experience. It may occur immediately after the trauma or years later.

■ PTSD sufferers all share the experience of a profoundly traumatising event. **Classical conditioning** is involved to the extent that sufferers often show reactions to stimuli present at the time of the trauma. However, not everyone exposed to a traumatic event develops PTSD. This depends on the stressor's nature and severity, individual differences, and the **recovery environment**.

■ The return of memories years after a traumatic event suggests that socially valued life roles help people to avoid processing memories of the trauma. However, this prevents such memories being integrated into their world view. As a result, **extinction** of the associated responses cannot occur.

■ **Decreased opioid function** may occur in PTSD, and the **locus coeruleus** may act as an 'alarm centre', playing a crucial role in PTSD's genesis. When infused directly into the locus coeruleus, drugs which are effective in treating PTSD also prevent the development of **learned helplessness** in non-humans exposed to inescapable shock.

71

EATING DISORDERS

Introduction and overview

Eating disorders are characterised by physically and/or psychologically harmful eating patterns. In ICD-10, they are categorised as 'behavioural syndromes associated with physiological disturbances and physical factors'. Although there are several types of eating disorder (Brownell & Fairburn, 1995), two broad categories are *anorexia nervosa* and *bulimia nervosa*. This chapter describes the characteristics associated with these disorders and examines explanations of them.

Anorexia nervosa

Although the characteristics of what is now called anorexia nervosa have been known about for several hundred years (Hartley, 1997), it is only recently that the disorder has attracted much interest. This increased attention is the result of a greater public knowledge of the disorder, and the recent increase in its incidence (although Fombonne, 1995, argues that this increase can be attributed to changes in the diagnostic criteria concerning weight loss: see below).

Anorexia nervosa occurs primarily in females, and female *anorectics* outnumber males by a factor of 15:1 (Hartley, 1997). The disorder usually has its onset in adolescence, the period between 14 and 16 being most common (Hsu, 1990). However, the onset sometimes occurs later in adult life or before adolescence. Lask & Bryant-Waugh (1992), for example, have reported cases of the disorder in children as young as eight. Estimates of anorexia nervosa's incidence vary. American data suggest that one in 250 females may experience the disorder (Lewinsohn *et al.*, 1993). In Britain, the figure is somewhat higher, ranging from one in 100 to four in 100 (Sahakian, 1987), with around 70,000 people recognised as anorectic (Brooke, 1996).

Box 71.1 A typical case of anorexia nervosa

Frieda had always been a shy, sensitive girl who gave little cause for concern at home or in school. She was bright and did well academically, although she had few friends. In early adolescence, she was somewhat over-weight and teased by her family that she would never get a boyfriend unless she lost some weight. She reacted to this by withdrawing and becoming very touchy. Her parents had to be careful about what they said. If offended, Frieda would throw a tantrum and march off to her room.

Frieda began dieting. Initially her family was pleased, but gradually her parents sensed that all was not well. Meal times became battle times. Frieda hardly ate at all. Under pressure, she would take her meals to her room and later, having said that she had eaten everything, her mother would find food hidden away untouched. When her mother caught her deliberately inducing vomiting after a meal, she insisted they go to the family doctor. He found that Frieda had stopped menstruating a few months earlier. Not fooled by the loose, floppy clothes that Frieda was wearing, he insisted on carrying out a full physical examination. Her emaciated body told him as much as he needed to know, and he arranged for Frieda's immediate hospitalisation.

(Adapted from Rosenhan & Seligman, 1984)

As Box 71.1 illustrates, anorexia nervosa is characterised by a prolonged refusal to eat adequate amounts of food which results in deliberate weight loss. As 'Frieda''s case shows, body weight loss is often accompanied by the cessation of menstruation (*amenorrhea*). For a diagnosis of anorexia nervosa to be considered, the individual must weigh less than 85 per cent of normal or expected weight for height, age and sex. As a result of their significant weight loss, anorectics look emaciated. They also show a decline in general health, which is accompanied by many physical problems (Sharp & Freeman, 1993). These include low blood pressure and body temperature, constipation and dehydration. In five to 15 per cent of cases, anorexia nervosa is fatal (Hsu, 1990).

Literally, anorexia nervosa means 'nervous loss of appetite'. However, anorectics are often both hungry and preoccupied with thoughts of food. For example, they may constantly read recipe books and prepare elaborate meals for their friends (Hartley, 1997). Anorectics themselves, however, will avoid most calorie-rich foods, such as meat, milk products, sweets and other desserts, and will often limit their consumption to little more than a lettuce leaf and carrot. They also show reduced pleasure in eating. Although anorectics do not experience deficiencies in taste, they do have a *low hedonic responsiveness* to taste and an aversion to the oral sensation of fat (Sunday & Halmi, 1990).

Box 71.2 Restricting and binge eating/purging types

Anorexia nervosa is also characterised by an intense fear of being overweight which does not diminish even when a large amount of weight has been lost. As a consequence of this fear, anorectics take extreme measures to lose weight. In DSM-IV, two sub-types of anorexia nervosa are identified, both of which contribute to the refusal to maintain a body weight above the minimum normal weight. The *restricting type* loses weight through constant fasting and engaging in excessive physical activity. The *binge eating/purging type* alternates between periods of fasting and 'binge eating' (see below) in which normally avoided food is consumed in large quantities. The guilt and shame experienced as a result of the 'binge' lead the anorectic to use laxatives or self-induced vomiting to expel ingested food from the system.

One other characteristic of anorexia nervosa is a *distorted body image* in which the individual does not recognise the body's thinness. Even though their appearance may show protruding bones, many anorectics still see themselves as being fat and deny that they are 'wasting away'. As Bruch (1978) has observed, anorectics:

'vigorously defend their gruesome emaciation as not being too thin ... they identify with the skeleton-like appearance, actively maintain it and deny its abnormality'.

The fact that many people who would be diagnosed as anorectic do not perceive themselves as having a problem, suggests that data relating to both the incidence and prevalence of the disorder should be treated with caution (Cooper, 1995).

EXPLANATIONS OF ANOREXIA NERVOSA

Simmonds (1914) described the case of a girl who was emaciated, had stopped menstruating and showed severe atrophy of the pituitary gland. At the time, and for the next quarter of a century, it was believed that pituitary gland damage caused anorexia nervosa. However, this belief was mistaken and what Simmonds had identified was, in fact, a disorder that actually produces very different symptoms from anorexia nervosa (Colman, 1987). In *Simmonds' disease*, pituitary gland damage is associated

with a loss of pubic and underarm hair. This does not happen in anorexia nervosa, and the emaciation Simmonds observed is unusual except in terminal cases. Not surprisingly, therefore, attempts to treat anorexia nervosa with pituitary extracts were unsuccessful.

It has, however, been suggested that anorexia nervosa has a biological basis. Instead of the pituitary gland, it has been proposed that dysfunction in the *hypothalamus* leads to the disorder. Certainly, the hypothalamus plays an important role in the regulation of eating (see Chapter 16). Kaplan & Woodside (1987) showed that when *noradrenaline* acts on part of the hypothalamus, non-humans begin eating and show a marked preference for carbohydrates. *Serotonin*, by contrast, apparently induces satiation and suppresses appetite, especially for carbohydrates. Any condition which increased serotonin's effects would decrease eating. However, there is not yet sufficient evidence to indicate whether hypothalamic dysfunction and changes in neurotransmitter levels are causes of anorexia nervosa, effects of it or merely correlates (Kaye *et al.*, 1993).

Box 71.3 Corticotrophin-releasing hormone and anorexia nervosa

Park *et al.* (1995) examined four females with severe restrictive anorexia nervosa who spontaneously volunteered histories of glandular fever-like illnesses immediately preceding their eating disorder's onset. Park *et al.* suggest that viral- or immune-induced alterations in central homeostasis, particularly involving *corticotrophin-releasing hormone*, could trigger and perpetuate a behavioural response leading to a particularly severe form of restrictive anorexia nervosa. This suggestion is speculative, but biologically plausible.

Anorexia nervosa may have a genetic basis. There is a tendency for the disorder to run in families, with first- and second-degree relatives of anorectic individuals being significantly more likely to develop the disorder compared with first- and second-degree relatives of a control group of non-anorectics (Strober & Katz, 1987).

Twin studies have also been used to investigate the role of genetic factors. Askevold & Heiberg (1979) reported a 50 per cent concordance rate for MZs brought up in the same environment, which they see as strong evidence that genes play an important role. However, in the absence of concordance rates for DZs and MZs reared apart, this claim is difficult to evaluate. Holland *et al.* (1984) reported a concordance rate of 55 per cent for MZs brought up in the same environment and seven per cent for DZs. Although this difference hints at genetic involvement, the concordance rate suggests that if genes do play a role, it is likely to be a small one (Treasure & Holland, 1991).

Box 71.4   Anorexia and the anterior temporal lobes

According to Lask (cited in Kennedy, 1997), a blood flow deficiency in the anterior temporal lobes, which interpret vision, explains why anorectics see themselves as fat when they are thin. However, people with the deficiency would need other triggers to develop the disorder. These might include stress, a perfectionist personality and a society that promoted thinness (see below).

Other theories of anorexia nervosa are more social and psychological in their orientation. The psychodynamic model proposes that the disorder represents an unconscious effort by a girl to remain pre-pubescent. As a result of overdependence on the parents, some girls might fear becoming sexually mature and independent. As noted earlier, anorexia nervosa is associated with amenorrhea, and psychodynamic theorists see this as enabling the anorectic to circumvent growing up and achieving adult responsibilities. Certainly, to achieve puberty, we must attain a particular level of body fat, and evidence suggests that anorectics will eat, provided they do not gain weight.

An alternative psychodynamic account proposes that the disorder may allow a girl to avoid the issue of her sexuality. The weight loss that occurs prevents the rounding of the breasts and hips, and the body takes on a 'boy-like' appearance. This might be a way of avoiding the issue of sexuality in general, and the prospect of pregnancy in particular.

Yet another psychodynamic account sees the disorder as attempts by adolescents to *separate* themselves from their parents and establish their own identities. Psychodynamic theorists argue that the parents of anorectics tend to be domineering, and that the disorder reflects an attempt to exert individuality. Many female anorectics are 'good girls', who do well in school and are cooperative and well-behaved (Bemis, 1978). Bemis argues that this leads them to feel they have no choices and are being controlled by the desires and demands of others. One way of exerting individuality is to assume control over what is most concretely one's self – the body. Thinness and starvation, then, are signs of self-control and independence.

Figure 71.1   The much publicised English anorectic twins, Samantha and Michaela Kendall. Despite receiving treatment in the USA, Samantha eventually died. Michaela died three years later

Although there may be some truth in psychodynamic accounts of anorexia nervosa, at least two observations challenge them. First, some seem to apply only to females. It is impossible to see how avoiding the prospect of pregnancy could apply to male anorectics. Second, all of the accounts have difficulty in explaining anorexia nervosa's occurrence after adolescence.

The behavioural model sees anorexia nervosa as a *phobia* (see Chapter 70) concerning the possibility of gaining weight. Indeed, anorexia nervosa might be more appropriately called *weight phobia* (Crisp, 1967). The phobia is assumed to be the result of the impact of social norms, values and roles. Garner *et al.* (1980) have claimed that the winners of Miss America and the centrefolds in *Playboy* magazine have consistently been below the average female weight and have become significantly more so since 1959. Thus, the *cultural idealisation* of the slender female (as represented by 'supermodels') may be one cause of the fear of being fat (Petkova, 1997). The pressures have become so great that, in America at least, normal eating for women is characterised by dieting! (Polivy & Herman, 1985).

In at least some occupations, such as ballet dancing and modelling, there is considerable pressure on women to be thin and the incidence of anorexia nervosa in these occupations is higher than in the population in general (Garfinkel & Garner, 1982). However, not all ballet dancers, models and so on, who diet to be slim develop eating disorders (Cooper, 1995). For Wooley & Wooley (1983):

'an increasingly stringent cultural standard of thinness for women has been accompanied by a steadily increasing incidence of serious eating disorders in women'.

Support for the claim that societal norms can be influential in this respect comes from evidence about eating disorders in other cultures. In at least some non-Western cultures (including China, Singapore and Malaysia), the incidence of anorexia nervosa is much lower than in Western societies (Lee *et al.*, 1992). Additionally, cases of anorexia nervosa reported in black populations of Western and non-Western cultures are significantly lower than those in white populations (Sui-Wah, 1989).

Box 71.5   Sindy and anorexia nervosa

According to Hill (cited in Uhlig, 1996a), women's fashion magazines play a part in shaping young girls' perceptions of desirable figures, but are not as influential as classmates, mothers and toys. According to Hill:

'[Sindy] is now unashamedly blonde, pointedly thin, [and] dressed immaculately ... Not only does 90s Sindy depict the ideal appearance and lifestyle of 90s women, she does so for girls only halfway to puberty'.

One consequence of young children's preoccupation with weight and shape is *osteoporosis* ('brittle bone' disease) more usually associated with elderly women (Hall, 1997). Some companies have withdrawn their advertising campaigns from magazines which feature 'skeletal' models on the grounds that it is 'irresponsible ... to have models of anorexic proportions' (Weaver, 1996).

One puzzling observation which is difficult for theories to account for is the development of anorexia nervosa in people unable to see. As noted earlier (see page 614), body image disturbance is one of the 'hallmarks' of anorexia nervosa. However, Yager *et al.* (1986) describe the case of a 28-year-old woman, blind from age two, who had become anorectic at age 21. Touyz *et al.* (1988) report a case of anorexia nervosa in a woman blind from birth. Although neither research team offered a satisfactory explanation for their findings, both agreed that blindness either from birth or a very early age does not

preclude anorexia nervosa's development, and that people do not have to be actually able to see themselves to desire a slimmer physique (see also Box 71.4).

Figure 71.2   Kate Moss (above), well-known supermodel, and two models from *Yes!* magazine (below), demonstrating that physical beauty or ideal body shape/size can be defined in more than one way, within the same culture and at the same point in time

Bulimia nervosa

Literally, bulimia comes from the Greek *bous* meaning 'ox' and *limos* meaning 'hunger'. The disorder was first extensively investigated by Russell (1979), who saw it as 'an ominous variant' of anorexia nervosa. Bulimia nervosa is characterised by periodic episodes of 'compulsive' or 'binge' eating, the rapid and seemingly uncontrolled consumption of food, especially that rich in carbohydrates.

The binge is terminated either by abdominal pain or, in the case of the *purging type*, by the expulsion of food using diuretics, laxatives or self-induced vomiting. Some bulimics begin their binges by eating coloured 'marker' foods and, after they have finished, will continue purging until the marker has re-emerged (Colman, 1987). A typical binge might include the consumption of a large amount of ice cream, packets of crisps, a pizza and several cans of fizzy drink. As well as their high calorific content, most foods consumed by bulimics have textures that aid rapid consumption. Thus, food tends to be 'wolfed down' rather than chewed properly. With the *non-purging type*, strict dieting or vigorous exercise (rather than regular purging) occurs.

'Binge eating' itself is actually quite common and many people admit to indulging occasionally (Polivy & Herman, 1985). In bulimia nervosa, however, the *frequency* of such behaviour is much higher, averaging at least two or three times a week, and sometimes as often as 30 times a week.

> **Box 71.6   A typical case of bulimia nervosa**
>
> Miss A. was a 22-year-old single clerk, who was referred by her doctor for treatment of 'psychiatric problems'. She had a three-year history of uncontrolled overeating. Although she was not originally obese, she disliked her 'square face' and developed a sensitive personality. After failing an examination and being unable to study in further education, she started to relieve her boredom and comfort herself by overeating. Her binges occurred four times per week and lasted one to three hours each.
>
> Triggers included feelings of emptiness and critical remarks from others. On average, she secretly consumed 800 g of bread and biscuits. Such episodes were followed by abdominal bloating, guilt and dysphoria (inappropriate emotional feelings). There was nausea, but no vomiting. She took excessive laxatives (usually prune juice) to purge and 'calm' herself, restricted food intake and exercised excessively in the next one to two days. Her body weight fluctuated by up to 4 kg per week, but her menstrual cycle was normal.

> Examination revealed a girl who was fully conscious of what she was doing and who felt helpless over the 'attacks of overeating'. She desired a body weight of 45 kg and disparaged her waistline and square face, which made her 'look like a pig'. She found food dominated her life, and likened her problem to heroin addiction. There was a persistent request for laxatives.
>
> (Adapted from Lee *et al.*, 1992)

Most bulimics are women, with fewer than five per cent of cases presenting for treatment being men (Cooper, 1995). The disorder usually begins in adolescence or early adulthood and generally appears later than in anorexia nervosa. Bulimia nervosa is also more frequent than anorexia nervosa and may affect as many as five per cent of the population. Like anorectics, bulimics have what ICD-10 calls 'an intrusive fear of fatness', and they are unduly concerned with their body weight and shape (hence they take the drastic steps described above to control their weight). Cutts & Barrios (1986), for example, asked bulimics to imagine gaining weight. Physiological measures indicated increased heart rate and muscle tension compared with non-bulimic controls performing the same task.

Whilst the discrepancy between actual body weight and desired body weight is generally no greater than among non-bulimics, the discrepancy between *estimations* of body size and desired size is substantial (Cooper, 1995). Although bulimics are mostly able to maintain a normal body weight, they tend to fluctuate between weight gain and weight loss. The binge–purge behaviour is typically accompanied by guilty feelings. The purging of food produces feelings of relief and a commitment to a severely restrictive diet which ultimately fails (Sue *et al.*, 1994).

Clearly, bulimics recognise their eating behaviour is abnormal and feel frustrated by it. However, they are unable to control the behaviour voluntarily. Because of the guilty feelings, bingeing and purging are usually carried out in secret and, consequently, many bulimics go unrecognised even to close friends and family. Moreover, because there is not a constant weight loss, and because the bulimic's eating habits may appear normal in public, the estimate given for the number of cases must be treated cautiously.

Purging does, however, produce some effects that might be noticeable to others. One of these is a 'puffy' facial appearance (a consequence of swollen parotid glands caused by vomiting). Another is a deterioration in tooth enamel (caused by the stomach acid produced when vomiting occurs). A third is the development of calluses over the back of the hand (caused by rubbing the hand against the upper teeth when the fingers are pushed into the throat to induce vomiting). Other associated physiological effects include digestive tract damage, dehydration and nutritional imbalances. Psychological effects include anxiety, sleep disturbances and depression (see below).

Associations between *self-mutilative* behaviour and bulimia nervosa have also been reported. Parry-Jones & Parry-Jones (1993) examined 25 bulimic cases reported from the late seventeenth to the late nineteenth centuries. They found four instances of self-mutilative behaviour and argue that such historical evidence offers some support for the suggested connection between eating disorders and self-mutilation.

Box 71.7   Blood-letting and bulimia

An unusual form of self-mutilation was reported by Parkin & Eagles (1993) who studied three cases of *blood-letting* in association with bulimia nervosa. All three had some medical training and began blood-letting after they had acquired sufficient expertise in the insertion of intravenous cannulae and the necessary implements. Each bulimic appeared to derive similar psychological benefit from the blood-letting which seemed to serve much the same function as bingeing and vomiting in that it relieved feelings of anxiety, tension and anger.

EXPLANATIONS OF BULIMIA NERVOSA

As with anorexia nervosa, there are several theoretical approaches to understanding the cause of bulimia nervosa. As mentioned previously (see page 614), certain neurotransmitters have been implicated in the regulation of eating behaviour. Neurotransmitters may also be implicated in bulimia nervosa. For example, abnormal neurotransmitter activity might account for the periodic carbohydrate bingeing.

Hormones and *endorphins* may also play a mediating role. Lydiard *et al.* (1993) reported that levels of *cholecystokinin octapeptide* (CCK-8: see Box 16.4, page 132) were significantly lower in 11 drug-free female bulimics than 16 age-matched controls. Since there was no correlation between the mean frequency of binge eating or vomiting and scores on the *eating disorders inventory*, the bulimics' unusual eating habits do not seem to be responsible for the decreased levels of CCK-8.

Other research has found that *plasma endorphins* are elevated in people with bulimia nervosa (and, interestingly, in those who self-mutilate: cf. Parkin & Eagles', 1993, study

described in Box 71.7). However, whether the elevated levels are a cause or a result of bulimia nervosa remains to be established. Additionally, the genetic evidence for bulimia nervosa is much weaker than that for anorexia nervosa. Kendler *et al.* (1991), for example, have reported a concordance rate of only 23 per cent for MZs and nine per cent for DZs (see page 614).

Box 71.8   The disinhibition hypothesis

One psychological approach to understanding bulimia nervosa is Ruderman's (1986) *disinhibition hypothesis*. This distinguishes between 'unrestrained' and 'restrained' eaters, the latter being people who constantly monitor their weight and constantly diet. Sometimes, 'restrained' eaters believe they have overeaten, a belief that may be accompanied by the thought that, since the diet has been broken, there is no reason why more should not be eaten. This *disinhibition* leads to the consumption of more food, which is followed by purging in an attempt to reduce the weight gained by the binge eating. As well as breaking a diet, other *disinhibiting factors* include alcohol. For Ruderman, the food intake pattern of highly weight-conscious people is characterised by an all-or-nothing rigidity which makes them susceptible to binge eating.

Because anorexia nervosa and bulimia nervosa share many characteristics, some researchers believe they can be explained in the same way. Garner (1986) has argued that it is seriously misleading to consider the disorders as being psychologically dissimilar. Echoing Garner, Bee (1992) describes them as 'variations on a basic theme' rather than distinctly different disorders. Garner has shown that as well as sharing many psychological traits (such as perfectionism), anorectics and bulimics also share the same goal of maintaining a sub-optimal body weight. Moreover, a particular individual may often move *between* the two disorders in the quest for thinness.

According to Waller (1993), sexual abuse is related to eating disorders, particularly those involving bulimic features. In a study of 100 women with eating disorders, Waller found that *borderline personality disorder* explains at least a small part of the link between sexual abuse and bulimic behaviour, especially as regards the frequency of bingeing. This alleged link has, however, been challenged (Cooper, 1995). Even if it exists, other factors are surely involved. For example, people with eating disorders often have a personal history of affective disorder (particularly depression: see Chapter 69). Piran *et al.* (1985) found that among 18 patients with a lifetime history of major depression, the depressive symptoms preceded the eating disorder's emergence by at least one year in eight cases, post-dated its onset in six, and occurred around the same time in the other four. Also, binge eating, mood and purging vary seasonally with bulimia nervosa. This might suggest that a vulnerability to depression (or seasonal affective disorder: see Chapter 69) increases the predisposition to eating disorders, and an episode of depression might contribute to either the initation of its symptoms or its maintenance (Cooper, 1995).

Conclusions

Several theories of anorexia nervosa and bulimia nervosa have been proposed. Although some are more plausible than others, and have more supporting evidence, no theory yet has explanatory power over all others. Possibly, the two eating disorders do not have single discrete causes, and there may be complex chains of events which interact to precipitate them.

Summary

■ **Anorexia nervosa** occurs more frequently in females than males and usually appears in adolescence. It is characterised by a prolonged refusal to eat adequate amounts of food, resulting in deliberate weight loss. To be diagnosed as anorectic, an individual must weigh less than 85 per cent of normal/expected weight for height, age and sex. In five to 15 per cent of cases, anorexia is fatal.

■ Because of their fear of being overweight, anorectics take extreme measures to lose weight. The **restricting type** engages in constant fasting/excessive physical activity, whilst the **binge eating/purging type** alternates between periods of fasting and 'binge eating', food being expelled by laxatives or self-induced vomiting.

■ Damage to the **hypothalamus** might cause anorexia nervosa. In non-humans, stimulation of the hypothalamus by **noradrenaline** produces eating and a preference for carbohydrates. **Serotonin** produces the opposite effect. **Corticotrophin-releasing hormone** and **anterior temporal lobe** deficiencies have also been implicated. However, whether brain dysfunction and/or changes in neurotransmitters are causes, effects or correlates is unclear. If **genetic** factors are involved, their role is likely to be small.

■ There are several **psychodynamic** accounts of anorexia nervosa. Whilst some observations are consistent with them, they apply only to females and focus on anorexia exclusively as an adolescent disorder.

■ The **behavioural** model sees anorexia as a **phobia** of gaining weight, resulting from the impact of social norms, values and roles. The current cultural idealisation of the 'slender female' may be one cause of the fear of being fat. A lower incidence of anorexia in other cultures supports this perspective.

■ One difficulty for all theories is in explaining anorexia's development in people blind from birth. This finding makes the importance of a distorted body image as one of the disorder's characteristics difficult to explain.

■ Most **bulimics** are women, and **bulimia nervosa** usually begins in adolescence or early adulthood. The **purging type** is characterised by frequent episodes of compulsive/binge eating, ended either by abdominal pain or the use of diuretics, laxatives, and/or self-induced vomiting. The **non-purging type** counteracts the food intake either by strict dieting or vigorous exercise.

■ Like anorectics, bulimics are unduly concerned with their body weight/shape. Although able to maintain a normal body weight, they tend to fluctuate between gain and loss. Bulimics recognise the abnormal nature of their eating behaviour, but are unable to control it. Bulimia is also associated with **self-mutilative behaviour**, one unusual form being **blood-letting**.

■ **Noradrenaline**, **serotonin**, **hormones** and **endorphins** may all play mediating roles in bulimia nervosa. For example, elevated **plasma endorphin** levels have been found in bulimics, although whether these are a cause, consequence or correlate of the disorder is not known.

■ The **disinhibition hypothesis** proposes that when 'restrained eaters' believe they have overeaten, their eating becomes 'disinhibited'. This is followed by purging to reduce the weight gained. Highly weight-conscious people display all-or-nothing rigidity, making them susceptible to binge eating.

■ Anorexia and bulimia may be distinct disorders or 'variations on a theme'. Anorectics and bulimics share many psychological traits, along with the goal of maintaining a sub-optimal body weight. The same person may also alternate between the two disorders.

■ Sexual abuse is correlated with some eating disorders, and **borderline personality disorder** partly links the two. However, seasonal affective disorder may increase a predisposition to eating disorders. A depressive episode might contribute to the initiation of an eating disorder or its maintenance.

PART 3

Therapeutic approaches

THERAPIES BASED ON THE MEDICAL MODEL

Introduction and overview

As noted in Chapter 66, the medical model views mental disorders as being caused largely, if not exclusively, by physical factors. As a result, the medical model's favoured therapeutic approaches are physical, and collectively known as *somatic therapy*. The early and middle parts of the twentieth century saw the introduction of a variety of extraordinary treatments for mental disorders, whose names conjure up disturbing images of what they involved (David, 1994). These include *carbon dioxide inhalation therapy, nitrogen shock therapy, narcosis therapy, insulin coma therapy* and *malaria therapy*.

Although many somatic therapies have been abandoned, three are still used (and their names too may conjure up disturbing images). These are *chemotherapy, electroconvulsive therapy* and *psychosurgery*. This chapter describes these therapies and considers some of the issues surrounding their use.

Chemotherapy

The use of *drugs* to treat mental disorders has been the most influential of the currently used somatic therapies. Indeed, according to SANE (1993b), a quarter of all medications prescribed in Britain through the National Health Service are *psychotherapeutic* drugs. The three main types of drug are *neuroleptics, antidepressants* and *antimanics*, and *anxiolytics*.

NEUROLEPTICS

Neuroleptics were the forerunners of the 'drug revolution' in the treatment of mental disorders. They were introduced in the 1950s following the accidental discovery that they calmed psychotic individuals. Since they lessened the need for the physical restraint (such as straitjackets) of seriously disturbed individuals, they were seen as a great advance in treatment. Neuroleptics are also known as *major tranquillisers*, although this term is misleading because they generally tranquillise without impairing consciousness. The term *antipsychotics* is also used to describe them, because they are mainly used to treat schizophrenia and other severe disorders, such as mania and amphetamine abuse.

Box 72.1   The neuroleptic drugs

Examples: The most widely used group are the *phenothiazines* and include *chlorpromazine* (marketed under the trade names *Thorazine* and *Largactil*). The *butyrophenone* group includes *haloperidol* (*Haldol*) and *droperidol* (*Droleptan*). One of the more recent neuroleptics is *clozapine* (*Clozaril*), a member of the *dibezazepines* group, which was developed to avoid the side-effects (see below) of the phenothiazines.

Mode of action: Most neuroleptics block D2 *dopamine* receptors in the brain with the result that dopamine cannot excite post-synaptic receptors (see Chapter 68, page 593). Neuroleptics also inhibit the functioning of the hypothalamus (which contains dopamine secreting neurons). The hypothalamus plays a role in arousal, and neuroleptic drugs prevent arousal signals from reaching

---

higher brain regions. Rather than blocking D2 receptors, clozapine blocks D4 receptors, and for that reason is known as an *atypical* neuroleptic.

Side-effects: Of many that have been reported, the more extreme include blurred vision, *neuroleptic malignant syndrome* (which produces delirium, coma and death) and *extrapyramidal symptoms*. These consist of *akathisia* (restlessness), *dystonia* (abnormal body movements, one of which is known as the 'Thorazine shuffle'), and *tardive dyskinesia*. Tardive (late onset) dyskinesia (movement disorder) is an irreversible condition resembling Parkinson's disease. Some side-effects can be controlled by the use of other drugs such as *procyclidine* (*Kemadrin*).

Attempts to limit side-effects include *targeted strategies* or *drug holidays*, in which the drugs are discontinued during periods of remission and reinstituted when early signs of relapse occur. *Agranulocytosis* (a decrease in the number of infection-fighting white blood cells) is a side-effect of clozapine and some other neuroleptics. It occurs in about two per cent of users, and is potentially fatal. Blood tests must be given on a regular basis. When the cell count drops too low, the drug's use must be permanently discontinued. Newer neuroleptics such as *risperidone* (*Risperdal*) may avoid many of the side-effects described above (NSF, 1994). *Olanzapine*, which has a similar action to clozapine but without the haematological complications, is marketed under the trade name *Zyprexa* (BNF, 1997).

Typical neuroleptics are effective in reducing schizophrenia's *positive* symptoms (see page 593), and allow other therapies to be used when the symptoms are in remission. However, some people fail to respond to the drugs, especially those displaying *negative* symptoms, such as apathy and withdrawal. Although *atypical* neuroleptics may treat negative symptoms, antipsychotic drugs do not *cure* schizophrenia, but reduce its prominent symptoms (Hutton, 1998). Relapse occurs after several weeks if the drugs are stopped. Additionally, neuroleptics are of little value in treating social incapacity and other difficulties in adjusting to life outside the therapeutic setting. As a result, relapse is common (Green, 1996c).

ANTIDEPRESSANTS AND ANTIMANICS

Antidepressants are classified as *stimulants* and were also introduced in the 1950s. As well as treating depression, they have been used in the treatment of anxiety, agoraphobia, obsessive–compulsive disorder and eating disorders (Hamilton & Timmons, 1995).

Box 72.2   Antidepressants

Examples: The *monoamine oxidase inhibitor* (MAOI) group includes *phenelzine* (marketed under the trade name *Nardil*). The *tricyclic* group includes *imipramine* (*Tofranil*). The *tetracyclic* group includes *fluoxetine* (*Prozac*). Because of their mode of action (see below), the tetracyclics are also known as *selective serotonin re-uptake inhibitors* (SSRIs).

Mode of action: MAOIs are so called because they inhibit (or block) the uptake of the enzyme that deactivates *noradrenaline* and *serotonin*. Thus, they are believed to act directly on these neurotransmitters (see page 33). The tricyclic group prevents the re-uptake of noradrenaline and serotonin by the cells that released them, making these neurotransmitters more likely to reach receptor sites. The tetracyclics block the action of an enzyme that removes serotonin from the synapses between neurons (hence serotonin levels are elevated).

Side-effects: MAOIs require adherence to a special diet. Amine-rich food (such as some cheeses, pickled herrings and yeast extracts) must be avoided. Failure to do so results in the accumulation of amines, which causes cerebral haemorrhage. Both MAOIs and the tricyclics are associated with cardiac arrhythmias and heart block, dry mouth, blurred vision and urinary retention. Tetracyclic drugs like Prozac are also not free from serious side-effects, including impairment of sexual function (Breggin, 1996) and abnormal aggression (Cornwell, 1996). The most recent antidepressants include *reboxetine* (*Edronax*), which exerts its effects exclusively on noradrenaline (Lemonick, 1997).

None of the antidepressants identified in Box 72.2 exerts immediate effects (Stevenson & Baker, 1996). For example, *tricyclics* can take up to four weeks before a noticeable change in behaviour is observed (and with individuals who are so depressed that they are contemplating suicide, this is clearly a drawback). However, when mood improves, psychological therapies can be used to try and get at the root of the depression. MAOIs are generally less effective than tricyclics, and because of dietary requirements and the fact that they have more side-effects than tricyclics, MAOIs are the least preferred antidepressant drug.

Prozac, an SSRI antidepressant, was introduced in 1987. It has been termed the 'happy pill' and its users 'the happy, shiny people'. Because Prozac was believed to have fewer side-effects than the tricyclics, it has been widely prescribed as a treatment for depression. The claim that Prozac can increase happiness and create a 'more interesting personality' has produced astonishing sales. More than 15 million people worldwide take the drug, including 500,000 in Britain (Costello *et al.*, 1995). In 1996, American *children* aged between six and 18 received 735,000 prescriptions for Prozac and other SSRIs (Laurence, 1997).

Although antidepressants are effective when used in the short term with severe depression, they are not useful on a long-term basis. Indeed, they do not alleviate depression in all people, and controlled studies suggest their effectiveness is no greater than psychotherapy and cognitive therapy (NIMH, 1987). As Box 72.2 illustrates, one side-effect (especially of the tricyclics) is *urinary retention*. Controversially, this has been used to treat *nocturnal enuresis* (bedwetting) in children, even when other simple measures have not been tried.

Lithium carbonate was approved as an antimanic drug in 1970, but was actually first used in the mid-nineteenth century for *gouty mania* (Garrod, 1859). It is used to treat bipolar disorder and unipolar depression, as well as mania. Lithium salts (such as *lithium carbonate* and *lithium citrate*) flatten out cycles of manic behaviour. Once the manic phase in bipolar disorder has been eliminated, the depressed phase does not return. Lithium salts appear to be 'miracle drugs', in that within two weeks of taking them, 70–80 per cent of manic individuals show an improvement in mood.

Box 72.3   Antimanics

Examples: The inorganic salts lithium carbonate and lithium citrate are marketed under a variety of trade names including *Camoclit* and *Liskanum* (both lithium carbonate) and *Litarex* and *Piradel* (both lithium citrate).

Mode of action: By increasing the re-uptake of *noradrenaline* and *serotonin*, it is believed that lithium carbonate decreases their availability at various synaptic sites.

Side-effects: These include depressed reactions, hand tremors, dry mouth, weight gain, impaired memory and kidney poisoning. If lithium becomes too concentrated in the bloodstream, side effects include nausea, diarrhoea and, at very high levels, coma and death. As a result, users' blood is regularly checked.

ANXIOLYTICS

These are classified as *depressants* and are also known as *anti-anxiety drugs* or *minor tranquillisers*. Anxiety was first treated with synthetic *barbiturates* (such as *phenobarbitol*). However, because of their side-effects and the introduction

of other anxiolytic drugs, their use gradually declined. Anxiolytics are used to reduce anxiety and tension in people whose disturbances are not severe enough to warrant hospitalisation. The drugs are effective in reducing the symptoms of GAD (see Chapter 70), especially when used in the short term and in combination with psychological therapies. They are also used to combat withdrawal symptoms associated with opiate and alcohol addiction. However, anxiolytics are of little use in treating the anxiety that occurs in sudden, spontaneous panic attacks.

Box 72.4   Anxiolytics

Examples: The *propanediol* group includes *meprobamate* (marketed under the trade name *Miltown*). The *benzodiazepine* group includes *chlordiazepoxide* (*Librium*) and *diazepam* (*Valium*).

Mode of action: Their general effect is to depress CNS activity, which causes a decrease in activity of the sympathetic branch of the ANS. This produces decreased heart and respiration rate and reduces feelings of nervousness and tension. Since benzodiazepine receptor sites exist in the brain, that group might exert their effect by mimicking or blocking a naturally occurring substance yet to be discovered.

Side-effects: These include drowsiness, lethargy, tolerance, dependence, withdrawal (manifested as tremors and convulsions) and toxicity. *Rebound anxiety* (anxiety which is even more intense than that originally experienced) can occur when their use is stopped. Rebound anxiety may be physiological *or* psychological in origin. Newer anxiolytics (such as *Busparin* and *Zopiclone*) seem to be as effective as established anxiolytics, although unpleasant side-effects have also been reported with them.

The term *minor tranquillisers* might suggest that anxiolytic drugs are 'safe'. However, one of their dangers is that overdose can lead to death, especially when taken with alcohol. As Box 72.4 shows, anxiolytics also produce addiction. Although it is generally agreed that anxiolytic use should be limited to people whose anxiety is clearly handicapping their work, leisure and family relationships, they are all too commonly prescribed. Indeed, Valium is the most prescribed of all drugs. An astonishing 8000 tons of *benzodiazepines* were consumed in the United States alone in 1977, and 21 million prescriptions issued in Britain alone in 1989 (Rassool & Winnington, 1993). As with other drugs, their use with children (to relieve acute anxiety and related insomnia caused by fear) is controversial, and the use of benzodiazepines during pregnancy has been linked with vascular and limb malformations in the offspring (MacDonald, 1996).

Electroconvulsive therapy

Sakel (1933, cited in Fink, 1984) found that inducing a hypoglycaemic coma by means of insulin seemed to be effective in treating certain psychoses. Later, von Meduna claimed that schizophrenia and epilepsy were *biologically incompatible*, that is, schizophrenia rarely occurred in epilepsy and vice versa. Drawing on his observation that psychotic individuals prone to epilepsy showed less severe symptoms following an epileptic fit, von Meduna advocated inducing major epileptiform fits in psychotics in order to 'drive out' and hence 'cure' their schizophrenia.

Von Meduna used *Cardiazol*, a cerebral stimulant, to induce the epileptic fit. However, this method was unsatisfactory, not least because it induced feelings of impending death during the conscious phase of its action! Various alternatives were tried until, after visiting an abattoir and seeing animals rendered unconscious by means of electric shocks, Cerletti and Bini (Bini, 1938) advocated passing an electric current across the temples to induce an epileptic fit. Although there have been refinements to Cerletti and Bini's original procedures, *electroconvulsive therapy* (ECT) is still administered in essentially the same way.

Box 72.5   The procedures used in ECT

Following a full physical examination (necessary because heart conditions, chest diseases and peptic ulcers can be accentuated by ECT), the person is required to fast for three to four hours prior to treatment and empty the bladder immediately before treatment. Whilst being psychologically prepared, dentures, rings and other metallic objects are removed and a loose-fitting gown worn.

Forty-five to sixty minutes before treatment, an *atropine sulphate* injection is given. This prevents the heart's normal rhythm from being disturbed and inhibits the secretion of mucus and saliva. An anxiolytic drug may also be given if a person is particularly apprehensive. With the person lying supine, head supported by a pillow, a short-acting anaesthetic followed by a muscle relaxant is given, the latter ensuring that a reduced convulsion will occur. Oxygen is given before and after treatment, and a mouth gag is applied to prevent the tongue or lips being bitten.

In *bilateral* ECT, saline-soaked lint-covered electrodes are attached to each temple. In *unilateral* ECT, two electrodes are attached to the temple and mastoid region of the non-dominant cerebral hemisphere. With the chin held still, a current of around 200 milliamps, flowing at 110 volts, is passed from one electrode to another for a brief period (around 0.5–4 seconds).

Because of the use of muscle relaxants, the only observable sign of the fit is a slight twitching of the eyelids, facial muscles, and toes. When the convulsion is complete and the jaw relaxed, an airway is inserted into the mouth and oxygen given until breathing resumes unaided. The person is turned into the left lateral position, head on the side, and is carefully observed until the effects of the muscle relaxant and anaesthetic have worn off and recovery is complete.

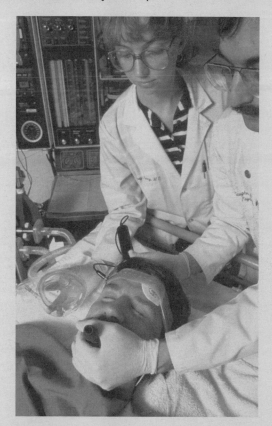

Figure 72.1   ECT as it is carried out today. Despite the technical improvements, ECT is a highly controversial treatment

Typically, a number of ECT treatments occurring over several weeks will be administered, the amount being gauged by the individual's response (Freeman, 1995). Although originally used to treat schizophrenia, ECT's usefulness with that disorder has been seriously questioned, and today it is primarily used to treat severe depression, bipolar disorder and certain obsessive–compulsive disorders. In Britain, around 20,000 people a year undergo ECT (Johnston, 1996). According to Wesseley (1993), ECT is 'highly effective' in the treatment of severe depression and particularly useful with those who harbour suicidal feelings because its effects are immediate (unlike the antidepressant drugs: see page 621).

Box 72.6 Explaining ECT's effectiveness

Whilst ECT's effectiveness in certain disorders is beyond dispute, its use has been questioned on the grounds that it is not known why the beneficial effects occur (Benton, 1981). It might be due to the *anterograde* and *retrograde amnesia* that occur as a side-effect (see Chapter 30). However, *unilateral ECT* (see Box 72.5), which minimises memory disruption, is also effective in reducing depression. As a result, a 'memory loss' theory is unlikely to be true.

Given ECT's nature and the negative publicity it has received, a person might deny his or her symptoms to avoid the 'punishment' the therapy is perceived as being, which extinguishes the abnormal behaviour. This possibility has been tested by applying *sub-convulsive shocks*. However, these do not seem to be beneficial and, since they are as unpleasant as convulsive shocks, a 'punishment' theory account is also unlikely to be true.

The most plausible account of ECT's effectiveness is that it produces a variety of *biochemical changes* in the brain which are greater than those produced by antidepressant drugs. However, many physiological changes occur when ECT is administered, and it is difficult to establish which of these are important. Since ECT appears to be most effective in the treatment of depression, and since both noradrenaline and serotonin have been strongly implicated in that disorder (see Chapter 69), it is most likely that these neurotransmitters are affected (Lilienfeld, 1995).

ECT has also been criticised on ethical grounds. Indeed, in 1982, it was outlawed in Berkeley, California by voter referendum, and its use was punishable by a fine of up to $500 and six months in jail. As noted earlier, ECT has a negative public image deriving from horrific descriptions in books and films. Some of its opponents have described the therapy as being 'about as scientific as kicking a television set because it is not working' (Heather, 1976). Certainly, the primitive methods once used were associated with bruises and bone fractures (a consequence of the restraint used by nursing staff during the convulsion), and with pain when an individual failed to lose consciousness during the treatment. However, the use of muscle relaxants minimises the possibility of fractures, and anaesthetics rule out the possibility of the individual being conscious during treatment (see Box 72.5).

Yet whilst ECT is now considered to be a 'low-risk' therapeutic procedure, Breggin (1979) has argued that brain damage can occur following its administration (at least in non-humans sacrificed immediately after receiving ECT). Breggin has also pointed out that whilst ECT is typically seen as a treatment of 'last resort', which should be preceded by a careful assessment of the costs and benefits for a particular individual, such assessments are not always routine. Although this may be true in the United States, under Section 58 of the Mental Health Act (1983), ECT's use in Britain requires an individual's consent or a second medical opinion before it can be administered.

Psychosurgery

Psychosurgery refers to surgical procedures that are performed on the brain to treat mental disorders. The term is properly used when the intention is to *purposely* alter psychological functioning. Thus, whilst removing a brain tumour might affect a person's behaviour, it would not constitute a psychosurgical procedure.

Psychosurgical techniques, albeit primitive ones, have been carried out for a long time (see Chapter 66 and *trephining*). In medieval times, psychosurgery involved 'cutting the stone of folly' from the brains of those considered to be 'mad'. Modern psychosurgical techniques can be traced to the Second International Neurological Conference held in London in 1935, when Jacobsen reported the effects of removing the pre-frontal areas (the forwardmost portion) of the frontal lobes in chimpanzees. The procedure apparently abolished the violent outbursts some of the chimpanzees had been prone to.

In the audience was Moniz, a Portugese neuropsychiatrist. Moniz was sufficiently impressed by Jacobsen's findings to persuade a colleague, Lima, to carry out surgical procedures on the frontal lobes of schizophrenics and other disturbed individuals in an attempt to reduce their aggressive behaviour. The procedure involved severing the neural connections between the pre-frontal areas and the hypothalamus and thalamus, the rationale being that thought (mediated by the cortex) would be disconnected from emotion (mediated by lower brain centres).

The *leucotomy* or *pre-frontal lobotomy* seemed to be successful in reducing aggressive behaviour in unmanageable patients. The original 'apple corer' technique involved drilling a hole through the skull covering on each side of the head and then inserting a blunt instrument which was rotated in a vertical arc. This procedure followed the unsuccessful technique of injecting alcohol to destroy areas of frontal lobe brain tissue. Moniz originally used the technique on schizophrenics and people who were compulsive and anxiety-ridden. After a year, a 70 per cent 'cure' rate was claimed by Moniz and Lima.

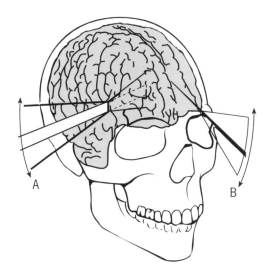

Figure 72.2   The 'apple corer' technique originally used by Moniz and Lima

Also at the 1935 conference was Freeman, a neurologist who was not trained as a surgeon. Freeman & Watts (1942) developed and popularised the 'standard' prefrontal lobotomy. In the absence of alternative therapeutic techniques, and with the seemingly high success rate claimed by Moniz and others, the operation became extremely common. Estimates vary as to the number of operations performed in the United States following Freeman and Watts' pioneering work. Kalinowsky (1975) puts it at around 40,000, whilst Valenstein's (1980) estimate is 25,000. Although not surgically trained, Freeman developed his own psychosurgical technique called the *transorbital lobotomy* (see Figure 72.3).

Psychosurgery was largely abandoned in the late 1950s following the introduction of the psychotherapeutic drugs, and various other reasons.

Box 72.7   Some reasons for the abandonment of psychosurgery

Lack of scientific basis: The theoretical rationale for Moniz's operation was vague and misguided, with researchers not *entirely* clear why beneficial effects should occur. Indeed, David (1994) has questioned whether even now knowledge of the frontal lobes (or what he calls 'frontal lobology') is anything more than 'psychiatry's new pseudoscience'. Moniz's reports of success were also exaggerated, and whilst he was awarded

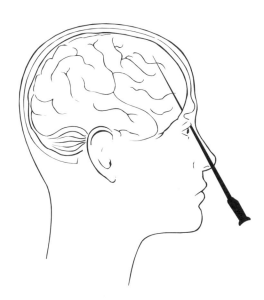

Figure 72.3   The transorbital lobotomy

the Nobel prize for medicine in 1949 'for his discovery of the therapeutic value of leucotomy in the treatment of some psychoses', it is ironic that he was shot and paralysed by a patient on whom he had performed a lobotomy! (Valenstein, 1990).

Consistency and irreversibility: Psychosurgery produces inconsistent outcomes. Behaviour change occurs in some individuals but not others, though who will be affected, and how, is difficult to predict. Psychosurgical procedures cannot be reversed.

Side-effects: Some of the severe and permanent side-effects associated with psychosurgery are (in no particular order):

apathy; impaired judgement; reduced creativity; epileptic-type seizures; severe blunting of emotions; intellectual impairments; hyperactivity; distractability; impaired learning ability; overeating; partial paralysis; memory loss; personal slovenliness; child-like behaviour; indifference to others; death.

Lack of evaluation: One surgeon noted that the *cingulotomy* (see below) produces 'little or no changes in intellectual and discriminative ability' using the ability to knit after the operation as the criterion for change (Winter, 1972).

Consent: Psychosurgical techniques were routinely used with people who could not give their consent to the operation. However, Section 58 of the revised Mental Health Act in Britain introduced stringent provisions regarding information to those referred for psychosurgery and their consent to treatment (Rappaport, 1992).

Given the reasons identified above, it is perhaps surprising to learn that, although controversial, psychosurgery is still performed today. However, it is very much a treatment of last resort used only when other treatment methods have failed. It is also occasionally used for pain control in the terminally ill. According to Snaith (1994), over 20 operations a year are conducted in Britain.

Modern lobotomies (*capsulotomies*) involve cutting two tiny holes in the forehead which allow radioactive electrodes to be inserted into the frontal lobe to destroy tissue by means of beta rays. Other psychosurgical techniques involve the destruction of small amounts of tissue in precisely located areas of the brain using a computer controlled electrode which is heated to 68°C. For example, the *tractotomy* interrupts the neural pathways between the limbic system and hypothalamus in the hope of alleviating depression.

Psychosurgical techniques reduce the risk of suicide in severe depression from 15 per cent to one per cent (Verkaik, 1995). The *cingulotomy* cuts the cingulum bundle (a small bundle of nerve fibres connecting the pre-frontal cortex with parts of the limbic system). This is used to treat obsessive–compulsive disorder, and evidently does so effectively (Hay *et al.*, 1993).

Even more controversial than ECT, psychosugery continues to have a negative image amongst both professionals and the public (Davison & Neale, 1994). However, according to Valenstein (1973):

'There are certainly no grounds for either the position that all psychosurgery necessarily reduces all people to a 'vegetable status' or that it has a high probability of producing miraculous cures. The truth, even if somewhat wishy-washy, lies in between these extreme positions'.

Conclusions

Somatic therapies, which derive from the medical model, have long been used to treat abnormal behaviour. This chapter has described and evaluated three somatic approaches to therapy. Although controversial, they continue to be used today in the treatment of mental disorders.

Summary

■ **Somatic approaches** are favoured by the medical model, and include **chemotherapy, electroconvulsive therapy** (ECT) and **psychosurgery**. The most influential somatic approach is chemotherapy. Three main types of psychotherapeutic drug are the **neuroleptics, antidepressants** and **antimanics,** and **anxiolytics**.

■ The neuroleptics (**major tranquillisers** or **antipsychotics**) are mainly used to treat schizophrenia, mania and amphetamine abuse. Most exert their effects by blocking D2 dopamine receptors, whilst atypical neuroleptics act on D4 receptors. Although effective, neuroleptics have many unpleasant and sometimes permanent side-effects. These include **neuroleptic malignant syndrome** and **extrapyramidal symptoms**.

■ Neuroleptics reduce schizophrenia's **positive** symptoms, but are less effective with its **negative** symptoms. They do not cure schizophrenia and are of little value in treating social incapacity and other difficulties in adjusting to life in the outside world. As a result, relapse is common.

■ **Antidepressants** are used to treat several disorders as well as depression. **Selective serotonin reuptake inhibitors** (SSRIs) are widely accepted as being more beneficial than **monoamine oxidase inhibitors** (MAOIs) and **tricyclics**. SSRIs affect serotonin levels, whilst MAOIs and tricylcics influence both serotonin and noradrenaline. Newer antidepressants (e.g. **reboxetine**) only influence noradrenaline.

■ Antidepressants take time to exert their effects, which limits their use with people who are suicidally depressed. Whilst they may be useful in the short-term, they are not useful on a long-term basis. All are associated with unpleasant side-effects, some of which are controversially used to treat other problems (such as bedwetting).

■ Salts of the metal lithium (**lithium carbonate** and **lithium citrate**) are used to treat bipolar disorder and unipolar depression as well as mania. Within two weeks of taking them, 70–80 per cent of manic individuals show an improvement in mood. They increase the re-uptake of noradrenaline and serotonin. However, unpleasant side-effects are also associated with their use.

■ **Anxiolytic drugs** (**anti-anxiety drugs** or **minor tranquillisers**) depress CNS activity, producing a decrease in activity in the sympathetic branch of the ANS. Some may mimic or block naturally occurring brain substances. Side-effects include **rebound anxiety**. They also produce **addiction**. Despite this, their use is still widespread.

■ **ECT** is used to treat depression, bipolar disorder, and certain obsessive–compulsive disorders. Typically, several treatments will be administered over a number of weeks. Although it is not known exactly why ECT is effective, the most plausible theory attributes its effectiveness to **biochemical changes** in the brain. Because it is not known how it works, ECT continues to be controversial.

■ **Psychosurgery** involves performing surgical procedures on the brain to purposely alter psychological functioning. Originally, the **leucotomy/pre-frontal lobotomy** was used with aggressive schizophrenics as was the **transorbital lobotomy**. At least 25,000 psychosurgical operations were performed in the United States alone.

■ Psychosurgery was largely abandoned in the 1950s following the introduction of psychotherapeutic drugs. Operations often lacked a sound theoretical rationale, did not produce consistent effects, and were associated with many side-effects. However, some surgical procedures are still performed, although only as a last resort. Around 20 operations are performed annually in Britain.

73

THERAPIES BASED ON THE PSYCHODYNAMIC MODEL

Introduction and overview

Chapter 66 noted that the psychodynamic model sees mental disorders as stemming from the demands of the id and/or the superego. If the ego is too weak to cope with these, it defends itself by repressing them into the unconscious. However, the conflicts do not disappear, but find expression through behaviour (and this is the disorder a person experiences).

For Freud, it is not enough to change a person's present behaviours. To bring about a permanent cure, the problems giving rise to the behaviours must also be changed. Because psychological problems have their origins in events that occurred earlier in life, Freud did not see present problems as the *psychoanalyst's* domain, because people will already have received sympathy and advice from family and friends. If such support was going to help, it would have done so already, and there would be no need for a psychoanalyst to be consulted.

According to Eisenberg (1995), there was a time 'when psychoanalysis was the only game in town'. However, whilst there are more than 400 psychotherapies (Holmes, 1996), the popularity of *psychodynamic* approaches (those based on psychoanalysis: see Chapter 1, pages 11–14) has declined over the years. For example, between 1961 and 1982, the proportion of therapists identifying themselves as psychoanalysts dropped from 41 to 14 per cent (Smith, 1982). Nonetheless, therapies based on the psychodynamic model are, 'one of Britain's most recession-proof industries' (Laurance, 1993), and more than 100,000 people are currently receiving some form of psychodynamically-based therapy. This chapter examines the processes involved in Freudian *psychoanalysis* and briefly considers some of the therapeutic variations on it.

Psychoanalysis

The purpose of *psychoanalysis* is to uncover the unconscious conflicts responsible for an individual's mental disorder. In Freud's words, psychoanalysis aims to 'drain the psychic abscess' and 'make the unconscious conscious'. The first step is thus to bring the conflicts into consciousness. Ultimately, this helps the *analysand* (the person undergoing psychoanalysis) to gain *insight* or conscious awareness of the repressed conflicts. The rationale is that once a person understands the reason for a behaviour, the ego can deal more effectively with it and resolve the conflict.

TECHNIQUES USED IN PSYCHOANALYSIS

Hypnosis

Ordinarily, the ego's defence mechanisms repress certain thoughts. As a result, bringing the unconscious into consciousness is difficult. Freud and his followers devised several methods to achieve this. Originally, Freud used *hypnosis*. This seemed to allow analysands to break through to things they were otherwise unaware of. However, Freud abandoned hypnosis because some of his analysands denied the accuracy of what they had revealed during it, whilst others found their revelations to be premature and painful.

Dream interpretation

As was seen in Chapter 13, Freud believed that the content of *dreams* is determined by unconscious processes as well as by the day's 'residues'. Unconscious impulses are expressed in dreams as a form of *wish fulfilment*. Freud believed dreams to be 'the royal road to the unconscious' and a rich source of information about hidden aspects of personality. Things that happened during the day evoked repressed childhood memories and desires. However, because some desires are too disturbing for an individual to face, even when asleep, these are expressed in symbolic form (the dream's *manifest content*). It is the analyst's task to unravel its hidden meaning (the dream's *latent content*).

Interpreting faulty actions and physiological cues

Two other methods used by psychoanalysts are the *interpretation of faulty actions* (or *parapraxes*) and the *interpretation of physiological cues*. Freud saw what others have called *Freudian slips* as a route to the unconscious, because the errors and mistakes we make in everyday life are unconscious thoughts finding their way into consciousness. Freud believed that repressed material could find expression through behaviour which is beyond conscious control, such as erroneous actions, forgetfulness and slips of the tongue and pen. The interpretation of physiological cues is used in conjunction with other methods. Blushing or pallor, and changes in the timbre of a person's voice, can all provide a useful indication of the unconscious significance of ideas touched on in therapy.

Free association

The most widely used technique in psychoanalysis is *free association*. In this, the analysand lies on a comfortable couch so that the analyst cannot be seen (which prevents the latter from distracting the former and interfering with concentration). The analysand is encouraged to say whatever comes to mind, no matter how trivial or frivolous it might seem. Freud called this the *basic rule* of psychoanalysis. He believed that the ego ordinarily acts as a censor, preventing threatening unconscious impulses from entering consciousness. By free-associating, the censor could be 'by-passed'. Although free association is the most widely used technique, it takes several sessions before analysands 'open up'.

Box 73.1   Introducing an analysand to free association

In ordinary conversation, you usually try to keep a connecting thread running through your remarks, excluding any intrusive ideas or side issues so as not to wander too far from the point, and rightly so. But in this case, you must talk differently. As you talk, various thoughts will occur to you which you would like to ignore because of certain criticisms and objections. You will be tempted to think, 'that is irrelevant or unimportant or nonsensical,' and to avoid saying it. Do not give in to such criticism. Report such thoughts in spite of your wish not to do so. Later, the reason for this injunction, the only one you have to follow, will become clear. Report whatever goes through your mind. Pretend that you are a traveller, describing to someone beside you the changing views which you see outside the train window.

(From Ford & Urban, 1963)

During analysis, the analyst remains '*anonymous*' and does not express emotion or evaluate the analysand's attitudes. The analyst does not reveal information about him- or herself, since whilst the analyst needs to learn a great deal about the analysand, the reverse is not true. This form of interaction ensures that the analysand does not form a close, personal relationship with the analyst, but views him or her purely as an 'anonymous and

ambiguous stimulus'. Whilst the analysand free-associates, the analyst acts as a sort of *sounding board*, often repeating and clarifying what the analysand has said. Thus, the analysand tells a story and the analyst helps interpret it in terms of repressed conflicts and feelings.

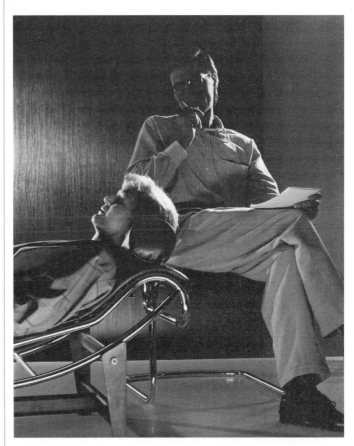

Figure 73.1   During psychoanalysis, the analysand usually reclines on a couch, while the analyst sits behind to avoid distracting the analysand. Although the analyst traditionally plays a passive role, occasionally he or she will offer an interpretation to help the analysand reach an insight

The main form of communication between the analyst and analysand is the analyst's *interpretive comments*. Sometimes, the analyst may need to draw attention to the analysand's *resistances*. Freud believed that what analysands do *not* say is as important as what they do say. During free association, analysands may express an unwillingness to discuss freely some aspects of their lives. For example, they may disrupt the session, change the subject whenever a particular topic comes up, joke about something as though it was unimportant, arrive late for a session, or perhaps miss it altogether.

Box 73.2 Freud's description of resistance

The analysand endeavours in every sort of way to extricate himself from [the rule of free association]. At one moment he declares that nothing occurs to him, at the next that so many things are crowding in on him that he cannot get hold of anything. Presently we observe with pained astonishment that he has given way first to one and then to another critical objection; he betrays this to us by the long pauses that he introduces into his remarks. He then admits that there is something he really cannot say – he would be ashamed to; and he allows this reason to prevail against his promise. Or he says that something has occurred to him, but it concerns another person and not himself and is therefore exempt from being reported. Or, what has now occurred to him is really too unimportant, too silly and senseless; I cannot possibly have meant him to enter into thoughts like that. So it goes on in innumerable variations.

(From Freud, 1894)

Freud saw resistance as natural because it is painful to bring unconscious conflicts into conscious awareness. It also indicates that the analyst is getting close to the source of the problem and that the unconscious is struggling to avoid 'giving up its secrets'. Although resistance hinders therapy, it provides useful information for both analysand and analyst in the form of clues about the repressed conflict's nature.

As therapy progresses, analysts may *privately deduce* the nature of what is behind the analysand's statements and attempt to generate further associations. For example, the analysand may apologise for saying something believed to be trivial. The analyst tells the analysand that what appears trivial might relate to something important. By appropriately timing this intervention, significant new associations may result. The analyst does not suggest what is important in what the analysand has said. The goal is to help the analysand discover this him- or herself.

Box 73.3 Confrontation and reconstruction

As therapy continues, the analyst may try to explain the analysand's behaviour in a way which is new to him or her. For example, analysands may be informed that their anger does not come from where they think it does, but rather that they are angry because the analyst reminds them of someone. In *confrontation*, the analyst tells the analysand exactly what is being revealed in the free associations. In *reconstruction*, the analyst provides hypothetical historical statements of hitherto buried

fragments of the analysand's past. For example, the analysand may be told that the anger is a repetition of feelings experienced as a child and that the analyst stands for the objects of that anger.

Transference

Once interpretation is complete and the unconscious conflict has been brought into consciousness, the analyst and the analysand repeat and 'live out' the conflict. The associated feelings which have been repressed for so long then become available for 'manipulation' by the analyst. Freud called this process *transference* or *transference neurosis*. In it, the original source of the conflict is displaced onto the analyst who now becomes the object of the analysand's emotional responses (see Box 73.3). Depending on the conflict's nature, the feelings may be positive and loving or negative and hostile. By exploring the transference relationship, psychoanalysis assumes that unconscious conflicts can be brought out into the open, understood and resolved. According to Thomas (1990):

'Over the years, it has become increasingly clear to practising analysts that the process of transference ... is one of the most important tools they have. It has become so central to theory and practice that many, though not all, analysts believe that making interpretations about transference is what distinguishes psychoanalysis from other forms of psychotherapy. When attention is focused on the transference and what is happening in the here and now, the historical reconstruction of childhood events and the search for the childhood origins of conflicts may take second place'.

Box 73.4 Countertransference

Freud discovered that transference operated in both directions and that he could transfer his own feelings onto his analysands. A male analysand, for example, could be viewed as a 'rebellious son'. Freud called the placing of clients into his own life *countertransference*. To avoid displacing their own repressed childhood feelings and wishes onto their patients, analysts undergo a *training analysis*. This permits them to understand their own conflicts and motivations, so they become *opaque* concerning their own behaviours and feelings to avoid countertransference with their analysands.

Whether the avoidance of countertransference is absolutely necessary is, however, debatable. As Thomas (1990) has observed:

'In Freud's time, countertransference feelings were considered to be a failing on the part of the analyst. These feelings were to be controlled absolutely. Now, counter-transference is considered an unavoidable outcome of the analytic process, irrespective of how well prepared the analyst is by analytic training and its years of required personal analysis ... most modern analysts are trained to observe their own countertransference feelings and to use these to increase their understanding of the analysand's transference and defences'.

The feelings associated with transference are the same for men and women. They include attachment to the analyst, overestimation of the analyst's qualities, and jealousy of those connected with the analyst. Sometimes, transference takes on an exaggerated form known as *acting out*, in which the analysand engages in the impulses stirred up by therapy. However, the analysand must be convinced that 'acting out' the conflict through transference does not constitute a true resolution of the problem. By itself, then, transference does not bring about the required change.

Quite clearly, transference is crucial, because without it the analyst's interpretations would not even be considered by the analysand. Freud believed that psychoanalysis was ineffective with disorders like schizophrenia and depression because people with these disorders could not produce transference. Whilst he believed that schizophrenia's and depression's origins could be explained in psychodynamic terms, they reduce the capacity for transference for some reason, and since people experiencing those disorders are completely indifferent to the analyst, the analyst cannot influence them.

Achieving insight and working through

Once an analysand consciously understands the roots of the conflict, *insight* has been achieved, and the analysand must be helped to deal with the conflict in a mature and rational way. Whilst insight sometimes comes from the recovery of the memory of a repressed experience, the notion of a psychoanalytic 'cure' resulting from the sudden recall of a single traumatic incident cannot be true, since psychodynamic therapists feel that troubles seldom stem from a single source. Instead, they are *over-determined*. For Freud, analysands gained insight through a gradual increase in self-knowledge (a process of *re-education*). This increase often involves repetitive consideration of all aspects of the conflict allowing the individual to face reality and deal with it effectively, rather than deny and distort it. This is called *working through*.

To break down the complex ego defences which have been developed to cope with the conflict, and to bring about a lasting personality change, the analysand and analyst need to work through every implication of the problem with complete understanding by the analysand. This is necessary to prevent the conflict from being

repressed into the unconscious again. As a result, the individual is strengthened and therefore becomes capable of handling different aspects of the conflict without having to resort to *defence mechanisms* (see page 570). The ultimate goal of psychoanalysis, then, is a deep-seated modification of personality so as to allow people to deal with problems on a realistic basis.

Box 73.5   Contemporary perspectives on classical psychoanalysis

Classical psychoanalysis is both intense, time-consuming and expensive (£25 to £35 per 50-minute session), involving perhaps three to six sessions per week over several years. Moreover, during its course, an analysand may be vulnerable and helpless for long periods. This occurs when the analysand's old defences and resistances are broken down, but the ego is still not strong enough to cope adequately with the conflict. Although some psychoanalysts still rigidly adhere to Freud's protracted techniques, there has been a shift in the theoretical basis of psychoanalysis and:

'the Aunt Sally of classical Freudianism is simply not relevant to present-day psychoanalysis' (Holmes, 1996).

For Garfield & Bergin (1994):

'The cornerstones of early Freudian metapsychology were repression, the unconscious, and infantile sexuality. Contemporary psychoanalysis views all three in a different light'.

Psychoanalytically oriented psychotherapies

Analysts who are more flexible in fitting the therapeutic sessions to a person's needs are known as *psychoanalytically oriented psychotherapists*. Most psychoanalytically oriented psychotherapies involve briefer treatment and use face-to-face interaction (*focal psychotherapies*). Although they also emphasise restructuring the entire personality, more attention is paid to the analysand's current life and relationships than to early childhood conflicts. Freudian principles are followed (the aim of therapy is still to gain insight and free expression is emphasised), but these therapies enable those who cannot afford protracted therapy or whose time is limited by other commitments to be treated (Cohn, 1994).

Perhaps the most influential of those who have revised Freudian therapeutic approaches are the *ego psychologists* or *ego analysts*. Rather than emphasising the id's role, these therapists focus on the ego and the way in which it acts as the *executive* of personality (see Chapters 44 and 66). As well as personality being shaped by inner conflicts, contemporary analysts believe that it may be shaped by the external environment.

Box 73.6   Contemporary therapeutic approaches derived from psychoanalysis

Ego analysts are sometimes referred to as the *second generation* of psychoanalysts. They believe that Freud over-emphasised the influence of sexual and aggressive impulses and underestimated the ego's importance. Erikson, for example, spoke to clients directly about their values and concerns and encouraged them to consciously fashion particular behaviours and characteristics. For Erikson, the ego's cognitive processes are constructive, creative and productive. This is different from Freud's therapeutic approach of establishing conditions in which patients could 'shore up' the ego's position.

Unlike Freud, who saw analysands as perpetual victims of their past who could not completely overcome their childhood conflicts, Horney saw them as capable of overcoming abuse and deprivation through self-understanding and productive adult relationships. Freud's emphasis on unconscious forces and conflicts was disputed by Anna Freud (Freud's daughter). She believed a better approach was to concentrate on the ways in which the ego perceives the world.

Klein and Mahler have stressed the child's separation from the mother and interpersonal relationships as being important in psychological growth. *Object relations theorists* believe that some people have difficulty in telling where the influences of significant others end and their 'real selves' begin. Mahler's approach to therapy is to help people separate their own ideas and feelings from those of others so they can develop as true individuals (see also Box 1.10).

As noted earlier, one of the major differences between classical psychoanalysis and psychoanalytically oriented psychotherapies is the *time* spent in therapy. Roth & Fonagy (1996) argue that there is a high 'relapse rate' in all types of brief therapies when those who have undergone treatment are not followed up for long periods of time. Therapy's ultimate goal must be good outcome sustained at follow-up, but as Holmes (1996) has remarked:

'Modern health services seem always to be in a hurry; time is money; but the cost of major cardiac surgery is still far greater than, say, the 100–200 hours of psychotherapy that are needed to make a significant impact on border-line personality disorder. An emphasis on sufficient *time* is a central psychoanalytic dimension that should be preserved at all costs'.

Psychodynamic approaches to group therapy

According to Roberts (1995), the power of the group process for change and healing has been discovered, forgotten and rediscovered on numerous occasions in Britain. One of the earliest uses of *group psychotherapy* was Bion's (1961) attempt to treat neurotic and psychotic soldiers. Since this pioneering work, various group approaches to psychodynamically-oriented therapy have been devised (Brown & Zinkin, 1994). Two of these are *psychodrama* and *transactional analysis*.

PSYCHODRAMA

Psychodrama was originated by Moreno (1946), who believed that most human problems arise from the need to maintain social roles which may conflict with each other and a person's essential self. For Moreno, this conflict is the source of a person's anxiety. In the therapy, participants and other group members act out their emotional conflicts. The individual dramatising the conflicts is the *protagonist*, and chooses other group members to represent the conflict's key figures. These *auxiliary egos* are briefed by being given full descriptions of their roles.

Once the protagonist has 'set the scene' by describing it in words and with the aid of very simple props, the interpersonal events are recreated by role play. For example, a male who is terrified of women may be literally 'put on stage' with a female group member who plays his mother. The two are then required to act out a childhood scene with, if necessary, other group members assuming the role of the father, brothers, sisters and so on. The aim is not for dramatic excellence but, in this example, to reveal the sources of the individual's fear of women (Kipper, 1992).

Box 73.7   Role reversal, doubling and mirroring

The basic pattern can be varied in several ways. In *role reversal*, the 'actors' switch roles, whilst in *doubling*, the therapist or group leader also acts out the protagonist's role and suggests feelings, motives and so on that might be operating within the protagonist, but which he or she has not yet identified. *Mirroring* involves group members minimising or exaggerating the protagonist's behaviour in order to provide feedback.

Psychodrama's goal is to reveal to the protagonist why he or she is behaving in a particular way. For Moreno, psychodrama is useful because (a) it helps to prevent destructive and irrational acting out in everyday life, (b) it enables feelings which cannot be adequately described or explained to be expressed more fully, and (c) it encourages individuals to reveal the deepest roots of their problems.

TRANSACTIONAL ANALYSIS

According to Berne (1964), personality is comprised of three *ego states*, and our behaviour at any given time is determined by one of these states. The *parent* state is that part of personality which stands for the cautions and prohibitions upheld by society and which we learn from our parents. The *child* state is the opposite, and is demanding, dependent and impulsive, seeking gratification of all its wishes *now*. The *adult* state is the mature, rational aspect of personality, which is flexible and adapts to new situations as they arise. Berne did not mean to imply that these three states equate with the id (child), ego (adult) and superego (parent), since the id, ego and superego are, to varying degrees, unconscious. For Berne, we are capable of being fully conscious of the child and parent ego states.

Box 73.8   Complementary and crossed interactions

Like Freud, Berne believed that mental disorders occur when one of the ego states comes to dominate the personality. Many interactions between people are *complementary*, that is, aspects of their personalities are matched. For example, the interaction between two people's adult states produces a rational and mature interaction, as when one person says, 'These data don't make any sense' and the other replies, 'I agree. Let's run them through the computer again'. When the aspects of personality operating do not match, the interactions are *crossed*, and this is when problems arise (Baron, 1989). For example, a passenger in a car operating in the child state, might say, 'Come on, let's see if we can get 100 mph out of this car'. The driver, operating in the adult state, might reply, 'No way. If the police are about, we'll be in big trouble'.

Berne argued that crossed interactions often take the form of 'games', interactions which leave both people feeling upset or angry and prevent spontaneous and appropriate behaviour. In *uproar*, one person baits another (Berne, 1976). The other responds in kind and the exchange escalates until one person storms off in anger. Transactional analysis concentrates on people's tendencies to manipulate others in destructive and non-productive ways.

However, unlike psychoanalysis, it focuses on the *present* rather than the past. Through role play, the ego states are identified as they are used in various personal transactions.

This *structural analysis* enables people to understand their behaviour and change it in a way which will give them greater control over their life. Although this is usually initially conducted on an individual basis, the person later participates in group *transactions* (or transactional analysis 'proper'). This involves experimenting, by enacting more appropriate ego states and observing the effects of these on the self and others. By analysing such games, basic conflicts may come to the surface, and these can then be discussed openly, the aim being to show that whilst people's coping patterns may feel natural, they are actually destructive and there are better ways of relating to others.

Therapies based on the psychodynamic model: some issues

At least some people who have undergone psychoanalysis claim that it has helped them achieve insight into their problems, and has provided long-term relief from the repressed feelings that were interfering with healthy functioning. However, although Freud's theories and his therapeutic approach have been influential, they have also been the subject of much criticism, and there have been numerous explanations of 'why Freud was wrong' (Webster, 1995) and several calls to 'bury Freud' (Tallis, 1996). Perhaps the major problem with Freud's work is that it is difficult to study scientifically, since concepts like transference, insight, unconscious conflicts and repression are either vague or difficult to measure.

Evaluating the effectiveness of any therapeutic approach is, as Chapter 77 illustrates, extremely difficult. With psychoanalysis, however, the problems are particularly acute. Much of the evidence favouring psychoanalysis derives from carefully selected case studies which may be biased. In cases where psychoanalysis fails to produce significant changes, analysts can blame the analysand. If an analysand accepts an insight into a behaviour but does not change that behaviour, the insight is said to be merely *intellectual* (Carlson, 1988).

Box 73.9   Psychoanalysis as a closed system

The 'escape clause' of intellectual insight makes the argument for insight's importance completely circular

---

and therefore illogical: if the analysand improves, the improvement is due to insight, but if the analysand's behaviour remains unchanged, then real insight did not occur. Carlson (1987) likens this to the logic of wearing a charm in the belief that it will cure an illness. If the illness is cured, then the charm works. If it is not cured, then the individual does not believe sufficiently in its power. Psychoanalysis is a *closed system*. A critic who raises questions about the validity of psychoanalysis is described as suffering from *resistance*, since the critic cannot recognise the therapy's 'obvious' value.

Conclusions

This chapter has examined psychodynamically-based therapies. Although less popular than they once were, such therapies are still used today. However, several important issues surround their use, and at least some professionals believe them to be of little help in the treatment of mental disorders.

Summary

■ The purpose of **psychoanalysis** is to uncover the unconscious conflicts responsible for an individual's mental disorder and make them conscious. By providing **insight** into these, the ego can deal more effectively with them.

■ Freud used a variety of techniques to break down an **analysand's** defences, including **hypnosis, dream interpretation, parapraxes (Freudian slips)** and the interpretation of **physiological cues**. However, the most widely used technique is **free association**.

■ The **basic rule** of psychoanalysis is that the analysand says whatever comes to mind, since this bypasses the ego's role as a **censor** of threatening unconscious impulses. The analyst acts as a **sounding board**, offering **interpretive comments** and drawing attention to the analysand's **resistances**.

■ As therapy progresses, the analyst may **privately deduce** what lies behind the analysand's free associations. Other techniques include **confrontation** and

reconstruction. When the unconscious conflict has been brought into consciousness, it can be manipulated by the analyst through the **transference/transference neurosis**. Transference may take the form of **acting out**.

■ The ultimate goal of psychoanalysis is a deep-seated modification of personality to allow people to deal with problems in a realistic way without having to resort to **defence mechanisms**. However, **insight** does not constitute a 'cure'. Insight is achieved through a process of 're-education' and increase in self-knowledge involving **working through**.

■ **Psychoanalytically oriented psychotherapies** are more flexible and briefer Freudian approaches and involve face-to-face interaction. Freudian principles are still followed, although more attention is paid to the analysand's current life and relationships.

■ Important revisions of Freudian approaches have been made by the **ego psychologists/ego analysts**, who focus on the ego rather than the id. Personality is seen as being shaped as much by the external environment as inner conflicts. This 'second generation' includes Erikson, Horney, Anna Freud, Klein and Mahler.

■ Psychodynamic approaches to **group psychotherapy** include Moreno's **psychodrama** and Berne's **transactional analysis**. Psychodrama helps to prevent destructive acting out in everyday life, and encourages individuals to reveal the deepest roots of their problems. Transactional analysis tries to show how 'natural' coping patterns can actually be destructive and that there are better ways of relating to others.

■ Although influential, Freud's theories and his therapeutic approach have been extensively criticised. Much of the evidence for Freud's approach comes from carefully selected case studies. When analysis fails, the analyst can blame the analysand. When an analysand accepts an insight but does not change behaviour, insight is only **intellectual**.

■ Critics contend that psychoanalysis is a **closed system**. A critic who raises questions about the validity of psychoanalysis is described as suffering from **resistance**, since he or she cannot recognise the therapy's 'obvious value'.

74

THERAPIES BASED ON THE BEHAVIOURAL MODEL

Introduction and overview

As Chapter 73 showed, psychodynamic therapies' attempts to produce insight into the causes of maladaptive behaviour *sometimes* result in it being replaced by adaptive behaviour. However, insight often does not result in behavioural change. Also, the majority of psychodynamically-oriented therapies insist on using *childhood* conflicts as a way of explaining present behaviours. According to the behavioural model, it is much better to focus on the behaviour giving rise to a problem rather than the historical reasons for its development.

Therapies based on the behavioural model therefore attempt to change behaviour by whatever means are most effective. The term *behaviour therapy* has been used to describe any therapeutic approach deriving from the behavioural model. However, this does not allow us to determine whether the principles of classical or operant conditioning are being used as the treatment method. Walker (1984) has suggested that the term *behaviour therapy* be confined to those therapies based on *classical conditioning*. Those techniques based on *operant conditioning* are more appropriately described as *behaviour modification techniques*. This chapter considers the application of therapies based on the behavioural model to the treatment of mental disorders.

Therapies based on classical conditioning: behaviour therapy

As was seen in Chapter 66 (see page 571), Watson & Rayner (1920) showed that by repeatedly pairing a neutral stimulus with an unpleasant one, a fear response to the neutral stimulus could be classically conditioned. If maladaptive behaviours can be learned, they can presumably be *unlearned*, since the same principles governing the learning of adaptive behaviours apply to maladaptive ones. Therapies based on classical conditioning concentrate on stimuli that elicit new responses which are contrary to the old, maladaptive ones. Three therapeutic approaches designed to treat phobic behaviour are *implosion therapy*, *flooding* and *systematic desensitisation*. Two therapies designed to treat other disorders (*aversion therapy* and *covert sensitisation*) exert their effects by *creating* phobias.

IMPLOSION THERAPY AND FLOODING

Implosion therapy and flooding both work on the principle that if the stimulus evoking a fear response is repeatedly presented without the unpleasant experience that accompanies it, its power to elicit the fear response will be lost.

Implosion therapy

In implosion therapy, the therapist repeatedly exposes the person to vivid mental images of the feared stimulus in the safety of the therapeutic setting. This is achieved by the therapist getting the person to imagine the most terrifying form of contact with the feared object using *stimulus augmentation* (vivid verbal descriptions of the feared stimulus, to supplement the person's imagery). After repeated trials, the stimulus eventually loses its anxiety-producing power and the anxiety extinguishes (or *implodes*) because no harm comes to the individual in the safe setting of the therapist's room.

Flooding

In flooding, the individual is forced to *confront* the object or situation eliciting the fear response. For example, a person with a fear of heights might be taken to the top of a tall building and physically prevented from leaving. By preventing avoidance of, or escape from, the feared object or situation, the fear response is eventually extinguished. Wolpe (1973) describes a case in which an adolescent girl afraid of cars was forced into the back of one. She was then driven around continuously for four hours. Initially, her fear reached hysterical heights. Eventually, it receded, and by the end of the journey had disappeared completely.

Implosion therapy and flooding are effective with certain types of phobia (Emmelkamp *et al.*, 1992). However, for some people, both lead to increased anxiety, and the procedures are too traumatic. As a result, they are used with considerable caution.

Box 74.1   Using virtual reality to treat phobias

Computer-generated virtual environments have been tested on people suffering from various phobias. The hardware consists of a head-mounted display and a sensor that tracks head and right hand movements so that the user can interact with objects in the virtual environment. The equipment is integrated with a square platform surrounded by a railing. This aids exposure by giving the user something to hold on to and an edge to feel.

Figure 74.1   Head-mounted display, similar to that used in the treatment of people with phobias

Software creates a number of virtual environments to confront different phobias. Those for acrophobia include:

- three footbridges hovering 7, 50 and 80 metres above water;

- four outdoor balconies with railings at various heights in a building ranging up to 20 floors high;

- a glass elevator simulating the one at Atlanta's Marriott Hotel which rises 49 floors.

People using virtual reality:

'had the same sensations and anxiety as they did *in vivo*. They were sweating, weak at the knees and had butterflies in the stomach. When the elevator went up and down, they really felt it. We are trying to help people confront what they are scared of' (Rothbaum, cited in Dobson, 1996).

Rothbaum sees virtual reality as holding the key to the treatment of phobia because it is easier to arrange and less traumatic than real exposure to phobia-causing situations. Compared with a control group of acrophobics, Rothbaum and her team reported a 100 per cent improvement in 12 participants after two months of 'treatment'.

SYSTEMATIC DESENSITISATION

Implosion therapy and flooding both use extinction to alter behaviour. However, neither trains people to substitute the maladaptive behaviour (such as fear) with an adaptive and *desirable* response. Jones (1924) showed that fear responses could be eliminated if children were given candy and other incentives in the presence of the feared object. Her method involved *gradually* introducing the feared object, bringing it closer and closer to the children whilst at the same time giving them candy, until no anxiety was elicited in its presence. For many years, Jones's work went unrecognised. Wolpe (1958) popularised and refined it under the name *systematic desensitisation* (SD).

The therapy requires that an individual initially constructs an *anxiety hierarchy* (a series of scenes or events rated from lowest to highest in terms of the amount of anxiety they elicit).

Box 74.2   An anxiety hierarchy generated by a person with thanatophobia (where 1 = no anxiety and 100 = extreme anxiety)

Ratings	Items
5	Seeing an ambulance
10	Seeing a hospital
20	Being inside a hospital
25	Reading an obituary notice of an old person
30–40	Passing a funeral home
40–55	Seeing a funeral
55–65	Driving past a cemetery
70	Reading the obituary of a young person who died of a heart attack
80	Seeing a burial assemblage from a distance
90	Being at a funeral
100	Seeing a dead man in a coffin

(Based on Wolpe & Wolpe, 1981)

Once the hierarchy has been constructed, *relaxation training* is given. This will be the adaptive substitute response and is the response most therapists use. Training aims to achieve complete relaxation, the essential task being to respond quickly to suggestions to feel relaxed and peaceful. After relaxation training, the person is asked to imagine, as vividly as possible, the scene at the bottom of the hierarchy, and is simultaneously told to remain calm and relaxed.

Box 74.3   Reciprocal inhibition and SD

Wolpe was influenced by the concept of *reciprocal inhibition* which, as applied to phobias, maintains that it is impossible to experience two incompatible emotional states (such as anxiety and relaxation) at the same time. If the individual finds that anxiety is *increasing*, the image is terminated, and the therapist attempts to help him or her regain the sense of relaxation. When thinking about the scene at the hierarchy's bottom no longer elicits anxiety, the next scene in the hierarchy is presented. *Systematically*, the hierarchy is worked through until the individual can imagine any of the scenes without experiencing discomfort. When this happens, the person is *desensitised*. Once the hierarchy has been worked through, the person is required to confront the anxiety-producing stimulus in the real world.

One problem with SD is its dependence on a person's ability to conjure up vivid images of encounters with a phobic object or situation. A way of overcoming this is to use photographs or slides displaying the feared object or situation. Another approach involves live (*in vivo*) encounters. For example, an arachnophobic may be desensitised by gradually approaching spiders, the method used by Jones (see above). *In vivo* desensitisation is almost always more effective and longer lasting than other desensitisation techniques (Wilson & O'Leary, 1978).

SD, implosion therapy and flooding are all effective in dealing with specific fears and anxieties. Compared with one another, flooding is more effective than SD (Marks, 1987) and implosion therapy (Emmelkamp *et al.*, 1992), whilst implosion therapy and SD do not differ in their effectiveness (Gelder *et al.*, 1989).

The fact that flooding is apparently the superior therapy suggests that *in vivo* exposure to the anxiety's source is crucial. Because implosion therapy and SD differ in their effectiveness, systematically working through a hierarchy might not be necessary. Indeed, presenting the hierarchy in reverse order (from most to least frightening), randomly, or in the standard way (from least to most frightening) does not influence SD's effectiveness (Marks, 1987).

AVERSION THERAPY

The therapies just considered are all appropriate in the treatment of phobias occurring in specific situations. Aversion therapy, by contrast, is used with people who want to *extinguish* the *pleasant* feelings associated with socially undesirable behaviours, like excessive drinking or smoking. SD tries to substitute a pleasurable response for an aversive one. Aversion therapy *reverses* this and pairs an unpleasant event with a desired but socially undesirable behaviour. If this unpleasant event and desired behaviour are repeatedly paired, the desired behaviour should eventually elicit negative responses.

Box 74.4   Aversion therapy and alcohol abuse

Perhaps aversion therapy's most well-known application has been in the treatment of alcohol abuse. In one method, the problem drinker is given a drug that induces nausea and vomiting, but *only* when combined with alcohol. When a drink is taken, the alcohol interacts with the drug to produce nausea and vomiting. It does not take many pairings before alcohol begins to elicit an aversive fear response (becoming nauseous).

In another method, the problem drinker is given a warm saline solution containing a drug which induces nausea and vomiting without alcohol. Immediately before vomiting begins, an alcoholic beverage is given, and the person is required to smell, taste and swill it around the mouth before swallowing it. The aversive fear response may generalise to other alcohol-related stimuli, such as pictures of bottles containing alcohol. However, to avoid *generalisation* to all drinks, the individual may be required to take a soft drink in between the aversive conditioning trials.

Aversion therapy has been used with some success in the treatment of alcohol abuse and other behaviours (most notably cigarette smoking, overeating and children's self-injurious behaviour). It has also found its way into popular culture. In Burgess's (1962) novel *A Clockwork Orange*, the anti-social 'hero', Alex, gains great enjoyment from rape and violent behaviour. When caught, he can choose between prison and therapy and opts for the latter. He is given a nausea-inducing drug and required to watch films of violence and rape. After his release, he feels nauseous whenever he contemplates violence and rape. However, because the therapy took place with Beethoven's music playing, Alex acquires an aversion towards Beethoven as well!

One of the most controversial (and non-fictional) applications of aversion therapy has been with sexual 'aberrations' such as homosexuality (Beresford, 1997). Male homosexuals, for example, are shown slides of nude males followed by painful but safe electric shocks. The conditioned response to the slides is intended to generalise to homosexual fantasies and activities beyond the therapeutic setting. Later, the individual may be shown slides of nude women and an electric shock terminated when a sexual response occurs (Adams *et al.*, 1981).

Whatever its use, aversion therapy is unpleasant, and not appropriate without an individual's *consent* or unless all other approaches to treatment have failed. As noted, evidence suggests that the therapy is effective. However, those undergoing it often find ways to continue with their problem behaviours. People have the cognitive abilities to discriminate between the situation in which aversive conditions occur and situations in the real world. In some cases, then, cognitive factors will 'swamp' the conditioning process, and this is one reason why aversion therapy is not always effective.

Aversion therapy does not involve classical conditioning alone and actually combines it with operant conditioning. Once the classically conditioned fear has been established, the person is inclined to avoid future contact with the problem stimulus (an *operant* response) in order to alleviate fear of it (which is *negatively reinforcing*). Critics see aversion therapy as being inappropriate unless the individual learns an *adaptive* response. For this reason, most behaviour therapists try to *shape* (see page 639) new adaptive behaviours at the same time as extinguishing existing maladaptive ones.

COVERT SENSITISATION

Silverstein (1972) has argued that aversion therapy is unethical and has the potential for misuse and abuse. As a response to this, some therapists use covert sensitisation (CS) as an alternative and 'milder' form of aversion therapy. CS is a mixture of aversion therapy and SD. Essentially, people are trained to punish themselves using their *imaginations* (hence the term *covert*). *Sensitisation* is achieved by associating the undesirable behaviour with an exceedingly disagreeable consequence.

Box 74.5 CS and alcohol abuse

A heavy drinker might be asked to imagine being violently sick all over him- or herself on entering a bar, and feeling better only after leaving and breathing fresh air. The individual is also instructed to rehearse an alternative 'relief' scene in which the decision not to drink is

accompanied by pleasurable sensations. CS can be helpful in controlling overeating and cigarette smoking as well as excessive drinking (Cautela, 1967).

Therapies based on operant conditioning: behaviour modification techniques

Behaviours under voluntary control are strongly influenced by their consequences. As noted in Chapter 32, actions producing positive outcomes tend to be repeated, whereas those producing negative outcomes tend to be suppressed. Therapies based on classical conditioning usually involve *emotional responses* (such as anxiety), although *observable behaviours* (such as gradually approaching an object that elicits anxiety) are also influenced. Therapies based on operant conditioning are aimed *directly* at observable behaviours.

There are several therapies based on operant conditioning, all involving three main steps. The first is to identify the undesirable or maladaptive behaviour. The next is to identify the reinforcers that maintain such behaviour. The final step is to restructure the environment so that the maladaptive behaviour is no longer reinforced. One way to eliminate undesirable behaviours is to *remove* the reinforcers that maintain them, the idea being that their removal will *extinguish* the behaviour they reinforce. Another way is to use aversive stimuli to *punish* voluntary maladaptive behaviours.

As well as eliminating undesirable behaviours, operant conditioning can be used to increase desirable behaviours. This can be achieved by providing *positive reinforcement* when a behaviour is performed, and making the reinforcement *contingent* on the behaviour being manifested voluntarily.

THERAPIES BASED ON EXTINCTION

The behavioural model proposes that people learn to behave in abnormal ways when they are unintentionally reinforced by others for doing so (see Chapter 68, page 590). For example, a child who receives parental attention when he or she shouts is likely to engage in this behaviour in the future, because attention is reinforcing. If abnormal behaviours can be *acquired* through operant conditioning, they can be *eliminated* through it. With a disruptive child, parents might be instructed to ignore the behaviour so that it is extinguished from the child's behavioural repertoire.

If this is to be effective, however, the therapist must be able to identify and eliminate the reinforcer that is maintaining the adaptive behaviour, and this is not always easy (Crooks & Stein, 1991).

Box 74.6   Behaviour modification using extinction

A 20-year-old woman reluctantly sought help for 'compulsive face-picking'. Whenever the woman found some little blemish or pimple, she would pick and scratch at it until it became a bleeding sore. As a result, her face was unsightly. Everyone was distressed except the individual herself, who seemed remarkably unconcerned. Her family and fiancé had tried several tactics to stop the face-picking, including appealing to her vanity, pleading and making threats.

The therapist felt that the face-picking was being maintained by the attention her family and fiancé were giving it. As long as she continued, the pattern of inadvertent reinforcement was maintained, and she would remain the centre of attention. Once the therapist had identified the behaviours that were reinforcing the face-picking, the parents and fiancé were instructed not to engage in these and to ignore the face-picking entirely. They were also told that it would probably get worse before it improved.

After a temporary increase in face-picking, it was quickly extinguished when attention was no longer given. To prevent the behaviour from reappearing, the parents and fiancé were encouraged to provide plenty of loving attention and to support the woman contingent upon a variety of healthy, adaptive behaviours.

(Based on Crooks & Stein, 1991)

THERAPIES BASED ON PUNISHMENT

In aversion therapy, an aversive stimulus, such as an electric shock, is used to classically condition a negative response to a desired but undesirable stimulus. Aversive stimuli can also be used to punish voluntary maladaptive behaviours. Cowart & Whaley (1971) studied an emotionally disturbed infant who was hospitalised because he persistently engaged in self-mutilating behaviour to such an extent that he had to be restrained in his crib. Electrodes were attached to the infant's leg, and he was placed in a room with a padded floor (the self-mutilation involved violently banging his head against the floor). When the infant began the self-mutilating behaviour, he was given an electric shock. Initially, he was startled, but continued self-mutilating, at which point another shock

was given. There were very few repetitions before self-mutilation stopped, and the infant could be safely let out of his crib.

Box 74.7   Punishment: effectiveness and ethics

It is generally agreed that therapies using punishment are not as effective as those employing positive reinforcement (see below) in bringing about behaviour change. At least one reason for not using punishment is the tendency for people to *overgeneralise* behaviour. Thus, behaviours which are *related* to the punished behaviour are also not performed. Moreover, punishment tends to produce only a temporary suppression of undesirable behaviour, and unless another reinforcement-inducing behaviour pattern is substituted for the punished behaviour, it will resurface (see Chapter 32, page 278).

There are also ethical issues surrounding punishment's use, particularly with very young children. In Cowart and Whaley's study, however, the infant was engaging in a behaviour which was clearly very harmful, and with these sorts of behaviour, punishment is actually extremely effective. Presumably, the physical well-being that occurred from not self-mutilating was sufficiently reinforcing to maintain the new behaviour pattern.

THERAPIES BASED ON POSITIVE REINFORCEMENT

Behaviour shaping

Isaacs *et al.* (1960) describe the case of a 40-year-old male schizophrenic who had not spoken to anyone for 19 years. Quite accidentally, a therapist discovered that the man loved chewing gum, and decided to use this as a way of getting him to speak.

Initially, the therapist held up a piece of gum. When the patient looked at it, it was given to him. The patient began to pay attention to the therapist and would look at the gum as soon as the therapist removed it from his pocket. Later, the therapist held up the gum and waited until the patient moved his lips. When this occurred, he was immediately given the gum. However, the therapist then began to give the gum *only* when the patient made a sound.

At the point when the patient reliably made a sound when the gum was shown, the therapist held the gum and instructed him to 'Say gum'. After 19 years of silence, the patient said the word. After six weeks, he spontaneously said 'Gum, please', and shortly afterwards began talking to the therapist. This approach is known as *behaviour shaping* and has been most notably used with the chronically disturbed and people with learning difficulties, who are extremely difficult to communicate with.

Box 74.8   Using positive reinforcement to treat anorexia nervosa

A young anorectic woman was in danger of dying because she had drastically curtailed her eating behaviour and weighed only 47 lbs. In the first stage of therapy, the therapist established an appropriate reinforcer that could be made contingent upon eating. The reinforcer chosen was social, and whenever the anorectic swallowed a bite of food, she was rewarded by the therapist talking to her and paying her attention. If she refused to eat, the therapist left the room and she remained alone until the next meal was served (which is 'time out' from positive reinforcement rather than punishment).

After a while, her eating behaviour gradually increased, and the therapist introduced other rewards contingent upon her continuing to eat and gain weight. These included having other people join her at meal times or being allowed to have her hair done. Eventually, the woman gained sufficient weight to be discharged from the hospital. Because people are likely to regress if returned to a non-supportive institutional setting, the woman's parents were instructed in ways to continue reinforcing her for appropriate eating behaviours. At follow-up nearly three years later, the woman was still maintaining an adequate weight.

(Based on Bachrach *et al.,* 1965)

Token economies

Ayllon & Haughton (1962) reported that staff at one hospital found it particularly difficult to get withdrawn schizophrenics to eat regularly. Ayllon and Haughton noticed that the staff were actually exacerbating the problem by coaxing the patients into the dining room and, in some cases, even feeding them. The researchers reasoned that the increased attention was reinforcing the patients' uncooperativeness and decided that the hospital rules should be changed. For example, if patients did not arrive at the dining hall within 30 minutes of being called, they were locked out. Additionally, staff were no longer permitted to interact with patients at meal times. Because their uncooperative behaviours were no longer being reinforced, the patients quickly changed their eating habits. Then, the patients were made to pay one penny in order to enter the dining hall. The pennies could be

earned by showing socially appropriate *target behaviours*, and their frequency also began to increase.

Ayllon and Haughton's approach was refined by Ayllon & Azrin (1968) in the form of a *token economy system*. In this, disturbed individuals are given tokens in exchange for desirable behaviour. The therapist first identifies what patients like (such as watching television or smoking cigarettes). When a productive activity occurs (such as making a bed or socialising with other patients), a patient is given tokens that can be exchanged for 'privileges'. The tokens therefore become conditioned reinforcers for desirable and appropriate behaviours.

Ayllon and Azrin showed that tokens were effective in eliciting and maintaining desired behaviours. The amount of time spent performing desired behaviours was highest when the reinforcement contingencies were imposed and lowest when they were not. Ayllon and Azrin also discovered that token economies had an effect on patient and staff morale, in that the patients were less apathetic and irresponsible, whilst the staff became more enthusiastic about their patients and the therapeutic techniques.

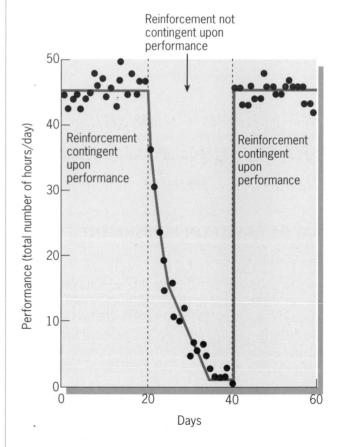

Figure 74.2   The effects of a token economy on hospitalised patients' performances of target behaviours

As well as being used with the chronically disturbed, token economies have also been used in programmes designed to modify the behaviour of children with *conduct disorders*. Schneider & Byrne (1987) awarded tokens to children who engaged in helpful behaviours and removed the tokens for inappropriate behaviours, such as arguing or not paying attention.

Box 74.9   Token economies: some issues

Despite their effectiveness in producing behaviour change with various disorders, issues have been raised about token economies. Eventually, tokens will have to be replaced by other social reinforcers, both within and outside the therapeutic setting. The individual is gradually 'weaned off' the tokens in the therapeutic setting, and can be transferred to a 'half-way house' or some other community live-in arrangement where more social reinforcers can be used. Unfortunately, this is not always successful, and there tends to be a high re-hospitalisation rate for discharged individuals.

Token economies can lead to 'token learning' (people might only indulge in a behaviour if they are directly rewarded for it: Baddeley, 1997). Whilst this might be effective within the confines of the therapeutic setting, Baddeley sees it as quite unproductive in other settings, where it is necessary to learn on a subtler and less immediate reward system.

Some general comments about therapies based on the behavioural model

One criticism of therapies based on the behavioural model is that they focus only on the observable aspects of a disorder. The behavioural model considers the maladaptive behaviour to be the disorder, and the disorder is 'cured' when the behaviour is changed. Although critics accept that therapies based on the behavioural model can alter behaviour, they argue that such therapies fail to identify a disorder's *underlying* causes. One consequence of this is *symptom substitution*, in which removing one symptom simply results in another, and perhaps one more serious, occurring in some other form.

As noted earlier, behaviours learnt under one set of conditions may not generalise to other conditions. The behavioural model sees behaviours as being controlled by the environment, so it is not surprising that behaviours altered in one context do not endure in a very different one. Indeed, Rimm (1976) sees this as behaviour therapy's major limitation. To avoid this, therapists attempt to extend the generality of changed behaviours by working (as far as possible) in environments which are representative of real life. They also encourage people to avoid environments that elicit maladaptive behaviours, to return for follow-up treatment, and teach them how to modify their behaviour on a continuing basis.

The most serious criticism of behaviour therapy and modification is ethical (see Chapter 85). Techniques involving punishment, in particular, have been criticised for exercising authoritarian control and for dehumanising and 'brainwashing' people. Another criticism is that behaviour therapists manipulate people and deprive them of their freedom (see Chapter 81). As has been seen, it is the therapist, rather than the person, who controls the reinforcers, and therapists do not encourage people to seek insight concerning their disorders.

However, supporters of the behavioural model argue that they do not treat disorders without consent and that, in a sense, we are all 'naïve behaviour therapists'. For example, when we praise people or tell them off for a particular behaviour, we are using behaviour modification techniques: all therapists are doing is using such approaches in a systematic and consistent way. Therapists who use behavioural methods are not attempting to control behaviour, but helping people to control their *own* behaviours.

Conclusions

Various behaviour therapies and behaviour modification techniques have been used to treat mental disorders. Although supporters of the behavioural model see the therapies as being highly effective, opponents believe that important criticisms can be made of them which limit their application.

Summary

■ Therapies based on the behavioural model try to change behaviour based on whatever means are most effective. **Behaviour therapies** use classical conditioning principles whilst **behaviour modification techniques** use operant conditioning.

■ If maladaptive behaviours can be acquired through classical conditioning, they can presumably be unlearned by the same principles. **Implosion therapy, flooding,** and **systematic desensitisation** (SD) are used to treat phobias, and attempt to produce new responses that are contrary to the old, maladaptive ones.

■ Neither implosion therapy nor flooding trains people to substitute maladaptive behaviour with adaptive/desirable behaviour. SD does, with **relaxation** being the adaptive substitute response used by most therapists.

■ Flooding is more effective than SD and implosion therapy. Implosion therapy and SD are equally effective. This suggests that **in vivo** exposure to the phobic stimulus is important, and that systematic progression through a hierarchy is unnecessary.

■ **Aversion therapy** is used to extinguish the pleasant feelings associated with an undesirable behaviour. This is achieved by repeatedly pairing an unpleasant stimulus with the undesirable behaviour until it eventually elicits an unpleasant response. This therapy uses both classical and operant conditioning

■ Although useful in the treatment of some problem behaviours, there are important ethical issues associated with aversion therapy's use. For that reason, **covert sensitisation** is sometimes employed. This method has been used to control excessive drinking, overeating and smoking.

■ Behaviour therapies usually involve emotional responses as well as observable behaviours. Therapies based on operant conditioning are aimed **directly** at observable behaviours. When the reinforcers that maintain an undesirable/maladaptive behaviour have been identified, the environment is restructured so that they are no longer reinforced.

■ Undesirable behaviours can be **extinguished** by removing the reinforcers that maintain them. Alternatively, aversive stimuli can be used to **punish** the behaviours. Desirable behaviours can be increased by making **positive reinforcement** contingent on voluntary behaviours being performed.

■ **Punishment** by electric shock has been used to treat self-mutilating behaviour. However, punishment only suppresses an undesirable behaviour, which will resurface unless substituted by a behaviour that is reinforced. Punishment also raises ethical issues, particularly when used to treat children.

■ **Behaviour shaping** and the **token economy** system both use **positive reinforcement** to change behaviour. These methods are effective in eliciting and maintaining desired behaviours. However, they are limited by a lack of generalisation beyond the therapeutic setting. Token economies, for example, can lead to 'token learning'. To avoid lack of generalisation, therapists try to work in environments that are as representative of real life as possible.

■ By focusing on a disorder's observable aspects, therapies based on the behavioural model fail to identify its underlying causes. One consequence of this is **symptom substitution**. Although critics accept that such therapies can be effective, they see therapists as manipulating, dehumanising, and controlling people and depriving them of their freedom. Therapists sees themselves helping people to control their own behaviour.

75

THERAPIES BASED ON THE COGNITIVE MODEL

Introduction and overview

The cognitive model sees mental disorders as resulting from distortions in people's cognitions. The aim of cognitively based therapies is to show people that their distorted or irrational thoughts are the main contributors to their difficulties. If faulty modes of thinking can be *modified* or *changed*, then disorders can be alleviated.

Therapies based on the cognitive model, then, have the goal of changing maladaptive behaviour by changing the way people think. Cognitive therapies have been viewed as a collection of techniques really belonging to the domain of the behavioural model (and thus the term *cognitive–behavioural therapies* is sometimes used to describe them). In some cases, the dividing line between a therapy based on the behavioural model and one based on the cognitive model is very fine and arbitrary. Indeed, therapists identifying their orientation as primarily behavioural or cognitive may actually be doing the same thing.

Supporters of the cognitive model, however, believe that behaviour change results from changes in cognitive processes, and hence cognitively based therapies can be separated from behavioural ones. Like psychodynamic therapies, cognitive therapies aim to produce *insight*. However, rather than focusing on the past, they try to produce insight into *current cognitions*. This chapter begins by looking at therapeutic approaches devised by Bandura who, whilst often considered a behaviour therapist, attempts to change behaviour by altering thoughts and perceptions. It continues with an examination of Ellis' *rational–emotive therapy*, Beck's *cognitive therapy for depression, attributional therapy*, Meichenbaum's *stress inoculation therapy*, and some more recent cognitively based applications.

Bandura's approaches to therapy

Many behavioural therapists incorporate cognitive processes into their theoretical outlook and cognitive procedures into their methodology (Wilson, 1982). Techniques like SD and covert sensitisation, for example, use *visual imagery*. The interface between behavioural methods and the cognitive model is called *cognitive–behavioural therapy*, and a leading researcher is Bandura.

As noted in Chapters 32 and 66, certain kinds of learning cannot be *solely* explained in terms of classical or operant conditioning. According to Bandura (1969) and other *social learning theorists*, humans and some non-humans can learn directly *without* experiencing an event, and can acquire new forms of behaviour from others simply by observing them (*observational learning*). Moreover, whether we see people being rewarded or punished can strengthen or reduce our own inhibitions against behaving in similar ways. If we see a positive outcome for a behaviour, our restraint against performing it is lowered (*response disinhibition*). However, if we see a negative outcome, our restraint is heightened (*response inhibition*).

Bandura argues that maladaptive behaviours can be altered by exposing those demonstrating them to appropriate *models* (others performing actions the person is afraid to perform). As well as changing behaviour, this approach aims to change thoughts and perceptions.

Box 75.1 illustrates *participant modelling* which involves the individual observing the therapist's behaviour and then imitating it. This method is more effective than having people watch filmed or video-taped models (*symbolic modelling*). Modelling has been successfully used with a variety of phobias and, as well as eliminating undesirable behaviours, has also been used to establish new and more appropriate behaviours.

Box 75.1   An application of modelling

The therapist performed the behaviour fearlessly at each step and gradually led participants into touching, stroking and then holding the snake's body with gloved and bare hands whilst the experimenter held the snake securely by the head and tail. If a participant was unable to touch the snake following ample demonstration, she was asked to place her hands on the experimenter's and to move her hand down gradually until it touched the snake's body. After the participants no longer felt any apprehension about touching the snake under these conditions, anxieties about contact with the snake's head area and entwining tail were extinguished.

The therapist again performed the tasks fearlessly, and then the experimenter and the participant performed the responses jointly. As participants became less fearful, the experimenter gradually reduced his participation and

---

Gross R & McIlveen R. 1998
Psychology: A New Introduction
Hodder & Stoughton.

control over the snake, until eventually participants were able to hold the snake in their laps without assistance, to let the snake loose in the room and retrieve it, and to let it crawl freely over their bodies. Progress through the graded approach tasks was paced according to the participants' apprehensiveness. When they reported being able to perform one activity with little or no fear, they were eased into a more difficult interaction.

(From Bandura, 1971)

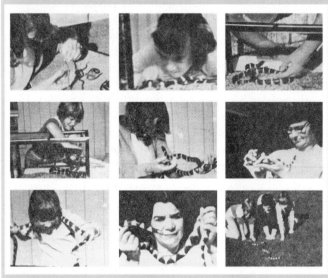

Figure 75.1   As this sequence of photographs shows, modelling can be an effective way of treating phobias

In *assertiveness training*, people with difficulty in asserting themselves in interpersonal situations are required to perform in the presence of a group who provide feedback about the adequacy of performance. Then, the therapist assumes the individual's role and models the appropriate assertive behaviour. The individual is asked to try again, this time imitating the therapist. The alternation between *behavioural rehearsal* and modelling continues until the assertive role has been mastered. When this occurs, the skills are tried out in real-life situations. This approach has also been widely used in *social skills training*, in which people who lack the ability to function effectively in certain situations observe others performing the desired behaviours and then attempt to imitate them.

Bandura (1977) believes that one reason for modelling's effectiveness is the development of *self-efficacy*. Being able to perform a behaviour that was previously impossible raises a person's evaluation of the degree to which he or she can cope with difficult situations. According to Bandura, when people encounter new situations in which they have difficulty, they are much more willing to engage in behaviours that were previously avoided.

Ellis' rational–emotive therapy (RET)

Rational–emotive therapy (RET) was developed in the 1950s by Ellis. After becoming dissatisfied with what he called the 'passivity of psychoanalysis', Ellis, a trained psychoanalyst, developed his own therapeutic approach. For several years, this therapy was regarded as being on the periphery. However, RET is now practised by a large number of therapists, particularly in the USA.

Box 75.2   The A–B–C model

Ellis (1958, 1962) argues that many emotional difficulties are due to the *irrational beliefs* people bring to bear on their experiences and the reinforcement these receive through being repeated. For Ellis (1991), irrational beliefs can be understood as part of the *A–B–C model*. According to this, a significant activating event (A) is followed by a highly charged emotional consequence (C). However, to say that A is the cause of C is not *always* correct, even though it may appear to be as far as a person is concerned. Rather, Ellis sees C occurring because of a person's belief system (B). Inappropriate emotions, such as depression and guilt, can only be abolished if a change occurs in beliefs and perceptions.

To illustrate this, suppose someone telephones several friends to invite them out for a drink, but finds that none is able to accept the invitation. This activating event (A) might produce the emotional consequence (C) that the person feels depressed, isolated and worthless. For Ellis, C occurs because of the person's belief system (B) which holds that because no one has accepted the invitation, it must mean that no one likes him or her.

The aim of RET is to help people find flaws in their thinking and 'to make mincemeat' of these maladaptive cognitions by creating D, a *dispute belief system* which has no severe emotional consequences. In the example used above, D might run along the lines of 'people have already made plans to go out and just because they can't accept my invitation doesn't mean they don't like me'.

Ellis proposes that two of the most common maladaptive cognitions people hold are (1) they are worthless unless they are perfectly competent at everything they try, and (2) they must be approved of and loved by everyone they meet. Because such beliefs make impossible demands on people who hold them, they lead to anxiety, failure and, frequently, abnormal behaviour.

Box 75.3   Some common irrational beliefs encountered in RET

- Certain people I must deal with are thoroughly bad and should be severely blamed and punished for it.

- It is awful and upsetting when things are not the way I would like them to be.

- My unhappiness is always caused by external events; I cannot control my emotional reactions.

- If something unpleasant might happen, I should keep dwelling on it.

- It is easier to avoid difficulties and responsibilities than to face them.

- I should depend on others who are stronger than I am.

- Because something once strongly affected my life, it will do so indefinitely.

- There is always a perfect solution to human problems, and it is awful if this solution is not found.

(Based on Rohsenow & Smith, 1982)

Box 75.4   Some rational alternatives to irrational beliefs

Irrational belief: I *must* prove myself to be thoroughly competent, adequate and achieving, or I *must* at least have real competence or talent at something important.

Rational alternative belief: What I do doesn't have to be perfect to be good. I will be happier if I achieve at a realistic level rather than strive for perfection.

Irrational belief: I *have* to view life as awful, terrible, horrible, or catastrophic when things do not go the way I would like them to go.

Rational alternative belief: If I can't change the situation, it may be unfortunate but not catastrophic. I can make plans for my life to be as enjoyable as possible.

Irrational belief: I *must* have sincere love and approval almost all the time from all the people who are significant to me.

Rational alternative belief: I would *like* to be approved, but I do not *need* such approval.

(Based on Lange & Jakubowksi, 1976)

Once the irrational beliefs have been identified, therapy continues by guiding the person to substitute more logical or realistic thoughts for the maladaptive ones, a task which Ellis believes can be accomplished 'by any therapist worth his or her salt'. Ellis sees the rational–emotive therapist as an *exposing and nonsense-annihilating scientist*. Therapists claim that the universe is logical and rational, and the appropriate means of understanding it is the scientific method of controlled observation. People have the *capacity* for rational understanding and the *resources* for personal growth. However, they also have the capacity to delude themselves and accept irrational beliefs.

As noted earlier, the first stage in therapy is for people to recognise and question their irrational beliefs. Rather than remaining 'anonymous', as a classical psychoanalyst would do, and occasionally offering some form of interpretation, the rational–emotive therapist will show the person how to ask questions like '*Where* is the evidence that I am a worthless person if I am not universally approved?', '*Who* says I must be perfect?' and '*Why* must things go exactly the way I would like them to go?'

Once people have recognised and analysed their beliefs, they are taught to substitute more realistic alternatives to engender *full acceptance*. Rather than measuring themselves against impossible standards, a rational–emotive therapist emphasises that failures should not be seen as 'disastrous', confirming a lack of self-worth, but merely as 'unfortunate' events.

Rational–emotive therapists use various approaches to minimise self-defeating beliefs. Rather than focusing on people's histories, they focus on the 'here and now'. As Ellis (1984) has put it:

'Therapists do not spend a great deal of time ... encouraging long tales of woe, sympathetically getting in tune with emotionalising or carefully and incisively reflecting feelings.'

Ellis is not interested in what he calls 'long-winded dialogues', which he sees as 'indulgent'. Rather, RET aims to help people *get* better rather than *feel* better during a therapy session, and to accept reality 'even when it is pretty grim'.

Indeed, by providing people with warmth, support, attention and caring, their need for love (which is usually the central core of their circumstances: Elkins, 1980) is reinforced. There is also the possibility that people become dependent on the therapy and the therapist. The direct approach used in RET is illustrated in Box 75.5, in which Ellis discusses the problems experienced by a 25-year-old female.

Box 75.5   RET in action

Therapist: The same crap! It's always the same crap. Now, if you would look at the crap – instead of 'Oh, how stupid I am! He hates me! I think I'll kill myself!' – then you'd get better right away.

Person: You've been listening! (laughs)

Therapist: Listening to what?

Person: (*laughs*) Those wild statements in my mind, like that, that I make.

Therapist: That's right! Because I know that you have to make those statements – because I have a good theory. And according to my theory, people couldn't get upset unless they made those nutty statements to themselves ... Even if I loved you madly, the next person you talk to is likely to hate you. So I like brown eyes and he likes blue eyes, or something. So then you're dead! Because you really think: 'I've got to be accepted! I've got to act intelligently!' Well, why?

Person: (*very soberly and reflectively*) True.

Therapist: You see?

Person: Yes.

Therapist: Now, if you will learn that lesson, then you've had a very valuable session. Because you don't have to upset yourself. As I said before: if I thought you were the worst [*expletive deleted*] who ever existed, well that's my opinion. And I'm entitled to it. But does that make you a turd?

Person: (*reflective silence*)

Therapist: Does it?

Person: No.

Therapist: What makes you a turd?

Person: *Thinking* that you are.

Therapist: That's right! Your *belief* that you are. That's the only thing that could ever do it. And you never have to believe that. See? You control your thinking. I control my thinking – *my* belief about you. But you don't have to be affected by that. You *always* control what you think.

(From Ellis, 1984)

RET seems to be effective for at least some types of disorder (Emmelkamp *et al.*, 1978). However, for other disorders (such as agoraphobia), RET is less effective than therapies derived from other models (Haaga & Davison, 1993). Clearly, RET is an active and directive therapeutic approach, and one in which the therapist's personal beliefs and values are an inevitable part of what goes on during therapy. However, Ellis' (1984) views that 'no one and nothing is supreme', that 'self-gratification' should be encouraged and that 'unequivocal love, commitment,

service and ... fidelity to any interpersonal commitment, especially marriage, leads to harmful consequences' have been disputed (e.g. Bergin, 1980).

The argumentative approach to therapy, in which the therapist attacks those beliefs regarded as foolish and illogical, has also been questioned, particularly by those who stress the importance of *empathy* in therapy (see Chapter 76). For example, Fancher (1995) believes that all cognitive therapies rely on a commonsense view of cognition, and falsely assume that therapists are capable of identifying 'faulty thinking': what is foolish and illogical to the therapist may not be foolish and illogical in terms of the individual's own experiences.

RET is effective in producing behaviour change amongst those who are self-demanding and feel guilty for not living up to their own standards of perfection (Brandsma *et al.*, 1978). For people with severe thought disorders (as in schizophrenia), however, the therapy is ineffective, since people with such disorders do not respond to an Ellis-type analysis of their problems (Ellis, 1993).

Beck's cognitive restructuring therapy

Like Ellis, Beck (1967) was originally trained as a psychoanalyst. As with RET, Beck's therapy assumes that disorders stem primarily from irrational beliefs that cause people to behave in maladaptive ways. Beck's approach is specifically designed to treat *depressed* people. Depressed people suffer from a *cognitive triad* of negative beliefs about themselves, their futures and their experiences (Beck *et al.*, 1979). Such beliefs are seen as arising from faulty information-processing and faulty logic.

Several types of faulty thinking that can contribute to depression were identified in Chapter 66 (see pages 572–573). As noted, Beck's therapy aims to identify the implicit and self-defeating assumptions depressed people make about themselves, change their validity and substitute more adaptive assumptions. Box 75.6 illustrates an exchange between a therapist using Beck's cognitive approach and a student who believed that she would not get into the college she had applied to.

Box 75.6 Beck's approach to therapy in action

Therapist: Why do you think you won't be able to get into the university of your choice?

Student: Because my grades were not really so hot.

Therapist: Well, what was your grade average?

Student: Well, pretty good up until the last semester in high school.

Therapist: What was your grade average in general?

Student: As and Bs.

Therapist: Well, how many of each?

Student: Well, I guess, almost all of my grades were As but I got terrible grades my last semester.

Therapist: What were your grades then?

Student: I got two As and two Bs.

Therapist: Since your grade average would seem to come out to almost all As, why do you think you won't be able to get into the university?

Student: Because of competition being so tough.

Therapist: Have you found out what the average grades are for admissions to the college?

Student: Well, somebody told me that a B+ average would suffice.

Therapist: Isn't your average better than that?

Student: I guess so.

(From Beck *et al.*, 1979)

Note how the therapist attempts to reverse the 'catastrophising beliefs' held by the student concerning herself, her situation and her future. Note also how the therapist takes a gentler, less confrontational and more experiential approach to the student than a rational–emotive therapist would.

Box 75.6 illustrates the strategy of identifying a person's self-impressions which, although not recognised as such, are misguided. Once the self-impressions have been identified, the therapist's role is to attempt to disprove rather than confirm the negative self-image (Williams, 1992). By sharing knowledge of the cognitive model, the person undergoing therapy may then understand the origins of the disorder and ultimately develop skills to apply effective interventions independently.

Given its original purpose, it is not surprising that Beck's approach to therapy is most successful in treating depression (Andrews, 1991). However, the therapy has also been used successfully with eating disorders (Fairburn *et al.*, 1993). Whether Beck's approach can be applied to schizophrenia and personality disorders is the subject of much debate (Beck & Freeman, 1990; Tarrier *et al.*, 1993).

Attributional therapy

Attributional therapy is a relatively recent cognitive approach to the treatment of depression which derives from the research described in Chapter 69 concerning the revised theory of learned helplessness (see page 598). Attributions are our beliefs about the causes of our own and other people's behaviours (see Chapter 51). Attributional therapists hold that, in some cases, depressed people make unrealistic or faulty attributions concerning their own behaviours and that these can cause considerable distress.

When asked to explain successful or unsuccessful outcomes, most people show the *self-serving bias* (see page 451). However, this is reversed in depressed people, who attribute failures to internal causes even when there is no evidence to support such an attribution. Successful outcomes, by contrast, tend to be attributed to external causes. For example, a depressed individual who passes an examination may attribute the success to 'an easy examination paper that anybody could have passed', when in fact it was the individual's own ability that produced the positive outcome.

Attributional therapists attempt to break the vicious circle that people low in self-esteem experience. This involves training them to perceive successes as resulting from internal factors and at least some failures from external factors beyond their control. Changing attributions can result in increased self-esteem, greater confidence and better performance. Moreover, beneficial changes can occur after only a small number of therapy sessions, which is clearly advantageous (Brockner & Guare, 1983).

Box 75.7   Attributional therapy and depression

Rabin *et al.* (1986) gave 235 depressed adults a ten-session programme that initially explained the advantages of interpreting events in the way that non-depressed people do. After this, they were trained to reform their habitually negative patterns of thinking and labelling by, for example, being given 'homework assignments' in which they recorded each day's positive events and the contributions they had made to them. Compared with a group of depressed people given no programme, the group receiving the ten-session programme reported experiencing significantly less depression.

Gross R. & McIlveen R.   1998
Psychology: A New Introduction
Hodder & Stoughton

Meichenbaum's stress inoculation therapy

Meichenbaum's (1976, 1985) *stress inoculation therapy* assumes that people sometimes find situations stressful because they think about them in catastrophising ways. Stress inoculation therapy aims to train people to cope more effectively with potentially stressful situations. The therapy consists of three stages. The first, *cognitive preparation* (or *conceptualisation*) involves the therapist and person exploring the way in which stressful situations are thought about. Typically, people react to stress by offering negative self-statements like 'I can't handle this'. This exacerbates an already stressful situation. The second stage, *skill acquisition and rehearsal*, attempts to replace negative self-statements with incompatible positive coping statements. These are then learned and practised.

Box 75.8   Some coping and reinforcing self-statements used in stress inoculation therapy

Preparing for a stressful situation

- What is it you have to do?
- You can develop a plan to deal with it.
- Just think about what you can do about it; that's better than getting anxious.
- No negative self-statements; just think rationally.
- Don't worry; worry won't help anything.
- Maybe what you think is anxiety is eagerness to confront it.

Confronting and handling a stressful situation

- Just 'psych' yourself up – you can meet this challenge.
- One step at a time; you can handle the situation.
- Don't think about fear; just think about what you have to do. Stay relevant.
- This anxiety is what the therapist said you would feel. It's a reminder to use your coping exercises.
- This tenseness can be an ally, a cue to cope.
- Relax; you're in control. Take a slow deep breath.
- Ah, good.

Coping with the feeling of being overwhelmed

- When fear comes, just pause.
- Keep the focus on the present; what is it that you have to do?

- Label your fear from 0 to 10 and watch it change.
- You should expect your fear to rise.
- Don't try to eliminate fear totally; just keep it manageable.
- You can convince yourself to do it. You can reason fear away.
- It will be over shortly.
- It's not the worst thing that can happen.
- Just think about something else.
- Do something that will prevent you from thinking about fear.
- Describe what is around you. That way you won't think about worrying.

Reinforcing self-statements

- It worked; you did it.
- Wait until you tell your therapist about this.
- It wasn't as bad as you expected.
- You made more out of the fear than it was worth.
- Your damn ideas – that's the problem. When you control them, you control your fear.
- It's getting better each time you use the procedures.
- You can be pleased with the progress you're making.
- You did it!

(From Meichenbaum, 1976)

The final stage of therapy, *application and follow-through*, involves the therapist guiding the person through progressively more threatening situations that have been rehearsed in actual stress-producing situations. Initially, the person is placed in a situation that is moderately easy to cope with. Once this has been mastered, a more difficult situation is presented. According to Meichenbaum *et al.* (1982), the 'power of positive thinking' approach advocated by stress inoculation therapy can be successful in bringing about effective behaviour change, particularly in relation to anxiety and pain.

Some other applications of therapies derived from the cognitive model

Like other therapies, therapies based on the cognitive model have received considerable scrutiny as to their worth (Andrews, 1993). Cognitively based therapies can be particularly helpful in the treatment of *panic disorder*. As noted in Chapter 70, Clark (1993) has argued that the core disturbance in this disorder is an abnormality in thinking in which people interpret normal bodily signs and symptoms as indications of an impending mental or physical catastrophe (such as a heart attack). Because of their fears, people become *hypervigilant* and repeatedly scan their body for signs of danger, which results in their noticing sensations which other people would not be aware of. Additionally, subtle *avoidance behaviours* prevent them from disconfirming their negative beliefs. For example, people convinced that they are suffering from cardiac disease may avoid exercise and rest whenever a palpitation occurs in the belief that this will prevent a fatal heart attack.

Clark *et al.* (1994) and Shear *et al.* (1994) have shown that cognitively based therapies can be highly effective in changing the cognitions and behaviour of 90 per cent of those treated. However, whether therapies derived from the cognitive model can and should be used with other disorders is less clear-cut. For example, in a review of research concerning obsessive–compulsive disorder, James & Blackburn (1995) found that of the few well-controlled studies examining cognitively based therapies' effectiveness, there was little evidence to suggest that improvement occurred. Against that, however, are findings indicating that cognitively-based therapies can have a significant impact on many medical conditions such as chronic fatigue syndrome (Sharpe *et al.*, 1996) and in reducing the psychological impact of unemployment (Proudfoot *et al.*, 1997).

Conclusions

Therapies based on the cognitive model have been used to treat several types of mental disorder, particularly depression. Although useful in the treatment of this disorder, their usefulness with other disorders is less clear-cut.

Summary

■ Therapies based on the cognitive model attempt to show people that their distorted/irrational thoughts are the main contributors to their disorder. By changing faulty thinking, disorders can be alleviated.

■ Bandura's approach to therapy uses **modelling**. As well as changing behaviour, models aim to change thoughts and perceptions. Modelling is useful in the treatment of phobias and is also effective in **assertiveness** and **social skills training**. One reason for this is the development of **self-efficacy**.

■ Ellis sees emotional difficulties as a result of 'irrational beliefs'. People have the capacity for rational understanding, but are also capable of deluding themselves and thinking irrationally. **Rational–emotive therapy** (RET) aims to help people find flaws in their thinking by creating a **dispute belief system**.

■ When irrational beliefs have been identified, they are substituted by more realistic ones. RET is an active, direct and argumentative approach, which has been questioned by those who stress **empathy's** importance in therapy. However, it seems to be effective for certain disorders.

■ Beck's **cognitive restructuring therapy** also sees disorders as stemming from irrational beliefs. The therapy is specifically designed to treat **depression**, and is effective in this. In a less confrontational way than RET, it identifies depressed people's implicit and self-defeating assumptions.

■ **Attributional therapy** is derived from the revised theory of learned helplessness and also treats depression. Attributional therapists try to break down the vicious circles that low self-esteem people experience. Changing attributions like this can lead to increased self-esteem, greater confidence and better performance.

■ Meichenbaum's **stress inoculation therapy** assumes that people sometimes find situations stressful because of their misperceptions about them. The therapy trains people to cope more effectively with potentially stressful situations through **cognitive preparation, skill acquisition and rehearsal**, and **application and practice**.

■ Cognitively based therapies are particularly helpful in treating **panic disorder**. They have also been shown to have a significant impact on many medical conditions and to reduce the psychological impact of unemployment. Their effectiveness with other disorders is, however, less clear-cut.

649

76

THERAPIES BASED ON THE HUMANISTIC MODEL

Introduction and overview

Chapter 66 noted that the humanistic model sees people as *sets of potentials* who are basically 'good' and strive for growth, dignity and self-determination. Mental disorders arise when external factors somehow block the potential for personal growth. Therapies based on the humanistic model attempt to remove such blocks and put people 'in touch' with their true selves. This chapter examines some of the therapeutic approaches based on the humanistic model. It considers Rogers' *client-* (or *person-*) *centred therapy*, Perls' *Gestalt therapy* and some *humanistic approaches to group therapy*.

Rogers' client- (or person-) centred therapy

Humanistic therapy was introduced in the 1940s by Rogers (1951) who originally called his approach *client-centred therapy*. However, in 1974, he and his colleagues changed its name to *person-centred therapy* in order to focus more clearly on the human values the approach emphasises (Meador & Rogers, 1984). The therapy was also called *non-directive therapy* because Rogers refused to tell people what to do or think (but see also page 652). Instead of directing therapy, the Rogerian approach is to clarify feelings by rephrasing what people say and repeatedly asking what they really believe and feel. Rather than looking at earlier parts of life, Rogers believed in focusing on the present.

Many people regard it as unusual for a therapist to refuse to offer expert advice. For example, a woman who sought advice on what to tell her daughter about relationships with men was repeatedly asked by Rogers what *she* thought. After several direct questions, Rogers replied:

'I feel this is the kind of very private thing that I couldn't possibly answer for you, but I sure as anything will try to help you work towards your own answer' (Meador & Rogers, 1973).

For Rogers (1986), the central premise of person-centred therapy is that:

'the individual has within him or herself vast resources of self-understanding, for altering his or her self-concept, attitudes and self-directing behaviour, and ... these resources can be tapped if only a definable climate of facilitative psychological attitudes can be provided'.

ENCOURAGING PERSONAL GROWTH

There are three major elements in the 'definable climate' or 'therapeutic atmosphere' which Rogers believed would encourage personal growth in his clients. These are *genuineness*, *unconditional positive regard* and *empathy*.

Genuineness

Genuineness (*authenticity* or *congruence*) refers to real human relationships in which therapists honestly express their own feelings. According to Rogers, it would be harmful to clients if a therapist could not be 'dependably real', that is, truly accept and like them, even though their values might differ from the therapist's. Therapists who tried to manufacture a fake concern or hid their own beliefs would actually *impede* their clients' true personal growth. Rogers admitted that he sometimes had negative feelings about his clients. The most common feeling was boredom, and he expressed this rather than holding it in (Bennett, 1985). If the therapist says one thing, but somehow communicates a different feeling, the client will pick this up and believe the therapist cannot be trusted.

Box 76.1   Genuineness

Rogers (1980) sees genuineness as the most important of the three elements:

'Sometimes [in therapy] a feeling 'rises up in me' which seems to have no particular relationship to what is going on. Yet I have learned to accept and trust this feeling in my awareness and to try to communicate it to my client. For example, a client is talking to me, and I suddenly feel an image of him as a pleading little boy, folding his hands in supplication, saying 'Please let me have this, please let me have this'. I have learned that if I can be real in the relationship with him and express this feeling that has occurred in me, it is very likely to strike some deep note in him and advance our relationship.'

Unconditional positive regard

This means respecting clients as important human beings with values and goals, and accepting people for what they are without reservation. Rogers believed that therapists should not judge clients' worth by their behaviours. Rather, they should provide a sense of security that encourages clients to follow their own feelings and recognise each person's essential dignity. Therapists must therefore convince clients that they actually like and respect them, and that the positive regard they give does not depend on what the client says or does.

Empathy

Empathy (or *empathic understanding*) is the process of perceiving the world from the client's perspective and understanding what he or she is experiencing. It is not to be confused with sympathy. For example, a therapist who says, 'I'm sorry you feel insecure', may be genuine, but not empathic because empathy involves an attempt to 'get inside the client's head' and to fully understand why the client lacks security. Thus, the client must be convinced that he or she is *understood* by the therapist. Without such understanding, a client might think, 'Sure, this therapist says he likes me and respects me, but that's because he really doesn't know me. If he really knew me, he wouldn't like me'.

Box 76.2   Empathic understanding

Client: I was thinking about this business of standards. I somehow developed a sort of knack, I guess, of, well, habit, of trying to make people feel at ease around me, or to make things go along smoothly.

Therapist: In other words, what you did was always in the direction of trying to keep things smooth and to make other people feel better and to smooth the situation.

Client: Yes. I think that's what it was. Now the reason why I did it probably was – I mean, not that I was a good little Samaritan going around making other people happy, but that was probably the role that felt easiest for me to play. I'd been doing it around the home so much. I just didn't stand up for my own convictions, until I don't know whether I have any convictions to stand up for.

Therapist: You feel that for a long time you've been playing the role of kind of smoothing out the frictions or differences or what not …

Client: Mm-hmm.

Therapist: Rather than having any opinion or reaction of your own in the situation. Is that it?

Client: That's it. Or that I haven't been really honestly being myself, or actually knowing what my real self is, and that I've been playing a sort of false role. Whatever role no one else was playing, and that needed to be played at the time, I'd try to fill it in.

(From Rogers, 1951)

Genuineness, unconditional positive regard and empathy are interconnected. Changes in a client's moment-to-moment feelings require that the therapist accepts and values the client (shows both empathy and unconditional positive regard). As noted, genuineness is the most important of all, because a meaningful relationship demands that empathy and unconditional positive regard are honest and real.

TECHNIQUES USED IN ROGERIAN THERAPY

Typically, Rogerian therapy sessions are held once a week with the client and therapist facing each other. One way of achieving empathic understanding is through *active listening* in which the therapist attempts to grasp both the *content* of what the client says and the *feeling* behind it. To communicate empathy, the therapist uses *reflection*, summarising the client's message (in terms of its content and feeling) and feeding this back. For example, a client who says 'I'm depressed', might have the therapist respond with 'Sounds like you're really down'.

Although empathy requires a great deal of skill, Rogers (1986) sees active listening as 'one of the most potent forces for change that I know'. As well as helping clients understand or clarify their feelings, active listening also lets them know that the therapist both understands and accepts what is being said. According to Thorne (1984), empathy is the most 'trainable' of the three major elements, but is also remarkably rare. As noted previously, therapists do not offer direct advice or interpretations, but may ask for clarifications now and again.

The therapist's passive reflection is gradually replaced by *active interpretation*. By going beyond the overt content of what the client says, the therapist responds to what is sensed to be the client's true feelings. The therapist starts to confront the client with inconsistencies in what is said, and may, for example, point out that the client is failing to take responsibility for personal actions.

In an atmosphere where anything that is felt may be expressed, the focus is more on *present* than past feelings. During therapy, clients begin to realise that, perhaps for the first time, someone is listening to them, and they become more aware of long-denied feelings and thoughts, and learn to accept these and incorporate them into their self-concept. In Rogers' terms, clients 'get it together' and experience *congruence*.

APPLICATION AND EVALUATION OF ROGERIAN THERAPY

As well as being used with individuals, Rogerian therapy is also used in human relations training for professionals of all kinds, including nurses, crisis workers and counsellors. In universities, for example, the approach has been used with students who have not yet made career choices. The therapy helps decision-making by providing an encouraging atmosphere in which clients can explore various choices and paths. As noted, Rogerian therapists do not tell clients what to do, but help them to arrive at their own decisions.

Box 76.3   Client-centred therapy in action

Client: I guess I do have problems at school ... You see, I'm the chairman of the Science department, so you can imagine what kind of a department it is.

Therapist: You sort of feel that if *you're* in something that it can't be too good. Is that ...?

Client: Well, it's not that I ... It's just that I'm ... I don't think that I could run it.

Therapist: You don't have any confidence in yourself?

Client: No confidence, no confidence in myself. I never had any confidence in myself. I – like I told you that – like when even when I was a kid, I didn't feel I was capable and I always wanted to get back with the intellectual group.

Therapist: This has been a long-term thing, then. It's gone on a long time.

Client: Yeah, the *feeling* is – even though I know it isn't, it's the feeling that I have, that I haven't got it, that ... that ... that ... people will find out that I'm dumb or ... or ...

Therapist: Masquerade ...

Client: Superficial, I'm just superficial. There's nothing below the surface. Just superficial generalities, that ...

Therapist: There's nothing really deep and meaningful to you.

Client: No – they don't know it, and ...

Therapist: And you're terrified they're going to find out.

Client: My wife has a friend, and – and she and the friend got together so we could go out together with her and my wife and her husband ... And the guy, he's an engineer and he's, you know – he's got it, you know; and I don't want to go, I don't want to go because ... because if ... if we get together he's liable to start to ... to talk about something I don't know, and I'll ... I won't know about that.

Therapist: You're terribly frightened in this sort of thing.

Client: I ... I'm afraid to be around people who ... who I feel are my peers. Even in pool ... now I ... I play pool very well and ... if I'm playing with some guy that I ... I know I can beat, *psychologically*, I can run 50, but ... but if I start playing with somebody that's my level, I'm done. I'm done. I ... I ... I'll miss a ball every time.

Therapist: So the ... the fear of what's going on just immobilises you, keeps you from doing a good job.

(From Hersher, 1970)

Rogers & Dymond (1954) published studies detailing person-centered therapy's success. Unlike supporters of some other therapies who rely on their own judgements, Rogers recorded therapeutic sessions so that his techniques could be evaluated. Truax (1966) obtained permission from Rogers and his clients to record therapy sessions in order to determine their effectiveness. Truax found that only those clients who showed progress were regularly followed by positive responses from Rogers, and that during their therapy, they made more statements indicating progress.

What this suggests is that social reinforcement is very powerful. This does not discredit client-centred therapy, but shows that Rogers was very effective in adopting a strategy for altering a person's behaviour. Although the term *non-directive* was initially used to describe Rogerian therapy, when Rogers realised he was reinforcing positive statements, he stopped referring to it as non-directive, because it quite clearly was not.

Box 76.4   Q-sorts

One method used by Rogers to validate client-centred therapy empirically was the *Q-sort*. This consists of cards which have statements relating to the self, such as 'I am a domineering person'. Clients are required to arrange them in a series of ten piles ranging from 'very characteristic of me' to 'not at all characteristic of me' to describe the self-image. The process is then repeated to describe the 'ideal self'. After this, the two Q-sorts are correlated to determine the discrepancy between actual self-image and ideal self-image. During therapy, the procedure is repeated several times, the idea being that if therapy is having a beneficial effect, the discrepancy between actual self-image and ideal self-image should narrow (and the correlation between them increase: see Chapter 46, page 403).

Critics of Rogerian therapy have objected to its methods on the grounds that it treats people in the same way irrespective of their disorder (a point which also applies to some other therapies). It has also been suggested that giving people unconditional positive regard might actually be harmful, because they could leave therapy with the unrealistic expectation that anything they do will meet with society's approval (Bandura, 1969). Also, Rogerian therapy is not appropriate for disorders like schizophrenia, and seems to be most effective for people who want to change and who are intelligent enough to gain some sort of insight concerning their problems.

Other critics have argued that the humanistic model is simply wrong in viewing humans as being basically 'good' (see Chapter 66). Whether a person who has exhibited signs of dissocial personality disorder should be provided with unconditional positive regard is debatable. The therapy is, however, more affordable and less time-consuming than, say, psychodynamic therapies.

According to Barker (1998), the core emphasis on the experience of mental distress has found its way into almost all contemporary therapies through working in the 'here and now'. This legacy:

'... will live on, long after many other forms of popular therapy have been consigned to the footnotes of history'.

Perls' Gestalt therapy

Like Rogers, Perls believed that therapy should help people integrate conflicting parts of their personalities. Perls was dissatisfied with psychoanalysis and called it 'a disease that pretends to be a cure'. However, whilst Perls agreed with Rogers that people are free to make choices and affect their growth, Gestalt therapy is highly *directive*, and the therapist leads the client through *planned experiences*.

Despite his dissatisfaction with psychoanalysis, Perls agreed with Freud that mental disorders result from unconscious conflicts and, like Freud, he stressed the importance of dream analysis. However, whereas Freud

saw dreams as the 'royal road to the unconscious', Perls saw them as 'disowned parts of the personality'. Another difference between them was that Perls believed current problems (the 'here and now') could be focused on, and that people have responsibility for the direction of their own lives (which is, of course, consistent with the humanistic model).

Perls called his therapy Gestalt therapy, referring to the German word that means 'pattern' or 'organised whole' (see Chapter 21), because he believed that when therapy was complete, a person became 'whole' and could resume normal growth. The approach was particularly influential in the 1960s, especially in the USA. According to Gestalt therapists, psychologically healthy people are *aware* of themselves so fully that they can detect whatever requires their attention. Mental disorders occur as a result of a blockage of awareness. Perls saw awareness as being critical, because if people are unaware of what they want or feel at any time or moment, then they have limited control over their feelings and behaviours. At times, we act out of habit rather than choice, and the habits may become self-defeating.

Figure 76.1   Frederick (Fritz) Perls (1893–1970), founder of Gestalt therapy

Gestalt therapists, then, see mental disorders as arising because the various aspects of personality (such as thoughts, feelings and actions) cannot be integrated into a healthy, well-organised whole. The aim of therapy is therefore to help a person bring together the 'alienated fragments' of the self into an integrated, unified whole (the sense of wholeness is called *organismic self-regulation*). Gestalt therapists believe that by achieving a sense of wholeness, people can relate more fully to others and live more spontaneous lives.

The development of awareness allows an individual to confront and make choices, an assumption being that when allowed to make choices, people choose self-enhancing and growthful options instead of self-defeating ones that have been used before. So, by being aware of inner conflicts, people can accept reality, rather than deny and repress it. This can help productive choices to be made despite misgivings and fear.

Gestalt therapy's primary focus is on moment-to-moment *self-awareness*. The therapist's role is that of an *active co-explorer* with clients, encouraging them to break through whatever defences are preventing full experience of their feelings and thoughts. The client–therapist relationship has been likened to that between an apprentice and master (Kempler, 1973). The skill the master teaches the apprentice is that of awareness. As the relationship between them develops, the therapist uses awareness to enhance growth in the client.

Perls did not believe there was any set formula for achieving this. However, Levitsky & Perls (1970) provided guidelines for therapists. In many ways, Gestalt therapists behave like psychoanalysts by, for example, directing clients' attention to conflicts and dreams. But as noted, Gestalt therapists interpret dreams differently. For them, fragments of dreams are aspects of personality, and the aim is to help clients piece together dream fragments as they relate to current problems.

Typically, therapy is conducted in a *group setting* (see page 655) with the focus on one person at a time. Various techniques are used to help people become aware of who they are and what they are feeling and of personal responsibility. According to Gestalt therapists, any action implies a choice, and with choice goes responsibility. On some occasions, a therapist will deliberately frustrate clients, especially if clients are trying to lean on the therapist when support is not really necessary. The therapist's job is to emphasise awareness on the client's part and this can be achieved in various ways.

Box 76.5   Some techniques used in Gestalt therapy

The following techniques or 'directed experiments' are usually carried out in a consulting room or group setting.

Role playing: A person who is angry at his or her mother, say, first plays him- or herself talking to the mother and then reverses the roles and becomes the mother. In the *empty chair exercise*, the client moves back and forth between two chairs to play the roles. Perls believed that by acting out both sides to a conflict, a person would complete *unfinished business*, that is, become aware of unexpressed feelings that had been carried around for many years. This allows a sense of completion to be gained which frees the individual to deal with present-day problems rather than those from the past. Note how different this is to Rogers' therapy. Indeed, unlike a Rogerian, a Gestalt therapist might even become involved and join in the role playing.

Amplification: The therapist asks the client to exaggerate some behaviour or feeling in order to become more aware of it. A man who responds to a question about his wife, for example, might talk favourably about her, but draw his fingers towards his palm slightly. When asked to exaggerate this, the client might make a fist, strike the table and offer revealing comments about his wife.

Dialogue: In this, the client undertakes verbal confrontations between opposing wishes and ideas. One example of clashing personality elements is *underdog* and *top dog*. The former, and its suggestions of 'don't take chances' is confronted with the latter and its suggestions that 'you'll never progress if you don't take chances'. A heightened awareness of the elements of conflict can clear the path towards resolution, perhaps through compromise.

Speaking in the first person: This approach helps people recognise and take responsibility for their own actions. A person who says 'sometimes people are afraid to take the first step in initiating a relationship for fear of being rejected' is encouraged to restate this in the first person: '*I* am afraid to take the first step ... because *I* fear being rejected'.

The ultimate aim of therapy is to make people aware of their problems, and teach them *how* to become aware so they can do this independently. When this has been achieved, therapy is complete.

Box 76.6   The moral injunctions of Gestalt therapy

- Live now. Be concerned with the present rather than the past or future.

- Live here. Deal with what is present rather than what is absent.

- Stop imagining. Experience the real.
- Stop unnecessary thinking. Rather, taste and see.
- Express rather than manipulate, explain, justify or judge.
- Give in to unpleasantness and pain just as to pleasure. Do not restrict your awareness.
- Accept no 'should' or 'ought' other than your own. Adore no graven image.
- Take full responsibility for your actions, feelings and thoughts.
- Surrender to being as you are.

One way of evaluating Gestalt therapy's effectiveness and appropriateness is in terms of the number of people who have adopted it. Proponents argue that its growth is one indicator of its effectiveness. However, there have been few controlled studies to validate Gestalt therapy, and so it is not known how effective it is (Rimm & Masters, 1979). Gestalt therapists argue that controlled research is not necessary because the direct experiences of those who have received it are overwhelming evidence of its effectiveness. Moreover, because the therapy is so individualised, it cannot be evaluated in the same way as other therapies (a point returned to in Chapter 77). Evidence suggests, however, that techniques like amplification can be effective (Simkin & Yontef, 1984), though clearly Gestalt therapy, like other therapies, is more effective with some populations than others.

Humanistic approaches to group therapy

Although group approaches to therapy were described in Chapter 73, the humanistic model has contributed most to the group therapy movement. The major therapeutic gains of group approaches are believed to be the development of intimacy and co-operation through being part of a mutually supportive group, and finding out about oneself through candid interactions with others.

ENCOUNTER GROUPS

The earliest form of humanistic group therapy (which laboured under the generic term *human potential movement*), was the *encounter group*, part of the American (and, in particular, Californian) culture of the 1960s and 1970s.

Encounter groups were originally developed by Rogers to be what Graham (1986) has called:

> 'a means whereby people can break through the barriers erected by themselves and others in order to react openly and freely with one another'.

Participants (rather than *clients*) are encouraged to act out their emotions, rather than just talk about them, through bodily contact and structured 'games'. The group leader (or *facilitator*) attempts to create an atmosphere of mutual trust in which group members, usually numbering between eight and 18, feel free to express their feelings irrespective of whether these are positive or negative. According to Rogers (1973), this expression reduces defensiveness and promotes self-actualisation.

SENSITIVITY TRAINING GROUPS

Sensitivity training groups (or *T-groups*) were first introduced in the late 1940s with the intention of helping group leaders improve the functioning of groups by democratic methods. Later, the approach was used to help business executives improve their relations with co-workers. Unlike encounter groups, in which feelings are expressed by yelling, weeping, touching exercises, and other unrestrained displays of emotion, T-groups were originally limited to 'subtler' emotional expressions. However, whether such groups can bring about change is questionable, and some have warned against their dangers.

It has been claimed that such groups can precipitate, if not cause, various sorts of psychological disturbances. Aggressive, highly charismatic and authoritarian leaders were the most likely to have 'casualties' (people who suffered a severe psychological disturbance lasting up to six months after the group experience). One destructive characteristic is the pressure to have some ecstatic, (what Maslow, 1968, calls *peak*), experience which is viewed as necessary for continuing mental health. Maslow himself, however, would argue that such experiences are relatively uncommon and certainly cannot be produced 'on demand' (see Chapter 17).

Box 76.7   T-groups, encounter groups and Gestalt therapy

It was noted on page 654 that Gestalt therapy is typically conducted in a group setting with the focus on one person at a time. However, in its pure group form, participants in Gestalt therapy *help one another* work through their emotional crises. Unlike T-groups, but like encounter groups, unrestrained emotional outpouring is encouraged, with emphasis on the participants' present experiences. For Perls (1967), such group approaches are helpful because:

'in the safe emergency of the therapeutic situation, the (individual) discovers that the world does not fall to pieces if he or she gets angry, sexy, jealous or mournful'.

Conclusions

Therapies based on the humanistic model of abnormality aim to put people in touch with their true selves. They have attracted considerable interest, and evidence suggests that they can be effective in the treatment of certain disorders.

Summary

■ Humanistic therapies aim to remove blocks to personal growth and put people 'in touch' with their true selves. Rogers' **client/person-centred therapy** involves clarifying feelings by repeating what people say and repeatedly asking what they really believe/feel **without** offering any expert advice.

■ The three major elements which Rogers believes encourage personal growth are **genuineness (authenticity/congruence)**, **unconditional positive regard** and **empathy**. Of these, genuineness is the most important, because a meaningful relationship demands that empathy and unconditional positive regard are honest and real.

■ Rogerian therapy typically involves a once-weekly session with client and therapist facing each other. Passive reflection is gradually replaced by **active interpretation**, in which the therapist goes beyond the overt content of what the client says and responds to the client's true feelings. The outcome of this is **congruence**.

■ Evaluations of Rogers' therapy indicate that social reinforcement by the therapist is a very powerful strategy for changing people's behaviour. This does not discredit the therapy, but shows that it is not non-directive. Another way of evaluating the therapy is through **Q-sorts**.

■ Rogerian therapy is not helpful in disorders like schizophrenia. It is most effective with people who want to change and are capable of gaining insight into their problems. It is also much more affordable and less time-consuming than psychodynamic approaches.

■ **Gestalt therapy** also tries to help people integrate conflicting parts of their personalities. However, it is highly **directive** and the therapist leads the client through 'planned experiences'. Mental disorders are seen as blockages of **awareness**. Therapy tries to bring together the 'alienated fragments' of the self into an integrated unified whole (**organismic self-regulation**).

■ There is no set formula for achieving awareness. Therapy usually takes place in a **group setting** with the focus on one person at a time. Various techniques ('directed experiments') are used. These include **role playing, amplification, dialogue** and **speaking-in-the-first-person**.

■ The ultimate aim of Gestalt therapy is to teach people **how** to become aware of their problems, so they can deal with them independently. The **moral injunctions** of Gestalt therapy are rules to live one's life by.

■ The humanistic model has contributed more than any other to **group therapy** (the **human potential movement**). Rogers developed **encounter groups** in which participants are encouraged to act out their positive and negative emotions through bodily contact and structured 'games'. The 'facilitator' creates an air of mutual trust.

■ **Sensitivity training groups (T-groups)** were originally intended to help group leaders improve group functioning by democratic methods. However, their effectiveness in producing change has been questioned, and critics claim that they may actually cause mental disturbances.

77

ASSESSING THE EFFECTIVENESS OF THERAPIES

Introduction and overview

Chapters 72–76 described therapeutic approaches that either have been or currently are used to treat mental disorders. Although the procedures and disorders they are used with were described in detail, their effectiveness was not. This chapter looks at attempts to assess the effectiveness of therapies and considers major issues surrounding such attempts.

Early attempts at assessing therapy's effectiveness

Eysenck (1952) made the first systematic attempt to evaluate therapy's effectiveness. He examined psychoanalysis and *eclectic* psychotherapy (psychotherapy incorporating a variety of approaches rather than the single approach used in psychoanalysis). Prior to Eysenck's findings being published, the value and effectiveness of psychotherapeutic approaches had not been seriously questioned since, at least as far as therapists were concerned, many people seeking treatment improved and reported themselves satisfied with its effects.

Box 77.1   Eysenck's assessment of therapy's effectiveness

According to Eysenck, Freudian therapeutic approaches were 'unsupported by any scientifically acceptable evidence'. Looking at studies conducted between 1920 and 1951, Eysenck discovered that in only 44 per cent of cases using psychoanalysis could the person be considered 'cured', 'much improved' or 'improved'. Using the same criteria to assess people treated by means of eclectic psychotherapy, the figure was higher, at 64 per cent.

Eysenck argued that many people with psychological problems actually improve without any professional treatment (*spontaneous remission*). To assess the effectiveness of the two psychotherapies, it was necessary to compare the above figures with a *control group* of people with similar problems to those who received therapy, but who did not themselves receive any form of professional treatment (by, for example, being treated only custodially in an institution). Eysenck located two such

studies (Landis, 1938; Denker, 1946) and found that 66 per cent satisfied the 'cured', 'much improved' or 'improved' criteria. On the basis of these data, he concluded that:

'There thus appears to be an inverse correlation between recovery and psychotherapy: the more psychotherapy, the smaller the recovery rate'.

Eysenck's claim that no treatment is at least as effective, if not more effective, than professional treatment was not greeted enthusiastically by psychoanalysts or eclectic psychotherapists. Nor was his additional claim that it was unethical for therapists to charge people for their services, when the evidence suggested they were paying for nothing (Eysenck, 1992).

Following the publication of Eysenck's controversial article, several critiques were made of his conclusions and much research was conducted on assessing therapy's effectiveness. For example, some researchers questioned Eysenck's inclusion as 'failures' those people who 'dropped out' of therapy, on the grounds that somebody who leaves therapy cannot necessarily be counted as 'not cured'. When Eysenck's figures were reanalysed taking this into account, the figure of 44 per cent for psychoanalysis rose to a considerably higher 66 per cent (Oatley, 1984).

Other researchers argued that the success rate for psychoanalysis increased to 83 per cent if 'improvement' was measured differently (Bergin, 1971). Yet others argued that the people in Eysenck's 'control' group differed in important ways from those who received treatment (a point acknowledged by Eysenck). Malan *et al.* (1975), for example, noted that 'untreated' individuals actually had one assessment interview which some of them perceived as a powerful impetus for *self-induced change*. Since the interview clearly influenced at least some people, they could hardly be considered to have 'spontaneously' recovered. Even Landis (1938), whose article was one of those from which Eysenck derived his figure for spontaneous remission, noted that there were differences between those who received therapy and those who did not.

The issue of measurement

To evaluate a therapy, it is clearly necessary to have some way of *measuring* its effectiveness, that is, there should be a *criterion of success* (Crooks & Stein, 1991). Unfortunately, it is not easy to determine what the most appropriate criterion should be. Some therapists would argue that the most appropriate and straightforward measurement is an observable change in behaviour. After all, if a person has a phobia before a course of therapy begins but does not have one after it has ended, then the therapy has surely been successful (Guscott & Taylor, 1994).

Those who use therapies based on the behavioural model (see Chapter 74) define their therapeutic goals in such terms, and would certainly want observable change to be used as the criterion of success. However, with some other therapies, this criterion would be considered inappropriate. Psychoanalysts argue that for therapy to be effective, unconscious conflicts must be resolved and a restructuring of personality produced (see Chapter 73). Since these cannot be directly measured, they would argue that an observable change in behaviour cannot be the *only* criterion of success (Krebs & Blackman, 1988).

Box 77.2   The problem of therapist bias

Even if behaviour change were an appropriate criterion, *who* should be the judge of whether such a change has occurred? To use the therapist would surely be a mistake. What therapist, who has seen a person over a long period of time (and in all probability receiving payment), would conclude that therapy has been ineffective? Therapists clearly have a stake in believing that their therapies are positive and they cannot possibly be unbiased.

Being unable to directly measure outcomes, psychoanalysts would argue that their analysands' reports must be relied on. However, this assumes that people are always excellent judges of their own behaviours, an assumption unlikely to be true. Moreover, since the insights gained in psychoanalysis are, by their nature, unique, it is impossible to measure objectively how much insight has been gained.

Using the family and friends of the person who has received treatment is also problematic, since in at least some cases, family members and/or friends may actually be the *cause* of a person's problems! Consider, for example, a woman who has sought therapy to be more assertive but is married to an overbearing husband. The husband would hardly be expected to approve of his previously submissive wife's increased assertiveness (Krebs & Blackman, 1988).

Perhaps the most objective assessors would be therapists who were not involved in an individual's treatment and who would, presumably, not be biased in their judgements. This approach was used by Sloane *et al.* (1975) who compared the effectiveness of psychotherapy, behaviour therapy and no therapy at all. The participants were 90 people suffering from various anxiety and personality disorders. They were carefully matched according to age, sex and their mental disorders, and then randomly assigned to a course of psychotherapy, behaviour therapy or were placed on a waiting list for therapy without actually receiving any treatment.

Highly experienced clinicians, who were experts in either psychotherapy or behaviour therapy, interviewed the participants before the study began and, without knowing which group they had been assigned to, at various times later on. After four months, 80 per cent of those treated using behaviour therapy *or* psychotherapy had either improved or recovered. For the control group, the figure was 48 per cent, suggesting that, contrary to Eysenck's (1952) claim, psychotherapy *did* have a significant effect compared with no treatment at all.

When the participants were assessed one year later, those treated with psychotherapy or behaviour therapy had maintained their improvement, whereas control group participants had made small but significant gains towards the levels of the two treatment groups. So, whilst spontaneous remission may occur (as Eysenck had claimed), both of the therapeutic techniques were still better than no treatment at all.

Box 77.3   Experimental studies of the effectiveness of therapy – some important questions

Although Sloane *et al.*'s (1975) study was methodologically sound, it raises several important questions. As noted, the participants were assigned to one of two therapeutic groups or a 'control' group. Suppose a similar study were conducted which extended over a lengthy time period, such as ten years. Should those in the 'control' group, who might (for example) be suicidal, be kept away from treatment? What if a person specifically sought out a particular therapy, but was assigned to either an alternative therapy or the control group?

In an ideal experiment, a person would be 'blind' to the therapy he or she was receiving to control for expectations about the treatment. Even if this could be done,

---

would we really want to do it? Would it be ethical to deceive a person into thinking that another form of therapy was the same as the therapy being given?

Whilst carefully controlled research is essential, many important questions can be asked about this sort of research.

Durham *et al.* (1994) compared cognitive therapy, analytic psychotherapy and anxiety management training for GAD (see Chapter 70) using an *assessor* who was 'blind' to the individual's therapist and treatment condition. Individuals were rated according to *symptom change*, a criterion devised by Jacobson *et al.* (1984) for determining the proportion of outpatients returning to normal functioning. Cognitive therapy was significantly more effective than analytic psychotherapy, with anxiety management training falling in between these two.

As well as an observable change in behaviour, many other measures could be used to assess a therapy's effectiveness. These include scores obtained on psychometric tests, and *recidivism rates* (whether or not a person is readmitted for therapy or seeks additional therapy in a period of time after an initial course has ended). Using these measures, Luborsky *et al.* (1975) claimed that improvements following a course of psychotherapy were significantly higher than in people who received no treatment at all. Luborsky *et al.* also reported that the outcome was better the more sessions that took place (the *dose–effect relationship*). However, because more treatment requires more *time*, the possibility that the mere passage of time contributes to improvement cannot be ruled out.

Meta-analytic studies

One way of overcoming the possibility that certain types of measurement may 'favour' certain therapies is to look at *all* types of measurement used by researchers. This approach was taken by Smith *et al.* (1980), who examined 475 studies concerned with therapy effectiveness. Some of these compared differences between therapies with respect to their effectiveness, whilst others compared a therapy's effectiveness against no treatment at all. Because researchers sometimes used several criteria of success, Smith *et al.* actually had 1776 outcome measures which varied from being highly subjective (some were supplied by therapists) to much more objective (the use of physiological measures).

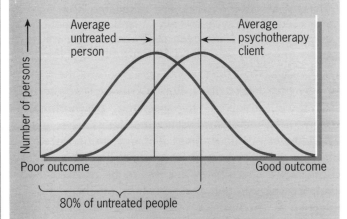
On the basis of their findings, Smith *et al.* concluded that psychodynamic therapies are effective and that such therapies:

'benefit people of all ages as reliably as schooling educates them, medicine cures them or business turns a profit. The average person who receives therapy is better off at the end of it than 80 per cent of persons who do not'.

However, they also acknowledged that the case for psychotherapy's effectiveness was far from proven:

'This does not mean that everyone who receives psychotherapy improves. The evidence suggests that some people do not improve, and a small number get worse [Smith *et al.* report a figure of nine per cent]'.

Smith *et al.*'s conclusions were a far cry from Eysenck's (1965) remark that:

'current psychotherapeutic procedures have not lived up to the hopes which greeted their emergence 50 years ago'.

However, Smith *et al.*'s meta-analysis attracted considerable criticism. For example, over half the people receiving treatment in the 475 studies were *students*, who are hardly representative of the general population. Also, in some of the studies, the psychological problems being treated were not particularly serious, including smoking, overeating and performance anxieties (Shapiro & Shapiro, 1982).

More important was the inclusion of studies which were seriously methodologically flawed. In a reanalysis of the original meta-analysis, Prioleau *et al.* (1983) found only 32 studies free from methodological defects and otherwise sound. Analysis of these led Prioleau *et al.* to a different conclusion from that reached by Smith *et al.*:

'Thirty years after Eysenck first raised the issue of the effectiveness of psychotherapy ... and after about 500 outcome studies have been reviewed, we are still not aware of a single convincing demonstration [of] the benefits of psychotherapy'.

In a lengthy debate that followed Prioleau *et al.*'s reanalysis, those involved in assessing psychotherapy's effectiveness, including Eysenck and Smith, were invited to comment on the findings. The only thing agreed was that no agreement could be reached! The issue of psychotherapy's effectiveness has yet to be resolved. Some evidence suggests that psychotherapy can be at least as effective as chemotherapy in treating certain disorders (Garfield, 1992). Andrews (1993), by contrast, has argued that dynamic psychotherapy is no better than routine clinical care. In his view:

'The lack of evidence for efficacy despite considerable research, the real possibility of harm and the high cost all make dynamic psychotherapy unlikely to be a preferred option of the health service'.

Meta-analyses of research into the effectiveness of other therapies have also been conducted. Piccinelli *et al.* (1995) looked at the effectiveness of chemotherapy (see Chapter 72) in the treatment of obsessive–compulsive disorder (OCD). They found that with various outcome measures (such as *global clinical improvement* and *psychosocial adjustment*), drugs were far superior to *placebo* (see Box 77.5) treatment, with non-SSRI antidepressant drugs (see Chapter 72) being by far the most effective in the short-term treatment of OCD.

Comparing the relative effectiveness of therapies

We have encountered several studies which, at least in part, aimed to compare the effectiveness of various therapies. Another study of this sort was conducted by May (1975), who assigned schizophrenics not previously hospitalised to one of five groups. One received individual psychoanalytic-type psychotherapy, whilst a second was given *phenothiazine* drugs alone. The third was given a combination of psychotherapy and drugs, and the fourth ECT. The fifth received *milieu therapy*, a form of treatment that attempts to make a disturbed person's total environment a *therapeutic community*.

May's criteria of success were assessments of improvement made by nurses and clinicians, measures of 'release' rates, and the duration of hospitalisation. Drugs alone, and psychotherapy plus drugs, were the two most effective treatments. Since these two forms of treatment did not differ from one another, May concluded that psychotherapy had little or no tangible effects.

Faced with findings such as May's, it is tempting to conclude that some types of therapy *are* more effective than others. Despite methodological problems relating to their meta-analysis, Smith *et al.* (1980) argued that whilst all therapies produced beneficial changes, no particular type of therapy was significantly better than any other. A similar conclusion had been reached by Luborsky *et al.* (1975) some years earlier. Borrowing from Lewis Carroll's *Alice in Wonderland*, Luborsky *et al.* suggested that as far as effectiveness was concerned, 'everybody has won and all must have prizes'.

Box 77.5 Explaining divergent findings about effectiveness

Explaining the different conclusions about the relative effectiveness of therapies is difficult. However, one potential explanation is in terms of the measurements taken. As noted earlier, different therapies have different goals and therefore define 'improvement' in different ways. When an observable behaviour change is used as the criterion of success, behaviour therapy (which focuses on overt behaviour) is far superior to psychodynamic therapies (Shapiro & Shapiro, 1982). It could be argued that it would be much 'fairer' to examine the extent to which a therapy satisfies its *own* goals, but then there is the problem of whether everybody would consider the goals a therapeutic approach sets to be satisfactory ones.

Kiesler (1966) anticipated the problems outlined in Box 77.5 when he argued that the question, 'Which type of therapy is better?', is actually inappropriate. A much better question is:

'what type of treatment by what type of therapist is most effective in dealing with specific problems among specific persons?'.

Kiesler's question may be a more appropriate one, since it avoids the pitfalls of using *general outcome measures* which may mask differences between therapies, but it is also much more difficult to answer (Wilson & Barkham, 1994).

DO THERAPISTS INFLUENCE A THERAPY'S EFFECTIVENESS?

Although they may practise the same therapeutic procedure, not all therapists are equally effective, implying that any benefits cannot be solely attributable to the therapy itself (Wolpe, 1985). Irrespective of the therapy they use, experienced therapists are generally (but not always) more effective than novice therapists (Russell, 1981). This suggests that therapists have something to learn, which means that therapeutic processes are not entirely futile (Carlson, 1987). One reason for experienced therapists' effectiveness is their willingness to embrace *technical eclecticism* or *multi-modal therapy*, in which techniques are borrowed from different therapies to tailor treatment to individual patients (Beitman *et al.*, 1989).

Experience alone, however, is not sufficient. With psychotherapy, research has consistently found that the most effective therapists genuinely care about those they treat and aim to establish relationships which are empathic and foster respect and trust. By contrast, a lack of these qualities seems to be associated with *client deterioration*. As Truax & Carkhuff (1964) have observed:

'[People] whose therapists offered a high level of unconditional positive warmth, self-congruence or genuineness, and empathic understanding showed significant positive personality and behaviour changes on a wide variety of indices, and … [people] whose therapists offered relatively low levels of these conditions during therapy exhibited significant deterioration in personality and behaviour functioning' (see also Chapter 76).

The qualities described by Truax and Carkhuff are not, of course, exclusive to therapists. Strupp & Hadley (1979) asked university professors who were not professionally trained in psychotherapy, but were known to be warm, trustworthy and empathic, to 'treat' students experiencing depression and anxiety. Despite their lack of professional training, the professors were able to bring about a significant improvement in some students which was just as great as that produced in others by professional therapists.

Luborsky (1984) calls the ability to establish a warm and understanding relationship, in which the person seeking treatment and the person providing it believe they are working together, a *therapeutic alliance*. On the basis of Strupp and Hadley's findings, it seems that it is the therapeutic alliance, rather than a knowledge of psychopathology and its treatment, which is most impor-

tant at least for some disorders. The possibility that a treatment effect can be attributable solely to a therapist suggests that a therapy's effectiveness may have little more value than the *placebo effect*.

Box 77.6   The placebo effect

According to London (1964):

'Whatever is new and enthusiastically introduced and pursued seems, for the time, to work better than what previously did, whether or not it is more valid scientifically. Eventually, these novelties too join the Establishment of Techniques and turn out [to be] nothing more than went before'.

London was commenting on the fact that, in some cases, the mere belief or expectation that a treatment will be effective can be sufficient to convince a person that he or she has been helped, and to thus show signs of improvement. Shapiro (1971) has described the apparently successful use by faith healers and physicians centuries ago of drugs made from crocodile dung, human perspiration and pigs' teeth to treat illnesses they did not understand with ingredients that had no medicinal value.

Today, the media are constantly hailing new treatments as 'wonder cures' and it is possible that the therapeutic benefits associated with such cures are derived simply from the media attention they are given. To try to assess a therapy's effectiveness and overcome the placebo effect, researchers use *double blind control* (see Chapter 2, page 20). In this, the person administering the treatment and the person receiving it are kept ignorant as to the exact nature of the treatment being studied. Since neither knows what has actually been given, the expectations of both are minimised.

In studies assessing the effectiveness of drugs, the placebo treatment is an inert pill or injection. In psychotherapy, a person receiving a placebo is given relaxation therapy without any attempt to address the psychological problem. Achieving satisfactory double blind control is not always straightforward. For example, in studies of psychotherapeutic drugs, people can sometimes tell if they are receiving a placebo because of the *absence* of side-effects (see Chapter 72). However, this problem can be overcome by using *active placebos* which mimic a drug's side-effects but exert no other effect (Fisher & Greenberg, 1980).

Smith *et al.*'s (1980) meta-analytic study revealed that there was a significant placebo effect in therapy, confirming that when people *believe* they are receiving therapeutic attention, they tend to show some sort of improvement.

DOES THE TYPE OF DISORDER INFLUENCE A THERAPY'S EFFECTIVENESS?

Some types of therapy are more effective for certain disorders. For example, drugs are essential in the treatment of schizophrenia, whereas psychodynamically based forms of therapy contribute little additional benefit (Pines, 1982). Behavioural treatments are significantly better than other approaches for treating agoraphobia (Berman & Norton, 1985). However, even within a therapeutic approach, differences have been observed. Recall from Chapter 74 that one type of behaviour therapy (flooding) is more effective than others (SD and implosion therapy) in the treatment of some phobias.

The meta-analytic studies described earlier also indicate that all therapies are not equally effective with different disorders. Amongst other things, Smith *et al.* (1980) found that whilst therapies derived from the psychodynamic model are effective, they are much more effective with anxiety disorders than with schizophrenia (see above). The rate of spontaneous remission has also been shown to vary considerably depending on the disorder. For example, people experiencing depression and GAD were more likely to recover spontaneously than those experiencing phobic or obsessive–compulsive disorders (Bergin & Lambert, 1978).

DOES THE TYPE OF PERSON RECEIVING THERAPY INFLUENCE ITS EFFECTIVENESS?

Some people have a choice about the sort of therapy they would prefer to undergo (Carlson, 1988). In at least some cases, then, people *self-select* a particular therapy. This makes it very difficult to assess therapies, because some people will either change therapists or leave therapy completely. As well as making it difficult to assess effectiveness, it makes comparisons between therapies difficult, since in both cases we are left with the evaluation *only* of those people who remain.

Despite this, some research findings should be mentioned. Garfield (1980) reported that therapies derived from the psychodynamic model are most effective with well-educated, articulate, strongly motivated and confident people experiencing light to moderate depression, anxiety disorders or interpersonal problems. Researchers call this the *YAVIS effect*, since such people tend to be **y**oung, **a**ttractive, **v**erbal, **i**ntelligent and **s**uccessful.

Also, since no two people will ever present *exactly* the same set of problems, no two people will ever receive exactly the same treatment. Precisely what will happen in a given therapeutic session is very hard to specify or assess even in those therapies (like behaviour therapy) where the therapist operates much more to a 'script' as far as the therapeutic session is concerned (Vallis *et al.*, 1986).

Box 77.7   Culture and therapy

At least some therapies *must* take into account the fact that people seeking treatment will come from diverse cultural or ethnic backgrounds. Rogler *et al.* (1987), for example, suggest that psychoanalysis or other therapies requiring high levels of verbal skills would be inappropriate for a person from a community whose members had completed little formal education.

In Hispanic societies, views concerning gender roles are different from those held by most members of Western societies. A therapeutic approach which did not take into account the established values and traditions of other cultures would lack *cultural sensitivity* and probably be of little benefit to a person seeking help (Baron, 1989).

Similarly, compared with American schizophrenics, Asian schizophrenics require significantly smaller amounts of neuroleptics for optimal treatment (Linn *et al.*, 1991). The reason for this is unclear, but it is likely that differences in metabolic rates, body fat and cultural practices (in, for example, eating) might be responsible.

Conclusions

Assessing the effectiveness of therapies and comparing their relative effectiveness is much more difficult than it might at first appear to be. The principal difficulty relates to measurement. Since there is no *criterion of success* which satisfies everybody, it is impossible to make judgements about effectiveness with which everyone would agree.

Summary

■ Based on his assessment of psychoanalysis and eclectic psychotherapy, Eysenck concluded that neither was as effective as **no** treatment at all. Eysenck found that 66 per cent of people who had a similar problem to those who received therapy showed **spontaneous remission**. The cure/improvement figures for psychoanalysis and eclectic psychotherapy were 44 per cent and 64 per cent respectively.

■ Eysenck's assessment has several methodological weaknesses, however. When the data are analysed using different measurements of 'improvement', the success rate for psychoanalysis increases dramatically.

Eysenck's spontaneous remission figure has also been challenged.

■ It is difficult to determine what the most appropriate **criterion for success** should be when trying to measure a therapy's effectiveness. Different therapies favour different measurements. Another issue concerns **who** determines whether a therapy has been effective. One approach is to use assessors who are not involved in the therapy being assessed.

■ **Meta-analyses** look at **all** measurements of effectiveness in order to assess a therapy and combine the results of all research relating to it. This provides an 'average estimate' of the size of the therapy's effectiveness. Smith *et al.*'s meta-analysis indicated that psychodynamic therapies are effective, although some people show no improvement and a small percentage actually gets worse.

■ Smith *et al.*'s meta-analysis has itself been criticised. When methodologically flawed studies are removed, Eysenck's original claim of no convincing evidence for psychotherapy's effectiveness is confirmed.

■ Some studies comparing relative effectiveness indicate that therapies differ. Others indicate that no type of therapy is significantly better than any other. One reason for these different conclusions is that improvement is defined in different ways. However, to ask 'Which type of therapy is better?' is inappropriate since it assumes 'general outcome measures' which may mask differences between therapies.

■ Kiesler argues that it is much better to ask about the effectiveness of different therapies in relation to different therapists, different disorders, and different individuals. This, however, is a more complex question to answer.

■ Not all therapists are equally effective, and experienced therapists are usually more effective than inexperienced ones. The possibility that a treatment may be effective solely because of the therapist suggests that a therapy's effectiveness may have little more value than the **placebo effect**.

■ Some therapies are more effective for certain disorders. For example, drugs are essential in the treatment of schizophrenia, and behaviour therapies are significantly better than other approaches for the treatment of agoraphobia. Additionally, even within a therapeutic approach there may be differences. Flooding is more effective than SD and implosion therapy in treating some phobias.

■ The type of person receiving a therapy also influences effectiveness. Psychodynamic therapies are most effective with well-educated, articulate, motivated and confident people with non-severe depression, anxiety disorders or interpersonal problems. Therapies must also consider the diversity of clients' cultural/ethnic backgrounds: they must display **cultural sensitivity** if they are to be of benefit.

PART 4

Atypical development

78

LEARNING DIFFICULTIES

Introduction and overview

As Chapter 65 showed, defining 'abnormal' is difficult. Similarly, distinguishing between 'typical' and 'atypical' development is not straightforward. According to Bee (1997), a child's development is 'atypical' if a problem persists for six months or longer or if it is at the extreme end of the continuum for that behaviour.

Chapters 79 and 80 look at physical and sensory impairments and emotional disturbances and behavioural problems in childhood and adolescence. This chapter concentrates on theories and research relating to the major causes and problems associated with learning difficulties, including dyslexia as a specific learning difficulty.

Defining learning difficulties

One way of defining learning difficulties is in terms of measured intelligence (see Chapter 43). In both ICD-10 and DSM-IV, an individual is designated *mentally retarded* if his or her IQ is less than 70. Originally, terms like 'feeble-minded', 'idiot', 'imbecile' and 'moron' were used to identify different levels of retardation. However, these gradually disappeared and were replaced by the terms 'mild' (IQ score 50–55 to 70), 'moderate' (35–40 to 50–55), 'severe' (20–25 to 35–40) and 'profound' (below 20 or 25) mental retardation. Today, the terms 'mild', 'moderate' and 'severe and profound' *learning difficulties* or *special needs* are used, although it is not easy to find terms which are acceptable to everyone (Frude, 1998).

Whilst the use of IQ scores to define learning difficulties is common, other criteria include using the discrepancy between performance on intellectual functioning and achievement tests, and the ability to live independently (such as being able to dress oneself relative to one's age). Indeed, the American Association of Mental Retardation (AAMR) no longer classifies mental retardation on the basis of IQ scores. Its classification is based on the *intensity of needed support* (the amount of support a person needs to function in the environment). Consequently, the AAMR uses 75 rather than 70 as the IQ cut-off point (Sue *et al.*, 1994).

The use of an IQ score of 70 has been criticised on several grounds. For example, if an ability is normally distributed in a population, then about two per cent of people will lie beyond two standard deviations from the mean. This is about the percentage of children who actually attend special schools (see Box 78.5) and corresponds to the IQ score of 70. However, this percentage was originally advocated by Burt (1921), London's first educational psychologist, who argued that:

'for immediate practical purposes, the only satisfactory definition of mental deficiency is a percentage definition based on the amount of existing accommodation'.

Since then, an IQ of 70 has been taken to *imply* a critical level of need, even though it is essentially an arbitrary point based on circular logic (Gipps & Stobart, 1990).

Categories of learning difficulties

Prior to the Warnock report (*Special Educational Needs*, 1978), children were grouped into categories which described their general ability levels (such as 'Educationally Sub-Normal [Severe]'). The Warnock report's recommendation was that the children's learning *needs* be emphasised. Hence the terms 'mild', 'moderate' and 'severe' learning difficulties were introduced.

Box 78.1   Characteristics of children with mild, moderate and severe learning difficulties

- **Mild learning difficulties:** These children have some difficulties with normal school work, but can cope with the normal curriculum. If work is differentiated and support is available, their needs can be met.

- **Moderate learning difficulties:** These children make very limited progress in basic academic skills such as literacy and numeracy, despite support being given. As a result, they need additional help, achieved by a statement of their special educational needs (see Box 78.5, pages 667–668).

- **Severe learning difficulties:** These children function at a low level in terms of basic skills. Communication skills and academic attainment are normally very limited. Such children may attend special schools (see Box 78.6, page 668), although they may experience some integration during their early schooling when the curriculum is more child-centred and developmental.

(Based on Coopers & Lybrand, 1996)

In addition to the categories identified above, some children are also identified as having a *specific learning difficulty*, often called *dyslexia*. This is discussed on pages 668–670.

Box 78.2   Cognitive abilities in people with learning difficulties

People with learning difficulties are generally poorer in acquiring, retrieving and manipulating information. According to the *delay model*, these differences are quantitative (the skills develop in the same way, but more slowly). The *difference model* proposes that learning difficulties are qualitatively different (a different type). Which of these models is most accurate has yet to be resolved. People with learning difficulties may even be both cognitively delayed *and* different.

(From Frude, 1998)

The causes of learning difficulties

Frude (1998) distinguishes between two broad types of cause, *pathological* (or *organic*) and *familial* (or *subcultural*). Pathological causes reflect some form of organic pathology which may be a result of genetic abnormalities or non-genetic biological factors. Familial causes reflect an individual's family background (genetically and sometimes environmentally).

PATHOLOGICAL CAUSES
Genetic abnormalities

Normally, there are 23 pairs of chromosomes in every body cell, giving 46 in all. Half of these are contributed by the mother, and half by the father. In the vast majority of *Down's syndrome* cases, there is an extra chromosome 21 (*trisomy 21*). The likelihood of a woman giving birth to a child with Down's syndrome increases with her age, although the reasons for this are not precisely understood. At age 25, the likelihood is one in 1400. After age 35, however, it is one in 380, and after age 45, one in 65.

Down's syndrome can be tested for by diagnostic and screening tests. The former identify whether an unborn child has the syndrome, whilst the latter provide an estimate of the likelihood that the baby will have it. Two diagnostic tests are *amniocentesis*, in which a sample of amniotic fluid containing the foetus's cells is tested, and *chorionic villi sampling* (CVF), in which a tiny piece of placenta is removed and the cells on its hair-like projections (villi) tested. Although accurate, these tests increase the risk of miscarriage, whereas screening tests do not.

Because of the availability of these various tests, the incidence of Down's syndrome has decreased significantly in recent years. This is because many couples decide to terminate the pregnancy when the syndrome is detected. Also, women now tend to have their last child at an age when the likelihood of it having the syndrome is low (Frude, 1998).

Box 78.3   Characteristics associated with Down's syndrome

Around 40 per cent of people with Down's syndrome have heart problems at birth. Babies tend to have reduced muscle tone, which results in floppiness (*hypotonia*), although this improves with age. The mouth tends to be smaller and the tongue larger than average, which can lead to speech difficulties. Other unusual

---

characteristics include short in-curving fingers, short broad hands, slanted eyes, a flat and broad face, and incomplete or delayed sexual development.

Many people with Down's syndrome enjoy healthy lives, and a lifespan of 40–60 years is not unusual. However, some medical conditions are more common in those with Down's syndrome. Ability levels vary, but progress in physical and mental skills is typically slower than in people who do not have the syndrome. At least some people with Down's syndrome have been very successful in their academic and other pursuits.

Because it is identifiable at birth and of known genetic origin, Down's syndrome provides invaluable information regarding the nature of the interaction between genes and the environment in determining developmental outcome (Wishart, 1995). Since stimulating environmental interventions can significantly affect the cognitive development of children with Down's syndrome (Lewis, 1987), genetic factors may set a limit on intellectual development in it, whilst environmental factors determine how close to that limit eventual development actually is (as is the case in non-affected children).

Interestingly, children with Down's syndrome characteristically show a decline in their developmental rate with increasing age. According to Wishart (1995), the children themselves contribute to their failure to maintain a developmental rate by becoming progressively more reluctant learners as they grow older. They often actively avoid opportunities for learning and make inefficient use of their existing skills. Presumably, facilitative intervention would help these children reach their full developmental potential.

After Down's syndrome, the next most common cause of moderate and severe learning difficulties is *fragile X syndrome*, which is characterised by hyperactive behaviour and early learning and memory difficulties. Fragile X syndrome is caused by a defect of the X chromosome, and males are particularly vulnerable to the disorders caused by X chromosome defects since they have only one X chromosome, whereas females have two (one of which can exert an overriding influence: see Chapter 45).

The 'fragile site' where the X chromosome 'loops out' in an affected child was revealed in 1977. However, it was not until 1992 that the gene responsible (*FMR-1*) was identified. The gene contains a particular sequence (a 'triplet repeat'), of which most people have up to 50 copies. When the gene is passed on, the repeat can expand to up to 200 copies and becomes unstable. Although the person with

this pre-mutation has no symptoms, when the gene is next passed on it expands further, and the repeat increases to several thousand copies which shuts it off. This causes the syndrome. In 1993, another fragile site nearer the tip of the X chromosome was identified. This is also associated with a triplet repeat, but on a gene active mainly in parts of the brain associated with learning and memory (Ferry, 1997).

Phenylketonuria (PKU) is a rare genetic disorder in which an offspring inherits a recessive gene from both parents. This results in a deficiency of the enzyme phenylalanine hydroxylase which metabolises phenylalanine, an amino acid. This leads to a build-up of phenylalanine, which is toxic to the developing brain. If detected early, learning difficulties can be avoided by placing the child on a phenylalanine-free diet for the first six years of life. However, unless treatment begins within the first few months of life, retardation is permanent and IQ scores of 30 and below are not uncommon (Bee, 1997).

Clearly, genetic factors play an important role in learning difficulties. At least 50 anomalies have been identified, including Turner's syndrome, Klinefelter's syndrome (both sex chromosome anomalies) and Tay–Sachs disease (which, like PKU, is a single gene anomaly).

Non-genetic biological factors

Learning difficulties can also be the result of various environmental factors (*teratogens*) occurring pre-natally, peri-natally or post-natally, although pre-natal factors account for by far the largest proportion of biologically caused learning difficulties. Known pre-natal teratogens include certain infections (e.g. maternal rubella), toxic chemicals in the mother's body (e.g. drugs like heroin, cocaine and alcohol), radiation and pollutants. Whilst some toxins are environmental, others are produced as a result of the mother's own faulty metabolism, or as a consequence of incompatibility between the rhesus factors in the mother's body and that of her developing foetus (Frude, 1998).

Box 78.4 Foetal alcohol syndrome

Children with foetal alcohol syndrome (FAS) are typically smaller than normal and suffer from *microcephaly* (an unusually small head and brain). Such children often have heart defects, short noses, and low nasal bridges. The eyes, too, have a distinctive appearance. FAS children are generally mildly retarded, though some may be moderately retarded and others of average intelligence. However, in those of average intelligence, there are significant academic and attentional difficulties (Sue *et al.*, 1994).

Jones *et al.* (1973) identified the syndrome, which is a consequence of the mother's excessive alcohol use during pregnancy. *Behavioural teratologists* do not agree on a 'safe' level of maternal drinking during pregnancy, although there appears to be a linear relationship between the amount of alcohol consumed and the risk of the foetus developing FAS. Binge drinking during pregnancy may be as dangerous as regular drinking.

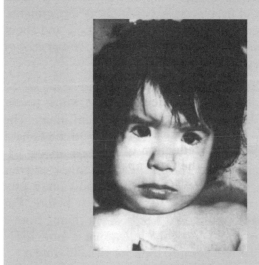

Figure 78.1   A child with FAS (From Bee, 1992)

Peri-natal influences on subsequent learning difficulties include birth trauma, prematurity (and associated low birth weight) and asphyxiation. *Post-natal* influences include exposure to various toxins (such as pesticides and lead from car exhaust fumes), malnutrition, tumours and infections (particularly bacterial meningitis and encephalitis). They also include brain damage caused by violent child abuse. According to Buchanan & Oliver (1977):

'children rendered mentally handicapped as a result of abuse may account for more cases than PKU. The consequences are frequently more severe than those of Down's syndrome'.

FAMILIAL CAUSES

About one-third of people with severe learning difficulties have a known genetic abnormality, about one-fifth have multiple congenital abnormalities, and just under one half have some clear evidence of brain damage (Simonoff *et al.*, 1996). In the majority of children with mild and moderate learning difficulties, however, there are no known pathological problems.

Assuming that a proportion of the variation in measured intelligence can be attributed to genetic differences (see Chapter 43, pages 373–376), some learning difficulties will be a result of normal genetic variation. As Sue *et al.* (1994) have observed:

'In a normal distribution of traits ... some individuals have lower intelligence than others. No organic or physiological anomaly associated with [learning difficulties] is found ... The normal range of intelligence lies between the IQ scores of 50 and 150 and ... some individuals simply lie at the lower end of this normal range'.

Relatives of people with mild learning difficulties also tend to have low IQs, which suggests a genetic basis (Frude, 1998). In families where the parents have low IQs, however, there is often serious family disorganisation and emotional/cognitive deprivation (in the form of a lack of attention and reinforcement from others), along with poverty, inadequate health care, poor nutrition and a lack of education. These factors can operate simultaneously with genetic factors to produce learning difficulties (Bee, 1997).

Rutter & Madge (1976) call the effects of the interaction between environmental and genetic factors a *cycle of disadvantage*, in which parents with low abilities provide unstimulating environments for their children, who in turn raise their own children similarly. Equally, children's environments can be modified by genetic potential. So, a child who is unresponsive by virtue of an inherited disorder might lead his or her parents to reduce their involvement (Plomin, 1995).

Special education

If moderate learning difficulties are mainly the product of non-pathological factors such as social deprivation, the process of segregated special education is not justified (Dunn, 1968). However, compensatory education programmes for disadvantaged children can produce beneficial effects (see Chapter 43). Special education is the most widespread form of intervention for those with learning difficulties (Frude, 1998), and exists to support such children and, if possible, prevent difficulties from developing.

Box 78.5   Statementing

There are five stages in identifying and providing for children with special needs. These involve the class teacher, the school's special educational needs co-ordinator (SENCO), external agents (e.g. peripatetic learning support teachers and educational psychologists) and the special needs section of the local education authority (LEA).

Following various reports and assessments, the LEA issues a *statement of special educational needs*, and provides appropriate support or school placement. The statement summarises the child's functioning, educational needs, how the needs will be met, and the nature of any additional provision. Parents are involved at all stages, and the child's statement is reviewed regularly to see if changes need to be made to the support being given.

Parents who disagree with a formal assessment's outcome can appeal to a *special educational needs tribunal* which is independent of the LEA. The tribunal, chaired by a lawyer, focuses on how the child's needs can be properly met in the future.

The largest category of special needs is mild learning difficulties, embracing those failing in the classroom. One-to-one teaching can be highly effective (Bloom, 1984), but economically unsustainable. Alternatives include the use of other children, parents, and non-teaching assistants, all of whom are beneficial (Topping, 1992). Structured learning programmes delivered on a regular basis also produce improvements, especially when undertaken early in a child's school life in a small (and ideally one-to-one) group setting (Beckett, 1995).

Box 78.6 Special schools

Some statemented children are separated from the rest of the school population and educated in special schools. Class sizes are much smaller, the children are taught by teachers with specialist qualifications, and the curriculum is more closely matched to the children's rate of learning. The cost of educating children in this way is approximately three times that of normal education (Audit Commission, 1992: see also Chapter 79, page 677).

Whether segregated provision is necessary has been extensively debated. Proponents argue that children who have evidently failed in ordinary schools need help in different and separate schools (Hall, 1996). Opponents believe that such schooling does not necessarily result in better learning outcomes, and isolates children socially by separating them from their local peer groups. Some parents of children with learning difficulties prefer *mainstreaming* (educating a child with learning difficulties in an ordinary school). However, whilst there are social and emotional benefits from integrating children as much as possible, those who are mainstreamed may fail to realise their academic potentials precisely because their special educational needs are not being met (Frude, 1998).

Specific learning difficulties

As noted earlier (see page 665), the terms 'specific learning difficulty' and *dyslexia* (which literally means 'non-reading') are often used interchangeably. People with dyslexia have normal general cognitive abilities, as assessed by intelligence tests, and have no visual or auditory impairments. Around ten per cent of the world's population, and about 350,000 British schoolchildren are dyslexic, 75 per cent of these being boys.

Researchers distinguish between *acquired* and *developmental* dyslexia. The former identifies a condition which occurs in previously literate people following brain injury. The latter occurs in children as they get older. Both types have several different forms. *Phonological dyslexia* affects letter–sound conversion. The individual cannot convert written words to their sounds directly, and cannot pronounce written words they have not seen before. For example, if asked to pick two words which rhyme from a list of 'rite', 'rit' and 'knight' the individual is more likely to select the first two because they are visually similar.

Surface dyslexia affects whole word recognition. So, the individual can only recognise a word by sounding it out rather than reading it by sight. Words which break standard pronunciation rules, such as 'broad', cannot be read correctly, and people with dyslexia often regularise the pronunciation ('broad' may be pronounced 'brode'). Finally, *deep dyslexia* affects reading for meaning. The individual is unable to pronounce aloud non-words, has problems with function words (sometimes substituting one for another), and often responds to real words with words of similar meaning (Coltheart *et al.*, 1983).

Diagnosis of dyslexia is usually made by an educational psychologist, who looks at the individual's behaviour and attainment (see Chapter 1, page 7). Young sufferers may have trouble remembering two or more instructions in sequence or catching a ball, despite an ability to manipulate toys like Lego, remember nursery rhymes, and clap out a rhythm. Their speech develops slowly and they are often clumsy, inattentive, and unable to concentrate (Fawcett & Nicolson, 1994). In school, the individual might reverse letters or numbers, find multiplication and musical notation difficult, and confuse left and right (Kingston, 1996).

Box 78.7   Diagnosing dyslexia

Until recently, dyslexia was not commonly recognised until age nine to 12, and many LEAs refused to accept that a problem existed until a child's reading age fell *two years* behind its chronological age. One diagnostic tool which can be used with the minimum amount of supervision with five-year-olds (whether or not they have begun to read) is the cognitive profiling system (CoPS). This is an interactive CD-ROM consisting of ten skills tests presented as games. At the end of a session, CoPS produces a psychometric profile identifying a child's cognitive weaknesses and the remedial action needed to overcome them.

In 'Zoid's Friends' (Zoid is a cartoon character from another world), the child must recall the colours of cartoon characters in the order they appear on the screen. In 'Rabbits', the screen displays ten holes out of which a rabbit appears periodically and randomly. The child is required to replicate the sequence by using a 'mouse' to click on the right holes in the right order. Both of these test visual sequential memory. Other games test associated and verbal memory, phonological awareness, and auditory discrimination skills.

Since the profile identifies remedial action, a child's school (which has a statutory responsibility under the 1981 Education Act to identify and assess pupils with special educational needs early and effectively) is in a position to help overcome learning difficulties. A similar diagnostic tool is the dyslexia early screening test (DEST) for use with children aged four-and-a-half to six-and-a-half (Nicolson, 1996). Like CoPS, DEST is intended for use in school by teachers, and provides a profile of cognitive abilities. It also gives a numerical 'at risk' index for dyslexia.

(Adapted from Clare, 1995 and Nicolson, 1996)

The causes of dyslexia

Because developmental and acquired dyslexia share characteristics, it has been suggested that developmental dyslexia may also have an underlying physical basis. Some evidence supports the view that specific learning difficulties are a result of *minimal brain damage* or *dysfunction*. For example, in acquired dyslexia there is damage to the left posterior hemisphere. In some people with developmental dyslexia, there is atypical asymmetry in the *plenum temporale* (in Wernické's area: see Chapter 8).

The plenum temporale is evidently directly associated with phonological coding deficits, which may be responsible for reading difficulties. However, these neurological problems are also common in children who are generally poor readers and do not show a reading-IQ discrepancy (Whittaker, 1992). Moreover, whilst the forms of acquired dyslexia are present in developmental dyslexia, they are also present in both normal and generally delayed readers (Ellis *et al.*, 1996).

There may also be a genetic basis to dyslexia, since a child is 17 times more likely to be dyslexic if either parent is a sufferer. Cardon *et al.*, (1996) have linked dyslexia to a specific section of DNA on chromosome 6. However, whether the gene (or genes) involved is necessary or sufficient for reading difficulties is disputed, and at best accounts for only a small proportion of reading difficulties (Gifford & Rodda, 1998).

Another approach has been to identify specific processing deficits. Several sub-skills have been the focus of research, including visual sequential memory, transient information processing (which might reflect an impairment in STM), phoneme processing, and deficits in automaticity (Fawcett & Nicolson, 1994). Presently, it is unclear whether dyslexia is a sub-skill deficit or not.

Rack *et al.* (1994) have provided data consistent with the view that dyslexia is a sub-skill deficit, whilst Stanovich (1994) argues that people with dyslexia cannot be distinguished from the normal continuum of reading failure on any sub-skills. For example, difficulties with underlying phonological awareness have been identified as the main characteristic of children with *all* types of reading failure, whether they were just behind or specifically delayed (Fletcher *et al.*, 1994: see Chapter 28).

Box 78.8   Dyslexia: purely a visual processing disorder?

A.S. is a 17-year-old boy who lives in Japan with his English mother and Australian father. His first language is English, which is used exclusively at home. However, at age six, he went to a Japanese-speaking school. A.S. has no difficulty with Japanese, and can use university textbooks. His English, though, is behind that of his classmates, and at age 13 it was confirmed that he was dyslexic in English but not Japanese.

Japanese has two written forms – kanji and kana. Kanji symbols have meaning but no phonetic values. If A.S.'s dyslexia were a result of a visual processing problem, he should have more difficulties with kanji than English, but he clearly does not. A.S. appears to suffer from a form of dyslexia that could be unique to English. The many pronunciation and spelling irregularities in English apparently confuse the method by which A.S. assigns sounds to letters (Wydell & Butterworth, cited in Uhlig, 1996b).

Dealing with dyslexia

Presland (1991) believes that whilst dyslexic children may be a conceptual sub-type, they do not require any specific remedial techniques. Others (e.g. Hornaby & Miles, 1980) have argued that such children require teaching which integrates visual, auditory and physical work (the *multisensory approach*). One teaching approach derives from the finding that some people with dyslexia have difficulty distinguishing sounds that change rapidly in frequency or begin and end suddenly (e.g. 'ba' and 'da'). When these words are presented more slowly, however, they can be processed.

Research with monkeys indicates that they can be trained to improve their skills in identifying rapidly changing sounds and that this produces dramatic changes in how the brain processes information contained in sounds. These findings suggest that dyslexic children's language learning histories could underlie a different form of brain organisation and that improvements in distinguishing fast sounds should result from retraining of this skill (Merzenich *et al.*, cited in Highfield, 1996f).

Box 78.9 Retraining discrimination skills

Merzenich *et al.* devised a programme of exercises, in the form of computer games, to retrain how the brain perceives sound. The four games incorporate the strategies developed in experiments with monkeys (see text), and modify speech to help children distinguish between sounds, and perceive speech as normal. The computer-modified speech and sounds were used to train the children to discriminate rapidly changing parts of speech.

This approach is evidently successful with some children who, after a month, had caught up with their friends whose language abilities were two years ahead. According to Merzenich:

'There may be no fundamental defect in the learning machinery in at least the substantial majority of these children, because they so rapidly learn the same skills at which they were defined to be deficient. It seems unlikely that [they] learned the equivalent of approximately two years of language in one month. Rather, it appears that they had already developed considerably more language comprehension than they were able to use under normal listening and speaking conditions' (cited in Highfield, 1996f).

Dyslexia: a cultural and political phenomenon?

Uncertainty about dyslexia at the theoretical level is reflected in confusion at the practical level (Bee, 1997).

The Department for Education and Employment's code of practice for children with special needs was established under the 1993 Education Act, and requires LEAs to monitor whether schools have taken appropriate steps to help children with learning difficulties. According to Booth & Goodey (1996), dyslexia is 'the cuckoo in the nest' of special educational needs, accounting for over 40 per cent of cases coming before the SEN Appeals Tribunal. It has a distorting effect on a school's special needs budget:

'at the expense of children who have genuine disabilities or difficulties worthy of being covered by a statement'.

Booth and Goody argue that the dyslexia label says to parents 'your child has a problem, but your child is normal'. As they note, this is reflected in the SEN code of practice, where 'special learning difficulties (dyslexia)' is listed separately from 'learning difficulties'. In their view, it is hard to see what is specific about the first category by contrast with the second, unless it is just the absence of stigma.

Accusations that dyslexia is a convenient label for middle class parents to excuse their children's poor academic performance, and that the dyslexia lobby uses resources which should go to children with other special needs, are strongly refuted by the British Dyslexia Association (Kingston, 1996). According to the Association's director:

'The undiagnosed dyslexic can become the class clown or school failure even though he or she might be perfectly able. To understand how an undiagnosed dyslexic feels, imagine yourself in China unable to read or write the language. You are surrounded by symbols you don't understand – it puts you outside society' (Brooks, cited in Kingston, 1996).

Conclusions

Many causes of learning difficulties exist. Some are pathological and others familial. Whether children with learning difficulties should receive special education or be 'mainstreamed' is the subject of much debate. There are several explanations of dyslexia and various practical approaches to it, although its existence as a specific learning difficulty has been questioned.

Summary

■ ICD-10 and DSM-IV designate individuals with IQs below 70 as **mentally retarded**, although 'mild', 'moderate' and 'profound' **learning difficulties/special**

needs are preferred terms today, reflecting the Warnock report's influence. Another criterion of learning difficulties is the ability to live independently.

■ Children with mild learning difficulties can manage the curriculum with appropriate support. Those with moderate learning difficulties need support with basic academic skills. Children with severe learning difficulties may attend special schools.

■ According to the **delay model**, cognitive skills develop more slowly in people with learning difficulties. The **difference model** proposes a qualitative difference. Both models may be valid.

■ **Pathological/organic** causes of learning difficulties include genetic and non-genetic biological factors. **Familial/subcultural** causes reflect family background factors.

■ People with **Down's syndrome** typically display slower progress than non-affected individuals in physical and mental skills, although some are very successful academically. As with non-affected individuals, genetic factors may set a limit on intellectual development whilst environmental factors determine how close to the limit development actually is. The characteristic decline in developmental rate with age may be due to decreased motivation to learn and inefficient use of existing skills.

■ **Fragile X syndrome** and **phenylketonuria** (PKU) are also genetic. The former is caused by a defective X chromosome, whilst the latter is the result of inheriting a defective gene from both parents. Other genetic abnormalities include Turner's and Klinefelter's syndromes, and Tay–Sachs disease.

■ **Pre-natal teratogens** include maternal infections, drug abuse, radiation and pollutants. Children with foetal alcohol syndrome (FAS) have **microcephaly**, and even those of average intelligence have academic and attentional difficulties.

■ **Peri-natal** teratogens include birth trauma, prematurity and asphyxiation. **Post-natal** teratogens include exposure to toxins, malnutrition, tumours, infections and brain damage.

■ Most children with mild and moderate learning difficulties have no identifiable pathological problems. Their relatives tend to have low IQs and their families are often disorganised and emotionally, materially, and cognitively deprived. Hence, environmental and genetic factors operate simultaneously to create a **cycle of disadvantage** which produces learning difficulties.

■ A range of **special education** provision is available in both mainstream and segregated schools. **Mainstreaming** offers social and emotional advantages but at the potential expense of failing to meet special educational needs.

■ Different types of **acquired** and **developmental dyslexia** include **phonological**, **surface** and **deep**. Diagnosis of dyslexia involves assessment of behaviour and attainment, in particular **reading age**. Assessment techniques include the **cognitive profiling system** (CoPs) and **dyslexia early screening test** (DEST).

■ Dyslexia may be caused by **minimal brain damage/dysfunction**, and there is also evidence suggesting a genetic basis. The view that dyslexia involves specific sub-skills difficulties has not been consistently supported, and some types of dyslexia may be unique to English.

79

PHYSICAL AND SENSORY IMPAIRMENTS

Introduction and overview

According to the National Council for Civil Liberties (1996), about four million people have mobility problems. Over half a million use wheelchairs on a daily basis, and up to a million use wheelchairs some of the time. Half a million people have hearing impairments, one million are blind, and a further two million are partially sighted. This chapter looks at research into the psychological effects of some physical and sensory impairments and the problems of coping with them.

Impairments, disability and handicap

Although it has been challenged (Johnson, 1996), the World Health Organisation (WHO) has made a useful distinction between impairment, disability and handicap. An *impairment* is the objective pathology or psychological difficulty. A *disability* is the effects that the impairment has on everyday activities. A *handicap* is the effect of the impairment on social and occupational roles. For example, a travelling salesman who breaks a leg (an impairment) might be disabled by this (he cannot drive), and so is handicapped (because he cannot get to work). The same impairment can lead to different levels of handicap depending on how crucial the impairment is to a person's social and occupational roles (Kent, 1995).

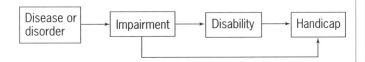

Figure 79.1   The World Health Organisation model of disability

Many people with physical impairments do not define themselves as disabled, and are not regarded as such by society because their impairments do not lead to social exclusion. Some impairments can be easily corrected (short-sightedness, for example) and others (such as colour blindness) do not prevent people from participating in

most areas of society on generally equal terms (National Council for Civil Liberties, 1996).

PHYSICAL IMPAIRMENTS

Chronic illnesses

As many as 30 per cent of children may be affected by *chronic illnesses* and disabilities. In the case of congenital heart disease, only two-thirds of affected children survive to age 20. With other illnesses, such as cystic fibrosis and diabetes, advances in medical technology have significantly increased survival rates and increased quality of life expectations (Elander & Midence, 1997).

> **Box 79.1   The effects of chronic illnesses**
>
> Most children and their families show remarkable resilience and seem to cope well with illness. However, many chronic childhood illnesses are associated with increased behavioural problems and greater difficulties in coping and adjustment among affected children, as well as adverse effects on family members and overall family functioning. Emotional disturbances are about twice as high among children with chronic physical illnesses compared with healthy peers. Factors such as social/family circumstances, and children's perceptions of their illnesses and their consequences, play a greater role in predicting adjustment than a condition's physical aspects.
>
> Supportive psychological intervention in the home, school, community and clinical environment can contribute to improved functioning and quality of life. One such contribution is in facilitating decision-making in the difficult choices that affected individuals and their families have to make about conditions and their treatment. Using *psychological decision theory*, affected individuals and their families can be helped to reach illness-related decisions in a systematic way which optimises their own needs and values.
>
> *Problem-focused approaches* prepare children to cope better with painful or stressful medical procedures or an illness's symptoms. *Cognitive approaches* (coping strategies) promote adjustment more generally by altering thought and behaviour patterns presumed to mediate outcomes in terms of health, relationships, happiness and achievement. *Social approaches* include administrative interventions in delivery of care, programmes aimed

at improving prospects in areas such as education and the work place, and interventions aimed more broadly at the family or community of an affected child. (See Chapter 20, page 167.)

(From Elander & Midence, 1997)

Cerebral palsy

Cerebral palsy (CP) is a term applied to various neurological defects from brain damage arising either before birth (as the result of congenital abnormality) or early in life. It affects around 2.3 children per 1000 and is characterised by motor patterns not usually seen in other children, a delay in acquiring new skills, and the persistence of certain infant behaviour patterns (such as infantile reflexes).

The commonest type involves movement difficulties on one side of the body (*hemiplegia*), resulting from damage to the opposite cerebral hemisphere. In some cases, however, all four limbs are affected (*quadriplegia*). In *ataxic cerebral palsy*, the individual has difficulty with balance, and voluntary movements are often clumsy. *Atheoid cerebral palsy* is characterised by unusual and uncontrollable movements of the face and hands. CP is also associated with impairments in cognitive process and visual and auditory perception. However, in some individuals, normal cognitive processes are masked by physical difficulties in communication.

Box 79.2 Neuropsychological impairment in CP and its implications for schools

According to Davies (1995), students with CP have a visual (performance) IQ two or three standard deviations below their verbal IQ. Without being aware of this, teachers sometimes assume that failure to produce work equivalent to their able-bodied peers is evidence of learning difficulties. In other cases, students with CP who have no or limited speech, no adequate hand control and no or limited mobility, are also sometimes labelled as having learning difficulties.

Students with adequate speech, but no adequate hand control and no or limited mobility can be assessed, but their work in the classroom may not match the potential described in their assessments. Students with speech, hand control and mobility, but nevertheless obvious physical disability, may well be the equals of the best in their class. However, their study and organisation skills may be affected because of visuo-perceptual problems: work may be presented messily, handwriting untidy, and work rate significantly slower than their peers. For Davies (1995):

'the teaching and learning implications of the neurological sequelae of CP beyond the physical disability must be appreciated and fully considered in the management of the curriculum for the student with CP'.

SENSORY IMPAIRMENTS

Hearing impairments

Sensory impairments are usually less evident than physical impairments, but can have an enormous effect on children's education. Hearing loss is divided up into quartiles. Most people can hear sounds in the lowest quartile, at 10–25 decibels (dB). People who can only hear sounds at 25–50 dB plus are *moderately hearing impaired*, whilst at 50–75 dB plus they are *severely hearing impaired*. At 75–100 dB plus, they are *profoundly hearing impaired*.

There are two main types of hearing impairment. In *conductive deafness*, sound waves are not conducted efficiently enough through the external and middle ears, and do not reach the inner ear. *Perceptive* (or *sensorineural*) *deafness* is a result of damage to the inner ear, auditory nerve, or brain.

The most common causes of conductive deafness are wax or foreign bodies, blocking of the Eustachian tube in upper respiratory infections, and acute *otitis media* (inflammation of the middle ear). Chronic otitis media can lead to permanent deafness. Perceptive deafness is commonly caused by infection of the middle ear, Ménière's disease and, in old age, degeneration of auditory nerve endings. In new-borns, rhesus blood incompatibility, jaundice or labour complications are often associated with inner ear defects.

Some infants are born with serious hearing loss or are totally deaf. The most obvious sign of hearing loss in an infant is congenital absence or abnormality of the external ear. There may also be abnormality of the middle or inner ear. These abnormalities have several causes including viral infections (e.g. maternal rubella) and the mother taking certain drugs in the first three months of pregnancy.

Another sign of hearing loss is the absence of the startle reflex in response to a sudden loud noise (see Chapter 23). This can be detected within the first six months. At around nine months, hearing infants can localise sound quite well, and this forms the basis for the *distraction test*, the most widely used method for assessing hearing impairments in infancy.

Box 79.3   The distraction, otoacoustic emission (OAE) and auditory brainstem response (ABR) tests

The distraction test is carried out by health visitors with babies of seven or eight months. One health visitor plays with the child, whilst another makes various sounds nearby and notes whether they attract the infant's attention. However, it is not always reliable because some hearing impaired children can pick up visual 'cues' from the health visitors and create the impression they have noticed a sound.

The OAE and ABR tests are advantageous because they can be used with babies as young as two- or three-days-old. Although slightly different, both tests involve inserting a sound-emitting probe into a baby's ear. Special equipment determines whether the sounds are being correctly detected by the auditory cortex. The OAE and ABR tests have a success rate of more than 90 per cent compared with 30 per cent for the distraction test, and neither relies on the health visitor's subjective judgement.

(Based on Ferriman, 1997)

Babies may be born with normal hearing but acquire an impairment after birth as a consequence of mumps, measles, scarlet fever, and other infections or injuries. Impaired hearing in children, as in adults, may be conductive or perceptive. Whilst the former can often be improved by surgery or a *hearing aid* (see below), the latter is more serious if the infant has no or almost no ability to hear sounds. Unlike the outer and middle ear, the inner ear has few powers of recovery. As a result, deafness is often incurable.

Box 79.4   Language development in the hearing impaired

Of those hearing impaired children born every year, half are detected by age 18 months, and a quarter by age three. The rest are detected after that. Like hearing babies, hearing impaired babies babble. However, they stop at around nine months, probably because hearing the noises produced is necessary to continue making them. Words are acquired at a much slower rate (200 at age four to six) than in hearing children (2000 or more at the same age: see Chapter 33). Up to age 11, hearing impaired children show little improvement in language proficiency (Kyle, 1981), and nearly half of those referred for special help with reading have middle ear disorders (Gottlieb *et al.*, 1980).

As with reading, spoken language is less developed, and the greater the hearing loss the poorer the development (though both reading and language development in the hearing impaired are correlated with measured intelligence). The average reading age of school leavers with profound hearing impairment is two years behind non-hearing impaired school leavers (Conrad, 1977). Written language also differs from that of the non-hearing impaired. Hearing impaired children use shorter and simpler sentences, more nouns and verbs, and often omit function words like 'is'.

Interestingly, hearing impaired children of hearing impaired parents acquire sign language (see text below) at a similar, if not faster, rate than oral language (Harris, 1991). Left alone, profoundly hearing impaired children produce their own sign language (Goldin-Meadow & Feldman, 1977: see Chapter 34).

Hearing impairments are actually quite prevalent in young children, and as many as 20 per cent of primary age suffer from temporary conductive hearing loss. Around one in 25 children has a mild hearing impairment, usually conductive middle ear deafness due to 'glue ear', in which the auditory tube becomes blocked as a result of middle ear secretions becoming thick and interfering with ossicle vibration. One in 500 children has a moderate hearing impairment, sufficient to require the use of a hearing aid. One child in 1000 is profoundly hearing impaired and requires special education.

Box 79.5   What is it like to be hearing impaired?

Along with our other senses, we take hearing for granted. Empathising with someone who is hearing impaired depends in part on knowing what it is like to be hearing impaired. Try watching your favourite TV programme without the sound on and without subtitles. How long can you do this for? Was the experience frustrating? Now think about speaking to a hearing impaired person. Should your speed be normal, slower than normal, or very slow? Should your rhythm be staccato or regular? (see Box 79.6).

Hearing impaired children may be educated in either special residential schools or mainstream schools. Residential schools, in which class sizes are smaller, take such children as early as possible. Speech, lip-reading, sign language and finger spelling (see page 675) are taught as the usual means of communication, and attempts are made to use whatever remains of the child's hearing. Hearing aids and other devices are often used. As noted in Chapter 78, there are advantages and disadvantages associated with special and mainstream schools. Mixing with normally hearing peers is socially and emotionally advantageous, but the difficulties of hearing in a large class, poor acoustics, and being taught by teachers with no special knowledge of hearing impairment are obvious limitations.

Without a hearing aid, a severely impaired child does not hear speech, although he or she will respond to a shout at close range. A profoundly hearing impaired child reacts only when heavy objects are dropped or vibration is caused by heavy banging. A hearing aid enables the child to become aware of some street noises and, in a quiet environment, the rhythm of a voice can be detected provided the aid is set to maximum.

Box 79.6   Speaking to a child with a hearing impairment

Box 79.5 asked how you should speak to a hearing impaired person. Speech which is too loud will be distorted, and speech which is too quiet will not be heard. Speech at normal loudness is best up to a distance of four feet. The nearer one approaches the child, the quieter the voice should become. At distances greater than four feet, a hearing aid will pick up other sounds in the environment and drown some speech. Breaking up speech upsets rhythm and intonation, and it is better to speak distinctly if a little slower than normal.

Various communication systems exist for use with hearing impaired individuals. These include oral English, sign language (e.g. British Sign Language) and manually-coded English (e.g. finger spelling). The *Makaton language programme* (Walker, 1996) is a sign language consisting of a special selection of essential words, structured in stages of increasing complexity. Only key words are signed, accompanied by normal grammatical speech. Signs communicate facts, needs and emotions, and are accompanied by appropriate facial expressions (see Figure 79.2).

Other communication systems for children who cannot talk intelligibly (as a result of a hearing impairment, autism, CP and other disorders) include *Blissymbols*. The symbols are pictures translatable into any language, and can be used to create sentences, represent needs, and so on (see Figure 79.3).

Oralists maintain that effective communication by hearing impaired children is best achieved through lip-reading, hearing aids, and attempts to produce spoken language, rather than sign language and signing. Evidence concerning

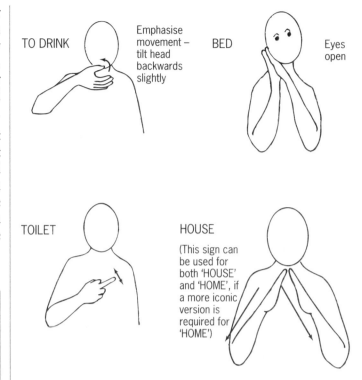

Figure 79.2   Examples from stage 1 of the Makaton language programme (From Walker, 1996)

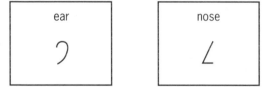

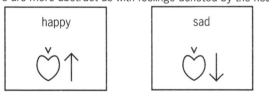

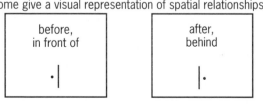

Figure 79.3   Blissymbols are printed on cards and can be laid out to represent needs, create sentences, and produce highly creative language

their relative effectiveness is mixed, but an important feature appears to be the *quality* of the interaction whatever mode is used (Webster & Wood, 1989). *Total communication* (using any effective communication method) appears to benefit the hearing rather than the hearing impaired (Stewart, 1992).

Visual impairments

Various forms of visual impairment exist. Some individuals have *residual vision* (partial sight). Others have no vision at all (they are blind). In the school age population, there are around four partially sighted and three blind children per 10,000 children. Visual impairment has many causes. These include infection (such as severe infection of the conjunctivae during birth, caused by the *Gonococcus*), trauma, congenital cataracts, pituitary gland tumours, and occipital lobe or optic fibre damage.

Box 79.7   Types of residual vision

- Lack of peripheral vision (which impairs mobility and alertness to movement) but good central vision.

- Lack of central vision but good peripheral vision.

- Scanning difficulties, or the inability to focus and follow movement.

- Reduced monocular vision (which makes speed, distance and depth estimation a problem and also impairs accuracy of reach).

- Difficulty in identifying two-dimensional representations.

- Diminished colour vision.

Children without sight must depend on their other senses for information. Although there is no automatic compensation for loss of vision, children learn to make efficient use of their other senses. Hence, reading is achieved through *Braille* (a writing system using patterns of raised dots to represent letters, words, numbers or musical notation, which enables material to be read by touch).

Like hearing impaired children, the vocabularies of visually impaired children do not grow as quickly as those of non-impaired children, although the difference is not major. However, reversal of the meaning of personal pronouns ('you' and 'I') is common, and words concerned with locations may be used interchangeably (Andersen *et al.*, 1993).

Box 79.8   What is it like to be visually impaired?

Sight helps us identify objects' properties quickly, because a large amount of information is received simultaneously. The other senses receive information more slowly and sequentially, and such information has to be acted on in sequence. Compare the speed at which you can identify one object from a selection of ten with and without a blindfold.

Next, ask a friend to take you blindfolded to a busy area (such as a canteen) and seat you in a chair at a table. Listen to the sounds in the environment and then try to obtain a meal and make your way back to the table and chair. Try to eat the meal. Now sit in front of a television without the picture when your favourite programme is on. If it's football and the commentator screams' You'll never see a better goal than that!', how would you feel? Finally, ask a friend to rearrange the furniture in a room you're familiar with. Can you find your way around the room wearing a blindfold?

Coping with impairments: employment and education

EMPLOYMENT

Legislation exists to prevent discrimination in employment. For example, it is against the law to treat a person disabled by virtue of a physical or mental impairment less favourably than someone else, solely on the basis of his or her disability, *unless there is good reason*. This applies to all employment matters including recruitment, training, promotion, and dismissal. Less favourable treatment can only be justified when it is relevant to the individual's circumstances *and* there is a 'substantial' reason. For example, if an employer required a typist with a particular speed, and received an application from someone with arthritis who could not type at that speed, the employer would be justified in not employing the person, provided no reasonable adjustment to the job's parameters could be made.

To help disabled people do a job, employers have to look at the changes they could make to the work place or to the way the work is done, and make any reasonable changes. However, people with disabilities (PWDs) are *vulnerable*, not only by their own limitations, but also by the barriers created by others (Martin & Kearns, 1995).

Box 79.9 Some barriers to equal opportunities in employment

- Able-bodied candidates are more likely to receive a positive response to their job application than those expressing a disability.

- The unsuitability of a post with a company is just one factor used to legitimise discrimination against disabled people. Others include unsuitable premises and difficult access/journey to work.

- Non-disabled workers often discriminate against their disabled colleagues.

- Employers tend to associate disability with illness, and assume that disabled applicants will be absent much of the time.

- The nature and cause of a disability can influence recruitment decisions. People with mental disorders are less likely than the physically disabled to be offered employment, and those whose disability is attributed to an internal cause (e.g. drug addiction) are less likely to be recommended for employment than those whose disability is attributed to factors beyond the applicant's control.

- The disabled may also be disadvantaged in terms of career progression, given a career trend amongst employers to expect 'multi-functioning' workforces.

(From Martin & Kearns, 1995)

Evidently, visual and hearing impairments are bigger obstacles to getting a job than having a criminal record or a history of drug abuse (Brindle, 1997). However, discrimination is not in an employer's interests, since PWDs stay in the same job longer (reducing recruitment and training costs), and are less likely to take sick leave or sustain industrial injuries. For Martin & Kearns (1995), psychologists have a role to play in bringing about attitude change with respect to PWDs, and can influence how personnel decisions are made and ensure equal opportunities for all (see Box 1.3, page 6).

EDUCATION

All children are entitled to access to appropriate educational experience and to the company of their peer groups in their own communities. However, educational choice is not as available to children and adults with impairments (Coopers & Lybrand, 1992), who are likely to leave school with fewer qualifications and face numerous discriminatory barriers to higher education.

Mainstream education is largely inaccessible to people with impairments. Many school facilities, such as playgrounds, libraries and toilets are inaccessible at both primary and secondary levels. Undergraduates have to apply to the few universities that are accessible and have appropriate facilities, rather than those with the most suitable courses (Cornwall, 1995).

As noted in Chapter 78 (see Box 78.6 and page 688), there has been much debate over whether mainstream or special schools are best for children with learning difficulties. A survey by the charity SCOPE indicates that discrimination is prevalent in mainstream schools. Fifty three per cent of impaired respondents who had been to mainstream schools felt they had been treated differently, and 41 per cent believed that teachers had underestimated their abilities. Disturbingly, 47 per cent reported that they were bullied at school because of their impairments, and 36 per cent of those who had been to special schools felt they had lower academic standards than other schools in the area (Donnellan, 1996). Clearly, much needs to be done to reduce discrimination against those with impairments.

Conclusions

There are important psychological effects arising from physical and sensory impairments. Coping with such impairments is made more difficult by the existence of discriminatory practices in settings to which physically and sensorily impaired people should have equal access.

Summary

■ The World Health Organisation distinguishes between **impairment**, **disability**, and **handicap**. The same impairment can produce different degrees of handicap depending on how much social participation/exclusion it produces.

■ **Physical impairments** include **chronic illnesses** and disabilities. Whilst most chronically ill children and their families show great resilience, they are more likely to have behavioural and emotional problems. Children's perceptions of their illnesses and their consequences are a greater influence on adjustment than the illnesses themselves.

■ The commonest type of **cerebral palsy** (CP) involves **hemiplegia**. Other types include **quadriplegia, ataxic** and **atheoid** CP. Normal cognitive processes are sometimes masked by physical difficulties, but neuropsychological impairments are quite common and may be mistaken for learning difficulties.

■ **Sensory impairments** are usually less evident than physical impairments, but can have considerable impact on children's education.

■ **Hearing impairments** can be **moderate**, **severe** or **profound**. A distinction is made between **conductive** and **perceptual/sensorineural deafness**, each of which is associated with different causes. The former can be improved by surgery or a **hearing aid**. The latter is often incurable.

■ Hearing loss may be indicated by abnormality of the external and/or middle or inner ear, absence of the startle reflex, and failure on the distraction, otoacoustic emission (OAE) and auditory brainstem response (ABR) tests.

■ Hearing impaired children's language development (speech, reading and writing) is slower than hearing children's. Those born to hearing impaired parents rapidly acquire sign language, and will spontaneously produce their own sign language.

■ Hearing impaired children may be educated in mainstream or special residential schools. There are both advantages and disadvantages to mainstreaming.

■ Communication systems used with the hearing impaired include British Sign Language, manually-coded English (such as finger spelling), and the **Makaton language programme**. Other systems (also used with autistic children and those with CP) include **Blissymbols**. The effectiveness of different methods apparently depends on the **quality** of the interaction, rather than the particular communication mode(s).

■ **Visual impairments** include **residual vision** (partial sight) and total blindness. Different types of residual vision include lack of peripheral or central vision, scanning difficulties, and reduced monocular or colour vision.

■ Blind children learn to use their other senses to compensate for their lack of vision, as in **Braille** reading. Vocabulary develops more slowly than in sighted children, and they often display personal pronoun reversal.

■ Legislation exists to prevent discrimination at work regarding recruitment, training, promotion and dismissal, unless there is good reason. Employers are obliged to make reasonable changes to the workplace or job to help disabled people, who are vulnerable due to their own limitations and barriers to equal opportunities created by others.

■ Visual and hearing impairments are bigger obstacles to employment than a criminal record or history of drug abuse. However, people with disabilities are more likely to stay in the same job longer and less likely to go sick or suffer industrial injuries.

■ Many schools and universities are inaccessible for people with impairments. At school, discrimination occurs in the form of underestimating abilities, bullying, and lower academic standards at special schools.

80

EMOTIONAL DISTURBANCES AND BEHAVIOURAL PROBLEMS IN CHILDHOOD AND ADOLESCENCE

Introduction and overview

There are several emotional disturbances and behavioural problems whose onset usually occurs in childhood and adolescence, and both ICD-10 and DSM-IV have categories identifying them (see Chapter 67, pages 576–577). One is *attentional-deficit/hyperactivity disorder* (ADHD), which is called *hyperkinetic disorder* in ICD-10. Another is *autism*. DSM-IV classifies autism as a disorder usually first diagnosed in infancy, childhood or adolescence, whilst ICD-10 classifies it as a disorder of psychological development. This chapter examines theory and research relating to the causes and effects of these two disorders.

Attention-deficit/ hyperactivity disorder (ADHD)

ADHD was once called 'hyperactivity' and was first recognised by Still, an English paediatrician, in 1902. Both ICD-10 and DSM-IV identify two broad types, one characterised by *attentional problems* and the other by *hyperactivity*, although both may occur in the same individual. Attentional problems include being easily distracted, failing to follow instructions or respond to commands, difficulty in completing tasks, and paying little attention to detail. Hyperactivity problems include excessive or exaggerated motor activity (such as aimless or haphazard running or fidgeting), impulsiveness, and a lack of self-control.

> **Box 80.1 ADHD: Some classificatory issues**
>
> - Whether attentional problems and hyperactivity are the same or different disorders is unclear. The latter is more common, but the term 'hyperactivity' refers to both a diagnostic category and behavioural characteristics.
>
> - Children with 'short attention spans' are often referred to as 'hyperactive', even though they may not meet the diagnostic criteria for this disorder. So, children may be *overactive* without meeting the criteria for being *hyperactive*.
>
> - Attentional deficit or hyperactivity is not always evident or displayed in all situations, and 'pervasive' ADHD (displayed in different situations) may be different from 'true' ADHD (displayed in all situations).
>
> - According to some experts, the diagnosis is too readily applied to children whom parents and teachers find difficult to control.
>
> (Based on Bootzin & Acocella, 1984, and Sue *et al.*, 1994)

Estimates of ADHD's prevalence differ, but around five per cent of the school-age population may be affected (Prentice, 1996), and ADHD is the most common behaviour disorder seen by child psychiatrists. It is much more prevalent in boys than girls, and occurs with greatest frequency before age ten. Some of the difficulties associated with it (such as motor restlessness) persist into adolescence and adulthood. Whilst children with ADHD may be of average or above average intelligence, they have severe learning problems because of their inability to sustain attention in the classroom (Boyd, 1996).

ADHD children are extremely disruptive in structured situations. They also show poor social and emotional adjustment, disrupting games, getting into fights and throwing temper tantrums when they do not get their own way. As a result, they are often disliked by their peers (Prentice, 1996). The attention deficits are typically variable, and a child may appear greatly improved one week, but very much worse the next. As a result of their poor academic performance and problems with peer relations, ADHD-children often become adults with continuing academic difficulties, poor self-image, and social difficulties.

THE CAUSES OF ADHD

One theory implicates *family variables*. According to this, the home environment, especially the parent–child relationship is influential in ADHD's development (Paternite & Loney, 1980). For example, many parents of hyperactive

Figure 80.1   Michael Oliver as 'Junior" in the film
Problem Child

children have clinical diagnoses of personality disorder or hysteria (Morrison, 1980). However, whilst family relationships may be a factor, children's disruptive behaviours could be the *cause* of particular types of parental behaviour as much as the result of them (see Chapter 40). Nonetheless, family stability and positive parent–child relationships predict positive outcomes in adolescence, whilst family instability and punitive parent–child relationships are associated with adolescent antisocial behaviour. At the very least, then, family variables may be associated with ADHD's *course*, if not its cause.

One theoretical perspective that received much public attention was proposed by Feingold (1975), who argued that hyperactivity was produced by *dietary factors*, and could be treated by means of a suitable diet.

Box 80.2   Food additives and ADHD

According to Feingold, food additives (artificial flavours and colours) are chemically similar to *salicylate* (a substance found in apples, tomatoes and certain other natural foods) and produce physiological changes which cause disruptiveness and hyperactivity. Feingold placed hyperactive children on a diet free of food additives and salicylates, and reported a complete remission in the symptoms of some of them. Feingold also found that a slight deviation from the diet caused an immediate relapse.

Although Feingold's hypothesis received wide media attention and a large amount of anecdotal support, studies testing it have produced mixed results. Some research has found that children show poorer learning after taking large amounts (100 mg) of food dye (Bootzin & Acocella, 1984), but other research has failed to find significant effects. For example, Harley *et al.* (1978) placed 36 school-age boys and their families on experimental and control diets. The food was provided by the researchers, and the boys' behaviours were rated by teachers and trained raters who visited their classrooms. At the end of the diet period, the boys were tested for intelligence, memory, concentration, motor speed and motor coordination.

Around 30 per cent were rated by their parents as being less hyperactive when on the experimental diet. However, there were no differences between the experimental and control diet groups on all other measures, leading the researchers to conclude that Feingold's claims were 'seriously overstated'. Notwithstanding this caution, the general finding that some children show very clear effects after consuming food dyes suggests that Feingold's hypothesis cannot be completely discounted.

Genetic factors have also been implicated in ADHD. For example, the concordance rate is higher for MZs than DZs (Gillis *et al.*, 1992), and at least some parents of hyperactive children have themselves had long histories of hyperactivity (Dendy, 1995). Because ADHD's central problem is in sustaining attention, the disorder might be due to inadequate or impaired neurological development. Factors involved in such neurological impairment include lead poisoning, foetal alcohol syndrome, and chromosomal abnormalities (Farrington, 1995: see Box 43.3, page 376).

The reticular activating system (attention), frontal lobes (voluntary control of attention) and temporal–parietal regions of the cortex (involuntary attention) have all been implicated in ADHD (Sue *et al.*, 1994). Zametkin (1990) used PET to examine glucose metabolism in hyperactive and normal adults. They found that hyperactive adults showed much slower glucose metabolism in the brain structure involved in attention and the inhibition of inappropriate responses.

TREATING ADHD

One line of support for a neurological perspective comes from the success of certain drugs in ADHD's treatment. Some children, with *and* without ADHD, show marked reductions in activity when given stimulant drugs, particularly *amphetamines* (see Box 15.2, page 124).

Box 80.3   Using stimulant drugs with ADHD

The idea that stimulant drugs can help an already over-stimulated child runs counter to common sense. Whereas amphetamines would be expected to 'speed up' people who do not have ADHD so that they behave hyperactively, the same drugs produce a paradoxical effect and *slow down* hyperactive children. Drugs like methylphenidate hydrochloride (*Ritalin*) reduce excess motor activity and increase the ability to pay attention and concentrate. This enhances ADHD-children's learning ability (Gadow, 1991).

Exactly why stimulants are effective in ADHD's treatment is not known, but it may be linked to underarousal or complex deficits in the regulation of arousal (Campbell & Werry, 1986). According to this, the brains of ADHD-children lack arousal, and their behaviours are an attempt to seek more stimulation to enable them to function at an optimum level of arousal (see Chapter 19). Ritalin, then, has a 'normalising' effect on their brains. Dopamine may play an important role because of its apparent effects on attention, motivation and the motor system, all of which are affected in ADHD (Prentice, 1996).

However, stimulant medication is effective only in around 70 per cent of children with ADHD (Whalen & Henker, 1991), Also, it appears to treat only the symptoms rather than ADHD's causes, because behaviour changes that do occur are short-lived (Sue *et al.*, 1994). Finally, although several brain structures have been implicated, there is no compelling evidence of brain impairment. However, this might just reflect the possibility that there are actually several different types of ADHD, only some of which are linked to neurological deficits (Schachar, 1991).

Box 80.4   Drug therapies and children with ADHD

As well as the caution that Ritalin does not cure ADHD, but merely reduces its symptoms, several other cautions must be exercised when drugs are used with children.

- Drug treatment can have adverse side effects including insomnia, weight loss, high blood pressure and growth suppression. The long-term effects of these is not known.

- If drugs are routinely administered with 'problem children', as a way of 'keeping peace in the classroom', there is the potential for abuse, with medication being administered to *all* 'problem children' including those whose behaviours stem from family conflict, for instance.

- Drugs are a *social handicap*. Children who must take pills are likely to be labelled as 'sick' by others, and eventually by themselves, leading to lower self-esteem. Ross & Ross (1976) describe the case of an eight-year-old boy about whom one of his peers had written the following poem:

> David Hill
> Did you take the pill
> That makes you work
> And keeps you still?
> Take your pill, Hill

In the boy's own words, 'sometimes I wish I could go to another school and start over'.

(Adapted from Bootzin & Acocella, 1984)

In view of the cautions identified in Box 80.4, many researchers have advocated different approaches to treatment, or the use of drugs in conjunction with other approaches (DuPaul & Barkley, 1993). Behaviour modification, particularly token economies (see Chapter 74, pages 640–641) has been used successfully with ADHD (Weeks & Laver-Bradbury, 1997), whilst relaxation training (see Chapter 20, page 165) has been effective in reducing hyperactivity (Dunn & Howell, 1982). Cognitive–behavioural therapy (see Chapter 75) has also been used. Children are taught to stop and think before they undertake behaviours, and guide their own performance by deliberate self-instructions that are first made overtly and then covertly.

Also important in ADHD's management is counselling, specialist schooling, and parent training (Straw & Anderson, 1996). Parent training involves supervising medication and developing behavioural coping strategies. Most of these are good parenting strategies, and include things like dividing long assignments into small parts and giving lots of praise for effort. However, whilst most parents are often lax in implementing such strategies, parents of ADHD-children *must* adhere strictly to them (Prentice, 1996).

Clearly, ADHD is a complex disorder which may have multiple causes and effects. It could be that it is best explained in *interactionist* terms. Some children may have a biological predisposition for ADHD which is triggered in certain types of environment (Moffit, 1990). Interestingly, though, it has been suggested that ADHD is simply a label used to 'pathologise' children who are boisterous. Certainly, some parents of ADHD-children claim to be:

'frustrated by a wall of ignorance and often prejudice from the medical, educational and social services' (Sloan, 1995).

There are few specialist schools in Britain, and parents have sometimes moved to other countries (such as Australia) because the provision for ADHD-children is significantly better. However, the behaviours in ADHD *are* very different from 'normal' and can be identified as such by most observers (Boyd, 1996).

Autism

The term *early infantile autism* was coined by Kanner (1943). Literally, autism means 'selfism'. Kanner's use of the word came from his research with eleven children who were unresponsive and apparently oblivious to others, preferred non-social objects, either did not talk or repeated words, phrases and noises, and regularly engaged in self-stimulating and self-destructive behaviours, often for hours at a time. They also became upset when objects they had arranged in a special order were moved or changed. Some displayed incredible rote memory, particularly with respect to the arrangement of objects.

Kanner believed that the children's disorder was inborn and could be distinguished from other childhood psychoses. Both beliefs have been challenged. What is now called *childhood autism* in ICD-10 and *autistic disorder* in DSM-IV can be acquired at any time during the first three years of life, and some researchers have argued that autism and childhood schizophrenia are earlier and later manifestations of the same childhood psychosis (Bender, 1969). However, it is generally accepted that Kanner was right in his view that autism can be distinguished from childhood schizophrenia.

Box 80.5   Characteristics of autism

- **Social and interpersonal isolation:** Autistic children largely ignore other people, show little attachment even to their parents, and retreat into a 'private world' (*extreme autistic aloneness*).

- **Stereotyped behaviour:** Autistic children engage in ritualistic behaviours such as rocking back and forth or engaging in other repetitive behaviours for long, uninterrupted time periods. Each autistic child has an individualised repertoire of preferred stereotyped behaviours.

- **Disturbances of movement:** Varying among autistic children, and from one time to another, there may be hyperactivity or prolonged inactivity. However, autistic children have remarkable agility and dexterity. There may be a preoccupation with mechanical objects (e.g. light switches).

- **Resistance to changes in routine:** Autistic children establish strong habits and insist on sameness.

- **Abnormal responses to sensory stimuli:** Autistic children may ignore visual stimuli and sounds, especially speech, sometimes to the extent that they appear deaf. At other times, they may show 'startle reactions' to very mild stimuli.

- **Insensitivity to pain:** Autistic children are insensitive to cuts, burns, extreme hot or cold, and other pain, at least some of the time.

- **Inappropriate emotional expression:** Autistic children are inaccessible and emotionally unresponsive to people. Sometimes, they have sudden bouts of fear and crying for no obvious reason. At other times, they display utter fearlessness and unprovoked laughter.

- **Poor speech development:** Some autistic children never develop any spoken language (*mutism*). Others begin to develop speech and then lose it. They may learn the names of many common objects and develop good pronunciation. *Echolalic repetition* (repetition of words or phrases from TV commercials, songs, and so on) is common. However, language is literal, never used to ask for anything, or to interact socially. 'I' and 'yes' are absent until age six. Pronoun reversal also occurs. A boy might refer to himself as 'you', 'he', or his own name, but not as 'I'.

- **Specific, limited intellectual problems:** Many autistic children do well, sometimes extraordinarily well, on some tasks. These include remembering names and dates, performing complex calculations, drawing, and playing musical instruments. In general, though, their performance is very poor. It is often difficult to assess intelligence because autistic children generally do not follow the directions for completing IQ tests.

(Based on Rimland, 1964, and Kalat, 1984)

Figure 80.2   An example of the artistic abilities of a three-and-a-half-year-old autistic girl (Selfe, 1978)

Autistic disorder is rare (about one case per 5000 children), more frequently observed in boys, and usually identified by age 30 months. Contrary to popular belief, autism is not more prevalent in children from upper socioeconomic levels, and autistic children come from all ethnic backgrounds. Although the prognosis is generally poor, children who have developed some meaningful speech by age five are most likely to benefit from treatment.

THE CAUSES OF AUTISM

As noted previously, Kanner (1943) believed that autism was inborn. However, he also believed that it could be exacerbated by cold, detached, and unresponsive parents (what Kanner & Eisenberg, 1955, called 'emotional refrigerators'). Kanner argued that the parents' failure to form a relationship with the child resulted in the child never forming relationships with anyone else.

Kanner's theory was expanded by Bettelheim (1967), who proposed that autism is the result of parental failure to provide stimulation during the first nine months of life. The absence of stimulation means that the child is without a base on which to form emotional attachments (see Chapter 38) and develop speech and motor skills. It also feels unable to control the world as a result of parental unresponsiveness, and so withdraws into a private world, imposing order and constancy through the insistence on sameness (Bootzin & Acocella, 1984).

At least four lines of evidence indicate that this explanation of autism is invalid. First, autistic children's parents are not significantly different from those of children with other disorders. Second, brothers and sisters of autistic children are typically not autistic. Third, children who are seriously neglected do not usually show the characteristics of autism. Fourth, even if parents are unresponsive, it is not clear whether the unresponsiveness is a cause, consequence, or correlate of autism.

According to Ferster's (1961) behavioural account, autism can be explained in terms of parents' unresponsiveness resulting in children failing to learn adaptive responses. Despite the lack of evidence for the behavioural model, it has been helpful in the treatment of autism (see page 685) in the same way that behavioural techniques have been used to treat schizophrenia (see Chapter 74).

Whilst theorists like Kanner acknowledged the existence of cognitive deficits in autism, they saw them as the secondary consequence of primary social disturbances. Others, however, see the cognitive deficits as being primary and the social disturbances as a secondary consequence. Several such theories have been advanced. These implicate the impaired comprehension of sounds (Rutter, 1971), the modulation and integration of input from different sensory pathways (Hermelin & O'Connor, 1970), and overselectiveness of attention (Lovaas, 1978). One of the most promising cognitive approaches came from developmental psychologists' interest in the question 'How does a child become social?' and their answer to it, 'By becoming a proficient mindreader' (Baron-Cohen, 1997).

Box 80.6   'Mindreading'

We spend a great deal of our waking lives thinking about what other people might be thinking. The term 'mindreading' comes from primatology, and refers to our attempts to make sense of the social world around us. When normal children and adults see a social situation, they interpret it in terms of people's mental states – their thoughts, desires, intentions, beliefs, and so on. By age two, normally developing children understands that people might be pretending, and by age three they understand that people might know something or be ignorant of it. By age four, they understand that different people can have different, and even false, beliefs about the same situation.

Baron-Cohen *et al.* (1985) were the first to suggest that autistic children might have serious deficiencies in their abilities to 'mindread', and that this might account for their social difficulties. They used variations on a task devised by Wimmer & Perner (1983) to assess 'mindreading' in normally developing children. In one of these, the child is shown two dolls, 'Sally' and 'Anne'. Sally has a marble under her yellow box, and whilst Sally goes away, Anne moves the marble and places it under her blue box. Sally then returns, and the child is asked where she will look for her marble.

Baron-Cohen *et al.* (1985) found that when this task and others were given to autistic children, they failed to take into account the other person's mental model of the world, and referred only to their *own* model of it (most autistic children said that Sally would look under Anne's box). In Baron-Cohen *et al.*'s view, autistic children lack a *theory of mind* (ToM) and suffer from a specific form of '*mindblindness*' (the inability to perceive mental states in themselves and others). 'Specific' means that the autistic child's difficulty is not related to his or her general intelligence or language levels. It is also specific because autistic children can perform non-social tasks involving reasoning and logic at a level appropriate for their measured intelligence (Baron-Cohen, 1997).

Box 80.7   What must the world be like without a theory of mind?

Consider a quite ordinary situation: You are sitting with Mary, at the breakfast table and she suddenly leaps out of her chair and runs into another room. You might make sense of this by interpreting her behaviour as follows: Mary forgot something important in the other room, and wanted to get it. Or maybe she thought there was something in the room and wanted to show it to everyone. Referring to her thoughts or mental states gives us a way of making sense of her otherwise odd behaviour.

How would a child with autism react to Mary's behaviour? One reaction might be to withdraw from the social world because it is too confusing without a mindreading ability. Another might be to behave in a stereotyped and stilted manner (such as asking a person the same question) as a way of attempting to understand a complex and unpredictable world. Both reactions are typical of autistic children in social situations.

(Adapted from Baron-Cohen, 1997)

Baron-Cohen (1995) sees 'mindreading' as a universally human and evolutionarily advantageous behaviour. As a result of the pressures to survive in social environments,

a specific neural-based mechanism for representing what the individual and other people are thinking would have evolved. The benefits would include being able to recognise others' intentions, monitoring what others know or need to know, and being able to deceive them. What Baron-Cohen calls 'mindreading' has been called 'self-consciousness' and 'Machiavellian intelligence' by others.

Figure 80.3   The self-absorption displayed by this autistic girl prevents her from developing a normal 'theory of mind'

Baron-Cohen (1995) proposed the existence of four modules involved in 'mindreading'. These are the *intentionality detector* (ID), *eye-direction detector* (EDD), *shared-attention mechanism* (SAM) and the *theory of mind mechanism* (ToMM). Several studies have implicated genetic factors in autism. For example, a higher concordance rate for MZs than DZs has been found (Folstein & Rutter, 1977), and it is possible that genetic mechanisms build neural mechanisms for understanding the world in mentalistic ways (Baron-Cohen, 1997). The modules might have evolved because, as noted earlier, they would enable us to survive and succeed in social environments.

Evidence also suggests that mothers of autistic children suffer more complications during pregnancy, such as congenital rubella (Piggott, 1979), and these may damage the hypothesised modules, or produce some other neuro-cognitive deficit essential for mindreading's development. However, whilst some autistic children suffer from brain abnormalities (Courchesne *et al.*, 1988), there is no consistent evidence for one part of the brain being abnormal in all cases of the disorder (Garber & Ritvo, 1992).

Box 80.8   Autism and endorphins

Kalat (1984) has proposed that autistic children suffer from the over-production of *endorphins* (see Chapter 3, page 33), and this explains why, for example, they often show diminished reactions to extremely painful stimuli (see Box 80.5). Research with non-humans indicates that when they are given endorphins, they behave in ways similar to those seen in autistic children. Moreover, when substances which block endorphin production are given to autistic children, they apparently become more responsive to their social environment, show improved speech patterns, and reduce self-mutilative behaviour (McAuliffe, 1987).

TREATING AUTISM

As a result of their research, Baron-Cohen *et al.* (1992) have been able to improve the early diagnosis of autism, and in one study were able to predict which of a group of 'at risk' 18-month-olds would be diagnosed as autistic by age three. Several approaches to the treatment of autism have been developed. Biologically-based treatments include the neuroleptic drug *haloperidol* and serotonin-reducing drugs such as *fenfluramine* (Geller *et al.*, 1982). However, results have been disappointing and, of course, the drugs are associated with side-effects (see Chapter 72, pages 620–621).

Other biological approaches derive from the observation that certain allergies produce behaviours similar to those seen in autism, such as headbanging and screaming. As a result, *orthomolecular therapy*, in which autistic children are placed on low carbohydrate diets, and *megavitamin therapy*, in which large daily doses of vitamin B6 are given, have been tried. However, in those studies where the results have been encouraging, serious methodological criticisms have been made.

Behavioural approaches, particularly behaviour modification (see Chapter 74), have been used to eliminate some aspects of autism such as self-mutilative behaviour. Typically, these approaches use positive reinforcement or extinction, although these can be time-consuming (Harris *et al.*, 1991). For example, Simmons & Lovaas (1969) found that it took 1800 head bangs over an eight day period before that behaviour was extinguished by the withdrawal of social attention. Controversially, punish-

ment (in the form of electric shocks) has been used with autistic children (see also Chapter 74). This is evidently extremely effective in eliminating self-mutilative behaviour. For Lovaas (1977):

> 'Seemingly independently of how badly the child is mutilating himself or how long he has been doing so, we can essentially remove the self-destructive behaviour within the first minute'.

Autistic children are clearly not transformed into 'normal' children by behavioural methods. However, these methods may provide them with enough adaptive behaviours to cope more efficiently in the world, even though such approaches suffer from the problems of stimulus substitution (replacing one maladaptive behaviour with another) and generalising the changes from the therapeutic to other settings.

More cognitively based therapies involve *structural therapy*, in which the environment is structured to provide the child with spontaneous physical and verbal stimulation in the form of play and games. By increasing the amount of stimulation children receive, the therapy aims to make them more aware of themselves and their environment, and more related to it. Bartak (1978) views this therapy 'with qualified optimism'. Other approaches involve including the parents of autistic children in the treatment programme (which acknowledges their role as potential agents for change) and teaching children sign language. This takes advantage of their sensitivity to touch and movement, and circumvents their insensitivity to spoken language (Webster *et al.*, 1973). However despite the various attempts to treat autism and the improvements seen in *some* children, effective treatment still appears to be a long way off.

Conclusions

Both ADHD and autism are disorders whose causes are not yet clearly established. Although various approaches have been taken to their treatment, none is completely effective.

Summary

■ Two broad types of **attention deficit/hyperactivity disorder (ADHD)** are characterised by **hyperactivity** and **attentional problems**, although both may occur in the same individual.

■ ADHD is more prevalent in boys and occurs with greatest frequency before age ten. ADHD-children show poor social and emotional adjustment, and some of the difficulties associated with the disorder persist into adolescence and adulthood.

■ **Family variables** play a role in the course of ADHD, if not its cause. Stability and positive parent–child relationships predict positive outcomes in adolescence, whilst instability and punitive relationships are associated with anti-social behaviour in adolescence.

■ **Dietary factors** (e.g. food additives) have also been proposed to play a causal role in ADHD. Although the role of diet appears to have been overstated, the fact that some children are affected by food dyes suggests that this proposal cannot be completely discounted.

■ There is a higher concordance rate for ADHD in MZs than DZs, suggesting that genetic factors may be involved. ADHD may result from impaired neurological development, and several brain structures and cortical regions have been implicated. Although there is no compelling evidence of brain impairment, there might be several types of ADHD, only some of which are linked to neurological deficits.

■ A neurological perspective on ADHD is supported by the finding that stimulant drugs (such as *Ritalin*) are effective in treating ADHD. However, exactly why such drugs are effective is not known, and the use of drug therapies with children is controversial.

■ **Behaviour modification**, **relaxation training**, and **cognitive–behavioural therapy**, often in conjunction with drugs, have also been shown to be effective in ADHD's treatment. **Counselling**, **specialist schooling** and **parent training** are important in ADHD's management.

■ Literally, 'autism' means 'selfism'. **Childhood autism/autistic disorder** can develop at any time during the first three years of life. It is more frequent in boys, but not related to social class or ethnic background. The prognosis is generally poor, with those who have developed some speech by age five being most likely to benefit from treatment.

■ The characteristics of autism include **social and interpersonal isolation**, **stereotyped behaviour**, **poor speech development**, **insensitivity to pain**, and **inappropriate emotional expression**.

■ A promising approach to understanding autism's causes is based on the concept of **mindreading**, which refers to our attempts to make sense of the social world around us. Autistic children have serious deficiencies in their abilities to mindread.

■ Autistic children apparently lack a **theory of mind (ToM)** and suffer from a specific form of **mindblindness**, the ability to perceive mental states in themselves and others. Mindreading is universally human and evolutionarily advantageous.

■ 'Modules' involved in mindreading are the **intentionality detector**, **eye-direction detector**, **shared-attention mechanism** and **theory of mind mechanism**. Genetic mechanisms may build neural mechanisms for understanding the world in mentalistic ways. However, whilst some autistic children suffer from brain abnormalities, there is no consistent evidence for one part of the brain being abnormal in all cases of the disorder.

■ Biologically-based treatments include **drug therapies**, **orthomolecular therapy**, and **megavitamin therapy**. However, there is no compelling evidence of their effectiveness. **Behavioural approaches** are effective in providing autistic children with enough adaptive behaviours to cope more efficiently in the world.

■ **Structural therapy** is cognitively based and aims to make children more aware of themselves and their environments. Other approaches include involving parents in the treatment programme and teaching autistic children sign language, which makes use of their sensitivity to touch and movement.

UNIT 7

Perspectives

PART 1

Approaches to psychology

81

THE NATURE OF THE PERSON IN PSYCHOLOGY: FREE WILL AND DETERMINISM, AND REDUCTIONISM

Introduction and overview

As Chapter 83 shows, any discussion of psychology's scientific status raises fundamental questions about the nature of the person or, at least, the image of the person that underlies major psychological theories (see Chapter 1) and which is implicit in much of the study of human behaviour. This chapter discusses two of these fundamental questions. One, debated by Western philosophers for centuries, is whether we choose to act as we do, or whether behaviours are caused by influences beyond our control (*free will versus determinism*). The other, which has a shorter history and is debated by philosophers of science, concerns the validity of attempts to explain complex wholes in terms of their constituent parts (*reductionism*). One example of this is the relationship between the mind or consciousness and the brain (the '*mind–body problem*').

Free will and determinism

WHAT IS FREE WILL?

One way of approaching this question is to consider examples of behaviour where 'free will' (however defined) is clearly *absent*.

> **Box 81.1   A case of Tourette's disorder**
>
> Tim is 14 and displays a variety of twitches and tics. His head sometimes jerks and he often blinks and grimaces. Occasionally, he blurts out words, usually vulgarities. He does not mean to do it and is embarrassed by it, but he cannot control it. Because of his strange behaviour, most other children avoid him. His isolation and embarrassment are interfering with his social development. Tim suffers from a rare condition called Tourette's disorder.
>
> (From Holmes, 1994)

Exercise 1

What specific aspects of Tim's disorder are relevant to understanding the concept of 'free will'? If you think Tim lacks it, what led you to this conclusion? Think of other behaviours (normal or abnormal) that demonstrate a lack of free will.

Intuition tells us that people have the ability to choose their own courses of action, determine their behaviours and, to this extent, have *free will*. Simultaneously, though, this freedom is exercised only within certain physical, political, sociological and other environmental constraints. However, the positivistic, mechanistic nature of scientific psychology (see Chapter 83) implies

688

that behaviour is *determined* by external (or internal) events or stimuli and that people are passive responders. To this extent, people are *not* free. *Determinism* also implies that behaviour occurs in a regular, orderly manner which (in principle) is totally predictable. For Taylor (1963), determinism maintains that:

'in the case of everything that exists, there are antecedent conditions, known or unknown, given which that thing could not be other than it is ... More loosely, it says that everything, including every cause, is the effect of some cause or causes; or that everything is not only determinate but causally determined'.

'Everything that exists' includes people and their thoughts and behaviours, so a 'strict determinist' believes that thought and behaviours are no different from (other) 'things' or events in the world. However, this begs the question of whether thoughts and behaviours are the same *kind of thing or event* as, say, chemical reactions in a test tube, or neurons firing in the brain. We don't usually ask if the chemicals 'agreed' to combine in a certain way, or if the neurons 'decided' to fire. Unless we were trying to be witty, we would be guilty of *anthropomorphism* (attributing human abilities and characteristics to non-humans).

It is only *people* who can agree and make decisions. These abilities and capacities are part of our concept of a person, which, in turn, forms an essential part of 'everyday' or commonsense psychology (see Chapter 1). Agreeing and deciding are precisely the kinds of things we do *with our minds* (they are mental processes or events), and to be able to agree and make decisions, it is necessary to 'have a mind'. So, free will implies having a mind. However, having a mind does not imply free will: it is possible that decisions and so on are themselves *caused* (determined), even though they seem to be freely chosen.

Exercise 2

Try to explain what someone means when he or she says: 'I had no choice but to ...' or 'You leave me no choice ...'. Can you interpret this in a way that is consistent with a belief in free will?

DIFFERENT MEANINGS OF 'FREE WILL'

One of the difficulties with the free will versus determinism debate is the ambiguity of the concepts involved.

Having a choice

The 'actor' could have behaved differently, given the same circumstances. This contrasts sharply with a common definition of determinism, namely that things could only have happenend as they did, given everything that happened previously.

Not being coerced or constrained

If someone puts a loaded gun to your head and tells you to do something, your behaviour is clearly not free: you have been *forced* to act this way. This is usually where the philosophical debate about 'free' will *begins*. It is also related to what James (1890) called *soft determinism* (see pages 691–692).

Voluntary

If 'involuntary' conveys reflex behaviour (such as the eye-blink response to a puff of air directed at the eye), then 'voluntary' implies 'free' (the behaviour is not automatic). By definition, most behaviour (human and non-human) is *not* reflex, nor is it usually the result of coercion. So is most behaviour free?

Box 81.2   Evidence for the distinction between voluntary and involuntary behaviour

Penfield's (1947) classic experiments involved stimulating the cortex of patients about to undergo brain surgery (see Chapter 6). Even though the cortical area being stimulated was the same as that which is involved when we normally ('voluntarily') move our limbs, patients reported feeling that their arms and legs were being moved passively, quite a different experience from initiating the movement themselves. This demonstrates that the *subjective experience* (phenomenology) of the voluntary movement of one's limbs cannot be *reduced* to the stimulation of the appropriate brain region (otherwise Penfield's patients should not have reported a difference). Doing things voluntarily simply *feels* different from the 'same' things 'just happening'. Similarly, see Delgado's (1969) study, (page 60).

If this is true for bodily movements, then it adds weight to the claim that having free will is an undeniable part of our subjective experience of ourselves as people. The sense of self is most acute (and important and real for us) where moral decisions and feelings of responsibility for past actions are involved (Koestler, 1967). See text and Box 81.3 for further discussion of free will and moral responsibility.

One demonstration of people's belief in their free will is *psychological reactance* (Brehm, 1966; Brehm & Brehm, 1981: see Chapter 17). A common response to the feeling that our freedom is being threatened is the attempt to regain or reassert it, which is related to the need to be free from others' controls and restrictions, to determine our own actions, and not be dictated to. A good deal of contrary (resistant) behaviour, otherwise known as 'bloody-mindedness' ('Don't tell me what to do!') seems to reflect this process (Carver & Scheier, 1992).

Similar to this need to feel free from others' control is *intrinsic motivation* or *self-determination* (Deci, 1980; Deci & Ryan, 1987). This refers to people's intrinsic interest in things, such that they do not need to be offered extrinsic incentives for doing them. Engaging in such activities is motivated by the desire for competence and self-determination.

So what happens if someone is offered an extrinsic reward for doing something which is already interesting and enjoyable in itself? Lepper *et al.* (1973) found that the activity loses its intrinsic appeal, and motivation is reduced (the *paradox of reward*: see Chapter 17, page 141). This has implications for accounts of moral development based on learning theory principles, especially operant conditioning (see Chapters 32 and 44).

Exercise 3

How could you account for the 'paradox of reward' in terms of attributional principles, specifically, internal and external causes? (See Chapter 52.)

Deliberate control

Norman & Shallice (1986) define divided attention as an upper limit to the amount of processing that can be performed on incoming information at any one time. They propose three levels of functioning, namely *fully automatic processing*, *partially automatic processing*, and *deliberate control* (see Chapter 26, pages 223–224). Deliberate control corresponds to free will.

Driving a car is a sensory–motor skill, performed by experienced drivers more-or-less automatically. It does not require deliberate, conscious control, unless some unexpected event disrupts the performance (such as putting your foot on the brake when there is an obstacle ahead: this is a 'rule of the game'). However, on an icy road, this can be risky, since the steering wheel has a different 'feel' and the whole driving strategy must be changed. After doing it several times, this too may become a semi-automatic routine:

'but let a little dog amble across the icy road in front of the driver, and he will have to make a 'top-level decision' whether to slam down the brake, risking the safety of his passengers, or run over the dog. And if, instead of a dog, the jaywalker is a child, he will probably resort to the brake, whatever the outcome. It is at this level, when the pros and cons are equally balanced, that the subjective experience of freedom and moral responsibility arises' (Koestler, 1967).

As we move downwards from conscious control, the subjective experience of freedom diminishes. According to Koestler:

'Habit is the enemy of freedom ... Machines cannot become like men, but men can become like machines'.

Koestler also maintains that the second enemy of freedom is very powerful (especially negative) emotion:

'When [emotions] are aroused, the control of decisions is taken over by those primitive levels of the hierarchy which the Victorians called 'the Beast in us' and which are in fact correlated to phylogenetically older structures in the nervous system'.

The arousal of these structures results in 'diminished responsibility' and 'I couldn't help it' (Koestler, 1967).

Exercise 4

In Koestler's quote above, (a) what does 'phylogenetically older structures' mean? and (b) what are the major 'primitive levels of the hierarchy' correlated with these structures? (See Chapter 4, page 40 and Chapter 18.)

WHY SHOULD PSYCHOLOGISTS BE INTERESTED IN THE CONCEPT OF FREE WILL?

As noted in the *Introduction and overview*, the philosophical debate about free will and determinism is centuries old. It can be traced back at least to the French philosopher Descartes (1596–1650), whose ideas had a great influence on both science in general and psychology in particular. For much of its history as a separate, scientific discipline, psychology has operated as if there were no difference between natural, physical phenomena and human thought and behaviour (see pages 694–695).

During the period 1913–1956, psychology (at least in the USA) was dominated by behaviourism, Skinner being particularly influential. Skinner's beliefs about the influence of mental phenomena on behaviour, and those concerning free will, are discussed on pages 693–694.

Exercise 5

Try to identify some (other) ways in which the issue of free will is relevant to psychological theory and practice. For example, how does the notion of free will relate to criteria for defining and diagnosing mental disorders? (See Chapter 65.)

FREE WILL AND PSYCHOLOGICAL ABNORMALITY

Definitions of abnormality, and the diagnosis and treatment of mental disorders, often involve implicit or explicit judgements about free will and determinism. In a general sense, mental disorders can be seen as the partial or complete breakdown of the control people normally have over their thoughts, emotions and behaviours. For example, *compulsive* behaviour, by definition, is behaviour which a person cannot help but do: he or she is 'compelled' to do it. People are *attacked* by panic, *obsessed* by thoughts of germs, or become the *victims* of thoughts which are *inserted* into their mind from outside and are under external influence (see Chapter 68, page 586). In all these examples, things are happening to, or being done to, the individual (instead of the individual *doing them*), both from the individual's perspective and that of a psychologist or psychiatrist.

Being judged to have lost control (possession of which is usually thought of as a major feature of normality), either temporarily or permanently, is a legally acceptable defence in cases of criminal offences.

Box 81.3 Forensic psychiatry, diminished responsibility and the law

Forensic psychiatry deals with assessment and treatment of mentally disturbed offenders. The 1983 Mental Health Act has several clauses providing for the compulsory detention of prisoners (either while awaiting trial or as part of their sentences) in hospital. Psychiatrists, as expert witnesses, can play important roles in advising the Court about:

1 fitness to plead;

2 mental state at the time of the offence;

3 diminished responsibility.

The defence of *diminished responsibility* (for murder) was introduced in England and Wales in the 1957 Homicide Act, largely replacing the plea of 'not guilty by reason of insanity', which was based on the 'McNaughton Rules' of 1843.

If accepted, there is no trial and a sentence of manslaughter is passed. If not accepted, a trial is held and the jury must decide whether the accused (at the time the crime was committed) was suffering from an abnormality of mind, and if so, whether it was such as to substantially impair his or her responsibility.

Peter Sutcliffe, the 'Yorkshire Ripper', was found guilty of the murder of 13 women and the attempted murder of seven others, despite his defence that he heard God's voice telling him to 'get rid' of prostitutes. In finding him guilty of murder, the jury did not necessarily reject the defence's argument that he was suffering from paranoid schizophrenia, only that it did not constitute an abnormality of mind of sufficient degree to substantially impair his mental responsibility for his acts.

Sutcliffe was sentenced to 20 concurrent terms of life imprisonment, which he served initially in an ordinary prison before being sent to Broadmoor Special Hospital.

(Based on Gelder *et al.*, 1989, and Prins, 1995)

FREE WILL AND MORAL ACCOUNTABILITY

Underlying the whole question of legal (and moral) responsibility is the presupposition that people are, at least some of the time, able to control their behaviours and choose between different courses of action. How else could we ever be held responsible for *any* of our actions? In most everyday situations and interactions, we attribute responsibility, both to ourselves and others, unless we have reason to doubt it. According to Flanagan (1984):

'it seems silly to have any expectations about how people ought to act, if everything we do is the result of some inexorable causal chain which began millenia ago. 'Ought', after all, seems to imply 'can', therefore, by employing a moral vocabulary filled with words like 'ought' and 'should', we assume that humans are capable of rising above the causal pressures presented by the material world, and, in assuming this we appear to be operating with some conception of freedom, some notion of free will'.

FREE WILL AS AN ISSUE IN MAJOR PSYCHOLOGICAL THEORIES

Most major theorists in psychology have addressed the issue of free will and determinism, including James, Freud, Skinner, and Rogers.

James and soft determinism

As was seen in Chapter 1, James pioneered psychology as a separate, scientific discipline. In *The Principles of Psychology* (1890), he devoted a whole chapter to the 'will', which he related to attention:

'The most essential achievement of the will ... when it is most 'voluntary' is to *attend* to a different object and hold it fast before the mind ... Effort of attention is thus the essential phenomenon of will'.

For James, there was a conflict. Belief in determinism seemed to fit best with the scientific view of the world, whilst belief in free will seemed to be required by our social, moral, political, and legal practices, as well as by our personal, subjective experience (see above). His solution to this conflict was two-fold.

First, he distinguished between the scientific and non-scientific worlds. Psychology as a science could only progress by assuming determinism, but this does not

691

mean that belief in free will must be abandoned in other contexts. So, scientific explanation is not the only useful kind of explanation.

Second, he drew a further distinction between *soft* and *hard* determinism. According to *soft determinism*, the question of free will depends on the type(s) of cause(s) our behaviour has, not whether it is caused or not caused (the opposite of 'not caused' is 'random', not 'free'). If our actions have, as their immediate (proximate) cause, processing by a system such as *conscious mental life* (or CML, which includes consciousness, purposefulness, personality and personal continuity), then they count as free, rational, voluntary, purposive actions.

According to *hard determinism*, CML is itself caused, so that the immediate causes are only part of the total causal chain which results in the behaviour we are trying to explain. Therefore, as long as our behaviour is caused at all, there is no sense in which we can be described as acting freely.

Freud and psychic determinism

Although in most respects their ideas about human behaviour are diametrically opposed, Freud and Skinner shared the fundamental belief that free will is an illusion. However, in keeping with their theories as a whole, their reasons are radically different.

Exercise 6

Based on what you already know about Freud's psychoanalytic theory, try to identify those parts which are most relevant to his rejection of free will.

According to Strachey (1962):

'Behind all of Freud's work ... we should posit his belief in the universal validity of the law of determinism ... Freud extended the belief (derived from physical phenomena) uncompromisingly to the field of mental phenomena'.

Similarly, Sulloway (1979) maintains that all of Freud's work in science (and Freud saw himself very much as a scientist) was characterised by an abiding faith in the notion that all vital phenomena, including psychical (psychological) ones, are rigidly and lawfully determined by the principle of cause and effect. One major example of this was the extreme importance he attached to the technique of *free association*.

Box 81.4　How 'free' is Freud's 'free association'?

'Free association' is a misleading translation of the German *'freier Einfall'*, which conveys much more accurately the intended impression of an uncontrollable 'intrusion' (*'Einfall'*) by pre-conscious ideas into conscious thinking. In turn, this pre-conscious material reflects *unconscious* ideas, wishes and memories (what Freud was really interested in), since here lay the principal cause(s) of neurotic problems.

It is a great irony that 'free' association should refer to a technique used in psychoanalysis meant to reveal the *unconscious causes* of behaviour (see Chapter 73, page 629). It is because the causes of our thoughts, actions and supposed choices are unconscious (mostly *actively repressed*), that we *think* we are free. Freud's application of this general philosophical belief in causation to mental phenomena is called *psychic determinism*.

(Based on Sulloway, 1979)

For Freud, part of what 'psychic determinism' conveyed was that in the universe of the mind. there are no 'accidents'. No matter how apparently random or irrational behaviour may be (such as 'parapraxes' or 'Freudian slips'), unconscious causes can always account for them, and this also applies to hysterical symptoms and dreams. As Gay (1988) states, '... Freud's theory of the mind is ... strictly and frankly deterministic'. However:

- Freud accepted that true accidents, in the sense of forces beyond the victim's control (e.g. being struck by lightning), can and do occur, and are not unconsciously caused by the victim.

- One of the aims of psychoanalysis is to 'give the patient's ego *freedom* to decide one way or another' (Freud, quoted in Gay, 1988), so therapy rests on the belief that people *can* change. However, Freud saw the extent of possible change as being very limited.

- One aspect of psychic determinism is *overdetermination*, that is, much of our behaviour has *multiple* causes, both conscious and unconscious. So, although our conscious choices, decisions and intentions may genuinely influence behaviour, they never tell the whole story.

- Despite never having predicted in advance what choice or decision a patient would make, Freud maintained that these are not arbitrary and can be understood as revealing personality characteristics (Rycroft, 1966). What Freud often did was to explain his patients' choices, neurotic symptoms, and so on *not* in terms of causes (the *scientific* argument), but by trying to make sense of them and give them meaning (the *semantic* argument). Indeed, the latter is supported by the title of, arguably, his greatest book, *The Interpretation of Dreams* (1900) (as opposed to *The 'Cause' of Dreams*).

Skinner and the illusion of free will

Like Freud, Skinner sees free will as an illusion. However, whilst Freud focused on 'the mind', especially unconscious thoughts, wishes, and memories, Skinner's *radical behaviourism* eliminates all reference to mental or private states as part of the explanation of behaviour (including theories like Freud's!).

Although Skinner does not deny that pain and other internal states exist, they have no 'causal teeth' and hence no part to play in scientific explanations of (human) behaviour (Garrett, 1996). Free will (and other '*explanatory fictions*') cannot be defined or measured objectively, nor are they needed for successful prediction and control of behaviour (for Skinner, the primary aims of a science of behaviour). It is only because the causes of human behaviour are often hidden from us in the environment, that the myth or illusion of free will survives.

Exercise 7

Given what you know about Skinner's theory of operant conditioning and his 'analysis of behaviour', try to identify the causes of human behaviour which he believes are often hidden from us in the environment (see Chapters 1 and 32).

Skinner argues that when what we do is dictated by force or punishment, or by their threat (negative reinforcement), it is obvious to everyone that we are not acting freely. For example, when the possibility of prison stops us committing crimes, there is clearly no choice involved, because we know what the environmental causes of our behaviour are. Similarly, it may sometimes be very obvious which positive reinforcers are shaping behaviour (a bonus for working over-time, for example).

However, most of the time we are unaware of environmental causes, and it looks (and feels) as if we are behaving freely. Yet all this means is that we are free of punishments or negative reinforcement, and behaviour is still determined by the pursuit of things that have been positively reinforced in the past. When we perceive others as behaving freely, we are simply unaware of their reinforcement histories (Fancher, 1996).

Box 81.5   The freedom myth and the rejection of punishment

In *Beyond Freedom and Dignity*, Skinner (1971) argued that the notion of 'autonomous man', upon which so many of Western society's assumptions are based, is both false and has many harmful consequences. In particular, the assumption that people are free *requires* that they are constantly exposed to punishment and its threat as a negative reinforcer (Fancher, 1996).

Based on experiments with rats and pigeons, Skinner argued that positive reinforcement is more effective than negative reinforcement or punishment in producing lasting conditioning effects. In Skinner's version of Utopia (described in his novel *Walden Two*, 1948), negative reinforcement is completely abandoned as a means of social control. Children are reared only to seek positive reinforcement contingent upon their showing socialised, civilised behaviour. Inevitably, they grow up to be cooperative, intelligent, sociable and happy.

Exercise 8

What *ethical* issues are raised by Skinner's advocacy of a utopian society like *Walden Two*? In what ways does this Utopia reflect Skinner's beliefs about the aims of a scientific psychology?

Skinner and moral responsibility

Clearly, Skinner's belief that free will is an illusion conflicts with the need to attribute people with free will if we are to hold them (and ourselves) morally (and legally) responsible for their behaviour. Skinner (1971) himself acknowledges that freedom and dignity are:

'essential to practices in which a person is held responsible for his conduct and given credit for his achievements'.

However, Skinner equates 'good' and 'bad' with 'beneficial to others' (what is rewarded) and 'harmful to others' (what is punished) respectively, thus removing morality from human behaviour. For Skinner, 'oughts' are not 'moral imperatives': they reflect *practical*, rather than moral, guidelines and rules (Morea, 1990).

According to Garrett (1996), if we are rational, thinking creatures capable of assessing ethical rules and principles and evaluating the goodness of our lives, then we have all the freedom needed to reasonably prefer democratic to non- (or anti-) democratic forms of government (as expressed in *Walden Two* and *Beyond Freedom and Dignity*).

A further consequence of Skinner's rejection of the notion of 'autonomous man' is what Ringen (1996) calls *the behaviour therapist's dilemma*, which is closely related to

693

some of the most fundamental *ethical* issues faced by psychologists as *agents of change* (see Chapter 85, pages 746–748).

Box 81.6   The behaviour therapist's dilemma

Ringen (1996) claims that there is a deep tension between two features of modern clinical psychology. On the one hand, Skinner (1971) argues that scientific considerations support radical behaviourism as the most appropriate framework for understanding and facilitating the development of effective behaviour therapy (including methods based on both classical and operant conditioning). On the other hand, an increasingly significant ethical and legal constraint on therapeutic practice, the doctrine of informed consent, obliges behaviour therapists (and other practitioners in the helping professions, including psychiatry) to acknowledge the autonomy of those who come to them for help.

The behaviour therapist's dilemma describes a widely accepted assessment of why these two aspects of modern clinical psychology are in tension, namely, that *either* radical behaviourism is false *or* human beings never act autonomously. This involves having to choose between alternatives that many contemporary behaviour therapists would find it difficult to defend.

(From Ringen, 1996)

Rogers, freedom and the fully functioning person

As was seen in Chapter 1, Rogers was perhaps the most influential *humanistic, phenomenological* psychologist. As such, he stressed the process of self-actualisation and the necessity of adopting the other person's perspective if we are to understand that person, and in particular, his or her self-concept.

Understanding the self-concept is also central to Rogers' *client-centred therapy* (see Chapter 76, pages 650–653). His experience as a therapist convinced him that real change does occur in therapy: people choose to see themselves and their life situations differently. Therapy and life are about free human beings struggling to become more free. Personal experience is important, but it does not imprison us. How we react to our experience is something we ourselves choose and decide (Morea, 1990).

Exercise 9

According to Rogers, in what ways are individuals prevented from recognising their *true* feelings and behaviour? In what respects is Rogers' view of human beings a more optimistic one than, say, Freud's?

Rogers' deep and lasting trust in human nature did not, however, blind him to the reality of evil *behaviour*:

'In my experience, every person has the capacity for evil behaviour. I, and others, have had murderous and cruel impulses ... feelings of anger and rage, desires to impose our wills on others ... Whether I ... will translate these impulses into behaviour depends ... on two elements: social conditioning and voluntary choice' (Rogers, 1982, cited in Thorne, 1992).

By making the distinction between 'human nature' and behaviour, Rogers retains his optimistic view of human beings. However, this did not exclude altogether a deterministic element in his later writings. In *Freedom to Learn for the '80s* (1983), he states that it is becoming clear from science that human beings are complex machines and not free. So how can this be reconciled with self-actualisation, psychological growth, and the freedom to choose?

One proposed solution is in the form of a version of soft determinism. Unlike neurotic and incongruent people (see Chapter 76), whose defensiveness forces them to act in ways they would prefer not to, the healthy, fully functioning person:

'not only experiences, but utilises, the most absolute freedom when he spontaneously, freely and voluntarily chooses and wills that which is absolutely determined'.

The fully functioning person chooses to act and be the way he or she has to. It is the most satisfying way to behave (Morea, 1990).

Reductionism

WHAT IS REDUCTIONISM?

Together with positivism, mechanism, determinism, and empiricism, reductionism represents part of 'classical' science (see Chapter 83). Luria (1987) traces the origins of reductionism to the mid-nineteenth century view within biology that the organism is a complex of organs and the organs are complexes of cells. To explain the basic laws of the living organism, we have to study as carefully as possible the features of separate cells.

From its biological origins, reductionism was extended to science in general. For example, the properties of a protein molecule could be uniquely determined or predicted in terms of properties of the electrons or protons making up its atoms. Consistent with this view is Garnham's (1991) definition of reductionism as:

'the idea that psychological explanations can be replaced by explanations in terms of brain functioning or even in terms of physics and chemistry'.

Although reductionism's ultimate aim (according to its supporters) is to account for all phenomena in terms of microphysics, *any* attempt to explain something in terms of its components or constituent parts may be thought of as reductionist. A useful definition, which is consistent with this broader view, is that of Rose *et al.* (1984), for whom reductionism is:

'the name given to a set of general methods and modes of explanation both of the world of physical objects and of human societies. Broadly, reductionists try to explain the properties of complex wholes – molecules, say, or societies – in terms of the units of which those molecules or societies are composed'.

Exercise 10

There are many examples of psychological theories and concepts which fit either or both of Garnham's and Rose *et al.*'s definitions. These can be found in all areas of the syllabus, but below are a few of the more 'obvious' examples. For each one, try to explain (a) *why* the theory or concept is reductionist, and (b) what are the strengths and/or weaknesses of such an approach.

i According to *structuralism* (e.g. Wundt), perception is simply a series of sensations. (see Chapter 83).
ii According to Watson's *peripheralism*, thought consists of tiny movements of the vocal chords (see Chapter 37).
iii Intelligence is a person's performance on a standardised intelligence test (his or her IQ score: see Chapter 43).
iv Psychological sex differences are caused by biological factors (such as hormones: see Chapter 45).
v According to Freud, personality development involves progress through a series of *psychosexual* stages (see Chapter 66).
vi Schizophrenia is caused by an excess of the neurotransmitter, dopamine (see Chapter 68).
vii According to Adorno *et al.*, anti-semitism (and other forms of racism) are symptomatic of the *authoritarian personality* (see Chapter 53).

THE MIND–BODY PROBLEM: WHAT IS THE RELATIONSHIP BETWEEN MIND AND BRAIN?

Perhaps the oldest and most frequently debated example of reductionism is the mind–body problem (or the problem of mind and brain). Originally a philosophical issue, it continues to be discussed, often passionately, by neurophysiologists, biologists, neuropsychologists and psychologists in general.

While it is generally agreed that the mind (or consciousness) is a property of human beings (as is walking upright on two legs), and that without the human brain there would be no consciousness, a 'problem' remains.

Box 81.7   The problem of the mind–brain relationship

- How can two 'things' be related when one of them is physical (the brain has size, weight, shape, density, exists in space and time) and the other apparently lacks all these characteristics?

- How can something that is non-physical/non-material (the mind) influence or produce changes in something that is physical (the brain/body)?

The 'classic' example given by philosophers to illustrate the problem is the act of deciding to lift one's arm. (This example also illustrates the exercise of [free] will: see text.) From a strictly scientific perspective, this kind of causation should be impossible, and science (including psychology and neurophysiology) has traditionally rejected any brand of *philosophical dualism*, that is, the belief in the existence of two essentially different kinds of 'substance', the physical body and the non-physical mind (see Table 81.8).

From an evolutionary perspective, could consciousness have equipped human beings with survival value *unless* it had causal properties (Gregory, 1981), that is, unless it could actually bring about changes in behaviour? Our subjective experiences tell us that our minds *do* affect behaviour and that consciousness does have causal properties (just try lifting your arm). However, many philosophers and scientists from various disciplines have not always shared the layperson's common sense understanding.

Whilst there are many theories of the mind–brain relationship, most are not strictly relevant to the debate about reductionism. Box 81.8 and Figure 81.1 summarise most of the major theories, but emphasis will be given to reductionist approaches, especially as they impinge on *psychological* theories.

Box 81.8   Some major theories of the mind–brain relationship

- Theories fall into two main categories: *dualism* (which distinguishes between mind and brain), and *monism* (which claims that only mind *or* matter is real).

- According to Descartes' seventeenth century dualist theory (which first introduced the mind–body problem into philosophy), the mind can influence the

---

695

brain, but not vice versa. Whilst *epiphenomenology* sees the mind as a kind of by-product of the brain (the mind has no influence on the brain), *interactionism* sees the influence as two-way.

- *Psychophysical parallelists* are dualists who believe that there is no mind–brain interaction at all: mental and neural events are merely perfectly synchronised or correlated.

- According to *mentalism/idealism*, only mental phenomena are real. *Phenomenological* theories, such as that of Rogers, and *constructionist* explanations of behaviour, have a mentalist 'flavour'.

- Most monist theories take one or other form of *materialism*.

- The *peripheralist* version of materialism is illustrated by Skinner's *radical behaviourism* (see Chapter 1, pages 9–10). During the 1930s, Skinner denied the existence of mental phenomena (as Watson, the founder of behaviourism, had done). However, from 1945 he began to adopt a less extreme view, recognising their existence, but defining them as *covert/internal actions*, subject to the same laws as overt behavioural events (those of conditioning). This *is* a form of reductionism.

- *Centralist materialism* (or *mind–brain identity theory*) identifies mental processes with purely physical processes in the central nervous system. Whilst it is logically possible that there might be separate, mental, non-physical phenomena, it just turns out that, as a matter of fact, mental states are identical with physical states of the brain. We are, simply, very complicated physico-chemical mechanisms.

- *Eliminative materialism* represents an extreme reductionist form of (centralist) materialism: see text.

(Based on Flanagan, 1984; Gross, 1995, and Teichman, 1988)

Exercise 11

Using your knowledge of biopsychology, try to relate the examples below to the theories outlined in Box 81.8 and Figure 81.1. Specifically, do these examples involve *interactions* between mind and brain, and, if so, in what direction is the influence taking place?

a The effects of psychoactive drugs (see Chapters 15 and 72).
b Electrical stimulation of the brain (see Chapter 6).
c Sperry's study of split-brain patients (see Chapter 9).
d Stress (see Chapter 20).

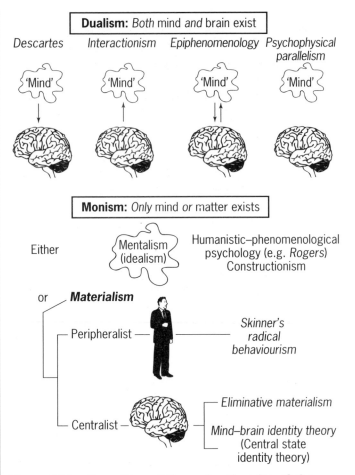

Figure 81.1   An outline of the major theories of the mind–brain relationship

REDUCTIONIST THEORIES OF THE MIND–BRAIN RELATIONSHIP

As Box 81.8 shows, *eliminative materialism* is an extreme form of reductionist materialism. What makes it reductionist is the attempt to *replace* a psychological account of behaviour with an account in terms of neurophysiology. An example of this approach is Crick's (1994) *The Astonishing Hypothesis: The Scientific Search for the Soul*. According to Crick:

'You, your joys and your sorrows, your memories and your ambitions, your sense of personality and free will, are in fact no more than the behaviour of a vast assembly of nerve cells and their associated molecules'.

But is this a valid equation to make? According to Smith (1994), the mind and brain problem is radically different from other cases of *contingent identity* (identical as a matter of fact) with which it is usually compared, such as 'a gene is a section of the DNA molecule'. What is different is reductionism and the related issue of exactly what is meant by *identity*.

Box 81.9   Different meanings of 'identity' relevant to the mind–brain relationship

Whilst it is generally agreed that we cannot have a mind without a brain, mind states and brain states are not systematically correlated, and the neurophysiological and neurological evidence points towards *token identity*. For example, we cannot just assume that the same neurophysiological mechanisms will be used by two different people both engaged in the 'same' activity of reading (Broadbent, 1981). There are many ways that 'the brain' can perform the same task.

But it is precisely this kind of systematic correlation that mind–brain identity has been taken to imply, whereby whenever a mind state of a certain type occurs, a brain state of a certain type occurs (*type identity*). Token identity means that there must always be a place for an autonomous psychological account of human thought and action.

(Based on Harré *et al.*, 1985)

According to Penrose (1990), there is a built-in indeterminacy in the way that individual neurons and their synaptic connections work (their responses are inherently unpredictable). Yet, despite this unpredictability at the level of the individual units or components, the system as a whole is predictable. The 'nervous system' (or subsystems within it) does not operate randomly, but in a highly organised, structured way.

Consciousness, intelligence, and memory are properties of the brain as a system, *not* properties of the individual units, and they could not possibly be predicted from analysing the units. Instead, they 'emerge' from interactions between the units that compose the system (and so are called *emergent properties*). The whole is greater than the sum of its parts (see Chapter 21, page 173).

CAN YOU BE A MATERIALIST WITHOUT BEING A REDUCTIONIST?

According to Rose (1992):

'the mind is never replaced by the brain. Instead we have two distinct and legitimate languages, each describing the same unitary phenomena of the material world'.

Rose speaks as a materialist and an *anti-reductionist*, who believes that we should learn how to translate between mind language and brain language (although this may be impossibly difficult). Whilst most materialists are also reductionists, and vice versa, this is not necessarily so. Freud, for example, was a materialist who believed that no single scientific vocabulary (such as anatomy) could adequately describe (let alone explain) all facets of the material world. He believed in the *autonomy of psychological explanation*.

The fact that there are different 'languages' for describing minds and brains (or different *levels of description* or *universes of discourse*) relates to the question of the relevance of knowing, say, what is going on inside our brains when we think or are aware. For Eiser (1994):

'The firing of neurons stands to thought in the same relation as my walking across the room (etc.) stands to my getting some coffee. It is absolutely essential in a causal or physical sense, and absolutely superfluous ... to the logic of the higher-order description. In short, I can accept that it happens, and then happily ignore it'.

This explains how it is possible to be simultaneously a materialist (the brain is necessarily implicated in everything we do and the mind does not represent a different kind of reality) *and* an anti-reductionist (we can describe and explain our thinking without having to 'bring my brain into it'). Two separate levels of description are involved.

Conclusions

Given psychology's intellectual and historical roots in philosophy and natural science, it is hardly surprising that psychological theories have contributed to the debate about free will versus determinism, and reductionism. The possession of free will is a fundamental aspect of our common sense concept of a person. Therefore, any theory calling itself psychological must have something to say about this issue. Equally, belief (or not) in the independence of psychological from neurophysiological explanations of behaviour, is crucial to the survival of psychology itself as a separate discipline. This chapter has tried to capture some of the essential features of both these issues.

Summary

■ Our intuitive belief in free will conflicts with the scientific belief in determinism. Determinism also implies behaviour's complete predictability and that everything (including thoughts and behaviour) has a cause. Whilst free will implies having a mind, the things we do with our minds may themselves be determined, despite appearing to be freely chosen.

■ Free will is an ambiguous concept and can denote having a choice, not being coerced or constrained, voluntary (as opposed to reflex), and deliberate control (as opposed to automatic information processing). The more automatic our behaviours, the weaker our subjective experience of freedom becomes.

■ Penfield demonstrated that voluntarily moving one's limbs involves a different **subjective experience** compared with brain stimulation causing one's limbs to move. This supports the view that free will is part of our experience of being a person, which is demonstrated by **psychological reactance**. Similar to this need to feel free from others' control is **intrinsic motivation/self-determination**.

■ Definitions of abnormality, and the diagnosis and treatment of mental disorders, often involve judgements about free will. Temporary or permanent loss of control is a legally acceptable defence in criminal cases, as in the **diminished responsibility** defence (for murder). Legal and moral responsibility presuppose free will.

■ For James, a conflict exists between science's belief in determinism and belief in free will as required by other social institutions. He proposed that psychology as a science could only progress by assuming determinism, but belief in free will could be maintained in other contexts. James also distinguished between **soft** and **hard determinism**, the former allowing **conscious mental life** to be the immediate cause of behaviour.

■ Freud extended the law of determinism to mental phenomena (**psychic determinism**). Ironically, 'free' association was used in psychoanalysis to reveal the **unconscious causes** of behaviour, our ignorance of which creates an **illusion** of freedom.

■ However, Freud recognised the occurrence of 'true' accidents, and argued that therapy enables people to change in limited ways. His concept of **overdetermination** allows the **conscious** mind a role in influencing behaviour, and he often tried to interpret the **meaning** of patients' thoughts and behaviours (rather than look for causes).

■ Skinner's radical behaviourism involves a rejection of **explanatory fictions**, such as free will and other mentalistic terms. The illusion of free will survives because the environmental causes of behaviour are often hidden from us. He advocated that negative reinforcement and punishment should be abandoned as means of social control, with only positive reinforcement being used for socialised, civilised behaviour.

■ Skinner rejects the notion of 'autonomous man' and removes morality from human behaviour by equating 'good' and bad' with what is rewarded and punished respectively. One consequence of this is **the behaviour therapist's dilemma**.

■ Rogers stressed self-actualisation, psychological growth and the freedom to choose. The need to understand people's self-concepts is central to his **client-centred therapy**, which enables people to change and become more free.

■ However, whilst remaining optimistic about 'human nature', Rogers argued that science shows people to be complex machines and not free. The fully functioning person chooses to act the way he or she must.

■ Originating in biology, **reductionism** became part of science in general. Although its supporters see reductionism's ultimate aim as accounting for all phenomena (including psychological) in terms of microphysics, **any** attempt to explain something in terms of its components is reductionist. A long-debated example is the **mind–body problem**.

■ Whilst it is generally agreed that a brain is necessary for consciousness, the problem remains of how the non-physical mind can influence the physical brain. From a strictly scientific perspective, such influence should be impossible. However, from an evolutionary perspective, consciousness should be able to produce behaviour change, which is what our subjective experience tells us.

■ Theories of the mind–brain relationship are either **dualist** or **monist**. Dualist theories include Descartes' original dualism, epiphenomenology, interactionism, and psychophysical parallelism. Monist theories include mentalism/idealism, **peripheralist materialism** (such as Skinner's radical behaviourism) and **centralist materialism/mind–brain identity theory**.

■ Skinner's definition of mental phenomena as **covert/internal actions** is reductionist, as is **eliminative materialism**, which attempts to **replace** psychological accounts of behaviour with neurophysiological ones. The latter confuses **type identity** with **token identity**.

■ Whilst individual neurons and their synaptic connections are unpredictable, the nervous system overall is highly organised. **Emergent properties** (such as intelligence and consciousness) reflect the activity of the brain as a system and could not possibly be predicted from analysis of its components.

■ Whilst most materialists are also reductionists, some argue that psychology and neurophysiology constitute distinct **levels of description/universes of discourse**, which cannot replace each other. Freud, for example, believed in the **autonomy of psychological explanation**.

PART 2

Controversies in psychology

CONTROVERSIAL APPLICATIONS

Introduction and overview

Whilst all scientific knowledge can be abused or used in controversial ways, psychology is, perhaps, especially open to such abuse. Since its subject matter includes human beings, people's lives are likely to be influenced, directly or indirectly, by what psychologists believe about human behaviour and cognitive processes.

Sometimes this influence is passive, in the sense that people may come to think about themselves differently (and hence act differently) simply by knowing something about a particular theory (such as Freud's psychoanalytic theory: see Chapters 1 and 66). More controversially, the influence can be active, as when psychologists (or others) use theories and research findings to deliberately *change* people's attitudes and behaviours (as in advertising), or when individuals' performances on psychometric tests (such as intelligence tests) can determine educational and occupational opportunities.

This chapter considers some of the most controversial applications of psychological theory and research, in particular advertising, propaganda and warfare, and sychometric testing (with an emphasis on intelligence and personality testing). A common thread linking the first three is *persuasion*, which is one form of social influence (see Figure 82.1, page 700).

Social influence, behaviour change and ethics

Having identified the concept of *change* as essential for trying to understand what is controversial about these applications, it is necessary to distinguish between different kinds of change and different kinds of influence. Much of social psychology is concerned with *social influence* (see Chapters 58–61), but most of this is not considered controversial, since it is seen as an inevitable feature of social interaction. It only becomes controversial when psychologists apply their knowledge to influence those who do not share it ('the general public') in ways that are not necessarily in the latter's best interests.

Not knowing that you are being influenced is dubious enough, but changing your behaviour in ways you may not have chosen to makes the influence even more unethical. This has some parallels with participants in field experiments (see Chapter 2), who not only cannot give their informed consent, but cannot give any consent at all, since they do not realise that there is an experiment taking place! Hence, 'controversial' in this context really means 'ethically dubious'.

The ethics of attitude and behaviour change also apply to clinical psychology, psychotherapy and psychiatry (see Chapter 1). Controversies still arise even when people voluntarily seek help from one or other of these professions. These, and other ethical issues, are discussed in Chapter 85.

699

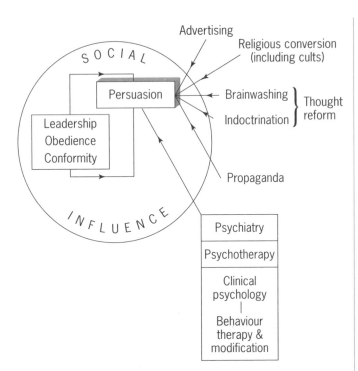

Figure 82.1   Different kinds of attempt to change people's attitudes and behaviour. These range from professional help for emotional and behavioural problems, through inevitable features of social interaction/social influence, to deliberate attempts to manipulate and control others for the benefit of the manipulator

Psychology, propaganda and warfare

PSYCHOLOGY AND WAR

According to Richards (1996b), war presents psychology with a dilemma. Since the vast majority of modern psychologists accept that war is an evil pathology, their task should, apparently, be to diagnose its psychological roots. However, such principled opposition is offset by the fact that most psychologists, no less than anyone else, usually feel bound to support the war efforts of their host societies.

Psychologists have increasingly been called upon to use their professional skills in such tasks as selection and training, propaganda and the design of military technology. Psychology (like other disciplines) has been happy to exploit the abundant scientific funding and research opportunities that war provides, which Richards (1996b) believes does not imply cynicism since, in the final analysis, psychologists' own fundamental identifications are generally with their countries' national war aims.

Beginning with the First World War (1914–18), psychology has been shaped, to a significant degree, by its wartime roles. Some of the best known and influential theories and research areas have been stimulated, directly or indirectly, by these roles.

Exercise 1

Before reading Box 82.1, try to think of theories and areas of research that you have previously read about and/or discussed which are in some way linked to war. These examples are most likely to be found in the cognitive and social sections of the syllabus.

Box 82.1   Psychological theory and research stimulated by war

- Gibson's (1950) *theory of (direct) perception* arose from his research during the Second World War (1939–45), when he was asked by the US Army Air Force to prepare training films that would describe the problems pilots experience when taking off and landing. His theory is discussed in Chapter 22.

- The *intelligence tests* introduced in America for army recruits during the First World War (the army alpha and beta tests) by Yerkes, Goddard and Terman, represented the beginning of mass intelligence testing. Colonel Yerkes supervised the testing of no fewer than 1.75 million recruits (Gould, 1981).

- American psychologists (and sociologists) initially studied *persuasion/persuasive communication* out of concern about the influence on the individual (seen as an isolated being in a 'mass society') of the mass media (as instruments of totalitarian European regimes). However, the American government was also interested in knowing how the media could be used more effectively in advertising, politics, and putting across its policies (especially during the Second World War). The long-term Yale research programme on communications was a direct descendent of the research branch of the US War Department's Information and Education Division. Hovland, who headed the Yale programme, started his experimental work whilst employed by the US War Department, where he was concerned with the practical problems of briefing American military personnel (Brown, 1985).

- Milgram's obedience studies were originally intended to test the view, popular with historians, that Hitler could not have put into operation his plan to systematically destroy millions of Jews and others, without the co-operation of an abnormally obedient German nation. Milgram's research is discussed in detail in Chapter 59.

700

- Since the First World War, psychologists have become involved in the treatment of those suffering war-related mental disturbances, primarily military personnel traumatised by combat, victims of 'shell shock' (First World War) or 'combat fatigue' (Second World War). These categories were created by psychologists undertaking this work (Richards, 1996b). As was seen in Chapter 70 (see pages 609–610), these categories have been replaced by (and fall within) the more general 'post-traumatic stress disorder' (PTSD). One of the most intensively studied groups of people with PTSD are combat veterans from the Vietnam War. Of 2.8 million Vietnam-era veterans who served in combat, 0.5–1.2 million may suffer from PTSD (Wilson *et al.*, 1996)

- Eysenck's identification of *introversion–extroversion* and *neuroticism–stability* as universal dimensions of human personality occurred whilst he was treating Second World War soldiers at the Mill Hill Emergency Hospital in London (see Gross, 1996).

- According to Brown (1985), the use of 'thought reform' ('brainwashing' plus indoctrination) by Chinese Communists against Allied prisoners of war (PoWs) during the Korean War (1950–53) caused great anxiety in the West, and raised questions about the nature of loyalty and treason and the preparation of soldiers for captivity. Returning PoWs were extensively studied by the military, psychologists and psychiatrists in several countries and considerable research was undertaken, often financed by military authorities. This included Hebb's (1952) studies of sensory deprivation and sleep deprivation (see Chapter 12) for the Defence Research Board in Canada, and Zimbardo *et al.*'s (1973) prison simulation experiment for the US Office of Naval Research (see Chapter 60). From such research, lessons were learned as to how to resist indoctrination and the stresses of captivity (Brown, 1985). These techniques of thought reform mirror those used by past and present religious groups, and so-called 'cults'.

The examples given in Box 82.1 represent one basic kind of involvement of psychology with war (Richards, 1996b). By the Second World War, a sub-discipline called 'military psychology' had emerged in the US, concerned with applying psychology for military purposes. According to Geuter (1992), the demands of *Wehrmacht* (armed forces) psychology in the 1930s was crucial in professionalising German psychology, as were the 1917–18 army IQ tests for American psychology (see Box 82.1).

A different kind of involvement took the form of trying to diagnose the psychological roots of war (Richards, 1996b). Freud (1920, 1923) came to see aggression as a separate instinct from sexuality following the horrific carnage of the First World War. He distinguished between the life instinct (or *Eros*), which included sexuality, and the death instinct (or *Thanatos*: see Chapter 63). Another theory of aggression that has much in common with Freud's is Lorenz's *ethological* theory.

Exercise 2

Try to identify some of the similarites and differences between Freud's and Lorenz's theories of aggression. How valid is it to regard war as simply a form of instinctive aggression? In answering the second question, try to use the concept of *reductionism* (see Chapter 81, pages 694–697).

This kind of involvement of psychology with war has, more recently, taken the form of research into the psychological aspects of the effects of nuclear weapon development during the mid-1980s Cold War. In fact, there is a much longer history of psychological study of the effects of war, especially on children.

Box 82.2   Some research findings concerning the effects of war on children

- Several early reports dealt with children's adjustment during World War II, but their findings were inconsistent. Some researchers concluded that children who experienced air raids generally suffered minimal psychological effects (Freud & Burlingham, 1942), whilst others described both acute and chronic post-traumatic stress reactions (Dunsdon, 1941).

- Reports on British children evacuated from cities to the countryside pointed to certain consistent effects, such as impaired concentration, anxiety and delinquency (Dunsdon, 1941; Burt, 1943).

- Significant increases in anxiety were also found in Israeli children following the Yom Kippur War in 1973, the greatest increases occurring in those children who had the lowest levels of peace time anxiety (Milgram & Milgram, 1976). Interestingly, Israeli children living in border communities exposed to shelling over prolonged periods showed no more anxiety than those in communities that were never under fire (Ziv & Israeli, 1973). This was possibly because of the cohesiveness and social support provided in the former, and also the fact that the experience of being shelled had become a part of the children's way of life (Udwin, 1993). However, the

---

adaptation that allows effective functioning in a combat situation may be *maladaptive* under peaceful conditions (Newman *et al.*, 1997).

- Working for UNICEF's psychosocial support programme for children and families in Mostar, Bosnia in 1994, Udwin (1995) identified significant psychological difficulties in many of the 6000 children studied. These included high levels of anxiety, sleeping and concentration problems, depression, withdrawal and behavioural difficulties. Increasingly, children and other civilians are innocent victims, representing a change in twentieth century warfare compared with earlier periods.

(Based on Ladd & Cairns, 1996)

PROPAGANDA AND WAR

'Propaganda' comes from the Latin 'propagare', which refers to the gardener's practice of pinning the fresh shoots of a plant into the earth in order to reproduce new plants which will later take on lives of their own. So, one implication of the term (as originally used in the seventeenth century) is the spread of ideas through their deliberate cultivation or artificial generation.

However, in the twentieth century, propaganda implies something sinister, a deliberate attempt to manipulate, often by concealed or underhand means, the minds of other people for ulterior ends (Brown, 1963). Whilst this change can be dated from the official use of propaganda as a weapon in the total warfare of modern times, beginning with World War I, this was itself an effect of changes in the nature of communication within technically advanced societies. Pratkanis & Aronson (1991) define propaganda as:

'mass suggestion or influence, through the manipulation of symbols and the psychology of the individual. Propaganda is the communication of a point of view with the ulterior goal of having the recipient of the appeal come to 'voluntarily' accept this position as if it were his or her own'.

The aims of propaganda

According to Brown (1963), the chief aims of wartime propaganda are the same regardless of the particular war or the media used (such as pamphlets, leaflets, newspapers, posters, films and public speeches during World War I). These aims were:

- to mobilise and direct hatred against the enemy and undermine the enemy's morale;

- to convince the home public of the rightness of the Allied cause and to increase and maintain fighting spirit;
- to develop the friendship of neutrals and strengthen in their minds the belief that not only were the Allies in the right but they would be victorious in the end and, if possible, to enlist their active support and co-operation;
- to promote a picture of the enemy (as brutal, committing atrocities, wholly responsible for the war in the first place and so on) that justifies the entry of a (usually) peaceable nation into war to '… clear the conscience of the whole nation …' (Brown, 1963);
- to develop and strengthen the friendship of the Allies;
- to build up strong in-group attitudes and feelings and opposed feelings of hatred towards the enemy as a dangerous out-group. As Brown (1963) claims:

'There is nothing like a war for breaking down class and other barriers and creating feelings of friendship and co-operation within a country because all its previously inwardly-directed aggression and resentment comes to be directed against an external enemy, and it is only in the last stages of a losing effort or after a war has been won that disunity begins to show itself once more'.

Exercise 3

How does Brown's quote relate to Tajfel's social identity theory as an explanation of prejudice and discrimination (see Chapter 53), and to Allport's advocacy of equal status contact and the pursuit of common goals as means of reducing them? (See Chapter 54.)

If freedom of choice presupposes a full appreciation of all the alternatives involved, then a feature of propaganda is that it tries to limit our choices deliberately.

Box 82.3 Some specific techniques used in propaganda

The use of stereotypes: The Nazi portrayal of Jews (as shown below) is a good illustration of how a generalised belief about an entire group of people is exaggerated in the form of a caricatured portrayal of that group – the negative characteristics are taken to an extreme form (see Chapter 53).

The substitution of names: Favourable or unfavourable names, with emotional connotations, are substituted for neutral ones. For example, 'Red' (Communist or Russian), 'Union bosses' (presidents of trade unions), 'Huns'/'Krauts' (Germans), and 'Yids' (Jews). Conversely, 'free enterprise' sounds better than 'capitalism'.

Selection: From a mass of complex facts, selection is made for propaganda purposes. Censorship is one way of achieving this and so is a form of propaganda.

Repetition: If a statement or slogan is repeated often enough, it will eventually come to be accepted by the audience, such as Hitler's 'Ein Volk, ein Reich, ein Führer' ('One People, one Empire, one Leader'). During the First World War, there were demands for 'A War to End War' and to 'Make the World Safe for Democracy'.

Assertion: Instead of argument, bald assertions are used to support the propagandist's case, as in the presentation of only one side of the picture, and the deliberate limitation of free thought and questioning.

Pinpointing the enemy: It is useful to present a message not only *for* something but also *against* some real or imagined enemy who is supposedly frustrating the audience's will. This is demonstrated by the Nazi campaign against the Jews (the scapegoats for Germany's humiliation and economic hardships following World War I – see Chapter 53), which pervaded every aspect of German life in the 1930s. An example of this is the beer mat with the inscription 'Whoever buys from a Jew is a traitor to his people'. (The caricatured face also illustrates the use of stereotypes – see above.)

Appeal to authority: This may be a religious or political figure, science and the professions (also used widely in advertising) or 'the crowd' (the 'band wagon effect').

(Based on Brown, 1963)

Propaganda versus education

Although public health campaigns (such as those for safe sex, and anti-drink-driving) fit Pratkanis and Aronson's definition of propaganda, they are not usually what we have in mind when we use the term, probably because

they are aimed at *benefiting* the audience. Similarly, education is often contrasted with propaganda. The former aims to encourage independence of judgement, individual responsibility and an open mind, as well as *how* to think. The latter provides ready-made judgements for the un-thinking, promotes a closed mind and tells people *what* to think.

However, what about the vast majority of high-school textbooks in USA history that virtually ignore the contributions of blacks and other minorities 'to the US scene' (Aronson, 1992)? Such books may not be merely imparting knowledge. This parallels the view that psychology discovers 'facts' about human behaviour which exist objectively (see Chapters 83 and 84). Box 82.4 describes a recent demonstration of 'history as doctrine'.

Box 82.4   Changing the history of war

In 1997, a history professor in Japan won a 32-year fight to expose one of the darkest chapters in his country's wartime history. Saburo Ienaga won a Supreme Court ruling that censorship of references in his books to a germ warfare group (Unit 731) were 'unlawful'. Unit 731 conducted biological warfare experiments, including injecting prisoners with anthrax and cholera, exposing them to sub-zero temperatures, and manufacturing bubonic plague bombs (the latter killing thousands of Chinese civilians). None of the 3000 Chinese, Korean, Russian and Mongolian prisoners survived, many being dismembered alive to monitor the progress of the diseases through their bodies.

The Japanese government has never acknowledged these activities, let alone apologised for them. In August, 1997, the Supreme Court in Tokyo ruled that the Japanese education ministry acted illegally when it censored a proposed textbook by Mr Ienaga, but it upheld its right to continue screening all textbooks and removing anything it finds objectionable, including references to war crimes.

(From *The Daily Mail*, August 30, 1997)

Advertising

An interesting link between psychology and advertising comes in the form of Watson, the founder of behaviourism (see Chapters 1, 32, 75 and 84). After leaving his academic position at Johns Hopkins University, Watson joined the J. Walter Thompson advertising agency, becoming one of the first and most successful applied psychologists (Banyard & Hayes, 1994).

Scott (1909, cited in Brown, 1963) wrote the first textbook published in Britain on advertising. In it, he identified several principles, the most fundamental being *association*. Not until the late 1930s did advertisers discover Freud – but little came of it until the late 1940s and early 1950s (Brown, 1963).

Exercise 4

Taking some advertisments with which you are familiar, try to identify the way that (a) *association* (as demonstrated by classical conditioning), and (b) aspects of Freud's psychoanalytic theory are used. Are these 'techniques' more likely to influence (following Banyard, 1996b):

- developing a need (convincing people that they want or need the product);
- noticing the product;
- purchasing the product;
- behaviour after the purchase (encouraging repeat purchases)?

SUBLIMINAL ADVERTISING

This is by far the most controversial aspect of advertising. It originated with Jim Vicary, an American market researcher, who arranged with the owner of a New Jersey cinema to install a second special projector which, during a film, flashed on the screen phrases such as 'Hungry? Eat Popcorn' and 'Drink Coca-Cola'. These were either flashed so quickly or printed so faintly that they could not be consciously perceived ('subliminal perception' means perception *without* awareness), even after a warning that they were about to appear.

Films treated in this way were alternated with untreated ones throughout the summer of 1956. In the former, sales of popcorn rose by about 50 per cent and soft-drinks by about 18 per cent. Although Vicary himself believed it unlikely that a subliminal stimulus could produce any response at all unless prospective customers already intended buying the product, subliminal advertising caused a storm of protest in the American press, and, later on, in the UK too.

Seeking to scare, rather than sell, a movie producer used a similar technique to Vicary's to flash pictures of a skull and the word 'blood' at key points in pairs of horror movies (Packard, 1957). Despite subliminal messages being legally outlawed (even before it was established whether they really worked), they made a comeback in the mid-1970s. In *The Exorcist* (1974), for example, a death mask was flashed on to the screen subliminally and, more recently, in order to reduce theft, several department stores in America began mixing barely audible and

rapidly repeated whispers (such as 'I am honest. I will not steal') with their piped music. Many stores reported dramatic decreases in shoplifting. Also, audio cassette tapes are readily available which supposedly cure stress with soothing sub-audible messages covered by mood music or the ambient sounds of nature (Zimbardo & Leippe, 1991).

More recently still, in 1990, the heavy-metal band Judas Priest went on trial for causing the suicides of two young fans through, allegedly, recording the subliminal message 'Do it' in one of their tracks. They won their case on the grounds that there is no scientific evidence that subliminal messages, even if perceived, could produce such extreme behaviour. It was *this* aspect of the trial which the media emphasised, rather than details of the troubled lives of the two young people concerned (Wadeley, 1996).

Box 82.5   Are subliminal messages effective?

To be effective, subliminal stimuli:

- must be able to influence judgements when superimposed on consciously attended-to material. Subliminals *can* have an impact, even when presented simultaneously with something that dominates conscious attention (Greenwald *et al.*, 1989);

- must affect general reactions (so that in the popcorn/Coca-Cola example, Vicary did not want the audience to *like* the words 'Hungry? Eat Popcorn' more than they did before, but to have an increased desire to eat popcorn that would lead to buying more). Subliminal priming studies (e.g. Bargh & Pietromonaco, 1982) show that evaluations of *other* stimuli are influenced by subliminal ones;

- need to be strong and persistent enough to affect the mental processes that lead to subsequent directed behaviour. There is little relevant evidence.

Subliminal *sounds* are less likely to be effective than visual messages, since they are apt to go *totally* unregistered if attention is given to other sounds. According to Pratkanis *et al.* (1990), subliminal 'self-help' tapes have little, if any, therapeutic effect (not even a potentially beneficial placebo effect: see Chapter 77).

According to Zimbardo & Leippe (1991):

'so far none of the more fabulous claims for subliminals have been borne out by well-controlled and replicable studies. And while some of the touted subliminal techniques merit scientific study, others are simply not possible given what is known about the functioning of the human mind'.

Are subliminal messages ethically unacceptable?

Exercise 5

Before reading on, try to identify some of the ethical objections to any form of subliminal advertising. How relevant is the evidence presented in Box 82.5 to the question of ethics?

As noted earlier, exposure of subliminal advertising in the 1950s caused great controversy, resulting in its ban in both the UK and the USA. The British Institute of Practitioners in Advertising published a booklet (*Subliminal Communication*, 1958, cited in Brown, 1963) and banned all its 243 affiliated agencies from using it:

'The free choice by the public to accept or reject is an integral part of all forms of professionally accepted advertising and does not appear to be available to recipients of subliminal communication'.

Whether subliminal messages are unethical depends on the ethics of social influence and persuasion in general (Zimbardo & Leippe, 1991). It is widely agreed that any technique used to influence others (excluding physical coercion) is unethical if it (a) relies on deception, (b) prohibits exposure to opposing messages ('denial of the other side'), and (c) unfairly prevents efforts to resist it.

As far as (a) is concerned, subliminals are deceptive to the extent that their users keep their use a secret, but, conceivably, they might still be effective even when it is openly announced that they are present. Regarding (b), this does not apply to subliminals (but is relevant for evaluating attempts to indoctrinate people, as used by the Moonies, for example: see above).

It is with regard to (c) that subliminals can be viewed as extremely unethical. We cannot defend against something we do not know about and, by definition, we do not know about subliminals. Unlike other forms of influence, such as the image processing of political candidates, or classical conditioning, we cannot resist the influence of subliminals through being observant and mindful. It is only later on – at the time of behavioural decision – that we may ask ourselves why we feel a certain way:

'if subliminal influence should prove to work outside the laboratory in advertising contexts, it would seem highly unethical to use it – mainly because it deprives people of much of their opportunity to resist it' (Zimbardo & Leippe, 1991).

Psychometric testing

Measurement has always been central to experimental science, but trying to quantify *psychological* phenomena ('psychometric' means 'mental measurement') has always proved problematical (Richards, 1996b).

> **Box 82.6   Some problems associated with trying to measure psychological phenomena**
>
> - At a fairly abstract level, and in keeping with other sciences, there is the problem of how something can be measured without being changed. In physics (where the riddle first arose), the answer is unambiguously 'it can't'. The nature of measurement is far less straightforward and logical than traditionally assumed.
>
> - How can psychologists identify overt, publicly measurable 'indices' of the essentially inaccessible phenomena such as memory, motivation, the structure of personality, and intelligence (and other *hypothetical constructs*: see Chapter 1)? Psychologists tend to assume that these exist in some objective form, but this assumption is a false and a dangerous one to make (see Chapter 83). A good example of a measure that is obviously historically and culturally embedded is the F(Fascism)-scale of authoritarianism (Adorno *et al.*, 1950: see Chapter 53).
>
> - Once a measuring instrument exists, we can be misled into inferring that what is being measured has a concrete or objective status (this is called *reification*). This is especially likely to occur when performance using the instrument is expressed as a numerical value (as in an IQ score – see text).

As far as psychometrics in general is concerned, there are two major issues that need to be addressed:

1 *Is the test a good test?* Essentially, this refers to the test's *reliability* (consistency), *validity* (whether it measures what it claims to measure), *discriminatory power* (its ability to produce a wide distribution of scores) and *standardisation* (a standardised test is one that has been used with a large, representative sample of the population, which enables individual scores to be compared with appropriate group norms).

2 The above properties are essentially *statistical* and *theoretical* criteria, and a more detailed discussion is beyond the scope of this chapter. However, even if they were all fulfilled in every case (which they certainly are not), this would have no direct bearing on the *practical* issue, that is, *what is the test being used for*

705

and *how will a person's performance affect his or her educational or occupational future?*

PERSONALITY MEASUREMENT

Kline (1995) identifies three main types of personality test. These are *personality questionnaires and inventories* (the terms are interchangeable), *projective tests* (in which people are presented with ambiguous stimuli, their interpretations of which are taken to reflect unconscious motives), and *objective tests* (in which the test's true purpose is hidden but which provides an objective measurement, such as the circumference of a blown-up balloon as a measure of 'timidity'). There are many examples of each type and each individual test's reliability, validity and so on need to be considered separately.

Box 82.7   Some advantages of personality questionnaires/inventories compared with other types of personality tests

- They are easy and quick to use, which is especially important in applied settings. Even the longest (the Minnesota Multiphasic Personality Inventory) only takes about 30 minutes.

- They can be given to many people at the same time, by people without special training in psychology (and the same is true of scoring).

- They can be standardised so as to produce norms, without which individual scores are almost impossible to interpret.

- They can be computerised: all responses to each item are stored in the computer, which simplifies later statistical analysis. Scoring is automatic and error-free, making possible an almost immediate print-out of scores. This can be a great advantage in certain applied settings, such as clinical assessment, vocational guidance, and career counselling.

(Based on Kline, 1995)

The use of personality testing in occupational assessment

The use of personality testing in occupational assessment has been steadily increasing over the past 20 years, with some recent surveys suggesting that up to two-thirds of large organisations in the UK use personality tests for selecting managers (Drakeley, 1997). The vast majority – but not all – use tests responsibly and wisely.

The British Psychological Society has promoted responsible test use by developing the Certificate of Competence

in Occupational Testing in order to raise standards. To reach the highest ('Full Level B') standard, those wishing to use personality tests have to demonstrate that they know how to use such instruments for selection, promotion, redundancy, individual personal development, team development, career guidance, and counselling. Of these, promotion and redundancy are especially controversial.

Exercise 6

Before reading on, think about *why* the use of personality tests for promotion and redundancy is more controversial than their other uses as listed above.

With promotion and redundancy, the individual is already employed by the organisation. His or her behaviour and 'personality' could be readily observed at work and the normal appraisal system should be sufficient without the use of tests ('Doesn't my track record speak for itself?'). Many employees feel that personality testing is unnecessary and an insensitive intrusion into their private lives (Drakeley, 1997).

Box 82.8   Arguments for and against the use of personality tests for promotion and redundancy

The case for

- Tests are patently fairer than many of the flawed, informal procedures (such as favouritism, and the 'old-boy' network) used within some organisations.

- They provide standardised, numerical information allowing easy comparison of people on the same criteria.

- Good tests produce explicit and specific indications of temperament (a 'score') as opposed to vague, ambiguous, coded platitudes (such as 'satisfactory', 'high-flyer') often found in annual appraisals.

- Good tests are 'scientific', that is, they have soundly based theoretical and empirical foundations.

The case against

- Personality measurement usually involves profiling an individual on several 'traits', but these can range from 15 to 30. How many are needed to describe personality with any degree of precision? For any given job, several different combinations of traits could be equally effective.

- A person's performance is likely to be influenced by the situation he or she works in, and often the most salient aspect of the situation is other people. Relatively little is known about the dynamic and complex

---

706

ways in which different personalities might interact to affect a particular individual's behaviour.

(From Drakeley, 1997)

For the reasons given in Box 82.8, Drakeley believes that personality tests should be used with caution. For example, should tests alone be used for redundancy selection? He concludes that this can only be justified:

'when future job performance cannot reasonably be predicted from current or past job performance. In the particular case of redundancy, this limits the use of such procedures to situations involving real and substantial job redesign'.

THE MEASUREMENT OF INTELLIGENCE

Intelligence (or IQ/Intelligence Quotient) tests form one kind of *ability* test, designed to measure underlying constructs that are not a direct result of training (Coolican, 1996). They are contrasted with *attainment* (or achievement) tests (such as tests of reading and comprehension, spelling and numeracy) designed to assess *specific* information learned in school. *Aptitude* tests form a third kind of test, aimed at measuring *potential* performance (such as a general logic test designed to predict how good someone would be at computer programming). As will be seen, these distinctions are problematical and controversial.

One widely used test is the Wechsler Intelligence Scale for Children (WISC), originally constructed in the USA but now standardised on the UK population (WISC-III UK: Wechsler, 1992). Like Wechsler's tests (which include the Wechsler Adult Intelligence Scale/WAIS), the British Ability Scales (BAS: Elliot *et al.*, 1979, revised 1983) include a battery of verbal and non-verbal tests, and several visual perceptual and cognitive tests.

Through the introduction of a new statistical procedure, the BAS can now be used either as a *criterion-referenced* assessment (indicating whether a child has successfully achieved a given objective or not, irrespective of whether this is appropriate for its age), or as a *norm-referenced* assessment (involving a comparison between an individual's score and the typical score on the test for that individual's age group). Typically, IQ tests are norm-referenced and administered (at least in the case of *individual tests*, such as the WAIS and the BAS) only by those with special training, such as educational psychologists. However, assessment under the National Curriculum, for example, is criterion-referenced, with standard assessment tests (SATs) administered by class teachers.

For and against IQ tests

One argument in favour of the use of IQ assessment is that it has *prevented* some children from being segregated into special schools or classes. Thus, there are cases where a child's IQ score indicates a *higher* level of ability than is reflected in his or her attainments or the teacher's perceptions (Quicke, 1982). This is particularly relevant to areas of learning difficulty which, by definition, relate to a discrepancy between the child's actual cognitive ability (as reflected in the IQ score) and his or her (more limited) specific attainments (Coolican, 1996).

Conversely, Bee (1994) claims that the most important use of IQ tests is in identifying children who might need or benefit from special education. Children whose speed of learning is much faster or slower than normal may be given an IQ test to see if they are gifted or retarded. However, Bee also argues that, whilst it is generally agreed that schools need to diagnose and sort children, what is most controversial about IQ tests is their use as a *central basis* for such sorting.

Exercise 7

Before reading on, think about some of the limitations of IQ tests. Is the distinction (made above) between ability and attainment tests valid, and how might this relate to the argument that IQ tests do not measure what they claim to measure?

Box 82.9   Some arguments against the use of IQ tests

- IQ tests were designed to measure children's basic capacity or underlying *competence*, whilst achievement/attainment tests are supposed to measure what they have actually learned (*performance*). Each of us presumably has some upper limit of ability (what we could do under ideal conditions, when we are maximally motivated, well and rested). However, everyday conditions are rarely ideal and we typically perform below this hypothetical ability. In fact, it is not *possible* to measure competence and so we are *always* measuring 'today's' performance. According to Bee (1994), logically:

  'all IQ tests are really achievement tests to some degree. The difference between tests called IQ tests and those called achievement tests is really a matter of degree'.

- Whilst IQ scores do become quite stable in late childhood, individual children's IQ scores can and do fluctuate, especially in response to any life stress (see Chapter 43).

- Traditional tests simply fail to measure a whole host of cognitive and social skills likely to be highly significant for getting on in the world, such as creativity/divergent thinking, insight, 'street smarts', and social intelligence (reading other people's emotional states and social behaviour: Gardner, 1983; Sternberg, 1990). IQ tests, in keeping with why they were originally designed, have an excessively narrow focus on the specific range of skills needed for school success ('school intelligence'), which includes convergent, logical thinking. Intellectual ability is *reduced* to a single (IQ) number (see Chapter 81).

- If IQ score alone is used as a measure of a child's functioning, then a child who is categorised as having learning difficulties (IQ below 70), but who nonetheless has sufficient social skills to function well in a regular classroom, would be inappropriately excluded (see Chapter 78).

- Knowing a child's IQ score can result in a *self-fulfilling prophecy*. Based on the belief that IQ is a measure of 'true' – and fixed – ability, the child is treated accordingly (such as placement in remedial classes or special schools), which could actually influence its development, including its IQ score.

(Based on Bee, 1994; and Cernovsky, 1997).

Bee (1994) argues that the most serious objection to the use of IQ tests is the fact that they are *biased*, especially against minority groups (see Chapter 84). Taking such tests and doing well may also require certain test-taking skills, motivations and attitudes that are less common especially among African–American children. Despite attempts to eliminate all types of bias:

'When IQ tests are used for diagnosis in schools, proportionately more minority than white children continue to be diagnosed as retarded or slow' (Bee, 1994).

As a result of several lawsuits, there are many places in the USA (such as California) where the use of IQ tests for diagnosis and placement of African–American and other minority children is forbidden.

Conclusions

This chapter has highlighted some of those areas where 'psychological technology' has been (and still is) used – the mass media, international relations, commerce and industry and education – and has discussed how these applications are controversial. Many of the controversies are based on the belief that people are manipulated into behaving in particular ways, their freedom curtailed, or their lives shaped by their performance on tests that claim to measure highly complex aspects of human functioning.

Summary

■ Psychology is especially open to abuse because of its subject matter. Active forms of social influence, in which psychologists apply their knowledge to influence people who do not share this knowledge in ways that may not be in their best interests, are controversial and ethically dubious. This also applies to the consequences for people of their performance on psychometric tests.

■ Psychology has been shaped, since the First World War, by its wartime roles, which have stimulated many influential theories and areas of research. These include Gibson's theory of perception, the army alpha and beta intelligence tests, persuasive communication, Milgram's obedience studies, and Eysenck's personality tests.

■ Attempts to diagnose the psychological roots of war include Freud's distinction between the life and death instincts. There is also a long history of research into the effects of war, especially on children.

■ Propaganda was first officially used as a weapon in the First World War. Regardless of which particular communication media are used, wartime propaganda has several aims. These include undermining the enemy's morale, maintaining fighting spirit, promoting a picture of the enemy that justifies involvement in the war, and building strong pro-in-group and anti-out-group feelings.

■ Propaganda deliberately tries to limit people's choices, either through presenting one viewpoint and excluding all others (as in censorship), or through use of caricature, stereotypes, emotive names, repetitive slogans, and the appeal to authority.

■ Propaganda is usually contrasted with education, the latter encouraging independent thinking, individual responsibility and an open mind. However, textbooks can be very biased, as in the case of the Japanese government's censorship of school history books for reference to that country's war crimes.

■ The first textbook on advertising published in Britain identified **association** as the fundamental principle, and Watson, the founder of behaviourism in America, became one of the first and most successful applied psychologists when he joined a major advertising agency. Advertisers later began using principles derived from Freud's psychoanalytic theory.

■ **Subliminal advertising** was originally used in cinemas to increase sales of popcorn and Coca-Cola. Subliminal messages have also been used in other ways, both before and since being made illegal. They can influence judgements when superimposed on consciously-attended to material, and produce general reactions (such as increasing the desire to eat popcorn). However, their influence on behaviour is much less certain. Subliminals remain highly controversial mainly because, unlike other forms of influence, they deprive people of the opportunity to resist them.

■ A good **psychometric test** should be reliable, valid, have discriminatory power and be standardised. These statistical and theoretical properties are distinct from what the tests are used for.

■ Personality questionnaires/inventories have clear advantages compared with projective and objective tests, including the automatic and error-free scoring useful in applied settings, such as clinical assessment, vocational guidance, and career counselling.

■ Personality testing in occupational assessment is increasingly being used by UK organisations, the most controversial uses of such tests being for promotion and redundancy. The only justification for using a test as the sole basis for redundancy selection is when future job performance cannot be predicted from current or past performance.

■ Intelligence (IQ) tests are usually defined as **ability** tests, as opposed to **attainment** or **aptitude** tests. The British Ability Scales (BAS) comprise a battery of verbal and non-verbal tests, plus several visual perceptual and cognitive tests. The BAS can be used either as **criterion-referenced** or **norm-referenced**, as **individual** IQ tests typically are.

■ IQ assessment can prevent children from being placed in special schools or classes. Conversely, they can identify children who might **benefit** from special education. Although it is generally agreed that schools need to diagnose and sort children, it is controversial to use IQ tests as the basis for doing this.

■ Since it is impossible to measure **competence** (as IQ tests claim to do), the difference between competence and **performance** (as measured by attainment tests) is only one of **degree**. Traditional tests fail to measure a variety of cognitive and social skills important for everyday life and are narrowly focused on 'school intelligence'. Also, knowing a child's IQ score can result in a **self-fulfilling prophecy**. Most seriously of all, IQ tests are **biased**, especially against minority groups.

83

PSYCHOLOGY AS A SCIENCE

Introduction and overview

As was seen in Chapter 1, psychology is commonly defined as the *scientific* study of behaviour and cognitive processes (or mind or experience). In effect, the book as a whole has been looking at how different psychologists have put this definition into practice, through their use of various investigative methods to study a wide variety of behaviours and cognitive processes.

This chapter turns the spotlight once more on that definition of psychology. It does this by examining the nature of science (including the major features of scientific method), and by tracing some of the major developments in psychology's history as a scientific discipline. This enables the question of how appropriate it is to use scientific method to study human behaviour and cognitive processes to be addressed, and the validity of this widely accepted definition to be assessed.

Figure 83.1   René Descartes (1596–1650)

Some philosophical roots of science and psychology

As noted in Chapter 81, Descartes was the first to distinguish formally between mind and matter (*philosophical dualism*), which had an enormous impact on the development of both psychology as a science and science in general. Dualism allowed scientists to treat matter as inert and completely distinct from themselves, which meant that the world could be described *objectively*, without reference to the human observer. Objectivity became the ideal of science, and was extended to the study of human behaviour and social institutions by Comte in the mid-1800s, calling it *positivism*.

Descartes also promoted *mechanism*, the view that the material world comprises objects which are assembled like a huge machine and operated by mechanical laws. He extended this view to living organisms, including, eventually, the human body. Because the mind is non-material, Descartes believed that, unlike the physical world, it can be investigated only through introspection (observing one's own thoughts and feelings). He was also one of the first advocates of *reductionism* (see Chapter 81).

Empirism refers to the ideas of the seventeenth and eighteenth century British philosophers, Locke, Hume and Berkeley. They believed that the only source of true knowledge about the world is sensory experience (what comes to us through our senses or what can be inferred about the relationship between such sensory facts.) Empirism is usually contrasted with *nativism* (or *rationalism*), according to which knowledge of the world is largely innate or inborn (see, for example, Chapter 23).

Exercise 1

Try to identify examples of psychological theory and research which reflect empirist or nativist views. (Another way of doing this is to ask where in psychology the *nature–nurture* or *heredity and environment* debate takes place.)

The word 'empirical' ('through the senses') is often used to mean 'scientific', implying that what scientists do, and what distinguishes them from non-scientists, is carry out experiments and observations as ways of collecting data or 'facts' about the world (hence, 'empirical methods' for 'scientific methods': see Chapter 2). Empirism proved to be one of the central influences on the development of physics and chemistry.

EMPIRISM AND PSYCHOLOGY

Prior to the 1870s, there were no laboratories specifically devoted to psychological research, and the early scientific psychologists had trained mainly as physiologists, doctors, philosophers, or some combination of these. The two professors who set up the first two psychological laboratories deserve much of the credit for the development of academic psychology. They were Wundt (1832–1920) in Germany and James (1842–1910) in the USA (Fancher, 1979).

WUNDT'S CONTRIBUTION

A physiologist by training, Wundt is generally regarded as the 'founder' of the new science of experimental psychology, or what he called 'a new domain of science' (1874). Having worked as Helmholtz's assistant (see Chapter 22, page 183), Wundt eventually became professor of 'scientific philosophy' at Leipzig University in 1875, illustrating the lack of distinct boundaries between the various disciplines which combined to bring about psychology's development (Fancher, 1979).

Figure 83.2   Wilhelm Wundt (1832–1920)

In 1879, Wundt converted his 'laboratory' at Leipzig into a 'private institute' of experimental psychology. For the first time, a place had been set aside for the explicit purpose of conducting psychological research and hence 1879 is widely accepted as the 'birthdate' of psychology as a discipline in its own right. From its modest beginnings, the institute began to attract people from all over the world, who returned to their own countries to establish laboratories modelled on Wundt's.

Box 83.1   Wundt's study of the conscious mind: introspective psychology and structuralism

Wundt believed that conscious mental states could be scientifically studied through the systematic manipulation of antecedent variables (those that occur before some other event), and analysed by carefully controlled techniques of introspection. *Introspection* was a rigorous and highly disciplined technique for analysing conscious experience into its most basic elements (*sensations* and *feelings*). Participants were always advanced psychology students who had been carefully trained to introspect properly.

Sensations are the raw sensory content of consciousness, devoid of all 'meaning' or interpretation, and all conscious thoughts, ideas, perceptions and so on were assumed to be combinations of sensations. Based on his experiment in which he listened to a metronome beating at varying rates, Wundt concluded that *feelings* could be analysed in terms of *pleasantness–unpleasantness, tension–relaxation,* and *activity–passivity*.

Wundt believed that introspection made it possible to cut through the learned categories and concepts that define our everyday experience of the world, and so expose the 'building blocks' of experience. Because of introspection's central role, Wundt's early brand of psychology was called *introspective psychology* (or *introspectionism*), and his attempt to analyse consciousness into its elementary sensations and feelings is known as *structuralism*.

(Based on Fancher, 1979)

Exercise 2

1 Consider the difficulties that might be involved in relying on introspection to formulate an account of the nature of conscious experience (i.e. an account that applies to *people in general*).
2 In what ways is structuralism *reductionist*? (see Chapter 81).
3 Which major theory of perception rejects this structuralist approach? Outline its principal features (see Chapter 21).

JAMES' CONTRIBUTION

James taught anatomy and physiology at Harvard University in 1872, and by 1875 was calling his course *The Relations between Physiology and Psychology*. In the same year, he established a small laboratory, used mainly for teaching purposes. In 1878, he dropped anatomy and physiology and for several years taught 'pure psychology'.

His view of psychology is summarised in *The Principles of Psychology* (1890), which includes discussion of instinct, brain function, habit, the stream of consciousness, the self (see Chapter 46), attention (Chapters 25 and 26), memory (Chapter 27), perception (Chapters 23 and 24), free will (Chapter 81) and emotion (Chapter 19).

Figure 83.3   William James (1842–1910)

Principles provided the famous definition of psychology as 'the Science of Mental Life' (see Chapter 1). Ironically, however, James was very critical both of his book and of what psychology could offer as a science. He became increasingly interested in philosophy and disinterested in psychology, although in 1894 he became the first American to call favourable attention to the recent work of the then little known Viennese neurologist, Sigmund Freud (Fancher, 1979).

James proposed a point of view (rather than a theory) which directly inspired *functionalism* which emphasises behaviour's purpose and utility (Fancher, 1979). Functionalism, in turn, helped to stimulate interest in individual differences, since they determine how well or poorly individuals will adapt to their environments. These attitudes made Americans especially receptive to Darwin's (1859) ideas about individual variation, evolution by natural selection, and the 'survival of the fittest'.

WATSON'S BEHAVIOURIST REVOLUTION: A NEW SUBJECT MATTER FOR PSYCHOLOGY

Watson took over the psychology department at Johns Hopkins University in 1909 and immediately began cutting psychology's ties with philosophy and strengthening those with biology. At that time, Wundt's and James's studies of consciousness were still the 'real' psychology, but Watson was doing research on non-humans and became increasingly critical of the use of introspection.

Figure 83.4   John Broadus Watson (1878–1958)

In particular, Watson argued that introspective reports were unreliable and difficult to verify. It is impossible to check the accuracy of such reports because they are based on purely private experience, to which the investigator has no possible means of access. As a result, Watson (1913) redefined psychology in his famous 'behaviourist manifesto' of 1913.

> **Box 83.2   Watson's (1913) 'behaviourist manifesto'**
>
> Watson's article 'Psychology as the behaviourist views it' is often referred to as the 'behaviourist manifesto', a charter for a truly scientific psychology. It was *behaviourism* which was to represent a rigorous empirist approach within psychology for the first time. According to Watson:
>
> 'Psychology as the behaviourist views it is a purely objective natural science. Its theoretical goal is the prediction and control of behaviour. Introspection forms no essential part of its methods, nor is the scientific value of its data dependent upon the readiness with which they lend themselves to interpretation in terms of consciousness. The behaviourist ... recognises no dividing line between man and brute. The behaviour of a man ... forms only a part of the behaviourist's total scheme of investigation.'
>
> Three features of this 'manifesto' deserve special mention:
>
> - Psychology must be purely objective, excluding all subjective data or interpretations in terms of conscious experience. This redefines psychology as the 'science of behaviour' (rather than the 'science of mental life').
>
> - The goals of psychology should be to predict and control behaviour (as opposed to describing and explaining conscious mental states), a goal later endorsed by Skinner's *radical behaviourism* (see Chapter 1).

- There is no fundamental (*qualitative*) distinction between human and non-human behaviour. If, as Darwin had shown, humans evolved from more simple species, then it follows that human behaviour is simply a more complex form of the behaviour of other species (the difference is merely *quantitative*, one of degree). Consequently, rats, cats, dogs and pigeons became the major source of psychological data: since 'psychological' now meant 'behaviour' rather than 'consciousness', non-humans that were convenient to study, and whose environments could easily be controlled, could replace people as experimental subjects.

(Based on Fancher, 1979, and Watson, 1913)

Exercise 3

Try to formulate arguments for *and* against Watson's claim that there is only a *quantitative* difference between the behaviour of humans and non-humans.

In his 1915 Presidential address to the American Psychological Association, Watson talked about his recent 'discovery' of Pavlov's work on conditioned reflexes in dogs. He proposed that the conditioned reflex could become the foundation for a full-scale human psychology.

The extreme environmentalism of Locke's empiricism (see page 710) lent itself well to the behaviourist emphasis on learning (through the process of Pavlovian or classical conditioning). Whilst Locke had described the mind at birth as a *tabula rasa* ('blank slate') on which experience writes, Watson, in rejecting the mind as suitable for a scientific psychology, simply swapped mind for behaviour: it is now behaviour that is shaped by the environment.

According to Miller (1962), empiricism provided psychology with both a *methodology* (stressing the role of observation and measurement) and a *theory*, including analysis into elements (such as stimulus–response units) and *associationism* (which explains how simple elements can be combined to form more complex ones).

Behaviourism also embodied positivism, in particular the emphasis on the need for scientific rigour and objectivity. Humans were now conceptualised and studied as 'natural phenomena', with subjective experience, consciousness and other characteristics (traditionally regarded as distinctive human qualities) no longer having a place in the behaviourist world.

THE COGNITIVE REVOLUTION

Academic psychology in the USA and the UK was dominated by behaviourism for the next 40 years. However, criticism and dissatisfaction with it culminated in a number of 'events', all taking place in 1956, which, collectively, are referred to as the 'cognitive revolution'.

This new way of thinking about and investigating people was called the *information-processing approach*. At the centre of this is the *computer analogy*, the view that human cognition can be understood by comparing it with the functioning of a digital computer. It was now acceptable to study the mind again, although its conceptualisation was very different from that of Wundt, James and the other pioneers of the 'new psychology' prior to Watson's 'behaviourist revolution'.

Box 83.3   The 1956 'cognitive revolution'

- At a meeting at the Massachusetts Institute of Technology (MIT), Chomsky introduced his theory of language (see Chapter 34), Miller presented a paper on the 'magical number seven' in short-term memory (see Chapter 27), and Newell and Simon presented a paper on the logical theory machine (or logic theorist), with a further paper by Newell *et al.* (1958), which Newell & Simon (1972) extended into the general problem solver (GPS: see Chapter 36).

- The first systematic attempt to investigate concept formation (in adults) from a cognitive psychological perspective was reported (Bruner *et al.*, 1956).

- At Dartmouth College, New Hampshire (the 'Dartmouth Conference'), ten academics met to discuss the possibilities of producing computer programs that could 'behave' or 'think' intelligently. These academics included McCarthy (generally attributed with having coined the term 'artificial intelligence'), Minsky, Simon, Newell, Chomsky and Miller.

(Based on Eysenck & Keane, 1995)

SCIENCE, SCIENTISM AND MAINSTREAM PSYCHOLOGY

Despite this major change in psychology after 1956, certain central assumptions and practices within the discipline have remained essentially the same, and these are referred to as *mainstream psychology*. Harré (1989) refers to the mainstream as the 'old paradigm', which he believes continues to be haunted by certain 'unexamined presuppositions', one of which is *scientism*, defined by Van Langenhove (1995) as:

'the borrowing of methods and a characteristic vocabulary from the natural sciences in order to discover causal mechanisms that explain psychological phenomena'.

Scientism maintains that all aspects of human behaviour can and should be studied using the methods of natural science, which claims to be the sole means of establishing 'objective truth'. This can be achieved by studying phenomena removed from any particular context ('context-stripping' exposes them in their 'pure' form), and in a *value-free* way (there is no bias on the investigator's part). The most reliable way of doing this is through the laboratory experiment, the method providing the greatest degree of control over relevant variables (see Chapter 2 and pages 719–721). As noted above, these beliefs and assumptions add up to the traditional view of science known as positivism.

Exercise 4

Try to find examples of experimental studies of human behaviour that fit the definition of 'context-stripping' given above. Probably the 'best' examples will come from social psychology, which in itself should suggest criticisms of this approach to studying behaviour. (See also Chapter 84, page 724.)

Although much research has moved beyond the confines of the laboratory experiment, the same positivist logic is still central to how psychological inquiry is conceived and conducted. Method and measurement still have a privileged status:

'Whether concerned with mind or behaviour (and whether conducted inside or outside the laboratory), research tends to be constructed in terms of the separation (or reduction) of entities into independent and dependent variables and the measurement of hypothesised relationships between them' (Smith *et al.*, 1995).

Despite the fact that since the mid-1970s the natural sciences model has become the subject of vigorous attacks, psychology is still to a large extent dominated by it. The most prominent effect of this is the dominance of experiments (Van Langenhove, 1995). This has far-reaching effects on the way psychology *pictures* people as more or less passive and mechanical information-processing devices, whose behaviour can be split up into variables. It also affects the way psychology *deals* with people. In experiments, people are not treated as single individuals, but as interchangeable 'subjects'. There is no room for individualised observations.

What do we mean by 'science'?

THE MAJOR FEATURES OF SCIENCE

Most psychologists and philosophers of science would probably agree that for a discipline to be called a science, it must possess certain characteristics. These are summarised in Box 83.4 and Figure 83.5.

Box 83.4   The major features of science

- **A definable subject matter:** This changed from conscious human thought to human and non-human behaviour, then to cognitive processes within psychology's first 40 years as a separate discipline.

- **Theory construction:** This represents an attempt to explain observed phenomena, such as Watson's attempt to account for (almost all) human and non-human behaviour in terms of classical conditioning, and Skinner's subsequent attempt to do the same with operant conditioning.

- **Hypothesis testing:** This involves making specific predictions about behaviour under certain specified conditions (for example, predicting that by combining the sight of a rat with the sound of a hammer crashing down on a steel bar just behind his head, a small child will learn to fear the rat: see the case of Little Albert, page 571.

- **The use of empirical methods:** These are used to collect data (evidence) relevant to the hypothesis being tested.

WHAT IS 'SCIENTIFIC METHOD'?

The account given in Box 83.4 and Figure 83.5 of what constitutes a science is non-controversial. However, it fails to tell us how the *scientific process* takes place, the sequence of 'events' involved (such as where the theory comes from in the first place, and how it is related to observation of the subject matter), or the exact relationship between theory construction, hypothesis testing and data collection.

Collectively, these 'events' and relationships are referred to as (the) *scientific method*. Table 83.1 summarises some common beliefs about both science and scientific method, as identified by Medawar (1963) and Popper (1972), together with some alternative views.

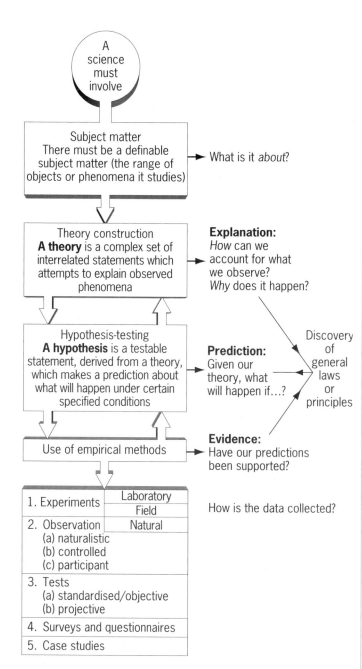

Figure 83.5 A summary of the major features of a science

Table 83.1 Some common beliefs, and alternative views about, 'science' and 'scientific method'

Common beliefs

- Scientific discovery begins with simple, unbiased, unprejudiced observation (i.e. the scientist simply 'samples' the world without any preconceptions, expectations or predetermined theories).

- ■ From the resulting sensory evidence ('data'/sense-data), generalised statements of fact will take shape (i.e. we gradually build up a picture of what the world is like based on a number of separate 'samples').

- ▲ The essential feature of scientific activity is the use of empirical methods, through which the sensory evidence is gathered (i.e. what distinguishes science from non-science is performing experiments and so on).

- + The truth about the world (the objective nature of things, what the world is 'really like') can be established through properly controlled experiments and other ways of collecting 'facts' (i.e. science can tell us about reality as it is *independently* of the scientist or the activity of observing it).

- ✗ Science involves the steady accumulation of knowledge, so that each generation of scientists adds to the discoveries of previous generations.

Alternative views

- There is no such thing as 'unbiased' or 'unprejudiced' observation. Our observation is always selective, interpretative, pre-structured and directed (i.e. we must have at least some idea of what we are looking for, otherwise we cannot know when we have found it).

- ■ 'Data' do not constitute 'facts': evidence usually implies measurement, numbers, recordings and so on which need to be interpreted in the light of a theory. Facts do *not* exist objectively and cannot be discovered through 'pure observation'. 'Fact' = Data + Theory (Deese, 1972).

- ▲ Despite the central role of data collection, data alone do not make a science. Theory is just as crucial, because without it, data have no meaning (see second bullet above).

- + Scientific theory and research reflect the biases, prejudices, values and assumptions of the individual scientist, as well as of the scientific community to which he or she belongs. Science is *not* value-free (see text).

- ✗ Science involves an endless succession of long, peaceful periods ('normal science') and 'scientific revolutions' (Kuhn, 1962: see Table 83.3).

- Science has a warm, human, exciting, argumentative, creative 'face' (Collins, 1994: see Box 83.5).

(Based on Medawar, 1963, and Popper, 1972)

Box 83.5   The inner world of scientists

According to Richards & Wolpert (1997), scientists, outside their own habitat, are a poorly understood species. If they feature in popular awareness at all, it is through a limited set of media stereotypes. With a few exceptions, if scientists are not mad or bad, they are perceived as personality-free, their measured tones and formal reports implying ways of thinking and working far removed from the intellectual and emotional messiness of other human activities.

Richards and Wolpert engaged in a series of conversations with several eminent scientists (including chemists, immunologists, biologists, biochemists, neuro- and evolutionary biologists) in an attempt to redress the balance, and give a rare glimpse of the human reality of scientific life.

Scientists think and feel about their work using the same psychological apparatus as the rest of us. The human qualities of science come over very strongly: its energy and imaginative richness, the frustration, love and despair which enslaves its practitioners.

For example, Mitchison (an immunologist) says that experiments start with 'the act of creation':

> '... Not all experiments you think of are good experiments, but thinking of one is just wonderful, eureka! It's fantastic'.

According to Edelman (an immunologist and neurobiologist), stumbling upon the solution to a problem when you least expect to find it is a '... remarkable pleasure ...'. Some scientists are like voyeurs, with '... almost a lustful feeling of excitement when a secret of nature is revealed ...'.

(Adapted from Richards & Wolpert, 1997)

Table 83.2   Comparison between the classical, inductive view of science and Popper's revised version

Inductive method	Popper's version
Observation and method	Problem (usually a refutation of an existing theory or prediction)
Inductive generalisation	Proposed solution or new theory
Hypothesis	Deduction of testable statements (hypotheses) from the new theory. This relates to the *hypothetico-deductive method*, which is usually contrasted with/opposed to the inductive method. In practice, both approaches are involved in the scientific process and are complementary.
Attempted verification of hypothesis	Tests or attempts to refute by methods including observation and experiment
Proof or disproof	Establishing a preference between competing theories
Knowledge	

(Based on Popper, 1972)

been seen that each approach rests upon a different image of what people are like, which in turn determines what is important to study, as well as the methods of study that can and should be used.

Exercise 5

What is the underlying image of the person associated with each of the major theoretical approaches within psychology? Which of these do you consider captures your own experience, and your experience of others, most accurately, and why? (You might find it helpful to refer to both Chapters 1 and 66.)

Consequently, different approaches can be seen as self-contained disciplines, as well as different facets of the same discipline (Kuhn, 1962; Kline, 1988).

Kuhn argues that a field of study can only legitimately be considered a science if a majority of its workers subscribe to a common, global perspective or *paradigm*. According to Kuhn, this means that psychology is *pre-paradigmatic*: it lacks a paradigm, without which it is still in a state (or stage) of *pre-science*. Whether psychology has, or has ever had, a paradigm, is hotly debated (see Table 83.3).

As a result of the first two beliefs identified in Table 83.1, Popper (1972) has revised the stages of the scientific process as proposed by the classical view (the *inductive method*). This, together with Popper's revised version, is shown in Table 83.2.

CAN PSYCHOLOGY BE A SCIENCE IF PSYCHOLOGISTS CANNOT AGREE WHAT PSYCHOLOGY IS?

As previously noted, definitions of psychology have changed during its lifetime, largely reflecting the influence and contributions of its major theoretical *approaches* or orientations. In this chapter (and Chapter 1) it has

Table 83.3   Kuhn's three stages in the development of a science, and some views about how they apply to psychology

Stages in the development of a science (●) and their application to psychology (■)

- ● *Pre-science:* No paradigm has evolved and there are several schools of thought or theoretical orientations.
- ■ Like Kuhn, Joynson (1980) and Boden (1980) argue that psychology is pre-paradigmatic. Kline (1988) sees its various approaches as involving different paradigms.
- ● *Normal science:* A paradigm has emerged, dictating the kind of research that is carried out and providing a framework for interpreting results. The details of the theory are filled in and workers explore its limits. Disagreements can usually be resolved within the limits allowed by the paradigm.
- ■ According to Valentine (1982), behaviourism comes as close as anything could to a paradigm. It provides: (i) a clear definition of the subject matter (behaviour, as opposed to 'the mind'); (ii) fundamental assumptions, in the form of the central role of learning (especially conditioning), and the analysis of behaviour into stimulus–response units, which allow prediction and control; (iii) a methodology, with the controlled experiment at its core.
- ● *Revolution:* A point is reached in almost all established sciences where the conflicting evidence becomes so overwhelming that the old paradigm has to be abandoned and is replaced by a new one (*paradigm shift*). For example, Newtonian physics was replaced by Einstein's theory of relativity. When this paradigm shift occurs, there is a return to *normal science*.
- ■ Palermo (1971) and LeFrancois (1983) argue that psychology has already undergone several paradigm shifts. The first paradigm was *structuralism*, represented by Wundt's introspectionism. This was replaced by Watson's *behaviourism*. Finally, *cognitive psychology* largely replaced behaviourism, based on the computer analogy and the concept of information processing. Glassman (1995) disagrees, claiming that there never has been a complete reorganisation of the discipline as has happened in physics.

(Based on Gross, 1996)

Is a theoretical approach the same as a paradigm?

As Table 83.3 shows, Kuhn (a philosopher of science), along with some psychologists, maintains that psychology is still a pre-science. Others believe that psychology has already undergone at least two revolutions, and is in a stage of normal science, with cognitive psychology the current paradigm. A third view, which represents a blend of the first two, is that psychology currently, and simultaneously, has a number of paradigms.

For example, Smith & Cowie (1991) identify psychoanalysis, behaviourism, sociobiology, the information-processing, and cognitive–developmental approaches as paradigms, with the last being the most important as far as child development is concerned (see Chapter 41). For Davison & Neale (1994) there are 'four major paradigms of contemporary abnormal psychology', namely, the biological, psychoanalytic, learning (behaviourist) and cognitive (see Chapter 65).

Lambie (1991) believes that it is a mistake to equate 'paradigm' with 'approach'. As noted in Table 83.2, whilst theory is an essential part of a paradigm, there is much more involved than this. For example, different theories can coexist within the same overall approach, such as classical and operant conditioning within 'learning theory' (the behaviourist approach), and Freud's and Erikson's theories within the psychodynamic approach.

One of the 'ingredients' that makes a paradigm different from an approach is its *social psychological* dimension. Paradigms refer to assumptions and beliefs held in common by most, if not all, the members of a given scientific community. This issue is discussed further in the following section.

Is it appropriate to study human behaviour using scientific methods?

THE SOCIAL NATURE OF SCIENCE: THE PROBLEM OF OBJECTIVITY

'Doing science' is part of human behaviour. When psychologists study what people do, they are engaging in some of the very same behaviours they are trying to understand (such as thinking, perceiving, problem-solving and explaining). This is what is meant by the statement that psychologists are part of their own subject matter, which makes it even more difficult for them to be objective than other scientists.

According to Richards (1996b):

'Whereas in orthodox sciences there is always some external object of enquiry – rocks, electrons, DNA, chemicals – existing essentially unchanging in the non-human world (even if never finally knowable 'as it really is' beyond human conceptions), this is not so for Psychology. 'Doing Psychology' is the human activity of studying human activity; it is human psychology examining itself – and what it produces by way of new theories, ideas and beliefs about itself is also part of our psychology!'.

Knowable 'as it really is' refers to objectivity, and Richards is claiming that it may be impossible for *any* scientist to achieve complete objectivity. One reason for this relates to the social nature of scientific activity. Does this mean that 'the truth' only exists 'by agreement'? Does science tell us not about what things are 'really' like, but only what scientists happen to believe is the truth at any particular time?

Exercise 6

Given what was said earlier about the sometimes very intense feelings aroused in individual scientists during the course of their work (see Box 83.5), in what ways do you think science can be described as a social activity? (It might be useful to think about why you do practicals – other than because you have to!)

According to Richardson (1991), whatever the *logical* aspects of scientific method may be (deriving hypotheses from theories, the importance of refutability and so on):

'science is a very *social* business. Yet this exposure of scientific activities to national and international comment and criticism is what distinguishes it from the 'folklore' of informal theories'.

Research must be qualified and quantified to enable others to replicate it, and in this way the procedures, instruments and measures become standardised, so that scientists anywhere in the world can check the truth of reported observations and findings. This implies the need for universally agreed conventions for reporting these observations and findings (Richardson, 1991).

Collins (1994) takes a more extreme view, arguing that the results of experiments are more ambiguous than they are usually taken to be, whilst theory is more flexible than most people imagine:

'This means that science can progress only within communities that can reach consensus about what counts as plausible. Plausibility is a matter of social context so science is a "social construct"' (Collins, 1994).

Kuhn's concept of a paradigm also stresses the role of agreement or consensus among fellow scientists working within a particular discipline. Accordingly, 'truth' has more to do with the popularity and widespread acceptance of a particular framework within the scientific community than with its 'truth value'. The fact that revolutions do occur (paradigm shifts: see Table 83.3) demonstrates that 'the truth' can and does change.

For example, the change from Newtonian to Einsteinian physics reflected the changing popularity of these two accounts. For Planck, who helped to shape the 'Einsteinian revolution':

'a new scientific theory does not triumph by convincing its opponents and making them see the light, but rather because its opponents eventually die, and a new generation grows up that is familiar with it' (Cited in Kuhn, 1970).

However, the popularity or acceptability of a theory must be at least partly determined by how well it explains and predicts the phenomena in question. In other words, *both* social and 'purely' scientific or rational criteria are relevant.

However, even if there are widely accepted ways of 'doing science', 'good science' does not necessarily mean 'good psychology'. Is it valid to study human behaviour and experience as part of the natural world, or is a different kind of approach needed altogether? After all, it is not just psychologists who observe, experiment and theorise (Heather, 1976).

THE PSYCHOLOGY EXPERIMENT AS A SOCIAL SITUATION

To regard empirical research in general, and the experiment in particular, as objective involves two related assumptions. The first is that researchers only influence the *participant's* behaviour (the outcome of the experiment) to the extent that they decide what hypothesis to test, how the variables are to be operationalised, what design to use, and so on. The second assumption is that the only factors influencing the participants' performance are the objectively defined variables manipulated by the experimenter.

Exercise 7

Try to formulate some arguments *against* these two assumptions. What do the experimenter and participant bring with them into the experimental situation that is not directly related to the experiment, and how may this (and other factors) influence what goes on in the experimental situation? (See Chapters 2 and 84.)

Experimenters are people too: the problem of experimenter bias

According to Rosenthal (1966), what the experimenter is *like* is correlated with what he or she *does*, as well as influencing the participant's perception of, and response to, the experimenter. This is related to *experimenter bias*.

Box 83.6   Some examples of experimenter bias

According to Valentine (1992), experimenter bias has been demonstrated in a variety of experiments, including reaction time, psychophysics, non-human learning,

---

verbal conditioning, personality assessment, person perception, learning and ability, as well as in everyday life situations.

What these experiments consistently show is that if one group of experimenters has one hypothesis about what it expects to find and another group has the opposite hypothesis, both groups will obtain results that support their respective hypotheses. The results are *not* due to the mishandling of data by biased experimenters, but the experimenter's bias somehow creates a changed environment, in which participants actually behave differently.

Experimenters who had been informed that rats learning mazes had been specially bred for this ability ('maze-bright'), obtained better learning from their rats than did experimenters who believed that their rats were 'maze-dull' (Rosenthal & Fode, 1963; Rosenthal & Lawson, 1961). In fact, both groups of rats were drawn from the *same* population and were *randomly* allocated to the 'bright' or 'dull' condition. The crucial point is that the 'bright' rats did actually learn faster. The experimenters' expectations in some way concretely changed the situation, although *how* this happened is far less clear.

In a natural classroom situation, children whose teachers were told that they would show academic 'promise' during the next academic year, showed significantly greater IQ gains than children for whom such predictions were not made (although this group also made substantial improvements). The children were, in fact, *randomly* allocated to the two conditions, but the teachers' expectations actually produced the predicted improvements in the 'academic promise' group, that is, there was a *self-fulfilling prophecy* (Rosenthal & Jacobson, 1968).

(Based on Valentine, 1992, and Weisstein, 1993)

Exercise 8

How could you explain the findings from the studies described in Box 83.6? How could experimenter expectations actually bring about the different performances of the two groups of rats and children?

Participants are psychologists too: demand characteristics

Instead of seeing the person being studied as a passive responder to whom things are done ('subject'), Orne (1962) stresses what the person *does*, implying a far more active role. Participants' performance in an experiment could be thought of as a form of problem-solving behaviour. At some level, they see the task as working out the true purpose of the experiment and responding in a way which will support (or not support, in the case of the unhelpful participant: see Chapter 2, page 20) the hypothesis being tested.

In this context, the cues which convey the experimental hypothesis to participants represent important influences on their behaviour, and the sum total of those cues are called *demand characteristics* of the experimental situation. These cues include:

'the rumours or campus scuttlebut [gossip] about the research, the information conveyed during the original situation, the person of the experimenter, and the setting of the laboratory, as well as all explicit and implicit communications during the experiment proper' (Orne, 1962).

This tendency to identify the demand characteristics is related to the tendency to play the role of a 'good' (or 'bad') experimental subject.

Box 83.7   The lengths that some people will go to to please the experimenter

Orne points out that if people are asked to do five push-ups as a favour, they will ask 'Why?', but if the request comes from an experimenter, they will ask 'Where?' Similarly, he reports an experiment in which people were asked to add sheets of random numbers, then tear them up into at least 32 pieces. Five-and-a-half hours later, they were still at it and the experimenter had to stop them!

This demonstrates very clearly the strong tendency to want to please the experimenter, and not to 'upset the experiment'. It is mainly in this sense that Orne sees the experiment as a social situation, in which the people involved play different but complementary roles. In order for this interaction to proceed fairly smoothly, each must have some idea of what the other expects of him or her.

The expectations referred to in Box 83.7 are part of the culturally shared understandings of what science in general, and psychology in particular, involves and without which the experiment could not 'happen' (Moghaddam *et al.*, 1993). So not only is the experiment a social situation, but science itself is a *culture-related phenomenon*. This represents another respect in which science cannot claim complete objectivity.

THE PROBLEM OF REPRESENTATIVENESS

Traditional, mainstream experimental psychology adopts a *nomothetic* ('law-like') approach. This involves generalisation from limited samples of participants to 'people in general', as part of the attempt to establish general 'laws' or principles of behaviour (see Figure 83.5, page 715).

Exercise 9

Figure 83.6 captures a fairly typical scene as far as participant characteristics in mainstream psychological research are concerned.

Figure 83.6

In this photograph of one of Asch's famous conformity experiments (see Chapter 58, pages 499–502), what are the most apparent characteristics of the experimental participants, and how are they similar to/different from those of Asch (who is pictured furthest right)?

Despite the fact that Asch's experiments were carried out in the early 1950s, very little has changed as far as participant samples are concerned. In American psychology, at least, the typical participant is a psychology undergraduate, who is obliged to take part in a certain number of studies as a course requirement and who receives 'course credit' for so doing (Krupat & Garonzik, 1994).

Mainstream British and American psychology has implicitly equated 'human being' with 'member of Western culture'. Despite the fact that the vast majority of research participants are members of Western societies, the resulting findings and theories have been applied to 'human beings' as if culture made no difference. This Anglocentric or Eurocentric bias (a form of *ethnocentrism*) is matched by the androcentric or masculinist bias (a form of *sexism*), according to which the behaviours and experiences of men are taken as the standard against which women are judged (see Chapter 84).

In both cases, whilst the bias remains implicit and goes unrecognised (and is reinforced by psychology's claim to be objective and value-free), research findings are taken as providing us with an objective, scientifically valid, account of what 'women/people in general are like'. Once we realise that scientists, like all human beings, have prejudices, biases and values, their research and theory begin

to look less objective, reliable and valid than they did before (see Chapter 84).

THE PROBLEM OF ARTIFICIALITY

Criticisms of traditional empirical methods (especially the laboratory experiment) have focused on their *artificiality*, including the often unusual and bizarre tasks that people are asked to perform in the name of science (see Box 83.7). Yet we cannot be sure that the way people behave in the laboratory is an accurate indication of how they are likely to behave outside it (Heather, 1976).

What makes the laboratory experiment such an unnatural and artificial situation is the fact that it is almost totally structured by one 'participant' – the experimenter. This relates to *power differences* between experimenters and their 'subjects', which is as much an *ethical* as a practical issue and is discussed further in Chapter 85.

Traditionally, participants have been referred to as 'subjects', implying something less than a person, a dehumanised and depersonalised 'object'. According to Heather (1976), it is a small step from reducing the person to a mere thing or object (or experimental 'subject'), to seeing people as machines or machine-like ('mechanism' = 'machine-ism' = mechanistic view of people). This way of thinking about people is reflected in the popular definition of psychology as the study of 'what makes people tick' (see Chapter 1 and page 710).

THE PROBLEM OF INTERNAL VERSUS EXTERNAL VALIDITY

If the experimental setting (and task) is seen as similar or relevant enough to everyday situations to allow us to generalise the results, we say that the study has high *external* or *ecological validity*. But what about *internal validity*? Modelling itself on natural science, psychology attempts to overcome the problem of the complexity of human behaviour by using *experimental control*. This involves isolating an independent variable (IV) and ensuring that extraneous variables (variables other than the IV likely to affect the dependent variable) do not affect the outcome (see Chapter 2). But this begs the crucial question: *how do we know when all the relevant extraneous variables have been controlled?*

Box 83.8   Some difficulties with the notion of experimental control

- Whilst it is relatively easy to control the more obvious *situational variables*, this is more difficult with *participant variables* (such as age, gender and culture), either for practical reasons (such as the availability of

---

these groups), or because it is not always obvious exactly what the relevant variables are. Ultimately, it is down to the experimenter's judgement and intuition: what he or she believes is important (and possible) to control (Deese, 1972).

- If judgement and intuition are involved, then control and objectivity are matters of degree, whether it is in psychology or physics (see Table 83.1).

- It is the *variability/heterogeneity* of human beings that makes them so much more difficult to study than, say, chemicals. Chemists don't usually have to worry about how two samples of a particular chemical might be different from each other, but psychologists definitely do have to allow for individual differences between participants.

- We cannot just assume that the IV (or 'stimulus' or 'input') is identical for every participant, and can be defined in some objective way, independently of the participant, exerting a standard effect on everyone. The attempt to define IVs (and DVs) in this way can be regarded as a form of reductionism (see Chapter 81).

- Complete control would mean that the IV alone was responsible for the DV, so that experimenter bias and the effect of demand characteristics were irrelevant. But even if complete control were possible (even if we could guarantee the *internal validity* of the experiment), a fundamental dilemma would remain. The greater the degree of control over the experimental situation, the more different it becomes from real-life situations (the more artificial it gets and the lower its *external validity*).

As Box 83.8 indicates, in order to discover the relationships between variables (necessary for understanding human behaviour in natural, real-life situations), psychologists must 'bring' the behaviour into a specially created environment (the laboratory), where the relevant variables can be controlled in a way that is impossible in naturally-occurring settings. However, in doing so, psychologists have constructed an artificial environment and the resulting behaviour is similarly artificial. It is no longer the behaviour they were trying to understand!

Conclusions

Psychology as a separate field of study grew out of several other disciplines, both scientific (such as physiology), and non-scientific (in particular philosophy). For much of its life as an independent discipline, and through what some call revolutions and paradigm shifts, it has taken the natural sciences as its model (scientism). This chapter has highlighted some of the major implications of adopting methods of investigating the natural world and applying them to the study of human behaviour and experience. In doing this, the chapter has also examined what are fast becoming out-dated and inaccurate views about the nature of science. Ultimately, whatever a particular science may claim to have discovered about the phenomena it studies, scientific activity remains just one more aspect of human behaviour.

Summary

■ **Philosophical dualism** enabled scientists to describe the world **objectively**, which became the ideal of science. Its extension by Comte to the study of human behaviour and social institutions is called **positivism**. Descartes extended **mechanism** to the human body, but the mind remained accessible only through **introspection**.

■ **Empirism** emphasises the importance of sensory experience, as opposed to **nativism's** claim that knowledge is innate. 'Empirical' implies that the essence of science is collecting data/'facts' through experiments and observations. Empirism influenced psychology through its influence on physiology, physics and chemistry.

■ **Wundt** is generally regarded as the founder of the new science of experimental psychology, establishing its first laboratory in 1879. He used **introspection** to study conscious experience, analysing it into its basic elements (**sensations** and **feelings**). This is called **structuralism**.

■ **James** is the other pioneer of scientific psychology. He influenced several important research areas, and helped make Freud's ideas popular in America. His views influenced **functionalism** which, in turn, stimulated interest in individual differences.

■ **Watson's** criticisms of introspection culminated in his 1913 'behaviourist manifesto'. He argued that for psychology to be objective, it must study behaviour rather than mental life, its goals should be the prediction and control of **behaviour**, and there are only **quantitative** differences between human and non-human behaviour. The conditioned reflex could become the basis of a full-scale human psychology.

■ Instead of the mind being influenced by experience (as Locke believed), Watson saw **behaviour** as shaped by the environment. Empirism provided for psychology both a **methodology** and a **theory** (including analysis into elements and **associationism**). Consciousness and subjective experience had no place in the behaviourist world and people were studied as 'natural phenomena'.

■ Dissatisfaction with behaviourism culminated in the 1956 'cognitive revolution'. At the centre of this new **information-processing approach** lay the **computer analogy**.

■ Despite this major change, **mainstream** psychology (the 'old paradigm') has survived. **Scientism** maintains that all aspects of human behaviour can and should be studied using the methods of natural science, and involves 'context-stripping' and the **value-free**, objective use of laboratory experiments in particular. People are seen as passive and mechanical information-processing devices and treated as interchangeable 'subjects'.

■ A science must possess a definable **subject matter**, involve **theory construction** and **hypothesis testing**, and use **empirical methods** for data collection. However, these characteristics fail to describe the **scientific process** or **scientific method**, about which there are several common misconceptions. Whilst the classical view of science is built around the **inductive method**, Popper's revised view stresses the **hypothetico-deductive method**. The two methods are complementary.

■ Different theoretical **approaches** can be seen as self-contained disciplines, making psychology **pre-paradigmatic** and so still in a stage of **pre-science**. According to Kuhn, only when a discipline possesses a paradigm has it reached the stage of **normal science**, after which **paradigm shifts** result in **revolution** (and a return to normal science). However, 'paradigm' and 'approach' are different, with the former involving a **social psychological** dimension.

■ Even where there are external objects of scientific enquiry (as in chemistry), complete objectivity may be impossible. Whatever the **logical** aspects of scientific method may be, science is a very **social** activity. Consensus among colleagues is paramount, as shown by the fact that revolutions involve re-defining 'the truth'.

■ **Experimenter bias** and **demand characteristics** make psychological research (especially experiments) even less objective than natural sciences. Environmental changes are somehow produced by experimenters' expectations, and demand characteristics influence participants' behaviours by helping to convey the experimental hypothesis. Their performance is a form of problem-solving behaviour and reflects their playing the roles of 'good' (or 'bad') experimental subjects. The experiment is a social situation and science itself is **culture-related**.

■ The **artificiality** of laboratory experiments is largely due to their being totally structured by experimenters. Also, the higher an experiment's **internal validity**, the lower its **external validity** becomes. Whilst certain **situational variables** can be controlled quite easily, this is more difficult with **participant variables**.

84

BIAS IN PSYCHOLOGICAL THEORY AND RESEARCH

Introduction and overview

As was seen in Chapter 83, mainstream academic psychology, modelling itself on classical, orthodox, natural science (such as physics and chemistry), claims to be *objective*, *unbiased*, and *value-free* (collectively referred to as the *positivist* view of science, or *positivism*). As applied to the study of humans, this implies that it is possible to study people as they 'really are', without the psychologist's characteristics influencing the outcome of the investigation in any way.

This chapter shows that a view of psychology as unbiased and value-free is mistaken. It discusses two major forms of bias (namely, *sexism* and *ethnocentrism*, relating to gender and culture respectively) which permeate much psychological theory and research.

Much of this chapter's content is relevant to the topic of prejudice and discrimination. As Chapters 53 and 54 showed, prejudice and discrimination can be understood as characteristics of *individuals* or of *social groups*, *institutions* and even *whole societies*. With bias in psychological theory and research, it is sometimes individual psychologists, and sometimes 'psychology as a whole' that are being accused.

Gender bias: feminist psychology, sexism and androcentrism

Not surprisingly, most of the criticism of mainstream psychology regarding its gender bias has come from *feminist psychology*, which Wilkinson (1997) defines as:

'... psychological theory and practice which is explicitly informed by the political goals of the feminist movement ...'.

Whilst feminism can take a variety of forms, two common themes are the valuation of women as worthy of study in their own right (not just in comparison with men), and recognition of the need for social change on behalf of women.

Feminist psychology is openly political (Unger & Crawford, 1992) and sets out to challenge the discipline of psychology for its inadequate and damaging theories about women, and for its failure to see power relations as central to social life. More specifically, it insists on exposing and challenging the operation of male power in psychology:

'... psychology's theories often exclude women, or distort our experience by assimilating it to male norms or man-made stereotypes, or by regarding "women" as a unitary category, to be understood only in comparison with the unitary category "men" ... Similarly, psychology [screens out] ... the existence and operation of social and structural inequalities between and within social groups ... ' (Wilkinson, 1991).

Psychology obscures the social and structural operation of male power by concentrating its analysis on people as individuals *(individualism)*. Responsibility (and pathology: see Chapter 69) are located within the individual, to the total neglect of social and political oppression. By ignoring or minimising the *social context*, psychology obscures the mechanisms of oppression. For example, the unhappiness of some women after childbirth is treated as a problem in individual functioning (with possible hormonal causes), thus distracting attention away from the difficult material situation in which many new mothers find themselves (Wilkinson, 1997: see Chapter 69).

> **Box 84.1 Some major feminist criticisms of psychology**
>
> - Much psychological research is conducted on all-male samples, but then either fails to make this clear or reports the findings as if they applied equally to women and men.
>
> - Some of the most influential theories within psychology as a whole are based on studies of males only, but are meant to apply equally to women and men.
>
> - If women's behaviour differs from men's, the former is often judged to be pathological, abnormal or deficient in some way *(sexism)*, since the behaviour of men is, implicitly or explicitly, taken as the 'standard' or norm against which women's behaviour is compared

(*androcentrism*, male-centredness, or the *masculinist bias*).

- Psychological explanations of behaviour tend to emphasise biological (and other internal) causes, as opposed to social (and other external) causes (*individualism*). This gives (and reinforces) the impression that psychological sex differences are inevitable and unchangeable. This reinforces widely held stereotypes about men and women, contributing to the oppression of women (another form of *sexism*).

- Heterosexuality (both male and female) is taken, implicitly or explicitly, as the norm, so that homosexuality is seen as abnormal (*heterosexism*).

Exercise 1

Try to think of (at least) one example for each of the five major criticisms of psychological theory and research made in Box 84.1. Regarding the fourth point, how does this relate to attribution theory as discussed in Chapter 52?

THE FEMINIST CRITIQUE OF SCIENCE

In many ways, a more fundamental criticism of psychology than those listed in Box 84.1 is feminists' belief that scientific enquiry itself (whether this be within psychology or not) is biased.

Psychology's claims to be a science are based on its methods (especially the experiment) and the belief that it is a value-free discipline (see Chapter 83). However, as far as the latter is concerned, can scientific enquiry be neutral, wholly independent of the value system of the human scientists involved? According to Prince & Hartnett (1993):

'Decisions about what is, and what is not, to be measured, how this is done, and most importantly, what constitutes legitimate research are made by individual scientists within a socio-political context, and thus science is ideological ...'.

As far as scientific method is concerned, many feminist psychologists argue that it is itself gender-biased. For example, Nicolson (1995) identifies two major problems associated with adherence to the 'objective' investigation of behaviour for the way knowledge claims are made about women and gender differences.

First, the experimental environment takes the individual 'subject's *behaviour*' as distinct from the 'subject' herself as the unit of study. Therefore, it becomes deliberately blind to the behaviour's *meaning*, including the social, personal and cultural contexts in which it is enacted. As a result, claims about gender differences in competence

and behaviour are attributed to intrinsic (either the product of 'gender role socialisation' or biology) as opposed to contextual qualities. This is another reference to *individualism* (see page 723).

Second, experimental psychology, far from being context-free, takes place in a very specific context which typically disadvantages women (Eagly, 1987). In an experiment, a woman becomes anonymous, stripped of her social roles and accompanying power and knowledge she might have achieved in the outside world. She is placed in this 'strange', environment, and expected to respond to the needs of (almost inevitably) a male experimenter who is in charge of the situation, with all the social meaning ascribed to gender power relations.

The belief that it is possible to study people 'as they really are', removed from their usual socio-cultural context (in a 'de-contextualised' way), is completely invalid:

'Psychology relies for its data on the practices of socialised and culture-bound individuals, so that to explore 'natural' or 'culture-free' behaviour (namely that behaviour unfettered by cultural, social structures and power relations) is by definition impossible ...' (Nicolson, 1995).

Feminist psychologists offer a critical challenge to psychological knowledge on gender issues by drawing on other disciplines, such as sociology. According to Giddens (1979), for example:

'There is no static knowledge about people to be 'discovered' or 'proved' through reductionist experimentation, and thus the researcher takes account of context, meaning and change over time'.

Exercise 2

Do you agree with Nicolson's claim that all human behaviour is 'culture-bound? What about 'instinctive' behaviours, such as eating, drinking and sex: does culture play a part here too? If so, in what ways? (These questions are equally relevant to the section on culture bias.)

SOME PRACTICAL CONSEQUENCES OF GENDER BIAS

For Prince & Hartnett (1993), scientific psychology has *reified* concepts such as personality and intelligence (treating abstract or metaphorical terms as if they were 'things' or entities):

'... and the scientific psychology which 'objectively' and 'rationally' produced means of measuring these reifications has been responsible for physical assaults on women such as forced abortions and sterilisations'.

Between 1924 and 1972, more than 7500 women in the state of Virginia alone were forcibly sterilised, in particular, 'unwed mothers, prisoners, the feeble-minded, children with discipline problems'. The criterion used in all cases was mental age as measured by the Stanford–Binet intelligence test (Gould, 1981).

Having convinced society that intelligence 'exists' in some objective way, and having produced a means of measuring it, psychologists could then promote and justify discrimination against particular social groups. Another example of the use of intelligence tests to justify blatant discrimination (although not specifically against women) involved the army alpha and beta tests (see Chapter 82), which influenced the passing of the 1924 Immigration Restriction Act in the USA.

Box 84.2   Psychology's influence on immigration policy in the USA

Debates in Congress leading to passage of the Immigration Restriction Act of 1924 continually made reference to data from the army alpha and beta tests. Eugenicists (those who advocate 'selective breeding' in humans in order to 'improve' genetic stock) lobbied for immigration limits and for imposing harsh quotas against nations of inferior stock. In short, Southern and Eastern Europeans, who scored lowest on the army tests, should be kept out. The eugenicists battled and won one of the greatest victories of scientific racism in American history. 'America must be kept American', proclaimed President Coolidge as he signed the bill.

Throughout the 1930s, Jewish refugees, anticipating the Holocaust, sought to emigrate, but were refused admission. Estimates suggest that the quotas barred up to six million Southern, Central and Eastern Europeans between 1924 and 1939.

'We know what happened to many who wished to leave, but had nowhere to go. The paths to destruction are often indirect, but ideas can be agents as sure as guns and bombs' (Gould, 1981).

(From Gould, 1981)

In the 1993 preface to *In a Different Voice* (1982), Gilligan says that at the core of her work on moral development in women and girls (see below) was the realisation that within psychology, and in society at large, 'values were taken as facts'. She continues:

' ... in the aftermath of the Holocaust ... it is not tenable for psychologists or social scientists to adopt a position of ethical neutrality or cultural relativism ... Such a hands-off stance in the face of atrocity amounts to a kind of complicity'.

Whilst the example she gives is clearly extreme, it helps to illustrate the argument that not only do psychologists (and other scientists) have a responsibility to make their values explicit about important social and political issues, but failure to do so may (unwittingly) contribute to prejudice, discrimination and oppression. These considerations are as relevant to a discussion of the ethics of psychological research as they are to gender (and culture) bias, and are discussed in more detail in Chapter 85.

THE MASCULINIST BIAS AND SEXISM: A CLOSER LOOK

Box 84.1 identified the masculinist bias (*androcentrism*) and sexism as two major criticisms of mainstream psychology made by feminist psychologists. Whilst each of these can take different forms, emphasis here will be given to (a) the argument that men are taken as some sort of standard or norm, against which women are compared and judged, and (b) gender bias in psychological research.

The male norm as the standard

According to Tavris (1993):

'In any domain of life in which men set the standard of normalcy, women will be considered abnormal, and society will debate woman's 'place' and her 'nature'. Many women experience tremendous conflict in trying to decide whether to be 'like' men or 'opposite' from them, and this conflict is itself evidence of the implicit male standard against which they are measuring themselves. This is why it is normal for women to feel abnormal'.

She gives two examples of why it is normal for women to feel abnormal. First, in 1985, the American Psychiatric Association proposed two new categories of mental disorder for inclusion in the revised (third) edition of the *Diagnostic and Statistical Manual of Mental Disorders* (DSM-III-R: see Chapter 67). One was *masochistic personality*. In DSM-II this was described as one of the psychosexual disorders in which sexual gratification requires being hurt or humiliated. The proposal was to extend the term so that it became a more pervasive personality disorder, in which one seeks failure at work, at home, and in relationships, rejects opportunities for pleasure, puts others first, thereby sacrificing one's own needs, plays the martyr, and so on.

Whilst not intended to apply to women exclusively, these characteristics are associated predominantly with the female role. Indeed, according to Caplan (1991), it represented a way of calling psychopathological the behaviour of women who conform to social norms for a 'feminine woman' (the 'good wife syndrome').

In short, such a diagnostic label was biased against women and perpetuated the myth of women's masochism. The label was eventually changed to *self-defeating personality disorder* and was put in the appendix of DSM-III-R.

Exercise 3

If you were proposing a parallel diagnosis for men who conform to social norms for a 'masculine man', what characteristics would this have to include, and what would you call it? Could you justify extending *sadism* to conformist men?

Tavris's second example of why it is normal for women to feel abnormal concerns causal attributions made about men's and women's behaviours. When men have problems, such as drug abuse, and behave in socially unacceptable ways, as in rape and other forms of violence, the causes are looked for in their upbringings. Women's problems, however, are seen as the result of their psyches or hormones. This is another form of *individualism*, with the further implication that it could have been different for men (they are the victims of their childhood, for example), but not for women ('that's what women are like').

The 'mismeasure of woman'

According to Tavris, the view that man is the norm and woman is the opposite, lesser or deficient (the problem) constitutes one of three currently competing views regarding the 'mismeasure of woman' (meant to parallel Gould's, 1981, the *Mismeasure of Man*, a renowned critique of intelligence testing: see Chapter 82). It is the view that underpins so much psychological research designed to discover why women aren't 'as something' (moral, intelligent, rational) as men. It also underlies the enormous self-help industry, whereby women consume millions of books and magazines advising them how to become more beautiful, independent and so on. Men, being normal, feel no need to 'fix' themselves in corresponding ways (Tavris, 1993).

Box 84.3 A demonstration of the 'mismeasure of woman'

Wilson (1994) states that the reason 95 per cent of bank managers, company directors, judges and university professors in Britain are men is that men are 'more competitive' and because 'dominance is a personality characteristic determined by male hormones'.

He also argues that women in academic jobs are less productive than men: 'objectively speaking, women

may already be over-promoted'. Women who *do* achieve promotion to top management positions 'may have brains that are masculinised'.

The research cited by Wilson to support these claims comes partly from the psychometric testing industries (see Chapter 82) which provide 'scientific' evidence of women's inadequacies, such as (compared with men) their lack of mathematical and spatial abilities. Even if women are considered to have the abilities to perform well in professional jobs, they have personality defects (in particular, low self-esteem and lack of assertiveness) which impede performance.

According to Wilson (1994):

'These differences [in mental abilities, motivation, personality and values] are deep-rooted, based in biology, and not easily dismantled by social engineering. Because of them we are unlikely to see the day when the occupational profiles of men and women are the same ...'.

(From Wilson, 1994, and Wilkinson, 1997)

Exercise 4

In Box 84.3, try to identify examples of *individualism*. Can you formulate some arguments *against* Wilson's claims?

Sexism in research

The American Psychological Association's Board of Social and Ethical Responsibility set up a Committee on Nonsexist Research, which reported its findings as *Guidelines for Avoiding Sexism in Psychological Research* (Denmark *et al.*, 1988). This maintains that gender bias is found at all stages of the research process: (i) question formulation (ii) research methods and design (iii) data analysis and interpretation, and (iv) conclusion formulation. The principles set out in the *Guidelines* are meant to apply to other forms of bias too: race, ethnicity, disability, sexual orientation and socio-economic status.

Box 84.4 Examples of gender bias at each stage of the research process

- **Question formulation:** It is assumed that topics relevant to white males are more important and 'basic' (e.g. the effects of TV violence on aggression in boys: see Chapter 64), whilst those relevant to white females, or ethnic minority females or males, are more marginal, specialised, or applied (e.g. the psychological correlates of pregnancy or the menopause).

- **Research methods and design:** Surprisingly often, the sex and race of the participants, researchers, and any confederates who may be involved, are not specified. As a consequence, potential interactions between these variables are not accounted for. For example, men tend to display more helping behaviour than women in studies involving a young, female confederate 'victim' (see Chapter 62). This could be a function of either the sex of the confederate or an interaction between the confederate and the participant, rather than sex differences between the participants (which is the conclusion usually drawn).

- **Data analysis and interpretation:** Significant *sex differences* may be reported in very misleading ways, because the wrong sorts of comparisons are made. For example:

  'The spatial ability scores of women in our sample is significantly lower than those of men, at the 0.01 level'. You might conclude from this that women cannot or should not become architects or engineers. However, 'Successful architects score above 32 on our spatial ability test ... engineers score above 31 ... 12 per cent of women and 16 per cent of men in our sample score above 31; 11 per cent of women and 15 per cent of men score above 32'. What conclusions would you draw now? (Denmark *et al.*, 1988)

- **Conclusion formulation:** Results based on one sex only are then applied to both. This can be seen in some of the major theories within developmental psychology, notably Erikson's psychosocial theory of development (1950), Levinson *et al.*'s (1978) *Seasons of a Man's Life* (see Chapter 48), and Kohlberg's theory of moral development (1969: see Chapter 44). These are discussed further below.

(Based on Denmark *et al.*, 1988)

Sexism in theory

Gilligan (1982) gives Erikson's theory of lifespan development (based on the study of males only) as one example of a sexist theory, which portrays women as 'deviants' (see Chapters 47 and 48). In one version of his theory, Erikson (1950) describes a series of eight *universal* stages, so that, for both sexes, in all cultures, the conflict between *identity* and *role confusion* (adolescence) precedes that between *intimacy* and *isolation* (young adulthood). In another version, he acknowledges that the sequence is *different* for the female, who postpones her identity as she prepares to attract the man whose name she will adopt, and by whose status she will be defined (Erikson, 1968). For women, intimacy seems to go along with identity: they come to know themselves through their relationships with others (Gilligan, 1982).

Despite his observation of sex differences, Erikson's *epigenetic chart* of the life-cycle remains unchanged. As Gilligan points out:

'identity continues to precede intimacy as male experience continues to define his [Erikson's] life-cycle concept'.

Similarly, Kohlberg's (1969) six-stage theory of moral development was based on a 20-year longitudinal study of 84 boys, but he claims that these stages are universal (see Chapter 44). Females rarely attain a level of moral reasoning above stage three ('Good boy–nice girl' orientation), which is supposed to be achieved by most adolescents and adults. This leaves females looking decidedly morally deficient.

Like other feminist psychologists, Gilligan argues that psychology speaks with a 'male voice', describing the world from a male perspective and confusing this with absolute truth. The task of feminist psychology is to listen to women and girls who speak in a 'different voice' (Gilligan, 1982; Brown & Gilligan, 1992). Gilligan's work with females has led her to argue that men and women have qualitatively different conceptions of morality, with moral dilemmas being 'solved' in terms of care, responsibility and relationships. Men are more likely to stress rights and rules.

Exercise 5

In what ways is Freud's psychoanalytic theory (especially the psychosexual stages of development) sexist (or what Grosz, 1987, calls 'phallocentric')? (Repeat this exercise for Levinson *et al.*'s theory of adult development, and any other theory you are familiar with.)

Culture bias

In discussing gender bias, several references have been made to cultural bias. Denmark *et al.*'s (1988) report on sexism is meant to apply equally to all other major forms of bias, including cultural (see Box 84.4). Ironically, many feminist critics of Gilligan's ideas have argued that women are not a cohesive group who speak in a single voice, a view which imposes a false sameness upon the diversity of women's voices across differences of age, ethnicity, (dis)ability, class and other social divisions (Wilkinson, 1997).

Exercise 6

Before reading on, ask yourself what is meant by the term 'culture'. How is it related to 'race', 'ethnicity' and 'sub-cultures'?

CROSS-CULTURAL PSYCHOLOGY AND ETHNOCENTRISM

According to Smith & Bond (1993), cross-cultural psychology studies variability in behaviour among the various societies and cultural groups around the world. For Jahoda (1978), its additional goal is to identify what is similar across different cultures, and thus likely to be our common human heritage (the universals of human behaviour).

Cross-cultural psychology is important because it helps to correct *ethnocentrism*, the strong human tendency to use our own ethnic or cultural groups' norms and values to define what is 'natural' and 'correct' for everyone ('reality': Triandis, 1990). Historically, psychology has been dominated by white, middle class males in the USA. Over the last century, they have enjoyed a monopoly as both the researchers and the 'subjects' of the discipline (Moghaddam & Studer, 1997). They constitute the core of psychology's First World (Moghaddam, 1987).

> ## Box 84.5 Psychology's First, Second and Third Worlds
>
> - The USA, the *First World* of psychology, dominates the international arena and monopolises the manufacture of psychological knowledge, which it exports to other countries around the globe, through control over books and journals, test manufacture and distribution, training centres and so on.
>
> - The *Second World* countries comprise Western European nations and Russia. They have far less influence in shaping psychology around the world, although, ironically, it is in these countries that modern psychology has its philosophical roots (see Chapter 83). Just as the countries of the Second World find themselves overpowered by US pop culture, they also find themselves overwhelmed by US-manufactured psychological knowledge.
>
> - *Third World* countries are mostly importers of psychological knowledge, first from the USA but also from the Second World countries with which they historically had colonial ties (such as Pakistan and England). India is the most important Third World 'producer' of psychological knowledge, but even there most research follows the lines established by the US and, to a lesser extent, Western Europe.
>
> (From Moghaddam & Studer, 1997)

According to Moghaddam *et al.* (1993), American researchers and participants:

> 'have shared a lifestyle and value system that differs not only from that of most other people in North America, such as ethnic minorities and women, but also the vast majority of people in the rest of the world'.

Yet the findings from this research, and the theories based upon it, have been applied to *people in general*, as if culture makes no difference. An implicit equation is made between 'human being' and 'human being from Western culture' (the *Anglocentric* or *Eurocentric bias*).

When members of other cultural groups have been studied, it has usually been to compare them with Western samples, using the behaviour and experience of the latter as the 'standard'. As with androcentrism, it is the failure to acknowledge this bias which creates the misleading and false impression that what is being said about behaviour can be generalised without qualification.

Cross-cultural psychologists do *not* equate 'human being' with 'member of Western culture', because for them, cultural background is the crucial *independent variable*. In view of the domination of First World psychology, this distinction becomes crucial. At the same time, the search for universal principles of human behaviour is quite valid (and is consistent with the 'classical' view of science: see Chapter 83).

WHAT IS CULTURE?

Herskovits (1955) defines culture as 'the human-made part of the environment'. For Triandis (1994):

> 'Culture is to society what memory is to individuals. In other words, culture includes the traditions that tell 'what has worked' in the past. It also encompasses the way people have learned to look at their environment and themselves, and their unstated assumptions about the way the world is and the way people should act'.

The 'human-made' part of the environment can be broken down into *objective* aspects (such as tools, roads, radio stations) and *subjective* aspects (such as categorisations, associations, norms, roles, values). This allows us to examine how subjective culture influences behaviour (Triandis, 1994). Whilst culture is made by humans, it also helps to 'make' them: humans have an interactive relationship with culture (Moghaddam *et al.*, 1993).

Much cross-cultural research is actually based on 'national cultures', often comprising a number of sub-cultures, which may be demarcated by religion (as in

Northern Ireland), language (Belgium), or race (Malaysia and Singapore). However, such research often fails to provide any more details about the participants than the name of the country (national culture) in which the study was done. When this happens, we pay two 'penalties'.

First, when we compare national cultures, we can lose track of the enormous diversity found within many of the major nations of the world, and differences found *between* any two countries might well also be found between carefully selected subcultures *within* those countries. Second, there is the danger of implying that national cultures are unitary systems, free of conflict, confusion and dissent. This is rarely the case (Smith & Bond, 1993).

HOW DO CULTURES DIFFER?

Definitions of culture such as those above stress what *different cultures* have in common. To evaluate research findings and theory that are culturally biased, it is even more important to consider the ways in which *cultures are different* from each other. Triandis (1990) identifies several *cultural syndromes*, which he defines as:

'a pattern of values, attitudes, beliefs, norms and behaviours that can be used to contrast a group of cultures to another group of cultures'.

Box 84.6   Three major cultural syndromes used to contrast different cultures

Three major cultural syndromes are *cultural complexity*, *individualism–collectivism*, and *tight vs. loose cultures*.

- **Cultural complexity** refers to how much attention people must pay to *time*. This is related to the number and diversity of the roles that members of the culture typically play. More industrialised and technologically advanced cultures, such as Japan, Sweden and the USA are more complex in this way. (The *concept* of time also differs between cultures: see Chapter 37 , page 318).

- **Individualism–collectivism** refers to whether one's identity is defined by personal choices and achievements (the autonomous individual: *individualism*) or by characteristics of the collective group to which one is more or less permanently attached, such as the family, tribal or religious group, or country (*collectivism*). Whilst people in every culture display both, the *relative* emphasis in the West is towards individualism and in the East towards collectivism. Broadly, *capitalist* politico-economic systems are associated with individualism, while *socialist* societies are associated with collectivism.

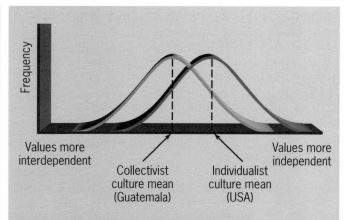

Figure 84.1   Hypothetical distributions of interdependent/independent value scores in a collectivist and an individualist national culture (From Smith & Bond, 1993)

- **Tight** cultures expect their members to behave according to clearly defined norms, and there is very little tolerance of deviation from those norms (see the criteria of normality/abnormality in Chapter 65). Japan is a good example of a tight culture, and Thailand an example of a loose culture.

(Based on Smith & Bond, 1993, and Triandis, 1990, 1994)

The emic–etic distinction

Research has to begin somewhere and, inevitably, this usually involves an instrument or observational technique rooted in the researcher's own culture (Berry, 1969). These can be used for studying *both* cross-cultural differences *and* universal aspects of human behaviour (or the 'psychic unity of mankind').

Exercise 7

Try to identify some behaviours (both normal and abnormal) which can be considered to have both universal (i.e. common to all cultures) *and* culture-specific features.

The distinction between culture-specific and universal behaviour is related to what cross-cultural psychologists call the *emic–etic distinction*, first made by Pike (1954) to refer to two different approaches to the study of behaviour. The *etic* looks at behaviour from outside a particular cultural system, the *emic* from the inside. This derives from the distinction made in linguistics between phon*etics* (the study of universal sounds, independently of their meaning) and phon*emics* (the study of universal sounds as they contribute to meaning: see Chapter 33, page 285).

'Etics' refers to culturally general concepts, which are easier to understand (because they are common to all cultures), whilst 'emics' refers to culturally specific concepts, which include all the ways that particular cultures deal with etics. It is the emics of another culture that are often so difficult to understand (Brislin, 1993).

The research tools that the 'visiting' psychologist brings from 'home' are an emic for the home culture, but when they are assumed to be valid in the 'alien' culture and are used to compare them, they are said to be an *imposed etic* (Berry, 1969). Many attempts to replicate American studies in other parts of the world involve an imposed etic: they all assume that the situation being studied has the same meaning for members of the alien culture as it does for members of the researcher's own culture (Smith & Bond, 1993).

The danger of imposed etics is that they are likely to involve imposition of the researcher's own cultural biases and theoretical framework which simply may not 'fit' the phenomena being studied, resulting in their distortion. A related danger is ethnocentrism (see above).

Box 84.7   Intelligence as an imposed etic

Brislin (1993) gives the example of the concept of intelligence. The etic is 'solving problems, the exact form of which hasn't been seen before', a definition which at least recognises that what constitutes a 'problem' differs between cultures. However, is the emic of 'mental quickness' (as measured by IQ tests, for example) universally valid? Among the Baganda people of Uganda, for example, intelligence is associated with slow, careful, deliberate thought (Wober, 1974). Nor is quick thinking necessarily a valid emic for all schoolchildren within a culturally diverse country like the USA (Brislin, 1993).

Psychologists need to adapt their methods, so that they are studying the same processes in different cultures (Moghaddam *et al.*, 1993). But how do we know that we are studying the same processes? What does 'same' mean in this context? For Brislin (1993), this is the problem of *equivalence*. For a detailed discussion of different kinds of equivalence, see Gross (1995).

Advantages of cross-cultural research

It may now seem obvious (almost 'common sense') to state that psychological theories must be based on the study of people's behaviours from all parts of the world. However, it is important to give specific reasons and examples in support of this argument.

Box 84.8   Major advantages of cross-cultural research

- **Highlighting implicit assumptions:** Cross-cultural research allows investigators to examine the influence of their own beliefs and assumptions, revealing how human behaviour cannot be separated from its cultural context.

- **Separating behaviour from context:** Being able to stand back from their own cultural experiences allows researchers to appreciate the impact of situational factors on behaviour. They are thus less likely to make the *fundamental attribution error* (see Chapter 51), or to use a 'deficit model' to explain the performances of minority group members.

- **Extending the range of variables:** Cross-cultural research expands the range of variables and concepts that can be explored. For example, people in individualist and collectivist cultures tend to explain behaviour in different ways, with the latter less likely to make *dispositional attributions* (see Chapter 51).

- **Separating variables:** Cross-cultural research allows the separation of the effects of variables that may be confounded within a particular culture. For example, studying the effects of television on school achievement is very difficult using just British or American samples, since the vast majority of these families own (at least) one TV set!

- **Testing theories:** Only by conducting cross-cultural research can Western psychologists be sure whether their theories and research findings are relevant outside of their own cultural contexts. For example, Thibaut and Kelley's exchange theory of relationships (see Chapter 56, pages 488), and Sherif *et al.*'s 'Robber's Cave' field experiment on intergroup conflict (see Chapter 53, pages 464–465) have all failed the replication test outside of North American settings.

(Based on Rogoff & Morelli, 1989; Brislin, 1993; Moghaddam *et al.*, 1993, and Smith & Bond, 1993)

Conclusions

This chapter has considered many different examples of how mainstream psychology is biased and, therefore, much less objective and value-free than is required by the positivist view of science it has traditionally modelled itself on. Whilst gender and culture bias are often discussed separately, this chapter has shown that they are actually quite closely related. Despite its shortcomings, Moghaddam & Studer (1997) believe that cross-cultural psychology is one of the avenues through which minorities have begun to have their voices heard in psychology and that:

' there has been a demand that psychology make good its claim to being the science of *humankind* by including women and non-whites as research participants ...'.

Summary

■ A **positivist** study of people implies an objective, value-free psychology, in which the psychologist's characteristics have no influence on the investigation's outcome. However, **sexism** and **ethnocentrism** pervade much psychological theory and research.

■ **Feminist psychologists** challenge mainstream psychology's theories about women, who are either excluded from research studies or whose experiences are assimilated to/matched against male norms (**androcentrism/the masculinist bias**). Male power and social and political oppression are screened out through **individualism,** thus playing down the **social context**. This reinforces popular gender stereotypes, contributing to women's oppression.

■ Feminist psychologists also challenge psychology's claim to be an objective, value-free science. Decisions about what constitutes legitimate research are made by individual scientists within a socio-political context, making science ideological. Scientific method itself is gender-biased, concentrating on the 'subject's' behaviour, rather than its meaning, and ignoring contextual influences. These typically include a male experimenter who controls the situation.

■ One consequence of the **reification** of concepts such as personality and intelligence is enforced sterilisation and abortions among various groups of women. Another is the use of the army alpha and beta tests to justify restricting immigration to the USA in the 1920s and 30s. Psychologists have a responsibility to make their values explicit about important social and political issues, and failure to do so may contribute to discrimination and oppression.

■ Tavris argues that it is normal for women to feel abnormal. An example is the proposal to include **masochistic personality** within DSM-111-R. Although not intended to apply to women exclusively, changing the disorder from a psychosexual to a general personality disorder effectively made 'feminine' behaviour psychopathological. Similarly, whilst men's problems are usually explained in terms of external influences beyond their control, women's problems are attributed to internal factors, such as hormones.

■ Wilson claims that men's success in commerce and academic life is due to their hormonally-determined dominance, and women who are successful may have masculinised brains. Using psychometric test results, he argues that men and women differ in terms of mental abilities, motivation, personality, and values, which are based in biology.

■ According to Denmark *et al.*, gender bias is found at all stages of the **research process**. The last stage (conclusion formulation) is related to **theory construction**. Levinson *et al.'s*, Erikson's, and Kohlberg's theories all claim to present **universal** accounts of development. In fact, they are based on all-male samples and describe the world from male perspectives. Freud's psychoanalytic theory is also 'phallocentric'.

■ Cross-cultural psychology is concerned both with behavioural variability between cultural groups and behavioural universals. It also helps to correct **ethnocentrism**. Historically, psychology has been dominated by white, middle class American males, who constitute the core of psychology's **First World**. The USA exports psychological knowledge to the rest of the world, including **Second World** countries, which are also producers. **Third World** countries are almost exclusively importers.

■ American researchers and participants share a lifestyle and value system which differ from those of both most other North Americans and the rest of the world's population. Yet the research findings are applied to **people in general**, disregarding culture's relevance (the **Anglocentric/Eurocentric bias**). Cross-cultural psychologists take cultural background to be the crucial **independent variable**.

■ Culture is the human-made part of the environment, comprising both **objective** and **subjective** aspects. When cross-cultural researchers compare national cultures, they fail to recognise the great diversity often found **within** them, implying that national cultures are free of conflict and dissent.

■ Cultural differences can be assessed in terms of three major **cultural syndromes**, namely, **cultural complexity, individualism–collectivism**, and **tight vs. loose cultures**. Whilst members of every culture display both individualism and collectivism, the relative emphasis in the West is towards the former, and in the East towards the latter. This also applies to capitalist and socialist politico-economic systems respectively.

■ The distinction between culture-specific and universal behaviour corresponds to the **emic–etic distinction**. When Western psychologists study non-Western cultures, they often use research tools which are emic for them but an **imposed etic** for the culture being studied. This involves imposition of the researcher's own cultural biases and theoretical framework, producing distortion of the phenomenon under investigation.

■ Cross-cultural research allows researchers to examine the influence of their own beliefs and assumptions, and to appreciate the impact of situational factors on behaviour. It also allows separation of the effects of variables that may usually be confounded within the researchers' own cultures. Only by doing cross-cultural research can Western psychologists be sure that their theories and research findings are relevant outside their own cultural contexts.

PART 3

Ethical issues

ETHICAL ISSUES IN PSYCHOLOGY

Introduction and overview

In Chapter 83, it was noted that one of psychology's unique features is that people are both the investigators and the subject matter. This means that the 'things' studied in a psychological investigation are capable of thoughts and feelings. Biologists and medical researchers share this problem of subjecting living, sentient things to sometimes painful, stressful or strange and unusual experiences.

Just as Orne (1962) regards the psychological experiment as primarily a *social situation* (which raises questions of objectivity: see Chapter 83), so every psychological investigation is an *ethical situation* (raising questions of propriety and responsibility). Similarly, just as *methodological* issues permeate psychological research, so do *ethical* issues. For example, the *aims* of psychology as a science (see Chapters 1 and 83) concern what is *appropriate* as much as what is *possible*. Social psychology's use of stooges to deceive naïve participants (see Chapters 58, 59, 62 and 63), and the surgical manipulation of animals' brains in biopsychology (Chapters 3–7) are further examples of the essential difference between the study of the physical world and that of humans and non-humans. What psychologists can and cannot do is determined by the effects of the research on those being studied, as much as by what they want to find out.

However, psychologists are *practitioners* as well as scientists and investigators. They work in practical and clinical settings where people with psychological problems require help (see Chapters 1 and 72–76). Whenever the possibility of *changing* people arises, ethical issues also arise, just as they do in medicine and psychiatry. This chapter looks at

the ethical issues faced by psychologists as scientists/investigators, both of humans and non-humans, and as practitioners.

Codes of conduct and ethical guidelines

Whilst there are responsibilities and obligations common to both the scientist and practitioner roles, there are also some important differences. These are reflected in the *codes of conduct* and *ethical guidelines* published by the major professional bodies for psychologists – the British Psychological Society (BPS) and the American Psychological Association (APA).

The *Code of Conduct for Psychologists* (BPS, 1985: see Figure 85.1) applies to both the major areas of research and practice, and there are additional documents designed for the two areas separately. The *Ethical Principles for Conducting Research with Human Participants* (BPS, 1990, 1993) and the *Guidelines for the Use of Animals in Research* (BPS and the Committee of the Experimental Psychological Society, 1985) obviously apply to the former, whilst, for example, the *Guidelines for the Professional Practice of Clinical Psychology* (BPS, 1983) apply to the latter.

The BPS's *Ethical Principles for Conducting Research with Human Participants* (for the rest of this chapter abbreviated to '*Ethical Principles*') identifies several guiding principles, the most important being *consent/informed consent, withdrawal from the investigation, deception, protection of participants, debriefing*, and *confidentiality*.

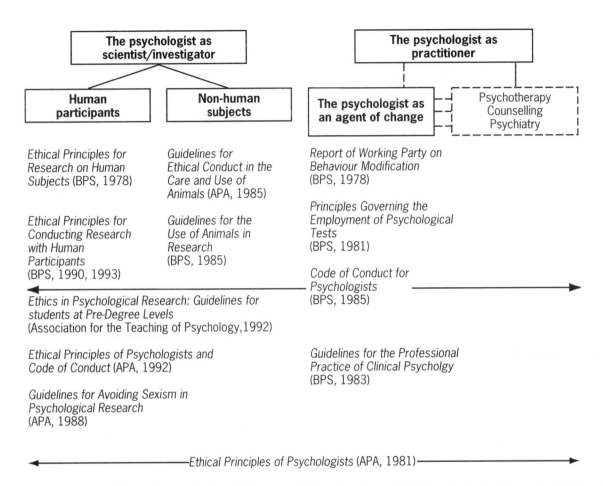

Figure 85.1   Major codes of conduct/ethical guidelines published by the British Psychological Society (BPS) and the American Psychological Association (APA)

Exercise 1

Do you think it is necessary for psychologists to have written codes of conduct and ethical guidelines? What do you consider to be their major functions?

Psychologists as scientists/investigators

The problem of ethics in psychological research is daunting (Gale, 1995). Guidelines are difficult to apply in a hard-and-fast way in any particular research context. Most journals *assume* that researchers have considered ethical issues, rather than requiring formal statements to that effect. The fact that both the BPS and APA codes are periodically reviewed and revised indicates that at least some aspects do not depend on absolute or universal ethical truths (Gale, 1995). Guidelines need to be updated in light of the changing social and political context of

psychological research. For example, new issues, such as sexual behaviour in the context of AIDS, might highlight new ethical problems, and, more importantly, changing views about the nature of individual rights will call into question the extent to which psychological research respects or is insensitive to such rights.

Human participants

Figure 85.1 shows that the 1978 *Ethical Guidelines* used the term 'subject', whilst later documents use 'participant'. Gale (1995) believes that this reflects a genuine shift in how the individual is perceived within psychology, from object (a more appropriate term than 'subject') to person. In part, this change can be attributed to the influence of *feminist* psychologists (see Chapters 83 and 84), who have also helped to bring about the removal of sexist language from BPS and APA journals as a matter of policy.

The introduction to the *Ethical Principles* states that:

'Psychological investigators are potentially interested in all aspects of human behaviour and conscious experience. However, for ethical reasons, some areas of human experience and behaviour may be beyond the reach of experiment, observation or other form of psychological investigation. Ethical guidelines are necessary to clarify the conditions under which psychological research is acceptable' [paragraph 1.2].

Psychologists are urged to encourage their colleagues to adopt the Principles and ensure that they are followed by all researchers whom they supervise (including *all* students, GCSE, A/AS level, undergraduate and beyond):

'In all circumstances, investigators must consider the ethical implications and psychological consequences for the participants in their research. The essential principle is that the investigation should be considered from the standpoint of all participants; foreseeable threats to their psychological well-being, health, values or dignity should be eliminated' [paragraph 2.1].

Exercise 2

In the above quote from paragraph 2.1, what do you understand by '... threats to their psychological well-being, health, values and dignity ... '? Try to identify examples of research studies which have breached this principle. (See Chapters 59 and 66.)

CONSENT, INFORMED CONSENT AND THE RIGHT TO WITHDRAW

According to the *Ethical Principles*:

'Participants should be informed of the objectives of the investigation and all other aspects of the research which might reasonably be expected to influence their willingness to participate – only such information allows *informed consent* to be given [paragraph 3.1] ... Special care needs to be taken when research is conducted with detained persons (those in prison, psychiatric hospital, etc.), whose ability to give free informed consent may be affected by their special circumstances' [paragraph 3.5].

'Investigators must realise that they often have influence over participants, who may be their students, employees or clients: this relationship must not be allowed to pressurise the participants to take part or remain in the investigation' [paragraph 3.6].

In relation to paragraph 3.6, it is standard practice in American universities for psychology students to participate in research as part of their course requirements (see Chapter 83, page 720). Whilst they are free to choose which research to participate in, they are *not* free to opt out.

Box 85.1 Is there more to informed consent than being informed?

Although informed consent clearly requires being informed of the procedure, participants will not have full knowledge until they have *experienced* it. Indeed, there is no guarantee that the investigators fully appreciate the procedure without undergoing it themselves. In this sense, it is difficult to argue that full prior knowledge can ever be guaranteed. How much information should be given beforehand, how much information can young children, elderly people, infirm or disabled people, or those in emotional distress be expected to absorb?

Even if a potential participant fulfils this 'informational' criterion of consent, the status of the experimenter, the desire to please others and not let them down, the desire not to look foolish by insisting on withdrawing when an experiment is already underway, all seem to detract from the idea that the participant is truly choosing *freely* in a way that is assumed by the *Ethical Principles*.

(From Gale, 1995)

Milgram's obedience experiments

As noted in Chapter 59, Milgram's obedience experiments (1963, 1965) were ethically controversial. Baumrind (1964) accused Milgram of failing to protect his participants from the stress and emotional conflict they experienced.

Exercise 3

How did Milgram respond to Baumrind's criticism and was this a justifiable defence?

Although Milgram, arguably, met Baumrind's original criticism, it does not remove the charge of *deception* (a feature of much social psychological research). If participants were deceived as to the study's true purpose (which they unquestionably were), they could not give informed consent (see below).

Box 85.2 Zimbardo *et al.*'s prison simulation experiment and informed consent

Like Milgram's experiments, this is often cited as an example of ethically unacceptable research (see Chapter 59). However, in Zimbardo's (1973) words:

'The legal counsel of Stanford University was consulted, drew up a formal 'informed consent' statement and told us of work, fire, safety and insurance requirements we had to satisfy (which we did). The 'informed

---

consent' statement signed by every participant specified that there would be an invasion of privacy, loss of some civil rights and harassment. Neither they, nor we, however, could have predicted in advance the intensity and extent of these aspects of the prison experience. We did not, however, inform them of the police arrests, in part, because we did not secure final approval from the police until minutes before they decided to participate and, in part, because we did want the mock arrests to come as a surprise. This was a breach, by omission, of the ethics of our informed consent contract. The staff of the university's Student Health Department was alerted to our study and prior arrangements made for any medical care which might be required.'

'Approval was officially sought and received in writing from the sponsoring agency ONR [see Box 82.1, pages 700–701], the Psychology Department and the University Committee of Human Experimentation'.

Zimbardo *et al.*'s study was planned to last for two weeks but was abandoned after six days because of the prisoners' distress (see Chapter 59). Why didn't Milgram call a halt to *his* experiments when he saw how much distress his 'teachers' were experiencing? This relates to the issue of *withdrawal from the investigation*:

' ... investigators should make plain to the participants their right to withdraw from the study at any time, regardless of any payment or other inducement offered ... [paragraph 6.1]. In the light of experience of the investigation, or as a result of debriefing [see below], participants have the right to withdraw their consent retrospectively and to require their own data (including any recordings) to be destroyed' [paragraph 6.2].

Milgram flagrantly contravened this principle. Each time a participant expressed the wish to stop giving shocks he or she was urged to continue, with the prods and prompts becoming increasingly harsh (Coolican, 1990).

An APA ethics committee investigated Milgram's research shortly after its first publication (during which time Milgram's APA membership was suspended), and eventually found it ethically acceptable (Colman, 1987). In 1965, Milgram was awarded the prize for outstanding contribution to social psychological research by the American Association for the Advancement of Science.

DECEPTION

The *Ethical Principles* state that:

'Intentional deception of the participants over the purpose and general nature of the investigation should be avoided whenever possible. Participants should never be deliberately misled without extremely strong scientific or medical justification. Even then there should be strict controls and the disinterested approval of independent advisors' [paragraph 4.2].

The decision that deception is necessary should only be taken after determining that alternative procedures avoiding concealment or deception are unavailable, ensuring that the participants will be *debriefed* at the earliest opportunity, and consulting on how the withholding of information and deliberate deception will be received.

Some cases of deception are less serious than others. Perhaps most serious are those likely to affect the participant's *self-image*, particularly self-esteem, which is why Milgram's and Zimbardo *et al.*'s studies were so controversial. Arguably, the most potentially damaging deception goes on in social psychological research, where people are most likely to learn things about themselves *as people*. This will be of much greater emotional significance than, say, one's ability to perceive, remember or solve problems.

A form of deception used almost exclusively in social psychology is the stooge (or confederate) who (usually) pretends to be another participant (as in Milgram's experiments). An elaborate 'staging' of events occurs into which the naïve participant has to fit, without realising that any pretence is being staged.

Exercise 4

Drawing on field experiments such as Piliavin *et al.*'s (1969) 'New York subway' study (see Chapter 62), weigh up their *methodological advantages* (compared with laboratory experiments) against their *ethical disadvantages* (compared with laboratory experiments). Regarding the latter, try focusing on the relationship between deception and debriefing. Repeat this, using examples of *naturalistic observation* and the principle of *invasion of privacy*.

Can deception ever be justified?

In Chapter 59 (see page 515), Aronson's (1988) defence of Milgram's use of deception was considered. Assuming it is important to understand the processes involved in obedience (the *end*), can deception be justified as a *means* of studying it, and even if it can, is it a *sufficient* justification?

Box 85.3   How do participants feel about being deceived?

- Mannucci (1977, cited in Milgram, 1992) asked 192 laypeople about ethical aspects of psychology experiments. They regarded deception as a relatively minor issue, and were far more concerned about the quality of the experience they would undergo as participants.

- Most participants deceived in Asch's conformity experiments (see Chapter 58) were very enthusiastic and expressed their admiration for the elegance and significance of the experimental procedure (Milgram, 1992).

- In defence of his own obedience experiments, Milgram (1974) reports that his participants were all thoroughly debriefed. This involved receiving a comprehensive report which detailed the procedure and results of all the experiments, and a follow-up questionnaire concerning their participation (see Chapter 59, page 515). More specifically, the 'technical illusions' (a morally neutral term Milgram prefers to the morally biased 'deception') are justified because they are in the end accepted and endorsed by those who are exposed to them:

  'The central moral justification for allowing a procedure of the sort used in my experiment is that it is judged acceptable by those who have taken part in it. Moreover, it was the salience of this fact throughout that constituted the chief moral warrant for the continuation of the experiments' (Milgram, 1974).

- In a review of studies focusing on the ethical acceptability of deception experiments, Christensen (1988) reports that, as long as deception is not extreme, participants don't seem to mind. Christensen suggests that the widespread use of mild forms of deception is justified, first because no one is apparently harmed, and second, because there seem to be few, if any, acceptable alternatives.

- Among 255 university psychology students, those who had been deceived at least once while participating in psychological research were significantly more likely to expect to be deceived again compared with those who had not been deceived (Krupat & Garonzik, 1994). The experience of being deceived does *not*, however, have a significant impact on their evaluation of other aspects of participation, such as enjoyment and interest, and consistent with Christensen and Mannucci's findings, previously deceived participants were not particularly upset at the prospect of being deceived again. Indeed, those who had been deceived at least once said they would be *less* upset at being lied to or misled again.

PROTECTION OF PARTICIPANTS

'Investigators have a primary responsibility to protect participants from physical and mental harm during the investigation. Normally, the risk of harm must be no greater than in ordinary life, i.e. participants should not be exposed to risks greater than or additional to those encountered in their normal life styles' [paragraph 8.1].

Exercise 5

Try to identify experiments in which participants have been exposed to harmful (painful or aversive) stimuli. What safeguards are there for participants in such cases? (see Chapters 62 and 63).

Debriefing (together with *confidentiality* and the *right to withdraw*) represents a major means of protecting participants where emotional suffering has occurred. Participants must also be protected from the stress that might be produced by disclosing highly personal and private information. They must be reassured that they are *not* obliged to answer such questions.

DEBRIEFING

According to Aronson (1988):

'The experimenter must take steps to ensure that subjects leave the experimental situation in a frame of mind that is at least as sound as it was when they entered. This frequently requires post-experimental 'debriefing' procedures that require more time and effort than the main body of the experiment'.

Where no undue suffering is experienced but participants are deceived regarding the real purpose of the experiment:

'the investigator should provide the participant with any necessary information to complete their understanding of the nature of the research. The investigator should discuss with the participants their experience of the research in order to monitor any unforeseen negative effects or misconceptions' [paragraph 5.1].

However:

'some effects which may be produced by an experiment will not be negated by a verbal description following the research. Investigators have a responsibility to ensure that participants receive any necessary de-briefing in the form of active intervention before they leave the research setting' [paragraph 5.3].

This is more like a 'therapeutic' measure than just 'good manners'. Examples of this second kind of debriefing (which also incorporates the first) can be found in both the Zimbardo *et al.* and Milgram experiments.

Box 85.4 Some examples of 'therapeutic' debriefing

- Following Zimbardo *et al.*'s experiment, there were group and individual de-briefing sessions. All participants returned post-experimental questionnaires several weeks later, several months later, and at yearly intervals. Many submitted retrospective diaries and personal analyses of the effects of their participation. Most subsequently met with the investigators singly or in small groups, or discussed their reactions by telephone:

  'We are sufficiently convinced that the suffering we observed and were responsible for, was stimulus-bound and did not extend beyond the confines of the basement prison' (Zimbardo, 1973).

- In Milgram's experiments, a very thorough debriefing ('dehoax') was carefully carried out with all participants during which they: (i) were reunited with the unharmed actor/victim, (ii) were assured that no shock had been delivered, and (iii) had an extended discussion with Milgram. Obedient participants were assured that their behaviours were entirely normal and their feelings of conflict and tension were shared by others, whilst defiant participants were supported in their decisions to disobey the experimenter. One year after the experiments, an impartial psychiatrist interviewed 40 participants, several of whom had experienced extreme stress. None showed any signs of having been psychologically harmed or having suffered traumatic reactions.

Debriefing also provides the experimenter with an opportunity to acquire additional information about the topic under investigation, so the experiment can become an educational experience for participants (Aronson, 1988). In addition, the experimenter can determine to what extent the procedure worked:

'and find out from the one person who knows best (the subject) how the procedure might be improved. In short, the prudent experimenter regards subjects as colleagues – not as objects' (Aronson, 1988).

CONFIDENTIALITY

'Subject to the requirements of legislation, including the Data Protection Act, information obtained about a participant during an investigation is confidential unless otherwise agreed in advance ... Participants in psychological research have a right to expect that information they provide will be treated confidentially, and, if published, will not be identifiable as theirs' [paragraph 7.1].

Apart from the ethical considerations, a purely pragmatic argument for guaranteeing anonymity is that members of the public would soon stop volunteering if their identities were disclosed without their permission. If participants have been seriously deceived, they have the right to witness destruction of any such records they don't wish to be kept. Results are usually made anonymous as early as possible by use of a letter/number instead of name (Coolican, 1994).

In special circumstances, the investigator might contravene the confidentiality rule. For example, where there are clear or direct dangers to human life, as in participant observation of gang life where a serious crime is planned, or a psychiatrist's patient plans to kill him or herself:

'The ethical principles involved here are broader than those involved in conducting scientific research' (Coolican, 1994).

WIDENING THE ETHICAL DEBATE: PROTECTING THE INDIVIDUAL VERSUS HARMING THE GROUP

So far, the discussion of the ethics of psychological research has focused on the vulnerability of individual participants and psychologists' responsibilities to ensure that they do not suffer in any way from their experience of participating. Whilst 'protection of participants' is one of the specific principles included in the *Ethical Principles*, *all* the principles (informed consent, avoidance of deception and so on) are designed to prevent any harm coming to the participant, or the avoidance of overt 'sins' (Brown, 1997).

As important as this is, little attention is paid to errors of omission or covert expressions of damaging assumptions, attitudes and values which are, often unconsciously, helping to shape the research questions (see Chapters 83 and 84). Whilst individual participants may be protected from overt harm, the *social groups* to which they belong (and which they represent in the research context) may be harmed as a consequence of the research findings.

Exercise 6

Re-read Chapter 84. Try to identify some fundamental values and biases that are potentially damaging to particular social groups. In what ways are these values/biases harmful to these groups?

Box 85.5   The ethics of ethical codes: underlying assumptions

According to Brown (1997), one core assumption underlying ethical codes is that what psychologists do as researchers, clinicians, teachers and so on is basically harmless and inherently valuable because it is based on 'science' (defined as *positivism*: see Chapter 83). Consequently, it is possible for a psychologist to conduct technically ethical research but still do great harm. For example, a researcher can adhere strictly to 'scientific' research methodologies, get technically adequate informed consent from participants (and not breach any of the other major prescribed principles), but still conduct research which claims to show the inferiority of a particular group. Because it is conducted according to 'the rules' (both methodological and ethical), the question of whether it is ethical in the broader sense to pursue such matters is ignored.

For example, neither Jensen (1969) nor Herrnstein (1971) were ever considered by mainstream psychology to have violated psychology's ethics by the questions they asked regarding the intellectual inferiority of African Americans (see Chapter 43). Individual black participants were not harmed by being given IQ tests and might even have found them interesting and challenging. However, the way the findings were interpreted and used:

'weakened the available social supports for people of colour by stigmatising them as genetically inferior, thus strengthening the larger culture's racist attitudes. Research ethics as currently construed by mainstream ethics codes do not require researchers to put the potential for this sort of risk into their informed consent documents' (Brown, 1997).

Jensen's and Herrnstein's research (highlighted by Herrnstein & Murray, in '*The Bell Curve*', 1994) has profoundly harmed black Americans. Ironically, the book has received much *methodological* criticism, but only black psychologists (such as Hilliard, 1995, and Sue, 1995) have raised the more fundamental question of whether simply conducting such studies might be ethically dubious. As Brown observes:

'To ask this question about the risks of certain types of inquiry challenges science's hegemony as the source of all good in psychology'.

Herrnstein and Murray, Rushton (1995), Brand (cited in Richards, 1996a) and others, like the Nazi scientists of the 1930s, claim that the study of race differences is a purely 'objective' and 'scientific' enterprise (Howe, 1997).

If it is thought unethical to deceive individual black or female participants about the purposes of some particular study, but ethically acceptable to use the results to support the claim that blacks or women are genetically inferior, then this narrow definition of ethics makes it an ineffective way of guiding research into socially sensitive issues (Howitt, 1991). Formal codes continue to focus narrowly on risks to the individual participant, in the specific context of the investigation, but neglect questions about the risks to the group to which the participant belongs.

'As long as research ethics avoid the matter of whether certain questions ethically cannot be asked, psychologists will conduct technically ethical research that violates a more general ethic of avoiding harm to vulnerable populations' (Brown, 1997).

PROTECTING THE INDIVIDUAL VERSUS BENEFITING SOCIETY

If the questions psychologists ask are limited and shaped by the values of individual researchers, they are also limited and shaped by considerations of *methodology* (what it is *possible* to do, practically, when investigating human behaviour and experience). For example, in the context of intimate relationships (see Chapters 55–57), Brehm (1992) claims that, by its nature, the laboratory experiment is extremely limited in the kinds of questions it allows psychologists to investigate.

Conversely, and just as importantly, there are certain aspects of behaviour and experience which *could* be studied experimentally, although it would be unethical to do so, such as 'jealousy between partners participating in laboratory research' (Brehm, 1992). Indeed:

'all types of research in this area involve important ethical dilemmas. Even if all we do is to ask subjects to fill out questionnaires describing their relationships, we need to think carefully about how this research experience might affect them and their partner' (Brehm, 1992).

So, what it may be *possible* to do may be *unacceptable*, but equally, what may be *acceptable* may not be *possible*. However, just as focusing on protection of individual participants can work to the detriment of whole groups (see above), so it can discourage psychologists from carrying out *socially meaningful* research (what Brehm, 1992, calls the *ethical imperative*) which, potentially, may improve the quality of people's lives. Social psychologists in particular have a *two-fold* ethical obligation, to individual participants *and* to society at large (Myers, 1994). This relates to discussion of psychology's *aims* as a science (see Chapters 1 and 83). Similarly, Aronson (1992) argues that social psychologists are:

'obligated to use their research skills to advance our knowledge and understanding of human behaviour for the ultimate aim of human betterment. In short, social psychologists have an ethical responsibility to the society as a whole'.

Talking about the aim of 'human betterment' raises important questions about basic *values*. It opens out the ethical debate in such a way that values must be addressed and recognised as part of the research process (something advocated very strongly by feminist psychologists: see above and Chapter 84).

Exercise 7

Before reading on, try to think of some examples of how research findings that you are familiar with might be used to *benefit people in general*. You may find it useful to focus on social psychology.

Box 85.6   An example of the benefits of social psychological research

In many bystander intervention studies (e.g. Latané & Darley, 1968: see Chapter 62), people are deceived into believing that an 'emergency' is taking place. Many of Latané and Darley's participants were very distressed by their experiences, especially those in the experiment in which they believed another participant was having an epileptic fit. Yet when asked to complete a post-experimental questionnaire (which followed a very careful debriefing), *all* said they believed the deception was justified and would be willing to participate in similar experiments again. None reported any feelings of anger towards the experimenter.

Beaman *et al.* (1978) built on these earlier experiments. They used a lecture to inform students about how bystanders' refusals to help can influence both one's interpretation of an emergency and feelings of responsibility. Two other groups of students heard either a different lecture or no lecture at all. Two weeks later, as part of a different experiment in a different location, the participants found themselves (accompanied by an unresponsive stooge) walking past someone who was slumped over or sprawled under a bike. Of those who had heard the lecture about helping behaviour, 50 per cent stopped to offer help compared with 25 per cent who had not.

This suggests that the results of psychological research can be used to make us more aware of influences on behaviour, making it more likely that we will act differently armed with that knowledge from how we might otherwise have done. In the case of bystander intervention, this 'consciousness-raising' is beneficial in a tangible way to the person who is helped. Being more sensitive to

the needs of others and feeling satisfied by having helped another person, may also be seen as beneficial to the helper.

The 'double obligation dilemma'

The dilemma faced by social psychologists (regarding their obligations to society and individual participants) is greatest when investigating important areas such as conformity, obedience and bystander intervention (Aronson, 1992). In general, the more important the issue, (i) the greater the potential benefit for society, and (ii) the more likely an individual participant is to experience distress and discomfort. This is because the more important the issue, the more essential the use of *deception* (or 'technical illusion') becomes.

Psychologists want to know how people are likely to behave if they found themselves in that situation *outside the laboratory*. This raises several crucial *methodological* questions (such as experimental realism, external validity or mundane realism: see Chapters 2 and 59). However, the key *ethical* issue hinges on the fact that the use of deception *both* contributes enormously (and perhaps irreplaceably) to our understanding of human behaviour (helping to satisfy the obligation to society), and at the same time significantly increases individual participants' distress (detracting from the responsibility to protect individuals).

Box 85.7   Some proposed solutions to the 'double obligation dilemma'

- Having accepted that, under certain circumstances, deception is permissible, most psychologists still advocate that it should not be used unless it is considered *essential* (Milgram, 1992; Aronson, 1992). This is consistent with the *Ethical Principles*.

- Aronson (1992) advocates a *cost–benefit analysis*: weighing how much 'good' (benefits to society) will derive from doing the research against how much 'bad' will happen to the participants.

- Milgram (1992) believes that if the experimental creation of stress or conflict were excluded on principle, and only studies which produced positive emotions were allowed, this would produce

  '... a very lopsided psychology, one that caricatured rather than accurately reflected human experience'.

Traditionally, the most deeply informative experiments in social psychology include those examining how participants resolve *conflicts*, such as Asch's studies of conformity (truth versus conformity: see Chapter 58),

Latané and Darley's bystander intervention studies (getting involved in another's troubles versus not getting involved: see Chapter 62), and Milgram's own obedience experiments (internal conscience versus external authority: Chapter 59).

- Two compromise solutions to the problem of not being able to obtain informed consent are *presumptive consent* (of 'reasonable people') and *prior general consent*. In the former, the views of many people are obtained about an experimental procedure's acceptability. These people would not participate in the actual experiment (if it went ahead), but their views could be taken as evidence of how people in general would react to participation.

Prior general consent could be obtained from people who might, subsequently, serve as experimental participants. Before volunteering to join a pool of research volunteers, people would be explicitly told that sometimes participants are misinformed about a study's true purpose and sometimes experience emotional stress. Only those agreeing would be chosen (Milgram, 1992). This is a compromise solution, because people would be giving their 'informed consent' (a) well in advance of the actual study, (b) only in a very general way, and (c) without knowing what specific manipulations/deceptions will be used in the particular experiment in which they participate. It seems to fall somewhere between 'mere' consent and full 'informed consent' (and could be called *semi- or partially informed consent*).

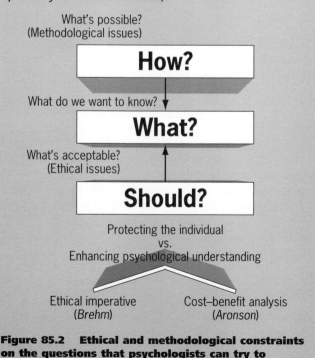

Figure 85.2 Ethical and methodological constraints on the questions that psychologists can try to answer through the research process.

Non-human subjects

The BPS Scientific Affairs Board published its *Guidelines for the Use of Animals in Research* (1985), in conjunction with the Committee of the Experimental Psychological Society. It offers a checklist of points which investigators should carefully consider when planning experiments with living non-humans. Researchers have a general obligation to:

'avoid, or at least to minimise, discomfort to living animals ... discuss any future research with their local Home Office Inspector and colleagues who are experts in the topic ... seek ... Widespread advice as to whether the likely scientific contribution of the work ... justifies the use of living animals, and whether the scientific point they wish to make may not be made without the use of living animals' [BPS, 1985].

This raises two fundamental questions: (a) how do we know non-humans suffer? and (b) what goals can ever justify subjecting them to pain and suffering?

HOW DO WE KNOW THAT NON-HUMANS SUFFER?

Exercise 8

Identify examples of experiments involving non-humans in which they suffered pain and distress. Try to specify *in what ways* suffering occurred.

Box 85.8   Some criteria for judging non-human suffering

- Disease and injury are generally recognised as major causes of suffering. Consequently, experiments like Brady's (1958) 'executive monkey' experiments would probably not even be debated in the current climate (Mapstone, 1991). Brady attached pairs of monkeys to an apparatus which gave electric shocks, such that one monkey (the 'executive': see Figure 85.3) could prevent the shock by pressing a lever but the other could not. The former developed ulcers and eventually died.

Figure 85.3

- Even if we are sure that non-humans are not suffering physically, their confinement might cause mental suffering not affecting their external condition (Dawkins, 1980). For example, apparently healthy zoo and farm animals often show bizarre behaviours.

- We must *find out* about non-human suffering by careful observation and experimentation. Because different species have different requirements, lifestyles, and, perhaps, emotions, we cannot assume that we know about their suffering or well-being without studying them species by species (Dawkins, 1980).

Drawing on the Institute of Medical Ethics (IME) Working Party's report (Haworth, 1992), Bateson (1986, 1992) has proposed criteria for assessing animal suffering, including:

- possessing receptors sensitive to noxious or painful stimulation, and

- having brain structures comparable to the human cerebral cortex.

Bateson (1992) tentatively concludes that insects probably do not experience pain, whereas fish and octopi probably do. However, the boundaries between the presence and absence of pain are 'fuzzy'.

Exercise 9

Try to formulate arguments for and against the use of non-humans in research. This should not be confined to *psychological* research, since much of the debate takes place in relation to medicine, pharmacology and so on.

HOW CAN WE JUSTIFY EXPERIMENTS WITH NON-HUMANS?

The question of suffering wouldn't arise if non-humans were not being used in experiments in the first place. According to Gray (1987), the main justifications for non-human experimentation are the pursuit of scientific knowledge and the advancement of medicine.

To justify the use of non-humans, especially when very stressful procedures are used, the research must be rigorously designed and the potential results must represent a significant contribution to our knowledge of medicine, pharmacology, biopsychology or psychology as a whole. This is a safeguard against distressing research being carried out for its own sake, or at the researcher's whim.

The *Guidelines* state that if the non-humans are confined, constrained, harmed or stressed in any way, the experimenter must consider whether the knowledge to be

gained justifies the procedure. Some knowledge is trivial and experiments must not be done simply because it is possible to do them. To take the executive monkeys experiments again (see Box 85.8), the medical justification (to discover why business executives develop ulcers) was insufficient to justify their continuation. The monkeys' obvious suffering superseded even the combination of scientific and medical justification. However, there are other cases where, whilst the scientific justification may be apparent, the medical justification is much less so, such as Olds & Milner's (1954) experiments where non-humans' brains are stimulated via implantation of a permanent electrode (electrical self-stimulation of the brain/ESSB: see Box 17.5, page 140).

SAFEGUARDS FOR NON-HUMAN SUBJECTS

Whatever practical application Olds and Milner's ESSB experiments may have subsequently had (such as pain/anxiety relief in psychotics, epileptics and cancer patients), they don't seem to have been conducted with such human applications in mind. Can the scientific knowledge gained about ESSB as a very powerful positive reinforcer *on its own* justify the rats' eventual 'sacrifice'? The very least required of researchers is that the minimum of suffering is caused, both during and following any surgical procedure and by any electric shock or food deprivation, the most objected-to treatments (Gray, 1987). Rats are the most commonly used experimental subjects in psychology.

Box 85.9   Some safeguards for non-human subjects

- Gray (1987) claims that food deprivation is *not* a source of suffering, and that the rats are either fed once a day when experimentation is over, or maintained at 85 per cent of their free-feeding (*ad lib.*) body weight. Both are actually *healthier* than allowing them to eat *ad lib*. Electric shock may cause *some* but not *extreme* pain (based on observations of the animals' behaviour). The level permitted is controlled by the Home Office (HO) inspectors, who monitor implementation of The Animals (Scientific Procedures) Act (1986). The average level used in the UK is 0.68 milliamperes, for an average of 0.57 seconds. This produces an unpleasant tickling sensation in humans.

- Procedures causing pain or distress are illegal, unless the experimenter holds an HO licence and relevant certificates. Even then, there should be no alternative ways of conducting the experiment without the use of aversive stimulation. Similarly, it is illegal in the UK to perform any surgical or pharmacological procedure

---

on vertebrates without an HO licence and relevant certification. Such procedures must be performed by experienced staff.

- The *Guidelines* stress the importance of understanding *species differences* in relation to (i) caging and social environment, (ii) the stress involved in marking wild animals for identification or attaching them with radio transmitters, and (iii) the duration of food/drink deprivation. Field workers should disturb non-humans as little as possible. Even simple observation of non-humans in the wild can have marked effects on their breeding and survival.

- The number of non-humans used in laboratory experiments is declining. For example, in the UK, the Netherlands, Germany and several other European countries, the numbers have fallen by half since the 1970s (Mukerjee, 1997).

- The UK, Australia, Germany and several other countries require a utilitarian *cost–benefit analysis* (non-human pain, distress and death versus acquisition of new knowledge and the development of new medical therapies for humans) to be performed before any non-human experiment can proceed (Mukerjee, 1997; Rowan, 1997).

THE MEDICAL JUSTIFICATION ARGUMENT

The strongest argument for non-human experiments is undoubtedly the advancement of medical knowledge and treatments. However, it is easy for *scientific* and *ethical* issues to become confused. Demonstrations of what has been achieved in a practical sense from non-human experiments represents only a *minimum* requirement for their justification. So, only if it can be convincingly shown, for example, that many drugs used in the treatment of human diseases (including anti-cancer drugs, AIDS treatments, anti-epileptic and anti-depressant drugs: Green, 1994) have been developed using non-humans and could not have been developed otherwise, can the ethical debate begin.

Box 85.10   Are non-human experiments scientifically useful?

The case for

- Non-human experiments have played a crucial role in the development of modern medical treatments, and will continue to be necessary as researchers seek to alleviate existing ailments and respond to the emergence of new diseases.

- The causes of and vaccines for dozens of infectious diseases, including diphtheria, tetanus, rabies, whooping cough, tuberculosis, poliomyelitis, measles, mumps, and rubella, have been determined largely through non-human experimentation. It has also led to the development of antibacterial and antibiotic drugs.

- Non-human research has also been vital to areas of medicine such as open-heart surgery, kidney failure and organ transplantation, diabetes, malignant hypertension, and gastric ulcers.

- There are no basic differences between the physiologies of laboratory animals and humans. Both control their internal biochemistries by releasing the same basic endocrine hormones (see Chapter 5), both send out similar chemical transmitters from neurons in the CNS and PNS (see Chapter 3), and both react in the same way to infection or tissue injury. Non-human models of disease (see below) are intended to provide a means of studying a particular procedure (such as gene therapy for cystic fibrosis).

The case against

- Through genetic manipulation, surgical intervention, or injection of foreign substances, researchers produce diseases in laboratory animals that 'model' human diseases. However, evolutionary pressures have produced innumerable subtle differences between species, and the knock-on effect of applying a stimulus to one particular organ system on the non-human's overall physiological functioning is often unpredictable and not fully understood.

- Important medical advances have been delayed because of misleading results from non-human experiments. Cancer research is especially sensitive to physiological differences between species. Rats and mice, for example, synthesise about 100 times the recommended daily allowance of vitamin C believed to help the (human) body ward off cancer.

- The stress of handling, confinement, and isolation alters a non-human's physiology, introducing a variable that makes extrapolating results to humans even more difficult. Laboratory stress can increase non-humans' susceptibility to infectious disease and certain tumours, as well as influencing hormone and antibody levels.

- Non-human experiments to test the safety of drugs are confounded by the fact that tests on different species often produce conflicting results.

(Based on Barnard & Kaufman, 1997, Botting & Morrison, 1997, and Mukerjee, 1997)

Green (1994), Carlson (1992) and many other biopsychologists believe that the potential benefits of non-human experiments is sufficient to justify their use.

Speciesism: extending the medical justification argument

According to Gray (1991), whilst most people (both experimenters and animal rights activists) would accept the ethical principle that inflicting pain is wrong, we are sometimes faced with having to choose between different ethical principles, which may mean having to choose between human and non-human suffering. Gray believes that *speciesism* (discriminating against and exploiting animals because they belong to a particular [non-human] species: Ryder, 1990) *is* justified, and argues that:

'not only is it not wrong to give preference to the interests of one's own species, one has a duty to do so'.

Such a moral choice involves establishing a calculus (Dawkins, 1990), which pits the suffering of non-humans against the human suffering which the former's use will alleviate. For Gray (1991):

'In many cases the decision not to carry out certain experiments with animals (even if they would inflict pain or suffering) is likely to have the consequence that more people will undergo pain or suffering that might otherwise be avoided'.

One of the problems associated with the pro-speciesism argument is that medical advance may only become possible after extensive development of knowledge and scientific understanding in a particular field (Gray, 1991). In the meantime, scientific understanding may be the only specific objective that the experiment can readily attain. It is at this interim stage that the suffering imposed on experimental animals will far outweigh any (lesser) suffering eventually avoided by people, and this is at the core of the decisions that must be made by scientists and ethical committees.

Psychologists as practitioners

Clinical psychologists (as well as educational psychologists, psychotherapists, psychiatrists, social workers, nurses, counsellors and other professionals) are concerned with bringing about *psychological change*. It is in their capacities as *agents of change* that clinical psychologists face their greatest ethical challenges (see Chapter 1).

Exercise 10

Consider some of the ethical issues faced by psychologists attempting to change other people's behaviours. Some are of a general nature, such as freedom versus determinism (see Chapter 81), others will overlap with ethical principles governing research (such as confidentiality and informed consent), and yet others may be specific to particular therapeutic approaches (see Chapters 73–77).

According to Fairbairn & Fairbairn (1987), clinical psychologists:

'must decide how they will interact with those who seek their help; for example, whether in general they will regard them as autonomous beings with rights and responsibilities, or rather as helpless individuals, incapable of rational choice'.

Fairbairn and Fairbairn argue that two quite common beliefs likely to detract from an explicit consideration of professional ethics and values in psychological practice are (a) that psychology is a value-free science, and (b) that therapists should be value-neutral or 'non-directive'.

PSYCHOLOGY AS VALUE-FREE SCIENCE

Central to clinical (and counselling) psychology is the *scientist–practitioner model* of helping (Dallos & Cullen, 1990). This sees clinical psychology as being guided by, and operating within, the framework of the general scientific method (see Chapters 83 and 84). If clinical psychologists view clinical psychology as having firm foundations in positivist science, they may disregard ethics because these are not amenable to objective consideration. However, even if the psychological knowledge used in clinical practice was always the result of the application of an objective scientific method, moral questions of an interpersonal kind are bound to arise *at the point at which it is applied* (Fairbairn & Fairbairn, 1987).

This distinction between possession of knowledge and its application ('science' versus 'technology') is fundamental to any discussion of ethics, because it is related to the notion of *responsibility*. Presumably, clinical psychologists *choose* which techniques to use with clients and how to use them. The mere existence (and even the demonstrated effectiveness) of certain techniques does not *in itself* mean that they must be used. Similarly, the kind of research which clinical psychologists consider worth doing (and which then provides the scientific basis for the use of particular techniques) is a matter of choice, and reflects views regarding the nature of people and how they can be changed (see Chapters 1 and 66).

Box 85.11 Criticisms of scientific behaviour therapy and modification

- Because of (rather than despite) its espoused status as a value-free, applied science, behaviour therapy and modification tend to devalue and thereby dehumanise their clients by treating people for 'scientific' purposes as if they were 'organisms' as opposed to 'agents', helpless victims of forces outside their control. This criticism also applies to medical psychiatry and classical psychoanalysis, except that both see the controlling forces as being internal (organic abnormalities or intra-psychic forces, respectively) as opposed to environmental contingencies (see Chapter 66).

- Clients soon come to believe that they are abnormal, helpless and also worthless, because this is part of the culture-wide stereotype of 'mental illness' and related terms (see Chapter 65). Negative self-evaluation and passivity characterise many, if not most, mental health clients, who think and behave like passive organisms. The solution lies in helping people recover, or discover, their agency.

(Based on Trower, 1987)

THERAPISTS AS VALUE-NEUTRAL AND NON-DIRECTIVE

If psychology as a value-free science involves not regarding or treating clients fully as human beings, this second major issue is about the therapist or psychologist functioning as something less than a complete person within the therapeutic situation. Providing help and support in a non-directive, value-free way is a tradition for psychotherapists and counsellors (Fairbairn & Fairbairn, 1987: see Chapter 76). However, such an approach may seem to require remaining aloof and distant from the client which, in turn, may entail not treating the client with respect as a person, since this requires the therapist to recognise that the client is a person like him- or herself.

Exercise 11

Evaluate the claim that it is possible for therapists not to have any influence over their clients/patients.

The influence of the therapist

Adopting what is thought to be a value-free position in therapy may lead therapists to deny the importance or influence of their own moral values, which are often hidden in therapy. This kind of influence is much more subtle and covert than the coercion that can operate on hospitalised psychiatric patients – even voluntary ones.

The in-patient is subjected to strong persuasion to accept the treatment recommendations of professional staff. As Davison & Neale (1994) observe:

'even a 'voluntary' and informed decision to take psychotropic medication or to participate in any other therapy regimen is often (maybe usually) less than free'.

Box 85.12 Therapist influence in psychodynamic and behaviour therapy

The issue of the therapist's influence on the patient/client has been central to a long-standing debate between traditional (psychodynamic) psychotherapists and behaviour therapists (who are usually clinical psychologists by training: see Chapters 73 and 74). Psychotherapists regard behaviour therapy as unacceptable (even if it works), because it is manipulative and demeaning of human dignity. By contrast, their own methods are seen as fostering the autonomous development of the patient's inherent potential, helping the patient to express his or her true self, and so on. Instead of influencers, they see themselves as 'psychological midwives', present during the birth, possessing useful skills, but there primarily to make sure that a natural process goes smoothly.

However, this is an exaggeration and misrepresentation of both approaches. For many patients, the 'birth' would probably not happen at all without the therapist's intervention, and he or she undoubtedly influences the patient's behaviour. Conversely, behaviour therapists are at least partly successful because they establish active, cooperative relationships with the patients, who play much more active roles in the therapy than psychotherapists believe.

All therapists, of whatever persuasion, if they are at all effective, influence their patients. Both approaches comprise a situation in which one human being (the therapist) tries to act in a way that enables another human being to act and feel differently, and this is as true of psychoanalysis as it is of behaviour therapy.

(From Wachtel, 1977)

The crucial issue is the *nature* of the therapist's influence rather than whether or not influence occurs. One ethical issue is whether the influence is exerted in a direction that is in the patient's interest, or in the service of the therapist's needs. Another is whether the patient is fully informed about the kind of influence the therapist wishes to exert and the kind of ends being sought (the issue of *informed consent*). Therapist *neutrality* is a myth. Therapists influence their clients in subtle yet powerful ways. According to Davison & Neale (1994):

'Unlike a technician, a psychiatrist cannot avoid communicating and at times imposing his own values upon his patients. The patient usually has considerable difficulty in finding the way in which he would wish to change his behaviour, but as he talks to the psychiatrist his wants and needs become clearer. In the very process of defining his needs in the presence of a figure who is viewed as wise and authoritarian, the patient is profoundly influenced. He ends up wanting some of the things the psychiatrist thinks he should want'.

In the above quotation, we can add 'psychologist' and 'psychotherapist' to 'psychiatrist'.

Freedom and behavioural control

Whilst a behavioural technique such as *systematic desensitisation* is mainly limited to anxiety reduction, this can at least be seen as enhancing the patient's freedom, since anxiety is one of the greatest restrictions on freedom. By contrast, methods based on *operant conditioning* can be applied to almost any aspect of a person's behaviour. Those who use operant methods (such as the *token economy*) often describe their work rather exclusively in terms of *behavioural control*, subscribing to Skinner's (1971) view of freedom as an illusion (see Chapter 81, pages 693–694).

Wachtel (1977) believes that, when used in institutional settings (such as with long-term schizophrenic patients in psychiatric hospitals), the token economy is so subject to abuse that its use is highly questionable. It may be justifiable if it works, and if there is clearly no alternative way of rescuing the patient from an empty and destructive existence. However, as a routine part of how society deals with deviant behaviour, this approach raises very serious ethical questions. One of these relates to the question of *power*. Like the experimental 'subject' relative to the experimenter, the patient is powerless relative to the institutional staff responsible for operating the token economy programme:

'reinforcement is viewed by many – proponents and opponents alike – as somehow having an inexorable controlling effect upon the person's behaviour and rendering him incapable of choice, reducing him to an automaton or duly wound mechanism' (Wachtel, 1977).

It is the reinforcing agent's power to physically deprive uncooperative patients of 'privileges' that is the alarming feature of the token economy (see Chapter 74, pages 640–641).

The abuse of patients by therapists

In recent years, there has been considerable criticism of psychotherapy (especially Freudian psychoanalysis), including its ethical shortcomings. Masson (1988) believes that there is an imbalance of power involved in the therapeutic relationship, and individuals who seek therapy need protection from the therapist's constant temptation to abuse, misuse, profit from and bully the client. The therapist has almost absolute emotional power over the patient and Masson catalogues many examples of patients' emotional, sexual and financial abuse at their therapists' hands.

Not surprisingly, Masson's attack has stirred up an enormous controversy. Holmes (1992) agrees with the core of Masson's (1992) argument, namely that:

'no therapist, however experienced or distinguished, is above the laws of the unconscious, and all should have access to supervision and work within a framework of proper professional practice'.

However, in psychotherapy's defence, Holmes points out that exploitation and abuse are by no means confined to psychotherapy: lawyers, university teachers, priests and doctors are also sometimes guilty. All these professional groups have ethical standards and codes of practice (often far more stringent than the law of the land), with disciplinary bodies which impose severe punishments (usually expulsion from the profession). We should not condemn an entire profession because of the transgressions of a small minority.

Conclusions

This chapter has considered the ethics of psychological research, with both human participants and non-human subjects, as well as ethical issues arising from the psychologist's role as a professional involved in behaviour change. Discussion of ethical issues has, in various ways, struck at the heart of psychology itself, requiring us to ask what psychology is *for*. According to Hawks (1981), prevention rather than cure should be a primary aim of psychology, enabling people to cope by themselves, without professional help, thus 'giving psychology away' to people/clients. For Bakan (1967), the significant place in society of the psychologist is more that of the teacher than expert or technician.

Summary

■ Psychology's subject matter consists of sentient things with thoughts and feelings. This makes every psychological investigation an ethical situation, with research determined as much by its effects on those being studied, as by what psychologists want to find out. Clinical psychologists also face ethical issues in their roles as agents of behavioural change.

■ Various codes of conduct and ethical guidelines exist to regulate psychological research with humans and non-humans, as well as the practice of clinical and other applied branches of psychology. The BPS's *Ethical Principles* identifies several guiding principles for research with human participants, including consent/informed consent and withdrawal from the investigation, deception, protection of participants, debriefing, and confidentiality.

■ The fact that codes of conduct are periodically revised means that they are not based on any absolute or universal ethical truths. However, the use of 'participant' rather than 'subject' reflects a change in psychology's perception of the individual. Ethical principles apply to all professional psychologists and to all psychology students.

■ One of the controversial features of Milgram's obedience experiments was **deception** of participants, thereby preventing them from giving **informed consent**. Zimbardo *et al.*'s prison experiment provided many safeguards, including an 'informed consent' statement signed by every participant, and approval was obtained from various bodies.

■ Full prior knowledge (necessary for informed consent) may not be possible without having actually experienced the procedure, and this may apply to experimenters as much as participants. Even if this were possible, the **interpersonal** nature of the experimental situation makes it unlikely that participants **freely** choose to participate.

■ Zimbardo *et al.* abandoned their experiment prematurely because of the prisoners' distress, but Milgram failed to do the same in response to his participants' distress. This relates to the principle of **withdrawal from the investigation**.

■ Deception should only be used as a last resort and be followed by immediate debriefing. The most potentially damaging deception occurs in social psychology, where participants are most likely to learn things about themselves **as people**. Field experiments and naturalistic observation studies present their own ethical problems, which need to be weighed against their methodological advantages.

■ Research indicates that participants accept deception, provided it is not extreme, and they are not deterred from participating again. Asch's and Milgram's participants expressed very positive feelings about the experiments during their debriefings, and for Milgram this justified his use of 'technical illusions'.

■ Investigators have a primary responsibility to protect participants from physical and mental harm. **Debriefing, confidentiality** and the right to withdraw are ways of protecting participants who have suffered emotionally. Sometimes, debriefing needs to assume a 'therapeutic' form.

■ Whilst ethical codes serve to protect individual participants, underlying assumptions may harm the **social groups** they represent. For example, technically ethical research (which protects individuals) may reinforce racist attitudes (thereby harming social groups). Formal codes neglect wider issues regarding the ethical acceptability of **socially sensitive research**.

■ Psychological research must be **socially meaningful** (the **ethical imperative**). This applies particularly to social psychologists, such as those engaged in bystander intervention studies. Using results from earlier studies to make participants more aware of situational influences on behaviour can increase the likelihood that they will subsequently offer help.

■ The dual obligation to individual participants and to society produces a dilemma regarding the use of deception. Three possible solutions are conducting a **cost–benefit analysis**, and obtaining **presumptive** or **prior general consent**.

■ Two fundamental issues relating to the use of non-humans in research are how we assess their suffering, and the goals used to justify any suffering that is produced. Whilst physical suffering is obvious, mental suffering is less overt. Species need to be studied individually, but more general criteria (such as possessing pain receptors) can also be applied.

■ The main justifications for non-human experimentation are the pursuit of scientific knowledge and the advancement of medicine. Safeguards exist to minimise pain and distress in experiments, include the BPS *Guidelines* and the Animals (Scientific Procedures) Act monitored by Home Office inspectors. Several countries (including the UK) require a cost–benefit analysis to be performed.

■ The medical justification argument presupposes that medical benefits have actually resulted from non-human experiments. Scientific opinion is divided about this, with some researchers stressing the biological similarities between species, others stressing subtle differences which can result in misleading and conflicting results.

■ Gray advocates **speciesism** by arguing that we are morally obliged to inflict pain on non-humans in order to reduce potential human suffering. This is often a long-term goal, and ethical decisions centre around justifying non-human suffering in the short-term when only scientific knowledge is achievable.

■ Clinical psychologists and other **agents of change** are likely to neglect professional ethics because of the twin beliefs that psychology is a value-free science (as embodied in the **scientist–practitioner model** of helping) and that therapists should be value-neutral/'non-directive'.

■ However effective a particular technique may be, clinical psychologists still **choose** which techniques to use and what research is worth doing. Behaviour therapy and modification treat people as helpless organisms, reinforcing stereotypes of the 'mentally ill' which clients then internalise, resulting in low self-esteem and passivity.

■ Psychiatric in-patients are subjected to subtle coercion to accept particular treatments, and therapists may exert an even more covert influence over their clients. Whilst psychodynamic therapists have traditionally accused behaviour therapists of manipulating and dehumanising their clients/patients, **all** therapists influence their clients/patients. The crucial issue is the **nature** of that influence.

■ The **token economy** is often described in terms of **behavioural control** (based on Skinner's rejection of free will). Within institutions, staff have the **power** to deprive patients of 'privileges'. There is also a power imbalance between therapists and their clients. In both situations, abuse of power may occur.

REFERENCES

ABERNATHY, E.M. (1940) The effect of changed environmental conditions upon the results of college examinations. *Journal of Psychology*, 10, 293–301.

ABRAHAM, K. (1911) Notes on the psychoanalytical investigation and treatment of manic-depressive insanity and allied conditions. Originally written in 1911 and later published in E. Jones (Ed.) *Selected Papers of Karl Abraham, MD*. London: The Hogarth Press.

ABRAHAMS, C. & STANLEY, E. (1992) *Social Psychology for Nurses*. London: Edward Arnold.

ABRAMS, D. & MANSTEAD, A.S.R. (1981) A test of theories of social facilitation using a musical task. *British Journal of Social Psychology*, 20, 271–278.

ABRAMS, D., WETHERELL, M., COCHRANE, S., HOGG, M.A. & TURNER, J.C. (1990) Knowing what to think by knowing who you are: Self-categorization and the nature of norm formation. *British Journal of Social Psychology*, 29, 97–119.

ABRAMSON, L.Y., SELIGMAN, M.E.P. & TEASDALE, J.D. (1978) Learned helplessness in humans: Critique and reformulation. *Journal of Abnormal Psychology*, 87, 49–74.

ADAM, K. & OSWALD, I. (1977) Sleep is for tissue restoration. *Journal of the Royal College of Physicians*, 11, 376–388.

ADAM, K. & OSWALD, I. (1983) Protein synthesis, bodily renewal and the sleep-wake cycle. *Clinical Science*, 65, 561–567.

ADAM, M.N. (1983) 'Time of Day Effects in Memory for Text.' (D.Phil. thesis, University of Sussex.)

ADAMS, H.E., TOLLISON, C.S. & CARSON, T.P. (1981) Behaviour therapy with sexual preventative medicine. In S.M. Turner, K.S. Calhoun & H.E. Adams (Eds) *Handbook of Clinical Behaviour Therapy*. New York: Wiley.

ADAMS, J.A. (1976) Issues for a closed-loop theory of motor learning. In G.E. Stelmach (Ed.) *Motor Control: Issues and Trends*. London: Academic Press.

ADAMS, R.J. (1987) Visual acuity from birth to five months as measured by habituation: A comparison to forced-choice preferential looking. *Infant Behaviour and Development*, 10, 239–244.

ADAMS, R.J. & MAURER, D. (1984) Detection of contrast by the new-born and two-month-old infant. *Infant Behaviour and Development*, 7, 415–422.

ADEY, P., SHAYER, M. & YATES, C. (1989) Cognitive acceleration: The effects of two years of intervention in science classes. In P. Adey (Ed.) *Adolescent Development and School Science*. Lewes: Falmer Press.

ADLER, A. (1927) *The Practice and Theory of Individual Psychology*. New York: Harcourt Brace Jovanovich.

ADORNO, T.W., FRENKEL-BRUNSWICK, E., LEVINSON, J.D. & SANFORD, R.N. (1950) *The Authoritarian Personality*. New York: Harper & Row.

AINSWORTH, M.D.S. (1985) Patterns of infant-mother attachments: Antecedents and effects on development. *Bulletin of the New York Academy of Medicine*, 61, 771–791.

AINSWORTH, M.D.S., BELL, S.M.V. & STAYTON, D.J. (1971) Individual differences in strange-situation behaviour of one-year-olds. In H.R. Schaffer (Ed.) *The Origins of Human Social Relations*. New York: Academic Press.

AINSWORTH, M.D.S., BLEHAR, M.C., WATERS, E. & WALL, S. (1978) *Patterns of Attachment: A Psychological Study of the Strange Situation*. Hillsdale, NJ: Lawrence Erlbaum Associates Inc.

AITCHISON, J. (1983) *The Articulate Mammal*. London: Hutchinson.

AITCHISON, J. (1996) Wugs, woggles and whatsits. *The Independent*, Section Two, 28 February, 8.

ALBA, J.W. & HASHER, L. (1983) Is memory schematic? *Psychological Bulletin*, 93, 203–231.

ALDEN, P. (1995) Hypnosis – the professional's perspective. *The Psychologist*, 8, 78.

ALEXANDER, F. (1946) Individual psychotherapy. *Psychosomatic Medicine*, 8, 110–115.

ALLEN, M. (1976) Twin studies of affective illness. *Archives of General Psychiatry*, 33, 1476–1478.

ALLEN, V.L. & LEVINE, J.M. (1971) Social support and conformity: The role of independent assessment of reality. *Journal of Experimental Social Psychology*, 7, 48–58.

ALLPORT, D.A. (1980) Attention and performance. In G. Claxton (Ed.) *Cognitive Psychology: New Directions*. London: Routledge & Kegan Paul.

ALLPORT, D.A. (1989) Visual attention. In M. Posner (Ed.) *Foundations of Cognitive Science*. Cambridge, MA: MIT Press.

ALLPORT, D.A. (1993) Attention and control. Have we been asking the wrong questions? A critical review of twenty-five years. In D.E. Meyer & S.M. Kornblum (Eds) *Attention and Performance*, Volume XIV. London: MIT Press.

ALLPORT, D.A., ANTONIS, B. & REYNOLDS, P. (1972) On the division of attention: A disproof of the single-channel hypothesis. *Quarterly Journal of Experimental Psychology*, 24, 225–235.

ALLPORT, G.W. (1954) *The Nature of Prejudice*. Reading, MA: Addison-Wesley.

ALLPORT, G.W. (1955) *Theories of Perception and the Concept of Structure*. New York: Wiley.

ALLPORT, G.W. & PETTIGREW, T.F. (1957) Cultural influences on the perception of movement: The trapezoidal illusion among Zulus. *Journal of Abnormal and Social Psychology*, 55, 104–113.

ALLPORT, G.W. & POSTMAN, L. (1947) *The Psychology of Rumour*. New York: Holt, Rinehart & Winston.

AMATO, P.R. (1983) Helping behaviour in urban and rural environments: Field studies based on a taxonomic organisation of helping episodes. *Journal of Personality and Social Psychology*, 45, 571–586.

AMATO, P.R. (1993) Children's adjustment to divorce: Theories, hypotheses and empirical support. *Journal of Marriage and the Family*, 55, 23–28.

AMERICAN PSYCHIATRIC ASSOCIATION (1952) *Diagnostic and Statistical Manual of Mental Disorders*. Washington: American Psychiatric Association.

AMERICAN PSYCHIATRIC ASSOCIATION (1968) *Diagnostic and Statistical Manual of Mental Disorders* (2nd edition). Washington, D.C. American Psychiatric Association.

AMERICAN PSYCHIATRIC ASSOCIATION (1980) *Diagnostic and Statistical Manual of Mental Disorders* (3rd edition). Washington, D.C. American Psychiatric Association.

AMERICAN PSYCHIATRIC ASSOCIATION (1987) *Diagnostic and Statistical Manual of Mental Disorders* (3rd edition, revised). Washington, D.C. American Psychiatric Association.

AMERICAN PSYCHIATRIC ASSOCIATION (1994) *Diagnostic and Statistical Manual of Mental Disorders* (4th edition). Washington: American Psychiatric Association.

AMERICAN PSYCHOLOGICAL ASSOCIATION (1985) *Guidelines for Ethical Conduct in the Care and Use of Animals*. Washington, DC: American Psychological Association.

AMERICAN PSYCHOLOGICAL ASSOCIATION (1992) Ethical principles of psychologists and code of conduct. *American Psychologist*, 47 (12), 1597–1612.

AMICE, V., BERCOVI, J., NAHOUL, K., HATAHET, M. & AMICE, J. (1989) Increase in H-Y antigen positive lymphocytes in hirsute women: Effects of cyproterone acetate and estradiol treatment. *Journal of Clinical Endocrinology and Metabolism*, 68, 58–62.

AMIR, Y. (1969) Contact hypothesis in ethnic relations. *Psychological Bulletin*, 71, 319–342.

AMIR, Y. (1994) The contact hypothesis in intergroup relations. In W.J. Lonner & R.S. Malpass (Eds) *Psychology and Culture*. Boston: Allyn & Bacon.

ANAND, B.K. & BROBECK, J.R. (1951) Hypothalamic control of food intake in rats and cats. *Yale Journal of Biological Medicine*, 24, 123–140.

ANCONA, L. & PAREYSON, R. (1968) Contributo allo studio della a aggressione: la dinimica della obbedienza distructiva. *Archivio di Psicologia Neurologia e Psichiatria*, 29, 340–372.

ANDERSEN, E.S., DUNLEA, A. & REKELIS, L. (1993) The impact of input: Language acquisition in the visually impaired. *First Language*, 13, 23–49.

ANDERSON, D.R., LORCH, E.P., FIELD, D.E., COLLINS, P.A. & NATHAN, J.G. (1986) Television viewing at home: Age trends in visual attention and time with TV. *Child Development*, 57, 1024–1033.

ANDERSON, J. (1974) Bystander intervention in an assault. Paper presented at the meeting of the Southeastern Psychological Association, Hollywood, FL.

ANDERSON, J.R. (1983) *The Architecture of Cognition* (2nd edition). Cambridge, MA: Harvard University Press.

ANDERSON, J.R. (1995a) *Learning and Memory: An Integrated Approach*. Chichester: Wiley.

ANDERSON, J.R. (1995b) *Cognitive Psychology and its Implications*. New York: W.H. Freeman & Company.

ANDREWS, G. (1991) The evaluation of psychotherapy. *Current Opinions of Psychotherapy*, 4, 379–383.

ANDREWS, G. (1993) The essential psychotherapies. *British Journal of Psychiatry*, 162, 447–451.

ANNIS, R.C. & FROST, B. (1973) Human visual ecology and orientation anisotropies in acuity. *Science*, 182, 729–731.

ANSHEL, M.H. (1996) Effects of chronic aerobic exercise and progressive relaxation on motor performance and affect following acute stress. *Behavioural Medicine*, 21, 186–196.

APPLEBEE, A.N. (1984) Writing and reasoning. *Review of Educational Research*, 54, 577–596.

ARENDT, H. (1965) *Eichmann in Jerusalem: A Report on the Banality of Evil*. New York: Viking.

ARGYLE, M. (1983) *The Psychology of Interpersonal Behaviour* (4th edition). Harmondsworth: Penguin.

ARGYLE, M. (1988) *Bodily Communication* (2nd edition). London: Methuen.

ARGYLE, M. (1989) *The Social Psychology of Work* (2nd edition). Harmondsworth: Penguin.

ARGYLE, M. & HENDERSON, M. (1984) The rules of friendship. *Journal of Social and Personal Relationships*, 1, 211–237.

ARKIN, R., COOPER, H. & KOLDITZ, T. (1980) A statistical review of the literature concerning the self-serving bias in interpersonal influence situations. *Journal of Personality and Social Psychology*, 48, 435–448.

ARMS, R.L., RUSSELL, G.W. & SANDILANDS, M.I. (1980) Effects of viewing aggressive sports on the hostility of spectators. In R.M. Suinn (Ed.) *Psychology in Sport: Methods and Applications*. Minneapolis: Burgess.

ARMSBY, R.E. (1971) A re-examination of the development of moral judgement in children. *Child Development*, 42, 1241–1248.

ARMSTRONG, S. (1997) 'Ello, 'ello: Where did all those bodies go? *The Sunday Times*, 19 January, 4–5.

ARONFREED, J. (1963) The effects of experimental socialisation paradigms upon two moral responses to transgression. *Journal of Abnormal and Social Psychology*, 66, 437–438.

ARONFREED, J. (1976) Moral development from the standpoint of a general psychological theory. In T. Lickona (Ed.) *Moral Development and Behaviour*. New York: Holt, Rinehart & Winston.

ARONSON, E. (1980) *The Social Animal* (3rd edition). San Francisco: W.H. Freeman.

ARONSON, E. (1988) *The Social Animal* (5th edition). New York: Freeman.

ARONSON, E. (1992) *The Social Animal* (6th edition). New York: Freeman.

ARONSON, E., BRIDGEMAN, D.L. & GEFFNER, R. (1978) The effects of a co-operative classroom structure on student behaviour and attitudes. In D. Bar-Tal & L. Saxe (Eds) *Social Psychology of Education*. New York: Wiley.

ARONSON, E. & LINDER, D. (1965) Gain and loss of esteem as determinants of interpersonal attraction. *Journal of Experimental Social Psychology*, 1, 156–171.

ARONSON, E., WILLERMAN, B. & FLOYD, J. (1966) The effect of a pratfall on increasing attractiveness. *Psychonomic Science*, 4, 227–228.

ASCH, S.E. (1946) Forming impressions of personality. *Journal of Abnormal and Social Psychology*, 41, 258–290.

ASCH, S.E. (1951) Effect of group pressure upon the modification and distortion of judgements. In H. Guetzkow (Ed.) *Groups, Leadership and Men*. Pittsburgh, PA: Carnegie Press.

ASCH, S.E. (1952) *Social Psychology*. Englewood Cliffs, NJ: Prentice Hall.

ASCH, S.E. (1955) Opinions and social pressure. *Scientific American*, 193, 31–35.

ASCH, S.E. (1956) Studies of independence and submission to group pressure: 1: A minority of one against a unanimous majority. *Psychological Monographs*, 70, Whole No. 416.

ASCHOFF, J. & WEVER, R. (1981) The circadian system in man. In J. Aschoff (Ed.) *Handbook of Behavioural Neurology* (Volume 4). New York: Plenum Press.

ASERINSKY, E. & KLEITMAN, N. (1953) Regularly occurring periods of eye motility and concomitant phenomena during sleep. *Science*, 118, 273–274.

ASHER, J. (1987) Born to be shy? *Psychology Today*, April, 56–64.

ASHMORE, R. & DEL BOCA, F. (1976) Psychological approaches to understanding intergroup conflicts. In P. Katz (Ed.) *Towards the Elimination of Racism*. New York: Pergamon.

ASKEVOLD, F. & HEIBERG, A. (1979) Anorexia nervosa: Two cases in discordant MZ twins. *Psychological Monographs*, 70, 1–70.

ASLIN, R.N., PISONI, D.B. & JUSCZYK, P.W. (1983) Auditory development and speech perception in infancy. In P.H. Mussen (Ed.) *Handbook of Child Psychology* (4th edition). New York: Wiley.

ASSOCIATION FOR THE TEACHING OF PSYCHOLOGY (1992) Ethics in psychological research: Guidelines for students at pre-degree levels. *Psychology Teaching*, 4–10, New Series, No. 1.

ATCHLEY, R.C. (1982) Retirement: Leaving the world of work. *Annals of the American Academy of Political and Social Science*, 464, 120–131.

ATCHLEY, R.C. (1985) *Social Forces and Ageing: An Introduction to Social Gerontology*. Belmont, California: Wadsworth.

ATCHLEY, R.C. & ROBINSON, J.L. (1982) Attitudes towards retirement and distance from the event. *Research on Ageing*, 4, 288–313.

ATKINSON, R.C. (1975) Mnemonotechnics in second-language learning. *American Psychologist*, 30, 821–828.

ATKINSON, R.C. & SHIFFRIN, R.M. (1968) Human memory: A proposed system and its control processes. In K.W. Spence & J.T. Spence (Eds) *The Psychology of Learning and Motivation*, Volume 2. London: Academic Press.

ATKINSON, R.C. & SHIFFRIN, R.M. (1971) The control of short-term memory. *Scientific American*, 224, 82–90.

ATKINSON, R.L., ATKINSON, R.C., SMITH, E.E. & BEM, D.J. (1990) *Introduction to Psychology* (10th edition). New York: Harcourt Brace Jovanovich.

ATKINSON, R.L., ATKINSON, R.C., SMITH, E.E. & BEM, D.J. (1993) *Introduction to Psychology* (11th edition). London: Harcourt Brace Jovanovich.

ATTNEAVE, F. (1954) Some informational aspects of visual perception. *Psychological Review*, 61, 183–193.

ATWELL, M. (1981) The evolution of text: The inter-relationship of reading and writing in the composing process. Paper presented at the Annual Meeting of the National Council of Teachers of English, Boston, MA.

ATWOOD, M.E. & POLSON, P.G. (1976) A process model for water-jug problems. *Cognitive Psychology*, 8, 191–216.

AUDIT COMMISSION (1992) *Getting in on the Act*. HMI. London: HMSO.

AX, A.F. (1953) The physiological differentiation of fear and anger in humans. *Psychosomatic Medicine*, 15, 422–433.

AYLLON, T. & AZRIN, N.H. (1968) *The Token Economy: A Motivational System for Therapy and Rehabilitation*. New York: Appleton Century Crofts.

AYLLON, T. & HAUGHTON, E. (1962) Control of the behaviour of schizophrenic patients by food. *Journal of the Experimental Analysis of Behaviour*, 5, 343–352.

AZRIN, N.H. & HOLZ, W.C. (1966) Punishment. In W.K. Honig (Ed) *Operant Behaviour: Areas of Research and Application*. New York: Appleton-Century-Crofts.

BACHRACH, A., ERWIN, W. & MOHN, J. (1965) The control of eating behaviour in an anorexic by operant conditioning. In L. Ullman & L. Krasner (Eds) *Case Studies in Behaviour Modification*. New York: Holt, Rinehart & Winston.

BADDELEY, A.D. (1966) The influence of acoustic and semantic similarity on long-term memory for word sequences. *Quarterly Journal of Experimental Psychology*, 18, 302–309.

BADDELEY, A.D. (1968) Closure and response bias in short-term memory for form. *British Journal of Psychology*, 59, 139–145.

BADDELEY, A.D. (1976) *The Psychology of Memory*. New York: Basic Books.

BADDELEY, A.D. (1981) The concept of working memory: A view of its current state and probable future development. *Cognition*, 10, 17–23.

BADDELEY, A.D. (1986) *Working Memory*. Oxford: Oxford University Press.

BADDELEY, A.D. (1990) *Human Memory*. Hove: Lawrence Erlbaum Associates.

BADDELEY, A.D. (1995) Memory. In C.C. French & A.M. Colman (Eds) *Cognitive Psychology*. London: Longman.

BADDELEY, A.D (1997) *Human Memory: Theory and Practice* (revised edition). East Sussex: Psychology Press.

BADDELEY, A.D. & HITCH, G. (1974) Working memory. In G.H. Bower (Ed.) *Recent Advances in Learning and Motivation*, Volume 8. New York: Academic Press.

BADDELEY, A.D. & SCOTT, D. (1971) Short-term forgetting in the absence of proactive inhibition. *Quarterly Journal of Experimental Psychology*, 23, 275–283.

BADDELEY, A.D., THOMSON, N. & BUCHANAN, M. (1975) Word length and the structure of short-term memory. *Journal of Verbal Learning and Verbal Behaviour*, 14, 575–589.

BAHRICK, H.P. (1984) Semantic memory content in permastore: Fifty years of memory for Spanish learned in school. *Journal of Experimental Psychology: General*, 113, 1–29.

BAHRICK, H.P. & HALL, L.K. (1991) Lifetime maintenance of high-school mathematics content. *Journal of Experimental Psychology: General*, 120, 20–33.

BAHRICK, L.E., WALKER, A.S. & NEISSER, U. (1981) Selective looking by infants. *Cognitive Psychology*, 13, 377–390.

BAILEY, C.L. (1979) Mental illness – a logical misrepresentation? *Nursing Times*, May, 761–762.

BAILEY, S. (1993) Fast forward to violence. *Criminal Justice Matters*, 3, 6–7

BAILLARGEON, R. (1987) Object permanence in 3½- and 4½-month-old infants. *Developmental Psychology*, 33, 655–664.

BAKAN, D. (1967) *On Method*. San Francisco: Jossey-Bass Inc.

BALASUBRAMAMIAM, V., KANATA, T.S. & RAMAMURTHI, B. (1970) Surgical treatment of hyperkinetic and behaviour disorders. *International Surgery*, 54, 18–23.

BALES, J. (1986) New studies cite drug use dangers. *APA Monitor*, 17 (11), 26.

BALES, R.F. (1950) *Interactional Process Analysis: A Method for the Study of Small Groups*. Reading, MA: Addison Wesley.

BALES, R.F. & SLATER, P. (1955) Role differentiation in small decision-making groups. In T. Parsons & R.F. Bales (Eds) *Family, Socialisation and Interaction Processes*. New York: Free Press.

BALL, S. & NUKI, P. (1996) Most under-11s watch violent videos. *The Sunday Times*, 23 July, 1.

BALON, R., JORDAN, M., PHOL, R. & YERAGNI, V. (1989) Family history of anxiety disorders in control subjects with lactate-induced panic attacks. *American Journal of Psychiatry*, 146, 1304–1306.

BALTES, P.B. (1987) Theoretical propositions of life-span developmental psychology: On the dynamics of growth and decline. *Developmental Psychology*, 23, 611–626.

BALTES, P.B. & BALTES, M.M. (1993) *Successful Ageing: Perspectives from the Behavioural Sciences*. Cambridge: Cambridge University Press.

BANAJI, M.R. & CROWDER, R.G. (1989) The bankruptcy of everyday memory. *American Psychologist*, 44, 1185–1193.

BANDURA, A. (1965) Influence of model's reinforcement contingencies on the acquisition of imitative responses. *Journal of Personality & Social Psychology*, 1, 589–595.

BANDURA, A. (1969) *Principles of Behaviour Modification*. New York: Holt, Rinehart & Winston.

BANDURA, A. (1971) *Social Learning Theory*. Morristown, NJ: General Learning Press.

BANDURA, A. (1973) *Aggression: A Social Learning Analysis*. London: Prentice Hall.

BANDURA, A. (1974) Behaviour theory and models of man. *American Psychologist*, 29, 859–869.

BANDURA, A. (1977) *Social Learning Theory* (2nd edition). Englewood Cliffs, NJ: Prentice-Hall.

BANDURA, A. (1984) Recycling misconceptions of perceived self-efficacy. *Cognitive Therapy and Research*, 8, 231–235.

BANDURA, A. (1994) Social cognitive theory of mass communication. In J. Bryant & D. Zillman (Eds) *Media Effects: Advances in Theory and Research*. Hove: Erlbaum.

BANDURA, A., ROSS, D. & ROSS, S.A. (1961) Transmission of aggression through imitation of aggressive models. *Journal of Abnormal and Social Psychology*, 63, 575–582.

BANDURA, A., ROSS, D. & ROSS, S.A. (1963) Imitation of film-mediated aggressive models. *Journal of Abnormal and Social Psychology*, 66, 3–11.

BANDURA, A. & WALTERS, R. (1959) *Social Learning and Personality Development*. New York: Holt.

BANNISTER, D., SALMON, P. & LIEBERMAN, D.M. (1964) Diagnosis–treatment relationships in psychiatry: A statistical analysis. *British Journal of Psychiatry*, 110, 726–732.

BANYAI, E.I. & HILGARD, E.R. (1976) A comparison of active-alert hypnotic induction with traditional relaxation induction. *Journal of Abnormal Psychology*, 85, 218–224.

BANYARD, P. (1996a) *Applying Psychology to Health*. London: Hodder & Stoughton.

BANYARD, P. (1996b) Psychology and advertising. *Psychology Review*, 3 (1), September, 24–27.

BANYARD, P. & HAYES, N. (1994) *Psychology: Theory and Applications*. London: Chapman & Hall.

BARBER, M. (1996) The long shadow of the IQ empire. *Times Educational Supplement*, 13 September, 152.

BARBER, T.X. (1969) *Hypnosis: A Scientific Approach*. New York: Von Nostrand.

BARBER, T.X. (1970) *LSD, Marijuana, Yoga And Hypnosis*. Chicago: Aldine Press.

BARBER, T.X. (1979) Suggested ('hypnotic') behaviour: The trance paradigm versus an alternative paradigm. In E. Fromm & R.E. Shor (Eds) *Hypnosis: Developments in Research and New Perspectives*. Chicago: Aldine Press.

BARD, P. (1928) Diencephalic mechanism for the expression of rage with special reference to the sympathetic nervous system. *American Journal of Physiology*, 84, 490–515.

BARGH, J.A. & PIETROMONACO, P. (1982) Automatic information processing and social perception: The influence of trait information presented outside of conscious awareness on impression formation. *Journal of Personality & Social Psychology*, 43, 437–449.

BARKER, M. & PETLEY. J. (1997) (Eds) *Ill Effects: The Media/Violence Debate*. London: Routledge.

BARKER, P. (1998) The humanistic therapies. *Nursing Times*, 94, 52–53.

BARKER, R., DEMBO, T. & LEWIN, K. (1941) Frustration and regression: An experiment with young children. *University of Iowa Studies in Child Welfare*, 18, 1–314.

BARNARD, N.D. & KAUFMAN, S.R. (1997) Animal research is wasteful and misleading. *Scientific American*, February, 64–66.

BARON, M., RISCH, N., HAMBURGER, R., MANDEL, B., KUSHNER, S., NEWMAN, M., DRUMER, D. & BELMAKER, R. (1987) Genetic linkage between X-chromosome markers and bipolar affective illness. *Nature*, 326, 289–292.

BARON, R.A. (1977) *Human Aggression*. New York: Plenum.

BARON, R.A. (1983) The reduction of human aggression: An incompatible response strategy. In R.G. Geen & E. Donnerstein (Eds) *Aggression: Theoretical and Empirical Reviews*. New York: Academic Press.

BARON, R.A. (1989) *Psychology: The Essential Science*. London: Allyn & Bacon.

BARON, R.A. & BYRNE, D.S. (1984) *Social Psychology: Understanding Human Interaction* (4th edition). London: Allyn & Bacon.

BARON, R.A. & BYRNE, D.S. (1994) *Social Psychology: Understanding Human Interaction* (7th edition). London: Allyn & Bacon.

BARON, R.A. & RICHARDSON, D.R. (1994) *Human Aggression* (2nd edition). New York: Plenum.

BARON-COHEN, S. (1995) *Mind Blindness: An Essay on Autism and the Theory of Mind*. Cambridge, MA: MIT Press.

BARON-COHEN, S. (1997) Autism: First lessons in mind-reading. *Psychology Review*, 3, 30–33.

BARON-COHEN, S., ALLEN, J. & GILLBERG, C. (1992) Can autism be detected at 18 months? The needle, the haystack and the CHAT. *British Journal of Psychiatry*, 161, 839–843.

BARON-COHEN, S, LESLIE, A.M. & FRITH, U. (1985) Does the autistic child have a 'Theory of Mind'? *Cognition*, 21, 37–46.

BARR, C.E., MEDNICK, S.A. & MUNK-JORGENSON, P. (1990) Exposure to influenza epidemics during gestation and adult schizophrenia: A forty-year study. *Archives of General Psychiatry*, 47, 869–874.

BARRETT, M.D. (1989) Early language development. In A. Slater & G. Bremner (Eds) *Infant Development*. Hove: Erlbaum.

BARROW, G. & SMITH, P. (1979) *Aging, Ageism and Society*. St. Paul, MN: West.

BARRY, H. (1980) Description and uses of the Human Relations Area Files. In H.C. Triandis & J.W. Berry (Eds) *Handbook of Cross-Cultural Psychology*, Volume 2, *Methodology*. Boston: Allyn & Bacon.

BARRY, H., CHILD, I. & BACON, M. (1959) Relation of child training to subsistence economy. *American Anthropologist*, 61, 51–63.

BARTAK, L. (1978) Educational approaches. In M. Rutter & E. Schopler (Eds) *Autism: A Reappraisal of Concepts and Treatments*. New York: Plenum.

BARTLETT, F.C. (1932) *Remembering*. Cambridge: Cambridge University Press.

BATES, B.L. (1993) Individual differences in response to hypnosis. In J.W. Rhue, S.J. Lynn & I. Kirsch (Eds) *Handbook of Clinical Hypnosis*. Washington, D.C.: American Psychological Association.

BATESON, G., JACKSON, D., HALEY, J. & WEAKLAND, J. (1956) Toward a theory of schizophrenia. *Behavioural Science*, 1, 251–264.

BATESON, P. (1986) When to experiment on animals. *New Scientist*, 109 (14960), 30–32.

BATESON, P. (1992) Do animals feel pain? *New Scientist*, 134 (1818), 30–33.

BATSON, C.D. & COKE, J.S. (1981) Empathy: A source of altruistic motivation for helping? In J.P. Rushton & R.M. Sorentino (Eds) *Altruism and Behaviour: Social, Personality, and Development Prespectives*. Hillsdale, NJ: Erlbaum.

BAUMRIND, D. (1964) Some thoughts on the ethics of research: After reading Milgram's behavioural study of obedience. *American Psychologist*, 19, 421–423.

BAUMRIND, D. (1967) Child care practices anteceding three patterns of preschool behaviour. *Genetic Psychology Monographs*, 75, 43–88.

BAUMRIND, D. (1971) Current patterns of parental authority. *Developmental Psychology Monograph*, 4 (1, Part 2).

BAUMRIND, D. (1975) Early socialisation and adolescent competence. In S.E. Dragustin & G.H. Elder (Eds) *Adolescence in the Life Cycle*. Washington, DC: Hemisphere.

BAUMRIND, D. (1983) Rejoinder to Lewis' reinterpretation of parental firm control effects: Are authoritative families really harmonious? *Psychological Bulletin*, 94, 132–142.

BAUMRIND, D. (1991) Parenting styles and adolescent development. In R. Lerner, A.C. Petersen & J. Brooks-Gunn (Eds) *The Encyclopaedia of Adolescence*. New York: Garland.

BAYLEY, N. (1969) *Bayley Scales of Infant Development*. New York: Psychological Corporation.

BEACH, R. & BRIDWELL, L.S. (1984) *New Directions in Composition Research*. New York: Guildford.

BEAMAN, A.L., BARNES, P.J., KLENTZ, B., & MCQUIRK, B. (1978) Increasing helping rates through information dissemination: Teaching pays. *Personality & Social Psychology Bulletin*, 4, 406–411.

BEAUMONT, J.G. (1988) *Understanding Neuropsychology*. Oxford: Blackwell.

BEAUMONT, P. (1996) Thirtysomethings who won't grow up. *The Observer*, 19 May, 11.

BECK, A.T. (1967) *Depression: Causes and Treatment*. Philadelphia: University of Philadelphia Press.

BECK, A.T. (1974) The development of depression: A cognitive model. In R.J. Friedman & M.M. Katz (Eds) *The Psychology of Depression: Contemporary Theory and Research*. New York: Wiley.

BECK, A.T. & FREEMAN, A. (1990) *Cognitive Therapy of Personality Disorders*. New York: Guilford Press.

BECK, A.T., RUSH, A.J., SHAW, B.F. & EMORY, G. (1979) *Cognitive Therapy of Depression*. New York: Guilford Press.

BECK, A.T. & WEISHAAR, M.E. (1989) Cognitive therapy. In R.J. Corsini & D. Wedding (Eds) *Current Psychotherapies*. Itasca, ILL: Peacock.

BECK, A.T. & YOUNG, J.E. (1978) College blues. *Psychology Today*, September, 80–92.

BECKETT, F. (1995) Pioneer's fears are realised. *The Times Educational Supplement*, 21 April, 5.

BEE, H. (1992) *The Developing Child* (7th edition). New York: HarperCollins.

BEE, H. (1994) *Lifespan Development*. New York: HarperCollins.

BEE, H. (1997) *The Developing Child* (8th edition). New York: Longman.

BEE, H. & MITCHELL, S.K. (1980) *The Developing Person: A Lifespan Approach*. New York: Harper & Row.

BEITMAN, B., GOLDFRIED, M. & NORCROSS, J. (1989) The movement toward integrating the psychotherapies: An overview. *American Journal of Psychiatry*, 146, 138–147.

BEKERIAN, D.A. & BOWERS, J.M. (1983) Eye-witness testimony: Were we misled? *Journal of Experimental Psychology: Learning, Memory and Cognition*, 9, 139–145.

BELEZZA, F.S. (1981) Mnemonic devices: Classification, characteristics and criteria. *Review of Educational Research*, 51, 247–275.

BELFER, P.L. & GLASS, C.R. (1992) Agoraphobic anxiety and fear of fear: Test of a cognitive–attentional model. *Journal of Anxiety Disorders*, 6, 133–146.

BELL, P.A. & BARON, R.A. (1974) Effects of heat, noise and provocation on retaliatory evaluative behaviour. *Bulletin of the Psychonomic Society*, 4, 479–481.

BELL, S.M. & AINSWORTH, M.D.S. (1972) Infant crying and maternal responsiveness. *Child Development*, 43, 1171–1190.

BELLUR, R. (1995) Interpersonal attraction revisited: Cross-cultural conceptions of love. *Psychology Review*, 1, 24–26.

BEM, D.J. (1967) Self-perception: An alternative interpretation of cognitive dissonance phenomena. *Psychological Review*, 74, 183–200.

BEM, D.J. (1972) Self-perception theory. In L. Berkowitz (Ed.) *Advances in Experimental Social Psychology*, Volume 6. New York: Academic Press.

BEM, S.L. (1985) Androgyny and gender schema theory: A conceptual and empirical integration. In T.B. Sonderegger (Ed.) *Nebraska Symposium on Motivation*. Nebraska, NE: University of Nebraska Press.

BEMIS, K.M. (1978) Current approaches to the aetiology and treatment of anorexia nervosa. *Psychological Bulletin*, 85, 593–617.

BENDER, L. (1969) Longitudinal study of schizophrenic children with autism. *Hospital Community Psychiatry*, 20, 230–237.

BENDER, M. (1995) The war goes on. *The Psychologist*, 8, 78–79.

BENEWICK, R. & HOLTON, R. (1987) The peaceful crowd: Crowd solidarity and the Pope's visit to Britain. In G. Gaskell & R. Benewick (Eds) *The Crowd in Contemporary Britain*. London: Sage.

BENNETT, D. (1985) Rogers: More intuition than therapy. *APA Monitor*, 16, 3.

BENNETT, M. (1993) Introduction. In M. Bennett (Ed.) *The Child as Psychologist: An Introduction to the Development of Social Cognition*. Hemel Hempstead: Harvester Wheatsheaf.

BENNETT, W. (1997) Daughter dead after living like a monk in a room for 14 years. *The Daily Telegraph*, 5 September, 3.

BENTALL, R. (1996) The illness that defies diagnosis. *The Times*, 20 May, 14.

BENTON, D. (1981) ECT. Can the system take the shock? *Community Care*, 12 March, 15–17.

BEREITER, C. & ENGELMAN, S. (1966) *Teaching Disadvantaged Children in The Pre-School*. Englewood Cliffs, NJ: Prentice-Hall.

BERESFORD, D. (1997) Army gave gays shock treatment. *The Guardian*, 17 June, 13.

BERGIN, A.E. (1971) The evaluation of therapeutic outcomes. In A.E. Bergin & S.L. Garfield (Eds) *Handbook of Psychotherapy and Behaviour Change: An Empirical Analysis*. New York: Wiley.

BERGIN, A.E. (1980) Psychotherapy and religious values. *Journal of Consulting and Clinical Psychology*, 48, 642–645.

BERGIN, A.E. & LAMBERT, M.J. (1978) The evaluation of therapeutic outcomes. In S.A. Garfield & A.E. Bergin (Eds) *Handbook of Psychotherapy and Behaviour Change: An Empirical Analysis* (2nd edition). New York: Wiley.

BERKMAN, L.F. (1984) Assessing the physical health of social networks and social support. *Annual Review of Public Health*, 5, 413–432.

BERKO, J. (1958) The child's learning of English morphology. *Word*, 14, 150–177.

BERKOWITZ, L. (1966) On not being able to aggress. *British Journal of Clinical and Social Psychology*, 5, 130–139.

BERKOWITZ, L. (1968) Impulse, aggression and the gun. *Psychology Today*, September, 18–22.

BERKOWITZ, L. (1978) Whatever happened to the frustration–aggression hypothesis? *American Behavioural Scientist*, 21, 691–708.

BERKOWITZ, L. (1983) Aversively stimulated aggression: Some parallels and differences in research with humans and animals. *American Psychologist* 38, 1135–1144.

BERKOWITZ, L. (1986) *A Survey of Social Psychology* (3rd edition). New York: Holt, Rinehart & Winston.

BERKOWITZ, L. (1989) The frustration–aggression hypothesis: an examination and reformation. *Psychological Bulletin*, 106, 59–73.

BERKOWITZ, L. (1990) On the formation and regulation of anger and aggression – a cognitive neoassociationistic analysis. *American Psychologist*, 45, 494–503.

BERKOWITZ, L. (1993) *Aggression: Its Causes, Consequences and Control*. New York: McGraw-Hill.

BERKOWITZ, L. (1995) A career on aggression. In G.G. Brannigan & M.R. Merrens (Eds) *The Social Psychologists: Research Adventures*. New York: McGraw-Hill.

BERKOWITZ, L. & GEEN, R.G. (1966) Film violence and the cue properties of available targets. *Journal of Personality and Social Psychology*, 3, 525–530.

BERKOWITZ, L. & LEPAGE, A. (1967) Weapons as aggression-eliciting stimuli. *Journal of Personality and Social Psychology*, 7, 202–207.

BERLIN, B. & KAY, P. (1969) *Basic Colour Terms: Their Universality and Evolution*. Berkeley, CA: University of California Press.

BERMAN, J.S. & NORTON, N.C. (1985) Does professional training make a therapist more effective? *Psychological Bulletin*, 98, 401–407.

BERNE, E. (1964) *Games People Play: The Psychology of Human Relationships*. New York: Grove Press.

BERNE, E. (1976) *Beyond Games and Scripts*. New York: Grove Press.

BERNSTEIN, B. (1961) Social class and linguistic development: A theory of Social Learning. In A.H. Halsey, J. Floyd & C.A. Anderson (Eds) *Education, Economy and Society*. London: Collier-Macmillan Ltd.

BERRY, D.T.R. & WEBB, W.B. (1983) State measures and sleep stages. *Psychological Reports*, 52, 807–812.

BERRY, J.W. (1969) On cross-cultural compatability. *International Journal of Psychology*, 4, 119–128.

BERRY, J.W., POOTINGA, Y.H., SEGALL, M.H. & DASEN, P.R. (1992) *Cross-Cultural Psychology: Research and Applications*. Cambridge: Cambridge University Press.

BERSCHEID, E., DION, K., HATFIELD, E. & WALSTER, G.W. (1971) Physical attractiveness and dating choice: A test of the matching hypothesis. *Journal of Experimental and Social Psychology*, 7, 173–189.

BERSCHEID, E. & WALSTER, E.M. (1974) Physical attractiveness. In L. Berkowitz (Ed.) *Advances in Experimental Social Psychology*, Volume 7. New York: Academic Press.

BERSCHEID, E. & WALSTER, E.M. (1978) *Interpersonal Attraction* (2nd edition). Reading, MA: Addison-Wesley.

BERTENTHAL, B.I. & FISCHER, K.W. (1978) Development of self-recognition in the infant. *Developmental Psychology*, 14, 44–50.

BETTELHEIM, B. (1967) *The Empty Fortress*. New York: Free Press.

BIANCHI, A. (1992) Dream chemistry. *Harvard Magazine*, September–October, 21–22.

BICK, P.A. & KINSBOURNE, M. (1987) Auditory hallucinations and subvocal speech in schizophrenic patients. *American Journal of Psychiatry*, 32, 297–306.

BICKMAN, L. (1971) The effects of another bystander's ability to help on bystander intervention in an emergency. *Journal of Experimental Social Psychology*, 7, 367–379.

BICKMAN, L. (1974) The social power of a uniform. *Journal of Applied Social Psychology*, 1, 47–61.

BIEDERMAN, I. (1987) Recognition-by-components: A theory of human image understanding. *Psychological Review*, 94, 115–147.

BIEDERMAN, I., COOPER, E.E., MAHDEVAN, R.S. & FOX, P.W. (1992) Unexceptional spatial memory in an exceptional mnemonist. *Journal of Experimental Psychology: Learning, Memory and Cognition*, 18, 654–657.

BIERHOFF, H.W. & KLEIN, R. (1988) Prosocial behaviour. In M. Hewstone, W. Stroebe, J.P. Codol & G.M. Stephenson (Eds) *Introduction to Social Psychology*. Oxford: Blackwell.

BIFULCO, A., HARRIS, T. & BROWN, G.W. (1992) Mourning or early inadequate care? Re-examining the relationship of maternal loss in childhood with adult depression and anxiety. *Development and Psychopathology*, 4, 433–449.

BINI, L. (1938) Experimental researches on epileptic attacks induced by electric current. *American Journal of Psychiatry*, Supplement 94, 172–183.

BION, W.R. (1961) *Experiences in Groups*. London: Tavistock.

BIRCH, B. (1985) *A Question of Race*. London: Macdonald and Co.

BIRNBAUM, J.C. (1982) The reading and composing behaviours of selected fourth- and seventh-grade students. *Research in the Teaching of English*, 16, 241–260.

BLACKMAN, D.E. (1980) Images of man in contemporary behaviourism. In A.J. Chapman and D.M. Jones (Eds) *Models of Man*. Leicester: British Psychological Society.

BLAIR, R.J.R., JONES, L., CLARK, F. & SMITH, M (1997) The psychopathic individual: A Lack of responsiveness to distress cues? *Psychophysiology*, 34, 192–198.

BLAKE, M.J.F. (1971) Temperament and time of day. In W.P. Colquhoun (Ed.) *Biological Rhythms and Human Performance*. London: Academic Press.

BLAKEMORE, C. (1988) *The Mind Machine*. London: BBC Publications.

BLAKEMORE, C. & COOPER, G.F. (1970) Development of the brain depends on the visual environment. *Nature*, 228, 477–478.

BLANEY, P. (1975) Implications of the medical model and its alternatives. *American Journal of Psychiatry*, 132, 911–914.

BLASI, A. (1980) Bridging moral cognition and moral action: A critical review of the literature. *Psychological Bulletin*, 88, 1–44.

BLAU, P.M. (1964) *Exchange and Power in Social Life*. New York: Wiley.

BLEULER, E. (1911) *Dementia Praecox or the Group of Schizophrenias*. New York: International University Press.

BLEULER, M.E. (1978) The long-term course of schizophrenic psychoses. In L.C. Wynne, R.L. Cromwell & S. Mathyse (Eds) *The Nature of Schizophrenia: New Approaches to Research and Treatment*. New York: Wiley.

BLIESZNER, R. & ADAMS, R. (1992) *Adult Friendships*. Newbury Park: Sage.

BLOCH, V. (1976) Brain activation and memory consolidation. In Rosenzweig, M.A. & Bennett, E.L. (Eds) *Neural Mechanisms of Learning and Memory*. Cambridge, MA: MIT Press.

BLOCK, J. (1978) Review of H.J. Eysenck and S.B.G. Eysenck, The Eysenck Personality Questionnaire. In O. Buros (Ed.) *The Eighth Mental Measurement Yearbook*. Highland Park, NJ: Gryphon.

BLOCK, J. (1979) Another look at sex differentiation in the socialisation behaviours of mothers and fathers. In F. Denmark & J. Sherman (Eds) *Psychology of Women: Future Directions of Research*. New York: Psychological Dimensions.

BLOOD, R.O. & WOLFE, D.M. (1969) *Husbands and Wives: The Dynamics of Married Lives*. New York: Free Press.

BLOOM, B. (1984) The 2 sigma problem: The search for methods of group instruction as effective as one-to-one tutoring. *Educational Researcher*, June/July, 4–16.

BLOOM, B.S. (1964) *Stability and Change in Human Characteristics*. New York: Harcourt Brace Jovanovich.

BLUM, K. (1984) *Handbook of Abusable Drugs*. New York: Gardner Press.

BLUNDELL, J.E. & HILL, A.J. (1995) Hunger and appetite. In Parkinson, B. & Colman, A.M. (Eds) *Emotion and Motivation*. London: Longman.

BNF (1997) *British National Formulary*. Number 32. London: British Medical Association/Royal Pharmaceutical Society of Great Britain.

BODEN, M. (1980) Artificial intelligence and intellectual imperialism. In A.J. Chapman & D.M. Jones (Eds) *Models of Man*. Leicester: British Psychological Society.

BODEN, M. (1987) *Artificial Language and Natural Man* (2nd edition). Cambridge, MA: Harvard University Press.

BOGDONOFF, M.D., KLEIN, R.F., ESTES, E.H., SHAW, D.M. & BACK, K. (1961) The modifying effect of conforming behaviour upon lipid responses accompanying CNS arousal. *Clinical Research*, 9, 135.

BOGEN, J.E. (1969) The other side of the brain. *Bulletin of the Los Angeles Neurological Societies*, 34, 3.

BOKERT, E. (1970) The effects of thirst and related auditory stimulation on dream reports. Paper presented at the Association for the Physiological Study of Sleep, Washington DC.

BOLLES, R.C. (1967) *Theory of Motivation*. New York: Harper & Row.

BOLLES, R.C. (1980) Ethological learning theory. In G.M. Gazda & R.J. Corsini (Eds) *Theories of Learning: A comparative approach*. Itaska, ILL.: Free Press.

BOLTER, A., HEMINGER, A., MARTIN, G. & FRY, M. (1976) Outpatient clinical experience in a community drug abuse program with phencyclidine. *Clinical Toxicology*, 9, 593–600.

BOOTH, A. & AMATO, P.R. (1994) Parental marital quality, parental divorce and relations with parents. *Journal of Marriage and the Family*, 55, 21–34.

BOOTH, T. & GOODEY, C. (1996) Playing for the sympathy vote. *Education Guardian*, 21 May, 5.

BOOTZIN, R.R. & ACOCELLA, J.R. (1984) *Abnormal Psychology: Current Perspectives* (4th edition). New York: Random House.

BORBELY, A. (1986) *Secrets of Sleep*. Harmondsworth: Penguin.

BORKE, H. (1975) Piaget's mountains revisited: Changes in the egocentric landscape. *Developmental Psychology*, 11, 240–243.

BORNSTEIN, M.H. (1976) Infants are trichromats. *Journal of Experimental Child Psychology*, 19, 401–419.

BORNSTEIN, M.H. (1988) Perceptual development across the life-cycle. In M.H. Bornstein & M.E. Lamb (Eds) *Perceptual, Cognitive and Linguistic Development*. Hove: Erlbaum.

BORNSTEIN, M.H. (1989) Sensitive periods in development: Structural characteristics and causal interpretations. *Psychological Bulletin*, 105, 179–197.

BORNSTEIN, M.H. & MARKS, L.E. (1982) Colour revisionism. *Psychology Today*, 16 (1), 64–73.

BOTTING, J.H. & MORRISON, A.R. (1997) Animal research is vital to medicine. *Scientific American*, 67–79, February.

BOTVIN, G.J. & MURRAY, F.B. (1975) The efficacy of peer modelling and social conflict in the acquisition of conservation. *Child Development*, 46, 796–799.

BOUCHARD, T.J. & McGUE, M. (1981) Familial studies of intelligence: A review. *Science*, 212, 1055–1059.

BOUCHARD, T.J. & SEGAL, N.L. (1988) Heredity, environment and IQ. In Instructor's Resource Manual to accompany G. Lindzey, R. Thompson & B. Spring. *Psychology* (3rd edition). New York: Worth Publishers.

BOUCHARD, T.J., LYKKEN, D.T., McGUE, M., SEGAL, N.L. & TELLEGEN, A. (1990) Sources of human psychological differences: The Minnesota study of twins reared apart. *Science*, 250, 223–228.

BOURNE, L.E., DOMINOWSKI, R.L. & LOFTUS, E.F. (1979) *Cognitive Processes*. Englewood Cliffs, NJ: Prentice-Hall.

BOUSFIELD, W.A. (1953) The occurrence of clustering in the recall of randomly arranged associates. *Journal of General Psychology*, 49, 229–240.

BOWER, G.H. (1972) Mental imagery and associative learning. In L. Gregg (Ed.) *Cognition in Learning and Memory*. New York: Wiley.

BOWER, G.H. (1973) How to … uh … remember! *Psychology Today*, October, 63–70.

BOWER, G.H., BLACK, J.B. & TURNER, T.J. (1979) Scripts in memory for text. *Cognitive Psychology*, 11, 177–220.

BOWER, G.H. & CLARK, M.C. (1969) Narrative stories as mediators for serial learning. *Psychonomic Science*, 14, 181–182.

BOWER, G.H., CLARK, M.C., LESGOLD, A. & WINSENZ, D. (1969) Hierarchical retrieval schemes in recall of categorised word lists. *Journal of Verbal Learning and Verbal Behaviour*, 8, 323–343.

BOWER, G.H. & HILGARD, E.R. (1981) *Theories of Learning*. Englewood Cliffs, NJ: Prentice Hall.

BOWER, G.H. & MAYER, J. (1985) Failure to replicate mood-dependent retrieval. *Bulletin of the Psychonomic Society*, 23, 39–42.

BOWER, G.H. & SPRINGSTON, F. (1970) Pauses as recoding points in letter series. *Journal of Experimental Psychology*, 83, 421–430.

BOWER, T.G.R. (1966) The visual world of infants. *Scientific American*, 215, 80–92.

BOWER, T.G.R. (1971) The object in the world of the infant. *Scientific American*, 225, 38–47.

BOWER, T.G.R. (1979) *Human Development*. San Francisco: W.H. Freeman.

BOWER, T.G.R., BROUGHTON, J.M. & MOORE, M.K. (1970) Infant responses to approaching objects: An indicator of response to distal variables. *Perception and Psychophysics*, 9, 193–196.

BOWER, T.G.R. & WISHART, J.G. (1972) The effects of motor skill on object permanence. *Cognition*, 1, 28–35.

BOWERS, K.S. (1976) *Hypnosis for the Seriously Curious*. Monterey, CA: Brooks Cole.

BOWLBY, J. (1946) *Forty-Four Juvenile Thieves*. London: Balliere Tindall and Cox.

BOWLBY, J. (1951) *Maternal Care and Mental Health*. Geneva: World Health Organisation.

BOWLBY, J. (1953) *Child Care and the Growth of Love*. Harmondsworth: Penguin.

BOWLBY, J. (1969) *Attachment and Loss*. Volume 1: *Attachment*. Harmondsworth: Penguin.

BOWLBY, J. (1973) *Attachment and Loss*. Volume 2: *Separation*. Harmondsworth: Penguin.

BOWLBY, J. (1980) *Attachment and Loss*. Volume 3: *Loss, Sadness and Depression*. London: Hogarth Press.

BOWLBY, J., AINSWORTH, M., BOSTON, M. & ROSENBLUTH, D. (1956) The effects of mother-child separation: A follow-up study. *British Journal of Medical Psychology*, 29, 211.

BOYD, C. (Ed.) (1996) *Attention Deficit Disorder: BBC Watchdog Healthcheck Handbook*. London: BBC Books.

BRACHA, H.S., TORREY, E.F., BIGELOW, L.B., LOHR, J.B. & LININGTON, B.B. (1991) Subtle signs of prenatal maldevelopment of the head ectoderm in schizophrenia: A preliminary monozygotic twin study. *Biological Psychiatry*, 30, 719–725.

BRADBURY, T.N. & FINCHAM, F.D. (1990) Attributions in marriage: Review and critique. *Psychological Bulletin*, 107, 3–33.

BRADDOCK, J.H. (1985) School desegregation and black assimilation. *Journal of Social Issues*, 41, 9–29.

BRADLEY, R.H. & CALDWELL, B.M. (1976) The relation of infants' home environments to mental test performance at 54 months: A follow-up study. *Child Development*, 47, 1172–1174.

BRADLEY, R.H. & CALDWELL, B.M. (1984) The relation of infants' home environments to achievement test performance in first grade: A follow-up study. *Child Development*, 55, 803–809.

BRADY, J.V. (1958) Ulcers in executive monkeys. *Scientific American*, 199, 95–100.

BRADY, J.V. & NAUTA, W.J.H. (1953) Subcortical mechanisms in emotional behaviour: Affective changes following septal forebrain lesions in the albino rat. *Journal of Comparative and Physiological Psychology*, 46, 339–346.

BRAINERD, C.J. (1978) Neo-Piagetian training experiments revisited: Is there any support for the cognitive-developmental stage hypothesis? *Cognition*, 2, 349–370.

BRAINERD, C.J. (1983) Modifiability of cognitive development. In S. Meadows (Ed.) *Development of Thinking*. London: Methuen.

BRANDSMA, J.M., MAULTSBY, M.C. & WELSH, R. (1978) 'Self-help techniques in the treatment of alcoholism.' Unpublished manuscript cited in G.T. Wilson & K.D. O'Leary *Principles of Behaviour Therapy*. Englewood Cliffs, NJ: Prentice-Hall.

BRANSFORD, J.D. (1979) *Human Cognition: Learning, Understanding and Remembering*. Belmont, CA: Wadsworth.

BRANSFORD, J.D., FRANKS, J.J., MORRIS, C.D. & STEIN, B.S. (1979) Some general constraints on learning and memory research. In L.S. Cermak & F.I.M. Craik (Eds) *Levels of Processing in Human Memory*. Hillsdale, NJ: Erlbaum.

BRANSFORD, J.D. & JOHNSON, M.K. (1972) Contextual prerequisites for understanding: Some investigations of comprehension and recall. *Journal of Verbal Learning and Verbal Behaviour*, 11, 717–726.

BREGGIN, P. (1973) Psychosurgery (letter to the editor). *Journal of the American Medical Association*, 226, 1121.

BREGGIN, P. (1979) *Electroshock: Its Brain Disabling Effects*. New York: Springer.

BREGGIN, P. (1996) *Toxic Psychiatry*. London: Fontana.

BREHM, J.W. (1966) *A Theory of Psychological Reactance*. New York: Academic Press.

BREHM, S.S. (1992) *Intimate Relationships* (2nd edition). New York: McGraw-Hill.

BREHM, S.S. & BREHM, J.W. (1981) *Psychological Reactance: A Theory of Freedom and Control*. New York: Academic Press.

BRETHERTON, I. (1985) Attachment theory: Retrospect and prospect. In I. Bretherton & E. Walters (Eds) Growing points of attachment theory and research. *Child Development Monographs*, 50 (Serial No. 209), 1–2.

BREWER, M.B. & KRAMER, R.M. (1985) The psychology of intergroup attitudes and behaviour. *Annual Review of Psychology*, 36, 219–243.

BREWER, W.F. (1974) There is no convincing evidence for operant or classical conditioning in adult humans. In W.B. Weimar & D.S. Palermo (Eds) *Cognition and the symbolic processes*. Hillsdale, NJ: Lawrence Erlbaum.

BRIDWELL, L.S. (1980) Revising strategies in twelfth-grade students' transactional writing. *Research in the Teaching of English*, 14, 197–222.

BRIGHAM, J. (1986) *Social Psychology*. Boston: Little, Brown.

BRIGHAM, J. & MALPASS, R.S. (1985) The role of experience and contact in the recognition of faces of own- and other-race persons. *Journal of Social Issues*, 41, 139–155.

BRIGHAM, J. & WEISSBACH, T. (1972) *Racial Attitudes in America: Analyses and Findings of Social Psychology*. New York: Harper & Row.

BRINDLE, D. (1997) Deafness more of a bar in job market than criminal record. *The Guardian*, 12 December, 6.

BRISLIN, R. (1993) *Understanding Culture's Influence on Behaviour*. Orlando, FL: Harcourt Brace Jovanovich.

BRITISH PSYCHOLOGICAL SOCIETY (1978) Ethical principles for research on human subjects. *Bulletin of the British Psychological Society*, 31, 48–49.

BRITISH PSYCHOLOGICAL SOCIETY (1983) *Guidelines for the professional practice of clinical psychology*. Leicester: British Psychological Society.

BRITISH PSYCHOLOGICAL SOCIETY (1985) A code of conduct for psychologists. *Bulletin of the British Psychological Society*, 38, 41–43.

BRITISH PSYCHOLOGICAL SOCIETY (1990) Ethical principles for conducting research with human participants. *The Psychologist*, 3 (6), 269–272.

BRITISH PSYCHOLOGICAL SOCIETY (1993) Ethical principles for conducting research with human participants (revised). *The Psychologist*, 6 (1), 33–35.

BRITISH PSYCHOLOGICAL SOCIETY (1995) *Recovered Memories: The Report of the Working Party of the British Psychological Society*. Leicester: British Psychological Society.

BRITISH PSYCHOLOGICAL SOCIETY & THE COMMITTEE OF THE EXPERIMENTAL PSYCHOLOGICAL SOCIETY (1985) *Guidelines for the use of animals in research*. Leicester: British Psychological Society.

BROADBENT, D.E. (1954) The role of auditory localisation and attention in memory span. *Journal of Experimental Psychology*, 47, 191–196.

BROADBENT, D.E. (1958) *Perception and Communication*. Oxford: Pergamon.

BROADBENT, D.E. (1981) Non-corporeal explanations in psychology. In A.F. Heath (Ed.) *Scientific Explanation*. Oxford: Clarendon Press.

BROADBENT, D.E. (1982) Task combination and selective intake of information. *Acta Psychologica*, 50, 253–290.

BROADBENT, D.E., COOPER, P.J. & BROADBENT, M.H.P. (1978) A comparison of hierarchical and matrix retrieval schemes in recall. *Journal of Experimental Psychology: Human Learning and Memory*, 4, 486–497.

BROCKNER, J. & GUARE, J. (1983) Improving the performance of low self-esteem individuals: An attributional approach. *Academy of Management Journal*, 29, 373–384.

BROCKNER, J. & RUBIN, Z. (1985) *Entrapment in Escalating Conflict*. New York: Springer-Verlag.

BRODBECK, A. & IRWIN, O. (1946) The speech behaviour of infants without families. *Child Development*, 17, 145–146.

BROMLEY, D.B. (1988) *Human Ageing: An Introduction to Gerontology* (3rd edition). Harmondsworth: Penguin.

BRONFENBRENNER, U. (1960) Freudian theories of identification and their derivatives. *Child Development*, 31, 15–40.

BRONFENBRENNER, U. (1979) *The Ecology of Human Development*. Cambridge, MA: Harvard University Press.

BROOKE, S. (1996) The anorexic man. *The Sunday Times (Style Section)*, 11 February, 17.

BROOKS, J. & WATKINS, M. (1989) Recognition memory and the mere exposure effect. *Journal of Experimental Psychology: Learning, Memory and Cognition*, 15, 968–976.

BROOM, L. & SELZNICK, P. (1977) *Sociology* (6th edition). London: Harper & Row.

BROWN, B. & GROTBERG, J.J. (1981) *Headstart: A successful experiment*. Courrier (Paris International Children's Centre).

BROWN, G.W. & HARRIS, T.O. (1978) *Social Origins of Depression: A Study of Psychiatric Disorder in Women*. London: Tavistock.

BROWN, H. (1985) *People, Groups and Society*. Milton Keynes: Open University Press.

BROWN, J. (1996) Playing for time. *The Sunday Times Style Magazine*, 27 October, 36.

BROWN, J.A. (1958) Some tests of the decay theory of immediate memory. *Quarterly Journal of Experimental Psychology*, 10, 12–21.

BROWN, J.A.C. (1963) *Techniques of Persuasion: From Propaganda to Brainwashing*. Harmondsworth: Penguin.

BROWN, J.D. & SMART, S. (1991) The self and social conduct: Linking self-representations to prosocial behaviour. *Journal of Personality and Social Psychology*, 60, 368–375.

BROWN, L.M. & GILLIGAN, C. (1992) *Meeting at the Crossroads: Women's Psychology and Girls' Development*. Cambridge, MA.: Harvard University Press.

BROWN, L.S. (1997) Ethics in psychology: Cui bono? In D. Fox & I. Prilleltensky (Eds) *Critical Psychology: An Introduction*. London: Sage.

BROWN, R. (1954) Mass phenomena. In G. Lindzey (Ed.) *Handbook of Social Psychology*. London: Addison-Wesley.

BROWN, R. (1965) *Social Psychology*. New York: The Free Press.

BROWN, R. (1970) The first sentences of child and chimpanzee. In R. Brown (Ed.) *Psycholinguistics*. New York: Free Press.

BROWN, R. (1973) *A First Language: The Early Stages*. Cambridge, MA: Harvard University Press.

BROWN, R. (1986) *Social Psychology: The Second Edition*. New York: Free Press.

BROWN, R., CAZDEN, C.B. & BELLUGI, U. (1969) The child's grammar from one to three. In J.P. Hill (Ed.) *Minnesota Symposium on Child Psychology*, Volume 2. Minneapolis: University of Minnesota Press.

BROWN, R. & KULIK, J. (1977) Flashbulb memories. *Cognition*, 5, 73–99.

BROWN, R. & KULIK, J. (1982) Flashbulb memories. In U. Neisser (Ed.) *Memory Observed*. San Francisco: Freeman.

BROWN, R. & LENNEBERG, E.H. (1954) A study in language and cognition. *Journal of Abnormal and Clinical Psychology*, 49, 454–462.

BROWN, R. & McNEILL, D. (1966) The 'tip-of-the-tongue' phenomenon. *Journal of Verbal Learning and Verbal Behaviour*, 5, 325–337.

BROWN, R.J. (1988) Intergroup relations. In M. Hewstone, W. Stroebe, J.P. Codol & G.M. Stephenson (Eds) *Introduction to Social Psychology*. Oxford: Blackwell.

BROWN, R.J. (1996) Intergroup relations. In M. Hewstone, W. Stroebe & G.M. Stephenson (Eds) *Introduction to Social Psychology* (2nd edition). Oxford: Blackwell.

BROWN, R.J. & TURNER, J.C. (1981) Interpersonal and intergroup behaviour. In J.C. Turner & H. Giles (Eds) *Intergroup Behaviour*. Oxford: Blackwell.

BROWNELL, K.D. & FAIRBURN, C.G. (1995) *Eating Disorders and Obesity: A Comprehensive Handbook*. New York: Guildford.

BRUCE, V. & GREEN, P.R. (1990) *Visual Perception* (2nd edition). Hove: Erlbaum.

BRUCE, V., BURTON, A.M. & DENCH, N. (1994) What's distinctive about a distinctive face? *Quarterly Journal of Experimental Psychology*, 47A, 119–141.

BRUCH, H. (1978) *Eating Disorders: Obesity, Anorexia Nervosa and the Person Within*. New York: Basic Books.

BRUNER, J.S. (1957) On perceptual readiness. *Psychological Review*, 64, 123–152.

BRUNER, J.S. (1963) *The Process of Education*. Cambridge, MA: Harvard University Press.

BRUNER, J.S. (1966) On the conservation of liquids. In J.S. Bruner, R.R. Oliver & P.M. Greenfield (Eds) *Studies in Cognitive Growth*. New York: Wiley.

BRUNER, J.S. (1975) The ontogenesis of speech acts. *Journal of Child Language*, 2, 1–21.

BRUNER, J.S. (1978) Acquiring the uses of language. *Canadian Journal of Psychology*, 32, 204–218.

BRUNER, J.S. (1983) *Child's Talk: Learning to Use Language*. Oxford: Oxford University Press.

BRUNER, J.S., BUSIEK, R.D. & MINTURN, A.L. (1952) Assimilation in the immediate reproduction of visually perceived figures. *Journal of Experimental Psychology*, 44, 151–155.

BRUNER, J.S., GOODNOW, J.J., & AUSTIN, G.A. (1956) *A Study of Thinking*. New York: Wiley.

BRUNER, J.S. & KENNEY, H. (1966) *The Development of the Concepts of Order and Proportion in Children*. New York: Wiley.

BRUNER, J.S., OLIVER, R.R. & GREENFIELD, P.M. (1966) *Studies in Cognitive Growth*. New York: Wiley.

BRUNER, J.S. & POSTMAN, L. (1949) On the perception of incongruity. *Journal of Personality*, 18, 206–223.

BRUNER, J.S. & TAGIURI, R. (1954) The perception of people. In G. Lindzey (Ed.) *Handbook of Social Psychology*, Volume 2. London: Addison Wesley.

BRYANT, J. & ZILLMAN, D. (Eds) (1994) *Media Effects: Advances in Theory and Research*. Hove: Erlbaum.

BRYDEN, M. & SAXBY, L. (1985) Developmental aspects of cerebral lateralisation. In J. Obrzat & G. Hynd (Eds) *Child Neuropsychology*, Volume 1: *Theory and Research*. Orlando, FLA: Academic Press.

BUCHANAN, A. & OLIVER, J.E. (1977) Abuse and neglect as a cause of mental retardation. *British Journal of Psychiatry*, 131, 458–467.

BUEHLER, C. & LEGGE, B.H. (1993) Mothers' receipt of social support and their psychological well being following marital separation. *Journal of Social and Personal Relationships*, 10, 21–38.

BUNNEY, W., GOODWIN, F. & MURPHY, D. (1972) The 'switch process' in manic-depressive illness. *Archives of General Psychiatry*, 27, 312–317.

BURGER, F. (1982) The 46-hour-a-week habit. *The Boston Globe*, 2 May

BURGESS, A. (1962) *A Clockwork Orange*. Harmandsworth: Penguin.

BURLINGHAM, D. & FREUD, A. (1944) *Infants without Families: The Case for and against Residential Nurseries*. London: Allen & Unwin.

BURMAN, E. (1994) *Deconstructing Developmental Psychology*. London: Routledge.

BURNE, J. (1996) How to tell if you've really had a brain wave. *The Daily Telegraph*, 10 April, 16.

BURNSIDE, I.M., EBERSOLE, P. & MONEA, H.E. (1979) *Psychological Caring Throughout the Lifespan*. New York: McGraw-Hill.

BURR, V. (1995) *An Introduction to Social Constructionism*. London: Routledge.

BURR, W.R. (1970) Satisfaction with various aspects of marriage over the life cycle: A random middle class sample. *Journal of Marriage and the Family*, 32, 29–37.

BURT, C. (1921) *Mental and Scholastic Tests*. London: King and Son.

BURT, C. (1943) War neuroses in British children. *Nervous Child*, 2, 324–337.

BURT, C. (1966) The genetic determination of differences in intelligence: A study of monozygotic twins reared together and apart. *British Journal of Psychology*, 57, 137–153.

BUSHNELL, I.W.R. & SAI, F. (1987) Neonatal Recognition of the Mother's Face. *University of Glasgow Report* No.87/1.

BUSS, A.H. (1966) *Psychopathology*. New York: Wiley.

BUSS, A.H. & PLOMIN, R. (1984) *Temperament: Early Developing Personality Traits*. Hillsdale, NJ: Erlbaum.

BUSS, D.M. (1988) The evolutionary biology of love. In R.J. Sternberg & M.L. Barnes (Eds) *The Psychology of Love*. New Haven, CT: Yale University Press.

BUSS, D.M. (1989) Sex differences in human mate preferences: Evolutionary hypotheses tested in 37 cultures. *Behavioural and Brain Sciences*, 12, 1–49.

BUSS, D.M. (1994) Mate preference in 37 cultures. In W.J. Lonner & R.S. Malpass (Eds) *Psychology and Culture*. Boston: Allyn & Bacon.

BUTLER, R. (1963) The life review: An interpretation of reminiscence in the aged. *Psychiatry*, 26, 65–76.

BUUNK, B.P. (1996) Affiliation, attraction and close relationships. In M. Hewstone, W. Stroebe & G.M. Stephenson (Eds) *Introduction to Social Psychology* (2nd edition). Oxford: Blackwell.

BYRNE, D.S. (1971) *The Attraction Paradigm*. New York: Academic Press.

BYRNE, D.S. & MURNEN, S. (1988) Maintaining loving relationships. In R.J. Sternberg & M. Barnes (Eds) *The Psychology of Loving*. New Haven, CT: Yale University Press.

CALLAGHAN, P. & O'CARROLL, M. (1993) Making women mad. *Nursing Times*, 89, 26–29.

CALVIN, W.H. (1994) The emergence of language. *Scientific American*, October, 79–85.

CAMPBELL, A. (1981) *The Sense of Well-Being in America*. New York: McGraw-Hill.

CAMPBELL, A. & MUNCER, S. (1994) Men and the meaning of violence. In J. Archer (Ed.) *Male Violence*. London: Routledge.

CAMPBELL, B.A. & CHURCH, R.M. (1969) (Eds) *Punishment and aversive behaviour*. New York: Appleton-Century-Crofts.

CAMPBELL, D.T. (1967) Stereotypes and the perception of group differences. *American Psychologist*, 22, 817–829.

CAMPBELL, R. (1996) Cognitive skills and domain-specificity. Report on the Piaget-Vygotsky centenary conference. *The Psychologist*, 9, 369.

CAMPBELL, S. & WERRY, J. (1986) Attention deficit disorder (Hyperactivity). In H. Quay & J. Werry (Eds) *Psychological Disorders of Childhood* (3rd edition). New York: Wiley.

CAMPFIELD, L.A., BRANDON, P. & SMITH, F.J. (1985) On-line continuous measurement of blood-glucose and meal pattern in free-feeding rats: The role of glucose in meal initiation. *Brain Research Bulletin*, 14, 605–616.

CAMPOS, J.J., LANGER, A. & KROWITZ, A. (1970) Cardiac responses on the visual cliff in pre-locomotor human infants. *Science*, 170, 196–197.

CANNON, W.B. (1927) The James-Lange theory of emotions: A critical reexamination and an alternative theory. *American Journal of Psychology*, 39, 106–124.

CANNON, W.B. (1929) *Bodily Changes in Pain, Hunger, Fear, and Rage*. New York: Appleton.

CANNON, W.B. & WASHBURN, A.L. (1912) An explanation of hunger. *American Journal of Physiology*, 29, 441–454.

CANTIN, M. & GENEST, J. (1986) The heart as an endocrine gland. *Scientific American*, 254, 76–81.

CANTRIL, H. (1941) *The Psychology of Social Movements*. New York: Wiley.

CAPLAN, P.J. (1991) Delusional dominating personality disorder (DDPD). *Feminism & Psychology*, 1 (1), 171–174.

CAPRON, C. & DUYME, M. (1989) Assessment of effects of socio-economic status on IQ in full cross-fostering study. *Nature*, 340, 552–554.

CARLSON, N.R. (1977) *Physiology of Behaviour*. Boston: Allyn & Bacon.

CARLSON, N.R. (1987) *Discovering Psychology*. London: Allyn & Bacon.

CARLSON, N.R. (1988) *Foundations of Physiological Psychology*. Boston: Allyn & Bacon.

CARLSON, N.R. (1992) *Foundations of Physiological Psychology* (2nd edition). Boston: Allyn & Bacon.

CARLSON, N.R. & BUSKIST, W. (1997) *Psychology: The Science of Behaviour* (5th edition). Needham Heights, MA.: Allyn and Bacon.

CARNEGIE, D. (1937) *How To Win Friends and Influence People*. New York: Simon & Schuster.

CARROLL, D.W. (1986) *Psychology of Language*. Monterey, CA: Brooks/Cole Publishing Co.

CARROLL, J.B. & CASAGRANDE, J.B. (1958) The function of language classifications in behaviour. In E.E. Maccoby, T.M. Newcombe & E.L. Hartley (Eds) *Readings in Social Psychology* (3rd edition). New York: Holt, Rinehart & Winston.

CARSON, R. (1989) Personality. *Annual Review of Psychology*, 40, 227–248.

CARTWRIGHT, R.D. (1978) *A Primer on Sleep and Dreaming*. Reading, MA: Addison-Wesley.

CARVER, C.S. & SCHEIER, M.F. (1992) *Perspectives on Personality* (2nd edition). Boston: Allyn & Bacon.

CASE, R. (1985) *Intellectual Development*. London: Methuen.

CAUTELA, J.R. (1967) Covert sensitisation. *Psychology Reports*, 20, 459–468.

CAVANAUGH, J.C. (1995) Ageing. In P.E. Bryant & A.M. Colman (Eds) *Developmental Psychology*. London: Longman.

CERNOVSKY, Z.Z (1997) A critical look at intelligence research. In D. Fox & I. Prilleltensky (Eds) *Critical Psychology: An Introduction*. London: Sage.

CHAIKIN, A.L. & DARLEY, J.M. (1973) Victim or perpetrator? Defensive attribution of responsibility and the need for order and justice. *Journal of Personality and Social Psychology*, 25, 268–275.

CHALL, J. (1967) *Learning to Read: The Great Debate*. New York: McGraw Hill.

CHALL, J. (1983) *Stages of Reading Development*. New York: McGraw Hill.

CHANCE, P. (1984) I'm OK, you're a little odd. *Psychology Today*, September, 18–19.

CHANDLER, C. (1989) Specific retroactive interference in modified recognition tests: Evidence for an unknown cause of interference. *Journal of Experimental Psychology: Learning, Memory and Cognition*, 15, 256–265.

CHAPMAN, L.J. & CHAPMAN, J.P. (1969) Illusory correlation as an obstacle to the use of valid psychodiagnostic signs. *Journal of Abnormal Psychology*, 74, 271–280.

CHARLTON, B. (1996) How to get inside the thinking brain. *The Times*, 5 February, 12.

CHASE, M. & MORALES, F. (1990) The atonia and myoclonia of active (REM) sleep. *Annual Review of Psychology*, 41, 557–584.

CHERRY, E.C. (1953) Some experiments on the recognition of speech with one and two ears. *Journal of the Acoustical Society of America*, 25, 975–979.

CHERRY, E.C. & TAYLOR, W.K. (1954) Some further experiments on the recognition of speech with one and two ears. *Journal of the Acoustical Society of America*, 26, 554–559.

CHERRY, F. & BYRNE, D.S. (1976) Authoritarianism. In T. Blass (Ed.) *Personality Variables in Social Behaviour*. Hillsdale, NJ: Erlbaum.

CHOMSKY, N. (1957) *Syntactic Structures*. The Hague: Mouton.

CHOMSKY, N. (1965) *Aspects of the Theory of Syntax*. Cambridge, MA: MIT Press.

CHOMSKY, N. (1968) *Language and Mind*. New York: Harcourt Brace Jovanovich.

CHOMSKY, N. (1979) *Language and Responsibility*. Sussex: Harvester Press.

CHRISTENSEN, L. (1988) Deception in psychological research: When is its use justified? *Personality & Social Psychology*, 14, 665–675.

CHUA, S.E. & McKENNA, P.J. (1995) Schizophrenia – a brain disease? A critical review of structural and functional cerebral abnormality in the disorder. *British Journal of Psychiatry*, 166, 563–582.

CHUMLEA, W. (1982) Physical growth in adolescence. In B. Wolman (Ed.) *Handbook of Developmental Psychology*. Englewood Cliffs, NJ: Prentice-Hall.

CLAMP, A. & RUSSELL, J. (1998) *Comparative Psychology*. London: Hodder & Stoughton.

CLARE, J. (1995) Zoid's friends and other virtual teachers. *The Daily Telegraph*, January 16, 19.

CLARIDGE, G. (1987) The continuum of psychosis and the gene. *British Journal of Psychiatry*, 150, 129–133 (correspondence).

CLARK, D.M. (1993) Treating panic attacks. *The Psychologist*, 6, 73–74.

CLARK, D.M., SALKOVSKIS, P.M., HACKMANN, A., MIDDLETON, H., ANASTASIADES, P. & GELDER, M. (1994) A comparison of cognitive therapy, applied relaxation and imipramine in the treatment of panic disorder. *British Journal of Psychiatry*, 164, 759–769.

CLARK, K.B. & CLARK, M. (1947) Racial identification and preference in negro children. In T.M. Newcomb & E.L. Hartley (Eds) *Readings in Social Psychology*. New York: Holt.

CLARK, K.E. & MILLER, G.A. (Eds 1970) *Psychology: Behavioural and Social Sciences Survey Committee*. Englewood Cliffs, NF: Prentice Hall.

CLARK, M.S., MILLBERG, S. & ERBER, R. (1987) Arousal and state dependent memory: Evidence and some implications for understanding social judgements and social behaviour. In K. Fiedler & J.P. Forgas (Eds) *Affect, Cognition and Social Behaviour*. Toronto: Hogrefe.

CLARK, R.D. & MAASS, A. (1988) The role of social categorization and perceived source credibility in minority influence. *European Journal of Social Psychology*, 18, 381–394.

CLARK, R.D. & WORD, L.E. (1974) Where is the apathetic bystander? Situational characteristics of the emergency. *Journal of Personality and Social Psychology*, 29, 279–287.

CLARKE, A.M. & CLARKE, A.D.B. (1976) *Early Experience: Myth and Evidence*. New York: Free Press.

CLIFFORD, B. (1980) Recent developments in memory. In J. Radford & E. Govier (Eds) *A Textbook of Psychology*. London: Sheldon.

CLIFFORD, B. (1991) Memory. In J. Radford & E. Govier (Eds) *A Textbook of Psychology* (2nd edition). London: Routledge.

CLOPTON, N.A. & SORELL, G.T. (1993) Gender differences in moral reasoning: Stable or situational? *Psychology of Women Quarterly*, 17, 85–101.

CLORE, G.L. & BYRNE, D.S. (1974) A reinforcement-affect model of attraction. In T.L. Huston (Ed.) *Foundations of Interpersonal Attraction*. New York: Academic Press.

CLORE, G.L., BRAY, R.M., ITKIN, S.M. & MURPHY, P. (1978) Interracial attitudes and behaviour at a summer camp. *Journal of Personality and Social Psychology*, 36, 706–712.

COCHRANE, R. (1983) *The Social Creation of Mental Illness*. London: Longman.

COCHRANE, R. (1995) Women and depression. *Psychology Review*, 2, 20–24.

COCHRANE, R. (1996) Marriage and madness. *Psychology Review*, 3, 2–5.

COE, W.C. & YASHINSKI, E. (1985) Volitional experiences associated with breaching post-hypnotic amnesia. *Journal of Personality and Social Psychology*, 48, 716–722.

COHEN, D.B. (1973) Sex role orientation and dream recall. *Journal of Abnormal Psychology*, 82, 246–252.

COHEN, G. (1990) Memory. In I. Roth (Ed.) *Introduction to Psychology*, Volume 2. Milton Keynes: Open University Press.

COHEN, G. (1993) Everyday memory and memory systems: The experimental approach. In G. Cohen, G. Kiss & M. Levoi (Eds) *Memory: Current Issues* (2nd edition). Buckingham: Open University Press.

COHEN, J. (1958) *Humanistic Psychology*. London: Allen & Unwin.

COHEN, M. & DAVIS, N. (1981) *Medication Errors: Causes and Prevention*. Philadelphia: G.F. Stickley.

COHN, H.W. (1994) What is existential psychotherapy? *British Journal of Psychiatry*, 165, 699–701.

COLBY, A., KOHLBERG, L., GIBBS, J. & LIEBERMAN, M. (1983) A longitudinal study of moral development. *Monographs of the Society for Research in Child Development*, 48, (1–2, Serial No. 200).

COLEMAN, J.C. (1980) *The Nature of Adolescence*. London: Methuen.

COLEMAN, J.C. (1995) Adolescence. In P.E. Bryant & A.M. Colman (Eds) *Developmental Psychology*. London: Longman.

COLEMAN, J.C. & HENDRY, L. (1990) *The Nature of Adolescence* (2nd edition). London: Routledge.

COLLEE, J. (1993) Symbol minds. *The Observer Life Magazine*, 26 September, 14.

COLLETT, P. (1993) *Foreign Bodies*. London: Simon & Schuster.

COLLINS, A.M. & LOFTUS, E.F. (1975) A spreading-activation theory of semantic processing. *Psychological Review*, 82, 407–428.

COLLINS, A.M. & QUILLIAN, M.R. (1969) *Retrieval time for semantic memory*. *Journal of Verbal Learning and Verbal Behaviour*, 8, 240–247.

COLLINS, A.M. & QUILLIAN, M.R. (1972) How to make a language user. In E. Tulving & W. Donaldson (Eds) *Organisation of Memory*. New York: Academic Press.

COLLINS, H. (1994) *Times Higher Education Supplement*, 18, 30 September.

COLLINS, R.C. (1983) Headstart: An update on program effects. *Newsletter of the Society for Research in Child Development*. Summer, 1–2.

COLLIS, G.M. & SCHAFFER, H.R. (1975) Synchronization of visual attention in mother-infant pairs. *Journal of Child Psychology and Psychiatry*, 16, 315–320.

COLMAN, A.M. (1987) *Facts, Fallacies and Frauds in Psychology*. London: Unwin Hyman.

COLMAN, A.M., HARGREAVES, D.J., & SLUCKIN, W. (1981) Preferences for Christian names as a function of their experienced familiarity. *British Journal of Social Psychology*, 72, 363–369.

COLTHEART, M. (1979) When can children learn to read and what should they be taught? In T.G. Waller & G.E. McKinnon (Eds) *Reading Research: Advances in Theory and Practice*, Volume 1. New York: Academic Press.

COLTHEART, M., MASTERSON, J., BYNG, S., PRIOR, M. & RIDDOCH, J. (1983) Surface dyslexia. *Quarterly Journal of Experimental Psychology*, 35A, 469–495.

COMINGS, D.E. & COMINGS, B.G. (1987) Hereditary agoraphobia and obsessive-compulsive behaviour in relatives of patients with Gilles de la Tourette's syndrome. *British Journal of Psychiatry*, 151, 195–199.

COMSTOCK, G. & PAIK, H. (1991) *Television and the American Child*. New York: Academic Press.

CONDRY, J.C. & ROSS, D.F. (1985) Sex and aggression: The influence of gender label on the perception of aggression in children. *Child Development*, 56, 225–233.

CONNOR, S. (1997) Mute boy speaks after brain is halved. *The Sunday Times*, 4 May, 10.

CONNOR, S. (1998) Science finds a way of treating fear. *The Sunday Times*, 22 February, 11.

CONRAD, C. (1972) Cognitive economy in semantic memory. *Journal of Experimental Psychology*, 92, 148–154.

CONRAD, R. (1964) Acoustic confusion in immediate memory. *British Journal of Psychology*, 55, 75–84.

CONRAD, R. (1977) The reading ability of deaf school-leavers. *British Journal of Educational Psychology*, 47, 60–65.

CONSTANZO, P.R., COIE, J.D., GRUMET, J.F. & FARNHILL, D. (1973) Re-examination of the effects of intent and consequence of children's moral judgements. *Child Development*, 44, 154–161.

CONWAY, M.A., ANDERSON, S.J., LARSEN, S.F., DONNELLY, C.M., McDANIEL, M.A., McCLELLAND, A.G.R. & RAWLES, R.E. (1994). The formation of flashbulb memories. *Memory and Cognition*, 22, 326–343.

COOK, E. (1997) Is marriage driving women mad? Real Life. *Independent on Sunday*, 10 August, 1–2.

COOK, S.W. (1984) The 1954 social science statement and school desegregation. *American Psychologist*, 39, 819–832.

COOLEY, C.H. (1902) *Human Nature and the Social Order*. New York: Shocken.

COOLICAN, H. (1990) *Research Methods and Statistics in Psychology*. Sevenoaks: Hodder & Stoughton.

COOLICAN, H. (1994) *Research Methods and Statistics in Psychology* (2nd edition). London: Hodder & Stoughton.

COOLICAN, H. (1995) *Introduction to Research Methods and Statistics in Psychology*. London: Hodder & Stoughton.

COOLICAN, H. (1997) Thinking about prejudice. *Psychology Review*, 4, 26–29.

COOLICAN, H., CASSIDY, T., CHERCHER, A., HARROWER J., PENNY, G., SHARP, R., WALLEY, M. & WESTBURY, T. (1996) *Applied Psychology*. London: Hodder & Stoughton.

COOPER, G. (1994) Napoleon island to end TV exile. *Independent on Sunday*, 12 June, 7.

COOPER, G. (1996a) How nursery breeds bad behaviour. *Independent*, 13 September, 3.

COOPER, G. (1996b) The satisfying side of being home alone. *Independent*, 13 September, 3.

COOPER, H.M. (1979) Statistically combining independent studies: A meta-analysis of sex differences in conformity research. *Journal of Personality and Social Psychology*, 37, 131–146.

COOPER, J.E. (1995) On the publication of the Diagnostic and Statistical Manual of Mental Disorders (4th edition). *British Journal of Psychiatry*, 166, 4–8.

COOPER, J.E., KENDELL, R.E., GURLAND, B.J., SHARPE, L., COPELAND, J.R.M. & SIMON, R. (1972) *Psychiatric Diagnosis in New York and London*. Oxford: Oxford University Press.

COOPER, P.J. (1995) Eating disorders. In A.A. Lazarus & A.M. Colman (Eds) *Abnormal Psychology*. London: Longman.

COOPER, R. & ZUBEK, J. (1958) Effects of enriched and restricted early environments on the learning ability of bright and dull rats. *Canadian Journal of Psychology*, 12, 159–164.

COOPERS & LYBRAND (1992) *Within Reach: Access for Disabled Children to Mainstream Education*. National Union of Teachers in association with SCOPE.

COOPERS & LYBRAND (1996) *The SEN Initiative: Managing Budgets for Pupils with Special Educational Needs*. London.

COOPERSMITH, S. (1967) *The Antecedents of Self-Esteem*. San Francisco: Freeman.

COREN, S. (1996) *Sleep Thieves*. New York: Free Press.

COREN, S. & GIRGUS, J.S. (1978) *Seeing is Deceiving: The Psychology of Visual Illusions*. Hillsdale, NJ: Erlbaum.

COREY, G. (1991) *Theory and Practice of Counselling and Psychotherapy*. Pacific Groves, CA: Brooks/Cole.

CORNWALL, J. (1995) Psychology, disability and equal opportunity. *The Psychologist*, 8, 396–397.

CORNWELL, T. (1997) Board tones down Ebonics policy. *Times Educational Supplement*, 31 January, 14.

CORRIGAN, R. (1978) Language development as related to stage-6 object permanence development. *Journal of Child Language*, 5, 173–189.

CORSARO, W.A. (1993) Interpretive reproduction in the 'scuola materna'. *European Journal of Psychology of Education*, 8, 357–374.

CORTEEN, R.S. & WOOD, B. (1972) Autonomic responses to shock-associated words in an unattended channel. *Journal of Experimental Psychology*, 94, 308–313.

COSKY, M.J. (1976) The role of letter recognition in word recognition. *Memory and Cognition*, 4, 207–214.

COSTANTINI, E. & CRAIK, K.H. (1980) Personality and politicians: California party leaders, 1960–1976. *Journal of Personality and Social Psychology*, 38, 641–661.

COSTELLO, T.W., COSTELLO, J.T., & HOLMES, D.A. (Adapting author) (1995) *Abnormal Psychology*. London: HarperCollins.

COTMAN, C.W. & McGAUGH, J.L. (1980) *Behavioural Neuroscience*. New York: Academic Press.

COUCH, C.J. (1968) Collective behaviour: An examination of some stereotypes. *Social Problems*, 15, 310–322.

COUNCIL, J.R., KIRSCH, I. & HAFNER, L.P. (1986) Expectancy versus absorption in the prediction of hypnotic responding. *Journal of Personality and Social Psychology*, 50, 182–189.

COURCHESNE, I., YEUNG-COURCHESNE, R., PRESS, G.A., HESSELINK, J.R. & JERNIGAN, T.L. (1988) Hypoplasia of cerebellar vermal lobules VI and VII in autism. *New England Journal of Medicine*, 318, 1349–1354.

COWAN, N. (1984) On short and long auditory stores. *Psychological Bulletin*, 96, 341–370.

COWART, J. & WHALEY, D.L. (1971) Punishment of self-mutilation behaviour. Cited in D.L. Whaley & R.W. Malott *Elementary Principles of Behaviour*. New York: Appleton Century Crofts.

CRAIG, G.J. (1992) *Human Development* (6th edition). Englewood Cliffs, NJ: Prentice-Hall.

CRAIK, F.I.M. & LOCKHART, R. (1972) Levels of processing. *Journal of Verbal Learning and Verbal Behaviour*, 11, 671–684.

CRAIK, F.I.M. & TULVING, E. (1975) Depth of processing and retention of words in episodic memory. *Journal of Experimental Psychology: General*, 104, 268–294.

CRAIK, F.I.M. & WATKINS, M.J. (1973) The role of rehearsal in short-term memory. *Journal of Verbal Learning and Verbal Behaviour*, 12, 599–607.

CRAMB, A. (1997) Stress can be good for the heart, says study. *The Daily Telegraph*, 19 September, 11.

CRAMER, D. (1994) Personal relationships. In D. Tantam & M. Birchwood (Eds) *Seminars in Psychology and the Social Sciences*. London: Gaskell Press.

CRAMER, D. (1995) Special issue on personal relationships. *The Psychologist*, 8, 58–59.

CRATTY, B.J. (1970) *Perceptual and Motor Development in Children*. New York: MacMillan.

CRAWFORD, H.J. (1994) Brain dynamics and hypnosis: Attentional and disattentional processes. *International Journal of Clinical and Experimental Hypnosis*, 42, 204–231.

CRICK, F. (1994) *The Astonishing Hypothesis: The Scientific Search for the Soul*. London: Simon & Schuster.

CRICK, F. & MITCHISON, G. (1983) The function of dream sleep. *Nature*, 304, 111–114.

CRIDER, A.B., GOETHALS, G.R., KAVANAUGH, R.D. & SOLOMON, P.R. (1989) *Psychology* (3rd edition). London: Scott, Foresman and Company.

CRISP, A.H. (1967) Anorexia nervosa. *Hospital Medicine*, 1, 713–718.

CROCKER, J., THOMPSON, L., McGRAW, K. & INGERMAN, C. (1987) Downward comparison, prejudice, and evaluation of others: Effects of self-esteem and threat. *Journal of Personality and Social Psychology*, 52, 907–916.

CROMER, R.F. (1974) The development of language and cognition: The cognition hypothesis. In B.M. Foss (Ed.) *New Perspectives in Child Development*. Harmondsworth: Penguin.

CROOK, T. & ELIOT, J. (1980) Parental death during childhood and adult depression: A critical review of the literature. *Psychological Bulletin*, 87, 252–259.

CROOKS, R.L. & STEIN, J. (1991) *Psychology: Science, Behaviour and Life* (2nd edition). London: Holt, Rinehart & Winston Inc.

CROW, T.J. & DONE, D.J. (1992) Prenatal exposure to influenza does not cause schizophrenia. *British Journal of Psychiatry*, 161, 390–393.

CROW, T.J., CROSS, A.G., JOHNSTONE, E.C. & OWEN, F. (1982) Two syndromes in schizophrenia and their pathogenesis. In F.A. Henn & G.A. Nasrallah (Eds) *Schizophrenia as a Brain Disease*. New York: Oxford University Press.

CROWNE, D.P. & MARLOWE, D. (1964) *The Approval Motive*. New York: Wiley.

CRUTCHFIELD, R.S. (1954) A new technique for measuring individual differences in conformity to group judgement. *Proceedings of the Invitational Conference on Testing Problems*, 69–74.

CRUTCHFIELD, R.S. (1955) Conformity and character. *American Psychologist*, 10, 191–198.

CSIKSZENTMIHALYI, M. & LARSON, R. (1984) *Being Adolescent: Conflict and Growth in the Teenage Years*. New York: Basic Books.

CUMBERBATCH, G. (1987) *The Portrayal of Violence on British Television*. London: BBC Publications.

CUMBERBATCH, G. (1997) Media violence: Science and common sense. *Psychology Review*, 3, 2–7.

CUMMING, E. (1975) Engagement with an old theory. *International Journal of Ageing and Human Development*, 6, 187–191.

CUMMING, E. & HENRY, W.E. (1961) *Growing Old: The Process of Disengagement*. New York: Basic Books.

CURTIS, R. & MILLER, K. (1988) Believing another likes or dislikes you: Behaviour making the beliefs come true. *Journal of Personality and Social Psychology*, 51, 284–290.

CURTISS, S. (1977) *Genie: A Psycholinguistic Study of a Modern-Day 'Wild Child'*. London: Academic Press.

CUTTS, T.F. & BARRIOS, B.A. (1986) Fear of weight gain among bulimic and non-disturbed females. *Behaviour Therapy*, 17, 626–636.

DACEY, J.S. (1982) *Adolescents Today* (2nd edition). Glenview, Illinois: Scott, Foresman & Company.

DALE, P.S. (1976) *Language Development: Structure and Function* (2nd edition). New York: Holt, Rinehart and Winston.

DALLOS, R. & CULLEN, C. (1990) Clinical psychology. In I. Roth (Ed.) *Introduction to Psychology*, Volume 2. Hove/E.Sussex/Milton Keynes: Open University Press/Lawrence Erlbaum Associates Ltd.

DALTON, K. (1964) *The Premenstrual Syndrome*. Springfield, ILL: Charles C. Thomas.

DAMASIO, A.R. & DAMASIO, H. (1992) Brain and language. *Scientific American*, 267 (3), September, 63–71 (Special issue).

DAMON, W. & HART, D. (1988) *Self-Understanding in Childhood and Adolescence*. Cambridge: Cambridge University Press.

DARLEY, J.M. (1991) Altruism and prosocial behaviour research: Reflections and prospects. In M.S. Clark (Ed.) *Prosocial Behaviour, Review of Personality and Social Psychology*, 12. Newbury Park: CA: Sage.

DARLEY, J.M. & BATSON, C.D. (1973) From Jerusalem to Jericho: A study of situational and dispositional variables in helping behaviour. *Journal of Personality and Social Psychology*, 27, 100–108.

DARLEY, J.M. & HUFF, C.W. (1990) Heightened damage assessment as a result of the intentionality of the damage causing act. *British Journal of Social Psychology*, 29, 181–188.

DARLEY, J.M. & LATANÉ, B. (1968) Bystander intervention in emergencies: Diffusion of responsibility. *Journal of Personality and Social Psychology*, 8, 377–383.

DARLING, N. & STEINBERG, L. (1993) Parenting style as context: an integrative model. *Psychological Bulletin*, 113, 487–496.

DARWIN, C.J., TURVEY, M.T. & CROWDER, R.G. (1972) An auditory analogue of the Sperling partial report procedure: Evidence for brief auditory storage. *Cognitive Psychology*, 3, 225–267.

DARWIN, C.R. (1859) *The Origin of Species by Means of Natural Selection*. London: John Murray.

DASEN, P.R. (1994) Culture and cognitive development from a Piagetian perspective. In W.J. Lonner & R.S. Malpass (Eds) *Psychology and Culture*. Boston: Allyn & Bacon.

DATAN, N., RODEHEAVER, D. & HUGHES, F. (1987) Adult development and ageing. *Annual Review of Psychology*, 38, 153–180.

DAVEY, G.C.L. (1983) An associative view of human classical conditioning. In G.C.L. Davey (Ed.) *Animal models of human behaviour: Conceptual, evolutionary, and neurobiological perspectives*. Chichester: Wiley.

DAVID, A.S. (1994) Frontal lobology: Psychiatry's new pseudoscience. *British Journal of Psychiatry*, 161, 244–248.

DAVIDSON, J. (1992) Drug therapy of post-traumatic stress disorder. *British Journal of Psychiatry*, 160, 309–314.

DAVIDSON, R.J. (1992) Anterior cerebral asymmetry and the nature of emotion. *Brain and Cognition*, 20, 280–299.

DAVIES, D.L. (1956) Psychiatric illness in those enagaged to be married. *British Journal of Preventive and Social Medicine*, 10, 123–127.

DAVIES, J.C. (1969) The J-curve of rising and declining satisfactions as a cause of some great revolutions and a contained rebellion. In H.D. Graham & T.R. Gurr (Eds) *The History of Violence in America: Historical and Comparative Perspectives*. New York: Praeger.

DAVIES, M. (1995) Beyond physical access for students with cerebral palsy. *The Psychologist*, 8, 401–404.

DAVIS, D., CAHAN, S. & BASHI, J. (1977) Birth order and intellectual development: The confluence model in the light of cross-cultural evidence. *Science*, 196, 1470–1472.

DAVIS, J.A. (1959) A formal interpretation of the theory of relative deprivation. *Sociometry*, 22, 280–296.

DAVIS, J.M. (1974) A two-factor theory of schizophrenia. *Journal of Psychiatric Research*, 11, 25–30.

DAVIS, K. (1940) Extreme isolation of a child. *American Journal of Sociology*, 45, 554–565.

DAVIS, K.L., KAHN, R.S., KO, G. & DAVIDSON, M. (1991). Dopamine in schizophrenia; a review and reconceptualization. *American Journal of Psychiatry*, 148, 1474–1486.

DAVISON, G. & NEALE, J. (1990) *Abnormal Psychology* (5th edition). New York: Wiley.

DAVISON, G. & NEALE, J. (1994) *Abnormal Psychology* (6th edition). New York: Wiley.

DAWKINS, M.S. (1980) The many faces of animal suffering. *New Scientist*, November 20.

DAWKINS, M.S. (1990) From an animal's point of view: Motivation, fitness and animal welfare. *Behavioural and Brain Sciences*, 13, 1–9.

DAWKINS, R. (1976) *The Selfish Gene*. Oxford: Oxford University Press.

DAY, R & WONG, S. (1996) Anomalous perceptual asymmetries for negative emotional stimuli in the psychopath. *Journal of Abnormal Psychology*, 105, 648–652.

DE GROOT, A.D. (1966) Perception and memory versus thought: Some old ideas and recent findings. In B. Kleinmuntz (Ed.) *Problem-Solving: Research, Method and Theory*. New York: Wiley.

DE PAULO, B.M. & FISHER, J.D. (1981) Too tuned-out to take: The role of non-verbal sensitivity in help-seeking. *Personality and Social Psychology Bulletin*, 7, 201–205.

DE VILLIERS, P.A. & DE VILLIERS, J.G. (1979) *Early Language*. Cambridge, MA: Harvard University Press.

DEAUX, K., DANE, F.C. & WRIGHTSMAN, L.S. (1993) *Social Psychology in the 90s*. Pacific Grove, CA: Brooks/Cole.

DECI, E.L. (1980) *The Psychology of Self-determination*. Lexington, MA.: D.C. Heath.

DECI, E.L. & RYAN, R.M. (1987) The support of autonomy and the control of behaviour. *Journal of Personality & Social Psychology*, 53, 1024–1037.

DEESE, J. (1972) *Psychology as Science and Art*. New York: Harcourt Brace Jovanovich.

DEIN, S. (1994) Cross-cultural psychiatry. *British Journal of Psychiatry*, 165, 561–564.

DELBOEUF, J.L.R. (1892) Sur une nouvelle illusion d'optique. *Bulletin de L'Academie Royale de Belgique*, 24, 545–558.

DELGADO, J.M.R. (1969) *Physical Control of the Mind*. New York: Harper & Row.

DELK, J.L. & FILLENBAUM, S. (1965) Differences in perceived colour as a function of characteristic colour. *American Journal of Psychology*, 78, 290–293.

DEMENT, W.C. (1960) The effects of dream deprivation. *Science*, 131, 1705–1707.

DEMENT, W.C. (1974) *Some Must Watch While Some Must Sleep*. San Francisco: W.H. Freeman.

DEMENT, W.C. & KLEITMAN, N. (1957) Cyclical variations in EEG during sleep and their relation to eye movements, body motility and dreaming. *Electroencephalography and Clinical Neurophysiology*, 9, 673–690.

DEMENT, W.C. & WOLPERT, E. (1958) The relation of eye movements, body motility and external stimuli to dream content. *Journal of Experimental Psychology*, 55, 543–553.

DENDY, C.A.Z. (1995) *Teenagers with ADD: A Parent's Guide*. Bethesda, MA: Woodbine House.

DENKER, R. (1946) Results of treatment of psychoneuroses by the general practitioner: A follow-up study of 500 cases. *New York State Journal of Medicine*, 46, 356–364.

DENMARK, F., RUSSO, N.F., FRIEZE, I.H., & SECHZER, J.A. (1988) Guidelines for avoiding sexism in psychological research: A report of the ad hoc committee on nonsexist research. *American Psychologist*, 43 (7), 582–585.

DENNEY, N. & PALMER, A. (1981) Adult age differences on traditional problem-solving measures. *Journal of Gerontology*, 36, 323–328.

DENNIS, W. (1960) Causes of retardation among institutional children: Iran. *Journal of Genetic Psychology*, 96, 47–59.

DENZIN, N.K. (1995) Symbolic interactionism. In J.A. Smith, R. Harre & L.V. Langenhove (Eds) *Rethinking Psychology*. London: Sage Publications.

DEPARTMENT OF HEALTH (1994) *Drugs: A Parent's Guide*. Central Print Unit.

DEREGOWSKI, J. (1972) Pictorial perception and culture. *Scientific American*, 227, 82–88.

DERMER, M. & THIEL, D.L. (1975) When beauty may fail. *Journal of Personality and Social Psychology*, 31, 1168–1176.

DEUTSCH, F.M. & LAMBERTI, D.M. (1986) Does social approval increase helping? *Personality and Social Psychology Bulletin*, 12, 149–157.

DEUTSCH, J.A. & DEUTSCH, D. (1963) Attention: Some theoretical considerations. *Psychological Review*, 70, 80–90.

DEUTSCH, J.A. & DEUTSCH, D. (1967) Comments on 'Selective attention: Perception or response?' *Quarterly Journal of Experimental Psychology*, 19, 362–363.

DEUTSCH, M. & COLLINS, M.E. (1951) *Interracial Housing: A Psychological Evaluation of a Social Experiment*. Minneapolis, MN: University of Minnesota Press.

DEUTSH, M. & GERARD, H.B. (1955) A study of normative and informational social influence upon individual judgement. *Journal of Abnormal and Social Psychology*, 51, 629–636.

DEVALOIS, R.L. & JACOBS, G.H. (1984) Neural mechanisms of colour vision. In Darian-Smith, I. (Ed.) *Handbook of Physiology*, Volume 3. Bethesda, MD: American Physiological Society.

DEVLIN REPORT (1976) Report to the Secretary of State for the Home Development of the Departmental Committee on Evidence of Identification in Criminal Cases. London: HMSO.

DI GIACOMO, J.P. (1980) Intergroup alliances and rejections within a protest movement (analysis of social representations). *European Journal of Social Psychology*, 10, 329–344.

DIAMOND, M. (1978) Sexual identity and sex roles. *The Humanist*, March/April.

DIAMOND, M. (1982) Sexual identity, monozygotic twins reared in discordant roles, and a BBC follow-up. *Archives of Sexual Behaviour*, 11, 181–186.

DICARA, L.V. & MILLER, N.E. (1968) Instrumental learning of systolic blood pressure responses by curarized rats. *Psychosomatic Medicine*, 30, 489–494.

DIENER, E. (1980) Deindividuation: The absence of self-awareness and self-regulation in group members. In P.B. Paulus (Ed.) *Psychology of Group Influence.* Hillsdale, NJ: Erlbaum.

DIENER, E., FRASER, S.C., BEAMAN, A.L. & KELEM, R.T. (1976) Effects of deindividuation variables on stealing among Halloween trick-or-treaters. *Journal of Personality and Social Psychology*, 33, 178–183.

DIETCH, J.T. (1995) Old age. In D. Wedding (Ed.) *Behaviour and Medicine* (2nd edition). St Louis, MO: Mosby-Year Book.

DILLNER, L. (1997) Joint action. *The Guardian*, 15 April, 9.

DILSAVER, J. (1989) Panic disorder. *American Family Physician*, 39, 167–173.

DION, K.K. (1972) Physical attractiveness and evaluation of children's transgressions. *Journal of Personality and Social Psychology*, 24, 207–213.

DION, K.K. & BERSCHEID, E. (1974) Physical attractiveness and peer perception among children. *Sociometry*, 37, 1–12.

DION, K.K., BERSCHEID, E. & WALSTER, E. (1972) What is beautiful is good. *Journal of Personality and Social Psychology*, 24, 285–290.

DION, K.K. & DION, K.L. (1995) On the love of beauty and the beauty of love: Two psychologists study attraction. In G.G. Brannigan & M.R. Merrens (Eds) *The Social Psychologists: Research Adventures.* New York: McGraw-Hill.

DIXON, N.F. (1980) Humour: A cognitive alternative to stress? In Sarason, I.G. & Spielberger, C.D. (Eds) *Stress and Anxiety.* Washington, DC: Hemisphere.

DIXON, N.F. (1994) Disastrous decisions. *The Psychologist*, 7, 303–307.

DIXON, P., REHLING, G. & SHIWACH, R. (1993) Peripheral victims of the Herald of Free Enterprise disaster. *British Journal of Medical Psychology*, 66, 193–202.

DOANE, J.A., FALLOON, I.R.H., GOLDSTEIN, M.J. & MINTZ, J. (1985) Parental affective style and the treatment of schizophrenia: Predicting course of illness and social functioning. *Archives of General Psychiatry*, 42, 34–42.

DOBSON, R. (1996) Confront your phobias in virtual reality. *The Sunday Times*, 21 January, 14.

DOCKRAY, G.J., GREGORY, R.A. & HUTCHINSON, J.B. (1978) Isolation, structure and biological activity of two cholecystokinin octapeptides from the sheep brain. *Nature*, 274, 711–713.

DODWELL, P.C. (1995) Fundamental processes in vision. In R.L. Gregory & A.M. Colman (Eds) *Sensation and Perception.* London: Longman.

DOLLARD, J., DOOB, L.W., MOWRER, O.H. & SEARS, R.R. (1939) *Frustration and Aggression.* New Haven, CT: Harvard University Press.

DONALDSON, M. (1978) *Children's Minds.* London: Fontana.

DONCHIN, E. (1975) On evoked potentials, cognition and memory. *Science*, 190, 1004–1005.

DONNELLAN, C. (1996) *Living with Disabilities.* Cambridge: Independence.

DONNERSTEIN, E. & BERKOWITZ, L. (1981) Victim reactions in aggressive erotic films as a factor in violence against women. *Journal of Personality and Social Psychology*, 41, 710–724.

DONNERSTEIN, E. & DONNERSTEIN, M. (1976) Research in the control of interracial aggression. In R.G. Geen & E.O'Neil (Eds) *Perspectives on Aggression.* New York: Academic Press.

DONNERSTEIN, E., LINZ, D. & PENROD, S. (1987) *The Question of Pornography.* London: The Free Press.

DONNERSTEIN, E. & WILSON, W. (1976) Effects of noise and perceived control on ongoing and subsequent aggressive behaviour. *Journal of Personality and Social Psychology*, 34, 774–781.

DOOLEY, D. & PRAUSE, J. (1995) Effect of unemployment on school leavers' self-esteem. *Journal of Occupational and Organisational Psychology*, 68, 177–192.

DORNER, G. (1976) *Hormones and Brain Differentiation.* Amsterdam: Elsevier.

DOTY, R.M., PETERSON, W.E. & WINTER, D.G. (1991) Threat and authoritarianism in the United States 1978–1987. *Journal of Personality and Social Psychology*, 61, 629–640.

DOVIDIO, J.F. (1995) With a little help from my friends. In G.G. Brannigan & M.R. Merrens (Eds) *The Social Psychologists: Research Adventures.* New York: McGraw-Hill.

DOVIDIO, J.F., ALLEN, J.L. & SCHROEDER, D.A. (1990) Specificity of empathy-induced helping: Evidence for altruistic motivation. *Journal of Personality and Social Psychology*, 59, 249–260.

DOVIDIO, J.F., PILIAVIN, J.A., GAERTNER, S.L., SCHROEDER, D.A. & CLARK, R.D. (1991) The arousal: Cost-reward model and the process of intervention. In M.S. Clark (Ed.) *Prosocial Behaviour: Review of Personality and Social Psychology*, 12. Newbury Park, CA: Sage.

DOWD, J.J. (1975) Ageing as exchange: A preface to theory. *Journal of Gerontology*, 30, 584–594.

DOWD, M. (1984) Twenty years after the murder of Kitty Genovese, the question remains: Why? *The New York Times*, B1, B4.

DOWNEY, D.B. & POWELL, B. (1993) Do children in single-parent households fare better living with same sex parents? *Journal of Marriage and the Family*, 55, 65–71.

DRABMAN, R.S. & THOMAS, M.H. (1974) Does media violence increase children's toleration of real-life aggression? *Developmental Psychology*, 10, 418–421.

DRAKELEY, R. (1997) Psychometric testing. *Psychology Review*, 3 (3), 27–29, February.

DRIVER, J. (1996) Attention and segmentation. *The Psychologist*, 9, 119–123.

DUCK, S. (Ed.) (1982) *Personal Relationships 4: Dissolving Personal Relationships.* London: Academic Press.

DUCK, S. (1988) *Relating to Others.* Milton Keynes: Open University Press.

DUCK, S. (1992) *Human Relationships* (2nd edition). London: Sage.

DUCK, S. (1995) Repelling the study of attraction. *The Psychologist*, 8, 60–63.

DUGDALE, N. & LOWE, C.F. (1990) Naming and stimulus equivalence. In D.E. Blackman & H. Lejeune (Eds) *Behaviour analysis in theory and practice: Contributions and controversies.* Hillsdale, NJ: Lawrence Erlbaum.

DUNCAN, H.F., GOURLAY, N. & HUDSON, W. (1973) *A Study of Pictorial Perception among Bantu and White Primary-school Children in South Africa.* Johannesburg: Witwatersrand University Press.

DUNCAN, J. & HUMPHREYS, G.W. (1992) Beyond the search surface: Visual search and attentional engagement. *Journal of Experimental Psychology*: Human Perception and Performance, 18, 578–588.

DUNCKER, K. (1945) On problem-solving. *Psychological Monographs*, 58 (Whole No. 270).

DUNN, F.M. & HOWELL, R.J. (1982) Relaxation training and its relationship to hyperactivity in boys. *Journal of Clinical Psychology*, 38, 92–100.

DUNN, L. (1968) Special education for the mildly retarded: Is much of it justifiable? *Exceptional Children*, 35, 5–22.

DUNSDON, M.I. (1941) A psychologist's contribution to air raid problems. *Mental Health*, 2, 37–41.

DUPAUL, G.J. & BARKLEY, R.A. (1993) Behavioural contributions to pharmacotherapy: The utility of behavioural methodology in medication treatment of children with attention deficit hyperactivity disorder. *Behaviour Therapy*, 24, 47–65.

DURHAM, R.C., MURPHY, J., ALLAN, T., RICHARD, K., TRELIVING, L.R. & FENTON, G.W. (1994) Cognitive therapy, analytic psychotherapy and anxiety management training for generalised anxiety disorder. *British Journal of Psychiatry*, 165, 315–323.

DURKHEIM, E. (1898) Répresentations individuelles et représentations collectives. *Revue de Métaphysique et de Morale*, 6. 273–302.

DURKIN, K. (1995) *Developmental Social Psychology: From Infancy to Old Age.* Oxford: Blackwell.

DUTTON, D.G. & ARON, A.P. (1974) Some evidence for heightened sexual attraction under conditions of high anxiety. *Journal of Personality and Social Psychology*, 30, 510–517.

DWORETZKY, J.P. (1981) *Introduction to Child Development.* St Paul, Minnesota: West Publishing Co.

DYER, C. (1996) Parents could face new restrictions on smacking children. *The Guardian*, 10 September, 1.

DYSON, J. (1980) Sociopolitical influences on retirement. *Bulletin of the British Psychological Society*, 33, 128–130.

EAGLY, A.H. (1983) Gender and social influence: A social psychological analysis. *American Psychologist*, September.

EAGLY, A.H. (1987) *Sex Differences in Social Behaviour: A Social Role Interpretation.* Hillsdale, NJ.: Erlbaum.

EAGLY, A.H. & CROWLEY, M. (1986) Gender and helping behaviour: A meta-analytic review of the social psychological literature. *Psychological Bulletin*, 100, 232–308.

EAGLY, A.H. & STEFFEN, V.J. (1984) Gender stereotypes stem from the distribution of men and women into social roles. *Journal of Personality and Social Psychology*, 46, 735–754.

EASTERBROOKS, M. & GOLDBERG, W. (1984) Toddler development in the family: Impact of father involvement and parenting characteristics. *Child Development*, 55, 74–752.

EBBINGHAUS, H. (1885) *On Memory*. Leipzig: Duncker.

ECCLES, J.C. (1973) The cerebellum as a computer: Patterns in space and time. *Journal of Physiology*, 229, 1–32.

ECKENSBERGER, L.H. (1994) Moral development and its measurement across cultures. In W.J. Lonner & R.S. Malpass (Eds) *Psychology and Culture*. Boston: Allyn & Bacon.

EDLEY, N. & WETHERELL, M. (1995) *Men in Perspective: Practice, Power and Identity*. Hemel Hempstead: Harvester Wheatsheaf.

EGELAND, J., GERHARD, D., PAULS, D., SUSSEX, J., KIDD, K., ALLEN, C., HOSTETTER, A. & HOUSEMAN, D. (1987) Bipolar affective disorder linked to DNA markers on chromosome 11. *Nature*, 325, 783–787.

EHRENFELS, C. von (1890) Über Gestaltqualitäten. *Vierteljahresschrift für wissenschaftliche Philosophie und Soziologie*, 14, 249–292.

EICH, E. & METCALFE, J. (1989) Mood-dependent memory for internal versus external events. *Journal of Experimental Psychology: Learning, Memory and Cognition*, 15, 443–455.

EIMAS, P.D. (1975) Speech perception in early infancy. In L.B. Cohen and P. Salapatek (Eds) *Infant Perception: From Sensation to Cognition*, Volume 2. New York: Academic Press.

EISER, J.R. (1983) From attributions to behaviour. In M. Hewstone (Ed.) *Attribution Theory: Social and Functional Extensions*. Oxford: Blackwell.

EISER, J.R. (1994) *Attitudes, Chaos and the Connectionist Mind*. Oxford: Blackwell.

EKMAN, P., FRIESEN, W.V. & SIMONS, R.C. (1985) Is the startle reaction an emotion? *Journal of Personality and Social Psychology*, 49, 1416–1426.

ELANDER, J. & MIDENCE, K. (1997) Children with chronic illnesses. *The Psychologist*, 10, 211–215.

ELARDO, R., BRADLEY, R.H. & CALDWELL, B.M. (1975) The relation of infants' home environments to mental test performance from 6 to 36 months: A longitudinal analysis. *Child Development*, 46, 71–76.

ELKIND, D. (1970) Erik Erikson's eight ages of man. *New York Times Magazine*, 5 April.

ELKIND, D. (1976) *Child Development and Education: A Piagetian Perspective*. Oxford: Oxford University Press.

ELKINS, R.L. (1980) Covert sensitisation treatment of alcoholism. *Addictive Behaviours*, 5, 67–89.

ELLENBERG, L. & SPERRY, R.W. (1980) Lateralised division of attention in the commissurotomised and intact brain. *Neuropsychologia*, 18, 411–418.

ELLIOT, C.D., MURRAY, D.J., & PEARSON, L.S. (1979, revised 1983) *British Ability Scales*. Slough: National Foundation for Educational Research.

ELLIOTT, B.J. & RICHARDS, M.P.M. (1991) Children and divorce: Educational performance before and after parental separation. *International Journal of Law and the Family*, 5, 258–278.

ELLIOTT, J. (1977) The power and pathology of prejudice. In P. Zimbardo & F.L. Ruch (Eds) *Psychology and Life* (9th edition). Glenview, IL: Scott, Forseman and Co.

ELLIOTT, J. (1990) In *Discovering Psychology. Program 20 (PBS Video Series)*. Washington, DC: Annenberg/CPB Program.

ELLIS, A. (1958) *Rational Psychotherapy*. California: Institute for Rational Emotive Therapy.

ELLIS, A. (1962) *Reason and Emotion in Psychotherapy*. Secaucus, NJ: Lyle Stuart (Citadel Press).

ELLIS, A. (1984) Rational–emotive therapy. In R. Corsini (Ed.) *Current Psychotherapies* (3rd edition). Itasca, Il: Peacock.

ELLIS, A. (1991) The revised ABC of rational–emotive therapy. *Journal of Rational Emotive and Cognitive Behaviour Therapy*, 9, 139–192.

ELLIS, A. (1993) Reflections on rational–emotive therapy. *Journal of Consulting and Clinical Psychology*, 61, 199–201.

ELLIS, A., McDOUGALL, S. & MONK, A. (1996) Are dyslexics different? Individual differences among dyslexics, reading age controls, poor readers and precocious readers. *Dyslexia*, 2, 59–68.

ELLIS, A.W. (1993) *Reading, Writing and Dyslexia: A Cognitive Analysis* (2nd edition). Hove: Erlbaum.

ELLIS, A.W. & YOUNG, A.W. (1988) *Human Cognitive Neuropsychology*. Hove: Erlbaum.

ELLISON, G.D. & FLYNN, J.P. (1968) *Organised aggressive behaviour in cats after surgical isolation of the hypothalamus*. Archives Italiennes de Biologie, 106, 1–20.

EMLER, N., OHANA, J. & DICKINSON, J. (1990) Children's representations of social relations. In G. Duveen & B.Lloyd (Eds) *Social Representations and the Development of Knowledge*. Cambridge: Cambridge University Press.

EMMELKAMP, P.M.G., BOUMAN, T.K. & SCHOLING, A. (1992) *Anxiety Disorders: A Practitioner's Guide*. New York: Plenum.

EMMELKAMP, P.M.G., KUIPERS, A.C.M. & EGGERAAT, J.B. (1978) Cognitive modification versus prolonged exposure *in vivo*: A comparison with agoraphobics as subjects. *Behaviour Research and Therapy*, 16, 33–42.

EMPSON, J.A.C. (1989) *Sleep and Dreaming*. London: Faber and Faber.

EMPSON, J.A.C. & CLARKE, P.R.F. (1970) Rapid eye movements and remembering. *Nature*, 228, 287–288.

ENGEL, G. (1962) *Psychological Development in Health and Disease*. Philadelphia: Saunders.

ERIKSEN, C.W. (1990) Attentional search of the visual field. In D. Brogan (Ed.) *Visual Search*. London: Taylor & Francis.

ERIKSEN, C.W. & YEH, Y.Y. (1987) Allocation of attention in the visual field. *Journal of Experimental Psychology: Human Perception and Performance*, 11, 583–597.

ERIKSON, E.H. (1950) *Childhood and Society*. New York: Norton.

ERIKSON, E.H. (1963) *Childhood and Society* (2nd edition). New York: Norton.

ERIKSON, E.H. (1968) *Identity: Youth and Crisis*. New York: Norton.

ERLENMEYER-KIMLING, L. & JARVIK, L.F. (1963) Genetics and intelligence: A review. *Science*, 142, 1477–1479.

ERON, L.D. & HUESMANN, L.R. (1985) The role of television in the development of pro-social and anti-social behaviour. In D. Olweus, M. Radke-Yarrow, & J. Block (Eds) *Development of Anti-Social and Pro-Social Behaviour*. Orlando, FL: Academic Press.

ESTERLING, B. & RABIN, B. (1987) Stress-induced alteration of T-lymphocyte subsets and humoral immunity in mice. *Behavioural Neuroscience*, 101, 115–119.

ESTES, W.K. (1970) *Learning theory and mental develoment*. New York: Academic Press.

ESTES, W.K. (1972) An associative basis for coding and organisation in memory. In A. Melton & E. Martin (Eds) *Coding Processes in Human Memory*. Washington, DC: Winston.

EVANS, C. (1984) *Landscapes of the Night: How and Why We Dream*. New York: Viking.

EVANS, P., CLOW, A. & HUCKLEBRIDGE, F. (1997) Stress and the immune system. *The Psychologist*, 10, 303–307.

EVANS, P., HUCKLEBRIDGE, F., CLOW, A. & DOYLE, A. (1995) Secretory immunoglobulin A as a convenient bio-marker in mental health survey work. In J. Rodriguez-Marin (Ed.) *Health Psychology and Quality of Life Research*, Volume II. Alicante: University of Alicante Press.

EYSENCK, H.J. (1952) The effects of psychotherapy: An evaluation. *Journal of Consulting Psychology*, 16, 319–324.

EYSENCK, H.J. (1954) *The Psychology of Politics*. London: Routledge & Kegan Paul.

EYSENCK, H.J. (1964) *Crime and Personality*. London: Routledge & Kegan Paul.

EYSENCK, H.J. (1965) The effects of psychotherapy. *International Journal of Psychiatry*, 1, 97–142.

EYSENCK, H.J. (1967) *The Biological Basis of Personality*. Springfield, ILL: Charles C. Thomas.

EYSENCK, H.J. (1985) *Decline and Fall of the Freudian Empire*. Harmondsworth: Penguin.

EYSENCK, H.J. (1992) The outcome problem in psychotherapy. In W. Dryden & C. Feltham (Eds) *Psychotherapy and its Discontents*. Buckingham: Open University Press.

EYSENCK, H.J. & WAKEFIELD, J.A. (1981) Psychological factors as predictors of marital satisfaction. *Advances in Behaviour Research and Therapy*, 3, 151–192.

EYSENCK, H.J. & WILSON, G.D. (1973) *The Experimental Study of Freudian Theories*. London: Methuen.

EYSENCK, M.W. (1982) *Attention and Arousal: Cognition and Performance*. Berlin: Springer.

EYSENCK, M.W. (1984) *A Handbook of Cognitive Psychology*. London: Lawrence Erlbaum Associates.

EYSENCK, M.W. (1986) Working memory. In G. Cohen, M.W. Eysenck & M.A. Le Voi (Eds) *Memory: A Cognitive Approach*. Milton Keynes: Open University Press.

EYSENCK, M.W. (1993) *Principles of Cognitive Psychology*. Hove: Erlbaum.

EYSENCK, M.W. (1994) Attention. In C.C. French & A.M. Colman (Eds) *Cognitive Psychology*. London: Longman.

EYSENCK, M.W. (1997a) Doing two things at once. *Psychology Review*, 4 (1) 10–12.

EYSENCK, M.W. (1997b) Absent-mindedness. *Psychology Review*, 3, 16–18.

EYSENCK, M.W. & EYSENCK, M.C. (1980) Effects of processing depth, distinctiveness and word frequency on retention. *British Journal of Psychology*, 71, 263–274.

EYSENCK, M.W. & KEANE, M.J. (1990) *Cognitive Psychology: A Student's Handbook*. Sussex: Lawrence Erlbaum Associates.

EYSENCK, M.W. & KEANE, M.J. (1995) *Cognitive Psychology: A Student's Handbook* (2nd edition). Hove: Erlbaum.

FAGOT, B.I. (1978) The influence of sex of child on parental reactions to toddler children. *Child Development*, 49, 459–465.

FAGOT, B.I. (1985) Beyond the reinforcement principle: Another step toward understanding sex-role development. *Developmental Psychology*, 21, 1097–1104.

FAIGLEY, L. & WITTE, S. (1981) Analysing revision. *College Composition and Communication*, 32, 400–414.

FAIRBAIRN, G. & FAIRBAIRN, S. (1987) Introduction. In S. Fairbairn & G. Fairbairn (Eds) *Psychology, ethics and change*. London: Routledge & Kegan Paul.

FAIRBAIRN, R. (1952) *Psychoanalytical Studies of the Personality*. London: Tavistock.

FAIRBURN, C.G., JONES, R. & PEVELER, R.C. (1993) Psychotherapy and bulimia nervosa: The longer-term effects of interpersonal psychotherapy, behaviour therapy and cognitive behaviour therapy. *Archives of General Psychiatry*, 50, 419–428.

FALEK, A. & MOSER, H.M. (1975) Classification in schizophrenia. *Archives of General Psychiatry*, 32, 59–67.

FANCHER, R.E. (1979) *Pioneers of Psychology*. New York: Norton.

FANCHER, R.E. (1996) *Pioneers of Psychology* (3rd edition). New York: Norton.

FANTZ, R.L. (1961) The origin of form perception. *Scientific American*, 204, 66–72.

FARBER, S.L. (1981) *Identical Twins Reared Apart*. New York: Basic Books.

FARINA, A. (1982) The stigma of mental disorders. In A.G. Miller (Ed.) *In the Eye of the Beholder*. New York: Praeger.

FARR, R.M. & MOSCOVICI, S. (Eds) (1984) *Social Representations*. Cambridge: Cambridge University Press.

FARRINGTON, D.P. (1995) Intensive health visiting and the prevention of juvenile crime. *Health Visitor*, 68, 100–102.

FAWCETT, A. & NICOLSON, R. (1994) *Dyslexia in Children*. Hemel Hempstead: Harvester Wheatsheaf.

FEATHER, N.T. & SIMON, J.G. (1971) Attribution of responsibility and valence of success and failure in relation to initial confidence and task performance. *Journal of Personality and Social Psychology*, 18, 173–188.

FEIGENBAUM, E.A. & McCORDUCK, P. (1983) *The Fifth Generation*. New York: Addison-Wesley.

FEINGOLD, B. (1975) *Why Your Child is Hyperactive*. New York: Random House.

FELIPE, N.J. & SOMMER, R. (1966) Invasion of personal space. *Social Problems*, 14, 206–214.

FELMLEE, D.H. (1995) Fatal attractions: Affection and disaffection in intimate relationships. *Journal of Social and Personal Relationships*, 12, 295–311.

FERRIMAN, A. (1997) Impaired hearing. *Telegraph Magazine*, 6 December, 62.

FERRY, G. (1997) The fragile X files. *Oxford Today*, 9, 10–13.

FERSTER, C. (1961) Positive reinforcement and behavioural deficits of autistic children. *Child Development*, 32, 437–456.

FERSTER, C. (1965) Classification of behaviour pathology. In L. Krasner & L. Ullman (Eds) *Research in Behaviour Modification*. New York: Holt, Rinehart & Winston.

FERSTER, C.B. & SKINNER, B.F. (1957) *Schedules of Reinforcement*. New York: Appleton-Century-Crofts.

FESTINGER, L. (1954) A theory of social comparison processes. *Human Relations*, 7, 117–140.

FESTINGER, L., PEPITONE, A. & NEWCOMB, T. (1952) Some consequences of deindividuation in a group. *Journal of Abnormal and Social Psychology*, 47, 382–389.

FESTINGER, L., RIEKEN, H.W. & SCHACHTER, S. (1956) *When Prophecy Fails*. Minneapolis: University of Minnesota Press.

FESTINGER, L., SCHACHTER, S. & BACK, K. (1950) *Social Pressures in Informal Groups: A Study of Human Factors in Housing*. Stanford, CA: Stanford University Press.

FIEDLER, F.E. (1964) A contingency model of leadership effectiveness. In L. Berkowitz (Ed.) *Group Processes*. New York: Academic Press.

FIEDLER, F.E. (1967) *A Theory of Leadership Effectiveness*. New York: McGraw-Hill.

FIEDLER, F.E. (1981) Leadership effectiveness. *American Behavioural Scientist*, 24, 619–632.

FIEDLER, F.E. & CHEMERS, M. (1984) *Improving Leadership Effectiveness: The Leader Match Concept*. New York: Wiley.

FIELD, T. (1978) Interaction behaviours of primary versus secondary caretaker fathers. *Developmental Psychology*, 14, 183–184.

FIELDS, H. (1991) Depression and pain: A neurobiological model. *Neuropsychiatry, Neuropsychology and Behavioural Neurology*, 4, 83–92.

FINCHAM, F. (1997) Understanding marriage. From fish scales to milliseconds. *The Psychologist*, 10, 543–547.

FINK, M. (1984) Meduna and the origins of convulsive therapy in suicidal patients. *American Journal of Psychiatry*, 141, 1034–1041.

FISCHMAN, J. (1985) Mapping the mind. *Psychology Today*, September, 18–19.

FISHER, S. & GREENBERG, R. (1977) *Scientific Credibility of Freud's Theories*. New York: Basic Books.

FISHER, S. & GREENBERG, R. (Eds) (1980) *A Critical Appraisal of Biological Treatments for Psychological Distress: Comparisons with Psychotherapy and Placebo*. Hillsdale, NJ: Erlbaum.

FISKE, S.T. & NEUBERG, S.L. (1990) A continuum of impression formation, from category-based to individuating processes: Influences of information and motivation on attention and interpretation. In L. Berkowitz (Ed.) *Advances in Experimental Social Psychology*, Volume 23. New York: Academic Press.

FISKE, S.T. & TAYLOR, S.E. (1991) *Social Cognition* (2nd edition). New York: McGraw-Hill.

FLANAGAN, C. (1996) *Applying Psychology to Early Child Development*. London: Hodder & Stoughton.

FLANAGAN, O.J. (1984) *The Science of the Mind*. Cambridge, Mass.: MIT Press.

FLAVELL, J.H. (1971) First discussant's comments: What is memory development the development of? *Human Development*, 14, 272–278.

FLAVELL, J.H. (1982) Structures, stages and sequences in cognitive development. In W.A. Collins (Ed.) *The Concept of Development: The Minnesota Symposia on Child Development*, Volume 15. Hillsdale, NJ: Erlbaum.

FLAVELL, J.H., SHIPSTEAD, S.G. & CROFT, K. (1978) 'What young children think you see when their eyes are closed.' (Unpublished report, Stanford University.)

FLEISCHMAN, P.R. (1973) Letter to the editor. *Science*, 180, 356.

FLEMING, R., BAUM, A. & SINGER, J.E. (1984) Towards an integrative approach to the study of stress. *Journal of Personality and Social Psychology*, 46, 939–949.

FLETCHER, G.J. & WARD, C. (1988) Attribution theory and processes: Cross-cultural perspectives. In M.Bond (Ed.) *The Cross-Cultural Challenge to Psychology*. Newbury Park, CA: Sage.

FLETCHER, J., SHAYWITZ, S., SHANKWEILER, D., KATZ, L., LIEBERMAN, I., STEUBING, K., FRANCIS, D., FOWLER, A. & SBAYWITZ, B. (1994) Cognitive profiles of reading disability: Comparisons of discrepancy and low achievement definitions. *Journal of Educational Psychology*, 86, 6–23.

FLOWERS, J.H., WARNER, J.L. & POLANSKY, M.L. (1979) Response and encoding factors in ignoring irrelevant information. *Memory and Cognition*, 7, 86–94.

FODOR, J.A. & PYLYSHYN, Z.W. (1981) How direct is visual perception? Some reflections on Gibson's 'ecological approach'. *Cognition*, 9, 139–196.

FOGELMAN, K. (1976) *Britain's Sixteen-Year-Olds*. London: National Children's Bureau.

FOLSTEIN, S. & RUTTER, M. (1977) Genetic influences and infantile autism. *Nature*, 265, 726–728.

FOMBONNE, E. (1995) Anorexia nervosa: No evidence of an increase. *British Journal of Psychiatry*, 166, 462–471.

FOOT, H.C. (1994) *Group and Interactive Learning*. Computational Mechanics Publications.

FOOT, H.C. & CHEYNE, W. (1995) Collaborative learning: Putting theory into practice. *Psychology Review*, 1, 16–19.

FORD, C.S. & BEACH, F.A. (1951) *Patterns of Sexual Behaviour*. New York: Harper & Row.

FORD, D.H. & URBAN, H.B. (1963) *Systems of Psychotherapy: A Comparative Study*. New York: Wiley.

FORD, R. (1998) Study fails to link film violence to crime. *The Times*, 8 January, 9.

FOULKES, D. (1971) Longitudinal studies of dreams in children. In Masserman, J. (Ed.) *Science and Psychoanalysis*. New York: Grune & Stratton.

FOULKES, D. (1985) *Dreaming: A Cognitive-Psychological Analysis*. Hillsdale, NJ: Lawrence Erlbaum Associates.

FOX, J.L. (1984) The brain's dynamic way of keeping in touch. *Science*, 225, 82–821.

FREAN, A. (1994) Researchers study TV's arrival on media-free island. *The Times*, 6 June, 8.

FREAN, A. (1995) Getting a kick from TV violence. *The Times*, 23 August, 31.

FREDERIKSON, J.R. & KROLL, J.F. (1976) Approaches to the internal lexicon. *Journal of Experimental Psychology: Human Perception and Performance*, 2, 361–379.

FREEDMAN, F. (1984) Effects of television violence on aggression. *Psychological Bulletin*, 96, 227–246.

FREEMAN, C. (Ed.) (1995) *The ECT Handbook*. London: Gaskell.

FREEMAN, H. & WATTS, J.W. (1942) *Psychosurgery*. Springfield, Ill.: Thomas.

FRENCH, J.R.P. & RAVEN, B.H. (1959) The bases of social power. In D. Cartwright (Ed.) *Studies in Social Power*. Ann Arbour, MI: Institute for Social Research, University of Michigan.

FRESE, M. (1985) Stress at work and psychosomatic complaints: A causal interpretation. *Journal of Applied Psychology*, 70, 314–328.

FREUD, A. & BURLINGHAM, D. (1942) *Young Children in Wartime*. London: Allen & Unwin.

FREUD, A. & DANN, S. (1951) An experiment in group upbringing. *Psychoanalytic Study of the Child*, 6, 127–168.

FREUD, S. (1894) The defence neuropsychoses. In J. Strachey (Ed.) *The Standard Edition of the Complete Psychological Works of Sigmund Freud*, Volume 1. London: The Hogarth Press, 1953.

FREUD, S. (1900) *The Interpretation of Dreams*. London: Hogarth Press.

FREUD, S. (1901) The psychopathology of everyday life. In J. Strachey (Ed.) *The Standard Edition of the Complete Works of Sigmund Freud*, Volume 6. London: Hogarth Press.

FREUD, S. (1909) *Analysis of a Phobia in a Five-Year-Old Boy*. London: The Hogarth Press.

FREUD, S. (1914) Remembering, repeating and working through. *Standard Edition*, Volume XII. London: Hogarth Press.

FREUD, S. (1915) A case of paranoia running counter to the psychoanalytical theory of the disease. In *Collected Papers*, Volume 2. London: The Hogarth Press.

FREUD, S. (1917) *Mourning and Melancholia*. London: The Hogarth Press.

FREUD, S. (1920/1984) *Beyond the Pleasure Principle*. Pelican Freud Library (11). Harmondsworth: Penguin.

FREUD, S. (1921) *Group Psychology and the Analysis of the Ego. (Standard Edition*, Volume 18*).* London: The Hogarth Press (1955).

FREUD, S. (1923/1984) *The Ego and the Id*. Pelican Freud Library (11). Harmondsworth: Penguin.

FREUD, S. (1924) The passing of the Oedipus complex. In E. Jones (Ed.) *Collected Papers of Sigmund Freud*, Volume 5. New York: Basic Books.

FREUD, S. (1926) Inhibitions, symptoms and anxiety. In *Standard Edition of the Complete Psychological Works of Sigmund Freud*, Volume 20. London: Hogarth Press.

FREUD, S. (1933) *New Introductory Lectures on Psychoanalysis*. New York: Norton.

FREUD, S. (1949) *An Outline of Psycho-analysis*. London: Hogarth Press.

FRIEDMAN, M. & ROSENMAN, R.H. (1974) *Type A Behaviour and Your Heart*. New York: Harper Row.

FRIEDMAN, M. & ULMER, D. (1984) *Treating Type A Behaviour and Your Heart*. New York: Fawcett Crest.

FRIEDMAN, M.I. & STRICKER, E.M. (1976) The physiological psychology of hunger: A physiological perspective. *Psychological Review*, 83, 409–431.

FRITH, U. (1985) The usefulness of the concept of unexpected reading failure: Comments on 'Reading retardation revisited'. *British Journal of Developmental Psychology*, 3, 15–17.

FRODI, A. (1975) The effect of exposure to weapons on aggressive behaviour from a cross-cultural perspective. *International Journal of Psychology*, 10, 283–292.

FROMM, E. (1941) *Escape From Freedom*. New York: Farrar & Rinehart.

FROMM, E. (1962) *The Art of Loving*. London: Unwin Books.

FROMM-REICHMAN, F. (1948) Notes on the development of treatment of schizophrenics by psychoanalytic psychotherapy. *Psychiatry*, 11, 263–273.

FRUDE, N. (1998) *Understanding Abnormal Psychology*. Oxford: Blackwell.

FRUZZETTI, A.E., TOLAND, K., TELLER, S.A. & LOFTUS, E.F. (1992) Memory and eyewitness testimony. In M. Gruneberg & P.E. Morris (Eds) *Aspects of Memory: The Practical Aspects*. London: Routledge.

FRYER, D. (1992) Signed on at the 'beroo': Mental health and unemployment research in Scotland. *The Psychologist*, 5, 539–542.

FRYER, D. (1995) Benefit agency? *The Psychologist*, 8, 265–272.

FURTH, H.G. (1966) *Thinking Without Language*. New York: Free Press.

GABRIELI, J.D.E., COHEN, N.J. & CORKIN, S. (1988) The impaired learning of semantic knowledge following bilateral medial temporal lobe resection. *Brain*, 7, 157–177.

GADOW, J.D. & SPRAFKIN, J. (1989) Field experiments of television violence: Evidence for an environmental hazard? *Paediatrics*, 83, 399–405.

GADOW, J.D. & SPRAFKIN, J. (1993) Television violence and children. *Journal of Emotional and Behavioural Disorders*, 1, 54–63.

GAGNÉ, E.D. (1985) *The Cognitive Psychology of School Learning*. Boston: Little, Brown and Company.

GAHAGAN, J. (1980) Social interaction. In J. Rasford & E. Govier (Eds) *A Textbook of Psychology*. London: Sheldon Books.

GAHAGAN, J. (1991) Understanding other people, understanding self. In J. Radford & E. Govier (Eds) *A Textbook of Psychology* (2nd edition). London: Routledge.

GAINES, A. (1992) *Ethnopsychiatry: The Cultural Construction of Professional and Folk Psychiatries*. New York: New York State University.

GALE, A. (1990) *Thinking about Psychology?* (2nd edition). Leicester: British Psychological Society.

GALE, A. (1995) Ethical issues in psychological research. In A.M. Colman (Ed.) *Psychological research methods and statistics*. London: Longman.

GALLUP, C.G. (1977) Self-recognition in primates. *American Psychologist*, 32, 329–338.

GAMSON, W.B., FIREMAN, B. & RYTINA, S. (1982) *Encounters with Unjust Authority*. Hounwood, IL: Dorsey Press.

GARBER, H.J. & RITVO, E.R. (1992) Magnetic resonance imaging of the posterior fossa in autistic adults. *American Journal of Psychiatry*, 149, 245–247.

GARBER, H.L. (1988) *The Milwaukee Project: Preventing Mental Retardation in Children at Risk*. Washington, DC: American Association on Mental Retardation.

GARCIA, J., ERVIN, F.R. & KOELLING, R.A. (1966) Learning with prolonged delay of reinforcement. *Psychonomic Science*, 5 (3), 121–122.

GARCIA, J. & KOELLING, R.A. (1966) Relation of cue to consequence in avoidance learning. *Psychonomic Science*, 4, 123–124.

GARDINER, J.M., CRAIK, F.I.M. & BIRTWISTLE, J. (1972) Retrieval cues and release from proactive inhibition. *Journal of Verbal Learning and Verbal Behaviour*, 11, 778–783.

GARDNER, H. (1983) *Frames of Mind: The Theory of Multiple Intelligences*. New York: Basic Books.

GARDNER, H. (1985) *The Mind's New Science*. New York: Basic Books.

GARFIELD, S. (1980) *Psychotherapy: An Eclectic Approach*. New York: Wiley.

GARFIELD, S. (1992) Response to Hans Eysenck. In W. Dryden & C. Feltham (Eds) *Psychotherapy and its Discontents*. Buckingham: Open University Press.

GARFIELD, S. & BERGIN, A. (1994) Introduction and historical overview. In A. Bergin & S. Garfield (Eds) *Handbook of Psychotherapy and Behaviour Change*. Chichester: Wiley.

GARFINKEL, P.E. & GARNER, D.M. (1982) *Anorexia Nervosa: A Multidimensional Perspective*. New York: Basic Books.

GARLAND, C. & WHITE, S. (1980) *Children and Day Nurseries*. London: Grant McIntyre.

GARNER, D.M. (1986) Cognitive–behavioural therapy for eating disorders. *The Clinical Psychologist*, 39, 36–39.

GARNER, D.M., GARFINKEL, P.E., SCHWARZ, D. & THOMPSON, M. (1980) Cultural expectations of thinness in women. *Psychological Reports*, 47, 483–491.

GARNHAM, A. (1988) *Artificial Intelligence: An Introduction*. London: Routledge, Kegan Paul.

GARNHAM, A. (1991) *The Mind in Action*. London: Routledge.

GARRETT, R. (1996) Skinner's case for radical behaviourism. In W. O'Donohue & R.F. Kitchener (Eds) *The Philosophy of Psychology*. London: Sage.

GARROD, A.B. (1859) *The Nature and Treatment of Gout and Rheumatic Gout.* London: Walton & Maberly.

GATHERCOLE, S.E. & BADDELEY, A.D. (1990) Phonological memory deficits in language-disordered children: Is there a causal connection? *Journal of Memory and Language*, 29, 336–360.

GAUKER, C. (1990) How to learn language like a chimpanzee. *Philosophical Psychology*, 3, 31–53.

GAY, P. (1988) *Freud: A Life for our Time.* London: J.M. Dent & Sons.

GAZZANIGA, M.S. (1967) The split-brain in man. *Scientific American*, 221, 24–29.

GAZZANIGA, M.S. (1983) Right hemisphere language following brain bisection: A 2-year perspective. *American Psychologist*, 38, 525–537.

GEEN, R.G. (1995) Social motivation. In Parkinson, B. & Colman, A.M. (Eds) *Emotion and Motivation.* London: Longman.

GEEN, R.G. & BERKOWITZ, L. (1966) Some conditions facilitating the occurrence of aggression after the observation of violence. *Journal of Personality*, 35, 666–676.

GEEN, R.G., STONNER, D. & SHOPE, G.L. (1975) The facilitation of aggression: A study in response inhibition and disinhibition. *Journal of Personality and Social Psychology*, 31, 721–726.

GEISELMAN, P.J. (1983) 'The role of hexoses in hunger motivation.' (Unpublished doctoral dissertation, University of California, Los Angeles.)

GEISELMAN, R.E. (1988) Improving eyewitness memory through mental reinstatement of context. In G.M. Davies & D.M. Thomson (Eds) *Memory in Context: Context in Memory.* Chichester: Wiley.

GEISLER, C., KAUFER, D. & HAYES, J.R. (1985) Translating instruction into skill: Learning to write precisely. Paper presented at the Annual Meeting of the American Educational Research Association, Chicago (March).

GELDER, M., GATH, D. & MAYON, R. (1989) *The Oxford Textbook of Psychiatry* (2nd edition). Oxford: Oxford University Press.

GELMAN, R. (1978) Counting in the pre-schooler: What does and does not develop. In R.S. Siegler (Ed.) *Children's Thinking: What Develops?* Hillsdale, NJ: Erlbaum.

GELMAN, R. (1979) Preschool thought. *American Psychologist*, 34, 900–905.

GELMAN, R. & BAILLARGEON, R. (1983) A review of some Piagetian concepts. In J.H. Flavell & E.M. Markman (Eds) *Cognitive development*, Volume 3 in P.H. Mussen (Ed.) *Handbook of Child Psychology* (4th edition). New York: Wiley.

GEORGE, M.S. & BALLENGER, J.C. (1992) The neuropsychology of panic disorder: The emerging role of the right parahippocampal region. *Journal of Anxiety Disorders*, 6, 181–188.

GERBNER, G. (1972) Violence in television drama: Trends and symbolic functions. In G.A. Comstock & E.A. Rubenstein (Eds) *Television and Social Behaviour*, Volume 1, *Media Content and Control.* Washington, DC: US Government Printing Office.

GERBNER, G. & GROSS, L. (1976) Living with television: The violence profile. *Journal of Communication*, 26, 173–199.

GERBNER, G., GROSS, L., MORGAN, M. & SIGNORIELLI, N. (1980) The 'mainstreaming' of America: Violence profile No. II. *Journal of Communication*, 30, 10–29.

GERBNER, G., GROSS, L., SIGNORIELLI, N. & MORGAN, M. (1986) *Television's mean world: Violence profile No. 14–15.* Philadelphia: Annenberg School of Communications, University of Pennsylvania.

GERGEN, K.J. (1973) Social psychology as history. *Journal of Personality and Social Psychology*, 26, 309–320.

GERGEN, K.J. & GERGEN, M.M. (1981) *Social Psychology.* New York: Harcourt Brace Jovanovich,

GERGEN, K.J., GERGEN, M.M. & BARTON, W. (1973) Deviance in the dark. *Psychology Today*, 7, 129–130.

GERRARD, N. (1997) Nicaragua's deaf children. *The Observer Review*, 30 March, 5.

GESCHWIND, N. (1972) Language and the brain. *Scientific American*, 226, 76–83.

GESCHWIND, N. (1979) *The Brain.* San Francisco: Freeman.

GESCHWIND, N. & BEHAN, P. (1984) Laterality, hormones and immunity. In N. Geschwind & A. Galaburda (Eds) *Cerebral Dominance: The Biological Foundations.* Cambridge, MA: Harvard University Press.

GESCHWIND, N., QUADFASEL, F.A. & SEGARRA, J.M. (1968) Isolation of the speech area. *Neuropsychologia*, 6, 327–340.

GEUTER U. (1992) *The Professionalization of Psychology in Nazi Germany.* Cambridge: Cambridge University Press.

GIBBS, J.C. & SCHNELL, S.V. (1985) Moral development 'versus' socialisation. *American Psychologist*, 40, 1071–1080.

GIBSON, E.J. & WALK, P.D. (1960) The visual cliff. *Scientific American*, 202, 64–71.

GIBSON, E.J., SHAPIRO, F. & YONAS, A. (1968) 'Confusion matrices of graphic patterns obtained with a latency measure: A program of basic and applied research.' (*Final Report Project No. 5-1213*, Cornell University.)

GIBSON, H.B. (1967) Self-reported delinquency among schoolboys and their attitudes towards the police. *British Journal of Social and Clinical Psychology*, 6, 168–173.

GIBSON, J.J. (1950) *The Perception of the Visual World.* Boston: Houghton Mifflin.

GIBSON, J.J. (1966) *The Senses Considered as Perceptual Systems.* Boston: Houghton Mifflin.

GIBSON, J.J. (1979) *The Ecological Approach to Visual Perception.* Boston: Houghton Mifflin.

GIDDENS, A. (1979) *Central Problems in Social Theory.* Basingstoke: Macmillan.

GIDDENS, A. (1993) *Sociology.* Cambridge: Polity Press.

GIFFORD, L. & RODDA, M. (1998) British scientists find dyslexia gene. *Independent on Sunday*, 22 February, 1.

GILBERT, D.T. (1995) Attraction and interpersonal perception. In A. Tesser (Ed.) *Advanced Social Psychology.* New York: McGraw-Hill.

GILBERT, G.M. (1951) Stereotype persistence and change among college students. *Journal of Abnormal and Social Psychology*, 46, 245–254.

GILBERT, S.J. (1981) Another look at the Milgram obedience studies: The role of the graduated series of shocks. *Personality and Social Psychology Bulletin*, 7, 690–695.

GILFORD, R. & BENGSTON, V. (1979) Measuring marital satisfaction in three generations: Positive and negative dimensions. *Journal of Marriage and the Family*, 41, 387–398.

GILHOOLY, K. (1996) Working memory and thinking. *The Psychologist*, 9, 82.

GILLIE, O. (1976) Pioneer of IQ faked his research. *The Sunday Times*, 29 October, H3.

GILLIGAN, C. (1982) *In a Different Voice: Psychological Theory and Women's Development.* Cambridge, MA: Harvard University Press.

GILLIGAN, C. (1993) Letter to Readers (Preface) In *In A Different Voice.* Cambridge, MA.: Harvard University Press.

GILLING, D. & BRIGHTWELL, R. (1982) *The Human Brain.* London: Orbis Publishing.

GILLIS, J.J., GILGER, J.W., PENNINGTON, B.F. & DEFRIES, J.C. (1992) Attention deficit in reading-disabled twins: Evidence for a genetic etiology. *Journal of Abnormal Child Psychology*, 20, 303–315.

GILOVICH, T. (1983) Biased evaluation and persistence in gambling. *Journal of Personality and Social Psychology*, 44, 1110–1126.

GINSBERG, H.P. (1981) Piaget and education: The contributions and limits of genetic epistemology. In K. Richardson & S. Sheldon (Eds) *Cognitive Development to Adolescence.* Milton Keynes: Open University Press.

GIPPS, C. & STOBART, G. (1990) *Assessment: A Teacher's Guide to the Issues.* London: Hodder & Stoughton.

GLANZER, M. & CUNITZ, A.R. (1966) Two storage mechanisms in free recall. *Journal of Verbal Learning and Verbal Behaviour*, 5, 928–935.

GLANZER, M. & MEINZER, A. (1967) The effects of intralist activity on free recall. *Journal of Verbal Learning and Verbal Behaviour*, 6, 928–935.

GLASSMAN, W.E. (1995) *Approaches to Psychology* (2nd edition). Buckingham: Open University.

GLEASON, J. (1967) Do children imitate? *Proceedings of the International Conference on Oral Education of the Deaf*, 2, 1441–1448.

GLEITMAN, H. & JONIDES, J. (1978) The effect of set on categorisation in visual search. *Perception and Psychophysics*, 24, 361–368.

GLOVER, J.A. & BRUNING, R.H. (1987) *Educational Psychology: Principles and Applications.* Boston: Little, Brown and Company.

GLUCKSBERG, S. & COWAN, N. (1970) Memory for non-attended auditory material. *Cognitive Psychology*, 1, 149–156.

GLUCKSBERG, S. & WEISBERG, R. (1966) Verbal behaviour and problem-solving: Some effects of labelling upon availability of novel functions. *Journal of Experimental Psychology*, 71, 659–664.

GODDEN, D. & BADDELEY, A.D. (1975) Context-dependent memory in two natural environments: On land and under water. *British Journal of Psychology*, 66, 325–331.

GOFFMAN, E. (1959) *The Presentation of Self in Everyday Life*. Harmondsworth: Penguin.

GOFFMAN, E. (1968) *Asylums – Essay on the Social Situation of Mental Patients and Other Inmates*. Harmondsworth: Penguin.

GOFFMAN, E. (1971) *The Presentation of Self in Everyday Life*. Harmondsworth: Penguin.

GOLDFARB, W. (1943) The effects of early institutional care on adult personality. *Journal of Experimental Education*, 12, 106–129.

GOLDIN-MEADOW, S. & FELDMAN, H. (1977) The development of a language-like communication without a language model. *Science*, 197, 401–403.

GOLDSTEIN, A.P., CARR, E.D., DAVIDSON, W.S. & WEHR, P. (1981) *In Response to Aggression: Methods of Control and Prosocial Alternatives*. New York: Pergamon.

GOLDSTEIN, M. & PALMER, J. (1975) *The Experience of Anxiety: A Casebook* (2nd edition). New York: Oxford University Press.

GOLDWYN, E. (1979) The fight to be male. *The Listener*, 24 May, 709–712.

GOLOMBOK, S., SPENCER, A. & RUTTER, M. (1983) Children in lesbian and single-parent households: Psychosexual and psychiatric appraisal. *Journal of Child Psychology and Psychiatry*, 24, 551–572.

GOLOMBOK, S., TASKER, F., & MURRAY, C. (1997) Children Raised in Fatherless Families from Infancy: Family Relationships and the Socioemotional Development of Children of Lesbian and Single Heterosexual Mothers. *Journal of Child Psychology & Psychiatry*, 38 (7), 783–791.

GOMBRICH, E.H. (1960) *Art and Illusion*. London: Phaidon.

GOODWIN, R. (1991) A re-examination of Rusbult's responses to dissatisfaction typology. *Journal of Social and Personal Relationships*, 8, 569–574.

GOODWIN, R. (1995) Personal relationships across cultures. *The Psychologist*, 8, 73–75.

GORDON, I.E. (1989) *Theories of Visual Perception*. Chichester: Wiley.

GORDON, R.M. (1978) Emotion labelling and cognition. *Journal for the Theory of Social Behaviour*, 8, 125–135.

GORMAN, C. (1997) Anatomy of melancholy. *Time*, 12 May, 30.

GOSWAMI, U. (1993) Orthographic analogies and reading development. *The Psychologist*, 6, 312–316.

GOTLIB, I.A. & COLBY, C.A. (1995) *Psychological Aspects of Depression: Towards a Cognitive-Interpersonal Integration*. Chichester: Wiley.

GOTTESMAN, I. (1991) *Schizophrenia Genesis*. New York: W.H. Freeman.

GOTTESMAN, I.I. & SHIELDS, J. (1972) *Schizophrenia and Genetics: A Twin Study Vantage Point*. New York: Academic Press.

GOTTFRIED, A. (Ed.) (1984) *Home Environment and Early Cognitive Development: Longitudinal Research*. Orlando, FLA: Academic Press.

GOTTLEIB, G. (1975) Development of species identification in ducklings. III. Maturational rectification of perceptual deficit caused by auditory deprivation. *Journal of Comparative and Physiological Psychology*, 89, 899–912.

GOTTLIEB, M., ZINKUS, P. & THOMPSON, A. (1980) Chronic middle ear disease and auditory perceptual deficits. *Clinical Paediatrics*, 18, 725–732.

GOULD, R.L. (1978) *Transformations: Growth and Change in Adult Life*. New York: Simon & Schuster.

GOULD, R.L. (1980) Transformational tasks in adulthood. In S.I. Greenspan & G.H. Pollock (Eds) *The Course of Life: Psychoanalytic Contributions Toward Understanding Personality Development*, Volume 3: *Adulthood and the Ageing Process*. Washington, DC: National Institute for Mental Health.

GOULD, S.J. (1981) *The Mismeasure of Man*. Harmondsworth: Penguin.

GRAHAM, H. (1986) *The Human Face of Psychology*. Milton Keynes: Open University Press.

GRAY, J.A. (1975) *Elements of a two-process theory of learning*. London: Academic Press.

GRAY, J.A. (1987) The ethics and politics of animal experimentation. In H. Beloff & A.M. Colman (Eds) *Psychology Survey*, No.6. Leicester: British Psychological Society.

GRAY, J.A. (1991) On the morality of speciesism. *The Psychologist*, 4 (5), 196–198.

GRAY, J.A (1997) Obituary: Hans Eysenck 1916–1997. *The Psychologist*, 10, 510.

GRAY, J.A. & WEDDERBURN, A.A. (1960) Grouping strategies with simultaneous stimuli. *Quarterly Journal of Experimental Psychology*, 12, 180–184.

GREEN, B.L. (1994) Psychosocial research in traumatic stress: An update. *Journal of Traumatic Stress*, 7, 341–363.

GREEN, S. (1980) Physiological studies I and II. In Radford, J. & Govier, E. (Eds) *A Textbook of Psychology*. London: Sheldon Press.

GREEN, S. (1994) *Principles of Biopsychology*. Sussex: Lawrence Erlbaum Associates.

GREEN, S. (1996a) Drugs and behaviour. *Psychology Review*, 3, 14–17.

GREEN, S. (1996b) Ecstasy. *Psychology Review*, 3, 34.

GREEN, S. (1996c) Drugs and psychological disorders. *Psychology Review*, 3, 25–28.

GREENBERG, J. & BARON, R.A. (1995) *Behaviour in Organisations*. London: Prentice-Hall.

GREENBERG, J., PSYZCZYNSKI, T. & SOLOMON, S. (1982) The self-serving attributional bias: Beyond self-presentation. *Journal of Experimental Social Psychology*, 18, 56–67.

GREENBERG, M. & MORRIS, N. (1974) Engrossment: The newborn's impact upon the father. *American Journal of Orthopsychiatry*, 44, 520–531.

GREENBERG, R. & PEARLMAN, C. (1967) Delerium tremens and dreaming. *American Journal of Psychiatry*, 124, 133–142.

GREENBERG, R., PILLARD, R. & PEARLMAN, C. (1972) The effect of dream (stage REM) deprivation on adaptation to stress. *Psychosomatic Medicine*, 34, 257–262.

GREENE, J. (1975) *Thinking and Language*. London: Methuen.

GREENE, J. (1987) *Memory, Thinking and Language*. London: Methuen.

GREENE, J. (1990) Perception. In I. Roth (Ed.) *Introduction to Psychology*, Volume 2. Milton Keynes: Open University Press.

GREENFIELD, P.M. (1984) *Mind and the Media: The Effects of Television, Video Games and Computers*. Cambridge, MA: Harvard University Press.

GREENFIELD, P.M. & SMITH, J.H. (1976) *The Structure of Communication in Early Language Development*. New York: Academic Press.

GREENOUGH, W.T. & BLACK, J.E. (1992) Induction of brain structure by experience: substrates for cognitive development. In M. Gunnar & C.A. Nelson (Eds) *Behavioural Developmental Neuroscience*, Volume 24: *Minnesota Symposia on Child Psychology*. Hillsdale, NJ: Erlbaum.

GREENWALD, A.G., KLINGER M.R. & LIU, T.J. (1989) Unconscious processing of dichoptically masked words. *Memory & Cognition*, 17, 35–47.

GREGOR, A.J. & McPHERSON, D. (1965) A study of susceptibility to geometric illusions among cultural outgroups of Australian aborigines. *Psychologia Africana*, 11, 490–499.

GREGORY, R.L. (1966) *Eye and Brain*. London: Weidenfeld & Nicolson.

GREGORY, R.L. (1970) *The Intelligent Eye*. London: Weidenfeld & Nicolson.

GREGORY, R.L. (1972) Visual illusions. In B.M. Foss (Ed.) *New Horizons in Psychology 1*. Harmondsworth: Penguin.

GREGORY, R.L. (1973) *Eye and Brain* (2nd edition). New York: World Universities Library.

GREGORY, R.L. (1980) Perceptions as hypotheses. *Philosophical Transactions of the Royal Society of London, Series B*, 290, 181–197.

GREGORY, R.L. (1981) *Mind in Science*. Harmondsworth: Penguin.

GREGORY, R.L. (1983) Visual illusions. In J. Miller (Ed.) *States of Mind*. London: BBC Productions.

GREGORY, R.L. (1996) Twenty-five years after 'The Intelligent Eye'. *The Psychologist*, 9, 452–455.

GREGORY, R.L. & WALLACE, J. (1963) *Recovery from Early Blindness*. Cambridge: Heffer.

GRIER, W. & COBBS, P. (1968) *Black Rage*. New York: Basic Books.

GRIFFITHS, M. (1993) Are computer games bad for children? *The Psychologist*, 6, 401–407.

GRIFFITHS, M. (1997) Video games and aggression. *The Psychologist*, 10, 397–401.

GROSS, R. (1994) *Key Studies in Psychology* (2nd edition). London: Hodder & Stoughton.

GROSS, R. (1995) *Themes, Issues and Debates in Psychology*. London: Hodder & Stoughton.

GROSS, R. (1996) *Psychology: The Science of Mind and Behaviour* (3rd edition). London: Hodder & Stoughton.

GROSS, R. & McILVEEN, R. (1997) *Cognitive Psychology*. London: Hodder & Stoughton.

GROSZ, E.A. (1987) Feminist theory and the challenge of knowledges. *Women's Studies International Forum*, 10, 475–480.

GRUENDEL, J.M. (1977) Referential overextension in early language development. *Child Development*, 48, 1567–1576.

GRUNEBERG, M. (1992) *Linkword Language System: Greek*. London: Corgi Books.

GRUSH, J.E. (1976) Attitude formation and mere exposure phenomena: A non-artifactual explanation of empirical findings. *Journal of Personality and Social Psychology*, 33, 281–290.

GUERIN, B.J. (1993) *Social Facilitation*. Cambridge: Cambridge University Press.

GUNTER, B. (1986) *Television and Sex-Role Stereotyping*. London: IBA and John Libbey.

GUNTER, B., CLIFFORD, B. & BERRY, C. (1980) Release from proactive interference with television news items: Evidence for encoding dimensions within televised news. *Journal of Experimental Psychology*: Human Learning and Memory, 6, 216–223.

GUNTER, B. & HARRISON, J. (1995) *Violence on Television in the UK: A Content Analysis*. London: BBC/ITC.

GUNTER, B. & McALEER, J.L. (1990) *Children and Television – The One-Eyed Monster?* London: Routledge.

GUPTA, U. & SINGH, P. (1992) Exploratory study of love and liking and types of marriage. *Indian Journal of Applied Psychology*, 19, 92–97.

GUR, R.C., SKOLNICK, B.E. & GUR, R.E. (1994) Effects of emotional discrimination tasks on cerebral blood flow: Regional activation and its relation to performance. *Brain and Cognition*, 25, 271–286.

GUSCOTT, R. & TAYLOR, L. (1994) Lithium prophylaxis in recurrent affective illness: Efficacy, effectiveness and efficiency. *British Journal of Psychiatry*, 164, 741–746.

GUSTAFSON, G. & HARRIS, K. (1990) Women's responses to young infants' cries. *Developmental Psychology*, 26, 144–152.

GUTHRIE, E.R. (1938) *Psychology of Human Conflict*. New York: Harper & Row.

GWIAZDA, J., BRILL, S., MOHINDRA, I. & HELD, R. (1980) Preferential looking acuity in infants from two to 58 weeks of age. *American Journal of Optometry and Physiological Optics*, 57, 428–432.

HAAGA, D.A. & BECK, A.T. (1992) Cognitive therapy. In S. Pakyel (Ed.) *Handbook of Affective Disorders* (2nd edition). Cambridge: Cambridge University Press.

HAAGA, D.A. & DAVISON, G.C. (1993) An appraisal of rational-emotive therapy. *Journal of Consulting and Clinical Psychology*, 61, 215–220.

HABER, R.N. (1969) Eidetic images. *Scientific American*, 220, 36–44.

HABER, R.N. (1980) Eidetic images are not just imaginary. *Psychology Today*, November, 72–82.

HABER, R.N. & HERSHENSON, M. (1980) *The Physiology of Visual Perception*. New York: Holt, Rinehart & Winston.

HAGELL, A. & NEWBURN, T. (1994) *Young Offenders and the Media*. London: Batsford.

HALL, C. (1997) Mothers starve 'fat' babies. *The Daily Telegraph*, 16 April, 9.

HALL, C. & VAN DE CASTLE, R.L. (1966) *The Content Analysis of Dreams*. E. Norwalk, CT: Appleton-Century-Crofts.

HALL, C.S. (1966) *The Meaning of Dreams*. New York: McGraw-Hill.

HALL, E.T. (1959) *The Silent Language*. New York: Doubleday.

HALL, G.S. (1904) *Adolescence*. New York: Appleton & Company.

HALL, J. (1996) *Social Devaluation and Special Education: The Right to Full Mainstream Inclusion and an Honest Statement*. London: Routledge.

HALLIDAY, M.A.K. & HASAN, R. (1976) *Cohesion in English*. London: Longman.

HALLIGAN, P.W. (1995) Drawing attention to neglect: The contribution of line bisection. *The Psychologist*, 8, 257–264.

HALLORAN, J.D. & CROLL, P. (1972) Television programmes in Great Britain. In G.A. Comstock & E.A. Rubenstein (Eds) *Television and Social Behaviour, Volume 1, Media Content and Control*. Washington, DC: US Government Printing Office.

HALPIN, A. & WINER, B. (1952) *The Leadership Behaviour of the Airplane Commander*. Columbus, OH: Ohio State University Research Foundation.

HAMBURG, D. & TAKANISHI, R. (1989) Preparing for life: The critical transition of adolescence. *American Psychologist*, 44, 825–827.

HAMILTON, D.L. & GIFFORD, R.K. (1976) Illusory correlation in interpersonal perception: A cognitive basis of stereotypic judgements. *Journal of Experimental Social Psychology*, 12, 392–407.

HAMILTON, L.W. & TIMMONS, C.R. (1995) Psychopharmacology. In D. Kimble & A.M. Colman (Eds) *Biological Aspects of Behaviour*. London: Longman.

HAMILTON, V.L. (1978) Obedience and responsibility: A jury simulation. *Journal of Personality and Social Psychology*, 36, 126–146.

HAMILTON, W.D. (1964) The genetic evolution of social behaviour, I and II. *Journal of Theoretical Biology*, 7, 1–16, 17–52.

HAMMEN, C.L. (1985) Predicting depression: A cognitive-behavioural perspective. In P. Kendall (Ed.) *Advances in Cognitive-Behavioural Research and Therapy*, Volume 4. New York: Academic Press.

HAMPSON, P.J. (1989) Aspects of attention and cognitive science. *Irish Journal of Psychology*, 10, 261–275.

HAMPSON, P.J. & MORRIS, P.E. (1996) *Understanding Cognition*. Oxford: Blackwell.

HAMPSON, S.E. (1995) The construction of personality. In S.E. Hampson & A.M. Colman (Eds) *Individual Differences and Personality*. London: Longman.

HAMPTON, J.A. (1979) Polymorphous concepts in semantic memory. *Journal of Verbal Learning and Verbal Behaviour*, 18, 441–461.

HARBURG, E., ERFURT, J.C., HAUENSTEIN, L.S., CHAPE, C., SCHULL, W.J. & SCHORK, M.A. (1973) Socioecological stress, suppressed hostility, skin colour, and black-white male blood pressure: Detroit. *Psychosomatic Medicine*, 35, 276–296.

HARDIE, E.A. (1997) PMS in the workplace: Dispelling the myth of the cyclic dysfunction. *Journal of Occupational and Organisational Psychology*, 70, 97–102.

HARGREAVES, D., MOLLOY, C. & PRATT, A. (1982) Social factors in conservation. *British Journal of Psychology*, 73, 231–234.

HARLEY, J.P., RAY, R.S., TOMAS, L., EICHMAN, P.L., MATTHEWS, C.G., CHUN, R., CLEELAND, C. & TRAISMAN, E. (1978) Hyperkinesis and food additives: Testing the Feingold Hypothesis. *Paediatrics*, 61, 818–828.

HARLOW, H.F. (1959) Love in infant monkeys. *Scientific American*, 200, 68–74.

HARLOW, H.F. & SUOMI, S.J. (1970) The nature of love – simplified. *American Psychologist*, 25, 161–168.

HARLOW, H.F. & ZIMMERMAN, R.R. (1959) Affectional responses in the infant monkey. *Science*, 130, 421–432.

HARRÉ, R. (1983) *Personal Being*. Oxford: Blackwell.

HARRÉ, R. (1985) The language game of self-ascription: A note. In K.J. Gergen & K.E. Davis (Eds) *The Social Construction of the Person*. New York: Springer-Verlag.

HARRÉ, R. (1989) Language games and the texts of identity. In J. Shotter & K.J. Gergen (Eds) *Texts of Identity*. London: Sage.

HARRÉ, R., CLARKE, D., & De CARLO, N. (1985) *Motives and Mechanisms: An Introduction to the Psychology of Action*. London: Methuen.

HARRIS, A.J. & SIPEY, E.R. (1983) *Readings on Reading Instruction* (2nd edition). New York: Longman.

HARRIS, M. (1991) From gesture to language in hearing and deaf children. *First Language*, 11, 181–187.

HARRIS, M.G. & HUMPHREYS, G.W. (1995) Computational theories of vision. In R.L. GREGORY & A.M. COLMAN (Eds) *Sensation and Perception*. London: Longman.

HARRIS, S.L., HANDLEMAN, J.S., GORDON, R., KRISTOFF, B. & FUENTES, F. (1991) Changes in cognitive and language functioning of preschool children with autism. *Journal of Autism and Developmental Disorders*, 21, 281–290.

HARRISON, P. (1995) Schizophrenia: A misunderstood disease. *Psychology Review*, 2, 2–6.

HARROWER, J. (1998) *Applying Psychology to Crime*. London: Hodder & Stoughton.

HART, B.B., & ALDEN, P. (1994) Hypnotic techniques in the control of pain. In H.B. Gibson (Ed.) *Psychology, Pain and Anaesthesia*. London: Chapman & Hall.

HART, C. & HART, B.B. (1996) The use of hypnosis with children and adolescents. *The Psychologist*, 9, 506–509.

HART, J., BERNDT, R.S. & CARAMAZZA, A. (1985) Category-specific naming deficit following cerebral infarction. *Nature*, 316, 439–440.

HARTLEY, J. & BRANTHWAITE, A. (1997) Earning a crust. *Psychology Review*, 3 (3), 24–26.

HARTLEY, P. (1997) Eating disorders: myths and misconceptions. *Biological Sciences Review*, 9, 25–27.

HARTMANN, E.L. (1973) *The Functions of Sleep*. New Haven, CT: Yale University Press.

HARTSHORNE, H. & MAY, M. (1930) *Studies in the Nature of Character*. New York: MacMillan.

HARTSTON, W. (1996) A history of the world in 10½ inches: 21 – Alcohol. *The Independent (Section 2)*, 19 September, 30.

HARVEY, J.H. & WEARY, G. (1984) Current issues in attribution theory and research. *Annual Review of Psychology*, 35, 427–459.

HASSETT, J. & WHITE, M. (1989) *Psychology in Perspective* (2nd edition). Cambridge: Harper & Row.

HASTIE, R. & PARK, B. (1986) The relationship between memory and judgement depends on whether the judgement task is memory based or on-line. *Psychological Bulletin*, 93, 258–268.

HATFIELD, E. & RAPSON, R. (1987) Passionate love/sexual desire: Can the same paradigm explain both? *Archives of Sexual Behaviour*, 16, 259–278.

HAVIGHURST, R.J. (1964) Stages of vocational development. In H. Borrow (Ed.) *Man in a World of Work*. Boston: Houghton Mifflin.

HAVIGHURST, R.J., NEUGARTEN, B.L. & TOBIN, S.S. (1968) Disengagement and patterns of ageing. In B.L. Neugarten (Ed.) *Middle Age and Ageing*. Chicago: University of Chicago Press.

HAWKES, N. (1997) Where a cabbie keeps his A to Z. *The Times*, 17 September, 6.

HAWKINS, S.A. & HASTIE, R. (1990) Hindsight: Biased judgements of past events after the outcomes are known. *Psychological Bulletin*, 107, 311–327.

HAWKS, D. (1981) The dilemma of clinical practice – Surviving as a clinical psychologist. In I. McPherson & M. Sutton (Eds) *Reconstructing Psychological Practice*. London: Croom Helm.

HAWORTH, G. (1992) The use of non-human animals in psychological research: the current status of the debate. *Psychology Teaching*, 46–54. New Series, No.1.

HAY, P., SACHDEV, P. & CUMMING, S. (1993) Treatment of obsessive–compulsive disorder by psychosurgery. *Acta Psychiatrica Scandinavia*, 87, 197–207.

HAYES, J.R. & FLOWER, L.S. (1980) Identifying the organisation of writing processes. In L.W. Gregg & E.R. Sternberg (Eds) *Cognitive Processes in Writing*. Hillsdale, NJ: Erlbaum.

HAYES, J.R. & FLOWER, L.S. (1986) Writing research and the writer. *American Psychologist*, 41, 1106–1113.

HAYES, J.R., FLOWER, L.S., SCHRIVER, K., STRATMAN, J. & CAREY, L. (1985) Cognitive Processes in Revision. *Technical Report No.12*. Pittsburgh, PA: Carnegie Mellon University.

HAYES, N. (1994) *Foundations of Psychology: An Introductory Text*. London: Routledge.

HAYES, N. (1997) Social representations: A European theory. *Psychology Review*, 4, 13–17.

HAYSLIP, B. & PANEK, P.E. (1989) *Adult Development and Ageing*. New York: Harper & Row.

HEAP, B. (1996) The nature of hypnosis. *The Psychologist*, 9, 498–501.

HEARNSHAW, L. (1979) *Cyril Burt: Psychologist*. Ithaca, NY: Cornell University Press.

HEAROLD, S. (1986) A synthesis of 1043 effects of television on social behaviour. In G. Comstock (Ed.) *Public Communication and Behaviour*. New York: Academic Press.

HEATHER, N. (1976) *Radical Perspectives in Psychology*. London: Methuen.

HEBB, D.O. (1949) *The Organisation of Behaviour*. New York: Wiley.

HEBB, D.O. (1952) The effects of isolation upon attitudes, motivation and thought. *Fourth Symposium, Military Medicine, I. Defence Research Board*: Canada.

HEBER, R. & GARBER, H. (1975) The Milwaukee Project: A study of the use of familial retardation to prevent cultural retardation. In B.Z. Friedlander, G.M. Sterrit & G.E. Kirk (Eds) *Exceptional Infant*, Volume 3: *Assessment and Intervention*. New York: Brunner/Mazel.

HEIDER, E. (1972) Universals in colour naming and memory. *Journal of Experimental Psychology*, 93, 10–20.

HEIDER, E. & OLIVER, D. (1972) The structure of the colour space in naming and memory for two languages. *Cognitive Psychology*, 3, 337–354.

HEIDER, F. (1946) Attitudes and cognitive organisation. *Journal of Psychology*, 21, 107–112.

HEIDER, F. (1958) *The Psychology of Interpersonal Relations*. New York: Wiley.

HELD, R. & BOSSOM, J. (1961) Neonatal deprivation and adult rearrangement: Complementary techniques for analysing plastic sensory-motor co-ordinations. *Journal of Comparative and Physiological Psychology*, 54, 33–37.

HELD, R. & HEIN, A. (1963) Movement-produced stimulation in the development of visually guided behaviour. *Journal of Comparative and Physiological Psychology*, 56, 607–613.

HELLER, R.F., SALTZSTEIN, H.D. & CASPE, W.B. (1992) Heuristics in medical and non-medical decision-making. *Quarterly Journal of Experimental Psychology*, 44A, 211–235.

HENDERSON, A.S., JABLENSKY, A. & SARTORIUS, N. (1994) ICD-10: A neuropsychiatrist's nightmare? *British Journal of Psychiatry*, 165, 273–275.

HENDRICK, S.S., HENDRICK, C. & ADLER N.L. (1988) Romantic relationships. Love, satisfaction and staying together. *Journal of Personality & Social Psychology*, 54, 980–988.

HENDRIX, L. (1985) Economy and child training reexamined. *Ethos*, 13, 246–261.

HENSLEY, W.E. (1981) The effects of attire, location, and sex on aiding behaviour: A similarity explanation. *Journal of Non-Verbal Behaviour*, 6, 3–11.

HEPWORTH, J.T. & WEST, S.G. (1988) Lynchings and the economy: A time series analysis of Hovland and Sears (1940). *Journal of Personality and Social Psychology*, 55, 239–247.

HERBERT, T.B. & COHEN, S. (1993) Stress and immunity in humans: A meta-analytic review. *Psychosomatic Medicine*, 55, 364–379.

HERMAN, J. & ROFFWARG, H. (1983) Modifying oculomotor activity in awake subjects increases the amplitude of eye movement during REM sleep. *Science*, 220, 1074–1076.

HERMELIN, B. & O'CONNOR, N. (1970) *Psychological Experiments with Autistic Children*. Oxford: Pergamon Press.

HERRNSTEIN, R.J. (1971) IQ. *Atlantic Monthly*, September, 43–64.

HERRNSTEIN, R.J. & MURRAY, C. (1994) *The Bell Curve: Intelligence and Class Structure in American Life*. New York: Free Press.

HERSHENSON, M., MUNSINGER, H. & KESSEN, W. (1965) Preference for shapes of intermediate variability in the newborn human. *Science*, 147, 630–631.

HERSHER, L. (Ed.) (1970) *Four Psychotherapies*. New York: Appleton-Century-Crofts.

HERSKOVITS, M.J. (1958) *Cultural Anthropology*. New York: Knopf.

HESS, E.H. (1956) Space perception in the chick. *Scientific American*, July, 71–80.

HESS, E.H. (1958) Imprinting in animals. *Scientific American*, March, 71–80.

HESS, R.D. & SHIPMAN, V. (1965) Early experience and the socialisation of cognitive modes in children. *Child Development*, 36, 860–886.

HESTON, L.L. (1966) Psychiatric disorders in foster-home-reared children of schizophrenic mothers. *British Journal of Psychiatry*, 122, 819–825.

HESTON, L.L. (1970) The genetics of schizophrenia and schizoid disease. *Science*, 167, 249–256.

HETHERINGTON, A.W. & RANSON, S.W. (1942) The relation of various hypothalamic lesions to adiposity in the rat. *Journal of Comparative Neurology*, 76, 475–499.

HETHERINGTON, E.M. (1967) The effects of familial variables on sex-typing, on parent-child similarity, and on imitation in children. In J.P. Hill (Ed.) *Minnesota Symposium on Child Psychology*, Volume 1. Mineapolis, MN: University of Minnesota Press.

HETHERINGTON, E.M. & BALTES, P.B. (1988) Child psychology and life-span development. In E.M. Hetherington, R. Lerner, & M. Perlmutter (Eds) *Child Development in Life-Span Perspective*. Hillsdale, NJ: Erlbaum.

HEWSTONE, M. & BROWN, R.J. (1986) Contact is not enough: An intergroup perspective on the contact hypothesis. In M. Hewstone & R.J. Brown (Eds) *Contact and Conflict in Inter-group Encounters*. Oxford: Blackwell.

HEWSTONE, M. & FINCHAM, F. (1996) Attribution theory and research: Basic issues and applications. In M. Hewstone, W. Stroebe & G.M. Stephenson (Eds) *Introduction to Social Psychology* (2nd edition). Oxford: Blackwell.

HEWSTONE, M. & JASPARS, J.M.F. (1982) Explanations for racial discrimination: The effect of group discussion on intergroup attributions. *European Journal of Social Psychology*, 12, 1–16.

HEWSTONE, M., STROEBE, W. & STEPHENSON, G.M. (1996) *Introduction to Social Psychology* (2nd edition). Oxford: Blackwell.

HICKS, R. & PELLEGRINI, R. (1982) Sleep problems and Type A-B behaviour in college students. *Psychological Reports*, 51, 96.

HIGBEE, K.L. (1996) *Your Memory: How it Works and How to Improve it*. New York: Marlowe and Co.

HIGHFIELD, R. (1995a) Brain scans show sexes are not on the same wavelength. *The Daily Telegraph*, 5 January, 5.

HIGHFIELD, R. (1995b) Revealed: the source of those voices we hear. *The Daily Telegraph*, 28 June, 18.

HIGHFIELD, R (1996a) Want to know what she's thinking? *The Daily Telegraph*, 28 August, 12.

HIGHFIELD, R. (1996b) Scientists shed light on the origins of our body clock. *The Daily Telegraph*, 5 May, 6.

HIGHFIELD, R. (1996c) Working out how time flies. *The Daily Telegraph*, 21 February, 14.

HIGHFIELD, R. (1996d) While you were dreaming … *The Daily Telegraph*, 2 October, 14.

HIGHFIELD, R. (1996e) Don't worry, it's just in your genes. *The Daily Telegraph*, 20 November, 5.

HIGHFIELD, R. (1996f) Computer game helps dyslexia children. *The Daily Telegraph*, 5 January, 5.

HIGHFIELD, R. (1997a) Forgetfulness opens windows on the mind. *The Daily Telegraph*, 18 July, 3.

HIGHFIELD, R. (1997b) A new vision of the human brain. *The Daily Telegraph*, 16 April, 20.

HIGHFIELD, R. (1997c) Faulty gene linked to schizophrenia. *The Daily Telegraph*, 22 January, 11.

HIGHFIELD, R. (1997d) Depression in women due to 'chemistry'. *The Daily Telegraph*, 13 May, 5.

HILGARD, E.R. (1973) A neodissociation interpretation of pain reduction in hypnosis. *Psychological Review*, 80, 396–411.

HILGARD, E.R. (1977) *Divided Consciousness: Multiple Controls in Human Thought and Action*. New York: Wiley-Interscience.

HILGARD, E.R., ATKINSON, R.L. & ATKINSON, R.C. (1979) *Introduction to Psychology* (7th edition). New York: Harcourt Brace Jovanovich.

HILL, C.Y., RUBIN, Z. & PEPLAU, A. (1976) Breakups before marriage: The end of 103 affairs. *Journal of Social Issues*, 32, 147–167.

HILLIARD, A.G. (1995) The nonsense and nonsense of the bell curve. *Focus: Notes from the Society for the Psychological Study of Ethnic Minority Issues*, 10–12.

HILTON, D.J. & SLUGOSKI, B.R. (1986) Knowledge-based causal attribution: The Abnormal Conditions Focus model. *Psychological Review*, 93, 75–88.

HINDE, R.A. (1974) *Biological Bases of Human Social Behaviour*. New York: McGraw-Hill.

HINTON, J. (1975) *Dying*. Harmondsworth: Penguin.

HIRSCH, H. (1995) *Genocide and the Politics of Memory*. Chapel Hill, NC: The University of North Carolina Press.

HISCOCK, J. (1996) Schools recognise 'Black English'. *The Daily Telegraph*, 21 December, 12.

HOBBES, T. (1651) *Leviathan*. London: Dent, 1914.

HOBSON, J.A. (1988) *The Dreaming Brain*. New York: Basic Books.

HOBSON, J.A. (1989) Dream theory: A new view of the brain-mind. *The Harvard Medical School Mental Health Letter*, 5, 3–5.

HOBSON, J.A. & McCARLEY, R.W. (1977) The brain as a dream state generator: An activation-synthesis hypothesis of the dream process. *American Journal of Psychiatry*, 134, 1335–1348.

HOCHBERG, J.E. (1970) Attention, organisation and consciousness. In D.I. MOSTOFSKY (Ed.) *Attention: Contemporary Theory and Analysis*. New York: Appleton Century Crofts.

HOCHBERG, J.E. (1971) Perception. In J.W. Kling & L.A. Riggs (Eds) *Experimental Psychology*. New York: Holt.

HOCHBERG, J.E. (1978) Art and perception. In E.C. Carterette & H. Friedman (Eds) *Handbook of Perception*, Volume 10. London: Academic Press.

HODGES, J. & TIZARD, B. (1989) Social and family relationships of ex-institutional adolescents. *Journal of Child Psychology and Psychiatry*, 30, 77–97.

HODGKIN, J. (1988) Everything you always wanted to know about sex. *Nature*, 331, 300–301.

HODGSON, J.W. & FISHER, J.L. (1979) Sex differences in identity and intimacy development. *Journal of Youth and Adolescence*, 8, 37–50.

HODGSON, R.J. & RACHMAN, S. (1972) The effects of contamination and washing in obsessional patients. *Behaviour Research and Therapy*, 10, 111–117.

HODKIN, B. (1981) Language effects in assessment of class-inclusion ability. *Child Development*, 52, 470–478.

HOFFMAN, M.L. (1970) Conscience, personality and socialisation techniques. *Human Development*, 13, 90–126.

HOFFMAN, M.L. (1975) Altruistic behaviour and the parent-child relationship. *Journal of Personality and Social Psychology*, 31, 937–943.

HOFFMAN, M.L. (1976) Empathy, role-taking, guilt and development of altruistic motives. In T. Lickona (Ed.) *Moral Development and Behaviour*. New York: Holt, Rinehart & Winston.

HOFLING, K.C., BROTZMAN, E., DALRYMPLE, S., GRAVES, N. & PIERCE, C.M. (1966) An experimental study in the nurse–physician relationships. *Journal of Nervous and Mental Disorders*, 143, 171–180.

HOGG, M.A. & VAUGHAN, G.M. (1995) *Social Psychology: An Introduction*. Hemel Hempstead: Prentice Hall/Harvester Wheatsheaf.

HOHMANN, G.W. (1966) Some effects of spinal cord lesions on experienced emotional feelings. *Psychophysiology*, 3, 143–156.

HOLAHAN, C.K. & SEARS, R.R. (1995) *The Gifted Group in Later Maturity*. Stanford, CA: Stanford University Press.

HOLDAWAY, S. (1988) *Crime and Deviance*. London: Macmillan.

HOLLAND, A.J., HALL, A., MURRAY, R., RUSSELL, G.F.M. & CRISP, A.H. (1984) Anorexia nervosa: A study of 34 twin pairs and one set of triplets. *British Journal of Psychiatry*, 145, 414–418.

HOLLANDER, E.P. (1958) Conformity, status, and idiosyncrasy credit. *Psychological Review*, 65, 117–127.

HOLLANDER, E.P. (1985) Leadership and power. In G. Lindsay & E. Aronson (Eds) *Handbook of Social Psychology* (3rd edition). New York: Random House.

HOLLIN, C. & HOWELLS, K. (1997) Controlling violent behaviour. *Psychology Review*, 3, 10–14.

HOLLINGTON, S. (1995) Sweet dreams are made of this. *The Observer*, 12 March, 3.

HOLMES, D.S. (1994) *Abnormal Psychology* (2nd edition). New York: HarperCollins.

HOLMES, J. (1992) Response to Jeffrey Masson. In W. Dryden & C. Feltham (Eds) *Psychotherapy and its Discontents*. Buckingham: Open University Press.

HOLMES, J. (1993) *John Bowlby and Attachment Theory*. London: Routledge.

HOLMES, J. (1996) Psychoanalysis – An endangered species? *Psychiatric Bulletin*, 20, 321–322.

HOMANS, G.C. (1974) *Social Behaviour: Its Elementary Forms* (2nd edition). New York: Harcourt Brace Jovanovich.

HONZIK, M.P., MacFARLANE, H.W. & ALLEN, L. (1948) The stability of mental test performance between two and eighteen years. *Journal of Experimental Education*, 17, 309–324.

HOPSON, B. & SCALLY, M. (1980) Change and development in adult life: Some implications for helpers. *British Journal of Guidance and Counselling*, 8, 175–187.

HORGAN, J. (1993) Eugenics revisited. *Scientific American*, June, 92–100.

HORN, J.L. (1976) Human abilities: A review of research and theory in the early 1970s. *Annual Review of Psychology*, 27, 437–485.

HORN, J.L. (1982) The ageing of human abilities. In B. Wolman (Ed.) *Handbook of Developmental Psychology*. Englewood Cliffs, NJ: Prentice-Hall.

HORNABY, B. & MILES, T. (1980) The effects of a dyslexia centred teaching programme. *British Journal of Educational Psychology*, 51, 10–22.

HORNE, J.A. & OSTERBERG, O. (1976) A self-assessment questionnaire to determine morningness-eveningness in human circadian rhythms. *International Journal of Chronobiology*, 4, 97–190.

HORTON, P.B. & HUNT, C.L. (1976) *Sociology* (4th edition). New York: McGraw-Hill.

HOUSTON, J.P., HAMMEN, C., PADILLA, A. & BEE, H. (1991) *Invitation to Psychology* (3rd edition). London: Harcourt Brace Jovanovich.

HOVLAND, C.I. & SEARS, R.R. (1940) Minor studies in aggression, VI: Correlation of lynchings with economic indices. *Journal of Psychology*, 2, 301–310.

HOWARD, J.A., BLUMSTEIN, P. & SCHWARTZ, P. (1987) Social or evolutionary theories: Some observations on preferences in mate selection. *Journal of Personality and Social Psychology*, 53, 194–200.

HOWE, M. (1980) *The Psychology of Human Learning*. London: Harper & Row.

HOWE, M. (1990) *The Origins of Exceptional Abilities*. Oxford: Blackwell.

HOWE, M. (1995) Hothouse tots: Encouraging and accelerating development in young children. *Psychology Review*, 2, 2–4.

HOWE, M. (1997) *IQ in Question: The Truth about Intelligence*. London: Sage.

HOWE, M. & GRIFFEY, H. (1994) *Give Your Child a Better Start*. London: Michael Joseph.

HOWITT, D. (1991) *Concerning Psychology: Psychology Applied to Social Issues*. Milton Keynes: Open University Press.

768

HOYENGA, K.B. & HOYENGA, K.T. (1979) *The Question of Sex Differences.* Boston: Little Brown.

HSU, L.K. (1990) *Eating Disorders.* New York: Guilford.

HU, Y. & GOLDMAN, N. (1990) Morality differentials by marital status: An international comparison. *Demography*, 27, 233–250.

HUBBARD, P. (1991) Evaluating computer games for language learning. *Simulation and Gaming*, 22, 220–223.

HUBEL, D.H. & WIESEL, T.N. (1962) Receptive fields, binocular interaction and functional architecture in the cat's visual cortex. *Journal of Physiology*, 160, 106–154.

HUBEL, D.H. & WIESEL, T.N. (1965) Receptive fields of single neurons in the two non-striate visual areas, 18 and 19 of the cat. *Journal of Neurophysiology*, 28, 229–289.

HUBEL, D.H. & WIESEL, T.N. (1968) Receptive fields and functional architecture of monkey striate cortex. *Journal of Physiology*, 195, 215–243.

HUBEL, D.H. & WIESEL, T.N. (1977) Functional architecture of the macaque monkey visual cortex. *Proceedings of the Royal Society of London, Series B*, 198, 1–59.

HÜBER-WEIDMAN, H. (1976) *Sleep, Sleep Disturbances and Sleep Deprivation.* Cologne: Kiepenheuser & Witsch.

HUCZYNSKI, A. & BUCHANAN, D. (1991) *Organisational Behaviour: An Introductory Text* (2nd edition). Hemel Hempstead: Prentice-Hall.

HUDSON, W. (1960) Pictorial depth perception in sub-cultural groups in Africa. *Journal of Social Psychology*, 52, 183–208.

HUESMANN, L.R. & ERON, L.D. (Eds) (1986) *Television and the Aggressive Child: A Cross-National Comparison.* Hove: Erlbaum.

HUESMANN, L.R., ERON, L.D., KLEIN, R., BRICE, P. & FISCHER, P. (1983) Mitigating the imitation of aggressive behaviours by changing children's attitudes about media violence. *Journal of Personality and Social Psychology*, 44, 899–910.

HUGDAHL, K. & ÖHMAN, A. (1977) Effects of instruction on acquisition of electrodermal response to fear relevant stimuli. *Journal of Experimental Psychology*, 3, 608–618.

HUGGET, C. & ALDCROFT, C. (1996) The experience of living in a secluded cave for a month. *Proceedings of the British Psychological Society 27th Annual Student Conference, School of Education, University of Wales*, Cardiff, 27 April.

HUMPHREYS, G.W. & RIDDOCH, M.J. (1987) *To See But Not to See – A Case Study of Visual Agnosia.* London: Erlbaum.

HUMPHREYS, N. (Ed.) (1975) *Vital Statistics: A Memorial Volume of Selections from the Reports and Writings of William Farr.* Metuchen, NJ: Scarecrow Press.

HUMPHREYS, P.W. (1992) Prefaces to the experimental, observational and correlational methods. In R. Mcilveen, L. Higgins, A. Wadeley & P. Humphreys (Eds) *BPS Manual of Psychology Practicals.* Leicester: BPS Books.

HUMPHREYS, P.W. (1994) Obedience after Milgram. *Psychology Review*, 1, 2–5.

HUMPHREYS, P.W. (1997) (Ab)normality. *Psychology Review*, 3, 10–15.

HUNT, E. & AGNOLI, A. (1991) The Whorfian hypothesis: A cognitive psychological perspective. *Psychological Review*, 98, 377–389.

HUNT, J. McVicker (1961) *Intelligence and Experience.* New York: Ronald Press.

HUNT, J. McVicker (1969) Has compensatory education failed? Has it been attempted? *Harvard Educational Review*, 39, 278–300.

HUNT, J. McVicker (1982) Towards equalising the developmental opportunities of pre-school children. *Journal of Social Issues*, 38, 163–191.

HUNT, L. (1995) Why a fear of spiders is all in the genes. *The Independent*, 20 December, 17.

HUNT, N. (1997) Trauma of war. *The Psychologist*, 10, 357–360.

HUNTER, I.M.L. (1957) *Memory, Facts and Fallacies.* Harmondsworth: Penguin.

HUSTON, A.C. (1983) Sex-typing. In E.M. Hetherington (Ed.) *Socialisation, personality and social development*, Volume 4 in P.H. Mussen (Ed.) *Handbook of Child Psychology.* New York: Wiley.

HUSTON, T. & KORTE, C. (1976) The responsive bystander: Why he helps. In T. Lickona (Ed.) *Moral Development and Behaviour.* New York: Holt, Rinehart & Winston.

HUSTON, T., RUGGERIO, M., CONNER, R. & GEIS, G. (1981) Bystander intervention into crime: A study based on naturally occurring episodes. *Social Psychology* Quarterly, 44, 14–23.

HUTTON, A. (1998) Mental health: Drug update. *Nursing Times*, 94, February, 11.

HYDE, J.S., FENNEMA, E. & LAMON, S. (1990) Gender differences in mathematics performance: A meta-analysis. *Psychological Bulletin*, 107, 139–155.

HYDE, J.S. & LINN, M.C. (1988) Gender differences in verbal ability: A meta-analysis. *Psychological Bulletin*, 104, 53–69.

HYDE, T.S. & JENKINS, J.J. (1973) Recall for words as a function of semantic, graphic and syntactic orienting tasks. *Journal of Verbal Learning and Verbal Behaviour*, 12, 471–480.

IMPERATO-McGINLEY, J., PETERSON, R., GAUTIER, T. & STURLA, E. (1979) Androgens and the evolution of male-gender identity among pseudohermaphrodites with 5–alpha-reductase deficiency. *New England Journal of Medicine*, 300, 1233–1237.

INHELDER, B. & PIAGET, J. (1958) *The Growth of Logical Thinking.* London: Routledge & Kegan Paul.

INSKO, C.A., DRENAN, S., SOLOMON, M.R., SMITH, R. & WADE, T.J. (1983) Conformity as a function of the consistency of positive self-evaluation with being liked and being right. *Journal of Experimental Social Psychology*, 19, 341–358.

INTONS-PETERSON, M.J. & REDDEL, M. (1984) What do people ask about a neonate? *Developmental Psychology*, 20, 358–359.

IRWIN, A. (1996a) Five days go missing as student plays her bagpipes. *The Daily Telegraph*, 28 September, 1.

IRWIN, A. (1996b) Diet advice that's hard to follow. *The Daily Telegraph*, 17 September, 5.

IRWIN, A. (1997) People 'not designed for night work'. *The Daily Telegraph*, 22 September, 6.

IRWIN, F.W. & SEIDENFELD, M.A. (1937) The application of the method of comparison to the problem of memory change. *Journal of Experimental Psychology*, 21, 363–381.

ISAACS, W., THOMAS, J. & GOLDIAMOND, I. (1960) Application of operant conditioning to reinstate verbal behaviour in psychotics. *Journal of Speech and Hearing Disorders*, 25, 8–12.

ITTELSON, W.H. (1952) *The Ames Demonstrations in Perception.* Princeton, NJ: Princeton University Press.

IVERSEN, L.L. (1979) The chemistry of the brain. *Scientific American*, 241, 134–149.

JACKENDOFF, R. (1993) *Patterns in the Mind: Language and Human Nature.* Hemel Hempstead: Harvester-Wheatsheaf.

JACOB, R.G., KRAEMER, H.C. & AGRAS, W.S. (1977) Relaxation therapy in the treatment of hypertension: A review. *Archives of General Psychiatry*, 34, 1417–1427.

JACOBS, B.L. (1987) How hallucinogenic drugs work. *American Scientist*, 75, 386–392.

JACOBS, M. (1992) *Freud.* London: Sage Publications.

JACOBS, T.J. & CHARLES, E. (1980) Life events and the occurrence of cancer in children. *Psychosomatic Medicine*, 42, 11–24.

JACOBSON, E. (1938) *Progressive Relaxation.* Chicago: University of Chicago Press.

JACOBSON, N.S., FOLLETTE, W.C. & REVENSTORF, D. (1984) Psychotherapy outcome research: Methods for reporting variability and evaluating clinical significance. *Behaviour Therapy*, 15, 336–352.

JAHODA, G. (1966) Geometric illusions and the environment: A study in Ghana. *British Journal of Psychology*, 57, 193–199.

JAHODA, G. (1978) Cross-cultural perspectives. In H. Tajfel & C. Fraser (Eds) *Introducing Social Psychology.* Harmondsworth: Penguin.

JAHODA, G. (1988) Critical notes and reflections on 'social representations'. *European Journal of Social Psychology*, 18, 195–209.

JAHODA, M. (1958) *Current Concepts of Positive Mental Health.* New York: Basic Books.

JAMES, I.A. & BLACKBURN, I.-M. (1995) Cognitive therapy with obsessive-compulsive disorder. *British Journal of Psychiatry*, 166, 144–150.

JAMES, W. (1890) *The Principles of Psychology.* New York: Henry Holt & Company.

JAMISON, K. (1989) Mood disorders and patterns of creativity in British writers and artists. *Psychiatry*, 52, 125–134.

JANOWITZ, H.D. & GROSSMAN, M.I. (1949) Effects of variations in nutritive density on intake of food in dogs and cats. *American Journal of Physiology*, 158, 184–193.

JASNOS, T.M. & HAKMILLER, K.L. (1975) Some effects of lesion level and emotional cues on affective expression in spinal cord patients. *Psychological Reports*, 37, 859–870.

JELLISON, J.M. & OLIVER, D.F. (1983) Attitude similarity and attraction: An impression management approach. *Personality and Social Psychology Bulletin*, 9, 111–115.

JENKINS, J.G. & DALLENBACH, K.M. (1924) Oblivescence during sleep and waking. *American Journal of Psychology*, 35, 605–612.

JENSEN, A. (1969) How much can we boost IQ and scholastic achievement? *Harvard Educational Review*, 39, 1–23.

JENSEN-CAMPBELL, L.A., GRAZIANO, W.G. & WEST, S.G. (1995) Dominance, prosocial orientation and females preferences: Do nice guys really finish last? *Journal of Personality and Social Psychology*, 68, 427–440.

JOHANSSON, G. (1975) Visual motion perception. *Scientific American*, 14, 76–89.

JOHNSON, D. (1989) Schizophrenia as a brain disease. *American Psychologist*, 44, 553–555.

JOHNSON, J.T. & JUDD, C.M. (1983) Overlooking the incongruent: Categorization biases in the identification of political statements. *Journal of Personality and Social Psychology*, 45, 978–996.

JOHNSON, M. (1996) Models of disability. *The Psychologist*, 9, 205–210.

JOHNSON, R. (1997) This is not my beautiful wife ... *New Scientist*, 22 March, 19.

JOHNSON, R.D. & DOWNING, L.E. (1979) Deindividuation and valence of cues: Effects on prosocial and antisocial behaviour. *Journal of Personality and Social Psychology*, 37, 1532–1538.

JOHNSON, R.N. (1972) *Aggression in Man and Animals*. Philadelphia: Saunders.

JOHNSON, T.J., FEIGENBAUM, R. & WEIBY, M. (1964) Some determinants and consequences of the teacher's perception of causation. *Journal of Experimental Psychology*, 55, 237–246.

JOHNSON-LAIRD, P.N., HERRMAN, D.J. & CHAFFIN, R. (1984) Only connections: A critique of semantic networks. *Psychological Bulletin*, 96, 292–315.

JOHNSTON, L. (1996) Move to outlaw electro therapy. *The Observer*, 12 December, 14.

JOHNSTON, W.A. & DARK, V.J. (1986) Selective attention. *Annual Review of Psychology*, 37, 43–75.

JOHNSTON, W.A. & HEINZ, S.P. (1978) Flexibility and capacity demands of attention. *Journal of Experimental Psychology*: General, 107, 420–435.

JOHNSTON, W.A. & HEINZ, S.P. (1979) Depth of non-target processing in an attention task. *Journal of Experimental Psychology*, 5, 168–175.

JOHNSTON, W.A. & WILSON, J. (1980) Perceptual processing of non-targets in an attention task. *Memory and Cognition*, 8, 372–377.

JONES, E.E. & DAVIS, K.E. (1965) From acts to dispositions: The attribution process in person perception. In L. Berkowitz (Ed.) *Advances in Experimental Social Psychology*, Volume 2. New York: Academic Press.

JONES, E.E., DAVIS, K.E. & GERGEN, K. (1961) Role playing variations and their informational value for person perception. *Journal of Abnormal and Social Psychology*, 63, 302–310.

JONES, E.E. & NISBETT, R.E. (1971) *The Actor and the Observer: Divergent Perceptions of the Causes of Behaviour*. Morristown, NJ: General Learning Press.

JONES, K.L., SMITH, D.W., ULLELAND, C.N. & STREISSGUTH, A. (1973) Patterns of malformation in offspring of chronic alcoholic mothers. *Lancet*, 1, 1267–1271.

JONES, M. C. (1924) The elimination of children's fears. *Journal of Experimental Psychology*, 7, 382–390.

JONES, M.C. (1925) A laboratory study of fear: The case of Peter. *Pedagogical Seminary*, 31, 308–315.

JONES, W. & ANDERSON, J. (1987) Short- and long-term memory retrieval: A comparison of the effects of information load and relatedness. *Journal of Experimental Psychology: General*, 116, 137–153.

JOSEPH, S., YULE, W., WILLIAMS, R. & HODGKSINSON, P. (1993) Increased substance use in survivors of the Herald of Free Enterprise. *British Journal of Medical Psychology*, 66, 185–192.

JOUVET, M. (1967) Mechanisms of the states of sleep: A neuropharmacological approach. *Research Publications of the Association for the Research in Nervous and Mental Diseases*, 45, 86–126.

JOUVET, M. (1983) Hypnogenic indolamine-dependent factors and paradoxical sleep rebound. In Monnier, E. & Meulders, A. (Eds) *Functions of the Nervous System*, Volume 4: *Psychoneurobiology*. New York: Elsevier.

JOYNSON, R.B. (1980) Models of man: 1879–1979. In A.J. Chapman & D.M. Jones (Eds) *Models of Man*. Leicester: British Psychological Society.

JUDD, C.M. & PARK, B. (1988) Out-group homogeneity: Judgements of variability at the individual and group levels. *Journal of Personality and Social Psychology*, 54, 778–788.

JUDD, J (1997) Working mothers need not feel guilty. *Independent on Sunday*, 27 November, 5.

JUEL-NIELSEN, N. (1965) Individual and environment: A psychiatric and psychological investigation of monozygous twins raised apart. *Acta Psychiatrica et Neurologica Scandinavica*, (Suppl. 183).

JUST, M.A. & CARPENTER, P.A. (1980) A theory of reading: From eye fixations to comprehension. *Psychological Review*, 87, 329–354.

JUST, M.A. & CARPENTER, P.A. (1984) Eye movements and reading comprehension. In D.E. Kieras & M.A. Just (Eds) *New Methods in Reading Comprehension Research*. Hillsdale, NJ: Erlbaum.

JUST, M.A. & CARPENTER, P.A. (1992) A capacity theory of comprehension: Individual differences in working memory. *Psychological Review*, 99, 122–149.

KADUSHIN, A. (1970) *Adopting Older Children*. New York: Columbia University Press.

KAGAN, J. (1984) *The Nature of the Child*. New York: Basic Books.

KAGAN, J. (1989) *Unstable Ideas: Temperament, Cognition and Self*. Cambridge, MA: Harvard University Press.

KAGAN, J., KEARSLEY, R. & ZELAGO, P. (1978) *Infancy: Its Place in Human Development*. Cambridge, MA: Harvard University Press.

KAGAN, J., KEARSLEY, R.B. & ZELAZO, P. (1980) *Infancy: Its place in Human Development* (2nd edition). Cambridge, MA: Harvard University Press.

KAGAN, J. & KLEIN, R.E. (1973) Cross-cultural perspectives on early development. *American Psychologist*, 28, 947–961.

KAHNEMAN, D. (1973) *Attention and Effort*. Englewood Cliffs, NJ: Prentice-Hall.

KAHNEMAN, D. & HENIK, A. (1979) Perceptual organisation and attention. In M. Kubovy & J.R. Pomerantz (Eds) *Perceptual Organisation*. Hillsdale, NJ: Erlbaum.

KAHNEMAN, D. & TVERSKY, A. (1984) Changing views of attention and automaticity. In R. Parasuraman, D.R. Davies & J. Beatty (Eds) *Varieties of Attention*. New York: Academic Press.

KAIL, R.V. & NIPPOLD, M.A. (1984) Unrestrained retrieval from semantic memory. *Child Development*, 55, 944–951.

KALAT, J.W. (1984) *Biological Psychology* (2nd edition). Belmont, CA: Wadsworth.

KALES, A., KALES, J.D. & BIXLER, E.O. (1974) Insomnia: An approach to management and treatment. *Psychiatric Annals*, 4, 28–44.

KALINOWSKY, L. (1975) Psychosurgery. In A. Freedman, H. Kaplan & B. Sadock (Eds) *Comprehensive Textbook of Psychiatry*. Baltimore: Williams & Wilkins.

KALISH, R.A. (1982) *Late Adulthood: Perspectives on Human Development*. Monterey, CA: Brooks-Cole.

KALNINS, I.V. & BRUNER, J.S. (1973) The co-ordination of visual observation and instrumental behaviour in early infancy. *Perception*, 2, 307–314.

KAMIN, L.J. (1974) *The Science and Politics of IQ*. Harmondsworth: Penguin.

KAMINER, H. & LAVIE, P. (1991) Sleep and dreaming in Holocaust survivors: Dramatic decrease in dream recall in well-adjusted survivors. *Journal of Nervous and Mental Diseases*, 179, 664–669.

KANNER, L. (1943) Autistic disturbances of affective content. *Nervous Child*, 2, 217–240.

KANNER, L. & EISENBERG, L. (1955) Notes on the follow-up studies of autistic children. In P. Hoch & J. Zubin (Eds) *Psychopathology of Childhood*. New York: Grune & Stratton.

KANIZSA, A. (1976) Subjective contours. *Scientific American*, 234, 48–52.

KAPLAN, A. & WOODSIDE, D. (1987) Biological aspects of anorexia nervosa and bulimia nervosa. *Journal of Consulting and Clinical Psychology*, 55, 645–653.

KARLINS, M., COFFMAN, T.L. & WALTERS, G. (1969) On the fading of social stereotypes: Studies in three generations of college students. *Journal of Personality and Social Psychology*, 13, 1–16.

KASTENBAUM, R. (1979) *Growing Old – Years of Fulfilment*. London: Harper & Row.

KATONA, G. (1940) *Organising and Memorising*. New York: Columbia University Press.

KATZ, D. & BRALY, K. (1933) Racial stereotypes of one hundred college students. *Journal of Abnormal and Social Psychology*, 28, 280–290.

KAUFMAN, J. & ZIGLER, E. (1987) Do abused children become abused parents? *American Journal of Orthopsychiatry*, 57, 186–192.

KAUSHALL, P., ZETIN, M. & SQUIRE, L. (1981) A psychological study of chronic, circumscribed amnesia: Detailed report of a noted case. *Journal of Nervous and Mental Disorders*, 169, 383–389.

KAY, R.W. (1994) Geomagnetic storms: Association with incidence of depression as measured by hospital admission. *British Journal of Psychiatry*, 164, 403–409.

KAYE, W.H., WELTZIN, T.E. & HSU, L.G. (1993) Relationship between anorexia nervosa and obsessive and compulsive behaviours. *Psychiatric Annals*, 23, 365–373.

KEESEY, R.E. & POWLEY, T.L. (1975) Hypothalamic regulation of body weight. *American Scientist*, 63, 558–565.

KELLEY, H.H. (1967) Attribution theory in social psychology. In D. Levine (Ed.) *Nebraska Symposium on Motivation,* Volume 15. Lincoln, NE: Nebraska University Press.

KELLEY, H.H. (1972) Causal schemata and the attribution process. In E.E. Jones, D.E. Kanouse, H.H. Kelley, S. Valins & B. Weiner (Eds) *Attribution: Perceiving the Causes of Behaviour.* Morristown, NJ: General Learning Press.

KELLEY, H.H. (1983) Perceived causal structures. In J.M.F. Jaspars, F.D. Fincham & M. Hewstone (Eds) *Attribution Theory and Research: Conceptual, Developmental and Social Dimensions.* London: Academic Press.

KELMAN, H. & LAWRENCE, L. (1972) Assignment of responsibility in the case of Lt. Calley: Preliminary report on a national survey. *Journal of Social Issues*, 28, 177–212.

KELSOE, J.R., GINNS, E.I., EGELAND, J.A. & GERHARD, D.S. (1989) Re-evaluation of the linkage relationship between chromosome 11 loci and the gene for bipolar disorder in the Old Order Amish. *Nature*, 342, 238–243.

KEMPLER, W. (1973) Gestalt therapy. In R. Corsini (Ed.) *Current Psychotherapies.* Itasca, ILL: Peacock.

KENDELL, R.E. (1975) *The Role of Diagnosis in Psychiatry.* Oxford: Blackwell.

KENDLER, K.S., McLEAN, C., NEALE, M., KESSLER, R., HEATH, A. & EAVES, L. (1991) The genetic epidemiology of bulimia nervosa. *American Journal of Psychiatry*, 148, 1627–1637.

KENNEDY, D. (1997) Anorexia is linked to brain deficiency. *The Times*, 14 April, 5.

KENRICK, D.T. (1994) Evolutionary social psychology: From sexual selection to social cognition. *Advances in Experimental Social Psychology*, 26, 75–121.

KENT, G. (1995) Impairment, disability and psychological wellbeing. *The Psychologist*, 8, 412–413.

KEPPEL, G. & UNDERWOOD, B.J. (1962) Proactive inhibition in short-term retention of single items. *Journal of Verbal Learning and Verbal Behaviour*, 1, 153–161.

KERCKHOFF, A.C. (1974) The social context of interpersonal attraction. In T.L. Huston (Ed.) *Foundations of Interpersonal Attraction.* New York: Academic Press.

KERCKHOFF, A.C. & DAVIS, K.E. (1962) Value consensus and need complementarity in mate selection. *American Sociological Review*, 27, 295–303.

KERMIS, M.D. (1984) *The Psychology of Human Ageing.* Boston: Allyn & Bacon.

KERTESZ, A. (1979) Anatomy of jargon. In Brown, J. (Ed.) *Jargonapahasia.* New York: Academic Press.

KESSLER, R.C. & ESSEX, M. (1982) Marital status and depression: The importance of coping resources. *Social Forces*, 61, 484–507.

KETY, S.S. (1974) From rationalisation to reason. *American Journal of Psychiatry*, 131, 957–963.

KETY, S.S. (1975) Biochemistry of the major psychoses. In A. Freedman, H. Kaplan & B. Sadock (Eds) *Comprehensive Textbook of Psychiatry.* Baltimore: Williams & Wilkins.

KETY, S.S., ROSENTHAL, D., WENDER, P.H. & SCHULSINGER, F. (1968) The types and prevalence of mental illness in the biological and adoptive families of adopted schizophrenics. In D. Rosenthal & S.S. Kety (Eds) *The Transmission of Schizophrenia.* Elmsford, NY: Pergamon Press.

KIESLER, D.J. (1966) Some myths of psychotherapy research and the search for a paradigm. *Psychological Bulletin*, 65, 110–136.

KILHAM, W. & MANN, L. (1974) Level of destructive obedience as a function of transmitter and executant roles in the Milgram obedience paradigm. *Journal of Personality and Social Psychology*, 29, 696–702.

KIMBLE, D.P. (1988) *Biological Psychology.* New York: Holt, Rinehart & Winston.

KIMURA, D. (1992) Sex differences in the brain. *Scientific American*, 267 (3), September, 80–87 (Special issue).

KING, M.L. & RENTEL, V.M. (1981) Research update: Conveying meaning in written texts. *Language Arts*, 58, 721–728.

KINGSTON, P. (1996) Worthy cause or parental conspiracy? *Guardian Education*, 21 May, 4–5.

KINNUNEN, T., ZAMANSKY, H.S. & BLOCK, M.L. (1995) Is the hypnotised subject lying? *Journal of Abnormal Psychology*, 103, 184–191.

KINSEY, A.C., POMEROY, W.B. & MARTIN, C.E. (1948) *Sexual Behaviour in the Human Male.* Philadelphia: W.B. Saunders.

KIPPER, D. (1992) Psychodrama: Group therapy through role playing. *International Journal of Group Psychotherapy*, 42, 495–521.

KIRKPATRICK, S.A. & LOCKE, E.A. (1991) Leadership: Do traits matter? *Academy of Management Executives*, 5, 48–60.

KIRSCH, I. & COUNCIL, J.R. (1992) Situational and personality correlates of hypnotic responsiveness. In E. Fromm & M.R. Nash (Eds) *Contemporary Hypnosis Research.* New York: Guildford Press.

KITZINGER, C. & COYLE, A. (1995) Lesbian and gay couples: Speaking of difference. *The Psychologist*, 8, 64–69.

KLANING, U., MORTENSEN, P.B. & KYVIK, K.D. (1996) Increased occurrence of schizophrenia and other psychiatric illnesses among twins. *British Journal of Psychiatry*, 168, 688–692.

KLAUS, H.M. & KENNELL, J.H. (1976) *Maternal Infant Bonding.* St Louis: Mosby.

KLEBANOFF, L.D. (1959) A comparison of parental attitudes of mothers of schizophrenics, brain injured and normal children. *American Journal of Psychiatry*, 24, 445–454.

KLEINER, K.A. (1987) Amplitude and phase spectra as indices of infants' pattern preference. *Infant Behaviour and Development*, 10, 49–59.

KLEITMAN, N. (1963) *Sleep and Wakefulness* (2nd edition). Chicago: University of Chicago Press.

KLINE, P. (1988) *Psychology Exposed.* London: Routledge.

KLINE, P. (1989) Objective tests of Freud's theories. In A.M. Colman and J.G. Beaumont (Eds) *Psychology Survey No.7.* Leicester: British Psychological Society.

KLINE, P. (1995) Personality tests. In S.E. Hampson & A.M. Colman (Eds) *Individual Differences and Personality.* London: Longman.

KLÜVER, H. & BUCY, P. (1937) 'Psychic blindness' and other symptoms following bilateral temporal lobectomy in Rhesus monkeys. *American Journal of Physiology*, San Diego, CA: Edits.

KOBASA, S.C. (1979) Stressful life events, personality, and health: An inquiry into hardiness. *Journal of Personality and Social Psychology*, 37, 1–11.

KOESTLER, A. (1967) *The Ghost in the Machine.* London: Pan.

KOFFKA, K. (1935) *The Principles of Gestalt Psychology.* New York: Harcourt Brace and World.

KOHLBERG, L. (1963) The development of children's orientations toward a moral order: 1. Sequence in the development of moral thought. *Human Development*, 6, 11–33.

KOHLBERG, L. (1969) Stage and sequence: The cognitive developmental approach to socialisation. In D.A. Goslin (Ed.) *Handbook of Socialisation Theory and Research.* Chicago: Rand McNally.

KOHLBERG, L. (1978) Revisions in the theory and practice of moral development. *Directions for Child Development*, 2, 83–88.

KOHLBERG, L. (1984) Essays on Moral Development: *The Psychology of Moral Development,* Volume 2. New York: Harper & Row.

KOHLBERG, L. & ULLIAN, D.Z. (1974) Stages in the development of psychosexual concepts and attitudes. In R.C. Van Wiele (Ed.) *Sex Differences in Behaviour.* New York: Wiley.

KOHLER, I. (1962) Experiments with goggles. *Scientific American*, 206, 67–72.

KÖHLER, W. (1925) *The Mentality of Apes.* New York: Harcourt Brace Jovanovich.

KOHN, M. (1995) In two minds. *The Guardian* Magazine, 5 August, 13–16.

KOLB, L.C. (1987) A neuropsychological hypothesis explaining post-traumatic stress disorders. *American Journal of Psychiatry*, 144, 989–995.

KOLTZ, C. (1983) Scapegoating. *Psychology Today*, December, 68–69.

KOLUCHOVA, J. (1972) Severe deprivation in twins: A case study. *Journal of Child Psychology and Psychiatry*, 13, 107–114.

KOLUCHOVA, J. (1976) The further development of twins after severe and prolonged deprivation: A second report. *Journal of Child Psychology & Psychiatry*, 17, 181–188.

KOTELCHUCK, M. (1976) The infant's relationship to the father: Experimental evidence. In M.E. Lamb (Ed.) *The Role of the Father in Child Development.* New York: Wiley.

KOUKKOU, M. & LEHMAN, D. (1980) Psychophysiologie des Traumens und der Neurosentherapie: Das Zustands-Wechsel Modell, eine Synopsis. *Fortschritte der Neurologie, Psychiatrie unter ihrer Grenzgebiete*, 48, 324–350.

KOVEL, J. (1978) *A Complete Guide to Therapy.* Harmondsworth: Penguin.

KRAEPELIN, E. (1913) *Clinical Psychiatry: A Textbook for Physicians* (translated by A. Diffendorf). New York: Macmillan.

KRANTZ, D. & MANUCK, S. (1984) Acute psychophysiologic reactivity and risk of cardiovascular disease: A review and methodological critique. *Psychological Bulletin*, 96, 435–464.

KREBS, D. & BLACKMAN, R. (1988) *Psychology: A First Encounter*. New York: Harcourt Brace Jovanovich.

KREMER, J.F. & STEPHENS, L. (1983) Attributions and arousal as mediators of mitigation's effect on retaliation. *Journal of Personality and Social Psychology*, 45, 335–343.

KROGER, J. (1985) Separation-individuation and ego identity status in New Zealand university students. *Journal of Youth and Adolescence*, 14, 133–147.

KROGER, J. (1996) *Identity in Adolescence: The Balance between Self and Other* (2nd edition). London: Routledge.

KRUGER, A.C. (1992) The effect of peer and adult-child transactive discussions on moral reasoning. In M. Gauvain & M. Cole (Eds) *Readings on the Development of Children*. New York: W.H. Freeman & Company.

KRUPAT, E. & GARONZIK, R. (1994) Subjects' expectations and the search for alternatives to deception in social psychology. *British Journal of Social Psychology*, 33, 211–222.

KRYSTAL, J.H., KOSTEN, T.R. & SOUTHWICK, S. (1989) Neurobiological aspects of PTSD: A review of clinical and preclinical studies. *Behaviour Therapy*, 20, 177–198.

KÜBLER-ROSS, E. (1969) *On Death and Dying*. London: Tavistock/Routledge.

KUHN, H.H. (1960) Self attitudes by age, sex and professional training. *Sociology Quarterly*, 1, 39–55.

KUHN, H.H. & McPARTLAND, T.S. (1954) An empirical investigation of self attitudes. *American Sociology Review*, 47, 647–652.

KUHN, T.S. (1962) *The Structure of Scientific Revolutions*. Chicago: University of Chicago Press.

KUHN, T.S. (1970) *The Structure of Scientific Revolutions* (2nd edition). Chicago: University of Chicago Press.

KULIK, J.A. & BROWN, R. (1979) Frustration, attribution of blame and aggression. *Journal of Experimental Social Psychology*, 15, 183–194.

KULIK, J.A. & MAHLER, H.I.M. (1989) Stress and affiliation in a hospital setting: Pre-operative roommate preferences. *Personality and Social Psychology Bulletin*, 15, 183–193.

KYLE, J.G. (1981) Reading development in deaf children. *Journal of Research in Reading*, 3, 86–97.

LaBERGE, D. (1983) Spatial extent of attention to letters and words. *Journal of Experimental Psychology: Human Perception and Performance*, 9, 371–379.

LABOUVIE-VIEF, G. (1980) Beyond formal operations: uses and limits of pure logic in life-span development. *Human Development*, 22, 141–161.

LABOV, W. (1970) The logic of non-standard English. In F. Williams (Ed.) *Language and Poverty*. Chicago: Markham.

LABOV, W. (1973) The boundaries of words and their meanings. In C.J.N. Bailey & R.W. Shuy (Eds) *New Ways of Analysing Variations in English*. Washington, DC: Georgetown University Press.

LACHMAN, S.J. (1984) Processes in visual misperception: Illusions for highly structured stimulus material. Paper presented at the 92nd annual convention of the American Psychological Association, Toronto, Canada.

LADD, G.W. & CAIRNS, E. (1996) Children: Ethnic and political violence. *Child Development*, 67, 14–18.

LAKOFF, G. (1987) *Women, Fire and Dangerous Things: What Categories Reveal About The Mind*. Chicago: University of Chicago Press.

LAMB, M.E. (1976) Twelve-month-olds and their parents: Interactions in a laboratory playroom. *Developmental Psychology*, 12, 237–244.

LAMB, M.E., THOMPSON, R.A., GANDER, W. & CHARNOV, E.L. (1985) *Infant-mother Attachment: The Origins and Significance of Individual Differences in Strange Situation Behaviour*. Hillsdale, NJ: Earlbaum.

LAMBERT, W.E., HAMERS, J. & FRASURE-SMITH, N. (1979) *Child Rearing Values*. New York: Praeger.

LAMBERT, W.W., SOLOMON, R.L. & WATSON, P.D. (1949) Reinforcement and extinction as factors in size estimation. *Journal of Experimental Psychology*, 39, 637–641.

LAMBIE, J. (1991) The misuse of Kuhn in psychology. *The Psychologist*, 4 (1), 6–11.

LAND, E.H. (1977) The retinex theory of colour vision. *Scientific American*, 237, 108–128.

LANDIS, C. (1938) Statistical evaluation of psychotherapeutic methods. In S.E. Hinde (Ed.) *Concepts and Problems of Psychotherapy*. London: Heineman.

LANG, K. & LANG, G.E. (1961) *Collective Dynamics*. New York: Thomas Y. Crowell Co.

LANGE, A.J. & JAKUBOWSKI, P. (1976) *Responsible Assertive Behaviour: Cognitive/Behavioural Procedures for Trainers*. Champaign, ILL: Research Press.

LANGLOIS, J. & ROGGMAN, L. (1994) Attractive faces are only average. *Psychological Science*, 1, 115–121.

LANGLOIS, J., ROGGMAN, L., CASEY, R., RITTER, J., RIESER-DANNER, L. & JENKINS, Y. (1987) Infant preferences for attractive faces: Rudiments of a stereotype. *Developmental Psychology*, 22, 363–369.

LANGLOIS, J., ROGGMAN, L. & RISER-DANNER, L. (1990) Infants' differential social responses to attractive and unattractive faces. *Developmental Psychology*, 26, 153–159.

LANSKY, L.M., CRANDALL, V.J., KAGAN, J. & BAKER, C.T. (1961) Sex differences in aggression and its correlates in middle-class adolescents. *Child Development*, 32, 45–58.

LARSEN, K.S. (1974) Conformity in the Asch experiment. *Journal of Social Psychology*, 94, 303–304.

LARSEN, K.S., TRIPLETT, J.S., BRANT, W.D. & LANGENBERG, D. (1979) Collaborator status, subject characteristics and conformity in the Asch paradigm. *Journal of Social Psychology*, 108, 259–263.

LARSEN, R.J. & DIENER, E. (1987) Affect intensity as an individual difference characteristic: A review. *Journal of Research in Personality*, 21, 1039.

LASHLEY, K. (1926) Studies of cerebral function in learning: VII The relation between cerebral mass, learning and retention. *Journal of Comparative Neurology*, 41, 1–48.

LASK, B. & BRYANT-WAUGH, R. (1992) Childhood onset of anorexia nervosa and related eating disorders. *Journal of Child Psychology and Psychiatry*, 3, 281–300.

LATANÉ, B. & DARLEY, J.M. (1968) Group inhibitions of bystander intervention in emergencies. *Journal of Personality and Social Psychology*, 10, 215–221.

LATANÉ, B., NIDA, S. & WILLIAMS, D.W. (1981) The effects of group size on helping behaviour. In J.P. Rushton & R.M. Sorrentino (Eds) *Altruism and Helping Behaviour*. Hillsdale, NJ: Erlbaum.

LATANÉ, B. & RODIN, J. (1969) A lady in distress: Inhibiting effects of friends and strangers on bystander intervention. *Journal of Experimental Social Psychology*, 5, 189–202.

LAU, R.R. & RUSSELL, D. (1980) Attributions in the sports pages. *Journal of Personality and Social Psychology*, 39, 29–38.

LAUGHLIN, H.P. (1967) *The Neuroses*. Washington, DC: Butterworth.

LAURANCE, J. (1993) Is psychotherapy all in the mind? *The Times*, 15 April, 7.

LAURANCE, J. (1996) Psychologists extol the benefits of divorce for all the family. *The Times*, 16 September, 6.

LAURENCE, C. (1997) Cheer up, son – take Prozac. *The Daily Telegraph*, 4 December, 27.

LAWSON, E.A. (1966) Decisions concerning the rejected channel. *Journal of Experimental Psychology*, 18, 260–265.

LAZARUS, R.S. (1982) Thoughts on the relations between emotion and cognition. *American Psychologist*, 37, 1019–1024.

LAZARUS, R.S. & FOLKMAN, S. (1984) *Stress, Appraisal, and Coping*. New York: Springer.

LE BON, G. (1879) *The Crowd: A Study of the Popular Mind*. London: Unwin.

LE FANU, J. (1994) May I examine your dream? *The Times*, 13 January, 15.

LEA, M. & SPEARS, R. (1995) Love at first byte: Relationships conducted over electronic systems. In J.T. Wood & S. Duck (Eds) *Understanding Relationship Processes 6: Understudied Relationships: Off the Beaten Track*. Thousand Oaks, CA: Sage.

LEA, S.E.G. (1984) *Instinct, Environment and Behaviour*. London: Methuen.

LEACH, M.P. (1993) Should parents hit their children? *The Psychologist*, 6, 216–220.

LE DOUX, J.E. (1989) Cognitive-emotional interactions in the brain. *Cognition and Emotion*, 3, 267–289.

LEE, A. (1996) St. Helena study shows benefit of television. *The Times*, 3 August, 7.

LEE, A.M. & HUMPHREY, N.D. (1943) *Race Riot*. New York: Holt, Rinehart & Winston.

LEE, L. (1984) Sequences in separation: A framework for investigating endings of the personal (romantic) relationship. *Journal of Social and Personal Relationships,* 1, 49–74.

LEE, S., HSU, L.K.G. & WING, Y.K. (1992) Bulimia nervosa in Hong Kong Chinese patients. *British Journal of Psychiatry,* 161, 545–551.

LEFKOWITZ, M.M., ERON, L.D., WALDER, L.O. & HUESMANN, L.R. (1972) Television violence and child aggression: A follow-up study. In G.A. Comstock & E.A. Rubenstein (Eds) *Television and Social Behaviour,* Volume 3. *Television and Adolescent Aggressiveness.* Washington, DC: US Government Printing Office.

LeFRANCOIS, G.R. (1983) *Psychology.* Belmont, CA: Wadsworth Publishing Co.

LeFRANCOIS, G.R. (1986) *Of Children: An Introduction to Child Development.* Belmont, CA: Wadsworth.

LEGGE, D. (1975) *An Introduction to Psychological Science.* London: Methuen.

LEMONICK, M.D. (1997) The Mood Molecule. *Time,* September 29, 67–73.

LENNEBERG, E.H. (1967) *Biological Foundations of Language.* New York: Wiley.

LEON, G.R. (1990) *Case Histories of Psychopathology.* Boston: Allyn & Bacon.

LEPPER, M.R., GREENE, D., & NISBETT, R.E. (1973) Undermining children's intrinsic interest with extrinsic reward: A test of the overjustification hypothesis. *Journal of Personality & Social Psychology,* 28, 129-137.

LERNER, R.M. & SHEA, J.A. (1982) Social behaviour in adolescence. In B.B. Wolman (Ed.) Handbook of *Developmental Psychology.* Englewood Cliffs, NJ: Prentice-Hall.

LEVIN, I.P. & GAETH, G.J. (1988) How consumers are affected by the framing of attribution information before and after consuming the product. *Journal of Consumer Research,* 15, 374–378.

LEVINE, J.D., GORDON, N.C. & FIELDS, H.L. (1979) Naloxone dose dependently produces analgesia and hyperalgesia in post-operative pain. *Nature,* 278, 740–741.

LEVINSON, D.J. (1986) A conception of adult development. *American Psychologist,* 41, 3–13.

LEVINSON, D.J., DARROW, D.N., KLEIN, E.B., LEVINSON, M.H. & McKEE, B. (1978) *The Seasons of a Man's Life.* New York: A.A. Knopf.

LEVITSKY, A. & PERLS, F.S. (1970) The rules and games of Gestalt therapy. In J. Fagan & I. Shephard (Eds) *Gestalt Therapy Now.* Palo Alto, CA: Science and Behaviour Books.

LEVY, B. & LANGER, E. (1994) Ageing free from negative stereotypes: Successful memory in China and among the American deaf. *Journal of Personality and Social Psychology,* 66, 989–997.

LEVY, J. (1983) Language, cognition and the right hemisphere: A response to Gazzaniga. *American Psychologist,* 38, 538–541.

LEVY, J., TREVARTHEN, C. & SPERRY, R.W. (1972) Perception of bilateral chimeric figures following hemispheric disconnection. *Brain,* 95, 61–78.

LEVY, R. (1996) Improving memory in old age through implicit self-stereotyping. *Journal of Personality & Social Psychology,* 71, 1092–1107.

LEVY, S. (1983) Death and dying: Behavioural and social factors that contribute to the process. In Burish, T. & Bradley, L. (Eds) *Coping with Chronic Illness: Research and Application.* New York: Academic Press.

LEWIN, K., LIPPITT, R. & WHITE, R. (1939) Patterns of aggressive behaviour in experimentally created 'social climates'. *Journal of Social Psychology,* 10, 271–299.

LEWINSOHN, P.M. (1974) A behavioural approach to depression. In R. Friedman & M. Katz (Eds) *The Psychology of Depression: Contemporary Theory and Research.* Washington, DC: Winston/Wiley.

LEWINSOHN, P.M. & HOBERMAN, H.M. (1982) Depression. In A.S. Bellack, M. Hersen & A.E. Kazdin (Eds) *International Handbook of Behaviour Modification and Therapy.* New York: Plenum.

LEWINSOHN, P.M., HOPS, H. & ROBERTS, R.E. (1993) Adolescent psychopathology: I. Prevalence and incidence of depression and other DSM-3-R disorders in high school students. *Journal of Abnormal Psychology,* 102, 133–144.

LEWIS, C. (1981) The effects of parental firm control: A reinterpretation of findings. *Psychological Bulletin,* 90, 547–563.

LEWIS, M. & BROOKS-GUNN, J. (1979) *Social Cognition and the Acquisition of Self.* New York: Plenum.

LEWIS, M. & ROWE, D. (1994) Good news. Bad news. *The Psychologist,* 7, 157–160.

LEWIS, S. (1994) ICD-10: A neuropsychiatrist's nightmare? *British Journal of Psychiatry,* 164, 157–158.

LEWIS, V. (1987) *Development and Handicap.* Oxford: Blackwell.

LEWONTIN, R. (1976) Race and intelligence. In N.J. Block & G. Dworkin (Eds) *The IQ Controversy: Critical Readings.* New York: Pantheon.

LEY, P. (1988) *Communicating with Patients: Improving Communication, Satisfaction and Compliance.* London: Chapman Hall.

LEY, R.G. & BRYDEN, M.P. (1979) Hemispheric differences in processing emotions and faces. *Brain and Language,* 7, 127–138.

LEYENS, J.P. & CODOL, J.P. (1988) Social cognition. In M. Hewstone, W. Stroebe, J.P. Codol & G.M. Stephenson (Eds) *Introduction to Social Psychology.* Oxford: Blackwell.

LEYENS, J.P. & DARDENNE, B. (1996) Basic concepts and approaches in social cognition. In M. Hewstone, W. Stroebe & G.M. Stephenson (Eds) *Introduction to Social Psychology* (2nd edition). Oxford: Blackwell.

LIDZ, T. (1973) Commentary on 'A critical review of recent adoption, twin and family studies of schizophrenia: Behavioural genetics perspectives'. *Schizophrenia Bulletin,* 2, 402–412.

LIEBERMAN, M.A. (1993) Bereavement self-help groups: Review of conceptual and methodological issues. In M.S. Stroebe, W. Stroebe & R.O. Hansson (Eds) *Handbook of Bereavement: Theory, Research and Intervention.* New York: Cambridge University Press.

LIEBERT, R.M. & BARON, R.A. (1972) Some immediate effects of televised violence on children's behaviour. *Developmental Psychology,* 6, 469–475.

LIEBERT, R.M. & SPRAFKIN, J. (1988) *The Early Window: Effects of Television on Children and Youth.* New York: Pergamon Press.

LIGHT, P. (1986) Context, conservation and conversation. In M. Richards & P. Light (Eds) *Children of Social Worlds.* Cambridge: Polity Press.

LIGHT, P., BUCKINGHAM, N. & ROBBINS, A.H. (1979) The conservation task as an interactional setting. *British Journal of Educational Psychology,* 49, 304–310.

LIGHT, P. & GILMOUR, A. (1983) Conservation or conversation? Contextual facilitation of inappropriate conservation judgements. *Journal of Experimental Child Psychology,* 36, 356–363.

LIKERT, R. (1961) *New Patterns of Management.* New York: McGraw-Hill.

LILIENFELD S.D. (1995) *Seeing Both Sides: Classic Controversies in Abnormal Psychology.* Pacific Grove: Brooks/Cole.

LIMBER, J. (1977) Language in child and chimp. *American Psychologist,* 32, 280–295.

LINDSAY, P.H. & NORMAN, D.A. (1977) *Human Information Processing: An Introduction to Psychology* (2nd edition). New York: Academic Press.

LINN, K.-M., MILLER, M.H., POLAND, R.E., NUCCIO, I. & YAMAGUCHI, M. (1991) Ethnicity and family involvement in the treatment of schizophrenic patients. *Journal of Nervous and Mental Disorder,* 179, 631–633.

LINN, R.L. (1982) Admissions testing on trial. *American Psychologist,* 29, 279–291.

LINVILLE, P.W., FISCHER, G.W. & SALOVEY, P. (1989) Perceived distributions of the characteristics of in-group and out-group members: Empirical evidence and a computer simulation. *Journal of Personality and Social Psychology,* 57, 165–188.

LIPPMANN, W. (1922) *Public Opinion.* New York: Harcourt.

LITTLEWOOD, R. (1992) Psychiatric diagnosis and racial bias: Empirical and interpretive approaches. *Social Science and Medicine,* 34, 141–149.

LITTLEWOOD, R. & LIPSEDGE, M. (1989) *Aliens and Alienists: Ethnic Minorities and Psychiatry.* London: Unwin Hyman.

LLEWELLYN-SMITH, J. (1996) Courses for gifted children are often 'a waste of time'. *The Sunday Telegraph,* 8 September, 5.

LLOYD, P., MAYES, A., MANSTEAD, A.S.R., MEUDELL, P.R. & WAGNER, H.L. (1984) *Introduction to Psychology – An Integrated Approach.* London: Fontana.

LOCKE, J. (1690) *An Essay Concerning Human Understanding.* New York: Mendon (reprinted, 1964).

LOFTUS, E.F. (1975) Leading questions and the eyewitness report. *Cognitive Psychology,* 1, 560–572.

LOFTUS, E.F. (1979) Reactions to blatantly contradictory information. *Memory and Cognition,* 7, 368–374.

LOFTUS, E.F. (1980) *Memory. Reading,* MA: Addison and Wesley.

LOFTUS, E.F. (1997) Creating False Memories. *Scientific American,* September 50–55.

LOFTUS, E.F. & LOFTUS, G. (1980) On the permanence of stored information in the human brain. *American Psychologist,* 35, 409–420.

LOFTUS, E.F. & PALMER, J.C. (1974) Reconstruction of automobile destruction: An example of the interaction between language and memory. *Journal of Verbal Learning and Verbal Behaviour,* 13, 585–589.

LOFTUS, E.F. & ZANNI, G. (1975) Eyewitness testimony: The influence of wording on a question. *Bulletin of the Psychonomic Society* 5, 86–88.

LOFTUS, G. (1974) Reconstructing memory: The incredible eyewitness. *Psychology Today*, December, 116–119.

LOFTUS, G. & LOFTUS, E.F. (1983) *Mind at Play: The Psychology of Video Games*. New York: Basic Books.

LOGAN, G.D. (1988) Toward an instance theory of automatisation. *Psychological Review*, 95, 492–527.

LONDON, P. (1964) *The Modes and Morals of Psychotherapy*. New York: Holt, Rinehart & Winston.

LOOMIS, A.L., HARVEY, E.N. & HOBART, A. (1937) Cerebral states during sleep as studied by human brain potentials. *Journal of Experimental Psychology*, 21, 127–144.

LOPATA, H.Z. (1988) Support systems of American urban widowhood. *Journal of Social Issues*, 44, 113–128.

LORD, B.J., KING, M.G. & PFISTER, H.P. (1976) Chemical sympathectomy and two-way escape and avoidance learning in the rat. *Journal of Comparative and Physiological Psychology*, 90, 303–316.

LORD, C.G., ROSS, L. & LEPPER, M.R. (1979) Biased assimilation and attitude polarisation: The effects of prior theories on subsequently considered evidence. *Journal of Personality and Social Psychology*, 37, 2098–2107.

LORENZ, K.Z. (1935) The companion in the bird's world. *Auk*, 54, 245–273.

LORENZ, K.Z. (1966) *On Aggression*. London: Methuen.

LOVAAS, O.I. (1977) *The Autistic Child: Language Development Through Behaviour Modification*. New York: Halste Press.

LOVAAS, O.I. (1978) Parents as therapists. In M. Rutter & E. Schopler (Eds) *Autism: A Reappraisal of Concepts and Treatments*. New York: Plenum.

LOVAAS, O.I. (1987) Behavioural treatment and normal educational and intellectual functioning in young autistic children. *Journal of Consulting and Clinical Psychology*, 55, 3–9.

LOWE, G. (1994) The mating game. *The Psychologist*, 7, 225.

LUBORSKY, L. (1984) *Principles of Psychoanalytic Psychotherapies: A Manual for Supportive–Expressive Treatment*. New York: Basic Books.

LUBORSKY, L., SINGER, B. & LUBORSKY, L. (1975) Comparative studies of psychotherapies: Is it true that 'everyone has won and all must have prizes'? *Archives of General Psychiatry*, 32, 49–62.

LUCE, G.G. (1971) *Body Time: The Natural Rhythms of the Body*. St. Albans: Paladin.

LUCE, G.G. & SEGAL, J. (1966) *Sleep*. New York: Coward, McCann & Geoghegan.

LUCE, T.S. (1974) Blacks, whites and yellows, they all look alike to me. *Psychology Today*, November, 105–6, 108.

LUCHINS, A.S. (1942) Mechanisation in problem-solving: The effect of Einstellung. *Psychological Monographs*, 54 (Whole No. 248).

LUCHINS, A.S. & LUCHINS, E.H. (1959) *Rigidity of Behaviour*. Eugene, OR: University of Oregon Press.

LUGARESSI, E., MEDORI, R., MONTAGNA, P., BARUZZI, A., CORTELLI, P., LUGARESSI, A., TINUPER, A., ZUCCONI, M. & GAMBETTI, P. (1986) Fatal familial insomnia and dysautonomia in the selective degeneration of thalamic nuclei. *New England Journal of Medicine*, 315, 997–1003.

LUMSDEN, C.J. & WILSON, E.O. (1983) *Promethean Fire*. Cambridge, MA: Harvard University Press.

LURIA, A.R. (1968) *The Mind of a Mnemonist*. New York: Basic Books.

LURIA, A.R. (1973) *The Working Brain: An Introduction to Neuropsychology* (translated by B. Haigh). New York: Basic Books.

LURIA, A.R. (1980) *Higher Cortical Functions in Man* (2nd edition, revised). New York: Basic Books.

LURIA, A.R. (1987) Reductionism. In R.L. Gregory (Ed.) *The Oxford Companion to the Mind*. Oxford: Oxford University Press.

LURIA, A.R. & YUDOVICH, F.I. (1971) *Speech and the Development of Mental Processes in the Child*. Harmondsworth: Penguin.

LYDIARD, R.B., BREWERTON, T.D., FOSSEY, M.D., LARAIA, M.T., STUART, G., BEINFIELD, M.C. & BALLENGER, J.C. (1993) CSF cholecystokinin octapeptide in patients with bulimia nervosa and in comparison with normal subjects. *American Journal of Psychiatry*, 150, 1099–1101.

LYKKEN, D.T. & TELLEGREN, A. (1993) Is human mating adventitious or the result of lawful choice?: A twin study of mate selection. *Journal of Personality and Social Psychology*, 65, 56–68.

LYONS, J. (1970) *Chomsky*. London: Fontana.

LYTTON, H. & ROMNEY, D.M. (1991) Parents' differential socialisation of boys and girls: A meta-analysis. *Psychological Bulletin*, 109, 267–296.

MACCOBY, E.E. (1980) *Social Development – Psychological Growth and the Parent-Child Relationship*. New York: Harcourt Brace Jovanovich.

MACCOBY, E.E. & JACKLIN, C.N. (1974) *The Psychology of Sex Differences*. Stanford, CA: Stanford University Press.

MACCOBY, E.E. & MARTIN, J.A. (1983) Socialisation in the context of the family: Parent-child interaction. In E.M. Hetherington (Ed.) *Handbook of Child Psychology: Socialisation, Personality and Social Development*, Volume 20. Orlando, FLA: Academic Press.

MacDONALD, V. (1996) Drug blunder resurfaces in children. *The Sunday Telegraph*, 15 December, 5.

MACKAY, D. (1975) *Clinical Psychology: Theory and Therapy*. London: Methuen.

MACKAY, D.C. & NEWBIGGING, P.L. (1977) The Poggendorf and its variants do arouse the same perceptual processes. *Perception and Psychophysics*, 21, 26–32.

MACKAY, D.G. (1973) Aspects of the theory of comprehension, memory and attention. *Quarterly Journal of Experimental Psychology*, 25, 22–40.

MACKINTOSH, N.J. (1978) Cognitive or associative theories of conditioning: implications of an analysis of blocking. In S.H. Hulse, M. Fowler, & W.K. Honig (Eds) *Cognitive processes in animal behaviour*. Hillsdale, NJ: Lawrence Erlbaum.

MACKINTOSH, N.J. (1995) Classical and operant conditioning. In N.J. Mackintosh & A.M. Colman (Eds) *Learning and Skills*. London: Longman.

MACLEAN, P.D. (1949) Psychosomatic disease and the 'visceral brain': Recent developments bearing on the Papez theory of emotion. *Psychosomatic Medicine*, 11, 338–353.

MACLEAN, P.D. (1973) *A Triune Concept of Brain and Behaviour*. Toronto: University of Toronto Press.

MACLEAN, P.D. (1982) On the origin and progressive evolution of the triune brain. In E. Armstrong & D. Falk (Eds) *Primate Brain Evolution*. New York: Plenum Press.

MacPHILLAMY, D. & LEWINSOHN, P.M. (1974) Depression as a function of levels of desired and obtained pleasure. *Journal of Abnormal Psychology*, 83, 651–657.

MADDOX, G.L. (1964) Disengagement theory: A critical evaluation. *The Gerontologist*, 4, 80–83.

MAHER, B. (1968) The shattered language of schizophrenia. *Psychology Today*, 30ff.

MAIER, N.R.F. (1931) Reasoning in humans II: The solution of a problem and its appearance in consciousness. *Journal of Comparative Psychology*, 12, 181–194.

MAIN, M. (1991) Metacognitive knowledge, metacognitive monitoring, and singular (coherent) versus multiple (incoherent) models of attachment: Findings and directions for future research. In C.M. Murray Parkes, J.M. Stephenson-Hinde & P. Marris (Eds) *Attachment Across the Life-Cycle*. London: Routledge.

MAJOR, B. (1980) Information acquisition and attribution processes. *Journal of Personality and Social Psychology*, 39, 1010–1023.

MALAN, D.H., HEATH, E.S., BACAL, H.A. & BALFOUR, F.H.G. (1975) Psychodynamic changes in untreated neurotic patients. *Archives of General Psychiatry*, 32, 110–126.

MALINOWSKI, B. (1929) *The Sexual Life of Savages*. New York: Harcourt Brace Jovanovich.

MALLICK, S.K. & McCANDLESS, B.R. (1966) A study of catharsis of aggression. *Journal of Personality and Social Psychology*, 4, 591–596.

MALMSTROM, P. & SILVA, M. (1986) Twin talk: Manifestations of twin status in the speech of toddlers. *Journal of Child Language*, 13, 293–304.

MANDLER, G. (1962) Emotion. In Brown, R. (Ed.) *New Directions in Psychology*. New York: Holt, Rinehart & Winston.

MANDLER, G. (1967) Organisation and memory. In K.W. Spence & J.T. Spence (Eds) *The Psychology of Learning and Motivation*, Volume 1. New York: Academic Press.

MANN, L. (1969) *Social Psychology*. New York: Wiley.

MANN, L. (1981) The baiting crowd in episodes of threatened suicide. *Journal of Personality and Social Psychology*, 41, 703–709.

MANSTEAD, A.S.R. & SEMIN, G.R. (1980) Social facilitation effects: Mere enhancement of dominant responses? *British Journal of Social and Clinical Psychology*, 19, 19–36.

MAPSTONE, E. (1991) Special issue on animal experimentation. *The Psychologist*, 4 (5), 195.

MARANON, G. (1924) Contribution à l'etude de l'action emotive de l'adrenaline. *Revue Française d'Endocrinologie*, 2, 301–325.

MARATSOS, M.P. (1983) Some current issues in the study of the acquisition of grammar. In J.H. Flavell & E.M. Markman (Eds) Cognitive Development, Volume 3. In P.H. Mussen (Ed.) *Handbook of Child Psychology* (4th edition). New York: Wiley.

MARCIA, J.E. (1980) Identity in adolescence. In J. Adelson (Ed.) *Handbook of Adolescent Psychology*. New York: Wiley.

MARCUS, D.E. & OVERTON, W.F. (1978) The development of cognitive gender constancy and sex-role preferences. *Child Development*, 49, 434–444.

MARK, V. & ERVIN, F. (1970) *Violence and the Brain*. New York: Harper & Row.

MARKS, I. (1987) *Fears, Phobias and Rituals*. New York: Oxford University Press.

MARKS, M. & FOLKHARD, S. (1985) Diurnal rhythms in cognitive performance. In J. Nicholson & H. Beloff (Eds) *Psychology Survey 5*. Leicester: British Psychological Society.

MARR, D. (1982) *Vision: A Computational Investigation into the Human Representation and Processing of Visual Information*. San Francisco, CA: W.H. Freeman.

MARR, D. & HILDRETH, E. (1980) Theory of edge detection. *Proceedings of the Royal Society of London, Series B*, 207, 187–217.

MARR, D. & NISHIHARA, K.H. (1978) Representation and recognition of the spatial organisation of three-dimensional shapes. *Proceedings of the Royal Society of London, Series B*, 200, 269–294.

MARSH, G., FRIEDMAN, M., WELCH, V. & DESBERG, P. (1981) A cognitive-developmental theory of language acquisition. In G.E. MacKinnon & T.G. Waller (Eds) *Reading Research: Advances in Theory and Practice*. New York: Academic Press.

MARSHALL, G. & ZIMBARDO, P. (1979) Affective consequences of inadequately explaining physiological arousal. *Journal of Personality and Social Psychology*, 37, 970–988.

MARSLAND, D. (1987) *Education and Growth*. London: Falmer.

MARSLEN-WILSON, W.D. (1984) Function and process in spoken-word recognition: A tutorial review. In H. Bouma & D.G. Bouwhuis (Eds) *Attention and Performance X: Control of Language Processes*. Hillsdale, NJ: Erlbaum.

MARTIN, B. (1975) Parent-child relations. In F.D. Horowitz (Ed.) *Review of Child Development Research*, Volume 4. Chicago: University of Chicago Press.

MARTIN, C.L. (1991) The role of cognition in understanding gender effects. *Advances in Child Development and Behaviour*, 23, 113–149.

MARTIN, S. & KEARNS, A. (1995) Disability and equal opportunities in employment. *The Psychologist*, 8, 398–400.

MARVIN, R.S. (1975) Aspects of the pre-school child's changing conception of his mother. Cited in C.G. Morris (1988) *Psychology: An Introduction* (6th edition). Englewood Cliffs, NJ: Prentice-Hall.

MASLACH, C. (1978) Emotional consequences of arousal without reason. In C.E. Izard (Ed.) *Emotions and Psychopathology*. New York: Plenum Publishing Company.

MASLACH, C., STAPP, J. & SANTEE, R.T. (1985) Individuation: Conceptual analysis and assessment. *Journal of Personality and Social Psychology*, 49, 729–738.

MASLING, J. (1966) Role-related behaviour of the subject and psychologist and its effects upon psychological data. In D. Levine (Ed.) *Nebraska Symposium on Motivation*. Lincoln, Nebraska: University of Nebraska Press.

MASLOW, A. (1954) *Motivation and Personality*. New York: Harper & Row.

MASLOW, A. (1968) *Towards a Psychology of Being* (2nd edition). New York: Van Nostrand Reinhold.

MASON, M.K. (1942) Learning to speak after six and one half years of silence. *Journal of Speech and Hearing Disorders*, 7, 295–304.

MASSARO, D.W. (1989) *Experimental Psychology: An Information Processing Approach*. New York: Harcourt Brace Jovanovich.

MASSON, J. (1988) *Against Therapy: Emotional Tyranny and the Myth of Psychological Healing*. New York: Athaneum.

MASSON, J. (1992) The tyranny of psychotherapy. In W. Dryden & C. Feltham (Eds) *Psychotherapy and its Discontents*. Buckingham: Open University Press.

MATLIN, M. (1989) *Cognition* (2nd edition). Fort Worth, TX: Holt, Rinehart & Winston.

MATTHEWS, R. (1996a) How anti-matter can go straight to a child's head. *The Sunday Telegraph*, 1 December, 16.

MATTHEWS, R. (1996b) Parents blamed for tantrums of Terrible Twos. *The Sunday Telegraph*, 8 September, 3.

MATTHEWS, R. (1997a) Why being a born loser is all in the mind. *The Sunday Telegraph*, 9 March, 16.

MATTHEWS, R. (1997b) Bad news poses health threat to TV audience. *The Sunday Telegraph*, 30 March, 3.

MAUNSELL, J.H.R. & NEWSOME, W.T. (1987) Visual processing in monkey extrastriate cortex. *Annual Review of Neuroscience*, 10, 363–401.

MAURER, D. & SALAPATEK, P. (1976) Developmental changes in the scanning of faces by young infants. *Child Development*, 47, 523–527.

MAY, P.R. (1975) A follow-up study of the treatment of schizophrenia. In R.L. Spitzer & D.F. Klein (Eds) *Evaluation of Psychological Therapies*. Baltimore: The Johns Hopkins University Press.

MAYALL, B. & PETRIE, P. (1983) *Childminding and Day Nurseries: What Kind of Care?* London: Heinemann Educational Books.

MAYER, J. & MARSHALL, N.B. (1956) Specificity of Gold Thioglucose for ventromedial hypothalamic lesions and obesity. *Nature*, 178, 1399–1400.

MAYKOVICH, M.K. (1975) Correlates of racial prejudice. *Journal of Personality and Social Psychology*, 32, 1014–1020.

MAYLOR, E.A. (1994) Ageing and the retrieval of specialised and general knowledge: Performance of ageing masterminds. *British Journal of Psychology*, 85, 105–114.

McARTHUR, L.A. (1972) The how and why of why: Some determinants and consequences of causal attribution. *Journal of Personality and Social Psychology*, 22, 171–193.

McAULIFFE, K. (1987) A drug that lets the world in. *U.S. News & World Report*, 2 February, 66.

McBURNEY, D.H. & COLLINS, V.B. (1984) *Introduction to Sensation and Perception* (2nd edition). Englewood Cliffs, NJ: Prentice-Hall.

McCALL, R.B., APPLEBAUM, M.I. & HOGARTY, P.S. (1973) Developmental changes in mental test performance. *Monographs for the Society of Research in Child Development*, 38, (3, Whole No. 150).

McCANN, J.J. (1987) Retinex theory and colour constancy. In R.L. Gregory (Ed.) *Oxford Companion to the Mind*. Oxford: Oxford University Press.

McCANNE, T.R. & ANDERSON, J.A. (1987) Emotional responding following manipulation of facial feedback. *Journal of Personality and Social Psychology*, 52, 759–768.

McCARTNEY, J. (1996) Yes it hurts … No, it doesn't work. *The Sunday Telegraph*, 8 September, 22.

McCAULEY, C. & STITT, C.L. (1978) An individual and quantitative measure of stereotypes. *Journal of Personality and Social Psychology*, 36, 929–940.

McCLELLAND, D.C. (1958) Methods of measuring human motivation. In J.W. Atkinson (Ed.) *Motives in Fantasy, Action and Society*. Princeton, NJ: Van Nostrand.

McCLELLAND, D.C. & ATKINSON, J.W. (1948) The projective expression of need: I. The effect of different intensities of the hunger drive on perception. *Journal of Psychology*, 25, 205–222.

McCLOSKEY, M. & ZARAGOZA, M. (1985) Misleading information and memory for events: Arguments and evidence against memory impairment hypothesis. *Journal of Experimental Psychology*: General, 114, 3–18.

McCORMICK, L.J. & MAYER, J.D. (1991) Mood-congruent recall and natural mood. Poster presented at the annual meeting of the New England Psychological Association, Portland, ME.

McCROHAN, C. (1996) Synapses: Their roles in learning and memory. *Biological Sciences Review*, 4, 26–29.

McCRYSTAL, C. (1997) Now you can live forever, or at least for a century. *The Observer*, 15 June, 3.

McCUTCHEN, D. & PERFETTI, C. (1982) Coherence and connectedness in the development of discourse production. *Text*, 2, 113–139.

McDONALD, S. & PEARCE, S. (1996) Clinical insights into pragmatic theory: frontal lobe deficits and sarcasm. *Brain and Language*, 53, 81–104.

McDOUGALL, W. (1908) *An Introduction to Social Psychology*. London: Methuen.

McGARRIGLE, J. & DONALSON, M. (1974) Conservation accidents. *Cognition*, 3, 341–350.

McGHEE, P. (1996) Make or break. *Psychology Review*, 2, 27–30.

McGHEE, P.E. (1976) Children's appreciation of humour: A test of the cognitive congruency principle. *Child Development*, 47, 420–426.

McGLONE, J. (1980) Sex differences in human brain asymmetry: A critical survey. *Behaviour and Brain Sciences*, 3, 215–227.

McGOVERN, L.P. (1976) Dispositional social anxiety and helping behaviour under three conditions of threat. *Journal of Personality*, 44, 84–97.

McGOWAN, R.J. & JOHNSON, D.L. (1984) The mother-child relationship and other antecedents of childhood intelligence: A causal analysis. *Child Development*, 55, 810–820.

McGUIRE, P.K., BENCH, C.J., FRITH, C.D., MARKS, I.M., FRACKOWIAK, R.S.J. & DOLAN, R.J. (1994) Functional asymmetry of obsessive–compulsive phenomena. *British Journal of Psychiatry*, 164, 459–468.

McGUIRE, W.J. (1969) The nature of attitudes and attitude change. In G. Lindzey & E. Aronson (Eds) *Handbook of Social Psychology*, Volume 3 (2nd edition). Reading, MA: Addison-Wesley.

McGURK, H. (1975) *Growing and Changing*. London: Methuen.

McILROY, A.J. (1994) Screen test for children of St. Helena. *The Daily Telegraph*, 19 September, 9.

McILVEEN, R.J., LONG, M. & CURTIS, A. (1994) *Talking Points in Psychology*. London: Hodder & Stoughton.

McLEOD, P., DRIVER, J., DIENES, Z. & CRISP, J. (1991) Filtering by movement in visual search. *Journal of Experimental Psychology: Human Perception and Performance*, 17, 55–64.

McNEILL, D. (1970) *The Acquisition of Language*. New York: Harper & Row.

McWILLIAMS, S.A. & TUTTLE, R.J. (1973) Long-term psychological effects of LSD. *Psychological Bulletin*, 79, 341–351.

MEAD, G.H. (1934) *Mind, Self and Society*. Chicago: Chicago University Press.

MEAD, M. (1935) *Sex and Temperament in Three Primitive Societies*. New York: Dell.

MEADOR, B.D. & ROGERS, C.R. (1973) Person-centred therapy. In R. Corsini (Ed.) *Current Psychotherapies*. Itasca, ILL: Peacock.

MEADOR, B.D. & ROGERS, C.R. (1984) Person-centred therapy. In R. Corsini (Ed.) *Current Psychotherapies* (3rd edition) Itasca, ILL: Peacock.

MEADOWS, S. (1993) *The Child as Thinker: The Acquisition and Development of Cognition in Childhood*. London: Routledge.

MEADOWS, S. (1995) Cognitive development. In P.E. Bryant & A.M. Colman (Eds) *Developmental Psychology*. London: Longman.

MEDAWAR, P.B. (1963) *The Art of the Soluble*. Harmondsworth: Penguin.

MEDDIS, R. (1975) *The Sleep Instinct*. London: Routledge, Kegan & Paul.

MEDDIS, R., PEARSON, A.J.D. & LANFORD, G. (1973) An extreme case of healthy insomnia. *Electroencephalography and Clinical Neurophysiology*, 35, 213–214.

MEDNICK, S. (1958) A learning theory approach to schizophrenia. *Psychological Bulletin*, 55, 316–327.

MEEUS, W.H.J & RAAIJMAKERS, Q.A.W. (1986) Administrative obedience: Carrying out orders to use psychological-administrative violence. *European Journal of Social Psychology*, 16, 311–324.

MEGARGEE, E.I. (1966) Uncontrolled and overcontrolled personality types in extreme antisocial aggression. *Psychological Monographs: General and Applied* (Whole No. 611).

MEGARGEE, E.I. & MENDELSOHN, G.A. (1962) A cross validation of twelve MMPI indices of hostility and control. *Journal of Abnormal and Social Psychology*, 65, 431–438.

MEHLER, J. & DUPOUX, E. (1994) *What Infants Know*. Oxford: Blackwell.

MEICHENBAUM, D.H. (1976) Towards a cognitive therapy of self-control. In G. Schawrtz & D. Shapiro (Eds) *Consciousness and Self-Regulation: Advances in Research*. New York: Plenum Publishing Co.

MEICHENBAUM, D.H. (1985) *Stress Inoculation Training*. New York: Pergamon.

MEICHENBAUM, D.H., HENSHAW, D. & HIMMEL, N. (1982) Coping with stress as a problem-solving process. In W. Krohne & L. Laux (Eds) *Achievement, Stress and Anxiety* . Washington, DC: Hemisphere.

MEILMAN, P.W. (1979) Cross-sectional age changes in ego identity status during adolescence. *Developmental Psychology*, 15, 230–231.

MELHUISH, E.C. (1982) Visual attention to mothers' and strangers' faces and facial contrast in one-month-olds. *Developmental Psychology*, 18, 299–333.

MELTZOFF, A. & MOORE, M. (1983) Newborn infants imitate adult facial gestures. *Child Development*, 54, 702–709.

MELTZOFF, A.N. & MOORE, M. (1992) Early imitation within a functional framework: The importance of person identity, movement and development. *Infant Behaviour and Development*, 15, 479–505.

MEMON, A. & VARTOUKIAN, R. (1996) The effect of repeated questioning on young children's eyewitness testimony. *British Journal of Psychology*, 87, 403–415.

MENNINGER, W.W. (Ed.) (1995) *Fear of Humiliation – Integrated Treatment of Social Phobia and Comorbid Conditions*. New Jersey: Jason Aronson.

MEREI, F. (1949) Group leadership and institutionalisation. *Human Relations*, 2, 18–30.

MESSER, D. (1995) Seeing and pulling faces. *The Psychologist*, 8, 77.

MEYER, J.P. & PEPPER, S. (1977) Need compatibility and marital adjustment in young married couples. *Journal of Personality and Social Psychology*, 35, 331–342.

MICHELINI, R.L. & SNODGRASS, S.R. (1980) Defendant characteristics and juridic decisions. *Journal of Research in Personality*, 14, 340–350.

MIDGLEY, C. (1998) TV violence has little impact on children, study finds. *The Times*, 12 January, 5.

MIELL, D. (1990) Issues in social psychology. In I. Roth (Ed.) *Introduction to Psychology*, Volume 2. Hove: Erlbaum/Open University.

MIHILL, C. (1997) Drugs turn friends into enemies of the young. *The Guardian*, February 25, 4.

MIKULA, G. (1994) Perspective-related defferences in interpretations of injustice by victims and victimizers: A test with close relationships. In M.J. Lerner & G. Mikula (Eds) *Injustice in Close Relationships: Entitlement and the Affectional Bond*. New York: Plenum.

MILAVSKY, J.R., KESSLER, R.C., STIPP, H. & RUBENS, W.S. (1982) *Television and Aggression: A Panel Study*. New York: Academic Press.

MILGRAM, R.M. & MILGRAM, N.A. (1976) The effect of the Yom Kippur War on anxiety level in Israeli children. *Journal of Psychology*, 94, 107–113.

MILGRAM, S. (1963) Behavioural study of obedience. *Journal of Abnormal and Social Psychology*, 67, 391–398.

MILGRAM, S. (1964) Issues in the study of obedience: A reply to Baumrind. *American Psychologist*, 19, 848–852.

MILGRAM, S. (1965) Liberating effects of group pressure. *Journal of Personality and Social Psychology*, 1, 127–134.

MILGRAM, S. (1974) *Obedience to Authority*. New York: Harper & Row.

MILGRAM, S. (1992) *The Individual in a Social World* (2nd edition). New York: McGraw-Hill.

MILGRAM, S. & TOCH, H. (1969) Collective behaviour: Crowds and social movements. In G. Lindzey & E. Aronson (Eds) *Handbook of Social Psychology*, Volume 4. Reading, MA: Addison-Wesley.

MILLAR, S. (1996) You are feeling sleepy. *The Guardian*, 30 July, 14.

MILLER, D.T. & ROSS, M. (1975) Self-serving biases in the attribution of causality: Fact or fiction? *Psychological Bulletin*, 82, 213–225.

MILLER, E. & MORLEY, S. (1986) *Investigating Abnormal Behaviour*. London: Erlbaum.

MILLER, E. & MORRIS, R. (1993) *The Psychology of Dementia*. Chichester: Wiley.

MILLER, G.A. (1956) The magical number seven, plus or minus two: Some limits on our capacity for processing information. *Psychological Review*, 63, 81–97.

MILLER, G.A. (1962) *Psychology: The Science of Mental Life*. Harmondsworth: Penguin.

MILLER, G.A. (1978) The acquisition of word meaning. *Child Development*, 49, 999–1004.

MILLER, G.A. & McNEILL, D. (1969) Psycholinguistics. In G. Lindzey & E. Aronson (Eds) *The Handbook of Social Psychology*, Volume 3. Reading, MA: Addison-Wesley.

MILLER, G.A. & SELFRIDGE, J.A. (1950) Verbal context and the recall of meaningful material. *American Journal of Psychology*, 63, 176–185.

MILLER, J.G. (1984) Culture and the development of everyday social explanation. *Journal of Personality and Social Psychology*, 46, 961–978.

MILLER, L. (1987) The emotional brain. *Psychology Today*, 22, 35–42.

MILLER, N., GOLD, M. & MILLIMAN, R. (1989) Cocaine. *American Family Physician*, 39, 115–121.

MILLER, N.E. (1941) The frustration–aggression hypothesis. *Psychological Review*, 48, 337–342

MILLER, N.E. & DOLLARD, J. (1941) *Social Learning and Imitation*. New Haven, CT.: Yale University Press.

MILLER, R.J., HENNESSY, R.T. & LEIBOWITZ, H.W. (1973) The effect of hypnotic ablation of the background on the magnitude of the Ponzo perspective illusion. *International Journal of Clinical and Experimental Hypnosis*, 21, 18–191.

MILLER, W.R., ROSELLINI, R.A. & SELIGMAN, M.E.P. (1977) Learned helplessness and depression. In J.D. Maser & M.E.P. Seligman (Eds) *Psychopathology: Experimental Models*. San Francisco: W.H. Freeman.

MILLS, J. & CLARK, M.S. (1980) 'Exchange in communal relationships.' (Unpublished manuscript.)

MILNER, B. (1971) Interhemispheric differences in the localisation of psychological processes in man. *British Medical Bulletin*, 27, 272–277.

MILNER, D. (1996) Children and racism: Beyond the value of the dolls. In W.P. Robinson (Ed.) *Social Groups and Identities*. Oxford: Butterworth/Heineman.

MILNER, D. (1997) Racism and childhood identity. *The Psychologist*, 10, 123–125.

MINARD, R.D. (1952) Race relations in the Pocohontas coalfield. *Journal of Social Issues*, 8, 29–44.

MINORS, D. (1997) Melatonin – hormone of darkness. *Biological Sciences Review*, 10, 39–41.

MINTURN, L. & LAMBERT, W.W. (1964) *Mothers of Six Cultures*, New York: Wiley.

MISCHEL, W. (1973) Toward a cognitive social learning reconceptualisation of personality. *Psychological Review*, 80, 252–283.

MISCHEL, W. & MISCHEL, H.N. (1976) A cognitive social learning approach to morality and self-regulation. In T. Lickona (Ed.) *Moral Development and Behaviour: Theory, Research and Social Issues*. New York: Holt, Rinehart & Winston.

MITA, T.H., DERMER, M. & KNIGHT, J. (1977) Reversed facial images and the mere exposure hypothesis. *Journal of Personality and Social Psychology*, 35, 597–601.

MITCHELL, D.E. & WILKINSON, F. (1974) The effect of early astigmatism on the visual recognition of gratings. *Journal of Psychology*, 243, 739–756.

MITCHELL, T.R. & LARSON, J.B. Jnr. (1987) *People in Organisations: An Introduction to Organisational Behaviour* (3rd edition). New York: McGraw-Hill.

MOERK, E.L. (1989) The LAD was a lady, and the tasks were ill-defined. *Developmental Review*, 9, 21–57.

MOERK, E.L. & MOERK, C. (1979) Quotations, imitations and generalisations: Factual and methodological analyses. *International Journal of Behavioural Development*, 2, 43–72.

MOFFIT, T.E. (1990) Juvenile delinquency and attention deficit disorder: Boys' developmental trajectories from age 3 to age 15. *Child Development*, 61, 893–910.

MOGHADDAM, F.M. (1987) Psychology in the Three Worlds: As Reflected by the Crisis in Social Psychology and the Move towards Indigenous Third World Psychology. *American Psychologist*, 42, 912–920.

MOGHADDAM, F.M. & STUDER, C. (1997) Cross-cultural psychology: The frustrated gladfly's promises, potentialities and failures. In D. Fox & D. Prilleltensky (Eds) *Critical Psychology: An Introduction*. London: Sage.

MOGHADDAM, F.M., TAYLOR, D.M. & WRIGHT, S.C. (1993) *Social Psychology in Cross-cultural Perspective*. New York: W.H. Freeman & Co.

MONEY, J. (1974) Prenatal hormones and postnatal socialisation in gender identity differentiation. In J.K. Cole & R. Dienstbier (Eds) *Nebraska Symposium on Motivation*. Lincoln: University of Nebraska Press.

MONEY, J. & ERHARDT, A. (1972) *Man and Woman, Boy and Girl*. Baltimore, MD: The Johns Hopkins University Press.

MONTEMAYOR, R. (1983) Parents and adolescents in conflict: All families some of the time and some families most of the time. *Journal of Early Adolescence*, 3, 83–103.

MOORE, C. & FRYE, D. (1986) The effect of the experimenter's intention on the child's understanding of conservation. *Cognition*, 22, 283–298.

MOOS, R.H. (1988) *Coping Response Inventory Manual*. Social Ecology Laboratory, Department of Psychiatry, Stanford University and Veterans Administration Medical Centers. Palo Alto, California.

MORAY, N. (1959) Attention in dichotic listening: Affective cues and the influence of instructions. *Quarterly Journal of Experimental Psychology*, 11, 56–60.

MOREA, P. (1990) *Personality: An Introduction to the Theories of Psychology*. Harmondsworth: Penguin.

MORELAND, R.L. & ZAJONC, R.B. (1982) Exposure effects in person perception: Familiarity, similarity, and attraction. *Journal of Experimental Social Psychology*, 18, 395–415.

MORENO, J.L. (1946) *Psychodrama*. New York: Beacon.

MORGAN, E. (1995) Measuring time with a biological clock. *Biological Sciences Review*, 7, 2–5.

MORGAN, M.J. (1969) Estimates of length in a modified Müller-Lyer figure. *American Journal of Psychology*, 82, 380–384.

MORLAND, J. (1970) A comparison of race awareness in northern and southern children. In M. Goldschmid (Ed.) *Black Americans and White Racism*. Monterey, CA: Brooks/Cole.

MORPHETT, M.V. & WASHBURNE, C. (1931) When should children begin to read? *Elementary School Journal*, 31, 496–503.

MORRIS, C.G. (1988) *Psychology: An Introduction* (6th edition). London: Prentice-Hall.

MORRIS, J.N. (1953) Coronary heart disease and physical activity of work. *The Lancet*, 2, 1053–1057.

MORRIS, P.E. (1977) On the importance of acoustic encoding in short-term memory: The error of studying errors. *Bulletin of the British Psychological Society*, 30, 380.

MORRIS, P.E. (1992) Prospective memory: Remembering to do things. In M. Gruneberg & P.E. Morris (Eds) *Aspects of Memory*, Volume 1: *The Practical Aspects*. London: Routledge.

MORRISON, J. (1980) Adult psychiatric disorders in parents of hyperactive children. *American Journal of Psychiatry*, 137, 825–827.

MORTON, J. (1964) A preliminary functional model for language behaviour. *International Audiology*, 3, 216–225.

MORTON, J. (1969) Interaction of information in word recognition. *Psychological Review*, 76, 165–178.

MORTON, J. (1970) A functional model for memory. In D.A. Norman (Ed.) *Models of Human Memory*. New York: Academic Press.

MORTON, J. (1979) Facilitation in word recognition: Experiments causing change in the logogen model. In P.A. Kolers, M.E. Wrolstadt & H. Bouma (Eds) *Processing of Visible Language*. New York: Plenum Press.

MORUZZI, G. & MAGOUN, H.W. (1949) Reticular formation and activation of the EEG. *Electroencephalography and Clinical Neurophysiology*, 1, 455–473.

MOSCOVICI, S. (1961) *La Psychoanalyse: Son Image et Son Public*. Paris: Presses Universitaires de France.

MOSCOVICI, S. (1976) *La Psychoanalyse: Son Image et Son Public* (2nd edition). Paris: Presses Universitaires de France.

MOSCOVICI, S. (1981) On social representations. In J.P. Forgas (Ed.) *Social Cognition: Perspectives on Everyday Understanding*. London: Academic Press.

MOSCOVICI, S. (1984) The phenomenon of social representations. In R.M. Farr & S. Moscovici (Eds) *Social Representations*. Cambridge: Cambridge University Press.

MOSCOVICI, S. (1985) Social influence and conformity. In G. Lindzey & E. Aronson (Eds) *Handbook of Social Psychology* (3rd edition). New York: Random House.

MOSCOVICI, S. & FAUCHEUX, C. (1972) Social influence, conforming bias and the study of active minorities. In L. Berkowitz (Ed.) *Advances in Experimental Social Psychology*, Volume 6. New York: Academic Press.

MOSCOVICI, S. & HEWSTONE, M. (1983) Social representations and social explanations: From the 'naive' to the 'amateur' scientist. In M. Hewstone (Ed.) *Attribution Theory: Social and Functional Extensions*. Oxford: Blackwell.

MOSCOVICI, S. & LAGE, E. (1976) Studies in social influence III: Majority versus minority influence in a group. *European Journal of Social Psychology*, 6, 149–174.

MOSER, K.A., FOX, A.J. & JONES, D.R. (1984) Unemployment and mortality in the OPCS longitudinal study. *Lancet*, 2, 1324–1329.

MOSHMAN, D.A., GLOVER, J.A. & BRUNING, R.H. (1987) *Developmental Psychology: A Topical Approach*. Boston: Little, Brown & Company.

MOWRER, O.H. (1947) On the dual nature of learning – a reinterpretation of 'conditioning' and 'problem-solving'. *Harvard Educational Review*, 17, 102–148.

MOWRER, O.H. (1960) *Learning Theory and Behaviour*. New York: John Wiley.

MOYER, K.E. (1976) *The Psychobiology of Aggression*. New York: Harper & Row.

MUKERJEE, M. (1997) Trends in animal research. *Scientific American*, 63, February.

MULLEN, B. (1983) Operationalising the effect of the group on the individual: A self-attentive perspective. *Journal of Experimental Social Psychology*, 19, 295–322.

MULLEN, B. & JOHNSON, C. (1990) Distinctiveness-based illusory correlations and stereotyping: A meta-analytic integration. *British Journal of Social Psychology*, 29, 11–28.

MULLER, H.J. & MAXWELL, J. (1994) Perceptual integration of motion and form information: Is the movement filter involved in form discrimination? *Journal of Experimental Psychology: Human Perception and Performance*, 20, 397–420.

MUMMENDEY, A. (1996) Aggressive behaviour. In M. Hewstone, W. Stroebe & G.M. Stephenson (Eds) *Introduction to Social Psychology* (2nd edition). Oxford: Blackwell.

MUNDY-CASTLE, A.C. & NELSON, G.K. (1962) A neuropsychological study of the Kuysma forest workers. *Psychologia Africana*, 9, 240–272.

MUNROE, R.H., SHIMMIN, H.S. & MUNROE, R.L. (1984) Gender understanding and sex-role preference in four cultures. *Developmental Psychology*, 20, 673–682.

MUNSINGER, H. (1975) The adopted child's IQ: A critical review. *Psychological Bulletin*, 82, 623–659.

MURDOCK, B.B. (1962) The serial position effect in free recall. *Journal of Experimental Psychology*, 64, 482–488.

MURDOCK, B.B. & WALKER, K.D. (1969) Modality effects in free recall. *Journal of Verbal Learning and Verbal Behaviour*, 8, 665–676.

MURDOCK, G.P. (1975) *Outline of World Cultures* (5th edition). New Haven: Human Relations Area Files.

MURDOCK, G.P., FORD, C.S. & HUDSON, A.E. (1971) *Outline of Cultural Materials* (4th edition). New Haven: Human Relations Area Files.

MURPHY, G. (1947) *Personality: A Bio-Social Approach to Origins and Structure*. New York: Harper & Row.

MURRAY, E.J. & FOOTE, F. (1979) The origins of fear of snakes. *Behaviour Research and Therapy*, 17, 489–493.

MURRAY, H.A. (1938) *Explorations in Personality*. New York: Oxford University Press.

MURRAY, I. (1997) Popeye phobia was no laughing matter. *The Times*, 4 August, 3.

MURRAY, J. (1995) *Prevention of Anxiety and Depression in Vulnerable Groups*. London: Gaskell.

MURRAY, R., OON, M., RODNIGHT, R., BIRLEY, J. & SMITH, A. (1979) Increased excretion of dimethyltryptamine and certain features of psychosis. *Archives of General Psychiatry*, 36, 644–649.

MURSTEIN, B.I. (1972) Physical attractiveness and marital choice. *Journal of Personality and Social Psychology*, 22, 8–12.

MURSTEIN, B.I. (1976) The stimulus-value-role theory of marital choice. In H. Grunebaum & J. Christ (Eds) *Contemporary Marriage: Structures, Dynamics and Therapy*. Boston: Little, Brown.

MURSTEIN, B.I. (1987) A clarification and extension of the SVR theory of dyadic parting. *Journal of Marriage and the Family*, 49, 929–933.

MURSTEIN, B.I. & MacDONALD, M.G. (1983) The relation of 'exchange orientation' and 'commitment' scales to marriage adjustment. *International Journal of Psychology*, 18, 297–311.

MURSTEIN, B.I., MacDONALD, M.G. & CERETO, M. (1977) A theory of the effect of exchange orientation on marriage and friendship. *Journal of Marriage and the Family*, 39, 543–548.

MYERS, D.G. (1990) *Exploring Psychology*. New York: Worth.

MYERS, D.G. (1994) *Exploring Social Psychology*. New York: McGraw-Hill.

NAHEMOW, L. & LAWTON, M.P. (1975) Similarity and propinquity in a friendship formation. *Journal of Personality and Social Psychology*, 32, 205–213.

NALIBOFF, B.D., SOLOMON, G.F., GILMORE, S.L., FAHEY, J.L., BENTON, D. & PINE, J. (1995) Rapid changes in cellular immunity following a confrontation role-play stresor. *Brain, Behaviour and Immunity*, 9, 207–219.

NAPOLITAN, D.A. & GOETHALS, G.R. (1979) The attribution of friendliness. *Journal of Experimental Social Psychology*, 15, 105–113.

NATHANS, J. (1989) The genes for colour vision. *Scientific American*, 226, 42–49.

NATIONAL COUNCIL FOR CIVIL LIBERTIES (1996) *Violence, Harassment and Discrimination Against Disabled People in Great Britain*. London: NCCL.

NATIONAL INSTITUTE OF MENTAL HEALTH (1982) *Television and Behaviour: Ten Years of Scientific Progress and Implications for the Eighties*, Volume 1. Washington, DC: US Government Printing Office.

NATIONAL TELEVISION VIOLENCE STUDY (1996). Los Angeles: Mediascope.

NAVON, D. (1977) Forest before trees: The precedence of global features in visual perception. *Cognitive Psychology*, 9, 353–383.

NAVON, D. (1984) Resources – A theoretical soup stone? *Psychological Review*, 91, 216–234.

NAVON, D. & GOPHER, D. (1979) On the economy of the human processing system. *Psychological Review*, 86, 214–255.

NEBES, R.D. (1974) Hemispheric specialisation in commissurotomised man. *Psychological Bulletin*, 81, 1–14.

NEEDLEMAN, H.L., SCHELL, A., BELLINGER, D., LEVITON, A. & ALLRED, E. (1990) Lead-associated intellectual deficit. *New England Journal of Medicine*, 322, 83–88.

NEILL, J. (1987) 'More than medical significance': LSD and American psychiatry 1953 to 1966. *Journal of Psychoactive Drugs*, 19, 39–45.

NEISSER, U. (1967) *Cognitive Psychology*. New York: Appleton Century Crofts.

NEISSER, U. (1976) *Cognition and Reality*. San Francisco, CA: W.H. Freeman.

NEISSER, U. (1981) John Dean's memory: A case study. *Cognition*, 9, 1–22.

NEISSER, U. (1982) *Memory Observed*. San Francisco: Freeman.

NEISSER, U. & BECKLEN, R. (1975) Selective looking: Attending to visually specified events. *Cognitive Psychology*, 7, 480–494.

NEISSER, U. & HARSCH, N. (1992) Phantom flashbulbs: False recollections of hearing news about Challenger. In E.O. Winograd & U. Neisser (Eds) *Affect and Accuracy in Recall: Studies of 'Flashbulb' Memories*. New York: Cambridge University Press.

NELSON, K. (1973) Structure and strategy in learning to talk. *Monographs of the Society for Research in Child Development*, 38, 149.

NELSON, S.A. (1980) Factors influencing young children's use of motives and outcomes as moral criteria. *Child Development*, 51, 823–829.

NEMETH, C. & WACHTLER, J. (1973) Consistency and modification of judgement. *Journal of Experimental Social Psychology*, 9, 65–79.

NEUGARTEN, B.L. (1975) The future of the young-old. *The Gerontologist*, 15, 4–9.

NEUGARTEN, B.L. & NEUGARTEN, D.A. (1987) The changing meanings of age. *Psychology Today*, 21, 29–33.

NEWCOMB, T.M. (1943) *Personality and Social Change*. New York: Holt, Rinehart & Winston.

NEWCOMB, T.M. (1953) An approach to the study of communication. *Psychological Review*, 60, 393–404.

NEWCOMB, T.M. (1961) *The Acquaintanceship Process*. New York: Holt, Rinehart & Winston.

NEWCOMB, T.M. (1978) The acquaintance process: Looking mainly backwards. *Journal of Personality and Social Psychology*, 36, 1075–1083.

NEWELL, A., SHAW, J.C. & SIMON, H.A. (1958) Elements of a theory of human problem-solving. *Psychological Review*, 65, 151–166.

NEWELL, A. & SIMON, H.A. (1956) IRE Trans. on Inform. Theory. *IT-2*, 3, 61.

NEWELL, A. & SIMON, H.A. (1972) *Human Problem-Solving*. Englewood Cliffs, NJ: Prentice-Hall.

NEWMAN, H.H., FREMAN, F.N. & HOLZINGER, K.J. (1937) *Twins: A Study of Heredity and the Environment*. Chicago, ILL: University of Chicago Press.

NEWMAN, M., BLACK, D. & HARRIS-HENDRIKS, J. (1997) Victims of disaster, war, violence, or homicide: Psychological effects on siblings. *Child Psychology & Psychiatry Review*, 2 (4), 140–149.

NEWSON, E. (1994) Video violence and the protection of children. *Psychology Review*, 1, 2–6.

NEWSTEAD, S. (1995) Language and thought: The Whorfian hypothesis. *Psychology Review*, 1, 5–7.

NIAS, D.B.K. (1979) Marital choice: Matching or complementation? In M. Cook & G. Wilson (Eds) *Love and Attraction*. New York: Pergamon Press.

NICHOLSON, J. (1977) *Habits*. London: Macmillan

NICOLSON, P. (1995) Feminism and psychology. In J.A.Smith, R. Harre, & L. Van Langenhove (Eds) *Rethinking Psychology*. London: Sage.

NICOLSON, R. (1996) Screening and diagnosis of SpLD/dyslexia. *The Psychologist*, 9, 81.

NIMH (1987) *The Switch Process in Manic-Depressive Illness* (DHHS Publication No. ADM 81–108). Washington, DC: Government Printing Office.

NISBETT, R.E. (1972) Hunger, obesity and the ventromedial hypothalamus. *Psychological Review*, 79, 433–453.

NISBETT, R.E. & BORGIDA, E. (1975) Attribution and the psychology of prediction. *Journal of Personality and Social Psychology*, 32, 923–943.

NOLLER, P. & CALLAN, V.J. (1990) Adolescents' perceptions of the nature of their communication with parents. *Journal of Youth and Adolescence*, 19, 349–362.

NORMAN, D.A. (1968) Toward a thaery of memory and attention. *Psychological Review*, 75, 522–536.

NORMAN, D.A. (1969) Memory while shadowing. *Quarterly Journal of Experimental Psychology*, 21, 85–93.

NORMAN, D.A. (1976) *Memory and Attention* (2nd edition). Chichester: Wiley.

NORMAN, D.A. (1981) Categorisation of action slips. *Psychological Review*, 88, 1–15.

NORMAN, D.A. & BOBROW, D.G. (1975) On data-limited and resource-limited processes. *Cognitive Psychology*, 7, 44–64.

NORMAN, D.A. & SHALLICE, T. (1986) Attention to action: Willed and automatic control of behaviour. In R.J. Davidson, G.E. Schwartz & D. Shapiro (Eds) *The Design of Everyday Things*. New York: Doubleday.

NORMAN, R., PEARLMAN, I., KOLB, H., JONES, J. & DALEY, S. (1984) Direct excitatory interactions between cones of different spectral types in the turtle retina. *Science*, 224, 625–627.

NOVAK, M.A. (1979) Social recovery of monkeys isolated for the first years of life: 2. Long-term assessment. *Developmental Psychology*, 15, 50–61.

NOVAK, M.A. & HARLOW, H.F. (1975) Social recovery of monkeys isolated for the first years of life: 1. Rehabilitation and therapy. *Developmental Psychology*, 11, 453–465.

NSF (1994) *National Schizophrenia Fellowship: A Guide to the Types of Drugs Available to Treat Schizophrenia*. London: National Schizophrenia Fellowship.

NUECHTERLEIN, K.H. & DAWSON, M.E. (1984) A heuristic vulnerability/stress model of schizophrenic episodes. *Schizophrenia Bulletin*, 10, 300–311.

NUTTALL, N. (1996) Missing ingredient may control gluttons' appetite. *The Times*, 4 January, 3.

NUTTIN, J.M. (1987) Affective consequences of mere ownership: The name-letter effect in twelve European languages. *European Journal of Social Psychology*, 17, 381–402.

NYDEGGER, R.V. (1975) Information processing complexity and leadership status. *Journal of Experimental Social Psychology*, 11, 317–328.

O'BRIEN, M., HUSTON, A.C. & RISLEY, T. (1983) Sex-typed play of toddlers in a day-care centre. *Journal of Applied Developmental Psychology*, 4, 1–9.

O'CALLAGHAN, E., SHAM, P.C. & TAKEI, N. (1993) Schizophrenia after prenatal exposure to 1957 A2 influenza epidemic. *The Lancet*, 337, 1248–1250.

O'CALLAGHAN, E., SHAM, P.C., TAKEI, N., MURRAY, G.K., GLOVER, G., HARE, E.H. & MURRAY, R.M. (1994) The relationship of schizophrenic births to sixteen infectious diseases. *British Journal of Psychiatry*, 165, 353–356.

O'CALLAGHAN, E., SHAM, P.C., TAKEI, N., MURRAY, G.K., HARE, E.H. & MURRAY, R.M. (1991) Schizophrenia following prenatal exposure to influenza epidemics between 1939 and 1960. *British Journal of Psychiatry*, 160, 461–466.

O'LEARY, K.D. & WILSON, G.T. (1975) *Behaviour Therapy: Application and Outcome*. Englewood Cliffs, NJ: Prentice-Hall.

O'NEILL, S. (1996) A little kindness goes a long way. *The Daily Telegraph*, 31 August, 1.

OAKES, P.J., HASLAM, S.A. & TURNER, J.C. (1994) *Stereotyping and Social Reality*. Oxford: Blackwell.

OAKHILL, J.V. (1984) Why children have difficulty reasoning with three-term series problems. *British Journal of Developmental Psychology*, 2, 223–230.

OAKLEY, D., ALDEN, P. & MATHER, M.M. (1996) The use of hypnosis in therapy with adults. *The Psychologist*, 9, 502–505.

OAKLEY, D.A. (1983) The varieties of memory: A phylogenetic approach. In A.R. Mayes (Ed.) *Memory in Humans and Animals*. Wokingham: Van Nostrand.

OATLEY, K. (1984) *Selves in Relation: An Introduction to Psychotherapy and Groups*. London: Methuen.

OFFER, D. (1969) *The Psychological World of the Teenager*. New York: Basic Books.

OFFER, D., OSTROV, E., HOWARD, K.I. & ATKINSON, R. (1988) *The Teenage World: Adolescents' Self-Image in Ten Countries*. New York: Plenum Press.

OGILVIE, A.D., BATTERSBY, S., BUBB, V.J., FINK, G., HARMAR, A.J., GOODWIN, G.M. & SMITH, C.A.D. (1996) Polymorphism in the serotonin transporter gene associated with susceptibility to major depression. *The Lancet*, 347, 731–733.

OHTSUKA, T. (1985) Relation of spectral types to oil droplets in cones of turtle retina. *Science*, 229, 874–877.

OKASHA, A., SADEK, A., AL-HADDAD, M.K. & ABDEL,–MAWGOUD, M. (1993) Diagnostic agreement in psychiatry: A comparative study between ICD-9, ICD-10 and DSM-III-R. *British Journal of Psychiatry*, 162, 621–626.

OLDS, J. & MILNER, P. (1954) Positive reinforcement produced by electrical stimulation of the septal area and other regions of the rat brain. *Journal of Comparative and Physiological Psychology*, 47, 419–427.

OLWEUS, D. (1980) Familial and temperamental determinants of aggressive behaviour in adolescent boys: A causal analysis. *Developmental Psychology*, 16, 644–666.

ONO, T., SQUIRE, L.R., RAICHLE, M.E., PERRETT, D.I. & FUKUDA, M. (Eds) (1993) *Brain Mechanisms of Perception and Memory. From Neurone to Behaviour*. New York: Oxford University Press.

OPTON, E.M. (1973) 'It never happened and besides they deserved it.' In W.E. Henry & N. Sanford (Eds) *Sanctions for Evil*. San Francisco: Jossey-Bass.

ORNE, M.T. (1962) On the social psychology of the psychological experiment – with particular reference to demand characteristics. *American Psychologist*, 17 (11), 776–783.

ORNE, M.T. & EVANS, F.J. (1965) Social control in the psychological experiment: Anti-social behaviour and hypnosis. *Journal of Personality and Social Psychology*, 1, 189–200.

ORNE, M.T. & HOLLAND, C.C. (1968) On the ecological validity of laboratory deceptions. *International Journal of Psychiatry*, 6, 282–293.

ORNE, M.T., SHEEHAN, P.W. & EVANS, F.J. (1968) Occurrence of posthypnotic behaviour outside the experimental setting. *Journal of Personality and Social Psychology*, 9, 189–196.

ORNSTEIN, R. (1986) *The Psychology of Consciousness* (2nd edition, revised). Harmondsworth: Penguin.

ORUM, A.L. (1972) *Black Students in Protest: A Study of the Origins of the Black Student Movement*. Washington, DC: American Sociological Association.

OSMOND, H. & SMYTHIES, J. (1953) Schizophrenia: A new approach. *The Journal of Mental Science*, 98, 309–315.

OSWALD, I. (1966) *Sleep*. Harmondsworth: Penguin.

OWUSU-BEMPAH, J. & HOWITT, D. (1994) Racism and the psychological textbook. *The Psychologist*, 7, 163–166.

PACKARD, V. (1957) *The Hidden Persuaders*. New York: McKay.

PAGE, D., MOSHER, R., SIMPSON, E., FISHER, E., MARDON, G., POLLOCK, J., McGILLIVRAY, B., CHAPPELLE, A. & BROWN, L. (1987) The sex-determining region of the human Y-chromosome encodes a finger protein. *Cell*, 51, 1091–1104.

PAIGE, K.E. (1973) Women learn to sing the menstrual blues. *Psychology Today*, 7, 41.

PAIVIO, A. (1979) Psychological processes in the comprehension of metaphor. In A. ORTONY (Ed.) *Metaphor and Thought*. New York: Cambridge University Press.

PAIVIO, A. (1986) *Mental Representations: A Dual-Coding Approach*. Oxford: Oxford University Press.

PALERMO, D.S. (1971) Is a scientific revolution taking place in psychology? *Psychological Review*, 76, 241–263.

PALMER, S., SCHREIBER, C. & FOX, C. (1991) Remembering the earthquake: 'Flashbulb' memory for experienced versus reproted events. Paper presented at the Annual Meeting of the Psychonomic Society, San Francisco.

PANTIN, H.M. & CARVER, C.S. (1982) Induced competence and the bystander effect. *Journal of Applied Social Psychology*, 12, 100–111.

PAPASTAMOU, S. (1979) 'Strategies d'influence minoritaires et majoritaires.' (Unpublished doctoral dissertation. Paris: Ecole des Hautes Etudes en Sciences Sociales.)

PAPEZ, J.W. (1937) A proposed mechanism of emotion. *Archives of Neurology and Psychiatry*, 38, 725–743.

PAPP, L.A., KLEIN, D.F., MARTINEZ, J., SCHNEIER, F., COLE, R., LIEBOWITZ, M.R., HOLLANDER, E., FYER, A.J., JORDAN, F. & GORMAN, J.M. (1993) Diagnostic and substance specificity of recent life-stress experience. *Journal of Consulting and Clinical Psychology*, 51, 467–469.

PARFIT, D. (1987) Divided minds and the nature of persons. In Blakemore, C. & Greenfield, S. (Eds) *Mindwaves*. Oxford: Blackwell.

PARK, R.J., LAWRIE, J.M. & FREEMAN, C.P. (1995) Post-viral onset of anorexia nervosa. *British Journal of Psychology*. 166, 386–389.

PARKE, R.D. (1981) *Fathering*. London: Fontana.

PARKE, R.D., BERKOWITZ, L., LEYENS, J.P., WEST, S.G. & SEBASTIAN, R.J. (1977) Some effects of violent and non-violent movies on the behaviour of juvenile delinquents. In L. Berkowitz (Ed.) *Advances in Experimental Social Psychology*, Volume 10. New York: Academic Press.

PARKE, R.D. & SWAIN, D.B. (1980) The family in early infancy. In F.A. Pederson (Ed.) *The Father-Infant Relationship: Observational Studies in a Family Context*. New York: Praeger.

PARKER, I., GEORGACA, E., HARPER, D., McLAUGHLIN, T. & STOWELL-SMITH, M. (1995) *Deconstructing Psychopathology*. London: Sage.

PARKES, C.M., BENJAMIN, B. & FITZGERALD, R.G. (1969) Broken heart: A statistical study of increased mortality among widowers. *British Medical Journal*, 1, 740–743.

PARKES, C.M. & WEISS, R.S. (1983) *Recovery From Bereavement*. New York: Basic Books.

PARKIN, A.J. (1987) *Memory and Amnesia: An Introduction*. Oxford: Blackwell.

PARKIN, A.J. (1993) *Memory: Phenomena, Experiment and Theory*. Oxford: Blackwell.

PARKIN, J.R. & EAGLES, J.M. (1993) Blood-letting in anorexia nervosa. *British Journal of Psychiatry*, 162, 246–248.

PARROTT, A. (1997) Ecstatic but memory depleted? *The Psychologist*, 10, 265.

PARROTT, A. & YEOMANS, M. (1995) Wobble, rave, inhale or crave. *The Psychologist*, 8, 305.

PARRY-JONES, W.Ll. & PARRY-JONES, B. (1993) Self-mutilation in four historical cases of bulimia. *British Journal of Psychiatry*, 163, 394–402.

PASCUAL-LEONE, J. (1980) Constructive problems for constructive theories: The current relevance of Piaget's work and a critique of information-processing simulation psychology. In R.H. Kluwe & H. Spads (Eds) *Developmental Models of Thinking*. New York: Academic Press.

PATERNITE, C.E. & LONEY, J. (1980) Childhood hyperkinesis: Relationships between symptomatology and home environment. In C.K. Whelan & B. Henker (Eds) *Hyperactive Children: The Social Ecology of Identification and Treatment*. New York: Academic Press.

PATON, D. (1992) Disaster research: The Scottish dimension. *The Psychologist*, 5, 535–538.

PATRICK, G.T.W. & GILBERT, J.A. (1898) On the effects of loss of sleep. The *Psychological Review*, 3, 469–483.

PATTERSON, G. (1986) Performance models for anti-social boys. *American Psychologist*, 41, 432–444.

PATTERSON, G.R. (1982) *Coercive Family Process*. Eugene, OR: Catalia Press.

PATTIE, F.A. (1937) The genuineness of hypnotically produced anaesthesia of the skin. *American Journal of Psychology*, 49, 435–443.

PAVLOV, I.P. (1927) *Conditioned reflexes*. London: Oxford University Press.

PECK, R.C. (1968) Psychological developments in the second half of life. In B.L. Neugarten (Ed.) *Middle Age and Ageing*. Chicago, Ill.: University of Chicago Press.

PENFIELD, W. (1947) Some observations on the cerebral cortex of man. *Proceedings of the Royal Society*, 134, 349.

PENFIELD, W. (1969) Consciousness, memory and man's conditioned reflexes. In K. PRIBRAM (Ed.) *On the Biology of Learning*. New York: Harcourt, Brace Jovanovich.

PENFIELD, W. & ROBERTS, L. (1959) *Speech and Brain Mechanisms*. Princeton: Princeton University Press.

PENGELLEY, E.T. & FISHER, K.C. (1957) Onset and cessation of hibernation under constant temperature and light in the golden-mantled ground squirrel, Citellus Lateralis. *Nature*, 180, 1371–1372.

PENNINGTON, D.C. (1986) *Essential Social Psychology*. London: Edward Arnold.

PENROD, S. (1983) *Social Psychology*. Englewood Cliffs, NJ: Prentice-Hall.

PENROSE, R. (1990) *The Emperor's New Mind*. Oxford: Oxford University Press.

PERIANI, D., BRESSI, S., CAPPA, S.F., VALLAR, G., ALBERONI, M., GRASSI, F., CALTAGIRONE, C., CIPLOTTI, L., FRANCESCHI, M., LENIZ, G.L. & FAZIO, F. (1993) Evidence of multiple memory systems in the human brain. *Brain*, 116, 903–919.

PERLBERG, M. (1979) Trauma at Tenerife: The psychic aftershocks of a jet disaster. *Human Behaviour*, 49–50.

PERLS, F.S. (1967) Group versus individual therapy. *ETC: A Review of General Semantics*, 34, 306–312.

PERRET, D.J., MAY, K.A. & YOSHIKAWA, S. (1994) Facial shape and judgements of female attractiveness. *Nature*, 368, 239–242.

PERRIN, S. & SPENCER, C. (1980) The Asch effect – A child of its time? *Bulletin of the British Psychological Society*, 33, 405–407.

PERRIN, S. & SPENCER, C. (1981) Independence or conformity in the Asch experiment as a reflection of cultural and situational factors. *British Journal of Social Psychology*, 20, 205–209.

PERRY, D.G. & BUSSEY, K. (1979) The social learning theory of sex differences: Imitation is alive and well. *Journal of Personality and Social Psychology*, 37, 1699–1712.

PERT, C.B. & SNYDER, S.H. (1973) Opiate receptor: Demonstration in the nervous tissue. *Science*, 179, 1011–1014.

PETERSON, L.R. & PETERSON, M.J. (1959) Short-term retention of individual items. *Journal of Experimental Psychology*, 58, 193–198.

PETKOVA, B. (1995) New views on the self: Evil women – witchcraft or PMS? *Psychology Review*, 2, 16–19.

PETKOVA, B. (1997) Understanding eating disorders: A perspective from feminist psychology. *Psychology Review*, 4, 2–7.

PETTIGREW, T.F. (1958) Personality and sociocultural factors in intergroup attitudes: A cross-national comparison. *Journal of Conflict Resolution*, 2, 29–42.

PHILLIPS, D.P. (1986) National experiments on the effects of mass media violence on fatal aggression: Strengths and weaknesses of a new approach. In L. Berkowitz (Ed.) *Advances in Experimental Social Psychology*, Volume 19. New York: Academic Press.

PHILLIPS, J.L. (1969) *The Origins of Intellect: Piaget's Theory*. San Francisco: W.H. Freeman.

PIAGET, J. (1932) *The Moral Judgement of the Child*. London: Routledge & Kegan Paul.

PIAGET, J. (1950) *The Psychology of Intelligence*. London: Routledge & Kegan Paul.

PIAGET, J. (1952) *The Child's Conception of Number*. London: Routledge & Kegan Paul.

PIAGET, J. (1963) *The Origins of Intelligence in Children*. New York: Norton.

PIAGET, J. (1973) *The Child's Conception of the World*. London: Paladin.

PIAGET, J. & INHELDER, B. (1956) *The Psychology of the Child*. London: Routledge & Kegan Paul.

PIAGET, J. & INHELDER, B. (1969) *The Psychology of the Child*. London: Routledge & Kegan Paul.

PIAGET, J. & SZEMINSKA, A. (1952) *The Child's Conception of Number*. London: Routledge & Kegan Paul.

PICCINELLI, M., PINI, S., BELLANTUONO, C. & WILKINSON, G. (1995) Efficacy of drug treatment in obsessive–compulsive disorder: A meta–analytic review. *British Journal of Psychiatry*, 166, 424–443.

PICKERING, J. (1981) Perception. *In Psychological Processes: Units 5 & 6–7*. Milton Keynes: The Open University Press.

PIGGOTT, L.R. (1979) Overview of selected basic research in autism. *Journal of Autism and Developmental Disorders*, 9, 199–218.

PIKE, K.L. (1954) Emic and etic standpoints for the description of behaviour. In K.L. Pike (Ed.) *Language in Relation to a Unified Theory of the Structure of Human Behaviour* (Prelim. edition). Glendale, CA.: Summer Institute of Linguistics.

PILIAVIN, I.M., RODIN, J. & PILIAVIN, J.A. (1969) Good Samaritanism: An underground phenomenon? *Journal of Personality and Social Psychology*, 13, 289–299.

PILIAVIN, J.A., DOVIDIO, J.F., GAERTNER, S.L. & CLARK, R.D. (1981) *Emergency Intervention*. New York: Academic Press.

PILIAVIN, J.A. & PILIAVIN, I.M. (1972) Effects of blood on reactions to a victim. *Journal of Personality and Social Psychology*, 23, 353–362.

PINEL, J.P.J. (1993) *Biopsychology* (2nd edition). Boston: Allyn & Bacon.

PINEO, P.C. (1961) Disenchantment in the later years of marriage. *Journal of Marriage and Family Living*, 23, 3–11.

PINES, A. (1984) Ma Bell and the Hardy Boys. *Across the Board*, July/August, 37–42.

PINES, M. (1982) Movement grows to create guidelines for mental therapy. *New York Times*, 4 May, C1, C6.

PIRAN, N., KENNEDY, S., GARFINKEL, P.E. & OWENS, M. (1985) Affective disturbance in eating disorders. *Journal of Nervous and Mental Disease*, 173, 395–400.

PLOMIN, R. (1988) The nature and nurture of cognitive abilities. In R.J. Sternberg (Ed.) *Advances in the Psychology of Human Intelligence*, Volume 4. Hillsdale, NJ: Erlbaum.

PLOMIN, R. (1995) Genetics and children's experiences in the family. *Journal of Child Psychology and Psychiatry*, 36, 33-68.

PLOMIN, R. & DeFRIES, J.C. (1980) Genetics and intelligence: Recent data. *Intelligence*, 4, 15–24.

POGGIO, T. & KOCH, C. (1987) Synapses that compute motion. *Scientific American*, 255, 46–92.

POLIVY, J. & HERMAN, C.P. (1985) Dieting and bingeing: Causal analysis. *American Psychologist*, 40, 193–201.

POLLATSEK, A., BOLOZKY, S., WELLS, A.D. & RAYNER, K. (1981) Asymmetries in the perceptual span for Israeli readers. *Brain and Language*, 14, 174–180.

POPPER, K. (1959) *The Logic of Scientific Discovery*. London: Hutchinson.

POPPER, K. (1972) Objective Knowledge: An Evolutionary Approach. Oxford: Oxford University Press.

POSNER, M.I. (1980) Orienting of attention. *Quarterly Journal of Experimental Psychology*, 32, 3–25.

POSNER, M.I., NISSEN, M.J. & OGDEN, W.C. (1978) Attended and unattended processing modes: The role of set for spatial location. In H.L. Pick & I.J. Saltzman (Eds) *Modes of Perceiving and Processing Information*. Hillsdale, NJ: Erlbaum.

POSNER, M.I., SNYDER, C.R.R. & DAVIDSON, B.J. (1980) Attention and the detection of signals. *Journal of Experimental Psychology: General*, 109, 160–174.

POST, F. (1994) Creativity and psychopathology. A study of 291 world-famous men. *British Journal of Psychiatry*, 165, 22–34.

POTTER, J. & WETHERELL, M. (1987) *Discourse and Social Psychology: Beyond Attitudes and Behaviour*. London: Sage Publications.

PRATKANIS, A. & ARONSON, E. (1991) *Age of Propaganda: Everyday Uses and Abuses of Persuasion*. New York: Freeman.

PRATKANIS, A.R., ESKENAZI, J. & GREENWALD A.G. (1990) *What you expect is what you believe (but not necessarily what you get): On the ineffectiveness of subliminal self-help audiotapes*. Paper presented at the Western Psychological Association, Los Angeles, CA, (April).

PRENTICE, P. (1996) Attention deficit hyperactivity disorder. *Psychology Review*, 3, 20–24.

PRENTICE-DUNN, S. & ROGERS, R.W. (1983) Deindividuation in aggression. In R.G. Geen & E.I. Donnerstein (Eds) *Aggression: Theoretical and Empirical Reviews*, Volume 2. New York: Academic Press.

PRESLAND, J. (1991) Explaining away dyslexia. *Educational Psychology in Practice*, 6, 215–221.

PRICE, R.A. & VANDENBERG, S.G. (1979) Matching for physical attractiveness in married couples. *Personality and Social Psychology Bulletin*, 5, 398–400.

PRINCE, J. & HARTNETT, O. (1993) From 'psychology constructs the female' to 'females construct psychology'. *Feminism & Psychology*, 3 (2), 219–224.

PRINGLE, M.L. KELLMER (1986) *The Needs of Children* (3rd edition). London: Hutchinson.

PRINS, H. (1995) *Offenders, Deviants or Patients?* (2nd edition) London: Routledge.

PRIOLEAU, L., MURDOCK, M. & BRODY, N. (1983) An analysis of psychotherapy versus placebo studies. *Behaviour and Brain Sciences*, 6, 273–310.

PROUDFOOT, J., GUEST, D., CARSON, J., DUNN, G. & GRAY, J. (1997) Effects of cognitive-behavioural training on job-find among long-term unemployed people. *Lancet*, 250, 96–100.

PUCETTI, R. (1977) Sperry on consciousness: A critical appreciation. *Journal of Medicine and Physiology*, 2, 127–146.

PUSHKIN, I. & VENESS, T. (1973) The development of racial awareness and prejudice in children. In P. Watson (Ed.) *Psychology and Race*. Harmondsworth: Penguin.

PYNOOS, R.S., GOENIJIAN, A., TASHJIAN, M., KARAKASHIAN, M., MANJIKAN, R., MANOUKIAN, G., STEINBERG, A.M. & FAIRBANKS, L.A. (1993) Post–traumatic stress reactions in children after the 1988 Armenian earthquake. *British Journal of Psychiatry*, 163, 239–247.

QUATTRONE, G.A. (1982) Overattribution and unit formation: When behaviour engulfs the person. *Journal of Personality and Social Psychology*, 42, 593–607.

QUATTRONE, G.A. (1986) On the perception of a group's variability. In S. Worchel & W. Austin (Eds) *The Psychology of Intergroup Relations*, Volume 2. New York: Nelson-Hall.

QUICKE, J. (1982) *The Cautious Expert*. Milton Keynes: Open University Press.

QUINTON, D. & RUTTER, M. (1988) *Parental Breakdown: The Making and Breaking of Intergenerational Links*. London: Gower.

RABBIT, P.M.A. (1967) Ignoring irrelevant information. *American Journal of Psychology*, 80, 1–13.

RABIN, A.S., KASLOW, N.J. & REHM, L.P. (1986) Aggregate outcome and follow-up results following self-control therapy for depression. Paper presented at the American Psychological Convention.

RACHMAN, S. (1977) *Fear and Courage*. San Francisco: W.H. Freeman.

RACHMAN, S. (1984) Agoraphobia – a safety signal perspective. *Behaviour Research and Therapy*, 22, 59–70.

RACK, J.P., HULME, C., SNOW, M.J. & WIGHTMAN, J. (1994) The role of phonology in young children's learning of sight words: The direct mapping hypothesis. *Journal of Experimental Child Psychology*, 57, 42–71.

RADFORD, T. (1997) Obesity gene found in cousins. *The Guardian*, 24 June, 8.

RAGLAND, D.R. & BRAND, R.J. (1988) Type A behaviour and mortality from coronary heart disease. *New England Journal of Medicine*, 318, 65–69.

RAMACHANDRON, V.S. & ANSTIS, S.M. (1986) The perception of apparent motion. *Scientific American*, 254, 80–87.

RAMSAY, R. & de GROOT, W. (1977) A further look at bereavement. Paper presented at EATI conference, Uppsala. Cited in P.E. Hodgkinson (1980) Treating abnormal grief in the bereaved. *Nursing Times*, 17 January, 126–128.

RAPER, A.F. (1933) *The Tragedy of Lynching*. Chapel Hill, NC: University of North Carolina Press.

RAPHAEL, B. (1984) *The Anatomy of Bereavement*. London: Hutchinson.

RAPHAEL, T.E. & KIRSCHNER, P. (1985) Improving expository writing ability: Integrating knowledge of information sources and text structures. Paper read to the Annual Meeting of the American Educational Research Association, Chicago (March).

RAPPAPORT, Z.H. (1992) Psychosurgery in the modern era: Therapeutic and ethical aspects. *Medicine and Law*, 11, 449–453.

RASSOOL, G.H. & WINNINGTON, J. (1993) Using psychoactive drugs. *Nursing Times*, 89, 38–40.

RATHUS, S.A. (1990) *Psychology* (4th edition). New York: Holt, Rinehart & Winston.

RAYNER, K. & POLLATSEK, A. (1989) *The Psychology of Reading*. London: Prentice-Hall.

RAYNER, K. & SERENO, S.C. (1994) Eye movements in reading: Psycholinguistic studies. In M.A. Gernsbacher (Ed.) *Handbook of Psycholinguistics*. New York: Academic Press.

RAZRAN, G. (1950) Ethnic dislikes and stereotypes: A laboratory study. *Journal of Abnormal and Social Psychology*, 45, 7–27.

REASON, J.T. (1979) Actions not as planned: The price of automatisation. In G. Underwood & R. Stevens (Eds) *Aspects of Consciousness:* Volume 1, *Psychological Issues*. London: Academic Press.

REASON, J.T. (1992) Cognitive underspecification: Its variety and consequences. In B.J. Baars (Ed.) *Experimental Slips and Human Error: Exploring the Architecture of Volition*. New York: Plenum Press.

REASON, J.T. & MYCIELSKA, K. (1982) *Absentmindedness: The Psychology of Mental Lapses and Everyday Errors*. Englewood Cliffs, NJ: Prentice-Hall.

REBER, A.S. (1985) *The Penguin Dictionary of Psychology*. Harmondsworth: Penguin.

REBOK, G. (1987) *Life-Span Cognitive Development*. New York: Holt, Rinehart & Winston.

RECHTSCHAFFEN, A., GILLILAND, M., BERGMANN, B. & WINTER, J. (1983) Physiological correlates of prolonged sleep deprivation in rats. *Science*, 221, 182–184.

RECHTSCHAFFEN, A. & KALES, A. (1968) A manual of standardised terminology, techniques, and scoring system for sleep stages of human subjects. *National Institute of Health Publication 204*. Washington, DC: US Government Printing Office.

REDER, L.M. & ANDERSON, J.R. (1980) A comparison of texts and their summaries: Memorial consequences. *Journal of Verbal Learning and Verbal Behaviour*, 19, 121–134.

REEDY, M.N. (1983) Personality and ageing. In D.S. Woodruff & J.E. Birren (Eds) *Ageing: Scientific Perspectives and Social Issues* (2nd edition). Monterey, CA: Brooks/Cole.

REEVES, A. & SPERLING, G. (1986) Attention gating in short-term retention of individual verbal items. *Psychological Review*, 93, 180–206.

REGAN, D.T. & TOTTEN, J. (1975) Empathy and attribution: Turning observers into actors. *Journal of Personality and Social Psychology*, 32, 850–856.

REICH, B. & ADCOCK, C. (1976) *Values, Attitudes and Behaviour Change*. London: Methuen.

REICHER, G.M. (1969) Perceptual recognition as a function of meaningfulness of stimulus material. *Journal of Experimental Psychology*, 81, 275–281.

REICHER, S.D. (1984) The St. Paul's riot: An explanation of the limits of crowd action in terms of a social identity model. *European Journal of Social Psychology*, 14, 1–21.

REINBERG, A. (1967) Eclairement et cycle menstruel de la femme. Rapport au Colloque International du CRNS, la photoregulation de la reproduction chez les oiseaux et les mammifères, Montpelier.

REISENZEIN, R. (1983) The Schachter theory of emotion: Two decades later. *Psychological Bulletin*, 94, 239–264.

REISER, M. & NIELSEN, M. (1980) Investigative hypnosis: A developing speciality. *American Journal of Clinical Hypnosis*, 23, 75–83.

REITMAN, J.S. (1974) Without surreptitious rehearsal, information in short-term memory decays. *Journal of Verbal Learning and Verbal Behaviour*, 13, 365–377.

RESCORLA, R.A. (1968) Probability of shock in the presence and absence of CS in fear conditioning. *Journal of Comparative & Physiological Psychology*, 66, 1–5.

REST, J.R. (1983) Morality. In J.H. Flavell & E. Markman (Eds) *Handbook of Child Psychology*, Volume 3. New York: Wiley.

RESTAK, R. (1975) Jose Delgado: Exploring inner space. *Saturday Review*, 9 August.

RESTAK, R. (1984) *The Brain*. New York: Bantam Books.

RESTLE, F. (1957) Discrimination of cues in mazes: A resolution of the 'place versus response' question. *Psychological Review*, 64, 217–228.

RHEINGOLD, H.L. (1961) The effect of environmental stimulation upon social and exploratory behaviour in the human infant. In B.M. Foss (Ed.) *Determinants of Infant Behaviour*, Volume 1. London: Methuen.

RHEINGOLD, H.L., GERWITZ, J.L. & ROSS, H.W. (1959) Social conditioning of vocalisations in the infant. *Journal of Comparative and Physiological Psychology*, 51, 68–73.

RICE, M. (1989) Children's language acquisition. *American Psychologist*, 44, 149–156.

RICE, R.W. (1978) Construct validity of the esteem for least preferred coworker (LPC) scale. *Psychological Bulletin*, 85, 1199–1237.

RICHARDS, A. & WOPERT, L. (1997) The Insiders' Story. *Independent on Sunday Review*, 27 September, 44–45.

RICHARDS, G. (1996a) Arsenic and old race. *Observer Review*, 5 May, 4.

RICHARDS, G. (1996b) *Putting Psychology in its Place*. London: Routledge.

RICHARDS, M.P.M. (1987) Children, parents and families: Developmental psychology and the re-ordering of relationships at divorce. *International Journal of Law and the Family*, 1, 295–317.

RICHARDS, M.P.M. (1995) The International Year of the Family – family research. *The Psychologist*, 8, 17–20.

RICHARDSON, J. (1993) The curious case of coins. *The Psychologist*, 6, 360–366.

RICHARDSON, K. (1991) *Understanding Intelligence*. Milton Keynes: Open University Press.

RIEGEL, K.F. (1976) The dialectics of human development. *American Psychologist*, 31, 689–700.

RIESEN, A.H. (1947) The development of visual perception in man and chimpanzee. *Science*, 106, 107–108.

RIESEN, A.H. (1965) Effects of early deprivation of photic stimulation. In S. Oster & R. Cook (Eds) *The Biosocial Basis of Mental Retardation*. Baltimore: Johns Hopkins University Press.

RIMLAND, B. (1964) *Infantile Autism*. New York: Appleton-Century-Crofts.

RIMM, D.C. (1976) Behaviour therapy: Some general comments and a review of selected papers. In R.L. Spitzer & D.F. Klein (Eds) *Evaluation of Psychological Therapies*. Baltimore: Johns Hopkins University Press.

RIMM, D.C. & MASTERS, J.C. (1979) *Behaviour Therapy: Techniques and Empirical Findings* (2nd edition). New York: Academic Press.

RINGEN, J. (1996) The behaviour therapist's dilemma: Reflections on autonomy, informed consent, and scientific psychology. In W. O'Donohue & R.F. Kitchener (Eds) *The Philosophy of Psychology*. London: Sage Publications.

RIPS, L.J., SHOBEN, E.H. & SMITH, E.E. (1973) Semantic distance and the verification of semantic relations. *Journal of Verbal Learning and Verbal Behaviour*, 12, 1–20.

RIVERS, W.H.R. (1901) Vision. In A.C. Haddon (Ed.) *Reports of the Cambridge Anthropological Expedition to the Torres Straits*, Volume 2, Part 1. Cambridge: Cambridge University Press.

ROBERTS, J.P. (1995) Group psychotherapy. *British Journal of Psychiatry*, 166, 124–129.

ROBERTS, R. & NEWTON, P.M. (1987) Levinsonian studies of women's adult development. *Psychology and Ageing*, 39, 165–174.

ROBERTSON, J. (1995) Recovery of brain function: People and nets. *The Psychologist*, 8, 253.

ROBERTSON, J.& ROBERTSON J. (1967–73) Film Series, *Young Children in Brief Separation:* No 3 (1969). John, 17 months, 9 days in a residential nursery. London: Tavistock.

ROBINSON, J.O. (1972) *The Psychology of Visual Illusions*. London: Hutchinson.

ROCHFORD, G. (1974) Are jargon aphasics dysphasic? *British Journal of Disorders of Communication*, 9, 35.

ROCK, I. (1983) *The Logic of Perception*. Cambridge, MA: MIT Press.

ROCK, I. (1984) *Perception*. New York: W.H. Freeman.

RODIN, F. & SLOCHOWER, J. (1976) Externality in the non-obese: Effects of environmental responsiveness on weight. *Journal of Personality and Social Psychology*, 33, 338–344.

ROGERS, B. (1994) Let them eat raw onions. *The Sunday Telegraph*, 13 November, 6.

ROGERS, C.R. (1951) *Client-Centred Therapy: Its Current Practice, Implications and Theory*. Boston: Houghton-Mifflin.

ROGERS, C.R. (1959) A theory of therapy, personality and interpersonal relationships as developed in the client-centred framework. In S. Koch (Ed.) *Psychology: A Study of Science*, Volume III, *Formulations of the Person and the Social Context*. New York: McGraw-Hill.

ROGERS, C.R. (1973) My philosophy of interpersonal relationships and how it grew. *Journal of Humanistic Psychology*, 13, 3–16.

ROGERS, C.R. (1980) *A Way of Being*. Boston: Houghton-Mifflin.

ROGERS, C.R. (1983) *Freedom to Learn in the '80s*. Columbus, OH.: Charles Merrill.

ROGERS, C.R. (1986) Client-centred therapy. In I. Kutash & A. Wolf (Eds) *Psychotherapist's Casebook*. San Francisco: Jossey-Bass.

ROGERS, C.R. & DYMOND, R.F. (Eds) (1954) *Psychotherapy and Personality Change*. Chicago: University of Chicago Press.

ROGERS, J., MEYER, J. & MORTEL, K. (1990) After reaching retirement age physical activity sustains cerebral perfusion and cognition. *Journal of the American Geriatric Society*, 38, 123–128.

ROGERS, M., DUBEY, D. & REICH, P. (1979) The influence of the psyche and the brain on disease immunity and disease susceptibility: A critical review. *Psychosomatic Medicine*, 41, 147–164.

ROGLER, L.H., MALGADY, R.G., CONSTANTINO, G. & BLUMENTHAL, R. (1987) What do culturally sensitive mental health services mean? The case of Hispanics. *American Psychologist*, 42, 565–570.

ROGOFF, B. (1990) *Apprenticeship in Thinking: Cognitive Development in a Social Context*. New York: Oxford University Press.

ROGOFF B. & MORELLI, G. (1989) Perspectives on children's development from cultural psychology. *American Psychologist*, 44, 343–348.

ROHLFING, M. (1995) 'Doesn't anybody stay in one place any more?': An exploration of the understudied phenomenon of long-distance relationships. In J.T. Wood & S. Duck (Eds) *Understanding Relationship Processes 6: Understanding Relationships: Off the Beaten Track*. Thousand Oaks, CA: Sage.

ROHSENOW, D.J. & SMITH, R.E. (1982) Irrational beliefs as predictors of negative affective states. *Motivation and Emotion*, 6, 299–301.

ROKEACH, M. (1948) Generalised mental rigidity as a factor in ethnocentrism. *Journal of Abnormal and Social Psychology*, 43, 254–278.

ROKEACH, M. (1960) *The Open and Closed Mind*. New York: Basic Books.

ROLLS, B.J., WOOD, R.J. & ROLLS, E.T. (1980) The initiation, maintenance and termination of drinking. In J.M. Sprague. & A.N. Epstein (Eds) *Progress in Psychobiology and Physiological Psychology*, Volume 9. New York: Academic Press.

ROSE, M. (1980) Rigid rules, inflexible plans and the stifling of language: A cognitivist analysis of writer's block. *College Composition and Communication*, 31, 389–401.

ROSE, P. & PLATZER, H. (1993) Confronting prejudice. *Nursing Times*, 89, 52–54.

ROSE, S. (1992) *The Making of Memory: From molecule to mind*. London: Bantam Books.

ROSE, S., LEWONTIN, R.C., & KAMIN, L.J. (1984) *Not in our Genes: Biology, Ideology and Human Nature*. Harmondsworth: Penguin.

ROSE, S.A. & BLANK, M. (1974) The potency of context in children's cognition: an illustration through conservation. *Child Development*, 45, 499–502.

ROSENBAUM, M.E. (1986) The repulsion hypothesis: On the non-development of relationships. *Journal of Personality and Social Psychology*, 51, 1156–1166.

ROSENBERG, M. (1965) *Society and the Adolescent Self-Image*. Princeton, NJ: Princeton University Press.

ROSENHAN, D.L. (1973) On being sane in insane places. *Science*, 179, 365–369.

ROSENHAN, D.L. & SELIGMAN, M.E. (1984) *Abnormal Psychology*. New York: Norton.

ROSENKILDE, C.E. & DIVAC, I. (1976) Time-discrimination performance in cats with lesions in prefrontal cortex and caudate nucleus. *Journal of Comparative and Physiological Psychology*, 90, 343–352.

ROSENTHAL, A.M. (1964) *Thirty-Eight Witnesses*. New York: McGraw-Hill.

ROSENTHAL, D. (Ed.) (1963) *The Genain Quadruplets*. New York: Basic Books.

ROSENTHAL, R. (1963) On the social psychology of the psychological experiment: The experimenter's hypothesis as unintended determinant of experimental results. *American Scientist*, 51, 268–283.

ROSENTHAL, R. (1966) *Experimenter Effects in Behavioural Research*. New York: Appleton-Century-Crofts.

ROSENTHAL, R. & FODE, K.L. (1963) The effects of experimenter bias on the performance of the albino rat. *Behavioural Science*, 8, 183–189.

ROSENTHAL, R. & JACOBSON, L. (1968) *Pygmalian in the Classroom*. New York: Holt, Rinehart, Winston.

ROSENTHAL, R. & LAWSON, R. (1961) 'A longitudinal study of the effects of experimenter bias on the operant learning of laboratory rats.' (Unpublished manuscript, Harvard University.)

ROSENTHAL, R. & ROSNOW, R.L. (1966) *The Volunteer Subject*. New York: Wiley.

ROSS, D.M. & ROSS, S.A. (1976) *Hyperactivity: Research, Theory and Action*. New York: Wiley.

ROSS, E.D. (1981) The aprosodias: Functional-anatomic organisation of the affective components of language in the right hemisphere. *Archives of Neurology*, 38, 561–569.

ROSS, L. (1977) The intuitive psychologist and his shortcomings. In L. Berkowitz (Ed.) *Advances in Experimental Social Psychology*, Volume 10. New York: Academic Pres.

ROSS, M. & FLETCHER, G.J.O. (1985) Attribution and social perception. In G. Lindzey & E. Aronson (Eds) *Handbook of Social Psychology*, Volume 2 (3rd edition). New York: Random House.

ROSSI, E.I. (1973) The dream protein hypothesis. *American Journal of Psychiatry*, 130, 1094–1097.

ROSSI, P.J. (1968) Adaptation and negative after-effect to lateral optical displacement in newly hatched chicks. *Science*, 160, 430–432.

ROTH, A. & FONAGY, P. (1996) *Research on the efficacy and effectiveness of the psychotherapies: A report to the Department of Health*. London: HMSO.

ROTH, I. (1986) An introduction to object perception. In I. Roth & J.P. Frisby (Eds) *Perception and Representation*. Milton Keynes: Open University Press.

ROTH, I. (1995) Object recognition. In I. Roth & V. Bruce (Eds) *Perception and Representation: Current Issues* (2nd edition). Buckingham: Open University Press.

ROTTER, J.B. (1966) Generalised expectancies for internal versus external control of reinforcement. *Psychological Monographs*, 30 (1), 1–26.

ROWAN, A.N. (1997) The benefits and ethics of animal research. *Scientific American*, 64–66, February.

ROWAN, J. (1978) *The Structured Crowd*. London: Davis Poynter.

ROY, A. (1981) Role of past loss in depression. *Archives of General Psychiatry*, 38, 301–302.

ROY, D.F. (1991) Improving recall by eyewitnesses through the cognitive interview: Practical applications and implications for the police service. *The Psychologist*, 4, 398–400.

RUBENSTEIN, C. (1983) The modern art of courtly love. *Psychology Today*, June, 39–49.

RUBIN, D.C. & OLSON, M.J. (1980) Recall of semantic domains. Memory and Cognition, 8, 354–366.

RUBIN, E. (1915) *Synsoplevede Figurer*. Kobenhaun: Gyldendalske Boghandel.

RUBIN, F. (Ed.) (1968) *Current Research in Hypnopaedia*. New York: Elsevier.

RUBIN, J.Z., PROVENZANO, F.J. & LURIA, Z. (1974) The eye of the beholder: Parents' views on sex of new-borns. *American Journal of Orthopsychiatry*, 44, 512–519.

RUBIN, Z. (1973) *Liking and Loving*. New York: Holt, Rinehart & Winston.

RUBIN, Z. & McNEIL, E.B. (1983) *The Psychology of Being Human* (3rd edition). London: Harper & Row.

RUBLE, D.N. (1984) Sex-role development. In M.C. Bornstein & M.E. Lamb (Eds) *Developmental Psychology: An Advanced Textbook*. Hillsdale, NJ: Erlbaum.

RUDERMAN, A.J. (1986) Dietary restraint: A theoretical and empirical review. *Psychological Bulletin*, 99, 247–262.

RUDOLPH, K., WIRZ-JUSTICE, A. & KRAUCHI, K. (1993) Static magnetic fields decrease nocturnal pineal cAMP in the rat. *Brain Research*, 446, 159–160.

RUMELHART, D.E. (1975) Notes on a schema for stories. In D.G. Bobrow & A. Collins (Eds) *Representation and Understanding: Studies in Cognitive Science*. New York: Academic Press.

RUMELHART, D.E. & McCLELLAND, J.L. (1982) An interactive activation model of context effect in letter recognition. Part 2: The contextual enhancement effect and some tests and extensions of the model. *Psychological Review*, 89, 60–94.

RUNCIMAN, W.G. (1966) *Relative Deprivation and Social Justice*. London: Routledge & Kegan Paul.

RUNDUS, D. & ATKINSON, R.C. (1970) Rehearsal procedures in free recall: A procedure for direct observation. *Journal of Verbal Learning and Verbal Behaviour*, 9, 99–105.

RUSBULT, C. (1987) Responses to dissatisfaction in close relationships: The exit–voice–loyalty–neglect model. In D. Perlman & S. Duck (Eds) *Intimate Relationships: Development, Dynamics and Deterioration*. London: Sage.

RUSHTON, J.P. (1995) *Race, Evolution and Behaviour*. New Brunswick, NJ: Transaction Publishers.

RUSSEK, M. (1971) Hepatic receptors and the neurophysiological mechanisms in controlling feeding behaviour. In S. Ehrenpreis (Ed.) *Neurosciences Research*, Volume 4. New York: Academic Press.

RUSSELL, G.F.M. (1979) Bulimia nervosa: An ominous variant of anorexia nervosa. *Psychological Medicine*, 9, 429–448.

RUSSELL, R. (1981) Report on effective psychotherapy: Legislative testimony. Paper presented at a public hearing on the Regulation of Mental Health Practitioners, New York (March).

RUTTER, M. (1971) Autism: A critical disorder of cognition and language? In M. Rutter (Ed.) *Infantile Autism: Concepts, Characteristics and Treatment*. London: Churchill Livingstone.

RUTTER, M. (1981) *Maternal Deprivation Reassessed* (2nd edition). Harmondsworth: Penguin.

RUTTER, M. (1989) Pathways from childhood to adult life. *Journal of Child Psychology and Psychiatry*, 30, 23–25.

RUTTER, M., GRAHAM, P., CHADWICK, D.F.D. & YULE, W. (1976) Adolescent turmoil: Fact or fiction? *Journal of Child Psychology and Psychiatry*, 17, 35–56.

RUTTER, M. & MADGE, N. (1976) *Cycles of Disadvantage*. London: Heinemann.

RUTTER, M. & RUTTER, M. (1992) *Developing Minds: Challenge and Continuity Across The Life-Span*. Harmondsworth: Penguin.

RYBACK, R.S. & LEWIS, O.F. (1971) Effects of prolonged bed rest on EEG sleep patterns in young, healthy volunteers. *Electroencephalography and Clinical Neurophysiology*, 31, 395–399.

RYCROFT, C. (1966) Introduction: Causes and Meaning. In C. Rycroft (Ed.) *Psychoanalysis Observed*. London: Constable & Co. Ltd.

RYDER, R. (1990) Open reply to Jeffrey Gray. *The Psychologist*, 3, 403.

SABBAGH, K. & BARNARD, C. (1984) *The Living Body*. London: Macdonald.

SACKHEIM, H.A. (1982) Hemispheric asymmetry in the expression of positive and negative emotions. *Archives of Neurology*, 39, 210–218.

SACKS, O. (1985) *The Man who Mistook his Wife for a Hat and Other Clinical Tales*. New York: Summit Books.

SAHAKIAN, B. (1987) Anorexia nervosa and bulimia nervosa. In R.L. Gregory (Ed.) *The Oxford Companion to the Mind*. Oxford: Oxford University Press.

SALAME, P. & BADDELEY, A.D. (1982) Disruption of short-term memory by unattended speech: Implications for the structure of working memory. *Journal of Verbal Learning and Verbal Behaviour*, 21, 150–164.

SALAPATEK, P. (1975) Pattern perception in early infancy. In L.B. Cohen & P. Salapatek (Eds) *Infant Perception: From Sensation to Cognition*, Volume 1. *Basic Visual Processes*. London: Academic Press.

SAMEROFF, A.J. & SEIFER, R. (1989) Social Regulation of Developmental Communities. Paper presented at the annual meeting of the American Association for the Advancement of Science, San Francisco.

SAMUEL, J. & BRYANT, P. (1984) Asking only one question in the conservation experiment. *Journal of Child Psychology and Psychiatry*, 25, 315–318.

SANAVIO, E. (1988) Obsessions and compulsions: The Padua Inventory. *Behaviour Research and Therapy*, 26, 169–177.

SANBONMATSU, D.M., SHAVITT, S., SHERMAN, S.J. & ROSKO-EWOLDSEN, D.R. (1987) Illusory correlation in the perception of performance by self or a salient other. *Journal of Experimental Social Psychology*, 23, 518–543.

SANDE, G.N., GOETHALS, G.R. & RADLOFF, C.E. (1988) Perceiving one's own traits and others': The multifaceted self. *Journal of Personality and Social Psychology*, 54, 13–20.

SANDERS, G.S. (1984) Effects of context cues on eyewitness identification responses. *Journal of Applied Social Psychology*, 14, 386–397.

SANE (1993a) *Depression and Manic Depression: The Swings and Roundabouts of the Mind*. London: SANE Publications.

SANE (1993b) *Medical Methods of Treatment: A Guide to Psychiatric Drugs*. London: SANE Publications.

SANFORD, R.N. (1937) The effects of abstinence from food upon imaginal processes. A further experiment. *Journal of Psychology*, 3, 145–159.

SANGIULIANO, I. (1978) *In Her Time*. New York: Morrow.

SANTEE, R. & MASLACH, C. (1982) To agree or not to agree: Personal dissent amid social pressure to conform. *Journal of Personality and Social Psychology*, 42, 690–700.

SANTROCK, J.W. (1986) *Psychology: The Science of Mind and Behaviour*. Dubuque, IA: William C. Brown.

SAPIR, E. (1929) The study of linguistics as a science. *Language*, 5, 207–214.

SARAFINO, E.P. & ARMSTRONG, J.W. (1980) *Child and Adolescent Development*. Glenview, Ill.: Scott, Foresman and Company.

SARBIN, T.R. (1992) The social construction of schizophrenia. In W. Flack, D.R. Miller & M. Wiener (Eds) *What is Schizophrenia?* New York: Springer-Verlag.

SARTORIUS, N., KAELBER, C.T. & COOPER, J.E. (1993) Progress toward achieving a common language in psychiatry. Results from the field trials accompanying the clinical guidelines of mental and behavioural disorders in ICD-10. *Archives of General Psychiatry*, 50, 115–124.

SARTRE, J.P. (1948) *Anti-Semite and Jew*. New York: Shocken.

SATZ, P. (1979) A test of some models of hemispheric speech organisation in the left- and right-handed. *Science*, 203, 1131–1133.

SAVAGE-RUMBAUGH, E.S. (1990) Language as a cause-effect communication system. *Philosophical Psychology*, 3, 55–76.

SAVAGE-RUMBAUGH, E.S., RUMBAUGH, D.M. & BOYSEN, S.L. (1980) Do apes have language? *American Scientist*, 68, 49–61.

SAYERS, J. (1982) *Biological Politics: Feminist and Anti-Feminist Perspectives*. London: Tavistock.

SAYLES, S.M. (1966) Supervisory style and productivity: Reward and theory. *Personnel Psychology*, 19, 275–286.

SCARDAMALIA, M. & BEREITER, C. (1987) Written composition. In M. Wittrock (Ed.) *Third Handbook of Research on Testing*. New York: Macmillan.

SCARDAMALIA, M., BEREITER, C. & GOLEMAN, H. (1982) The role of productive factors in writing ability. In M. Nystrand (Ed.) *What Writers Know: The Language, Process and Structure of Written Discourse*. New York: Academic Press.

SCARR, S. & WEINBERG, R. (1976) IQ test performance of black children adopted by white families. *American Psychologist*, 31, 726–739.

SCARR, S. & WEINBERG, R. (1978) Attitudes, interests, and IQ. *Human Nature*, April, 29–36.

SCARR, S. (1984) *Mother Care/Other Care*. New York: Basic Books.

SCHACHAR, R. (1991) Childhood hyperactivity. *Journal of Child Psychology and Psychiatry*, 32, 155–191.

SCHACHTER, S. (1951) Deviation, rejection and communication. *Journal of Abnormal and Social Psychology*, 46, 190–207.

SCHACHTER, S. (1959) *The Psychology of Affiliation: Experimental Studies of the Sources of Gregariousness*. Stanford, CA: Stanford University Press.

SCHACHTER, S. (1964) The interaction of cognitive and physiological determinants of emotional state. In L. Berkowitz (Ed.) *Advances in Experimental Social Psychology*, Volume 1. New York: Academic Pres.

SCHACHTER, S. & SINGER, J.E. (1962) Cognitive, social and physiological determinants of emotional state. *Psychological Review*, 69, 379–399.

SCHAFFER, H.R. (1966) The onset of fear of strangers and the incongruity hypothesis. *Journal of Child Psychology and Psychiatry*, 7, 95–106.

SCHAFFER, H.R. (1971) *The Growth of Sociability*. Harmondsworth: Penguin.

SCHAFFER, H.R. (1989) Early social development. In A. Slater & G. Bremner (Eds) *Infant Development*. Hove: Erlbaum.

SCHAFFER, H.R. (1996a) *Social Development* Oxford: Blackwell.

SCHAFFER, H.R. (1996b) Is the child father to the man? *Psychology Review*, 2, 2–5.

SCHAFFER, H.R. & EMERSON, P.E. (1964) The development of social attachments in infancy. *Monographs of the Society for Research in Child Development*, 29 (Whole No. 3).

SCHAIE, K.W. & HERTZOG, C. (1983) Fourteen-year cohort-sequential analysis of adult intellectual development. *Developmental Psychology*, 19, 531–543.

SCHANK, R.C. (1975) *Conceptual Information Processing*. Amsterdam: North-Holland.

SCHANK, R.C. (1982) *Dynamic Memory*. New York: Cambridge University Press.

SCHANK, R.C. & ABELSON, R.P. (1977) *Scripts, Plans, Goals and Understanding*. Hillsdale, NJ: Erlbaum.

SCHEERER, M. (1963) Problem-solving. *Scientific American*, 208, 118–128.

SCHEPER-HUGHES, N. (1991) *Death Without Weeping: The Violence of Everyday Life in Brazil*. Los Angeles: University of California Press.

SCHIFF, N., DUYME, M., DUMARET, A., STEWART, J., TOMKIEWICZ, S. & FEINGOLD, J. (1978) Intellectual status of working-class children adopted early into upper-middle-class families. *Science*, 200, 1503–1504.

SCHIFFMAN, R. & WICKLUND, R.A. (1992) The minimal group paradigm and its minimal psychology. *Theory and Psychology*, 2, 29–50.

SCHILDKRAUT, J. (1965) The catecholamine hypothesis of affective disorders: A review of supporting evidence. *American Journal of Psychiatry*, 122, 509–522.

SCHLOSSBERG, N.K., TROLL, L.E. & LEIBOWITZ, Z. (1978) *Perspectives on Counselling Adults: Issues and Skills*. Monterey, CA: Brooks/Cole.

SCHNEIDER, B.H. (1991) A comparison of skill-building and desensitisation strategies for intervention with aggressive children. *Aggressive Behaviour*, 17, 301–311.

SCHNEIDER, B.H. & BYRNE, B.M. (1987) Individualising social skills training for behaviour-disordered children. *Journal of Consulting and Clinical Psychology*, 55, 444–445.

SCHNEIDER, K. (1959) *Clinical Psychopathology*. New York: Grune & Stratton.

SCHNEIDER, W. & FISK, A.D. (1982) Degree of consistent training: Improvements in search performance and automatic process development. *Perception and Psychophysics*, 31, 160–168.

SCHNEIDER, W. & SHIFFRIN, R.M. (1977) Controlled and automatic human information processing: I. Detection, search and attention. *Psychological Review*, 84, 1–66.

SCHROEDER, D.A., PENNER, L.A., DOVIDIO, J.F. & PILIAVIN, J.A. (1995) *The Psychology of Helping and Altruism: Problems and Puzzles*. New York: McGraw-Hill.

SCHUMAN, H. & RIEGER, C. (1992) Collective memory and collective memories. In M.A. Conway, D.C. Rubin, H. Spinnler & W. Wagenaar (Eds) *Theoretical Perspectives on Autobiographical Memory*. Dordecht: Kluwer Academic Publishers.

SCHWARTZ, G.E., WEINBERGER, D.A. & SINGER, J.A. (1981) Cardiovascular differentiation of happiness, sadness, anger, and fear following imagery and exercise. *Psychosomatic Medicine*, 43, 343–364.

SCHWEINHART, L.J. & WEIKART, D.P. (1980) Young children grow up: The effects of the Perry Preschool Program on youths through age 15. *Monographs of the High/Scope Educational Research Foundation* (Series No. 7).

SCODEL, A. (1957) Heterosexual somatic preference and fantasy dependence. *Journal of Consulting Psychology*, 21, 371–374.

SCOLLON, R. (1976) *Conversations With a One-Year-Old*. Honolulu: University of Hawaii Press.

SCOTT, J. (1994) Cognitive therapy. *British Journal of Psychiatry*, 164, 126–130.

SEARS, D.O. & McCONAHAY, J.B. (1969) Participation in the Los Angeles riot. *Social Problems*, 17, 3–20.

SEARS, D.O., PEPLAU, L.A. & TAYLOR, S.E. (1991) Social Psychology (7th edition). Englewood Cliffs, NJ: Prentice-Hall.

SEARS, R.R., MACCOBY, E.E. & LEVIN, H. (1957) Patterns of Child Rearing. New York: Harper & Row.

SEGAL, M.W. (1974) Alphabet and attraction: An unobtrusive measure of the effect of propinquity in the field setting. *Journal of Personality and Social Psychology*, 30, 654–657.

SEGALL, M.H., CAMPBELL, D.T. & HERSKOVITS, M.J. (1963) Cultural differences in the perception of geometrical illusions. *Science*, 139, 769–771.

SELFE, L. (1978) *Nadia: A Case of Extraordinary Drawing Ability in an Autistic Child.* New York: Academic Press.

SELFRIDGE, O.G. (1959) Pandemonium: A paradigm for learning. *Symposium on the Mechanisation of Thought Processes.* London: HMSO.

SELIGMAN, M.E.P. (1970) On the generality of the laws of learning. *Psychological Review*, 77, 406–418.

SELIGMAN, M.E.P. (1972) *Biological Boundaries of Learning.* New York: Academic Press.

SELIGMAN, M.E.P. (1973) Fall into hopelessness. *Psychology Today*, 7, 43–47.

SELIGMAN, M.E.P. (1975) *Helplessness: On Depression, Development and Death.* San Francisco: W.H. Freeman.

SELIGMAN, M.E.P. & MAIER, S.F. (1967) Failure to escape traumatic shock. *Journal of Experimental Psychology*, 74, 1–9.

SELLEN, A.J. & NORMAN, D.A. (1992) The psychology of slips. In B.J. Baars (Ed.) *Experimental Slips and Human Error: Exploring the Architecture of Volition.* New York: Plenum Press.

SELLERI, P., CARUGATI, F. & SCAPPINI, E. (1995) What marks should I give? A model of the organisation of teachers' judgements of their pupils. *European Journal of Psychology of Education*, 10, 25–40.

SELYE, H. (1936) A syndrome produced by diverse nocuous agents. *Nature*, 138, 32.

SELYE, H. (1976) *The Stress of Life* (revised edition). New York: McGraw-Hill.

SELYE, H. (1980) The stress concept today. In I.L. Kutash (Ed.) *Handbook on Stress and Anxiety.* San Francisco: Jossey-Bass.

SEM-JACOBSEN, C.W. (1968) *Depth-Electrographic Stimulation of the Human Brain and Behaviour.* Springfield, ILL: Charles C. Thomas.

SERPELL, R.S. (1976) *Culture's Influence on Perception.* London: Methuen.

SHAFFER, D.R. (1985) *Developmental Psychology.* Monterey, CA: Brooks/Cole.

SHAFFER, L.H. (1975) Multiple attention in continuous verbal tasks. In P.M.A. Rabbitt & S. Dornic (Eds) *Attention and Performance,* Volume V. London: Academic Press.

SHALLICE, T. (1967) Paper presented at NATO symposium on short-term memory, Cambridge, England.

SHALLICE, T. & WARRINGTON, E.K. (1970) Independent functioning of verbal memory stores: A neurophysiological study. *Quarterly Journal of Experimental Psychology*, 22, 261–273.

SHAPIRO, A.K. (1971) Placebo effects in medicine, psychotherapy and psychoanalysis. In A.E. Bergin & S.L. Garfield (Eds) *Handbook of Psychotherapy and Behaviour Change: An Empirical Analysis.* New York: Wiley.

SHAPIRO, C.M., BORTZ, R., MITCHELL, D., BARTEL, P. & JOOSTE, P. (1981) Slow-wave sleep: A recovery period after exercise. *Science*, 214, 1253–1254.

SHAPIRO, D.A. & SHAPIRO, D. (1982) Meta-analysis of comparative therapy outcome studies: A replication and refinement. *Psychological Bulletin*, 92, 581–604.

SHARP, C.W. & FREEMAN, C.P.L. (1993) The medical complications of anorexia nervosa. *British Journal of Psychiatry*, 162, 452–462.

SHARPE, M. (1994) 30 just watched as drunk yobs did this to Sgt. Gary. *The Sun*, 30 April, 7.

SHARPE, M., HAWTON, K., SIMKIN, S., HACKMANN, A., KLIMES, I., PETO, T., WARRELL, S., & SEAGROAT, V. (1996) Cognitive-behavioural therapy for the chronic fatigue syndrome: A randomised controlled trial. *British Medical Journal*, 312, 22–26.

SHATZ, M. (1994) *A Toddler's Life: Becoming a Person.* Oxford: Oxford University Press.

SHAW, M.E. (1981) *Group Dynamics: The Psychology of Small Group Behaviour.* New York: McGraw-Hill.

SHAW, M.E., ROTHSCHILD, G.H. & STRICKLUND, J.F. (1957) Decision processes in communication nets. *Journal of Abnormal and Social Psychology*, 54, 323–330.

SHEAR, K.K., PILKONIS, P.A., CLOITRE, M. & LEON, A.C. (1994) Cognitive behavioural treatment compared with nonprescriptive treatment of panic disorders. *Archives of General Psychiatry*, 51, 395–401.

SHEEHY, G. (1976) *Passages – Predictable Crises of Adult Life.* New York: Bantam Books.

SHEEHY, G. (1996) *New Passages.* New York: HarperCollins.

SHEFFIELD, F.D. & ROBY, T.B. (1950) Reward value of a non-nutritive sweet taste. *Journal of Comparative and Physiological Psychology*, 43, 471–481.

SHELLOW, R. & ROEMER, D.V. (1966) No heaven for 'Hell's Angels'. *Transaction*, July–August, 12–19.

SHERIDAN, C.L. & KING, R.G. (1972) Obedience to authority with an authentic victim. Proceedings of the 80th Annual Convention, *American Psychological Association, Part 1*, 7, 165–166.

SHERIF, M. (1935) A study of social factors in perception. *Archives of Psychology*, 27, Whole No. 187.

SHERIF, M. (1936) The *Psychology of Social Norms.* New York: Harper & Row.

SHERIF, M. (1966) *Group Conflict and Co-operation: Their Social Psychology.* London: Routledge & Kegan Paul.

SHERIF, M., HARVEY, O.J., WHITE, B.J., HOOD, W.R. & SHERIF, C.W. (1961) *Intergroup Conflict and Co-operation: The Robber's Cave Experiment.* Norman, OK: University of Oklahoma Press.

SHIBUTANI, T. (1966) *Improvised News: A Sociological Study of Rumour.* Indianapolis: Bobbs-Merrill Co.

SHIELDS, J. (1962) *Monozygotic Twins Brought Up Apart and Brought Up Together.* London: Oxford University Press.

SHIFFRIN, R.M. & SCHNEIDER, W. (1977) Controlled and automatic human information processing: II. Perceptual learning, automatic attending and a general theory. *Psychological Review*, 84, 127–190.

SHORTLIFFE, E.H. (1976) *Computer-Based Medical Consultations: MYCIN.* New York: American Elsevier.

SHOTLAND, R.L. & HEINOLD, W.D. (1985) Bystander response to arterial bleeding: Helping skills, the decision-making process, and differentiating the helping response. *Journal of Personality and Social Psychology*, 49, 347–356.

SHOTLAND, R.L. & STRAW, M.K. (1976) Bystander response to an assault: When a man attacks a woman. *Journal of Personality and Social Psychology*, 34, 990–999.

SHULMAN, H.G. (1970) Encoding and retention of semantic and phonemic information in short-term memory. *Journal of Verbal Learning and Verbal Behaviour*, 9, 499–508.

SHWEDER, R.A. (1991) *Thinking Through Cultures: Expeditions in Cultural Psychology.* Cambridge, MA: Harvard University Press.

SHWEDER, R.A., MAHAPATRA, M. & MILLER, J.G. (1987) Culture and moral development. In J. Kagan & S. Lamb (Eds) *The Emergence of Morality in Young Children.* Chicago: University of Chicago Press.

SIANN, G. (1985) *Accounting for Aggression – Perspectives on Aggression and Violence.* London: Allen & Unwin.

SIDDIQUE, C.M. & D'ARCY, C. (1984) Adolescence, stress and psychological well-being. *Journal of Youth and Adolescence*, 13, 459–474.

SIEGEL, R.K. (1982) Quoted by Hooper, J. in 'Mind tripping'. *Omni*, October, 155.

SIGALL, H. & LANDY, D. (1973) Radiating beauty: Effects of having a physically attractive partner on person perception. *Journal of Personality and Social Psychology*, 28, 218–224.

SILVERMAN, I. (1971) Physical attractiveness and courtship. *Sexual Behaviour*, September, 22–25.

SILVERN, S.B. (1986) Classroom use of video games. *Education Research Quarterly*, 10, 10–16.

SILVERSTEIN, C. (1972) Behaviour modification and the gay community. Paper presented at the annual conference of the Association for the Advancement of Behaviour Therapy, New York.

SIMKIN, J.S. & YONTEF, G.M. (1984) Gestalt therapy. In R.J. Corsini (Ed.) *Current Psychotherapies* (3rd edition). Itasca, ILL: Peacock.

SIMMONDS, M. (1914) Über Hypophysisschwund mit todlichem Ausung. *Deutsche Medizinische Wochenschrift*, 40, 332–340.

SIMMONS, J.Q. & LOVAAS, O.I. (1969) Use of pain and punishment as treatment techniques with childhood schizophrenia. *American Journal of Psychotherapy*, 23, 23–36.

SIMMONS, R. & BLYTH, D.A. (1987) *Moving Into Adolescence.* New York: Aldine de Gruyter.

SIMMONS, R. & ROSENBERG, S. (1975) Sex, sex-roles and self-image. *Journal of Youth and Adolescence*, 4, 229–256.

SIMON, H.A. & HAYES, J.R. (1976) The understanding process: Problem isomorphs. *Cognitive Psychology*, 8, 165–190.

SIMONOFF, E., BOLTON, P. & RUTTER, M. (1996) Mental retardation: Genetic findings, clinical implications and research agenda. *Journal of Child Psychology and Psychiatry*, 37, 259–280.

SIMS, A.C.P. & GRAY, P. (1993) The Media, Violence and Vulnerable Viewers. Document presented to the Broadcasting Group, House of Lords.

SINCLAIR-de-ZWART, H. (1969) Developmental psycholinguistics. In D. Elkind & J. Flavell (Eds) *Handbook of Learning and Cognitive Processes*, Volume 5. Hillsdale, NJ: Erlbaum.

SINGER, D. (1989) Children, adolescents, and television – 1989. *Paediatrics*, 83, 445–446.

SINGER, J.E., BRUSH, C.A. & LIBLIN, J.C. (1965) Some aspects of deindividuation: Identification and conformity. *Journal of Experimental Social Psychology*, 1, 356–378.

SINGH, B.R. (1991) Teaching methods for reducing prejudice and enhancing academic achievement for all children. *Educational Studies*, 17, 157–171.

SISTRUNK, F. & McDAVID, J.W. (1971) Sex variable in conforming behaviour. *Journal of Personality and Social Psychology*, 2, 200–207.

SKEELS, H.M. & DYE, H.B. (1939) A study of the effects of differential stimulation on mentally retarded children. *Proceedings of the American Association of Mental Deficiency*, 44, 114–136.

SKEELS, H.M. (1966) Adult status of children with contrasting early life experiences. *Monographs of the Society for Research in Child Development*, 31, (Whole No. 3).

SKINNER, B.F. (1938) *The Behaviour of Organisms*. New York: Appleton-Century-Crofts.

SKINNER, B.F. (1948) Superstition in the pigeon. *Journal of Experimental Psychology*, 38, 168–172.

SKINNER, B.F. (1948) *Walden Two*. New York: Macmillan.

SKINNER, B.F. (1957) *Verbal Behaviour*. New York: Appleton-Century-Crofts.

SKINNER, B.F. (1971) *Beyond Freedom and Dignity*. New York: Knopf.

SKINNER, B.F. (1974) *About Behaviourism*. New York: Alfred Knopf.

SKINNER, B.F. (1985) 'Cognitive science and behaviourism.' (Unpublished manuscript. Harvard University.)

SKINNER, B.F. (1987) Skinner on Behaviourism. In R.L. Gregory (Ed.) *The Oxford Companion to the Mind*. Oxford: Oxford University Press.

SKINNER, B.F. (1990) Can psychology be a science of mind? *American Psychologist*, 45, 1206–1210.

SKRIVER, J. (1996) Naturalistic decision-making. *The Psychologist*, 9, 321–322.

SKUSE, P. (1984) Extreme deprivation in early childhood – I. Diverse outcome for three siblings from an extraordinary family. *Journal of Child Psychology and Psychiatry*, 25, 523–541.

SLABY, R.G. & FREY, K.S. (1975) Development of gender constancy and selective attention to same-sex models. *Child Development*, 46, 839–856.

SLATER, A. (1989) Visual memory and perception in early infancy. In A. Slater & G. Bremner (Eds) *Infant Development*. Hove: Erlbaum.

SLATER, A. (1994) Perceptual development in infancy. *Psychology Review*, 1, 12–16.

SLATER, A. & MORISON, V. (1985) Shape constancy and slant perception at birth. *Perception*, 14, 337–344.

SLATER, E. & ROTH, M. (1969) *Clinical Psychiatry* (3rd edition). Ballière-Tindall and Cassell.

SLATER, E. & SHIELDS, J. (1969) Genetic aspects of anxiety. In M. Lader (Ed.) *Studies of Anxiety*. Ashford, England: Headley Brothers.

SLAVIN, R. & MADDEN, N. (1979) School practices that improve race relations. *American Edcuation Research Journal*, 16, 169–180.

SLAVIN, R.E. (1985) Cooperative learning: Applying contact theory in desegregated schools. *Journal of Social Issues*, 41, 45–62.

SLOAN, D. (1995) The hidden handicap. *The Guardian*, 30 January, 10–11.

SLOANE, R., STAPLES, F., CRISTOL, A., YORKSTON, N. & WHIPPLE, K. (1975) *Psychotherapy Versus Behaviour Therapy*. Cambridge, MA: Harvard University Press.

SLOBIN, D.I. (1975) On the nature of talk to children. In E.H. Lenneberg & E. Lenneberg (Eds) *Foundations of Language Development*, Volume 1. New York: Academic Press.

SLOBIN, D.I. (1979) *Psycholinguistics* (2nd edition). Glenview, ILL: Scott, Foresman and Company.

SLOBIN, D.I. (1986) *The Cross-Linguistic Study of Language Acquisition*. Hillsdale, NJ: Erlbaum.

SLUCKIN, W. (1965) *Imprinting and Early Experiences*. London: Methuen.

SMEDSLUND, J. (1961) The acquisition of conservation of substance and weight in children. *Scandinavian Journal of Psychology*, 2, 11–20.

SMELSER, N.J. (1963) *Theory of Collective Behaviour*. New York: The Free Press.

SMETANA, J.G. (1990) Morality and conduct disorders. In M. Lewis & S.M. Miller (Eds) *Handbook of Developmental Psychopathology*. New York: Plenum.

SMITH, C. & LLOYD, B.B. (1978) Maternal behaviour and perceived sex of infant. *Child Development*, 49, 1263–1265.

SMITH, C.U.M. (1994) You are a group of neurons. *The Times Higher Educational Supplement*, 27 May, 20–21.

SMITH, D. (1982) Trends in counselling and psychotherapy. *American Psychologist*, 37, 802–809.

SMITH, D.E., WESSON, D.R., BUXTON, M.E., SEYMOUR, R. & KRAMER, H.M. (1978) The diagnosis and treatment of the PCP abuse syndrome. In R.C. Peterson & R.C. Stillman (Eds) *Phencyclidine (PCP) Abuse: An Appraisal*. NIDA Research Monograph No. 21, DHEW Publication No. ADM 78–728. Washington, DC: US Government Printing Office.

SMITH, E.E., SHOBEN, E.J. & RIPS, L.J. (1974) Structure and process in semantic memory: A feature model of semantic decisions. *Psychological Review*, 81, 214–241.

SMITH, E.M., BROWN, H.O., TOMAN, J.E.P. & GOODMAN, L.S. (1947) The lack of cerebral effects of D-tubo-curarine. *Anaesthesiology*, 8, 1–14.

SMITH, J.A., HARRÉ, R., & VAN LANGENHOVE, L. (1995) Introduction. In J.A.Smith, R. Harré, & L. Van Langenhove (Eds) *Rethinking Psychology*. London: Sage.

SMITH, K.A., FAIRBURN, C.G. & COWEN, P.J. (1997) Relapse of depression after rapid depletion of tryptophan. *The Lancet*, 349, 915–919.

SMITH, M.L., GLASS, G.V. & MILLER, T.I. (1980) *The Benefits of Psychotherapy*. Baltimore: Johns Hopkins University Press.

SMITH, M.M., COLLINS, A.F., MORRIS, P.E. & LEVY, P. (1994) *Cognition in Action* (2nd edition). Hove: Erlbaum.

SMITH, P.B. (1995) Social influence proceses. In M. Argyle & A.M. Colman (Eds) *Social Psychology*. London: Longman.

SMITH, P.B. & BOND, M.H. (1993) *Social Psychology Across Cultures: Analysis and Perspectives*. Hemel Hempstead: Harvester Wheatsheaf.

SMITH, P.B. & PETERSON, M.F. (1988) *Leadership, Organisations and Culture*. London: Sage.

SMITH, P.K. & COWIE, H. (1991) *Understanding Children's Development* (2nd edition). Oxford: Basil Blackwell.

SMITH, P.K. & DAGLISH, L. (1977) Sex differences in parent and infant behaviour in the home. *Child Development*, 48, 1250–1254.

SMITH, S.M. (1979) Remembering in and out of context. *Journal of Experimental Psychology: Human Learning and Memory*, 5, 460–471.

SMYTHIES, J. (1976) Recent progress in schizophrenia research. *The Lancet*, 2, 136–139.

SNAITH, R.P. (1994) Psychosurgery: Controversy and enquiry. *British Journal of Psychiatry*, 161, 582–584.

SNAREY, J.R. (1987) A question of morality. *Psychology Today*, June, 6–8.

SNOW, C.E. (1977) Mother's speech research: From input to interaction. In C.E. Snow and C.A. Ferguson (Eds) *Talking to children: Language input and acquisition*. New York: Cambridge University Press.

SNOW, C.E. (1983) Saying it again: The role of expanded and deferred imitations in language acquisition. In K.E. Nelson (Ed.) *Children's Language*, Volume 4. New York: Gardner Press.

SNOWMAN, J., KREBS, E.V. & LOCKHART, L. (1980) Improving information of recall from prose in high-risk students through Learning Strategy Training. *Journal of Instructional Psychology*, 7, 35–40.

SNYDER, F.W. & PRONKO, N.H. (1952) *Vision with Spatial Inversion*. Wichita, Kansas: University of Wichita Press.

SNYDER, S. (1977) Opiate receptors and internal opiates. *Scientific American*, 236, 44–56.

SOBER, E. (1992) The evolution of altruism: Correlation, cost and benefit. *Biology and Philosophy*, 7, 177–188.

SOBESKY, W. (1983) The effects of situational factors on moral judgements. *Child Development*, 54, 575–584.

SOLOMON, M. (1987) Standard issue. *Psychology Today*, December, 30–31.

SOLOMON, R. & CORBIT, J. (1974) An opponent-process theory of motivation. *Psychological Review*, 81, 119–145.

SOLSO, R.L. (1995) *Cognitive Psychology* (4th edition). Boston: Allyn & Bacon.

SOMMER, R. (1969) *Personal Space: The Behavioural Basis of Design.* Englewood Cliffs, NJ: Prentice-Hall.

SONSTROEM, R.J. (1984) Exercise and self-esteem. *Exercise and Sport Sciences Review*, 12, 123–155.

SORRENTINO, R.M. & FIELD, N. (1986) Emergent leadership over time: The functional value of positive motivation. *Journal of Personality and Social Psychology*, 50, 1091–1099.

SPACHE, G.B. (1981) *Diagnosing and Correcting Reading Disabilities.* Boston: Allyn & Bacon.

SPANIER, G.B. & LEWIS, R.A. (1980) Marital quality: A review of the seventies. *Journal of Marriage and the Family*, 42, 825–840.

SPANOS, N.P. (1986) Hypnotic behaviour: A social-psychological interpretation of amnesia, analgesia, and 'trance logic'. *The Behavioural and Brain Sciences*, 9, 499–502.

SPANOS, N.P. (1991) A sociocognitive approach to hypnosis. In S.J. Lynn & J.W. Rhue (Eds) *Theories of Hypnosis: Current Models and Perspectives.* New York: Guildford Press.

SPANOS, N.P., GWYNN, M.I. & STAM, H.J. (1983) Instructional demands and ratings of overt and hidden pain during hypnotic analgesia. *Journal of Abnormal Psychology*, 92, 479–488.

SPANOS, N.P., JONES, B. & MALFARA, A. (1982) Hypnotic deafness: Now you hear it – now you still hear it. *Journal of Abnormal Psychology*, 91, 75–77.

SPECIAL EDUCATIONAL NEEDS (1978) (The Warnock report). London: HMSO.

SPELKE, E.S., HIRST, W.C. & NEISSER, U. (1976) Skills of divided attention. *Cognition*, 4, 215–230.

SPERLING, G. (1960) The information available in brief visual presentation. *Psychological Monographs*, 74 (Whole No. 498).

SPERLING, H.G. (1946) 'An experimental study of some psychological factors in judgement.' (Master's thesis, New School for Social Research.)

SPERRY, R.W. (1943) The effect of 180-degree rotation in the retinal field on visuo-motor co-ordination. *Journal of Experimental Zoology*, 92, 263–279.

SPERRY, R.W. (1964) The great cerebral commissure. *Scientific American*, 210, 42–52.

SPERRY, R.W. (1974) Lateral specialisation in the surgically separated hemispheres. In F.O. Schmitt & F.G. Worden (Eds) *The Neurosciences: Third Study Program.* Cambridge, MA: MIT Press.

SPERRY, R.W. (1982) Some effects of disconnecting the cerebral hemispheres. *Science*, 217, 1223–1226.

SPINNEY, L. (1997a) Now, reshape your brain. *The Daily Telegraph*, 22 January, 16.

SPINNEY, L. (1997b) Brain operation left woman with no sense of fear. *The Daily Telegraph*, 11 January, 7.

SPITZ, R.A. (1945) Hospitalisation: An inquiry into the genesis of psychiatric conditions in early childhood. *Psychoanalytic Study of the Child*, 1, 53–74.

SPITZ, R.A. (1946) Hospitalism: A follow-up report on investigation described in Vol. 1, 1945. *Psychoanalytic Study of the Child*, 2, 113–117.

SPITZ, R.A. & WOLF, K.M. (1946) Anaclitic depression. *Psychoanalytic Study of the Child*, 2, 313–342.

SPITZER, R.L. (1975) On pseudoscience in science, logic in remission and psychiatric diagnosis: A critique of Rosenhan's 'On being sane in insane places'. *Journal of Abnormal Psychology*, 84, 442–452.

SPITZER, R.L., SKODAL, A.E., GIBBON, M. & WILLIAMS, J.B.W. (Eds) (1981) *DSM-III Case Book.* Washington, DC: American Psychiatric Association.

SPOCK, B. (1946) *Baby and Child Care.* New York: Pocket Books.

SPROTT, W.J.H. (1958) *Human Groups.* Harmondsworth: Penguin.

SQUIRE, L.R. (1987) *Memory and Brain.* Oxford: Oxford University Press.

SROUFE, L.A., FOX, N.E. & PANCAKE, V.R. (1983) Attachment and dependency in developmental perspective. *Child Development*, 54, 1615–1627.

STACEY, M., DEARDEN, R., PILL, R. & ROBINSON, D. (1970) *Hospitals, Children and Their Families: The Report of a Pilot Study.* London: Routledge & Kegan Paul.

STANOVICH, K. (1994) Annotation: Does dyslexia exist? *Journal of Child Psychology and Psychiatry*, 35, 579–595.

STAUB, E. (1979) Understanding and predicting social behaviour – with emphasis on prosocial behaviour. In E. Staub (Ed.) *Personality: Basic Issues and Current Research.* Englewood Cliffs, NJ: Prentice-Hall.

STEPHAN, C.W. & LANGLOIS, J. (1984) Baby beautiful: Adult attributions of infant competence as a function of infant attractiveness. *Child Development*, 55, 576–585.

STEPHAN, W.G. & ROSENFIELD, D. (1978) Effects of desegregation on racial attitudes. *Journal of Personality and Social Psychology*, 36, 795–804.

STERN, D. (1977) *The First Relationship: Infant and Mother.* Cambridge, MA: Harvard University Press.

STERNBERG, R.J. (1986a) Cognition and instruction: Why the marriage sometimes ends in divorce. In R.F. Dillon & R.J. Sternberg (Eds) *Cognition and Instruction.* London: Academic Press.

STERNBERG, R.J. (1986b) A triangular theory of love. *Psychological Review*, 93, 119–135.

STERNBERG, R.J. (1988) Triangulating love. In R.J. Sternberg & M.L. Barnes (Eds) *The Psychology of Love.* New Haven, CT: Yale University Press.

STERNBERG, R.J. (1990) *Metaphors of Mind.* Cambridge: Cambridge University Press.

STEVENS, J.R. (1982) Neurology and neuropathology of schizophenia. In F.A. Henn & G.A. Nasrallah (Eds) *Schizophrenia as a Brain Disease.* New York: Oxford University Press.

STEVENS, R. (1995) Freudian theories of personality. In S.E. Hampson & A.M. Colman (Eds) *Individual Differences and Personality.* London: Longman.

STEVENSON, G.I. & BAKER, R. (1996) Brain Chemistry. *Education in Chemistry*, 33, 124–128.

STEWART, D.A. (1992) Initiating reform in total communication programmes. *Journal of Special Education*, 26, 68–84.

STEWART, V.M. (1973) Tests of the 'carpentered world' hypothesis by race and environment in America and Africa. *International Journal of Psychology*, 8, 83–94.

STOCK, M.B. & SMYTHE, P.M. (1963) Does malnutrition during infancy inhibit brain growth and subsequent intellectual development? *Archives of Disorders in Childhood*, 38, 546–552.

STOGDILL, R.M. (1974) *Handbook of Leadership.* New York: Free Press.

STORMS, M.D. (1973) Videotape and the attribution process: Reversing actors' and observers' points of view. *Journal of Personality and Social Psychology*, 27, 165–175.

STOUFFER, S.A., SUCHMAN, E.A., DeVINNEY, L.C., STARR, S.A. & WILLIAMS, R.M. (1949) *The American Soldier: Adjustment During Army Life*, Volume 1. Princeton, NJ: Princeton University Press.

STRACHEY, J. (1962–1977) *Sigmund Freud: A sketch of his life and ideas.* This appears in each volume of the Pelican Freud Library: originally written for the *Standard Edition of the Complete Psychological Works of Sigmund Freud, 1953–1974.* London: Hogarth Press.

STRATTON, G.M. (1896) Some preliminary experiments on vision. *Psychological Review*, 3, 611–617.

STRATTON, G.M. (1897) Vision without inversion of the retinal image. *Psychological Review*, 4, 341–481.

STRAUS, M., GELLES, R. & STEINMETZ, S. (1980) *Behind Closed Doors: Violence in the American Family.* Garden City, NY: Anchor Press.

STRAW, J. & ANDERSON, A. (1996) *Parenting: A Discussion Paper.* London: House of Commons.

STROBER, M. & KATZ, J.L. (1987) Do eating disorders and affective disorders share a common aetiology? *International Journal of Eating Disorders*, 6, 171–180.

STROEBE, M.S., STROEBE, W. & HANSSON, R.O. (1993) Contemporary themes and controversies in bereavement research. In M.S. Stroebe, W. Stroebe & R.O. Hansson (Eds) *Handbook of Bereavement: Theory, Research and Intervention.* New York: Cambridge University Press.

STROOP, J.R. (1935) Studies of interference in serial verbal reactions. *Journal of Experimental Psychology*, 18, 643–662.

STRUPP, H.H. & HADLEY, S.W. (1979) Specific versus non-specific factors in psychotherapy: A controlled study of outcome. *Archives of General Psychiatry*, 36, 1125–1136.

STUART-HAMILTON, I. (1994) *The Psychology of Ageing: An Introduction* (2nd edition). London: Jessica Kingsley.

STUART-HAMILTON, I. (1997) Adjusting to Later Life. *Psychology Review*, 4 (2), 20–23, November.

SUE, D., SUE, D. & SUE, S. (1994) *Understanding Abnormal Behaviour* (4th edition). Boston: Houghton-Mifflin.

SUE, S. (1995) Implications of the Bell curve: Whites are genetically inferior in intelligence? *Focus: Notes from the Society for the Psychological Study of Ethnic Minority Issues*, 16–17.

SUI–WAH, L. (1989) Anorexia nervosa and Chinese food. *British Journal of Psychiatry*, 155, 568.

SULLOWAY, F.J. (1979) *Freud, Biologist of the Mind: Beyond the Psychoanalytic Legend*. New York: Basic Books.

SULSER, F. (1979) Pharmacology: New cellular mechanisms of anti-depressant drugs. In S. Fielding & R.C. Effland (Eds) *New Frontiers in Psychotropic Drug Research*. Mount Kisco, NY: Futura.

SUMNER, W.G. (1906) *Folkways*. Boston: Ginn.

SUNDAY, S.R. & HALMI, K.A. (1990) Taste perceptions and hedonics in eating disorders. *Physiology and Behaviour*, 48, 587–594.

SUOMI, S.J. & HARLOW, H.F. (1977) Depressive behaviour in young monkeys subjected to vertical chamber confinement. *Journal of Comparative and Physiological Psychology*, 80, 11–18.

SURREY, D. (1982) 'It's like good training for life'. *Natural History*, 91, 71–83.

SUTHERLAND, P. (1992) *Cognitive Development Today: Piaget and his Critics*. London: Paul Chapman Publishing.

SUTHERLAND, S. (1991) *Macmillan Dictionary of Psychology*. London: The Macmillan Press.

SWEENEY, K. (1995) Stay calm and heal better. *The Times*, 21 December, 5.

SWEET, W.H., ERVIN, F. & MARK, V.H. (1969) The relationship of violent behaviour to focal cerebral disease. In Garattini, S. & Sigg, E.B. (Eds) *Aggressive Behaviour*. New York: Wiley.

SWENSEN, C.H. (1983) A respectable old age. *American Psychologist*, 46, 1208–1221.

SYAL, R. (1997) Doctors find pick-me-up for SAD people. *The Sunday Times*, 19 January, 4.

SYLVA, K. (1996) Education: Report on the Piaget-Vygotsky centenary conference. *The Psychologist*, 9, 370–372.

SZASZ, T.S. (1960) The myth of mental illness. *American Psychologist*, 15, 113–118.

SZASZ, T.S. (1962) *The Myth of Mental Illness*. New York: Harper & Row.

SZASZ, T.S. (1974) *Ideology and Insanity*. Harmondsworth: Penguin.

SZASZ, T.S. (1994) *Cruel Compassion – Psychiatric Control of Society's Unwanted*. New York: Wiley.

TACHE, J., SELYE, H. & DAY, S. (1979) *Cancer, Stress, and Death*. New York: Plenum Press.

TAJFEL, H. (1969) Social and cultural factors in perception. In G. Lindzey & E. Aronson (Eds) *Handbook of Social Psychology*, Volume 3. Reading, MA: Addison-Wesley.

TAJFEL, H. (Ed.) (1978) *Differentiation Between Social Groups: Studies in the Social Psychology of Intergroup Relations*. London: Academic Press.

TAJFEL, H. & BILLIG, M. (1974) Familiarity and categorization in inter-group behaviour. *Journal of Experimental Social Psychology*, 10, 159–170.

TAJFEL, H., BILLIG, M.G. & BUNDY, R.P. (1971) Social categorization and intergroup behaviour. *European Journal of Social Psychology*, 1, 149–178.

TAJFEL, H. & TURNER, J.C. (1986) The social identity theory of intergroup behaviour. In S. Worchel & W. Austin (Eds) *Psychology of Intergoup Relations*. Chicago: Nelson-Hall.

TAKAHASHI, K. (1990) Are the key assumptions of the strange situation procedure universal?: A view from Japanese research. *Human Development*, 33, 23–30.

TALLIS, F. (1994) Obsessive-compulsive disorder. *The Psychologist*, 7, 312.

TALLIS, F. (1995) *Obsessive Compulsive Disorder: A Cognitive and Neuropsychological Perspective*. Chichester: Wiley.

TALLIS, R. (1996) Burying Freud. *The Lancet*, 347, 669–671.

TANFORD, S. & PENROD, S. (1984) Social influence model: A formal investigation of research on majority and minority influence proceses. *Psychological Bulletin*, 95, 189–225.

TANNER, J.M. (1978) *Fetus into Man: Physical Growth from Conception to Maturity*. Cambridge, MA: Harvard University Press.

TANNER, J.M. & WHITEHOUSE, R.H. (1976) Clinical longitudinal standards for height, weight, height velocity, weight velocity and stages of puberty. *Archives of Disorders in Childhood*, 51, 170–179.

TARRIER, N., BECKETT, R. & HARWOOD, S. (1993) A trial of two cognitive behavioural methods of treating drug-resistant residual psychotic symptoms in schizophrenic patients. *British Journal of Psychiatry*, 162, 524–532.

TARTTER, V. (1986) *Language Processes*. New York: Holt, Rinehart & Winston.

TAVRIS, C. (1993) The mismeasure of woman. *Feminism & Psychology*, 3 (2), 149–168.

TAVRIS, C. & WADE, C. (1995) *Psychology in Perspective*. New York: HarperCollins.

TAYLOR, D.M. & PORTER, L.E. (1994) A multicultural view of stereotyping. In W.J. Lonner & R.S. Malpass (Eds) *Psychology and Culture*. Boston: Allyn & Bacon.

TAYLOR, R. (1963) *Metaphysics*. Englewood Cliffs, NJ: Prentice-Hall.

TAYLOR, S. (1990) Health psychology: The science and the field. *American Psychologist*, 45, 40–50.

TAYLOR, S.E., PEPLAU, L.A. & SEARS, D.O. (1994) *Social Psychology* (8th edition). Englewood Cliffs, NJ: Prentice-Hall.

TEASDALE, J. (1988) Cognitive vulnerability to persistent depression. *Cognition and Emotion*, 2, 247–274.

TEICHMAN, J. (1988) *Philosophy and the Mind*. Oxford: Blackwell.

TEITELBAUM, P.H. (1955) Sensory control of hypothalamic hyperphagia. *Journal of Comparative and Physiological Psychology*, 48, 156–163.

TEITELBAUM, P.H. & EPSTEIN, A.N. (1962) The lateral hypothalamic syndrome: Recovery of feeding and drinking after hypothalamic lesions. *Psychological Review*, 67, 74–90.

TEMPLIN, M.C. (1957) *Certain Language Skills in Children: Their Development and Interrelationships*. Minneapolis: University of Minnesota Press.

TETLOCK, P.E. & LEVI, A. (1982), Attribution bias: On the inconclusiveness of the cognition–motivation debate. *Journal of Experimental Social Psychology*, 18, 68–88.

TEUTING, P., ROSEN, S. & HIRSCHFELD, R. (1981) *Special Report on Depression Research*. Washington, DC: NIMH-DHHS Publication No. 81–1085.

THATCHER, R., WALKER, R. & GUIDICE, S. (1978) Human cerebral hemispheres develop at different rates and ages. *Science*, 236, 1110–1113.

THE DAILY MAIL (1997) Japan germ war censor overruled. 30 August, 31.

THIBAUT, J.W. & KELLEY, H.H. (1959) *The Social Psychology of Groups*. New York: Wiley.

THOMAS, E.L. & ROBINSON, H.A. (1972) *Improving Reading in Every Class: A Sourcebook for Teachers*. Boston: Allyn & Bacon.

THOMAS, J.C. (1974) An analysis of behaviour in the 'hobbit-orcs' problem. *Cognitive Psychology*, 28, 167–178.

THOMAS, K. (1990) Psychodynamics: The Freudian approach. In I. Roth (Ed.) *Introduction to Psychology*. Hove: Lawrence Erlbaum Associates Ltd.

THOMAS, R.M. (1985) *Comparing Theories of Child Development* (2nd edition). Belmont, CA: Wadsworth Publishing Company.

THOMPSON, L.A., DETTERMAN, D.K. & PLOMIN, R. (1991) Associations between cognitive abilities and scholastic achievement: Genetic overlap but environmental differences. *Psychological Science*, 2, 158–165.

THOMPSON, S.B.N. (1997) War experiences and post-traumatic stress disorder. *The Psychologist*, 10, 349–350.

THORNDIKE, E. L. (1898) Animal intelligence: An experimental study of the associative processes in animals. *Psychological Review Monograph Supplement 2* (Whole No. 8).

THORNDIKE, E.L. (1911) *Animal Intelligence*. New York: Macmillan.

THORNE, B. (1984) Person-centred therapy. In W. Dryden (Ed.) *Individual Therapy in Britain*. London: Harper Row.

THORNE, B. (1992) *Rogers*. London: Sage Publications.

THORNTON, D. & REID, D.L. (1982) Moral reasoning and type of criminal offence. *British Journal of Social Psychology*, 21, 231–238.

TILLEY, A.J. & EMPSON, J.A.C. (1978) REM sleep and memory consolidation. *Biological Psychology*, 6, 293–300.

TIMONEN, S., FRANZAS, B. & WISCHMANN, K. (1964) Photosensibility of the human pituitary. *Annales Chirurgiae et Gynaecologiae Feminae*, 53, 156–172.

TINBERGEN, N. (1951) *The Study of Instinct*. Oxford: Clarendon Press.

TIPPER, S.P. & DRIVER, J. (1988) Negative priming between pictures and words: Evidence for semantic analysis of ignored stimuli. *Memory and Cognition*, 16, 64–70.

TITCHENER, E.B. (1903) *Lectures on the Elementary Psychology of Feeling and Attention*. New York: Macmillan.

TIZARD, B. (1977) *Adoption: A Second Chance*. London: Open Books.

TIZARD, B. & HODGES, J. (1978) The effects of early institutional rearing on the development of eight-year-old children. *Journal of Child Psychology and Psychiatry*, 19, 99–118.

TIZARD, B., JOSEPH, A., COOPERMAN, O. & TIZARD, J. (1972) Environmental effects on language development: A study of young children in long-stay residential nurseries. *Child Development,* 43, 337–358.

TIZARD, B. & REES, J. (1974) A comparison of the effects of adoption, restoration to the natural mother and continued institutionalisation on the cognitive development of four-year-old children. *Child Development,* 45, 92–99.

TOCH, H. (1980) *Violent Men* (revised edition). Cambridge, MA: Schenkman.

TOLMAN, E.C. (1923) The nature of instinct. *Psychological Bulletin,* 20, 200–216.

TOLMAN, E.C. (1948) Cognitive maps in rats and man. *Psychological Review,* 55, 189–208.

TOLMAN, E.C. & HONZIK, C.H. (1930) Introduction and removal of reward and maze-learning in rats. *University of California Publications in Psychology,* 4, 257–275.

TOLMAN, E.C., RITCHIE, B.F., & KALISH, D. (1946) Studies in spatial learning. 1: Orientation and the short-cut. *Journal of Experimental Psychology,* 36, 13–25.

TOMARKEN, A.J. & DAVIDSON, R.J. (1994) Frontal brain activation in repressors and non-repressors. *Journal of Abnormal Psychology,* 103, 334–349.

TOMKINS, S.S. (1962) *Affect, Imagery, and Consciousness,* Volume 1: *The Positive Affects.* New York: Springer-Verlag.

TOMLINSON-KEASEY, C. (1985) *Child Development: Psychological, Sociocultural, and Biological Factors.* Chicago: Dorsey Press.

TOPPING, K. (1992) Cooperative learning and peer tutoring: An overview. *The Psychologist,* 5, 151–157.

TORREY, E.F. (1988) *Surviving Schizophrenia* (revised edition). New York: Harper & Row.

TORREY, E.F., TORREY, B.B. & PETERSON, M.R. (1977) Seasonality of schizophrenic births in the United States. *Archives of General Psychiatry,* 34, 1065–1070.

TOUYZ, S.W., O'SULLIVAN, B.T., GERTLER, R. & BEAUMONT, P.J.V. (1988) Anorexia nervosa in a woman blind since birth. *British Journal of Psychiatry,* 153, 248–249.

TRABASSO, T. (1977) The role of memory as a system in making transitive inferences. In R.V. Kail & J.W. Hagen (Eds) *Perspectives on the Development of Memory and Cognition.* Hillsdale, NJ: Erlbaum.

TREASURE, J.L. & HOLLAND, A.J. (1991) Genes and the aetiology of eating disorders. In P. McGuffin & R. Murray (Eds) *The New Genetics of Mental Illness.* Oxford: Butterworth.

TREDRE, R. (1996) Untitled article. *Observer Life,* 12 May, 16–19.

TREISMAN, A.M. (1960) Contextual cues in selective listening. *Quarterly Journal of Experimental Psychology,* 12, 242–248.

TREISMAN, A.M. (1964) Verbal cues, language and meaning in selective attention. *American Journal of Psychology,* 77, 206–219.

TREISMAN, A.M. (1988) Features and objects: The fourteenth Bartlett memorial lecture. *Quarterly Journal of Experimental Psychology,* 40A, 201–237.

TREISMAN, A.M. & GEFFEN, G. (1967) Selective attention: Perception or response. *Quarterly Journal of Experimental Psychology,* 19, 1–18.

TREISMAN, A.M. & GELADE, G. (1980) A feature-integration theory of attention. *Cognitive Psychology,* 12, 97–136.

TREISMAN, A.M. & RILEY, J.G.A. (1969) Is selective attention selective perception or selective response?: A further test. *Journal of Experimental Psychology,* 79, 27–34.

TREISMAN, A.M. & SATO, S. (1990) Conjunction search revisited. *Journal of Experimental Psychology: Human Perception and Performance,* 16, 459–478.

TREISMAN, A.M. & SCHMIDT, H. (1982) Illusory conjunctions in the perception of objects. *Cognitive Psychology,* 14, 107–141.

TRIANDIS, H.C. (1990) Theoretical concepts that are applicable to the analysis of ethnocentrism. In R.W. Brislin (Ed.) *Applied Cross-Cultural Psychology.* Newbury Park, CA.: Sage.

TRIANDIS, H.C. (1994) *Culture and Social Behaviour.* New York: McGraw-Hill.

TRIESCHMANN, R.B. (1980) *Spinal Cord Injuries.* New York: Pergamon Press.

TRISELIOTIS, J. (1980) Growing up in foster care and after. In J. Triseliotis (Ed.) *New Developments in Foster Care and Adoption.* London: Routledge & Kegan Paul.

TRIVERS, R.L. (1971) The evolution of reciprocal altruism. *Quarterly Review of Biology,* 46, 35–57.

TRONICK, E., ALS, H., ADAMSON, L., WISE, S. & BRAZELTON, T.B. (1978) The infant's response to entrapment between contradictory messages in face-to-face interaction. *Journal of the American Academy of Child Psychiatry,* 17, 1–13.

TROWER, P. (1987) On the ethical bases of 'scientific' behaviour therapy. In S. Fairbairn & G. Fairbairn (Eds) *Psychology, Ethics and Change.* London: Routledge & Kegan Paul.

TROWLER, P. (1988) *Investigating the Media.* London: Unwin Hyman Limited.

TRUAX, C.B. (1966) Reinforcement and non-reinforcement in Rogerian therapy. *Journal of Abnormal Psychology,* 71, 1–9.

TRUAX, C.B. & CARKHUFF, R.R. (1964) Significant developments in psychotherapy research. In L.E. Abt & B.F. Reiss (Eds) *Progress in Clinical Psychology.* New York: Grune & Stratton.

TRYON, R.C. (1940) Genetic differences in maze-learning abilities in rats. In *39th Yearbook, Part 1.* National Society for the Study of Education. Chicago: University of Chicago Press.

TULVING, E. (1968) Theoretical issues in free recall. In T.R. Dixon & D.L. Horton (Eds) *Verbal Behaviour and General Behaviour Theory.* Englewood Cliffs, NJ: Prentice-Hall.

TULVING, E. (1972) Episodic and semantic memory. In E. Tulving & W. Donaldson (Eds) *Organisation of Memory.* London: Academic Press.

TULVING, E. (1974) Cue-dependent forgetting. *American Scientist,* 62, 74–82.

TULVING, E. (1985) How many memory systems are there? *American Psychologist,* 40, 395–398.

TULVING, E. & PEARLSTONE, Z. (1966) Availability versus accessibility of information in memory for words. *Journal of Verbal Learning and Verbal Behaviour,* 5, 389–391.

TULVING, E. & THOMSON, D.M. (1973) Encoding specificity and retrieval processes in episodic memory. *Psychological Review,* 80, 352–373.

TURNBULL, C.M. (1961) *The Forest People.* New York: Simon & Schuster.

TURNBULL, S.K. (1995) The middle years. In D. Wedding (Ed.) *Behaviour and Medicine* (2nd edition). St. Louis, MO: Mosby-Year Book.

TURNER, J.C. (1991) *Social Influence.* Milton Keynes: Open University Press.

TURNER, J.S. & HELMS, D.B. (1989) *Contemporary Adulthood* (4th edition). Fort Worth, FL: Holt, Rinehart & Winston.

TURNER, R.H. (1964) Collective behaviour. In R.E.L. Faris (Ed.) *Handbook of Modern Sociology.* Chicago: Rand McNally.

TURNER, R.H. & KILLIAN, L.M. (1957) *Collective Behaviour.* Englewood Cliffs, NJ: Prentice-Hall.

TURNER, R.H. & KILLIAN, L.M. (1972) *Collective Behaviour* (revised edition). Englewood Cliffs, NJ: Prentice-Hall.

TVERSKY, A. (1972) Elimination by aspects: A theory of choice. *Psychological Review,* 79, 281–299.

TVERSKY, A. & KAHNEMAN, D. (1973) Judgement under uncertainty: Heuristics and biases. *Science,* 185, 1124–1131.

TVERSKY, A. & KAHNEMAN, D. (1986) Rational choice and the framing of decisions. *Journal of Business,* 59, 5251–5278.

TVERSKY, A. & TUCHIN, M. (1989) A reconciliation of the evidence on eyewitness testimony: Comments on McCloskey and Zaragoza. *Journal of Experimental Psychology:* General, 118, 86–91.

TYERMAN, A. & SPENCER, C. (1983) A critical test of the Sherifs' Robber's Cave experiment: Intergroup competition and co-operation between groups of well-acquainted individuals. *Small Group Behaviour,* 14, 515–531.

TYLER, T.R. & COOK, F.L. (1984) The mass media and judgement of risk: Distinguishing impact on personal and societal level judgements. *Journal of Personality and Social Psychology,* 47, 693–708.

UDWIN, O. (1993) Children's reactions to traumatic events. *Journal of Child Psychology & Psychiatry,* 34 (2), 115–127.

UDWIN, O. (1995) Psychological intervention with war-traumatized children in Bosnia: A consultation model. *Association for Child Psychology & Psychiatry Review & Newsletter,* 17 (4), 195–200.

UHLIG, R. (1996a) Superwaif Sindy 'is shaping future of girls aged eight'. *The Daily Telegraph,* 14 September, 9.

UHLIG, R. (1996b) Boy challenging dyslexia theory. *The Daily Telegraph,* 19 January, 11.

UHLIG, R. (1997) Man 'now at the limit of his intelligence'. *The Daily Telegraph,* 23 January, 14.

ULLMAN, L.P. & KRASNER, L. (1969) *A Psychological Approach to Abnormal Behaviour.* Englewood Cliffs, NJ: Prentice-Hall.

UNDERWOOD, G. (1974) Moray vs. the rest: The effects of extended shadowing practice. *Quarterly Journal of Experimental Psychology,* 26, 368–372.

UNGER, R. (1979) *Female and Male*. London: Harper & Row.

UNGER, R. & CRAWFORD, M. (1992) *Women and Gender: A Feminist Psychology*. New York: McGraw-Hill.

VALENSTEIN, E.S. (1973) *Brain Control*. New York: John Wiley and Sons.

VALENSTEIN, E.S. (1977) The brain and behaviour control. In E.S. Valenstein (Ed.) *Master Lectures on Behaviour Control*. Washington, DC: American Psychological Association.

VALENSTEIN, E.S. (1980) Rationale and psychosurgical procedures. In E.S. Valenstein (Ed.) *The Psychosurgery Debate*. San Francisco: W.H. Freeman.

VALENSTEIN, E.S. (1990) The prefrontal area and psychosurgery. *Progress in Brain Research*, 85, 539–554.

VALENTINE, E.R. (1982) *Conceptual Issues in Psychology*. London: Routledge.

VALENTINE, E.R. (1992) *Conceptual Issues in Psychology* (2nd edition). London: Routledge.

VALENTINE, E.R. & WILDING, J.M. (1994) Memory expertise. *The Psychologist*, 7, 405–408.

VALLIS, M., McCABE, S.B. & SHAW, B.F. (1986) The relationships between therapist skill in cognitive therapy and general therapy skill. Paper presented to the Society for Psychotherapy Research, Wellesley, MA. (June).

VAN AVERMAET, E. (1996) Social influence in small groups. In M. Hewstone, W. Stroebe & G.M. Stephenson (Eds) *Introduction to Social Psychology* (2nd edition). Oxford: Blackwell.

VAN DER KOLK, B.A., PITMAN, R.K. & ORR, S.P. (1989) Endogenous opioids, stress-induced analgesia and post-traumatic stress disorder. *Psychopharmacology Bulletin*, 25, 108–112.

VAN ESSEN, D.C. (1985) Functional organisation of primate visual cortex. In A. Peters. & E.G. Jones (Eds) *Cerebral Cortex*, Volume 2 – *Visual Cortex*. New York: Plenum Press.

VAN LANGENHOVE, L. (1995) The theoretical foundations of experimental psychology and its alternatives. In J.A.Smith, R. Harré, & L. Van Langenhove (Eds) *Rethinking Psychology*. London: Sage.

VAN LEHN, K. (1983) On the representation of procedures in repair theory. In H.P. Ginsburg (Ed.) *The Development of Mathematical Thinking*. London: Academic Press.

VANNEMAN, R.D. & PETTIGREW, T.F. (1972) Race and relative deprivation in the urban United States. *Race*, 13, 461–486.

VAUGHN, B.E., GOVE, F.L. & EGELAND, B.R. (1980) The relationship between out-of-home care and the quality of infant-mother attachment in an economically disadvantaged population. *Child Development*, 51, 1203–1214.

VERKAIK, R. (1995) The kindest cut of all? *The Sunday Times*, 30 July, 18–19.

VERNON, M.D. (1955) The functions of schemata in perceiving. *Psychological Review*, 62, 180–192.

VISINTAINER, M., SELIGMAN, M. & VOLPICELLI, J. (1983) Helplessness, chronic stress and tumor development. *Psychosomatic Medicine*, 45, 75–76.

VITELLI, R. (1988) The crisis issue reassessed: An empirical analysis. *Basic and Applied Social Psychology*, 9, 301–309.

VIVIAN, J. & BROWN, R. (1995) Prejudice and intergroup conflict. In M. Argyle & A.M. Colman (Eds) *Social Psychology*. London: Longman.

VIVIAN, J., BROWN, R.J. & HEWSTONE, M. (1994) 'Changing attitudes through intergroup contact: The effects of membership salience.' (Unpublished manuscript, Universities of Kent and Wales, Cardiff.)

VON SENDEN, M. (1932) *Space and Sight. The Perception of Space and Shape in the Congenitally Blind Before and After Operations* (translated by P. Heath, 1960). London: Methuen.

VON WRIGHT, J.M., ANDERSON, K. & STENMAN, U. (1975) Generalisation of conditioned GSRs in dichotic listening. In P.M.A. Rabbitt & S. Dornic (Eds) *Attention and Performance*, Volume 1. London: Academic Press.

VOSS, J.F., VESONDER, G.T. & SPILICH, G.J. (1980) Text generation and recall by high-knowledge and low-knowledge individuals. *Journal of Verbal Learning and Verbal Behaviour*, 19, 651–667.

VYGOTSKY, L. (1962) *Thought and Language*. Cambridge, MA: MIT Press (originally published in 1934).

VYGOTSKY, L.S. (1978) *Mind in Society*. Cambridge, MA: Harvard University Press.

VYGOTSKY, L.S. (1981) The genesis of higher mental functions. In J.V. Wertsch (Ed.) *The Concept of Activity in Soviet Psychology*. Armonk, NY: Sharpe.

WACHTEL, P.L. (1977) *Psychoanalysis and Behaviour Therapy: Towards an Integration*. New York: Basic Books.

WADE, C. & TAVRIS, C. (1993) *Psychology* (3rd edition). New York: HarperCollins.

WADELEY, A. (1996) Subliminal perception. *Psychology Review*, 3 (1), September.

WAGSTAFF, G.F. (1991) Compliance, belief, and semantics in hypnosis: A non-state sociocognitive perspective. In S.J. Lynn & J.W. Rhue (Eds) *Theories of Hypnosis: Current Models and Perspectives*. New York: Guildford Press.

WAHBA, N. & BRIDWELL, L. (1976) Maslow reconsidered: A review of research on the need hierarchy theory. *Organisation Behaviour and Human Performance*, 15, 212–240.

WALKER, M. (1996) *Book of Signs (Line Drawings)* (revised edition). Camberley: The Makaton Vocabulary Development Project.

WALKER, S. (1984) *Learning Theory and Behaviour Modification*. London: Methuen.

WALLACE, B. & FISHER, L.E. (1987) *Consciousness and Behaviour* (second edition). Boston: Allyn & Bacon.

WALLACE, P. (1974) Complex environments: Effects on brain development. *Science*, 185, 1035–1037.

WALLAS, G. (1926) *The Art of Thought*. London: Cape.

WALLER, G. (1993) Sexual abuse and eating disorders. *British Journal of Psychiatry*, 162, 771–775.

WALSTER, E., ARONSON, E. & ABRAHAMS, D. (1966) On increasing the persuasiveness of a low prestige communicator. *Journal of Experimental Social Psychology*, 2, 325–342.

WALSTER, E., ARONSON, E. & ABRAHAMS, D. & ROTTMAN, L. (1966) Importance of physical attractiveness in dating behaviour. *Journal of Personality and Social Psychology*, 4, 508–516.

WARD, S.H. & BRAUN, J. (1972) Self-esteem and racial preference in Black children. *American Journal of Orthopsychiatry*, 42 (4), 644–647.

WARK, P. & BALL, S. (1996) Death of innocence. *The Sunday Times*, 23 June, 12.

WARR, P.B. (1984) Work and unemployment. In P.J.D. Drenth (Ed.) *Handbook of Work and Organisational Psychology*. Chichester: Wiley.

WARR, P.B. (1987) *Work, Unemployment and Mental Health*. Oxford: Clarendon Press.

WASON, P.C. (1960) On the failure to eliminate hypotheses in a conceptual task. *Quarterly Journal of Experimental Psychology*, 12, 129–140.

WATSON, J.B. (1913) Psychology as the behaviourist views it. *Psychological Review*, 20, 158–177.

WATSON, J.B. (1919) *Psychology from the Standpoint of a Behaviourist*. Philadelphia: J.B. Lippincott.

WATSON, J.B. (1928) *Psychological Care of Infant and Child*. New York: Norton.

WATSON, J.B. & RAYNER, R. (1920) Conditioned emotional responses. *Journal of Experimental Psychology*, 3, 1–14.

WATSON, R.J. (1973) Investigation into deindividuation using a cross-cultural survey technique. *Journal of Personality & Social Psychology*, 25, 342–345.

WAUGH, N.C. & NORMAN, D.A. (1965) Primary memory. *Psychological Review*, 72, 89–104.

WEARY, G. & ARKIN, R.M. (1981) Attributional self-presentation. In J.H. Harvey, W.J. Ickes & R.F. Kidd (Eds) *New Directions in Attributional Research*, Volume 3. Hillsdale, NJ: Erlbaum.

WEATHERLEY, D. (1961) Anti-semitism and expression of fantasy aggression. *Journal of Abnormal and Social Psychology*, 62, 454–457.

WEAVER, M. (1996) We are watching your weight, skinny Vogue models warned. *The Daily Telegraph*, 31 May, 3.

WEBB, W.B. (1975) *Sleep: The Gentle Tyrant*. Englewood Cliffs, NJ: Prentice-Hall.

WEBB, W.B. (1982) Sleep and biological rhythms. In Webb, W.B. (Ed.) *Biological Rhythms, Sleep and Performance*. Chichester: John Wiley & Sons.

WEBB, W.B. & CAMPBELL, S. (1983) Relationships in sleep characteristics of identical and fraternal twins. *Archives of General Psychiatry*, 40, 1093–1095.

WEBB, W.B. & CARTWRIGHT, R.D. (1978) Sleep and dreams. *Annual Review of Psychology*, 29, 223–252.

WEBSTER, A. & WOOD, D. (1989) *Children with Hearing Difficulties*. London: Cassell.

WEBSTER, C.D., McPHERSON, H., SLOMAN, L, EVANS, M.A. & KUCHAR, E. (1973) Communicating with an autistic boy by gestures. *Journal of Autism and Childhood Schizophrenia*, 3, 337–346.

WEBSTER, R. (1995) *Why Freud was Wrong: Sin, Science and Psychoanalysis*. London: HarperCollins.

WECHSLER, D. (1992) Wechsler Intelligence Scale for Children (3rd edition) UK (WISC-III-UK). *The Psychological Corporation*, Sidcup, Kent: Harcourt Brace & Co.

WEEKS, A. & LAVER-BRADBURY, C. (1997) Behaviour modification in hyperactive children. *Nursing Times*, 93, 56–58.

WEGNER, D.M., BENEL, D.C. & RILEY, E.N. (1976) Changes in perceived inter-trait correlations as a function of experience with persons. Paper presented at the meeting of the SouthWestern Psychological Association, Alberquerque (April).

WEGNER, D.M. & VALLACHER, R.R. (1976) *Implicit Psychology: An Introduction to Social Cognition*. Oxford: Oxford University Press.

WEHR, T. & ROSENTHAL, N. (1989) Seasonability and affective illness. *American Journal of Psychiatry*, 146, 201–204.

WEIL, A. & ROSEN, W. (1983) *Chocolate to Morphine: Understanding Mind-Active Drugs*. Boston: Houghton Mifflin.

WEIL, A. & ZINBERG, N.E. (1969) Acute effects of marijuana on speech. *Nature*, 222, 434–437.

WEINBERG, R. (1989) Intelligence and IQ: Landmark issues and great debates. *American Psychologist* 44, 98–104.

WEINER, B. (1986) *An Attributional Theory of Motivation and Emotion*. New York: Springer-Verlag.

WEINER, B. (1992) *Human Motivation: Metaphors, Theories and Research*. Newbury Park, CA: Sage.

WEINER, M.J. & WRIGHT, F.E. (1973) Effects of undergoing arbitrary discrimination upon subsequent attitudes toward a minority group. *Journal of Applied Social Psychology*, 3, 94–102.

WEISFELD, G. (1994) Aggression and dominance in the social world of boys. In J. Archer (Ed.) *Male Violence*. London: Routledge.

WEISKRANTZ, L. (1956) Behavioural changes associated with ablation of the amygdaloid complex in monkeys. *Journal of Comparative and Physiological Psychology*, 49, 381–391.

WEISKRANTZ, L. (1986) *Blindsight: A Case Study and Implications*. Oxford: Oxford University Press.

WEISKRANTZ, L. (1988) *Thought Without Language*. Oxford: Oxford University Press.

WEISS, R.S. (1993) Loss and recovery. In M.S. Stroebe, W. Stroebe & R.O. Hansson (Eds) *Handbook of Bereavement: Theory, Research and Intervention*. New York: Cambridge University Press.

WEISSMAN, M. (1987) Advances in psychiatric epidemiology: Rates and risks for major depression. *American Journal of Public Health*, 77, 445–451.

WEISSMAN, M. & PAYKEL, E. (1974) *The Depressed Woman*. Chicago: University of Chicago Press.

WEISSTEIN, N. (1993) Psychology constructs the female; or, The fantasy life of the male psychologist (with some attention to the fantasies of his friend, the male biologist and the male anthropologist). *Feminism & Psychology*, 3 (2), 195–210.

WELLS, G.L. (1993) What do we know about eyewitness identification? *American Psychologist*, 48, 553–571.

WELLS, G.L. & HARVEY, J.H. (1977) Do people use consensus information in making causal attributions? *Journal of Personality and Social Psychology*, 35, 279–293.

WELLS, P.A., WILLMOTH, T. & RUSSELL, R.J.H. (1995) Does fortune favour the bald?: Psychological correlates of hair loss in males. *British Journal of Psychology*, 86, 337–344.

WENDER, P.H., KETY, S.S., ROSENTHAL, D., SCHULSINGER, F., ORTMANN, J. & LUNDE, I. (1986) Psychiatric disorders in the biological and adoptive families of individuals with affective disorders. *Archives of General Psychiatry*, 43, 923–929.

WENDER, P.H. & KLEIN, D.F. (1981) The promise of biological psychiatry. *Psychology Today*, 15, 25–41.

WERTHEIMER, M. (1970) *A Brief History of Psychology*. New York: Holt Rinehart & Winston.

WESSELEY, S. (1993) Shocking treatment. *The Times*, 18 November, 22.

WESSLER, R.L. (1986) Conceptualising cognitions in the cognitive-behavioural therapies. In W. Dryden & W. Golden (Eds) *Cognitive-Behavioural Approaches to Psychotherapy*. London: Harper & Row.

WESTHEAD, R. (1996) Power line link to the baby blues. *The Sunday Telegraph*, 15 September, 2.

WETHERELL, M. (1982) Cross-cultural studies of minimal groups: Implications for the social identity theory of intergroup relations. In H. Tajfel (Ed.) *Social Identity and Intergroup Relations*. Cambridge: Cambridge University Pres.

WHALEN, C.R. & HENKER, B. (1991) Therapies for hyperactive children: Comparisons, combinations and compromises. *Journal of Consulting and Clinical Psychology*, 59, 126–137.

WHITE, B.L. (1971) *Human Infants: Experience and Psychological Development*. Englewood Cliffs, NJ: Prentice-Hall.

WHITE, G.L. (1980) Physical attractiveness and courtship progress. *Journal of Personality and Social Psychology*, 39, 660–668.

WHITE, J., DAVISON, G.C. & WHITE, M. (1985) 'Cognitive distortions in the articulated thoughts of depressed patients.' (Unpublished manuscript, University of Southern California, Los Angeles.)

WHITE, K.M. & FERSTENBERG, A. (1978) Professional specialisation and formal operations: The balance task. *Journal of Genetic Psychology*, 133, 97–104.

WHITEHURST, G.J. (1982) Language development. In B.B. Woolman (Ed.) *Handbook of Developmental Psychology*. Englewood Cliffs, NJ: Prentice-Hall.

WHITEHURST, G.J., FALCO, F.L., LONIGAN, C.J. & FISCHEL, J.E. (1988) Accelerating language development through picture-book reading. *Developmental Psychology*, 24, 552–559.

WHITING, B.B. (Ed.) (1963) *Six Cultures: Studies in Child Rearing*. New York: Wiley.

WHITING, J.W. & CHILD, I. (1953) *Child Training and Personality*. New Haven: Yale University Press.

WHITTAKER, E. (1992) Specific learning difficulty (dyslexia) and neurological research. *Educational Psychology in Practice*, 8, 139–144.

WHITTELL, G. (1995) Spectacular northern lights linked to suicidal depression. *The Times*, 15 April, 9.

WHITTELL, G. (1996) Black American slang wins place in classroom. *The Times*, 21 December, 11.

WHORF, B.L. (1956) *Language, Thought and Reality*. Cambridge, MA: MIT Press.

WHYTE, W.F. (1943) *Street Corner Society: The Social Structure of an Italian Slum*. Chicago: University of Chicago Press.

WHYTE, W.W. (1956) *The Organization Man*. New York: Simon and Schuster.

WICKENS, C.D. (1972) Characteristics of word encoding. In A. Melton & E. Martin (Eds) *Coding Processes in Human Memory*. Washington, DC: Winston.

WICKENS, C.D. (1992) *Engineering Psychology and Human Performance* (2nd edition). New York: HarperCollins.

WIESEL, T.N. (1982) Post-natal development of the visual cortex and the influence of environment. *Nature*, 229, 583–591.

WILDER, D.A. (1977) Perceptions of groups, size of opposition and influence. *Journal of Experimental Social Psychology*, 13, 253–268.

WILDER, D.A. (1984) Intergroup contact: The typical member and the exception to the rule. *Journal of Experimental Social Psychology*, 20, 177–194.

WILDING, J.M. (1982) *Perception: From Sense to Object*. London: Hutchinson.

WILDING, J.M. & VALENTINE, E.R. (1994) Memory champions. *British Journal of Psychology*, 85, 231–244.

WILKINSON, S. (1991) Feminism & psychology: From critique to reconstruction. *Feminism & Psychology*, 1 (1), 5–18.

WILKINSON, S, (1997) Feminist Psychology. In D. Fox & D. Prilleltensky (Eds) *Critical Psychology: An Introduction*. London: Sage.

WILLIAMS, J.E. & BEST, D.L. (1994) Cross-cultural views of women and men. In W.J. Lonner & R.S. Malpass (Eds) *Psychology and Culture*. Boston: Allyn & Bacon.

WILLIAMS, J.M.G. (1992) *The Psychological Treatment of Depression*. London: Routledge.

WILLIAMS, J.M.G. & HARGREAVES, I.R. (1995) Neuroses: Depressive and anxiety disorders. In A.A. Lazarus & A.M. Colman (Eds) *Abnormal Psychology*. London: Longman.

WILLIAMS, K.B. & WILLIAMS, K.D. (1983) Social inhibition and asking for help: The effects of number, strength and immediacy of potential help givers. *Journal of Personality and Social Psychology*, 44, 67–77.

WILLIAMS, M. (1981) *Brain Damage, Behaviour and the Mind*. Chichester: John Wiley & Sons.

WILLIAMS, T.M. (Ed.) (1986) *The Impact of Television: A National Experiment in Three Communities*. New York: Academic Press.

WILLIS, R.H. (1963) Two dimensions of conformity–nonconformity. *Sociometry*, 26, 499–513.

WILNER, D.M., WALKLEY, R. & COOK, S.W. (1955) *Human Relations in Interracial Housing: A Study of the Contact Hypothesis*. Minneapolis: University of Minnesota Press.

WILSON, C.O. (1996) Children are out of control, says Spock. *The Sunday Telegraph*, 20 October, 22.

WILSON, E.O. (1978) *On Human Nature*. Cambridge, MA: Harvard University Press.

WILSON, G. (1994) Biology, sex roles and work. In C. Quest (Ed.) *Liberating Women from Modern Feminism*. London: Institute of Economic Affairs, Health & Welfare Unit.

WILSON, G.T. & O'LEARY, K.D. (1978) *Principles of Behaviour Therapy*. Englewood Cliffs, NJ: Prentice-Hall.

WILSON, G.T., O'LEARY, K.D., NATHAN, P.E. & CLARK, L.A. (1996) *Abnormal Psychology: Integrating Perspectives*. Needham Heights, MA.: Allyn and Bacon.

WILSON, J.E. & BARKHAM, M. (1994) A practitioner-scientist approach to psychotherapy process and outcome research. In P. Clarkson & M. Pokorny (Eds) *The Handbook of Psychotherapy*. London: Routledge.

WILSON, P. (1982) Combined pharmacological and behavioural treatment of depression. *Behaviour Research and Therapy*, 20, 173–184.

WILSON, R.S. (1983) The Louisville Twin Study: Developmental synchronies in behaviour. *Child Development*, 54, 298–316.

WIMMER, H. & PERNER, J. (1983) Beliefs about beliefs: Representation and constraining function of wrong beliefs in young children's understanding of deception. *Cognition*, 13, 103–128.

WINCH, R.F. (1958) *Mate Selections: A Study of Complementary Needs*. New York: Harper.

WINEBERG, H. (1994) Marital reconciliation in the United States: Which couples are successful? *Journal of Marriage and the Family*, 56, 80–88.

WING, J.K., COOPER, J.E. & SARTORIUS, N. (1974) *Measurement and Classification of Psychiatric Symptoms*. Cambridge: Cambridge University Press.

WINGFIELD, A. (1979) *Human Learning and Memory*. New York: Harper & Row.

WINNICOTT, D.W. (1958) *Through Paediatrics to Psychoanalysis*. London: The Hogarth Press.

WINTER, A. (1972) Depression and intractible pain treated by modified prefrontal lobotomy. *Journal of Medical Sociology*, 69, 757–759.

WISHART, J. (1995) Learning the hard way? *The Psychologist*, 8, 253–254.

WITKIN, H.A., DYK, R.B., FATERSON, H.F., GOODENOUGH, D.R. & KARP, S.A. (1962) *Psychological Differentiation*. London: Wiley.

WITTGENSTEIN, L. (1961) *Tractatus Logico-Philosophicus* (translated by D.F. PEARS & B.F. McGUINNESS). London: Routledge & Kegan Paul (originally published in 1921).

WOBER, J.M., REARDON, G. & FAZAL, S. (1987) *Personality, Character Aspirations and Patterns of Viewing Among Children*. London: IBA Research Papers.

WOBER, M. (1974) Towards an understanding of the Kiganda concept of intelligence. In J.W. Berry & P.R. Dasen (Eds) *Culture and Cognition*. London: Methuen.

WOLF, S. & BRUHN, J. (1993) *The Power of the Clan: The Influence of Human Relationships on Heart Disease*. New York: Transaction.

WOLF, S. & WOLFF, H.G. (1947) *Human Gastric Function*. New York: Oxford University Press.

WOLPE, J. (1958) *Psychotherapy by Reciprocal Inhibition*. Stanford, CA: Stanford University Press.

WOLPE, J. (1969) For phobia: A hair of the hound. *Psychology Today*, 3, 34–37.

WOLPE, J. (1973) *The Practice of Behaviour Therapy*. New York: Pergamon Press.

WOLPE, J. (1985) Existential problems and behaviour therapy. *The Behaviour Therapist*, 8, 126–127.

WOLPE, J. & RACHMAN, S. (1960) Psychoanalytic evidence: A critique based on Freud's case of Little Hans. *Journal of Nervous and Mental Disease*, 131, 135–145.

WOLPE, J. & WOLPE, D. (1981) *Our Useless Years*. Boston: Houghton-Mifflin.

WOOD, D.J., BRUNER, J.S. & ROSS, G. (1976) The role of tutoring in problem-solving. *Journal of Child Psychology and Psychiatry*, 17, 89–100.

WOOD, J.T. & DUCK, S. (1995) *Understanding Relationship Processes 6: Understudied Relationships: Off the Beaten Track*. Thousand Oaks, CA: Sage.

WOOD, W., LUNDGREN, S., OUELLETTE, J.A., BUSCEME, S. & BLACKSTONE, T. (1994) Minority influence: A meta-analytic review of social influence processes. *Psychological Bulletin*, 115, 323–345.

WOODWORTH, R.S. (1918) *Dynamic Psychology*. New York: Columbia University Press.

WOODWORTH, R.S. (1938) *Experimental Psychology*. New York: Holt.

WOOLEY, S. & WOOLEY, O. (1983) Should obesity be treated at all? *Psychiatric Annals*, 13, 884–885.

WORCHEL, S., COOPER, J. & GOETHALS, G.R. (1988) *Understanding Social Psychology* (4th edition). Chicago: The Dorsey Press.

WRIGHT, D. (1971) *The Psychology of Moral Behaviour*. Harmondsworth: Penguin.

WRIGHT, D.B. (1993) Recall of the Hillsborough disaster over time: Systematic biases of 'flashbulb' memories. *Applied Cognitive Psychology*, 7, 129–138.

WRIGHT, L. (1988) The Type A behaviour pattern and coronary artery disease: Quest for the active ingredients and the elusive mechanism. *American Psychologist*, 43, 2–14.

WULF, F. (1922) Über die Veränderung von Vorstellungen. *Psychologisch Forschung*, 1, 333–373.

WUNDT, W. (1974) *Grundzuge der Physiologischen Psychologie*. Leipzig: Engelmann.

WURTMAN, R. & WURTMAN, J. (1989) Carbohydrates and depression. *Scientific American*, 251, 68–75.

WYER, R.S. (1966) Effects of incentive to perform well, group attraction and group acceptance on conformity in a judgement task. *Journal of Personality and Social Psychology*, 4, 21–27.

WYNNE, L.C., SINGER, M.T., BARTKO, J.J. & TOOHEY, M.L. (1977) Schizophrenics and their families: Recent research on parental communication. In J.M. Tanner (Ed.) *Developments in Psychiatric Research*. London: Hodder & Stoughton.

YAGER, J., HATTON, C.A. & LAWRENCE, M. (1986) Anorexia nervosa in a woman totally blind since the age of two. *British Journal of Psychiatry*, 149, 506–509.

YARBUS, A.L. (1967) *Eye Movements and Vision* (translated by B. Haigh). New York: Plenum.

YESAVAGE, J.A. & ROSE, T.L. (1984) Semantic elaboration and the method of loci: A new trip for old learners. *Experimental Aging Research*, 10, 155–160.

YOGMAN, M., DIXON, S., TRONICK, E., ALS, H. & BRAZELTON, T.B. (1977) The goals and structure of face-to-face interaction between infants and fathers. Paper presented at the biennial meetings of the Society for Research in Child Development, New Orleans (March).

YOUNG, A. (1997) Finding the mind's construction in the face. *The Psychologist*, 10, 447–452.

YOUNG, A. & BRUCE, V. (1998) Pictures at an exhibition: The science of the face. *The Psychologist*, 11, 120–125.

YOUNG, C.V. (1971) *The Magic of a Mighty Memory*. West Nyack, NY: Parker Publishing Company.

YOUNG, K. (1946) *Handbook of Social Psychology*. London: Kegan Paul.

YUILLE, J.C. & CUTSHALL, J.L. (1986) A case study of eyewitness memory of a crime. *Journal of Applied Psychology*, 71, 291–301.

YULE, W. (1993) Children's trauma from transport disasters. *The Psychologist*, 7, 318–319.

YUSSEN, S.R. & SANTROCK, J.W. (1982) *Child Development* (2nd edition). Dubuque, IA: Wm. C. Brown.

ZAIDEL, E. (1983) A response to Gazzaniga. *American Psychologist*, 38, 542–546.

ZAJONC, R.B. (1968) Attitudinal effects of mere exposure. *Journal of Personality and Social Psychology*, Monograph Supplement 9, Part 2, 1–27.

ZAJONC, R.B. (1984) On the primacy of affect. *American Psychologist*, 39, 117–123.

ZAJONC, R.B. & MARKUS, G.B. (1975) Birth order and intellectual development. *Psychological Review*, 82, 74–88.

ZAMETKIN, A.J. (1990) Cerebral glucose metabolism in adults with hyperactivity of childhood onset. *New England Journal of Medicine*, 323, 1361–1366.

ZEBROWITZ, L.A. (1990) *Social Perception*. Milton Keynes: Open University Press.

ZIGLER, E., ABELSON, W.D., TRICKETT, P.K. & SEITZ, V. (1982) Is an intervention program necessary to improve economically disadvantaged children's IQ scores? *Child Development*, 53, 340–348.

ZIGLER, E. & PHILLIPS, L. (1961) Psychiatric diagnosis and symptomatology. *Journal of Abnormal Psychology*, 63, 69–75.

ZILBOORG, G. & HENRY, G.W. (1941) *A History of Medical Psychology*. New York: Norton.

ZILLMAN, D. (1978) Attribution and misattribution of excitatory reactions. In J.H. Harvey, W. Ickes & R.F. Kidd (Eds) *New Directions in Attribution Research*, Volume 2. New York: Erlbaum.

ZILLMAN, D. (1982) Transfer of excitation in emotional behaviour. In J.T. Cacioppo & R.E. Petty (Eds) *Social Psychophysiology: A Sourcebook*. New York: Guilford Press.

ZILLMAN, D. & BRYANT, J. (1974) Effect of residual excitation on the emotional response to provocation and delayed aggressive behaviour. *Journal of Personality and Social Psychology*, 30, 782–791.

ZILLMAN, D. & BRYANT, J. (1984) Effects of massive exposure to pornography. In M.N. Malamuth & E. Donnerstein (Eds) *Pornography and Sexual Aggression*. New York: Academic Press.

ZIMBARDO, P.G. (1969) The human choice: Individuation, reason, and order versus deindividuation, impluse, and chaos. In W.J. Arnold & D. Levine (Eds) *Nebraska Symposium on Motivation*. Lincoln: University of Nebraska Press.

ZIMBARDO, P.G. (1973) On the ethics of intervention in human psychological research with special refernce to the 'Stanford Prison Experiment'. *Cognition*, 2 (2), 243–255.

ZIMBARDO, P.G. (1992) *Psychology and Life* (13th edition) New York: Harper Collins.

ZIMBARDO, P.G., BANKS, W.C., CRAIG, H. & JAFFE, D. (1973) A Pirandellian prison: The mind is a formidable jailor. *New York Times Magazine*, 8 April, 38–60.

ZIMBARDO, P.G. & LEIPPE, M. (1991) *The Psychology of Attitude Change and Social Influence*. New York: McGraw-Hill.

ZIMBARDO, P.G. & WEBER, A.L. (1994) *Psychology*. New York: HarperCollins.

ZINBERG, D.S. (1997) Ebonics unleashes tongues. *The Times Higher Education Supplement*, 14 February, 14.

ZIV, A. & ISRAELI, R. (1973) Effects of bombardment on the manifest anxiety level of children living in kibbutzim. *Journal of Consulting & Clinical Psychology*, 40, 287–291.

ZUCKERMAN, M. (1979) *Sensation Seeking: Beyond the Optimum Level of Arousal*. Hillsdale, NJ: Erlbaum.

INDEX

Please note that page numbers in **bold** refer to definitions and (main) explanations of particular concepts.

PICTURE CREDITS

The publishers would like to thank the following for permission to reproduce photographs and other illustrations in this book:

Page 5, Corbis-Bettman; p.9 (Fig. 1.4), Corbis-Bettman; p.13 (Figs 1.5, 1.6a,c,d), Corbis-Bettman; (Fig. 1.6b) Olive Pearce/Robert Hunt Library; p.14, Times Newspapers Ltd, London; p.15 (Figs 1.8, 1.9), Corbis-Bettman; p.44, from *Psychology in Perspective* by James Hassett. Copyright © 1984 by Harper and Row Publishers, Inc. Reprinted by permission of Addison-Wesley Educational Publishers, Inc.; p.52, from Penfield, W. & Boldrey, E. (1937) 'Somatic, motor and sensory representation in the cerebral cortex as studies by electrical stimulation'. *Brain*, 60, 389–442. By permission of Oxford University Press; p.55, The Guardian, 1996; p.85, Isia Leviant; p.86, from *Psychology*, Fourth Edition by Spencer A. Rathus, copyright © 1990 Holt, Rinehart & Winston, reproduced by permission of the publisher; p.94 (Fig. 11.2), Dr D. Cohen; p.97, Steve Goldberg/Monkmeyer Press Photo Service; p.100, from *Psychology: Science, Behaviour and Life*, Second Edition, by Robert L. Crooks, copyright © 1991 Holt, Rinehart & Winston, reproduced by permission of the publisher; p.108 (Table 13.1), from *Psychology*, Fourth Edition by Spencer A. Rathus, copyright © 1990 Holt, Rinehart & Winston, reproduced by permission of the publisher; p.112, The Telegraph Group Limited, London, 1996; p.131, from *Psychology: Science, Behaviour and Life*, Second Edition, by Robert L. Crooks, copyright © 1991 Holt, Rinehart & Winston, reproduced by permission of the publisher; p.171 (Fig. 21.2), Weidenfeld & Nicolson Ltd; (Fig. 21.4a) Kaiser Porcelain Ltd; p.172 (Fig. 21.4b), Cordon Art, M.C. Escher's *Circle Limit IV* © 1997 Cordon Art – Baarn-Holland; (Box 21.1, shell) Worth Publishers Inc from David G. Myers *Exploring Psychology* (1993) Second Edition, New York: Worth Publishers; p.176 (Fig. 21.6f), The British Journal of Psychology; p.177 (21.8d), Cordon Art, M.C. Escher's *Relativity* © 1997 Cordon Art – Baarn-Holland; p.180, from Biederman, I. Computer Vision, Graphics and Image Processing, 1985, 32, 29–73. Academic Press Inc.; p.184, Professor Richard L. Gregory; p.188, Eastern Counties Newspapers Ltd; p.190, The Open University from Roth I. and Bruce V. (1995) *Perception and Representation*, Second Edition; p.195 (Figs 23.1, 23.2), Alex Semenoick; p.196, Alex Semenoick; p.206, from *The Journal of Social Psychology*, 52, 183–208 (1960).

Reprinted with permission of the Helen Dwight Reid Educational Foundation, published by Heldref Publications 1319, 18th St., N.W., Washington D.C. 20036–1802. Copyright © 1960; p.207, Scientific American; p.215, from Neisser, U. & Becklen, R. *Cognitive Psychology*, 1975, 7, 480–494. Academic Press, Inc.; p.217, Professor Jon Driver from *The Psychologist*, 1996, 3, 120; p.222, Life File © Emma Lee; p.225, Private Eye; p.263, Polygram/Pictorial Press; p.295, Times Newspapers Limited © Peter Brookes/The Times; p.310, Prentice-Hall; p.312, BBC Worldwide Ltd; p.314, Corbis-Bettman/UPI; p.318, David Gaskill; p.331 (Figs 38.1, 38.2), Harlow Primate Laboratory, University of Winsconsin; p.332, John L. Howard for Scientific American; p.334, Sally and Richard Greenhill; p.337, Concord Films Council/Joyce Robertson; p.339, The Ronald Grant Film Archive; p.341, Associated Press/Topham; p.343, Ashgate Publishing Limited; p.350, The Telegraph Group Limited; p.366, Paul Chapman Publishing Ltd, from Sutherland, P. (1992) *Cognitive Development Today: Piaget and His Critics*, copyright © Paul Chapman Publishing Ltd, London; p.375, Rex Features Ltd; p.383, Edward Arnold /© Antony McAvoy; p.385, ZEFA; p.386, Alpha Press Agency Ltd; p.389, Associated Press/Topham; p.390, Topham Picture Point; p.393, Popperfoto; p.395, The Johns Hopkins University Press, from Money J. and Ehrhardt A. (1972) *Man and Woman, Boy and Girl* © 1972, The Johns Hopkins University Press; p.398 (top), Life File © Nicola Sutton; (bottom) Sally and Richard Greenhill, © Sally Greenhill; p.405, Owen Franken/Corbis; p.411 (Fig. 47.1), Castlemead Publications; (Fig. 47.2) The Kobal Collection; p.416, Routledge, from Coleman J.C. and Hendry L. *The Nature of Adolescence*, Second Edition, published 1990 by Routledge; p.420, BBC Worldwide Ltd; p.423, The Ronald Grant Archive; p.424, The Mc-Graw–Hill Companies from *Psychology*, Fifth Edition by Santrock, J. *et al.*, copyright © 1997 The McGraw–Hill Companies, reproduced by permission of the publishers; p.428, BBC Worldwide Ltd; p.431, Sally and Richard Greenhill © Kate Mayers; p.433, Sally and Richard Greenhill © Kate Mayers; p.438, Times Newspapers Limited © Peter Brookes/ The Times, 1996; p.440 (top), Topham Picture Point; (bottom) Sally and Richard Greenhill; p.450, Copyright House of Viz/John Brown Publishing Ltd; p.454, Copyright House of Viz/John Brown Publishing Ltd; p.463, Camera Press Ltd; p.464, Associated Press; p.466, Action Images; p.470,

Concord Video and Film Council; p.471, Private Eye; p.473, Tony Stone Images. Chip Henderson; p.477 (Fig. 55.1), from Festinger, L. *et al.* (1950), *Social Pressures in Informal Groups: A Study of Human Factors in Housing*. Stanford University Press; (Box 55.2) from Nicholson, J. (1977) *Habits*. London: Macmillan; p.478, from the *Journal of Social Psychology*, 21, 107–112 (1946). Reprinted with permission of the Helen Dwight Reid Educational Foundation. Published by Heldref Publications, 1319 Eighteenth Street., N.W., Washington, C.C. 20036–1802. Copyright © 1946; p.480, The British Psychological Society from *The Psychologist*, 1995, 8, 77; p.487, Ken Pyne, from *The Relationship – A Cartoon Novel of Romance in the 80s*, (1981) Little, Brown & Co (UK), © Ken Pyne, 1981; p.489, Rex Features, London by Mike Daines; p.497, from McGhee, P. (1996) Make or break. *Psychology Review*, 2, 27–30. Reprinted by permission of Philip Allan Publishers; p.499, Private Eye; p.509 (Fig 59.1) Pinter & Martin Ltd, HarperCollins Publishers, Inc., New York; (Figs 59.2, 59.3), from the film *Obedience*, copyright © 1965 by Stanley Milgram and distributed by Penn State Media Sales; p.511, from *Psychology* by Zimbardo P.G. & Weber A.L. (1994), Copyright © 1994 by Philip G Zimbardo and Ann L. Weber. Reprinted by permission of Addison-Wesley Educational Publishers Inc; p.522, AKG photo London; p.525, Camera Press Ltd; p.527, Corbis-Bettman; p.528, Prentice-Dunn, S. & Rogers, R.W. (1983) *Journal of Personality and Social Psychology*, 43, 503–513. Copyright © 1983 by the American Psychological Association. Reprinted with permission. p.532, © 1994 Phil Callaghan/The Sun; p.535, from Darley J.M. & Latané B. (1968) Bystander intervention in emergencies: Diffusion of responsibility. *Journal of Personality and Social Psychology*, 8, 377–383. Copyright © 1968 by the American Psychological Association. Reprinted with permission; p.537, from Piliavin J.A. *et al.* (1981) *Emergency Intervention*. Academic Press, Inc.; p.538, Associated Press; p.543, (top) FLPA © by T. Whittaker; (bottom) National Film Archive. Ronald Grant Collection; p.546, Albert Bandura, Stanford University; p.552 (Fig. 64.1), BFI Stills; p.558, Telegraph Colour Library. Photograph: Elke Hesser; p.562, Associated Press/Kathy Willens; p.563, Big Pictures/ © Jamie Budge; p.566, Rex Features, London, Charles Ommaney; p.568, Mary Evans Picture Library; p.579, The Kobal Collection; p.587, The Bridgeman Art Library, *The Garden of Earthly Delights: Hell*, right wing of triptych, detail of 'Tree Man', c1500, (panel) by Hieronymous Bosch (c1450–1516); p.606, Science Photo Library; p.606, Life File © Mike Maidment; p.610, Rex Features, London © SIPA-PRESS;

p.615, Rex Features, London, Robin Palmer; p.616 (top), Rex Features, London; (bottom) Yes! Magazine/Richard Barnes; p.623, Science Photo Library, Will and Deni Mcintyre; p.629, The Telegraph Photo Library; p.636, Colorific/ Mark Richards/ Dot Pictures; p.659, The Johns Hopkins University Press from Smith, M.L. *et al.* (1980) *The Benefits of Psychotherapy* © 1980 The Johns Hopkins University Press; p.672, Dr Gerry Kent from *The Psychologist*, 1995, 8, 412–413; p.675 (top), from Walker, M. (1996) *Book of Signs* (revised edition). © Makaton Vocabulary Development Project 1997; p.675 (bottom), Blissymbols used herein derived from the symbols described in the work, Semantography, original copyright © C.K. Bliss 1949. Blissymbolics Communication International, Toronto, Canada, exclusive licensee, 1982. All rights reserved; p.680, Ronald Grant Collection; p.683, from Selfe, L. *A Case of Extraordinary Drawing Ability in An Autistic Child*. Academic Press, Inc; p.703 (Box 82.3), from M Gilbert, (1986) *The Holocaust: The Jewish Tragedy*. HarperCollins Publishers Ltd; p.710, Corbis; p.711, Wide World Photo, Inc.; p.712 (Figs 83.3, 83.4), The Bettman Archive; p.729 (Box 84.6), from Hofstede G. (1980) *Culture Consequences*, copyright © 1980 Sage Publications Inc., reprinted by permission of Sage Publications.

The publisher would also like to thank the following for permission to reproduce text extracts:

p.458 (Box 52.8), from Durkin, K. *Developmental Social Psychology, From Infancy to Old Age* (1995) Blackwell Publishers; p.526 (Box 61.4), from *Race Riot* by A.M. Lee and N.D. Humphrey, Copyright © 1943 by A.M. Lee and N.D. Humphrey. Reprinted by permission of Henry Holt & Company, Inc.; p549 (Box 63.7), from Hollins, C. & Howells, K. (1997) Controlling violent behaviour. *Psychology Review*, 3 (3), Reprinted by permission of Philip Allan Publishers; p.552 (Box 64.3), © Times Newspapers Limited, 1997; p.557 (Box 64.9), from Gunter B. and McAleer J.L. (1990) *Children and Television – The One-Eyed Monster?* Reprinted by permission of Routledge; p.558 (Box 64.10), Mark Griffiths from *The Psychologist*, 9, 410–407.

Every effort has been made to obtain necessary permission with reference to copyright material. The publishers apologise if inadvertently any sources remain unacknowledged and will be glad to make the necessary arrangements at the earliest opportunity.

Index compiled by Frank Merrett, Cheltenham, Gloucester.